Educational Psychology

SEVENTH EDITION

Anita E. Woolfolk

The Ohio State University

Allyn and Bacon

Boston ▪ London ▪ Toronto ▪ Sydney ▪ Tokyo ▪ Singapore

Senior Vice President & Publisher, Education: Nancy Forsyth
Development Editor: Alicia Reilly
Editorial Assistant: Cheryl Ouellette
Marketing Manager: Kris Farnsworth
Senior Editorial Production Administrator: Susan McIntyre
Editorial Production Service: Kathy Smith
Composition and Prepress Buyer: Linda Cox
Manufacturing Buyer: Megan Cochran
Cover Administrator: Linda Knowles
Photo Research: Susan Duane
Electronic Composition: Omegatype East

Copyright © 1998, 1995, 1993, 1990, 1987, 1984, 1980 by Allyn & Bacon
A Viacom Company
160 Gould Street
Needham Heights, MA 02194

Internet: www.abacon.com
America Online: keyword: College Online

Library of Congress Cataloging-in-Publication Data

Woolfolk, Anita
    Educational psychology / Anita E. Woolfolk. — 7th ed.
       p.   cm.
    Includes bibliographical references and indexes.
    ISBN 0-205-26335-6
    1. Educational psychology.   I. Title.
  LB1051.W74 1998
  370.15--dc21   97-11670
                                            CIP

Printed in the United States of America
10 9 8 7 6 5 4 3 2 1 VHP 04 03 02 01 00 99 98 97

In memory of my father,
Charles Goodwin Pratt,
who taught me to love learning and put away my tools,

and my brother-in-law,
Thomas C. Hoy,
a gifted teacher and principal

Contents

Student Preface   *xvii*

1 Teachers, Teaching, and Educational Psychology   2

OVERVIEW   3

What Would You Do?   4

WHAT IS GOOD TEACHING?   4

Inside Five Classrooms   5
  A Bilingual First Grade
  A Suburban Sixth Grade
  An Inner-City Middle School
  Two Advanced Math Classes

Expert Knowledge   7

TEACHING: ARTISTRY, TECHNIQUE, AND A LOT OF WORK   8

Concerns of Beginning Teachers   8

POINT■COUNTERPOINT: Whose Classroom Is It Anyway? 9

What about the Students?   10

THE ROLE OF EDUCATIONAL PSYCHOLOGY   11

Is It Just Common Sense?   11
  Taking Turns
  Classroom Management
  Skipping Grades

Using Research to Understand and Improve Teaching   13

Descriptive Research
Correlations
Experimentation
Theories for Teaching

THE CONTENTS OF THIS BOOK   16

A Quick Tour of the Topics   16

How This Book Can Help You Learn   17
  Getting Ready to Learn
  Aids to Understanding
  Applying Knowledge
  Becoming a Good Beginning Teacher

SUMMARY   19

KEY TERMS   19

TEACHERS' CASEBOOK:
  What Would They Do?   20

Part One
Human Development: A Framework for Teachers

2 Cognitive Development and Language   22

OVERVIEW   23

What Would You Do?   24

A DEFINITION OF DEVELOPMENT   24

General Principles of Development   25

The Brain and Cognitive Development   25

**PIAGET'S THEORY OF COGNITIVE
DEVELOPMENT**   27

Influences on Development   27

Basic Tendencies in Thinking   28

Organization
Adaptation
Equilibration

Four Stages of Cognitive Development   29

Infancy: The Sensorimotor Stage
Early Childhood to the Early Elementary Years:
  The Preoperational Stage
Later Elementary to the Middle School Years:
  The Concrete-Operational Stage
Junior and Senior High: Formal Operations
Do We All Reach the Fourth Stage?

**IMPLICATIONS OF PIAGET'S THEORY
FOR TEACHERS**   39

Understanding Students' Thinking   39

Matching Strategies to Abilities   40

Constructing Knowledge   40

Some Limitations of Piaget's Theory   41

The Trouble with Stages

POINT ■ COUNTERPOINT: Can Cognitive
Development Be Accelerated? 42

Underestimating Children's Abilities
Cognitive Development and Information Processing
Cognitive Development and Culture

**VYGOTSKY'S SOCIOCULTURAL
PERSPECTIVE**   44

The Role of Language and Private
Speech   45

Vygotsky's and Piaget's Views Compared
Self-Talk and Learning

The Role of Adults and Peers   47

**IMPLICATIONS OF VYGOTSKY'S THEORY
FOR TEACHERS**   47

Assisted Learning   48

The Zone of Proximal Development   49

Assessment
Teaching

THE DEVELOPMENT OF LANGUAGE   51

How Do We Learn Language?   51

Stages in the Process of Language
Acquisition   52

First Words
First Sentences

Learning Grammar
Learning Vocabulary

Language Development in the School
Years   54

Pronunciation
Syntax
Vocabulary and Meaning
Pragmatics
Metalinguistic Awareness

LANGUAGE, LITERACY, AND TEACHING   57

Teachers and Literacy   58

Partnerships with Families   58

SUMMARY   60

KEY TERMS   61

CHECK YOUR UNDERSTANDING   61

TEACHERS' CASEBOOK:
  What Would They Do?   62

GUIDELINES: Teaching the Preoperational Child   33
        Teaching the Concrete-Operational
          Child   36
        Helping Students to Use Formal
          Operations   39
        Applying Vygotsky's Ideas in Teaching   50
        Family and Community Partnerships for
          Literacy Programs   59

3 *Personal, Social, and
     Emotional Development*   64

OVERVIEW   65

What Would You Do?   66

THE WORK OF ERIKSON   66

The Preschool Years: Trust, Autonomy, and
Initiative   67

Elementary and Middle School Years:
Industry versus Inferiority 69

Adolescence: The Search for Identity   70

Identity Statuses

Beyond the School Years   72

**UNDERSTANDING OURSELVES AND
OTHERS**   73

Self-Concept and Self-Esteem   73

How Self-Concept Develops

School Life and Self-Esteem   75

Gender, Ethnicity, and Self-Esteem   76

Gender and Self-Esteem
Personal and Collective Self-Esteem

The Self and Others   79

Intention
Taking the Perspective of Others

MORAL DEVELOPMENT   80

Kohlberg's Stages of Moral
Development   81

Alternatives to Kohlberg's Theory   83

Social Conventions versus Moral Issues
Cultural Differences in Moral Reasoning

The Morality of Caring   84

Empathy
Friendships

POINT■ COUNTERPOINT: Should Schools Teach
Values? 87

A Curriculum of Caring

Moral Behavior   89

Cheating
Aggression

SOCIALIZATION: THE HOME AND THE SCHOOL   91

American Families Today   92

Growing Up Too Fast
Developmentally Appropriate Preschools
Children of Divorce

New Roles for Teachers   96

CHALLENGES FOR CHILDREN   98

Physical Development   98

The Preschool Years
Elementary School
Adolescence

Children and Youth at Risk   100

Child Abuse
Teenage Sexuality and Pregnancy
Eating Disorders
Drug Abuse
AIDS
Suicide

SUMMARY   106

KEY TERMS   107

CHECK YOUR UNDERSTANDING   107

TEACHERS' CASEBOOK:
What Would They Do?   108

GUIDELINES: Encouraging Initiative in the Preschool
Child   69
Encouraging Industry   70
Supporting Identity Formation   72
Family and Community Partnerships to
Strengthen Student Self-Esteem   79
Dealing with Aggression and Encouraging
Cooperation   91
Helping Children of Divorce   95
Supporting Personal and Social
Development   97
Dealing with Differences in Growth and
Development   100

Part Two
Individual Variations

4 Learning Abilities and Learning Problems   110

OVERVIEW   111

What Would You Do?   112

LANGUAGE AND LABELING   112

INDIVIDUAL DIFFERENCES IN INTELLIGENCE   113

What Does Intelligence Mean?   113

Intelligence: One Ability or Many?
Multiple Intelligences
Intelligence as a Process

How Is Intelligence Measured?   118

Binet's Dilemma
Group versus Individual IQ Tests

What Does an IQ Score Mean?   119

Intelligence and Achievement
Intelligence: Heredity or Environment?

ABILITY DIFFERENCES AND TEACHING   121

Ability Grouping   122

Between-Class Ability Grouping
Within-Class Ability Grouping

Mental Retardation   123

Gifted and Talented   126

Who Are the Gifted?
What Problems Do the Gifted Face?

Recognizing Students' Special Abilities
Giftedness and Formal Testing
Teaching Gifted Students

CREATIVITY 129

  Creativity and Cognition 129

  Assessing Creativity 130
    Paper-and-Pencil Tests of Creativity
    Teachers' Judgments of Creativity

  Creativity in the Classroom 131
    The Brainstorming Strategy
    Take Your Time—and Play!

COGNITIVE AND LEARNING STYLES 134

  Cognitive Styles 134
    Field Dependence and Field Independence
    Impulsive and Reflective Cognitive Styles

  Learning Styles and Preferences 135

STUDENTS WITH LEARNING CHALLENGES 136

  Students with Physical and Sensory Challenges 137
    Seizure Disorders (Epilepsy)
    Cerebral Palsy
    Hearing Impairment
    Vision Impairment

  Communication Disorders 139
    Speech Impairments
    Language Disorders

  Emotional or Behavioral Disorders 140

  Hyperactivity and Attention Disorders 141

  Learning Disabilities 142
    Students with Learning Disabilities
    Teaching Students with Learning Disabilities

INTEGRATION, MAINSTREAMING, AND INCLUSION 146

  Changes in the Law 146
    Least Restrictive Placement

POINT■COUNTERPOINT: Is Full Inclusion a Reasonable Approach to Teaching Exceptional Students? 147
    Individual Education Program
    The Rights of Students and Parents

  Effective Teaching in Inclusive Classrooms 148
    Resource Rooms, Collaborative Consultation, and Cooperative Teaching

  Making a Referral
  Including Families

  Computers and Exceptional Students 153

  SUMMARY 154

  KEY TERMS 156

  CHECK YOUR UNDERSTANDING 156

  TEACHERS' CASEBOOK:
    What Would They Do? 158

GUIDELINES: Interpreting IQ Scores 120
    Grouping by Achievement 123
    Teaching Students with Mental
      Retardation 125
    Encouraging Creativity 133
    Family and Community Partnerships for
      Productive Conferences 152

5 The Impact of Culture and Community *160*

  OVERVIEW 161

What Would You Do? 162

TODAY'S MULTICULTURAL CLASSROOMS 162

  Individuals, Groups, and Society 162

  American Cultural Diversity 163

POINT■COUNTERPOINT: Should Multicultural Education Emphasize Similarities or Differences? 164
    Culture and Group Membership
    Cautions in Interpreting Cultural Differences

SOCIAL CLASS DIFFERENCES 166

  Who Are the Poor? 167

  SES and Achievement 167
    Low Expectations—Low Self-Esteem
    Learned Helplessness
    Resistance Cultures
    Tracking
    Childrearing Styles

ETHNIC AND RACIAL DIFFERENCES 170

  The Changing Demographics 171

  Cultural Differences 171
    Cultural Conflicts
    Cultural Compatibility
    Working with Families and Communities

Ethnic and Racial Differences in School Achievement   174

The Legacy of Discrimination   175

Continuing Prejudice
The Development of Prejudice
Continuing Discrimination

WOMEN AND MEN: DIFFERENCES IN THE CLASSROOM   178

Gender-Role Identity   178

Gender-Role Stereotyping in the Preschool Years
Gender Bias in the Curriculum
Sex Discrimination in Classrooms

Sex Differences in Mental Abilities   182

Sex and Mathematics

Eliminating Gender Bias   184

LANGUAGE DIFFERENCES IN THE CLASSROOM   185

Dialects   185

Dialects and Language Skills
Dialects and Teaching

Bilingualism   187

What Does Bilingualism Mean?
Becoming Bilingual
Bilingual Education
Research on Bilingual Programs

CREATING CULTURALLY COMPATIBLE CLASSROOMS   192

Social Organization   192

Learning Styles   192

Hispanic Americans
African Americans
Native Americans
Asian Americans
Criticisms of Learning-Styles Research

Sociolinguistics   194

Participation Structures
Sources of Misunderstandings

Bringing It All Together: Teaching Every Student   195

Know Your Students
Respect Your Students
Teach Your Students

SUMMARY   198

KEY TERMS   199

CHECK YOUR UNDERSTANDING   199

TEACHERS' CASEBOOK:

What Would They Do?   200

GUIDELINES: Family and Community Partnerships for Building Learning Communities   173
Avoiding Sexism in Teaching   185
Teaching Dialect-Dominant Students   187
Creating Culturally Compatible Classrooms   197

Part Three
Learning: Theory and Practice

6 *Behavioral Views of Learning*   202

OVERVIEW   203

What Would You Do?   204

UNDERSTANDING LEARNING   204

Learning: A Definition   204

Learning Is Not Always What It Seems   205

EARLY EXPLANATIONS OF LEARNING: CONTIGUITY AND CLASSICAL CONDITIONING   207

Pavlov's Dilemma and Discovery: Classical Conditioning   207

Generalization, Discrimination, and Extinction   208

OPERANT CONDITIONING: TRYING NEW RESPONSES   208

The Work of Thorndike and Skinner   209

Types of Consequences   210

Reinforcement
Punishment

Reinforcement Schedules   212

Summarizing the Effects of Reinforcement Schedules   213

Extinction

Antecedents and Behavior Change   214

Cueing
Prompting

APPLIED BEHAVIOR ANALYSIS   216

Methods for Encouraging Behaviors   216

Reinforcing with Teacher Attention

Selecting Reinforcers: The Premack Principle
Shaping
Positive Practice

Coping with Undesirable Behavior   221

Negative Reinforcement
Satiation
Reprimands
Response Cost
Social Isolation
Some Cautions

SOCIAL LEARNING THEORY   225

Elements of Social Cognitive Theory   225

Learning by Observing Others   226

Elements of Observational Learning   226

Attention
Retention
Production
Motivation and Reinforcement

Factors That Influence Observational Learning   228

Observational Learning in Teaching   228

Teaching New Behaviors
Encouraging Already-Learned Behaviors
Strengthening or Weakening Inhibitions
Directing Attention
Arousing Emotion

SELF-REGULATION AND COGNITIVE BEHAVIOR MODIFICATION   231

Self-Management   232

Goal Setting
Recording and Evaluating Progress
Self-Reinforcement

Cognitive Behavior Modification and Self-Instruction   235

PROBLEMS AND ISSUES   236

Ethical Issues   237

Goals
Strategies

Criticisms of Behavioral Methods   237

POINT■COUNTERPOINT: Should Students Be Rewarded for Learning? 238

SUMMARY   239

KEY TERMS   240

CHECK YOUR UNDERSTANDING   240

TEACHERS' CASEBOOK:
What Would They Do?   242

GUIDELINES: Using Principles of Classical
Conditioning   209
Using Praise Appropriately   217
Using Positive Reinforcement   220
Using Punishment   224
Using Observational Learning   231
Family and Community Partnerships for
Student Self-Management Programs   234

7 Cognitive Views of Learning   244

OVERVIEW   245

What Would You Do?   246

ELEMENTS OF THE COGNITIVE PERSPECTIVE   246

Comparing Cognitive and Behavioral Views   247

The Importance of Knowledge in Learning   247

General and Specific Knowledge
Declarative, Procedural, and Conditional Knowledge

THE INFORMATION PROCESSING MODEL OF MEMORY   249

An Information Processing Model   249

Sensory Memory   250

Capacity, Duration, and Contents of Sensory Memory
Perception
The Role of Attention
Attention and Teaching

Working Memory   254

Capacity, Duration, and Contents of Working Memory
Retaining Information in Working Memory
Forgetting

Long-Term Memory   257

Capacity and Duration of Long-Term Memory
Contents of Long-Term Memory
Propositions and Propositional Networks
Images
Schemas
Episodic Memory
Procedural Memory

Storing and Retrieving Information in Long-Term Memory   261

Levels of Processing Theories
Retrieving Information from Long-Term Memory

Forgetting and Long-Term Memory

Connectionism: An Alternative View of Memory 266

METACOGNITION, REGULATION, AND INDIVIDUAL DIFFERENCES 266

Metacognitive Knowledge and Regulation 267

Individual Differences in Metacognition 267

Individual Differences and Working Memory 268

Developmental Differences
Individual Differences

Individual Differences and Long-Term Memory 269

BECOMING KNOWLEDGEABLE: SOME BASIC PRINCIPLES 270

Development of Declarative Knowledge 270

Rote Memorization
Mnemonics

POINT■COUNTERPOINT: What's Wrong with Memorizing? 273

Making It Meaningful

Becoming an Expert: Development of Procedural and Conditional Knowledge 274

Automated Basic Skills
Domain-Specific Strategies
Learning Outside School

CONSTRUCTIVISM AND SITUATED LEARNING: CHALLENGING SYMBOLIC PROCESSING MODELS 277

Constructivist Views of Learning 277

Types of Constructivism

Knowledge: Accuracy versus Usefulness 278

Situated Learning 279

SUMMARY 282

KEY TERMS 283

CHECK YOUR UNDERSTANDING 283

TEACHERS' CASEBOOK:
What Would They Do? 284

GUIDELINES: Gaining and Maintaining Attention 253
Using Information Processing Ideas in the Classroom 265
Family and Community Partnerships for Students' Learning 276

8 Complex Cognitive Processes 286

OVERVIEW 287

What Would You Do? 288

THE IMPORTANCE OF THINKING AND UNDERSTANDING 288

LEARNING AND TEACHING ABOUT CONCEPTS 289

Views of Concept Learning 289

Prototypes and Exemplars
Concepts and Schemas

Strategies for Teaching Concepts 290

An Example Concept-Attainment Lesson
Lesson Components
Lesson Structure
Extending and Connecting Concepts

PROBLEM SOLVING 294

Problem Solving: General or Domain-Specific? 295

A General Problem-Solving Strategy 295

Defining Goals and Representing the Problem 296

Focusing Attention
Understanding the Words
Understanding the Whole Problem
Translation and Schema Training
The Results of Problem Representation

Exploring Possible Solution Strategies 300

Algorithms
Heuristics

Anticipating, Acting, and Looking Back 301

Factors That Hinder Problem Solving 302

Functional Fixedness
Response Set
The Importance of Flexibility

Effective Problem Solving: What Do the Experts Do? 304

Expert Knowledge
Expert Teachers
Novice Knowledge

BECOMING AN EXPERT STUDENT: LEARNING STRATEGIES AND STUDY SKILLS 307

Learning Strategies and Tactics 307

Underlining and Highlighting
Taking Notes
Visual Tools   311
PQ4R   311

TEACHING AND LEARNING ABOUT THINKING   314
Stand-Alone Programs for Developing Thinking   315
Developing Thinking in Every Class   315

POINT■COUNTERPOINT: **Should Schools Teach Critical Thinking and Problem Solving? 316**

The Language of Thinking
Critical Thinking
Thinking as a "State of Mind"

TEACHING FOR TRANSFER   319
Defining Transfer   319
A Contemporary View of Transfer   320
Teaching for Positive Transfer   321
What Is Worth Learning?
How Can Teachers Help?
Stages of Transfer for Strategies
SUMMARY   324
KEY TERMS   325
CHECK YOUR UNDERSTANDING   325
TEACHERS' CASEBOOK:
What Would They Do?   326

GUIDELINES: Problem Solving   306
            Study Skills and Learning Strategies   313
            Family and Community Partnerships for
                Encouraging Transfer   323

9   *Learning and Instruction*   328

OVERVIEW   329

What Would You Do?   330

CONTRIBUTIONS OF BEHAVIORAL LEARNING   330
Objectives for Learning   330
Mager: Start with the Specific
Gronlund: Start with the General
Bloom's Taxonomy of Objectives
Are Objectives Useful?   333

Mastery Learning   334
Advantages and Problems
Direct Instruction   335
Rosenshine's Six Teaching Functions
Criticisms of Direct Instruction

COGNITIVE MODELS OF TEACHING   338
Discovery Learning   338
Structure and Discovery
Discovery in Action
Expository Teaching/Reception Learning   341
Advance Organizers

POINT■COUNTERPOINT: **Is Discovery Learning Effective? 342**

Steps in an Expository Lesson
Making the Most of Expository Teaching
The Instructional Events Model   345

CONSTRUCTIVIST AND SITUATED LEARNING   346
Elements of Constructivist Perspectives   346
Complex Learning Environments and Authentic Tasks
Social Negotiation
Multiple Representations of Content
Understanding the Knowledge Construction Process
Inquiry and Problem-Based Learning   348
Group Work and Cooperation in Learning   349
Working in Groups
Beyond Groups to Cooperation
Elements of Cooperative Learning Groups
Setting Up Cooperative Groups
Jigsaw
Reciprocal Questioning
Scripted Cooperation
What Can Go Wrong: Misuses of Group Learning
Instructional Conversations   355
Cognitive Apprenticeships   355

COGNITIVE AND CONSTRUCTIVIST APPROACHES TO READING, MATHEMATICS, AND SCIENCE   357
Learning to Read and Write   357
Whole Language
Integrated Curriculum
Do Students Need Skills and Phonics?
Being Sensible about Reading and Writing
Reciprocal Teaching   360
An Example of Reciprocal Teaching
Applying Reciprocal Teaching

Learning and Teaching Mathematics   362

Learning Science   364

Working with Families   365

SUMMARY   366

KEY TERMS   367

CHECK YOUR UNDERSTANDING   367

TEACHERS' CASEBOOK:

   What Would They Do?   368

GUIDELINES: Developing Instructional Objectives   333
                      Applying Bruner's Ideas in the
                         Classroom   340
                      Applying Ausubel's Ideas in the
                         Classroom   344
                      Family and Community Partnerships for
                         Innovative Teaching Approaches   365

Part Four

Motivation, Management, and Teaching

10 Motivation: Issues and Explanations   370

OVERVIEW   371

What Would You Do?   372

WHAT IS MOTIVATION?   372

Intrinsic and Extrinsic Motivation   373

Four General Approaches to
Motivation   375

   Behavioral Approaches to Motivation
   Humanistic Approaches to Motivation

POINT■COUNTERPOINT: What Should Schools
Do to Encourage Students' Self-Esteem?   376

   Cognitive Approaches to Motivation
   Social Learning Approaches to Motivation

Motivation to Learn in School   378

GOALS AND MOTIVATION   379

Types of Goals   379

Feedback and Goal Acceptance   380

Goals: Lessons for Teachers   382

NEEDS AND MOTIVATION   382

Maslow's Hierarchy   382

Achievement Motivation   384

The Need for Self-Determination   385

The Need for Relatedness   386

Needs and Motivation: Lessons for
Teachers   386

ATTRIBUTIONS, BELIEFS, AND
MOTIVATION   387

Attribution Theory   387

   Dimensions: Locus, Stability, Responsibility
   Learned Helplessness
   Attributions and Student Motivation
   Cues about Causes

Beliefs about Ability   390

Beliefs about Self-Efficacy 392

   Efficacy and Motivation
   Teacher Efficacy

Attributions, Achievement Motivation, and
Self-Worth   394

Attributions and Beliefs: Lessons for
Teachers   395

ANXIETY AND COPING IN THE
CLASSROOM   396

What Causes Anxiety at School?   397

Helping Anxious Students   397

Anxiety: Lessons for Teachers   398

SUMMARY   399

KEY TERMS   400

CHECK YOUR UNDERSTANDING   401

TEACHERS' CASEBOOK:

   What Would They Do?   402

GUIDELINES: Family and Community Partnerships for
                      Setting Goals   381
                      Supporting Autonomy and
                         Self-Determination   385
                      Encouraging Students' Self-Worth   396
                      Dealing with Anxiety   398

11 Motivation, Teaching, and Learning   404

OVERVIEW   405

What Would You Do?   406

AN ULTIMATE GOAL OF TEACHING:
LIFELONG LEARNING   406

Self-Regulated Learning   406
Knowledge
Motivation
Volition

On TARGETT for Self-Regulated
Learning   408

TASKS FOR LEARNING   409

Tapping Interests and Arousing
Curiosity   410

Task Operations: Risk and
Ambiguity   411

Task Value   412

SUPPORTING AUTONOMY AND
RECOGNIZING ACCOMPLISHMENT   414

Advantages of Autonomy in the
Classroom   414

Information and Control   414

Autonomy Supporting Class Climates   415

Recognizing Accomplishment   416

GROUPING, EVALUATION, AND TIME   416

Grouping and Goal Structures   417
STAD
TGT

Evaluation   420

Time   421

TEACHER EXPECTATIONS 421

Two Kinds of Expectation Effects   421

POINT■COUNTERPOINT: Do Teachers'
Expectations Affect Students' Learning? 422

Sources of Expectations   423

Teacher Behavior and Student
Reaction   423
Instructional Strategies
Teacher-Student Interactions

STRATEGIES TO ENCOURAGE MOTIVATION
AND THOUGHTFUL LEARNING   427

Necessary Conditions in Classrooms   427

Can I Do It? Building Confidence and
Positive Expectations   427

Do I Want to Do It? Seeing the Value of
Learning   428
Attainment and Intrinsic Value
Instrumental Value

What Do I Need to Do to Succeed? Staying
Focused on the Task   430

How Do Beginning Teachers Motivate
Students?   432

Students' Views of Motivation   433

SUMMARY   434

KEY TERMS   435

CHECK YOUR UNDERSTANDING   435

TEACHERS' CASEBOOK:
What Would They Do?   436

GUIDELINES: Supporting Autonomy in the
Classroom   415
Avoiding the Negative Effects of Teacher
Expectations   425
Family and Community Partnerships to
Encourage Motivation to Learn   431

12 Creating Learning Environments   438

OVERVIEW   439

What Would You Do?   440

THE NEED FOR ORGANIZATION   440

The Ecology of Classrooms   440
Characteristics of Classrooms
The Basic Task: Gain Their Cooperation
Age-Related Needs

The Goals of Classroom Management   442
More Time for Learning
Access to Learning
Management for Self-Management

CREATING A POSITIVE LEARNING
ENVIRONMENT   445

Some Research Results   445

Rules and Procedures Required   445
Procedures
Rules
Rules for Elementary School
Rules for Secondary School
Consequences

Planned Spaces for Learning   449
Interest-Area Arrangements
Personal Territories

Getting Started: The First Weeks of
Class   454
Effective Managers for Elementary Students
Effective Managers for Secondary Students

MAINTAINING A GOOD ENVIRONMENT FOR LEARNING   455

Encouraging Engagement   455

Prevention Is the Best Medicine   457

Withitness
Overlapping and Group Focus
Movement Management

Dealing with Discipline Problems   459

Special Problems with Secondary Students   460

SPECIAL PROGRAMS FOR CLASSROOM MANAGEMENT   461

Group Consequences   461

Token Reinforcement Programs   462

Contingency Contract Programs   463

THE NEED FOR COMMUNICATION   463

Message Sent—Message Received   464

Diagnosis: Whose Problem Is It?   465

Counseling: The Student's Problem   466

Confrontation and Assertive Discipline   467

"I" Messages
Assertive Discipline
Confrontations and Negotiations

POINT■COUNTERPOINT: Does Assertive Discipline Work? 469

Student Conflicts and Confrontations   470

Conflicts: Goals and Needs
Violence in the Schools
Peer Mediation

Communicating with Families about Classroom Management   473

SUMMARY   474

KEY TERMS   474

CHECK YOUR UNDERSTANDING   475

TEACHERS' CASEBOOK:
   What Would They Do?   476

GUIDELINES: Establishing Class Procedures   446
   Designing Learning Spaces   451
   Keeping Students Engaged   456
   Imposing Penalties   459
   Family and Community Partnerships for
      Classroom Management   473

13   *Teaching for Learning*   478

OVERVIEW   479

What Would You Do?   480

THE FIRST STEP: PLANNING   480

Flexible and Creative Plans—Using Taxonomies   481

The Cognitive Domain
The Affective Domain
The Psychomotor Domain

Planning from a Constructivist Perspective   484

An Example of Constructivist Planning
Integrated and Thematic Plans
Assessment

TEACHING: WHOLE GROUP AND DIRECTIVE   488

Lecturing and Explaining   488

Recitation and Questioning   489

Kinds of Questions
Fitting the Questions to the Students
Responding to Student Answers

Seatwork and Homework   492

TEACHING: SMALL GROUP AND STUDENT-CENTERED   494

An Example of Constructivist Teaching   495

Group Discussion   496

Humanistic Education   498

Computers, Videodiscs, and Beyond   498

Computers as Learning Environments
Computers and Learning
Videodiscs

SUCCESSFUL TEACHING: FOCUS ON THE TEACHER   502

Characteristics of Effective Teachers   503

Teachers' Knowledge
Organization and Clarity
Planning for Clarity
Clarity during the Lesson
Warmth and Enthusiasm

Putting It All Together:
The Effective Teacher   506

SUCCESSFUL UNDERSTANDING: FOCUS ON
THE STUDENT   506
The New Zealand Studies   507
Some Findings
Conditions for Learning from Teaching
Learning Functions: The Effective
Student   508

INTEGRATIONS: BEYOND MODELS TO
OUTSTANDING TEACHING   508
Matching Methods to Learning Goals   508

POINT■COUNTERPOINT: What Is the Best Way
to Help Students at Risk of Failing? 510
APA's Learner-Centered Psychological
Principles   511
SUMMARY   514
KEY TERMS   515
CHECK YOUR UNDERSTANDING   515
TEACHERS' CASEBOOK:
What Would They Do?   516

GUIDELINES: Family and Community Partnerships for
Homework   494
Leading Class Discussions   497
Using Computers and Other
Technology   501
Teaching Effectively   505

Part Five

Assessing Student Learning

14 *Standardized Testing* *518*

OVERVIEW   519

What Would You Do?   520

MEASUREMENT AND EVALUATION   520
Norm-Referenced Tests   521

Criterion-Referenced Tests   521

WHAT DO TEST SCORES MEAN?   523
Basic Concepts   523
Frequency Distributions
Measurements of Central Tendency and Standard
Deviation
The Normal Distribution
Types of Scores   526
Percentile Rank Scores
Grade-Equivalent Scores
Standard Scores
Interpreting Test Scores   529
Reliability
True Score
Confidence Interval
Validity

TYPES OF STANDARDIZED TESTS   532
Achievement Tests: What Has the Student
Learned?   533
Using Information from a Norm-Referenced
Achievement Test
Interpreting Achievement Test Scores
Diagnostic Tests: What Are the Student's
Strengths and Weaknesses?   536
Aptitude Tests: How Well Will the Student
Do in the Future?   537
Scholastic Aptitude
IQ and Scholastic Aptitude
Discussing Test Results with Families

ISSUES IN STANDARDIZED TESTING   539
The Uses of Testing in American
Society   539
Readiness Testing

POINT■COUNTERPOINT: To Test or Not
to Test? 541
Minimum and World-Class Standards
Testing Teachers
Advantages in Taking Tests—Fair and
Unfair   544
Bias in Testing
Coaching and Test-Taking Skills

NEW DIRECTIONS IN STANDARDIZED
TESTING   547
Assessing Learning Potential   547
Authentic Assessment   548

SUMMARY 549

KEY TERMS 550

CHECK YOUR UNDERSTANDING 551

TEACHERS' CASEBOOK:
What Would They Do? 552

GUIDELINES: Increasing Test Reliability and Validity
533
Family and Community Partnerships
for Discussing Standardized Test
Results 538
Taking a Test 546

15 *Classroom Assessment and Grading* 554

OVERVIEW 555

What Would You Do? 556

FORMATIVE AND SUMMATIVE ASSESSMENT 556

GETTING THE MOST FROM TRADITIONAL ASSESSMENT APPROACHES 558

Planning for Testing 558
Using a Behavior-Content Matrix
When to Test?
Judging Textbook Tests

Objective Testing 560
Using Multiple-Choice Tests
Writing Multiple-Choice Questions

Evaluating Objective Test Items 563

Essay Testing 564
Constructing Essay Tests
Evaluating Essays: Dangers
Evaluating Essays: Methods

INNOVATIONS IN ASSESSMENT 566

POINT■COUNTERPOINT: To Test or Not to
Test, Part II 567

Authentic Classroom Tests 568

Performance in Context: Portfolios
and Exhibitions 568
Portfolios
Exhibitions

Evaluating Portfolios and
Performances 572
Scoring Rubrics
Reliability, Validity, and Equity

EFFECTS OF GRADES AND GRADING ON STUDENTS 575

Effects of Failure 575

Effects of Feedback 576

Grades and Motivation 577

GRADING AND REPORTING: NUTS AND BOLTS 578

Criterion-Referenced versus Norm-
Referenced Grading 578
Criterion-Referenced Systems
Norm-Referenced Systems

Preparing Report Cards 581

The Point System 582

Percentage Grading 583

The Contract System and Grading
Rubrics 584

Grading on Effort and Improvement 585

Cautions: Being Fair 586

BEYOND GRADING: COMMUNICATION 587

SUMMARY 590

KEY TERMS 590

CHECK YOUR UNDERSTANDING 591

TEACHERS' CASEBOOK:
What Would They Do? 592

GUIDELINES: Writing Objective Test Items 561
Creating Portfolios 571
Minimizing the Detrimental Effects of
Grading 577
Using Any Grading System 586
Family and Community Partnerships for
Successful Parent-Teacher Conferences
589

GLOSSARY G-1

REFERENCES R-1

NAME INDEX I-1

SUBJECT INDEX I-10

Student Preface

Many of you reading this book will be enrolled in an educational psychology course as part of your professional preparation for teaching, counseling, speech therapy, or psychology. Others of you, while not planning to become teachers, are reading this book because you are interested in what educational psychology has to say about teaching and learning in a variety of settings. The material in this text should be of interest to everyone who is concerned about education and learning, from the nursery school volunteer to the instructor in a community program for disabled adults. No background in psychology or education is necessary to understand this material. It is as free of jargon and technical language as possible, and many people have worked to make this edition clear, relevant, and interesting.

Since the first edition of *Educational Psychology* appeared, there have been many exciting developments in the field. This edition incorporates new insights and current trends while retaining the best features of the previous work. The seventh edition continues to emphasize the educational implications and applications of research on child development, cognitive science, learning, and teaching. Theory and practice are not separated but are considered together; the text shows how information and ideas drawn from research in educational psychology can be applied to solve the everyday problems of teaching. To explore the connections between knowledge and practice, there are many examples, lesson segments, case studies, guidelines, and practical tips from experienced teachers. Throughout the text you will be challenged to think about the value and use of the ideas in each chapter and you will see principles of educational psychology in action. Professors and students who used the first six editions found these features very helpful. But what about the new developments?

The study of teaching has taken a very logical turn to focus on the person being taught—the student doing the learning. In this revision, there is a new chapter on *learning and instruction*. In this chapter we will explore what is known about how to encourage and support students' learning as we consider instruction based on different models of teaching—behavioral, cognitive, constructivist, and situated learning.

Over 200 new citations have been added to this edition to bring prospective teachers the most current information. Topics include the following:

- assisted learning and scaffolding,
- the role of adults and peers in cognitive development,
- literacy partnerships with families,
- personal and collective self-esteem
- collaborative teaching for inclusion classrooms,
- learning styles,
- parent conferences,

- the development of prejudice,
- observational learning,
- types of constructivism,
- visual tools for learning,
- situated learning,
- cognitive apprenticeships,
- cooperative learning,
- learning to read,
- conceptual change teaching in science,
- constructivist approaches in mathematics,
- learning functions,
- grading rubrics,
- authentic assessment, and
- portfolios.

The Plan of the Book.   The introductory chapter begins with you, the prospective teacher, and the questions you may be asking yourself about a teaching career. What is good teaching, and what does it take to become an excellent teacher? How can educational psychology help you to become such a teacher? Part One, "Human Development: A Framework for Teachers" focuses on the students. How do they develop mentally, physically, emotionally, and socially, and how do all these aspects fit together? Part Two, "Individual Variations," addresses questions such as: Where do individual differences come from, and what do they mean for teachers? How can teachers adapt instruction for students with special needs? What does it mean to create a culturally compatible classroom, one that makes learning accessible to all students? Part Three, "Learning: Theory and Practice," looks at learning from three major perspectives, behavioral, cognitive, and constructivist, with an emphasis on the last two. Learning theories have important implications for instruction at every level. Cognitive research is particularly vital right now and promises to be a wellspring of ideas for teaching in the immediate future. The new chapter, "Learning and Instruction," explores the contributions of different views of learning for the creation of teaching. Part Four, "Motivation, Management, and Teaching" discusses the ever-present, linked issues of motivating, managing, and teaching today's students. The material in these chapters is based on the most recent research in real classrooms and includes information on both teacher-centered and student-centered approaches to teaching. Part Five, "Assessing Student Learning" looks at many types of testing and grading, providing a sound basis for determining how well students have learned.

Aids to Understanding.   At the beginning of each chapter you will find an *Outline* of the key topics with page numbers for quick reference. An *Overview* begins with a question asking about a subject related to the chapter. Before you read each chapter, take a moment to reflect on the questions raised. Your answers to the questions and the Overview, along with a list of *Learning Objectives* (also useful for review later) provide an "orientation" to the chapter topics.

When you turn the page you confront another question, "What Would You Do?" about a real-life classroom situation related to the information in the chapter. By the time you reach the Teachers' Casebook at the end of the chapter, you should have even more ideas about how to solve the problem raised, so be alert as you read.

Within the chapter, headings point out themes, questions, and problems as they arise, so you can look up information easily. These can also serve as a quick review of important points. When a new term or concept is introduced, it appears in boldface type along with a brief margin definition. These *Key Terms* are also defined in a *Glossary* at the end of the book. After every major section of the chapter, *Focus on Learning* asks questions that check your understanding of the material. Can you answer these questions? If not, you might review the material. Throughout the book, graphs, tables, photos, and cartoons have been chosen to clarify and extend the text material—and to add to your enjoyment.

Each chapter ends with a *Summary* of the key ideas in each main heading and an alphabetical list of the Key Terms from the chapter, along with the page number where each is discussed. With the information from the chapter as a base, you are ready to solve the problems posed in the *Check Your Understanding* application exercises at the end of each chapter. These questions cover both elementary and secondary classrooms and include a cooperative learning activity.

Other Text Features.   As in the previous editions, every chapter in the seventh edition includes *Guidelines,* the *Teachers' Casebook,* and *Point/Counterpoints* on such issues as supported inclusion, values in the schools, "paying" kids to learn, and alternatives to direct teaching.

Guidelines.   An important reason for studying educational psychology is to gain skills in solving classroom problems. Often texts give pages of theory and research findings, but little assistance in translating theory into practice. This text is different. Included in each chapter are several sets of *Guidelines,* teaching tips and practical suggestions based on the theory and research discussed in the chapter. Each suggestion is clarified by two or three specific examples. Although the *Guidelines* cannot cover every possible situation, they do provide a needed bridge between knowledge and practice and should help you transfer the text's information to new situations. New in this edition, every chapter after the first has one set of Guidelines that gives ideas for *working with families and the community*—an area of growing importance today.

Teachers' Casebook.   This highly acclaimed and popular feature from the first six editions is back, but with a new twist. At the end of each chapter, master teachers from all over the country offer their own solutions to the problem you encountered at the beginning of each chapter. *Teachers' Casebook: What Would They Do?* gives you insights into the thinking of expert teachers; compare their solutions to the ones you devised. Their ideas truly show educational psychology at work in a range of everyday situations. The *Teachers' Casebook* brings to life the topics and principles discussed in each chapter.

Point/Counterpoint.   There is a section in every chapter called *Point/Counterpoint,* a debate that examines two contrasting perspectives on an important question or controversy related to research or practice in educational psychology. Many of the topics considered in these *Point/Counterpoints* have "made the news" recently and are central to the discussions of educational reformers.

Student Supplements.   A *Study Guide* designed to help you master the material in the text is also available. The *Study Guide* includes concept maps, case study applications, lists of key points, exercises with key terms and concepts, and practice tests.

Student Responses.   You are invited to respond to any aspect of this text. We welcome your feedback. You may wish to criticize the solutions in the *Teachers' Casebook,* for example, or suggest topics or materials you think should be added to future editions. We would also like to know what you think of the text features and student supplements. Please send letters to:

Woolfolk
EDUCATIONAL PSYCHOLOGY, 7/E
Allyn & Bacon
160 Gould Street
Needham Heights, MA 02194

ACKNOWLEDGMENTS

During the years I have worked on this book, from initial draft to this most recent revision, many people have supported the project. Without their help, this text simply could not have been written.

Many educators contributed to this project. Carol Weinstein (Rutgers University) wrote the section in Chapter 12 on spaces for learning. Kathryn Linden (Purdue University) is responsible for the *Test Bank* and the answer feedback material that accompanies each item. The *Instructor's Resource Manual* was created by Angela O'Donnell (Rutgers University) and the *Study Guide* was written by Beth Mowrer-Popiel (University of Idaho). The summaries of research for the *Instructor's Resource Manual* were written by Wayne K. Hoy II, now Vice President of Advanced Software Products. Chapters 8 and 9 on learning benefited from the comments of James Applefield, *University of North Carolina, Wilmington;* Kathryn Biacindo, *California State University, Fresno;* Kay S. Bull, *Oklahoma State University;* Ali Iran-Nejad, *University of Alabama;* Pamela Manners, *Troy State University;* Peter V. Oliver, *University of Hartford;* and Dale H. Schunk, *Purdue University.*

My writing was guided by extensive and thoughtful reviews from the following individuals:

Frank D. Adams
    Wayne State College
Julius Gregg Adams
    *State University of
    New York at
    Fredonia*
Joyce Alexander
    *Indiana University,
    Bloomington*
Richard Aslett
    *Utah Valley Community
    College*
Kathleen Beauvais
    *Eastern Michigan
    University*
Kathryn Biacindo
    *California State
    University, Fresno*

Kay Bull
    *Oklahoma State
    University*
Maureen Sherry Carr
    Oregon State University
Charles Carter
    *William Patterson
    College*
Peggy Dettmer
    Kansas State University
Carlos Diaz
    *Florida Atlantic
    University*
Lynne Díaz-Rico
    California State University, San Bernardino
Miranda D'Amico
    McGill University

Roberta Dimord
    *Delaware Valley
    College*
Kathy Farber
    *Bowling Green State
    University*
Ricardo Garcia
    University of Idaho
Teresa Garcia
    *University of Texas at
    Austin*
Karl Haberlandt
    Trinity College
Daniel P. Hallahan
    University of Virginia
Sharon Lee Hiett
    *University of Central
    Florida*

Robert L. Hohn
University of Kansas
Dianne Horgan
The University of Memphis
Ali Iran-Nejad
The University of Alabama
Sharon Lamb
Bryn Mawr College
Kathryn Linden
Purdue University
Susan G. Magliaro
Virginia Polytechnic Institute and State University
Pamela Manners
Troy State University
Hermine Marshall
University of California, Berkeley
Marion Mason
Bloomsburg University
Catherine McCartney
Bemidji State University

John R. McClure
Northern Arizona University
Suzanne Morin
Shippensburg University
Peter V. Oliver
University of Hartford
Stephen A. Parker
Chicago State University
Suzanne H. Pasch
University of Wisconsin
Michael Piechowski
Northland College
Johnmarshall Reeve
University of Wisconsin
Leslie Rescorla
Bryn Mawr College
Steven Richman
Nassau Community College
Dianne Rivera
Florida Atlantic University
Harry Robinson
Muskegon Community College

Barak Rosenshine
University of Illinois
Ruth Sandlin
California State University, San Bernardino
Dale H. Schunk
Purdue University
Elizabeth M. Street
Central Washington University
David E. Tanner
California State University, Fresno
Julianne Turner
Indiana University
Michael P. Verdi
Grand Canyon
Jeffrey J. Walczyk
Illinois State University
Jerry Willis
University of Houston
James Young
Brigham Young University

As I made decisions about how to revise this edition, I benefited from the ideas of professors around the country who took the time to complete surveys and answer my questions. Thanks to:

Elaine Ackerman
Eastern Washington University
Frank D. Adams
Wayne State University
Martha Wilson Alcock
Capital University
Jo Alexander
Auburn University
Jeanne T. Amlund
Pennsylvania State University
Padma Anand
Slippery Rock University
Eric Anderman
University of Kentucky
Arthur Bangs
La Salle University
Denouse M. Bartolo
Plymouth State College
Brenna Beedle
Eastern Washington University
Herman Behling
Western Maryland College

Paul Berghoff
Pembroke State University
Bonnie Billingsley
Virginia Polytechnic Institute and State University
Sally Bing
University of Maryland, Eastern Shore
Loren J. Blanchard
Xavier University of Louisiana
Joe Bordeaux
Lindenwood College
Lyn Boulter
Catawba College
Allan Brandhurst
Valparaiso University
Michael B. Brown
East Carolina University
Jim Burns
John Wood Community College
Ann Calahan
Tarleton State University

Charles Carter
William Patterson College
Jerrell Cassady
Purdue University
Ann Chapman
Eastern Kentucky University
Anne Marie Coffey
Long Island University
Theodore Coladarci
University of Maine
Hazel Colebank
Northern Arizona University
Joan Collins
St. Cloud State University
Kathleen Cornell
Loyola College
Anthony Dallmann–Jones
Marian College
Betty Davenport
Campbell University
Pam Davis
Rockhurst College

(continued)

Cynthia J. B. DeCorse
LeMoyne College
Victor Delclos
*University of New
Mexico*
Peter Denner
Idaho State University
Carl L. Denti
*Tontchess Community
College*
B. R. Dunn
Marietta College
Paul Egan
Marist College
Daniel Fasko, Jr.
*Morehead State
University*
P. Federici
North Idaho College
Jack Fennema
Dordt College
Sarah Ferguson
University of Dayton
Evelyn Finn
Long Island University
Lynn Fox
American University
William Franzen
*University of Missouri–
St. Louis*
Arnold Fraese
Sterling College
John Gambro
College of St. Francis
Patricia Gandara
*University of California–
Davis*
Judy Grouix
*Texas Christian
University*
Nancy Grausam
*Pennsylvania College of
Technology*
Nancy Hall
Minot State University
Julie Harper
Oregon State University
Jo-Ann Harvey
Franklin Pierce College
Judith Hassel
Ohio Wesleyan University
Jerald Hauser
St. Norbert College
Phillip Hocker
East Central University
Dianne Horgan
University of Memphis

Lynne E. Houtz
*Nebraska Wesleyan
University*
John J. Hudak
Marist College
Joe Huffman
*Belleville Area
College*
Randy Isaacson
*Indiana University–
South Bend*
Paula Jacobs
Saddlebrook College
Jean Johnson
*Governors State
University*
Irwin Kahn
Ferris State University
Beatrice Kachuk
Brooklyn College
Charles Kaplan
*University of North
Carolina–Charlotte*
Gloria Karin
*State University of
New York–New Paltz*
John E. Keefer
*University of
Pittsburgh*
Nancy Keese
*Tennessee State
University*
Cynthia S. Kelley
*West Virginia University
of Parkersburg*
M. W. Kelly
*Kean College of New
Jersey*
Jennifer Kinsley
*The Ohio State
University*
Kathleen Kleissler
Kutztown University
Eileen Kobrin
Rutgers University
Kurt L. Kraus
University of Maine
Lynn LaVenture
University of Wisconsin
Gail Lawson
Rhode Island College
Jon Leffingwell
*The University of Texas
at Austin*
Izzy Linoner
*St. Mary of the Woods
College*

Leonard Lock
*Pennsylvania State
University*
John Lockney
*New Mexico State
University*
Edward Lonky
*State University of New
York–Oswego*
Linda N. Lucksinger
Schreiner College
Cheri Manning
*Des Moines Area
Community College*
Mary F. Maples
University of Nevada
Peter H. McCandless
Park College
J. Victor Mcguire
Sonoma State University
Mary Ann McLaughlin
*Clarion University of
Pennsylvania*
Linda Melzbe
Lyndon State College
Charles Miron
*Catonsville Community
College*
Lilian Mitchell
Ohio University
Sidney Moon
Purdue University
Lee Morganett
*Indiana University–
Southeast*
Anthony Murphy
*Hillsborough Com-
munity College*
Brian Edward Nicoll
Towson State University
Peter Oliver
University of Hartford
Daniel Olympia
University of Utah
Hagob S. Pambookian
*Shawnee State
University*
Elizabeth M. Penn
Thomas More College
Cummings Piatt
*East Stroudsburg
University*
Beth Mowrer-Popiel
University of Idaho
Jay Pozner
*Jackson Community
College*

Roy Richardson
Montgomery County
Community College
Lawrence R. Rogien
Boise State University
Teri Rollins
Miami University
Kail Ruffner
Kentucky Christian
College
B. Satory
University of Wisconsin–
La Crosse
Geoffrey Scheurman
University of Wisconsin–
River Falls
Beth Silhanek
Marshalltown
Community College
R.E. Simpson
Western Kentucky
University
P. Smeaton
East Stroudsberg
University
Barbara Smith
Radford University
Glenn E. Snelbecker
Temple University

Charles J. Stanley
Florida University
Judith A. Stechly
West Liberty State
University
Jean Strait
Augsburg College
Gary B. Stuck
University of North
Carolina–Chapel Hill
Timothy Sullivan
University of Central
Florida
John J. Sweeder
La Salle University
Gary Taylor
University of Arkansas
J. William Turner
University of North
Texas
Mike Tylo
University of South
Florida
Lani Van Dusen
Utah State University
Jonatha Vare
Winthrop University
Donna Waechter
John Carroll University

Earl Wellborn, Jr.
Missouri Valley College
David Wendler
Martin Luther College
P. Whang
Auburn University
John Wheeler
Southwest Baptist
University
B. D. Whetstone
Birmingham Southern
College
Deborah White
Northwest College
Faye Wisner
Florida Community
College at Jacksonville
Lisa Wolf
Felician College
Jane Wolfle
Bowling Green State
University
Arnold M. Zeagler
New Mexico State
University
O. John Zillman
Concordia University

Many classroom teachers across the country contributed their experience, creativity, and expertise to the *Teachers' Casebook*. I have thoroughly enjoyed my association with these master teachers and I am grateful for the perspective they brought to the book.

Diane Batty, *Orono High School, Orono, Maine*
Suzy L. Boswell, *Pickens County Middle School, Jaspers, Georgia*
Nancy Cambridge, *Orono High School, Orono, Maine*
Constance Carter, *Orono High School, Orono, Maine*
Mary Ellen Casey, *Snug Harbor Community School, Quincy, Massachusetts*
Valerie A. Chilcoat, *Glenmount School, Baltimore, Maryland*
Elizabeth Chouinard, *MacGregor Elementary School, Houston, Texas*
Nicole DePalma Cobb, *Sterling Middle School, Quincy, Massachusetts*
Michael J. Ellis, *Quincy High School, Quincy, Massachusetts*
Aimee Fredette, *Fisher Elementary School, Walpole, Massachusetts*
Fran Garland, *Winship School, Boston, Massachusetts*

Linda Glisson, *St. James Episcopal Day School, Baton Rouge, Louisiana*
Jeff Horton, *Colton School, Colton, Washington*
Jeffrey Hovermill, *Seabury Hall, Makaiwao, Hawaii*
Kelly L. Hoy, *Faber Elementary School, Dunellen, New Jersey*
Mitchell D. Klett, *A. C. New Middle School, Springs, Texas*
Regina M. LaRose, *Hillside School, Needham, Massachusetts*
Peggy McDonnell, *West Park School, Moscow, Idaho*
Sandra T. McNeice, *Sterling Middle School, Quincy, Massachusetts*
Sue Middleton, *St. James Episcopal Day School, Baton Rouge, Louisiana*
Brenda Miller, *Yucca Elementary, Alamogordo, New Mexico*
Thomas O'Donnell, *Malden High School, Malden, Massachusetts*

(continued)

James O'Kelly, *Eisenhower Elementary School, Sayreville, New Jersey*

Allan Osborne, *Snug Harbor Community School, Quincy, Massachusetts*

Mary Phillips, *Orono High School, Orono, Maine*

Katie Piel, *West Park School, Moscow, Idaho*

Martha J. Pond, *Timberlane High School, Plaistow, New Hampshire*

Denise Ready, *Snug Harbor Community School, Quincy, Massachusetts*

Ann Sande, *Henry Viscardi School, Albertson, New York*

Andrea Santoro, *Snug Harbor Community School, Quincy, Massachusetts*

Nancy Sheehan–Melzack, *Snug Harbor Community School, Quincy Massachusetts*

Susan Strauss, *Lincoln High School, Lincoln, Rhode Island*

Trish Sullivan, *Snug Harbor Community School, Quincy, Massachusetts*

Anne Worth, *Clardy School, Kansas City, Missouri*

In a project of this size so many people make essential contributions. Laurie Frankenthaler, Permissions Coordinator, worked diligently to obtain permissions for the material reproduced in this text and the supplements. Susan Duane guided the collection of photographs. The text designer, Debbie Schneck, and cover coordinator, Linda Knowles, made the look of this book the best yet. They make it seem easy to produce a beautiful book—it isn't. Kathy Smith, Editorial Production Services, Susan McIntyre, Production Administrator, and Elaine Ober, Production Manager coordinated all aspects of the project, including the *Annotated Instructor's Edition,* with amazing skill and grace. Somehow they brought order to what could have been chaos and fun to what might have been drudgery. Now the book is in the able hands of Jeff Lasser, Director of Marketing, Kris Farnsworth, Marketing Manager, Lou Kennedy, Director of Advertising, and their staff. I can't wait to see what they are planning for me now! What a talented and creative group—I am honored to work with them all.

On this edition, I was privileged to work with an outstanding editorial group. Bill Barke, President of Allyn and Bacon, brought his distinctive style and leadership to the project, making the effort a pleasure. Sandi Kirshner, Editorial Director, provided wisdom, wit, and encouragement throughout this and the past three revisions. I was once again privileged to work with Nancy Forsyth, Senior Vice-President and Publisher. Her intelligence, creativity, sound judgment, style, and enduring commitment to quality can be seen on every page of this text. She will always have my deepest respect and enduring friendship. Cheryl Ouellette, Editorial Assistant, kept everything running smoothly and kept my fax machine and e-mail humming. On this edition I was fortunate again to have the help of Alicia Reilly, an outstanding developmental editor with just the right combination of knowledge and organizational ability. She guided this revision in all its many aspects, always staying just ahead of whatever had to happen next—remarkable! The supplements package and the excellent pedagogical supports would not exist without her tireless efforts.

Finally, I want to thank my family and friends for their kindness and support during the long days and nights that I worked on this book. Again, to my daughter, Liz, thanks for your insights about teachers and students, shared over the years. You have been my teacher—the source of my greatest joy and deepest sadness. To my family, Anita Wieckert; Marion, Bob, Lucas, Geoffrey, Eric, and Suzie Pratt; Claudia Casser; and Wayne C., Elsie, Wayne K., Kelly, Tom, and Mike Hoy—you are the best.

And finally, to Wayne Hoy, my friend, colleague, inspiration, passion, husband—you have taught me about working, and playing, and living. There will never be enough time to be with you.

Anita Woolfolk Hoy

Educational Psychology

1

Teachers, Teaching, and Educational Psychology

Overview | *What Would You Do?*

WHAT IS GOOD TEACHING? 4
   Inside Five Classrooms | Expert Knowledge

TEACHING: ARTISTRY, TECHNIQUE, AND A LOT OF WORK 8
   Concerns of Beginning Teachers | What about the Students?

THE ROLE OF EDUCATIONAL PSYCHOLOGY 11
   Is It Just Common Sense? | Using Research to Understand and Improve Teaching

THE CONTENTS OF THIS BOOK 16
   A Quick Tour of the Topics | How This Book Can Help You Learn

Summary | *Key Terms* | *Teachers' Casebook: What Would They Do?*

*T*ake a minute to remember the names of the best teachers you ever had, inside or outside a classroom. What was it about these teachers that made you remember them over the years? What effects did they have on you?

If you are like many students, you begin this course with a mixture of anticipation and wariness. Perhaps you are required to take educational psychology as part of a program in teacher education, speech therapy, nursing, or counseling. You may have chosen this class as an elective because you are interested in education or psychology. Whatever your reason for enrolling, you probably have questions about teaching, schools, students—or even about yourself—that you hope this course may answer. I have written the seventh edition of *Educational Psychology* with questions such as these in mind.

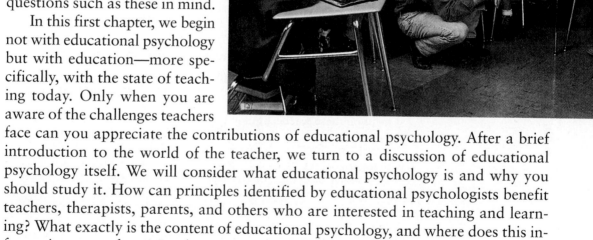

In this first chapter, we begin not with educational psychology but with education—more specifically, with the state of teaching today. Only when you are aware of the challenges teachers face can you appreciate the contributions of educational psychology. After a brief introduction to the world of the teacher, we turn to a discussion of educational psychology itself. We will consider what educational psychology is and why you should study it. How can principles identified by educational psychologists benefit teachers, therapists, parents, and others who are interested in teaching and learning? What exactly is the content of educational psychology, and where does this information come from? By the time you have finished this chapter, you will be in a much better position to answer these questions and many others such as:

- What is good teaching?
- Would teaching be a good career for me?
- What do expert teachers know?
- What are the greatest concerns of beginning teachers?
- Why should I study educational psychology?
- What roles do theory and research play in this field?
- What kinds of problems will the study of educational psychology help me to solve?

What Would You Do?

It is your second year as a teacher at the Riverside Combined Campus (Kindergarten–eighth grade). The district has just received money from the state and a private foundation to give three awards in your school for "excellence in teaching." The principal wants the teachers' recommendations about how to choose the recipients of these awards, so a committee is formed, composed of experienced teachers and one beginner—you. When the principal asked you to serve on the committee, you felt you had to say yes. All week the Teachers' Lounge has been buzzing with discussion about the awards. Some teachers are suspicious— they fear the decisions will be purely political. Others are glad to see teaching honored. Names are mentioned as "sure winners" and a few teachers who seldom speak to you have become very friendly ever since the committee membership was announced. It's clear that the job of determining how to choose winners will not be as easy as you had hoped. The first meeting is next week. How will you prepare for it?

- What do you need to know about teaching to complete this task?

- What are some indicators of excellent teaching? Do different philosophies of teaching provide different answers to this question?

- What are your recommendations, and how would you back them up?

Describing teachers who made a difference in his life, Harvard professor Robert Coles (1990) said:

> I mention these teachers in my life because, in fact, they continue to be a great big part of it still. Their voices are in my head and are part of my voice, I am sure. Their thoughts and values inform what I consider and call my own thoughts and values. Their example—the things they did, the style of their teaching, the strategies they employed—continue to inform the way I work. . . .
>
> In a sense, then, all good teachers rescue us from the death of boredom, apathy, self-preoccupation, and self-satisfaction: the teacher as an intellectual and moral life saver who fortunately has come our way and, of course, the teacher as one who is rescued by rescuing others. (p. 59)

What Is Good Teaching?

There are hundreds of answers to this question, including ideas based on your own experience. This question has been examined by educators, psychologists, philosophers, novelists, journalists, mathematicians, scientists, historians, policy makers, and parents, to name only a few groups. And good teaching is not confined to classrooms—it occurs in homes and hospitals, museums and sales meetings, therapists' offices and summer camps. In this book, we are primarily concerned with teaching in classrooms, but much of what you will learn applies to other settings as well.

Inside Five Classrooms

To begin our examination of good teaching, let's step inside the classrooms of several outstanding teachers. All the situations that follow are real. The first two teachers worked with my student teachers in local elementary schools. I have chosen them because one of my former colleagues at Rutgers, Carol Weinstein, has written about them in her book on classroom management (Weinstein & Mignano, 1997). The next three are secondary-school teachers who have been studied by other educational psychologists.

A Bilingual First Grade. There are 25 students in Viviana's class. Most have recently emigrated from the Dominican Republic; the rest come from Nicaragua, Mexico, Puerto Rico, and Honduras. Even though the children speak little or no English when they begin school, by the time they leave in June, Viviana has helped them master the normal first-grade curriculum for their district. She accomplishes this by teaching in Spanish early in the year to aid understanding, then gradually introducing English as the students are ready. Viviana does not want her students segregated or labeled as disadvantaged. She encourages them to take pride in their Spanish-speaking heritage while using every available opportunity to support their developing English proficiency.

Viviana's expectations for her students are high, and she makes sure the students have the resources they need. She provides materials—pencils, scissors, crayons—so no child lacks the means to learn. And she supplies constant encouragement. "Viviana's commitment to her students is evident in her first-grade bilingual classroom. With an energy level that is rare, she motivates, prods, instructs, models, praises, and captivates her students. . . . The pace is brisk and Viviana clearly has a flair for the dramatic; she uses music, props, gestures, facial expressions, and shifts in voice tone to communicate the material" (Weinstein & Mignano, 1997, p. 13).

Viviana's expectations for herself are high as well. She continually expands her knowledge of teaching through graduate work and participation in special training programs. To know more about her students each year, she spends hours in their homes. For Viviana, teaching is a not just a job; it is a way of life.

A Suburban Sixth Grade. Ken teaches sixth grade in a suburban elementary school in central New Jersey. Ken emphasizes "process writing." His students complete first drafts, discuss them with others in the class, revise, edit, and "publish" their work. The students also keep daily journals and often use these to share personal concerns with Ken. They tell him of problems at home, fights, and fears; he always takes the time to respond in writing. The study of science is also placed in the context of the real world. The students use a National Geographic Society computer network to link with other schools in order to identify acid rain patterns around the world. For social studies, the class played two simulation games that focused on the first half of the 1800s. They "lived" as trappers collecting animal skins, and as pioneers heading west to search for gold.

Throughout the year Ken is very interested in the social and emotional development of his students—he wants them to learn about responsibility and fairness as well as science and social studies. This concern is evident in the way he develops his class rules at the beginning of the year. Rather than specifying dos and don'ts, Ken and his students devise a "Bill of Rights" for the class, describing the rights of the students and of the teacher. These rights cover most of the situations that might need a "rule."

An Inner-City Middle School. Another excellent teacher is described in the *Harvard Education Letter.*

> Robert Moses, founder of the Algebra Project at the Martin Luther King School in Cambridge, Massachusetts, teaches students the concept of number and sign through a physical event: they go for a ride on a subway. Choosing one subway stop as a starting point, students relate inbound and outbound to positive and negative numbers. They translate their subway ride into mathematical language by considering both the number of stops and their direction. By giving students such experiences before introducing the formal language of algebra, Moses . . . has made math more enjoyable and accessible. (Ruopp & Driscoll, 1990, p. 5)

Two Advanced Math Classes. Hilda Borko and Carol Livingston (1989) describe two expert secondary-school mathematics teachers. In one lesson for her advanced mathematics class, Ellen had her students identify any three problems about ellipses from their text. She asked if there were any questions or uncertainties about these problems. Ellen answered student questions, worked two of the problems, and then used the three problems to derive all the concepts and equations the students needed to understand the material. Ellen's knowledge of the subject and of her students was so thorough that she could create the explanations and derive the formulas on the spot, no matter which problems the students chose.

Another teacher, Randy, worked with his students' confusion to construct a review lesson about strategies for doing integrals. When one student said that a particular section in the book seemed "haphazard," Randy led the class through a process of organizing the material. He asked the class for general statements about useful strategies for doing integrals. He clarified their suggestions, elaborated on some, and helped students improve others. He asked the students to tie their ideas to passages in the text. Even though he accepted all reasonable suggestions, he listed only the key strategies on the board. By the end of the period, the students had transformed the disorganized material from the book into an ordered and useful outline to guide their learning. They also had a better idea about how to read and understand difficult material.

What do you see in these classrooms? The teachers are committed to their students. They must deal with a wide range of student abilities and challenges: different languages, different home lives, different needs. These teachers must understand their subjects and their students' thinking so well that they can spontaneously create new examples and explanations when students are confused. They must make the most abstract concepts, such as negative numbers, real and understandable for their particular students. And then there is the challenge of new technologies and techniques. The teachers must use them appropriately to accomplish important goals, not just to entertain the students. The whole time that these experts are navigating through the academic material, they also are taking care of the emotional needs of their students, propping up sagging self-esteem and encouraging responsibility. If we followed these individuals from the first day of class, we would see that they carefully plan and teach the basic procedures for living and learning in their classes. They can efficiently correct and collect homework, regroup students, give directions, distribute materials, collect lunch money, and deal with disruptions—do all of this while also making a mental note to check why one of their students is so tired.

Viviana, Ken, Robert, Ellen, and Randy are examples of **expert teachers,** the focus of much recent research in education and psychology. For another perspective on the question "What is good teaching?" let's examine this research on what expert teachers know.

Expert Knowledge

Expert teachers have elaborate *systems of knowledge* for understanding problems in teaching. For example, when a beginning teacher is faced with students' wrong answers on math or history tests, all the wrong answers may seem about the same—wrong. The inexperienced teacher may have trouble connecting other facts or ideas with the students' wrong answers. But for an expert teacher, wrong answers are part of a rich system of knowledge that could include how to recognize several types of wrong answers, the misunderstanding or lack of information behind each kind of mistake, the best way to reteach and correct the misunderstanding, materials and activities that have worked in the past, and several ways to test whether the reteaching was successful (Floden & Klinzing, 1990; Leinhardt, 1988). Peterson and Comeaux (1989) argue that it is the quality of teachers' professional knowledge and their ability to be aware of their own thinking that make them expert.

What do expert teachers know that allows them to be so successful? Lee Shulman (1987) has studied this question, and he has identified seven areas of professional knowledge. Expert teachers know:

1. The academic subjects they teach.

2. General teaching strategies that apply in all subjects (such as the principles of classroom management, effective teaching, and evaluation that you will discover in this book).

3. The curriculum materials and programs appropriate for their subject and grade level.

4. Subject-specific knowledge for teaching: special ways of teaching certain students and particular concepts, such as the best ways to explain negative numbers to lower-ability students.

5. The characteristics and cultural backgrounds of learners.

6. The settings in which students learn—pairs, small groups, teams, classes, schools, and the community.

7. The goals and purposes of teaching.

This is quite a list. Obviously, one course cannot give you all the information you need to teach. In fact, a whole program of courses won't make you an expert. That takes time and experience. But studying educational psychology can add to your professional knowledge. In this book we will focus on general teaching strategies, the characteristics of students, and settings for learning. We will also touch on learning goals and subject-specific knowledge for teaching.

Expert Teachers Experienced, effective teachers who have developed solutions for common classroom problems. Their knowledge of teaching process and content is extensive and well organized.

Expert teachers not only know the content of the subjects they teach, they also know how to relate this content to the world outside the classroom and how to keep students involved in learning.

How do you grow from beginning teacher to expert? Can you learn to be an expert teacher, or are really great teachers just born? Is good teaching an art or a science? Answers to this last question provide another perspective on good teaching.

Teaching: Artistry, Technique, and a Lot of Work

Because researchers have identified a number of effective teaching techniques, some educators argue that all teachers should learn these practices and be tested on them to earn or to keep their teaching certificates. Other educators believe that the mark of an excellent teacher is not the ability to apply techniques but the artistry of being **reflective**—thoughtful and inventive—about teaching (Schon, 1983). Educators who adopt this view tend to be more concerned with how teachers plan, solve problems, create instruction, and make decisions than they are with the specific techniques teachers apply. They believe teaching is a complicated, demanding activity that requires creative thinking and a commitment to lifelong learning (Borko, 1989; Peterson & Comeaux, 1989).

Most people agree that teachers must be both technically competent and inventive. They must be able to use a range of strategies, and they must also be able to invent new strategies. They must have some simple routines that work for managing classes, but they must also be willing and able to break from the routine when the situation calls for change. New problems arise all the time, and when the old solutions do not work, something else is needed.

With the growing understanding that teaching is a complex problem-solving activity has come a call to give teachers more freedom and responsibility. A number of educational reform movements seek to involve teachers in designing the curriculum and making the decisions for their own students, as you can see in the Point/Counterpoint section.

You may be thinking that all this talk about expert teachers and expert knowledge, artistry, and technique is a bit idealistic and abstract. Right now, you may have other, more down-to-earth, concerns about becoming a teacher. You are not alone!

Concerns of Beginning Teachers

Reflective Thoughtful and inventive. Reflective teachers think back over situations to analyze what they did and why and to consider how they might improve learning for their students.

Beginning teachers everywhere share many concerns. A review of studies conducted around the world found that beginning teachers regard maintaining classroom discipline, motivating students, accommodating differences among students, evaluating student work, and dealing with parents as the most serious challenges they face. Many teachers also experience what has been called "reality shock" when they take their first job and confront the "harsh and rude reality of everyday classroom life" (Veenman, 1984, p. 143). One source of shock may be that teachers really cannot ease into their responsibilities. On the first day of their first job, beginning teachers face the same tasks as teachers with years of experience. Student teaching, while a critical element, does not really prepare prospective teachers for starting off a school year with a new

POINT COUNTERPOINT

Whose Classroom Is It Anyway?

The Carnegie Forum on Education and the Economy report, *A Nation Prepared: Teachers for the 21st Century* (1986), introduced a new word to the vocabulary of educational reform—*restructuring*. The report argued that we must "restructure schools to provide a professional environment for teachers, freeing [teachers] to decide how to best meet the state and local goals for children" (p. 57). Is this recommendation becoming a reality? Is the structure of schools changing so teachers can use their expertise in deciding how to teach their students?

POINT　Teachers have a bigger say.

The National Governors' Association, the National Education Association, and the National Association of Secondary School Principals have issued reports supporting teacher participation in school decisions. The National Governors' Association (1989) states that restructuring should involve (1) modifying curriculum to support higher-order thinking and problem solving, creativity, and cooperation; (2) bringing together teachers, administrators, and parents at each school to make instructional decisions; (3) creating new staff roles to make better use of the teachers' expertise; and (4) holding schools accountable for students' achievement.

The April 1990 issue of *Educational Leadership* describes many elementary and secondary schools that have radically altered curriculum, decision-making, roles, and accountability systems. For example, the staff of Central Park East Secondary School decided to limit the number of class periods for its students to allow more in-depth study:

A typical week for students in grades 7–10, for example, includes several two-hour blocks of humanities and math-science, daily one-hour classes in Spanish, two to three hours of community service, and several advisory periods. During an extended lunch period and after school, students may participate in clubs, music, physical education, sports, and other activities. (O'Neil, 1990b, p. 7)

In 119 Dade County, Florida, schools, administrator/teacher/parent councils have been created to redesign the schools. Three of the innovations established by these councils are Saturday classes providing extra help, enrichment, and even ballet instruction; satellite schools in local businesses; and lead teachers who receive extra pay to support and guide their colleagues.

COUNTERPOINT　Restructuring is not working.

In 1987 the Carnegie Foundation for the Advancement of Teaching surveyed teachers across the United States to see if they felt involved in decisions at their schools. Most teachers—about 79 percent—participated in choosing textbooks, and a good number (63 percent) felt they were involved in shaping the curriculum. But only 47 percent helped to set standards for students' behavior, only 43 percent participated in designing staff development programs, and a mere 20 percent had a say in school budgets.

Some researchers suggest that teachers must be so focused on their classrooms and students that they have little time or energy for participating in schoolwide decisions (Lortie, 1977). Other researchers suggest that teachers and administrators have a kind of agreement not to interfere in each other's "territory." In return for leaving school-level decisions to the administrators, teachers get to be autonomous in their classrooms (Corwin, 1981). Some critics fear that restructuring will require teachers to take on more responsibilities without giving them more time or resources to meet these new obligations (Conley, 1991).

Evidently, the problems persist. David Clark and Terry Astuto (1994) ask these questions about restructuring schools so that teachers are more involved in making decisions about their individual students:

Why do we focus on implementing site-based management systems for high schools while we retain the daily schedule of six to eight 50-minute class periods, which ensures that most high school teachers will never get to know about the lives of the 150 to 200 students whom they see each day? Does anyone believe that such an organizational structure provides the time for English teachers to tutor their students in writing? . . . Or that it provides an opportunity for individualized instruction and counseling? (p. 514)

Teaching is one of the few professions in which a new teacher is expected to assume all the responsibilities of an experienced "pro" during the first week on the job. Veteran teachers can be a source of support and guidance to new teachers during these early weeks.

class. And schools usually offer little chance for helpful contact between novice and experienced teachers, making mutual support and assistance difficult. If you have had any of these concerns, you shouldn't be troubled. It comes with the job of being a beginning teacher (Calderhead & Robson, 1991; Cooke & Pang, 1991; Veenman, 1984).

With experience, however, most teachers meet the challenges that seem difficult for beginners. They have more time to experiment with new methods or materials. Finally, as confidence grows, seasoned teachers can focus on the students' needs. Are my students learning? Are they developing positive attitudes? Is this the best way to teach the slower learners to write a persuasive essay? At this advanced stage, teachers judge their success by the successes of their students (Feiman-Nemser, 1983; Fuller 1969).

What about the Students?

I have talked about good teachers because that is what many of you are planning to become. But all good teaching begins with an understanding of students and learning. As you will see throughout this text, today there is great interest in studying how people understand and apply knowledge. Just as educational psychologists have investigated how expertise develops in teaching, they have also explored how students come to be experts in particular subjects. Many of the chapters in this book are concerned with these issues.

Focus on...

Good Teaching

- What are some of the characteristics of expert teachers?
- What aspects of teachers' professional knowledge can you hope to develop by studying educational psychology?
- How are your concerns about teaching similar to or different from those reported in studies of beginning teachers?

I tell my class the first day of the semester that I hope they will "take educational psychology personally." By this I mean I want them to apply the ideas to their own lives as students. If you can become a more expert learner by applying the knowledge from this text about study strategies, motivation, active learning, and understanding, then you will be a better teacher as well. Years ago a wonderful principal told me that teachers are the *professional learners* and students are the *amateurs*. She encouraged the teachers in her school to be good guides and learning coaches so that their students would become expert learners too.

Of course, all experts were once beginners. How can educational psychology give you a basis for being an expert learner now and a good beginning teacher in the future?

The Role of Educational Psychology

We begin our consideration of the role of educational psychology by defining the term. For as long as educational psychology has existed—about 90 years—there have been debates about what it really is. Some people believe educational psychology is simply knowledge gained from psychology and applied to the activities of the classroom. Others believe it involves applying the methods of psychology to study classroom and school life (Clifford, 1984a; Grinder, 1981).

The view generally accepted today is that **educational psychology is a distinct discipline with its own theories, research methods, problems, and techniques.** "Educational psychology is distinct from other branches of psychology because it has the understanding and improvement of education as its primary goal" (Wittrock, 1992, p. 138). Educational psychologists "study what people think and do [I would add *feel*] as they teach and learn a particular curriculum in a particular environment where education and training are intended to take place" (Berliner, 1992, p. 145). Merle Wittrock sums it up well, saying that educational psychology focuses on "the psychological study of the everyday problems of education, from which one derives principles, models, theories, teaching procedures, and practical methods of instruction and evaluation, as well as research methods, statistical analyses, and measurement and assessment procedures appropriate for studying the thinking and affective processes of learners and the socially and culturally complex processes of schools." But are the findings of educational psychologists really that helpful for teachers? After all, most teaching is just common sense, isn't it? Let's take a few minutes to examine these questions.

Is It Just Common Sense?

In many cases, the principles set forth by educational psychologists—after spending much thought, research, and money—sound pathetically obvious. People are tempted to say, and usually do say, "Everyone knows that!" Consider these examples:

Taking Turns. What method should a teacher use in selecting students to participate in a primary-grade reading class?

Educational Psychology The discipline concerned with teaching and learning processes; applies the methods and theories of psychology and has its own as well.

Common Sense Answer.   Teachers should call on students randomly so that everyone will have to follow the lesson carefully. If a teacher were to use the same order every time, the students would know when their turn was coming up.

Answer Based on Research.   Research by Ogden, Brophy, and Evertson (1977) indicates that the answer to this question is not so simple. In first-grade reading classes, for example, going around the circle in order and giving each child a chance to read led to better overall achievement than calling on students randomly. The critical factor in going around the circle may be that each child gets a chance to participate. Without some system for calling on everyone, many students can be overlooked or skipped. Research suggests there are better alternatives for teaching reading than going around the circle, but if teachers choose this alternative, they should make sure that everyone has the chance for practice and feedback (Tierney, Readence, & Dishner, 1990).

Classroom Management.   Students are engaged in an appropriate and educationally meaningful task, but still, some students are repeatedly out of their seats without permission, wandering around the room. What should the teacher do?

Common Sense Answer.   Each time they get up, the teacher should remind students to remain in their seats. These repeated reminders will help overactive students remember the rule. If the teacher does not remind them and lets them get away with breaking the rules, both the out-of-seat students and the rest of the class may decide the teacher is not really serious about the rule.

Answer Based on Research.   In a now-classic study, Madsen, Becker, Thomas, Koser, and Plager (1968) found that the more a teacher told students to sit down when they were out of their seats, the more often the students got out of their seats without permission. When the teacher ignored students who were out of their seats and praised students who were sitting down, the rate of out-of-seat behavior dropped greatly. When the teacher returned to the previous system of telling students to sit down, the rate of out-of-seat behavior increased once again. It seems that—at least under some conditions—the more a teacher says "Sit down!" the more the students stand up!

Skipping Grades.   Should a school encourage exceptionally bright students to skip grades or to enter college early?

Common Sense Answer.   No! Very intelligent students who are a year or two younger than their classmates are likely to be social misfits. They are neither physically nor emotionally ready for dealing with older students and would be miserable in the social situations that are so important in school, especially in the later grades.

Answer Based on Research.   Maybe. According to Samuel Kirk and his colleagues (1993), "From early admissions to school to early admissions to college, research studies invariably report that children who have been accelerated have adjusted as well as or better than have children of similar ability who have not been accelerated" (p. 105). Whether acceleration is the best solution for a student depends on many specific individual characteristics, including the intelligence and maturity of the student, and on the other available options. For some students, moving quickly through the material and working in advanced courses with older students is a very good idea.

Lily Wong (1987) demonstrated that just seeing research results in writing can make them seem obvious. She selected 12 findings from research on teaching; one of them was the "taking turns" result noted above. She presented six of the findings in their correct form and six in *exactly the opposite form* to college students and to experienced teachers. Both the college students and teachers rated about half of the *wrong* findings as "obviously" correct. In a follow-up study, another group of subjects was shown the 12 findings and their opposites and was asked to pick which ones were correct. For 8 of the 12 findings, the subjects chose the wrong result more often than the right one.

You may have thought that educational psychologists spend their time discovering the obvious. The examples above point out the danger of this kind of thinking. When a principle is stated in simple terms, it can sound simplistic. A similar phenomenon takes place when we see a gifted dancer or athlete perform; the well-trained performer makes it look easy. But we see only the results of the training, not all the work that went into mastering the individual movements. And bear in mind that any research finding—or its opposite—may sound like common sense. The issue is not what *sounds* sensible, but what is demonstrated when the principle is put to the test (Gage, 1991).

Using Research to Understand and Improve Teaching

Conducting research to test possible answers is one of two major tasks of educational psychology. The other is combining the results of various studies into theories that attempt to present a unified view of such things as teaching, learning, and development.

Descriptive Research. Educational psychologists design and conduct many different kinds of research studies in their attempts to understand teaching and learning. Some of these studies are "descriptive," that is, their purpose is simply to describe events in a particular class or several classes. Reports of **descriptive research** often include survey results, interview responses, samples of actual classroom dialogue, or records of the class activities.

One descriptive approach, classroom **ethnography,** is borrowed from anthropology. Ethnographic methods involve studying the naturally occurring events in the life of a group and trying to understand the meaning of these events to the people involved. For example, the descriptions of expert high school mathematics teachers in the opening pages of this chapter were taken from an ethnographic study by Hilda Borko and Carol Livingston (1989). The researchers made detailed observations in the teachers' classes and analyzed these observations, along with audio recordings and information from interviews with the teachers, in order to describe differences between novice and expert teachers.

In some descriptive research, researchers carefully analyze videotapes of classes to identify recurring patterns of teacher and student behaviors. In other

Descriptive Research Studies that collect detailed information about specific situations, often using observation, surveys, interviews, recordings, or a combination of these methods.

Ethnography A descriptive approach to research that focuses on life within a group and tries to understand the meaning of events to the people involved.

These students are conducting field observations and measurements as part of a science lesson. What will they learn using this approach? Can research shed light on this question?

studies, the researcher uses **participant observation** and works within the class or school to understand the actions from the perspectives of the teacher and the students. Researchers also may employ case studies. A **case study** investigates in depth how a teacher plans courses, for example, or how a student tries to learn specific material.

Correlations.   Often the results of descriptive studies include reports of correlations. We will take a minute to examine this concept, because you will encounter many correlations in the coming chapters. A **correlation** is a number that indicates both the strength and the direction of a relationship between two events or measurements. Correlations range from 1.00 to –1.00. The closer the correlation is to either 1.00 or –1.00, the stronger the relationship. For example, the correlation between height and weight is about .70 (a strong relationship); the correlation between height and number of languages spoken is about .00 (no relationship at all).

The sign of the correlation tells the direction of the relationship. A **positive correlation** indicates that the two factors increase or decrease together. As one gets larger, so does the other. Height and weight are positively correlated because greater height tends to be associated with greater weight. A **negative correlation** means that increases in one factor are related to decreases in the other. For example, the correlation between outside temperature and the weight of clothing worn is negative, since people tend to wear clothing of increasing weight as the temperature decreases.

It is important to note that correlations do not prove cause and effect (see Figure 1.1). Height and weight are correlated—taller people tend to weigh more than shorter people. But gaining weight obviously does not cause you to grow taller. Knowing a person's height simply allows you to make a general prediction about that person's weight. Educational psychologists identify correlations so they can make predictions about important events in the classroom.

FIGURE 1.1

Correlations Do Not Show Causation

When research shows that broken homes and crime are correlated, it does not show causation. Poverty, a third variable, may be the cause of both crime and broken homes.

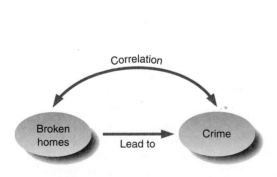

Faulty Assumption

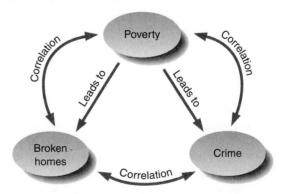

More Likely Assumption

Experimentation.   A second type of research—experimentation—allows educational psychologists to go beyond predictions and actually study cause and effect. Instead of just observing and describing an existing situation, the investigators introduce changes and note the results. First, a number of comparable groups of subjects are created. In psychological research, the term **subjects** generally refers to the people being studied—such as teachers or eighth graders—not to subjects like math or science. One common way to make sure that groups of subjects are essentially the same is to assign each subject to a group using a random procedure. **Random** means each subject has an equal chance to be in any group.

In one or more of these groups, the experimenters change some aspect of the situation to see if this change or "treatment" has an expected effect. The results in each group are then compared. Usually statistical tests are conducted to see if the differences between the groups are significant. When differences are described as **statistically significant,** it means that they probably did not happen simply by chance. A number of the studies we will examine attempt to identify cause-and-effect relationships by asking questions such as this: If teachers ignore students who are out of their seats without permission and praise students who are working hard at their desks (cause), will students spend more time working at their desks (effect)?

In many cases, both descriptive and experimental research occur together. The study by Ogden, Brophy, and Evertson (1977) described at the beginning of this section is a good example. In order to answer questions about the relationship between how students are selected to read in a primary-grade class and their achievement in reading, these investigators first observed students and teachers in a number of classrooms and then measured the reading achievement of the students. They found that having students read in a predictable order was associated, or correlated, with gains in reading scores. With a simple correlation such as this, however, the researchers could not be sure that the strategy was actually causing the effect. In the second part of the study, Ogden and her colleagues asked several teachers to call on each student in turn. They then compared reading achievement in these groups with achievement in groups where teachers used other strategies. This second part of the research was thus an experimental study.

Theories for Teaching.   The major goal of educational psychology is understanding teaching and learning, and research is a primary tool. Reaching this goal is a slow process; there are very few landmark studies that answer a question once and for all. Human beings are too complicated. Instead, research in educational psychology examines limited aspects of a situation—perhaps a few variables at a time or life in one or two classrooms. If enough studies are completed in a certain area and findings repeatedly point to the same conclusions, we eventually arrive at a **principle.** This is the term for an established relationship between two or more factors—between a certain teaching strategy, for example, and student achievement.

Another tool for building a better understanding of the teaching and learning processes is **theory.** The common sense notion of theory (as in "Oh well, it was only a theory") is "a guess or hunch." But the scientific meaning of theory is quite different. "A theory in science is an interrelated set of concepts that

---

Participant Observation A method for conducting descriptive research in which the researcher becomes a participant in the situation in order to better understand life in that group.

Case Study Intensive study of one person or one situation.

Correlation Statistical description of how closely two variables are related.

Positive Correlation A relationship between two variables in which the two increase or decrease together. Example: calorie intake and weight gain.

Negative Correlation A relationship between two variables in which a high value on one is associated with a low value on the other. Example: height and distance from top of head to the ceiling.

Experimentation Research method in which variables are manipulated and the effects recorded.

Subjects People or animals studied.

Random Without any definite pattern; following no rule.

Statistically Significant Not likely to be a chance occurrence.

Principle Established relationship between factors.

Theory Integrated statement of principles that attempts to explain a phenomenon and make predictions.

is used to explain a body of data and to make predictions about the results of future experiments" (Stanovich, 1992, p. 21). Given a number of established principles, educational psychologists have developed explanations for the relationships among many variables and even whole systems of relationships. There are theories to explain how language develops, how differences in intelligence occur, and, as noted earlier, how people learn.

Few theories explain and predict perfectly. In this book, you will see many examples of educational psychologists taking different theoretical positions and disagreeing on the overall explanations of such issues as learning and motivation. Because no one theory offers all the answers, it makes sense to consider what each has to offer.

So why, you may ask, is it necessary to deal with theories? Why not just stick to principles? The answer is that both are useful. Principles of classroom management, for example, will give you help with specific problems. A good theory of classroom management, on the other hand, will give you a new way of thinking about discipline problems; it will give you tools for creating solutions to many different problems and for predicting what might work in new situations. A major goal of this book is to provide you with the best and the most useful theories for teaching—those that have solid evidence behind them. Although you may prefer some theories over others, consider them all as ways of understanding the challenges teachers face.

> **Focus on . . .**
>
> ### Educational Psychology
>
> - What is your definition of educational psychology?
> - What would you say to someone who asserts that "teaching is just common sense"?
> - What methods are used to study learning and teaching in educational psychology?

The Contents of This Book

Now that we have explored the role of theory and research, let us turn to a consideration of the topics studied by educational psychologists.

A Quick Tour of the Topics

At the heart of educational psychology is a concern with learning wherever it occurs—in classrooms and corporations, in the military, and in medical internships, wherever people strive to become more knowledgeable and competent. No person can learn for another; students create their own knowledge and skills. The teacher's role is to orchestrate materials, tasks, environments, conversations, and explorations that encourage and support learning and the increasing independence of their students.

Parts One and Two of this text focus on the students. In Part One, we examine the ways in which students develop. Because children may differ from adolescents and adults in their thinking, language, and images about themselves, they may require different kinds of teaching. As a teacher, you will want to take into account the mental, physical, emotional, and social abilities and limitations of your students.

Part Two explores how children differ in their abilities, previous learning, learning styles, and in the ways that they have been prepared for schools by their cultural experiences. Classrooms today are becoming more and more diverse. Teachers are expected to work with students with learning disabilities and visual or hearing impairments, for example, and with both the retarded and the gifted. And most classrooms today are multicultural, with students who speak different languages and come from a variety of cultural backgrounds. Teachers must be able to recognize, respect, and adapt to these individual and group differences and to create classroom communities that allow students to belong and to thrive.

Having introduced the students, we will move to one of the most important topics in both educational psychology and the classroom: human learning. Part Three explores the three main approaches to the study of learning, behavioral, information processing, and constructivist perspectives. We will also see how these approaches can be applied in a number of very practical ways, including strategies for teaching and classroom management and instruction in various subject areas. An understanding of how students learn is the basis for teachers' professional knowledge about both general and specific teaching strategies.

Having covered the dual foundations of teaching—the students and the processes of learning—we can concentrate in Parts Four and Five on actual practice. Part Four examines theories of motivation and their applications to teaching. There is no learning without attention and engagement, so teachers and students must understand and incorporate the motivational factors that support active, engaged, independent learning. Because most learning and teaching happen in groups, we will examine how to organize and manage a classroom full of active learners. And because teachers deal with individuals as well as groups, we will spend some time discussing communication and interpersonal relationships. In this Part, we also look at instruction from two perspectives: a teacher-focused view that emphasizes the teacher's role in planning, providing, and monitoring instruction, and a student-centered view that emphasizes the students' active construction of understanding. Teachers owe it to their students to design powerful environments for learning, so the teachers must understand how different approaches can influence students' learning.

In Part Five, we consider how to evaluate what has been taught. Because to learn is to become more knowledgeable and competent, teachers must have at their disposal ways to assess knowledge and competence in order to guide students and give them useful information so they can guide themselves. We will look at standardized tests, teacher-made tests, grading systems, and various alternatives to the traditional systems of evaluation and grading.

How This Book Can Help You Learn

Earlier, I encouraged you to "take this book personally"—to use it to learn more about learning, motivation, goal setting, studying, test-taking, and self-regulation so you can apply the knowledge to your life now. In addition, if you are a teacher or prospective teacher, I have written the text to help you build a knowledge base for teaching. The structure as well as the content support learning. Here is how you might use the different elements of the book to help you develop a base of knowledge for use as a student now and always and as a teacher later.

Getting Ready to Learn.   Each chapter begins with several features to help you get ready for learning. You are asked several questions to start you thinking about a topic related to the chapter. Your answers may bring to mind information you already know about the topics in the chapter. You will soon see that all learning begins with what students already know and believe. The chapter *Outline* and the *Overview* give you a snapshot of the organization of the material to come. Next you encounter a *"What would you do?"* scenario, asking you to project yourself into a classroom and decide how you would handle a problem situation. As you consider possible actions, you will be confronting issues from the upcoming chapter. So, as you read the chapter, you can check out and perhaps expand your ideas for handling the situation. Reading with a purpose in mind aids comprehension. I hope the "What would you do?" problem gives you good reasons and purposes for reading that tie knowledge in educational psychology to classroom practice.

Aids to Understanding.   Throughout the chapters, you will find other aids to understanding and application. Use them fully to get the most from this book. Notice the headings and subheadings as you read. These headings show the structure of the chapter, the main ideas and the related ideas under each main idea. Key terms are highlighted in bold and defined in the margin the first time they are used. There is a list of key terms at the end of each chapter. When you finish reading, test yourself to see if you can briefly explain these terms in your own words. Also, after each main section of the chapter are *"Focus on"* boxes, asking you to check your understanding of higher-level principles. At the end of the chapter are a *Summary* and several other scenarios. *Check your understanding*—asks you to use the ideas from the chapters you have read (and from other courses) to solve problems of practice.

Applying Knowledge.   If the ideas in this book are to be valuable, they need to be used to think about and act on problems of teaching and learning—both your own and those of your students. That emphasis is clear at the beginning of each chapter when I ask you to consider, *"What would you do?"* Throughout every chapter after this one are *Guidelines,* principles that can be applied in teaching. Each principle includes a few examples. These examples are intended to encourage your thinking about applications. One set of Guidelines focuses on families as partners in teaching—a very important consideration today. Every chapter also contains a *Point/Counterpoint* debate about a critical issue in educational psychology. You will see that educators do not always agree about the meaning of research findings or how those findings should be applied. Finally, at the end of every chapter we return to the "What would you do?" situation to see what several experienced teachers around the country would do. Compare your ideas with theirs and with the information in the chapter. Do you agree? What would you add?

The study of educational psychology involves both content and process. The content of facts, principles, and theories adds to the store of your professional knowledge for teaching. The process aspect of educational psychology helps you think critically about teaching so you can become a researcher on your own effectiveness.

Becoming a Good Beginning Teacher.   Becoming an expert teacher takes time and experience, but you can start now by becoming a good beginner. You can develop a repertoire of effective principles and practices for your first years of teaching so that some activities quickly become automatic. You can also develop the habit of questioning and analyzing these accepted practices and your own teaching so you can solve new problems when they arise. You can learn to look behind the effective techniques identified in research to ask: Why did this approach work with these students? What else might be as good or better? The answers to these questions and your ability to analyze the situations are much more important than the specific techniques themselves. As you ask and answer questions, you will be refining your personal theories of teaching.

My goal in writing this book is to help you become an excellent beginning teacher, one who can both apply and improve many techniques. Even more important, I hope this book will cause you to think about students and teaching in new ways, so you will have the foundation for becoming an expert as you gain experience.

SUMMARY

In this introductory chapter we have examined good teaching by looking in the classrooms of expert teachers and considering the research on what distinguishes experts from beginners. There was also an overview of the field of educational psychology.

What Is Good Teaching?

It takes time and experience to become an expert teacher. These teachers have a rich store of well-organized knowledge about the many specific situations of teaching. This includes knowledge about the subjects they teach, their students, general teaching strategies, subject-specific ways of teaching, settings for learning, curriculum materials, and the goals of education.

Teaching is both an art and a science. Effective teaching requires an understanding of research findings on learning and instruction and knowledge of effective techniques and routines. Teaching also calls for the creativity, talent, and judgment of an artist.

Learning to teach is a gradual process. The concerns and problems of teachers change as they progress. During the beginning years, attention tends to be focused on survival. Maintaining discipline, motivating students, evaluating students' work, and dealing with parents are universal concerns for beginning teachers. The more experienced teacher can move on to concerns about professional growth and effectiveness with a wide range of students.

Becoming a good teacher means being a good learner. Much of the information in this text will help you become a more expert learner if you take the ideas personally and apply them to your own life.

The Role of Educational Psychology

The goals of educational psychology are to understand and to improve the teaching and learning processes. Educational psychologists develop knowledge and methods; they also use the knowledge and methods of psychology and other related disciplines to study learning and teaching in everyday situations.

Both descriptive studies and experimental research can provide valuable information for teachers. Correlations allow you to predict events that are likely to occur in the classroom; experimental studies can indicate cause-and-effect relationships and should help you implement useful changes.

Educational psychology involves content and process. The findings from research offer a number of possible answers to specific problems, and the theories offer perspectives for analyzing almost any situation that may arise. The process of analyzing research and theory will encourage you to think critically about teaching.

KEY TERMS

case study, p. 14
correlation, p. 14
descriptive research, p. 13
educational psychology, p. 11
ethnography, p. 13
experimentation, p. 15

expert teachers, p. 7
negative correlation, p. 14
participant observation, p. 14
positive correlation, p. 14
principle, p. 15

random, p.15
reflective, p. 8
statistically significant, p. 15
subjects, p. 15
theory, p. 15

What Would They Do?

It is your second year as a teacher at the Riverside Combined Campus (Kindergarten–eighth grade). The district has just received money from the state and a private foundation to give three awards in your school for "excellence in teaching." The principal wants the teachers' recommendations about how to choose the recipients of these awards, so a committee is formed, composed of experienced teachers and one beginner—you. The first meeting is next week. How will you prepare?

DENISE READY

Second Grade Teacher
Snug Harbor Community School, Quincy, Massachusetts

There are many qualities that contribute to excellent teaching. Different philosophical teaching backgrounds bring a variety of what would be considered valuable teaching assets. Teachers with different philosophies each have individual opinions as to what they view as "quality teaching." The job of the committee members would be to take the values agreed on and use them as a measurement to determine who should receive the award.

My preparation for this meeting would have been to come up with the following list of what I believe are indicators of excellent teaching. An excellent teacher:

- Loves children.
- Respects all children and parents under all circumstances.
- Creates a classroom atmosphere that makes children feel safe and secure—an atmosphere in which they feel the importance of classroom ownership.
- Sees potential in all children.
- Motivates students to reach their highest potential.
- Has a wealth of knowledge on child growth and development, along with the ability to use that knowledge to meet individual children's needs.
- Has an in-depth knowledge of classroom management as well as behavior management.
- Is a spontaneous and creative educator. A good teacher should be able to see a teachable moment and seize the opportunity to go with it.
- Is a good role model and mentor for less experienced teachers.
- Has a sense of belonging to a team and a willingness to share responsibilities.

- Uses new educational ideas and insights and has the ability and desire to change so that the field of education can continue to grow.
- Has a sense of humor.
- Is willing to take the "extra time" and go the "extra mile"—the desire to be the best teacher that he or she can be.

AIMEE FREDETTE

Second Grade Teacher
Fisher Elementary School, Walpole, Massachusetts

There are many facets to being an effective teacher, the foremost being that the teacher will reach all children no matter what it takes. Effective teachers will modify curriculum and instruction to allow all ability levels to feel success and to foster a learning environment that builds the self-esteem of their students. This environment and confidence will encourage children to succeed at their own attempts to learn.

Another indicator of an effective teacher would be the ability to relate to and work with other staff members. Strong communication skills among the administration, peers, parents, and students is essential. When a teacher is able to positively and clearly inspire a class, those students will become curious investigators of the world. If this happens, the parents of these children will become a strong asset to the teacher. Now the child has a foundation on which to grow in both the school and the home environment.

In today's world, a teacher is a critical professional, and, in order to fulfill this role, a continuous effort of self-improvement and professional development must be undertaken. There are many effective means to improve oneself, from attending workshops and conferences, to enrolling in classes, reading trade journals and articles, and conducting peer focus groups and curriculum reviews. A professional who realizes that growth and learning are lifelong and who works to attain new ideas and skills is a valuable asset to any classroom.

There are a variety of teaching philosophies, and each teacher may have a different interpretation of each teaching approach. The teaching philosophies should always arrive at the same outcomes: the growth of student knowledge and the desire of teachers to learn more on their own. Each philosophy that has these goals in mind will use a different way to obtain success.

Effective teachers, regardless of philosophy, will excite and spark the children's interest. This will help the children to develop their own motivation for learning. I also feel that teachers should fully support the placement of all children into their classroom, regardless of abilities. To be effective, teachers will appropriately modify and implement assignments to meet those levels. A positive learning experience is created with a cooperative relationship among teachers, students, and home.

To reinforce recommendations for the indicators of an effective teacher, researching in professional books and journals would be beneficial. Another suggestion would be to brainstorm a list of things that you feel indicate an effective educator.

Cognitive Development and Language

Overview | *What Would You Do?*

A DEFINITION OF DEVELOPMENT   24
General Principles of Development | The Brain and Cognitive
Development

PIAGET'S THEORY OF COGNITIVE DEVELOPMENT   27
Influences on Development | Basic Tendencies in Thinking | Four
Stages of Cognitive Development

IMPLICATIONS OF PIAGET'S THEORY FOR TEACHERS   39
Understanding Students' Thinking | Matching Strategies to Abilities |
Constructing Knowledge | Some Limitations of Piaget's Theory

VYGOTSKY'S SOCIOCULTURAL PERSPECTIVE   44
The Role of Language and Private Speech | The Role of Adults
and Peers

IMPLICATION OF VYGOTSKY'S THEORY FOR TEACHERS   47
Assisted Learning | The Zone of Proximal Development

THE DEVELOPMENT OF LANGUAGE   51
How Do We Learn Language? | Stages in the Process of Language
Acquisition | Language Development in the School Years

LANGUAGE, LITERACY, AND TEACHING   57
Teachers and Literacy | Partnerships with Families

Summary | *Key Terms* | *Check Your Understanding* |
Teachers' Casebook: What Would They Do?

*T*hink for a moment about how you would explain the concept of "symbol" to a 6-year-old and to a 14-year-old. Would you use words? Pictures? Specific examples? What kind? What do you know about how younger and older children differ in their thinking?

The material in this chapter will help you answer these questions and many others about how young people think and how their thinking changes over time. These changes in thinking and understanding are called *cognitive development*.

In this chapter, we begin with a discussion of the general principles of human development and a brief look at the human brain. Then we will examine the ideas of two of the most influential cognitive developmental theorists, Jean Piaget and Lev Vygotsky. Piaget's ideas have implications for teachers about what their students can learn and when the students are ready to learn it. We will examine important criticisms of his ideas as well.

The work of Lev Vygotsky, a Russian psychologist, is becoming more and more influential. His theory highlights the important role teachers and parents play in the cognitive development of the child. Finally, we will explore language development and discuss the role of the school in developing and enriching language skills.

By the time you have completed this chapter, you should be able to:

- State three general principles of human development, and give examples of each.
- Explain how children's thinking differs at each of Piaget's four stages of development.
- Summarize the implications of Piaget's theory for teaching students of different ages.
- Contrast Piaget's and Vygotsky's ideas about cognitive development.
- Give implications of Vygotsky's theory for teaching students of any age.
- Describe briefly the stages of language development.
- Suggest ways a teacher can help children expand their language use and comprehension.

What Would You Do?

The district curriculum guide calls for a unit on poetry, including lessons on *symbolism* in poems. You are concerned that many of your fifth-grade students may not be ready to understand this abstract concept. To test the waters, you ask a few students what a symbol is.

"It's sorta like a big metal thing that you bang together." Tracy waves her hands like a drum major.

"Yeah," Sean adds, "My sister plays one in the high school band."

You realize they are on the wrong track here, so you try again. "I was thinking of a different kind of symbol, like a ring as a symbol of marriage or a heart as a symbol of love, or . . . "

You are met with blank stares.

Trevor ventures, "You mean like the Olympic torch?"

"And what does that symbolize, Trevor?" you ask.

"I said, the torch." Trevor wonders how you could be so dense.

- What do these students' reactions tell you about children's thinking?

- How would you approach this unit?

- What more would you do to "listen" to your students' thinking so you could match your teaching to their level of thinking?

- How would you give your students concrete experience with symbolism?

- How will you decide if the students are not developmentally ready for this material?

Development Orderly, adaptive changes we go through from conception to death.

Physical Development Changes in body structure and function over time.

Personal Development Changes in personality that take place as one grows.

Social Development Changes over time in the ways we relate to others.

Cognitive Development Gradual, orderly changes by which mental processes become more complex and sophisticated.

A Definition of Development

The term **development** in its most general psychological sense refers to certain changes that occur in human beings (or animals) between conception and death. The term is not applied to all changes, but rather to those that appear in orderly ways and remain for a reasonably long period of time. A temporary change caused by a brief illness, for example, is not considered a part of development. Psychologists also make a value judgment in determining which changes qualify as development. The changes, at least those that occur early in life, are generally assumed to be for the better and to result in behavior that is more adaptive, more organized, more effective, and more complex (Mussen, Conger, & Kagan, 1984).

Human development can be divided into a number of different aspects. **Physical development,** as you might guess, deals with changes in the body. **Personal development** is the term generally used for changes in an individual's personality. **Social development** refers to changes in the way an individual relates to others. And **cognitive development** refers to changes in thinking.

Many changes during development are simply matters of growth and maturation. **Maturation** refers to changes that occur naturally and spontaneously and that are, to a large extent, genetically programmed. Such changes emerge over time and are relatively unaffected by environment, except in cases of malnutrition or severe illness. Much of a person's physical development falls into this category. Other changes are brought about through learning, as individuals interact with their environment. Such changes make up a large part of a person's social development. But what about the development of thinking and personality? Most psychologists agree that in these areas, both maturation and interaction with the environment (or nature and nurture, as they are sometimes called) are important, but they disagree about the amount of emphasis to place on each.

General Principles of Development

Although there is disagreement about what is involved in development and about the way it takes place, there are a few general principles almost all theorists would support.

1. *People develop at different rates*. In your own classroom, you will have a whole range of examples of different developmental rates. Some students will be larger, better coordinated, or more mature in their thinking and social relationships. Others will be much slower to mature in these areas. Except in rare cases of very rapid or very slow development, such differences are normal and to be expected in any large group of students.

2. *Development is relatively orderly*. People develop certain abilities before others. In infancy they sit before they walk, babble before they talk, and see the world through their own eyes before they can begin to imagine how others see it. In school, they will master addition before algebra, Bambi before Shakespeare, and so on. Theorists may disagree on exactly what comes before what, but they all seem to find a relatively logical progression.

3. *Development takes place gradually*. Very rarely do changes appear overnight. A student who cannot manipulate a pencil or answer a hypothetical question may well develop this ability, but the change is likely to take time.

The Brain and Cognitive Development

If you have taken an introductory psychology class, you have read about the brain and nervous system. You probably remember, for example, that there are several different areas of the brain and that certain areas are involved in particular functions. For example, the feathery-looking cerebellum seems to coordinate and orchestrate smooth, skilled movements—from the graceful gestures of the dancer to the everyday action of eating without stabbing yourself in the nose with a fork. The thalamus is involved in our ability to learn new information, particularly if it is verbal. The reticular formation plays a role in attention and arousal, blocking some messages and sending others on to higher brain centers for processing (Wood & Wood, 1993).

The outer 1/8-inch-thick covering of the cerebrum is the wrinkled-looking cerebral cortex—the largest area of the brain. The cerebral cortex accounts for about 85% of the brain's weight and contains the greatest number of nerve

Maturation Genetically programmed, naturally occurring changes over time.

FIGURE 2.1

A View of the Cerebral Cortex

This is a simple representation of the left side of the human brain, showing the cerebral cortex. The cortex is divided into different areas or lobes, each having a variety of regions with different functions. A few of the major functions are indicated here.

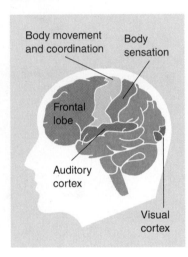

Body movement and coordination

Body sensation

Frontal lobe

Auditory cortex

Visual cortex

cells—the tiny structures that store and transmit information; this part of the brain allows the greatest human accomplishments. This crumpled sheet of neurons serves three major functions: receiving signals from sense organs such as visual or auditory signals, controlling voluntary movement, and forming associations. In humans, this area of the brain is much larger than in lower animals. The cortex is the last part of the brain to develop, so it is believed to be more susceptible to environmental influences than other areas of the brain (Berk, 1996, 1997). Different areas of the cortex seem to have different functions, as shown in Figure 2.1.

Even though areas of the cortex are somewhat specialized, they must work together. For example, many areas of the cortex are necessary in processing language. To answer a question, you must first hear it. This involves the primary auditory cortex. Movements controlled by the motor cortex are required to speak your response. Broca's area (near the area that controls the lips, jaw, and tongue) has a role in setting up a grammatically correct way of expressing an idea, and Wernicke's area (near the auditory cortex) is necessary for connecting meaning with particular words. A person with a functioning Broca's area but a damaged Wernicke's area will say meaningless things in a grammatically correct structure. Damage limited to Broca's area, on the other hand, is associated with short, ungrammatical sentences, but the words are appropriate (Anderson, 1995a).

Another aspect of brain functioning that has implications for cognitive development is *lateralization,* or the specialization of the two hemispheres of the brain. We know that each half of the brain controls the opposite side of the body. Damage to the right side of the brain will affect movement of the left side of the body and vice versa. In addition, certain areas of the brain affect particular behaviors. For most of us, the left hemisphere of the brain is the major factor in language processing, and the right hemisphere handles most of the spatial-visual information and emotions (nonverbal information). For some left-handed people, the relationship may be reversed, but for most left-handers there is less hemispheric specialization altogether (Berk, 1996, 1997).

Developmental psychologists are concerned about when lateralization occurs, because before specializations are established in particular areas of the brain, the brain is very adaptable, or *plastic*. If one area is damaged, other areas can take over functioning. So when very young children experience damage to part of their brain, other parts of the brain can handle the tasks usually accomplished by the damaged area—to a point. It appears that lateralization begins even before birth and proceeds for several years. Thus, the younger the child, the more he or she is able to recover from damage or deprivation.

Lateralization does not mean that one side or the other of the brain is in complete control, depending on the task. For people who have normal intact brains, both hemispheres are involved in all learning tasks, even if one side may be more or less involved at any given moment (Bjorklund, 1989). It is possible that researchers will trace certain learning problems to aspects of hemispheric specialization, but the evidence is not yet conclusive. In fact, some preliminary research indicates that the front-

---

Focus on...

Development

- Distinguish between development and maturation.
- Summarize three principles of how development takes place.
- Give an example of the way different areas of the brain work together to produce language.
- What aspect of development is involved in Trevor's understanding of "symbolism" at the opening of this chapter?

to-back functioning of the brain may be as important as left/right functioning in understanding learning disabilities (Jordan & Goldsmith-Phillips, 1994).

In the next decade we should see increasing research on the brain, development, learning, and teaching. Until recently, implications of brain research for teaching were not widely recognized, but we are moving into a time when this could change dramatically. For example, in 1992 there was a special issue of the *Educational Psychologist* on "Brain and Education." In it were articles describing research on variations in the development of different working brain systems that can affect learning to read and write and several models of learning and teaching based on brain research. A message of many of the authors of this volume is that the brain is a complex collection of systems working together to construct understanding, detect patterns, create rules, and make sense of experience. These systems change over the lifetime as the individual matures and learns.

The first theory of cognitive development we will consider was developed by a biologist turned psychologist, Jean Piaget.

Piaget's Theory of Cognitive Development

During the past half-century, the Swiss psychologist Jean Piaget devised a model describing how humans go about making sense of their world by gathering and organizing information (Piaget, 1954, 1963, 1970a, b). We will examine Piaget's ideas closely, because they provide an explanation of the development of thinking from infancy to adulthood.

According to Piaget (1954), certain ways of thinking that are quite simple for an adult are not so simple for a child. Sometimes all you need to do to teach a new concept is to give a student a few basic facts as background. At other times, however, all the background facts in the world are useless. The student simply is not ready to learn the concept. With some students, you can discuss the general causes of civil wars and then ask why they think the American Civil War broke out in 1861. But suppose the students respond with "When is 1861?" Obviously their concepts of time are different from your own. They may think, for example, that they will some day catch up to a sibling in age, or they may confuse the past and the future.

Influences on Development

As you can see, cognitive development is much more than the addition of new facts and ideas to an existing store of information. According to Piaget, our thinking processes change radically, though slowly, from birth to maturity, because we constantly strive to make sense of the world. How do we do this? Piaget identified four factors—biological maturation, activity, social experiences, and equilibration—that interact to influence changes in thinking (Piaget, 1970a). Let's briefly examine the first three factors. We'll return to a discussion of equilibration in the next section.

One of the most important influences on the way we make sense of the world is *maturation,* the unfolding of the biological changes that are genetically programmed in each human being at conception. Parents and teachers

Jean Piaget was a Swiss psychologist whose insightful descriptions of children's thinking changed the way we understand cognitive development.

have little impact on this aspect of cognitive development, except to be sure that children get the nourishment and care they need to be healthy.

Activity is another influence. With physical maturation comes the increasing ability to act on the environment and learn from it. When a young child's coordination is reasonably developed, for example, the child may discover principles about balance by experimenting with a seesaw. So as we act on the environment—as we explore, test, observe, and eventually organize information—we are likely to alter our thinking processes at the same time.

As we develop, we are also interacting with the people around us. According to Piaget, our cognitive development is influenced by *social transmission*, or learning from others. Without social transmission, we would need to reinvent all the knowledge already offered by our culture. The amount people can learn from social transmission varies according to their stage of cognitive development.

Maturation, activity, and social transmission all work together to influence cognitive development. How do we respond to these influences?

Basic Tendencies in Thinking

As a result of his early research in biology, Piaget concluded that all species inherit two basic tendencies, or "invariant functions." The first of these tendencies is toward **organization**—the combining, arranging, recombining, and rearranging of behaviors and thoughts into coherent systems. The second tendency is toward **adaptation**, or adjusting to the environment.

Organization.   People are born with a tendency to organize their thinking processes into psychological structures. These psychological structures are our systems for understanding and interacting with the world. Simple structures are continually combined and coordinated to become more sophisticated and thus more effective. Very young infants, for example, can either look at an object or grasp it when it comes in contact with their hands. They cannot coordinate looking and grasping at the same time. As they develop, however, infants organize these two separate behavioral structures into a coordinated higher-level structure of looking at, reaching for, and grasping the object. They can, of course, still use each structure separately (Ginsburg & Opper, 1988).

Piaget gave a special name to these structures. In his theory, they are called schemes. **Schemes are the basic building blocks of thinking.** They are organized systems of actions or thought that allow us to mentally represent or "think about" the objects and events in our world. Schemes may be very small and specific, for example, the sucking-through-a-straw scheme or the recognizing-a-rose scheme. Or they may be larger and more general—the drinking scheme or the categorizing-plants scheme. As a person's thinking processes become more organized and new schemes develop, behavior also becomes more sophisticated and better suited to the environment.

Adaptation.   In addition to the tendency to organize their psychological structures, people also inherit the tendency to adapt to their environment. Two basic processes are involved in adaptation: assimilation and accommodation.

Assimilation takes place when people use their existing schemes to make sense of events in their world. Assimilation involves trying to understand some-

Organization Ongoing process of arranging information and experience into mental systems or categories.

Adaptation Adjustment to the environment.

Schemes Mental systems or categories of perception and experience.

Assimilation Fitting new information into existing schemes.

thing new by fitting it into what we already know. At times, we may have to distort the new information to make it fit. For example, the first time many children see a skunk, they call it a "kitty." They try to match the new experience with an existing scheme for identifying animals.

Accommodation occurs when a person must change existing schemes to respond to a new situation. If data cannot be made to fit any existing schemes, then more appropriate structures must be developed. We adjust our thinking to fit the new information, instead of adjusting the information to fit our thinking. Children demonstrate accommodation when they add the scheme for recognizing skunks to their other systems for identifying animals.

People adapt to their increasingly complex environments by using existing schemes whenever these schemes work (assimilation) and by modifying and adding to their schemes when something new is needed (accommodation). In fact, both processes are required most of the time. Even using an established pattern like sucking through a straw may require some accommodation if the straw is of a different size or length than the type you are used to. If you have tried drinking juice from box packages, you know that you have to add a new skill to your sucking scheme—don't squeeze the box or you will shoot juice through the straw, straight up into the air and into your lap. Whenever new experiences are assimilated into an existing scheme, the scheme is enlarged and changed somewhat, so assimilation involves some accommodation.

There are also times when neither assimilation nor accommodation is used. If people encounter something that is too unfamiliar, they may ignore it. Experience is filtered to fit the kind of thinking a person is doing at a given time. For example, if you overhear a conversation in a foreign language, you probably will not try to make sense of the exchange unless you have some knowledge of the language.

How are assimilation and accommodation involved in using this straw? Can the girl respond to this straw exactly as she does to a conventional one?

Equilibration.   According to Piaget, organizing, assimilating, and accommodating can be seen as a kind of complex balancing act. In his theory, the actual changes in thinking take place through the process of **equilibration**—the act of searching for a balance. Piaget assumed that people continually test the adequacy of their thinking processes in order to achieve that balance.

Briefly, the process of equilibration works like this: If we apply a particular scheme to an event or situation and the scheme works, then equilibrium exists. If the scheme does not produce a satisfying result, then **disequilibrium** exists, and we become uncomfortable. This motivates us to keep searching for a solution through assimilation and accommodation, and thus our thinking changes and moves ahead. In order to maintain a balance between our schemes for understanding the world and the data the world provides, we continually assimilate new information using existing schemes, and we accommodate our thinking whenever unsuccessful attempts to assimilate produce disequilibrium.

Four Stages of Cognitive Development

Now we turn to the actual differences that Piaget hypothesized for children as they grow. Piaget's four stages of cognitive development are called sensorimotor, preoperational, concrete operational, and formal operational. Piaget believed that all people pass through the same four stages in exactly the same

Accommodation Altering existing schemes or creating new ones in response to new information.

Equilibration Search for mental balance between cognitive schemes and information from the environment.

Disequilibrium In Piaget's theory, the "out-of-balance" state that occurs when a person realizes that his or her current ways of thinking are not working to solve a problem or understand a situation.

	TABLE 2.1	Piaget's Stages of Cognitive Development	
Stage	**Approximate Age**	**Characteristics**	
Sensorimotor	0–2 years	Begins to make use of imitation, memory, and thought.	*sensory motor*
		Begins to recognize that objects do not cease to exist when they are hidden.	*object permanence*
		Moves from reflex actions to goal-directed activity.	
Preoperational	2–7 years	Gradually develops use of language and ability to think in symbolic form.	
		Able to think operations through logically in one direction.	
		Has difficulties seeing another person's point of view.	
Concrete operational	7–11 years	Able to solve concrete (hands-on) problems in logical fashion.	
		Understands laws of conservation and is able to classify and seriate.	
		Understands reversibility.	
Formal operational	11–adult	Able to solve abstract problems in logical fashion.	
		Becomes more scientific in thinking.	
		Develops concerns about social issues, identity.	

Source: From *Piaget's Theory of Cognitive and Affective Development,* 4/e by Barry J. Wadsworth. Copyright © 1971, 1979, 1984, 1989. Adapted by permission of Addison-Wesley Educational Publishers Inc.

order. These stages are generally associated with specific ages, as shown in Table 2.1. When you see ages linked to stages, remember that these are only general guidelines, not labels for all children of a certain age. Piaget was interested in the kinds of thinking abilities people are able to use, not in labeling. Often, people can use one level of thinking to solve one kind of problem and a different level to solve another. Piaget noted that individuals may go through long periods of transition between stages and that a person may show characteristics of one stage in one situation but characteristics of a higher or lower stage in other situations. Therefore, knowing a student's age is never a guarantee that you know how the child will think (Ginsburg & Opper, 1988).

Infancy: The Sensorimotor Stage.   The earliest period is called the **sensorimotor** stage, because the child's thinking involves seeing, hearing, moving, touching, tasting, and so on. During this period, the infant develops **object permanence**, the understanding that objects in the environment exist whether the

Sensorimotor Involving the senses and motor activity.

Object Permanence The understanding that objects have a separate, permanent existence.

baby perceives them or not. As most parents discover, before infants develop object permanence, it is relatively easy to take something away from them. The trick is to distract them and remove the object while they are not looking— "out of sight, out of mind." The older infant who searches for the ball that has rolled out of sight is indicating an understanding that the objects still exist even though they can't be seen.

A second major accomplishment in the sensorimotor period is the beginning of logical, **goal-directed actions**. Think of the familiar container toy for babies. It is usually plastic, has a lid, and contains several colorful items that can be dumped out and replaced. A 6-month-old baby is likely to become frustrated trying to get to the toys inside. An older child who has mastered the basics of the sensorimotor stage will probably be able to deal with the toy in an orderly fashion. Through trial and error the child will slowly build a "container toy" scheme: (1) get the lid off; (2) turn the container upside down; (3) shake if the items jam; (4) watch the items fall. Separate lower-level schemes have been organized into a higher-level scheme to achieve a goal.

The child is soon able to reverse this action by refilling the container. Learning to reverse actions is a basic accomplishment of the sensorimotor stage. As we will soon see, however, learning to reverse thinking—that is, learning to imagine the reverse of a sequence of actions—takes much longer.

Early Childhood to the Early Elementary Years: The Preoperational Stage.

By the end of the sensorimotor stage, the child can use many action schemes. As long as these schemes remain tied to physical actions, however, they are of no use in recalling the past, keeping track of information, or planning. For this, children need what Piaget called **operations**, or actions that are carried out and reversed mentally rather than physically. The stage after sensorimotor is called **preoperational**, because the child has not yet mastered these mental operations but is moving toward mastery.

According to Piaget, the first step from action to thinking is the internalization of action, performing an action mentally rather than physically. The first type of thinking that is separate from action involves making action schemes symbolic. The ability to form and use symbols—words, gestures, signs, images, and so on—is thus a major accomplishment of the preoperational period and moves children closer to mastering the mental operations of the next stage. This ability to work with symbols, such as using the word "bicycle" or a picture of a bicycle to stand for a real bicycle that is not actually present, is called the **semiotic function**.

The child's earliest use of symbols is in pretending or miming. Children who are not yet able to talk will often use action symbols—pretending to drink from an empty cup or touching a comb to their hair, showing that they know what each object is for. This behavior also shows that their schemes are becoming more general and less tied to specific actions. The eating scheme, for example, may be used in playing house. During the preoperational stage, we also see the rapid development of that very important symbol system, language. Between the ages of 2 and 4, most children enlarge their vocabulary from about 200 to 2,000 words.

As the child moves through the preoperational stage, the developing ability to think about objects in symbolic form remains somewhat limited to think-

Goal-Directed Actions Deliberate actions toward a goal.

Operations Actions a person carries out by thinking them through instead of literally performing the actions.

Preoperational The stage before a child masters logical mental operations.

Semiotic Function The ability to use symbols—language, pictures, signs, or gestures—to represent actions or objects mentally.

Being able to manipulate concrete objects helps children understand abstract relationships such as the connection between symbols and quantity.

Reversible Thinking Thinking backward, from the end to the beginning.

Conservation Principle that some characteristics of an object remain the same despite changes in appearance.

Decentering Focusing on more than one aspect at a time.

Egocentric Assuming that others experience the world the way you do.

Collective Monologue Form of speech in which children in a group talk but do not really interact or communicate.

ing in one direction only, or using *one-way logic*. It is very difficult for the child to "think backwards," or imagine how to reverse the steps in a task.

Reversible thinking is involved in many tasks that are difficult for the preoperational child, such as the conservation of matter. Conservation is the principle that the amount or number of something remains the same even if the arrangement or appearance is changed, as long as nothing is added and nothing is taken away. You know that if you tear a piece of paper into several pieces, you will still have the same amount of paper. To prove this, you know that you can reverse the process by taping the pieces back together.

A classic example of difficulty with conservation is found in the preoperational child's response to the following Piagetian task. Leah, a 5-year-old, is shown two identical glasses, both short and wide in shape. Both have exactly the same amount of colored water in them. The experimenter asks Leah if each glass has the same amount of water, and she answers, "Yes." The experimenter then pours the water from one of the glasses into a tall, narrow glass and asks Leah again if each glass has the same amount of water. Now she is likely to insist that there is more water in the tall, narrow glass, because the water level is higher. Notice, by the way, that Leah shows a basic understanding of identity (it's the same water) but not an understanding that the *amounts* are identical (Ginsburg & Opper, 1988).

Piaget's explanation for Leah's answer is that she is focusing, or centering, attention on the dimension of height. She has difficulty considering more than one aspect of the situation at a time, or decentering. The preoperational child cannot understand that increased diameter compensates for decreased height, since this would require taking into account two dimensions at once. Thus, children at the preoperational stage have trouble freeing themselves from their own perceptions of how the world appears.

This brings us to another important characteristic of the preoperational stage. Preoperational children, according to Piaget, are very egocentric; they tend to see the world and the experiences of others from their own viewpoint. Egocentric, as Piaget intended it, does not mean selfish; it simply means children often assume that everyone else shares their feelings, reactions, and perspectives. For example, if a little boy at this stage is afraid of dogs, he may assume that all children share this fear. Very young children center on their own perceptions and on the way the situation appears to them. This is one reason it is difficult for these children to understand that your right hand is not on the same side as theirs when you are facing them.

Egocentrism is also evident in the child's language. You may have seen young children happily talking about what they are doing even though no one is listening. This can happen when the child is alone or, even more often, in a group of children—each child talks enthusiastically, without any real interaction or conversation. Piaget called this the collective monologue.

Recent research has shown that young children are not totally egocentric in every situation, however. Children as young as age 4 change the way they talk to 2-year-olds by speaking in simpler sentences, and even before age 2 children show toys to adults by turning the front of the toy to face the other person. So young children do seem quite able to take the needs and different perspectives of others into account, at least in certain situations (Gelman, 1979; Gelman & Ebeling, 1989). The Guidelines give ideas for working with preoperational thinkers.

Use concrete props and visual aids whenever possible.

Examples

1. When you discuss concepts such as "part," "whole," or "one-half," use shapes on a felt board or cardboard "pizzas" to demonstrate.
2. Let children add and subtract with sticks, rocks, or colored chips.

Make instructions relatively short, using actions as well as words.

Examples

1. When giving instructions about how to enter the room after recess and prepare for social studies, ask a student to demonstrate the procedure for the rest of the class by walking in quietly, going straight to his or her seat, and placing the text, paper, and a pencil on his or her desk.
2. Explain a game by acting out one of the parts.
3. Show students what their finished papers should look like. Use an overhead projector or display examples where students can see them easily.

Don't expect the students to be consistent in their ability to see the world from someone else's point of view.

Examples

1. Avoid social studies lessons about worlds too far removed from the child's experience.
2. Avoid long lectures on sharing. Be clear about rules for sharing or use of materials, but avoid long explanations of the rationales for the rules.

Be sensitive to the possibility that students may have different meanings for the same word or different words for the same meaning. Students may also expect everyone to understand words they have invented.

Examples

1. If a student protests, "I won't take a nap. I'll just rest!," be aware that a nap may mean something like "changing into pajamas and being in my bed at home."
2. Ask children to explain the meanings of their invented words.

Give children a great deal of hands-on practice with the skills that serve as building blocks for more complex skills like reading comprehension.

Examples

1. Provide cut-out letters to build words.
2. Supplement paper-and-pencil tasks in arithmetic with activities that require measuring and simple calculations—cooking, building a display area for class work, dividing a batch of popcorn equally.

Provide a wide range of experiences in order to build a foundation for concept learning and language.

Examples

1. Take field trips to zoos, gardens, theaters, and concerts; invite storytellers to the class.
2. Give students words to describe what they are doing, hearing, seeing, touching, tasting, and smelling.

Later Elementary to the Middle School Years: The Concrete-Operational Stage. Piaget coined the term **concrete operations** to describe this stage of "hands-on" thinking. The basic characteristics of the stage are the recognition of the logical stability of the physical world, the realization that elements can be changed or transformed and still conserve many of their original characteristics, and the understanding that these changes can be reversed.

Figure 2.2 shows examples of the different tasks given to children to assess conservation and the approximate age ranges when most children can

FIGURE 2.2

Some Piagetian Conservation Tasks

In addition to the tasks shown here, other tasks involve the conservation of number, length, weight, and volume. These tasks are all achieved over the concrete-operational period.

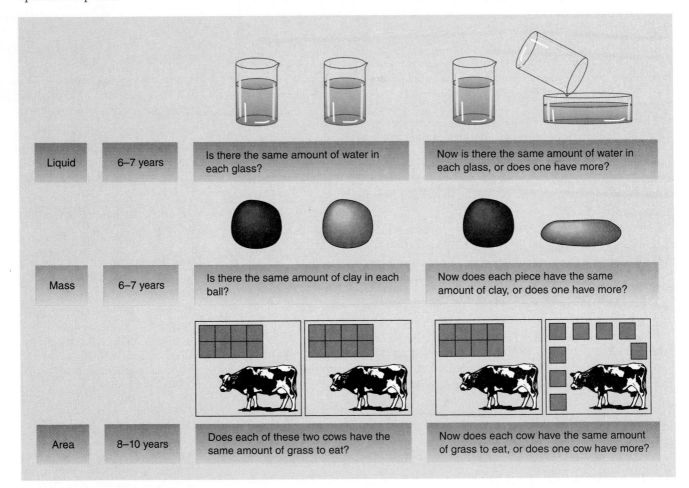

Source: From Laura E. Berk, *Child Development,* 4/e. Copyright © 1997. All rights reserved. Adapted by permission of Allyn & Bacon.

solve these problems. According to Piaget, a student's ability to solve conservation problems depends on an understanding of three basic aspects of reasoning: identity, compensation, and reversibility. With a complete mastery of **identity,** the student knows that if nothing is added or taken away, the material remains the same. With an understanding of **compensation, the student knows that an apparent change in one direction can be compensated for by a change in another direction.** That is, if the liquid rises higher in the glass, the glass must be narrower. And with an understanding of **reversibility, the student can mentally cancel out the change that has been made.**

Another important operation mastered at this stage is **classification.** Classification depends on a student's abilities to focus on a single characteristic of objects in a set and group the objects according to that characteristic. Given 12 objects of assorted colors and shapes, the concrete-operational student can invariably pick out the ones that are round.

More advanced classification at this stage involves recognizing that one class fits into another. A city can be in a particular state or province and also in a particular country. As children apply this advanced classification to locations, they often become fascinated with "complete" addresses such as Lee Jary, 5116 Forest Hill Drive, Richmond Hill, Ontario, Canada, North America, Northern Hemisphere, Earth, Solar System, Milky Way, Universe.

Classification is also related to reversibility. The ability to reverse a process mentally now allows the concrete-operational student to see that there is more than one way to classify a group of objects. The student understands, for example, that buttons can be classified by color, then reclassified by size or by the number of holes.

Seriation is the process of **making an orderly arrangement from large to small or vice versa.** This understanding of sequential relationships permits a student to construct a logical series in which A < B < C (A is less than B is less than C) and so on. Unlike the preoperational child, the concrete-operational child can grasp the notion that B can be larger than A but smaller than C.

With the abilities to handle operations like conservation, classification, and seriation, the student at the concrete-operational stage has finally developed a complete and very logical system of thinking. This system of thinking, however, is still tied to physical reality. The logic is based on concrete situations that can be organized, classified, or manipulated. Thus, children at this stage can imagine several different arrangements for the furniture in their rooms before they act. They do not have to solve the problem strictly through trial and error by actually making the arrangements. But the concrete-operational child is not yet able to reason about hypothetical, abstract problems that involve the coordination of many factors at once. This kind of coordination is part of Piaget's next and final stage of cognitive development.

In any grade you teach, a knowledge of concrete-operational thinking will be helpful. In the early grades, the students are moving toward this logical system of thought. In the middle grades, it is in full flower, ready to be applied and extended by your teaching. In the high school years, it is often used by students whose thinking may not have fully developed to the next stage—the stage of formal operations. The Guidelines on page 36 should give you ideas for teaching children who can apply concrete operations.

Concrete Operations Mental tasks tied to concrete objects and situations.

Identity Principle that a person or object remains the same over time.

Compensation The principle that changes in one dimension can be offset by changes in another.

Reversibility A characteristic of Piagetian logical operations—the ability to think through a series of steps, then mentally reverse the steps and return to the starting point; also called reversible thinking.

Classification Grouping objects into categories.

Seriation Arranging objects in sequential order according to one aspect, such as size, weight, or volume.

Guidelines

Teaching the Concrete-Operational Child

Continue to use concrete props and visual aids, especially when dealing with sophisticated material.

Examples

1. Use time lines in history and three-dimensional models in science.
2. Use diagrams to illustrate hierarchical relationships like branches of government and the agencies under each branch.

Continue to give students a chance to manipulate and test objects.

Examples

1. Set up simple scientific experiments like the following involving the relationship between fire and oxygen. What happens to a flame when you blow on it from a distance? (If you don't blow it out, the flame gets larger briefly, because it has more oxygen to burn.) What happens when you cover the flame with a jar?
2. Have students make candles by dipping wicks in wax, weave cloth on a simple loom, bake bread, set type by hand, or do other craft work that illustrates the daily occupations of people in the colonial period.

Make sure presentations and readings are brief and well organized.

Examples

1. Assign stories or books with short, logical chapters, moving to longer reading assignments only when students are ready.
2. Break up a presentation with a chance to practice the first steps before introducing the next.

Use familiar examples to explain more complex ideas.

Examples

1. Compare students' lives with those of characters in a story. After reading *Island of the Blue Dolphins* (the true story of a girl who grew up alone on a deserted island), ask "Have you ever had to stay alone for a long time? How did you feel?"
2. Teach the concept of area by having students measure two rooms in the school that are different sizes.

Give opportunities to classify and group objects and ideas on increasingly complex levels.

Examples

1. Give students slips of paper with individual sentences written on each paper and ask the students to group the sentences into paragraphs.
2. Compare the systems of the human body to other kinds of systems: the brain to a computer, the heart to a pump. Break down stories into components, from the broad to the specific: author; story; characters, plot, theme; place, time; dialogue, description, actions.

Present problems that require logical, analytical thinking.

Examples

1. Use mind twisters, brain teasers, Master Mind, and riddles.
2. Discuss open-ended questions that stimulate thinking: "Are the brain and the mind the same thing?" "How should the city deal with stray animals?" "What is the largest number?"

Junior and Senior High: Formal Operations.   Some students remain at the concrete-operational stage throughout their school years, even throughout life. However, new experiences, usually those that take place in school, eventually present most students with problems that they cannot solve using concrete operations. What happens when a number of variables interact, as in a laboratory experiment? Then a mental system for controlling sets of variables and working through a set of possibilities is needed. These are the abilities Piaget called **formal operations.**

At the level of formal operations, all the earlier operations and abilities continue in force; that is, formal thinking is reversible, internal, and organized in a system of interdependent elements. The focus of thinking shifts, however, from what *is* to what *might be*. Situations do not have to be experienced to be imagined. Ask a young child how life would be different if people did not sleep, and the child might say, "People have to sleep!" In contrast, the adolescent who has mastered formal operations can consider contrary-to-fact questions. In answering, the adolescent demonstrates the hallmark of formal operations—**hypothetico-deductive reasoning.** The formal thinker can consider a hypothetical situation (people do not sleep) and reason deductively (from the general assumption to specific implications, such as longer workdays, more money spent on lighting, or new entertainment industries). Formal operations also include inductive reasoning, or using specific observations to identify general principles. For example, the economist observes many specific changes in the stock market and attempts to identify general principles about economic cycles. Formal-operational thinkers can form hypotheses, set up mental experiments to test them, and isolate or control variables in order to complete a valid test of the hypotheses.

The ability to consider abstract possibilities is critical for much of mathematics and science. After elementary school, most math is concerned with hypothetical situations, assumptions, and givens: "Let $x = 10$," or "Assume $x^2 + y^2 = z^2$," or "Given two sides and an adjacent angle . . . ." Young children cannot reason based on symbols and abstractions, but this kind of reasoning is expected in the later grades (Bjorklund, 1989). Work in social studies and literature requires abstract thinking, too: "What did Wilson mean when he called World War I the 'war to end all wars'?" "What are some metaphors for hope and despair in Shakespeare's sonnets?" "What symbols of old age does T. S. Eliot use in *The Waste Land*?" "How do animals symbolize human character traits in Aesop's fables?"

The organized, scientific thinking of formal operations requires that students systematically generate different possibilities for a given situation. For example, if a child capable of formal operations is asked, "How many different meat/vegetable/salad meals can you make using three meats, three vegetables, and three salads?" the child can systematically identify the 27 possible combinations. A concrete thinker might name just a few meals, focusing on favorite foods or using each food only once. The underlying system of combinations is not yet available.

The ability to think hypothetically, consider alternatives, identify all possible combinations, and analyze one's own thinking has some interesting consequences for adolescents. Since they can think about worlds that do not exist, they often become interested in science fiction. Because they can reason from general principles to specific actions, they often are critical of people whose ac-

Formal Operations Mental tasks involving abstract thinking and coordination of a number of variables.

Hypothetico-Deductive Reasoning A formal operations problem-solving strategy in which an individual begins by identifying all the factors that might affect a problem and then deduces and systematically evaluates specific solutions.

tions seem to contradict their principles. Adolescents can deduce the set of "best" possibilities and imagine ideal worlds (or ideal parents and teachers, for that matter). This explains why many students at this age develop interests in utopias, political causes, and social issues. They want to design better worlds, and their thinking allows them to do so. Adolescents can also imagine many possible futures for themselves and may try to decide which is best. Feelings about any of these ideals may be strong.

Another characteristic of this stage is **adolescent egocentrism.** Unlike egocentric young children, adolescents do not deny that other people may have different perceptions and beliefs; the adolescents just become very focused on their own ideas. They analyze their own beliefs and attitudes. They reflect on others' thinking as well but often assume that everyone else is as interested as they are in their thoughts, feelings, and behavior. This can lead to what Elkind (1981) calls the sense of an *imaginary audience*—the feeling that everyone is watching. Thus, adolescents believe that others are analyzing them: "Everyone noticed that I wore this shirt twice this week." "The whole class thought my answer was dumb!" "Everybody is going to love my new CD." You can see that social blunders or imperfections in appearance can be devastating if "everybody is watching." Luckily, this feeling of being "on stage" seems to peak in early adolescence by age 14 or 15.

Do We All Reach the Fourth Stage?   As we have just seen, most psychologists agree that there is a level of thinking more sophisticated than concrete operations. But the question of how universal formal-operational thinking actually is, even among adults, is a matter of debate. According to Neimark (1975), the first three stages of Piaget's theory are forced on most people by physical realities. Objects really are permanent. The amount of water doesn't change when it is poured into another glass. Formal operations, however, are not so closely tied to the physical environment. They may be the product of experience and of practice in solving hypothetical problems and using formal scientific reasoning. These abilities tend to be valued and taught in literate cultures, particularly in colleges and universities.

Piaget himself (1974) suggested that most adults may be able to use formal-operational thought in only a few areas where they have the greatest experience or interest. So do not expect every student in your junior high or high school class to be able to think hypothetically about all the problems you present. Students who have not learned to go beyond the information given to them are likely to fall by the wayside. Sometimes students find shortcuts for dealing with problems that are beyond their grasp; they may memorize formulas or lists of steps. These systems may be helpful for passing tests, but real understanding will take place only if students are able to go beyond this superficial use of memorization—only, in other words, if they learn to use formal-operational thinking. The Guidelines may help you support the development of formal operations with your students.

Focus on...

Piaget's Theory

- What is a scheme?
- Distinguish between assimilation and accommodation.
- As children move from sensorimotor to formal-operational thinking, what are the major changes?
- What are the characteristics of concrete-operational thinking? Is Trevor's thinking concrete (p. 24)?

Adolescent Egocentrism Assumption that everyone else shares one's thoughts, feelings, and concerns.

Continue to use concrete-operational teaching strategies and materials.

Examples

1. Use visual aids such as charts and illustrations as well as somewhat more so-phisticated graphs and diagrams.

2. Compare the experiences of characters in stories to students' experiences.

Give students the opportunity to explore many hypothetical questions.

Examples

1. Have students write position papers, then exchange these papers with the opposing side and have debates about topical social issues—the environment, the economy, national health insurance.

2. Ask students to write about their personal vision of a utopia; write a description of a universe that has no sex differences; write a description of Earth after humans are extinct.

Give students opportunities to solve problems and reason scientifically.

Examples

1. Set up group discussions in which students design experiments to answer questions.

2. Ask students to justify two different positions on animal rights, with logical arguments for each position.

Whenever possible, teach broad concepts, not just facts, using materials and ideas relevant to the students' lives.

Examples

1. When discussing the Civil War, consider other issues that have divided the United States since then.

2. Use lyrics from popular songs to teach poetic devices, to reflect on social problems, and to stimulate discussion on the place of popular music in our culture.

Implications of Piaget's Theory for Teachers

Piaget has taught us that we can learn a great deal about how children think by listening carefully, by paying close attention to their ways of solving problems. If we understand children's thinking, we will be better able to match teaching methods to children's abilities.

Understanding Students' Thinking

The students in any class will vary greatly both in their level of cognitive development and in their academic knowledge. As a teacher, how can you determine whether students are having trouble because they lack the necessary thinking abilities or because they simply have not learned the basic facts? To do this, Case (1985b) suggests you observe your students carefully as they try to solve the problems you have presented. What kind of logic do they use? Do they focus on only one aspect of the situation? Are they fooled by appearances? Do they suggest solutions systematically or by guessing and forgetting what they have already tried? Ask your students how they tried to solve the problem. Listen to their strategies. What kind of thinking is behind repeated mistakes or problems? The students are the best sources of information about their own thinking abilities (Confrey, 1990a).

Matching Strategies to Abilities

An important implication of Piaget's theory for teaching is what Hunt years ago (1961) called "the problem of the match." Students must be neither bored by work that is too simple nor left behind by teaching they cannot understand. According to Hunt, disequilibrium must be kept "just right" to encourage growth. Setting up situations that lead to errors can help create an appropriate level of disequilibrium. When students experience some conflict between what they think should happen (a piece of wood should sink because it is big) and what actually happens (it floats!), they may rethink their understanding, and new knowledge may develop.

It is worth pointing out, too, that many materials and lessons can be understood at several levels and can be "just right" for a range of cognitive abilities. Classics such as *Alice in Wonderland,* myths, and fairy tales can be enjoyed at both concrete and symbolic levels. It is also possible for students to be introduced to a topic together, then work individually on follow-up activities matched to their level. Tom Good and Jere Brophy (1994) describe activity cards for three or four ability levels. These cards provide different readings and assignments, but all are directed toward the overall class objectives. One of the cards should be a good "match" for each student.

Constructing Knowledge

Piaget's fundamental insight was that individuals *construct* their own understanding; learning is a constructive process. At every level of cognitive development, you will also want to see that students are actively engaged in the learning process. They must be able to incorporate the information you present into their own schemes. To do this, they must act on the information in some way. Schooling must give the students a chance to experience the world. This active experience, even at the earliest school levels, should not be limited to the physical manipulation of objects. It should also include mental manipulation of ideas that arise out of class projects or experiments (Ginsburg & Opper, 1988). For example, after a social studies lesson on different jobs, a primary-grade teacher might show the students a picture of a woman and ask, "What could this person be?" After answers such as "teacher," "doctor," "secretary," "lawyer," "saleswoman," and so on, the teacher could suggest, "How about a daughter?" Answers such as "sister," "mother," "aunt," and "granddaughter" may follow. This should help the children switch dimensions in their classification and center on another aspect of the situation. Next, the teacher might suggest "American," "jogger," or "blonde." With older children, hierarchical classification might be involved: it is a picture of a woman, who is a human being; a human being is a primate, which is a mammal, which is an animal, which is a life form.

All students need to interact with teachers and peers in order to test their thinking, to be challenged, to receive feedback, and to watch how others work out problems. Disequilibrium is often set in motion quite naturally when the teacher or another student suggests a new way of thinking about something. As a general rule, students should act, manipulate, observe, and then talk and/ or write (to the teacher and each other) about what they have experienced. Concrete experiences provide the raw materials for thinking. Communicating with others makes students use, test, and sometimes change their thinking abilities. Discussions about the implications of Piaget's theory often center on the question of whether cognitive development can be accelerated, as you can see in the Point/Counterpoint on page 42.

Some Limitations of Piaget's Theory

Piaget's influence on developmental psychology and education has been enormous, even though recent research has not supported all his ideas. Although most psychologists agree with Piaget's insightful descriptions of how children think, many disagree with his explanations of why thinking develops as it does.

The Trouble with Stages. Some psychologists have questioned the existence of four separate stages of thinking, even though they agree that children do go through the changes that Piaget described (Gelman & Baillargeon, 1983). One problem with the stage model is the lack of consistency in children's thinking. Psychologists reason that if there are separate stages, and if the child's thinking at each stage is based on a particular set of operations, then once the child has mastered the operations, he or she should be somewhat consistent in solving all problems requiring those operations. In other words, once you can conserve, you ought to know that the number of blocks does not change when they are rearranged (conservation of number) and that the weight of a ball of clay does not change when you flatten it (conservation of weight). But it doesn't happen this way. Children can conserve *number* a year or two before they can conserve *weight*. Piagetian theorists have tried to deal with these inconsistencies, but not all psychologists are convinced by their explanations (Siegler, 1991).

Some psychologists have pointed to research on the brain to support Piaget's stage model. Epstein observed changes in rates of growth in brain weight and skull size and changes in the electrical activity of the brain between infancy and adolescence. These growth spurts occur at about the same time as transitions between the stages described by Piaget (Epstein, 1978, 1980). Evidence from animal studies indicates that infant rhesus monkeys show dramatic increases in synaptic (nerve) connections throughout the brain cortex at the same time that they master the kinds of sensorimotor problems described by Piaget (Berk, 1997). This may be true in human infants as well. Transition to the higher cognitive states in humans has also been related to changes in the brain, such as production of additional synaptic connections.

Can Cognitive Development Be Accelerated?

Ever since Piaget described his stages of cognitive development, some people have asked if progress through the stages could be accelerated. More recently, the question has focused on whether we should accelerate learning for preschoolers and young children at risk of academic failure. Can learning be accelerated, and if so, is this a good idea?

POINT **Every child deserves a head start.**

Some of the strongest arguments in favor of "speeding up" cognitive development are based on the results of cross-cultural studies of children (studies that compare children growing up in different cultures). These results suggest that certain cognitive abilities are indeed influenced by the environment and education. Children of pottery-making families in one area of Mexico, for example, learn conservation of substance earlier than their peers in families who do not make pottery (Ashton, 1978). Furthermore, children in non-Western cultures appear to acquire conservation operations later than children in Western cultures. It seems likely that factors in the environment contribute to the rate of cognitive development.

But even if cognitive development can be accelerated, is this a good idea? Two of the most vocal (and heavily criticized) advocates of early academic training are Siegfried and Therese Engelmann (1981). In their book, *Give Your Child a Superior Mind*, they suggest that children who learn academic skills as preschoolers will be smarter throughout their school years, are less likely to fail, and are more likely to enjoy school. They contend:

> Children respond to the environment. Their capacity to learn and what they learn depends on what the environment teaches. . . . Instead of relying on the traditional environment that is rich in learning opportunities for the child, we can take the environment a step further and mold it into a purposeful instrument that teaches and that guarantees your child will have a superior mind. (p. 10)

COUNTERPOINT **Acceleration is ineffective and may be harmful.**

The position of Piagetian psychologists who attempt to apply his theory to education is that development should not be speeded up. This traditional view has been well summarized by Wadsworth (1978):

> The function of the teacher is not to accelerate the development of the child or speed up the rate of movement from stage to stage. The function of the teacher is to insure that development within each stage is thoroughly integrated and complete. (p. 117)

According to Piaget, cognitive development is based on the self-selected actions and thoughts of the student, not on the teacher's action. If you try to teach a student something the student is not ready to learn, he or she may learn to give the "correct" answer. But this will not really affect the way the student thinks about this problem. Therefore, why spend a long time teaching something at one stage when students will learn it by themselves much more rapidly and thoroughly at another stage?

Today the pressure is on parents and preschool teachers to create "superkids," 3-year-olds who read, write, and speak a second language. David Elkind (1991) asserts that pushing children can be harmful. Elkind believes that preschool children who are given formal instruction in academic subjects often show signs of stress such as headaches. These children may become dependent on adults for guidance. Early focus on "right" and "wrong" answers can lead to competition and loss of self-esteem. Elkind asserts:

> The miseducation of young children, so prevalent in the United States today, ignores well-founded and noncontroversial differences between early education and formal education. As educators, our first task is to reassert this difference and insist on its importance. (p. 31)

Underestimating Children's Abilities. It now appears that Piaget underestimated the cognitive abilities of children, particularly younger ones. The problems he gave young children may have been too difficult and the directions too confusing. His subjects may have understood more than they could show on these problems. For example, work by Gelman and her colleagues (Gelman,

Meck, & Merkin, 1986; Miller & Gelman, 1983) shows that preschool children know much more about the concept of number than Piaget thought, even if they sometimes make mistakes or get confused. As long as preschoolers work with only three or four objects at a time, they can tell that the number remains the same, even if the objects are spread far apart or clumped close together. Recent studies of infants show us that they too are much more competent than Piaget thought. Instead of having to learn that objects are permanent, they may just have to learn how to look for them. In other words, we may be born with a greater store of cognitive tools than Piaget suggested. Some basic understandings, like the permanence of objects or the sense of number, may be part of our evolutionary equipment, ready for use in our cognitive development.

Piaget's theory does not explain how even young children can perform at an advanced level in certain areas where they have highly developed knowledge and expertise. An expert 9-year-old chess player may think abstractly about chess moves, while a novice 20-year-old player may have to resort to more concrete strategies to plan and remember moves (Siegler, 1991). As John Flavell (1985) noted, "the expert [child] looks very, very smart—very 'cognitively mature'—when functioning in her area of expertise" (p. 83).

Cognitive Development and Information Processing.   As you will see in Chapter 7, there are alternative explanations for why children have trouble with conservation and other Piagetian tasks. These explanations focus on the child's developing information processing skills such as attention, memory capacity, and learning strategies. Siegler (1991) proposes that, as children grow older, they develop better and better rules for solving problems and for thinking logically. Teachers can help students develop their capacities for formal thinking by putting the students in situations that challenge their thinking and reveal the shortcomings of their logic. Seigler's approach is called *rule assessment* because it focuses on understanding, challenging, and changing the rules that students use for thinking. This approach assumes specific experiences, teaching, and other outside influences play a greater role children's cognitive development.

Cognitive Development and Culture.   A final criticism of Piaget's theory is that it overlooks the important effects of the child's cultural and social group. Children in Western cultures may master scientific thinking and formal operations because this is the kind of thinking required in Western schools (Artman & Cahan, 1993; Berk, 1996). Even basic concrete operations such as classification may not be so basic to people of other cultures. For example, when African subjects from among the Kpelle people were asked to sort 20 objects, they created groups that made sense to them—a hoe with a potato, a knife with an orange. The experimenter could not get the Kpelle to change their categories; they said this is how a wise man would do it. Finally the experimenter asked in desperation, "Well, how would a fool do it?" The subjects promptly created the four neat classification piles the experimenter had expected—food, tools, and so on (Rogoff & Morelli, 1989).

Focus on...

Implications of Piaget's Theory

- How can teachers get a sense of the kind of thinking (preoperational, concrete, or formal) their students use to solve problems?
- What is the "problem of the match" described by Hunt?
- What is active learning? Why is Piaget's theory of cognitive development consistent with active learning?
- How would you teach an abstract concept to students like Trevor (p. 24)?

There is an increasingly influential view of cognitive development. Proposed years ago by Lev Vygotsky and recently rediscovered, this theory ties cognitive development to culture.

Vygotsky's Sociocultural Perspective

Psychologists today recognize that the child's culture shapes cognitive development by determining what and how the child will learn about the world. For example, young Zinacanteco Indian girls of southern Mexico learn complicated ways of weaving cloth. In Brazil, without going to school, children who sell candy on the streets learn sophisticated mathematics in order to buy from wholesalers, sell, barter, and make a profit. Cultures that prize cooperation and sharing teach these skills early, whereas cultures that encourage competition nurture these abilities in their children (Bakerman et al., 1990; Childs & Greenfield, 1982; Saxe, 1988). The stages observed by Piaget are not necessarily "natural" for all children because to some extent they reflect the expectations and activities of the children's culture (Rogoff & Chavajay, 1995).

A major spokesperson for this **sociocultural theory** (also called sociohistoric) was a Russian psychologist who died more than 50 years ago. Lev Semenovich Vygotsky was only 38 when he died, but his ideas about language, culture, and cognitive development were very mature. Recent translations of his work show that he provided an alternative to many of Piaget's ideas. Whereas Piaget described the child as a little scientist, constructing an understanding of the world largely alone, Vygotsky (1978, 1986, 1987, 1993) suggested that cognitive development depends much more on interactions with the

Sociocultural Theory Emphasizes role in development of cooperative dialogues between children and more knowledgeable members of society. Children learn the culture of their community (ways of thinking and behaving) through these interactions.

Lev Vygotsky's theories emphasize the importance of social interaction and support in cognitive development.

people in the child's world and the *tools* that the culture provides to support thinking. Children's knowledge, ideas, attitudes, and values develop through interaction with others. Children learn not through solitary exploration of the world, but by *appropriating* or "taking for themselves" the ways of acting and thinking provided by their culture (Kozulin & Presseisen, 1995).

Vygotsky also believed that real and symbolic tools such as printing presses, pencils, (today, we would add computers), numbers and mathematical systems, signs and codes, and language play very important roles in cognitive development. For example, as long as the culture provides only Roman numerals for representing quantity, certain ways of thinking mathematically—from long division to calculus—are difficult or impossible. But with a number system that has a zero, fractions, positive and negative values, and an infinite number of numbers, much more is possible. The number system is a cultural tool that supports thinking, learning, and cognitive development. This system is passed from adult to child through formal and informal interactions and teachings.

In Vygotsky's theory, the most important symbol system supporting learning is language.

The Role of Language and Private Speech

Language is critical for cognitive development. It provides a means for expressing ideas and asking questions, the categories and concepts for thinking, and the links between the past and the future (Das, 1995). When we consider a problem, we generally think in words and partial sentences. Vygotsky placed much more emphasis than Piaget on the role of language in cognitive development. In fact, Vygotsky believed that language in the form of **private speech** (talking to yourself) guides cognitive development.

Vygotsky's and Piaget's Views Compared.   If you have spent much time around young children, you know that they often talk to themselves as they play. Piaget called children's self-directed talk "egocentric speech." He assumed that this egocentric speech is another indication that young children can't see the world through the eyes of others. They talk about what matters to them, without taking into account the needs or interests of their listeners. As they mature, and especially as they have disagreements with peers, Piaget believed, children develop socialized speech. They learn to listen and exchange ideas.

Vygotsky had very different ideas about young children's private speech. Rather than being a sign of cognitive immaturity, Vygotsky suggested that these mutterings play an important role in cognitive development. The children are communicating—they are communicating with themselves to guide their behavior and thinking. In any preschool room you might hear 4- or 5-year-olds saying, "No, it won't fit. Try it here. Turn. Turn. Maybe this one . . . " while they do puzzles. As these children mature, their self-directed speech goes underground, changing from spoken to whispered speech and then to silent lip movements. Finally, the children just "think" the guiding words. The use of private speech peaks at around 5 to 7 years of age and has generally disappeared by 9 years of age. Brighter children seem to make this transition earlier (Bee, 1992).

Vygotsky identified this transition from audible private speech to silent inner speech as a fundamental process in cognitive development. Through this process the child is using language to accomplish important cognitive activities

Private Speech Children's self-talk, which guides their thinking and action. Eventually these verbalizations are internalized as silent inner speech.

TABLE 2.2   Differences between Piaget's and Vygotsky's Theories of Egocentric or Private Speech

	Piaget	Vygotsky
Developmental Significance	Represents an inability to take the perspective of another and engage in reciprocal communication	Represents externalized thought; its function is to communicate with the self for the purpose of self-guidance and self-direction
Course of Development	Declines with age	Increases at younger ages and then gradually loses its audible quality to become internal verbal thought
Relationship to Social Speech	Negative; least socially and cognitively mature children use more egocentric speech	Positive; private speech develops out of social interaction with others
Relationship to Environmental Contexts	—	Increases with task difficulty. Private speech serves a helpful self-guiding function in situations where more cognitive effort is needed to reach a solution

Source: From L. E. Berk and R. A. Garvin. Development of private speech among low-income Appalachian children. *Developmental Psychology, 20,* p. 272. Copyright © 1984 by the American Psychological Association. Adapted by permission.

such as directing attention, solving problems, planning, forming concepts, and gaining self-control. Research supports Vygotsky's ideas (Berk & Spuhl, 1995; Bivens & Berk, 1990; Diaz & Berk, 1992; Kohlberg, Yaeger, & Hjertholm, 1969). Children tend to use more private speech when they are confused, having difficulties, or making mistakes. Inner speech not only helps us solve problems but also allows us to regulate our behavior. Have you ever thought to yourself something like, "Let's see, the first step is . . . " or "Where did I use my glasses last . . . ?" or "If I work to the end of this page, then I can . . . "? You were using inner speech to remind, cue, encourage, or guide yourself. In a really tough situation, you might even find that you return to muttering out loud. Table 2.2 contrasts Piaget's and Vygotsky's theories of private speech. We should note that Piaget accepted many of Vygotsky's arguments and came to agree that language could be used in both egocentric and problem solving ways (Piaget, 1962).

Self-Talk and Learning.   Because private speech helps students to regulate their thinking, it makes sense to allow, and even encourage, students to use private speech in school. Insisting on total silence when young students are working on difficult problems may make the work even harder for them. You may notice when muttering increases—this could be a sign that students need help. One approach, called **cognitive self-instruction,** teaches students to use self-talk to guide learning. For example, students learn to give themselves reminders to go slowly and carefully. They "talk themselves through" tasks, saying such things as "Okay, what is it I have to do? . . . Copy the picture with the different lines. I have to go slowly and carefully. Okay, draw the line down, down, good; then to the right, that's it; now . . . " (Meichenbaum, 1977, p. 32).

Cognitive Self-Instruction Approach in which students "talk themselves through" a learning task.

The Role of Adults and Peers

Language plays another important role in development. Vygotsky believed that cognitive development occurs through the child's conversations and interactions with more capable members of the culture, adults or more able peers. These people serve as guides and teachers, providing the information and support necessary for the child to grow intellectually. The adult listens carefully to the child and provides just the right help to advance the child's understanding. Thus, the child is not alone in the world "discovering" the cognitive operations of conservation or classification. This discovery is *assisted* or *mediated* by family members, teachers, and peers. Most of this guidance is communicated through language, at least in Western cultures. In some cultures, observing a skilled performance, not talking about it, guides the child's learning (Rogoff, 1990).

Jerome Bruner called this adult assistance **scaffolding** (Wood, Bruner, & Ross, 1976). The term aptly suggests that children use this help for support while they build a firm understanding that will eventually allow them to solve the problems on their own. For Vygotsky, social interaction was more than a method of teaching, it was the origin of higher mental processes such as problem solving. He assumed that "every function in a child's cultural development appears twice: first, on the social level and later on the individual level; first between people (*interpsychological*) and then inside the child (*intrapsychological*)" (Vygotsky, 1978, p. 57). Consider this example:

> A six-year-old has lost a toy and asks her father for help. The father asks her where she last saw the toy; the child says "I can't remember." He asks a series of questions—did you have it in your room? Outside? Next door? To each question, the child answers, "no." When he says "in the car?" she says "I think so" and goes to retrieve the toy. (Tharp & Gallimore, 1988, p. 14)

Who remembered? The answer is really neither the father nor the daughter, but the two together. The remembering and problem solving was *between people*—in the interaction, but the child may have internalized strategies to use next time something is lost. At some point, the child will be able to function independently to solve this kind of problem. Like the strategy for finding the toy, higher functions appear first between a child and a "teacher" before they exist within the individual child (Kozulin, 1990).

Implications of Vygotsky's Theory for Teachers

There are at least three ways that cultural tools can be passed from one individual to another—*imitative learning* (where one person tries to imitate the other), *instructed learning* (where learners internalize the instructions of the teacher and use these instructions to self-regulate), and *collaborative learning* (where a group of peers strives to understand each other and learning occurs

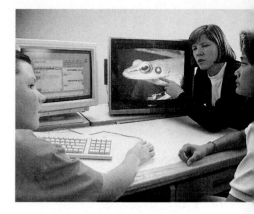

According to Vygotsky, much of children's learning is assisted or mediated by teachers and tools in their environment, and most of this guidance is communicated through language.

Focus on...

Vygotsky's Theory

- What are psychological tools and how do they support learning?
- What are the differences between Piaget's and Vygotsky's perspectives on private speech and its role in development?
- Explain how interpsychological development becomes intrapsychological development.

Scaffolding Support for learning and problem solving. The support could be clues, reminders, encouragement, breaking the problem down into steps, providing an example, or anything else that allows the student to grow in independence as a learner.

in the process) (Tomasello, Kruger, & Ratner, 1993). Vygotsky was most concerned with instructed learning though direct teaching or through structuring experiences that support another's learning, but his theory supports the other forms of cultural learning as well. Thus Vygotsky's ideas are relevant for educators who teach directly and also create learning environments (Das, 1995). One major aspect of teaching in either situation is assisted learning.

Assisted Learning

Assisted learning, or guided participation in the classroom, requires scaffolding—giving information, prompts, reminders, encouragement at the right time and in the right amounts, and then gradually allowing the students to do more and more on their own. Teachers can assist learning by adapting materials or problems to students' current levels; demonstrating skills or thought processes; walking students through the steps of a complicated problem; doing part of the problem (for example, in algebra, the students set up the equation and the teacher does the calculations or vice versa); giving detailed feedback and allowing revisions; or asking questions that refocus students' attention (Rosenshine & Meister, 1992). Meichenbaum's cognitive self-instruction described above is an example of assisted learning. Cognitive apprenticeships, reciprocal teaching, and instructional conversations (Chapter 9) are other examples. Table 2.3 gives examples of strategies that can be used in any lesson.

How can you know what kind of help to give and when to give it? One answer has to do with the student's zone of proximal development.

TABLE 2.3   Assisted Learning: Strategies to Scaffold Complex Learning

- *Procedural facilitators.* These provide a "scaffold" to help students learn implicit skills. For example, a teacher might encourage students to use "signal words" such as who, what, where, when, why, and how to generate questions after reading a passage.

- *Modeling use of facilitators.* The teacher, in the above example, might model the generation of questions about the reading.

- *Thinking out loud.* This models the teacher's expert thought processes, showing students the revisions and choices the learner makes in using procedural facilitators to work on problems.

- *Anticipating difficult areas.* During the modeling and presentations phase of instruction, for example, the teacher anticipates and discusses potential student errors.

- *Proving prompt or cue cards.* Procedural facilitators are written on "prompt cards" that students keep for

reference as they work. As students practice, the cards gradually become unnecessary.

- *Regulating the difficulty.* Tasks involving implicit skills are introduced by beginning with simpler problems, providing for student practice after each step, and gradually increasing the complexity of the task.

- *Providing half-done examples.* Giving students half-done examples of problems and having them work out the conclusions can be an effective way to teach students how to ultimately solve problems on their own.

- *Reciprocal teaching.* Having the teacher and students rotate the role of teacher. The teacher provides support to students as they learn to lead discussions and ask their own questions.

- *Providing checklists.* Students can be taught self-checking procedures to help them regulate the quality of their responses.

The Zone of Proximal Development

According to Vygotsky, at any given point in development there are certain problems that a child is on the verge of being able to solve. The child just needs some structure, clues, reminders, help with remembering details or steps, encouragement to keep trying, and so on. Some problems, of course, are beyond the child's capabilities, even if every step is explained clearly. The **zone of proximal development** is the area where the child cannot solve a problem alone, but can be successful under adult guidance or in collaboration with a more advanced peer (Wertsch, 1991). This is the area where instruction can succeed, because real learning is possible.

We can see how Vygotsky's beliefs about the role of private speech in cognitive development fit with the notion of the zone of proximal development. Often, an adult helps a child to solve a problem or accomplish a task using verbal prompts and structuring. This scaffolding may be gradually reduced as the child takes over the guidance, perhaps first by giving the prompts as private speech and finally as inner speech. Let's move forward to a future day in the life of the girl in the example above who had lost her toy and *listen to* her thoughts when she realizes that a schoolbook is missing. They might sound something like this:

> "Where's my math book? Used it in class. Thought I put it in my book-bag after class. Dropped my bag on the bus. That dope Larry kicked my stuff, so maybe . . . "

The girl can now systematically search for ideas about the lost book without help from anyone else.

Assessment.   One implication of Vygotsky's zone of proximal development has to do with assessment. Most standard tests simply measure what students can do alone. This is useful information, but may not tell teachers or parents how to help the students learn more. An alternative is dynamic assessment (Spector, 1992) or learning potential assessment (Feuerstein, 1979, 1990). The goal of these approaches is to identify the zone of proximal development by asking a child to solve a problem, then giving prompts and hints to see how he or she learns, adapts, and uses the guidance. These prompts are systematically increased to see how much support is needed and how the child responds. The teacher watches, listens, and takes careful notes about how the child uses the help and what level of support is necessary, and then applies this information to plan instructional groupings, peer tutoring, learning tasks, assignments, and so on.

Teaching.   A second implication of Vygotsky's work relates to teaching, but assessment and teaching are closely connected. Students should be put in situations where they have to reach to understand, but where support from other students or from the teacher is also available. Sometimes the best teacher is another student who has just figured out the problem, because this student is probably operating in the learner's zone of proximal development. Vygotsky's theory suggests that teachers need to do more than just arrange the environment

---

Focus on...

Vygotsky and Teaching

- What is assisted learning, and what role does scaffolding play?
- Think of some kinds of scaffolding that would help you learn about Vygotsky.
- How would you identify a student's zone of proximal development in an area you will teach?
- In the situation at the beginning of the chapter, how would you use peer learning to move students toward an understanding of symbolism?

Assisted Learning Providing strategic help in the initial stages of learning, gradually diminishing as students gain independence.

Zone of Proximal Development Phase at which a child can master a task if given appropriate help and support.

*S*ometimes the best teachers are other students who have just understood a particular concept. These "teachers" may be operating in the zone of proximal development for their fellow students.

so that students can discover on their own. The students should be guided by explanations, demonstrations, and work with other students—opportunities for cooperative learning. Having a student work with someone who is just a bit better at the activity would also be a good idea. In addition, students should be encouraged to use language to organize their thinking and to talk about what they are trying to accomplish. Dialogue and discussion are important avenues to learning (Karpov & Bransford, 1995; Kozulin & Presseisen, 1995). The Guidelines give more ideas.

Guidelines

Applying Vygotsky's Ideas in Teaching

Tailor scaffolding to the needs of students.

Examples

1. When students are beginning new tasks or topics, provide models, prompts, sentence starters, coaching, and feedback. As the students grow in competence, give less support and more opportunities for independent work.

2. Give students choices about the level of difficulty or degree of independence in projects; encourage them to challenge themselves but to seek help when they are really stuck.

Make sure students have access to powerful tools that support thinking.

Examples

1. Teach students to use learning and organizational strategies, research tools, language tools (dictionaries or computer searches), spreadsheets, and word processing programs.

2. Model the use of tools; show students how you use an appointment book or electronic notebook to make plans and manage time, for example.

Capitalize on dialogue and group learning.

Examples

1. Experiment with peer tutoring; teach students how to ask good questions and give helpful explanations.
2. Experiment with cooperative learning strategies described in Chapters 9 and 11.

The Development of Language

All children in every culture master the complicated system of their native language, unless severe deprivation or physical problems interfere. This knowledge is remarkable. At the least, sounds, meanings, words and sequences of words, volume, voice tone, inflection, and turn-taking rules must all be coordinated before a child can communicate effectively in conversations. As you might expect, there are different theories about how people master the complex process of communication.

How Do We Learn Language?

One early view of language development assumed that children learn language just as they learn anything else, by repeating those behaviors that lead to some kind of positive result. The child makes a sound, the parent smiles and replies. The child says, "Mmm," in the presence of milk, and the parent says, "Yes, milk, milk," and gives the child a drink. The child learns to say "milk" because it leads to a happy parent and a drink of milk. Children add new words by imitating the sounds they hear and improve their use of language when they are corrected by the adults around them. This explanation of language learning is based on the behavioral perspective described in Chapter 6.

Such a theory is appealing, but research has shown that many of a child's earliest utterances are not imitations but original creations. And they are unlikely to be rewarded, because they are "incorrect," even though they make sense to the people involved. Examples are such phrases as "paper find," "car mosquito," "tooth-guy" (dentist), or "all gone kitty" (Moshman, Glover, & Bruning, 1987). In addition, researchers studying interactions between young children and their parents have discovered that parents rarely correct pronunciation and grammar during the early stages of language development. They are much more likely to respond to the content of a child's remarks (Brown & Hanlon, 1970; Demetras & Post, 1985). In fact, if parents spent all their time correcting a child's language and never "heard" what the child was trying to say, the child might give up trying to master a system as complicated as language.

Adults caring for children seem continually to adapt their language to stay just ahead of the child. Before children begin talking, adults may direct long, complicated sentences to them, but as soon as a child utters identifiable words, adults simplify their language. As the child progresses, adults tend to change their language to stay just a bit more advanced than the child's current level of development, thus encouraging new understanding (Bohannon & Warren-

Leubecker, 1989; Fernald, 1993). It seems that in order to stretch the child's language development, adults give the kind of support, or scaffolding, that Vygotsky has recommended. Adults, by staying slightly more advanced in their language, may also create disequilibrium and encourage development as a result.

But even this rich learning environment cannot explain how children learn so much language so quickly and correctly. Think of all the sounds that could be combined in different orders and linked with many different meanings. Why don't children create wild languages or make crazy associations between a sound and a meaning? Why, for example, when their parents say, "Look, a rabbit," do children learn to connect the word *rabbit* with the whole animal, not with the animal's ears, or movements, or size, or fur? Some psychologists explain this amazing accomplishment by assuming that humans are born with a special capacity for processing, understanding, and creating language (Chomsky, 1965, 1986; Eimas, 1985; Maratsos, 1989). Humans may have built-in biases, rules, and constraints about language that restrict the number of possibilities considered. For example, young children seem to have a constraint specifying that a new label refers to a whole object, not just a part. Another built-in bias leads children to assume that the label refers to a class of similar objects. So the child learning about the rabbit is equipped naturally to assume that *rabbit* refers to the whole animal (not just its ears) and that other similar-looking animals are also rabbits. These built-in constraints simplify language learning (Markman, 1990). Also, humans may share a universal grammar, a set of specifications and rules that limit the range of language created. In other words, only certain possibilities are considered as the child figures out the puzzle of language (Chomsky, 1980).

It is likely that many factors—biological and experiential—play a role in language development. The important point is that children develop language as they develop other cognitive abilities by actively trying to make sense of what they hear and by looking for patterns and making up rules to put together the jigsaw puzzle of language. In this process, built-in biases and rules may limit the search and guide the pattern recognition. Reward and correction play a role in helping children learn correct language use, but the child's thinking and creativity in putting together the parts of this complicated system are very important (Rosser, 1994). In the process a child makes some very logical "mistakes," as you will see.

Stages in the Process of Language Acquisition

Before they learn to speak, children communicate through crying, smiling, and body movements. By the end of the first year, more or less, most children have spoken their first word. They have entered what psychologists call the one-word stage.

First Words.   After the first word, for the next three or four months, children add slowly to their vocabulary until they have about ten words. After this, words are added rapidly. By about 20 months, the vocabulary includes approximately 50 words (Nelson, 1981).

Even at this early stage, language is more complex than it might appear. One word can be used to communicate a variety of sophisticated ideas. For example, my daughter's first word was *ite* (translated: light). Said loudly while reaching toward the light switch on the wall, "ITE!" meant "I want to flip the switch on and off (and on and off, and on and off)." When someone else flipped the switch while she was playing on the floor, Elizabeth might remark "Ite," meaning "You turned on the light." When single words are used in this way, they are called **holophrases,** because they express whole phrases or complex ideas.

A second, related characteristic of this period is **overextension.** Children may use one word to cover a range of concepts. For example, on a trip to the zoo, the 13-month-old son of a friend pointed excitedly at every animal, including peacocks and elephants, saying "Dug, dug" (translated: dog, dog). This was the only word he had that came close to being adequate. He wisely rejected his other possibilities: "bye-bye," "more," "Mama," and "Dada." He used the language tools available to him to make sense of his world and to communicate. Children sometimes show **underextension** as well; they use words too specifically. For example, Siegler (1991) tells about the child who used the word "bottle" only for her baby bottle and not for soda bottles or water bottles.

First Sentences.   At about 18 months, many children enter the two-word stage. They begin to string words together in two-word sentences such as "Daddy book," "Play car," "Allgone milk," and "More light." This is **telegraphic speech** (R. Brown, 1973). The nonessential details are left out, and the words that carry the most meaning are included, as in a telegram. Even though sentences are short, semantics can be complex. Children can express possession ("Daddy book"), recurrence ("More light"), action on an object ("Play car"), and even disappearance or nonexistence ("Allgone milk").

For about one year, children continue to focus on the essential words even as they lengthen their sentences. At a certain point that varies from child to child, new features are added. Children begin to elaborate their simple language by adding plurals, endings for verbs such as *-ed* and *-ing,* and small words like *and, but,* and *in.* In the process of figuring out the rules governing these aspects of language, children make some very interesting mistakes.

Learning Grammar.   For a brief time, children may use irregular forms of particular words properly, as if they are saying what they have heard. Then, as they begin to learn rules, they **overregularize** words by applying the rules to everything. Children who once said, "Our car is broken" begin to insist, "Our car is broked." Parents often wonder why their child seems to be "regressing." Actually, these "mistakes" show how logical and rational children can be as they try to assimilate new words into existing schemes. Because most languages have many irregular words, accommodation is necessary in mastering language.

Another aspect of overregularizing language involves the order of words in a sentence. Since the usual order in English is subject–verb–object, preschoolers just mastering the rules of language have trouble with sentences in any different order. For example, if they hear a statement in the passive voice, like "The truck was bumped by the car," they usually think the truck did the bumping to the car (Berger, 1986). So in talking with young children, it is generally better to use direct language.

Learning Vocabulary.   During the preschool years, children learn new words very rapidly, doubling their vocabulary about every six months between

Holophrases Single words that express complex ideas.

Overextension Using one word to cover a range of concepts.

Underextension Being too specific in using a word, limiting the word's meaning to a narrow range of possible examples.

Telegraphic Speech Children's speech using only essential words, as in a telegram.

Overregularize Apply a learned rule to all situations, including inappropriate ones.

ages 2 and 4, from about 200 to 2,000 words. During this time they may enjoy making up words. Because their thinking is egocentric, they may assume you know exactly what these words mean. They also tend to center on one meaning for a word.

Preschool children like to play with language. They enjoy sounds and silliness. The young son of a friend of mine wanted to name his new baby sister "Brontosaurus" because he "just liked to say it!" Think of all the language games, rhymes, taunts, chants, secret languages (pig Latin, Obish), and rituals that filled your early days. In my time it was "Sticks and stones may break my bones, but words will never hurt me," and the ever-popular "School's out, school's out. . . ."

Language Development in the School Years

By about age 5 or 6, most children have mastered the basics of their native language. As noted earlier, the language of these children can still be quite egocentric. Preschoolers may have special meanings for words. They may talk to themselves as they work, first clearly, then in a whisper, and finally silently. What remains for the school-age child to accomplish?

Pronunciation.   The majority of first graders have mastered most of the sounds of their native language, but a few may remain unconquered. As you can see from Figure 2.3, the *j, v, th,* and *zh* sounds are the last to develop. About 10 percent of 8-year-olds still have some trouble with *s, z, v, th,* and *zh* (Rathus, 1988). Young children may understand and be able to use many words but prefer to use the words they can pronounce easily.

Intonation or word emphasis may also cause problems for young children. If the meaning of a sentence is ambiguous and intonation makes the difference, then children as old as 8 or 9 may misunderstand. Moshman, Glover, and Bruning (1987) give this example. Consider the sentence, "George gave the book to David, and he gave one to Bill." If you emphasize the *he*, then the meaning is "George gave the book to David, and David gave another book to Bill." With a different intonation, emphasizing the *and*, for example, the meaning is changed to "George gave the book to David, and George also gave one to Bill." Don't expect early elementary-school students to pick up subtle meanings in intonation.

Syntax.   Children master the basics of word orders, or **syntax,** in their native language early. But the more complicated forms, such as the passive voice, take longer to master. By early elementary school, many children can understand the meaning of passive sentences, yet they do not use such constructions in their normal conversations. Other accomplishments during elementary school include first understanding and then using complex grammatical structures such as extra clauses, qualifiers, and conjunctions.

Vocabulary and Meaning.   Between the ages of 2 and 6, the average child learns between six and ten words a day. This means the average 6-year-old has a vocabulary of 8,000 to 14,000 words. From ages 9 to 11, about 5,000 new words are added to this repertoire. It seems that the time before puberty, especially the preschool years, is a sensitive period for language growth.

"WHEN I SAY 'RUNNED,' YOU KNOW I MEAN 'RAN.' LET'S NOT QUIBBLE."

© 1994 by Sidney Harris

Syntax The order of words in phrases or sentences.

FIGURE 2.3

Acquisition of the Sounds of Speech

The solid bar for each sound of speech begins at the age by which 50 percent of children pronounce it properly. The bar ends at the age by which 90 percent of children are pronouncing the sound correctly.

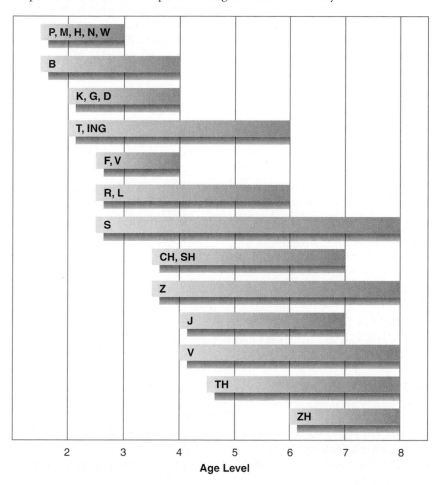

Source: Figure from *Understanding Child Development* by Spencer A. Rathus and Peter Favaro, copyright © 1988 by Holt, Rinehart and Winston, Inc., reproduced by permission of the publisher.

Research has shown that we can learn much about language after puberty, but that very positive or very negative conditions during the sensitive period before puberty can greatly help or hinder language development (Anglin, 1993; Johnson & Newport, 1989).

In the early elementary years, some children may have trouble with abstract words such as *justice* or *economy*. They may also take statements literally and thus misunderstand sarcasm or metaphor. Many children are in their preadolescent years before they are able to distinguish being kidded from being taunted or before they know that a sarcastic remark is not meant to be taken literally (Gardner, 1982b).

Pragmatics.   **Pragmatics** involves the appropriate use of language to communicate. Children show an understanding of pragmatics when they talk in simpler sentences to younger children or command their pets to "Come here!" in louder, deeper voices (Rice, 1984). But there is much more to successful communicating. For instance, children must learn the rules of turn-taking in conversation. The conversations of young children tend to follow the rules of turn-taking, even if the children don't seem to listen to each other, as illustrated in Figure 2.4. What seem to adults to be disjointed, unrelated remarks do not bother young children at all. They are paying attention to their own remarks, not the other children's, and they probably assume that everyone else is doing the same.

When children begin to have arguments, you can tell that they are listening to each other. In later elementary school, children's conversations start to sound like conversations. Contributions are usually on the same topic. By adolescence, students become interested in analyzing the feelings and views of others. They want to understand the perspective of the other speakers. You will hear "How did you feel when she did that?" or "Why aren't you sitting with Jonah? Did you have a fight?" (Dorval & Eckerman, 1984).

Focus on...

Language Development

- How are humans predisposed to develop language? What role does learning play?
- What do children's mistakes in using irregular verbs (i.e., "broked" for broken or "goed" for went) tell about the way they learn language?
- How can teachers extend and enrich students' language development?

FIGURE 2.4

Conversational Pragmatics

Young children know the structure of conversations—how to take turns—even though the "talk" is not always related.

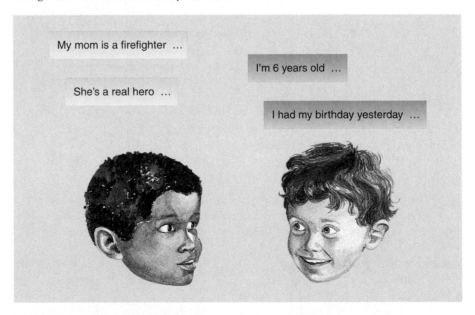

Source: From *Children's Thinking* by Robert Siegler, p. 35, © 1986. Adapted by permission of Prentice-Hall, Inc., Saddle River, NJ.

Pragmatics Area of language involving the effects of contexts on meaning.

Metalinguistic Awareness.   Around the age of 5, students begin to develop **metalinguistic awareness.** This means their understanding about language and how it works becomes explicit. They have knowledge about language itself. They are ready to study and extend the rules that have been implicit—understood but not consciously expressed. This process continues throughout life, as we all become better able to manipulate and comprehend language. Teachers can develop the language abilities and knowledge of their students in a variety of ways.

Language, Literacy, and Teaching

One goal of schooling is the development of language and literacy. Literacy includes oral language as well as reading and writing. Today we know that children know a great deal about written language long before they can read or write in conventional ways:

- A make-believe grocery store in a preschool has a sign announcing the daily special, "APLS BNS 5¢" (apples and bananas 5¢) (Berk, 1996).
- A 4-year-old announces to his mother as they drive into the mall parking lot, "Look Mommy, I can read those letters, M . . . A . . . C . . . Y . . . S— Sears!" (Morrow, 1997).
- A 4-year-old writes a story (a) and a grocery list (b) in Figure 2.5.

These students know a great deal about reading and writing. They know that letters have different forms; that letters are associated with sounds and go together to make words; that words communicate meaning and make sentences; that writing goes from left to right and lists go down the page; and that stories look different from shopping lists. Teachers should strive to build on this emerging literacy understanding (Paris & Cunningham, 1996).

FIGURE 2.5

A Story and a Grocery List

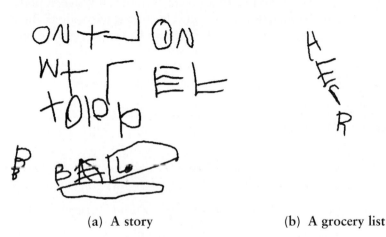

(a) **A story**   (b) **A grocery list**

Source: Lea M. McGee and Donald J. Richgels, *Literacy's Beginnings* (2nd ed.), p. 81. Copyright © 1990 by Allyn & Bacon. Reprinted by permission.

Metalinguistic Awareness Understanding about one's own use of language.

Teachers and Literacy

In its publication, *Literacy Development in Early Childhood (Preschool through Grade 3),* the International Reading Association (1995) lists the following basic premises of a sound prefirst-grade reading program:

- Reading and writing at school should permit children to build upon their existing knowledge of oral and written language.
- Learning should take place in a supportive environment where children can build a positive attitude toward themselves and toward language and literacy.
- For optimal learning, teachers should involve children actively in many meaningful, functional language experiences, including *speaking, listening, writing,* and *reading.*
- Teachers of young children should be prepared in ways that acknowledge differences in language and cultural backgrounds, and should emphasize reading as an integral part of language arts as well as the total curriculum.*

Teachers can enrich students' language environment by focusing not just on correct or incorrect usage, but on the idea expressed. Probe and extend students' ideas. For example, if a student says, "I writed my name on my picture," the teacher could respond, "You wrote your name above the rocket. Where is your astronaut going?" In this way, the teacher maintains the student's interest and at the same time expands the complexity of the statement and recasts the language to a more mature form (Rice, 1989). Parents who use these strategies have children who make rapid progress in language learning (Farrar, 1990).

Cazden (1988) suggests that word meanings are most easily learned through interactions and conversations with an adult in which the adult introduces new words. For example, when a student complains, "He does that on purpose, just to make me mad!" the teacher might respond, "So you think he is intentionally tripping by your desk just to irritate you? What's your evidence for that conclusion?" Reading aloud is also a potent form of language stimulation. Reading to students often leads to conversations about the pictures or ideas in the books. The importance of one-to-one interaction with an adult in developing language abilities has been stressed by many educators and psychologists (Morrow, 1997; Rice, 1989). This is in keeping with Vygotsky's theory of cognitive development.

> **Focus on...**
>
> ### Language, Literacy, and Teaching
>
> - How do young children reveal their emerging literacy understandings?
> - Describe teacher actions and responses that encourage language development.
> - Name two things you could do to form literacy partnerships with your students' families.
> - How could you elaborate on and extend Trevor's understanding of "symbolism" (p. 24)?

Partnerships with Families

Especially in the early years, the students' home experiences are central in the development of language and literacy (Roskos & Neuman, 1993; Snow, 1993; Whitehurst et al., 1994). In homes that promote literacy, parents and

*From *Literacy development and early childhood (preschool through grade 3).* (1990). A position statement prepared by the Early Childhood and Literacy Development Committee of the International Reading Association. Copyright © 1985 by the International Reading Association. All rights reserved. Reprinted by permission.

other adults value reading as a source of pleasure, and there are books and other printed materials everywhere. Parents read to their children, take them to bookstores and libraries, and limit the amount of television everyone watches (Pressley, 1996; Sulzby & Teale, 1991). Of course, not all homes provide this literacy-rich environment, but teachers can help, as you will see in the Guidelines.

Guidelines

Family and Community Partnerships for Literacy Programs

Communicate with families about the goals and activities of your program.

Examples

1. At the beginning of school, send home a description of the goals to be achieved in your class—make sure it is a clear and readable format.

2. As you start each unit, send home a newsletter describing what students will be studying—give suggestions for home activities that support the learning.

Involve families in decisions about curriculum.

Examples

1. Have planning workshops at times family members can attend—provide child care for younger siblings, but let children and families work together on projects.

2. Invite parents to come to class to read to students, take dictation of stories, tell stories, record or bind books, and demonstrate skills.

Provide home activities to be shared with family members.

Examples

1. Encourage family members to work with children to read and follow simple recipes, play language games, keep diaries or journals for the family, and visit the library. Get feedback from families or students about the activities.

2. Give families feedback sheets and ask them to help evaluate the child's school work.

3. Provide lists of good children's literature available locally—work with libraries, clubs, and churches to identify sources.

Source: From Lesley Mandel Morrow, *Literacy Development in the Early Years: Helping Children Read and Write,* 3/e, pp. 68–70. Copyright © 1997 by Allyn & Bacon. Adapted by permission.

Throughout this text you will read about other ways that teachers can encourage language development for both younger and older students. For example, we will discuss bilingual education in Chapter 5, reciprocal teaching, whole language, the language of thinking in Chapter 8, and instructional conversations in Chapter 9.

A Definition of Development

Theorists differ greatly in their approach to the study of development, but all tend to agree that people develop at different rates, that development is an orderly process, and that development takes place gradually. The brain begins to lateralize soon after birth and thus to specialize certain functions in certain areas. The younger the child, the more plastic the brain and the more easily the child's brain can adapt to damage. Even though certain functions are associated with certain parts of the brain, the various parts and working systems of the brain work together to learn and perform complex human activities and to construct understanding.

Piaget's Theory of Cognitive Development

Piaget's theory of cognitive development is based on the assumption that people try to make sense of the world and actively create their knowledge through direct experience with objects, people, and ideas. Maturation, activity, social transmission, and the need for equilibrium all influence the way thinking processes and knowledge develop. In response to these influences, according to Piaget's theory, thinking processes and knowledge develop through adaptation (including the complementary processes of assimilation and accommodation) and changes in the organization of thought (the development of schemes).

Piaget believed that young people pass through four stages as they develop: sensorimotor, preoperational, concrete-operational, and formal-operational. In the sensorimotor stage, infants explore the world through their senses and motor activity, and work toward mastering object permanence and performing goal-directed activities. In the preoperational stage, symbolic thinking and logical operations begin. Children in the stage of concrete operations can think logically about tangible situations and can demonstrate conservation, reversibility, classification, and seriation. The ability to perform hypothetico-deductive reasoning, coordinate a set of variables, and imagine other worlds marks the stage of formal operations.

Implications of Piaget's Theory for Teachers

Teachers can use Piaget's theory of cognitive development to understand students' thinking, to match instructional strategies to students' abilities, and to directly foster students' cognitive development. Piaget's theory has been criticized because children and adults often think in ways that are inconsistent with the notion of invariant stages. It also appears that Piaget underestimated children's cognitive abilities. Alternative explanations place greater emphasis on students' developing information processing skills and how

teachers can enhance their development. Piaget's work is also criticized for overlooking cultural factors in child development. Critics often point to the work of Vygotsky as an example of a theory of cognitive development that does include the important role of culture.

Vygotsky's Sociocultural Perspective

Vygotsky's sociocultural view asserts that cognitive development hinges on social interaction and the development of language. As an example, Vygotsky describes the role of children's self-directed talk in guiding and monitoring thinking and problem solving. Vygotsky, more than Piaget, emphasized the significant role played by adults and more able peers in children's learning. This adult assistance provides early support while students build the understanding necessary to solve problems on their own later.

Implications of Vygotsky's Theory for Teachers

Vygotsky proposed the concept of a zone of proximal development, in which children in challenging situations can develop their own thinking abilities through timely, appropriate guidance and support from teachers or peers, called scaffolding. Assisted learning is the process of providing appropriate scaffolding within the student's zone of proximal development. Assessment procedures designed to analyze a student's zone of proximal development can be applied to plan instructional groupings, learning tasks, and so on. Vygotsky's work implies that students should be given opportunities for cooperative learning and should be encouraged to use language to organize their thinking.

The Development of Language

Closely linked to cognitive development are the development of language and metalinguistic awareness. Children try to understand and apply language rules. Chomsky and others suggest that some of these rules are inborn in humans. Using their capacity for language, children try to solve the puzzle of the language they hear, moving from holophrasic to telegraphic speech through overextension, underextension, and overregularization to a basic understanding of pronunciation, vocabulary, grammar and syntax, semantics, and pragmatics by around age 5 or 6. Metalinguistic awareness typically begins at around this age, and continues throughout life.

Language, Literacy, and Teaching

Teachers have a significant role in helping children develop language ability and knowledge about language. Teachers can focus on effective communication, meaning, comprehension, and respect for language in the classroom. Reading aloud and one-on-one interactions with adults are significant in developing language abilities. Parents can play a key role in promoting literacy at home, and teachers can form partnerships with parents to capitalize on this role.

KEY TERMS

accommodation, p. 29
adaptation, p. 28
adolescent egocentrism, p. 38
assimilation, p. 28
assisted learning, p. 48
classification, p. 35
cognitive development, p. 24
cognitive self-instruction, p. 46
collective monologue, p. 32
compensation, p. 35
concrete operations, p. 34
conservation, p. 32
decentering, p. 32
development, p. 24
disequilibrium, p. 29
egocentric, p. 32

equilibration, p. 29
formal operations, p. 37
goal-directed actions, p. 31
holophrases, p. 53
hypothetico-deductive reasoning, p. 37
identity, p. 35
maturation, p. 25
metalinguistic awareness, p. 57
object permanence, p. 30
operations, p. 31
organization, p. 28
overextension, p. 53
overregularize, p. 53
personal development, p. 24
physical development, p. 24

pragmatics, p. 56
preoperational, p. 31
private speech, p. 45
reversibility, p. 35
reversible thinking, p. 32
scaffolding, p. 47
schemes, p. 28
semiotic function, p. 31
sensorimotor, p. 30
seriation, p. 35
social development, p. 24
sociocultural theory, p. 44
syntax, p. 54
telegraphic speech, p. 53
underextension, p. 53
zone of proximal development, p. 49

CHECK YOUR UNDERSTANDING

Can you apply the ideas from this chapter on cognitive development to solve the following problems of practice?

Preschool and Kindergarten

- A group of vocal parents wants you to introduce workbooks to teach basic arithmetic in your class for 4- and 5-year-olds. They seem to think that "play" with blocks, water, sand, clay, and so on is "wasted time." How would you respond?

Elementary and Middle School

- Two very concerned parents want to have a conference with you about their son's "language problems." He is in first grade and has some trouble with pronunciation. How would you prepare for the conference?

Junior High and High School

- The students in your class persist in memorizing definitions for many of the important abstract concepts in your class. They insist, "That's what you have to do to make a good grade in this class." Even though they can repeat the definitions precisely, they seem to have no conception of what the terms mean; they can't recognize examples of the concept in problems or give their own examples. It is almost as if they don't believe there is any real hope of understanding the ideas. Pick one important, difficult concept in your field, and design a lesson to teach it to students who believe only in memorization.

- It seems as if every fourth word from the mouths of your students is *like* or *you know*. Also, their understanding of the material in your class is limited, because they don't know the meaning of many words that you assumed high school students would certainly understand, such as *former* and *latter*. What would you do to encourage language development along with teaching your subject?

Cooperative Learning Activity

- Working with four or five other members of your educational psychology class, solve either the "pronunciation" or the "memorization" problem described above. Then pair up with another group and take turns teaching the lessons you designed.

What Would They Do?

The district curriculum guide calls for a unit on poetry, including lessons on *symbolism* in poems. You are concerned that many of your fifth-grade students may not be ready to understand this abstract concept. To test the waters, you ask a few students what a symbol is.

"It's sorta like a big metal thing that you bang together." Tracy waves her hands like a drum major.

You realize they are on the wrong track here, so you try again. "I was thinking of a different kind of symbol, like a ring as a symbol of marriage or a heart as a symbol of love, or . . . "

You are met with blank stares.

LINDA GLISSON AND SUE MIDDLETON

Fifth Grade Team Teachers
St. James Episcopal Day School, Baton Rouge, Louisiana

While most eleven-year-olds are in the beginning cognitive stage of understanding abstractions, it seems that these students have not reached that level of readiness. However, with use of controlled instruction designed to guide children from the concrete to the abstract, these students can learn that they actually know more about abstractions and symbolism than they realize.

In order to "listen" to my students' thinking to match my teaching to their level of thinking, I would keep a notepad handy for an entire day to jot down any ideas regarding symbolism that the children might unknowingly express during class time, lunch, and recess. I would then incorporate their personal experiences in a lesson on symbolism before deciding whether to move into the unit on symbolism in poetry.

To begin the lesson, I would have the students use a dictionary to define the word *symbolism* (root word—*symbol*) to discover that it means "something that stands for or represents something else." I would then give them a brief "across the curriculum" exercise in ways they incorporate symbols and symbolism into their thinking every day. For example: (social studies, American history): The American flag is just a piece of cloth. Why then do we recite a pledge to it? Stand at attention when it passes in a parade? What does it stand for? (English, literature—fables and fairy tales): What does the wolf usually represent (stand for)? The lion? The lamb? (Art): What color stands for a glorious summer day? Evil? Goodness and purity? I would continue with math symbols, scientific symbols, and music symbols and lead the students toward contributing other examples such as symbols representing holidays. I would then tell them about their own examples of symbolism that I had recorded. The students' participation in and enthusiasm for the exercises would serve to determine whether they were ready for the material.

DR. NANCY SHEEHAN-MELZACK

Art and Music Teacher
Snug Harbor Community School, Quincy, Massachusetts

Even very young children can recognize symbols *if* the symbol is presented first and explanation required second. A drawing of an octagon on a pole has always elicited the answer, "A stop sign," whenever I have shown it. Note that the word STOP was not mentioned in the drawing, because the octagon is left blank.

Children recognize symbols, but the teacher needs to work from their concrete knowledge to the more abstract concept, and there are a great many symbols in their daily life on which one can draw. It is important in your discussion of symbolism with children to explain that symbols are usually something that a group agrees will stand for an idea or concept. Children as young as first graders can recognize traffic sign shapes, letters of the alphabet, and numbers, and further recognize that they stand for directions, sounds, and how many. When they talk about these very common symbols they can also realize they all use them for the same meaning.

Starting from the most concrete examples and progressing to less concrete ones will help you to determine where on the continuum a child is in understanding the concept of symbol. Make an effort to point out symbolism wherever it occurs during the school day until the children are comfortable with the notion and begin pointing symbols out to you. From their comments, you can judge when symbolic language can be introduced. Begin with the poetry of others and then move on to their own original symbolic poetry. Some of the following questions may help: (1) What can you think of that is as cold as ice that you could use to describe the winter wind? (2) Sometimes we hear about people being a rainbow of colors. Is there anything else that comes in many colors that we could use to describe people? (3) What would you like to use to describe how strong you are? What part of you is strongest? Does this help you decide?

VALERIE A. CHILCOAT

Fifth/Sixth Grade Advanced Academics
Glenmount School, Baltimore, Maryland

Concrete examples of symbolism must come from the students' own world. Street signs, especially those with pictures and not words, are a great example. The writing of the students' own names is a more abstract example of a symbol. Statues, photographs, and drawings are more examples of concrete symbols.

These concrete symbols, however, are not exactly the same as symbolism used in poetry. The link has to be made from the concrete to the abstract. Silly poetry is one way to do this. It is motivating to the students to read or listen to, and it can provide many examples of one thing acting as another. This strategy can also be used in lower grades to simply expose children to poetry containing symbolism.

Finally, I would read aloud as the children read silently a brief selection containing a blatant example of poetic symbolism. I would then re-ask the question "What is symbolism?" and require an example from the text. By using response cards or every pupil response, I could gauge the overall level of understanding in the room. If, at this point, many students still do not understand, I would chalk it up to exposure, leave it for a while, and return to it at a later time.

3

Personal, Social, and Emotional Development

Overview | *What Would You Do?*

THE WORK OF ERIKSON   66
   The Preschool Years: Trust, Autonomy, and Initiative | Elementary
   and Middle School Years: Industry versus Inferiority | Adolescence:
   The Search for Identity | Beyond the School Years

UNDERSTANDING OURSELVES AND OTHERS   73
   Self-Concept and Self-Esteem | School Life and Self-Esteem | Gender,
   Ethnicity, and Self-Esteem | The Self and Others

MORAL DEVELOPMENT   80
   Kohlberg's Stages of Moral Development | Alternatives to Kohlberg's
   Theory | The Morality of Caring | Moral Behavior

SOCIALIZATION: THE HOME AND THE SCHOOL   91
   American Families Today | New Roles for Teachers

CHALLENGES FOR CHILDREN   98
   Physical Development | Children and Youth at Risk

Summary | *Key Terms* | *Check Your Understanding* |
Teachers' Casebook: What Would They Do?

*R*eflect *on a teacher who helped to shape your sense of who you are—your abilities, aspirations, or values. What did the teacher do or say that influenced you? Do you know someone whose career choice was affected by a teacher?*

Schooling involves more than cognitive development. In this chapter we examine emotional, social, and moral development.

We begin with the work of Erik Erikson, whose comprehensive theory provides a framework for studying personal and social development. Next, we explore ideas about how we come to understand ourselves and others. What is the meaning of the self-concept, and how is it shaped? How do our views of others change as we grow? What factors determine our views about morality? What can teachers do to foster such personal qualities as honesty, cooperation, empathy, and self-esteem? We then consider the two major influences on children's personal and social development: families and schools. Families today have gone through many transitions, and these changes affect the roles of teachers. With an understanding of these aspects of personal and social development, we can consider a pressing question: "What is a developmentally appropriate education for students?"

We end the chapter by examining several challenges for children—the problems and opportunities of physical development and the many risks that confront students today—such as child abuse, drugs, and AIDS.

By the time you have completed this chapter, you should be able to:

- Describe Erikson's stages of psychosocial development and list several of his theory's implications for teaching.
- Suggest how teachers can foster self-esteem in their students.
- Describe the child's changing view of friendship.
- Describe Kohlberg's stages of moral reasoning and give an example of each.
- Evaluate alternatives to Kohlberg's theory.
- Explain the factors that encourage cheating and aggression in classrooms and discuss possible responses to each.
- Describe a number of challenges and risks that students face today and suggest roles for teachers in helping students respond.

What Would You Do?

TEACHERS' CASEBOOK

One of the girls in your 10th-grade class is desperate for friends. Vanesa seems so lonely and depressed—no one ever joins her at lunch or walks with her to class. She is a reasonably good student, but just doesn't seem to fit in. On several occasions she has tried to join a group by offering help or asking questions, but these initiations never go anywhere. Even when a friendship begins, it never lasts. It seems like Vanesa gets so excited about the possibility of a developing relationship that she pushes the newfound friend away by overwhelming her with attention, showering her with special gifts, pouring out her heart, and sharing her deepest secrets and worries. Then Vanesa always seems to be the one exploited, abandoned, or hurt. Lately her schoolwork is careless and incomplete; she looks tired and pale.

- What are your concerns for this student?
- How do you think Vanesa feels about herself?
- What are some danger signs you might watch for?
- How would you help her form some genuine relationships?
- Consider the same situation, except the child is a third-grade student.

The Work of Erikson

Like Piaget, Erik Erikson did not start out as a psychologist. In fact, Erikson never graduated from high school. He spent his early adult years studying art and traveling around Europe. A meeting with Sigmund Freud in Vienna led to an invitation from Freud to study psychoanalysis. Erikson then emigrated to America to practice his profession and to escape the threat of Hitler.

In his influential *Childhood and Society* (1963), Erikson offered a basic framework for understanding the needs of young people in relation to the society in which they grow, learn, and later make their contributions. His later books, *Identity, Youth, and Crisis* (1968) and *Identity and the Life Cycle* (1980), expanded on his ideas. Although Erikson's approach is not the only explanation of personal and social development, I have chosen it to organize our discussion because Erikson emphasizes the emergence of the self, the search for identity, and the individual's relationships with others throughout life.

After studying child-rearing practices in several cultures, Erikson came to the conclusion that all humans have the same basic needs and that each society must provide in some way for those needs. Emotional changes and their relation to the social environment follow similar patterns in every society. This emphasis on the relationship of culture and the individual led Erikson to propose a **psychosocial** theory of development.

Like Piaget, Erikson saw development as a passage through a series of stages, each with its particular goals, concerns, accomplishments, and dangers.

Erik Erikson proposed a theory of psychosocial development that describes tasks to be accomplished at different stages of life.

Psychosocial Describing the relation of the individual's emotional needs to the social environment.

TABLE 3.1   Erikson's Eight Stages of Psychosocial Development

Stages	Approximate Age	Important Event	Description
1. Basic trust versus basic mistrust	Birth to 12–18 months	Feeding	The infant must form a first loving, trusting relationship with the caregiver or develop a sense of mistrust
2. Autonomy versus shame/doubt	18 months to 3 years	Toilet training	The child's energies are directed toward the development of physical skills, including walking, grasping, controlling the sphincter. The child learns control but may develop shame and doubt if not handled well.
3. Initiative versus guilt	3 to 6 years	Independence	The child continues to become more assertive and to take more initiative but may be too forceful, which can lead to guilt feelings.
4. Industry versus inferiority	6 to 12 years	School	The child must deal with demands to learn new skills or risk a sense of inferiority, failure, and incompetence.
5. Identity versus role confusion	Adolescence	Peer relationships	The teenager must achieve identity in occupation, gender roles, politics, and religion.
6. Intimacy versus isolation	Young adulthood	Love relationships	The young adult must develop intimate relationships or suffer feelings of isolation.
7. Generativity versus stagnation	Middle adulthood	Parenting/Mentoring	Each adult must find some way to satisfy and support the next generation.
8. Ego integrity versus despair	Late adulthood	Reflection on and acceptance of one's life	The culmination is a sense of acceptance of oneself as one is and a sense of fulfillment.

Source: Adapted from Lester A. Lefton, *Psychology,* 5/e. Copyright © 1994 by Allyn & Bacon. Reprinted by permission.

The stages are interdependent: accomplishments at later stages depend on how conflicts are resolved in the earlier years. At each stage, Erikson suggests, the individual faces a **developmental crisis.** Each crisis involves a conflict between a positive alternative and a potentially unhealthy alternative. The way in which the individual resolves each crisis will have a lasting effect on that person's self-image and view of society. An unhealthy resolution of problems in the early stages can have potential negative repercussions throughout life, although sometimes damage can be repaired at later stages. We will look briefly at all eight stages in Erikson's theory—or, as he calls them, the "eight ages of man." Table 3.1 presents the stages in summary form.

The Preschool Years: Trust, Autonomy, and Initiative

Erikson identifies *trust versus mistrust* as the basic conflict of infancy. In the first months of life, babies begin to find out whether they can depend on the world around them. According to Erikson, the infant will develop a sense of trust if its needs for food and care are met with comforting regularity. Closeness and responsiveness on the part of the parents at this time contribute greatly

Developmental Crisis A specific conflict whose resolution prepares the way for the next stage.

Children need opportunities to learn things for themselves in order to develop a sense of initiative.

to this sense of trust (Bretherton & Waters, 1985; Isabella & Belsky, 1991). In this first year, infants are in Piaget's sensorimotor stage and are just beginning to learn that they are separate from the world around them. This realization is part of what makes trust so important: infants must trust the aspects of their world that are beyond their control (Bretherton & Waters, 1985).

Erikson's second stage, **autonomy** *versus shame and doubt,* marks the beginning of self-control and self-confidence. Young children are capable of doing more and more on their own. They must begin to assume important responsibilities for self-care like feeding, toileting, and dressing.

During this period parents must tread a fine line; they must be protective—but not overprotective. If parents do not maintain a reassuring, confident attitude and do not reinforce the child's efforts to master basic motor and cognitive skills, children may begin to feel shame; they may learn to doubt their abilities to manage the world on their own terms. Erikson believes that children who experience too much doubt at this stage will lack confidence in their own powers throughout life.

For Erikson, "initiative adds to autonomy the quality of undertaking, planning, and attacking a task for the sake of being active and on the move" (Erikson, 1963, p. 255). But with **initiative** comes the realization that some activities are forbidden. At times, children may feel torn between what they want to do and what they should (or should not) do. The challenge of this period is to maintain a zest for activity and at the same time understand that not every impulse can be acted on.

Again, adults must tread a fine line, this time in providing supervision without interference. If children are not allowed to do things on their own, a sense of guilt may develop; they may come to believe that what they want to do is always "wrong." The Guidelines suggest ways of encouraging initiative.

Autonomy Independence.

Initiative Willingness to begin new activities and explore new directions.

Guidelines

Encourage children to make and to act on choices.

Examples

1. Have a free-choice time when children can select an activity or game.
2. As much as possible, avoid interrupting children who are very involved in what they are doing.
3. When children suggest an activity, try to follow their suggestions or incorporate their ideas into ongoing activities.
4. Offer positive choices: instead of saying, "You can't have the cookies now," ask, "Would you like the cookies after lunch or after naptime?"

Make sure that each child has a chance to experience success.

Examples

1. When introducing a new game or skill, teach it in small steps.
2. Avoid competitive games when the range of abilities in the class is great.

Encourage make-believe with a wide variety of roles.

Examples

1. Have costumes and props that go along with stories the children enjoy. Encourage the children to act out the stories or make up new adventures for favorite characters.
2. Monitor the children's play to be sure no one monopolizes playing "teacher," "Mommy," "Daddy," or other heroes.

Be tolerant of accidents and mistakes, especially when children are attempting to do something on their own.

Examples

1. Use cups and pitchers that make it easy to pour and hard to spill.
2. Recognize the attempt, even if the product is unsatisfactory.

Elementary and Middle School Years: Industry versus Inferiority

In the early school years, students are developing what Erikson calls a sense of **industry**. They are beginning to see the relationship between perseverance and the pleasure of a job completed. The crisis at this stage is *industry versus inferiority*. For children in modern societies, the school and the neighborhood offer a new set of challenges that must be balanced with those at home. Interaction with peers becomes increasingly important as well. The child's ability to move between these worlds and to cope with academics, group activities, and friends will lead to a growing sense of competence. Difficulty with these challenges can result in feelings of inferiority. The Guidelines on page 70 give ideas for encouraging industry.

Industry Eagerness to engage in productive work.

Guidelines

Encouraging Industry

Make sure that students have opportunities to set and work toward realistic goals.

Examples

1. Begin with short assignments, then move on to longer ones. Monitor student progress by setting up progress checkpoints.
2. Teach students to set reasonable goals. Write down goals and have students keep a journal of progress toward goals.

Give students a chance to show their independence and responsibility.

Examples

1. Tolerate honest mistakes.
2. Delegate to students tasks like watering class plants, collecting and distributing materials, monitoring the computer lab, grading homework, keeping records of forms returned, and so on.

Provide support to students who seem discouraged.

Examples

1. Use individual charts and contracts that show student progress.
2. Keep samples of earlier work so students can see their improvements.
3. Have awards for most improved, most helpful, most hardworking.

Adolescence: The Search for Identity

The central issue for adolescents is the development of an **identity** that will provide a firm basis for adulthood. The individual has of course been developing a sense of self since infancy. But adolescence marks the first time that a conscious effort is made to answer the now-pressing question, "Who am I?" The conflict defining this stage is *identity versus role confusion.*

Exactly what do we mean by identity, and what does the crisis of this adolescent stage involve? Identity refers to the organization of the individual's drives, abilities, beliefs, and history into a consistent image of self. It involves deliberate choices and decisions, particularly about work, values, ideology, and commitments to people and to ideas (Marcia, 1987; Penuel & Wertsch, 1995). If adolescents fail to integrate all these aspects and choices, or if they feel unable to choose at all, role confusion threatens.

Identity Statuses.   Elaborating on Erikson's work, James Marcia and his colleagues have suggested that there are four alternatives for adolescents as they confront themselves and their choices (Marcia, 1980; Schiedel & Marcia, 1985). The first is **identity achievement.** This means that after considering the realistic options, the individual has made choices and is pursuing them. It appears that few students achieve this status by the end of high school. Most are not firm in their choices for several more years; students who attend college

Identity The complex answer to the question, "Who am I?"

Identity Achievement Strong sense of commitment to life choices after free consideration of alternatives.

Identity Foreclosure Acceptance of parental life choices without consideration of options.

Identity Diffusion Uncenteredness; confusion about who one is and what one wants.

Moratorium Identity crisis; suspension of choices because of struggle.

*T*he search for identity is the hallmark of adolescent development. Adolescents often "try on" different roles and behaviors during this period.

may take a bit longer to decide (Archer, 1982). **Identity foreclosure** describes the situation of adolescents who do not experiment with different identities or consider a range of options, but simply commit themselves to the goals, values, and lifestyles of others, usually their parents. **Identity diffusion,** on the other hand, occurs when individuals reach no conclusions about who they are or what they want to do with their lives; they have no firm direction. Adolescents experiencing identity diffusion may have struggled unsuccessfully to make choices, or they may have avoided thinking seriously about the issues at all.

Finally, adolescents in the midst of struggling with choices are experiencing what Erikson called a **moratorium.** Erikson used the term *moratorium* to describe a delay in the adolescent's commitment to personal and occupational choices. This delay is very common, and probably healthy, for modern adolescents. Marcia expands the meaning of moratorium to include the adolescent's active efforts to deal with the crisis of shaping an identity. Erikson believed that adolescents in complex societies experience this *identity crisis,* or temporary period of moratorium and confusion. Today, the period is no longer referred to as a crisis because, for most people, the experience is a gradual exploration rather than a traumatic upheaval (Baumeister, 1990).

Both identity achievement and moratorium are considered healthy alternatives. The natural tendency of adolescents to "try on" identities, experiment with lifestyles, and commit to causes is an important part of establishing a firm

> **Focus on . . .**
>
> ## The Work of Erikson
>
> - Why is Erikson's theory considered a psychosocial perspective?
> - Describe the capabilities of a preschool child who has successfully emerged from Erikson's first three stages of personal-social development.
> - How might an adolescent experiencing identity foreclosure answer the question, "Why did you choose that major?"
> - How might Vanesa's difficulties making friends (described at the beginning of this chapter) influence her identity achievement?

identity. But adolescents who can't get past either the identity diffusion or fore-closure stage have difficulties adjusting. For example, identity-diffused adolescents and young adults often give up, trust their lives to fate, or go along with the crowd, so they are more likely to abuse drugs (Archer & Waterman, 1990). Foreclosed adolescents tend to be rigid, intolerant, dogmatic, and defensive (Frank, Pirsch, & Wright, 1990). The Guidelines suggest approaches that support identity formation in adolescents.

Guidelines

Supporting Identity Formation

Give students many models for career choices and other adult roles.
Examples
1. Point out models from literature and history. Have a calendar with the birthdays of eminent women, minority leaders, or people who made a little-known contribution to the subject you are teaching. Briefly discuss the person's accomplishments on his or her birthday.
2. Invite guest speakers to describe how and why they chose their professions. Make sure all kinds of work and workers are represented.

Help students find resources for working out personal problems.
Examples
1. Encourage them to talk to school counselors.
2. Discuss potential outside services.

Be tolerant of teenage fads as long as they don't offend others or interfere with learning.
Examples
1. Discuss the fads of earlier eras (neon hair, powdered wigs).
2. Don't impose strict dress or hair codes.

Give students realistic feedback about themselves.
Examples
1. When students misbehave or perform poorly, make sure they understand the consequences of their behavior—the effects on themselves and others.
2. Give students model answers or show them other students' completed projects so they can compare their work to good examples.
3. Since students are "trying on" roles, keep the roles separate from the person. You can criticize behavior without criticizing the student.

Beyond the School Years

The crises of Erikson's stages of adulthood all involve the quality of human relations. The first of these stages is *intimacy versus isolation*. Intimacy in this sense refers to a willingness to relate to another person on a deep level, to have a relationship based on more than mutual need. Someone who has not achieved a sufficiently strong sense of identity tends to fear being overwhelmed or swallowed up by another person and may retreat into isolation.

The conflict at the next stage is *generativity versus stagnation*. **Generativity** extends the ability to care for another person and involves caring and guidance for the next generation and for future generations. While generativity frequently refers to having and nurturing children, it has a broader meaning. Productivity and creativity are essential features.

The last of Erikson's stages is *integrity versus despair*, coming to terms with death. Achieving **integrity** means consolidating one's sense of self and fully accepting its unique and now unalterable history. Those unable to attain a feeling of fulfillment and completeness sink into despair.

With Erikson's theory of psychosocial development as a framework, we can now examine several aspects of personal and social development that are issues throughout childhood and adolescence.

Understanding Ourselves and Others

What is self-concept? How do we come to understand ourselves and other people? How do we develop a sense of right and wrong—and do these beliefs affect our behavior? You will see that developments in these areas follow patterns similar to those noted in Chapter 2 for cognitive development. Children's understandings of themselves are concrete at first, and then become more abstract. Early views of self and friends are based on immediate behaviors and appearances. Children assume that others share their feelings and perceptions. Their thinking about themselves and others is simple, segmented, and rule-bound, not flexible and integrated into organized systems. In time, children are able to think abstractly about internal processes—beliefs, intentions, values, motivations. With these developments, knowledge of self, others, and situations can incorporate more abstract qualities (Berk, 1996, 1997).

Self-Concept and Self-Esteem

When you considered Vanesa's situation at the beginning of this chapter, was the idea of self-concept part of your analysis? The term *self-concept* is part of our everyday conversation. We talk about people who have a "low" self-concept or individuals whose self-concept is not "strong," as if self-concept were fluid levels in a car or a muscle to be developed. These actually are misuses of the term. In psychology, **self-concept** generally refers to "the composite of ideas, feelings, and attitudes people have about themselves" (Hilgard, Atkinson, & Atkinson, 1979, p. 605). We could also consider the self-concept to be our attempt to explain ourselves to ourselves, to build a scheme (in Piaget's terms) that organizes our impressions, feelings, and attitudes about ourselves. But this model or scheme is not permanent, unified, or unchanging. Our self-perceptions vary from situation to situation and from one phase of our lives to another.

Self-concept and self-esteem are often used interchangeably, even though they have distinct meanings. Self-concept is a cognitive structure—a belief about who you are. **Self-esteem** is an affective reaction—an evaluation of who you are.

Generativity Sense of concern for future generations.

Integrity Sense of self-acceptance and fulfillment.

Self-Concept Our perceptions about ourselves.

Self-Esteem The value each of us places on our own characteristics, abilities, and behaviors.

FIGURE 3.1

Structure of Self-Concept

Students have many separate but sometimes related concepts of themselves. The overall sense of self appears to be divided into at least three separate, but slightly related, self-concepts—English, mathematics, and nonacademic.

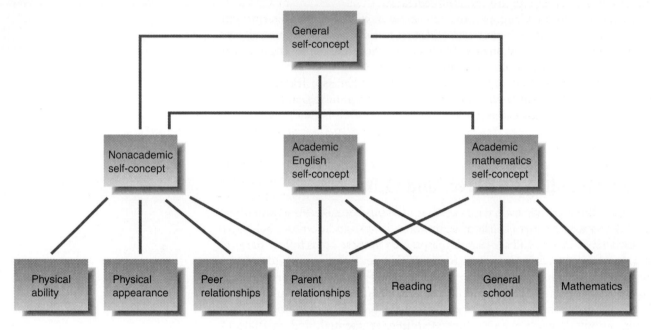

Source: From H.W. Marsh and R.J. Shavelson (1985). Self-concept: Its multifaceted, hierarchical structure. *Educational Psychologist, 20,* p. 114. Adapted by permission of the publisher and authors.

If people evaluate themselves positively—if they "like what they see"—we say that they have high *self-esteem.* (Pintrich & Schunk, 1996).

The model shown in Figure 3.1 suggests that the general view of self is made up of other, more specific concepts, including the nonacademic self-concept, self-concept in English, and self-concept in mathematics. Recent research indicates that self-concept for artistic abilities is another separate area (Vispoel, 1995). These self-concepts at the second level are themselves made up of more specific, separate conceptions of the self, such as conceptions about physical ability, appearance, relations with peers, and relations with family (particularly parents). These conceptions are based on many experiences and events such as: sports performance; assessment of body, skin, or hair; friendships; artistic abilities; contributions to community groups, and so on.

The hierarchical structure of self-concept shown in Figure 3.1 is strongest for early adolescents. Older adolescents and adults seem to have separate, specific self-concepts, but these are not necessarily integrated into an overall self-concept. Perhaps young adolescents, faced with the challenges of different academic subjects in school and the "life task" of forming an identity, try to integrate across their many "selves" to achieve that identity. Adults are not actively involved in *all* the academic domains (math, science, social studies) and can define themselves in terms of their current interests and activities, so self-concept is more situation-specific in adults (Byrne & Worth Gavin, 1996; Pintrich & Schunk, 1996).

How Self-Concept Develops.   The self-concept evolves through constant self-evaluation in different situations (Shavelson & Bolus, 1982). Children and adolescents are continually asking themselves, in effect, "How am I doing?" They gauge the verbal and nonverbal reactions of significant people—parents and other family members in the early years and friends, schoolmates, and teachers later—to make judgments. Students compare their performance with their own standards and with the performances of peers. Both personal (internal) and social (external) comparisons are important (Marsh, 1994). Students compare their performance in math to their performance in English and science, for example, to form self-concepts in these areas. If math is their best subject, their math self-concept may be the most positive, even if their actual performance in math is poor. But social comparisons are influential, too. Students' self-concepts in math are also shaped by how their performance compares to that of other students in their math classes. Students who are strong in math in an average school feel better about their math skills than students of equal ability in high-achieving schools. Marsh (1990) calls this the "Big-Fish-Little-Pond Effect." Participation in a gifted and talented program seems to have an opposite "Little-Fish-in-a-Big-Pond" effect—students who participate in gifted programs, compared to similar students who remain in regular classes, tend to show *declines* in academic self-concepts over time, but no changes in nonacademic self-concepts (Marsh, Chessor, Craven, & Roche, 1995).

There is another trend in the development of self-concept. Just after a transition to a new school, especially the transition to junior high school, students' self-concepts seem to become more negative and less stable. During the middle-school or junior high years, students grow more self-conscious (remember, adolescent egocentrism and Elkind's imaginary audience discussed in Chapter 2). At this age, feelings of self-worth are more closely tied to physical appearance and social acceptance, so these years can be exceedingly difficult for students like Vanesa, described at the opening of this chapter (Wigfield, Eccles, & Pintrich, 1996).

School Life and Self-Esteem

We turn now to self-esteem—the students' evaluations and feelings about themselves. For teachers, there are at least two questions to ask about self-esteem: (1) How does self-esteem affect a student's behavior in school? (2) How does life in school affect a student's self-esteem?

In answer to the first question, it appears that students with higher self-esteem are somewhat more likely to be successful in school (Marsh, 1990), although the strength of the relationship varies greatly, depending on the characteristics of the students and the research methods used (Hansford & Hattie, 1982; Marsh & Holmes, 1990). In addition, higher self-esteem is related to more favorable attitudes toward school, more positive behavior in the classroom, and greater popularity with other students (Cauley & Tyler, 1989; Metcalfe, 1981; Reynolds, 1980). Of course, as we discussed in Chapter 1, knowing that two variables are related (correlated) does not tell us that one is causing

Research indicates that awards such as "author of the week" have less impact on students' self-esteem than feedback and evaluation from the teacher or interactions with other students in class.

the other. It may be that high achievement and popularity lead to self-esteem, or vice versa. In fact, it probably works both ways (Marsh, 1987; Shavelson & Bolus, 1982).

This leads us to the second question of how school affects self-esteem. Good and Weinstein (1986) make this observation:

> School is a place where children develop or fail to develop a variety of competencies that come to define self and ability, where friendships with peers are nurtured, and where the role of the community member is played out, all during a highly formative period of development. Thus the building of self-esteem, interpersonal competence, social problem solving, and leadership becomes important in its own right and as a critical underpinning of success in academic learning. (p. 1095)

Is school really so important? A recent study that followed 322 sixth-grade students for two years would say yes. Hoge, Smit, and Hanson (1990) found that students' satisfaction with the school, their sense that classes were interesting and that teachers cared, and teacher feedback and evaluations influenced students' self-esteem. Teacher feedback and grades in particular subjects affected self-concepts in those subjects. In physical education, teachers' opinions were especially powerful in shaping students' conceptions of their athletic abilities. Interestingly, special programs like "Student of the Month" or admission to advanced math classes had little effect on self-esteem. (Relate this to the "Big-Fish-Little-Pond Effect.")

Over 100 years ago, William James (1890) suggested that self-esteem is determined by how *successful* we are in accomplishing tasks or reaching goals we *value*. If a skill or accomplishment is not important, incompetence in that area doesn't threaten self-esteem. Susan Harter (1990) has found evidence that James was right. Children who believe an activity is important and who feel capable in that area have higher self-esteem than students who think the activity is important, but question their competence. Students must have legitimate success on tasks that matter to them. The way individuals explain their successes or failures also is important. Students must attribute their successes to their own actions, not to luck or to special assistance, in order to build self-esteem.

Teachers' feedback, grading practices, evaluations, and communication of caring for students can make a difference in how students feel about their abilities in particular subjects. But the greatest increases in self-esteem probably come when students grow more competent in areas they value—including the social areas that become so important in adolescence. Thus a teacher's greatest challenge is to help students achieve important understandings and skills. Given this responsibility, what can teachers do? The recommendations in Table 3.2 are a beginning.

Gender, Ethnicity, and Self-Esteem

Younger children tend to have positive and optimistic views of themselves. In one study, over 80% of the first graders surveyed thought they were the best student in class. As they mature, students become more realistic, but many are not accurate judges of their own abilities (Paris & Cunningham, 1996). In fact,

TABLE 3.2   Suggestions for Encouraging Self-Esteem

1. Value and accept all pupils, for their attempts as well as their accomplishments.

2. Create a climate that is physically and psychologically safe for students.

3. Become aware of your own personal biases (everyone has some biases) and expectations.

4. Make sure that your procedures for teaching and grouping students are really necessary, not just a convenient way of handling problem students or avoiding contact with some students.

5. Make standards of evaluation clear; help students learn to evaluate their own accomplishments.

6. Model appropriate methods of self-criticism, perseverance, and self-reward.

7. Avoid destructive comparisons and competition; encourage students to compete with their own prior levels of achievement.

8. Accept a student even when you must reject a particular behavior or outcome. Students should feel confident, for example, that failing a test or being reprimanded in class does not make them "bad" people.

9. Remember that positive self-concept grows from success in operating in the world *and* from being valued by important people in the environment.

10. Encourage students to take responsibility for their reactions to events; show them that they have choices in how to respond.

11. Set up support groups or "study buddies" in school and teach students how to encourage each other.

12. Help students set clear goals and objectives; brainstorm about resources they have for reaching their goals.

13. Highlight the value of different ethnic groups—their cultures and accomplishments.

Sources: Information from J. Canfield (1990). Improving students' self-esteem, *Educational Leadership, 48*(1) pp. 48–50; M. M. Kash and G. Borich (1978). *Teacher behavior and student self-concept.* (Menlo Park, CA: Addison-Wesley); H. H. Marshall (1989). The development of self-concept. *Young Children, 44*(5) pp. 44–51.

some students suffer from "illusions of incompetence"—they seriously underestimate their own competence (Phillips & Zimmerman, 1990). Gender and ethnic stereotypes can play roles here.

Gender and Self-Esteem.   In the elementary grades, girls and boys have comparable perceptions of their own abilities. But by ninth grade and continuing through high school, on average, girls gradually lower their perceptions of their own abilities compared to boys (Phillips & Zimmerman, 1990). Similar trends were noted by the American Association of University Women (1991). Girls, aged 8 and 9, reported feeling confident, assertive, and authoritative about themselves. But they emerged from adolescence with a poor self-image, constrained views of their future and their place in society, and much less confidence about themselves and their abilities. Other studies indicate that for most ethnic groups (except African Americans) males are more confident about their abilities in school, particularly in math and science (Grossman & Grossman, 1994).

Personal and Collective Self-Esteem.   To this point we have discussed self-esteem as a purely individual characteristic. A number of psychologists have suggested that there is another basis for self-worth and identity. "The other level of identity, the collective self, involves those aspects of the individual that connect her or him with others—group memberships" (Wright & Taylor, 1995,

p. 242). Perhaps our self-esteem is influenced by both individual qualities and our group memberships—family, peer groups, ethnic heritage, and class or team memberships. This second dimension is called **collective self-esteem,** or a sense of the worth of the groups to which we belong. When students are faced with daily reminders, subtle or blatant, that their ethnic or family group has less status and power, the basis for collective self-esteem erodes.

Unfortunately, there is evidence that children from different ethnic groups hear and accept messages that devalue their group. When confronted with a light-skinned and a dark-skinned doll, African American children tended to choose the light-skinned doll as prettier and better on a number of dimensions (Clark & Clark, 1939). There is more recent evidence that Mexican American children (Weiland & Coughlin, 1979), Chinese American children (Aboud & Skerry, 1984), and Canadian Native children (Corenblum & Annis, 1987) have similar negative feelings about their ethnic groups.

For all students, pride in family and community is part of the foundation for a stable identity and collective self-esteem. Because ethnic-minority students are members of both a majority culture and a subculture, it is sometimes difficult for them to establish a clear identity. Values, learning styles, and communication patterns of the students' subculture may be inconsistent with the expectations of the school and the larger society. Special efforts to encourage **ethnic pride** are particularly important so these students do not get the message that differences are deficits. For example, differences in skin color, hair length, dress, dialect, or accent are just that—differences, not inferior or superior qualities (Spencer & Markstrom-Adams, 1990).

Research indicates that members of minority groups who have achieved an identity by exploring and adopting values from both their ethnic heritage and the dominant culture have a stronger sense of self-esteem, feel more competent, and have more positive relations with others (Phinney & Alipuria, 1990). Each of us has an ethnic heritage. When majority adolescents are knowledgeable and secure about their own heritage, they are also more respectful of the heritage of others. So exploring the ethnic roots of all students should foster both self-esteem and acceptance of others (Rotherham-Borus, 1994).

There is a particular aspect of ethnic heritage and pride that affects schooling—language. In Chapter 5 we will examine bilingual education in greater depth. But while we are talking about self-esteem, consider the results of a recent study of the impact of heritage language on personal and collective self-esteem by Stephen Wright and Donald Taylor (1995). These researchers found that when Canadian Native (Inuit) children were educated in their heritage language for the first three years of school, they had more positive personal and collective self-esteem than the Canadian Native children in the same school who received second-language instruction (English or French) from kindergarten on. When schools value the language of all students, ethnic pride and collective self-esteem may be enhanced.

One very important group membership for all students is their family. A recent study by John Fantuzzo, Gwendolyn Davis, and Marika Ginsburg (1995) capitalized on the power of families to improve students' self-esteem. The Guidelines list the strategies from their study that proved effective in increasing self-esteem and mathematics achievement for the fourth- and fifth-grade African American urban-school students who participated.

Collective Self-Esteem The sense of the value of a group, such as an ethnic group, that you belong to.

Ethnic Pride A positive self-concept about one's racial or ethnic heritage.

1. Work with families to co-create methods for family involvement. Offer a range of possible participation methods. Make sure the plans are realistic and fit the lives of the families.

2. Maintain regular home–school contact through telephone calls or notes. If a family has no telephone, identify a contact person (relative or friend) who can take messages. If literacy is a problem, use pictures, symbols, and codes for written communication.

3. Make all communications positive, emphasizing growth, progress, and accomplishments.

4. With the families, design family–student celebrations of the student's efforts and successes (a movie, special meal, trip to the park or library, going out for ice cream or pizza).

5. On a regular basis, send home a note in word or picture form that describes the student's progress. Ask families to indicate how they celebrated the success and to return the note.

6. Follow up with a telephone call to discuss progress, answer questions, solicit family suggestions, and express appreciation for the families' contributions.

7. Encourage families to visit the classroom.

Source: Adapted from Fantuzzo, J., Davis, G., & Ginsburg, M. (1995). Effects of parent involvement in isolation or in combination with peer tutoring on student self-concept and mathematics achievement. *Journal of Educational Psychology, 87,* 272–281.

The Self and Others

As we seek our own identity and form images of ourselves in various academic and social situations, we are also seeking and forming ways to understand the "significant others" around us. Children learn to see themselves as separate and to see others as separate people as well, with their own identities. How do we learn to interpret what others are thinking and feeling?

Intention.   Around the age of 2, children have a sense of intention, at least of their own intentions. They will announce, "I'm gonna get a puppy" or "I wanna peanut butter sandwich." They can say firmly, "I didn't break it on purpose!" By 2-1/2 or 3 years old, children extend the understanding of intention to others. Older preschoolers who get along well with their peers are able to separate intentional from unintentional actions and react accordingly. For example, they will not get angry when another child accidentally knocks over their block tower. But aggressive children have more trouble assessing intention. They are likely to attack anyone who topples their tower, even accidentally (Berk, 1997; Dodge & Somberg, 1987). As children mature, they are more able to assess and consider the intentions of others.

Taking the Perspective of Others.   Very young children don't understand that other people have different feelings and experiences. But this **perspective-taking ability** develops over time until it is quite sophisticated in adults. Robert Selman has developed a five-stage model to describe the development of perspective-taking. Consider this situation:

Focus on...

Understanding Ourselves and Others

- Distinguish between self-concept and self-esteem.
- How does self-concept change as children develop?
- Describe the changes in perspective-taking that occur as students mature.
- How might Vanesa's (p. 66) experiences with peers influence her self-concept, given her age?

Holly is an 8-year-old girl who likes to climb trees. She is the best tree climber in the neighborhood. One day while climbing a tree she falls off the bottom branch but does not hurt herself. Her father sees her fall. He is upset and asks her to promise not to climb trees anymore. Holly promises.

Later that day, Holly and her friends meet Sean. Sean's kitten is caught up in a tree and cannot get down. Something has to be done right away or the kitten may fall. Holly is the only one who climbs trees well enough to reach the kitten and get it down, but she remembers her promise to her father. (Selman & Byrne, 1974, p. 805)

If children of different ages are presented with this problem and asked such questions as, "If Holly climbs the tree, should she be punished?" "Will her father understand if she climbs the tree?" "Will Sean understand why Holly has trouble deciding what to do?" the children will give answers such as those in Table 3.3. As children mature, they take more information into account. They realize that different people can react differently to the same situation. They develop the ability to analyze the perspectives of several people involved in a situation from the viewpoint of an objective bystander, and they can even imagine how different cultural or social values would influence the perceptions of the bystander (Berk, 1996).

Moral Development

If you have spent time with young children, you know that there is a period when you can say, "Eating in the living room is not allowed!" and get away with it. For young children, rules simply exist. Piaget (1965) called this the state of **moral realism.** At this stage, the child of 5 or 6 believes that rules about conduct or rules about how to play a game are absolute and can't be changed. If a rule is broken, the child believes that the punishment should be determined by how much damage is done, not by the intention of the child or by other circumstances. So accidentally breaking three cups is worse than intentionally breaking one, and in the child's eyes, the punishment for the three-cup offense should be greater.

As children interact with others, develop perspective-taking abilities, and see that different people have different rules, there is a gradual shift to a **morality of cooperation.** Children come to understand that people make rules and people can change them. When rules are broken, both the damage done and the intention of the offender are taken into account. These developmental changes and others are reflected in Kohlberg's theory of moral development, based in part on Piaget's ideas.

Perspective-Taking Ability Understanding that others have different feelings and experiences.

Moral Realism Stage of development wherein children see rules as absolute.

Morality of Cooperation Stage of development wherein children realize that people make rules and people can change them.

TABLE 3.3   Selman's Five Stages of Perspective-Taking

Children's responses to Holly's dilemma show developmental changes in perspective-taking—the ability to imagine what other people are thinking and feeling.

Stage	Age	Description	Typical Response to the "Holly" Dilemma
Undifferentiated perspective-taking	3–6	Children recognize that the self and others can have different thoughts and feelings, but they frequently confuse the two.	The child predicts that Holly will save the kitten because she does not want it to get hurt and believes that Holly's father will feel just as she does about her climbing the tree: "Happy, he likes kittens."
Social-informational perspective-taking	5–9	Children understand that different perspectives may result because people have access to different information.	When asked how Holly's father will react when he finds out that she climbed the tree, the child responds, "If he didn't know anything about the kitten, he would be angry. But if Holly shows him the kitten, he might change his mind."
Self-reflective perspective-taking	7–12	Children can "step in another person's shoes" and view their own thoughts, feelings, and behavior from the other person's perspective. They also recognize that others can do the same.	When asked whether Holly thinks she will be punished, the child says, "No. Holly knows that her father will understand why she climbed the tree." This response assumes that Holly's point of view is influenced by her father being able to "step in her shoes" and understand why she saved the kitten.
Third-party perspective-taking	10–15	Children can step outside a two-person situation and imagine how the self and other are viewed from the point of view of a third, impartial party.	When asked whether Holly should be punished, the child says, "No, because Holly thought it was important to save the kitten. But she also knows that her father told her not to climb the tree. So she'd only think she shouldn't be punished if she could get her father to understand why she had to climb the tree." This response steps outside the immediate situation to view both Holly's and her father's perspectives simultaneously.
Societal perspective-taking	14–Adult	Individuals understand that third-party perspective-taking can be influenced by one or more systems of larger societal values.	When asked if Holly should be punished, the individual responds, "No. The value of humane treatment of animals justifies Holly's action. Her father's appreciation of this value will lead him not to punish her."

Source: From Laura E. Berk, *Infants, Children, and Adolescents,* 2/e, p. 475. Copyright © 1996 by Allyn & Bacon. Reprinted by permission.

Kohlberg's Stages of Moral Development

Lawrence Kohlberg (1963, 1975, 1981) proposed a detailed sequence of stages of **moral reasoning,** or judgments about right and wrong, and has led the field in studying their evolution. He divided moral development into three levels: (1) preconventional, where judgment is based solely on a person's own needs and perceptions; (2) conventional, where the expectations of society and law are

Moral Reasoning The thinking processes involved in judgments about questions of right and wrong.

TABLE 3.4   Kohlberg's Stage Theory of Moral Reasoning

Level 1. Preconventional Moral Reasoning

Judgment is based on personal needs and others' rules.

Stage 1   Punishment-Obedience Orientation
Rules are obeyed to avoid punishment. A good or bad action is determined by its physical consequences.

Stage 2   Personal Reward Orientation
Personal needs determine right and wrong. Favors are returned along the lines of "You scratch my back, I'll scratch yours."

Level 2. Conventional Moral Reasoning

Judgment is based on others' approval, family expectations, traditional values, the laws of society, and loyalty to country.

Stage 3   Good Boy–Nice Girl Orientation
Good means "nice." It is determined by what pleases, aids, and is approved by others.

Stage 4   Law and Order Orientation
Laws are absolute. Authority must be respected and the social order maintained.

Level 3. Postconventional Moral Reasoning

Stage 5   Social Contract Orientation
Good is determined by socially agreed-upon standards of individual rights. This is a morality similar to that of the U.S. Constitution.

Stage 6*   Universal Ethical Principle Orientation
Good and right are matters of individual conscience and involve abstract concepts of justice, human dignity, and equality.

*In later work Kohlberg questioned whether Stage 6 exists separately from Stage 5.

Source: Adapted by permission of the *Journal of Philosophy.* From L. Kohlberg (1975). "The cognitive-developmental approach to moral education." *Phi Delta Kappan, 56,* p. 671.

---

taken into account; and (3) postconventional, where judgments are based on abstract, more personal principles that are not necessarily defined by society's laws. Each of these three levels is then subdivided into stages, as shown in Table 3.4.

Kohlberg has evaluated the moral reasoning of both children and adults by presenting them with **moral dilemmas,** or hypothetical situations in which people must make difficult decisions. Subjects are asked what the person who is caught in the dilemma should do, and why. In these situations there is no obvious answer; no action will provide a complete solution.

One of the most commonly used moral dilemmas can be summarized as follows: A man's wife is dying. There is one drug that could save her, but it is

Moral Dilemmas Situations in which no choice is clearly and indisputably right.

very expensive, and the druggist who invented it will not sell it at a price low enough for the man to buy it. Finally, the man becomes desperate and considers stealing the drug for his wife. What should he do, and why?

At level 1 (preconventional), the child's answer might be, "It is wrong to steal because you might get caught." This answer reflects the child's basic egocentrism. The reasoning might be: "What would happen to me if I stole something? I might get caught and punished."

At level 2 (the conventional level), the subject is able to look beyond the immediate personal consequences and consider the views, and especially the approval, of others. Laws, religious or civil, are very important and are regarded as absolute and unalterable. One answer stressing adherence to rules is, "It is wrong to steal because it is against the law." Another answer, placing high value on loyalty to family and loved ones but still respecting the law, is, "It's right to steal because the man means well—he's trying to help his wife. But he will still have to pay the druggist when he can or accept the penalty for breaking the law."

At level 3 (the postconventional level), an answer might be, "It is not wrong to steal because human life must be preserved. The worth of a human life is greater than the worth of property." This response considers the underlying values that might be involved in the decision. Abstract concepts are no longer rigid, and, as the name of this level implies, principles can be separated from conventional values. A person reasoning on this level understands that what is considered right by the majority may not be considered right by an individual in a particular situation. Rational, personal choice is stressed.

Moral reasoning is related to both cognitive and emotional development. As we have seen, abstract thinking becomes increasingly important in the higher stages of moral development, as children move from decisions based on absolute rules to decisions based on principles such as justice and mercy. The ability to see another's perspective and to imagine alternative bases for laws and rules also enters into judgments at the higher stages.

Alternatives to Kohlberg's Theory

Kohlberg's stage theory has been criticized, first, because the stages do not seem in reality to be separate, sequenced, and consistent. People often give reasons for moral choices that reflect several different stages simultaneously. Or a person's choices in one instance may fit one stage and in a different situation may reflect another stage. When asked to reason about helping someone else versus meeting their own needs, both children and adolescents reason at higher levels than when they are asked to reason about breaking the law or risking punishment (Eisenberg et al., 1987; Sobesky, 1983).

Social Conventions versus Moral Issues.   Another criticism is that Kohlberg's theory does not differentiate between social conventions and true moral issues until the higher stages of moral reasoning. Social conventions are the social rules and expectations of a particular group or society—for example, "It is rude to eat with your hands." Such behavior would not be inappropriate if there were no social convention prohibiting it. True moral issues, on the other hand, involve the rights of individuals, the general welfare of the group, or the avoidance of harm. "Stealing" would be wrong, even if there were no "rule" against it. Children as young as 3 can distinguish between social conventions and moral issues. They know, for example, that being noisy in school would be fine if there were no rule requiring quiet, but that it would not be right to hit another child, even if there were no rule against it. So even very young children can reason based on moral principles that are not tied to social conventions and rules (Nucci, 1987; Smetana & Braeges, 1990; Turiel, 1983).

Cultural Differences in Moral Reasoning.   Another criticism of Kohlberg's stage theory is that stages 5 and 6 in moral reasoning are biased in favor of Western, male values that emphasize individualism. In cultures that are more family centered or group oriented, the highest moral value might involve putting the opinions of the group before decisions based on individual conscience. There has been much disagreement over the "highest" moral stage. Kohlberg himself has questioned the applicability of stage 6. Few people other than trained philosophers reason naturally or easily at this level. Kohlberg (1984) suggested that for all practical purposes, stages 5 and 6 might be combined.

The Morality of Caring

One of the most hotly debated criticisms of Kohlberg's theory is that the stages are biased in favor of males and do not represent the way moral reasoning develops in women. Because the stage theory was based on a longitudinal study of men only, it is very possible that the moral reasoning of women and the stages of women's development are not adequately represented (Gilligan, 1982; Gilligan & Attanucci, 1988). Carol Gilligan (1982) has proposed a different sequence of moral development, an "ethic of care." Gilligan suggests that individuals move from a focus on self-interests to moral reasoning based on commitment to specific individuals and relationships, and then to the highest level of morality based on the principles of responsibility and care for all people.

The highest stage in Kohlberg's theory of moral development involves decisions based on universal principles of justice and fairness. Reasoning based on caring for others and maintaining relationships is scored at a lower level. Many of Kohlberg's early studies of moral reasoning found that most men progressed to stages 4 and 5 by adulthood, while most women "stayed" at stage 3. This makes it appear as if women are moral midgets. But recent studies find few significant differences between men and women, or boys and girls, in their level of moral reasoning as measured by Kohlberg's procedures (Thoma, 1986).

In order to study moral reasoning as it actually happens in real life, and to get an idea about the basis for decisions, Walker and his colleagues (Walker, 1991; Walker, de Vries, & Trevarthan, 1987) asked children, adolescents, and adults to describe a personal moral problem and to analyze a traditional moral dilemma. For both types of problems, males and females revealed both a morality of caring and a concern with justice. Andrew Garrod and his colleagues (1990) used fables to study the moral reasoning of first, third, and fifth graders and found that both boys and girls tended to adopt a care orientation. With the exception of a few fifth-grade boys who suggested solutions involving violence or tricks, there were no differences between first- and third-grade boys and girls. So justice and caring seem to be important bases for moral reasoning for both men and women. Even though men and women both seem to

Carol Gilligan has challenged traditional conceptions of moral development with her work on the "ethic of care."

value caring and justice, there is some evidence that in everyday life, women feel more guilty about violating caring norms (being inconsiderate or untrustworthy) and men feel more guilty when they show violent behaviors (fighting or damaging property) (Williams & Bybee, 1994). Gilligan's criticisms and ideas have broadened the view of what constitutes morality.

Empathy.   **Empathy** is the ability to feel an emotion as it is experienced by another person—to put yourself in another's shoes. Both adults and children respond emotionally to signs of distress in others. But the emotional reaction of a young child is not based on an understanding of how another feels, since the child cannot yet see the other's emotions as separate. Very young children may respond to seeing another child hurt as if they had been hurt themselves. A little later, children begin to be aware that others' feelings are separate but assume that those feelings must be the same as their own. For example, a young boy might give his "blankie" to a friend who is crying, assuming that the friend would want exactly the same comfort he himself usually wants in a time of trouble. Children eventually become more and more able to imagine how other people would feel in a given situation. As they develop perspective-taking skills, their sense of empathy develops as well.

Empathy plays an important part in our ability to understand and get along with one another (Chapman, Zahn-Waxler, Cooperman, & Iannotti, 1987). Children who are empathetic are more compassionate and more likely to help others (Eisenberg & Miller, 1987; Eisenberg et al., 1987). Teachers can encourage the development of empathy by allowing students to work together and discuss emotional reactions to various experiences. When disputes arise in the later elementary and the secondary grades, teachers can resist the temptation to quote rules or act as a judge; instead, they can help the students see one another's point of view.

The ability to empathize with others and respect their views is critical in professional relationships and collaborations among teachers.

Empathy Ability to feel emotion as experienced by others.

Should Schools Teach Values?

For years, educators, parents, religious leaders, and politicians have debated whether the schools are responsible for moral education. Should the schools teach students about morality, or is this the sole responsibility of families and the community? Should values be transmitted to students by direct teaching, modeling, and exhortation, or should students be taught to make judgments and decisions, and clarify their own values?

POINT Moral education belongs in the schools.

According to Edward Wynne (1986):

The transmission of moral values has been the dominant educational concern of most cultures throughout history. Most educational systems have been simultaneously concerned with the transmission of cognitive knowledge—skills, information, and techniques of intellectual analysis—but these admittedly important educational aims have rarely been given priority over moral education. The current policies in American education that give secondary priority to transmitting morality represent a sharp fracture with the great tradition. (p. 4)

Wynne goes on to argue that all societies must socialize young people to work for the good of the society and not to act on purely selfish instincts. Children must be taught not just to mouth abstract moral principles, but to conduct themselves morally in the everyday spaces of their lives. No one segment of society has the sole responsibility for this teaching. In fact, all the people and institutions of a society—the family, the schools, religious institutions, community organizations, the media—must model and teach moral values. In the 1990s, as we are dismayed by rising crime, rampant drug use, violence, racial hatred, and the disintegration of the family, we cannot leave moral education to any one group: all institutions, including the schools, must assume this responsibility.

Are there other things teachers can do to promote moral development and values? As you can see in the Point/Counterpoint, opinions vary.

Friendships. Psychologists have found that as children mature, the meaning of friendship changes for them (Damon, 1977; Selman, 1981; Youniss, 1980). Damon has described three levels of friendship. At the first level, friends are the other children a child plays with often. But friendships can begin and end quickly, based on acts of kindness or "meanness." There is little sense that friends have stable characteristics, so moment-to-moment actions define the friendship (Berndt & Perry, 1986). Teachers working with young children should be aware that these rapidly changing allegiances are a normal part of development. Note, too, that a child's view of friends at this level may be related to the level of cognitive development: young children have difficulty seeing beyond the immediate situation.

Friendships at the next level are defined by a willingness to help when help is needed. Friends are playmates and companions. Children begin to base their choices for friends on concrete but stable personal qualities in another child, such as, "She always shares her lunch with me." This level of friendship may be linked to concrete operational cognitive abilities and the development of empathy and perspective-taking.

At the highest level, as children move into adolescence, friends are seen as people who share common interests and values, faithfully keep one's most pri-

COUNTERPOINT The schools should not teach morality or values.

There are two very different arguments against the direct teaching of morals and values in schools. The first argument is that moral education is the sole responsibility of the family. If schools teach values, whose values will they teach? Which culture or religion, if any, should be the guide? What if the school's teachings contradict the values of a child's family? Of course, we might all agree on the values of honesty, equality, and justice, but what do these values mean when applied to issues such as school prayer, abortion, divorce, safe sex, gun control, or capital punishment? If the school has no position on these issues, it has no moral authority. It seems to communicate that "anything goes." But if the school takes a position, how can it help but offend some students and their families?

The second argument often made against moral education in the schools is that schools should not teach values directly but should instead "help students *clarify their own values,* learn higher levels of *moral reasoning,* and learn the skills of *value analysis*" (Kirschenbaum, 1992, p. 771). In a pluralistic society there is no consensus about the "best" values. In addition, the moral dilemmas of the future cannot be anticipated today. So it is better for students to learn *how to reason* about moral issues than *what to think.*

Howard Kirschenbaum (1992) suggests that schools take a comprehensive approach to moral education by both teaching moral values and helping students learn to reason about morality.

Young people deserve to be exposed to the inculcation of values by adults who care: family members, teachers, and the community. They deserve to see models of adults with a joy for living. And they deserve to have opportunities that encourage them to learn the skills of guiding their own lives. (p. 775)

vate revelations a secret, and provide psychological support when necessary. The personal qualities of a friend—loyalty, similar philosophy of life—are more abstract and less tied to behaviors (Furman & Bierman, 1984). The cognitive abilities required to understand abstract concepts and to base judgments on them may come into play here. Friendship is now a long-term proposition and usually cannot be destroyed by one or even several incidents. At this stage, friendships can be very intense, especially for girls. At every stage, girls are more likely than boys to have one "best" friend and are more reluctant than boys to admit new members to a tight group of friends (Berndt & Perry, 1990).

At every level, friendships play a very significant role in healthy personal and social development. There is strong evidence that adults who had close friends as children have higher self-esteem and are more capable of maintaining intimate relationships than adults who spent lonely childhoods. Adults who were rejected as children tend to have more problems, such as dropping out of school or committing crimes (Hartup, 1989; Kupersmidt, Coie, & Dodge, 1990). Teachers sometimes forget just how central friendships are to their students' lives. When a student is having a problem with a friend, when there has been a falling-out or an argument, when one child is not invited to a sleep-over, when rumors are started and pacts are made to ostracize someone, the results can be devastating to the children involved. Even when students begin to mature and know intellectually that rifts will soon be healed, they may still be emotionally crushed by temporary trouble in the friendship.

A teacher should also be aware of how each student gets along with the group. Are there outcasts? Do some students play the bully role? Careful adult intervention can often correct such problems, especially at the middle elementary-school level.

A Curriculum of Caring. Caring for students and helping students learn to care has become a theme for many educators. The May 1995 issue of *Phi Delta Kappan* had a special section on "Youth and Caring." Articles emphasized connections with parents and communities, changes in school organization, and curriculum changes. For example, Nel Noddings (1995) urged that "themes of care" be used to organize the curriculum. Possible themes include "Caring for Self," "Caring for Family and Friends," and "Caring for Strangers and the World." Using the theme of "Caring for Strangers and the World," there could be units on crime, war, poverty, tolerance, ecology, or technology. Table 3.5 shows how a focus on crime and caring for strangers could be integrated into several high school classes.

TABLE 3.5   Using "Caring for Strangers and the World" as a Teaching Theme

As part of a unit on "Caring for Strangers and the World," high school students examine the issue of crime in several classes. In every class, the study of aspects of crime would be continually tied to the theme of caring and to discussions of safety, responsibility, trust in each other and in the community, and commitment to a safer future.

Subject	Elements
Mathematics	Statistics: Gather data on the location and rates of crimes, ages of offenders, and costs of crime to society. Is there a correlation between severity of punishment and incidence of crime? What is the actual cost of a criminal trial?
English and Social Studies	Read *Oliver Twist*. Relate the characters to their social and historical context. What factors contributed to crime in 19th century England?
	Read popular mysteries. Are they literature? Are they accurate depictions of the criminal justice system?
Science	Genetics: Are criminal tendencies heritable? Are there sex differences in aggressive behavior? Are women less competent than men in moral reasoning (and why did some social scientists think so)? How would you test this hypothesis?
Arts	Is graffiti art really art?

Source: From Nel Noddings. "Teaching Themes of Care." *Phi Delta Kappan, 76,* pp. 675–679. Copyright © 1995 by Phi Delta Kappan. Reprinted by permission of Phi Delta Kappan and the author.

Moral Behavior

As people move toward higher stages of moral reasoning, they also evidence more sharing, helping, and defending of victims of injustice. This relationship between moral reasoning and moral behavior is not very strong, however (Berk, 1997). Many other factors besides reasoning affect behavior. Two important influences on moral behavior are internalization and modeling.

Most theories of moral behavior assume that young children's moral behavior is first controlled by others through direct instruction, supervision, rewards and punishments, and correction. But in time, children **internalize** the moral rules and principles of the authority figures who have guided them; that is, children adopt the external standards as their own. If children are given reasons when they are corrected or instructed about their actions, then they are more likely to internalize moral principles. They can then behave morally even when "no one is watching." Reasons that highlight the effects of actions on others, stated in language the child can understand, are helpful (Berk, 1997; Hoffman, 1988).

A second important influence on the development of moral behavior is modeling. Children who have been consistently exposed to caring, generous adult models will tend to be more concerned for the rights and feelings of others (Lipscomb, MacAllister, & Bregman, 1985). Let's consider several moral issues that arise in classrooms.

Cheating.   Early research indicates that cheating seems to have more to do with the particular situation than with the general honesty or dishonesty of the individual (R. Burton, 1963). A student who cheats in math class is probably more likely to cheat in other classes, but may never consider lying to a friend or taking candy from the store. Most students will cheat if the pressure to perform well is great and the chances of being caught are slim. When asked why students cheat, the 1,100 high school subjects in a study by Schab (1980) listed three reasons: laziness about studying, fear of failure, and parental pressure for good grades. These students were very pessimistic about the incidence of cheating. Both boys and girls in the survey believed that over 97% of their peers had cheated at one time or another. However, this estimate may have been high; figures depend partly on how cheating is defined.

There are some individual differences in cheating. Most studies of older and college-age students find that males are more likely to cheat than females, lower achieving students are more likely to cheat than higher achievers, students focusing on performance goals (making good grades, looking smart) as opposed to learning goals are likely to cheat, and college students in engineering, business, and science are more likely to cheat than students in the arts and humanities (Davis, Grover, Becker, & McGregor, 1992; Newstead, Franklyn-Stokes, Armstead, 1996). Students also are particularly likely to cheat when they are behind or "cramming for tests."

The implications for teachers are straightforward. To prevent cheating, try to avoid putting students in high-pressure situations. Make sure they are well prepared for tests, projects, and assignments so they can do reasonably well without cheating. Focus on learning and not on grades. Make extra help available for those who need it. Be clear about your policies in regard to cheating,

Internalize Process whereby children adopt external standards as their own.

"SCOTT, YOU'VE BEEN
WATCHING TOO MUCH TV."

(© Stan Fine—From Phi Delta
Kappan*)*

and enforce them consistently. Help students resist temptation by monitoring carefully during testing.

Aggression.   **Aggression** is not to be confused with assertiveness, which means affirming or maintaining a legitimate right. Helen Bee (1981) gives this example of the difference between the two types of behavior: "A child who says, 'That's my toy!' is showing assertiveness. If he bashes his playmate over the head to reclaim it, he has shown aggression" (p. 350).

Modeling plays an important role in the expression of aggression (Bandura, Ross, & Ross, 1963). Children who grow up in homes filled with harsh punishment and family violence are more likely to use aggression to solve their own problems (Emery, 1989; Holden & Ritchie, 1991).

One very real source of aggressive models is found in almost every home in America—television. In the United States, 82% of programs have at least some violence. The rate for children's programs is especially high—an average of 32 violent acts per hour, with cartoons being the worst (Waters, 1993). Most children spend more time watching television than they do in any other activity except sleep (Timmer, Eccles, & O'Brien, 1988). You can reduce the negative effects of TV violence by stressing three points with your students: most people do not behave in the aggressive ways shown on television; the violent acts on TV are not real, but are created by special effects and stunts; and there are better ways to resolve conflicts, and these are the ways most real people use to solve their problems (Huessmann, Eron, Klein, Brice, & Fischer, 1983).

But television is not the only source of violent models. Many popular films and video games are also filled with graphic depictions of violence, sometimes performed by the "hero." Students growing up in the inner cities see street gangs and drug deals. Newspapers, magazines, and the radio are filled with stories of murders, rapes, and robberies. In some preschools the children don't play "Mommy" and "Daddy"; they pretend to sell "nickel bags" of heroin to their playmates. This description appeared in the *Washington Post* (June 2, 1988):

> As children huddle, drug games begin. From one child's pocket comes chalk, crushed to resemble cocaine, inside plastic sandwich bags smuggled from home. Soon another child passes cash—thick knots of Monopoly money, or notebook paper, wrapped with rubber bands and dubbed "bankroll."

In addition to being surrounded by violence, some children, particularly boys, have difficulty reading the intentions of others. As we saw earlier, they assume the another child "did it on purpose" when their block tower is toppled, they are pushed on the bus, or some other mistake is made. Retaliation follows and the cycle of aggression continues. Sandra Graham has successfully experimented with approaches that help aggressive, fifth- and sixth-grade African American boys become better judges of others' intentions. Strategies include engaging in role play, participating in group discussions of personal experiences, interpreting social cues from photographs, playing pantomime games, making videos, and writing endings to unfinished stories. The boys in the 12-session training group showed

---

Focus on . . .

Moral Development

- Distinguish the key differences among the preconventional, conventional, and postconventional levels of moral reasoning.
- Describe Gilligan's levels of moral reasoning.
- How can teachers encourage moral behavior and caring?
- How might Vanesa's (p. 66) teacher support Vanesa's attempts to make and keep friends?

Aggression   Bold, direct action that is intended to hurt someone else or take property; unprovoked attack.

clear improvement in reading the intentions of others and responding with less aggression (Graham, 1996). The Guidelines may give you ideas for handling aggression and encouraging cooperation.

Guidelines

Dealing with Aggression and Encouraging Cooperation

Present yourself as a nonaggressive model.

Examples

1. Do not use threats of aggression to win obedience.
2. When problems arise, model nonviolent conflict-resolution strategies.

Ensure that your classroom has enough space and appropriate materials for every student.

Examples

1. Prevent overcrowding.
2. Make sure prized toys or resources are plentiful.
3. Remove or confiscate materials that encourage personal aggression, such as toy guns.

Make sure students do not profit from aggressive behaviors.

Examples

1. Comfort the victim of aggression and ignore the aggressor.
2. Use reasonable punishment, especially with older students.

Teach directly about positive social behaviors.

Examples

1. Incorporate lessons on social ethics/morality through reading selections and discussions.
2. Discuss the effects of antisocial actions such as stealing, bullying, and spreading rumors.

Provide opportunities for learning tolerance and cooperation.

Examples

1. Emphasize the similarities among people rather than the differences.
2. Set up group projects that encourage cooperation.

Socialization: The Home and the School

Socialization is the process by which the mature members of a society, such as parents and teachers, influence the beliefs and behaviors of children, enabling them to fully participate in and contribute to the society. In this section we will consider two of the most important influences on the development and socialization of children—the family and the school.

Socialization The ways in which members of a society encourage positive development for the immature individuals of the group.

American Families Today

The most appropriate expectation to have about your students' families is no expectation at all. The idea of two parents, 2.2 children, Dad with the only job, and Mom in the kitchen is no longer the norm. In fact, this pattern held true for only 7% of American families in the mid-1980s, down from 60% in the 1950s (Hodgkinson, 1985).

More students today will have only one or no sibling, or they may be part of **blended families,** with stepbrothers or stepsisters who move in and out of their lives. Some of your students may live with an aunt, with grandparents, with one parent, in foster or adoptive homes, or with an older brother or sister. The best advice is to drop the phrases "your parents" and "your mother and father" and to speak of "your family" when talking to students.

Many middle-class couples are waiting longer to have children and are providing more material advantages. Children in these homes may have more "things," but they may also have less time with their parents. Of course, not all students are middle-class. About one-quarter of all children under 18 live with one parent, usually their mother, and almost half of these families have incomes below the poverty level (U.S. Bureau of the Census, 1990). Your students are likely to be alone or unsupervised much of the day. The growing number of these *latchkey children* has prompted many schools to offer before- and after-school programs.

Growing Up Too Fast.   Joan Isenberg (1991) summarizes the situation confronting children in this way:

> Today's youth live in a fast-paced, changing world characterized by social pressures that push them to grow up too fast. They are pressured to adapt to changing family patterns, to achieve academically at early ages, and to participate and compete in sports and specialized skills. Moreover, they are pressured to cope with adult information in the media before they have mastered the problems of childhood. Such pressure places increased responsibility and stress on children while simultaneously redefining the essence of childhood itself. (p. 38)

David Elkind (1986) talks about the "hurried child," and other psychologists note the "adultification" of children's television and literature. An article in *Newsweek* (1991) on "The End of Innocence" began with this story:

> A 16-year-old Houston girl was babysitting for two boys, 6 and 9 years old. The kids were glued to the George Michael "I Want Your Sex" video on MTV. Singing along, the boys came to the words "sex with you alone." The younger one looked a little puzzled. "What's that thing when it isn't alone, when lots of people do it?" he asked. "A borney?" "No," his older brother shot back contemptuously. "You're so dumb. It's an orgy." (p. 62)

Student teachers in my classes are amazed at the seeming sophistication of their young students. Every night on the news, these children hear about drugs, sex, AIDS, and other "adult" subjects. But don't assume that because your students know the vocabulary, they really understand these subjects or are emotionally ready to deal with them.

One antidote to "hurried children" is developmentally appropriate schooling.

© 1989 M. Twohy—From *Phi Delta Kappan.*

Blended Families Parents, children, and stepchildren merged into families through remarriages.

Developmentally Appropriate Preschools.   David Elkind (1989, 1991) also has been a vocal critic of formal education for preschool children. He suggests that before 1960 there were few preschools as we know them today. But changing family styles and pressure on education to improve sinking test scores led to an emphasis on teaching children more, sooner. Middle-class working parents paid for preschool experiences that promised to make up for time lost with Mom and Dad. Elkind (1989) believes that "teaching young children in a didactic way, as if they were miniature second or third graders, can have lasting negative effects on their academic careers and their successful adaptation to the larger society" (p. 47).

These negative effects include stress reactions such as headaches, stomach aches, and behavior problems. In addition, children who are given too much teacher direction at a time when they need to follow their own direction may develop a sense of guilt rather than initiative (in Erikson's terms), diminished self-confidence, and decreased motivation for academic learning later in life. They may learn to wait to be told what to learn and how to learn it. Furthermore, after a few years of elementary school, they will be no further ahead than children who spent their preschool years playing instead of "studying."

What is a **developmentally appropriate education** for preschoolers—one that fits their physical, social, emotional, and cognitive needs? Many suggestions echo the ideas we examined in the Guidelines in Chapter 2 for teaching preoperational children and in this chapter for encouraging initiative. Because young children are so variable in their development at this time, Elkind suggests grouping several ages together so that slower 5-year-olds can play and interact with more advanced 4-year-olds, and so on. If children must be grouped by age, then activities and materials must take into account the wide range of

Ideally, developmentally appropriate schools group children of different ages together and provide materials and activities suited to a wide range of development.

Developmentally Appropriate Education Educational programs and activities designed to meet the cognitive, emotional, social, and physical needs of students.

development. Materials should be nongraded, that is, appropriate for a range of ages. You have seen these before: blocks, water, sand, dolls, pretend props, a range of books, animals, cars, and playdough. A 2-year-old can stack three blocks and improve motor development. A 4-year-old can use the same blocks with a friend to develop some basic idea about counting and cooperating. The teacher is a matchmaker between child and materials, understanding what children are ready to learn and providing situations that support that learning (Bredekemp, 1986).

Children of Divorce.   Many of your students, ready or not, have to deal with one very adult issue—divorce. The divorce rate in the United States is the highest in the world, almost double that of the second-ranked nation, Sweden. By the year 2000, only about 30 percent of the students in the United States will live with both of their biological parents throughout their teen years (Nielsen, 1993).

As many of us know from experiences in our own families, separation and divorce are stressful events for all participants, even under the best circumstances. The actual separation of the parents may have been preceded by years of conflict in the home or may come as a shock to all, including friends and children. During the divorce itself, conflict may increase as property and custody rights are being decided.

After the divorce, more changes may disrupt the children's lives. Today, as in the past, the mother is most often the custodial parent, but the number of father-headed households is increasing and is now about 15% (Meyer & Garasky, 1993). The parent who has custody may have to move to a less-expensive home, find new sources of income, go to work for the first time, or work longer hours. For the child, this can mean leaving behind important friendships in the old neighborhood or school, just when support is needed the most. It may mean having just one parent, who has less time than ever to be with the children. About two-thirds of parents remarry and half of them divorce again, so there are more adjustments ahead for the children (Furstenburg & Cherlin, 1991; Nelson, 1993).

The economic hardships of divorce seem particularly great for women who take over as heads of their households. Only one in 19 two-parent families lives below the poverty level, but almost one in two female single-parent families is in this category (Hetherington, 1989; Moshman, Glover, & Bruning, 1987). To make matters worse, about three-quarters of women who are supposed to receive child support from absent fathers don't get the full share (Children's Defense Fund, 1994). Money shortages lead to fewer toys and trips, and less recreation in general. Children may also be asked to accept their parents' new lovers or even new stepparents. In some divorces there are few conflicts, ample resources, and the continuing support of friends and extended family. But divorce is never easy for anyone.

The first two years after the divorce seem to be the most difficult period for both boys and girls. During this time, children may have problems in school, lose or gain an unusual amount of weight, develop difficulties sleep-

Focus on...

Socialization

- What are some examples of the ways that children are pressured to grow up quickly?
- What challenges face children whose parents are divorced?
- What is developmentally appropriate education?
- As Vanesa's (p. 66) teacher, would you involve her family in dealing with her social problems? How would you decide what to do?

ing, and so on. They may blame themselves for the breakup of their family or hold unrealistic hopes for a reconciliation (Hetherington, 1989; Pfeffer, 1981). Long-term adjustment is also affected. Boys tend to show a higher rate of behavioral and interpersonal problems at home and in school than girls in general or boys from intact families. Girls may have trouble in their dealings with males. They may become more sexually active or have difficulties trusting males (Wallerstein & Blakeslee, 1989). But living with one fairly content, if harried, parent may be better than living in a conflict-filled situation with two unhappy parents (Nielsen, 1993). And adjustment to divorce is an individual matter; some children respond with increased responsibility and maturity.

Judith Wallerstein (1991) suggests that all children of divorce must face several tasks. They must separate real changes brought by the divorce from fantasy fears of abandonment or losing their parents. They must separate themselves from their parents' pain and get on with their own lives. Parents often make this very difficult by inflicting their own anger and loneliness on their children. Students experiencing divorce must deal with the very real loss of their family unit and usually lose the company of one parent as well. Ultimately, students have to accept that the divorce is permanent, that their family system is forever changed. Yet they must still be willing to take a chance on loving in this uncertain world of relationships. The Guidelines should help you help your students during these difficult times.

Guidelines

Helping Children of Divorce

Take note of any sudden changes in behavior that might indicate problems at home.

Examples

1. Be alert to physical symptoms like repeated headaches or stomach pains, rapid weight gain or loss, fatigue or excess energy.
2. Be aware of signs of emotional distress, like moodiness, temper tantrums, difficulty in paying attention or concentrating.
3. Let parents know about the students' signs of stress.

Talk individually to students about their attitude or behavior changes. This gives you a chance to find out about unusual stress such as divorce.

Examples

1. Be a good listener. Students may have no other adult willing to hear their concerns.
2. Let students know you are available to talk, and let the student set the agenda.

Watch your language to make sure you avoid stereotypes about "happy" (two-parent) homes.

Examples

1. Simply say "your families" instead of "your mothers and fathers" when addressing the class.

(continued)

2. Avoid statements such as "We need volunteers for room mother" or "Your father can help you."

Help students maintain self-esteem.

Examples

1. Recognize a job well done.

2. Make sure the student understands the assignment and can handle the workload. This is not the time to pile on new and very difficult work.

3. The student may be angry at his or her parents, but may direct the anger at teachers. Don't take the student's anger personally.

Find out what resources are available at your school.

Examples

1. Talk to the school psychologist, guidance counselor, social worker, or principal about students who seem to need outside help.

2. Consider establishing a discussion group, led by a trained adult, for students going through a divorce.

Be sensitive to both parents' rights to information.

Examples

1. When parents have joint custody, both are entitled to receive information and attend parent-teacher conferences.

2. The noncustodial parent may still be concerned about the child's school progress. Check with your principal about state laws regarding the noncustodial parent's rights.

New Roles for Teachers

When we consider the high rate of divorce, we see that teachers today are dealing with issues that once stayed outside the walls of the school. The first and most important task of the teacher is to educate, but student learning suffers when there are problems with personal and social development.

Teachers are sometimes the best source of help for students facing emotional or interpersonal problems. When students have chaotic and unpredictable home lives, they need a caring, firm structure in school. They need teachers who set clear limits, are consistent, enforce rules firmly but not punitively, respect students, and show genuine concern. As a teacher, you can be available to talk about personal problems without requiring that your students do so. One of my student teachers gave a boy in her class a journal entitled "Very Hard Thoughts" so that he could write about his parents' divorce. Sometimes he talked to her about the journal entries, but at other times he just recorded his feelings. The student teacher was very careful to respect the boy's privacy about his writings. What can teachers do to encourage personal and social growth in school? The Guidelines give some other ideas.

Guidelines

Help students examine the kinds of dilemmas they are currently facing or will face in the near future.

Examples

1. In elementary school, discuss sibling rivalries, teasing, stealing, prejudice, treatment of new students in the class, behavior toward handicapped classmates.

2. In high school, discuss cheating, letting friends drive when they are intoxicated, conforming to be more popular, protecting a friend who has broken a rule.

Help students see the perspectives of others.

Examples

1. Ask a student to describe his or her understanding of the views of another, then have the other person confirm or correct the perception.

2. Have students exchange roles and try to "become" the other person in a discussion.

Help students make connections between expressed values and actions.

Examples

1. Follow a discussion of "What should be done?" with "How would you act? What would be your first step? What problems might arise?"

2. Help students see inconsistencies between their values and their own actions. Ask them to identify inconsistencies, first in others, then in themselves.

Safeguard the privacy of all participants.

Examples

1. Remind students that in a discussion they can "pass" and not answer questions.

2. Intervene if peer pressure is forcing a student to say more than he or she wants to.

3. Don't reinforce a pattern of telling "secrets."

Make sure students are really listening to each other.

Examples

1. Keep groups small.

2. Be a good listener yourself.

3. Recognize students who pay careful attention to each other.

Make sure that as much as possible your class reflects concern for moral issues and values.

Examples

1. Make clear distinctions between rules based on administrative convenience (keeping the room orderly) and rules based on moral issues.

2. Enforce standards uniformly. Be careful about showing favoritism.

Source: Adapted with permission from J. W. Eiseman (1981). What criteria should public school moral education programs meet? *The Review of Education, 7,* pp. 226–227.

Challenges for Children

In the next few pages we examine a number of challenges children face as they mature. The first is as old as the human species—growing up—meeting the challenges of physical development. The remaining challenges are all too modern and have put students at great risk today. We will end by considering just a few of these risks.

Physical Development

For most children, at least in the early years, growing up means growing bigger, stronger, more coordinated. It also can be frightening, disappointing, exciting, and puzzling.

The Preschool Years.   Preschool children are very active. Their **gross-motor skills,** which involve control of the large muscles, improve greatly over the years from ages 2 to 5, as you can see in Table 3.6. Between ages 2 and about 4 or 5, preschoolers' muscles grow stronger, their balance improves, and their center of gravity moves lower, so they are able to run, jump, climb, and hop. Most of these movements develop naturally if the child has normal physical abilities and the opportunity to play. Children with physical problems, however, may need special training to develop these skills. For young children, physical activity can be an end in itself. It is fun just to improve. But preschoolers may literally run till they drop. They need periods of rest scheduled after physical exertion.

Fine-motor skills such as tying shoes or fastening buttons, which require the coordination of small movements, also improve greatly during the preschool years, as shown in Table 3.6. Children need to work with large paintbrushes, fat pencils and crayons, large pieces of drawing paper, and soft clay or playdough to accommodate their developing skills. During this time, children will begin to show a preference for their right or left hand. Most students, about 85% during this time, will prefer their right hand, but those who prefer

Gross-Motor Skills Voluntary body movements that involve the large muscles.

Fine-Motor Skills Voluntary body movements that involve the small muscles.

TABLE 3.6 Motor Skills Improve throughout the Preschool Years		
Approximate Age	**Gross-Motor Skills**	**Fine-Motor Skills**
Birth to 3 years	sits and crawls; walks; begins to run	picks up, grasps, stacks, and releases objects
3 to 4.5 years	walks up and down stairs; jumps with both feet; throws ball	holds crayon; uses utensils; buttons; copies shapes
4.5 to 6 years	skips; rides two-wheel bicycle; catches ball; plays sports	uses pencil; makes representational drawings; cuts with scissors; prints letters

their left should not be forced to change. This means that there must be a good supply of left-handed scissors for preschool classes.

Elementary School.   During the elementary-school years, physical development is fairly steady for most children. They become taller, leaner, and stronger, so they are better able to master sports and games. There is tremendous variation, however. A particular child can be much larger or smaller than average and still be perfectly healthy. Because children at this age are very aware of physical differences but are not the most tactful people, you may hear comments like "You're too little to be in fifth grade. What's wrong with you?" or "How come you're so fat?"

Throughout elementary school, many of the girls are likely to be as large as or larger than the boys in their classes. Between the ages of 11 and 14, girls are, on the average, taller and heavier than boys of the same age (Tanner, 1990). The size discrepancy can give the girls an advantage in physical activities, though some girls may feel conflict over this and, as a result, downplay their physical abilities.

Adolescence.   **Puberty** marks the beginning of sexual maturity. It is not a single event, but a series of changes involving almost every part of the body. The outcome of the changes is the ability to reproduce. The sex differences in physical development we saw during the later elementary years become even more pronounced at the beginning of puberty. Generally, girls begin puberty about two years ahead of boys and reach their final height by age 16; most boys continue growing until about age 18. For the typical girl, the adolescent growth spurt begins with breast development between the ages of 10 and 11 and continues for about three years. While this is the average time frame for girls, the actual range is from 9 to 16 years. Eighty percent of American girls have their first menstrual period between the ages of 11-1/2 and 14-1/2. For the typical boy, the growth spurt begins between the ages of 12 and 13.

The physical changes of adolescence have significant effects on the individual's identity. Psychologists have been particularly interested in the academic, social, and emotional differences they have found between adolescents who mature early and those who mature later. Early maturation seems to have certain special advantages for boys. The early maturers' taller, broader-shouldered body type fits the cultural stereotype for the male ideal. Early-maturing boys are more likely to enjoy high social status; they tend to be popular and to be leaders. On the other hand, boys who mature late have an especially difficult time. These late-maturing boys tend to be less popular, more talkative, and hungrier for attention (Kaplan, 1984). However, some studies show that in adulthood, males who matured later tend to be more creative, tolerant, and perceptive. Perhaps the trials and anxieties of maturing late teach some boys to be better problem solvers (Brooks-Gunn, 1988; Seifert & Hoffnung, 1991).

For girls, these effects are reversed. Maturing way ahead of classmates can be a definite disadvantage. Being larger than everyone else in the class is not a valued characteristic for girls in many cultures (Simmons & Blythe, 1987). A girl who begins to mature early probably will be the first in her peer group to start the changes of puberty. This can be very upsetting to some girls, especially if they have not been prepared for the changes or if friends tease them. Later-

Puberty The period in early adolescence when individuals begin to reach physical and sexual maturity.

maturing girls seem to have fewer problems, but they may worry that something is wrong with them. All students can benefit from knowing that the "normal" range in rates of maturation is great and that there are advantages for both early and late maturers. The Guidelines give a few ideas for dealing with physical differences in the classroom.

Guidelines

Dealing with Differences in Growth and Development

Do not call unnecessary attention to physical differences among students.

Examples

1. Avoid seating arrangements that are obviously based on height, but try to seat smaller students so they can see and participate in class activities.
2. Avoid games that call attention to differences in height, size, or strength.
3. Don't use or allow students to use nicknames based on physical traits.

Help students obtain factual information on differences in physical development.

Examples

1. Set up science projects on sex differences in growth rates.
2. Have readings and discussions that focus on differences between early and late maturers. Make sure that you present the positives and the negatives of each.
3. Find out the school policy on sex education and on informal guidance for students. Some schools, for example, encourage teachers to talk to girls who are upset about their first menstrual period, while other schools expect teachers to send the girls to talk to the school nurse.
4. Give the student models in literature or in their community of high-achieving individuals who do not fit the ideal physical stereotypes.

Accept that concerns about appearance and the opposite sex will occupy much time and energy for adolescents.

Examples

1. Allow students a few moments at the end of class to socialize.
2. Deal with some of these issues in curriculum-related materials.

Children and Youth at Risk

It is a difficult time to become an adult. Many of the challenges children face threaten their safety as well as their personal and social development. We will consider only a few of the risks that students encounter. In each of these areas teachers can play a role in helping students cope with their situations. In the first area—child abuse—teachers have legal responsibilities to consider.

Child Abuse.   Accurate information about the number of abused children in the United States is difficult to find; in 1992, 2.9 million cases were reported, an increase of 132% over the level in the 1980s. However, most ex-

TABLE 3.7 Factors Related to Child Abuse

Factor	Description
Parent characteristics	Psychological disturbance; substance abuse; history of abuse as a child; belief in harsh, physical discipline; desire to satisfy unmet emotional needs through the child; unreasonable expectations for child behavior; young age (most under 30); low educational level
Child characteristics	Premature or very sick baby; difficult temperament; inattentiveness and overactivity; and other developmental problems
Family characteristics	Low income; poverty; homelessness; marital instability; social isolation; physical abuse of mother by husband or boyfriend; frequent moves; large, closely spaced families; overcrowded living conditions; disorganized household; lack of steady employment; other signs of high life stress
Community	Characterized by social isolation; few parks, day care centers, preschool programs, recreation centers, and churches to serve as family supports
Culture	Approval of physical force and violence as ways to solve problems

Source: From Laura E. Berk, *Infants, children, and adolescents,* 2/e, p. 386. Copyright © 1996 by Allyn & Bacon. Reprinted by permission.

perts agree that an enormous number of cases go unreported (Children's Defense Fund, 1994). About half of all abusive parents could change their destructive behavior patterns if they received help. Without assistance, probably only about 5% of abusing parents improve (Starr, 1979). Of course, parents are not the only people who abuse children. Siblings, other relatives, and even teachers have been responsible for the physical and sexual abuse of children. Table 3.7 summarizes the factors related to child abuse.

As a teacher, you must alert your principal, school psychologist, or school social worker if you suspect abuse. In all 50 states of the United States, in the District of Columbia and the U.S. territories, the law requires certain professionals, often including teachers, to report suspected cases of child abuse. The legal definition of abuse has been broadened in many states to include neglect and failure to provide proper care and supervision. Most laws also protect teachers who report suspected neglect in good faith (Beezer, 1985). Be sure that you understand the laws in your state or province on this important issue as well as your own moral responsibility. Several thousand children die of abuse or neglect each year in the United States, in many cases because no one would "get involved." Table 3.8 on page 102 lists possible indicators of abuse.

It has always been difficult to navigate the adolescent years, but today the waters seem more dangerous than ever. Many challenges confront junior and senior high school students today. We will touch on only a few.

TABLE 3.8   Indicators of Child Abuse

The following are some of the signs of abuse. Not every child with these signs is abused, but these indicators should be investigated.

	Physical Indicators	Behavioral Indicators	
Physical Abuse	▪ unexplained bruises (in various stages of healing) welts, human bite marks, bald spots ▪ unexplained burns, especially cigarette burns or immersion-burns (glove-like) ▪ unexplained fractures, lacerations, or abrasions	▪ self-destructive ▪ withdrawn and aggressive—behavioral extremes ▪ uncomfortable with physical contact ▪ arrives at school early or stays late, as if afraid	▪ chronic runaway (adolescents) ▪ complains of soreness or moves uncomfortably ▪ wears clothing inappropriate to weather, to cover body
Physical Neglect	▪ abandonment ▪ unattended medical needs ▪ consistent lack of supervision ▪ consistent hunger, inappropriate dress, poor hygiene ▪ lice, distended stomach, emaciation	▪ regularly displays fatigue or listlessness, falls asleep in class ▪ steals food, begs from classmates ▪ reports that no caretaker is at home	▪ frequently absent or tardy ▪ self-destructive ▪ school dropout (adolescents)
Sexual Abuse	▪ torn, stained, or bloodied underclothing ▪ pain or itching in genital area ▪ difficulty walking or sitting ▪ bruises or bleeding in external genitalia ▪ venereal disease ▪ frequent urinary or yeast infections	▪ withdrawn, chronic depression ▪ excessive seductiveness ▪ role reversal, overly concerned for siblings ▪ poor self-esteem, self-devaluation, lack of confidence ▪ peer problems, lack of involvement ▪ massive weight change	▪ suicide attempts (especially adolescents) ▪ hysteria, lack of emotional control ▪ sudden school difficulties ▪ inappropriate sex play or premature understanding of sex ▪ threatened by physical contact, closeness ▪ promiscuity

Source: From T. Bear, S. Schenk, and L. Buckner. "Supporting victims of child abuse." *Educational Leadership, 50*(4), p. 44. Reprinted with permission of the Association for Supervision and Curriculum Development. Copyright © 1993 by ASCD. All rights reserved.

Teenage Sexuality and Pregnancy.   Today, about 80 percent of American men and 75 percent of American women have had sexual intercourse by age 19 (Guttmacher Institute, 1991). *Newsweek* (1991) reported that 50% of 15-year-old girls have had intercourse. The emotional impact of these early sexual experiences may have repercussions in the school, both for the students involved and for fellow students who hear about the experiences. One consequence of this early sexual activity is unexpected and unwanted pregnancy.

Naiveté about the possible consequences of early sexual activity, unwanted pregnancy, and sexually transmitted disease gives many adolescents a false sense of invincibility: "It won't happen to me."

Each year, more than 1 million teenage girls become pregnant—30,000 of them are younger than 15 years old (DeRidder, 1993; Scarr, Weinberg, & Levine, 1986). The adolescent pregnancy rate in the United States is twice that of England, France, and Canada, three times that of Sweden, and six times as high as the Netherlands (Berk, 1996).

A remarkable number of American adolescents have little information, or indeed the wrong information, about birth control. For example, about one-half of the adolescent girls who become pregnant do so in their first six months of sexual activity; often, they haven't decided yet what to do about birth control, partly because they don't expect anything to happen so quickly. It can! In fact, many teenage girls don't know when in their menstrual cycle they can become pregnant. They fear that they will "lose" their boyfriends if they don't have sex, but don't prepare for intercourse because they don't want to appear "sex crazed." Some adults fear that giving adolescents accurate information about sex will encourage them to experiment. Research indicates that this is not a danger. The main effect of providing the facts appears to be fewer unwanted pregnancies (Brooks-Gunn & Furstenberg, 1989; DeRidder, 1993).

Eating Disorders.   Adolescents going through the changes of puberty are very concerned about their bodies. This has always been true, but today, the emphasis on fitness and appearance makes adolescents even more likely to worry about how their bodies "measure up." For some, the concern becomes excessive. One consequence is eating disorders such as **bulimia** (binge eating) and **anorexia nervosa** (self-starvation), both of which are much more common in females than in males. Bulimics often binge, eating an entire gallon of ice cream or a whole cake. Then, to avoid gaining weight, they force themselves

Bulimia   Eating disorder characterized by overeating, then getting rid of the food by self-induced vomiting or laxatives.

Anorexia Nervosa   Eating disorder characterized by very limited food intake.

to vomit, or they use strong laxatives, to purge themselves of the extra calories. Bulimics tend to maintain a normal weight, but their digestive systems can be permanently damaged. Anorexia is an even more dangerous disorder, for anorexics refuse to eat or eat practically nothing. In the process they may lose 20 to 25% of their body weight, and some (about 5%) literally starve themselves to death. Anorexic students may appear pale, have brittle fingernails, and fine, dark hairs developing all over their bodies. They are easily chilled because they have so little fat to insulate their bodies. These eating disorders often begin in adolescence and require professional help (Harris, 1991). Again, a teacher may be the person who begins the chain of help for students with these tragic problems.

Drug Abuse. Modern society makes growing up a very confusing process. Notice the messages from films and billboards. "Beautiful," popular people drink alcohol and smoke cigarettes with little concern for their health. We have over-the-counter drugs for almost every common ailment. Coffee wakes us up, and a pill helps us sleep. And then we tell students to "Just say no!" to drugs.

For many reasons, not just because of these contradictory messages, drug use has become a problem for students. Accurate statistics are hard to find, but estimates from the National Center for Education Statistics indicate that 92% of high school seniors report some experience with alcohol—66% using it in the past month. About 20% of seniors are daily smokers, and 30% have tried at least one illegal drug.

What can be done about drug use among our students? First, we should distinguish between experimentation and abuse. Many students try something at a party but do not become regular users. The best way to help students who have trouble saying no appears to be through peer programs that teach how to say no assertively. The successful programs also teach general social skills and build self-esteem (Newcomb & Bentler, 1989). Also, the older students are when they experiment with drugs, the more likely they are to make responsible choices, so helping younger students say no is a clear benefit.

AIDS. A growing health risk for everyone, but especially for adolescents, is the spread of AIDS (acquired immune deficiency syndrome). As of 1992, only about 3% of all AIDS cases were individuals under the age of 21, and many of these were young children. But the frightening fact is that this percentage is growing rapidly, especially among adolescents. About one-fifth of all AIDS cases in the United States occur between ages 20 and 29 (Berk, 1996). In most cases, adolescents contract AIDS through intimate sexual contact or intravenous drug use. For the virus to be transmitted, people have to exchange bodily fluids without the fluids coming into contact with the air first. Obviously, this can happen a number of ways, but contact has to be more than casual. Many students do not understand that the AIDS virus is unable to survive in air or water, so AIDS cannot be transmitted by casual day-to-day touching, hugging, or sharing food—or even by being spit on (Seifert & Hoffnung, 1991). The Task Force on Pediatric AIDS of the American Psychological Asso-

Focus on...

Challenges Students Face

- How do students develop physically during the elementary years?
- Describe the worlds of the late-maturing adolescent boy and girl.
- How would you recognize a child who is being abused?
- What are some of the danger signs of eating disorders? of potential for suicide?
- How might you assess the physical and emotional risks Vanesa (p. 66) faces?

ciation (1989) recommends education about AIDS for students, beginning in the early years and continuing through high school. In this area, education can be life-saving and does not appear to encourage experimentation.

Suicide.   For young people ages 15 to 24, the suicide rate has tripled in the past 30 years. Figure 3.2 shows a steady climb in the number of suicides among all males and among white females.

Suicide often comes as a response to life problems—problems that parents and teachers sometimes dismiss. There are a number of warning signs that trouble is brewing. Watch for changes in eating or sleeping habits, weight, grades, disposition, activity level, or interest in friends. Students at risk sometimes suddenly give away prized possessions such as stereos, CDs, clothing, or pets. They may seem depressed or hyperactive and may say things like "Nothing matters anymore," "You won't have to worry about me anymore," or I wonder what dying is like." They may start missing school or quit doing work. It is especially dangerous if the student not only talks about suicide, but also has a plan for acting.

If you suspect that there is a problem, talk to the student directly. One feeling shared by many people who attempt suicide is that no one really takes them seriously. "A question about suicide does not provoke suicide. Indeed, teens (and adults) often experience relief when someone finally cares enough to ask" (Range, 1993, p. 145). Be realistic, not poetic, about suicide. Ask about specifics, and take the student seriously. Also, beware that teenage suicides often occur in clusters. After one student acts or when stories about a suicide are reported in the media, other teens are more likely to copy the suicide (Lewinsohn, Rohde, & Seeley, 1994). Table 3.9 lists common myths and facts about suicide.

FIGURE 3.2

Increasing Suicide Rates among Adolescents

From 1960 through 1987 the number of suicides per 100,000 adolescents has steadily increased for all groups except nonwhite females. The increase for white males has been the greatest.

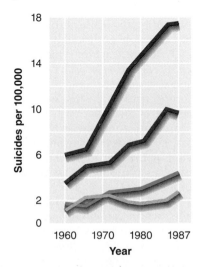

■ White males
■ Males, all other races
■ White females
■ Females, all other races

Source: U.S. Department of Health and Human Services, as reported in *Newsweek Special Issue, Education: A Consumer's Handbook* (Fall–Winter 1990–1991), p. 15.

TABLE 3.9   Myths and Facts about Suicide

Myth: People who talk about suicide don't kill themselves.

Fact: Eight out of ten people who commit suicide tell someone that they're thinking about hurting themselves before they actually do it.

Myth: Only certain types of people commit suicide.

Fact: All types of people commit suicide—male and female, young and old, rich and poor, country people and city people. It happens in every racial, ethnic, and religious group.

Myth: When a person talks about suicide, you should change the subject to get his or her mind off it.

Fact: You should take them seriously. Listen carefully to what they are saying. Give them a chance to express their feelings. Let them know you are concerned. And help them get help.

Myth: Most people who kill themselves really want to die.

Fact: Most people who kill themelves are confused about whether they want to die. Suicide is often intended as a cry for help.

Source: From R. Bell (1980). *Changing bodies, changing lives: A book for teens on sex and relationships.* New York: Random House, p. 142.

This has been a brief, selective look at the needs of children. As we saw earlier, educators and psychologists are concerned about providing a developmentally appropriate education for preschool students. All students, whatever their age, require an education that fits their physical, cognitive, personal, and social levels of development.

SUMMARY

The Work of Erikson

According to Erik Erikson's theory of emotional development, people go through eight life stages between infancy and old age, each of which involves a central crisis. Adequate resolution of each crisis leads to greater personal and social competence and a stronger foundation for solving future crises. In the first two stages, an infant must develop a sense of trust over mistrust and a sense of autonomy over shame and doubt. In early childhood, the focus of the third stage is on developing initiative and avoiding feelings of guilt. In the child's elementary-school years, the fourth stage involves achieving a sense of industry and avoiding feelings of inferiority.

In Erikson's fifth stage, identity versus role confusion, adolescents consciously attempt to solidify their identity. According to James Marcia, these efforts may lead to identity achievement, foreclosure, diffusion, or moratorium. Erikson's three stages of adulthood involve struggles to achieve intimacy, generativity, and integrity.

Understanding Ourselves and Others

Our self-concept and self-esteem—our definition and evaluation of ourselves—become increasingly complex, differentiated, and abstract as we mature. Self-concept evolves through constant self-evaluation, social interaction, and experiences in and out of school. The degree to which this evaluation is positive determines whether someone has high or low self-esteem. Teachers can have a profound effect on students' self-concept and self-esteem.

Students develop a self-concept by comparing themselves to personal (internal) standards, and social (external) standards. The self-esteem of middle and junior high school students becomes more tied to physical appearance and social acceptance. High self-esteem is related to better overall school experience, both academically and socially. Gender and ethnic stereotypes are significant factors as well.

An understanding of intentions develops as children mature, but aggressive students often have trouble understanding the intentions of others. Social-perspective-taking also changes as we mature. Young children believe that everyone has the same thoughts and feelings they do. Later, they learn that others have separate identities and therefore separate feelings and perspectives on events.

Moral Development

Lawrence Kohlberg's theory of moral development includes three levels: (1) a preconventional level, where judgments are based on self-interest; (2) a conventional level, where judgments are based on traditional family values and social expectations; and (3) a postconventional level, where judgments are based on more abstract and personal ethical principles. Critics suggest that Kohlberg's view does not account for possible sex differences in moral reasoning or differences between moral reasoning and moral behavior. Moral behavior is influenced by the internalization of rules (made easier if children are given reasons for rules) and by modeling. At every level, friendships play a significant role in healthy personal and social development. Many school programs have adopted programs to increase students' capacity to care for others. Cheating and aggression are two common behavior problems in the schools that involve moral issues.

Socialization: The Home and the School

Changes in family structures, childhood stress, and divorce profoundly affect development. Today's children exist in a fast-paced, changing world characterized by social pressures that push them to grow up too fast. Developmentally appropriate education does not hurry a child's progress but responds to unfolding needs. In light of social challenges, teachers are faced with new roles, including supporting the affective development of their students.

Challenges for Children

During the preschool years there is rapid development of children's gross- and fine-motor skills. Physical development continues throughout the elementary-school years, with girls often ahead of boys in size. With adolescence comes puberty and emotional struggles to cope with all the related changes. Females mature about two years ahead of males. Early maturation is generally beneficial for males, though it is not without its disadvantages. Early maturation is not generally beneficial for girls. Children face many risks today, including abuse, pregnancy, eating disorders, drug abuse, AIDS, and suicide. Teachers must report suspected cases of child abuse and can be instrumental in helping students cope with other risks as well. At all stages of development, teachers must address students' needs for education that is appropriate to their physical, cognitive, personal, and social levels of development.

KEY TERMS

aggression, p. 90
anorexia nervosa, p. 103
autonomy, p. 68
blended families, p. 92
bulimia, p. 103
collective self-esteem, p. 78
developmental crisis, p. 67
developmentally appropriate
    education, p. 93
empathy, p. 85
ethnic pride, p. 78

fine-motor skills, p. 98
generativity, p. 73
gross-motor skills, p. 98
identity, p. 70
identity achievement, p. 70
identity diffusion, p. 71
identity foreclosure, p. 71
industry, p. 69
initiative, p. 68
integrity, p. 73
internalize, p. 89

moral dilemmas, p. 82
moral realism, p. 80
moral reasoning, p. 81
morality of cooperation, p. 80
moratorium, p. 71
perspective-taking ability, p. 80
psychosocial, p. 66
puberty, p. 99
self-concept, p. 73
self-esteem, p. 73
socialization, p. 91

CHECK YOUR UNDERSTANDING

Can you apply the ideas from this chapter on personal/social development to solve the following problems of practice?

Preschool and Kindergarten

■ Elise and Donis have always been two of the most cooperative students in your 4-year-old group. But both will soon have new babies in their families, and as the time draws nearer, they are becoming more and more disruptive. What would you do?

Elementary and Middle School

■ You notice a fairly dramatic change in one of your students. This boy seems very tired and anxious, and he is not doing his homework. The situation has gone on for a few weeks now. How would you approach this problem?

Junior High and High School

■ Several of your junior high school students are afraid to go to gym class because a gang of students has been extorting money and personal possessions. What steps would you take to end this situation?

■ You hear from one of your students that a group of seniors has a small "business" selling college applications essays. What would you do?

Cooperative Learning Activity

■ With four or five other members of your class, select a social skill and develop a plan for integrating discussion of that skill into a lesson for the age level you will teach. How would you assess the effectiveness of your lesson?

What Would They Do?

One of the girls in your 10th-grade class is desperate for friends. Vanesa seems so lonely and depressed—no one ever joins her at lunch or walks with her to class. She is a reasonably good student, but just doesn't seem to fit in. On several occasions she has tried to join a group by offering help or asking questions, but these initiations never go anywhere. Even when a friendship begins, it never lasts. Lately her schoolwork is careless and incomplete; she looks tired and pale.

CONSTANCE CARTER
MARY PHILLIPS
DIANE BATTY

Orono High School, Orono, Maine

We've all had students like Vanesa in our classes. Our concerns for her would be that in spite of being a reasonably good student, it might not be enough to compensate for losing out on the social aspect of school. Social issues are very important, almost a matter of life or death, for students at this age. Vanesa might go overboard trying to come up with friends and make choices she wouldn't ordinarily make simply to impress peers.

With a student like this, teachers should watch for certain warning signals such as absences from school and decreased quality of work. If Vanesa feels like a failure already, a drop in her grades will only make her feel more like one. Listen for talk about feelings of hopelessness, of "not fitting in." Other danger signs might be low affect, weight loss, or a drop in personal care. Watch her demeanor in class and in the halls.

A student like this might substitute risk-taking attempts, especially if she feels that academic risk taking hasn't worked for her. She might substitute more dangerous risk-taking attempts, such as substance abuse or delinquent activities, to impress other students.

Many schools have resources available to help students like Vanesa. Our school has a student assistance team, which is a group of faculty that meets with students who are having difficulty surviving: the team takes a supportive, not a punitive, standpoint. We would encourage Vanesa to get involved in peer groups to develop healthy friendships and to keep in touch with a guidance counselor. Extracurricular activities can also be a wonderful way to develop self-esteem and a sense of belonging in students who otherwise feel cut off from school life.

A student like this might benefit from developing a one-on-one relationship with a counselor who could serve as her advocate. A job at school, even being responsible for one simple errand a day, can be an excellent way to encourage a student's feeling of worthiness. If Vanesa can be helped to feel that her presence each day at school is important, that her being there made the day better, it could have a very positive impact on her.

SUSAN B. STRAUSS

Principal
Lincoln High School, Lincoln, Rhode Island

Any time a student's work, attitude, or appearance show a continuing change from their regular appearance and routine, it is a "heads-up" notice for concern. Her neediness of others may be an indicator of problems at home—a dysfunctional family, neglect, or abuse. A student such as Vanesa, who relies on others for her feelings of self-worth, may start to question whether there is any point to trying to get good grades, keeping up a good appearance or even, at the extreme, living at all. It is likely that Vanesa has very negative feelings about herself, and probably doubts that she has any value to anyone.

Whenever a student displays behaviors that are attention seeking, it is because something is missing and/or wrong in his or her own life. These described behaviors are, in themselves, "danger signs," and having been alerted by them, I would be sure to monitor Vanesa for any increasing displays of the behaviors already observed, as well as being watchful for any signs of withdrawal, self-inflicted injury, or radical mood swings. Utilizing a strategy of collegial brainstorming for student support, I would contact the student's guidance counselor to arrange a meeting of Vanesa's teachers as well as the school social worker and psychologist. Have her behaviors been observed in all classes? Is there any other student who seems to take a genuine interest in Vanesa? Is there a teacher with whom Vanesa has bonded? Such a meeting can help to focus on what the observable behaviors have been and to identify a variety of creative options to help address the issue. It is also an opportunity for the social worker to determine if a social history is needed. At the classroom level, I would seek out the assistance of peer leaders—students, who by their nature, have an interest in helping others—and find ways to provide for cooperative learning activities that will, through the natural classroom learning environment, offer nonthreatening opportunities for interaction.

THOMAS O'DONNELL

Social Studies Chairperson, Grades 7–12
Malden High School, Malden, Massachusetts

The concerns are Vanesa's self-image and interpersonal relationships. I would turn to adjustment personnel, guidance personnel, and parents to alert them and have them use their expertise.

I might try counseling her one-on-one if I felt confident and comfortable under the circumstances. Seating arrangements and cooperative learning situations might help Vanesa develop some relationships. I might encourage her to join extracurricular activities where she can make contributions and form some attachments.

4

Learning Abilities and Learning Problems

Overview | *What Would You Do?*

LANGUAGE AND LABELING   112

INDIVIDUAL DIFFERENCES IN INTELLIGENCE   113
What Does Intelligence Mean? | How Is Intelligence Measured? |
What Does an IQ Score Mean?

ABILITY DIFFERENCES AND TEACHING   121
Ability Grouping | Mental Retardation | Gifted and Talented

CREATIVITY   129
Creativity and Cognition | Assessing Creativity | Creativity in
the Classroom

COGNITIVE AND LEARNING STYLES   133
Cognitive Styles | Learning Styles and Preferences

STUDENTS WITH LEARNING CHALLENGES   136
Students with Physical and Sensory Challenges | Communication
Disorders | Emotional or Behavioral Disorders | Hyperactivity and
Attention Disorders | Learning Disabilities

INTEGRATION, MAINSTREAMING, AND INCLUSION   146
Changes in the Law | Effective Teaching in Inclusive Classrooms |
Computers and Exceptional Students

Summary | *Key Terms* | *Check Your Understanding* |
Teachers' Casebook: What Would They Do?

*H*ave *you ever had the experience of being the only one in a group who had trouble doing something? How would you feel if every day in school you faced the same kind of difficulty, while everyone else seemed to find the work easier than you? What kind of support and teaching would you need to keep trying?*

So far we have talked little about individuals. We have discussed principles of development that apply to everyone—stages, processes, conflicts, and tasks. Our development as human beings is similar in many ways—but not in every way. Even among members of the same family, there are marked contrasts in appearance, interests, abilities, and temperament.

We will begin our discussion of individual differences in learning with a look at the names and labels that have been applied to some students. Then we turn to an extended examination of intellectual abilities, which vary so greatly from individual to individual and have proved so difficult to define and measure. How can teachers work with such a wide range of abilities? Is ability grouping a good answer? What are the special needs of the gifted and the retarded? How do individual cognitive styles and learning preferences affect learning?

Next we explore the kinds of learning problems students may have. As we discuss each problem area, we will consider how a teacher might recognize problems, seek help from school and community resources, and plan instruction based on individuals' needs. Recent changes in federal legislation mean that you probably will have at least one exceptional student in your class, whatever grade you teach. We will discuss the laws and how to cope with their effects.

By the time you have completed this chapter, you should be able to:

- Discuss the potential problems in categorizing and labeling students.
- Begin to develop a personal concept of intelligence to aid you in your teaching.
- Discuss how you might recognize and teach students who are mildly retarded or who are gifted.
- Adapt lessons to make them appropriate for students with varying learning styles.
- List indicators of hearing, vision, language, and behavior problems, as well as indicators of specific learning disabilities.
- Adapt teaching methods to meet the needs of exceptional students.
- Discuss the implications of the Individuals with Disabilities Act for your teaching.

What Would You Do?

Stuffed in your (undersized) mail box in the school office is a large, official-looking envelope. There seems to be one in almost every box. Inside are computer printouts with the results of the fall testing, including scores on a group test of intelligence for all the seventh- and eighth-grade students in your advisory section. Also in your box are notes from two parents who must have already heard that the test results are in. They want to meet with you to see their child's scores, and especially, as one parent put it, "To find out how smart Jason really is." You look at the printouts and at the notes, wondering what you should do with the results.

- How will you use this information?

- What do the intelligence test scores tell you about your students?

- How would you respond to the notes from the parents? Will you share the scores with the parents?

Language and Labeling

Every child is a distinctive collection of talents, abilities, and limitations. In that sense we all are "exceptional." But some students are called exceptional because they have learning abilities or problems and require special education or other services to reach their potential. **Exceptional students** may have mental retardation, learning disabilities, communication disorders, emotional or behavioral disorders, physical disabilities, autism, traumatic brain injury, impaired hearing, impaired vision, or special abilities and talents. Even though we will use these terms throughout the chapter, a caution is in order: labeling students is a controversial issue.

A label does not tell which methods to use with individual students. For example, few specific "treatments" automatically follow from a "diagnosis" of mental retardation—many different teaching strategies and materials are appropriate. Further, the labels can become self-fulfilling prophecies. Everyone—teachers, parents, classmates, and even the students themselves—may see a label as a stigma that cannot be changed. Finally, labels are mistaken for explanations, as in, "Chris gets into fights because he has a behavior disorder." "How do you know he has a behavior disorder?" "Because he gets into fights."

On the other hand, some educators argue that for younger students, at least, being labeled as "special" protects the child. For example, if classmates know a student is retarded, they will be more willing to accept his or her behaviors. Of course, labels still open doors to some special programs, needed information, or financial assistance. Labels probably both stigmatize and help students (Heward & Orlansky, 1992; Keogh & MacMillan, 1996). But until we are able to make diagnoses with greater accuracy, we should be very cautious about describing a whole human being with one or two words.

This caution also applies to many of the common descriptions heard in schools every day. Today some people object to labels such as "the mentally

Exceptional Students Students who have abilities or problems so significant that the students require special education or other services to reach their potential.

retarded" or "at-risk student," because describing a complex person with one or two words implies that the condition labeled is the most important aspect of the person. Actually the individual has many abilities, and to focus on the disability is to misrepresent the individual. An alternative is to speak of "students with mental retardation" or "students placed at risk." Here the emphasis is on the students first, not on the special challenges they face.

In the next section we consider a concept that has provided the basis for many labels—intelligence.

Individual Differences in Intelligence

Because the concept of intelligence is so important in education, so controversial, and so often misunderstood, we will spend quite a few pages discussing it. Let us begin with a basic question.

What Does Intelligence Mean?

The idea that people vary in what we call intelligence has been with us for a long time. Plato discussed similar variations over 2,000 years ago. Most early theories about the nature of intelligence involved one or more of the following three themes: (1) the capacity to learn; (2) the total knowledge a person has acquired; and (3) the ability to adapt successfully to new situations and to the environment in general.

In this century, there has been considerable controversy over the meaning of intelligence. In 1986 at a symposium on intelligence, 24 psychologists offered 24 different views about the nature of intelligence (Neisser et al., 1996; Sternberg & Detterman, 1986). Over half of the experts did mention higher-level thinking processes such as abstract reasoning, problem solving, and decision making as important aspects of intelligence, but they disagreed about the structure of intelligence—whether it is a single ability or many separate abilities (Gustafsson & Undheim, 1996).

Intelligence: One Ability or Many?   Some theorists believe intelligence is a basic ability that affects performance on all cognitively oriented tasks. An "intelligent" person will do well in computing mathematical problems, analyzing poetry, taking history essay examinations, and solving riddles. Evidence for this position comes from correlational evaluations of intelligence tests. In study after study, moderate to high positive correlations are found among all the different tests that are designed to measure separate intellectual abilities (Lohman, 1989; McNemar, 1964). What could explain these results?

Charles Spearman (1927) suggested there is one factor or mental attribute, which he called *g* or *general intelligence,* that is used to perform any mental test, but that each test also requires some specific abilities in addition to *g*. For example, performance on a test of memory for numbers probably involves both *g* and some specific ability for immediate recall of what is heard. Spearman assumed that individuals vary in both general intelligence and specific abilities, and that together these factors determine performance on mental tasks. A current version of the general and specific abilities theory is John Carroll's (1993) work identifying a few broad abilities and at least 70 specific abilities.

Howard Gardner's model of multiple intelligences broadened our view of intelligent behavior to include such factors as creativity and the ability to coordinate body movements.

Multiple Intelligences.   In spite of the correlations among the various tests of "specific abilities," some psychologists insist that there are several separate "primary mental abilities." Years ago, Thurstone (1938) listed verbal comprehension, memory, reasoning, ability to visualize spatial relationships, numerical ability, word fluency, and perceptual speed as the major mental abilities underlying intellectual tasks. J. P. Guilford (1988) and Howard Gardner (1983) are the most prominent modern proponents of the concept of multiple cognitive abilities.

Guilford suggests that there are three basic categories, or **faces of intellect:** *mental operations,* or the processes of thinking; *contents,* or what we think about; and *products,* or the end results of our thinking. Mental operations are divided into six subcategories: cognition (recognizing old information and discovering new), convergent thinking (finding one answer), divergent thinking (finding many possible solutions), evaluation (judgments about accuracy, value, etc.), immediate memory, and memory over time. The contents on which people operate are divided into five subcategories: visual content, auditory content, word meanings, symbols, and behaviors. The different products that may result are units, classes, relations, systems, transformations, and implications.

According to this view, carrying out a cognitive task is essentially performing a mental operation on some specific content to achieve a product. For example, listing the next number in the sequence 3, 6, 12, 24, . . . requires a *convergent operation* (there is only one right answer) with *symbolic content* (numbers) to achieve a *relationship product* (each number is double the one before). There are 180 combinations of operations, contents, and products—6 × 5 × 6.

Guilford's model of intelligence broadens our view of the nature of intelligence by adding such factors as social judgment (the evaluation of others' behavior) and creativity (divergent thinking). But, when people are tested on these different abilities, the abilities prove to be related. The problem of explaining the positive correlations among all these supposed separate mental abilities remains unsolved.

Faces of Intellect In Guilford's theory, the three basic categories of thinking—operations, contents, and products.

FIGURE 4.1

Seven Intelligences

Howard Gardner's theory of multiple intelligences suggests that there are seven different categories of human abilities. An individual might have strengths or weaknesses in one or several areas. The figure gives explanations of each capacity and examples of occupations that draw upon that ability.

Intelligence	End States	Core Components
Logical-mathematical	Scientist Mathematician	Sensitivity to, and capacity to discern, logical or numerical patterns; ability to handle long chains of reasoning.
Linguistic	Poet Journalist	Sensitivity to the sounds, rhythms, and meanings of words; sensitivity to the different functions of language.
Musical	Composer Violinist	Abilities to produce and appreciate rhythm, pitch, and timbre; appreciation of the forms of musical expressiveness.
Spatial	Navigator Sculptor	Capacities to perceive the visual-spatial world accurately and to perform transformations on one's initial perceptions.
Bodily-kinesthetic	Dancer Athlete	Abilities to control one's body movements and to handle objects skillfully.
Interpersonal	Therapist Salesman	Capacities to discern and respond appropriately to the moods, temperaments, motivations, and desires of other people.
Intrapersonal	Person with detailed, accurate self-knowledge	Access to one's own feelings and the ability to discriminate among them and draw on them to guide behavior; knowledge of one's own strengths, weaknesses, desires, and intelligence.

Source: From H. Gardner and T. Hatch. "Multiple intelligences go to school." *Educational Researcher, 18,* 8, Figure p. 6. Copyright 1989 by the American Educational Research Association. Reprinted by permission of the publisher.

Howard Gardner (1983, 1993c) has proposed a theory of **multiple intelligences.** According to Gardner there are at least seven separate kinds of intelligences: linguistic (verbal), musical, spatial, logical-mathematical, bodily-kinesthetic, understanding of others (interpersonal), and understanding of self (intrapersonal) (see Figure 4.1). Gardner has based his notion of separate abilities in part on evidence that brain damage (from a stroke, for example) often interferes with functioning in one area, such as language, but does not affect functioning in other areas. Gardner has also noted that individuals often excel in one of these seven areas but have no remarkable abilities in the other six. Gardner stresses that there may be more kinds of intelligence—seven is not a

Multiple Intelligences In Gardner's theory of intelligence, a person's seven separate abilities: logical-mathematical, verbal, musical, spatial, bodily-kinesthetic, interpersonal, intrapersonal.

magic number. For example, in some recent interviews, Gardner describes the eighth intelligence of Naturalist—the ability to recognize species of animals and plants (Gardner, 1995).

Inspired in part by children's museums, Gardner and his colleagues have designed "Project Spectrum," an environment for assessing and developing the multiple intelligences of young children (Gardner, 1991, 1993b). The Spectrum assessment tasks that examine seven areas of cognitive abilities (intelligences) are described Table 4.1.

In Project Spectrum classrooms there are materials and activities designed to develop students' abilities in each of the seven areas. For example, there is a naturalist corner where students examine biological specimens, thus drawing on their powers of logic, language, and visual observation. Theme-related kits, such as "Day and Night" or "About Me," provide a variety of activities for home and school. These themes can be enhanced by trips to local museums. For example, students learning about day and night might visit a planetarium.

Gardner describes a student whose life may have been changed as his multiple intelligences were recognized. Donnie, a 6-year-old boy from an abusive home, was about to be retained in first grade. Donnie's teacher saw him as slow, almost unable to learn. But in Project Spectrum, Donnie was able to take apart and rebuild everything in the assembly corner. He was a mechanical marvel! When his classroom teacher saw videotapes of Donnie rebuilding food grinders and door knobs, she was overwhelmed. Her entire view of him changed, and she was able to find ways to reach him in class.

Intelligence as a Process.   As you can see, the theories of Spearman, Thurstone, Guilford, and Gardner tend to describe how individuals differ in the *content* of intelligence—the different abilities. Recent work in cognitive psychology has emphasized instead the thinking *processes* that may be common to all people. How do humans gather and use information to solve problems and behave intelligently? New views of intelligence are growing out of this work.

Robert Sternberg's (1985, 1990) **triarchic theory of intelligence** is a cognitive process approach to understanding intelligence. As you might guess from the name, this theory has three parts—analytic, creative, and practical.

Analytic intelligence involves the mental processes of the individual that lead to more or less intelligent behavior. These processes are defined in terms of **components**—elementary information processes that are classified by the functions they serve and by how general they are. There are at least three different functions served. The first function—higher-order planning, strategy selection, and monitoring—is performed by *metacomponents.* A second function—executing the strategies selected—is handled by *performance components.* The third function—gaining new knowledge—is performed by *knowledge-acquisition components,* such as separating relevant from irrelevant information as you try to understand a new concept (Sternberg, 1985).

Some components are specific; that is, they are necessary for only one kind of task, such as solving analogies. Other components are very general and may be necessary in almost every cognitive task. For example, metacomponents are always operating to select strategies and keep track of progress. This may help to explain the persistent correlations among all types of mental tests. People who are effective in selecting good problem-solving strategies, monitoring progress, and moving to a new approach when the first one fails are more likely to be

Triarchic Theory of Intelligence A three-part description of the mental abilities (thinking processes, coping with new experiences, and adapting to context) that lead to more or less intelligent behavior.

Components In an information-processing view, basic problem-solving processes underlying intelligence.

TABLE 4.1   Areas of Cognitive Ability Examined in Project Spectrum

One goal of Project Spectrum is to develop students' abilities in all seven areas of cognitive ability identified by Howard Gardner

Numbers

Dinosaur Game: designed as a measure of a child's understanding of number concepts, counting skills, ability to adhere to rules, and use of strategy.

Bus Game: assesses a child's ability to create a useful notation system, perform mental calculations, and organize number information for one or more variables.

Science

Assembly Activity: designed to measure a child's mechanical ability. Successful completion of the activity depends on fine-motor skills and visual-spatial, observational, and problem-solving abilities.

Treasure Hunt Game: assesses a child's ability to make logical inferences. The child is asked to organize information to discover the rule governing the placement of various treasures.

Water Activity: used to assess a child's ability to generate hypotheses based on observations and to conduct simple experiments.

Discovery Area: includes year-round activities that elicit a child's observations, appreciation, and understanding of natural phenomena.

Music

Music Production Activity: designed to assess a child's ability to maintain accurate pitch and rhythm while singing and to recall a song's musical properties.

Music Perception Activity: assesses a child's ability to discriminate pitch. The activity consists of song recognition, error recognition, and pitch discrimination.

Language

Storyboard Activity: measures a range of language skills including complexity of vocabulary and sentence structure, use of connectors, use of descriptive language and dialogue, and ability to pursue a story line.

Reporting Activity: assesses a child's ability to describe an event with regard to the following criteria: ability to report content accurately, level of detail, sentence structure, and vocabulary.

Visual Arts

Art Portfolios: reviewed twice a year, and assessed on criteria that include use of lines and shapes, color, space, detail, and representation and design. Children also participate in three structured drawing activities. The drawings are assessed on criteria similar to those used in the portfolio assessment.

Movement

Creative Movement: the ongoing movement curriculum focuses on children's abilities in five areas of dance and creative movement: sensitivity to rhythm, expressiveness, body control, generation of movement ideas, and responsiveness to music.

Athletic Movement: an obstacle course focuses on the types of skills found in many different sports, such as coordination, timing, balance, and power.

Social

Classroom Model: assesses a child's ability to observe and analyze social events and experiences in the classroom.

Peer Interaction Checklist: a behavioral checklist is used to assess the behaviors in which children engage when interacting with peers. Different patterns of behavior yield distinctive social roles such as facilitator and leader.

Source: Table 6.1 Areas of Cognitive Ability from *Multiple intelligences: The theory in practice* by Howard Gardner pp. 91–92. Copyright © 1993 by Howard Gardner. Reprinted by permission of BasicBooks, a division of HarperCollins Publishers, Inc.

successful on all types of tests. Metacomponents may be a modern-day version of Spearman's *g*.

The second part of Sternberg's triarchic theory, *creativity*, involves coping with new experiences. Intelligent behavior is marked by two characteristics: (1) **insight,** or the ability to deal effectively with novel situations, and

Insight The ability to deal effectively with novel situations.

FIGURE 4.2

Sternberg's Triarchic Theory of Intelligence

Sternberg suggests that intelligent behavior is the product of applying thinking strategies, handling new problems creatively and quickly, and adapting to contexts by selecting and reshaping our environment.

	Contextual Intelligence	Experiential Intelligence	Componential Intelligence
Definition	Ability to adapt to a changing environment and shape the environment to make the most of opportunities—problem solving in specific situations.	Ability to formulate new ideas and combine unrelated facts; creativity—ability to deal with novel situations and make solutions automatic.	Ability to think abstractly, process information; verbal abilities.
Examples	Taking your telephone off the hook or putting a "do not disturb" sign on the door while studying to limit distractions.	Diagnosing a problem with a car engine; finding resources for a new project.	Solving analogies or syllogisms, learning vocabulary.

(2) **automaticity**—the ability to become efficient and automatic in thinking and problem solving. Thus intelligence involves solving new problems as well as quickly turning new solutions into routine processes that can be applied without much cognitive effort.

The third part of Sternberg's theory, practical intelligence, highlights the importance of choosing an environment in which a person can succeed, adapting to that environment, and reshaping it if necessary. Here, culture is a major factor in defining successful choice, adaptation, and shaping. What works in one cultural group will not work in another. For example, abilities that make a person successful in a rural farm community may be useless in the inner city or at a country club in the suburbs. People who are successful often seek situations in which their abilities will be valuable, then work hard to capitalize on those abilities and compensate for any weaknesses. Thus, intelligence in this third sense involves practical matters such as career choice or social skills (Sternberg, Wagner, Williams, & Horvath, 1995). Figure 4.2 summarizes the elements of Sternberg's triarchic theory of intelligence.

How Is Intelligence Measured?

Even though psychologists do not agree about what intelligence is, they do agree that intelligence, as measured by standard tests, is related to learning in school. Why is this so? It has to do in part with the way intelligence tests were first developed.

Binet's Dilemma.   In 1904, Alfred Binet was confronted with the following problem by the minister of public instruction in Paris: How can stu-

Automaticity The result of learning to perform a behavior or thinking process so thoroughly that the performance is automatic and does not require effort.

dents who will need special teaching and extra help be identified early in their school careers, before they fail in regular classes? Binet was also a political activist, very concerned with the rights of children. He believed that having an objective measure of learning ability could protect students from poor families who might be forced to leave school because they were the victims of discrimination and assumed to be slow learners.

Binet and his collaborator Theophile Simon wanted to measure not merely school achievement, but the intellectual skills students needed to do well in school. After trying many different tests and eliminating items that did not discriminate between successful and unsuccessful students, Binet and Simon finally identified 58 tests, several for each age group from 3 to 13. Binet's tests allowed the examiner to determine a **mental age** for a child. A child who succeeded on the items passed by most 6-year-olds, for example, was considered to have a mental age of 6, whether the child was actually 4, 6, or 8 years old.

The concept of **intelligence quotient,** or **IQ,** was added after Binet's test was brought to the United States and revised at Stanford University to give us the Stanford-Binet test. An IQ score was computed by comparing the mental-age score to the person's actual chronological age. The formula was

Alfred Binet developed a systematic procedure for assessing learning aptitudes. His goal was to understand intelligence and use this knowledge to help children.

$$\text{intelligence quotient} = \frac{\text{mental age}}{\text{chronological age}} \times 100$$

The early Stanford-Binet has been revised four times, most recently in 1986 (Thorndike, Hagen, & Sattler, 1986). The practice of computing a mental age has proven to be problematic because IQ scores calculated on the basis of mental age do not have the same meaning as children get older. To cope with this problem, the concept of **deviation IQ** was introduced. The deviation IQ score is a number that tells exactly how much above or below the average a person scored on the test, compared to others in the same age group.

Group versus Individual IQ Tests.   The Stanford-Binet is an individual intelligence test. It has to be administered to one student at a time by a trained psychologist and takes about two hours. Most of the questions are asked orally and do not require reading or writing. A student usually pays closer attention and is more motivated to do well when working directly with an adult. Psychologists also have developed group tests that can be given to whole classes or schools. Compared to an individual test, a group test is much less likely to yield an accurate picture of any one person's abilities. When students take tests in a group, they may do poorly because they do not understand the instructions, because their pencils break, because they are distracted by other students, or because they do not shine on paper-and-pencil tests. *As a teacher, you should be very wary of IQ scores based on group tests.*

What Does an IQ Score Mean?

Most intelligence tests are designed so that they have certain statistical characteristics. For example, the average score is 100; 50% of the people from the general population who take the tests will score 100 or above, and 50% will score below 100. About 68% of the general population will earn IQ scores

Mental Age In intelligence testing, a score based on average abilities for that age group.

Intelligence Quotient (IQ) Score comparing mental and chronological ages.

Deviation IQ Score based on statistical comparison of individual's performance with the average performance of others in that age group.

between 85 and 115. Only about 16% of the population will receive scores below 85, and only 16% will score above 115. Note, however, that these figures hold true for white, native-born Americans whose first language is Standard English. Whether IQ tests should even be used with ethnic minority-group students is hotly debated. The Guidelines will help you interpret IQ scores realistically.

Guidelines

Interpreting IQ Scores

Check to see if the score is based on an individual or a group test. Be wary of group test scores.

Examples

1. Individual tests include the Wechsler Scales (WPPSI, WISC-III, WAIS-R), the Stanford-Binet, the McCarthy Scales of Children's Abilities, the Woodcock-Johnson Psycho-Educational Battery, and the Kaufman Assessment Battery for Children.

2. Group tests include the Lorge-Thorndike Intelligence Tests, the Analysis of Learning Potential, the Kuhlman-Anderson Intelligence Tests, the Otis-Lennon Mental Abilities Tests, and the School and College Ability Tests (SCAT).

Remember that IQ tests are only estimates of general aptitude for learning.

Examples

1. Ignore small differences in scores among students.

2. Bear in mind that even an individual student's scores may change over time for many reasons, including measurement error.

3. Be aware that a total score is usually an average of scores on several kinds of questions. A score in the middle or average range may mean that the student performed at the average on every kind of question or that the student did quite well in some areas (for example, on verbal tasks) and rather poorly in other areas (for example, on quantitative tasks).

Remember that IQ scores reflect a student's past experiences and learning.

Examples

1. Consider these scores as predictors of school abilities, not measures of innate intellectual abilities.

2. If a student is doing well in your class, do not change your opinion or lower your expectations just because one score seems low.

3. Be wary of IQ scores for minority students and for students whose first language was not English. Even scores on "culture-free" tests are lower for disadvantaged students.

Intelligence and Achievement.   Intelligence test scores predict achievement in schools quite well, at least for large groups. For example, the correlation is about .65 between school achievement and scores on a popular individual intelligence test, the revised Wechsler Intelligence Scale for Children

(WISC-III) (Sattler, 1992). This isn't surprising because the tests were designed to predict school achievement. Remember, Binet threw out test items that did not discriminate between good and poor students.

But do people who score high on IQ tests achieve more in life? Here the answer is less clear. There is evidence that *g*, or general intelligence, correlates with "real-world academic, social, and occupational accomplishments" (Ceci, 1991), but there is great debate about the size and meaning of these correlations (*Current Directions in Psychological Science*, Controversies, February 1993; McClelland, 1993). People with higher intelligence-test scores tend to complete more years of school and to have higher-status jobs. However, when the number of years of education is held constant, IQ scores and school achievement are not highly correlated with income and success in later life. Other factors like motivation, social skills, and luck may make the difference (Neisser et al., 1996; Sternberg & Wagner, 1993).

> **Focus on...**
>
> ### Intelligence
>
> - Explain your personal definition of intelligence.
> - Give an original example of each of Gardner's seven intelligences.
> - What roles do new experiences play in Sternberg's theory of intelligence?
> - What do IQ scores predict?

Intelligence: Heredity or Environment? Nowhere, perhaps, has the nature-versus-nurture debate raged so hard as in the area of **intelligence**. Should intelligence be seen as a potential, limited by our genetic makeup, that once fulfilled cannot be exceeded? Or does intelligence simply refer to an individual's current level of intellectual functioning, as fed and influenced by experience and education? In fact, it is almost impossible to separate intelligence "in the genes" from intelligence "due to experience." Today, most psychologists believe that differences in intelligence are due to both heredity and environment, probably in about equal proportions for children. "Genes do not fix behavior. Rather they establish a range of possible reactions to the range of possible experiences that the environment can provide" (Weinberg, 1989, p. 101). And environmental influences include everything from the health of a child's mother during pregnancy to the amount of lead in the child's home to the quality of teaching a child receives.

As a teacher, it is especially important for you to realize that cognitive skills, like any other skills, are always improvable. *Intelligence is a current state of affairs,* affected by past experiences and open to future changes. Even if intelligence is a limited potential, the potential is still quite large, and a challenge to all teachers. For example, Japanese and Chinese students know much more mathematics than American students, but their intelligence test scores are quite similar. This superiority in math probably is related to differences in the way mathematics is taught and studied in the three countries (Stevenson & Stigler, 1992).

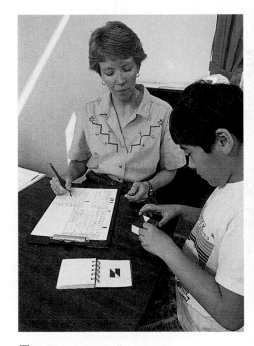

This boy is trying to arrange the red and white blocks so that they match the pattern in the booklet. His performance is timed. This subtest of the Wechsler Intelligence Scale for Children assesses spatial ability.

Intelligence Ability or abilities to acquire and use knowledge for solving problems and adapting to the world.

Ability Differences and Teaching

In this section we consider how you might handle differences in academic ability in your classes. First we examine a commonly used approach—ability grouping. Is this a solution to the challenge of ability differences? If so, when and for whom? Then we turn our attention to students who represent the extremes in ability, the retarded and the gifted. Both groups need teachers who understand their particular needs.

Ability Grouping

The expressed goal of ability grouping is to make teaching more appropriate for students. As we will see, this does not always happen.

Between-Class Ability Grouping.   When whole classes are formed based on ability, the process is called **between-class ability grouping** or tracking—a common practice in secondary schools and some elementary schools as well. Most high schools have "college prep" courses and "general" courses or, for example, high-, middle-, and low-ability classes in a particular subject. Although this seems on the surface to be an efficient way to teach, research has consistently shown that segregation by ability may benefit high-ability students slightly, but it causes problems for low-ability students (Garmon, Nystrand, Berends, & LePore, 1995; Good & Marshall, 1984; Slavin, 1987, 1990a).

Low-ability classes seem to receive lower-quality instruction in general. Teachers tend to emphasize lower-level objectives and routine procedures, with less academic focus. Often there are more management problems and, along with these problems, increased stress and decreased enthusiasm. These differences in instruction and the teachers' negative attitudes may mean that low expectations are communicated to the students. Student self-esteem suffers almost as soon as the assignment to "dummy" English or math is made. Attendance may drop along with self-esteem. The lower tracks often have a disproportionate number of minority-group and economically disadvantaged students, so ability grouping, in effect, becomes resegregation in school. Possibilities for friendships become limited to students in the same ability range. Assignments to classes are often made on the basis of group IQ tests instead of tests in the subject area itself. Yet group IQ tests are not good guides for what someone is ready to learn in a particular subject area (Corno & Snow, 1986; Garmon, Nystrand, Berends, & LePore, 1995; Kulik & Kulik, 1982; Slavin, 1987, 1990a).

There are two exceptions to the general finding that between-class ability grouping leads to lower achievement. The first is found in honors or gifted classes, where high-ability students tend to perform better than comparable students in regular classes. The second exception is the **nongraded elementary school** and the related **Joplin Plan.** In these arrangements, students are grouped by ability in particular subjects, regardless of their age or grade. A reading class might therefore have students from several grades, all working on the same level on reading. This cross-grade grouping seems to be effective for students of all abilities as long as the grouping allows teachers to give more direct instruction to the groups. When cross-age grouping is used to implement individualized instruction, the effects are much less positive (Gutierrez & Slavin, 1992).

Within-Class Ability Grouping.   A second method, **within-class ability grouping,** clustering students by ability within the same class, is another story. Many elementary-school classes are grouped for reading, and some are grouped for math, even though there is no clear evidence that this approach is superior to other approaches. If you use homogeneous small groups in your class, the following Guidelines should make the approach more effective (Good & Brophy, 1994; Slavin, 1987).

Between-Class Ability Grouping
System of grouping in which students are assigned to classes based on their measured ability or their achievements.

Nongraded Elementary School/ The Joplin Plan Arrangement wherein students are grouped by ability in particular subjects, regardless of their ages or grades.

Within-Class Ability Grouping
System of grouping in which students in a class are divided into two or three groups based on ability in an attempt to accommodate student differences.

Guidelines

Grouping by Achievement

Form and reform groups on the basis of students' *current performance* **in the subject being taught.**

Examples

1. Use scores on the most recent reading assessments to establish reading groups, and rely on current math performance to form math groups.
2. Change group placement frequently when students' achievement changes.

Discourage comparisons between groups and encourage students to develop a whole-class spirit.

Examples

1. Don't seat groups together outside the context of their reading or math group.
2. Avoid naming ability groups—save the names for mixed-ability or whole-class teams.

Group by ability for one or, at the most, two subjects.

Examples

1. Make sure there are many lessons and projects that mix members from the groups.
2. Experiment with learning strategies in which cooperation is stressed (described in Chapters 9 and 11).
3. Keep the number of groups small (two or three at most) so that you can provide as much direct teaching as possible—leaving students alone for too long leads to less learning.

Make sure teachers, methods, and pace are adjusted to fit the needs of the group.

Examples

1. Organize and teach groups so that low-achieving students get appropriate extra instruction—not just the same material again.
2. Experiment with alternatives to grouping. There are alternatives to within-class grouping that appear more effective for some subjects. DeWayne Mason and Tom Good (1993) found that supplementing whole-class instruction in math with remediation and enrichment for students when they needed it worked better than dividing the class into two ability groups and teaching these groups separately.

What should teachers do when they face more extreme differences in student ability? We turn to this question next.

Mental Retardation

According to the American Association on Mental Deficiency (AAMD Ad Hoc Committee on Terminology and Classification, 1992, p. 5), **mental retardation** refers to:

> substantial limitations in present intellectual functioning. It is characterized by significantly subaverage intellectual functioning existing concurrently with related limitations in two or more of the following applicable

Mental Retardation Significantly below-average intellectual and adaptive social behavior, evident before age 18.

adaptive skill areas: communication, self-care, home living, social skills, community use, self-direction, health and safety, functional academics, leisure, and work. Mental retardation manifests before age 18.

Intellectual function is usually measured by IQ tests with a cutoff score of 70 to 75 as one indicator of retardation. But remember, an IQ score below the 70 to 75 range is *not* enough to diagnose a child as having mental retardation. There must also be problems with adaptive behavior, day-to-day independent living, and social functioning. This caution is especially important when interpreting the scores of students from different cultures. Defining retardation based on test scores alone can create what some critics call "6-hour retardates"—students who are seen as retarded only for the part of the day they attend school.

Only about 1 to 1.5% of the population fit the AAMD's definition of retarded in both intellectual functioning and adaptive behavior (Hallahan & Kauffman, 1997). For years, retardation was further divided into mild, moderate, severe, and profound levels, with each level keyed to a particular range of IQ scores. Most school districts still use this system. However, the IQ ranges are not perfect predictors of individuals' abilities to function, so the AAMR now recommends a classification scheme based on the amount of support that a person requires to function at his or her highest level. Table 4.2 summarizes this new classification system.

Organic (physical) causes of retardation have been identified for only about 10 to 25% of the individuals involved. Still, it appears that up to 50% of all

---

TABLE 4.2   AAMR Classification Scheme for Mental Retardation

This new scheme for classification is based on the level of support a student would need to function as completely as possible.

Intermittent	Supports on an "as needed basis." Characterized by episodic nature, person not always needing the support(s), or short-term supports needed during life-span transitions (e.g., job loss or an acute medical crisis). Intermittent supports may be high or low intensity when provided.
Limited	An intensity of supports characterized by consistency over time and time-limited but not of an intermittent nature, may require fewer staff members and less cost than more intense levels of support (e.g., time-limited employment training or transitional supports during the school-to-adult period).
Extensive	Supports characterized by regular involvement (e.g., daily) in at least some environments (such as work or home) and not time-limited (e.g., long-term home living support).
Pervasive	Supports characterized by their constancy, high intensity, provided across environments; potential life-sustaining nature. Pervasive supports typically involve more staff members and intrusiveness than do extensive or time-limited supports.

Source: From AAMR Ad Hoc Committee on Terminology and Classification (1992). *Mental retardation: Definition, classification, and systems of support.* Copyright © 1992 by American Association on Mental Retardation. Reprinted with permission.

cases of retardation could be prevented by providing better prenatal care, improving nutrition and disease prevention for mothers and young children, preventing accidents, improving the physical and educational environment for young children, and providing high-quality parent training and preschool services for young children at risk (Campbell & Ramey, 1994; Hardman, Drew, & Egan, 1996; Smith & Luckasson, 1995).

As a regular teacher, you may not have contact with retarded children needing extensive or pervasive support, unless your school is participating in a full inclusion program for exceptional students (described later in this chapter), but you probably will work with mildly retarded children. In the early grades, these students may simply learn more slowly than their peers. By the third or fourth grade, they will probably have fallen far behind.

The Guidelines list suggestions for teaching students with below-average general intelligence.

Guidelines

Teaching Students with Mental Retardation

1. Determine readiness: however little a child may know, he or she is ready to learn a next step.

2. State and present objectives simply.

3. Base specific learning objectives on an analysis of the child's learning strengths and weaknesses.

4. Present material in small, logical steps. Practice extensively before going on to the next step.

5. Work on practical skills and concepts based on the demands of adult life.

6. Do not skip steps. Students with average intelligence can form conceptual bridges from one step to the next, but retarded children need every step and bridge made explicit. Make connections for the student. Do not expect him or her to "see" the connections.

7. Be prepared to present the same idea in many different ways.

8. Go back to a simpler level if you see the student is not following.

9. Be especially careful to motivate the student and maintain attention.

10. Find materials that do not insult the student. A junior high boy may need the low vocabulary of "See Spot run" but will be insulted by the age of the characters and the content of the story.

11. Focus on a few target behaviors or skills so you and the student have a chance to experience success. Everyone needs positive reinforcement.

12. Be aware that retarded students must overlearn, repeat, and practice more than children of average intelligence. They must be taught how to study, and they must frequently review and practice their newly acquired skills in different settings.

13. Pay close attention to social relations. Simply including retarded students in a regular class will not guarantee that they will be accepted or that they will make and keep friends.

Learning goals for many retarded students between the ages of 9 and 13 include basic reading, writing, arithmetic, learning about the local environment, social behavior, and personal interests. In junior and senior high school, the emphasis is on vocational and domestic skills, literacy for living (using the telephone book; reading signs, labels, and newspaper ads; completing a job application), job-related behaviors like courtesy and punctuality, health self-care, and citizenship skills. Today there is a growing emphasis on **transition programming**—preparing the retarded student to live and work in the community. As you will see later in the chapter, the law requires that schools design an IEP, or individualized educational program, for every disabled child. An ITP, or individualized transition plan, may be part of the retarded student's IEP (Hallahan & Kauffman, 1997).

Gifted and Talented

There is another group of students with special educational needs that is often overlooked by the schools: the gifted and talented. In the past, providing an enriched education for extremely bright or talented students was seen as undemocratic and elitist. Now there is a growing recognition that **gifted students** are being poorly served by most public schools. A national survey found that more than one-half of all gifted students do not achieve in school at a level equal to their ability (Tomlinson-Keasey, 1990).

Who Are the Gifted?   There is no agreement about what constitutes a gifted student. Individuals can have many different gifts. Remember that Gardner (1983) identified seven separate kinds of "intelligences," and Guilford (1988) claims there are 180. Renzulli and Reis (1991) have defined giftedness as a combination of three basic characteristics: above-average general ability, a high level of creativity, and a high level of task commitment or motivation to achieve in certain areas. Truly gifted children are not the students who simply learn quickly with little effort. The work of gifted students is original, extremely advanced for their age, and potentially of lasting importance.

What do we know about these remarkable individuals, whom former U.S. Commissioner of Education Sidney P. Marland has called "our most neglected students"? A classic study of the characteristics of the gifted was started decades ago by Lewis Terman and colleagues (1925, 1947, 1959). This huge project is following the lives of 1,528 gifted males and females and will continue until the year 2010. The subjects all have IQ scores in the top 1% of the population (140 or above on the Stanford-Binet individual test of intelligence). They were identified on the basis of teacher recommendations and IQ tests, so they probably fall into Renzulli's academically gifted category.

Terman and colleagues found that these gifted children were larger, stronger, and healthier than the norm. They often walked sooner and were more athletic. They were more emotionally stable than their peers and became better-adjusted adults than the average. They had lower rates of delinquency, emotional difficulty, divorce, drug problems, and so on. Of course, the teachers in Terman's study who made the nominations may have selected students who were better adjusted initially.

What Problems Do the Gifted Face?   In spite of Terman's findings, it would be incorrect to say that every gifted student is superior in adjustment

---

Transition Programming Gradual preparation of exceptional students to move from high school into further education or training, employment, or community involvement.

Gifted Student A very bright, creative, and talented student.

TABLE 4.3 The Eight Great Gripes of Gifted Students

Being gifted is not all positive. Here are the eight biggest complaints of gifted students.

1. No one explains what being gifted is all about—it's kept a big secret.
2. The stuff we do in school is too easy and it's boring.
3. Parents, teachers, and friends expect us to be perfect, to "do our best" all the time.
4. Kids often tease us about being smart.
5. Friends who really understand us are few and far between.
6. We feel too different and wish people would accept us for what we are.
7. We feel overwhelmed by the number of things we can do in life.
8. We worry a lot about world problems and feel helpless to do anything about them.

Source: From J. Galbraith (1985). The eight great gripes of gifted kids: Responding to special needs, *Roeper Review, 8,* p. 15. Copyright 1995. Reprinted with permission of *Roeper Review,* Bloomfield Hills, MI.

and emotional health. Many problems confront a gifted child, including boredom and frustration in school as well as isolation (sometimes even ridicule) from peers. Schoolmates may be consumed with baseball or worried about failing math, while the gifted child is fascinated with Mozart, focused on a social issue, or totally absorbed in computers, drama, or geology. Gifted children may also find it difficult to accept their own emotions, because the mismatch between mind and emotion can be great. They may be impatient with friends, parents, and even teachers who do not share their interests or abilities. Adjustment problems seem to be greatest for the most gifted, those in the highest range of academic ability (e.g., above 180 IQ) (Keogh & MacMillan, 1996). Table 4.3 lists the most frequent complaints of gifted students.

A follow-up of Terman subjects 60 years later reached some surprising conclusions about the relationship between popularity as a student and intellectual accomplishment as an adult. Terman's subjects who were popular and outgoing as children were less likely to maintain serious intellectual interests as adults. The authors of the study speculate that gifted students who became more accomplished as adults may have preferred adult company as children, or may have been comfortable being alone. It is possible that an active social life diverts interest away from intellectual pursuits (Tomlinson-Keasey & Little, 1990). Each path has its benefits and its liabilities for the individual.

Recognizing Students' Special Abilities. Identifying a gifted child is not always easy. Many parents provide early educational experiences for their children. A preschool or primary student coming to your class may read above grade level, play an instrument quite well, or whiz through every assignment. But even very advanced reading in the early grades does not guarantee that students will still be outstanding readers years later (Mills & Jackson, 1990). How do you separate gifted students from hardworking or parentally pres-

Current definitions of giftedness include the characteristics of above-average ability, creativity, and motivation to achieve. They also acknowledge that individuals, rather than being "superhumans," may be gifted in some areas and average in others.

sured students? In junior high and high school, some very able students deliberately earn lower grades, making their abilities even harder to recognize.

Teachers are successful only about 10 to 50% of the time in picking out the gifted children in their classes (Fox, 1981). These seven questions, taken from an early study of gifted students, are still good guides today (Walton, 1961):

- Who learns easily and rapidly?
- Who uses a lot of common sense and practical knowledge?
- Who retains easily what he or she has heard?
- Who knows about many things that the other children don't?
- Who uses a large number of words easily and accurately?
- Who recognizes relations and comprehends meanings?
- Who is alert and keenly observant and responds quickly?

Based on Renzulli and Reis's (1991) definition of giftedness, we might add:

- Who is persistent and highly motivated on some tasks?
- Who is creative, often has unusual ideas, or makes interesting connections?

Giftedness and Formal Testing.   The best single predictor of academic giftedness is still the individual IQ test, but these tests are costly and time-consuming—and far from perfect. Group achievement and intelligence tests tend to underestimate the IQs of very bright children. Group tests may be appropriate for screening, but they are not appropriate for making placement decisions. Many psychologists recommend a *case study* approach to identifying gifted students. This means gathering many kinds of information, test scores, grades, examples of work, projects and portfolios, letters or ratings from teachers, self-ratings, and so on (Renzulli & Reis, 1991; Sisk, 1988). Especially for recognizing artistic talent, experts in the field can be called in to judge the merits of a child's creations. Science projects, exhibitions, performances, auditions, and interviews are all possibilities. Creativity tests (discussed in the next section) may identify some children not picked up by other measures, particularly minority students who may be at a disadvantage on the other types of tests (Maker, 1987).

Teaching Gifted Students.   Some educators believe that gifted students should be *accelerated*—moved quickly through the grades or through particular subjects. Other educators prefer *enrichment*—giving the students additional, more sophisticated, and more thought-provoking work, but keeping them with their age-mates in school. Actually, both may be appropriate (Torrance, 1986).

Many people object to acceleration, but most careful studies indicate that truly gifted students who begin primary, elementary, junior high, high school, college, or even graduate school early do as well as, and usually better than, nongifted students who are progressing at the normal pace. Social and emotional adjustment does not appear to be impaired. Gifted students tend to prefer the company of older playmates and may be miserably bored if kept with children of their own age. Skipping grades may not be the best solution for a particular student, but it does not deserve the bad name it has received (Jones & Southern, 1991; Kulik & Kulik, 1984; Richardson & Benbow, 1990). An alternative to skipping grades is to accelerate students in one or two particular subjects but keep them with peers for most classes (Reynolds & Birch, 1988). For students who are extremely advanced intellectually (for example, those scoring 160 or higher on an individual intelligence test), the only practical solution may be to accelerate their education (Gross, 1992; Keogh & MacMillan, 1996).

Teaching methods for gifted students should encourage abstract thinking (formal-operational thought), creativity, and independence, not just the learning of greater quantities of facts. In working with gifted and talented students, a teacher must be imaginative, flexible, and unthreatened by the capabilities of these students. The teacher must ask; What does this child need most? What is she or he ready to learn? Who can help me to challenge them? Answers might come from faculty members at nearby colleges, retired professionals, books, museums, or older students. Strategies might be as simple as letting the child do math with the next grade. Increasingly, more flexible programs are being devised for gifted students: summer institutes; courses at nearby colleges; classes with local artists, musicians, or dancers; independent research projects; selected classes in high school for younger students; honors classes; and special-interest clubs. All are options for offering gifted students appropriate learning experiences (Mitchell, 1984).

We have spent quite a bit of time considering differences in cognitive ability. However, there are many more differences among students that have implications for teachers. We turn to these next.

Focus on...

Ability Differences

- If you have a wide range of academic abilities in your class, what are your options in grouping students for learning?
- How would you teach the concept of "safety" to a moderately retarded student?
- You have two students in your class who are way ahead of the others in their understanding. How would you help these two learn?

Creativity

Howard Gardner (1993a) defines the creative individual as "a person who regularly solves problems, fashions products, or defines new questions in a domain in a way that is initially considered novel but that ultimately becomes accepted in a particular cultural setting" (p. 35). This conception suggests that there is no such thing as "all-purpose creativity"; people are creative *in a particular area.* But to be creative, the "invention" must be intended. An accidental spilling of paint that produces a novel design is not creative unless the artist recognizes the potential of the "accident" or uses the spilling technique intentionally to create new works (Weisberg, 1993). Although we frequently associate the arts with **creativity,** any subject can be approached in a creative manner.

Creativity and Cognition

Having a rich store of knowledge in an area is the basis for creativity, but something more is needed. For many problems, that "something more" is the ability to break set—**restructuring** the problem to see things in a new way, which leads to a sudden insight. Often this happens when a person has struggled with a problem or project, then sets it aside for a while. Some psychologists believe that time away from the problem allows for *incubation,* a kind of unconscious working through the problem. But it is more likely that leaving

Creativity Imaginative, original thinking or problem solving.

Restructuring Conceiving of a problem in a new or different way.

What is creativity, and how can it be measured?

FIGURE 4.3

A Graphic Assessment of the Creativity of an 8-Year-Old Girl

Source: Test form copyright © 1980 by Scholastic Testing Service, Inc. Reprinted by permission of Scholastic Testing Service, Inc., Bensenville, IL 60106 from *The Torrance Tests of Creative Thinking* by E. P. Torrance.

the problem for a time interrupts rigid ways of thinking so you can restructure your view of the situation (Gleitman, 1991).

Howard Gardner's (1982a) description of Charles Darwin's creativity downplays sudden, dramatic insight but still highlights the role of knowledge restructuring.

> Darwin experienced no sudden epiphany of inspiration, no wholly novel thoughts or theories. Instead, Darwin marshalled endless lists of thoughts, images, questions, dreams, sketches, comments, arguments, and notes to himself, all of which he continually organized and reorganized. . . . Pivotal insights were anticipated in earlier scribbles, and occasionally discovered twice. (p. 353)

So it seems that creativity requires extensive knowledge, flexibility, and the continual reorganizing of ideas. Darwin's work also shows that motivation and persistence play important roles in the creative process.

Assessing Creativity

Psychologists and educators confront all the usual research problems when they attempt to study creativity. "How shall we define creativity?" becomes "How shall we measure creativity?" One answer has been to equate creativity with divergent thinking. As we saw when we discussed Guilford's faces of intellect, *divergent thinking* is the ability to propose many different ideas or answers. *Convergent thinking* is the more common ability to identify only one answer.

Paper-and-Pencil Tests of Creativity.   E. P. Torrance has developed two types of creativity tests, verbal and graphic (Torrance, 1972; Torrance & Hall, 1980). In the verbal test, you might be instructed to think up as many uses as possible for a tin can or asked how a particular toy might be changed to make it more fun to play with. On the graphic test, you might be given 30 circles and asked to create 30 different drawings, each drawing including at least one circle (Sattler, 1992). Figure 4.3 shows the creativity of an 8-year-old girl in completing this task. The titles she gave her drawings, from left to right, are as follows: "Dracula," "one-eyed monster," "pumpkin," "Hula-Hoop," "poster," "wheelchair," "earth," "moon," "planet," "movie camera," "sad face," "picture," "stoplight," "beach ball," "the letter O," "car," "glasses."

Responses to all these tasks are scored for *originality, fluency,* and *flexibility,* three aspects of divergent thinking. *Originality* is usually determined statistically. To be original, a response must be given by fewer than 5 or 10 people out of every 100 who take the test. *Fluency* is the number of different responses. *Flexibility* is generally measured by the number of different categories of responses. For instance, if you drew 30 circle pictures, but each was a face, your fluency score might be high, but your flexibility score would be quite low. Of the three measures, fluency—the number of responses—is the best predictor of divergent thinking, but there is more to real-life creativity than divergent thinking (Bjorklund, 1989).

Teachers' Judgments of Creativity.   Teachers are not always the best judges of creativity. In fact, Torrance (1972) reports data from a 12-year follow-up study indicating no relationship between teachers' judgments of their students' creative abilities and the actual creativity these students revealed in their adult lives. Jerome Sattler (1992) recommends the rating scale in Table 4.4

TABLE 4.4 Rating Scale to Identify Creative Students

Some of the possible characteristics of creative students are listed on this form.

Rating Scale: 1 Not present   4 Moderately present
                2 Minimally present   5 Strongly present
                3 Somewhat present

Trait	Rating (circle one number)	Trait	Rating (circle one number)
1. Ability to concentrate	1 2 3 4 5	19. Internal locus of control and evaluation	1 2 3 4 5
2. Ability to defer judgment	1 2 3 4 5	20. Inventiveness	1 2 3 4 5
3. Above-average IQ	1 2 3 4 5	21. Lack of tolerance for boredom	1 2 3 4 5
4. Adaptability	1 2 3 4 5	22. Need for supportive climate	1 2 3 4 5
5. Aesthetic appreciation	1 2 3 4 5	23. Nonconformism	1 2 3 4 5
6. Attraction to the complex and mysterious	1 2 3 4 5	24. Openness to experience	1 2 3 4 5
7. Curiosity	1 2 3 4 5	25. Playfulness	1 2 3 4 5
8. Delight in beauty of theory	1 2 3 4 5	26. Willingness to take risks	1 2 3 4 5
9. Delight in invention for its own sake	1 2 3 4 5	27. Self-confidence	1 2 3 4 5
10. Desire to share products and ideas	1 2 3 4 5	28. Sense of identity as originator	1 2 3 4 5
11. Eagerness to resolve disorder	1 2 3 4 5	29. Sense of mission	1 2 3 4 5
12. Extensive knowledge background	1 2 3 4 5	30. Sensitivity	1 2 3 4 5
13. Flexibility	1 2 3 4 5	31. Ability to see that solutions generate new problems	1 2 3 4 5
14. Good memory, attention to detail	1 2 3 4 5	32. Spontaneity	1 2 3 4 5
15. High energy level, enthusiasm	1 2 3 4 5	33. Commitment to task	1 2 3 4 5
16. Humor (perhaps bizarre)	1 2 3 4 5	34. Tolerance for ambiguity and conflict	1 2 3 4 5
17. Imagination, insight	1 2 3 4 5	35. Willingness to face social ostracism	1 2 3 4 5
18. Independence	1 2 3 4 5	36. Willingness to daydream and fantasize	1 2 3 4 5

Source: From J. Sattler (1988). *Assessment of children* (3rd. ed.) p. 682. San Diego: Jerome M. Sattler Publisher. Reprinted by permission.

to identify creative students. As you can see, many of the traits of creative individuals can make them a challenge in the classroom.

Creativity in the Classroom

Even though creative students may be difficult to identify (and sometimes difficult to handle), creativity is worth fostering. Certainly the many social, environmental, and economic problems facing our society will require creative solutions. How can teachers promote creative thinking?

Perhaps the most important step teachers can take to encourage creativity is to make sure students know that their creativity will be appreciated. "Individuals who ultimately make creative breakthroughs tend from their earliest days to be explorers, innovators, and tinkers. . . . Often this adventurousness is interpreted as insubordination, though more fortunate tinkerers receive from teachers or peers some form of encouragement for their experimentation" (Gardner, 1993a, pp. 32–33). All too often, in the crush of day-to-day classroom life, teachers stifle creative ideas without realizing what they are doing. Teachers are in an excellent position to encourage or discourage creativity through their acceptance or rejection of the unusual and imaginative.

The Brainstorming Strategy.   In addition to encouraging creativity through everyday interactions with students, teachers can try **brainstorming.** The basic tenet of brainstorming is to separate the process of creating ideas from the process of evaluating them because evaluation often inhibits creativity (Osborn, 1963). Evaluation, discussion, and criticism are postponed until all possible suggestions have been made. In this way, one idea inspires others; people do not withhold potentially creative solutions out of fear of criticism. John Baer (1997, p. 43) gives these rules for brainstorming:

1. *Defer judgment.*
2. *Avoid ownership of ideas.* When people feel that an idea is "theirs," egos sometimes get in the way of creative thinking. They are likely to be more defensive later when ideas are critiqued, and they are less willing to allow their ideas to be modified.
3. *Feel free to "hitchhike" on other ideas.* This means that it's okay to borrow elements from ideas already on the table, or to make slight modifications of ideas already suggested.
4. *Encourage wild ideas.* Impossible, totally unworkable ideas may lead someone to think of other, more possible, more workable ideas. It's easier to take a wildly imaginative bad idea and tone it down to fit the constraints of reality than to take a boring bad idea and make it interesting enough to be worth thinking about.

Individuals as well as groups may benefit from brainstorming. In writing this book, for example, I have sometimes found it helpful to list all the different topics that could be covered in a chapter, then leave the list and return to it later to evaluate the ideas.

Take Your Time—and Play!   Years ago, Sigmund Freud (1959) linked creativity and play: "Might we not say that every child at play behaves like a creative writer, in that he creates a world of his own, or, rather, rearranges the things of his world in a new way which pleases him? . . . The creative writer does the same as the child at play. He creates a world of phantasy which he takes very seriously—that is, which he invests with large amounts of emotion . . . " (pp. 143–144). There is some evidence that preschool children who spend more time in fantasy and pretend play are more creative. In fact, playing before taking a creativity test resulted in higher scores on the test for the young students in one study (Bjorklund, 1989). Teachers can encourage students of all ages to be more reflective—to take time for ideas to grow, develop, and be re-

---

Focus on . . .

Creativity

- Think of a time that you solved a problem in a creative way. What helped you see a different approach?
- What can teachers do to support creativity?

Brainstorming Generating many ideas without stopping to evaluate each one.

structured. Working in Logo computer environments can enhance both visual and verbal creativity in young children (Clements, 1991). The Guidelines, adapted from Frederiksen (1984) and Sattler (1992), describe other possibilities for encouraging creativity.

Guidelines

Encouraging Creativity

Accept and encourage divergent thinking.

Examples

1. During class discussion, ask: "Can anyone suggest a different way of looking at this question?"
2. Reinforce attempts at unusual solutions to problems, even if the final product is not perfect.

Tolerate dissent.

Examples

1. Ask students to support dissenting opinions.
2. Make sure nonconforming students receive an equal share of classroom privileges and rewards.

Encourage students to trust their own judgment.

Examples

1. When students ask questions you think they can answer, rephrase or clarify the questions and direct them back to the students.
2. Give ungraded assignments from time to time.

Emphasize that everyone is capable of creativity in some form.

Examples

1. Avoid describing the feats of great artists or inventors as if they were superhuman accomplishments.
2. Recognize creative efforts in each student's work. Have a separate grade for originality on some assignments.

Be a stimulus for creative thinking.

Examples

1. Use a class brainstorming session whenever possible.
2. Model creative problem solving by suggesting unusual solutions for class problems.
3. Encourage students to delay judging a particular suggestion for solving a problem until all the possibilities have been considered.

Cognitive and Learning Styles

In this section we examine individual differences that have very little to do with intelligence but can influence students' learning in school. These differences have been called *cognitive styles* or *learning styles*. Be aware that you may hear these terms used interchangeably. In general, educators prefer the term *learn-*

ing styles, and include many kinds of differences in this broad category. Psychologists tend to prefer the term *cognitive styles,* and to limit their discussion to differences in the ways people process information (Bjorklund, 1989).

Cognitive Styles

The notion of **cognitive styles** is fairly new. It grew out of research on how people perceive and organize information from the world around them. Results from these studies suggest that individuals differ in how they approach a task, but these variations do not reflect levels of intelligence or patterns of special abilities. Instead, they have to do with "characteristic modes of perceiving, remembering, thinking, problem solving, and decision making, reflective of information-processing regularities that develop . . . around underlying personality trends" (Messick, 1994, p. 122). For example, certain individuals respond very quickly in most situations. Others are more reflective and slower to respond, even though both types of people may be equally knowledgeable about the task at hand.

Field Dependence and Field Independence.   In the early 1940s, Herman Witkin became intrigued by the observation that certain airline pilots would fly into a bank of clouds and fly out upside down, without realizing that they had changed position. His interest led to a great deal of research on how people separate one factor from the total visual field. Based on his research, Witkin identified the cognitive styles of field dependence and field independence (Davis, 1991; Witkin, Moore, Goodenough, & Cox, 1977).

People who are **field dependent** tend to perceive a pattern as a whole, not separating one element from the total visual field. They have difficulty focusing on one aspect of a situation, picking out important details, analyzing a pattern into different parts, or monitoring their use of strategies to solve problems. They tend to work well in groups, have a good memory for social information, and prefer subjects such as literature and history. **Field-independent** people, on the other hand, are more likely to monitor their own information processing. They perceive separate parts of a total pattern and are able to analyze a pattern according to its components. They are not as attuned to social relationships as field-dependent people, but they do well in math and science, where their analytical abilities pay off.

Although you will not necessarily be able to determine all the variations in your students' cognitive styles, you should be aware that students approach problems in different ways. Some may need help learning to pick out important features and to ignore irrelevant details. They may seem lost in less-structured situations and need clear, step-by-step instructions. Other students may be great at organizing but less sensitive to the feelings of others and not as effective in social situations.

Impulsive and Reflective Cognitive Styles.   Another aspect of cognitive style is impulsivity versus reflectiveness. An **impulsive** student works very quickly but makes many mistakes. The more **reflective** student, on the other hand, works slowly and makes fewer errors. As with field dependence/independence, impulsive and reflective cognitive styles are not highly related to intelligence within the normal range. However, as children grow older, they generally become more reflective, and for school-age children, being more re-

---

Cognitive Styles Different ways of perceiving and organizing information.

Field Dependence Cognitive style in which patterns are perceived as wholes.

Field Independence Cognitive style in which separate parts of a pattern are perceived and analyzed.

Impulsive Characterized by cognitive style of responding quickly but often inaccurately.

Reflective Characterized by cognitive style of responding slowly, carefully, and accurately.

flective does seem to improve performance on school tasks such as reading (Kogan, 1983; Smith & Caplan, 1988).

Students can learn to be more reflective, however, if they are taught specific strategies. One that has proved successful in many situations is **self-instruction,** described in Chapter 2. This approach capitalizes on the beneficial use of private speech described by Vygotsky (Meichenbaum, 1986). Another possibility is learning scanning strategies. For example, students taking multiple-choice tests might be encouraged to cross off each alternative as they consider it, so that no possibilities will be ignored. They might work in pairs and talk about why each possibility is right or wrong. In math classes, impulsive children need to be given specific strategies for checking their work. Just slowing down is not enough. These students must be taught effective strategies for solving the problem at hand by considering each reasonable alternative. I have also encountered several bright students who seem too reflective. They turn 30 minutes of homework into an all-night project.

*P*eople have different preferences for how and where they like to learn. Students who are distracted by noise may work better in a quiet space, even if that place is on the floor in the hall.

Learning Styles and Preferences

Learning styles are approaches to learning and studying. Although many different learning styles have been described, one theme that unites most of the styles is differences between deep and surface approaches to processing information in learning situations (Snow, Corno, & Jackson, 1996). Individuals who have a *deep-processing approach* to learning see the learning materials or activities as a means for understanding some underlying concepts or meanings. These students tend to learn for the sake of learning and are less concerned about how their performance is evaluated, so motivation plays a role as well. Students who take a *surface-processing* approach focus on memorizing the learning materials, not understanding them. These students tend to be motivated by rewards, grades, external standards, and the desire to be evaluated positively by others. Of course, the situation can encourage deep or surface processing, but there is evidence that individuals have tendencies to approach learning situations in characteristic ways (Pintrich & Schrauben, 1992; Tait & Entwistle, in press).

Since the late 1970s a great deal has been written about differences in students' learning preferences (Dunn, 1987; Dunn & Dunn, 1978, 1987; Gregorc, 1982; Keefe, 1982). Workshops and in-service training sessions around the country focus on this topic. Learning preferences are usually called *learning styles* in these workshops, but I believe preferences is a more accurate label. **Learning preferences** are individual preferences for particular learning environments. They could be preferences for where, when, with whom, or with what lighting, food, or music you like to study. Think for a minute about how you learn best. I like to study and write during large blocks of time, late at night. I usually make some kind of commitment or deadline every week so that I have to work under pressure in long stretches to finish the work before that deadline. Then I take a day off. When I plan or think, I have to see my thinking in writing. I have a colleague who draws diagrams of relationships when she listens to a speaker or plans a paper. You may be similar or very different, even though we all work effectively.

There are a number of instruments for assessing students' learning preferences—for example, *The Learning Style Inventory* (Renzulli & Smith, 1978), *The*

Self-Instruction Talking oneself through the steps of a task.

Learning Styles An individual's characteristic approaches to learning and studying, usually involving deep versus superficial processing of information.

Learning Preferences Preferred ways of studying and learning, such as using pictures instead of text, working with other people versus alone, learning in structured or in unstructured situations, and so on.

Learning Style Inventory (Dunn, Dunn, & Price, 1984), and the *Learning Style Profile* (Keefe & Monk, 1986). Tests of learning style have been criticized for lacking evidence of reliability and validity. This led Snider (1990) to conclude, "People are different, and it is good practice to recognize and accommodate individual differences. It is also good practice to present information in a variety of ways through more than one modality, but it is not wise to categorize learners and prescribe methods solely on the basis of tests with questionable technical qualities. . . . The idea of learning styles is appealing, but a critical examination of this approach should cause educators to be skeptical" (p. 53).

It may be too much to expect the teacher to provide every student with his or her preferred setting and support for learning. But the teacher can make options available. Having quiet, private corners as well as large tables for working; comfortable cushions as well as straight chairs; brightly lighted desks along with darker areas; headphones for listening to music as well as earplugs; structured as well as open-ended assignments; information available from films and tapes as well as in books—all these options will allow students to work and learn in their preferred mode at least some of the time.

Will making these alterations lead to greater learning? Here the answer is not clear. Results of some research indicate that students learn more when they study in their preferred setting and manner (Dunn, Beaudry, & Klavas, 1989; Dunn & Dunn, 1987). There is some evidence that very bright students need less structure and prefer quiet, solitary learning (Torrance, 1986). But before you try to accommodate all your students' learning styles, remember that students, especially younger ones, may not be the best judges of how they should learn. Preference for a particular style may not always guarantee that using the style will be effective. Sometimes students, particularly poorer students, prefer what is easy and comfortable; real learning can be hard and uncomfortable. Sometimes students prefer to learn in a certain way because they have no alternatives; it is the only way they know how to approach the task. These students may benefit from developing new—and perhaps more effective—ways to learn (Weinstein & McCombs, in press).

Focus on . . .

Cognitive Styles

- Distinguish between cognitive style and learning preference.
- Are you more field dependent or field independent? How do you know?
- What are the advantages and disadvantages of matching teaching to individual learning styles?

Students with Learning Challenges

Thus far we have focused mostly on teachers' responses to the varying abilities and styles of students. For the rest of the chapter we will consider several kinds of problems that can interfere with learning. Before we continue, though, let's analyze the difference between a disability and a handicap. A **disability** is just what the word implies—an inability to do something specific such as see or walk. A **handicap** is a disadvantage in certain situations. Some disabilities lead to handicaps. For example, being blind (a visual disability) is a handicap if you are doing work that requires sight. But this disability is not a handicap when you are doing work that requires other skills, such as composing music, finding your way around in complete darkness, or talking on the telephone. Not all disabilities are handicaps in every situation. And not all handicaps are caused by disabilities; they may be the result of lack of experience or training.

Disability The inability to do something specific such as walk or hear.

Handicap A disadvantage in a particular situation, sometimes caused by a disability.

It is important that we do not *create* handicaps for people by the way we react to their disabilities.

Students with Physical and Sensory Challenges

Some students must have special **orthopedic devices** such as braces, special shoes, crutches, or wheelchairs to participate in a normal school program. If the school has the necessary architectural features, such as ramps, elevators, and accessible rest rooms, and if teachers allow for the physical limitations of students, little needs to be done to alter the usual educational program.

Seizure Disorders (Epilepsy).   A seizure is "an abnormal discharge of electrical energy in certain brain cells" (Hallahan & Kauffman, 1997, p. 405). The effects of the seizure depend on where the discharge of energy starts in the brain and how far it spreads. People with **epilepsy** have recurrent seizures, but not all seizures are the result of epilepsy; temporary conditions such as high fevers or infections can also trigger seizures.

Seizures take many forms and differ with regard to the length, frequency, and movements involved. A **partial seizure** involves only a small part of the brain, whereas a **generalized seizure** includes much more of the brain. Most generalized seizures (once called *grand mal*) are accompanied by uncontrolled jerking movements that ordinarily last two to five minutes, followed by a deep sleep or coma. On regaining consciousness the student may be very weary, confused, and in need of extra sleep. Most seizures can be controlled by medication. If a student has a seizure accompanied by convulsions in class, the teacher must take action so the student will not be injured. The major danger to a student having such a seizure is getting hurt by striking a hard surface during the violent jerking. But do not try to restrain the child's movements—you can't stop the seizure once it starts. Lower the child gently to the floor, away from furniture or walls. Move hard objects away. Turn the child's head gently to the side and loosen any tight clothing. Never put anything in the student's mouth. Find out from the student's parents how the seizure is usually dealt with. If one seizure follows another and the student does not regain consciousness in between or if the seizure goes on more than 10 minutes, get medical help right away (Hallahan & Kauffman, 1997).

Not all seizures are dramatic. Sometimes the student just loses contact briefly. The student may stare, fail to respond to questions, drop objects, and miss what has been happening for 1 to 30 seconds. These were once called *petit mal,* but they are now referred to as *absence seizures* and can easily go undetected. If a child in your class appears to daydream frequently, does not seem to know what is going on at times, or cannot remember what has just happened when you ask, you should consult the school psychologist or nurse. The major problem for students with absence seizures is that they miss the continuity of the class interaction. If their seizures are frequent, they will find the lessons confusing. Question these students to be sure they are understanding and following the lesson. Be prepared to repeat yourself periodically.

Cerebral Palsy.   Damage to the brain before or during birth or during infancy can cause a child to have difficulty moving and coordinating his or her body. The problem may be very mild, so the child simply appears a bit clumsy,

Orthopedic Devices Devices such as braces and wheelchairs that aid people with physical disabilities.

Epilepsy Disorder marked by seizures and caused by abnormal electrical discharges in the brain.

Partial Seizure A seizure beginning in a localized area and involving only a small part of the brain.

Generalized Seizure A seizure involving a large portion of the brain.

or so severe that voluntary movement is practically impossible. The most common form of **cerebral palsy** is characterized by **spasticity** (overly tight or tense muscles). But many children with cerebral palsy have secondary handicaps (Kirk, Gallagher, & Anastasiow, 1993). In the classroom, these secondary handicaps are the greatest concern—and these are generally what the regular teacher can help with most. For example, many children with cerebral palsy also have hearing impairments, speech problems, or mild mental retardation. The strategies described in this chapter should prove helpful in such situations.

Hearing Impairment.   Signs of hearing problems are turning one ear toward the speaker, favoring one ear in conversation, or misunderstanding conversation when the speaker's face cannot be seen. Other indications include not following directions, seeming distracted or confused at times, frequently asking people to repeat what they have said, mispronouncing new words or names, and being reluctant to participate in class discussions. Take note particularly of students who have frequent earaches, sinus infections, or allergies.

In the past, educators have debated whether oral or manual approaches are better for children with hearing impairments. Oral approaches involve **speech reading** (also called lip reading) and training students to use whatever limited hearing they may have. Manual approaches include **sign language** and **finger spelling.** Research indicates that children who learn some manual method of communicating perform better in academic subjects and are more socially mature than students who are exposed only to oral methods. Today, the trend is to combine both approaches (Hallahan & Kauffman, 1997). Technological innovations such as teletypewriters in homes and public phones and the many avenues of communication through e-mail and the Internet have expanded communication possibilities for all people with hearing impairments.

Vision Impairment.   Students who have difficulty seeing often hold books either very close to or very far from their eyes. They may squint, rub their eyes frequently, or complain that their eyes burn or itch. The eyes may actually be swollen, red, or encrusted. Students with vision problems may misread material on the chalkboard, describe their vision as being blurred, be very sensitive to light, or hold their heads at an odd angle (De Mott, 1982). Any of these signs should be reported to a qualified school professional.

Mild vision problems can be overcome with corrective lenses. Only about 1 in 1,000 children in this country have visual impairments so serious that special educational services are needed. Most of this group needing special services is classified as having **low vision.** This means they can read with the aid of a magnifying glass or large-print books. A small group of students, about 1 in every 2,500, is **educationally blind.** These students must use hearing and touch as the predominant learning channels (Kirk, Gallagher, & Anastasiow, 1993).

Special materials and equipment that help visually impaired students to function in regular classrooms include large-print typewriters; variable-speed tape recorders (allowing teachers to make time-compressed tape recordings, which speed up the rate of speech without changing the voice pitch); special calculators; the abacus; three-dimensional maps, charts, and models; and special measuring devices. For students with visual problems, the quality of the print is often more important than the size, so watch out for hard-to-read handouts and ditto sheets. The Instructional Materials Reference Center of the

Cerebral Palsy Condition involving a range of motor or coordination difficulties due to brain damage.

Spasticity Overly tight or tense muscles, characteristic of some forms of cerebral palsy.

Speech Reading Using visual cues to understand language.

Sign Language Communication system of hand movements that symbolize words and concepts.

Finger Spelling Communication system that "spells out" each letter with a hand position.

Low Vision Vision limited to close objects.

Educationally Blind Needing Braille materials in order to learn.

American Printing House for the Blind (1839 Frankfort Avenue, Louisville, KY 40206) has catalogs of instructional materials for visually impaired students.

Communication Disorders

Language is a complex learned behavior. Language disorders may arise from many sources, because so many different aspects of the individual are involved in learning language. A child with a hearing impairment will not learn to speak normally. A child who hears inadequate language at home will learn inadequate language. Children who are not listened to, or whose perception of the world is distorted by emotional problems, will reflect these problems in their language development. Because speaking involves movements, any impairment of the motor functions involved with speech can cause language disorders. And because language development and thinking are so interwoven, any problems in cognitive functioning can affect ability to use language.

Speech Impairments.   Students who cannot produce sounds effectively for speaking are considered to have a **speech impairment.** About 5% of school-age children have some form of speech impairment. Articulation problems and stuttering are the two most common problems.

Articulation disorders include substituting one sound for another (*thunthine* for *sunshine*), distorting a sound (*shoup* for *soup*), adding a sound (*ideer* for *idea*), or omitting sounds (*po-y* for *pony*) (Cartwright, Cartwright, & Ward, 1981). But keep in mind that most children are 6 to 8 years old before they can successfully pronounce all English sounds in normal conversation. The sounds of the consonants *l, r, y, s,* and *z* and the consonant blends *sh, ch, zh,* and *th* are the last to be mastered.

All students can benefit from learning alternative ways of communicating, for example, sign language systems. This encourages understanding and mutual respect among students of all abilities.

Speech Impairment Inability to produce sounds effectively for speaking.

Articulation Disorders Any of a variety of pronunciation difficulties, such as the substitution, distortion, or omission of sounds.

TABLE 4.5   Encouraging Language Development

- Talk about things in which the child is interested.
- Follow the child's lead. Reply to the child's initiations and comments. Share his/her excitement.
- Don't ask too many questions. If you must, use questions such as *how did/do . . . , why did/do . . . , and what happened . . .* that result in longer explanatory answers.
- Encourage the child to ask questions. Respond openly and honestly. If you don't want to answer a question, say so and explain why. *(I don't think I want to answer that question; it's very personal.)*
- Use a pleasant tone of voice. You need not be a comedian, but you can be light and humorous. Children love it when adults are a little silly.

- Don't be judgmental or make fun of a child's language. If you are overly critical of the child's language or try to catch and correct all errors, he/she will stop talking to you.
- Allow enough time for the child to respond.
- Treat the child with courtesy by not interrupting when he/she is talking.
- Include the child in family and classroom discussions. Encourage participation and listen to his/her ideas.
- Be accepting of the child and of the child's language. Hugs and acceptance can go a long way.
- Provide opportunities for the child to use language and to have that language work for him/her to accomplish his/her goals.

Source: From Robert E. Owens, Jr., *Language disorders: A functional approach to assessment and intervention,* 2/e, p. 416. Copyright © 1995 by Allyn & Bacon. Reprinted by permission.

Stuttering generally appears between the ages of 3 and 4. It is not yet clear what causes stuttering, but it can cause embarrassment and anxiety for the sufferer. In about 50% of cases, stuttering disappears during early adolescence (Wiig, 1982). If stuttering continues more than a year or so, the child should be referred to a speech therapist. Early intervention is critical (Onslow, 1992).

Voicing problems, a third type of speech impairment, include speaking with an inappropriate pitch, quality, or loudness or in a monotone (Hallahan & Kauffman, 1997). A student with any of these problems should be referred to a speech therapist. Recognizing the problem is the first step. Be alert for students whose pronunciation, loudness, voice quality, speech fluency, expressive range, or rate is very different from that of their peers. Pay attention also to students who seldom speak. Are they simply shy, or do they have difficulties with language?

Language Disorders.   Language differences are not necessarily language disorders. Students with language disorders are those who are markedly deficient in their ability to understand or express language, compared with other students of their own age and cultural group (Owens, 1995). Students who seldom speak, who use few words or very short sentences, or who rely only on gestures to communicate should be referred to a qualified school professional for observation or testing. Table 4.5 gives ideas for promoting language development for all students.

Emotional or Behavioral Disorders

Students with emotional and behavioral disorders can be among the most difficult to teach in a regular class. Behavior becomes a problem when it deviates so greatly from what is appropriate for the child's age group that it significantly interferes with the child's own growth and development and/or the lives

Stuttering Repetitions, prolongations, and hesitations that block flow of speech.

Voicing Problems Inappropriate pitch, quality, loudness, or intonation.

of others. Clearly, deviation implies a difference from some standard, and standards of behavior differ from one situation, age group, culture, and historical period to another. Thus, what passes for team spirit in the football bleachers might be seen as disturbed behavior in a bank or restaurant. In addition, the deviation must be more than a temporary response to stressful events; it must be consistent across time and in different situations.

Quay and Peterson (1987) describe six dimensions of emotional/behavioral disorders. Children who have *conduct disorders* are aggressive, destructive, disobedient, uncooperative, distractible, disruptive, and persistent. They have been corrected and punished for the same misbehavior countless times. Many of these children are disliked by the adults and even the other children in their lives. The most successful strategies for helping these children are the behavior management approaches described in Chapter 6. These students need very clear rules and consequences, consistently enforced. The future is not promising for students who never learn to control their behavior and who also fail academically. Waiting for the students to "outgrow" their problems is seldom effective (O'Leary & Wilson, 1987).

Children who are extremely anxious, withdrawn, shy, depressed, and hypersensitive, who cry easily and have little confidence, are said to have an *anxiety-withdrawal disorder*. These children have few social skills and consequently very few friends. The most successful approaches with them appear to involve the direct teaching of social skills (Gresham, 1981).

The third category is *attentional problems immaturity*. Characteristics include a short attention span, frequent daydreaming, little initiative, messiness, and poor coordination. If an immature student is not too far behind others in the class, she or he may respond to the behavior management strategies described in Chapter 6. But if these approaches fail or if the problem is severe, you should consult the school psychologist, guidance counselor, or another mental health professional. Related to this dimension is the category of *motor excess*. These students are restless and tense; they seem unable to sit still or stop talking.

The fifth category of behavior disorders is *socialized aggression*. Students in this group are often members of gangs. They may steal or vandalize because their peer culture expects it.

Finally, some students exhibit *psychotic behavior*. You are not likely to work with many of these students. Their behavior may be bizarre, and they may express very farfetched ideas. These six categories are very general. If you are concerned about the behavior of one of your students, it is best to consult the school psychologist or guidance counselor.

Hyperactivity and Attention Disorders

You have probably heard and may even have used the term **hyperactivity**. The notion is a modern one; there were no hyperactive children 30 to 40 years ago. Today, if anything, the term is applied too often and too widely. Hyperactivity is not one particular condition; it is "a set of behaviors—such as excessive restlessness and short attention span—that are quantitatively and qualitatively different from those of children of the same sex, mental age, and SES [socioeconomic status]" (O'Leary, 1980, p. 195).

Today most psychologists agree that the main problem for children labeled hyperactive is directing and maintaining attention, not simply controlling their

Hyperactivity Behavior disorder marked by atypical, excessive restlessness and inattentiveness.

FIGURE 4.4

Ritalin's Rise

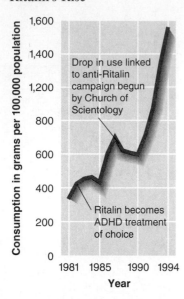

Source: From J. Leavy, "Mother's Little Helper," *Newsweek, 127,* March 18, 1996, p. 52. © 1996, Newsweek Inc. All rights reserved. Reprinted by permission.

Attention-Deficit/Hyperactivity Disorder Current term for disruptive behavior disorders marked by overactivity, excessive difficulty sustaining attention, or impulsiveness.

Learning Disability Problem with acquisition and use of language; may show up as difficulty with reading, writing, reasoning, or math.

restlessness and physical activity. The American Psychiatric Association has established a diagnostic category called **attention-deficit/hyperactivity disorder (ADHD)** to identify children with this problem.

Hyperactive children are not only more physically active and inattentive than other children; they also have difficulty responding appropriately and working steadily toward goals (even their own goals), and they may not be able to control their behavior on command, even for a brief period. The problem behaviors are generally evident in all situations and with every teacher. It is difficult to know how many children should be classified as hyperactive. The most common estimate is 5% of the elementary-school population (O'Leary, 1980). More boys than girls are identified as hyperactive. Just a few years ago, most psychologists thought that ADHD diminished as children entered adolescence, but now there are some researchers who believe that the problems can persist into adulthood (Hallowell & Ratey, 1994).

Today there is an increasing reliance on drug therapy for ADHD. According to a *Newsweek* headline (Leavy, 1996, March), 1.3 million American children take Ritalin—a 250% increase since 1990, as you can see in Figure 4.4.

Ritalin and other prescribed drugs such as Dexedrine are stimulants, but in particular dosages they tend to have paradoxical effects on many ADHD children: short-term effects include possible improvements in social behaviors such as cooperation, attention, and compliance. Research suggests that about 70% of hyperactive children are more manageable when on medication. But for many there are negative side effects such as increased heart rate and blood pressure, interference with growth rate, insomnia, weight loss, and nausea (Pelham & Murphy, 1986; Weiss & Hechtman, 1993). In addition, little is known about the long-term effects of drug therapy. There also is no evidence that the drugs lead to improvement in academic learning or peer relationships, two areas where hyperactive children have great problems. Because students appear to improve dramatically in their behavior, parents and teachers, relieved to see change, may assume the problem has been cured. It hasn't. The students still need special help in learning.

The methods that have proved most successful in helping students with attention deficits are based on the behavioral principles described in Chapter 6. One promising approach combines instruction in learning and memory strategies with motivational training. The goal is to give students the "skill and will" (Paris, 1988) to improve their achievement. Students learn how and when to apply learning strategies and study skills. They are also encouraged to be persistent and to see themselves as "in control" (Reid & Borkowski, 1987). These methods should be thoroughly tested with the student before drugs are used. Even if students in your class are on medication, it is critical that they also learn the academic and social skills they will need to survive. Again, this will not happen by itself, even if behavior improves with medication (Kneedler, 1984).

Learning Disabilities

How do you explain what is wrong with a student who is not mentally retarded, emotionally disturbed, or educationally deprived; who has normal vision, hearing, and language capabilities; and who still cannot learn to read, write, or compute? One explanation is that the student has a **learning disability.** This is a relatively new and controversial category of exceptional students.

There is no fully agreed upon definition. In fact, Cartwright, Cartwright, and Ward (1981) list 38 different definitions. A group of parents and professionals, the National Joint Committee on Learning Disabilities (1989), proposes the following definition:

> Learning disabilities is a general term that refers to a heterogeneous group of disorders manifest by significant difficulties in the acquisition and use of listening, speaking, reading, writing, reasoning, or mathematical abilities. These disorders are intrinsic to the individual, presumed to be due to central nervous system dysfunction, and may occur across the life span. (p. 1)

"YOUR FEELINGS OF INSECURITY SEEM TO HAVE STARTED WHEN MARY LOU GURNBLATT SAID, 'MAYBE I DON'T HAVE A LEARNING DISABILITY—MAYBE YOU HAVE A TEACHING DISABILITY.'"

(© 1975 Tony Saltzman. From Phi Delta Kappan.)

This definition eliminates references to older terms such as *brain injury* or *minimal brain dysfunction,* and indicates that learning disabilities may pose a lifelong challenge. Most definitions agree that learning-disabled students are at least average in intelligence, but have significant academic problems and perform significantly below what would be expected.

Some educators and psychologists believe the learning disability label is overused and abused. Almost one-half of all students receiving some kind of special education services in the public schools are diagnosed as learning disabled. This is by far the largest category of disabled student. Some researchers have suggested that many of the students called learning disabled are really slow learners in average schools, average learners in high-achieving schools, students with second-language problems, or that they may simply be behind in their work because they are absent frequently or have to change schools often (Gartner & Lipsky, 1987).

Students with Learning Disabilities.   As with any of the groups of disabled students described thus far, students with learning disabilities are not all alike. The most common characteristics are specific difficulties in one or more academic areas; poor coordination; problems paying attention; hyperactivity and impulsivity; problems organizing and interpreting visual and auditory information; disorders of thinking, memory, speech, and hearing; and difficulties making and keeping friends (Hallahan & Kauffman, 1997). As you can see, many students with other disabilities (such as ADHD) and many normal students may have some of the same characteristics. To complicate the situation even more, not all students with learning disabilities will have these problems, and few will have all of the problems.

Most students with learning disabilities have difficulties reading. These difficulties appear to be due to problems with relating sounds to letters that make up words, making spelling hard as well (Stanovich, 1991). Math, both computation and problem solving, is the second most common problem for learning-disabled students. The writing of some learning-disabled students is virtually unreadable, and their spoken language can be halting and disorganized. Many researchers trace some of these problems to the students' inability to use effective learning strategies like those we will discuss in Chapter 7. Learning-disabled students often lack effective ways to approach academic tasks. They

---

Focus on...
Learning Challenges
■ Distinguish between a disability and a handicap.
■ How can schools accommodate the needs of physically disabled students?
■ What are some signs of hearing impairment?
■ What are the advantages and disadvantages of drug therapy for attention deficit disorders?
■ Describe some teaching strategies that have been successful for learning-disabled students.

don't know how to focus on the relevant information, get organized, apply learning strategies and study skills, change strategies when one isn't working, or evaluate their learning. They tend to be passive learners, in part because they don't know *how* to learn. Working independently is especially trying, so homework and seatwork are often left incomplete (Hallahan & Kauffman, 1997; Hallahan, Kauffman, & Lloyd, 1995).

Early diagnosis is important so that learning-disabled students do not become terribly frustrated and discouraged. The students themselves do not understand why they are having such trouble, and they may become victims of **learned helplessness.** This condition was first identified in learning experiments with animals. The animals were put in situations where they received punishment (electric shocks) that they could not control. Later, when the situation was changed and they could have escaped the shocks or turned them off, the animals didn't even bother trying (Seligman, 1975). They had learned to be helpless victims. Learning-disabled students may also come to believe that they cannot control or improve their own learning. This is a powerful belief. The students never exert the effort to discover that they can make a difference in their own learning, so they remain passive and helpless.

TABLE 4.6   Learning Disabilities across the Life Span

Learning disabilities are not limited to the school years. This table lists the problems that may occur during different phases of life and the treatments that have the strongest support from research or from expert teachers in the field.

	Preschool	Grades K–1
Problem Areas	Delay in developmental milestones (e.g., walking) Receptive language Expressive language Visual perception Auditory perception Short attention span Hyperactivity	Academic readiness skills (e.g., alphabet knowledge, quantitative concepts, directional concepts, etc.) Receptive language Expressive language Visual perception Auditory perception Gross and fine motor Attention Hyperactivity Social skills
Treatments with Most Research and/or Expert Support	Direct instruction in language skills Behavioral management Parent training	Direct instruction in academic and language areas Behavioral management Parent training

Source: From Cecil D. Mercer, *Students with learning disabilities,* 5/e. Copyright © 1997. Adapted by permission of Prentice-Hall Inc., Saddle River, NJ.

Learned Helplessness The expectation, based on previous experiences with a lack of control, that all one's efforts will lead to failure.

Learning-disabled students may also try to compensate for their problems and develop bad learning habits in the process, or they may begin avoiding certain subjects out of fear of not being able to handle the work. To prevent these things from happening, the teacher should refer the students to the appropriate professionals in the school.

Teaching Students with Learning Disabilities. There is also controversy over how best to help these students. A promising approach seems to be to emphasize study skills and methods for processing information in a given subject like reading or math. Many of the principles of cognitive learning from Chapters 7 and 8 can be applied to help all students improve their attention, memory, and problem-solving abilities (Sawyer, Graham, & Harris, 1992). *The Kansas Learning Strategies Curriculum* is one example of this approach (Deshler & Schumaker, 1986). No set of teaching techniques will be effective for every learning-disabled child. You should work with the special education teachers in your school to design appropriate instruction for individual students. Table 4.6 summarizes problem areas and the most effective teaching approaches for learning-disabled students across the life span.

Grades 2–6	Grades 7–12	Adult
Reading skills	Reading skills	Reading skills
Arithmetic skills	Arithmetic skills	Arithmetic skills
Written expression	Written expression	Written expression
Verbal expression	Verbal expression	Verbal expression
Receptive language	Listening skills	Listening skills
Attention span	Study skills (meta-cognition)	Study skills
Hyperactivity	Social-emotional	Social-emotional
Social-emotional	Social-emotional-delinquency	
Direct instruction in academic areas	Direct instruction in academic areas	Direct instruction in academic areas
Behavioral management	Tutoring in subject areas	Tutoring in subject (college) or job area
Self-control training	Direct instruction in learning strategies (study skills)	Compensatory instruction (i.e., using aids such as tape recorder, calculator, computer, dictionary)
Parent training	Self-control training	
	Curriculum alternatives	

Integration, Mainstreaming, and Inclusion

We have been discussing in detail the many special problems of exceptional students because, no matter what grade or subject you teach, you will encounter these students in your classroom. The trend to integrate exceptional students into regular education began in the 1960s and led to legal actions in the 1970s.

Changes in the Law

In 1975 a law was passed that began revolutionary changes in the education of disabled children. The Education for All Handicapped Children Act (Public Law 94–142) required states to provide "a free, appropriate public education for every child between the ages of 3 and 21 (unless state law does not provide free public education to children 3 to 5 or 18 to 21 years of age) regardless of how, or how seriously, he may be handicapped." In 1986, PL 99–457 extended the requirement for a free, appropriate education to all handicapped children ages 3 to 5, even in states that do not have public schooling for children this age. Also in the mid-1980s, some special educators and educational policymakers suggested that regular and special education should be merged so that regular teachers would have to take even more responsibility for the education of exceptional students. This movement is called the **regular education initiative.**

In 1990, PL 94–142 was amended by the **Individuals with Disabilities Education Act (IDEA).** This legislation replaced the word "handicapped" with "disabled," and expanded the services for disabled students. Also in 1990, the **Americans with Disabilities Act (ADA)** extended civil rights protection in employment, transportation, public accommodations, state and local government, and telecommunications to people with disabilities.

Let's examine the requirements in these laws. There are three major points of interest to teachers: the concept of "least restrictive placement"; the individualized education program (IEP); and the protection of the rights of disabled students and their parents.

Least Restrictive Placement. The laws require states to develop procedures for educating each child in the **least restrictive placement.** This means a setting that is as normal as possible. Earlier interpretations of this requirement led to **mainstreaming**—bringing exceptional students into general educational settings when they could meet expectations for that setting—for example allowing them to participate in recess or art or music (Friend & Bursuck, 1996). In most schools severely disabled students were not integrated into regular classes; but in some districts there is a movement toward **full inclusion**—integrating all students, even those with severe disabilities, into regular classes. Advocates of inclusion believe that disabled students can benefit from involvement with their nondisabled peers and should be educated with them in their regular home-district school, even if doing so calls for changes in educational requirements, special aids, services, and training or consultation for the regular teaching staff (Stainback & Stainback, 1992). But some researchers caution that inclusion classrooms are not the best placement for every child. For example, Naomi Zigmond and her colleagues (1995) report that in their study of six elementary

Regular Education Initiative An educational movement that advocates giving regular education teachers, not special education teachers, responsibility for teaching mildly (and sometimes moderately) handicapped students.

Individuals with Disabilities Education Act (IDEA) Amendment to PL 94-142.

Americans with Disabilities Act (ADA) Legislation prohibiting discrimination against persons with disabilities in employment, transportation, public access, local government, and telecommunications.

Least Restrictive Placement Placement of each child in as normal an educational setting as possible.

Mainstreaming Teaching disabled children in regular classes for part or all of their school day.

Full Inclusion The integration of all students, including those with severe disabilities, into regular classes.

Is Full Inclusion a Reasonable Approach to Teaching Exceptional Students?

In his booklet entitled *Inclusion: Issues of educating students with disabilities in regular educational settings,* Michael Hardman (1994) summarizes the arguments for and against full inclusion.

POINT Full inclusion makes sense.

Supporters of full inclusion, such as Marsha Forest, believe that:

> All children need to learn with and from other children. . . . All children need to belong and feel wanted. . . . All children need to have fun and enjoy noise and laughter in their lives. . . . All children need to take risks and fall and cry and get hurt. . . . All children need to be in real families and real schools and real neighborhoods. (p. 403)

These opportunities are limited in special class placements. No matter how good the teaching, disabled students will never learn to cope with the world outside their special classroom if they are not allowed to live in that world. Furthermore, many researchers believe that special education has failed. For example, only 56% of students in special education earn a high school diploma and only 21% of these graduates go on to pursue any kind of post-secondary education. Segregation away from the mainstream, in special classes, robs disabled students of the opportunity to learn to participate fully in society, robs nondisabled students of the opportunity to develop understanding and acceptance of the disabled, and increases the likelihood that disabled individuals will be stigmatized.

COUNTERPOINT Full inclusion will not work.

Just because a disabled student is physically present in a class does not mean that student feels a sense of belonging. Disabled students can be just as socially isolated and alone in a regular class as they would be in a "special" class across the hall or across the state. Children can be cruel, and they may not necessarily provide opportunities for their disabled peers to "have fun and enjoy noise and laughter in their lives." Furthermore, many researchers believe that special education has been quite successful. Seventy-seven percent of parents of students with disabilities are satisfied with the education programs of their children (Harris, 1989). In fact, parents of children with disabilities are more satisfied with the public schools than are parents of school-age children in general (Robert Wood Johnson, 1988). And special classes cannot be held responsible for low graduation and high drop-out rates among special education students. Ninety-two percent of all students with disabilities spend at least some of their time in regular classes already. Shouldn't these classes be held responsible too?

Finally, can we really expect regular teachers who are already overburdened with responsibilities for low-achieving students, students coping with family crises, and students who speak little or no English to also handle the wide range of disabilities that could confront them? Regular educators are unprepared, unsupported, and unable to handle all these challenges at once. The idea that extra support and consultation will be provided is good in theory, but will it actually come to pass in practice? Albert Shanker, President of the American Federation of Teachers (AFT), speaking to members of his union during an AFT conference, *Inclusion: Where We Stand,* said the following:

I do believe very large numbers of students now separated into special education could be included and integrated into regular classes and it would be beneficial. . . . [But] We must put the brakes on the helter-skelter, even tumultuous rush toward full inclusion so that everyone involved—parents, school boards, legislators, Congress, and even the Clinton administration—can develop a policy based on what is best for all children in our public schools. . . . Full inclusion is becoming more widely practiced based on budgetary and social motivation and not on what most Americans think classrooms ought to be about, which is education. (Inclusive Education Programs, 1994, p. 1+)

schools that had implemented full inclusion, only about half of the learning disabled students in these schools were able to benefit. As you can see in the Point/Counterpoint, inclusion is a hotly debated issue.

Individual Education Program.   The drafters of the laws recognized that each student is unique and may need a specially tailored program to make progress. The **individualized education program,** or **IEP,** is written by a team that includes the student's teacher or teachers, a qualified school psychologist or special education supervisor, the parent(s) or guardian(s), and (when possible) the student. The program must be updated each year and must state in writing:

1. The student's present level of functioning.

2. Goals for the year and short-term measurable instructional objectives leading to those goals.

3. A list of specific services to be provided to the student and details of when those services will be initiated.

4. A description of how fully the student will participate in the regular school program.

5. A schedule telling how the student's progress toward the objectives will be evaluated and approximately how long the services described in the plan will be needed.

6. Beginning at age 16 (and as young as 14 for some students), a statement of needed transitional services to move the student toward further education or work in adult life.

Figure 4.5 is an exerpt from the IEP of a 9-year-old mildly retarded girl. This section of the IEP focuses on one behavior problem and on reading.

The Rights of Students and Parents.   Several stipulations in these laws protect the rights of parents and students. Schools must have procedures for maintaining the confidentiality of school records. Testing practices must not discriminate against students from different cultural backgrounds. Parents have the right to see all records relating to the testing, placement, and teaching of their child. If they wish, parents may obtain an independent evaluation of their child. Parents may bring an advocate or representative to the meeting at which the IEP is developed. Students whose parents are unavailable must be assigned a surrogate parent to participate in the planning. Parents must receive written notice (in their native language) before any evaluation or change in placement is made. Finally, parents have the right to challenge the program developed for their child, and are protected by due process of law.

Effective Teaching in Inclusive Classrooms

When you think about working with disabled students, what are your concerns? Do you have enough training? Will you get the support you need from school administrators or specialists? Will working with the disabled students take time away from your other responsibilities? These are common questions, and sometimes concerns are justified. But effective teaching for exceptional students does not require a unique set of skills. It is a combination of good teaching practices and sensitivity to all your students. Disabled students need to *learn the academic material,* and they need to be *full participants in the day-to-day life of the classroom.*

Individualized Education Program (IEP) Annually revised program for an exceptional student, detailing present achievement level, goals, and strategies, drawn up by teachers, parents, specialists, and (if possible) student.

FIGURE 4.5

An Excerpt from an Individualized Educational Program (IEP)

This IEP was developed for a 9-year-old girl. This section of the plan focuses on following the teacher's directions and on reading.

Student: _____ Amy North _____ Age: __ 9 __ Grade: __ 1 __ Date: _ Oct. 17, 1995 _

1. Unique Characteristics or Needs: Noncompliance

Frequently noncompliant with teacher's instructions.

1. Present Levels of Performance
   Complies with about 50% of teacher requests/commands.

2. Special Education, Related Services, and Modifications
   Implemented immediately, strong reinforcement for compliance with teacher's instructions (Example: "Sure I will!" plan including precision requests and reinforcer menu for points earned for compliance, as described in The Tough Kid Book, by Rhode, Jenson, and Reavis, 1992); within 3 weeks, training of parents by school psychologist to use precision requests and reinforcement at home.

3. Objectives (Including Procedures, Criteria, and Schedule)
   Within one month, will comply with teacher requests/commands 90% of the time; compliance monitored weekly by the teacher.

4. Annual Goals
   Will become compliant with teacher's requests/commands.

2. Unique Characteristics or Needs: Reading

2a. Very slow reading rate
2b. Poor comprehension
2c. Limited phonics skills
2d. Limited sight-word vocabulary

1. Present Levels of Performance
   2a. Reads stories of approximately 100 words of first-grade level at approximately 40 words per min.
   2b. Seldom can recall factual information about stories immediately after reading them.
   2c. Consistently confuses vowel sounds, often misidentifies consonants, and does not blend sounds.
   2d. Has sight-word vocabulary of approximately 150 words.

2. Special Education, Related Services, and Modifications
   2a–2c. Direct instruction 30 minutes daily in vowel discrimination, consonant identification, and sound blending: begin immediately, continue throughout schoolyear.
   2a & 2d. Sight word drill 10 minutes daily in addition to phonics instruction and daily practice; 10 minutes practice in using phonics and sight-word skills in reading story at her level; begin immediately, continue for schoolyear.

3. Objectives (Including Procedures, Criteria, and Schedule)
   2a. Within 3 months, will read stories on her level at 60 words per minute with 2 or fewer errors per story; within six months, 80 words with 2 or fewer errors; performance monitored daily by teacher or aide.
   2b. Within 3 months will answer oral and written comprehension questions requiring recall of information from stories she has just read with 90% accuracy (e.g., Who is in the story? What happened? When? Why?) and be able to predict probably outcomes with 80% accuracy; performance monitored daily by teacher or aide.
   2c. Within 3 months, will increase sight-word vocabulary to 200 words, within 6 months to 250 words, assessed by flashcard presentation.

4. Annual Goals
   2a–2c. Will read fluently and with comprehension at beginning-second-grade level.

Source: From Daniel P. Hallahan and James M. Kauffman, *Exceptional learners: Introduction to special education,* 7/e, p. 37. Copyright © 1995 by Allyn & Bacon. Reprinted by permission.

To accomplish the first goal of academic learning, Larrivee (1985) concluded that effective teachers of mainstreamed students do the following:

1. Use time efficiently by having smooth management routines, avoiding discipline problems, and planning carefully.

2. Ask questions at the right level of difficulty.

3. Give supportive, positive feedback to students, helping them figure out the right answer if they are wrong but on the right track.

To accomplish the second goal of integrating disabled students into the day-to-day life of the classroom, Ferguson, Ferguson, and Bogdan (1987) give the following guidelines:

1. Mix students with disabilities into groups with nondisabled students. Avoid resegregating the disabled students into separate groups.

2. Instead of sending students out for special services like speech therapy, remedial reading, or individualized instruction, try to integrate the special help into the class setting, perhaps during a time when the other students are working independently too.

3. Make sure your language and behavior with disabled students is a good model for everyone.

4. Teach about differences among people as part of the curriculum. Let students become familiar with aids for the disabled, such as hearing aids, sign language, communication boards, and so on.

5. Have students work together in cooperative groups or on special projects such as role plays, biographical interviews, or lab assignments.

6. Try to keep the schedules and activity patterns of disabled and nondisabled students similar.

Resource Rooms, Collaborative Consultation, and Cooperative Teaching. Many schools provide additional help for classroom teachers working with disabled students. A **resource room** is a classroom with special materials and equipment and a specially trained teacher. Students may come to the resource room each day for several minutes or several hours and receive instruction individually or in small groups. The rest of the day the students are in regular classes.

The resource room can also be used as a crisis center. Individual students may spend an hour, a day, or a week there during a crisis, when their regular teacher is unable to give them the necessary attention and guidance. Besides working with students directly, a resource teacher may also work with them indirectly by giving the regular teacher ideas, materials, or actual demonstrations of teaching techniques.

Increasingly, special and regular educators are working together, collaborating to assume equal responsibility for the education of disabled students. The collaboration may work through consultation, planning, and problem solving about how to teach specific students or the special education teacher might work directly alongside the regular teacher in a class made up of students with and without disabilities. The latter is called **cooperative teaching.** The teachers assume different roles, depending on the age of the students and their needs. For example, in a secondary class the regular teacher might be re-

Resource Room Classroom with special materials and a specially trained teacher.

Cooperative Teaching Collaboration between regular and special education teachers.

sponsible for academic content, while the special instructor teaches study skills and learning strategies. In another classroom the regular teacher might deal with core content, while the special teacher provides remediation, enrichment, or reteaching when necessary. The two teachers might also try team teaching, where each is responsible for different parts of the lesson.

When using cooperative teaching, it is important that regular and disabled students aren't resegregated in the class, with the regular teacher always working with the "regular" students and the special teacher always working with the "mainstreamed" students. I observed one class in which the disabled students worked only with the special education teacher but often looked longingly over their shoulders at the activities of their classmates working with the regular teacher. Rather than integrating the disabled students into the class, this cooperative teaching arrangement accentuated their separateness. Figure 4.6 shows different ways to implement cooperative teaching.

FIGURE 4.6

Cooperative and Co-Teaching Approaches

There are many ways for teachers to work together in inclusion classrooms.

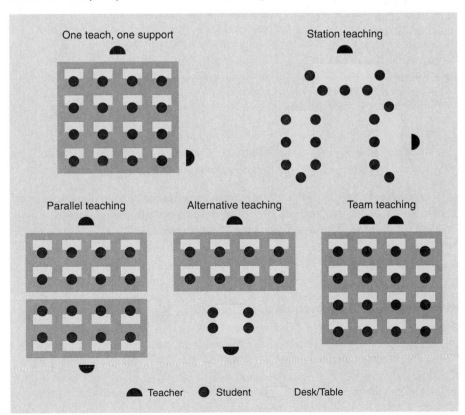

Source: From Marilyn Friend and William Bursuck, *Including students with special needs: A practical guide for classroom teachers,* p. 87. Copyright © 1996 by Allyn & Bacon. Reprinted by permission.

TABLE 4.7   Making a Referral

---

1. Contact the student's parents. It is very important that you discuss the student's problems with the parents *before* you refer.

2. Before making a referral, check *all* the student's school records. Has the student ever:

   - had a psychological evaluation?
   - qualified for special services?
   - been included in other special programs (e.g., for disadvantaged children; speech or language therapy)?
   - scored far below average on standardized tests?
   - been retained?

   Do the records indicate:

   - good progress in some areas, poor progress in others?
   - any physical or medical problem?
   - that the student is taking medication?

3. Talk to the student's other teachers and professional support personnel about your concern for the student. Have other teachers also had difficulty with the student? Have they found ways of dealing successfully with the student? Document the strategies that you have used in your class to meet the student's

educational needs. Your documentation will be useful as evidence that will be helpful to or required by the committee of professionals who will evaluate the student. Demonstrate your concern by keeping written records. Your notes should include items such as:

   - exactly what you are concerned about
   - why you are concerned about it
   - dates, places, and times you have observed the problem
   - precisely what you have done to try to resolve the problem
   - who, if anyone, helped you devise the plans or strategies you have used
   - evidence that the strategies have been successful or unsuccessful

Remember that you should refer a student only if you can make a convincing case that the student may have a handicapping condition and probably cannot be served appropriately without special education. Referral for special education begins a time-consuming, costly, and stressful process that is potentially damaging to the student and has many legal ramifications.

Source: P. L. Pullen and J. M. Kaufmann (1987). *What should I know about special education? Answers for classroom teachers.* Austin, Texas: Pro-Ed. Reprinted by permission.

Making a Referral.   If you wanted to refer a student for evaluation, how would you begin? Table 4.7 guides you through the referral process.

Including Families.   To create supportive learning environments for exceptional students, collaboration should extend outside the classroom to the students' families. The Guidelines give some ideas.

Guidelines

Family and Community Partnerships for Productive Conferences

Plan and prepare for a productive conference.

Examples

1. Have a clear purpose and gather the needed information. If you want to discuss student progress, have work samples.

2. Send home a list of questions and ask families to bring the information to the conference. Sample questions from Friend and Bursuck (1996) are:

   1. What is your child's favorite class activity?

   2. Does your child have worries about any class activities? If so, what are they?

3. What are your priorities for your child's education this year?

4. What questions do you have about your child's education in my class this year?

5. How could we at school help make this the most successful year ever for your child?

6. Are there any topics you want to discuss at the conference that I might need to prepare for? If so, please let me know.

7. Would you like other individuals to participate in the conference? If so, please give me a list of their names.

8. Is there particular school information you would like me to have available? If so, please let me know. (p. 101)

During the conference, create and maintain an atmosphere of collaboration and respect.

Examples

1. Arrange the room for private conversation. Put a sign on your door to avoid interruptions. Meet around a conference table for better collaboration. Have tissues available.

2. Address families as "Mr." and "Ms.," not "Mom" and "Dad" or "Grandma." Use students' names.

3. Listen to families' concerns and build on their ideas for their children.

After the conference, keep good records and follow-up on decisions.

Examples

1. Make notes to yourself and keep them organized.

2. Summarize any actions or decisions in writing and send a copy to the family and any other teachers or professionals involved.

3. Communicate with families on other occasions, especially when there is good news to share.

Computers and Exceptional Students

Computers have improved the education of exceptional children in countless ways. Given the record keeping and program planning needed to meet federal regulations, teachers can use computers to manage instruction. For students who require small steps and many repetitions to learn a new concept, computers are the perfect patient tutors, repeating steps and lessons as many times as necessary. A well-designed computer instructional program is engaging and interactive—two important qualities for students with problems paying attention or with a history of failure that has eroded motivation. For example, a math or spelling program might use images, sounds, and gamelike features to maintain the attention of a student with an attention-deficit disorder. Interactive videodisc programs are being developed to help hearing people use sign language. Many programs do not involve sound, so hearing-impaired students can get the full benefit from the lessons. Students who have trouble reading can use programs that will "speak" a word for them if they touch the unknown word with a light pen or the cursor. With this immediate access to help, the

Computers and other technology can support learning for disabled students so that the disabilities are less handicapping.

students are much more likely to get the reading practice they need to prevent falling further and further behind. And for the learning-disabled student whose writing can't be read, word processors produce perfect penmanship so the ideas can finally get on paper. Once the ideas are on paper, the student can reorganize and improve the writing without the agony of rewriting by hand (Hallahan & Kauffman, 1997; Hardman, Drew, & Egan, 1996; Reynolds & Birch, 1988).

For gifted students, computers can be a connection with databases and computers in universities, museums, and research labs. Computer networks allow students to work on projects and share information with others across the country. It is also possible to have gifted students write programs for students and teachers. Quite a few principals around the country rely on their students to make the technology in the school work. These are just a few examples of what technology can do. Check with the resource teachers in your district to find out what is available in your school.

Focus on...

Mainstreaming and Inclusion

- Describe the main legal requirements in the Individuals with Disabilities Act.
- What is your position on full inclusion?
- What should you do before referring a child for evaluation by special education professionals?

SUMMARY

Language and Labels

Exceptional learners have learning abilities or problems that require special education. In the past, education for children with learning problems or physical disabilities often meant segregating children in separate classes or programs.

Labels and diagnostic classifications of exceptional students can easily become both stigmas and self-fulfilling prophecies, but can also open doors to special programs and help teachers develop appropriate instructional strategies.

Individual Differences in Intelligence

Psychologists disagree on what intelligence is—a collection of discrete abilities; a general mental ability to learn new information and cope with the world; abilities for problem solving; or an array of multiple intelligences that include, for example, social judgment and creativity. The models of Spearman, Guilford, and Gardner describe the content of intelligence, while Sternberg's triarchic theory views intelligence as a process consisting of three components: analytic, creative, and practical.

IQ, as it is measured today through individually administered tests such as the Stanford-Binet and the Wechsler Scales, is closely related to success in school, but not necessarily to success in life. In the past, IQ compared mental age with chronological age, but today these tests compare the individual's performance with average scores for the same age group. IQ scores must be interpreted with caution, because many factors other than intelligence influence scores. Both heredity and environment play a role in intelligence, which is never fixed but is continually open to change.

Ability Differences and Teaching

Academic ability groupings can have both disadvantages and advantages for students and teachers. For low-ability students, however, between-class ability grouping generally has a negative effect on achievement, social adjustment, and self-esteem. Cross-age grouping by subject can be an effective way to deal with ability differences in a school. Within-class ability grouping, if handled sensitively and flexibly, can have positive effects, but alternatives such as cooperative learning are also possible.

Mentally retarded students have significantly below-average intellectual skills and difficulty adapting adequately to social norms. Classification of individuals with retardation has become less tied to IQ measurements than to determination of the level of support needed. Transition programming prepares retarded students to live and work in the community. Gifted students—those who are exceptionally bright, creative, or talented—also may have social adjustment problems and are often unable to fulfill their potential in public schools. Acceleration, enrichment, or out-of-school programs can help meet the needs of exceptionally able students.

Creativity

Creativity is a process that involves independently restructuring problems to see things in new, imaginative ways. Creativity is difficult to measure, but tests of divergent thinking can assess originality, fluency, and flexibility. Teachers can encourage creativity by providing opportunities for play, using brainstorming techniques, and accepting divergent ideas.

Cognitive and Learning Styles

Individuals have characteristic differences in personality, in the way they organize and process information, and in the conditions in which they learn best. Field dependence versus field independence and impulsive versus reflective cognitive styles are examples of these differences. A theme that unites many of the different learning styles is differences between deep and surface processing approaches to learning situations. While cognitive styles and learning preferences are not related to intelligence or effort, they do affect school performance. Applied with caution, learning style inventories can be used to modify instructional strategies and the classroom environment to take advantage of individual differences that help students learn.

Students with Learning Challenges

A disability and a handicap are not the same, and teachers must avoid imposing handicaps on disabled learners. Physically challenged students may rely on orthopedic devices, may have health problems such as epilepsy or cerebral palsy, or may be hearing or vision impaired to varying degrees. Communication disorders include speech impairments (articulation disorders, stuttering, and voicing problems) and oral language disorders. Behavioral and emotional problems include conduct disorders, anxiety-withdrawal, attentional problems/immaturity, motor excess, socialized aggression, and psychotic behavior. Attention-deficit/hyperactivity disorder (ADHD) is the term used to describe individuals of any age with hyperactivity and attention difficulties. Use of medication to address ADHD is controversial, but currently on the rise.

Specific learning disabilities often involve physical, behavioral, and emotional challenges. Learning-disabled students may become victims of learned helplessness when they come to believe that they cannot control or improve their own learning and therefore cannot succeed. A focus on learning strategies often helps students with learning disabilities.

Integration, Mainstreaming, and Inclusion

Public Law 94–142 (1975) requires that each exceptional learner or special-needs student be educated in the least restrictive environment according to an individualized education program. The law also protects the rights of special needs students and their parents. Public Law 99–457 extends the mainstreaming law to preschool-age children, and IDEA, the Individuals with Disabilities Act, extends services to include transition programming for exceptional learners 16 years old and older. The regular education initiative calls for regular classroom teachers to receive training in teaching exceptional learners. Well-developed instructional strategies and technologies exist for helping exceptional students to learn.

KEY TERMS

Americans with Disabilities Act (ADA), p. 146
articulation disorders, p. 139
attention-deficit/hyperactivity disorder, p. 142
automaticity, p. 118
between-class ability grouping, p. 122
brainstorming, p. 132
cerebral palsy, p. 138
cognitive styles, p. 134
components, p. 116
cooperative teaching, p. 150
creativity, p. 129
deviation IQ, p. 119
disability, p. 136
educationally blind, p. 138
epilepsy, p. 137
exceptional students, p. 112
faces of intellect, p. 114
field dependence, p. 134
field independence, p. 134

finger spelling, p. 138
full inclusion, p. 146
generalized seizure, p. 137
gifted student, p. 126
handicap, p. 136
hyperactivity, p. 141
impulsive, p. 134
Individuals with Disabilities Education Act (IDEA), p. 146
individualized education program (IEP), p. 148
insight, p. 117
intelligence, p. 121
intelligence quotient (IQ), p. 119
Joplin Plan, p. 122
learned helplessness, p. 144
learning disability, p. 142
learning preferences, p. 135
learning styles, p. 135
least restrictive placement, p. 146
low vision, p. 138

mainstreaming, p. 146
mental age, p. 119
mental retardation, p. 123
multiple intelligences, p. 115
nongraded elementary school, p. 122
orthopedic devices, p. 137
partial seizure, p. 137
reflective, p. 134
regular education initiative, p. 146
resource room, p. 150
restructuring, p. 129
self-instruction, p. 135
sign language, p. 138
spasticity, p. 138
speech impairment, p. 139
speech reading, p. 138
stuttering, p. 140
transition programming, p. 126
triarchic theory of intelligence, p. 116
voicing problems, p. 140
within-class ability grouping, p. 122

CHECK YOUR UNDERSTANDING

Can you apply the ideas from this chapter on individual differences to solve the following problems of practice?

Preschool and Kindergarten

- A little girl in your kindergarten class seldom speaks. When she does, she usually says only a word or two. She seems to understand when others talk, but almost never responds verbally. How would you approach this situation?

Elementary and Middle School

- The school psychologist tells you that one of your students is going to start taking medication designed to "calm him down." What would you want to know? How would you respond?

- The principal tells you that she is assigning two more students to your class because you are "new, and have more training in full inclusion than the older teachers." One student is retarded and has problems making friends. The other is blind. How will you respond to the principal's decision? How would you prepare your class and modify your teaching for these students?

Junior High and High School

- A student in your fifth-period class is failing. When you look at your grade book, you see that it is the written work that is giving the student trouble. Multiple-choice test scores and class participation are fine. But his writing is hardly legible and very disorganized. Sentences are started and never finished. Ideas fly in and out like frightened birds. How would you identify the source of the problem?

- How would you adapt your teaching to accommodate a hearing-impaired student in your biology lab class?

Cooperative Learning Activity

- Assume the faculty at your school has decided to reconsider how students are assigned to classes. The traditional way in the school has been between-class ability grouping, because your school serves a very wide range of students. Work with four or five members of your educational psychology class to design a new system; then present your recommendations to the entire class. Be prepared to justify your recommendations and explain how you would implement them.

What Would They Do?

Stuffed in your (undersized) mail box in the school office is a large, official-looking envelope. There seems to be one in almost every box. Inside are computer printouts with the results of the fall testing, including scores on a group test of intelligence for all the seventh- and eighth-grade students in your advisory section. Also in your box are notes from two parents who must have already heard that the test results are in. They want to meet with you to see their child's scores, and especially, as one parent put it, "To find out how smart Jason really is." You look at the printouts and at the notes, wondering what you should do with the results.

KELLY L. HOY

Third Grade Teacher
Faber Elementary School, Dunellen, New Jersey

Disclosing individual information about standardized tests is always a ticklish problem. Of course, parents want to know as much as they can about their children, but there are dangers of misinterpreting or misusing information, categorizing and stereotyping children, and invidious comparisons. I would be very careful about disclosing the specifics of IQ test scores to parents.

I certainly would meet with the parents who have written to explain the reasons for IQ testing in our school. Tests are aids to teachers to help us understand how to deal more effectively with our students—to challenge them, to help them, and to have high, but realistic expectations of them. For those parents who persist in wanting to know the results of an IQ test, in an individual conference I would sketch the meaning of IQ and emphasize the notion of multiple intelligences. I would avoid simple numbers and gross indices such as "your child has an IQ of 115." Rather, I would focus on the strengths of the student as I discussed the student's intelligence profile. All of my explanations would be in general terms, such has "your child is better than most of his peers in coping with new experiences, but about average in solving abstract word problems." Again, I would emphasize the positive and use other results to provide suggestions to parents about what they could do to help in areas in which the student seemed less advanced.

This real problem is a challenge because it forces me to do what I should be doing anyway—assessing each student as an individual to determine how strong the academic challenge should be and how much support is needed. The problem compels me to look for strengths while identifying areas where the child may need special help. I believe this process is fundamental to good teaching.

JEFF D. HORTON

Seventh–Twelfth Grade Teacher
Colton School, Colton, Washington

For the most part, intelligence testing can give some information about groups of students. It also can tell where individual students are positioned compared to a group. However, these tests are usually not a good instrument for determining how "smart" a student is or can be.

When presenting intelligence test scores to parents, it is important to be clear about what the information does and does not say. Parents should also be informed that they will be comparing their son(s) or daughter(s) score(s) against a group, not against individual students. This point is very important. Often teachers will be asked to compare one student's work with that of another student. This should never be done. Each student is unique and has a variety of abilities and limitations. Teachers must look at the individual abilities, skills, and knowledge of the student being assessed, as well as that student's effort in the subject(s) being taught. If the parent wants to see the actual scores, it maybe wise to have the school's counselor or an administrator available to help explain the results.

ELIZABETH CHOUINARD

Fourth Grade Teacher
MacGregor Elementary School, Houston, Texas

How smart is Jason? Can a standardized intelligence test give an accurate measure? From my personal experiences with standardized tests, I can say that they are not always accurate. One child might have an advantage over another because he or she has been exposed to that test's format before taking it, and the other child has not. Some students might score high on an intelligence test because they have been trained to use effective test-taking strategies. The students who have not been trained in these test-taking strategies would be at a great disadvantage and their test scores would reflect this.

A third concern is the actual test administration. Although the test would likely be administered using explicit directions, there is no way to ensure that test validity is being maintained. People giving the test could interpret the directions differently, they could follow the directions casually, or they could disregard them altogether. The obvious result would be intelligence scores that are not true reflections of the students involved. In addition, there are numerous emotional and physical factors that could affect test results, including amount of sleep the night before the test, awareness of the importance of the test, and whether there was adequate light in the test area, among others. The test results may not legitimately reflect the child's intelligence level.

With this in mind, I would cautiously analyze the test results and compare the results to other information on the child, such as different tests and classroom experiences. I would share the test results with parents of the children involved. However, I would caution them about possible sources of error in testing. I would also share other pertinent information with the parents that might present a more accurate rating of their child's intelligence level.

5

The Impact of Culture and Community

Overview | *What Would You Do?*

TODAY'S MULTICULTURAL CLASSROOMS   162
   Individuals, Groups, and Society | American Cultural Diversity

SOCIAL CLASS DIFFERENCES   166
   Who Are the Poor? | SES and Achievement

ETHNIC AND RACIAL DIFFERENCES   170
   The Changing Demographics | Cultural Differences | Ethnic and
   Racial Differences in School Achievement | The Legacy
   of Discrimination

WOMEN AND MEN: DIFFERENCES IN THE CLASSROOM   178
   Gender-Role Identity | Sex Differences in Mental Abilities |
   Eliminating Gender Bias

LANGUAGE DIFFERENCES IN THE CLASSROOM   185
   Dialects | Bilingualism

CREATING CULTURALLY COMPATIBLE CLASSROOMS   192
   Social Organization | Learning Styles | Sociolinguistics | Bringing It
   All Together: Teaching Every Student

Summary | *Key Terms* | *Check Your Understanding* |
Teachers' Casebook: What Would They Do?

_W_ere there students in your junior or senior high school who spoke a different language or who were from a different racial or ethnic group than
yours? How did you feel about these "different" students? Were they ever the butt
of jokes in your group? Are you prepared to dedicate yourself to teaching their children and the children of other racial or ethnic groups who may seem even more unlike you?

The face of American classrooms is changing. In this chapter we
examine the many cultures that form the fabric of our society. We
begin by tracing the schools' responses to different
ethnic and cultural groups and consider the concept of multicultural education. With a broad conception of culture as a basis, we then examine
three important dimensions of every student's
identity: social class, ethnicity, and gender.
For each dimension, we will explore the
experiences of the various groups in the
schools, possible differences in achievement and learning styles, and explanations for the lower achievement of some
groups. Then we turn to a consideration of language and bilingual education. The last section of the chapter
presents three general principles for
teaching every student.

By the time you have completed
this chapter you should be able to:

- Compare the notion of the melting pot with views about multicultural education.
- Define _culture_ and list the various groups that make up your own cultural identity.
- Explain why the school achievement of low-income students often falls below
  that of middle- and upper-income students.
- Give examples of conflicts and compatibilities between home and school cultures.
- Describe the school's role in the development of gender differences.
- Describe effective teaching in bilingual classrooms.
- Incorporate multicultural concepts into your teaching.

What Would You Do?

It has been a long week. One of the aides has been out all week with the flu and the weather has kept your 5-year-olds inside three of the last five days. Everyone is a bit tense. The noise level is higher than usual, but even so, you overhear a conversation that disturbs you coming from the block area.

"You can't play here. These toys are for boys and you're a girl. Girls can't build space stations!"

"Yes I can. Yes I can!"

"Go play with the dolls."

"Yeah, this place is for boys—no dumb girls here."

When you reach the block corner, Joshua and Mark are in a tug of war with Chrissy over a large red block. A few other children are watching as you walk up.

- What would you say to Joshua, Mark, and Chrissy?

- How would you help your whole class develop less stereotypic views of boys and girls?

- Do junior and senior high school students hold stereotypic views about gender roles? How do these issues arise among older students?

Today's Multicultural Classrooms

Who are the students in American classrooms today? Here are a few statistics:

- 1 in 4 Americans under the age of 18 lives in poverty. For children under age 3, the number is 1 in 3.
- Nearly 50 percent of all African American children are poor.
- 1 in 3 children lives with a single parent, usually a working mother.
- 15% of the children entering school in 1986 were immigrants who spoke little or no English; 10% had poorly educated or illiterate parents.
- By the year 2020, approximately 54% of all students will be whites and the rest will be students of color, many the children of new immigrants. (Banks, 1997; Grant & Sleeter, 1989; *Teacher Magazine,* April 1991)

Individuals, Groups, and Society

Since the beginning of the twentieth century, a flow of immigrants has entered the United Kingdom, western Europe, Canada, Australia, the United States, and many other developed countries. These new immigrants were expected to assimilate—that is, to enter the cultural **melting pot** and become like those who had arrived earlier. For years, the goal of American schools was to be the fire under the melting pot. Immigrant children who spoke different languages and had different religious and cultural heritages were expected to come to the schools, master standard English, and learn to become mainstream Americans.

In the 1960s and 1970s, some educators suggested that minority-group and poor students had problems in school because they had not fully "melted" or assimilated into mainstream American life. The students were described as

Melting Pot A metaphor for the absorption and assimilation of immigrants into the mainstream of society so that ethnic differences vanish.

"culturally disadvantaged" or "culturally handicapped." The assumption of this **cultural deficit model** was that the students' home culture was inferior because it had not prepared them to fit into the schools. Today most people reject the idea of cultural deficits. They believe that no culture is deficient, but rather that there may be incompatibilities between the student's home culture and the expectations of the school.

Also during the 1960s and 1970s, there was growing concern for civil and human rights and an increasing sense among many ethnic groups that they did not want to assimilate completely into mainstream American society. Rather, they wanted to maintain their culture and identity while still being a respected part of the larger society. Multicultural education is one response to the increasing diversity of the school population as well as to the growing demand for equality for all groups.

There are many definitions of and disagreements about **multicultural education.** A narrow definition of multicultural education is the expansion of educational curricula and activities to include the perspectives, histories, accomplishments, and concerns of non-European people (Hilliard, 1991/92). A broader conception of multicultural education is that "all students, regardless of the groups to which they belong, groups such as those related to gender, ethnicity, race, culture, social class, religion, or exceptionality, should experience educational equality in the schools" (Banks, 1993, p. 24). An examination of the alternative approaches to multicultural education is beyond the scope of an educational psychology text, but be aware that there is no general agreement about the "best" approach, as you can see in the Point/Counterpoint section on page 164.

James Banks (1994) suggests that multicultural education has five dimensions, as shown in Figure 5.1 on page 165. Many people are familiar only with the dimension of *content integration,* using examples and content from a variety of cultures when teaching a subject. Because they believe that multicultural education is simply a change in curriculum, many people assume that it is irrelevant for subjects such as science and mathematics. But if you consider the other four dimensions—helping students understand how knowledge is influenced by beliefs, reducing prejudice, creating social structures in schools that support learning and development for all students, and using teaching methods that reach all students—then you will see that this view of multicultural education is relevant to all subjects and all students.

Multicultural education rejects the idea of the melting pot. According to the multicultural ideal, America should be transformed into a society that values diversity (Banks, 1997; Casanova, 1987; Sleeter, 1995). Let's take a closer look at the differences that make up the mosaic of cultural diversity.

American Cultural Diversity

In this text we take a broad interpretation of culture and multicultural education, so we will examine social class, race, ethnicity, and gender as aspects of diversity. We begin with a look at the meaning of culture. Many people associate this concept with the "cultural events" section of the newspaper—art galleries, museums, Shakespeare, classical music, and so on. Culture has a much broader meaning; it embraces the whole way of life of a group of people.

Cultural Deficit Model A model that explains the school achievement problems of ethnic minority students by assuming that their culture is inadequate and does not prepare them to succeed in school.

Multicultural Education Education that teaches the value of cultural diversity.

Should Multicultural Education Emphasize Similarities or Differences?

In principle, virtually all of the experts who have studied, advocated, and criticized the various forms of multicultural education now taking shape in the United States agree on one point: Such education should provide students with a fuller, more balanced truth about their own history and culture than they have had up to now" (Viadero, 1990, p. 14). The question is how. Should education emphasize the similarities or the differences among people?

POINT Emphasize what is common among all students (traditional approaches).

Richard Rodriguez (1987), a well-known contemporary writer and editor, made a case for emphasizing what is common to all citizens in his criticism of a report by the Study Commission on Global Education:

Few words issue from the commission's 52-page report with more frequency or less precision than does the word, "diversity." The dilemma of our national diversity becomes, with a little choke on logic, the solution: American educators "must understand diversity." "Appreciate diversity." "Deal constructively with diversity." Pay "greater attention to . . . diversity . . . around the world and within the United States. . . ." Diversity is a liquid noun. Diversity admits everything, stands for nothing. . . .

I do not agree that the primary purpose of early education is to teach diversity. I believe something closer to the reverse—that education's primary purpose, its distinguishing obligation, is to foster commonality. It is in the classroom that the child comes to learn a public identity. The child learns the skills of numbers and words crucial to public survival, and learns to put on a public self, apart from family or ethnic community.

I submit that America is not a tale for sentimentalists. I read writings of 18th-century white men who powdered their wigs and kept slaves, because they were the men who shaped the country that shapes my life. I am brown and of Mexican ancestry, one generation into this country. I claim Thomas Jefferson as a cultural forefather.

COUNTERPOINT Emphasize diversity (ethnocentric approaches).

In response to Rodriguez's position, Alba Rosenman (1987) believes:

Education that values cultural diversity does not say that "diversity admits everything and stands for nothing," as Mr. Rodriguez puts it, but rather that a culture is not wrong because it is different. Knowledge of other societies and customs gives students choices that may be more meaningful to them than those offered in our society. It is possible that there are other and better ways to live than those we have grown to know and love. We might yet learn something from that imprecise mass called American "diversity." . . . A multicultural curriculum tries, while valuing differences, to teach a fair curriculum to students with diverse backgrounds. There is no threat to society here, simply a relevant education.

Rosenman agrees with Rodriguez that "the primary purpose of an early education should not be to 'teach diversity.' Its primary purposes are to teach students that in school they will learn how to survive in our society and to solidify their feelings of worth."

James Banks (1993) suggests that the notion that multicultural education will divide the nation "assumes that the nation is already united. While we are one nation politically, sociologically our nation is deeply divided along lines of race, gender, and class" (p. 23).

Sources: From "What Is an American Education?" by Richard Rodriguez. Copyright © 1987 by Richard Rodriguez. Reprinted by permission of Georges Borchardt, Inc. for the author. Reprinted with permission from Alba A. Rosenman (November 11, 1987). "The Value of Multicultural Curricula." *Education Week,* 7(10).

Culture The knowledge, values, attitudes, and traditions that guide the behavior of a group of people and allow them to solve the problems of living in their environment.

Culture and Group Membership. There are many definitions of **culture.** Most include the knowledge, rules, traditions, attitudes, and values that guide behavior in a particular group of people (Betancourt & Lopez, 1993). The group creates a culture—a program for living—and communicates the culture to members. Thus people are members of groups, they are not members of cultures. Groups can be defined along regional, ethnic, religious, racial, gender, social class, or other lines. Each of us is a member of many groups, so we all

FIGURE 5.1

Banks's Dimensions of Multicultural Education

Multicultural education is more than a change in the curriculum. To make education appropriate for all students, we must consider other dimensions as well. The way the athletics and counseling programs are structured, the teaching method used, lessons about prejudice, perspectives on knowledge—these and many more elements contribute to true multicultural education.

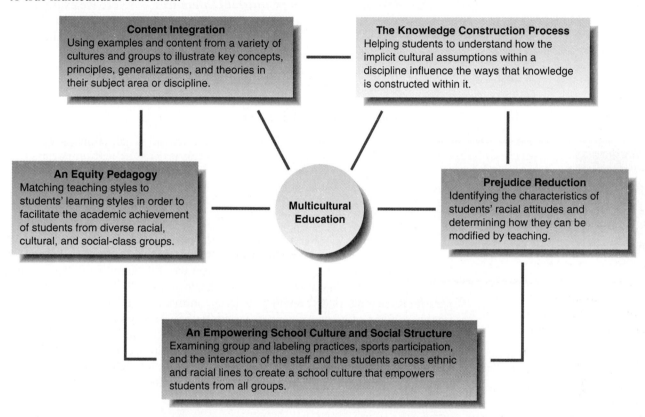

Source: From James A. Banks (1994). *Multiethnic education: Theory and practice,* 3/e, p. 5. Boston: Allyn & Bacon. Adapted with the permission of the author and the publisher.

are influenced by many different cultures. Sometimes the influences are incompatible or even contradictory. For example, if you are a feminist but also a Roman Catholic, you may have trouble reconciling the two different cultures' beliefs about the ordination of women as priests. Your personal belief will be based, in part, on how strongly you identify with each group (Banks, 1994).

There are many different cultures, of course, in every modern country. In the United States, students growing up in a small rural town in the Deep South are part of a cultural group that is very different from that of students in a large urban center or students in a West Coast suburb. In Canada, students living in the suburbs of Toronto certainly differ in a number of ways from students growing up in a Montreal high-rise apartment or on a farm in Quebec. Within those small towns in the Deep South or Quebec, the child of a gas station attendant grows up in a different culture from the child of the town doctor or dentist.

Individuals of African, Asian, Hispanic, Native American, or European descent have distinctive histories and traditions. The experiences of males and females are different in most ethnic and economic groups. Everyone living within a particular country shares many common experiences and values, especially because of the influence of the mass media. But other aspects of their lives are shaped by differing cultural backgrounds.

Cautions in Interpreting Cultural Differences. Before we examine the bases for cultural differences, two cautions are necessary. First, we will consider social class, ethnicity, and gender separately, because much of the available research focuses on only one of these variables. Of course, real children are not just African American, or middle class, or female; they are complex beings and members of many groups.

The second caution comes from James Banks (1993), who has written several books on multicultural education:

> Although membership in a gender, racial, ethnic, social-class, or religious group can provide us with important clues about an individual's behavior, it cannot enable us to predict behavior. . . . *Membership in a particular group does not determine behavior but makes certain types of behavior more probable.* (pp. 13–14)

Keep this in mind as you read about characteristics of economically disadvantaged students or Asian Americans or males. The information we will examine reflects tendencies and probabilities. It does not tell you about a specific person. Remember that you will be teaching individual students. Each child is a unique product of many influences, a member of a variety of groups. For example, if a minority-group student in your class consistently arrives late, you should not assume that the student's behavior reflects a cultural difference in beliefs about punctuality. It may be that the student has a job before school or must walk a long distance, or even that he or she hates school.

Focus on...

Multicultural Classrooms

- What group memberships particularly influence your identity?
- Explain the five aspects of multicultural education.

Social Class Differences

The term used by sociologists for variations in wealth, power, and prestige is **socioeconomic status,** or **SES.** In modern societies, levels of wealth, power, and prestige are not always consistent. Some people—for instance, university professors—are members of professions that are reasonably prestigious but provide little wealth or power. Other people have political power though they are not wealthy. No single variable, not even income, is an effective measure of SES. In spite of these inconsistencies, most researchers identify four general levels of SES: upper, middle, working, and lower. The main characteristics of these four levels are summarized in Table 5.1.

Social class is a powerful dimension of cultural differences, often overpowering other differences such as ethnicity or gender. For example, upper-class Anglo-Europeans, African Americans, and Hispanic Americans typically find that they have more in common with each other than they have with lower-class individuals from their own ethnic groups. (Gollnick & Chinn, 1994).

Socioeconomic Status (SES) Relative standing in the society based on income, power, background, and prestige.

	Upper Class	Middle Class	Working Class	Lower Class
Income	$100,000+	$40,000–$100,00 (1/3) $25,000–$39,999 (2/3)	$12,000–$40,000	Below $12,000
Occupation	Corporate, professional, family money	White-collar, skilled blue-collar	Blue-collar	Minimum-wage unskilled labor
Education	Prestigious colleges and professional schools	High school, college, or professional school	High school	High school or less
Home ownership	At least one home	Usually own home	About half own a home	No
Health coverage	Full	Usually	Limited	No
Neighborhoods	Exclusive or comfortable	Comfortable	Modest	Deteriorating
Afford children's college	Easily	Usually	Seldom	No
Political power	National, state, or local	State or local	Limited	No

TABLE 5.1   Selected Characteristics of Different Social Classes

Source: Information from J. J. Macionis (1993), *Sociology,* 4th ed. (Saddle River, NJ: Prentice-Hall), pp. 270–274.

Who Are the Poor?

Over one in four Americans under the age of 18 lives in poverty, defined in 1990 as an income below $13,359 for a family of four living in an urban area (Macionis, 1994). But these percentages don't tell the whole story. As you can see in Figure 5.2 on page 168, the absolute number of poor children will increase substantially. By 2020, schools will have to teach 5.4 million more poor students than they taught in 1984. The United States has the highest rate of poverty for children of all developed nations, as much as three times higher than most other industrialized countries. And these children are not concentrated in the inner cities. Twice as many poor children live outside large urban areas as within them (Reed & Sautter, 1990).

The majority of these poor children, about 65 percent, are white, because the total number of poor white families is greater than any other ethnic group. But even though the total number of poor African American and Hispanic American children is smaller than the number of poor white children, the percentages are higher. About 36% of all Hispanic American children and 44% of all African American children live in poverty. Compare this to an overall poverty rate of 20% for all children in the United States (Macionis, 1994).

SES and Achievement

There are many relationships between SES and school performance. For example, it is well documented that high-SES students of all ethnic groups show higher average levels of achievement on test scores and stay in school longer than low-SES students (Alwin & Thornton, 1984; Goleman, 1988; White, 1982).

FIGURE 5.2

Projected Number of Children in Poverty

The number of children who live in poverty in the United States grows each year and is projected to reach 20 million by the year 2020.

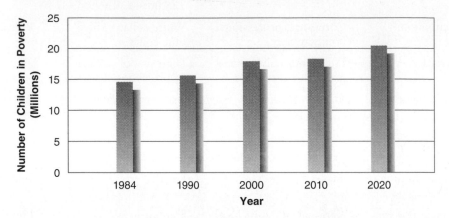

Source: From A. M. Pallas, G. Natriello, and E. L. McDill. "The changing nature of the disadvantaged population: Current dimensions and future trends." *Educational Researcher,* *18* (5), Figure p. 19. Copyright 1989 by the American Educational Research Association. Reprinted by permission of the publisher.

When SES is measured solely in terms of parents' education, income, or occupation, the relationship between SES and achievement is weaker. But when SES is measured in terms that include family atmosphere variables such as parents' attitudes toward education, their aspirations for their children, or the intellectual activities of the family, then the correlation is stronger (Laosa, 1984; Peng & Lee, 1992; White, 1982). This is an encouraging result. It indicates that lack of income may not be as important for school achievement as the actual attitudes and behaviors of the child's family life. In fact, many families with limited incomes do an excellent job of supporting their children's learning.

What are the effects of low socioeconomic status that might explain the lower school achievement of these low-SES students? Many factors maintain a cycle of poverty. Poor health care for mother and child, limited resources, family stress, interruptions in schooling, discrimination, and other factors lead to school failures, low-paying jobs—and another generation born in poverty. Garcia (1991), while cautioning that research on this question is meager, lists five other possible explanations. Let's take a closer look at each of them.

Low Expectations—Low Self-Esteem.   Because low-SES students may wear old clothes, speak ungrammatically, or be less familiar with books and school activities, teachers and other students may assume that these students are not bright. The teacher may avoid calling on them to protect them from the embarrassment of giving wrong answers or because they make the teacher uncomfortable. The children come to believe that they aren't very good at schoolwork (Elrich, 1994). The following true story shows how powerful this effect on self-esteem can be. Terrence Quinn, principal of an elementary school in New York, spends his mornings serving coffee and doughnuts in a welfare hotel six blocks from his school, trying to convince parents to send their children to school.

> Last spring, Jacqueline, a sixth-grader who had lived at the hotel, was se-
> lected as the school's valedictorian. One month before the official announce-
> ment, she entered Quinn's office and asked to speak to him in private.
> "Can someone on welfare actually be the valedictorian?" she asked. Quinn
> reassured Jacqueline, a youngster who has overcome many obstacles. . . .
> Why should a child such as Jacqueline feel so humiliated and ashamed of
> her predicament? (Reed & Sautter, 1990, p. K2)

Learned Helplessness.   Low-SES children may be the victims of learned helplessness, described in the previous chapter. That is, low-SES students (or any students who fail continually) may come to believe that doing well in school is hopeless. Many of their friends and relatives never finished school, so it seems normal to quit. In fact, about one-fourth of children from poor families drop out of school (Bennett, 1995). Without a high school diploma, these students find few rewards awaiting them in the work world. Many available jobs barely pay a living wage. If the head of a family of three works full time at the minimum wage, the family's income will still be below the poverty line (Reed & Sautter, 1990). Low-SES children, particularly those who also encounter racial discrimination, "become convinced that it is difficult if not impossible for them to advance in the mainstream by doing well in school" (Goleman, 1988).

Resistance Cultures.   Some researchers have suggested that low-SES students may become part of a **resistance culture.** To members of this culture, making it in school means selling out and trying to act "middle class." In order to maintain their identity and their status within the group, low-SES students must reject the behaviors that would make them successful in school—studying, cooperating with teachers, even coming to class (Bennett, 1995; Ogbu, 1987). John Ogbu linked identification in a resistance culture to poor Hispanic American, Native American, and African American groups, but similar reactions have been noted for poor white students both in the United States and in England (Willis, 1977).

Tracking.   Another explanation for the lower achievement of many low-SES students is that these students experience a different academic socialization, that is, they are actually taught differently. If they are tracked into "low-ability" or "general" classes, they may be taught to memorize and be passive. Their classes may be low-level and teacher-dominated. Middle-class students are more likely to be encouraged to think and create in their classes (Anyon, 1980). When low-SES students receive an inferior education, their academic skills are inferior and their life chances are limited. In an interview with Marge Scherer, Jonathan Kozol described the cruel predictive side of tracking:

> [T]racking is so utterly predictive. The little girl who gets shoved into the
> low reading group in 2nd grade is very likely to be the child who is urged
> to take cosmetology instead of algebra in the 8th grade, and most likely to
> be in vocational courses, not college courses, in the 10th grade, if she hasn't
> dropped out by then. (Scherer, 1993, p. 8)

Resistance Culture Group values and beliefs about refusing to adopt the behaviors and attitudes of the majority culture.

When families stress the value of reading, studying, and learning, their children are usually at an advantage in school.

Childrearing Styles.   The oldest explanation for the academic problems of low-SES children is that their home environment does not give them the head start in school provided by middle- and upper-class homes. Adjustment to school may be more difficult for these children, because schools tend to value and expect the behaviors more often taught in middle-class homes. Let's take a closer look at this last explanation.

Studies have shown that middle-class mothers talk more; give more verbal guidance; help their children understand the causes of events, make plans, and anticipate consequences; direct their children's attention to the relevant details of a problem; and, rather than impose solutions, encourage children to solve problems themselves (Hess & Shipman, 1965; L. Hoffman, 1984; Willerman, 1979). By assisting their children in these ways, mothers are actually following Vygotsky's advice to provide intellectual support, or scaffolding, in the children's zone of proximal development, as we discussed in Chapter 2. Contrast these two interactions as a mother works with a child on a puzzle:

> "What shape is that piece? Can you find a spot that is straight like the piece? Yes, that's straight, but look at the color. Does the color match? No? Look again for a straight, red piece. Yes—try that one. Good for you! You finished the corner."

> "No, that piece goes here!"

You can see how the first approach is more likely to encourage learning concepts (straight, shape, color, corner, match) and problem solving. Hess and McDevitt (1984) studied mothers and children over an eight-year period and found evidence that this "teaching as opposed to telling" style, often used by middle-class mothers, is related to higher achievement test scores for children ages 4 through 12. These differences in parental interaction styles may account for some of the differences among children from various SES groups.

You should be wary, however, of prejudging families based on their socioeconomic status. Many low-income families provide a rich learning environment for their children. When parents of any SES level support and encourage their children—by reading to them, providing books and educational toys, taking the children to the library, making time and space for learning—the children tend to become better, more enthusiastic readers (Morrow, 1983; Peng & Lee, 1992; Shields, Gordon, & Dupree, 1983). Remember, White (1982) found that the actual behaviors of the parents were more predictive of their children's school achievement than income level or parents' occupation.

Focus on...

Social Class Differences

■ Define socioeconomic status (SES).

■ Why might children from lower SES backgrounds have greater difficulties in school?

Ethnicity A cultural heritage shared by a group of people.

Race A group of people who share common biological traits that are seen as self-defining by the people of the group.

Ethnic and Racial Differences

Ethnicity is used to refer to "groups that are characterized in terms of a common nationality, culture, or language" (Betancourt & Lopez, 1993, p. 631). This shared sense of identity may be based on geography, religion, race, or language. We all have some ethnic heritage, whether our background is Italian, Jewish, Ukrainian, Hmong, Chinese, Japanese, Navajo, Hawaiian, Puerto Rican, Cuban, Eskimo, German, African, or Irish—to name only a few. **Race,** on the other hand, is defined as "a category composed of men and women who share biologically transmitted traits that are defined as socially significant" such as skin color or hair texture (Macionis, 1991, p. 308). Depending on the traits you measure and the theory you follow, there are between 3 and 300 races. In effect, race is a label people apply to themselves and to others based on appearances. There are no biologically pure races (Betancourt & Lopez, 1993).

Sociologists sometimes use the term **minority group** to label a group of people that receives unequal or discriminatory treatment. Strictly speaking, however, the term refers to a numerical minority compared to the total population. Referring to particular racial or ethnic groups as "minorities" is technically incorrect in some situations, because in certain places the "minority" group is actually the majority, for example, African Americans in Chicago or Mississippi. So the practice of referring to people as "minorities" because of their racial or ethnic heritage has been criticized because it is misleading—sometimes the "minority" is the "majority."

The Changing Demographics

Between 1981 and 1990, the number of immigrants entering the United States was the largest ever. Results of the 1990 census, shown in Table 5.2, reveal that the number of ethnic Americans has increased substantially. By the year 2020, almost half of the population of the country will be from African American, Asian, Hispanic, or other ethnic groups.

Cultural Differences

Ricardo Garcia (1991) compares culture to an iceberg. One-third of the iceberg is visible; the rest is hidden and unknown. The visible signs of culture, such as costumes and marriage traditions, represent only a small portion of the differences among cultures. Many of the differences are "below the surface." They are implicit, unstated, even unconscious biases and beliefs. Each cultural group teaches its members certain "lessons" about living (Casanova, 1987; Kagan, 1983).

Cultures differ in rules for conducting interpersonal relationships, for example. In some groups listeners give a slight affirmative nod of the head and perhaps an occasional "uh huh" to indicate they are listening carefully. But members of other cultures listen without giving acknowledgment, or with eyes downcast, as a sign of respect. In some cultures high-status individuals initiate

TABLE 5.2 Results of the 1990 Census for Selected Ethnic Groups

Group	Total Number	Increase Since 1980
African American	30.0 million	13.2%
Asian	7.3 million	107.8%
Native American	2.0 million	37.9%
Hispanic	22.4 million	53.0%
Other	9.8 million	

Source: U.S. Bureau of the Census, 1990.

Minority Group A group of people who have been socially disadvantaged—not always a minority in actual numbers.

The visible signs of cultural differences represent only a small portion of the differences among cultures. Many are "below the surface" and have more to do with beliefs and attitudes about life.

conversations and ask the questions, and low-status individuals only respond. In other cultures, the pattern is reversed.

Cultural influences are widespread and pervasive. Some psychologists even suggest that culture defines intelligence. For example, physical grace is essential in Balinese social life, so the ability to master physical movements is a mark of intelligence in that culture. Manipulating words and numbers is important in Western societies, so in these cultures such skills are indicators of intelligence (Gardner, 1983).

Cultural Conflicts.   The above are just a few areas where cultures may teach different lessons about living. The differences may be very obvious, such as holiday customs, or they may be very subtle, such as how to get your turn in conversations. The more subtle and unconscious the difference, the more difficult it is to change or even recognize (Casanova, 1987). Cultural conflicts are usually about below-the-surface differences, because when subtle cultural differences meet, misunderstandings are common. Thus, the members of a different culture may be misperceived as rude, slow, or disrespectful.

For example, Erickson and Shultz (1982) studied school counselors working with students from the same culture and students from different cultures. The researchers found that the culturally different students did not nod and say "uh huh" as they listened to the counselors. Not having received this expected feedback, the counselors assumed that the culturally different students had not understood, and so the counselors repeated their remarks in simpler form. Again no nod, so the counselors simplified and repeated once more. When the students were interviewed afterwards, many said that the counselors had made them feel stupid. In fact, the counselors had decided that these students were not very bright. Neither participant realized that a subtle cultural difference in how to listen was probably to blame for the impressions. In contrast, when students and counselors shared the same background, discussions proceeded smoothly, without the cycles of simplifying and repeating. The students knew the counselors' tacit rules for listening, because both counselor and student had learned from the same teacher—their common culture.

Cultural Compatibility.   Not all cultural differences lead to clashes, however. A study comparing mothers in the People's Republic of China, Chinese-American mothers, and Caucasian-American mothers found dramatic differences in beliefs about motivation and the value of education (Hess, Chih-Mei, & McDevitt, 1987). For example, the mothers from the Republic of China attributed school failure to lack of effort more often than the Caucasian-American mothers. The Chinese-American mothers were in the middle, attributing failure to lack of effort more often than the Caucasian-American mothers but less often than the Republic of China mothers.

This does not mean that all Chinese-American children are perfectly equipped for the American school, however. Children may perform well on tests and assignments but feel uncomfortable in social situations, where subtle rules for interacting are not second nature to them (Casanova, 1987; Yee, 1992).

Working with Families and Communities.   How can you get to know the cultures of your students? The Guidelines give some ideas. Later in this chapter, we will explore other ways to make classrooms compatible with the home cultures of students. First, however, we need to see some of the effects of cultural conflicts and discrimination on student achievement.

Guidelines

Family and Community Partnerships for Building Learning Communities

Joyce Epstein (1995) describes six types of family/school/community partnerships. The guidelines below are based on her six categories:

Parenting Partnerships: Help all families establish home environments to support children as students.

Examples

1. Offer workshops, videos, courses, family literacy fairs, and other informational programs to help parents cope with parenting situations that they identify as important.
2. Establish family support programs to assist with nutrition, health, and social services.
3. Find ways to help families share information with the school about the child's cultural background, talents, and needs—learn from the families.

Communication: Design effective forms for school-to-home and home-to-school communication.

1. Make sure communications fit the needs of families. Provide translations, visual support, large print—whatever is needed to make communication effective.
2. Visit families in their territory after gaining their permission. Don't expect family members to come to school until a trusting relationship is established.

(continued)

3. Balance messages about problems with communications of accomplishments and positive information.

Volunteering: Recruit and organize parent help and support.

Examples

1. Do an annual postcard survey to identify family talents, interests, times available, and suggestions for improvements.

2. Establish a structure (telephone tree, etc.) to keep all families informed. Make sure families without telephones are included.

3. If possible, set aside a room for volunteer meetings and projects.

Learning at home: Provide information and ideas for families about how to help children with schoolwork and learning activities.

Examples

1. Provide assignment schedules, homework policies, and tips on how to help with schoolwork without doing the work.

2. Get family input into curriculum planning—have idea and activity exchanges.

3. Send home learning packets and enjoyable learning activities, especially over holidays and summers.

Decision-making partnerships: Include families in school decisions, developing family and community leaders and representatives.

Examples

1. Create family advisory committees for the school with parent representatives.

2. Make sure all families are in a network with their representative.

Community partnerships: Identify and integrate resources and services from the community to strengthen school programs, family practices, and student learning and development.

Examples

1. Have students and parents research existing resources—build a database.

2. Identify service projects for students—explore service learning.

3. Identify community members who are school alumni and get them involved in school programs.

Source: From Joyce L. Epstein. "School/Family/Community partnerships: Caring for the children we share." *Phi Delta Kappan,* 76, pp. 704–705. Copyright © 1995 by Phi Delta Kappan. Reprinted by permission of Phi Delta Kappan and the author.

Ethnic and Racial Differences in School Achievement

A major concern in schools is that some ethnic groups consistently achieve below the average for all students. This pattern of results tends to hold for all standardized achievement tests, but the gaps have been narrowing over the past two to three decades, as shown in Figure 5.3.

FIGURE 5.3

White–Minority Difference in Math Achievement of 17-Year-Olds

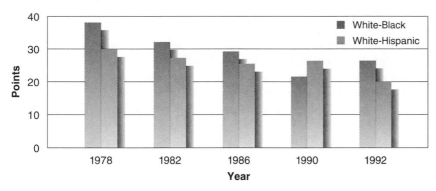

Source: National Center for Education Statistics (1994). *The Condition of Education.* Washington, D.C.: National Center for Education Statistics, U.S. Department of Education, p. VI.

Although there are consistent differences among ethnic groups on tests of cognitive abilities, most researchers agree that these differences are mainly the legacy of discrimination, the product of cultural mismatches, or a result of growing up in a low-SES environment. Because many minority-group students are also economically disadvantaged, it is important to separate the effects of these two sets of influences on school achievement. When we compare students from different ethnic and racial groups who are all at the same SES level, then their achievement differences diminish (Gleitman, 1991; Scarr & Carter-Saltzman, 1982).

The Legacy of Discrimination

When we considered explanations for why low-SES students have trouble in school, we listed the low expectations and biases of teachers and fellow students. This has been the experience of many ethnic minority students as well. Imagine that the child described below is your own. What would you do?

> Almost forty years ago, in the city of Topeka, Kansas, a minister walked hand in hand with his seven-year-old daughter to an elementary school four blocks from their home. Linda Brown wanted to enroll in the second grade, but the school refused to admit her. Instead, public school officials required her to attend another school two miles away. This meant that she had to walk six blocks to a bus stop, where she sometimes waited half an hour for the bus. In bad weather, Linda Brown would be soaking wet by the time the bus came; one day she became so cold at the bus stop that she walked back home. Why, she asked her parents, could she not attend the school only four blocks away? (Macionis, 1991, p. 307)

Her parents' answer to this question, with the help of other concerned families, was to file a suit challenging the school policy. You know the outcome of *Brown* v. *the Board of Education of Topeka.* "Separate but equal" schools for black children were declared inherently unequal. Even though segregation in schools became illegal in 1954, about two-thirds of all African American students still attend schools where members of minority groups make up at least

Nine-year-old Linda Brown, the plaintiff in Brown *v.* Topeka Board of Education.

50% of the student body. For about one-third of all black students, this figure is over 90% (Schofield, 1991). This is because segregation in housing and neighborhoods persists and because some areas have drawn school boundary lines deliberately to separate school enrollments along racial lines (Calmore, 1986; Kantor & Lowe, 1995).

Years of research on the effects of desegregation have mostly shown that legally mandated integration is not a quick solution to the detrimental effects of centuries of racial inequality. Too often, minority-group students are resegregated in low-ability tracks even in integrated schools. Simply putting people in the same building does not mean that they will come to respect each other or even that they will experience the same quality of education (Schofield, 1991). But when minority-group students are moved into high quality schools with a substantial proportion of middle-class peers and when these integrations start in early elementary school, the ethnic minority students benefit. They are more likely to achieve higher grades, attend integrated colleges, and earn more money as adults than comparable students who stayed in segregated schools. The quality of the school probably is the major factor influencing these positive outcomes (Schofield, 1995; Wells & Crain, 1994)

What is the legacy of unequal treatment and discrimination? Part of the testimony during the *Brown* v. *Board of Education* case in the 1950s was that when black children in a study were asked to pick the more attractive or smarter doll, they usually chose a white doll and rejected a black one. This test was repeated in 1990 with the same results (Pine & Hilliard, 1990).

Continuing Prejudice. The word *prejudice* is closely related to the word *prejudge*. **Prejudice** is a rigid and irrational generalization—a prejudgment—about an entire category of people (Macionis, 1994). Prejudice may be positive or negative, that is, you can have positive as well as negative irrational beliefs about a group, but the word usually refers to negative attitudes. Prejudice may target people in particular racial, ethnic, religious, political, geographic, or language groups, or it may be directed toward the sex or sexual orientation of the individual. Racial prejudice is pervasive. A 1991 survey by the National Opinion Research Center found that even though racial attitudes had improved somewhat since 1970, most of the groups surveyed felt at least some prejudice against all the other groups. For example, 78% of non-Hispanic Americans (whites, blacks, and Asian Americans) agreed with the statement that Hispanic Americans prefer to live off welfare, and 55% believed that Hispanic Americans are less intelligent. The results were virtually the same when whites were asked their opinions of African Americans. The United States is a racist society, and this racism is not confined to one group.

The Development of Prejudice. There are many theories about how and why prejudice develops. The different theories of prejudice focus on a wide variety of specific and different causal factors—and no framework has yet been proposed that provides a complete explanation of prejudice" (Duckitt, 1992, p. 1182). Current explanations of prejudice combine personal and social factors. Extreme prejudice may develop as part of an **authoritarian personality**— a person who rigidly conforms to conventional values and believes that society is naturally competitive, with the "better" people rightly reaping the rewards

Children do not instinctively dislike or mistrust people; they learn such attitudes from the words and actions of family and friends.

Prejudice Prejudgment, or irrational generalization about an entire category of people.

Authoritarian Personality Rigidly conforming to belief that society is naturally competitive, with "better" people reaping its rewards.

(Duckitt, 1992, 1994; Macionis, 1994). But prejudice is more than a personality trait—it is also a set of cultural values. Children learn about valued traits and characteristics from their families, friends, teachers, and the world around them. For years, most of the models presented in books, films, television, and advertising were middle- and upper-class European Americans. People of different ethnic and racial backgrounds were seldom the "heroes" (Gerbner, Gross, Signorelli, & Morgan, 1986). This is changing.

Prejudice is difficult to combat because it can be part of our thinking processes. You saw in Chapter 2 that children develop *schemas*—organized bodies of knowledge—about objects, events, and actions. We have schemas that organize our knowledge about drinking from a straw, people we know, the meaning of words, and so on. We can also form schemas about groups of people. If I were to ask you to list the traits most characteristic of college freshman, politicians, African Americans, Asian Americans, athletes, Buddhists, lesbians, or members of the National Rifle Association, you probably could generate a list. That list would show that you have a **stereotype**—a schema—that organizes what you know about the group (Wyler, 1988).

As with any schema, we use our stereotype to make sense of the world. You will see in Chapter 7 that having a schema allows you to process information more quickly and efficiently, but it also allows you to distort information to make it fit your schema better. This is the danger in racial and ethnic stereotypes. We notice information that confirms or agrees with our stereotype—our schema—and miss or dismiss information that does not fit. For example, if a juror has a negative stereotype of Asian Americans and is listening to evidence in the trial of an Asian American, the juror may interpret the evidence more negatively. The juror may actually forget testimony in favor of the defendant but remember more damaging testimony. Information that fits the stereotype is even processed more quickly (Anderson, Klatzky, & Murray, 1990; Baron, 1992).

Continuing Discrimination.   Prejudice consists of attitudes, feelings, and beliefs (usually negative) about an entire category of people. **Discrimination** is behavior, treating particular categories of people unequally. Clearly, ethnic Americans face prejudice and discrimination in subtle or blatant ways every day. One of the most discouraging findings I encountered while writing this chapter is that only 4% of the scientists, engineers, and mathematicians in the United States are either African American or Hispanic American—whereas more than 20% of the total population is from one of these groups. Even though their attitudes toward science and math are more favorable than the attitudes of white students, black and Hispanic students begin to lose out in science and math as early as elementary school. They are chosen less often for gifted classes and acceleration or enrichment programs. They are more likely to be tracked into "basic skills" classes. As they progress through junior high, high school, and college, their paths take them farther and farther out of the pipeline that produces our scientists. If they do persist and become scientists or engineers, they, along with women, will still be paid less than whites for the same work (National Science Foundation, 1988; Oakes, 1990).

> **Focus on...**
>
> ## Ethnic and Racial Differences
>
> - Explain how prejudice might develop.
> - Distinguish between prejudice and discrimination.
> - Describe some effects of discrimination.

Stereotype Schema that organizes knowledge or perceptions about a category.

Discrimination Treating particular categories of people unequally.

Prejudice and discrimination may cause particular problems for people of color in America. Stanley Gaines and Edward Reed (1995) describe

> a painful dilemma that every African American eventually must face: How do I tend to my unmistakably American self-oriented needs (i.e., individualistic strivings) while at the same time attend to my time-honored African, group-oriented needs (i.e., collectivist strivings)? (p. 102)

Gaines and Reed suggest that such choices and dilemmas are not part of the experience of European Americans. This message, "delivered to African Americans by a predominantly European American society, that African Americans must choose between White or Black" is "a choice they cannot win" (Gaines & Reed, 1995, p. 102).

Women and Men: Differences in the Classroom

While I was proofreading this very page for a previous edition, riding cross-country on a train, the conductor stopped beside my seat. He said, "I'm sorry, dear, for interrupting your homework, but do you have a ticket?" I had to smile at his (I'm sure unintended) sexism. I doubt that he made the same comment to the man across the aisle writing on his legal pad. Like racial discrimination, messages of sexism can be subtle. In this section we will examine how men and women are socialized and the role of teachers in providing an equitable education for both sexes.

Gender-Role Identity

Men and women are different. Years of research on personality indicates that men *on average* are more assertive and have slightly higher self-esteem than women. Women are more extroverted, anxious, trusting, and tender-minded (Feingold, 1994). There also appear to be some differences in spatial abilities between the sexes. The origins and meanings of these differences are hotly debated. Gender-role identify is part of the discussion.

The word *gender* usually refers to judgments about masculinity and femininity, judgments that are influenced by culture and context. In contrast, *sex* refers to biological differences (Deaux, 1993). **Gender-role identity** is the image each individual has of him- or herself as masculine or feminine in characteristics—a part of self-concept. People with a "feminine" identity would rate themselves high on characteristics usually associated with females, such as "sensitive" or "warm," and low on characteristics traditionally associated with males, such as "forceful" and "competitive." Most people see themselves in gender-typed terms, as high on *either* masculine or feminine characteristics. Some children and adults, however, are more **androgynous**—they rate themselves high on *both* masculine and feminine traits. They can be assertive or sensitive, depending on the situation. Having either a masculine or an androgynous identity is associated with higher self-esteem than having a feminine identity, possibly because feminine characteristics are not as valued (Bem, 1974; Boldizar, 1991).

How do gender-role identities develop? It is likely that biology plays a role. Very early, hormones affect activity level and aggression, with boys tending to

Gender-Role Identity Beliefs about characteristics and behaviors associated with one sex as opposed to the other.

Androgynous Having some typically male and some typically female characteristics apparent in one individual.

prefer active, rough, noisy play. Play styles lead young children to prefer same-sex play partners with similar styles, so by age 4, children spend three times as much play time with same-sex playmates as with opposite sex playmates and by age 6 the ratio is 11 to 1 (Benenson, 1993; Maccoby, 1990). Of course, these are averages and individuals do not always fit the average. In addition, many other factors—social and cognitive—affect gender-role identity.

All of us may learn very early what it means to be male or female because of the actions of our parents in the first years of our lives. Both parents play more roughly and vigorously with sons than they do with daughters. Parents tend to touch male infants more at first; later, they keep male toddlers at a greater distance than females. Parents also seem to spend more time interacting with sons, trying to get the babies to smile (Jacklin, DiPietro, & Maccoby, 1984). Parents are more likely to react positively to assertive behavior on the part of their sons and emotional sensitivity in their daughters (Fagot & Hagan, 1991; Lytton & Romney, 1991). When white middle-class parents are asked about what they value in their children, they list achievement, competitiveness, and emotional control for their sons and warmth and "ladylike" behavior for their daughters (Block, 1983; McGuire, 1988).

Through their interactions with family, peers, teachers, and the environment in general, children begin to form **gender schemas,** or organized networks of knowledge about what it means to be male or female (see Figure 5.4). These schemas help the children make sense of the world and guide their behavior. So a young girl whose schema for "girls" includes "girls play with dolls and not with trucks" or "girls can't be scientists" will pay attention to, remember, and interact more with dolls than trucks, and she may avoid science activities (Liben & Signorella, 1993; Martin & Little, 1990).

Gender-Role Stereotyping in the Preschool Years.   Different treatment of the sexes and gender-role stereotyping continue in early childhood. Boys are

FIGURE 5.4

Gender Schema Theory

According to *gender schema theory,* children and adolescents use gender as an organizing theme to classify and understand their perceptions about the world.

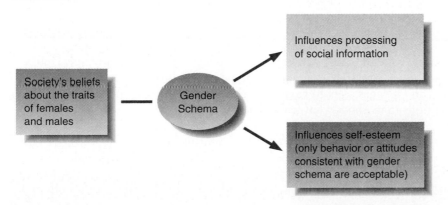

Gender Schemas Organized networks of knowledge about what it means to be male or female.

CATHY © 1987 *Cathy Guisewite. Reprinted with permission of Universal Press Syndicate. All rights reserved.*

encouraged to be more physically active; girls are encouraged to be affectionate and tender. Researchers have found that boys are given more freedom to roam the neighborhood, and they are not protected for as long a time as girls from potentially dangerous activities like playing with sharp scissors or crossing the street alone. Parents quickly come to the aid of their daughters, but are more likely to insist that their sons handle problems themselves (Block, 1983; Fagot, Hagan, Leinbach, & Kronsberg, 1985). Thus, independence and initiative seem to be encouraged more in boys than in girls.

Many of my student teachers are surprised when they hear young children talk about gender roles. Even in this era of great progress toward equal opportunity of the sexes, a preschool girl is more likely to tell you she wants to become a secretary than to say she wants to be an engineer. After she had given a lecture on the dangers of sex stereotyping in schools, a colleague of mine brought her young daughter to her college class. The students asked the little girl, "What do you want to be when you grow up?" The child immediately replied, "A doctor," and her professor/mother beamed with pride. Then the girl whispered to the students in the front row, "I really want to be a nurse, but my Mommy won't let me." Actually, this is a common reaction for young children. Preschoolers tend to have more stereotyped notions of sex roles than older children, and all ages seem to have more rigid and traditional ideas about male occupations than about what females do (Martin, 1989).

Gender Biases Different views of males and females, often favoring one gender over the other.

Gender Bias in the Curriculum.   During the elementary-school years, children continue to learn about what it means to be male or female. Unfortunately, schools often foster these **gender biases** in a number of ways. Most of the textbooks produced for the early grades before 1970 portrayed both males and females in sexually stereotyped roles. Materials for the later grades often omitted women altogether from illustrations and text. In a study of 2,760 stories in 134 books from 16 publishers, a group called *Women on Words and Images* (1975) found the total number of stories dealing with males or male animals to be four times greater than the number of stories dealing with females or female animals. They also found that females tended to be shown in the home, behaving passively and expressing fear or incompetence. Males were usually more dominant and adventurous; they often rescued the females.

In recent years textbook publishers have recognized these problems to some extent and established guidelines to prevent them. It still makes sense to check your teaching materials for such stereotypes, however. When Purcell and Stewart (1990) used the same design as *Women on Words and Images* to analyze 62 elementary readers, they found that the numbers of male and female characters were about equal. Girls were shown in a wide range of activities, but were still portrayed as more helpless than boys. And don't assume that books for older children are free of sexual stereotypes. Despite new publishers' guidelines, problems have not disappeared entirely (Powell, Garcia, & Denton, 1985).

The teacher's own attitude toward sex differences may be influential as well. One reason there have been more children's books and stories with male characters is the belief held by many teachers that boys like to read stories about boys and girls don't mind reading stories about boys—so why not assign stories about boys? It will help the boys be motivated to read, and it won't hurt the girls. Publishers seem to agree with this logic. When Scott O'Dell was looking for a publisher for his *Island of the Blue Dolphins,* he was told by several editors that he needed to make a small change—turn this story of a girl's courageous fight for survival into a story about a boy. O'Dell refused, and the book went on to win a Newbery Award for children's literature (Sadker, Sadker, & Klein, 1991).

The truth about reading preferences is not so simple. It appears that boys do like to read about male characters, but girls appear to prefer female characters. Both sexes find stories about nontraditional females to be at least as interesting as stories about traditional male characters (Sadker, Sadker, & Klein, 1991).

Sex Discrimination in Classrooms.   There has been quite a bit of research on teachers' treatment of male and female students. One of the best documented findings of the past 20 years is that teachers interact more with boys than with girls. This is true from preschool to college. Teachers ask more questions of males, give males more feedback (praise, criticism, and correction), and give more specific and valuable comments to boys. As girls move through the grades, they have less and less to say. By the time students reach college, men are twice as likely to initiate comments as women (Bailey, 1993; Sadker & Sadker, 1985, 1986b; Serbin & O'Leary, 1975; Wingate, 1986). The effect of these differences is that from preschool through college, girls, on the average, receive 1,800 fewer hours of attention and instruction than boys (Sadker, Sadker, & Klein, 1991). Of course, these differences are not evenly distributed. Some boys, generally high-achieving white students, receive more than their share. Minority-group boys, like girls, tend to receive much less attention from the teacher. The imbalances of teacher attention given to boys and girls are particularly dramatic in science classes. In one study, boys were questioned on the subject matter 80 percent more often than girls (Baker, 1986). Boys also dominate the use of equipment in science labs, often dismantling the apparatus before the girls in the class have a chance to perform the experiments (Rennie & Parker, 1987).

Stereotypes are perpetuated in many ways, some obvious, some subtle. Guidance counselors, parents, and teachers often do not protest at all when a bright girl says she doesn't want to take any more math or science courses, but when a boy of the same ability wants to forget about math or science, they will object. In these subtle ways, students' stereotyped expectations for themselves can be reinforced (Sadker & Sadker, 1985).

Sex Differences in Mental Abilities

From infancy through the preschool years, most studies find few differences between boys and girls in overall mental and motor development or in specific abilities. During the school years and beyond, psychologists find no differences in general intelligence on the standard measures—but these tests have been designed and standardized to minimize sex differences. The overall IQ scores of males and females are not significantly different on the average; however, scores on several subtests show sex differences.

Studies conducted before 1974 showed that males performed significantly better than females on tests of spatial ability. Since 1974 the differences have diminished, except on tests that require mental rotation of a figure in space, prediction of the trajectories of moving objects, and navigating. Here males are better. These skills have been related to males' more active play styles and to their participation in athletics (Linn & Hyde, 1989; Newcombe & Baenninger, 1990; Stumpf, 1995). Some researchers argue that evolution has favored these skills in males (Buss, 1995; Geary, 1995).

Sex and Mathematics. In studies conducted before 1974, males outperformed females in mathematics. Again, in studies conducted over the past 20 years, the differences are disappearing, though males still maintain an edge overall compared to females (Linn & Hyde, 1989; Mills, Ablard, & Stumpf, 1993). There is a caution, however. In most studies of sex differences, race and socioeconomic status are not taken into account. When racial groups are studied separately, African American females outperform African American males in high school mathematics; there is little or no difference in the performance of Asian American girls and boys in math or science (Grossman & Grossman, 1994; Yee, 1992).

It is important to realize that when differences are found between the average scores of boys and girls on tests of spatial and mathematical ability, the differences on many tests are small to moderate (Linn & Hyde, 1989). Some researchers have found that girls are better than boys on some kinds of problems—for example, on computational problems and logical, abstract problems—while boys do better than girls on other kinds of problems—for example, story problems and spatial relations problems (Hyde, Fennema, & Lamon, 1990; Mills, Ablard, & Stumpf, 1993).

The difference in mathematics performance between males and females is more pronounced among academically talented students. On the SAT quantitative tests, the highest scores still go to males (but again, these differences were not examined by race). For example, for the 1988–1989 administrations of the SAT math section, 89% of the students who earned a score of 750 or higher were males (National Center for Education Statistics, 1990). There is some evi-

TABLE 5.3   Who Finishes What Courses?

A government survey revealed the following data on the percentages of males and females who enrolled in and then completed high school courses in several areas.

Courses	Percent Males Completing	Percent Females Completing
Algebra	81.6	76.8
Trigonometry or geometry	60.1	50.3
Chemistry or physics	54.2	42.3
English, 3 years or more	92.8	94.1
Foreign language, 2 years or more	39.1	48.1

Source: National Center for Education Statistics (1990) *Digest of Education Statistics.* (Washington, D.C.: National Center for Education Statistics, U.S. Department of Education,) p. 130.

dence that male superiority on this test is related to males' ability to work quickly and to estimate answers (Linn & Hyde, 1989; Mills, Ablard, & Stumpf, 1993). Why this may be so is not fully understood, but confidence may play a role.

One controversial question is whether boys are better in mathematics because they take more math courses than girls. There appear to be few or no differences between boys and girls in math achievement at the beginning of high school (although differences show up earlier for academically gifted students), but during high school girls take fewer math courses (Pallas & Alexander, 1983). As soon as mathematics courses become optional, many girls avoid them, as you can see in Table 5.3. There is mounting evidence that the differences between boys and girls in math achievement decrease substantially or disappear altogether when the actual number of previous math courses taken by each student is considered (Fennema & Sherman, 1977; Oakes, 1990; Pallas & Alexander, 1983). But other researchers have reported that high-ability boys are superior to high-ability girls in mathematics reasoning, even when participation in previous math courses is taken into account (Benbow & Minor, 1986; Benbow & Stanley, 1980, 1983a & b; Kolata, 1980).

When Oakes (1990) analyzed the reasons why only 15% of the scientists, engineers, and mathematicians in the United States are women, she concluded that academically qualified girls choose not to take advanced science and math courses in high school. Thus, they don't develop their abilities in this area. In the process, they limit their college and career choices because colleges require applicants to possess some proficiency in mathematics and many jobs also demand abilities in this area.

Another controversial question is whether teachers are responsible, in part, for the lower participation of girls in math and science studies. There is some evidence that teachers treat girls and boys differently in mathematics classes. For example, some elementary-school teachers spend more academic time with boys in math and with girls in reading. In one study, high school geometry teachers directed most of their questions to boys, even though the girls asked questions and volunteered answers more often. Several researchers have found that some teachers tend to accept wrong answers from girls, saying, in effect, "Well, at least you

*T*he historical disparity between male and female performance is science and technical, or so-call "hard" subjects, has diminished over the past few decades. However, teachers must monitor classroom practices to encourage all students equally in all subjects.

tried." But when boys give the wrong answer, the teachers are more likely to say, "Try harder! You can figure this out." These messages, repeated time and again, can convince girls that they just aren't cut out for mathematics (Harvard University, 1986; Horgan, 1995). If you are like a few of the student teachers I have supervised who "really hate math," please don't pass this attitude on to your students. You may have been the victim of sex discrimination yourself.

Eliminating Gender Bias

We don't know what the situation would be like if all students, boys and girls, received appropriate instruction and encouragement in math. For example, Patricia Casserly of the Educational Testing Service studied 20 high schools where no sex differences in mathematics performance were found. Even though the schools were not alike in all ways, they shared several common features. The teachers had strong backgrounds in mathematics, engineering, or science, not just in general education. They were enthusiastic about mathematics. The brightest students, male and female, were grouped together for instruction in math, and there was heavy emphasis on reasoning in the classes (Kolata, 1980). The activities used to teach math may make a difference as well. Elementary-age girls may do better in math if they learn in cooperative as opposed to competitive activities. Certainly it makes sense to balance both cooperative and competitive approaches so that students who learn better each way have equal opportunities (Fennema & Peterson, 1988). The Guidelines provide additional ideas about avoiding sexism in your teaching.

Girls and Boys in the Classroom

- Distinguish between sex and gender.
- What are gender schemas and how do they develop?
- How do males and females differ in mathematical abilities?
- How can teachers promote gender equity in classrooms?

Check to see if textbooks and other materials you are using present an honest view of the options open to both males and females.

Examples

1. Are both males and females portrayed in traditional and nontraditional roles at work, at leisure, and at home?
2. Discuss your analyses with students, and ask them to help you find sex role biases in other materials—magazine advertising, TV programs, news reporting, for example.

Watch for any unintended biases in your own classroom practices.

Examples

1. Do you group students by sex for certain activities? Is the grouping appropriate?
2. Do you call on one sex or the other for certain answers—boys for math and girls for poetry, for example?

Look for ways in which your school may be limiting the options open to male or female students.

Examples

1. What advice is given by guidance counselors to students in course and career decisions?
2. Is there a good sports program for both girls and boys?

Use gender-free language as much as possible.

Examples

1. Do you speak of "law-enforcement officer" and "mail carrier" instead of "policeman" and "mailman"?
2. Do you name a committee "head" instead of a "chairman"?

Language Differences in the Classroom

In the classroom, quite a bit happens through language. Communication is at the heart of teaching, but as we have seen in this chapter, culture affects communication. In this section, we will examine two kinds of language differences —dialect differences and bilingualism.

Dialects

A **dialect** is a language variation spoken by a particular ethnic, social, or regional group. The rules for a language define how words should be pronounced, how meaning should be expressed, and the ways the basic parts of speech should be put together to form sentences. Dialects appear to differ in their rules

Dialect Rule-governed variation of a language spoken by a particular group.

in these areas, but it is important to remember that these differences are not errors. Each dialect within a language is just as logical, complex, and rule-governed as the standard form of the language (often called **standard speech**). An example of this is the use of the double negative. In Standard English the redundancy of the double negative is not allowed. But in many dialects, such as "black English," just as in many other languages (for instance, Russian, French, Spanish, and Hungarian), the double negative is required by the grammatical rules. To say "I don't want anything" in Spanish, you must literally say, "I don't want nothing," or "No quiero nada."

Dialects and Language Skills.   Another area in which nonstandard dialects differ from Standard English is pronunciation, which can lead to spelling problems. In "black English" and in Southern dialects, for instance, there is less attention paid to pronouncing the ends of words than in Standard English. A lack of attention to final consonants, such as *s*, can lead to failure to indicate possession, third-person singular verbs, and plurals in the standard way. So *John's book* might be *John book,* and words such as *thinks, wasps,* and *lists* may be difficult to pronounce. When endings are not pronounced, there are more *homonyms* (words that sound alike but have different meanings) in the student's language than the unknowing teacher may expect; *spent* and *spend* might sound alike, for example. Even without the confusions caused by dialect differences, there are many homonyms in English. Usually, special attention is given to words such as these when they come up in the spelling lesson. If the teacher is aware of the special homonyms in student dialects, direct teaching of these spelling differences is also possible.

Dialects and Teaching.   Now we turn to a very important issue. While the various dialects of a language may be equally logical, complex, and rule-governed, should teachers make learning easier for children by teaching in the dialect of the majority of students? To do this would show respect for the children's language, but the children would be robbed of the opportunity to learn the standard speech of the dominant culture. Being able to communicate effectively in standard speech allows adults to take advantage of many social and occupational opportunities.

The best teaching approach seems to be to focus on understanding the children and to accept their dialect as a valid and correct language system, but to teach as an alternative the standard form of English (or whatever the dominant language is in your country). Learning the standard speech is easy for most children whose original language is a dialect, as long as they have good models.

What does all of this mean for teachers? How can they cope with linguistic diversity in the classroom? First, they can be sensitive to their own possible negative stereotypes about children who speak a different dialect. Taylor (1983) found that teachers who held negative attitudes toward "black English" gave lower ratings for reading comprehension to students using that dialect, even when the accuracy of the students' performance was the same as that of Standard English speakers. Second, teachers can ensure comprehension by repeating instructions using different words and by asking students to paraphrase instructions or give examples. The Guidelines give more ideas.

Standard Speech The most generally accepted and used form of a given language.

1. Become familiar with features of the students' dialect. This will allow you to understand students better and to distinguish a reading miscue (a noncomprehension feature) from a comprehension error. Students should not be interrupted during the oral reading process. Correction of comprehension features is best done after the reading segment.

2. Allow students to listen to a passage or story first. This can be done in two ways: (a) finish the story and then ask comprehension questions, or (b) interrupt the story at key comprehension segments and ask students to predict the outcome.

3. Use predictable stories, which can be familiar episodes in literature, music, or history. They can be original works or experiential readers.

4. Use visual aids to enhance comprehension. Visual images, whether pictures or words, will aid word recognition and comprehension.

5. Use "cloze procedure" deletions to focus on vocabulary and meaning. Cloze procedures are selected deletions of words from a passage in order to focus on a specific text feature. *Examples:* (a) The little red hen found an ear of corn. The little red _____ said, "Who will dry the ear of _____ ?" (vocabulary focus) (b) Today I feel like a (*noun*). (grammar focus) (c) There was a (*pain*) in the pit of his stomach. (semantic focus)

6. Allow students to retell the story or passage in various speech styles. Have students select different people to whom they would like to retell the story (family member, principal, friend), and assist them in selecting synonyms most appropriate to each audience. This allows both teacher and student to become language authorities.

7. Integrate reading, speaking, and writing skills whenever possible.

8. Use the computer (if available) as a time-on-task exercise. The microcomputer can effectively assist in teaching the reading techniques of skimming (general idea), scanning (focused reference), reading for comprehension (mastery of total message), and critical reading (inference and evaluation).

Source: From Christine I. Bennett, *Comprehensive Multicultural Education, Theory and Practice, 2/e,* pp. 234–235. Copyright © 1990 by Allyn & Bacon. Reprinted by permission.

Bilingualism

Bilingualism is a topic that sparks heated debates and touches many emotions. One reason is the changing demographics discussed earlier in this chapter. In the United States in the late 1980s, 2.5 million school-age children were not native-English-speaking. This number is expected to double by the year 2000. In the past 10 years there has been a 65% increase in the number of Spanish speaking students and almost a 100% increase in students who speak Asian languages. In some states almost one-fourth of all students speak a first language other than English—usually Spanish (Gersten, 1996a).

Two terms that you will see associated with bilingualism are **English as a second language (ESL)**, describing classes for students whose primary language

Bilingualism The ability to speak two languages fluently.

English as a Second Language (ESL) Designation for programs and classes to teach English to students who are not native speakers of English.

is not English, and **limited English proficiency (LEP)**, referring to students whose English skills are limited.

What Does Bilingualism Mean?   There are disagreements about the meaning of *bilingualism*. Some definitions focus exclusively on a language-based meaning: bilingual people, or bilinguals, speak two languages. But this limited definition minimizes the significant problems that bilingual students face. Consider the words of these two students:

> A ninth-grade boy, who recently arrived in California from Mexico: "There is so much discrimination and hate. Even from other kids from Mexico who have been here longer. They don't treat us like brothers. They hate even more. It makes them feel more like natives. They want to be American. They don't want to speak Spanish to us, they already know English and how to act. If they are with us, other people will treat them more like wetbacks, so they try to avoid us." (Olsen, 1988, p. 36)

> A tenth-grade Chinese-American girl who had been in America for several years: "I don't know who I am. Am I the good Chinese daughter? Am I an American teenager? I always feel I am letting my parents down when I am with my friends because I act so American, but I also feel that I will never really be an American. I never feel really comfortable with myself anymore." (Olsen, 1988, p. 30)

The experiences of these two students show that there is more to being bilingual than just speaking two languages. You must also be able to move back and forth between two cultures while still maintaining a sense of your own identity (Hakuta & Garcia, 1989). Being bilingual and bicultural means mastering the knowledge necessary to communicate in two cultures as well as dealing with potential discrimination. As a teacher, you will have to help your students learn all these skills.

Becoming Bilingual.   Early research on bilingualism concluded that speaking two languages was so taxing on the mental development of the child that cognitive abilities suffered. Thus, the child should learn English as quickly as possible. Better designed studies today show that the opposite is true. Higher degrees of bilingualism are correlated with increased cognitive abilities in such areas as concept formation, creativity, knowledge of the workings of language, and cognitive flexibility. These findings seem to hold as long as there is no stigma attached to being bilingual and as long as students are not expected to abandon their first language to learn English (Galambos & Goldin-Meadow, 1990; Garcia, 1992; Hakuta & Garcia, 1989; Ricciardelli, 1992).

Learning a second language does not interfere with understanding in the first language. In fact, the more proficient the speaker is in the first language, the faster she or he will master a second language (Cummins, 1984, 1994). If children learn two languages simultaneously as toddlers, there is a period between ages 2 and 3 when they progress more slowly because they have not yet figured out that they are learning two different languages. They may mix up the grammar of the two. But researchers believe that by age 4, if they have enough exposure to both languages, they get things straight and speak as well as native **monolinguals** (Reich, 1986). The earlier we learn a second language, the more our pronunciation is near-native. After adolescence it is difficult to learn a new language without an accent (Anderson & Graham, 1994).

Limited English Proficiency (LEP) Descriptive term for students who have limited mastery of English.

Monolinguals Individuals who speak only one language.

Proficiency in a second language has two separate aspects: face-to-face communication (known as "contextualized language skills") and academic uses of language such as reading and doing grammar exercises ("decontextualized language skills") (Snow, 1987). It takes students about two years in a good-quality program to be able to communicate face-to-face in a second language, but mastering decontextualized, academic language skills in the new language takes five to seven years. So students who seem in conversation to "know" a second language may still have great difficulty with complex schoolwork in that language (Cummins, 1994; Ovando, 1989).

Bilingual Education.   Virtually everyone agrees that all citizens should learn the official language of their country. But when and how should instruction in that language begin? Here the debate is bitter at times, but it is clear the United States has not solved the problem. For example, "Spanish-speaking students—*even when taught and tested in Spanish*—still score at the [bottom] 32nd percentile in relation to a national comparison group (taught and tested in English)" (Goldenberg, 1996, p. 353).

Is it better to teach non–English-speaking and limited-English-proficiency students to read first in their native language or to begin reading instruction in English? Do these children need some oral lessons in English before reading instruction can be effective? Should other subjects, such as mathematics and social studies, be taught in the primary (home) language until the children are fluent in English? On these questions there are two basic positions, which have given rise to two contrasting teaching approaches, one that focuses on making the *transition* to English as quickly as possible and the other that attempts to *maintain* or improve the native language and use the native language as the primary teaching language until English skills are more fully developed.

*T*eachers in today's bilingual classrooms must help students learn skills to communicate in more than one culture.

Proponents of the first approach—transition—believe that English ought to be introduced as early as possible; they argue that valuable learning time is lost if students are taught in their native language. Most bilingual programs today follow this line of thinking. Proponents of native-language maintenance instruction, however, raise four important issues (Gersten, 1996b; Goldenberg, 1996; Hakuta & Garcia, 1989). First, children who are forced to try to learn math or science in an unfamiliar language are bound to have trouble. What if you had been forced to learn fractions or biology in a second language that you had studied for only a semester? Some psychologists believe students taught by this approach may become **semilingual,** inadequate speakers of both languages. Second, students may get the message that their home languages (and therefore, their families and cultures) are second class. You saw the seeds of these feelings in the stories of the two students at the beginning of this section. Third, the academic content (math, science, history, etc.) that students learn in their native language is learned—they do not forget the knowledge and skills when they are able to speak English.

Fourth, ironically, by the time students have mastered academic English and let their home language deteriorate, they reach secondary school and are encouraged to learn a second language. Had both the home language and English been developed all along, they would already be fluent in two languages without having to take French I or Introductory Spanish. Kenji Hakuta (1986) expresses this hope:

> Perhaps the rosiest future for bilingual education in the United States can be attained by dissolving the paradoxical attitude of admiration and pride for school-attained bilingualism on the one hand and scorn and shame for home-brewed immigrant bilingualism on the other. The goals of the educational system could be seen as the development of all students as functional bilinguals, including monolingual English speakers. (p. 229)

The maintenance approach to teaching advocates using the child's native language for some subject teaching while simultaneously developing English proficiency. Supporters believe that children have a right to be proficient speakers of their native language and to become fully competent speakers of the dominant language of their country. One new approach to reaching this goal is to create classes that mix students who are learning a second language with students who are native speakers. The goal is for both groups to become fluent in both languages (Snow, 1986). My daughter spent a summer in such a program in Quebec and has been ahead in every French class ever since. For truly effective bilingual education, we will need many bilingual teachers. If you have a competence in another language, you might want to develop it fully for your teaching.

Focus on...

Language Differences

- How should teachers deal with different dialects in the classroom?
- How does being bilingual affect learning?
- What are the advantages and disadvantages of the different approaches to bilingual education?

Semilingual Not proficient in any language; speaking one or more languages inadequately.

Research on Bilingual Programs.   It is difficult to separate politics from practice in the debate about bilingual education. It is clear that high quality bilingual education programs can have positive results. Students improve in the subjects that were taught in their native language, in their mastery of English, and in self-esteem as well (Hakuta & Gould, 1987; Willig, 1985; Wright & Taylor, 1995). English as a second language (ESL) pro-

TABLE 5.4 Ideas for Promoting Learning and Language Acquisition

Effective teaching for students in bilingual and ESL classrooms combines many strategies—direct instruction, mediation, coaching, feedback, modeling, encouragement, challenge, and authentic activities.

1. Structures, frameworks, scaffolds, and strategies

   - Provide support to students by "thinking aloud," building on and clarifying input of students
   - Use visual organizers, story maps, or other aids to help students organize and relate information

2. Relevant background knowledge and key vocabulary concepts

   - Provide adequate background knowledge to students and informally assess whether students have background knowledge
   - Focus on key vocabulary words and use consistent language
   - Incorporate students' primary language meaningfully

3. Mediation/feedback

   - Give feedback that focuses on meaning, not grammar, syntax, or pronunciation
   - Give frequent and comprehensible feedback
   - Provide students with prompts or strategies
   - Ask questions that press students to clarify or expand on initial statements
   - Provide activities and tasks that students can complete
   - Indicate to students when they are successful
   - Assign activities that are reasonable, avoiding undue frustration
   - Allow use of native language responses (when context is appropriate)
   - Be sensitive to common problems in second language acquisition

4. Involvement

   - Ensure active involvement of all students, including low-performing students
   - Foster extended discourse

5. Challenge

   - Implicit (cognitive challenge, use of higher-order questions)
   - Explicit (high but reasonable expectations)

6. Respect for—and responsiveness to—cultural and personal diversity

   - Show respect for students as individuals, respond to things students say, show respect for culture and family, and possess knowledge of cultural diversity
   - Incorporate students' experiences into writing and language arts activities
   - Link content to students' lives and experiences to enhance understanding
   - View diversity as an asset, reject cultural deficit notions

Source: From R. Gersten (1996). "Literacy instruction for language-minority students: The transition years." *The Elementary School Journal, 96,* pp. 241–242. Copyright © 1996. Adapted by permission of the University of Chicago Press.

grams seem to have positive effects on reading comprehension (Fitzgerald, 1995). But attention today is shifting from debate about general approaches to a focus on effective teaching strategies. As you will see many times in this book, a combination of clarity of learning goals and direct instruction in needed skills—including learning strategies and tactics, teacher- or peer-guided practice leading to independent practice, authentic and engaging tasks, opportunities for interaction and conversation that are academically focused, and warm encouragement from the teacher—seems to be effective (Chamot & O'Malley, 1996; Gersten, 1996b, Goldenberg, 1996). Table 5.4 is a set of constructs for promoting learning and language acquisition that capture many of theses ideas for effective instruction. We will revisit many of these ideas in later chapters.

We have dealt with a wide range of differences in this chapter. How can teachers provide an appropriate education for all their students? One response is to make the classroom compatible with the students' cultural heritage. Such a classroom is described as being culturally compatible.

Creating Culturally Compatible Classrooms

The goal of creating **culturally compatible classrooms** is to eliminate racism, sexism, and ethnic prejudice while providing equal educational opportunities for all students. Roland Tharp (1989) states that "two decades of data on cultural issues in classroom interactions and school outcomes have accumulated. When schools are changed, children's experiences and achievement also change" (p. 349). Tharp outlines several dimensions of classrooms that can be tailored to fit the needs of students. Three dimensions are social organization, learning style, and sociolinguistics.

Social Organization

Tharp states that "a central task of educational design is to make the organization of teaching, learning, and performance compatible with the social structures in which students are most productive, engaged, and likely to learn" (p. 350). Social structure or social organization in this context means the ways people interact to accomplish a particular goal. For example, the social organization of Hawaiian society depends heavily on collaboration and cooperation. Children play together in groups of friends and siblings, with older children often caring for the younger ones. When cooperative work groups of four or five boys and girls were established in Hawaiian classrooms, student learning and participation improved. The teacher worked intensively with one group while the children in the remaining groups helped each other. But when the same structure was tried in a Navajo classroom, students would not work together. These students are socialized to be more solitary and not to play with the opposite sex. By setting up same-sex working groups of only two or three Navajo students, teachers encouraged them to help each other.

Learning Styles

Some psychologists have found ethnic-group differences in students' cognitive styles. You may remember from the previous chapter that cognitive styles are the ways that individuals typically process information. The following are a few examples.

Hispanic Americans. Results of some research suggest that Mexican Americans tend to be field dependent, preferring holistic, concrete, social approaches to learning. Because being field independent is related to achievement in mathematics, the tendency to be field dependent may interfere with performance in mathematics if it is taught in the usual abstract, analytical way (Buenning & Tollefson, 1987). Other researchers have suggested that Hispanic American students are more oriented toward family and group loyalty and less individualistic. This may mean that Hispanic American students prefer coop-

Culturally Compatible Classrooms Classrooms in which procedures, rules, grouping strategies, attitudes, and teaching methods do not cause conflicts with the students' culturally influenced ways of learning and interacting.

crative activities and dislike being made to compete with fellow students (Garcia, 1992; Vasquez, 1990).

African Americans.   Bennett (1995) summarizes research that suggests the learning styles of African Americans may be inconsistent with teaching approaches in most schools. Some of the characteristics of this learning style are a visual/global rather than a verbal/analytic approach; a preference for reasoning by inference rather than formal logic; a focus on people and relationships; a preference for energetic involvement in several activities simultaneously rather than routine, step-by-step learning; a tendency to approximate numbers, space and time; and a greater dependence on nonverbal communication. To capitalize on these learning styles, Hale-Benson (1986) recommends the following strategies with young African-American children:

Use appropriate nonverbal cues, gestures, and eye contact

Allow equal "talking time" for teacher and students

Emphasize small-group learning and hands-on contact with the teacher

Use a variety of learning activities that include movement, games, poetry, and music.

Native Americans.   Native Americans also appear to have a more global, visual style of learning. For example, Navajo students prefer hearing a story all the way through to the end before discussing parts of the story. Teachers who stop to ask questions seem odd to these students and interrupt the learning process (Tharp, 1989). Also, these students sometimes show strong preferences for learning privately, through trial and error, rather than having their mistakes made public (Vasquez, 1990).

Asian Americans.   There has been little research on the learning styles of Asian Americans, perhaps because they are seen as "successful minorities." As we discussed earlier, many of the values and attitudes taught by some Asian cultures, such as respect for teachers, hard work, and persistent effort, can support academic achievement. Some educators suggest that Asian children tend to value teacher approval and to work well in structured, quiet learning environments where there are clear goals (Manning & Baruth, 1996). One recent study among refugee students found that they tended to be field dependent and global in their approach to problem solving. They tended to be more passive and learned best in cooperative settings with good support from peers and the teacher. Of course, strong support may be helpful for any group trying to cope with a new and very different culture.

> There are dangers when teachers stereotype Asian Americans as hardworking and passive. This practice tends to reinforce conformity and stifle creativity. Asian and Pacific American students, therefore, frequently do not develop the ability to assert and express themselves verbally and are channeled in disproportionate numbers into the technical/scientific fields. As a result, many Asian and Pacific American students undergo traumatic family/school discontinuities, suffer from low self-esteem, are overly conforming, and have their academic and social development narrowly circumscribed. (Suzuki, 1983, p. 9)

Suzuki's cautions are echoed by many critics of the research on ethnic differences in learning styles (Yee, 1992).

Criticisms of Learning-Styles Research.   In considering this research on learning styles, you should keep two points in mind. First, the validity of some of the learning-styles research has been strongly questioned, as we saw in the previous chapter. Second, there is a heated debate today about whether identifying ethnic-group differences in learning styles and preferences is a dangerous, racist, sexist exercise. In our society we are quick to move from the notion of "difference" to the idea of "deficit." Information about the "typical" learning styles of a given ethnic group can become just one more basis for stereotyping, as mentioned above (Gordon, 1991; O'Neil, 1990a). I have included the information about learning-style differences because I believe that, used sensibly, this information can help you better understand your students.

It is dangerous and incorrect, however, to assume that every individual in a group shares the same learning style. The best advice for teachers is to be sensitive to individual differences in all your students and to make available alternative paths to learning. Never prejudge how a student will learn best on the basis of assumptions about the student's ethnicity or race. Get to know the individual.

Sociolinguistics

Sociolinguistics is the study of "the courtesies and conventions of conversation across cultures" (Tharp, 1989, p. 351). A knowledge of sociolinguistics will help you understand why communication sometimes breaks down in classrooms. The classroom is a special setting for communicating; it has its own set of rules for when, how, to whom, about what subject, and in what manner to use language. Sometimes the sociolinguistic skills of students do not fit the expectations of teachers.

Participation Structures.   In order to be successful, students must know the communication rules; that is, they must understand the pragmatics of the classroom—when, where, and how to communicate. (See Chapter 2 for a discussion of pragmatics.) This is not such an easy task. As class activities change, rules change. Sometimes you have to raise your hand (during the teacher's presentation), but sometimes you don't (during storytime on the rug). Sometimes it is good to ask a question (during discussion), but other times it isn't so good (when the teacher is scolding you). The differing activity rules are called **participation structures.** These structures define appropriate participation for each class activity. Most classrooms have many different participation structures.

To be competent communicators in the classroom, students sometimes have to read very subtle, nonverbal cues telling them which participation structures are currently in effect. For example, in one classroom, when the teacher stood in a particular area of the room, put her hands on her hips, and leaned forward at the waist, the children in the class were signaled to "stop and freeze," look at the teacher, and anticipate an announcement (Shultz & Florio, 1979).

Sources of Misunderstandings.   Some children are simply better than others at reading the classroom situation because the participation structures of the school match the structures they have learned at home. The communication rules for most school situations are similar to those in middle-class homes, so children from these homes often appear to be more competent communicators.

Sociolinguistics The study of the formal and informal rules for how, when, about what, to whom, and how long to speak in conversations within cultural groups.

Participation Structures The formal and informal rules for how to take part in a given activity.

They know the unwritten rules. Students from different cultural backgrounds may have learned participation structures that conflict with the behaviors expected in school. For example, one study found that the home conversation style of Hawaiian children is to chime in with contributions to a story. In school, however, this overlapping style is seen as "interrupting." When the teachers in one school learned about these differences and made their reading groups more like their students' home conversation groups, the young Hawaiian children in their classes improved in reading (Au, 1980; Tharp, 1989).

The source of misunderstanding can be a subtle sociolinguistic difference, such as how long the teacher waits to react to a student's response. White and Tharp (1988) found that when Navajo students in one class paused in giving a response, their Anglo teacher seemed to think that they were finished speaking. As a result, the teacher often unintentionally interrupted students. In another study, researchers found that Pueblo Indian students participated twice as much in classes where teachers waited longer to react. Waiting longer also helps girls to participate more freely in math and science classes (Grossman & Grossman, 1994).

It seems that even students who speak the same language as their teachers may still have trouble communicating, and thus learning school subjects, if their knowledge of pragmatics does not fit the school situation. What can teachers do? Especially in the early grades, you should make communication rules for activities clear and explicit. Do not assume students know what to do. Use cues to signal students when changes occur. Explain and demonstrate appropriate behavior. I have seen teachers show young children how to "talk in your inside voice" or "whisper so you won't disturb others." One teacher said and then demonstrated, "If you have to interrupt me while I'm working with other children, stand quietly beside me until I can help you." Be consistent in responding to students. If students are supposed to raise their hands, don't call on those who break the rules.

Bringing It All Together: Teaching Every Student

The goal of this chapter is to give you a sense of the diversity in today's and tomorrow's schools and to help you meet the challenges of teaching in a multicultural classroom. How will you understand and build on all the cultures of your students? How will you deal with many different languages? Here are three general teaching principles to guide you in finding answers to these questions.

Know Your Students. Nothing you read in a chapter on cultural differences will teach you enough to understand the lives of all your students. If you can take other courses in college or read about other cultures, I encourage you to do it. But reading and studying are not enough. You should get to know your students' families and communities. Elba Reyes, a successful bilingual teacher for special needs children describes her approach:

Usually I find that if you really want to know a parent, you get to know them on their own turf. This is key to developing trust and understanding the parents' perspective. First, get to know the community. Learn where the local grocery store is and what the children do after school. Then schedule a home visit at a time that is convenient for the parents. . . . The home environment is not usually as ladened with failure. I sometimes observed the child being successful in the home, for example, riding a bicycle or helping with dinner. (Bos & Reyes, 1996, p. 349)

One goal of creating culturally compatible classrooms is to encourage mutual acceptance and respect among students from all backgrounds.

Try to spend time with students and parents on projects outside school. Ask parents to help in class or to speak to your students about their jobs, their hobbies, or the history and heritage of their ethnic group. In the elementary grades, don't wait until a student is in trouble to have the first meeting with a family member. Watch and listen to the ways that your students interact in large and small groups. Have students write to you, and write back to them. Eat lunch with one or two students. Spend some nonteaching time with them.

Respect Your Students.   From knowledge ought to come respect for your students' learning strengths—for the struggles they face and the obstacles they overcome. For a child, genuine acceptance is a necessary condition for developing self-esteem. Self-esteem and pride are important accomplishments of the school years. Sometimes the self-image and occupational aspirations of minority children actually decline in their early years in public school, probably because of the emphasis on majority culture values, accomplishments, and history. By presenting the accomplishments of particular members of an ethnic group or by bringing that group's culture into the classroom (in the form of, say, literature, art, or music), teachers can help students maintain a sense of pride in their cultural group. This integration of culture must be more than the "tokenism" of sampling ethnic foods or wearing costumes. Students should learn about the socially and intellectually important contributions of the various groups. There are many excellent references that provide background information, history, and teaching strategies for different groups of students (e.g., Banks, 1997).

Question 6

> **Focus on...**
>
> ## Culturally Compatible Classrooms
>
> - What are the advantages and dangers in assuming that different ethnic groups have different learning styles?
> - How do participation structures affect students' access to learning in classrooms?
> - How can you move "beyond the basics" in teaching all your students?

Teach Your Students.   The most important thing you can do for your students is teach them to read, write, speak, compute, think, and create. Too often, goals for low-SES or minority-group students have focused exclusively on basic skills. Students are taught words and sounds, but the meaning of the story is supposed to come later. Knapp, Turnbull, and Shields (1990) make these suggestions:

Focus on meaning and understanding from beginning to end—for example, by orienting instruction toward comprehending reading passages, communicating important ideas in written text, or understanding the concepts underlying number facts.

Balance routine skill learning with novel and complex tasks from the earliest stages of learning.

Provide context for skill learning that establishes clear reasons for needing to learn the skills.

Influence attitudes and beliefs about the academic content areas as well as skills and knowledge.

Eliminate unnecessary redundancy in the curriculum (e.g., repeating instruction in the same mathematics skills year after year). (p. 5)

And finally, teach students directly about how to be students. In the early grades this could mean directly teaching the courtesies and conventions of the classroom: how to get a turn to speak, how and when to interrupt the teacher, how to whisper, how to get help in a small group, how to give an explanation that is helpful. In the later grades it may mean teaching the study skills that fit your subject. You can ask students to learn "how we do it in school" without violating principle number two above—respect your students. Ways of asking questions around the kitchen table at home may be different from ways of asking questions in school, but students can learn both ways, without deciding that either way is superior. The Guidelines give more ideas.

Guidelines

Creating Culturally Compatible Classrooms

Experiment with different grouping arrangements to encourage social harmony and cooperation.

Examples

1. Try "study buddies" and pairs.

2. Organize heterogeneous groups of four or five.

3. Establish larger teams for older students.

Provide a range of ways to learn material to accommodate a range of learning styles.

Examples

1. Give students verbal materials at different reading levels.

2. Offer visual materials—charts, diagrams, models.

3. Provide tapes for listening and viewing.

4. Set up activities and projects.

Teach classroom procedures directly, even ways of doing things that you thought everyone would know.

Examples

1. Tell students how to get the teacher's attention.

2. Explain when and how to interrupt the teacher if students need help.

3. Show which materials students can take and which require permission.

4. Demonstrate acceptable ways to disagree with or challenge another student.

Learn the meaning of different behaviors for your students.

Examples

1. Ask students how they feel when you correct or praise them. What gives them this message?

2. Talk to family and community members and other teachers to discover the meaning of expressions, gestures, or other responses that are unfamiliar to you.

Emphasize meaning in teaching.

Examples

1. Make sure students understand what they read.

2. Try storytelling and other modes that don't require written materials.

3. Use examples that relate abstract concepts to everyday experiences; for instance, relate negative numbers to being overdrawn in your checkbook.

(continued)

Get to know the customs, traditions, and values of your students.

Examples

1. Use holidays as a chance to discuss the origins and meaning of traditions.
2. Analyze different traditions for common themes.
3. Attend community fairs and festivals.

Help students detect racist and sexist messages.

Examples

1. Analyze curriculum materials for biases.
2. Make students "bias detectives," reporting comments from the media.
3. Discuss the ways that students communicate biased messages about each other and what should be done when this happens.
4. Discuss expressions of prejudice such as anti-Semitism.

SUMMARY

Today's Multicultural Classrooms

Statistics point to increasing cultural diversity in American society. Old views—that minority-group members and immigrants should lose their cultural distinctiveness in the American "melting pot" or be regarded as culturally deficient —are being replaced by new emphases on multicultural education, equal educational opportunity, and the celebration of cultural diversity.

Everyone is a member of many cultural groups, defined in terms of geographic region, nationality, ethnicity, race, gender, social class, and religion. Membership in a particular group does not determine behavior or values but makes certain values and kinds of behavior more likely. Wide variations exist within each group.

Social Class Differences

Socioeconomic status (SES) is determined by several factors—not just income—and often overpowers other cultural differences. Disproportionate numbers of low-SES families are African American and Hispanic American.

Socioeconomic status and academic achievement are closely related. Low-SES students may suffer from teachers' lowered expectations of them, low self-esteem, learned helplessness, participation in resistance cultures, school tracking, and understimulating childrearing styles.

Ethnic and Racial Differences

Ethnicity (culturally transmitted behavior) and race (biologically transmitted physical traits) are socially significant categories people use to describe themselves and others. Minority groups (either numerically or historically unempowered) are rapidly increasing in population.

Conflicts between groups can arise from differences in culture-based beliefs, values, and expectations. Differences among ethnic groups in cognitive and academic abilities are largely the legacy of racial segregation and continuing prejudice and discrimination.

Women and Men: Differences in the Classroom

Educational equity for females and males is also an issue. Research shows that gender-role stereotyping begins in the preschool years and continues through gender bias in the school curriculum and sex discrimination in the classroom. Teachers often unintentionally perpetuate these problems.

Some measures on IQ and SAT tests have shown small sex-linked differences, especially in spatial abilities and mathematics. Research on the causes of these differences has been inconclusive, except to indicate that academic socialization and teachers' treatment of male and female students in mathematics classes do play a role. Teachers can use many strategies for reducing gender bias.

Language Differences in the Classroom

Language differences among students include dialects, bilingualism, and culture-based communication styles. Dialects are not inferior languages and should be respected, but Standard English should be taught for academic contexts.

Bilingual students speak a first language other than English, learn English as a second language, may have some degree of limitation in English proficiency, and also must often struggle with social adjustment problems relating to biculturalism. While there is much debate over the best way to help bilingual students master English, studies show it is best if they are not forced to abandon their first language.

The more proficient students are in their first language, the faster they will master the second. Mastering academic language skills in any new language takes five to seven years.

Creating Culturally Compatible Classrooms

Culturally compatible classrooms are free of racism, sexism, and ethnic prejudice and provide equal educational opportunities for all students. Dimensions of classroom life that can be modified to that end are social organization, learning-style formats, and participation structures. Teach-

ers, however, must avoid stereotypes of culture-based learning styles and must not assume that every individual in a group shares the same style.

Communication may break down in classrooms because of differences in sociolinguistic styles and skills. Teachers can directly teach appropriate participation structures and be sensitive to culture-based communication rules. To help create compatible multicultural classrooms, teachers must know and respect all their students, have high expectations of them, and teach them what they need to know to succeed.

KEY TERMS

androgynous, p. 178
authoritarian personality, p. 176
bilingualism, p. 187
cultural deficit model, p. 163
culturally compatible classrooms,
  p. 192
culture, p. 164
dialect, p. 185
discrimination, p. 177
English as a second language (ESL),
  p. 187

ethnicity, p. 170
gender biases, p. 180
gender-role identity, p. 178
gender schemas, p. 179
limited English proficiency (LEP),
  p. 188
melting pot, p. 162
minority group, p. 171
monolinguals, p. 188
multicultural education,
  p. 163

participation structures,
  p. 194
prejudice, p. 176
race, p. 170
resistance culture, p. 169
semilingual, p. 190
socioeconomic status (SES),
  p. 166
sociolinguistics, p. 194
standard speech, p. 186
stereotype, p. 177

CHECK YOUR UNDERSTANDING

Can you apply the ideas from this chapter on culture and community to solve the following problems of practice?

Elementary and Middle School

- Several of your students are from a public housing project in the district and clearly have fewer advantages than the other students in your class. You are concerned that the "project" students never seem to work or play with the others in the class. What would you do?

- Every year the number of non-English-speaking students in your class increases. This year there are four different language groups represented—and you know only about five words in each language. The school's resources are very limited. Pick one topic and tell how you would teach it to accommodate the limited English proficiency of your students.

Junior High and High School

- One day you notice that the males are doing most of the talking in your classes, particularly the advanced classes.

Just out of curiosity, you start to note each day how many girls and boys make contributions and ask questions. You are really surprised to see that your first impression was correct. What would you do to encourage more participation on the part of your female students?

- For some reason, this year there have been several racial incidents in your school. Each incident seems a bit nastier and more dangerous than the one before. What would you do in your classes to improve the situation?

Cooperative Learning Activity

- Your school has received a $30,000 grant from a private foundation to "improve cross-cultural communications in the school." Suggestions for accomplishing this include assessing the learning styles of all the students, hiring a consultant, buying new curriculum materials, sending teachers to multicultural workshops, and hiring more teachers' aides. With four or five other members of your educational psychology class, prepare a set of recommendations for spending the money so that the greatest benefit is achieved.

What Would They Do?

It has been a long week. One of the aides has been out all week with the flu and the weather has kept your 5-year-olds inside three of the last five days. Everyone is a bit tense. The noise level is higher than usual, but even so, you overhear a conversation that disturbs you coming from the block area.

"You can't play here. These toys are for boys and you're a girl. Girls can't build space stations!"

"Yes I can, Yes I can!"

"Go play with the dolls."

"Yeah, this place is for boys—no dumb girls here."

TRISH SULLIVAN

Kindergarten Teacher
Snug Harbor Community School, Quincy, Massachusetts

To help my class develop less stereotypical views of boys and girls, I would start with a simple lesson and divide the boys and the girls into two separate groups. I would have the children name all the ways the two groups are alike, from body parts to clothing, and write these responses on the blackboard.

I would then create a theme in the classroom entitled "What I want to be when I grow up." I would use the media specialist as a resource to gather information from books, software, and other media depicting various occupations with nontypical gender roles.

I would also set up a variety of centers in the classroom where children could experience dramatic play and hands-on learning with specific occupations such as astronaut, chef, or doctor. Parents of my students and other professionals would be invited to come share their work experiences with the class.

A senior high school math teacher shared his observations on this question with me. He is concerned that girls do not enroll in the advanced math and science classes because they have a poor self-image in this area. They view these courses in particular as being very technical. He has heard them say, "I can't because I'm a girl." Girls tend to not participate in the group classroom discussion during science lab because the boys take over the equipment and tend to take control. Boys also tend to show more confidence even if they get an answer wrong. However, in the drafting classes, the high school math teacher finds that girls are realizing they can meet the technical challenges and that they are actually more successful than the boys. He attributes this to the girls having more patience and neatness with the skills that are required in these classes.

200

JAMES O'KELLY

Kindergarten Teacher
Eisenhower Elementary School, Sayveville, New Jersey

This situation is one that demands two types of intervention: an immediate and direct one and a long-term, less direct intervention. I'd walk over to the block area and mention that I would like to help build the space station. I frequently join in center time activities, so this action would be no surprise. (The children are also usually delighted to have an adult join in their activities—they often invite me or the aide to do so.) As we work together to build the space station, I would ask a number of questions about the station, and I would elicit the children's advice about what I should do with my blocks. I would be sure to respond with favorable remarks about their ideas, being careful that Chrissy had a fair number of opportunities to respond. I would, however, be careful not to overdo things. The other children might sense a bias in favor of Chrissy and attribute it to her "being a girl." When I had the opportunity, I would have a meeting with the aide(s) to inform them of what I had witnessed. I would ask them to make it a practice of joining activities at some of the centers that might be viewed as "masculine" or "feminine" by the children (e.g., Tinkertoys, kitchen/home play area) and model what I had done. (The aides may very well have a few ideas of their own to consider.)

One reason I have few problems like this may be attributable to the way I handle center time. Each table in the class is identified by a color (red, blue, green, orange, yellow, purple). Each child in the class has a small plastic tag with his or her name on it that corresponds to the color of his or her table. Hanging on the wall I have a small bulletin board on which are photos of every center time area (coloring, blocks, computer, library, puppet stage, modeling clay, kitchen, jigsaw puzzles, piano, chalkboard, various manipulative toys, and so on—there are about 20 choices). Just above each photo are a number of pins on which I can hang the tags. The number of pins adjacent to the photo determines how many children may play in an area. (That number has been determined through experience—four kids are okay at blocks, four at the coloring area, two at Tinkertoys, two at the puppet theater, one at the Casio piano/keyboard, and so on.) Also hanging on the bulletin board on one pin are six tags (red, blue, green, orange, yellow, purple) that determine the order in which I call children to make their center time choices. We rotate the order of the tags each day; if red goes first today, then it will be last tomorrow, and so on. The system does several positive things: (1) It reinforces a notion of fairness between the teacher and the students. No children have the idea that the teacher favors one group of children when it comes to center time. (2) It prevents certain children from dominating certain toys. (3) It promotes a mixing of the children. Boys and girls have an equal opportunity to play in each area; the same is true for kids of different ethnic or racial backgrounds. (4) It "forces" children to go to areas that they might not typically choose. If you love to play with the blocks, but all the pins for blocks are filled, then you have to go somewhere else. At "somewhere else" you are likely to find someone with whom you do not normally play— and friendly relations usually result. (5) It also promotes the students' perceptions that they have some control over what goes on during the day.

I make a point of explaining this system to the parents at "back to school night." I think it reinforces their sense that their children are being treated fairly and respectfully.

6

Behavioral Views of Learning

Overview | *What Would You Do?*

UNDERSTANDING LEARNING   204
   Learning: A Definition | Learning Is Not Always What It Seems

EARLY EXPLANATIONS OF LEARNING: CONTIGUITY AND
CLASSICAL CONDITIONING   207
   Pavlov's Dilemma and Discovery: Classical Conditioning |
   Generalization, Discrimination, and Extinction

OPERANT CONDITIONING: TRYING NEW RESPONSES   208
   The Work of Thorndike and Skinner | Types of Consequences |
   Reinforcement Schedules | Summarizing the Effects of Reinforcement
   Schedules | Antecedents and Behavior Change

APPLIED BEHAVIOR ANALYSIS   216
   Methods for Encouraging Behaviors | Coping with Undesirable
   Behavior

SOCIAL LEARNING THEORY   225
   Elements of Social Cognitive Theory | Learning by Observing Others |
   Elements of Observational Learning | Factors That Influence
   Observational Learning | Observational Learning in Teaching

SELF-REGULATION AND COGNITIVE BEHAVIOR MODIFICATION   231
   Self-Management | Cognitive Behavior Modification and Self-
   Instruction

PROBLEMS AND ISSUES   236
   Ethical Issues | Criticisms of Behavioral Methods

Summary | *Key Terms* | *Check Your Understanding* | *Teachers'*
Casebook: What Would They Do?

A re you one of those people whose blood pressure goes up when it is taken in the doctor's office? Have you ever worn something new and received so many compliments that you found yourself wearing that outfit often? What happens when you tell a joke and no one laughs? Are you more or less likely to tell the joke in the future? If you see someone severely reprimanded for reading a newspaper in class, are you more or less likely to read the paper in that class? Does learning have an influence on your answers to these questions? We will spend the next four chapters looking at learning and its applications.

We begin this chapter with a general definition of learning that takes into account the opposing views of different theoretical groups. We will highlight one group, the behavioral theorists, in this chapter and the other major group, the cognitive theorists, in Chapters 7, 8, and 9.

Our discussion in this chapter will focus on four behavioral learning processes: contiguity, classical conditioning, operant conditioning, and observational learning, with the greatest emphasis on the last two processes. After examining the implications of applied behavior analysis for teaching, we look at three recent directions in behavioral approaches to learning —social learning theory, self-management, and cognitive behavior modification.

By the time you have completed this chapter, you should be able to:

- Define learning.
- Compare contiguity, classical conditioning, and operant conditioning, and give examples of each.
- Give examples of four different kinds of consequences that can follow any behavior and the effect each is likely to have on future behavior.
- Select a common academic or behavior problem and design an intervention based on applied behavior analysis.
- Describe situations in which a teacher may wish to use modeling.
- Compare self-management and cognitive behavior modification.

What Would You Do?

You were hired in January to take over the class of a teacher who moved away. This is a great district and a terrific school. If you do well, you might be in line for a full-time opening next fall. As you are introduced around the school, you get a number of sympathetic looks and many—too many—offers of help: "Let me know if I can do anything for you."

As you walk toward the class, you begin to understand why so many teachers volunteered their help. You hear the screaming when you are still halfway down the hall. "Give it back, it's MINE!" "No way—come and get it!" "I hate you." A crashing sound follows as a table full of books hits the floor. The first day is a nightmare. Evidently the previous teacher had no management system—no order. Several students walk around the room while you are talking to the class, interrupt you when you are working with a group, torment the class goldfish, and open their lunches (or other students') for a self-determined, mid-morning snack. Others listen, but ask a million questions off the topic. Simply taking roll and introducing the first activity takes an hour. You end the first day exhausted and discouraged, losing your voice and your patience.

- How would you approach the situation?

- Which problem behaviors would you tackle first?

- Would giving rewards or administering punishments be useful in this situation? Why or why not?

Understanding Learning

When we hear the word "learning," most of us think of studying and school. We think about subjects or skills we intend to master, such as algebra, Spanish, chemistry, or karate. But learning is not limited to school. We learn every day of our lives. Babies learn to kick their legs to make the mobile above their cribs move, teenagers learn the lyrics to all their favorite songs, middle-aged people like me learn to change their diet and exercise patterns, and every few years we all learn to find a new style of dress attractive when the old styles (the styles we once loved) go out of fashion. This last example shows that learning is not always intentional. We don't try to like new styles and dislike old; it just seems to happen that way. We don't intend to become nervous when we see the dentist fill a syringe with Novocain or when we step onto a stage, yet many of us do. So what is this powerful phenomenon called learning?

Learning Process through which experience causes permanent change in knowledge or behavior.

Learning: A Definition

In the broadest sense, **learning** occurs when experience causes a relatively permanent change in an individual's knowledge or behavior. The change may be deliberate or unintentional, for better or for worse. To qualify as learning, this

204

change must be brought about by experience—by the interaction of a person with his or her environment. Changes simply caused by maturation, such as growing taller or turning gray, do not qualify as learning. Temporary changes resulting from illness, fatigue, or hunger are also excluded from a general definition of learning. A person who has gone without food for two days does not learn to be hungry, and a person who is ill does not learn to run more slowly. Of course, learning plays a part in how we respond to hunger or illness.

Our definition specifies that the changes resulting from learning are in the individual's knowledge or behavior. While most psychologists would agree with this statement, some tend to emphasize the change in knowledge, others the change in behavior. Cognitive psychologists, who focus on changes in knowledge, believe learning is an internal mental activity that cannot be observed directly. As you will see in the next chapter, cognitive psychologists studying learning are interested in unobservable mental activities such as thinking, remembering, and solving problems (Schwartz & Reisberg, 1991).

The psychologists discussed in this chapter, on the other hand, favor **behavioral learning theories.** The behavioral view generally assumes that the outcome of learning is change in behavior and emphasizes the effects of external events on the individual. Some early behaviorists like J. B. Watson took the radical position that because thinking, intentions, and other internal mental events could not be seen or studied rigorously and scientifically, these "mentalisms," as he called them, should not even be included in an explanation of learning. Before we look in depth at behavioral explanations of learning, let's step into an actual classroom and note the possible results of learning.

Learning Is Not Always What It Seems

Elizabeth was beginning her first day of solo teaching. After weeks of working with her cooperating teacher in an eighth-grade social studies class, she was ready to take over. As she moved from behind the desk to the front of the room, she saw another adult approach the classroom door. It was Mr. Ross, her supervisor from college. Elizabeth's neck and facial muscles suddenly became very tense and her hands trembled.

"I've stopped by to observe your teaching," Mr. Ross said. "This will be my first of six visits. I tried to reach you last night to tell you."

Elizabeth tried to hide her reaction, but her hands trembled as she gathered the notes for the lesson.

"Let's start today with a kind of game. I will say some words, then I want you to tell me the first words you can think of. Don't bother to raise your hands. Just say the words out loud, and I will write them on the board. Don't all speak at once, though. Wait until someone else has finished to say your word. Okay, here is the first word: Slavery."

"Civil War." "Lincoln." "Freedom." "Emancipation Proclamation." The answers came very quickly, and Elizabeth was relieved to see that the students understood the game.

"All right, very good," she said. "Now try another one: South."

"South Carolina." "South Dakota." "South Street Seaport." "No, the Confederacy, you dummy." "*Gone with the Wind.*" "Clark Gable." With this last answer, a ripple of laughter moved across the room.

Behavioral Learning Theories Explanations of learning that focus on external events as the cause of changes in observable behaviors.

Are there experiences in your "learning history" that have made you anxious about speaking in public or taking tests? How might behavioral principals of learning help to explain the development of these anxieties?

"Clark Gable!" Elizabeth sighed dreamily. "*Gone with the Wind* was on television last month." Then she laughed too. Soon all the students were laughing. "Okay, settle down," Elizabeth said. "Here is another word: North."

"Bluebellies." The students continued to laugh. "Yellowbellies." "Bellydancers." More laughter and a few appropriate gestures.

"Just a minute," Elizabeth pleaded. "These ideas are getting a little off base!"

"Off base? Baseball," shouted the boy who had first mentioned Clark Gable. He stood up and started throwing balls of paper to a friend in the back of the room, simulating the style of Roger Clemens.

"The Atlanta Braves." "No, the Mets." "Shea Stadium." "Hot dogs." "Popcorn." "Home videos." "*Gone with the Wind.*" "Clark Gable." The responses now came too fast for Elizabeth to stop them. For some reason, the Clark Gable line got an even bigger laugh the second time around, and Elizabeth suddenly realized she had lost the class.

"Okay, since you know so much about the Civil War, close your books and take out a pen," Elizabeth said, obviously angry. She passed out the worksheet that she had planned as a cooperative, open-book project. "You have 20 minutes to finish this test!"

"You didn't tell us we were having a test!" "This isn't fair!" "We haven't even covered this stuff yet!" "I didn't do anything wrong!" There were moans and disgusted looks, even from the most mellow students. "I'm reporting you to the principal; it's a violation of students' rights!"

This last comment hit hard. The class had just finished discussing human rights as preparation for this unit on the Civil War. As she listened to the protests, Elizabeth felt terrible. How was she going to grade these "tests"? The first section of the worksheet involved facts about events during the Civil War, and the second section asked students to create a news-style program interviewing ordinary people touched by the war.

"All right, all right, it won't be a test. But you do have to complete this worksheet for a grade. I was going to let you work together, but your behavior this morning tells me that you are not ready for group work. If you can complete the first section of the sheet working quietly and seriously, you may work together on the second section." Elizabeth knew that her students would like to work together on writing the script for the news interview program.

It appears, on the surface at least, that very little learning of any sort was taking place in Elizabeth's classroom. In fact, Elizabeth had some good ideas; but she also made some mistakes in her application of learning principles. We will return to this episode later in the chapter to analyze various aspects of what took place. To get us started, four events can be singled out, each possibly related to a different learning process.

First, Elizabeth's hands trembled when her college supervisor entered the room. Second, the students were able to associate the words *Carolina* and *Dakota* with the word *South*. Third, one student continued to disrupt the class with inappropriate responses. And fourth, after Elizabeth laughed at a student comment, the class joined in her laughter. The four learning processes represented are classical conditioning, contiguity, operant conditioning, and observational learning. In the following pages we will examine these four kinds of learning, starting with contiguity.

Early Explanations of Learning: Contiguity and Classical Conditioning

One of the earliest explanations of learning came from Aristotle (384–322 B.C.). He said that we remember things together (1) when they are similar, (2) when they contrast, and (3) when they are *contiguous*. This last principle is the most important, because it is included in all explanations of *learning by association*. The principle of **contiguity** states that whenever two or more sensations occur together often enough, they will become associated. Later, when only one of these sensations (a **stimulus**) occurs, the other will be remembered too (a **response**) (Rachlin, 1991).

Some results of contiguous learning were evident in Elizabeth's class. When she said "South," students associated the words "Carolina" and "Dakota." They had heard these words together many times. Other learning processes may also be involved when students learn these phrases, but contiguity is a factor. Contiguity also plays a major role in another learning process best known as *classical conditioning*.

Pavlov's Dilemma and Discovery: Classical Conditioning

Classical conditioning focuses on the learning of *involuntary* emotional or physiological responses such as fear, increased heartbeat, salivation, or sweating, which are sometimes called **respondents** because they are automatic responses to stimuli. Through the process of classical conditioning, humans and animals can be trained to react involuntarily to a stimulus that previously had no effect—or a very different effect—on them. The stimulus comes to *elicit*, or bring forth, the response automatically.

Classical conditioning was discovered by Ivan Pavlov, a Russian physiologist, in the 1920s. In his laboratory, Pavlov was plagued by a series of setbacks in his experiments on the digestive system of dogs. He was trying to determine how long it took a dog to secrete digestive juices after it had been fed, but the intervals of time kept changing. At first, the dogs salivated in the expected manner while they were being fed. Then the dogs began to salivate as soon as they saw the food. Finally, they salivated as soon as they saw the scientist enter the room. The white coats of the experimenters and the sound of their footsteps all *elicited* salivation. Pavlov decided to make a detour from his original experiments and examine these unexpected interferences in his work.

In one of his first experiments, Pavlov began by sounding a tuning fork and recording a dog's response. As expected, there was no salivation. At this point, the sound of the tuning fork was a **neutral stimulus** because it brought forth no salivation. Then Pavlov fed the dog. The response was salivation. The food was an **unconditioned stimulus (US)** because no prior training or "conditioning" was needed to establish the natural connection between food and salivation. The salivation was an **unconditioned response (UR)**, again because it occurred automatically—no conditioning required.

Contiguity Association of two events because of repeated pairing.

Stimulus Event that activates behavior.

Response Observable reaction to a stimulus.

Classical Conditioning Association of automatic responses with new stimuli.

Respondents Responses (generally automatic or involuntary) elicited by specific stimuli.

Neutral Stimulus Stimulus not connected to a response.

Unconditioned Stimulus (US) Stimulus that automatically produces an emotional or physiological response.

Unconditioned Response (UR) Naturally occurring emotional or physiological response.

Using these three elements—the food, the salivation, and the tuning fork—Pavlov demonstrated that a dog could be conditioned to salivate after hearing the tuning fork. He did this by contiguous pairing of the sound with food. At the beginning of the experiment, he sounded the fork and then quickly fed the dog. After Pavlov repeated this several times, the dog began to salivate after hearing the sound but before receiving the food. Now the sound had become a **conditioned stimulus** (CS) that could bring forth salivation by itself. The response of salivating after the tone was now a **conditioned response** (CR).

Generalization, Discrimination, and Extinction

Pavlov's work also identified three other processes in classical conditioning: *generalization, discrimination,* and *extinction.* After the dogs learned to salivate in response to hearing one particular sound, they would also salivate after hearing similar tones that were slightly higher or lower. This process is called **generalization** because the conditioned response of salivating generalized or occurred in the presence of similar stimuli. Pavlov could also teach the dogs **discrimination**—to respond to one tone but not to others that are similar—by making sure that food always followed only one tone, not any others. **Extinction** occurs when a conditioned stimulus (a particular tone) is presented repeatedly but is not followed by the unconditioned stimulus (food). The conditioned response (salivating) gradually fades away and finally is "extinguished"—it disappears altogether.

Pavlov's findings and those of other researchers who have studied classical conditioning have implications for teachers. It is possible that many of our emotional reactions to various situations are learned in part through classical conditioning. For example, Elizabeth's trembling hands when she saw her college supervisor might be traced to previous unpleasant experiences. Perhaps she had been embarrassed during past evaluations of her performance, and now just the thought of being observed elicits a pounding heart and sweaty palms. Remember that emotions and attitudes as well as facts and ideas are learned in classrooms. This emotional learning can sometimes interfere with academic learning. Procedures based on classical conditioning also can be used to help people learn more adaptive emotional responses, as the Guidelines on page 209 suggest.

Operant Conditioning: Trying New Responses

So far we have concentrated on the automatic conditioning of involuntary responses such as salivation and fear. Clearly, not all human learning is so automatic and unintentional. Most behaviors are not *elicited* by stimuli, they are *emitted* or voluntarily enacted. People actively "operate" on their environment to produce different kinds of consequences. These deliberate actions are called **operants**. The learning process involved in operant behavior is called **operant conditioning** because we learn to behave in certain ways as we operate on the environment.

Focus on . . .

Classical Conditioning

- How does a neutral stimulus become a conditioned stimulus?
- Discriminate between generalization and discrimination.
- After several painful visits to the dentist, you feel your heart rate increase when you sit down in the dentist's chair to have your teeth cleaned. Analyze this situation in terms of classical conditioning.

Conditioned Stimulus (CS) Stimulus that evokes an emotional or physiological response after conditioning.

Conditioned Response (CR) Learned response to a previously neutral stimulus.

Generalization Responding in the same way to similar stimuli.

Discrimination Responding differently to similar, but not identical stimuli.

Extinction Gradual disappearance of a learned response.

Operants Voluntary (and generally goal-directed) behaviors emitted by a person or an animal.

Operant Conditioning Learning in which voluntary behavior is strengthened or weakened by consequences or antecedents.

Associate positive, pleasant events with learning tasks.

Examples

1. Emphasize group competition and cooperation over individual competition. Many students have negative emotional responses to individual competition that may generalize to other learning.

2. Make division drills fun by having students decide how to divide refreshments equally, then letting them eat the results.

3. Make voluntary reading appealing by creating a comfortable reading corner with pillows, colorful displays of books, and reading props such as puppets (see Morrow & Weinstein, 1986, for more ideas).

**Help students to risk anxiety-producing situations voluntarily
and successfully.**

Examples

1. Assign a shy student the responsibility of teaching two other students how to distribute materials for map study.

2. Devise small steps toward a larger goal. For example, give ungraded practice tests daily, and then weekly, to students who tend to "freeze" in test situations.

3. If a student is afraid of speaking in front of the class, let the student read a report to a small group while seated, then read it while standing, then give the report from notes instead of reading it verbatim. Next, move in stages toward having the student give a report to the whole class.

**Help students recognize differences and similarities among situations so they
can discriminate and generalize appropriately.**

Examples

1. Explain that it is appropriate to avoid strangers who offer gifts or rides but safe to accept favors from adults when parents are present.

2. Assure students who are anxious about taking college entrance exams that this test is like all the other achievement tests they have taken.

The Work of Thorndike and Skinner

Edward Thorndike and B. F. Skinner both played major roles in developing knowledge of operant conditioning. Thorndike's (1913) early work involved cats that he placed in problem boxes. To escape from the box and reach food outside, the cats had to pull out a bolt or perform some other task; they had to act on their environment. During the frenzied movements that followed the closing of the box, the cats eventually made the correct movement to escape, usually by accident. After repeating the process several times, the cats learned to make the correct response almost immediately. Thorndike decided, on the basis of these experiments, that one important law of learning was the law of effect: Any act that produces a satisfying effect in a given situation will tend to be repeated in that

*B.*F. *Skinner's work on operant conditioning changed the way we think about consequences and learning.*

situation. Because pulling out a bolt produced satisfaction (access to food), cats repeated that movement when they found themselves in the box again.

Thorndike thus established the basis for operant conditioning, but the person generally thought to be responsible for developing the concept is B. F. Skinner (1953). Skinner began with the belief that the principles of classical conditioning account for only a small portion of learned behaviors. Many human behaviors are operants, not respondents. Classical conditioning describes only how existing behaviors might be paired with new stimuli; it does not explain how new operant behaviors are acquired.

Behavior, like response or action, is simply a word for what a person does in a particular situation. Conceptually, we may think of a behavior as sandwiched between two sets of environmental influences: those that precede it (its **antecedents**) and those that follow it (its **consequences**) (Skinner, 1950). This relationship can be shown very simply as antecedent–behavior–consequence, or A–B–C. As behavior is ongoing, a given consequence becomes an antecedent for the next ABC sequence. Research in operant conditioning shows that operant behavior can be altered by changes in the antecedents, the consequences, or both. Early work focused on consequences, often using rats or pigeons as subjects.

Types of Consequences

According to the behavioral view, consequences determine to a great extent whether a person will repeat the behavior that led to the consequences. The type and timing of consequences can strengthen or weaken behaviors. We will look first at consequences that strengthen behavior.

Reinforcement.   While **reinforcement** is commonly understood to mean "reward," this term has a particular meaning in psychology. A **reinforcer** is any consequence that strengthens the behavior it follows. So, by definition, *reinforced behaviors increase in frequency or duration.* Whenever you see a behavior persisting or increasing over time, you can assume the consequences of that behavior are reinforcers for the individual involved. The reinforcement process can be diagrammed as follows:

	CONSEQUENCE		EFFECT
Behavior ⟶	Reinforcer	⟶	Strengthened or repeated behavior

We can be fairly certain that food will be a reinforcer for a hungry animal, but what about people? It is not clear why an event acts as a reinforcer for an individual, but there are many theories about why reinforcement works. For example, some psychologists suggest that reinforcers satisfy needs, while other psychologists believe that reinforcers reduce tension or stimulate a part of the brain (Rachlin, 1991). Whether the consequences of any action are reinforcing probably depends on the individual's perception of the event and the meaning it holds for her or him. For example, students who repeatedly get themselves sent to the principal's office for misbehaving may be indicating that something about this consequence is reinforcing for them, even if it doesn't seem desirable to you.

Reinforcers are those consequences that strengthen the associated behavior (Skinner, 1953, 1989). There are two types of reinforcement. The first, called **positive reinforcement,** occurs when the behavior produces a new stimulus. Ex-

Antecedents Events that precede an action.

Consequences Events that are brought about by an action.

Reinforcement Use of consequences to strengthen behavior.

Reinforcer Any event that follows a behavior and increases the chances that the behavior will occur again.

Positive Reinforcement Strengthening behavior by presenting a desired stimulus after the behavior.

amples include a peck on the red key producing food for a pigeon, wearing a new outfit producing many compliments, or falling out of your chair producing cheers and laughter from classmates.

Notice that positive reinforcement can occur even when the behavior being reinforced (falling out of a chair) is not "positive" from the teacher's point of view. In fact, positive reinforcement of inappropriate behaviors occurs unintentionally in many classrooms. Teachers help maintain problem behaviors by inadvertently reinforcing them. For example, Elizabeth may have unintentionally reinforced problem behavior in her class by laughing the first time the boy answered, "Clark Gable." The problem behavior may have persisted for other reasons, but the consequence of Elizabeth's laughter could have played a role.

When the consequence that strengthens a behavior is the *appearance* (addition) of a new stimulus, the situation is defined as positive reinforcement. In contrast, when the consequence that strengthens a behavior is the *disappearance* (subtraction) of a stimulus, the process is called **negative reinforcement.** If a particular action leads to stopping, avoiding, or escaping an **aversive** situation, the action is likely to be repeated in a similar situation. A common example is the car seatbelt buzzer. As soon as you attach your seatbelt, the irritating buzzer stops. You are likely to repeat this action in the future because the behavior made an aversive stimulus disappear. Consider students who continually "get sick" right before a test and are sent to the nurse's office. The behavior allows the students to escape aversive situations—tests—so getting "sick" is being maintained, in part, through negative reinforcement. It is negative because the stimulus (the test) disappears; it is reinforcement because the behavior that caused the stimulus to disappear (getting "sick") increases or repeats. It is also possible that classical conditioning plays a role. The students may have been conditioned to experience unpleasant physiological reactions to tests.

The "negative" in negative reinforcement does not imply that the behavior being reinforced is necessarily negative. The meaning is closer to that of "negative" numbers—something is subtracted. Associate positive and negative reinforcement with adding or subtracting something following a behavior.

Punishment.   Negative reinforcement is often confused with punishment. The process of reinforcement (positive or negative) always involves strengthening behavior. **Punishment,** on the other hand, involves *decreasing or suppressing behavior.* A behavior followed by a "punisher" is *less* likely to be repeated in similar situations in the future. Again, it is the effect that defines a consequence as punishment, and different people have different perceptions of what is punishing. One student may find suspension from school punishing, while another student wouldn't mind at all. The process of punishment is diagrammed as follows:

CONSEQUENCE   EFFECT

Behavior ──▶ Punisher ──▶ Weakened or decreased behavior

Like reinforcement, punishment may take one of two forms. The first type has been called Type I punishment, but this name isn't very informative, so I use the term **presentation punishment.** It occurs when the appearance of a stimulus following the behavior suppresses or decreases the behavior. When teachers assign demerits, extra work, running laps, and so on, they are using presen-

Negative Reinforcement Strengthening behavior by removing an aversive stimulus.

Aversive Irritating or unpleasant.

Punishment Process that weakens or suppresses behavior.

Presentation Punishment Decreasing the chances that a behavior will occur again by presenting an aversive stimulus following the behavior; also called Type I punishment.

FIGURE 6.1

Kinds of Reinforcement and Punishment

Negative reinforcement and punishment are often confused. It may help you to remember that reinforcement is always associated with increases in behavior, and punishment always involves decreasing or suppressing behavior.

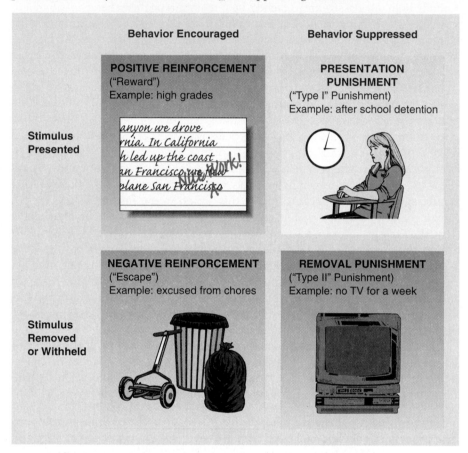

Removal Punishment Decreasing the chances that a behavior will occur again by removing a pleasant stimulus following the behavior; also called Type II punishment.

Continuous Reinforcement Schedule Presenting a reinforcer after every appropriate response.

Intermittent Reinforcement Schedule Presenting a reinforcer after some but not all responses.

Interval Schedule Length of time between reinforcers.

Ratio Schedule Number of responses between reinforcers.

tation punishment. The other type of punishment (Type II punishment) I call **removal punishment** because it involves removing a stimulus. When teachers or parents take away privileges after a young person has behaved inappropriately, they are applying removal punishment. With both types, the effect is to decrease the behavior that led to the punishment. Figure 6.1 summarizes the processes of reinforcement and punishment.

Reinforcement Schedules

When people are learning a new behavior, they will learn it faster if they are reinforced for every correct response. This is a **continuous reinforcement schedule.** Then, when the new behavior has been mastered, they will maintain it best if they are reinforced intermittently rather than every time. An **intermittent reinforcement schedule** helps students to maintain skills without expecting constant reinforcement.

TABLE 6.1   Reinforcement Schedules

Schedule	Definition	Example	Response Pattern	Reaction When Reinforcement Stops
Continuous	Reinforcement after every response	Turning on the television	Rapid learning of response	Very little persistence; rapid disappearance of response
Fixed-interval	Reinforcement after a set period of time	Weekly quiz	Response rate increases as time for reinforcement approaches, then drops after reinforcement	Little persistence; rapid drop in response rate when time for reinforcement passes and no reinforcer appears
Variable-interval	Reinforcement after varying lengths of time	Pop quizzes	Slow, steady rate of responding; very little pause after reinforcement	Greater persistence; slow decline in response rate
Fixed-ratio	Reinforcement after a set number of responses	Piece work Bake sale	Rapid response rate; pause after reinforcement	Little persistence; rapid drop in response rate when expected number of responses are given and no reinforcer appears
Variable-ratio	Reinforcement after a varying number of responses	Slot machines	Very high response rate; little pause after reinforcement	Greatest persistence; response rate stays high and gradually drops off

There are two basic types of intermittent reinforcement schedules. One—called an **interval schedule**—is based on the amount of time that passes between reinforcers. The other—a **ratio schedule**—is based on the number of responses learners give between reinforcers. Interval and ratio schedules may be either *fixed* (predictable) or *variable* (unpredictable). Table 6.1 summarizes the five possible reinforcement schedules (the continuous schedule and the four kinds of intermittent schedules).

Summarizing the Effects of Reinforcement Schedules

Speed of performance depends on control. If reinforcement is based on the number of responses you give, then you have more control over the reinforcement: the faster you accumulate the correct number of responses, the faster the reinforcement will come. A teacher who says, "As soon as you complete these ten problems correctly, you may go to the student lounge," can expect higher rates of performance than a teacher who says, "Work on these ten problems for the next 20 minutes. Then I will check your papers and those with ten correct may go to the lounge."

Persistence in performance depends on predictability. Continuous reinforcement and both kinds of fixed reinforcement (ratio and interval) are quite

Casino slot machines are a good example of the effectiveness of intermittent reinforcement: People "learn" to persist in losing their money on the chance that they will be rewarded with a jackpot.

predictable. We come to expect reinforcement at certain points and are generally quick to give up when the reinforcement does not meet our expectations. To encourage persistence of response, variable schedules are most appropriate. In fact, if the schedule is gradually changed until it becomes very "lean"—meaning that reinforcement occurs only after many responses or a long time interval—then people can learn to work for extended periods without any reinforcement at all. Just watch gamblers playing slot machines to see how powerful a lean reinforcement schedule can be.

Reinforcement schedules influence how persistently we will respond when reinforcement is withheld. What happens when reinforcement is completely withdrawn?

Extinction. In classical conditioning, we saw that the conditioned response was extinguished (disappeared) when the conditioned stimulus appeared but the unconditioned stimulus did not follow (tone, but no food). In operant conditioning, a person or an animal will not persist in a certain behavior if the usual reinforcer is withheld. The behavior will eventually be extinguished (stop). For example, if you go for a week without selling even one magazine door-to-door, you may give up. Removal of reinforcement altogether leads to extinction. The process may take a while, however, as you know if you have tried to extinguish a child's tantrums by withholding your attention. Often the child wins—you give up ignoring and instead of extinction, intermittent reinforcement occurs. This, of course, may encourage even more persistent tantrums in the future.

Focus on...

Consequences

- What defines a consequence as a reinforcer? As a punisher?
- How are negative reinforcement and punishment different?
- How can you encourage persistence in a behavior?

Antecedents and Behavior Change

In operant conditioning, antecedents—the events preceding behaviors—provide information about which behaviors will lead to positive consequences and which to negative. Skinner's pigeons learned to peck for food when a light was on, but not to bother when the light was off, because no food followed pecking when the light was off. In other words, they learned to use the antecedent light as a cue to discriminate the likely consequence of pecking. The pigeons' pecking was under **stimulus control**, controlled by the discriminative stimulus of the light. You can see that this idea is related to discrimination in classical conditioning, but here we are talking about voluntary behaviors like pecking, not reflexes like salivating.

We all learn to discriminate—to read situations. When should you ask to borrow your roommate's car, after a major disagreement or after you both have had a great time at a party? The antecedent cue of a school principal standing in the hall helps students discriminate the probable consequences of running or attempting to break into a locker. We often respond to such antecedent cues without fully realizing that they are influencing our behavior. But teachers can use cues deliberately in the classroom.

Stimulus Control Capacity for the presence or absence of antecedents to cause behaviors.

Cueing Providing a stimulus that "sets up" a desired behavior.

Prompt A reminder that follows a cue to make sure the person reacts to the cue.

ENVIROMENTAL
Cueing. By definition, **cueing** is the act of providing an antecedent stimulus just before a particular behavior is to take place. Cueing is particularly useful in setting the stage for behaviors that must occur at a specific time but are easily forgotten. In working with young people, teachers often find themselves correcting behaviors after the fact. For example, they may ask students,

"When are you going to start remembering to . . . ?" Such reminders often lead to irritation. The mistake is already made, and the young person is left with only two choices, to promise to try harder or to say, "Why don't you leave me alone?" Neither response is very satisfying. Presenting a nonjudgmental cue can help prevent these negative confrontations. When a student performs the appropriate behavior after a cue, the teacher can reinforce the student's accomplishment instead of punishing the student's failure.

Prompting. Sometimes students need help in learning to respond to a cue in an appropriate way so the cue becomes a discriminative stimulus. One approach is to provide an additional cue, called a **prompt,** following the first cue. There are two principles for using a cue and a prompt to teach a new behavior (Becker, Engelmann, & Thomas, 1975). First, make sure the environmental stimulus that you want to become a cue occurs immediately before the prompt you are using, so students will learn to respond to the cue and not rely only on the prompt. Second, fade the prompt as soon as possible so students do not become dependent on it.

An example of cueing and prompting is providing students with a checklist or reminder sheet. Figure 6.2 is a checklist for the steps in peer tutoring.

FIGURE 6.2

Written Prompts: A Peer-Tutoring Checklist

By using this checklist, students are reminded how to be effective tutors. As they become more proficient, the checklist may be less necessary.

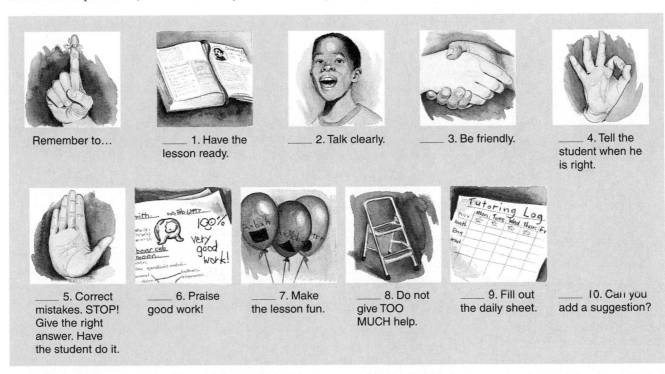

Remember to…

_____ 1. Have the lesson ready.

_____ 2. Talk clearly.

_____ 3. Be friendly.

_____ 4. Tell the student when he is right.

_____ 5. Correct mistakes. STOP! Give the right answer. Have the student do it.

_____ 6. Praise good work!

_____ 7. Make the lesson fun.

_____ 8. Do not give TOO MUCH help.

_____ 9. Fill out the daily sheet.

_____ 10. Can you add a suggestion?

Source: From B. Sulzer-Azaroff and G. R. Mayer. Figure from *Achieving educational excellence: Behavior analysis for school personnel,* p. 89. Copyright © 1994 by Beth Sulzer-Azaroff and G. Roy Mayer (San Marcos, CA: Western Image, P.O. Box 427). Reprinted by permission of the authors.

Focus on...

Antecedents

- What is the difference between a prompt and a cue?
- In what kinds of situations is cueing helpful?

Working in pairs is the cue; the checklist is the prompt. As students learn the procedures, the teacher may stop using the checklist, but may remind the students of the steps. When no written or oral prompts are necessary, the students have learned to respond appropriately to the environmental cue of working in pairs—they have learned how to behave in tutoring situations. But the teacher should continue to monitor the process, recognize good work, and correct mistakes. Before a tutoring session, the teacher might ask students to close their eyes and "see" the checklist, focusing on each step. As students work, the teacher could listen to their interactions and continue to coach students as they improve their tutoring skills.

Applied Behavior Analysis

Applied behavior analysis is the application of behavioral learning principles to change behavior. The method is sometimes called **behavior modification,** but this term has negative connotations for many people and is often misunderstood (Alberto & Troutman, 1990; Kaplan, 1991).

Ideally, applied behavior analysis requires clear specification of the behavior to be changed, careful measurement of the behavior, analysis of the antecedents and reinforcers that might be maintaining inappropriate or undesirable behavior, interventions based on behavioral principles to change the behavior, and careful measurement of changes. In research on applied behavior analysis, an ABAB design is common. That is, researchers take a baseline measurement of the behavior (A), then apply the intervention (B), then stop the intervention to see if the behavior goes back to the baseline level (A), and then reintroduce the intervention (B).

In classrooms, teachers usually cannot follow all the ABAB steps, but they can do the following:

1. Clearly specify the behavior to be changed and note the current level. For example, if a student is "careless," does this mean 2, 3, 4, or more computation errors for every 10 problems?

2. Plan a specific intervention using antecedents, consequences, or both. For example, offer the student one extra minute of computer time for every problem completed with no errors.

3. Keep track of the results, and modify the plan if necessary.

Let's consider some specific methods for accomplishing step 2—the *intervention.*

Methods for Encouraging Behaviors

As we discussed earlier, to encourage behavior is to reinforce it. There are several specific ways to encourage existing behaviors or teach new ones. These include praise, the Premack principle, shaping, and positive practice.

Reinforcing with Teacher Attention.   Based on early work such as that of Madsen, Becker, and Thomas (1968) demonstrating that teachers can im-

Applied Behavior Analysis The application of behavioral learning principles to understand and change behavior.

Behavior Modification Systematic application of antecedents and consequences to change behavior.

prove student behavior by ignoring rule-breakers and praising students who are following the rules, many psychologists advised teachers to "accentuate the positive"—liberally praise students for good behavior while ignoring mistakes and misbehavior. This *praise-and-ignore approach* can be helpful, but we should not expect it to solve all classroom management problems. Several studies have shown that disruptive behaviors persist when teachers use positive consequences (mostly praise) as their only classroom management strategy (Pfiffner, Rosen, & O'Leary, 1985; Rosen, O'Leary, Joyce, Conway, & Pfiffner, 1984).

There is a second consideration in using praise. The positive results found in research occur when teachers carefully and systematically praise their students. Unfortunately, praise is not always given appropriately and effectively. Merely "handing out compliments" will not improve behavior. To be effective, praise must (1) be contingent on the behavior to be reinforced, (2) specify clearly the behavior being reinforced, and (3) be believable (O'Leary & O'Leary, 1977). In other words, the praise should be sincere recognition of a well-defined behavior so students understand what they did to warrant the recognition. Teachers who have not received special training often violate these conditions (Brophy, 1981). Ideas for using praise effectively, based on Brophy's extensive review of the subject, are presented in the Guidelines.

Guidelines

Using Praise Appropriately

Be clear and systematic in giving praise.

Examples

1. Make sure praise is tied directly to appropriate behavior.
2. Make sure the student understands the specific action or accomplishment that is being praised. Say, "You returned this poster on time and in good condition," not, "You were very responsible."

Recognize genuine accomplishments.

Examples

1. Reward the attainment of specified goals, not just participation.
2. Do not reward uninvolved students just for being quiet and not disrupting the class.
3. Tie praise to students' improving competence or to the value of their accomplishment. Say, "I noticed that you double-checked all your problems. Your score reflects your careful work."

Set standards for praise based on individual abilities and limitations.

Examples

1. Praise progress or accomplishment in relation to the individual student's past efforts.
2. Focus the student's attention on his or her own progress, not on comparisons with others.

Attribute the student's success to effort and ability so the student will gain confidence that success is possible again.

Examples

1. Don't imply that the success may be based on luck, extra help, or easy material.

(continued)

2. Ask students to describe the problems they encountered and how they solved them.

Make praise really reinforcing.

Examples
1. Don't attempt to influence the rest of the class by singling out some students for praise. This tactic frequently backfires, since students know what's really going on. In addition, you risk embarrassing the student you have chosen to praise.
2. Don't give undeserved praise to students simply to balance failures. It is seldom consoling and calls attention to the student's inability to earn genuine recognition.

Some psychologists have suggested that teachers' use of praise tends to focus students on learning to win approval rather than on learning for its own sake. Perhaps the best advice is to be aware of the potential dangers of the overuse or misuse of praise and to navigate accordingly.

Selecting Reinforcers: The Premack Principle. In most classrooms, there are many readily available reinforcers other than teacher attention, such as the chance to talk to other students or feed the class animals. But teachers tend to offer these opportunities in a rather haphazard way. Just as with praise, by making privileges and rewards directly contingent on learning and positive behavior, the teacher may greatly increase both learning and desired behavior.

A helpful guide for choosing the most effective reinforcers is the Premack principle, named for David Premack (1965). According to the **Premack principle,** a high-frequency behavior (a preferred activity) can be an effective reinforcer for a low-frequency behavior (a less-preferred activity). This is sometimes referred to as "Grandma's rule": first do what I want you to do, then you may do what you want to do. Elizabeth used this principle in her class when she told them they could work together on their Civil War news program after they quietly completed the first section of the worksheet on their own.

If students didn't have to study, what would they do? The answers to this question may suggest many possible reinforcers. For most students, talking, moving around the room, sitting near a friend, being exempt from assignments or tests, reading magazines, or playing games are preferred activities. The best way to determine appropriate reinforcers for your students may be to watch what they do in their free time.

For the Premack principle to be effective, the low-frequency (less preferred) behavior must happen first. In the following dialogue, notice how the teacher loses a perfect opportunity to use the Premack principle:

Students: Oh, no! Do we have to work on grammar again today? The other classes got to discuss the film we saw in the auditorium this morning.

Teacher: But the other classes finished the lesson on sentences yesterday. We're almost finished too. If we don't finish the lesson, I'm afraid you'll forget the rules we reviewed yesterday.

Students: Why don't we finish the sentences at the end of the period and talk about the film now?

Teacher: Okay, if you promise to complete the sentences later.

Premack Principle Principle stating that a more-preferred activity can serve as reinforcer for a less-preferred activity.

TABLE 6.2   What Do You Like? Reinforcement Ideas from Students

Name _____ Grade _____ Date_____

Please answer all the questions as completely as you can.

1. The school subjects I like best are:
2. Three things I like most to do in school are:
3. If I had 30 minutes' free time at school each day to do what I really liked, it would be:
4. My two favorite snacks are:
5. At recess I like most to (three things):
6. If I had $1 to spend on anything, I would buy:
7. Three jobs I would enjoy in the class are:
8. The two people I most like to work with in school are:
9. At home I really enjoy (three things):

Source: From G. Blackham and A. Silberman (1979). *Modification of child and adolescent behavior,* 3rd ed., pp. 281–283. Copyright © 1979 by Wadsworth Publishing Co. Reprinted by permission of the publisher.

Discussing the film could have served as a reinforcer for completing the lesson. As it is, the class may well spend the entire period discussing the film. Just as the discussion becomes fascinating, the teacher will have to end it and insist that the class return to the grammar lesson.

Some teachers use questionnaires like the one in Table 6.2 to identify effective reinforcers for their students. Remember, what works for one student may not be right for another. And students can get "too much of a good thing"—reinforcers can lose their potency if they are overused.

Shaping.   What happens when students continually fail to gain reinforcement because they simply cannot perform a skill in the first place? Consider these examples:

> A fourth-grade student looks at the results of the latest mathematics test. "No credit on almost half of the problems again because I made one dumb mistake in each problem. I hate math!"

> A 10th-grade student tries each day to find some excuse for avoiding the softball game in gym class. The student cannot catch a ball and now refuses to try.

In both situations the students are receiving no reinforcement for their work because the end product of their efforts is not good enough. A safe prediction is that the students will soon learn to dislike the class, the subject, and perhaps the teacher and school in general. One way to prevent this problem is the strategy of **shaping,** also called **successive approximations.** Shaping involves reinforcing progress instead of waiting for perfection.

In order to use shaping, the teacher must break down the final complex behavior the student is expected to master into a number of small steps. One approach identifying the small steps is **task analysis,** originally developed by R. B.

"HEY, WAIT A MINUTE! YOU'RE CLEANING ERASERS AS A PUNISHMENT? I'M CLEANING ERASERS AS A REWARD!"

(© 1991 Tony Saltzman)

Shaping Reinforcing each small step of progress toward a desired goal or behavior.

Successive Approximations Small components that make up a complex behavior.

Task Analysis System for breaking down a task hierarchically into basic skills and subskills.

Miller (1962) to help the armed services train personnel. Miller's system begins with a definition of the final performance requirement, what the trainee (or student) must be able to do at the end of the program or unit. Then the steps that will lead to the final goal are specified. The procedure simply breaks skills and processes down into subskills and subprocesses.

Consider an example of task analysis in which students must write a position paper based on library research. If the teacher assigned the position paper without analyzing the task in this way, what could happen? Some of the students might not know how to use the card catalog. They might search through one or two encyclopedias, then write a summary of the issues based only on the encyclopedia articles. Another group of students might know how to use the card catalog, tables of contents, and indexes, but have difficulty reaching conclusions. They might hand in lengthy papers listing summaries of different ideas. Another group of students might be able to draw conclusions, but their written presentations might be so confusing and grammatically incorrect that the teacher could not understand what they were trying to say. Each of the groups would have failed in fulfilling the assignment, but for different reasons.

A task analysis gives a picture of the logical sequence of steps leading toward the final goal. An awareness of this sequence can help teachers make sure that students have the necessary skills before they move to the next step. In addition, when students have difficulty, the teacher can pinpoint problem areas.

Krumboltz and Krumboltz (1972) have described the following three methods of shaping: (1) reinforce each subskill, (2) reinforce improvements in accuracy, and (3) reinforce longer and longer periods of performance or participation.

Many behaviors can be improved through shaping, especially skills that involve persistence, endurance, increased accuracy, greater speed, or extensive practice to master. Because shaping is a time-consuming process, however, it should not be used if success can be attained through simpler methods like cueing.

Positive Practice.   A strategy for helping students replace one behavior with another is **positive practice**. This approach is especially appropriate for dealing with academic errors. When students make a mistake, they must correct it as soon as possible and practice the correct response (Gibbs & Luyben, 1985; Kazdin, 1984). The same principle can be applied when students break classroom rules. Instead of being punished, the student might be required to practice the correct alternative action.

The Guidelines summarize approaches encouraging positive behavior.

Positive Practice Practicing correct responses immediately after errors.

Guidelines

Using Positive Reinforcement

Make sure you recognize positive behavior in ways that students value.
Examples
1. When presenting class rules, set up positive consequences for following rules as well as negative consequences for breaking rules.
2. Recognize honest admissions of mistakes by giving a second chance: "Because you admitted that you copied your paper from a book, I'm giving you a chance to rewrite it."
3. Offer desired rewards for academic efforts, such as extra recess time, exemptions from homework or tests, extra credit on major projects.

When students are tackling new material or trying new skills, give plenty of reinforcement.

Examples

1. Find and comment on something right in every student's first life drawing.
2. Reinforce students for encouraging each other. "French pronunciation is difficult and awkward at first. Let's help each other by eliminating all giggles when someone is brave enough to attempt a new word."

After new behaviors are established, give reinforcement on an unpredictable schedule to encourage persistence.

Examples

1. Offer surprise rewards for good participation in class.
2. Start classes with a short, written extra-credit question. Students don't have to answer, but a good answer will add points to their total for the semester.
3. Make sure the good students get compliments for their work from time to time. Don't take them for granted.

Use cueing to help establish new behaviors.

Examples

1. Put up humorous signs in the classroom to remind students of rules.
2. At the beginning of the year, as students enter class, call their attention to a list on the board of the materials they should have with them when they come to class.

Make sure all students, even those who often cause problems, receive some praise, privileges, or other rewards when they do something well.

Examples

1. Review your class list occasionally to make sure all students are receiving some reinforcement.
2. Set standards for reinforcement so that all students will have a chance to be rewarded.

Establish a variety of reinforcers.

Examples

1. Let students suggest their own reinforcers or choose from a "menu" of reinforcers with "weekly specials."
2. Talk to other teachers or parents about ideas for reinforcers.

Use the Premack principle to identify effective reinforcers.

Examples

1. Watch what students do with their free time.
2. Notice which students like to work together. The chance to work with friends is often a good reinforcer.

Coping with Undesirable Behavior

No matter how successful you are at accentuating the positive, there are times when you must cope with undesirable behavior, either because other methods fail or because the behavior itself is dangerous or calls for direct action. For this purpose, negative reinforcement, satiation, reprimands, and punishment all offer possible solutions.

"OF COURSE YOU DON'T HAVE
TO GO TO SCHOOL, DEAR.
WOULD YOU GET SOME LIVER
OUT OF THE FREEZER TO
DEFROST FOR OUR LUNCH?"

(© *Martha Campbell*. From *Phi Delta Kappan*.)

Focus on...

Applied Behavior Analysis

- What are the steps in applied behavior analysis?
- How can the Premack principle help you identify reinforcers?
- When is shaping an appropriate approach?
- What are some of the possible side effects of punishment?

Satiation Requiring a person to repeat a problem behavior past the point of interest or motivation.

Negative Reinforcement.   Recall the basic principle of negative reinforcement: If an action stops or avoids something unpleasant, then the action is likely to occur again in similar situations. Negative reinforcement was operating in Elizabeth's classroom. When she gave in to the moans and complaints of her class and canceled the test, her behavior was being negatively reinforced. She escaped the unpleasant student comments by changing her assignment.

Negative reinforcement may also be used to enhance learning. To do this, you place students in mildly unpleasant situations so they can "escape" when their behavior improves. Consider these examples:

Teacher to a third-grade class: "When the supplies are put back in the cabinet and each of you is sitting quietly, we will go outside. Until then, we will miss our recess."

High school teacher to a student who seldom finishes in-class assignments: "As soon as you complete the assignment, you may join the class in the auditorium. But until you finish, you must work in the study hall."

You may wonder why these examples are not considered punishment. Surely staying in during recess or not accompanying the class to a special program is punishing. But the focus in each case is on strengthening specific behaviors (putting away supplies or finishing in-class assignments). The teacher strengthens (reinforces) the behaviors by removing something aversive *as soon as the desired behaviors occur.* Because the consequence involves removing or "subtracting" a stimulus, the reinforcement is negative.

Negative reinforcement also gives students a chance to exercise control. Missing recess and staying behind in study hall are unpleasant situations, but in each case the students retain control. As soon as they perform the appropriate behavior, the unpleasant situation ends. In contrast, punishment occurs after the fact, and a student cannot so easily control or terminate it.

There are several rules for negative reinforcement: Describe the desired change in a positive way. Don't bluff. Make sure you can enforce your unpleasant situation. Follow through despite complaints. Insist on action, not promises. If the unpleasant situation terminates when students promise to be better next time, you have reinforced making promises, not making changes (Krumboltz & Krumboltz, 1972; O'Leary, 1995).

Satiation.   Another way to stop problem behavior is to insist that students continue the behavior until they are tired of doing it. This procedure, called **satiation,** should be applied with care. Forcing students to continue some behaviors may be physically or emotionally harmful or even dangerous.

An example of an appropriate use of satiation is related by Krumboltz and Krumboltz (1972). In the middle of a ninth-grade algebra class, the teacher suddenly noticed four students making all sorts of unusual motions. In response to persistent teacher questioning, the students finally admitted they were bouncing imaginary balls. The teacher pretended to greet this idea with enthusiasm and suggested the whole class do it. At first, there was a great deal of laughing and joking. After a minute this stopped, and one student even quit. The teacher, however, insisted that all the students continue. After 5 minutes and a number of exhausted sighs, the teacher allowed the students to stop. No one bounced an imaginary ball in that class again.

Teachers also may allow students to continue some action until they stop by themselves, if the behavior is not interfering with the rest of the class. A teacher can do this by simply ignoring the behavior. Remember that responding to an ignorable behavior may actually reinforce it.

In using satiation, a teacher must take care not to give in before the students do. It is also important that the repeated behavior be the one you are trying to end. If the algebra teacher above had insisted that the students write, "I will never bounce imaginary balls in class again" 500 times, the students would have become satiated with writing rather than with bouncing balls.

Reprimands.   In the *Junction Journal,* my daughter's elementary-school newspaper, I read the following lines in a story called "Why I Like School," written by a fourth grader: "I also like my teacher. She helps me understand and learn. She is nice to everyone. . . . I like it when she gets mad at somebody, but she doesn't yell at them in front of the class, but speaks to them privately."

A study by Dan O'Leary and his associates examined the effectiveness of soft, private **reprimands** versus loud, public reprimands in decreasing disruptive behavior (O'Leary, Kaufman, Kass, & Drabman, 1970). Reprimanding a problem student quietly so that only the student can hear seems to be much more effective. When the teacher in the study spoke to offenders loudly enough for the entire class to hear, the disruptions increased or continued at a constant level. Some students enjoy public recognition for misbehavior. If reprimands are not used too often, and if the classroom is generally a positive, warm environment, then students usually respond quickly (Kaplan, 1991; Van Houten & Doleys, 1983).

Response Cost.   The concept of **response cost** is familiar to anyone who has ever paid a fine. For certain infractions of the rules, people must lose some reinforcer (money, time, privileges, pleasures). In a class, the concept of response cost may be applied in a number of ways. The first time a student breaks a class rule, the teacher gives a warning. The second time, the teacher makes a mark beside the student's name in the grade book. The student loses 2 minutes of recess for each mark accumulated. For older students, a certain number of marks might mean losing the privilege of working in a group or going on a class trip.

Social Isolation.   One of the most controversial behavioral methods for decreasing undesirable behavior is the strategy of **social isolation,** often called **time out** from reinforcement. The process involves removing a highly disruptive student from the classroom for 5 to 10 minutes. The student is placed in an empty, uninteresting room alone. It seems likely that the factor that actually decreases behavior is the punishment of brief isolation from other people (O'Leary & O'Leary, 1976). A trip to the principal's office or confinement to a chair in the corner of the regular classroom does not have the same effect as sitting alone in an empty room.

Some Cautions.   Punishment in and of itself does not lead to any positive behavior. Thus, whenever you consider the use of punishment, you should make

This student is in "social isolation." What conditions would help make this a useful intervention?

Reprimands Criticisms for misbehavior; rebukes.

Response Cost Punishment by loss of reinforcers.

Social Isolation Removal of a disruptive student for 5 to 10 minutes.

Time Out Technically, the removal of all reinforcement. In practice, isolation of a student from the rest of the class for a brief time.

it part of a two-pronged attack. The first goal is to carry out the punishment and suppress the undesirable behavior. The second goal is to make clear what the student should be doing instead and to provide reinforcement for those desirable actions. Thus, while the problem behaviors are being suppressed, positive alternative responses are being strengthened. The Guidelines give ideas for using punishment for positive purposes.

Guidelines

Using Punishment

Try to structure the situation so you can use negative reinforcement rather than punishment.

Examples

1. Allow students to escape unpleasant situations (completing additional workbook assignments, weekly tests of math facts) when they reach a level of competence.
2. Insist on actions, not promises. Don't let students convince you to change terms of the agreement.

Be consistent in your application of punishment.

Examples

1. Avoid inadvertently reinforcing the behavior you are trying to punish. Keep confrontations private, so that students don't become heroes for standing up to the teacher in a public showdown.
2. Let students know in advance the consequences of breaking the rules by posting major class rules for younger students or outlining rules and consequences in a course syllabus for older students.
3. Tell students they will receive only one warning before punishment is given. Give the warning in a calm way, then follow through.
4. Make punishment as unavoidable and immediate as is reasonably possible.

Focus on the students' actions, not on the students' personal qualities.

Examples

1. Reprimand in a calm but firm voice.
2. Avoid vindictive or sarcastic words or tones of voice. You might hear your own angry words later when students imitate your sarcasm.
3. Stress the need to end the problem behavior instead of expressing any dislike you might feel for the student.

Adapt the punishment to the infraction.

Examples

1. Ignore minor misbehaviors that do not disrupt the class, or stop these misbehaviors with a disapproving glance or a move toward the student.
2. Don't use homework as a punishment for misbehaviors like talking in class.
3. When a student misbehaves to gain peer acceptance, removal from the group of friends can be effective, since this is really time out from a reinforcing situation.
4. If the problem behaviors continue, analyze the situation and try a new approach. Your punishment may not be very punishing, or you may be inadvertently reinforcing the misbehavior.

Social Learning Theory

In recent years, most behavioral psychologists have found that operant conditioning offers too limited an explanation of learning. Many have expanded their view of learning to include the study of cognitive processes—such as expectations, thoughts, and beliefs—that cannot be directly observed. A prime example of this expanded view is Albert Bandura's (1986, 1997) **social cognitive theory.** Bandura believes that the traditional behavioral views of learning, while accurate, are incomplete. They give only a partial explanation of learning and overlook important elements, particularly the social influences on learning.

Elements of Social Cognitive Theory

Bandura distinguishes between the *acquisition of knowledge* (learning) and the *observable performance based on that knowledge* (behavior). In other words, Bandura suggests that we all may know more than we show. Students may have learned how to simplify fractions, but perform badly on a test because they are anxious or ill or have misread the problem. While learning may have occurred, it may not be demonstrated until the situation is right or there are incentives to perform. In social cognitive theory, therefore, both internal and external factors are important. Environmental events, personal factors and behaviors are seen as interacting in the process of learning. Personal factors (beliefs, expectations, attitudes, and knowledge), the environment (resources, consequences of actions, and physical setting), and behavior (individual actions, choices, and verbal statements) all influence and are influenced by each other. Bandura calls this interaction of forces **reciprocal determinism.**

> In the social cognitive view people are neither driven by inner forces nor automatically shaped and controlled by external stimuli. Rather, human functioning is explained in terms of a model of triadic reciprocality in which behavior, cognitive and other personal factors, and environmental events all operate as interacting determinants of each other. (Bandura, 1986, p. 18)

Bandura poses a second distinction, between *enactive* and *vicarious* learning. Enactive learning is learning by doing and experiencing the consequences of your actions. This may sound like operant conditioning all over again, but it is not, and the difference has to do with the role of consequences. Proponents of operant conditioning believe that consequences strengthen or weaken behavior. In enactive learning, however, consequences are seen as providing information about appropriate actions, creating expectations, and influencing motivation (Schunk, 1996).

Enactive learning is learning by doing; *vicarious learning* is learning by observing others. Bandura believed that traditional behavioral theories overlook the powerful effect that modeling and imitation can have on learning. People and animals can learn merely by observing another person or animal learn, and this fact challenges the behaviorist idea that cognitive factors are unnecessary in an explanation of learning. If people can learn by watching, they must be focusing their attention, constructing images, remembering, analyzing, and making decisions that affect learning.

Social Cognitive Theory Theory that emphasizes learning through observation of others.

Reciprocal Determinism An explanation of behavior that emphasizes the mutual effects of the individual and the environment on each other.

Learning by Observing Others

When Elizabeth laughed at the "Clark Gable" comment in class, she communicated that laughing was appropriate in this situation. Soon all the students were laughing along with her, and she did not try to stop them until it was too late. They were learning through modeling or observation, even though this was not the type of learning Elizabeth had intended. Elizabeth, through her behavior, provided a model for her students to imitate. Through modeling we learn not only how to perform a behavior but also what will happen to us in specific situations if we do perform it.

There are two main modes of **observational learning.** First, observational learning can take place through vicarious reinforcement. This happens when we see others being rewarded or punished for particular actions and then modify our behavior as if we had received the consequences ourselves. For example, if you compliment two students on the attractive illustrations in their lab reports, several other students who observe your compliments may turn in illustrated lab reports next time. This demonstrates vicarious reinforcement. Punishment can also be vicarious: you may slow down on a stretch of highway after seeing several people get speeding tickets there.

In the second kind of observational learning, the observer *imitates* the behavior of a model even though the model receives no reinforcement or punishment while the observer is watching. Often the model is demonstrating something the observer wants to learn and expects to be reinforced for mastering; for example, the proper way to position hands while playing a piano or the correct way to assemble laboratory equipment. But imitation can also occur when the observer simply wants to become more like an admired or high-status model. Models need not be real people. We may also use fictional characters or stereotypical images as models and try to behave as we imagine the model would (Hill, 1990; Pintrich & Schunk, 1996).

Observation can be a very efficient learning process. The first time children hold hairbrushes, cups, or tennis rackets, they usually brush, drink, or swing as well as they can, given their current muscle development and coordination. Let's take a closer look at how observational learning occurs.

Elements of Observational Learning

Bandura (1986) notes that there are four important elements to be considered in observational learning. They are *paying attention, retaining information or impressions, producing behaviors,* and *being motivated* to repeat the behaviors.

Attention.   In order to learn through observation, we have to pay attention. We typically pay attention to people who are attractive, popular, competent, or admired (Schunk, 1996; Sulzer-Azaroff & Mayer, 1986). For younger children this could mean parents, older brothers or sisters, or teachers. For older students it may mean popular peers, rock stars, or TV idols.

In teaching, you will have to ensure students' attention to the critical features of the lesson by making clear presentations and highlighting important points. In demonstrating a skill (for example, threading a sewing machine or operating a lathe), you may need to have students look over your shoulder as you work. Seeing your hands from the same perspective as they see their own directs their attention to the right features of the situation and makes observational learning easier.

Observational Learning Learning by observation and imitation of others.

*T*eachers must draw students' attention to the critical features of a lesson by making clear presentations and highlighting important details. Good demonstrations allow students to focus on the important features and make observational learning easier.

Retention.   In order to imitate the behavior of a model, you have to remember it. This involves mentally representing the model's actions in some way, probably as verbal steps ("Hwa-Rang, the eighth form in Tae Kwan Do karate, is a palm-heel block, then a middle riding stance punch, then . . . "), or as visual images, or both. Retention can be improved by mental rehearsal (imagining imitating the behavior) or by actual practice. In the retention phase of observational learning, practice helps us remember the elements of the desired behavior, such as the sequence of steps.

Production.   Once we "know" how a behavior should look and remember the elements or steps, we still may not perform it smoothly. Sometimes we need a great deal of practice, feedback, and coaching about subtle points before we can reproduce the behavior of the model. In the production phase, practice makes the behavior smoother and more expert.

Motivation and Reinforcement.   As mentioned earlier, social cognitive theory distinguishes between acquisition and performance. We may acquire a new skill or behavior through observation, but we may not perform that behavior until there is some motivation or incentive to do so. Reinforcement can play several roles in observational learning. If we anticipate being reinforced for imitating the actions of a model, we may be more motivated to pay attention, remember, and reproduce the behaviors. In addition, reinforcement is important in maintaining learning. A person who tries a new behavior is unlikely to persist without reinforcement (Barton, 1981; Ollendick, Dailey, & Shapiro, 1983). For example, if an unpopular student adopted the dress of the "in" group but was greeted with teasing and ridicule, it is unlikely that the imitation would continue.

Bandura identifies three forms of reinforcement that can encourage observational learning. First, of course, the observer may reproduce the behaviors of the model and receive direct reinforcement, as when a gymnast successfully executes a front flip/round-off combination and the coach/model says, "Excellent!" But the reinforcement need not be direct—it may be vicarious. As mentioned earlier, the observer may simply see others reinforced for a particular behavior and then increase his or her production of that behavior. Most TV ads hope for this kind of effect. People in commercials become deliriously happy when they drive a particular car or drink a specific juice, and the viewer is supposed to do the same; the viewer's behavior is reinforced vicariously by the actors' obvious pleasure. The final form of reinforcement is self-reinforcement, or controlling your own reinforcers. This sort of reinforcement is important for both students and teachers. We want our students to improve not because it leads to external rewards but because the students value and enjoy their growing competence. And as a teacher, sometimes self-reinforcement is all that keeps you going.

Factors That Influence Observational Learning

What causes an individual to learn and perform modeled behaviors and skills? Several factors play a role, as shown in Table 6.3. The developmental level of the observer makes a difference in learning. As children grow older, they are able to focus attention for longer periods of time, use memory strategies to retain information, and motivate themselves to practice. A second influence is the status of the model. Children are more likely to imitate the actions of others who seem competent, powerful, and prestigious—so parents, teachers, older siblings, Barney, athletes, action heroes, rock stars, or film personalities may serve as models—depending on the age and interests of the child. Third, by watching others, we learn about what behaviors are appropriate for people like ourselves, so models who are seen as similar are more readily imitated. All students need to see successful, capable models who look and sound like them, no matter what their ethnicity, socioeconomic status, or sex.

The last three influences involve goals and expectations. If observers expect that certain actions of models will lead to particular outcomes (such as particular practice regimens leading to improved athletic performance) and the observers value those outcomes or goals, then the observers are more likely to pay attention to the models and try to reproduce their behaviors. Finally, observers are more likely to learn from models if the observers have a high level of **self-efficacy**—that is, if they believe they are capable of doing the actions needed to reach the goals, or at least of learning how to do so (Bandura, 1995; Pintrich & Schunk, 1996). We will discuss goals, expectations, and self-efficacy in greater depth in Chapters 10 and 11 on motivation.

Observational Learning in Teaching

There are five possible outcomes of observational learning: teaching new behaviors and attitudes, encouraging existing behaviors, changing inhibitions, directing attention, and arousing emotions. Let's look at each of these as they occur in classrooms.

Self-Efficacy A person's sense of being able to deal effectively with a particular task.

TABLE 6.3	Factors That Affect Observational Learning
Characteristic	**Effects on Modeling**
Developmental status	Improvements with development include longer attention and increased capacity to process information, use strategies, compare performances with memorial representations, and adopt intrinsic motivators.
Model prestige and competence	Observers pay greater attention to competent, high-status models. Consequences of modeled behaviors convey information about functional value. Observers attempt to learn actions they believe they will need to perform.
Vicarious consequences	Consequences to models convey information about behavioral appropriateness and likely outcomes of actions. Valued consequences motivate observers. Similarity in attributes or competence signals appropriateness and heightens motivation.
Outcome expectations	Observers are more likely to perform modeled actions they believe are appropriate and will result in rewarding outcomes.
Goal setting	Observers are likely to attend to models who demonstrate behaviors that help observers attain goals.
Self-efficacy	Observers attend to models when they believe they are capable of learning or performing the modeled behavior. Observation of similar models affects self-efficacy ("If they can do it, I can too").

Source: From *Learning theories: An education perspective, 2/e,* by Dale H. Schunk, p. 121. © 1996. Adapted by permission of Prentice-Hall, Inc., Saddle River, NJ.

Teaching New Behaviors.   **Modeling** has long been used, of course, to teach dance, sports, and crafts, as well as skills in subjects such as home economics, chemistry, and shop. Modeling can also be applied deliberately in the classroom to teach mental skills and to broaden horizons—to teach new ways of thinking. Teachers serve as models for a vast range of behaviors, from pronouncing vocabulary words, to reacting to the seizure of an epileptic student, to being enthusiastic about learning. For example, a teacher might model sound critical thinking skills by thinking "out loud" about a student's question. Or a high school teacher concerned about girls who seem to have stereotyped ideas about careers might invite women with nontraditional jobs to speak to the class.

Modeling, when applied deliberately, can be an effective and efficient means of teaching new behavior (Bandura, 1986; Schunk, 1987). Studies indicate that modeling can be most effective when the teacher makes use of all the elements of observational learning described in the previous section, especially reinforcement and practice.

Models who are the same age as the students may be particularly effective. For example, Schunk and Hanson (1985) compared two methods for teaching

Modeling Changes in behavior, thinking, or emotions that occur through observing another person—a model.

subtraction to second graders who had difficulties learning this skill. One group of students observed other second graders learning the procedures, then participated in an instructional program on subtraction. Another group of students watched a teacher's demonstration, then participated in the same instructional program. Of the two groups, the students who observed peer models learning not only scored higher on tests of subtraction after instruction, but also gained more confidence in their own ability to learn. For students who doubt their own abilities, a good model is a low-achieving student who keeps trying and finally masters the material (Schunk, 1996).

Encouraging Already-Learned Behaviors.   All of us have had the experience of looking for cues from other people when we find ourselves in unfamiliar situations. Observing the behavior of others tells us which of our already-learned behaviors to use: the proper fork for eating the salad, when to leave a gathering, what kind of language is appropriate, and so on. Adopting the dress and grooming styles of TV idols is another example of this kind of effect.

Strengthening or Weakening Inhibitions.   If class members witness one student breaking a class rule and getting away with it, they may learn that undesirable consequences do not always follow rule breaking. The class may be less inhibited in the future about breaking this rule. If the rule breaker is a well-liked, high-status class leader, the effect of the modeling may be even more pronounced. One psychologist has called this phenomenon the **ripple effect** (Kounin, 1970). The ripple effect can work for the teacher's benefit. When the teacher deals effectively with a rule breaker, especially a class leader, the idea of breaking this rule may be inhibited for the other students viewing the interaction. This does not mean that teachers must reprimand each student who breaks a rule, but once a teacher has called for a particular action, following through is an important part of capitalizing on the ripple effect.

Directing Attention.   By observing others, we not only learn about actions, we also notice the objects involved in the actions. For example, in a preschool class, when one child plays enthusiastically with a toy that has been ignored for days, many other children may want to have the toy, even if they play with it in different ways or simply carry it around. This happens, in part, because the children's attention has been drawn to that particular toy.

Arousing Emotion.   Finally, through observational learning people may develop emotional reactions to situations they themselves have never experienced, such as flying or driving. A child who watches a friend fall from a swing and break an arm may become fearful of swings. Students may be anxious when they are assigned to a certain teacher because they've heard frightening stories about how "mean" that teacher is. Note that hearing and reading about a situation are also forms of observation. The Guidelines will give you some ideas about using observational learning in the classroom.

Focus on...

Social Learning Theory

- What is vicarious reinforcement?
- Describe the four elements of observational learning.
- What are the possible outcomes of observational learning? Give an example of each outcome from your own experience.

Ripple Effect "Contagious" spreading of behaviors through imitation.

Model behaviors and attitudes you want your students to learn.

Examples

1. Show enthusiasm for the subject you teach.

2. Be willing to demonstrate both the mental and the physical tasks you expect the students to perform. I once saw a teacher sit down in the sandbox while her 4-year-old students watched her demonstrate the difference between "playing with sand" and "throwing sand."

3. When reading to students, model good problem solving. Stop and say, "Now let me see if I remember what happened so far," or "That was a hard sentence. I'm going to read it again."

Use peers, especially class leaders, as models.

Examples

1. In group work, pair students who do well with those who are having difficulties.

2. Ask students to demonstrate the difference between "whispering" and "silence—no talking."

Make sure students see that positive behaviors lead to reinforcement for others.

Examples

1. Point out the connections between positive behavior and positive consequences in stories.

2. Be fair in giving reinforcement. The same rules for rewards should apply to the problem students as to the good students.

Enlist the help of class leaders in modeling behaviors for the entire class.

Examples

1. Ask a well-liked student to be friendly to an isolated, fearful student.

2. Let high-status students lead an activity when you need class cooperation or when students are likely to be reluctant at first. Popular students can model dialogues in foreign-language classes or be the first to tackle dissection procedures in biology.

Self-Regulation and Cognitive Behavior Modification

The most recent application of behavioral views of learning emphasizes **self-management**—helping students gain control of their own learning. As you will see throughout this book, the role of students in their own learning is a major concern of psychologists and educators today. This concern is not restricted to any one group or theory. Different areas of research and theory all converge on one important idea, that responsibility and the ability to learn rest within the student. No one can learn for someone else (Manning & Payne, 1996; Winne, 1995; Zimmerman, 1990; Zimmerman & Schunk, 1989).

Self-Management Use of behavioral learning principles to change your own behavior.

One reason that behavioral psychologists became interested in self-management is that students taught with classic behavioral methods seldom generalized their learning to new situations. For example, in my dissertation research I found that inattentive students could learn to pay excellent attention to lessons in a small group. But when they returned to the regular classroom, they did not take their new skill back with them (Woolfolk & Woolfolk, 1974). Many behavioral psychologists decided that generalization would be encouraged if students became partners in the behavior change procedures. About this same time, Donald Meichenbaum (1977) was having success teaching impulsive students to "talk themselves through" tasks, so there was evidence that students could benefit from what Meichenbaum termed "cognitive behavior modification" (Manning, 1991).

Self-Management

If one goal of education is to produce people who are capable of educating themselves, then students must learn to manage their own lives, set their own goals, and provide their own reinforcement. In adult life, rewards are sometimes vague and goals often take a long time to reach. Think how many small steps are required to complete an education and find your first job. Life is filled with tasks that call for this sort of self-management (Kanfer & Gaelick, 1986).

Students may be involved in any or all of the steps in implementing a basic behavior change program. They may help set goals, observe their own work, keep records of it, and evaluate their own performance. Finally, they can select and deliver reinforcement. Such involvement can help students master all the steps so they can perform these tasks in the future (Kaplan, 1991).

Self-management programs allow students to record and monitor their own progress and judge their performance.

Goal Setting.   It appears that the goal-setting phase is very important in self-management (Pintrich & Schunk, 1996; Reeve, 1996). In fact, some research suggests that setting specific goals and making them public may be the critical elements of self-management programs. For example, S. C. Hayes and his colleagues identified college students who had serious problems with studying and taught them how to set specific study goals. Students who set goals and announced them to the experimenters performed significantly better on tests covering the material they were studying than students who set goals privately and never revealed them to anyone (Hayes, Rosenfarb, Wulfert, Munt, Korn, & Zettle, 1985).

Higher standards tend to lead to higher performance (McLaughlin & Gnagey, 1981). Unfortunately, student-set goals have a tendency to become lower and lower. Teachers can help students maintain high standards by monitoring the goals set and reinforcing high standards. In one study, a teacher helped first-grade students raise the number of math problems they set for themselves to work on each day by praising them whenever they increased their objective by 10 percent. The students maintained their new, higher work standards, and the improvements even generalized to other subjects (Price & O'Leary, 1974).

Recording and Evaluating Progress.   Students may also participate in the recording and evaluation phases of a behavior change program. Some examples of behaviors that are appropriate for self-recording are the number of assignments completed, time spent practicing a skill, number of books read, and number of times out of seat without permission. Tasks that must be accomplished without teacher supervision, such as homework or private study, are also good candidates for self-monitoring. Students keep a chart, diary, or checklist recording the frequency or duration of the behaviors in question.

A progress record card can help older students break down assignments into small steps, determine the best sequence for completing the steps, and keep track of daily progress by setting goals for each day. The record card itself serves as a prompt that can be faded out (Jenson, Sloane, & Young, 1988). Because cheating on records is a potential problem, especially when students are rewarded for improvements, intermittent checking by the teacher plus bonus points for accurate recording may be helpful (Hundert & Bucher, 1978).

Self-evaluation is somewhat more difficult than simple self-recording because it involves making a judgment about quality. Very few studies have been conducted in this area, but it appears that students can learn to evaluate their behavior with reasonable accuracy (Rhode, Morgan, & Young, 1983). One key seems to be periodically checking students' self-evaluations and giving reinforcement for accurate judgments. Older students may learn accurate self-evaluation more readily than younger students. Again, bonus points can be awarded when the teachers' and students' evaluations match (Kaplan, 1991). I have worked with one teacher who found that his eighth-grade science class could learn to give themselves fair and accurate grades when he used such a system.

Self-Reinforcement.   The last step in self-management is **self-reinforcement**. There is some disagreement, however, as to whether this step is actually necessary. Some psychologists believe that setting goals and monitoring progress

Self-Reinforcement Providing yourself with positive consequences, contingent on accomplishing a particular behavior.

alone are sufficient and that self-reinforcement adds nothing to the effects (Hayes et al., 1985). Others believe that rewarding yourself for a job well done can lead to higher levels of performance than simply setting goals and keeping track of progress (Bandura, 1986). If you are willing to be tough and really deny yourself something you want until your goals are reached, then perhaps the promise of the reward can provide extra incentive for work. With that in mind, you may want to think of some way to reinforce yourself when you finish reading this chapter. A similar approach helped me write the chapter in the first place.

At times, families can be enlisted to help their children develop self-management abilities. Working together, teachers and parents can focus on a few goals and, at the same time, support the growing independence of the students. The Guidelines give some ideas.

Guidelines

Family and Community Partnerships for Student Self-Management Programs

Introduce the system to parents and students in a positive way.

Examples

1. Invite family participation and stress possible benefits to all family members.
2. Consider starting the program just with volunteers.
3. Describe how you use self-management programs yourself.

Help families and students establish reachable goals.

Examples

1. Have examples of possible self-management goals for students such as starting homework early in the evening, or keeping track of books read.
2. Show families how to post goals and keep track of progress. Encourage everyone in the family to work on a goal.

Give families ways to record and evaluate their child's progress (or their own).

1. Divide the work into easily measured steps.
2. Provide models of good work where judgments are more difficult, such as in creative writing.
3. Give families a record form or checklist to keep track of progress.

Encourage families to check the accuracy of student records from time to time, and help their children to develop forms of self-reinforcement.

Examples

1. Have many checkups when students are first learning, and fewer later.
2. Have siblings check one another's records.
3. Where appropriate, test the skills that students are supposed to be developing at home and reward students whose self-evaluations match their test performances.
4. Have students brainstorm ideas with their families for rewarding themselves for jobs well done.

Sometimes, teaching students self-management can solve a problem for teachers and provide fringe benefits as well. For example, the coaches of a competitive swim team with members aged 9 to 16 were having difficulty persuading swimmers to maintain high work rates. Then the coaches drew up four charts indicating the training program to be followed by each member and posted the charts near the pool. The swimmers were given the responsibility of recording their numbers of laps and completion of each training unit. Because the recording was public, swimmers could see their own progress and that of others, give and receive congratulations, and keep accurate track of the work units completed. Work output increased by 27%. The coaches also liked the system because swimmers could begin to work immediately without waiting for instructions (McKenzie & Rushall, 1974).

Cognitive Behavior Modification and Self-Instruction

Self-management generally means getting students involved in the basic steps of a behavior change program. **Cognitive behavior modification** adds an emphasis on thinking and self-talk. For this reason, many psychologists consider cognitive behavior modification more a cognitive than a behavioral approach. I present it here because it serves as a bridge to Chapters 7 and 8 on cognitive learning.

As noted in Chapter 2, there is a stage in cognitive development when young children seem to guide themselves through a task using private speech. They talk to themselves, often repeating the words of a parent or teacher. In cognitive behavior modification, students are taught directly how to use **self-instruction.** Meichenbaum (1977) outlined the steps:

> **Focus on...**
>
> ## Self-Management
>
> - How could you use the elements of self-management to study in this course?
> - What are the steps in self-instruction?

1. An adult model performs a task while talking to him- or herself out loud (cognitive modeling).

2. The child performs the same task under the direction of the model's instructions (overt, external guidance).

3. The child performs the task while instructing him- or herself aloud (overt, self-guidance).

4. The child whispers the instructions to him- or herself as he/she goes through the task (faded, overt self-guidance).

5. The child performs the task while guiding his/her performance via private speech (covert self-instruction). (p. 32)

Brenda Manning and Beverly Payne (1996) list four skills that can increase student learning: listening, planning, working, and checking. How might cognitive self-instruction help students develop these skills? One possibility is to use personal booklets or class posters that prompt students to "talk to themselves" about these skills. For example, one fifth-grade class designed the four posters in Figure 6.3 on page 236.

Cognitive Behavior Modification Procedures based on both behavioral and cognitive learning principles for changing your own behavior by using self-talk and self-instruction.

Self-Instruction Talking oneself through the steps of a task.

FIGURE 6.3

Posters to Remind Students to "Talk Themselves Through" Listening, Planning, Working, and Checking in School

These four posters were designed by a fifth-grade class to help them remember to use self-instruction. Some of the reminders reflect the special world of these preadolescents.

Poster 1	Poster 3
While Listening:	**While Working:**
1. Does this make sense?	1. Am I working fast enough?
2. Am I getting this?	2. Stop staring at my girlfriend and get back to work.
3. I need to ask a question now before I forget.	3. How much time is left?
4. Pay attention.	4. Do I need to stop and start over?
5. Can I do what he's saying to do?	5. This is hard for me, but I can manage okay.

Poster 2	Poster 4
While Planning:	**While Checking:**
1. Do I have everything together?	1. Did I finish everything?
2. Do I have my friends tuned out for right now?	2. What do I need to recheck?
3. Let me get organized first.	3. Am I proud of this work?
4. What order will I do this in?	4. Did I write all the words? Count them.
5. I know this stuff!	5. I think I finished. I organized myself. Did I daydream too much?

Source: From B. H. Manning and B. D. Payne, *Self-talk for teachers and students: Metacognitive strategies for personal and classroom use,* p. 125. Copyright © 1996 by Allyn & Bacon. Adapted by permission.

Actually, cognitive behavior modification as it is practiced by Meichenbaum and others has many more components than just teaching students to use self-instruction. Meichenbaum's methods also include dialogue and interaction between teacher and student, modeling, guided discovery, motivational strategies, feedback, careful matching of the task with the student's developmental level, and other principles of good teaching. The student is even involved in designing the program (Harris, 1990; Harris & Pressley, 1991). Given all this, it is no surprise that students do seem to generalize the skills developed with cognitive behavior modification to new learning situations (Harris, Graham, & Pressley, in press).

Problems and Issues

The preceding sections provide an overview of several strategies for changing classroom behavior. However, you should be aware that these strategies are tools that may be used responsibly or irresponsibly. What, then, are some issues you should keep in mind?

Ethical Issues

The ethical questions related to the use of the strategies described in this chapter are similar to those raised by any process that seeks to influence people. What are the goals? How do these goals fit with those of the school as a whole? Might students be rewarded for the "wrong" thing, though it seems "right" at first? By what criteria should strategies be chosen? What effect will a strategy have on the individuals involved? Is too much control being given to the teacher, or to a majority?

Goals.   The strategies described in this chapter could be applied exclusively to teaching students to sit still, raise their hands before speaking, and remain silent at all other times (Winett & Winkler, 1972). This certainly would be an unethical use of the techniques. It is true that a teacher may need to establish some organization and order, but stopping with improvements in conduct will not ensure academic learning. On the other hand, in some situations, reinforcing academic skills may lead to improvements in conduct. Whenever possible, emphasis should be placed on academic learning. Academic improvements generalize to other situations more successfully than do changes in classroom conduct.

Strategies.   Punishment can have negative side effects: It can serve as a model for aggressive responses, and it can encourage negative emotional reactions. Punishment is unnecessary and even unethical when positive approaches, which have fewer potential dangers, might work as well. When simpler, less-restrictive procedures fail, then more complicated procedures should be tried.

A second consideration in the selection of a strategy is the impact of the strategy on the individual student. For example, some teachers arrange for students to be rewarded at home with a gift or activities based on good work in school. But if a student has a history of being severely punished at home for bad reports from school, a home-based reinforcement program might be very harmful to that student. Reports of unsatisfactory progress at school could lead to increased abuse at home.

Criticisms of Behavioral Methods

Properly used, the strategies in this chapter can be effective tools to help students learn academically and grow in self-sufficiency. Effective tools, however, do not automatically produce excellent work. The indiscriminate use of even the best tools can lead to difficulties. Critics of behavioral methods point to two basic problems that may arise.

Some psychologists fear that rewarding students for all learning will cause them to lose interest in learning for its own sake (Deci, 1975; Deci & Ryan, 1985; Kohn, 1993, 1996; Lepper & Greene, 1978; Lepper, Keavney, & Drake, 1996; Ryan & Deci, 1996). Studies have suggested that using reward programs with students who are already interested in the subject matter may, in fact, cause students to be less interested in the subject when the reward program ends, as you can see in the Point/Counterpoint on page 238.

Should Students Be Rewarded for Learning?

For years educators and psychologists have debated whether students should be rewarded for school work and academic accomplishments. As a recent example, Judy Cameron and W. David Pierce (1996) published an article on reinforcement in the *Review of Educational Research* that precipitated extensive criticisms and rebuttals in the same journal from Mark Lepper, Mark Keavney, Michael Drake, Alfie Kohn, Richard Ryan, and Edward Deci. Earlier, Paul Chance and Alfie Kohn had exchanged opinions in several issues of *Phi Delta Kappan*: Kohn, A. (1991, March) "Caring kids: The role of the schools"; Chance, P. (1991, June) "Backtalk: A gross injustice"; Chance, P. (1992, November) "The rewards of learning"; Kohn, A. (1993, June) "Rewards versus learning: A response to Paul Chance"; Chance, P. (1993, June) "Sticking up for rewards." What are the arguments?

POINT Students are punished by rewards.

Alfie Kohn (1993) argues that "Applied behaviorism, which amounts to saying, 'do this and you'll get that,' is essentially a technique for controlling people. In the classroom it is a way of doing things *to* children rather than working *with* them" (p. 784). Kohn goes on to contend that rewards are ineffective because when the praise and prizes stop, the behaviors stop too. "Rewards (like punishments) can get people to do what we want: buckle up, share a toy, read a book.... But they rarely produce effects that survive the rewards themselves.... They do not create an enduring *commitment* to a set of values or to learning; they merely,

and temporarily, change what we do" (p. 784).

The problem with rewards does not stop here. According to Kohn, rewarding students for learning actually makes them less interested in the material:

All of this means that getting children to think about learning as a way to receive a sticker, a gold star, or a grade—or even worse, to get money or a toy *for* a grade, which amounts to an extrinsic motivator for an extrinsic motivator—is likely to turn learning from an end into a means. Learning becomes something that must be gotten through in order to receive the reward. Take the depressingly pervasive program by which children receive certificates for pizzas when they have read a certain number of books. John Nicholls of the University of Illinois comments, only half in jest, that the likely consequence of this program is "a lot of fat kids who don't like to read." (p. 785)

COUNTERPOINT Learning should be rewarding.

According to Paul Chance (1993):

Behavioral psychologists in particular emphasize that we learn by *acting on* our environment. As B. F. Skinner put it: "[People] act on the world, and change it, and are changed in turn by the consequences of their actions." Skinner, unlike Kohn, understood that people learn best in a responsive environment. Teachers who praise or otherwise reward student performance provide such an environment. . . . If it is immoral to let students know they have answered questions correctly, to pat students on the back for a good effort, to show joy at a student's understanding of a concept, or to recognize the achievement of a goal by provid-

ing a gold star or a certificate—if this is immoral, then count me a sinner. (p. 788)

Do rewards undermine interest? In their review of research, Cameron and Pierce concluded, "When tangible rewards (e.g., gold star, money) are offered contingent on performance on a task [not just on participation] or are delivered unexpectedly, intrinsic motivation is maintained" (p. 49). Even psychologists such as Edward Deci and Mark Lepper who suggest that rewards might undermine intrinsic motivation agree that rewards can also be used positively. When rewards provide students with information about their growing mastery of a subject or when the rewards show appreciation for a job well done, then the rewards bolster confidence and make the task more interesting to the students, especially students who lacked ability or interest in the task initially. Nothing succeeds like success. If students master reading or mathematics with the support of rewards, they will not forget what they have learned when the praise stops. Would they have learned without the rewards? Some would, but some might not. Would you continue working for a company that didn't pay you, even though you liked the work? Will freelance writer Alfie Kohn, for that matter, lose interest in writing because he gets paid fees and royalties?

Just as you must take into account the effects of a reward system on the individual, you must also consider the impact on other students. Using a reward program or giving one student increased attention may have a detrimental effect on the other students in the classroom. Is it possible that other students will learn to be "bad" in order to be included in the reward program? Most of the evidence on this question suggests that using individual adaptations such as reward programs does not have any adverse effects on students who are not participating if the teacher believes in the program and explains the reasons for using it to the nonparticipating students. After interviewing 98 students in grades 1 through 6, Cindy Fulk and Paula Smith (1995) concluded that "Teachers may be more concerned about equal treatment of students than students are" (p. 416). If the conduct of some students does seem to deteriorate when their peers are involved in special programs, many of the same procedures discussed in this chapter should help them return to previous levels of appropriate behavior (Chance, 1992, 1993).

Focus on...

Criticisms of Behavioral Approaches

- Is it ever appropriate to reward students for learning? Why or why not?
- What are the main criticisms of behavioral approaches?

SUMMARY

Understanding Learning

Although theorists disagree about the definition of learning, most would agree that learning occurs when experience causes a change in a person's knowledge or behavior. Behavioral theorists emphasize the role of environmental stimuli in learning and focus on behavior—observable responses. Behavioral learning processes include contiguity learning, classical conditioning, operant conditioning, and observational learning.

Early View of Learning: Contiguity and Classical Conditioning

In contiguity learning, two events that repeatedly occur together become associated in the learner's mind. Later, the presence of one event causes the learner to remember the other.

In classical conditioning, discovered by Pavlov, a previously neutral stimulus is repeatedly paired with a stimulus that evokes an emotional or physiological response. Later, the previously neutral stimulus alone evokes the response— that is, the conditioned stimulus brings forth a conditioned response. Conditioned responses are subject to the processes of generalization, discrimination, and extinction.

Operant Conditioning: Trying New Responses

In operant conditioning, a theory of learning developed by B. F. Skinner, people learn through the effects of their deliberate responses. Operant conditioning is most applicable to classroom learning. For an individual, the effects of consequences following an action may serve as reinforcement or punishment. Positive and negative reinforcement strengthens a response, while punishment decreases or suppresses the behavior. In addition, the scheduling of reinforcement influences the rate and persistence of responses. Ratio schedules encourage higher rates of response, and variable schedules encourage persistence of responses. In addition to controlling consequences of behavior, teachers can also control the antecedents of behavior through cueing and prompting.

Applied Behavior Analysis

Applied behavior analysis provides teachers with methods for encouraging positive behaviors and coping with undesirable ones. Teachers can reinforce positive, appropriate student behavior through attention, recognition, praise, and the judicious use of reinforcers. The Premack principle, that a more-preferred activity can be used as a reinforcer for a less-preferred one, can help teachers choose effective reinforcers for individuals as well as groups. Teachers can use shaping and positive practice to help students develop new responses. Negative reinforcement, satiation, and forms of punishment—such as reprimands, response cost, and social isolation—can also help change behavior but must be used with caution.

Social Learning Theory

Social learning theorists such as Bandura emphasize the role of observation in learning and in nonobservable cognitive processes, such as thinking and knowing. Observational learning occurs through reinforcement and imitation of high-status models and involves paying attention, retaining information or impressions, producing behaviors, and repeating behaviors through reinforcement or motivation. Teachers can use observational learning to teach new behaviors (providing peer models, for example), encourage already-learned behaviors, strengthen or weaken inhibitions, focus attention, or arouse emotions.

Self-Regulation and Cognitive Behavior Modification

Cognitive psychologists have influenced behavioral views, pointing, for example, to the importance of self-regulation in learning. Students can apply behavior analysis on their own to manage their own behavior. Teachers can encour-

age the development of self-management skills by allowing students to participate in setting goals, keeping track of progress, evaluating accomplishments, and selecting and giving their own reinforcements. Teachers can also use cognitive behavior modification, a behavior change program described by Meichenbaum in which students are directly taught how to use self-instruction.

Problems and Issues

The misuse or abuse of behavioral learning methods is unethical. Critics of behavioral methods also point out the danger that reinforcement could decrease interest in learning by overemphasizing rewards and could have a negative impact on other students. Guidelines do exist, however, for helping teachers use behavioral learning principles appropriately and ethically.

KEY TERMS

antecedents, p. 210
applied behavior analysis, p. 216
aversive, p. 211
behavioral learning theories, p. 205
behavior modification, p. 216
classical conditioning, p. 207
cognitive behavior modification,
    p. 235
conditioned response (CB), p. 208
conditioned stimulus (CS), p. 208
consequences, p. 210
contiguity, p. 207
continuous reinforcement schedule,
    p. 212
cueing, p. 214
discrimination, p. 208
extinction, p. 208
generalization, p. 208
intermittent reinforcement schedule,
    p. 212

interval schedule, p. 213
learning, p. 204
modeling, p. 229
negative reinforcement, p. 211
neutral stimulus, p. 207
observational learning, p. 226
operant conditioning, p. 208
operants, p. 208
positive practice, p. 220
positive reinforcement, p. 210
Premack principle, p. 218
presentation punishment,
    p. 211
prompt, p. 215
punishment, p. 211
ratio schedule, p. 213
reciprocal determinism, p. 225
reinforcement, p. 210
reinforcer, p. 210
removal punishment, p. 212

reprimands, p. 223
respondents, p. 207
response, p. 207
response cost, p. 223
ripple effect, p. 230
satiation, p. 222
self-efficacy, p. 228
self-instruction, p. 235
self-management, p. 231
self-reinforcement, p. 233
shaping, p. 219
social cognitive theory, p. 225
social isolation, p. 223
stimulus, p. 207
stimulus control, p. 214
successive approximations, p. 219
task analysis, p. 219
time out, p. 223
unconditioned response (UR), p. 207
unconditioned stimulus (US), p. 207

CHECK YOUR UNDERSTANDING

Can you apply the ideas from this chapter on learning to solve the following problems of practice?

Preschool and Kindergarten

- A student in your class is terrified of the class's pet guinea pigs. The child won't get close to the cages and wants you

to "give them away." How would you help the child overcome this fear?

Elementary and Middle School

- You want your students to improve their time management and self-management abilities so they will be prepared for the increased demands of high school next year. What would you do?

Junior High and High School

- You have been assigned an emotionally disturbed student. She seemed fine at first, but now you notice that when she encounters difficult work, she often interrupts or teases other students. How would you work with this student and the class to improve the situation?

- It takes you 10 minutes to get your class to settle down after the bell rings. Analyze this situation. What could be maintaining this problem? What could you do?

Cooperative Learning Activity

Work with two or three other members of your educational psychology class to develop a plan using applied behavior analysis to tackle one of the following problems:

- Three students who "hang out" together in your class repeatedly say insulting and disrespectful things to you, often in front of the entire class.

- Your class has gotten into the habit of ignoring due dates.

- One of the students in your class continues to attack other students verbally and physically.

What Would They Do?

You were hired in January to take over the class of a teacher who moved away. This is a great district and a terrific school. If you do well, you might be in line for a full-time opening next fall. As you are introduced around the school, you get a number of sympathetic looks and many—too many—offers of help.

As you walk toward the class, you begin to understand why so many teachers volunteered their help. You hear the screaming when you are still halfway down the hall. "Give it back, it's MINE!" "No way—come and get it!" "I hate you." A crashing sound follows as a table full of books hits the floor. The first day is a nightmare. Evidently the previous teacher had no management system—no order. Simply taking roll and introducing the first activity takes an hour. You end the first day exhausted and discouraged, losing your voice and your patience.

VALERIE A. CHILCOAT

Fifth/Sixth Grade Advanced Academics
Glenmount School, Baltimore, Maryland

BRIBERY!!! The only solution to a situation like this one is bribery. Ordinarily, I would never advocate this approach to classroom management, but in a case this extreme, extreme measures are called for.

I would begin by posting a laminated chart on which all of the students' names were written. Alongside would hang a washable transparency marker. I would explain to the class that any time a student gets caught doing something appropriate, he or she could go up and place a star next to his/her name. At the end of the week, students could then buy something from me at a predetermined cost. If the student desired, stars could be saved for several weeks in order to purchase a more expensive item. (You can get very inexpensive items from the dollar store or create homework passes or free time passes at no cost.)

The posting of the chart on the wall develops self-esteem by showing the students that no matter what the other staff members think of them, they are able to do something right. The purchasing of the items at the end of the week reinforces math skills when the students must subtract the price of the item from their "star account." It also provides the students with "pay" for doing their job. After all, we all want to get paid when we perform our respective jobs. For some students, the reward of a good education just isn't enough.

This token economy, however, will only get a tough situation in hand. It will not foster long-term changes in students' metacognitive processes or help the students to internalize the need or desire for appropriate behavior. Therefore, this system must be intermingled with several other classroom management strategies.

At first, when you begin the token economy, even very small, routine behaviors must be rewarded. Gradually, fewer and fewer stars are given as the teacher attempts to wean the students from the token economy. Meanwhile, other strategies will be filling the void. Begin to meet with each student individually at least once a week to find out what will motivate him or her and to discern special needs—both personal and academic. Use contracting to help students develop a sense of responsibility. Tape the contract to the desk as a reminder of the pledge. Allow students to develop their own consequences to inappropriate actions, making sure they identify the infraction, take responsibility, and create a consequence that is relevant to the undesired action.

ANNE WORTH

Fourth Grade Teacher
Clardy School, Kansas City, Missouri

After the first day of agony, it is obvious that something needs changing before any learning can occur. Have the students share their ideas about what rules are necessary at school and what a working classroom sounds and looks like. Try to call only on those who raise their hands and compliment those who do follow the rules. Before you begin this discussion say, "I think it is important that we establish the rules we will follow together, so for the next ten minutes we will share ideas about school rules. Please raise your hand to be called on so that everyone gets a chance to share." The time limit will keep this from getting away from the teacher. When the list is complete, or if the list needs additions, the teacher can add some basics.

Using a behavior tool such as marbles in a jar, the teacher can set up a system instantly. Tell the class that when each of the rules is followed, a marble will be dropped in the jar. When the jar is full there will be 15 minutes of free time. Drop a marble each time something good happens in the class. Hopefully by the end of the day or the next there will be a reward and you can begin to control the class and do some teaching.

BRENDA MILLER

Second Grade Teacher
Yucca Elementary School, Alamogordo, New Mexico

I would introduce this class to a reward system using classroom "bucks" and a "store" of items to be open each Friday. I would ask parents for various items to be sold in the store, such as toys, pencils, notepads, markers, and toiletries. I would describe the behaviors I expected to see and reward each good behavior with a "buck."

I believe rewards would be more useful at first because most children see discipline as negative, and this class has already seen too much negativism. After my reward system was established I would enlist the help of my students to determine the classroom rules. The key to the reward system's working is to be consistent, generous, and fair. I would price my items higher in the store and give "bucks" away often in reinforcement of good behavior. On the day of store I would have two students (different each week) be the shopkeepers. This reward system teaches responsibility, math, cooperation, and communication. I use this in my second grade classroom with much success.

243

Cognitive Views of Learning

Overview | *What Would You Do?*

ELEMENTS OF THE COGNITIVE PERSPECTIVE   246
Comparing Cognitive and Behavioral Views | The Importance of
Knowledge in Learning

THE INFORMATION PROCESSING MODEL OF MEMORY   249
An Information Processing Model | Sensory Memory | Working
Memory | Long-Term Memory | Storing and Retrieving Information
in Long-Term Memory | Connectionism: An Alternative View
of Memory

METACOGNITION, REGULATION, AND
INDIVIDUAL DIFFERENCES   266
Metacognitive Knowledge and Regulation | Individual Differences in
Metacognition | Individual Differences and Working Memory |
Individual Differences and Long-Term Memory

BECOMING KNOWLEDGEABLE: SOME BASIC PRINCIPLES   270
Development of Declarative Knowledge | Becoming an Expert:
Development of Procedural and Conditional Knowledge

CONSTRUCTIVISM AND SITUATED LEARNING: CHALLENGING
SYMBOLIC PROCESSING MODELS   277
Constructivist Views of Learning | Knowledge: Accuracy versus
Usefulness | Situated Learning

Summary | *Key Terms* | *Check Your Understanding* |
Teachers' Casebook: What Would They Do?

*W**hat makes a lesson easy to learn and remember? Think about the classes you are taking this semester. What have you studied in the last two or three days that you expect to remember next week? Next year? What is different about the memorable information? Did you learn it in a different way?*

In this chapter we turn from behavioral theories of learning to the cognitive perspective. This means a shift from "viewing the learners and their behaviors as products of incoming environmental stimuli" to seeing the learners as "sources of plans, intentions, goals, ideas, memories, and emotions actively used to attend to, select, and construct meaning from stimuli and knowledge from experience" (Wittrock, 1982, pp. 1–2). We will begin with a discussion of the general cognitive approach to learning and memory and the importance of knowledge in learning. To understand memory, we will consider a widely accepted cognitive model, information processing, which suggests that information moves through three different storage systems. We will briefly consider two alternatives to the three-store model of memory: depth of processing and connectionist views. Next we will explore metacognition, a field of study that may provide insights into individual and developmental differences in learning. Then we turn to ideas about how teachers can help their students become more knowledgeable. Finally, we consider recent challenges to the information processing view, constructivism and situated learning. By the time you have completed this chapter, you should be able to:

- ■ Discuss the role of knowledge in learning.
- ■ Describe three models of human information processing—the three-store model, levels of processing, and connectionism.
- ■ Give examples of the roles of perception and attention in learning.
- ■ Define declarative, procedural, and conditional knowledge.
- ■ Explain how schemas and scripts influence learning and remembering.
- ■ Explain why we remember some things and forget others.
- ■ Discuss individual differences in working and long-term memory.
- ■ Describe the stages in the development of cognitive skills.
- ■ Compare information processing, constructivist, and situated learning.

What Would You Do?

The students in your senior history classes seem to equate understanding with memorizing. They prepare for each unit test by memorizing the exact words of the textbook. Even the best students seem to think that flash cards are the only learning strategy possible. In fact, when you try to get them to think about history by reading some original sources, debating issues in class, or examining art and music from the time period you are studying, they rebel. "Will this be on the test?" "Why are we looking at these pictures—will we have to know who painted them and when?" "What's this got to do with history?" Even the students who participate in the debates seem to use words and phrases straight from the textbook without knowing what they are saying.

- What do these students "know" about history? What are their beliefs and expectations, and how do these affect their learning?

- Why do you think they insist on using the rote memory approach?

- How would you teach your students to learn in this new way?

- How will these issues affect the grade levels you will teach?

Elements of the Cognitive Perspective

The cognitive perspective is both the oldest and the youngest member of the psychological community. It is old because discussions of the nature of knowledge, the value of reason, and the contents of the mind date back at least to the ancient Greek philosophers (Hernshaw, 1987). From the late 1800s until a few decades ago, however, cognitive studies fell from favor and behaviorism thrived. Then, research during World War II on the development of complex human skills, the computer revolution, and breakthroughs in understanding language development all stimulated a resurgence in cognitive research. Evidence accumulated indicating that people do more than simply respond to reinforcement and punishment. For example, we plan our responses, use systems to help us remember, and organize the material we are learning in our own unique ways (Miller, Galanter, & Pribram, 1960; Shuell, 1986). With the growing realization that learning is an active mental process, educational psychologists became interested in how people think, learn concepts, and solve problems (e.g., Ausubel, 1963; Bruner, Goodnow, & Austin, 1956).

Interest in concept learning and problem solving soon gave way, however, to interest in how knowledge is represented in the mind and particularly how it is remembered. Remembering and forgetting became major topics for investigation in cognitive psychology in the 1970s and 1980s, and the information processing model of memory dominated research.

Today, there are other models of memory besides information processing. In addition, many cognitive theorists have a renewed interest in learning, thinking, and problem solving. The **cognitive view of learning** can best be described as a generally agreed-upon philosophical orientation. This means that cognitive theorists share basic notions about learning and memory. Cognitive theorists

Cognitive View of Learning
A general approach that views learning as an active mental process of acquiring, remembering, and using knowledge.

believe, for example, that learning is the result of our attempts to make sense of the world. To do this, we use all the mental tools at our disposal. The ways we think about situations, along with our knowledge, expectations, feelings, and interactions with others and the environment, influence how and what we learn (Anderson, 1995a,b; Bandura, 1986; Farnham-Diggory, 1994; Piaget, 1963).

Comparing Cognitive and Behavioral Views

The cognitive and behavioral views differ in their assumptions about what is learned. In the cognitive view, knowledge is learned, and changes in knowledge make changes in behavior possible. In the behavioral view, the new behaviors themselves are learned (Shuell, 1986). Both behavioral and cognitive theorists believe reinforcement is important in learning but for different reasons. The strict behaviorist maintains that reinforcement strengthens responses; cognitive theorists see reinforcement as a source of feedback about what is likely to happen if behaviors are repeated—as a source of information.

The cognitive view sees people as active learners who initiate experiences, seek out information to solve problems, and reorganize what they already know to achieve new insights. In fact, learning within this perspective is seen as "transforming significant understanding we already have, rather than simple acquisitions written on blank slates" (Greeno, Collins, & Resnick, 1996, p. 18). Instead of being passively influenced by environmental events, people actively choose, practice, pay attention, ignore, reflect, and make many other decisions as they pursue goals. Older cognitive views emphasized the *acquisition* of knowledge, but newer approaches stress its *construction* (Anderson, Reder, & Simon, 1996; Greeno, Collins, & Resnick, 1996; Mayer, 1992).

Differences between behavioral and cognitive views are also apparent in the methods each group has used to study learning. Much of the work on behavioral learning principles has been with animals in controlled laboratory settings. The goal is to identify a few general laws of learning that apply to all higher organisms (including humans, regardless of age, intelligence, or other individual differences). Cognitive psychologists, on the other hand, study a wide range of learning situations. Because of their focus on individual and developmental differences in cognition, they have not sought general laws of learning. This is one of the reasons that there is no single cognitive model or theory of learning representative of the entire field.

The Importance of Knowledge in Learning

Knowledge is the outcome of learning. When we learn a name, the history of cognitive psychology, or the rules of tennis, we know something new. But, knowledge is more than the end product of previous learning; it also guides new learning. The cognitive approach suggests that one of the most important elements in the learning process is what the individual brings to the learning situation. What we already know determines to a great extent what we will pay attention to, perceive, learn, remember, and forget (Greeno, Collins, & Resnick, 1996; Shuell, 1986). Pat Alexander (1996) notes that what we already know "is a scaffold that supports the construction of all future learning" (p. 31).

A study by Recht and Leslie (1988) shows the importance of knowledge in understanding and remembering new information. These psychologists identified junior high school students who were either very good or very poor readers.

The cognitive view sees people as active learners who initiate experiences, seek out information to solve problems, and reorganize what they already know to achieve new insights.

They tested the students on their knowledge of baseball and found that knowledge of baseball was not related to reading ability. So the researchers were able to identify four groups of students: *good readers/high baseball knowledge, good readers/low baseball knowledge, poor readers/high baseball knowledge,* and *poor readers/low baseball knowledge.* Then all the subjects read a passage describing a baseball game and were tested in a number of ways to see if they understood and remembered what they had read.

The results demonstrated the power of knowledge. Poor readers who knew baseball remembered more than good readers with little baseball knowledge and almost as much as good readers who knew baseball. Poor readers who knew little about baseball remembered the least of what they had read. So a good basis of knowledge can be more important than good learning strategies in understanding and remembering—but extensive knowledge plus good strategies is even better.

General and Specific Knowledge.

In the cognitive perspective, "knowledge emphasizes understanding of concepts and theories in different subject matter domains and general cognitive abilities, such as reasoning, planning, solving problems, and comprehending language" (Greeno, Collins, & Resnick, 1996, p. 16). So, there are different kinds of knowledge. Some is general—it applies to many different situations. For example, **general knowledge** about how to read or write or use a word processor is useful in and out of school. **Domain-specific knowledge,** on the other hand, pertains to a particular task or subject. For example, knowing that the shortstop plays between second and third base is specific to the domain of baseball. Of course, there is no absolute line between general and domain-specific knowledge. When you were first learning to read, you may have studied specific facts about the sounds of letters. At that time, knowledge about letter sounds was specific to the domain of reading. But now you can use both knowledge about sounds and the ability to read in more general ways (Alexander, 1992; Schunk, 1996).

Declarative, Procedural, and Conditional Knowledge.

Another way of categorizing knowledge is as declarative, procedural, or conditional (Paris & Cunningham, 1996; Paris, Lipson, & Wixson, 1983). **Declarative knowledge** is "knowledge that can be declared, usually in words, through lectures, books, writing, verbal exchange, Braille, sign language, mathematical notation, and so on" (Farnham-Diggory, 1994, p. 468). Declarative knowledge is "knowing that" something is the case. Robert Gagné (1985) calls this category *verbal information.* The history students in the opening "What Would You Do?" situation were focusing exclusively on declarative knowledge about history. The range of declarative knowledge is tremendous. You can know very specific facts (the atomic weight of gold is 196.967), or generalities (leaves of some trees change color in autumn), or personal preferences (I don't like lima beans), or personal events (what happened at my brother's wedding), or rules (to divide fractions, invert the divisor and multiply). Small units of declarative knowledge can be organized into larger units; for example, principles of reinforcement and punishment can be organized in your thinking into a theory of behavioral learning (Gagné, Yekovich, & Yekovich, 1993).

Procedural knowledge is "knowing how" to do something such as divide fractions or clean a carburetor—procedural knowledge must be demonstrated. Notice that repeating the rule "to divide fractions, invert the divisor and mul-

General Knowledge Information that is useful in many different kinds of tasks; information that applies to many situations.

Domain-Specific Knowledge Information that is useful in a particular situation or that applies only to one specific topic.

Declarative Knowledge Verbal information; facts; "knowing that" something is the case.

TABLE 7.1   Kinds of Knowledge

	General Knowledge	Domain-Specific Knowledge
Declarative	Hours the library is open Rules of grammar	The definition of "hypotenuse" The lines of the poem "The Raven"
Procedural	How to use your word processor How to drive	How to solve an oxidation-reduction equation How to throw a pot on a potter's wheel
Conditional	When to give up and try another approach When to skim and when to read carefully	When to use the formula for calculating volume When to rush the net in tennis

tiply" shows *declarative* knowledge—the student can state the rule. But to show *procedural* knowledge, the student must act. When faced with a fraction to divide, the student must divide correctly. Robert Gagné (1985) calls this kind of knowledge *intellectual skills*. Students demonstrate procedural knowledge when they translate a passage into Spanish or correctly categorize a geometric shape or craft a coherent paragraph.

Conditional knowledge is "knowing when and why" to apply your declarative and procedural knowledge. Robert Gagné (1985) calls this kind of knowledge *cognitive strategies*. Given many kinds of math problems, it takes conditional knowledge to know when to apply one procedure and when to apply another to solve each. It takes conditional knowledge to know when to read every word in a text and when to skim. For many students, conditional knowledge is a stumbling block. They have the facts and can do the procedures, but they don't seem to apply what they know at the appropriate time.

Table 7.1 shows that we can combine our two systems for describing knowledge. Declarative, procedural, and conditional knowledge can be either general or domain-specific.

To be used, knowledge must be remembered. What do we know about memory?

The Information Processing Model of Memory

There are a number of theories of memory, but the most common are the **information processing** explanations, including the newer neural-network or connectionist approaches (Martindale, 1991). We will use this well-researched framework for examining learning and memory.

An Information Processing Model

Information processing views of memory rely on the computer as a model. Like the computer, the human mind takes in information, performs operations on it to change its form and content, stores the information, retrieves it when needed,

Procedural Knowledge Knowledge that is demonstrated when we perform a task; "knowing how."

Conditional Knowledge "Knowing when and why" to use declarative and procedural knowledge.

Information Processing Human mind's activity of taking in, storing, and using information.

FIGURE 7.1

The Information Processing System

Information is encoded in the sensory register where perception determines what will be held in working memory for further use. Thoroughly processed information becomes part of long-term memory and can be activated at any time to return to working memory.

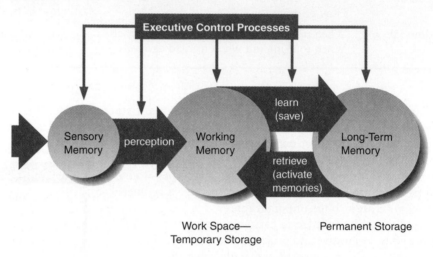

and generates responses to it. Thus, processing involves gathering and representing information, or *encoding;* holding information, or *storage;* and getting at the information when needed, or *retrieval.* The whole system is guided by *control processes* that determine how and when information will flow through the system.

For some cognitive psychologists, the computer model is only a metaphor for human mental activity. But other cognitive scientists, particularly those studying artificial intelligence, try to design and program computers to "think" and solve problems like human beings (Anderson, 1995a; Schunk, 1996). Some theorists suggest that the operation of the brain resembles a large number of very slow computers, all operating in parallel (at the same time), with each computer dedicated to a different, specific task (Martindale, 1991).

Figure 7.1 is a schematic representation of a typical information processing model of memory, derived from the ideas of several theorists (Atkinson & Shiffrin, 1968; R. Gagné, 1985). Other models have been suggested, but all of the models, despite their variations, resemble flow charts. In order to understand this model, let's examine each element.

Sensory Memory

Stimuli from the environment (sights, sounds, smells, etc.) constantly bombard our receptors. **Receptors** are the body's mechanisms for seeing, hearing, tasting, smelling, and feeling. The **sensory memory,** also called the *sensory register* or *sensory information store,* holds all these sensations—very briefly.

Capacity, Duration, and Contents of Sensory Memory.   The *capacity* of sensory memory is very large, more information than we can possibly handle

Receptors Parts of the human body that receive sensory information.

Sensory Memory System of receptors holding sensory information very briefly.

at once. But this vast amount of sensory information is fragile in *duration*. It lasts between one and three seconds. You can experience this brief holding of sensory information in your own sensory register. Wave a pencil (or your finger) back and forth before your eyes while you stare straight ahead. See the shadowy image that trails behind the object? The sensory input remains very briefly after the stimulus has left. You can see a trace of the pencil after the actual stimulus has been removed (Lindsay & Norman, 1977). The *content* of sensory memory resembles the sensations from the original stimulus. Visual sensations are coded briefly by the sensory register as images, almost like photographs. Auditory sensations are coded as sound patterns, similar to echoes. It may be that the other senses also have their own codes. Thus, for a second or so, a wealth of data from sensory experience remains intact. In these moments, we have a chance to select and organize information for further processing. Perception and attention are critical at this stage.

Perception.   The meaning we attach to the raw information received through our senses is called **perception.** This meaning is constructed based on both objective reality and our existing knowledge. For example, consider these marks: ⅓. If asked what the letter is, you would say "B." If asked what the number is, you would say "13." The actual marks remain the same; the perception of them—their meaning—changes in keeping with your expectation to recognize a number or a letter. To a child without appropriate knowledge to perceive either a number or a letter, the marks would probably be meaningless (F. Smith, 1975).

Some of our present-day understanding of perception is based on studies conducted in Germany (and later in the United States) early in this century by psychologists called *Gestalt theorists. Gestalt,* which means something like pattern or configuration in German, refers to people's tendency to organize sensory information into patterns or relationships. Instead of perceiving bits and pieces of unrelated information, we perceive organized, meaningful wholes. Figure 7.2 presents a few Gestalt principles.

The Gestalt principles are valid explanations of certain aspects of perception, but they are not the whole story. There are two current explanations

Perception Interpretation of sensory information.

FIGURE 7.2

Examples of Gestalt Principles

Gestalt principles of perception explain how we "see" patterns in the world around us.

a. *Figure-ground*
What do you see? Faces or a vase? Make one figure—the other ground.

b. *Proximity*
You see these lines as 3 groups because of the proximity of lines.

c. *Similarity*
You see these lines as an alternating pattern because of the similarity in height of lines.

d. *Closure*
You perceive a circle instead of dotted curved lines.

Source: From *Learning Theories: An Educational Perspective,* 2/e, by Dale H. Schunk. © 1996. Adapted by permission of Prentice-Hall, Inc., Saddle River, NJ.

in information processing theory for how we recognize patterns and give meaning to sensory events. The first is called *feature analysis,* or **bottom-up processing** because the stimulus must be analyzed into features or components and assembled into a meaningful pattern "from the bottom up." For example, a capital letter A consists of two relatively straight lines joined at a 45-degree angle $\wedge$ and a horizontal line (—) through the middle. Whenever we see these features, or anything close enough, including, Λ, ꓥ, **A**, *A*, *A*, and A, we recognize an A (Anderson, 1995a). This explains how we are able to read words written in other people's handwriting.

If all perception relied on feature analysis, learning would be very slow. Luckily, humans are capable of another type of perception, based on knowledge and expectation often called **top-down processing.** To recognize patterns rapidly, in addition to noting features, we use what we already know about the situation—what we know about words or pictures or the way the world generally operates. For example, you would not have seen the marks above as the letter A if you had no knowledge of the Roman alphabet. So, what you know also affects what you are able to perceive.

The Role of Attention.   If every variation in color, movement, sound, smell, temperature, and so on had to be perceived, life would be impossible. By paying attention to certain stimuli and ignoring others, we select from all the possibilities what we will process. But **attention** is a very limited resource. We can pay attention to only one demanding task at time (Anderson, 1995a). For example, there was a time when I was learning to drive when I couldn't listen to the radio and drive at the same time. After some practice, I could listen, but I had to turn the radio off when traffic was heavy. After years of practice, I can plan a class or talk on the phone as I drive. This is because many processes that initially require attention and concentration become automatic with practice.

Bottom-Up Processing Perceiving based on noticing separate defining features and assembling them into a recognizable pattern.

Top-Down Processing Perceiving based on the context and the patterns you expect to occur in that situation.

Attention Focus on a stimulus.

The first step in learning is paying attention; teachers must be able to gain and maintain students' attention.

Actually, **automaticity** probably is a matter of degree—we are not completely automatic but rather more or less automatic in our performances depending on how much practice we have had (Anderson, 1995a).

Attention and Teaching.   The first step in learning is paying attention. Students cannot process something that they do not recognize or perceive. Many factors in the classroom influence student attention. Eye-catching or startling displays or actions can draw attention at the beginning of a lesson. A teacher might begin a science lesson on air pressure by blowing up a balloon until it pops. Bright colors, underlining, highlighting of written or spoken words, calling students by name, surprise events, intriguing questions, variety in tasks and teaching methods, and changes in voice level, lighting, or pacing can all be used to gain attention. And students have to maintain attention—they have to stay focused on the important features of the learning situation. The Guidelines offer additional ideas for capturing and maintaining students' attention.

Guidelines

Gaining and Maintaining Attention

Use signals.

Examples

1. Develop a signal that tells students to stop what they are doing and focus on you. Some teachers move to a particular spot in the room, flick the lights, or play a chord on the class piano.
2. Avoid distracting behaviors such as tapping a pencil that interfere with both signals and attention to learning.
3. Give short, clear directions before, not during, transitions.

Make sure the purpose of the lesson or assignment is clear to students.

Examples

1. Write the goals or objectives on the board and discuss them with students before starting. Ask students to summarize or restate the goals.
2. Explain the reasons for learning, and ask students for examples of how they will apply their understanding of the material.
3. Tie the new material to previous lessons—show an outline or map of how the new topic fits with previous and upcoming material.

Emphasize variety, curiosity, and surprise.

Examples

1. Arouse curiosity with questions such as "What would happen if . . . ?"
2. Create shock by staging an unexpected event such as a loud argument just before a lesson on communication.
3. Alter the physical environment by changing the arrangement of the room or moving to a different setting.
4. Shift sensory channels by giving a lesson that requires students to touch, smell, or taste.
5. Use movements, gestures, and voice inflection—walk around the room, point, and speak softly and then more emphatically. (My husband has been known to jump up on his desk to make an important point in his college classes!)

(continued)

Automaticity The ability to perform thoroughly learned tasks without much mental effort.

Ask questions and provide frames for answering.

Examples

1. Ask students why the material is important, how they intend to study, and what strategies they will use.

2. Give students self-checking or self-editing guides that focus on common mistakes or have them work in pairs to improve each other's work—sometimes it is difficult to pay attention to your own errors.

Working Memory

Once noticed and transformed into patterns of images or sounds (or perhaps other types of sensory codes), the information in sensory memory is available for further processing. **Working memory** is the "workbench" of the memory system, the component of memory where new information is held temporarily and combined with knowledge from long-term memory. Working memory is like the workspace or screen of a computer—its *content* is activated information—what you are thinking about at the moment. For this reason, some psychologists consider the working memory to be synonymous with "consciousness."

Capacity, Duration, and Contents of Working Memory. Working memory *capacity* is limited—something many of your professors seem to forget as they race through a lecture. In experimental situations based on the information processing model, it appears that the capacity of working memory is only about five to nine separate new items at once (Miller, 1956). This limitation holds true to some degree in everyday life. It is quite common to remember a new phone number after looking it up, as you walk across the room to make the call. But what if you have two phone calls to make in succession? Two new phone numbers (14 digits) probably cannot be stored simultaneously.

Remember—put in your working memory—that we are discussing the recall of *new* information. In daily life we certainly can hold more than five to nine bits of information at once. While you are dialing that seven-digit phone number you just looked up, you are bound to have other things "on your mind"—in your memory—such as how to use a telephone, whom you are calling, and why. You don't have to pay attention to these things; they are not new knowledge. Some of the processes, such as dialing the phone, have become automatic. However, because of the working memory's limitations, if you were in a foreign country and were attempting to use an unfamiliar telephone system, you might very well have trouble remembering the phone number because you were trying to figure out the phone system at the same time.

Some psychologists argue that working memory is limited not by the number of bits of information it can store, but by the amount of information we can hold in an articulatory loop. The **articulatory loop** is a rehearsal system of about 1.5 seconds. Baddeley (1986) suggests that we can hold as much in working memory as we can rehearse (repeat to ourselves) in 1.5 seconds. The seven-digit telephone number fits this limitation.

No matter how the capacity of working memory is defined, by number of bits or by the amount you can keep in the articulatory (rehearsal) loop, it is clear that the *duration* of information is short, about 5 to 20 seconds. This is why working memory has been called *short-term* memory. It may seem to you

Working Memory The information that you are focusing on at a given moment.

Articulatory Loop A system for temporarily storing information that can hold as much information as can be repeated in about 1.5 seconds.

that a memory system with a 20-second time limit is not very useful. But without this system, you would have already forgotten what you read in the first part of this sentence before you came to these last few words. This would clearly make understanding sentences difficult.

The *contents* of information in working memory may be in the form of images that resemble the perceptions in sensory memory, or the information may be structured more abstractly, based on meaning. Some recent theories suggest that there are actually two working-memory systems—one for language-based information and another for nonverbal, spatial, visual information (Baddeley, 1986; Jurden, 1995).

Retaining Information in Working Memory.   Because information in working memory is fragile and easily lost, it must be kept activated to be retained. Activation is high as long as you are focusing on information, but activation decays or fades quickly when attention shifts away. Holding information in working memory is like keeping all the plates spinning on top of poles in a circus act. The performer gets one plate spinning, moves to the next, and the next, but has to return to the first before it slows down too much and falls off the pole. If we don't keep the information "spinning" in working memory—keep it activated—it will "fall off" (Anderson, 1995a, b). When activation fades, forgetting follows, as shown in Figure 7.3. To keep information activated in working memory for longer than 20 seconds, most people keep rehearsing the information mentally.

There are two types of rehearsal (Craik & Lockhart, 1972). **Maintenance rehearsal** involves repeating the information in your mind—in the articulatory

FIGURE 7.3

Working Memory

Information in working memory can be kept activated through maintenance rehearsal or transferred into long-term memory by being connected with information in long-term memory (elaborative rehearsal).

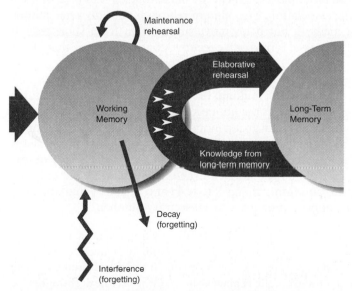

Maintenance Rehearsal Keeping information in working memory by repeating it to yourself.

*T*o learn the lines of a play, these students will use maintenance rehearsal. As long as they keep going over their lines, they'll probably remember them for the play. To the extent that they can connect this information with knowledge they already have in long-term memory, their recall of the lines may be stronger.

loop. As long as you repeat the information, it can be maintained in working memory indefinitely. Maintenance rehearsal is useful for retaining something you plan to use and then forget, like a phone number.

Elaborative rehearsal involves connecting the information you are trying to remember with something you already know, with information from long-term memory. For example, if you meet someone at a party whose name is the same as your brother's, you don't have to repeat the name to keep it in memory, you just have to make the association. This kind of rehearsal not only retains information in working memory but helps move information from short-term to long-term memory. Rehearsal is thus an "executive control process" that affects the flow of information through the information processing system.

The limited capacity of working memory can also be somewhat circumvented by the control process of **chunking**. Because the number of bits of information, not the size of each bit, is the limitation for working memory, you can retain more information if you can group individual bits of information. For example, if you have to remember the six digits 3, 5, 4, 8, 7, and 0, it is easier to put them together into three chunks of two digits each (35, 48, 70) or two chunks of three digits each (354, 870). With these changes, there are only two or three bits of information rather than six to hold at one time. Chunking helps you remember a telephone number or a social security number.

Forgetting.   Information may be lost from working memory through interference or decay (see Figure 7.3). Interference is fairly straightforward: remembering new information interferes with or gets in the way of remembering old information. The new thought replaces the old one. As new thoughts ac-

Elaborative Rehearsal Keeping information in working memory by associating it with something else you already know.

Chunking Grouping individual bits of data into meaningful larger units.

cumulate, old information is lost from working memory. Information is also lost by time **decay**. If you don't continue to pay attention to information, the activation level decays (weakens) and finally drops so low that the information cannot be reactivated—it disappears altogether.

Forgetting is very useful. Without forgetting, people would quickly overload their working memories and learning would cease. Also, it would be a problem if you remembered permanently every sentence you ever read. Finding a particular bit of information in all that sea of knowledge would be impossible. It is helpful to have a system that provides temporary storage.

Long-Term Memory

Working memory holds the information that is currently activated, such as a telephone number you have just found and are about to dial. **Long-term memory** holds the information that is well learned, such as all the other telephone numbers you know. Well-learned information is said to be high in memory strength or *durability* (Anderson, 1995b).

Capacity and Duration of Long-Term Memory.   There are a number of differences between working and long-term memory, as you can see in Table 7.2. Information enters working memory very quickly. To move information into long-term storage requires more time and a bit of effort. Whereas the capacity of working memory is limited, the capacity of long-term memory appears to be, for all practical purposes, unlimited. In addition, once information is securely stored in long-term memory, it can remain there permanently. Theoretically, we should be able to remember as much as we want for as long as we want. Of course, the problem is to find the right information when it is needed. Our access to information in working memory is immediate because we are thinking about the information at that very moment. But access to information in long-term memory requires time and effort.

Contents of Long-Term Memory.   Allan Paivio (1971, 1986; Clark & Paivio, 1991) suggests that information is stored in long-term memory as either visual images or verbal units, or both. Psychologists who agree with this point of view believe that information coded both visually and verbally is easiest to learn (Mayer & Sims, 1994). (This may be one reason why explaining

Decay The weakening and fading of memories with the passage of time.

Long-Term Memory Permanent store of knowledge.

TABLE 7.2 Working and Long-Term Memory					
Type of Memory	Input	Capacity	Duration	Contents	Retrieval
Working	Very fast	Limited	Very brief: 5–20 sec.	Words, images, ideas, sentences	Immediate
Long-term	Relatively slow	Practically unlimited	Practically unlimited	Propositional networks, schemata, productions, episodes, perhaps images	Depends on representation and organization

Source: Adapted by permission of the author from F. Smith (1975), *Comprehension and learning: A conceptual framework for teachers*, published by Holt, Rinehart and Winston.

FIGURE 7.4

A Propositional Network

The sentence "Ida borrowed the antique tablecloth" has two propositions: (1) Ida borrowed the tablecloth [in the past] and (2) The tablecloth is an antique.

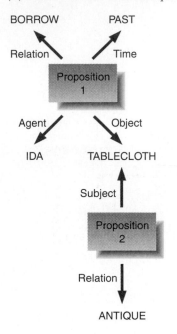

Source: Developed from material in J. Anderson (1985). *Cognitive psychology and its implications* (2nd ed.). San Francisco: W. H. Freeman; and D. Gentner (1975). Evidence for the psychological reality of semantic components: The verbs of possession. In D. Norman and D. Rumelhart (Eds.), *Explorations in Cognition*. San Francisco: W. H. Freeman.

Semantic Memory Memory for meaning.

Propositional Network Set of interconnected concepts and relationships in which long-term knowledge is held.

Images Representations based on the physical attributes—the appearance—of information.

an idea with words and representing it visually in a figure, as we do in textbooks, has proved helpful to students.) Paivio's ideas have some support, but critics contend that the capacity of the brain is not large enough to store all the images we can imagine. They suggest that many images are actually stored as verbal codes and then translated into visual information when an image is needed (Schunk, 1996). Most cognitive psychologists distinguish three categories of long-term memory: semantic, episodic, and procedural.

Semantic memory is memory for meaning. These memories are stored as *propositions, images,* and *schemas.* Because these are very important concepts for teaching, we will spend some extra time on them.

Propositions and Propositional Networks. A *proposition* is the smallest unit of information that can be judged true or false. The statement, "Ida borrowed the antique tablecloth," has two propositions:

1. Ida borrowed the tablecloth.

2. The tablecloth is an antique.

A **propositional network** is interconnected bits of information. Different cognitive psychologists have slightly different methods for diagramming propositional networks. Figure 7.4 is a common way of representing the relationships in the sentence "Ida (the *agent*) borrowed the antique tablecloth (the *object*)." Because the verb is in the past tense, the *time* of action is in the past. The same propositional network would apply to these sentences: "The antique tablecloth was borrowed by Ida," or "Ida borrowed the tablecloth, which was an antique." The meaning is the same, and it is this *meaning* that is stored in memory as a set of relationships.

It is possible that most information is stored and represented in propositional networks. When we want to recall a bit of information, we may translate its meaning (as represented in the propositional network) into familiar phrases and sentences, or mental pictures. Also, because of the network, recall of one bit of information can trigger or *activate* recall of another. We are not aware of these networks, for they are not part of our conscious memory (Anderson, 1995a). In much the same way, we are not aware of underlying grammatical structure when we form a sentence in our own language; we don't have to diagram a sentence in order to say it.

Images. **Images** are representations based on *perceptions*—on the structure or appearance of the information (Anderson, 1995a). As we form images we try to remember or recreate the physical attributes and spatial structure of information. For example, when asked how many window panes are in their living room, most people call up an image of the windows "in their mind's eye" and count the panes—the more panes, the longer it takes to respond. If the information were represented only in a proposition such as "my living room has seven window panes," then everyone would take about the same time to answer, whether the number was one or 24 (Mendell, 1971). Images are useful in making many practical decisions such as how a sofa might look in your living room or how to line up a golf shot. Images may also be helpful in abstract reasoning. Physicists, such as Faraday and Einstein, report creating images to reason about complex new problems (Gagné, Yekovich, & Yekovich, 1993).

FIGURE 7.5

A Schema for "Antique"

The concept of "antique" falls under the general category of "collectible object." It is related to other concepts, such as "hobby" and "traveling to flea markets," depending on the individual's experience.

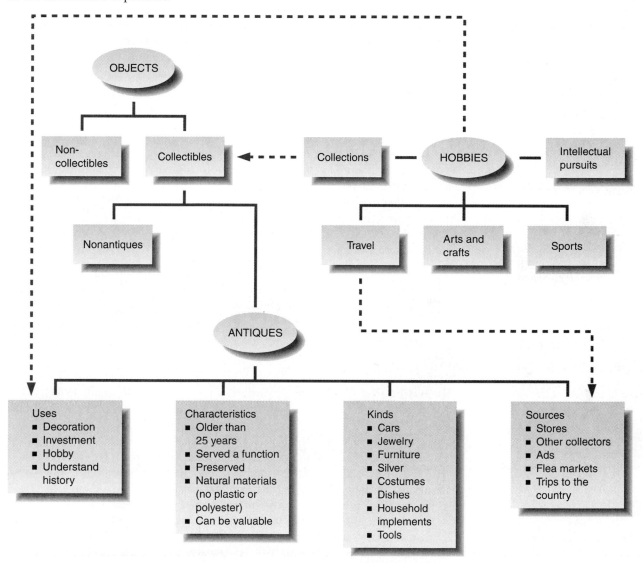

Schemas. As Ellen Gagné and her colleagues have noted, propositions and images are fine for representing single ideas and relationships. But often our knowledge about a topic combines images and propositions. "In order to deal with the fact that much of our knowledge seems integrated, psychologists have developed the idea of a schema" (Gagné, Yekovich, & Yekovich, 1993, p. 81). **Schemas** (sometimes called *schemata*) are abstract knowledge structures that organize vast amounts of information. A **schema** (the singular form) is a pattern or guide for understanding an event, concept, or skill. Figure 7.5 is a partial representation of a schema for knowledge about an "antique."

Schemas (singular, **Schema**) Basic structures for organizing information; concepts.

FIGURE 7.6

"Lunchtime" Script

This script is typical of ones generated by children 5 or 6 years of age. Younger children give scripts that are less detailed and that contain fewer main acts.

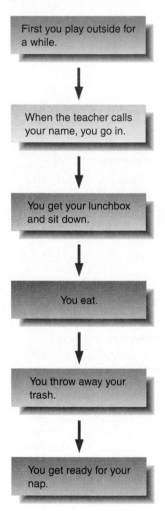

Source: From Laura E. Berk, *Child Development,* 2/e p. 282. Copyright © 1991 by Allyn & Bacon. Reprinted by permission.

Story Grammar Typical structure or organization for a category of stories.

The schema tells you what features are typical of a category, what to expect. The schema is like a pattern, specifying the "standard" relationships in an object or situation. The pattern has "slots" that are filled with specific information as we apply the schema in a particular situation. And schemas are individual. For example, my schema of an antique is less richly developed than the schema of an antique collector. You encountered the very similar concept of scheme in the discussion of Piaget's theory of cognitive development in Chapter 2.

When you hear the sentence, "Ida borrowed the antique tablecloth," you know even more about it than the propositions in Figure 7.4. This is because you have schemas about borrowing, tablecloths, antiques, and maybe even Ida herself. You know without being told, for example, that the lender does not have the tablecloth now, because it is in Ida's possession, and that Ida has an obligation to return the tablecloth to the lender (Gentner, 1975). None of this information is explicitly stated, but it is part of our schema for understanding the meaning of "borrow." Other schemas allow you to infer that the cloth is not plastic (if it is a real antique) and that Ida has probably invited guests for a meal. Your schema about Ida may even allow you to predict how promptly the cloth will be returned and in what condition.

Another type of schema, a **story grammar** (sometimes called a schema for text or **story structure**) helps students to understand and remember stories (Gagné, Yekovich, & Yekovich, 1993; Rumelhart & Ortony, 1977). A story grammar could be something like this: murder discovered, search for clues, murderer's fatal mistake identified, trap set to trick suspect into confessing, murderer takes bait . . . mystery solved! In other words, a story grammar is a typical general structure that could fit many specific stories. To comprehend a story, we select a schema that seems appropriate. Then we use this framework to decide which details are important, what information to seek, and what to remember. It is as though the schema is a theory about what should occur in the story. The schema guides us in "interrogating" the text, filling in the specific information we expect to find so that the story makes sense. If we activate our "murder mystery schema" we may be alert for clues or a murderer's fatal mistake (Resnick, 1981). Without the appropriate schema, trying to understand a story, textbook, or classroom lesson is a very slow, difficult process, something like finding your way through a new town without a map.

A schema representing the typical sequence of events in an everyday situation is called a **script** or an *event schema*. Children as young as 3 have basic scripts for the familiar events in their lives (Nelson, 1986). A kindergartner's script for "lunch" might be something like the one in Figure 7.6.

Storing knowledge of the world in schemas and scripts has advantages and disadvantages. A schema can be applied in many contexts, depending on what part of the schema is relevant. You can use what you know about antiques, for example, to plan trips, decide if a particular article is worth the price asked, or enjoy a museum display. Having a well-developed schema about Ida lets you recognize her (even as her appearance changes), remember many of her characteristics, and make predictions about her behavior. But it also allows you to be wrong. You may have incorporated incorrect or biased information into your schema of Ida. For example, if Ida is a member of an ethnic group different from yours and if you believe that group is dishonest, you may assume that Ida will keep the tablecloth. In this way, racial and ethnic stereotypes can function as schemas for misunderstanding individuals and for racial discrimination.

Episodic Memory.   Memory for information tied to a particular place and time, especially information about the events of your own life, is called **episodic memory**. Episodic memory keeps track of the order of things, so it is also a good place to store jokes, gossip, or plots from films. Martindale (1991) distinguishes between semantic and episodic memory as follows:

> Semantic memory contains the basic elements of knowledge, and episodic memory is made up from these elements. Semantic memory is like a dictionary containing the meanings of all of the words and images you know. Episodic memory is like a novel or movie that puts these concepts together in particular ways. (p. 181)

Procedural Memory.   Memory for how to do things is called **procedural memory**. It may take a while to learn a procedure—such as how to ski, serve a tennis ball, or factor an equation—but once learned, this knowledge tends to be remembered for a long time. Procedural memories are represented as *condition-action rules,* sometimes called productions. **Productions** specify what to do under certain conditions: if A occurs, then do B. A production might be something like, "If you want to snow ski faster, lean back slightly," or "If your goal is to increase student attention, and a student has been paying attention a bit longer than usual, then praise the student." People can't necessarily state all their condition-action rules, but they act on them nevertheless. The more practiced the procedure, the more automatic the action (Anderson, 1995a).

Storing and Retrieving Information in Long-Term Memory

Just what is done to "save" information permanently—to create semantic, episodic, or procedural, memories? How can we make the most effective use of our practically unlimited capacity to learn and remember? *The way you learn information in the first place*—the way you process it at the outset—seems to affect its recall later. One important requirement is that you integrate new material with information already stored in long-term memory as you construct an understanding. Here *elaboration, organization,* and *context* play a role.

Elaboration is the addition of meaning to new information through its connection with already existing knowledge. In other words, we apply our schemas and draw on already existing knowledge to construct an understanding and frequently change our existing knowledge in the process. We often elaborate automatically. For example, a paragraph about an historic figure in the seventeenth century tends to activate our existing knowledge about that period; we use the old knowledge to understand the new.

Material that is elaborated when first learned will be easier to recall later. First, as we saw earlier, elaboration is a form of rehearsal. It keeps the information activated in working memory long enough to have a chance for permanent storage in long-term memory. Second, elaboration builds extra links to existing knowledge. The more one bit of information or knowledge is associated with other bits, the more routes there are to follow to get to the original bit. To put it another way, you have several "handles," or retrieval cues, by which you can recognize or "pick up" the information you might be seeking (Schunk, 1996). Psychologists have also found that the more precise and sensible the elaborations,

Script Schema or expected plan for the sequence of steps in a common event such as buying groceries or ordering take-out pizza.

Episodic Memory Long-term memory for information tied to a particular time and place, especially memory of the events in a person's life.

Procedural Memory Long-term memory for how to do things.

Productions The contents of procedural memory; rules about what actions to take, given certain conditions.

Elaboration Adding and extending meaning by connecting new information to existing knowledge.

the easier recall will be (Bransford, Stein, Vye, Franks, Auble, Mezynski, & Perfetto, 1982; Stein, Littlefield, Bransford, & Persampieri, 1984).

The more students elaborate new ideas, the more they "make them their own"—the deeper their understanding and the better their memory for the knowledge. We help students to elaborate when we ask them to translate information into their own words, create examples, explain to a peer, draw the relationships, or apply the information to solve new problems. Of course, if students elaborate new information by making incorrect connections or developing misguided explanations, these misconceptions will be remembered too.

Organization is a second element of processing that improves learning. Material that is well organized is easier to learn and to remember than bits and pieces of information, especially if the information is complex or extensive. Placing a concept in a structure will help you learn and remember either general definitions or specific examples. The structure serves as a guide back to the information when you need it. For example, Table 7.1 on page 249 organizes information about types of knowledge; Table 7.2 on page 257 gives an organized view of the capacity, duration, contents, and retrieval of information from working and long-term memory; and Figure 7.5 on page 259 organizes my (limited) knowledge about antiques.

Context is a third element of processing that influences learning. Aspects of physical and emotional context—places, rooms, how we are feeling on a particular day, who is with us—are learned along with other information. Later, if you try to remember the information, it will be easier if the current context is similar to the original one. This has been demonstrated in the laboratory. Students who learned material in one type of room performed better on tests taken in a similar room than they did on tests taken in a very different-looking room (Smith, Glenberg, & Bjork, 1978). So studying for a test under "testlike" conditions may result in improved performance. Of course, you can't always go back to the same or to a similar place in order to recall something. But you can picture the setting, the time of day, and your companions, and you may eventually reach the information you seek.

Levels of Processing Theories.　Craik and Lockhart (1972) first proposed their **levels of processing theory** as an alternative to short-/long-term memory models, but levels of processing is particularly related to the notion of elaboration described above. Craik and Lockhart suggested that what determines how long information is remembered is *how completely* the information is analyzed and connected with other information. The more completely information is processed, the better are our chances of remembering it. For example, according to the levels of processing theory, if I ask you to sort pictures of dogs based on the color of their coats, you might not remember many of the pictures later. But if I ask you to rate each dog on how likely it is to chase you as you jog, you probably would remember more of the pictures. To rate the dogs you must pay attention to details in the pictures, relate features of the dogs to characteristics associated with danger, and so on. This rating procedure requires "deeper" processing and more focus on the *meaning* of the features in the photos.

Retrieving Information from Long-Term Memory.　When we need to use information from long-term memory, we search for it. Sometimes the search is conscious, as when you see a friend approaching and search for her name. At other times locating and using information from long-term memory is automatic,

Organization Ordered and logical network of relations.

Context The physical or emotional backdrop associated with an event.

Levels of Processing Theory Theory that recall of information is based on how deeply it is processed.

as when you dial a telephone or solve a math problem without having to search for each step. Think of long-term memory as a huge shelf full of tools and supplies ready to be brought to the workbench of working memory to accomplish a task. The shelf (long-term memory) stores an incredible amount, but it may be hard to find quickly what you are looking for. The workbench (working memory) is small, but anything on it is immediately available. Because it is small, however, supplies (bits of information) sometimes are lost when the workbench overflows or when one bit of information covers (interferes with) another (E. Gagné, 1985).

The size of the memory network is huge, but only one small area is activated at any one time. Only the information we are currently thinking about is in working memory. Information is retrieved in this network through the **spread of activation.** When a particular proposition or image is active—when we are thinking about it—other closely associated knowledge can be activated as well, and activation can spread through the network (Anderson, 1993; Gagné, Yekovich, & Yekovich, 1993). Thus, as I focus on the propositions, "I'd like to go for a drive to see the fall leaves today," related ideas such as, "I should rake leaves," and "The car needs an oil change," come to mind. As activation spreads from the "car trip" to the "oil change," the original thought, or active memory, disappears from working memory because of the limited space. So **retrieval** from long-term memory is partly through the spreading of activation from one bit of knowledge to related ideas in the network. We often use this spreading in reverse to retrace our steps in a conversation, as in, "Before we got onto the topic of where to get the oil changed, what were we talking about? Oh yes, seeing the leaves." (The learning and retrieving processes of long-term memory are diagrammed in Figure 7.7.)

FIGURE 7.7

Long-Term Memory

We activate information from long-term memory to help us understand new information in working memory. With mental work and processing (elaboration, organization, context) the new information can be stored permanently in long-term memory. Forgetting is caused by interference and time decay.

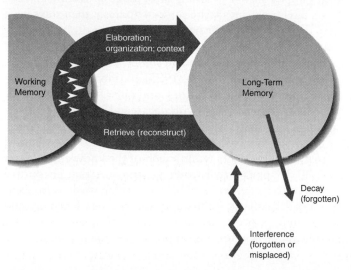

Spread of Activation Retrieval of pieces of information based on their relatedness to one another. Remembering one bit of information activates (stimulates) recall of associated information.

Retrieval Process of searching for and finding information in long-term memory.

In long-term memory the information is still available, even when it is not activated, even when you are not thinking about it at the moment. If spreading activation does not "find" the information we seek, then we might still come up with the answer through **reconstruction,** a problem-solving process that makes use of logic, cues, and other knowledge to *construct* a reasonable answer by filling in any missing parts. Sometimes reconstructed recollections are incorrect. For example, in 1932, F. C. Bartlett conducted a series of famous studies on remembering stories. He read a complex, unfamiliar Native-American tale to students at England's Cambridge University and, after various lengths of time, asked the students to recall the story. Students' recalled stories were generally shorter than the original and were translated into the concepts and language of the Cambridge student culture. The story told of a seal hunt, for instance, but many students remembered a "fishing trip," an activity closer to their experiences and more consistent with their schemas.

One area where reconstructed memory can play a major role is eyewitness testimony. Elizabeth Loftus and her colleagues have conducted a number of studies showing that misleading questions or other information during questioning can affect memory. For example, in a classic study, Loftus and Palmer (1974) showed subjects slides of a car wreck. Later, the experimenters asked some subjects, "How fast were the cars going when they *hit* each other?" while other subjects who saw the same slides were asked, "How fast were the cars going when they *smashed* into each other?" The difference in verbs was enough to bias the subjects' memories—the "hit" subjects estimated the cars were traveling an average of 34 miles per hour, but the "smashed" subjects estimated almost 41 miles per hour. And one week later, 32% of the "smashed" subjects remembered seeing broken glass at the scene of the wreck, while only 14% of the "hit" subjects remembered glass. (There was no broken glass visible in any of the slides.)

Forgetting and Long-Term Memory.   Information lost from working memory truly disappears. No amount of effort will bring it back. But information stored in long-term memory may be available, given the right cues. Some researchers believe that nothing is ever lost from long-term memory; however, recent research casts doubts on this assertion (Schwartz & Reisberg, 1991).

Information appears to be lost from long-term memory through time decay and **interference.** For example, memory for Spanish–English vocabulary decreases for about 3 years after a person's last course in Spanish, then stays level for about 25 years, then drops again for the next 25 years. One explanation for this decline is that neural connections, like muscles, grow weak without use. After 25 years, it may be that the memories are still somewhere in the brain, but they are too weak to be reactivated (Anderson, 1995a,b). Finally, newer memories may interfere with or obscure older memories, and older memories may interfere with memory for new material. Even with decay and interference, long-term memory is remarkable. In a recent review of almost 100 studies of memory for knowledge taught in school, George Semb and John Ellis (1994) concluded that, "contrary to popular belief, students retain much of the knowledge taught in the classroom" (p. 279). It appears that teaching strategies that encourage student engagement and lead to higher levels of *initial* learning (such as frequent reviews and tests, elaborated feedback, high standards, mastery learning, and active involvement in learning projects) are associated with longer retention. The Guidelines give applications of information processing for teaching.

Reconstruction Recreating information by using memories, expectations, logic, and existing knowledge.

Interference The process that occurs when remembering certain information is hampered by the presence of other information.

Make sure you have the students' attention.

Examples

1. Develop a signal that tells students to stop what they are doing and focus on you. Make sure students respond to the signal—don't let them ignore it. Practice using the signal.

2. Move around the room, use gestures, avoid speaking in a monotone.

3. Begin a lesson by asking a question that stimulates interest in the topic.

4. Regain the attention of individual students by walking closer to them, using their names, or asking them a question.

Help students separate essential from nonessential details and focus on the most important information.

Examples

1. Summarize instructional objectives to indicate what students should be learning. Relate the material you are presenting to the objectives as you teach: "Now I'm going to explain exactly how you can find the information you need to meet Objective One on the board—determining the tone of the story."

2. When you make an important point, pause, repeat, ask a student to paraphrase, note the information on the board in colored chalk, or tell students to highlight the point in their notes or readings.

Help students make connections between new information and what they already know.

Examples

1. Review prerequisites to help students bring to mind the information they will need to understand new material: "Who can tell us the definition of a quadrilateral? Now, what is a rhombus? Is a square a quadrilateral? Is a square a rhombus? What did we say yesterday about how you can tell? Today we are going to look at some other quadrilaterals."

2. Use an outline or diagram to show how new information fits with the framework you have been developing. For example, "Now that you know the duties of the FBI, where would you expect to find it in this diagram of the branches of the U.S. government?"

3. Give an assignment that specifically calls for the use of new information along with information already learned.

Provide for repetition and review of information.

Examples

1. Begin the class with a quick review of the homework assignment.

2. Give frequent, short tests.

3. Build practice and repetition into games, or have students work with partners to quiz each other.

(continued)

Present material in a clear, organized way.

Examples

1. Make the purpose of the lesson very clear.
2. Give students a brief outline to follow. Put the same outline on an overhead so you can keep yourself on track. When students ask questions or make comments, relate these to the appropriate section of the outline.
3. Use summaries in the middle and at the end of the lesson.

Focus on meaning, not memorization.

Examples

1. In teaching new words, help students associate the new word to a related word they already understand: "*Enmity* is from the same base as *enemy*. . . . "
2. In teaching about remainders, have students group 12 objects into sets of 2, 3, 4, 5, 6, and 7. Ask them to count the "leftovers" in each case.

Connectionism: An Alternative View of Memory

Some of the most recent explanations of how memory works are **connectionist models** that assume all knowledge is stored in patterns of connections among basic processing units in a vast network of the brain. The processing of information is assumed to be distributed across this network. So connectionist models use the brain's physical network of neurons as a metaphor for memory networks. Some connectionist models, such as **Parallel Distributed Processing** (PDP), stay at the metaphorical level and try to describe memory in a way that is consistent with human behavior. Brain-based theories, on the other hand, focus directly on how the nervous system might operate (Driscoll, 1994; Iran-Nejad, Marsh, & Clements, 1992).

Connectionist models have certain advantages. They can account for more than recall of information, and they can explain the slowly developing, incremental, ever-changing nature of human learning. As connections are constantly adjusted, learning occurs. When an output doesn't match a goal, the connections can be adjusted. However, connectionist models may not be developed enough to be useful for teachers except to remind us that learning involves the continued building, elaboration, and adjustment of knowledge (Driscoll, 1994; Iran-Nejad, Marsh, & Clements, 1992).

Focus on...

Information Processing

- Compare declarative, procedural, and conditional knowledge.
- Give two explanations for perception.
- How is information retained in working memory?
- How is information represented in long-term memory?
- A child from a large city has trouble understanding and remembering a story about endangered species in a national park. Explain this situation using information processing theory.

Connectionist Models Views of knowledge as being stored in patterns of connections among basic processing units in the brain.

Parallel Distributed Processing (PDP) Connectionist model that uses the brain's physical network of neurons as a metaphor for memory networks.

Metacognition, Regulation, and Individual Differences

One question that intrigues many cognitive psychologists is why some people learn and remember more than others. For those who hold an information processing view, part of the answer lies in the executive control processes shown in

Figure 7.1 on page 250. **Executive control processes** guide the flow of information through the information processing system. We have already discussed a number of control processes, including attention, maintenance rehearsal, elaborative rehearsal, organization, and elaboration. These executive control processes are sometimes called *metacognitive skills,* because the processes can be intentionally used to regulate cognition.

Metacognitive Knowledge and Regulation

Donald Meichenbaum and his colleagues describe **metacognition** as people's "awareness of their own cognitive machinery and how the machinery works" (Meichenbaum, Burland, Gruson, & Cameron, 1985, p. 5). Metacognition literally means cognition about cognition—or knowledge about knowledge. This knowledge is used to monitor and regulate cognitive processes—reasoning, comprehension, problem solving, learning, and so on. Because people differ in their metacognitive knowledge and skills, they differ in how well and how quickly they learn (Brown, Branford, Ferrara, & Campione, 1983; Morris, 1990).

Metacognition involves three kinds of knowledge: declarative knowledge about yourself as a learner, the factors that influence your learning and memory, and the skills, strategies, and resources needed to perform a task—knowing *what* to do; procedural knowledge or knowing *how* to use the strategies; and conditional knowledge to ensure the completion of the task—knowing *when* and *why* to apply the procedures and strategies (Schraw & Moshman, 1995).

Metacognitive knowledge is used to regulate thinking and learning (Brown, 1987; Nelson, 1996). There are three essential skills that allow us to do this: planning, monitoring, and evaluation. *Planning* involves deciding how much time to give to a task, which strategies to use, how to start, what resources to gather, what order to follow, what to skim and what to give intense attention, and so on. *Monitoring* is the on-line awareness of "how I'm doing." Monitoring entails asking, "Is this making sense? Am I trying to go too fast? Have I studied enough?" *Evaluation* involves making judgments about the processes and outcomes of thinking and learning. Should I change strategies? Get help? Give up for now? Is this paper (painting, model, poem, plan, etc.) finished? Many planning, monitoring, and evaluation processes are not necessarily conscious. Especially in adults, these processes can be automatic. Experts in a field may plan, monitor, and evaluate as second nature—they have difficulty describing their metacognitive knowledge and skills (Schraw & Moshman, 1995).

Computer menus provide a good analogy to metacognitive processes. In both cases, the individual decides what procedure is needed next, selects procedures from several choices, monitors the effect of making the choice, and returns to the menu if the results are unsatisfactory.

Individual Differences in Metacognition

Some differences in metacognitive abilities are the result of development. As children grow older they are more able to exercise executive control and use strategies. For example, they are more able to determine if they have understood instructions (Markman, 1977, 1979) or if they have studied enough to remember a set of items (Flavell, Friedrichs, & Hoyt, 1970). Metacognitive abilities begin to develop around ages 5 to 7 and improve throughout school (Flavell, 1985; Flavell, Green, & Flavell, 1995; Garner, 1990).

Not all differences in metacognitive abilities have to do with age or maturation. There is great variability even among students of the same developmental level, but these differences do not appear to be related to intellectual abilities.

Executive Control Processes Processes such as selective attention, rehearsal, elaboration, and organization that influence encoding, storage, and retrieval of information in memory.

Metacognition Knowledge about our own thinking processes.

In fact, superior metacognitive skills can compensate for lower levels of ability, so these metacognitive skills can be especially important for students who often have trouble in school (Swanson, 1990).

Some individual differences in metacognitive abilities are probably caused by biological differences or by variations in learning experiences. Students can vary greatly in their ability to attend selectively to information in their environment. In fact, many students diagnosed as learning disabled actually have attention disorders (Hallahan & Kauffman, 1997), particularly with long tasks (Pelham, 1981). Attention is also influenced by the individual and cultural differences we examined in Chapters 4 and 5, such as learning abilities and preferences, cognitive styles, and cultural background. Students who are field dependent, for example, have difficulty perceiving elements in a pattern and tend to focus on the whole.

Individual Differences and Working Memory

As you might expect, there are both developmental and individual differences in working memory. Let's examine a few.

Developmental Differences.   Research indicates that young children have very limited working memories, but their memory span improves with age. It is not clear whether these differences are the result of changes in memory *capacity* or improvements in *strategy* use. Case (1985a & b) suggests that the total amount of "space" available for processing information is the same at each age, but young children must use quite a bit of this space to remember how to execute basic operations, like reaching for a toy, finding the right word for an object, or counting. Using a new operation takes up a large portion of the child's working memory. Once an operation is mastered, however, there is more working memory available for short-term storage of new information. Biology may play a role too. As the brain and neurological system of the child mature, processing may become more efficient so that more working-memory space is available.

As children grow older, they develop more effective strategies for remembering information. Most children spontaneously discover rehearsal around age 5 or 6. Siegler (1991) describes a 9-year-old boy who witnessed a robbery, then mentally repeated the license number of the getaway car until he could give the number to the police. Younger children can be taught to rehearse, and will use the strategy effectively as long as they are reminded. But they will not apply the strategy spontaneously. Children are 10 to 11 years old before they have adultlike working memories.

According to Case (1985a, b), young children often use reasonable, but incorrect, strategies for solving problems because of their limited memories. They try to simplify the task by ignoring important information or skipping steps to reach a correct solution. This puts less strain on memory. For example, when comparing quantities, young children may consider only the height of the water in a glass, not the diameter of the glass, because this approach demands less of their memory. According to Case, this explains young children's inability to solve the classic Piagetian conservation problem. (See Figure 2.2 on page 34.)

There are several developmental differences in how students use organization, elaboration, and knowledge to process information in working memory.

Around age 6, most children discover the value of using *organizational strategies* and by 9 or 10 they use these strategies spontaneously. So, given the following words to learn:

> couch, orange, rat, lamp, pear, sheep, banana, rug, pineapple, horse, table, dog

an older child or an adult might organize the words into three short lists of furniture, fruit, and animals. Younger children can be taught to use organization to improve memory, but they probably won't apply the strategy unless they are reminded. Children also become more able to use elaboration as they mature, but this strategy is developed late in childhood. Creating images or stories to remember ideas is more likely for older elementary-school students and adolescents (Siegler, 1991).

Individual Differences.   Besides developmental differences, there are other individual variations in working memory. Some people seem to have more efficient working memories than others (Cariglia-Bull & Pressley, 1990; Dempster, 1981; Jurden, 1995), and differences in working memory may be associated with giftedness in math and verbal areas. For example, subjects in one research study were asked to remember lists of numbers, the locations of marks on a page, letters, and words (Dark & Benbow, 1991). Subjects who excelled in mathematics remembered numbers and locations significantly better than subjects talented in verbal areas. The verbally talented subjects, on the other hand, had better memories for words. Based on these results, Dark and Benbow believe that basic differences in information processing abilities play a role in the development of mathematical and verbal talent.

Individual Differences and Long-Term Memory

The major individual difference that affects long-term memory is knowledge. When students have more *domain-specific declarative* and *procedural knowledge,* they are better at learning and remembering material in that domain. Think what it is like for you to read a very technical textbook in an area you know little about. Every line is difficult. You have to stop and look up words or turn back to read about concepts you don't understand. It is hard to remember what you are reading because you are trying to understand and remember at the same time. But with a good basis of knowledge, learning and remembering become easier; the more you know, the easier it is to know more. This is true in part because having knowledge improves strategy use. Another factor is related to developing domain knowledge and remembering it—interest. Pat Alexander and her colleagues point out that to develop expert understanding and recall in a domain requires the "continuous interplay of skill (i.e., knowledge) and thrill (i.e., interest)" (Alexander, Kulikowich, & Schulze, 1994, p. 334).

> **Focus on...**
>
> ### Metacognition
>
> - Give some examples of your own metacognitive abilities.
> - How can using better metacognitive strategies improve memory?

Now that we have examined the information processing explanation of how knowledge is represented and remembered, let's turn to the really important question: How can teachers support the development of knowledge?

Becoming Knowledgeable: Some Basic Principles

Understanding a concept such as "antique" involves *declarative knowledge* about characteristics and images and *procedural knowledge* about how to apply rules to categorize specific antiques. We will discuss the development of declarative and procedural knowledge separately, but keep in mind that real learning is holistic and interrelated.

Development of Declarative Knowledge

Within the information processing perspective, to learn declarative knowledge is really to integrate new ideas with existing knowledge and construct an understanding. For example, a teacher says:

> "In vitro experiments show vitamin C increases the formation of white blood cells."

Students may ignore the phrase "in vitro" because they have no existing schemas for making sense of it. But through *spreading of activation* the concepts of "white blood cells" and "vitamin C" cue the retrieval of prior knowledge such as "vitamin C fights colds," "viruses cause colds," and "white blood cells destroy viruses." Using this prior knowledge about colds, viruses, and vitamin C, along with the new information that vitamin C increases white blood cells, the students may infer that "vitamin C fights colds *because* it increases the formation of the white blood cells." This information was neither in their long-term memories nor in the teacher's statement, but it was constructed by the students as they elaborated and organized their understanding of vitamin C. The resulting elaborated, reorganized network of knowledge includes the students' interpretations of the new information from the teacher in addition to their constructions and inferences (Gagné, Yekovich, & Yekovich, 1993). Let's examine factors that support the construction of declarative knowledge.

As you have seen, people learn best when they have a good base of knowledge in the area they are studying. With many well-elaborated schemas and scripts to guide them, new material makes more sense, and there are many possible networks for connecting new information with old. But students don't always have a good base of knowledge. In the early phases of learning, students of any age must grope around the landscape a bit, searching for landmarks and direction. Even experts in an area must use some learning strategies when they encounter unfamiliar material or new problems (Alexander, 1992, 1996; Garner, 1990; Perkins & Salomon, 1989; Shuell, 1990).

What are some possible strategies? First we will discuss **rote memorization** techniques, which help students remember information that, while it has little inherent meaning, may provide the basic building blocks for other learning—the populations of the 10 largest cities in the world, for example. Next we will examine *mnemonic strategies,* which build in meaning by connecting what is to be learned with established words or images. Then we explore approaches that build on *meaning.*

Rote Memorization.   Very few things need to be learned by rote. The greatest challenge teachers face is to help students think and understand, not

Rote Memorization. Remembering information by repetition without necessarily understanding the meaning of the information.

just memorize. Unfortunately, many students like those in the scenario opening this chapter, see memorizing and learning as the same thing (Iran-Nejad, 1990). But, there are times when we have to memorize something word-for-word, such as lines in a song, poem, or play.

If you must memorize, how would you do it? If you have tried to memorize a list of items that are all similar to one another, you may have found that you tended to remember items at the beginning and at the end of the list but forgot those in the middle. This is called the **serial-position effect. Part learning,** breaking the list into smaller segments, can help prevent this effect, because breaking a list into several shorter lists means there will be fewer middle items to forget.

Another strategy for memorizing a long selection or list is the use of **distributed practice.** A student who studies Hamlet's soliloquy intermittently throughout the weekend will probably do much better than a student who tries to memorize the entire speech on Sunday night. Studying for an extended period, rather than for briefer periods with rest time in between, is called **massed practice.** Distributed practice gives time for deeper processing and the chance to move information into long-term memory (Mumford, Costanza, Baughman, Threlfall, & Fleishman, 1994).

Mnemonics.   **Mnemonics** are systematic procedures for improving memory. Many of these mnemonic strategies use imagery (Levin, 1985; McCormick & Levin, 1987).

The **loci method** derives its name from the plural of the Latin word *locus,* meaning "place." To use loci, you must first imagine a very familiar place, such as your own house or apartment, and pick out particular locations. Every time you have a list to remember, the same locations serve as "pegs" to "hang" memories. Simply place each item from your list in one of these locations. For instance, let's say you want to remember to buy milk, bread, butter, and cereal at the store. Imagine a giant bottle of milk blocking the entry hall, a lazy loaf of bread sleeping on the living room couch, a stick of butter melting all over the dining room table, and dry cereal covering the kitchen floor. When you want to remember the items, all you have to do is take an imaginary walk through your house. Other **peg-type mnemonics** use a standard list of words (one is bun, two is shoe . . .) as pegs.

If you need to remember information for long periods of time, an acronym may be the answer. An **acronym** is a form of abbreviation—a word formed from the first letter of each word in a phrase, for example NAFTA (North American Free Trade Agreement). Another method forms phrases or sentences out of the first letter of each word or item in a list, for example, Every Good Boy Does Fine to remember the lines on the G clef—E, G, B, D, F. Because the words must make sense as a sentence, this approach also has some characteristics of **chain mnemonics,** methods that connect the first item to be memorized with the second, the second item with the third, and so on. In one type of chain method, each item on a list is linked to the next through some visual association or story. Another chain-method approach is to incorporate all the items to be memorized into a jingle like "i before e except after c," or "Thirty days hath September."

The mnemonic system that has been most extensively applied in teaching is the **keyword method.** The approach has two stages. To remember a foreign word, for example, you first choose an English word, preferably a concrete noun, that sounds like the foreign word or a part of it. Next, you associate the meaning of the foreign word with the English word through an image or sentence. For

Serial-Position Effect The tendency to remember the beginning and the end but not the middle of a list.

Part Learning Breaking a list of rote items into shorter lists.

Distributed Practice Practice in brief periods with rest intervals.

Massed Practice Practice for a single extended period.

Mnemonics Techniques for remembering; also, the art of memory.

Loci Method Technique of associating items with specific places.

Peg-Type Mnemonics Systems of associating items with cue words.

Acronym Technique for remembering names, phrases, or steps by using the first letter of each word to form a new, memorable word.

Chain Mnemonics Memory strategies that associate one element in a series with the next element.

Keyword Method System of associating new words or concepts with similar-sounding cue words.

FIGURE 7.8

Using the Keyword Method to Learn English Vocabulary

Here the keyword is "purse." It is a concrete noun that sounds like "persuade" (the vocabulary word to be learned). The keyword, definition, and vocabulary word are linked in an image.

Source: From J. R. Levin, C. B. McCormick, G. E. Miller, J. K. Berry, and M. Pressley. "Mnemonic versus nonmnemonic vocabulary—learning strategies for children." *American Educational Research Journal, 19,* pp. 121–136. Copyright 1982 by the American Educational Research Association. Reprinted by permission of the publisher.

"HOW MANY TIMES MUST I TELL YOU—IT'S 'CAT' BEFORE 'TEMPLE' EXCEPT AFTER 'SLAVE.'"

(By permission of Bo Brown, from Phi Delta Kappan*)*

example, the Spanish word *carta* (meaning "letter") sounds like the English word "cart." Cart becomes the keyword: you imagine a shopping cart filled with letters on its way to the post office, or you make up a sentence such as "The cart full of letters tipped over" (Pressley, Levin, & Delaney, 1982). Figure 7.8 offers another example of this method, this time used to learn English vocabulary.

One problem, however, is that the keyword method does not work well if it is difficult to identify a keyword for a particular item. Many words and ideas that students need to remember do not lend themselves to associations with keywords (Hall, 1991; Pressley, 1991). Also, vocabulary learned with keywords may be more easily forgotten than vocabulary learned in other ways, especially if students are given keywords and images instead of being asked to supply the words and images. When the teacher provides the memory links, these associations may not fit the students' existing knowledge and may be forgotten or confused later, so remembering suffers (Wang & Thomas, 1995; Wang, Thomas, & Ouelette, 1992). Younger students have some difficulty forming their own images. For them, memory aids that rely on auditory cues—rhymes like "i before e except after c," and "Thirty days hath September" seem to work better.

Many teachers use a mnemonic system to quickly learn their students' names. Until we have some knowledge to guide learning, it may help to use some rote memorization and mnemonic approaches to build vocabulary and facts. Not all educators agree, as is noted in the Point/Counterpoint.

What's Wrong with Memorizing?

For years students have relied on memorization to learn vocabulary, procedures, steps, names, and facts. Is this a bad idea?

POINT Rote memorization creates inert knowledge.

Years ago William James (1912) described the limitations of rote learning by telling a story about what can happen when students memorize but do not understand:

> A friend of mine, visiting a school, was asked to examine a young class in geography. Glancing at the book, she said: Suppose you should dig a hole in the ground, hundreds of feet deep, how should you find it at the bottom—warmer or colder than on top?" None of the class replying, the teacher said: "I'm sure they know, but I think you don't ask the question quite rightly. Let me try." So, taking the book, she asked: "In what condition is the interior of the globe?" And received the immediate answer from half the class at once. "The interior of the globe is in a condition of igneous fusion." (p. 150)

The students had memorized the answer, but they had no idea what it meant. Perhaps they didn't understand the meaning of "interior," "globe," or "igneous fusion." At any rate, the knowledge was useful to them only when they were answering test questions, and only then when the questions were phrased exactly as they had

been memorized. Students often resort to memorizing the exact words of definitions when they have no hope for actually understanding the terms or when teachers count off for definitions that are not exact.

Most recently, Howard Gardner has been a vocal critic of rote memorization and a champion of "teaching for understanding." In an interview in *Phi Delta Kappan* (Siegel & Shaughnessy, 1994), Gardner says:

> My biggest concern about American education is that even our better students in our better schools are just going through the motions of education. In *The Unschooled Mind,* I review ample evidence that suggests an absence of understanding—the inability of students to take knowledge, skills, and other apparent attainments and apply them successfully in new situations. In the absence of such flexibility and adaptability, the education that the students receive is worth little. (pp. 563–564)

COUNTERPOINT Rote memorization can be effective.

Memorization may not be such a bad way to learn new information that has little inherent meaning, such as foreign language vocabulary. Alvin Wang, Margaret Thomas, and Judith Ouellette (1992) compared learning Tagalog (the national language of the Philippines) using either rote memorization or the keyword approach. The

keyword method is a way of creating connections and meaning for associating new words with existing words and images. In their study, even though the keyword method led to faster and better learning initially, long-term forgetting was *greater* for students who had used the keyword method than for students who had learned by rote memorization.

There are times when students must memorize and we do them a disservice if we don't teach them how. Every discipline has its own terms, names, facts, and rules. As adults, we want to work with physicians who have memorized the correct names for the bones and organs of the body or the drugs needed to combat particular infections. Of course, they can look up some information or research certain conditions, but they have to know where to start. We want to work with accountants who give us accurate information about the new tax codes, information they probably had to memorize because it changes from year to year in ways that are not necessarily rational or meaningful. We want to deal with computer sales people who have memorized their stock and know exactly which printers will work with our computer. Just because something was learned through memorization does not mean it is inert knowledge. The real question, as Gardner points out above, is whether you can *use* the information flexibly and effectively to solve new problems.

Making It Meaningful.   Perhaps the best single method for helping students learn is to make each lesson as meaningful as possible. Meaningful lessons are presented in vocabulary that makes sense to the students. New terms are clarified through ties with more familiar words and ideas. Meaningful lessons

Meaningful lessons are presented in vocabulary that makes sense to the student. New terms are clarified through associations with more familiar words and ideas, as in these lists of solids, liquids, and gases.

are also well organized, with clear connections between the different elements of the lesson. Finally, meaningful lessons make natural use of old information to help students understand new information through examples or analogies.

The importance of meaningful lessons is emphasized in an example presented by Smith (1975). Consider the three lines below:

1. KBVODUWGPJMSQTXNOGMCTRSO

2. READ JUMP WHEAT POOR BUT SEEK

3. KNIGHTS RODE HORSES INTO WAR

Begin by covering all but the first line. Look at it for a second, close the book, and write down all the letters you remember. Then repeat this procedure with the second and third lines. Each line has the same number of letters, but the chances are great that you remembered all the letters in the third line, a good number of letters in the second line, and very few in the first line.

The first line makes no sense. There is no way to organize it in a brief glance. The second line is more meaningful. You do not have to see each letter because you bring prior knowledge of spelling rules and vocabulary to the task. The third line is the most meaningful. Just a glance and you can probably remember all of it because you bring to this task prior knowledge not only of spelling and vocabulary but also of rules about syntax and probably some historical information about knights (they didn't ride in tanks). This sentence is meaningful because you have existing schemas for assimilating it. It is relatively easy to associate the words and meaning with other information already in long-term memory.

The challenge for teachers is to make lessons less like learning the first line and more like learning the third line. Although this may seem obvious, think about the times when *you* have read a sentence in a text or heard an explanation from a professor that might just as well have been KBVODUWGPJMSQTXNOGMCTRSO. But remember, attempts to change the ways that students are used to learning—moving from memorizing to meaningful activities as in the opening "What Would You Do?" situation, are not always greeted with student enthusiasm. In Chapters 8 and 9 we will examine a variety of ways that teachers can support meaningful learning and understanding.

Becoming an Expert: Development of Procedural and Conditional Knowledge

Experts in a particular field have a wealth of domain-specific knowledge, that is, knowledge that applies specifically to their area or domain. They not only have *declarative knowledge* (facts and verbal information), but they also have at their command considerable *procedural knowledge,* an understanding of how to perform various cognitive activities. And they know when and why to apply their understandings; that is, they have *conditional knowledge,* so they can manipulate their declarative and procedural knowledge to solve problems.

Another characteristic distinguishes experts from novices in an area. Much of the expert's declarative knowledge has become "proceduralized," that is, incorporated into routines that can be applied automatically without making many demands on working memory. Skills that are applied without conscious thought are called **automated basic skills.** An example is shifting gears in a standard transmission car. At first you had to think about every step, but as you became more expert (if you did), the procedure became automatic. But not all procedures (sometimes called *cognitive skills*) can be automatic, even for experts in a particular domain. For example, no matter how expert you are in driving, you still have to consciously watch the traffic around you. This kind of conscious procedure is called a *domain-specific strategy.* Automated basic skills and domain-specific strategies are learned in different ways (Gagné, Yekovich, & Yekovich, 1993).

Automated Basic Skills.   Most psychologists identify three stages in the development of an automated skill: *cognitive, associative,* and *autonomous* (Anderson, 1995; Fitts & Posner, 1967). At the **cognitive stage,** when we are first learning, we rely on declarative knowledge and general problem-solving strategies to accomplish our goal. For example, to learn to assemble a bookshelf, we might try to follow steps in the instruction manual, putting a check beside each step as we complete it to keep track of progress. At this stage we have to "think about" every step and perhaps refer back to the pictures of parts to see what a "¼ inch metal bolt with lock nut" looks like. The load on working memory is heavy. There can be quite a bit of trial-and-error learning at this stage when, for example, the bolt we chose doesn't fit.

At the **associative stage,** individual steps of a procedure are combined, or "chunked" into larger units. We reach for the right bolt and put it into the right hole. One step smoothly cues the next. With practice, the associative stage moves to the **autonomous stage,** where the whole procedure can be accomplished without much attention. So if you assemble enough bookshelves, you can have a lively conversation as you do, paying little attention to the assembly task. This movement from the cognitive to the associative to the autonomous stage holds for the development of basic cognitive skills in any area, but science, medicine, chess, and mathematics have been most heavily researched.

What can teachers do to help their students pass through these three stages and become more expert? In general, it appears that two factors are critical: *prerequisite knowledge* and *practice with feedback*. First, if students don't have the essential prior knowledge (schemas, skills, etc.), the load on working memory will be too great. In order to compose a poem in a foreign language, for example, you must know some of the vocabulary and grammar of that language, and you must have some understanding of poetry forms. To learn the vocabulary, grammar, *and* forms as you also try to compose the poem would be too much.

Second, practice with feedback allows you to form associations, recognize cues automatically, and combine small steps into larger condition-action rules or *productions*. Even from the earliest stage, some of this practice should include a simplified version of the whole process in a real context. Practice in real contexts helps students learn not only *how* to do a skill but also *why* and *when* (Collins, Brown, & Newman, 1989; Gagné, Yekovich, & Yekovich, 1993). Of course, as every athletic coach knows, if a particular step, component, or process is causing trouble, that element might be practiced alone until it is more automatic, and then put back into the whole sequence, to lower the demands on working memory (Anderson, Reder, & Simon, 1996).

Automated Basic Skills Skills that are applied without conscious thought.

Cognitive Stage The initial learning of an automated skill when we rely on general problem-solving approaches to make sense of steps or procedures.

Associative Stage Individual steps of a procedure are combined or "chunked" into larger units.

Autonomous Stage Final stage in the learning of automated skills. The procedure is fine-tuned and becomes "automatic."

Domain-Specific Strategies.   As we saw earlier, some procedural knowledge, such as monitoring the traffic while you drive, is not automatic because conditions are constantly changing. Once you decide to change lanes, the maneuver may be fairly automatic, but the decision to change lanes was conscious, based on the traffic conditions around you. **Domain-specific strategies** are these consciously applied skills of organizing thoughts and actions to reach a goal.

To support this kind of learning, teachers need to provide opportunities for practice in many different situations—for example, practice reading with newspapers, package labels, magazines, books, letters, operating manuals, and so on. In the next chapter's discussion of problem solving, we will examine other ways to help students develop domain-specific strategies.

Learning Outside School.   The last several sections of this chapter have described many ideas for helping students become knowledgeable—memory strategies, mnemonics, metacognitive skills such as planning or monitoring comprehension, and cognitive skills. Some students have an advantage in school because they learn these strategies and skills at home. The Guidelines give ideas for working with families to give all your students more support and practice developing these skills.

Focus on...

Developing Knowledge

- How would you use the keyword method to teach the exports of foreign countries?
- Describe some procedures for developing procedural knowledge.

Guidelines

Family and Community Partnerships for Students' Learning

Give families specific strategies to help their children practice and remember.

Examples

1. Develop "super learner" homework assignments that include material to be learned and a "parent coaching card" with a description of a simple memory strategy—appropriate for the material—that parents can teach their child.
2. Provide a few comprehension check questions so a family member can review reading assignments and check the child's understanding.
3. Describe the value of distributed practice and give family members ideas for how and when to work skills practice into home conversations and projects.

Ask family members to share their strategies for organizing and remembering.

Examples

1. Create a family calendar.
2. Encourage planning discussions in which family members help students break large tasks into smaller jobs, identify goals, and find resources.

Discuss the importance of attention in learning.

Examples

1. Encourage families to create study spaces for children away from distractions.
2. Make sure parents know the purpose of homework assignments.

Domain-Specific Strategies Consciously applied skills to reach goals in a particular subject or problem area.

Constructivism and Situated Learning: Challenging Symbolic Processing Models

The information processing perspectives presented in this chapter share several features, even if they differ in their views of memory. All of these approaches regard the human mind as a symbol-processing system that converts sensory input into symbol structures (propositions, images, or schemas), and then processes those symbol structures so knowledge can be held in memory and retrieved. Learning leads to modifications in the internal symbol structures. The outside world is seen as a source of input, but once the sensations are perceived and enter working memory, the important work is assumed to be happening "inside the head" of the individual (Schunk, 1996; Vera & Simon, 1989). Today, there are challenges to these views of learning—the constructivist perspective and situated learning.

Constructivist Views of Learning

Even though information processing theorists believe that we actively *construct* knowledge based on what we already know and the new information we encounter, many constructivists believe that information processing does not take the idea of knowledge construction far enough (Derry, 1992; Garrison, 1995).

Constructivist perspectives are grounded in the research of Piaget, Vygotsky, the Gestalt psychologists, Bartlett, and Bruner as well as the educational philosophy of John Dewey, to mention just a few intellectual roots. As with information processing views, there is no one constructivist theory of learning. For example, there are constructivist approaches in science and mathematics education, in educational psychology and anthropology, and in computer-based education. Some constructivist views emphasize the *shared, social construction of knowledge;* others see social forces as less important (Driscoll, 1994; Iran-Nejad, 1990; Perkins, 1991; Spiro, Feltovich, Jacobson, & Coulson, 1991; Tobin, 1990; von Glaserfeld, 1990; Wittrock, 1992).

Types of Constructivism. Today, many psychologists and educators use the term "constructivism." It is helpful to organize the different approaches using Moshman's (1982) three categories of exogenous, endogenous, and dialectical constructivism. **Exogenous constructivism** focuses on the ways that individuals *reconstruct* outside reality by building accurate mental representations such as propositional networks, schemas, and condition-action production rules. Thus, in exogenous constructivism, learning is building accurate mental structures that reflect "the way things really are" in the world. (Think of *exo* as reflecting the *ex*ternal world). Many aspects of information processing are consistent with exogenous constructivism.

Endogenous constructivism is at the other extreme, and assumes that new knowledge is abstracted from old knowledge and is not shaped by accurately mapping the outside world. Knowledge develops as old cognitive structures are transformed to become more coordinated and useful. Piaget's stage theory of cognitive development is an example of endogenous constructivism.

Constructivist Perspective View that emphasizes the active role of the learner in building understanding and making sense of information.

Exogenous Constructivism A perspective that considers knowledge to be the reconstruction of structures that really exist in the external world.

Endogenous Constructivism The view emphasizing that learners construct their own knowledge through transforming and reorganizing their existing cognitive structures.

Constructivist and situated views of learning challenge other perspectives that see the learner as "receiver and processor of knowledge." Constructivist views see learners as having more interactive roles.

Finally, **dialectical constructivism** is a middle ground, suggesting that knowledge grows through the interactions of internal (cognitive) and external (environmental and social) factors. Vygotsky's description of cognitive development through the internalization and use of cultural tools such as language is an example of dialectical constructivism (Bruning, Schraw, & Ronning, 1995). Another example is Bandura's theory of reciprocal interactions between people, behaviors, and environments (Schunk, 1996). Table 7.3 summarizes the three kinds of constructivism.

Knowledge: Accuracy versus Usefulness

As you can see from Table 7.3, a fundamental difference between exogenous and other constructivists is that exogenous theorists assume the world is knowable; there is an objective reality "out there," and an individual can understand it. The understanding may be more or less accurate—knowledge constructions may be filled with misconceptions about how the world operates. For example, young children sometimes construct a subtraction procedure that says, "subtract the smaller number from the larger number, no matter which number in a problem is on top."

Many of the more extreme constructivist perspectives, on the other hand, do not assume that the world is knowable. They suggest that all knowledge is constructed and based not only on prior knowledge, but also the cultural and social context. They point out that what is true in one time and place—such as the "fact" before Columbus's time that the earth was flat—becomes false in

Dialectical Constructivism View that locates the source of knowledge in the interaction between learners and the environment.

TABLE 7.3	Three Types of Constructivism	
Type	Assumptions about Learning and Knowledge	Example Theories
Exogenous	Knowledge is acquired by constructing a representation of the outside world. Direct teaching, feedback, and explanation affect learning. Knowledge is accurate to the extent that it reflects the "way things really are" in the outside world.	Information Processing
Endogenous	Knowledge is constructed by transforming, organizing, and reorganizing previous knowledge. Knowledge is not a mirror of the external world, even though experience influences thinking and thinking influences knowledge. Exploration and discovery are more important than teaching.	Piaget
Dialectical	Knowledge is constructed based on social interactions and experience. Knowledge reflects the outside world as filtered through and influenced by culture, language, beliefs, interactions with others, direct teaching, and modeling. Guided discovery, teaching, models, and coaching as well as the individual's prior knowledge, beliefs, and thinking affect learning.	Vygotsky

another time and place. These constructivists are not concerned with accurate, "true" representations of the world, but only with *useful* constructions.

> Radical constructivists hold that we live in a relativistic world that can only be understood from individually unique perspectives, which are constructed through experimental activity in the social/physical world. No individual's viewpoint thus constructed should be viewed as inherently distorted or less correct than another's, although it is certainly true that one individual perspective can be more useful than another. (Derry, 1992, p. 415)

Particular ideas may be useful within a specific **community of practice,** such as fifteenth century navigation, but useless outside that community. What counts as new knowledge is determined in part by how well the new idea fits with current accepted practice. Over time, the current practice may be questioned and even overthrown, but until such major shifts occur, current practice will shape what is considered useful.

The idea of a community of practice brings us to another, related view of learning that is increasingly influential in teaching—situated learning.

Situated Learning

Information processing, as well as some constructivist perspectives such as that of Piaget, tends to focus on the individual information processor as he or she tries to make sense of the world. Thus, cognitive psychologists study individual and developmental differences, but may ignore the social situation in which learning occurs. In contrast, psychologists who emphasize the social construction of knowledge and **situated learning** affirm Vygotsky's notion that learning

Community of Practice Social situation or context in which ideas are judged useful or true.

Situated Learning The idea that skills and knowledge are tied to the situation in which they were learned and difficult to apply in new settings.

is inherently social and embedded in a particular cultural setting. Learning in the real world is not like studying in school. It is more like an apprenticeship where novices, with the support of an expert guide and model, take on more and more responsibility until they are able to function independently. For those who take a situated learning view, this explains learning in factories, around the dinner table, in high school halls, in street gangs, in the business office, and on the playground.

Situated learning is often described as "enculturation," or adopting the norms, behaviors, skills, beliefs, language, and attitudes of a particular community. The community might be mathematicians or gang members or readers or teachers or students in your eighth-grade class or Republicans—any group that has particular ways of thinking and doing. Knowledge is seen *not* as individual cognitive structures but as a creation of the community over time. The practices of the community—the ways of interacting and getting things done, as well as the tools the community has created—constitute the knowledge of that community. Learning means becoming more able to participate in those practices and use the tools (Derry, 1992; Garrison, 1995; Greeno, Collins, & Resnick, 1996).

At the most basic level, "situated learning . . . emphasizes the idea that much of what is learned is specific to the situation in which it is learned" (Anderson, Reder, & Simon, 1996, p. 5). Thus, some would argue, learning to do calculations in school may help students do more school calculations, but may not help them balance a checkbook, because the skills can be applied only in the context in which they were learned, namely school (Lave, 1988; Lave & Wenger, 1991). One implication is that students should learn skills and knowledge in meaningful contexts, with connections to the "real-life" situations in which the knowledge and skills will be useful.

There is evidence that much learning is tied to the situation in which it was learned. But it also appears that knowledge and skills can be applied across contexts that were not part of the initial learning situation, as when you use your ability to read and calculate to do your income taxes, even though income tax forms were not part of your high school curriculum (Anderson, Reder, & Simon, 1996). We will return many times in the upcoming chapters to these tensions surrounding *specific* and *general* knowledge and the *transfer* of knowledge from one situation to another.

Much of the work within constructivist perspectives has focused on teaching. Many of the new standards for teaching, such as the National Council of Teachers of Mathematics's *Curriculum and Evaluation Standards for School Mathematics* (NCTM, 1989) and the American Association for the Advancement of Science's *Benchmarks for Science Literacy* (AAAS, 1993) are based on constructivist assumptions and methods. Many of the efforts to reform and restructure schools are attempts to apply constructivist perspectives on teaching and learning to the curriculum and organization of entire schools. In Chapters 9 and 13 we consider many of these implications for teaching. As a summary of the different perspectives on learning, Table 7.4 presents the behavioral perspective and selected constructivist perspectives on learning.

Focus on...

Constructivism and Situated Learning

- Contrast exogenous, endogenous, and dialectical constructivist approaches to learning.
- How do communities of practice affect learning?
- What does it mean that learning is situated?

TABLE 7.4   Four Views of Learning

	Behavioral	Exogenous Constructivism	Endogenous Constructivism	Dialectical Constructivism/ Situated Learning
	Skinner	J. Anderson	Piaget	Vygotsky
Knowledge	Fixed body of knowledge to acquire	Fixed body of knowledge to acquire	Changing body of knowledge, individually constructed in social world	Socially constructed knowledge
	Stimulated from outside	Stimulated from outside Prior knowledge influences how information is processed	Built on what learner brings	Built on what participants contribute, construct together
Learning	Acquisition of facts, skills, concepts	Acquisition of facts, skills, concepts, and strategies	Active construction, restructuring prior knowledge	Collaborative construction of socially defined knowledge and values
	Occurs through drill, guided practice	Occurs through the effective application of strategies	Occurs through multiple opportunities and diverse processes to connect to what is already known	Occurs through socially constructed opportunities
Teaching	Transmission Presentation (Telling)	Transmission Guide students toward more "accurate" and complete knowledge	Challenge, guide thinking toward more complete understanding	Co-construct knowledge with students
Role of Teacher	Manager, supervisor	Teach and model effective strategies	Facilitator, guide	Facilitator, guide Co-participant
	Correct wrong answers	Correct misconceptions	Listen for student's current conceptions, ideas, thinking	Co-construct different interpretation of knowledge; listen to socially constructed conceptions
Role of Peers	Not usually considered	Not necessary but can influence information processing	Not necessary but can stimulate thinking, raise questions	Ordinary part of process of knowledge construction
Role of Student	Passive reception of information (little flexibility)	Active processor of information, strategy user	Active construction (within mind)	Active co-construction with others and self
	Active listener, direction-follower	Organizer and reorganizer of information Rememberer	Active thinker, explainer, interpreter, questioner	Active thinker, explainer, interpreter, questioner Active social participator

There are variations within each of these views of learning that differ in emphasis. There is also an overlap in constructivist views.

Source: Adapted by permission of the author from Hermine H. Marshall. *Reconceptualizing learning for restructured schools.* Paper presented at the Annual Meeting of the American Educational Research Association, April, 1992.

SUMMARY

Elements of the Cognitive Perspective

Cognitive learning theorists focus on the human mind's active attempts to make sense of the world. The ways we think about situations—along with our beliefs, expectations, and feelings—influence what and how we learn. Cognitivists view knowledge as the outcome of learning and the power of knowledge as the driving element in learning.

The Information Processing Model of Memory

Knowledge can be general or domain specific and can be classified as declarative, procedural, and conditional. Different kinds of knowledge require different teaching approaches.

One widely used cognitive model is information processing, based on the analogy between the mind and the computer. This model includes three storage systems: the sensory register, working memory, and long-term memory. Information processing involves encoding, retention, retrieval, and other processes. The sensory register takes in sensory stimuli and briefly holds the information. Perception is based on bottom-up processing (recognizing familiar elements) and top-down processing (using previous knowledge to fill in incomplete patterns).

Working memory, or short-term memory, holds five to nine bits of information at a time for 20 to 30 seconds. The duration of working memory can be extended through maintenance rehearsal, elaboration rehearsal, and chunking. Forgetting in working memory results from both interference and time decay.

Long-term memory seems to hold an unlimited amount of information permanently. Information may be part of our semantic, episodic, or procedural memories. In long-term memory, bits of information may be stored and interrelated in terms of propositional networks and schemas (such as story grammars and scripts)—data structures that allow us to represent large amounts of complex information, make inferences, and understand new information.

Information is retrieved from long-term memory through the spread of activation, as one memory activates other related information. Remembering is a reconstruction process leading to accurate, partly accurate, or inaccurate recall. Accurate retrieval depends on the extent to which information is elaborated, organized, and embedded in a context. As in working memory, forgetting in long-term memory occurs through interference and decay.

Another view of memory is the levels of processing theory, in which recall of information is determined by how completely it is processed. Recent connectionist models explain memory in terms of simple processing devices connected in a massive network, like many computers working simultaneously.

Metacognition, Regulation, and Individual Differences

Metacognition—knowledge about thinking—and monitoring are powerful executive controls in the information processing system. Metacognition involves an awareness of what thinking strategies to use and when, how, and why to apply them. There are both developmental and individual differences in metacognitive abilities. As children grow older they are more able to monitor and direct their attention and learning strategies. Teachers can teach metacognitive skills to help students become strategic learners.

Becoming Knowledgeable: Some Basic Principles

Declarative knowledge develops as we integrate new information with our existing understanding. The least effective way to accomplish this is rote memorization, which can best be improved by part learning and distributed practice. Mnemonics as memorization aids include peg-type approaches such as the loci method, acronyms, chain mnemonics, and the keyword method. The best way to learn and remember is to understand. Making the information to be remembered meaningful is important and often is the greatest challenge for teachers.

Constructivism and Situated Learning: Challenging Symbolic Processing Models

Today there are two related challenges to the information processing perspective—constructivism and situated learning. Grounded in the work of Piaget, Vygotsky, Bruner, Bartlett, and Dewey, the constructivist orientation emphasizes the individual's active construction of meaning. The focus is on meaning-making and knowledge construction, not memory for information. There are many constructivist theories, but they can be grouped into three categories: exogenous theories that include information processing and focus on "constructing" an accurate representation of external reality, endogenous constructivism that emphasizes transforming internal cognitive structures to construct unique personal understandings, and dialectical constructivism that asserts that both internal cognitive structures and external factors are important in constructing knowledge. Situated learning, like dialectical constructivism, emphasizes the importance of physical and social contexts in learning. What is learned is tied to the situation in which learning occurs and is difficult to apply in new settings.

KEY TERMS

acronym, p. 271
articulatory loop, p. 254
associative stage, p. 275
attention, p. 252
automated basic skills, p. 275
autonomous stage, p. 275
automaticity, p. 253
bottom-up processing, p. 252
chain mnemonics, p. 271
chunking, p. 256
cognitive stage, p. 275
cognitive view of learning,
    p. 246
community of practice, p. 279
conditional knowledge, p. 249
connectionist models, p. 266
constructivist perspective, p. 277
context, p. 262
decay, p. 257
declarative knowledge, p. 248
dialectical constructivism, p. 278
distributed practice, p. 271
domain-specific knowledge, p. 248

domain-specific strategies,
    p. 276
elaboration, p. 261
elaborative rehearsal, p. 256
endogenous constructivism, p. 277
episodic memory, p. 261
executive control processes, p. 267
exogenous constructivism, p. 277
general knowledge, p. 248
images, p. 258
information processing, p. 249
interference, p. 264
keyword method, p. 271
levels of processing theory, p. 262
loci method, p. 271
long-term memory, p. 257
maintenance rehearsal, p. 255
massed practice, p. 271
metacognition, p. 267
mnemonics, p. 271
organization, p. 262
parallel distributed processing
    (PDP), p. 266

part learning, p. 271
peg-type mnemonics, p. 271
perception, p. 251
procedural knowledge, p. 248
procedural memory, p. 261
productions, p. 261
propositional network, p. 258
receptors, p. 250
reconstruction, p. 264
retrieval, p. 263
rote memorization, p. 270
schemas; schema, p. 259
script, p. 260
semantic memory, p. 258
sensory memory, p. 250
serial-position effect, p. 271
situated learning, p. 279
spread of activation, p. 263
story grammar, p. 260
top-down processing, p. 252
working memory, p. 254

CHECK YOUR UNDERSTANDING

Can you apply the ideas from this chapter on cognitive views of learning to solve the following problems of practice?

Preschool and Kindergarten

■ The first-grade teachers believe that the kindergarten teachers could do a better job of preparing their students to "pay attention" in class. As a kindergarten teacher, what would you do? How would you justify your plans to the first-grade teachers?

Elementary and Middle School

■ Several students in your class are recent immigrants and have limited knowledge of the kinds of experiences described in your basal reader series (county fairs, zoos, trips to the beach, shopping malls, etc.). The students speak

and read English, but still have difficulty understanding and remembering what they read. What would you do?

Junior High and High School

■ You have reached a very complicated chapter in your text—one that is difficult for students every year. How would you make the highly abstract concepts (such as sovereignty and jurisprudence) understandable for your students?

Cooperative Learning Activity

■ With four or five other members of your class, develop a plan for helping your future students understand and remember three key concepts in your field.

What Would They Do?

The students in your senior history classes seem to equate understanding with memorizing. They prepare for each unit test by memorizing the exact words of the textbook. Even the best students seem to think that flash cards are the only learning strategy possible. In fact, when you try to get them to think about history by reading some original sources, debating issues in class, or examining art and music from the time period you are studying, they rebel. "Will this be on the test?" "Why are we looking at these pictures—will we have to know who painted them and when?" "What's this got to do with history?" Even the students who participate in the debates seem to use words and phrases straight from the textbook without knowing what they are saying.

ASHLEY DODGE

Ninth and Tenth Grade Teacher
Los Angeles Unified School District, Los Angeles, California

These students are obviously using strategies that have worked for them in the past (memorization and regurgitation of facts and dates), but they have not developed any critical thinking skills. Many students are very successful with these techniques up to a certain point. They become obsessed with learning only what is necessary to pass the class. At times it has seemed to me that they are attempting to conserve their energy for other things. Their insistence on using the rote memory approach may stem from unimaginative teachers in their past who have relied on tests of only facts and dates. These students may have received very good grades in the past, and thus now equate this type of learning with succeeding academically.

In order to give these students the opportunity to see history as something more than a time line, I would announce to the class that for the next unit, there would be no test. Instead, we would create projects reflective of the era. Perhaps we would produce a play, a fashion show with period clothing, or a festival. Some students may wish to construct a city at the time being studied, focusing on the differences in the city as it was then compared to now. The students would need to use the information in the text to incorporate their ideas into their project, but it would not need to be memorized. They would be graded on both the originality and the quality of their work, and the project grade would count as two unit grades.

Since I believe that it is important to give students reasonable assurance of success, especially when attempting something so foreign, I would try to give examples of successful similar projects, and to offer as much guidance and time as necessary. This requires a lot more personal time and energy on my part than simply lecturing on the text, but students are generally appreciative when they see a teacher working with them. In my experience students have worked very hard on these projects and have been pleased with the results.

MITCHELL D. KLETT

Twelfth Grade Teacher
A.C. New Middle School, Springs, Texas

Apparently, these students know historical events, including dates and places, but they don't comprehend the implications of these events to today's world. They seem to equate superficial knowledge with comprehension and conceptual understanding. Their beliefs indicate that the events in the past are "history" and of little or no relevance to the world today or specifically, to their world. Their learning consists of surface knowledge and rote memorization, probably because they've experienced history as series of disjointed, sequential events.

Students need to understand that the events of the past have a profound influence on the world today. The adage, "Those who don't know history are doomed to repeat it," rings true. As their teacher, I would emphasize cause and effect relationships throughout history and compare them with one another. By focusing on the causes of specific events, such as revolutions caused by economic rifts, students can better understand the cyclic nature of these types of revolutions. Events like the French Revolution and the Russian Revolution could be examined through inquiry learning, group discussion, or role playing. Students could be given the opportunity to explore the nature of revolutions and apply what they have learned to new situations. An example topic could be: Third World countries have increasing populations and diminishing resources—what will happen as the rift between the haves and the have nots is increased?

THOMAS O'DONNELL

Social Studies Chairperson
Grades 7–12
Malden High School, Malden, Massachusetts

These students "know" history as a set of factual events that happened in the past. Although much bias, prejudice, and myth have crept into the "known" history, the students don't realize this. Since they believe history is only a set of facts, they expect to learn them, know them, and be tested accordingly.

If their school experience has brought success through rote learning, it is logical for them to continue this approach to learning.

To help students break out of rote thinking I would test them on comprehension and assess them on that basis. Once they realize what the goal is, they will switch their approach in order to achieve success. I would also teach them to recognize any word in the reading that assumes "a truth" or accepts only one explanation of events. Finally, I would train students to ask Who? What? Where? How? and Why? for all situations.

Complex Cognitive Processes

Overview | *What Would You Do?*

THE IMPORTANCE OF THINKING AND UNDERSTANDING   288

LEARNING AND TEACHING ABOUT CONCEPTS   289
  Views of Concept Learning | Strategies for Teaching Concepts

PROBLEM SOLVING   294
  Problem Solving: General or Domain-Specific? | A General Problem-Solving Strategy | Defining Goals and Representing the Problem | Exploring Possible Solution Strategies | Anticipating, Acting, and Looking Back | Factors That Hinder Problem Solving | Effective Problem Solving: What Do the Experts Do?

BECOMING AN EXPERT STUDENT: LEARNING STRATEGIES AND STUDY SKILLS   307
  Learning Strategies and Tactics | Visual Tools | PQ4R

TEACHING AND LEARNING ABOUT THINKING   314
  Stand-Alone Programs for Developing Thinking | Developing Thinking in Every Class

TEACHING FOR TRANSFER   319
  Defining Transfer | A Contemporary View of Transfer | Teaching for Positive Transfer

Summary | *Key Terms* | *Check Your Understanding* | *Teachers' Casebook: What Would They Do?*

*T*hink of a concept you learned lately in a class. How did you learn it? If you learned from a text or a teacher, were there examples provided? What kinds? Do you understand the concept well enough to define it in your own words? Can you apply it to solve a problem?

In the previous chapter we focused on the development of knowledge—how people make sense of and remember information and ideas. In this chapter we will focus on understanding and thinking. We will be concerned with the implications of cognitive theories for the day-to-day practice of teaching, particularly for the development of students' thinking and understanding.

Because the cognitive perspective is a philosophical orientation and not a unified theoretical model, teaching methods derived from it are varied. In this chapter, we will first examine four important areas in which cognitive theorists have made suggestions for learning and teaching: concept learning, problem solving, learning strategies and tactics, and thinking. Finally, we will explore the question of how to encourage the transfer of learning from one situation to another to make learning more useful.

By the time you have completed this chapter, you should be able to:

- Design a lesson for teaching a key concept in your subject area.
- Describe the steps in solving complex problems and explain the role of problem representation.
- Apply new learning strategies and tactics to prepare for tests and assignments in your current courses.
- Discuss the implications of cognitive theories for teaching critical thinking.
- List three ways a teacher might encourage positive transfer of learning.

What Would You Do?

The directions seemed perfectly clear to you: Read two poems about nature (selected from the eight poems you read together last week), then write a one-page compare-and-contrast analysis of the two poems. The students enjoyed reading the poetry last week. But their first attempt to write about the poems is a disaster. They jot down a few lines, giving superficial descriptions of each poem and then tell which one they liked best. Most don't even give reasons why they chose one over the other. There is no comparison, no contrast, no critical thinking or analysis. The students must have spent all their time worrying about spelling and grammar. The form is fine, but the students don't really have anything to say. As you hand back the papers, you can see the disappointment in their faces. The grades are clearly lower that they expected.

- How would you explain what is missing in their papers?

- Where would you go from here?

- How would you encourage the students to think critically in analyzing the two poems?

- How will these issues affect the grades you will teach?

The Importance of Thinking and Understanding

The previous chapter examined basic learning and memory processes such as attention, knowledge representation, memory, and forgetting. In this chapter we consider complex cognitive processes that lead to understanding. Understanding is more than memorizing. It is more than retelling in your own words. Howard Gardner (1993b) defines understanding as:

> the capacity to take knowledge, skills, and concepts and apply them appropriately in new situations. If someone only parrots back what he or she has been taught, we do not know whether the individual understands. If that person applies the knowledge promiscuously, regardless of whether it is appropriate, then I would not say he or she understands either. . . . But if that person knows where to apply and where not to apply, and can do it to new situations, he or she understands. (p. 2)

David Perkins and Tina Blythe (1994) have a similar view of understanding. They believe that understanding means "being able to do a variety of thought-demanding things with a topic—like explaining, finding evidence and examples, generalizing, applying, analogizing, and representing the topic in new ways" (p. 6). So understanding involves appropriately *transforming* and *using* knowledge, skills, and ideas. You will see in the next chapter, that these understandings are considered "higher-level cognitive objectives" in a commonly used taxonomy of educational objectives (Bloom, Engelhart, Frost, Hill, & Krathwohl, 1956).

In the following sections we will explore what is known about different aspects of thinking: learning concepts, problem solving, critical thinking, using learning strategies, and how teachers can support these paths to understanding. We begin with a discussion of the building blocks of thinking—concepts.

Learning and Teaching about Concepts

Most of what we know about the world involves concepts and relations among concepts (Schwartz & Reisberg, 1991). But what exactly is a concept? A **concept** is a category used to group similar events, ideas, objects, or people. When we talk about a particular concept like *student,* we refer to a category of people who are similar to one another—they all study a subject. The people may be old or young, in school or not; they may be studying baseball or Bach, but they can all be categorized as students. Concepts are abstractions. They do not exist in the real world. Only individual examples of concepts exist. Concepts help us organize vast amounts of information into manageable units. For instance, there are about 7.5 million distinguishable differences in colors. By categorizing these colors into some dozen or so groups, we manage to deal with this diversity quite well (Bruner, 1973).

Views of Concept Learning

Traditionally, psychologists have assumed that members of a category share a set of **defining attributes,** or distinctive features. Students all study; books all contain pages that are bound together in some way. The defining attributes theory of concepts suggests that we recognize specific examples by noting key required features.

Since about 1970, however, these long-popular views about the nature of concepts have been challenged (Benjafield, 1992). While some concepts, such as equilateral triangle, have clear-cut defining attributes, most concepts do not. Take the concept of *party.* What are the defining attributes? You might have difficulty listing these attributes, but you probably recognize a party when you see or hear one (unless, of course we are talking about political parties, or the other party in a lawsuit, where the sound might not help you recognize the "party"). What about the concept of *bird*? Your first thought might be that birds are animals that fly. But is an ostrich a bird? What about a penguin?

Prototypes and Exemplars. According to critics of the traditional view of concept learning, we have in our minds a prototype of a party and a bird—an image that captures the essence of each concept. A **prototype** is the best representative of its category. For instance, the best representative of the "birds" category for many Americans might be a robin (Rosch, 1973). Other members of the category may be very similar to the prototype (sparrow) or similar in some ways but different in others (chicken, ostrich). At the boundaries of a category, it may be difficult to determine if a particular instance really belongs. For example, is a telephone a piece of "furniture"? Is an elevator a "vehicle"? Is an olive a "fruit"? Whether something fits into a category is a matter of degree. Thus, categories have fuzzy boundaries and **graded membership** (Schwartz & Reisberg, 1991). Some events, objects, or ideas are simply better examples of a concept than others.

Concept A general category of ideas, objects, people, or experiences whose members share certain properties.

Defining Attributes Distinctive features shared by members of a category.

Prototype Best representative of a category.

Graded Membership The extent to which something belongs to a category.

"CITY CHILDREN HAVE
TROUBLE WITH THE
CONCEPT OF HARVEST."

(© *Martha Campbell*—*From* Phi
Delta Kappan)

Another explanation of concept learning suggests that we identify members of a category by referring to exemplars. **Exemplars** are our actual memories of specific birds, parties, furniture, and so on that we use to compare with an item in question to see if that item belongs in the same category as our exemplar. For example, if you see a strange steel-and-stone bench in a public park, you may compare it to the sofa in your living room to decide if the uncomfortable-looking creation is still for sitting or if it has crossed a fuzzy boundary into "sculpture."

Prototypes probably are built from experiences with many exemplars. This happens naturally because episodic memories of particular events tend to blur together over time, creating an average or typical sofa prototype from all the sofa exemplars you have experienced (Schwartz & Reisberg, 1991).

Concepts and Schemas.   In addition to prototypes and exemplars, there is a third element involved when we recognize a concept—our schematic knowledge related to the concept. How do we know that counterfeit money is not "real" money, even though it perfectly fits our "money" prototype and exemplars? We know because of its history. It was printed by the "wrong" people. So our understanding of the concept of money is connected with concepts of crime, forgery, the federal treasury, and many others.

Strategies for Teaching Concepts

Most of the current approaches to teaching concepts still rely heavily on the traditional analysis of defining attributes. Interest is growing, however, in the prototypes view of concept learning, partly because children first learn many concepts in the real world from best examples or prototypes, pointed out by adults (Tennyson, 1981). The teaching of concepts can combine both distinctive features and prototypes.

One approach to teaching about concepts is called *concept attainment*—a way of helping students construct an understanding of specific concepts and practice thinking skills such as hypothesis testing (Joyce & Weil, 1996; Klausmeier, 1992).

✷An Example Concept-Attainment Lesson.   Here is how a fifth-grade teacher helped his students learn about a familiar concept and practice thinking skills at the same time (Eggen & Kauchak, 1996, pp. 105–107). The teacher began a lesson by saying that he had an idea in mind and wanted students to "figure out what it is." He placed two signs on a table—one said "Examples" and the other said "Nonexamples." Then from a bag he removed an apple and placed it in front of the "Examples" sign. Next he put a rock in front of the "Nonexamples" sign. He asked his students, "What do you think the idea might be?" "Things we eat" was the first suggestion. The teacher wrote "HYPOTHESES" on the board and, after a brief discussion of the meaning of "hypotheses," listed "things we eat" under this heading. Next he asked for other hypotheses—"living things" and "things that grow on plants" came next. After some discussion of the differences between living things and things that grow on plants, the teacher brought out two more objects, a tomato for the "Examples" side and a carrot for the "Nonexamples." Animated reconsideration of all the hypotheses followed these additions and a new hypothesis—"red things"—

Exemplar A specific example of a given category that is used to classify an item.

was suggested. Throughout the discussion, the teacher asked students to explain their conclusions—"We eat carrots, but a carrot is *not* an example, so the idea can't be things we eat." The teacher added an avocado as an example and celery as a nonexample (thus ruling out the "red" hypothesis). Through discussion of more examples (peach, squash, orange) and nonexamples (lettuce, artichoke, potato), the students narrowed their hypothesis to "things with seeds in the parts you eat." The students had "constructed" the concept of "fruit"—foods we eat with seeds in the edible parts (or, a more advanced definition, any engorged ovary, such as a pea pod, nut, tomato, pineapple, or the edible part of the plant developed from a flower).

Concept mapping has students "diagram" their understanding of a concept. What are examples of the concept of music for this student?

Lesson Components.   Whatever strategy you use for teaching concepts, you will need four components in any lesson: examples and nonexamples, relevant and irrelevant attributes, the name of the concept, and a definition (Joyce & Weil, 1996). In addition, visual aids such as pictures, diagrams, or maps can improve learning of many concepts (Anderson & Smith, 1987).

Examples are essential in teaching concepts. More examples are needed in teaching complicated concepts and in working with younger or less-able students. Both examples and nonexamples (sometimes called *positive* and *negative instances*) are necessary to make the boundaries of the category clear. So a discussion of why a bat (nonexample) is not a bird will help students define the boundaries of the bird concept.

The identification of relevant and irrelevant attributes is another aspect of teaching concepts. The ability to fly, as we've seen, is not a relevant attribute for classifying animals as birds. Even though many birds fly, some birds do not (ostrich, penguin), and some nonbirds do (bats, flying squirrels). The ability to fly would have to be included in a discussion of the bird concept, but students should understand that flying does not define an animal as a bird.

The name of the concept is important for communicating, but it is somewhat arbitrary. Simply learning a label does not mean the person understands the concept, although the label is necessary for the understanding. In the example above, students probably already used the "fruit" name, but may not have understood that squash and avocados are fruits.

A definition makes the nature of the concept clear. A good definition has two elements: a reference to any more *general category* that the new concept falls under, and a statement of the new concept's *defining attributes* (Klausmeier, 1976). For example, a fruit is food we eat (general category) with seeds in the edible parts (defining attributes). An equilateral triangle is a plane, simple, closed figure (general category), with three equal sides and three equal angles (defining attributes). This kind of definition helps place the concept in a schema of related knowledge.

In teaching some concepts "a picture is worth a thousand words"—or at least a few hundred. Seeing and handling specific examples, or pictures of examples, helps young children learn concepts. For students of all ages, the complex concepts in history, science, and mathematics can often be illustrated in diagrams or graphs. For example, Anderson and Smith (1983) found that when the students they taught just read about the concept, only 20% could understand the role of reflected light in our ability to see objects. But when the students worked with diagrams such as the one in Figure 8.1 on page 292, almost 80% understood the concept.

FIGURE 8.1

Understanding Complex Concepts

Illustrations can help students grasp a difficult concept.

Q. When sunlight strikes the tree it helps the boy to see the tree. How does it do this?

Q. When sunlight strikes the tree it helps the boy to see the tree. How does it do this?

A. Some of the light bounces (is reflected) off the tree and goes to the boy's eyes.

Source: From *The Educator's Handbook: A Research Perspective,* edited by Virginia Richardson-Koehler. Copyright © 1987. Reprinted by permission of Addison-Wesley Educational Publishers, Inc.

Lesson Structure.   The fruit lesson above is an example of good concept teaching for several reasons. First, it appears that it is more effective to examine examples and nonexamples *before* discussing attributes or definitions (Joyce & Weil, 1996). Start your concept lesson with prototypes, or best examples, to help the students establish the category. The teacher above began with the classic fruit example, an apple, then moved to less typical examples such as tomatoes and squash. These examples show the wide range of possibilities the category includes and the variety of irrelevant attributes within a category. This information helps students avoid focusing on an irrelevant attribute as a defining feature. The peach example tells students that fruit can have one seed as well as many. The squash and avocado examples indicate that fruits do not have to be sweet. Including fruits that have one seed or many, have a sweet taste or not, are different colors, and have thick or thin skin, will prevent **undergeneralization,** or the exclusion of some foods from their rightful place in the category *fruit.*

Nonexamples should be very close to the concept, but miss by one or just a few critical attributes. For instance, sweet potatoes and rhubarb are not fruits,

Undergeneralization Exclusion of some true members from a category; limiting a concept.

TABLE 8.1   Phases of the Concept Attainment Model

There are three main phases in concept attainment teaching. First the teacher presents examples/nonexamples and students identify the concept, then the teacher checks for understanding, and finally students analyze their thinking strategies.

Phase One: Presentation of Data and Identification of Concept	Phase Two: Testing Attainment of the Concept	Phase Three: Analysis of Thinking Strategies
Teacher presents labeled examples.	Students identify additional unlabeled examples as yes or no.	Students describe thoughts.
Students compare attributes in positive and negative examples.	Teacher confirms hypotheses, names concept, and restates definitions according to essential attributes.	Students discuss role of hypotheses and attributes.
Students generate and test hypotheses.		Students discuss type and number of hypotheses.
Students state a definition according to the essential attributes.	Students generate examples.	

Source: From Bruce R. Joyce and Marsha Weil, *Models of Teaching,* 5/e, p. 173. Copyright © 1996 by Allyn & Bacon. Reprinted by permission.

---

even though sweet potatoes are sweet and rhubarb is used to make pies. Including nonexamples will prevent **overgeneralization,** or the inclusion of substances that are not fruits.

After the students seem to have grasped the concept under consideration, it is useful to ask them to think about the ways that they formed and tested their hypotheses. Some students may consider one example at a time while other students may work with several simultaneously. Some older students may make systematic tests and eliminate one hypothesis at a time, keeping written records, while others are more global and scattered. Thinking back helps students develop their metacognitive skills and shows them that different people approach problems in different ways (Joyce & Weil, 1996). Table 8.1 summarizes the stages of concept teaching.

Extending and Connecting Concepts.   Once students have a good sense of a concept, they should use it. This might mean doing exercises, solving problems, writing, reading, explaining, or any other activity that requires them to apply their new understanding. This will connect the concept into the students' web of related schematic knowledge. One approach that you may see in some texts and workbooks for students above the primary grades is **concept mapping** (Novak & Musonda, 1991). Students "diagram" their understanding of the concept, as Amy has in Figure 8.2 on page 294. Amy's map shows a reasonable understanding of the concept of *molecule,* but also indicates that Amy holds one misconception. She thinks that there is no space between the molecules in solids.

Focus on...

Learning and Teaching about Concepts

- Distinguish between thinking and understanding.
- What are the defining attributes of the concept of "cup"? What attributes are irrelevant?
- What does it mean for a category to have graded membership?
- Distinguish between prototypes and exemplars.

Overgeneralization Inclusion of nonmembers in a category; overextending a concept.

Concept Mapping Students' diagramming their understanding of a concept.

FIGURE 8.2

Amy's Molecule

Amy, an eighth grader, has drawn a map to represent her understanding of the concept of "molecule." Her concept includes one misconception—that there is no space between molecules in solids.

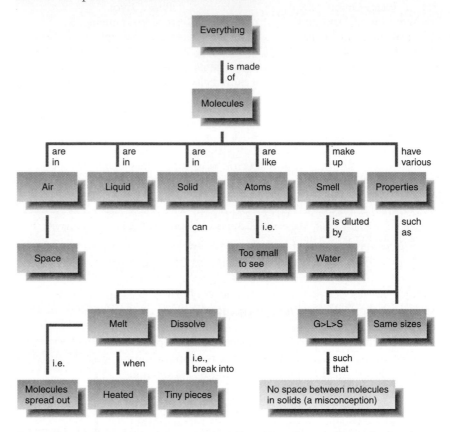

Source: From J. D. Novak and D. Musonda (1991). "A twelve-year longitudinal study of science concept learning." *American Educational Resource Journal, 28,* Figure p. 137. Copyright 1991 by the American Educational Research Association. Reprinted by permission of the publisher.

Problem Solving

"Educational programs," Robert Gagné has written, "have the important ultimate purpose of teaching students to solve problems—mathematical and physical problems, health problems, social problems, and problems of personal adjustment" (1977, p. 177). A **problem** has an initial state—the current situation, a goal—the desired outcome, and a path for reaching the goal, including operations or activities that move you toward the goal. Problem solvers often have to set and reach subgoals as they move toward the final solution. For example, if your goal is to drive to the beach, but at the first stop sign you skid through the intersection, you may have to reach a subgoal of fixing your brakes before you can continue toward the original goal (Schunk, 1996).

Problem Any situation in which you are trying to reach some goal and must find a means to do so.

Problem solving is usually defined as formulating new answers, going beyond the simple application of previously learned rules to achieve a goal. Problem solving is what happens when no solution is obvious—when, for example, you can't afford new brakes (Mayer & Wittrock, 1996). Some psychologists suggest that most human learning involves problem solving (Anderson, 1993).

Problem Solving: General or Domain-Specific?

There is an interesting debate about problem solving. Some psychologists believe that effective problem-solving strategies are specific to the problem area. That is, the problem-solving strategies in mathematics are unique to math, the strategies in art are unique to art, and so on. Becoming an expert problem solver in an area requires that you master the strategies of the area. The other side of the debate claims that there are some general problem-solving strategies that can be useful in many areas.

There is evidence for both sides of the argument. In fact, it appears that people move between general and specific approaches, depending on the situation and their level of expertise. Early on, when we know little about a problem area or domain, we may rely on general learning and problem-solving strategies to make sense of the situation. As we gain more domain-specific knowledge (particularly procedural knowledge about how to do things in the domain), we need the general strategies less and less. But if we encounter a problem outside our current knowledge, we may return to relying on general strategies to attack the problem (Alexander, 1992, 1996; Perkins & Salomon, 1989; Shuell, 1990).

A General Problem-Solving Strategy

Think of a general problem-solving strategy as a beginning point, a broad outline. Such strategies usually have five stages (Derry, 1991; Derry & Murphy, 1986; Gallini, 1991; Gick, 1986). John Bransford and Barry Stein (1993) use the acronym IDEAL to identify the five steps:

I   Identify problems and opportunities.

D   Define goals and represent the problem.

E   Explore possible strategies.

A   Anticipate outcomes and Act.

L   Look back and Learn.

The first step, identifying that a problem exists and treating the problem as an opportunity, begins the process. This is not always straightforward. There is a story describing tenants who were angry about the slow elevators in their building. Consultants hired to "fix the problem" reported that the elevators were no worse than average and that improvements would be very expensive. Then one day, as the building supervisor watched people waiting impatiently for an elevator, he realized that the problem was not slow elevators but the fact that people were bored; they had nothing to do while they waited. When the boredom problem was identified and seen as an opportunity to improve the "waiting experience," the simple solution of installing a mirror on each floor eliminated complaints.

Identifying a problem and turning it into an opportunity is the process behind many successful inventions, such as the ball point pen, garbage disposal,

Problem Solving Creating new solutions for problems.

appliance timer, alarm clock, self-cleaning oven, and thousands of others. A walk through stores such as Sharper Image or Brookstone will give you examples of problems turned into opportunities to sell you things you didn't know you needed—until you saw the creative solution!

Once a solvable problem is identified, what next? We will examine steps D, E, A, and L in some detail, because these are the heart of the process.

Defining Goals and Representing the Problem

Let's take a real problem: The machines designed to pick tomatoes are damaging the tomatoes. What to do? If we represent the problem as a faulty machine design, then the goal is to improve the machine. But if we represent the problem as a faulty design of the tomatoes, then the goal is to develop a tougher tomato. The problem solving process follows two entirely different paths, depending on which representation and goal are chosen (Bransford & Stein, 1993). To represent the problem and set a goal, you have to focus on relevant information, understand the elements of the problem, and activate the right *schema* to understand the whole problem.

Focusing Attention. Representing the problem often requires finding the relevant information and ignoring the irrelevant details. For example, consider the following problem adapted from Sternberg & Davidson (1982):

> If you have black socks and white socks in your drawer, mixed in the ratio of four to five, how many socks will you have to take out to make sure of having a pair the same color?

What information is relevant to solving this problem? Did you realize that the information about the four-to-five ratio of black socks to white socks is irrelevant? As long as you have only two different colors of socks in the drawer, you will have to remove only three socks before two of them have to match.

Understanding the Words. The second task in representing a story problem is **linguistic comprehension,** understanding the meaning of each sentence (Mayer, 1983a, b, 1992). Take, for example, the following sentence from an algebra story problem:

> The riverboat's rate in still water is 12 miles per hour more than the rate of the river current.

This is a *relational proposition*. It describes the relationship between two rates, that of the riverboat and that of the current. Here is another sentence from a story problem:

> The cost of the candy is $2.75 per pound.

This is an *assignment proposition*. It simply assigns a value to something, in this case the cost of one unit of candy.

Research shows that relational propositions are harder to understand and remember than assignment propositions. In one study, when students had to recall relational and assignment propositions like those above, the error rate for recalling relational propositions was about three times higher than the error rate for assignment propositions. (Mayer, 1982). If you misunderstand the meaning of individual statements in a problem, you will have a hard time representing the whole problem correctly and setting a goal.

Linguistic Comprehension Understanding of the meaning of sentences.

The main stumbling block in representing many word problems is the students' understanding of *part-whole relations* (Cummins, 1991). Students have trouble figuring out what is part of what, as evident in this dialogue between a teacher and a first grader:

Teacher: Pete has three apples; Ann also has some apples; Pete and Ann have nine apples altogether; how many apples does Ann have?

Student: Nine.

Teacher: Why?

Student: Because you just said so.

Teacher: Can you retell the story?

Student: Pete had three apples; Ann also had some apples; Ann had nine apples; Pete also has nine apples. (Adapted from De Corte & Verschaffel, 1985, p. 19)

The student interprets "altogether" (the whole) as "each" (the parts).

Understanding the Whole Problem.   The third task in representing a problem is to assemble all the relevant information and sentences into an accurate understanding or *translation* of the total problem. Even if you understand every sentence, you may still misunderstand the problem as a whole. Consider this example:

> Two train stations are 50 miles apart. At 2 P.M. one Saturday afternoon two trains start toward each other, one from each station. Just as the trains pull out of the stations, a bird springs into the air in front of the first train and flies ahead to the front of the second train. When the bird reaches the second train it turns back and flies toward the first train. The bird continues to do this until the trains meet. If both trains travel at the rate of 25 miles per hour and the bird flies at 100 miles per hour, how many miles will the bird have flown before the trains meet? (Posner, 1973)

Your interpretation of the problem is called a *translation* because you translate the problem into a schema that you understand. If you translate this as a *distance* problem and set a goal ("I have to figure out how far the bird travels before it meets the oncoming train and turns around, then how far it travels before it has to turn again, and finally add up all the trips back and forth . . . "), then you have a very difficult task on your hands. But there is a better way to structure the problem. You can represent it as a question of *time* and focus on the time the bird is in the air. If you figure out how long the bird is in the air, then you can easily determine the distance it will cover, because you know exactly how fast it flies. The solution could be stated like this:

> Because the stations are 50 miles apart and the trains are moving toward each other at the same speed, the trains will meet in the middle, 25 miles from each station. Because they are traveling 25 mph, it will take the trains one hour to reach the meeting point. In the one hour it takes the trains to meet, the bird will cover 100 miles because it is flying at 100 miles per hour. Easy!

Research shows that students can be too quick to decide what a problem is asking. The subjects in one study made their decisions about how to categorize standard algebra problems after reading only the first few sentences of a problem (Hinsley, Hayes, & Simon, 1977). Once a problem is categorized—"Aha, it's a distance problem!"—a particular schema is activated. The schema directs attention to relevant information and sets up expectations for what the right answer should look like (Robinson & Hayes, 1978).

When students do not have the necessary schemas to represent problems, they often rely on surface features of the situation and represent the problem incorrectly—like the student who wrote "15 + 24 = 39" as the answer to the question, "Joan has 15 bonus points and Louise has 24. How many more does Louise have?" This student saw two numbers and the word "more," so he applied the *add to get more* procedure. When students use the wrong schema, they overlook critical information, use irrelevant information, and may even misread or misremember critical information so that it fits the schema. Errors in representing the problem and difficulties in solving it are the results. But when students use the proper schema for representing a problem, they are less likely to be confused by irrelevant information or tricky wording, like *more* in a problem that really requires *subtraction* (Resnick, 1981). Figure 8.3 gives examples of different ways students might represent a simple mathematics problem.

Translation and Schema Training.   How can students improve translation and schema selection? To answer this question, we often have to move from general to area-specific problem-solving strategies. In mathematics, for example, it appears that students benefit from seeing many different kinds of example problems worked out correctly for them. The common practice of showing stu-

FIGURE 8.3

Four Different Ways to Represent a Problem

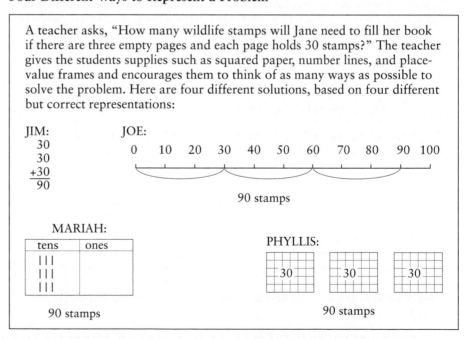

A teacher asks, "How many wildlife stamps will Jane need to fill her book if there are three empty pages and each page holds 30 stamps?" The teacher gives the students supplies such as squared paper, number lines, and place-value frames and encourages them to think of as many ways as possible to solve the problem. Here are four different solutions, based on four different but correct representations:

Source: From James E. Schwartz and C. Alan Riedesel. *Essentials of Classroom Teaching: Elementary Mathematics,* pp. 123–124. Copyright © 1994 by Allyn & Bacon. Reprinted by permission.

dents a few examples, then having students work many problems on their own, is less effective. Especially when problems are unfamiliar or difficult, worked-out examples are helpful (Cooper & Sweller, 1987). The most effective examples seem to be those that *do not* require students to integrate several sources of information, such as a diagram and a set of statements about the problem. This kind of attention splitting may put too much strain on the working memory. When students are learning, worked examples should deal with one source of information at a time (Ward & Sweller, 1990). Ask students to compare examples. What is the same about each solution? What is different? Why? The same procedures may be effective in areas other than mathematics.

How else might students develop the schemas they will need to represent problems in a particular subject area? Mayer (1983b) has recommended giving students practice in the following: (1) Recognizing and categorizing a variety of problem types; (2) representing problems—either concretely in pictures, symbols, or graphs, or in words; and (3) selecting relevant and irrelevant information in problems.

The Results of Problem Representation.   There are two main outcomes of the problem representation stage of problem solving, as shown in Figure 8.4. If your representation of the problem suggests an immediate solution, your task is done. In the language of the cognitive scientist, you have activated the right schema and the solution is apparent because it is part of the schema. In one sense, you haven't really solved a new problem, you have simply recognized the new problem as a "disguised" version of an old problem that you already know how to solve. This has been called **schema-driven problem solving,** a kind of matching between the situation and your store of systems for dealing with different problems (Gick, 1986). In terms of Figure 8.4, you have taken the *schema-activated route* and have proceeded directly to a solution. But what if you have no existing way of solving the problem or if your activated schema fails? Time to search for a solution!

Schema-Driven Problem Solving Recognizing a problem as a "disguised" version of an old problem for which one already has a solution.

FIGURE 8.4

Diagram of the Problem-Solving Process

There are two paths to a solution. In the first, the correct schema is activated and the solution is apparent. But if no schema is available, searching and testing may become the path to a solution.

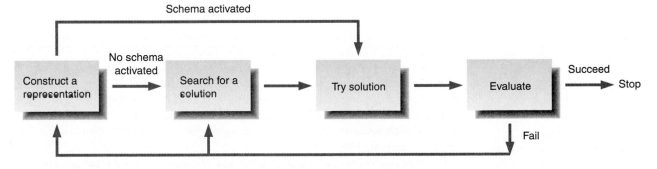

Source: From M. L. Gick (1986). Problem-solving strategies. *Educational Psychologist, 21,* p. 101. Adapted by permission of the publisher and author.

Exploring Possible Solution Strategies

If you do not have existing schemas that suggest an immediate solution, then you must take the *search-based route* indicated in Figure 8.4. Obviously, this path is not as efficient as activating the right schema, but sometimes it is the only way. In conducting your search for a solution, you have available two general kinds of procedures, algorithmic and heuristic.

Algorithms.   An **algorithm** is a step-by-step prescription for achieving a goal. It usually is domain-specific; that is, tied to a particular subject area. In solving a problem, if you choose an appropriate algorithm and implement it properly, a right answer is guaranteed. Unfortunately, students often apply algorithms haphazardly. They try first this, then that. They may even happen on the right answer, but not understand how they found it. For some students, applying algorithms haphazardly could be an indication that formal operational thinking and the ability to work through a set of possibilities systematically, as described by Piaget, is not yet developed.

In math classes you probably experienced some success applying algorithms. As long as you were careful in your computations, you were able to solve even complicated problems. Later, if you were given geometry proofs to verify or equations to differentiate, you soon discovered that there were no algorithms guaranteeing a solution. At that point, if you did not learn some heuristics, you probably bailed out of math classes as soon as possible.

Heuristics.   A **heuristic** is a general strategy that might lead to the right answer. Because many of life's problems are fuzzy, with ill-defined problem statements and no apparent algorithms, the discovery or development of effective heuristics is important. Let's examine a few.

In **means-ends analysis,** the problem is divided into a number of intermediate goals or subgoals and then a means of solving each is figured out. For example, writing a 20-page term paper can loom as an insurmountable problem for some students. They would be better off breaking this task into several intermediate goals, such as selecting a topic, locating sources of information, reading and organizing the information, making an outline, and so on. As they attack a particular intermediate goal, they may find that other goals arise. For example, locating information may require that they find someone to refresh their memory about using the library computer search system. Keep in mind that psychologists have yet to discover an effective heuristic for students who are just starting their term paper the night before it is due.

A second aspect of means-ends analysis is *distance reduction,* or pursuing a path that moves directly toward the final goal. People tend to look for the biggest difference between the current state of affairs and the goal and then search for a strategy that reduces the difference. We resist taking detours or making moves that are indirect as we search for the quickest way to reach the goal. So when you realize that reaching the goal of completing a term paper may require a detour of relearning the library computer search system, you may resist at first because you are not moving directly and quickly toward the final goal (Anderson, 1993).

Some problems lend themselves to a **working-backward strategy,** in which you begin at the goal and move back to the unsolved initial problem. Working backward is sometimes an effective heuristic for solving geometry proofs. It can

---

Algorithm Step-by-step procedure for solving a problem; prescription for solutions.

Heuristic General strategy used in attempting to solve problems.

Means-Ends Analysis Heuristic in which a goal is divided into subgoals.

Working-Backward Strategy Heuristic in which one starts with the goal and moves backward to solve the problem.

*O*ne advantage of working in groups is the opportunity to explain
your problem-solving strategy to someone else—putting solutions
into words often improves problem solving.

also be a good way to set intermediate deadlines ("Let's see, if I have to submit
this chapter in three weeks, then it has to be in the mail by the 28th, so I should
have a first draft by the 11th . . . ").

Another useful heuristic is **analogical thinking** (Copi, 1961), which limits
your search for solutions to situations that have something in common with the
one you currently face. When submarines were first designed, for example, engineers had to figure out how battleships could determine the presence and location of vessels hidden in the depths of the sea. Studying how bats solve an
analogous problem of navigating in the dark led to the invention of sonar.

Analogical reasoning can lead to faulty problem solving too. When they
were first learning to use a word processor, some people used the analogy of the
typewriter and failed to take advantage of the features of a computer. It seems
that people need knowledge both in the problem domain and the analogy domain in order to use an analogy effectively (Gagné, Yekovich, & Yekovich, 1993).

Putting your problem-solving plan into words and giving reasons for selecting it can lead to successful problem solving (Cooper & Sweller, 1987). You may
have discovered the effectiveness of this **verbalization** process accidentally, when
a solution popped into your head as you were explaining a problem to someone
else. Gagné and Smith (1962) found that when ninth- and tenth-grade students
were instructed to state a reason for each step they were taking, they were much
more successful in solving the problem than students who did not state reasons.

Anticipating, Acting, and Looking Back

After representing the problem and exploring possible solutions, the next step
is to select a solution and *anticipate the consequences*. For example, if you decide to solve the damaged tomato problem by developing a tougher tomato, how

Analogical Thinking Heuristic
in which one limits the search
for solutions to situations that
are similar to the one at hand.

Verbalization Putting your problem-solving plan and its logic into
words.

will consumers react? If you take time to learn a new graphics program to enhance your term paper (and your grade), will you still have enough time to finish the paper?

After you choose a solution strategy and implement it, evaluate the results by checking for evidence that confirms or contradicts your solution. Many people tend to stop working before reaching the best solution and simply accept an answer that works in some cases. In mathematical problems, evaluating the answer might mean applying a checking routine, such as adding to check the result of a subtraction problem or, in a long addition problem, adding the column from bottom to top instead of top to bottom. Another possibility is estimating the answer. For example, if the computation was 11×21, the answer should be around 200, since 10×20 is 200. A student who reaches an answer of 2,311 or 23 or 562 should quickly realize these cannot be correct. Estimating an answer is particularly important when students rely on calculators or computers, because they cannot go back and spot an error in the figures.

Factors That Hinder Problem Solving

Consider the following situation:

> You enter a room. There are two ropes suspended from the ceiling. You are asked by the experimenter to tie the two ends of the ropes together and assured that the task is possible. On a nearby table are a few tools, including a hammer and pliers. You grab the end of one of the ropes and walk toward the other rope. You immediately realize that you cannot possibly reach the end of the other rope. You try to extend your reach using the pliers but still cannot grasp the other rope. What can you do? (Maier, 1933)

Functional Fixedness. This problem can be solved by using an object in an unconventional way. If you tie the hammer or the pliers to the end of one rope and start swinging it like a pendulum, you will be able to catch it while you are standing across the room holding the other rope, as shown in Figure 8.5. You can use the weight of the tool to make the rope come to you instead of trying to stretch the rope. People often fail to solve this problem, because they seldom consider unconventional uses for materials that have a specific function. This difficulty is called **functional fixedness** (Duncker, 1945). Problem solving requires seeing things in new ways. In your everyday life, you may often exhibit functional fixedness. Suppose a screw on a dresser-drawer handle is loose. Will you spend 10 minutes searching for a screwdriver? Or will you think to use another object not necessarily designed for this function, such as a ruler edge or a dime?

Response set. Another block to effective problem solving is **response set**. Consider the following:

> In each of the four matchstick arrangements below, move only one stick to change the equation so that it represents a true equality such as V = V.
>
> $$\text{V}=\text{V}|| \quad \text{V}|=\text{X}| \quad \text{X}||=\text{V}|| \quad \text{V}|=||$$

You probably figured out how to solve the first example quite quickly. You simply move one matchstick from the right side over to the left to make $\text{V}|=\text{V}|$ Examples two and three can also be solved without too much difficulty by mov-

Functional Fixedness Inability to use objects or tools in a new way.

Response Set Rigidity; tendency to respond in the most familiar way.

FIGURE 8.5

Overcoming Functional Fixedness

In the two-string problem, the subject must set one string in motion in order to tie both strings together.

ing one stick to change the ∨ to an X or vice versa. But the fourth example (taken from Raudsepp & Haugh, 1977) probably has you stumped. To solve this problem you must change your response set or switch schemas, because what has worked for the first three problems will not work this time. The answer here lies in changing from Roman numerals to Arabic numbers and using the concept of square root. By overcoming response set, you can move one matchstick from the right to the left to form the symbol for square root; the solution reads ∨⊤ = I, which is simply the symbolic way of saying that the square root of 1 equals 1.

The Importance of Flexibility.   Functional fixedness and response set point to the importance of flexibility in understanding problems. If you get started with an inaccurate or inefficient representation of the true problem, it will be difficult—or at least very time-consuming—to reach a solution (Wessells, 1982). Sometimes it is helpful to "play" with the problem. Ask yourself: "What do I know? What do I need to know to answer this question? Can I look at this problem in other ways?" Try to think conditionally rather than rigidly and divergently rather than convergently. Ask, "What could this be?" instead of "What is it?" (Benjafield, 1992).

If you open your mind to multiple possibilities, you may have what the Gestalt psychologists called an insight. **Insight** is the sudden reorganization or reconceptualization of a problem that clarifies the problem and suggests a feasible solution. The supervisor described earlier, who suddenly realized that the problem in his building was not slow elevators but impatient, bored tenants, had an insight that allowed him to reach the solution of installing mirrors by the elevators.

Insight Sudden realization of a solution.

Effective Problem Solving: What Do the Experts Do?

Most psychologists agree that effective problem solving is based on an ample store of knowledge about the problem area. In order to solve the matchstick problem, for example, you had to understand Roman and Arabic numbers as well as the concept of square root. You also had to know that the square root of 1 is 1. Let's take a moment to examine this expert knowledge.

Expert Knowledge.   The modern study of expertise began with investigations of chess masters (Simon & Chase, 1973). Results indicated that masters can quickly recognize about 50,000 different arrangements of chess pieces. They can look at one of these patterns for a few seconds and remember where every piece on the board was placed. It is as though they have a "vocabulary" of 50,000 patterns. Michelene Chi (1978) demonstrated that third- through eighth-grade chess experts had a similar ability to remember chess piece arrangement. For all the masters, patterns of pieces are like words. If you were shown any word from your vocabulary store for just a few seconds, you would be able to remember every letter in the word in the right order (assuming you could spell the word).

But a series of letters arranged randomly is hard to remember, as you saw in Chapter 7. An analogous situation holds for chess masters. When chess pieces are placed on a board randomly, masters are no better than average players at remembering the positions of the pieces. The master's memory is for patterns that make sense or could occur in a game.

A similar phenomenon occurs in other fields. There may be an intuition about how to solve a problem based on recognizing patterns and knowing the "right moves" for those patterns. Experts in physics, for example, organize their knowledge around central principles, whereas beginners organize their smaller amounts of physics knowledge around the specific details stated in the problems. For instance, when asked to sort physics problems from a textbook in any way they wanted, novices sorted based on superficial features such as the kind of apparatus mentioned—a lever or a pulley—while the experts grouped problems according to the underlying physics principle needed to solve the problem, such as Boyle's or Newton's laws (Hardiman, Dufresne, & Mestre, 1989). And the experts can recognize the patterns needed to solve a particular problem very quickly, so they literally don't have to think as hard (Glaser, 1981).

In addition to representing a problem very quickly, experts know what to do next. They have a large store of productions or condition-action schemas about what action to take in various situations. Thus, the steps of understanding the problem and choosing a solution happen simultaneously and fairly automatically (Norman, 1982). Of course, this means that they must have many, many schemas available. A large part of becoming an expert is simply acquiring a great store of knowledge about a particular field. To do this, you must encounter many different kinds of problems in that field, see problems solved by others, and practice solving many yourself. Some estimates are that it takes 10 years or 10,000 hours of study to become an expert in most fields (Simon, 1995).

Experts' rich store of knowledge is *elaborated* and *well practiced*, so that it is easy to retrieve from long-term memory when needed (Anderson, 1993). Experts can use their extensive knowledge to *organize* information for easier learning and retrieval. Compared to fourth-graders with little knowledge of soccer, fourth-graders who were soccer experts learned and remembered far more new soccer terms, even though the abilities of the two groups to learn and remember nonsoccer terms were the same. The soccer experts organized and clustered the soccer terms to aid in recall (Schneider & Bjorklund, 1992). Even very young children who are experts on a topic can use strategies to organize their knowledge. To get an example of the use of category knowledge about dinosaurs I called my nephews, Lucas and Geoffrey (4 and 3 years old at the time), who promptly ran down the list of large and small plant- and meat-eating dinosaurs, from the well-known stegosaurus (large, plant eater) to the less familiar ceolophysis (small, meat eater).

With organization comes planning and monitoring. Experts spend more time analyzing problems, drawing diagrams, breaking large problems down into subproblems, and making plans. While a novice might begin immediately—writing equations for a physics problem or drafting the first paragraph of a paper, experts plan out the whole solution and often make the task simpler in the process. As they work, experts monitor progress, so time is not lost pursuing dead ends or weak ideas (Gagné et al., 1993).

Chi, Glaser, and Farr (1988) summarize the superior capabilities of experts. Experts (1) perceive large, meaningful patterns in given information, (2) perform tasks quickly and with few errors, (3) deal with problems at a deeper level, (4) have superior short- and long-term memories, and (5) take a great deal of time to analyze a given problem. When the area of problem solving is fairly well defined, such as chess or physics or computer programming, then these skills of expert problem solvers hold fairly consistently. But when the problem-solving area is less well-defined and has fewer clear underlying principles, such as problem solving in economics or psychology, then the differences between experts and novices are not as clear-cut (Alexander, 1992).

Expert Teachers.   Studies of expert teachers identify many of the characteristics described above. Expert teachers have a sense of what is typical in classrooms, of what to expect during certain activities or times of the day. Many of their teaching routines have become automatic—they don't even have to think about how to distribute materials, take roll, move students in and out of groups, or assign grades. This gives the teachers more mental and physical energy for being creative and focusing on their students' progress. For example, one study found that expert math teachers could go over the previous day's work with the class in two or three minutes, compared to 15 minutes for novices (Leinhardt, 1986).

Expert teachers work from integrated sets of principles instead of dealing with each new event as a new problem. They look for patterns revealing similarities in situations that seem quite different at first glance. Experts focus more than beginners on analyzing a problem and mentally applying different principles to develop a solution. In one study of solutions to discipline problems, the expert teachers spent quite a bit of time framing each problem, forming questions, deciding what information was necessary, and considering alternatives (Swanson, O'Conner, & Cooney, 1990).

Expert teachers have a deep and well-organized knowledge of the subjects they teach. They can improvise explanations and create new examples on the spot. They can turn students' confusion into understanding by helping the students organize and expand on what they know. Expert teachers are not bound by their plans, but can follow the needs of the students (Borko & Livingston,

1989; Sabers, Cushing, & Berliner, 1991; Tochon & Munby, 1993). And as we saw in Chapter 1, expert teachers also know a great deal about their students, the curriculum, teaching strategies, and ways to make the curriculum understandable and accessible to the students.

Novice Knowledge.   Studies of the differences between experts and novices in particular areas have revealed some surprising things about how novices understand and misunderstand a subject. Physics again provides many examples. Most beginners approach physics with a great deal of misinformation, partly because many of their intuitive ideas about the physical world are wrong. Most elementary-school children believe that light helps us see by brightening the area around objects. They do not realize that we see an object because the light is reflected by the object to our eyes. This concept does not fit with the everyday experience of turning on a light and "brightening" the dark area. Researchers from the Elementary Science Project at Michigan State University found that even after completing a unit on light in which materials explicitly stated the idea of reflected light and vision, most fifth-grade students—about 78%—continued to cling to their intuitive notions. But when new materials were designed that directly confronted the students' misconceptions, only about 20% of the students failed to understand (Eaton, Anderson, & Smith, 1984).

It seems quite important for science teachers to understand their students' intuitive models of basic concepts. If the students' intuitive model includes misconceptions and inaccuracies, then the students are likely to develop inadequate or misleading representations of a problem. In order to learn new information and solve problems, students must sometimes "unlearn" common sense ideas (Joshua & Dupin, 1987).

The Guidelines give some ideas for helping students become expert problem solvers.

Focus on...

Problem Solving

- What are the steps in the general problem-solving process?
- Why is the representation stage of problem solving so important?
- Describe factors that can interfere with problem solving.
- What are the differences between expert and novice knowledge in a given area?
- How do misconceptions interfere with learning?
- What are some common misconceptions about being an expert?

Guidelines

Problem Solving

Ask students if they are sure they understand the problem.

Examples

1. Can they separate relevant from irrelevant information?
2. Are they aware of the assumptions they are making?
3. Encourage them to visualize the problem by diagramming or drawing it.
4. Ask them to explain the problem to someone else. What would a good solution look like?

Encourage attempts to see the problem from different angles.

Examples

1. Suggest several different possibilities yourself and then ask students to offer some.
2. Give students practice in taking and defending different points of view on an issue.

Help students develop systematic ways of considering alternatives.

Examples

1. Think out loud as you solve problems.
2. Ask, "What would happen if . . . ?"
3. Keep a list of suggestions.

Teach heuristics.

Examples

1. Ask students to explain the steps they take as they solve problems.
2. Use analogies to solve the problem of limited parking in the downtown area. How are other "storage" problems solved?
3. Use the working backward strategy to plan a party.

Let students do the thinking; don't just hand them solutions.

Examples

1. Offer individual problems as well as group problems, so that each student has the chance to practice.
2. Give partial credit if students have good reasons for "wrong" solutions to problems.
3. If students are stuck, resist the temptation to give too many clues. Let them think about the problem overnight.

Becoming an Expert Student: Learning Strategies and Study Skills

As we saw in Chapter 7, the way something is learned in the first place greatly influences how readily we remember and how appropriately we can apply the knowledge later. First, students must be *cognitively engaged* in order to learn—they have to focus attention on the relevant or important aspects of the material. Second, they have to *invest effort*, make connections, elaborate, translate, organize, and reorganize in order to *think and process deeply*—the greater the practice and processing, the stronger the learning. Finally, students must *regulate and monitor* their own learning—keep track of what is making sense and notice when a new approach is needed. The emphasis today is on helping students develop effective learning strategies and tactics that *focus attention and effort, process information deeply, and monitor understanding.*

Learning Strategies and Tactics

Learning strategies are ideas for accomplishing learning goals, a kind of overall plan of attack. **Learning tactics** are the specific techniques that make up the plan (Derry, 1989). Your strategy for learning the material in this chapter might include the tactics of using mnemonics to remember key terms, skimming the chapter to identify the organization, and then writing answers to possible essay questions. Your use of strategies and tactics reflects metacognitive knowledge.

Learning Strategies General plans for approaching learning tasks.

Learning Tactics Specific techniques for learning, such as using mnemonics or outlining a passage.

*T*eachers can help students develop strategies and tactics for accomplishing learning goals—writing a story in this case.

Fortunately, teaching these procedural skills has become a high priority in education, and several important principles have been identified.

1. Students must be exposed to a number of *different strategies,* not only general learning strategies but also very specific tactics, such as the graphic strategies described later in this chapter.

2. *Teach conditional knowledge* about when, where, and why to use various strategies (Pressley, 1986). Although this may seem obvious, teachers often neglect this step, either because they do not realize its significance or because they assume students will make inferences on their own. A strategy is more likely to be maintained and employed if students know when, where, and why to use it.

3. Students may know when and how to use a strategy, but unless they also *develop the desire to employ these skills,* general learning ability will not improve. Several learning strategy programs (Borkowski, Johnston, & Reid, 1986; Dansereau, 1985) include a motivational training component. In Chapters 10 and 11 we look more closely at this important issue of motivation.

4. *Direct instruction in schematic knowledge* is often an important component of strategy training. In order to identify main ideas—a critical skill for a number of learning strategies—you must have an appropriate schema for making sense of the material. Table 8.2 summarizes several tactics for learning declarative (verbal) knowledge and procedural skills (Derry, 1989).

Underlining and Highlighting.   Do you underline or highlight key phrases in textbooks? Are my words turning yellow or pink at this very moment? What about outlining or taking notes? Underlining and note taking are probably two of the most commonly used strategies among college students. Yet few students receive any instruction in the best ways to take notes or underline, so it is not surprising that many students use ineffective strategies.

One common problem is that students underline or highlight too much. It is far better to be selective. In studies that limit how much students can underline—for example, only one sentence per paragraph—learning has improved (Snowman, 1984). In addition to being selective, you also should actively trans-

	Examples	Use When?
TABLE 8.2 Examples of Learning Tactics		

Tactics for Learning Verbal Information	1. Attention Focusing
	   ■ Making outlines, underlining
	   ■ Looking for headings and topic sentences
		With easy, structured materials; for good readers
		For poorer readers; with more difficult materials

	2. Schema Building
	   ■ Story grammars
	   ■ Theory schemas
	   ■ Networking and mapping
		With poor text structure, goal is to encourage active comprehension

	3. Idea Elaboration
	   ■ Self-questioning
	   ■ Imagery
		To understand and remember specific ideas

Tactics for Learning Procedural Information	1. Pattern Learning
	   ■ Hypothesizing
	   ■ Identifying reasons for actions
		To learn attributes of concepts
		To match procedures to situations

	2. Self-instruction ■ Comparing own performance to expert model	To tune, improve complex skills

	3. Practice
	   ■ Part practice
	
	   ■ Whole practice
		When few specific aspects of a performance need attention
		To maintain and improve skill

Source: Based on S. Derry (1989). Putting learning strategies to work, *Educational Leadership, 47*(5), pp. 5–6.

form the information into your own words as you underline or take notes. Don't rely on the words of the book. Note connections between what you are reading and other things you already know. Draw diagrams to illustrate relationships. Finally, look for organizational patterns in the material and use them to guide your underlining or note taking (Irwin, 1991; Kiewra, 1988).

Taking Notes.   As you sit in class, filling your notebook with words or furiously trying to keep up with a lecturer, you may wonder if taking notes makes a difference. The answer appears to be, yes—taking notes serves at least two important functions:

■ Taking notes focuses attention during class and helps encode information so it has a chance of making it to long-term memory. In order to record key ideas in your own words, you have to translate, connect, elaborate, and organize. Even if students don't review notes before a test, taking them in the first place appears to aid learning, especially for those who lack prior knowledge in an area. Of course, if taking notes distracts you from actually listening to and making sense of the lecture, then note taking may not be effective (DiVesta & Gray, 1972, Kiewra, 1989; Van Meter, Yokoi, & Pressley, 1994).

■ Notes provide extended external storage that allows you to return and review. Students who use their notes to study tend to perform better on tests, especially if they take many high quality notes—more is better as long as you are capturing key ideas, concepts, and relationships (Kiewra, 1985, 1989).

In a recent extensive interview study of 252 college students, Peggy Van Meter, Linda Yokoi, and Mike Pressley (1994) concluded that understanding is served when students use note taking to focus attention on important ideas and construct a representation in the notes that reflects the organization of the lecture. As the course progresses, the expert student matches notes to their anticipated use and makes modifications in strategies after tests or assignments; uses personal codes to flag material that is unfamiliar or difficult; fills in holes by consulting relevant sources (including other students in the class); records information verbatim only when a verbatim response will be required; and generally is strategic about taking and using notes.

To help students organize their note taking, some teachers provide matrices or maps, such as the one in Figure 8.6. If you use such an approach with your

FIGURE 8.6

A Map to Guide Note Taking

The compare/contrast map below allows students to organize their listening or reading as they consider two ideas, concepts, time periods, authors, experiments, theories, and so on.

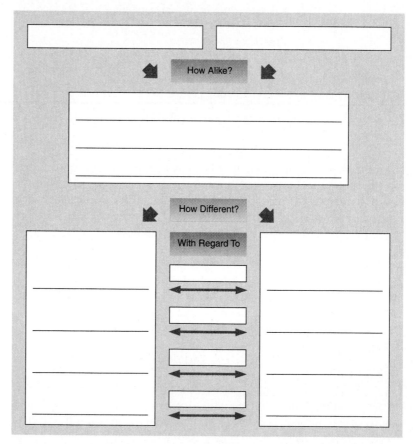

Source: From S. Parks and H. Black, *Organizing Thinking: Book 1.* 1992, published by Critical Thinking Books and Software. Reprinted by permission.

students, you might encourage students to exchange their filled-in maps and explain their thinking to each other.

Visual Tools

Effective use of underlining and note taking depends on an understanding of the organization of the text or lecture. Some visual strategies have been developed to help students with this key element. There is some evidence that creating graphic organizers such as maps or charts is more effective than outlining in learning from texts (Robinson & Kiewra, 1995). Armbruster and Anderson (1981) taught students specific techniques for diagramming relationships among ideas presented in a text. "Mapping" these relationships by noting causal connections, comparison/contrast connections, and examples improved recall. Davidson (1982) suggested that students compare one another's "maps" and discuss the differences. The map in Figure 8.7 on page 312 is a complex web about Holden Caufield, the main character of J. D. Salinger's *Catcher in the Rye,* developed using *Inspiration* software. Amy's molecule (Figure 8.2) is a hierarchical graphic depiction of the relationships among concepts. There are other ways to visualize organization such as *Venn diagrams* showing how ideas or concepts overlap or *tree diagrams* showing how ideas branch off of each other.

PQ4R

There have been many suggestions for understanding and remembering what you read. One of the most enduring systems is the SQ3R (Survey, Question, Read, Recite, Review) approach developed by F. P. Robinson (1961). You may have been exposed to this study strategy at some point during your academic career. A more recent variation is called **PQ4R** (Thomas & Robinson, 1972). In this system the extra R is for reflection, and the P stands for preview; so the acronym means Preview, Question, Read, Reflect, Recite, and Review. To use PQ4R to study this chapter, you would:

1. *Preview.* Introduce yourself to the chapter you are about to read by surveying the major topics and sections. Read the overview, the objectives, the section headings and subheadings, the summary, and perhaps the initial sentences of the major sections. All of these procedures will help activate schemas so you can interpret and remember the text that follows. Previewing also allows you to formulate your own general purpose for reading each section, whether it is to identify the main idea or to note the general biases of the author.

2. *Question.* For each major section, write questions that are related to your reading purposes. One way is to turn the headings and subheadings into questions. For example, in this chapter you might ask: "Why are thinking and understanding important in learning?"

3. *Read.* At last! The questions you have formulated can be answered through reading. Pay attention to the main ideas, supporting details, and other data in keeping with your purposes. You may have to adjust your reading speed to suit the difficulty of the material and your purpose in reading.

PQ4R A method for studying text that involves six steps: Preview, Question, Read, Reflect, Recite, Review.

FIGURE 8.7

A Map to Organize Studying and Learning

This map represents one student's (Brian Cooper) analysis of *Catcher in the Rye.* The map was produced using software called "Inspiration."

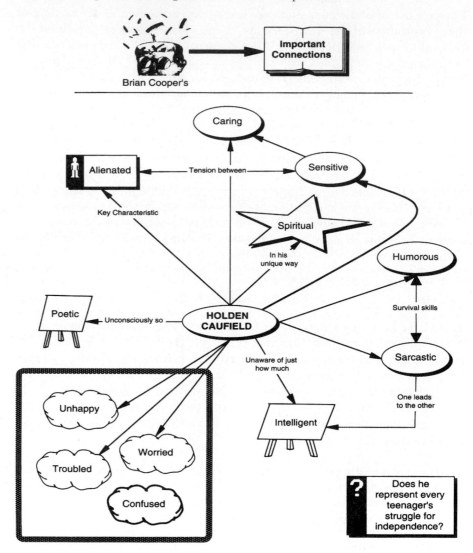

Source: From D. Helfgott, M. Westhaver, and B. Hoof, *Inspiration Software: User's Guide manual,* 1992, Inspiration Software, Inc., 1-800-877-4292 or 503-297-3004. Reprinted by permission.

4. *Reflect.* While you are reading, try to think of examples or create images of the material. Elaborate and try to make connections between what you are reading and what you already know.

5. *Recite.* After reading each section, sit back and think about your initial purposes and questions. Can you answer the questions without looking at the book? In doing this, you give your mind a second chance to connect what you

have read with what you already know. If your mind is blank after reading the section, it may have been too difficult to read comfortably, or you may have been daydreaming. Reciting helps you to monitor your understanding and tells you when to reread before moving on to the next section. Reciting should take place after each headed section, but you may need to do it more often when you are reading difficult material.

6. *Review.* Effective review incorporates new material more thoroughly into your long-term memory. As study progresses, review should be cumulative, including the sections and chapters you read previously. Rereading is one form of review, but trying to answer key questions without referring to the book is the best way. Wrong answers can direct you to areas that need more study, especially before an exam.

Anderson (1995a) suggests several reasons for PQ4R's effectiveness. First, following the steps makes students more aware of the organization of a given chapter. How often have you skipped reading headings entirely and thus missed major clues to the way the information was organized? Next, these steps require students to study the chapter in sections instead of trying to learn all the information at once. This makes use of distributed practice. Creating and answering questions about the material forces students to process the information more deeply and with greater elaboration (Doctorow, Wittrock, & Marks, 1978; Hamilton, 1985).

As you may have guessed, the PQ4R method is most appropriate for older children. Very little is known about teaching study skills to students before fifth grade. The effective application of study skills probably requires metacognitive development beyond the range of most very young children. And of course, young children are still focusing much of their attention on learning the basics of word recognition.

The Guidelines provide a summary of ideas about studying.

Focus on . . .

Study Strategies

- How could you improve your strategies for taking notes?
- Describe some procedures for developing procedural knowledge.
- How would you use study skills to study this chapter?

Guidelines

Study Skills and Learning Strategies

Make sure you have the necessary declarative knowledge (facts, concepts, ideas) to understand new information.

Examples

1. Keep definitions of key vocabulary available as you study.

2. Review required facts and concepts before attempting new material.

Find out what type of test the teacher will give (essay, short answer), and study the material with that in mind.

Examples

1. For a test with detailed questions, practice writing answers to possible questions.

2. For a multiple-choice test, use mnemonics to remember definitions of key terms.

(continued)

Make sure you are familiar with the organization of the materials to be learned.

Examples

1. Preview the headings, introductions, topic sentences, and summaries of the text.

2. Be alert for words and phrases that signal relationships, such as *on the other hand, because, first, second, however, since.*

Know your own cognitive skills and use them deliberately.

Examples

1. Use examples and analogies to relate new material to something you care about and understand well, such as sports, hobbies, or films.

2. If one study technique is not working, try another—the goal is to stay involved, not to use any particular strategy.

Study the right information in the right way.

Examples

1. Be sure you know exactly what topics and readings the test will cover.

2. Spend your time on the important, difficult, and unfamiliar material that will be required for the test or assignment.

3. Keep a list of the parts of the text that give you trouble and spend more time on those pages.

4. Process the important information thoroughly by using mnemonics, forming images, creating examples, answering questions, making notes in your own words, and elaborating on the text. Do not try to memorize the author's words —use your own.

Monitor your own comprehension.

Examples

1. Use questioning to check your understanding.

2. When reading speed slows down, decide if the information in the passage is important. If it is, note the problem so you can reread or get help to understand. If it is not important, ignore it.

3. Check your understanding by working with a friend and quizzing one another.

Source: Adapted from B. B. Armbruster and T. H. Anderson. "Research synthesis on study skills." *Educational Leadership, 39,* pp. 154–156. Reprinted by permission of the Association for Supervision and Curriculum Development. Copyright © 1981 by ASCD. All rights reserved.

Teaching and Learning about Thinking

Even if we are successful in teaching reading and problem solving, can we be sure that our students will be able to analyze and evaluate what they read? Will they be able to go beyond the information given to apply their knowledge, make judgments, and generate new ideas? In other words, will they be able to think (Prawat, 1991)? Many educational psychologists believe that good thinking can and should be developed in school. But clearly, teaching thinking entails much more than the standard classroom practices of answering "thought" questions at the end of the chapter or participating in teacher-led discussions. What else is needed?

One approach has been to focus on the development of *thinking skills,* either through stand-alone programs that teach skills directly, or through indirect methods that embed development of thinking in the regular curriculum.

Stand-Alone Programs for Developing Thinking

There are many different programs that teach thinking skills directly. A resource book for educators (Costa, 1985) lists over 15 different programs, including *de Bono's CoRT* system; *Odyssey: A Curriculum for Thinking; Winocur's Project Impact; Lipman's Philosophy for Children;* and *Meeker's SOI.* In these programs students learn skills such as comparing, ordering, classifying, and making inferences. The advantage of these **stand-alone thinking skills programs** is that students do not need extensive subject matter knowledge to master the skills. Students who have had trouble with the traditional curriculum may achieve success—and perhaps an enhanced sense of self-esteem—through these programs. The disadvantage is that the general skills often are not used outside the program unless teachers make a concerted effort to show students how to apply the skills in specific subjects, as you can see in the Point/Counterpoint discussion on page 316. You will see shortly when we discuss transfer, encouraging students to apply knowledge and skills to new situations is a challenge for all teachers (Mayer & Wittrock, 1996; Prawat, 1991).

"WE DID THAT LAST YEAR— HOW COME WE HAVE TO DO IT AGAIN THIS YEAR?"

(© W. A. Vanselow—From Phi Delta Kappan*)*

Developing Thinking in Every Class

Another way to develop students' thinking is to encourage analysis, problem solving, and reasoning through the regular lessons of the curriculum. David Perkins and his colleagues (Perkins, Jay, & Tishman, 1993) propose that teachers do this by creating a *culture of thinking* in their classrooms. This means that there is a spirit of inquisitiveness and critical thinking, a respect for reasoning and creativity, and an expectation that students will learn and understand. In such a classroom, education is seen as *enculturation,* a broad and complex process of acquiring knowledge and understanding. We all learned language by being a member of a particular cultural group. We also learned ways of interacting, norms of appropriate behavior, and many other complicated rules and procedures through living in a culture that supports certain knowledge and values. Just as our home culture taught us lessons about the use of language, the culture of a classroom can teach lessons about thinking by giving us *models* of good thinking; providing *direct instruction* in thinking processes; and encouraging *practice* of those thinking processes through *interactions* with others.

Let's consider how this might happen in a classroom described by Perkins, Jay, and Tishman (1993).

Suppose an eighth-grade teacher wants her students to learn how to construct explanations that involve *multiple causes.* The class is studying the agriculture

Stand-Alone Thinking Skills Programs Programs that teach thinking skills directly without need for extensive subject matter knowledge.

Should Schools Teach Critical Thinking and Problem Solving?

The question of whether schools should focus on process or content, problem-solving skills or core knowledge, higher-order thinking skills or academic information has been debated for years. Some educators suggest that students must be taught how to think and solve problems, while other educators assert that students cannot learn to "think" in the abstract. They must be thinking about something —some content. Should teachers focus on knowledge or thinking?

POINT **Problem Solving and Higher-Order Thinking Can and Should Be Taught**

An article in the April, 28, 1995, issue of the *Chronicle of Higher Education* makes this claim:

> Critical thinking is at the heart of effective reading, writing, speaking, and listening. It enables us to link together mastery of content with such diverse goals as self-esteem, self-discipline, multicultural education, effective cooperative learning, and problem solving. It enables all instructors and administrators to raise the level of their own teaching and thinking. (p. A-71)

How can students learn to think critically? Some educators recommend teaching thinking skills directly with widely used techniques such as the Productive Thinking Program or CoRT (Cognitive Research Trust). Other researchers argue that learning computer programming languages such as LOGO

will improve students' minds and teach them how to think logically. For example, Papert (1980) believes that when children learn through discovery how to give instructions to computers in LOGO, "powerful intellectual skills are developed in the process" (p. 60). Finally, because expert readers automatically apply certain metacognitive strategies, many educators and psychologists recommend directly teaching novice or poor readers how to apply these strategies. Michael Pressley's Good Strategy User model and Palincsar and Brown's (1984) reciprocal teaching approach—described in Chapter 9—are successful examples of direct teaching of metacognitive skills. Research on these approaches generally shows improvements in achievement and comprehension for students of all ages who participate (Pressley, Barkowski, & Schneider, 1987; Rosenshine & Meister, 1994).

COUNTERPOINT **Thinking and Problem-Solving Skills Do Not Transfer**

According to E. D. Hirsch, a vocal critic of critical thinking programs:

> But whether such direct instruction of critical thinking or self-monitoring *does* in fact improve performance is a subject of debate in the research community. For instance, the research regarding critical thinking is not reassuring. Instruction in critical thinking has been going on in several countries for over a hundred years. Yet re-

searchers found that students from nations as varied as Israel, Germany, Australia, the Philippines, and the United States, including those who have been taught critical thinking continue to fall into logical fallacies. (1996, p. 136)

The CoRT program has been used in over 5,000 classrooms in 10 nations. But Polson and Jeffries (1985) report that "after 10 years of widespread use we have no adequate evidence concerning . . . the effectiveness of the program" (p. 445). In addition, Mayer and Wittrock (1996) note that field studies of problem solving in real situations show that people often fail to apply the mathematical problem-solving approaches they learn in school to actual problems encountered in the grocery store or home.

Even though educators have been more successful in teaching metacognitive skills, critics still caution that there are times when such teaching hinders rather than helps learning. Robert Siegler (1993) suggests that teaching self-monitoring strategies to low-achieving students can interfere with the students' development of adaptive strategies. Forcing students to use the strategies of experts may put too much burden on working memory as the students struggle to use an unfamiliar strategy and miss the meaning or content of the lesson. For example, rather than teach students strategies for figuring out words from context, it may be helpful for students to focus on learning more vocabulary words.

of eastern Asia, specifically the important rice crops. The teacher introduces a lesson by *modeling* good thinking about multiple causes:

> Have you noticed that the roses in the park bloomed early this year? I'm asking myself why. What factors caused these early blooms? I recall it was a warm winter. That was probably an important factor. But certainly there are other factors involved—probably some hidden ones—and I know it is important to search for them. In fact, now that I have stopped to think, I remember that we had very heavy rains in March. This may be a factor too . . . (Perkins, Jay, & Tishman, 1993, p. 80)

After providing this model, the teacher points out other effects that have multiple causes such as winning a football game or staying healthy. Next, the teacher gives straightforward, *direct instruction* about how to analyze causes, such as considering how causal factors may work together or separately. She teaches the students to draw diagrams that depict multiple causes. Then she gives the students *practice* in analyzing multiple causes by asking them to diagram the causes involved in rice growth and how the causes work together or separately to produce rice. The teacher stimulates their thinking by suggesting that the students cast a wide net—consider many factors such as weather, soil, insects, and farming practices. One student's diagram is presented in Figure 8.8.

When the students finish their diagrams, the teacher asks them to discuss their analysis with a partner. She guides the *interaction* with questions such as "How did you identify causes?" "Was it hard to figure out if causes worked together or alone?" "What questions can you invent about this multifactor causal

This girl appears to be en-grossed in her reading, but how does her teacher know that she is making sense of what she is reading, or what her under-standing of the text is?

FIGURE 8.8

A Multicausal Analysis of Factors Affecting Rice Growth

Students are taught how to use the *and/or* convention to diagram causes that work together (*and*) or separately (*or*) to produce an effect, in this case, the growth of rice.

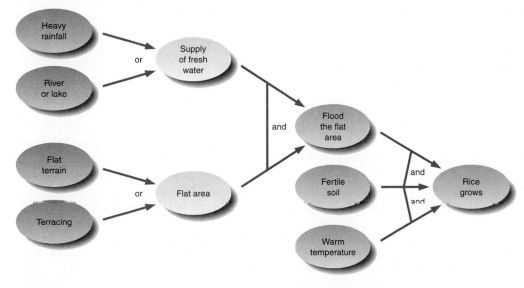

Source: From A. Collins and W. Ferguson (1993). Epistemic forms and epistemic games: Structures and strategies to guide inquiry. *Educational Psychologist, 28,* p. 35. Adapted by permission of the publisher and authors.

analysis game?" "Can you envision other situations where you could use this kind of causal analysis?"

In this lesson, the four factors of modeling, direct instruction, practice, and interaction help students become expert members of the thinking community.

The Language of Thinking. How many words can you find in the above lesson that describe aspects of thinking? A quick look finds "search," "asking why," "hidden factors," "analyze," "identify," "figure out," "envision," "effects," "contributing causes," and "invent." My computer's thesaurus just found over 100 more words when I highlighted "thinking." The language of thinking consists of natural language terms that refer to mental processes and mental products—"words like *think, believe, guess, conjecture, hypothesis, evidence, reasons, estimate, calculate, suspect, doubt,* and *theorize*—to name just a few" (Tishman, Perkins, & Jay, 1995, p. 8). The classroom should be filled with a clear, precise, and rich vocabulary of thinking. Rather than saying, "What do you think about Jamie's answer?" the teacher might ask questions that expand thinking such as, "What evidence can you give to refute or support Jamie's answer?" "What assumptions is Jamie making?" "What are some alternative explanations?" Students surrounded by a rich language of thinking are more likely to think deeply about thinking.

Critical Thinking. **Critical thinking** skills are useful in almost every life situation—even in evaluating the media ads that constantly bombard us. To evaluate the claim that 99 out of 100 dentists prefer a particular brand of toothpaste, you must consider such questions as: Which dentists were polled? How were they chosen? Was the toothpaste company involved in the polling process? If so, how could this bias the results of the poll? Or when you see a group of gorgeous people extolling the virtues of a particular brand of orange juice as they frolic in skimpy bathing suits, you must decide if sex appeal is a relevant factor in choosing a fruit drink. Psychologists have not been able to agree on the skills that constitute critical thinking, but Table 8.3 provides a representative list of skills.

No matter what approach you use to develop critical thinking, it is important to follow up with additional practice. One lesson is not enough. For example, if your class examined a particular historical document to determine if it reflected bias or propaganda, you should follow up by analyzing other written historical documents, contemporary advertisements, or news stories. Until thinking skills become overlearned and relatively automatic, they are not likely to be transferred to new situations. Instead, students will use these skills only to complete the lesson in social studies, not to evaluate the claims made by friends, politicians, toy manufacturers, or diet plans. What else is needed to apply good thinking?

Thinking as a "State of Mind." If people have a rich language for thinking and can be critical thinkers, they need one more quality to use their abilities—*mindfulness.* "Mindfulness is a state of mind that results from drawing novel distinctions, examining information from new perspectives, and being sensitive to context. It is an open, creative, probabilistic state of mind in which the individual might be led to finding differences among things thought

---

Focus on...

Thinking

- What is meant by a culture of thinking in the classroom?
- How is critical thinking required in your everyday life?
- How can a teacher encourage or discourage "mindfulness"?

Critical Thinking Evaluating conclusions by logically and systematically examining the problem, the evidence, and the solution.

TABLE 8.3   Examples of Critical Thinking Skills

Defining and Clarifying the Problem

1. Identify central issues or problems.
2. Compare similarities and differences.
3. Determine which information is relevant.
4. Formulate appropriate questions.

Judging Information Related to the Problem

5. Distinguish among fact, opinion, and reasoned judgment.
6. Check consistency.
7. Identify unstated assumptions.
8. Recognize stereotypes and clichés.
9. Recognize bias, emotional factors, propaganda, and semantic slanting.
10. Recognize different value systems and ideologies.

Solving Problems/Drawing Conclusions

11. Recognize the adequacy of data.
12. Predict probable consequences.

Source: From P. Kneedler. California assesses critical thinking. In A. Costa (Ed.), *Developing minds: A resource book for teaching thinking*, p. 277. Reprinted by permission of the Association for Supervision and Curriculum Development and the author. Copyright © 1985 by ASCD. All rights reserved.

to be similar and similarities among things thought to be different" (Langer, 1993, p. 44). The classroom culture should support the development of mindfulness by encouraging students to take intellectual risks, explore, inquire, seek challenges, and invest effort. Otherwise students will learn the language and skills of thinking, but seldom apply them outside the lessons of school. The challenge of transferring knowledge and understanding beyond the school house door has a long history of research in educational psychology.

Teaching for Transfer

Think back for a moment to a class in one of your high school subjects you did not go on to study in college. Imagine the teacher, the room, the textbook. Now remember what you actually studied in class. If it was a science class, what were some of the formulas you learned? Oxidation reduction? If you are like most of us, you may remember that you learned these things, but you will not be quite sure exactly what you learned. Were those hours wasted? These questions are about the transfer of learning.

Defining Transfer

Whenever something previously learned influences current learning or when solving an earlier problem affects how you solve a new problem, **transfer** has occurred (Mayer & Wittrock, 1996). If students learn a mathematical principle in first period and use it to solve a physics problem in fifth period, then positive

Transfer Influence of previously learned material on new material.

"I DON'T GET IT! THEY MAKE US LEARN READING, WRITING AND ARITHMETIC TO PREPARE US FOR A WORLD OF VIDEOTAPES, COMPUTER TERMINALS AND CALCULATORS!"

(Harley Schwadron—Phi Delta Kappan)*

transfer has taken place. Even more rewarding for teachers is when a math principle learned in October is applied to a physics problem in March. However, the effect of past learning on present learning is not always positive. *Functional fixedness* and *response set* are examples of negative transfer because they involve the attempt to apply familiar but *inappropriate* strategies to a new situation.

Specific transfer occurs when a rule, fact, or skill learned in one situation is applied in another, very similar situation; for example, applying rules of punctuation to write a job application letter or using knowledge of the alphabet to find a word in the dictionary. General transfer involves applying to new problems the principles and attitudes learned in other, often dissimilar situations. Thus, general transfer might mean using problem-solving heuristics to solve issues in your personal life—for example, applying working backward to decide when to call for an appointment to have a dentist check a sore tooth in time to get any necessary treatment done before you leave for spring break.

A Contemporary View of Transfer

Gavriel Salomon and David Perkins (1989) describe two kinds of transfer, termed low-road and high-road transfer. **Low-road transfer** "involves the spontaneous, automatic transfer of highly practiced skills, with little need for reflective thinking" (p. 118). The key to low-road transfer is practicing a skill often, in a variety of situations, until your performance becomes automatic. So if you worked one summer for a temporary secretarial service and were sent to many different offices to work on all kinds of typewriters and word processors, by the end of the summer you probably would be able to handle most machines easily. Your practice with many machines would let you transfer your skill automatically to a new situation.

High-road transfer, on the other hand, involves consciously applying abstract knowledge learned in one situation to a different situation. This can happen in one of two ways. You may learn a principle or a strategy, intending to use it in the future. For example, if you plan to apply what you learn in anatomy class this semester to work in a life-drawing course you will take next semester, you may search for principles about human proportions, muscle definition, and so on. This is called *forward-reaching transfer*, because you are looking forward to applying the knowledge gained. *Backward-reaching transfer* occurs when you are faced with a problem and look back on what you have learned in other situations to help you in this new one. Analogical thinking is an example of this kind of transfer. You search for other, related situations that might provide clues to the current problem. The key to high-road transfer is *mindful abstraction*, or the deliberate identification of a principle, main idea, strategy, or procedure that is not tied to one specific problem or situation but could apply to many. Such an abstraction becomes part of your metacognitive knowledge, available to guide future learning and problem solving.

There is one last kind of transfer that is especially important for students—the transfer of learning strategies. As we have seen several times in this book, students may learn new strategies for reading, studying, problem solving, or remembering, but fail to use those strategies outside the situations where they were learned. But the idea of learning strategies and tactics is that they be applied across a wide range of situations. What gets in the way of strategy transfer? Sometimes students simply don't understand that a particular strategy applies in new situations or they don't know how to adapt it to fit. Perhaps they

Low-Road Transfer Spontaneous and automatic transfer of highly practiced skills.

High-Road Transfer Application of abstract knowledge learned in one situation to a different situation.

TABLE 8.4	Kinds of Transfer	
	Low-Road Transfer	**High-Road Transfer**
Definition	Automatic transfer of highly practiced skill	Conscious application of abstract knowledge to a new situation
Key Conditions	Extensive practice Variety of settings and conditions Overlearning to automaticity	Mindful focus on abstracting a principle, main idea, procedure that can be used in many situations.
Examples	Driving many different cars Finding your gate in an airport	Applying PQ4R in reading texts Applying procedures from math in designing a page layout for the school newspaper

have practiced with only one kind of material or problem and never had the chance to apply the strategy to new material (Shunk, 1996). Table 8.4 summarizes the types of transfer.

Teaching for Positive Transfer

Years of research and experience show that teachers cannot expect students to automatically transfer what they learn to new problems. Students will master new knowledge, problem-solving procedures, and learning strategies, but not use them unless prompted or guided. For example, studies of real-world mathematics show that people do not always apply math procedures learned in school to solve practical problems in their homes or grocery stores (Lave, 1988; Lave & Wenger, 1991). This is because learning is *situated*, that is, learning happens in specific situations. We learn solutions to particular problems, not general all-purpose solutions that can fit any problem. Because knowledge is learned as a tool to solve particular problems, we may not realize that the knowledge is relevant when we encounter a problem that seems different, at least on the surface. We tend to use knowledge only in situations where it is obviously appropriate (Driscoll, 1994; Singley & Anderson, 1989). How can you make sure your students will use what they learn, even when situations change?

What Is Worth Learning?   First you must answer the question "What is worth learning?" The learning of basic skills like reading, writing, computing, cooperating, and speaking will definitely transfer to other situations, because these skills are necessary for later work both in and out of school—writing job applications, reading novels, paying bills, working on a team, locating and evaluating health care services, among others. All later learning depends on positive transfer of these basics to new situations.

Teachers must also be aware of what the future is likely to hold for their students, both as a group and as individuals. What will society require of them as adults? What will their careers require of them? As a child growing up in Texas in the 1950s and 1960s, I studied nothing about computers, even though my father was a computer systems analyst; yet now I spend hours at this word processor. Computer programming and word processing were not part of my high school curriculum, but learning to use a slide rule was taught. Now calculators and computers have made this skill obsolete. Undoubtedly changes as

A challenge for every generation of teachers and learners is to be able to transfer the knowledge they acquire in school and while growing up to situations they'll face in the future.

extreme and unpredictable as these await the students you will teach. For this reason, the general transfer of principles, attitudes, critical thinking ability, and problem-solving strategies will be just as important to these students as the specific transfer of basic skills.

How Can Teachers Help? To have something to transfer, students must first learn and understand. Students will be more likely to transfer information to new situations if they have been actively involved in the learning process. They must be encouraged to form abstractions that they will apply later. For example, Salomon and Perkins (1989) give this advice for teaching history:

> [The] history teacher can introduce direct discussion of contemporary events. To provoke forward-reaching transfer, the teacher can select an episode in history and encourage students to seek contemporary analogs. To provoke backward-reaching transfer, the teacher can choose a current phenomenon . . . and urge students to reach into their historical repertoires for analogies and disanalogies. (p. 136)

Greater transfer can also be ensured by **overlearning,** practicing a skill past the point of mastery. Many of the basic facts students learn in elementary school, such as the multiplication tables, are traditionally overlearned. Overlearning helps students retrieve the information quickly and automatically when it is needed.

Stages of Transfer for Strategies. Gary Phye (1992; Phye & Sanders, 1994) suggests we think of the transfer of learning strategies as a tool to be used in a "mindful" way to solve academic problems. He describes three stages in developing strategic transfer. In the *acquisition phase,* students should not only receive instruction about a strategy and how to use it, but they should also rehearse the strategy and practice being aware of when and how they are using

Overlearning Practicing a task past the point of mastery to combat forgetting and improve transfer.

it. In the *retention phase,* more practice with feedback helps students hone their strategy use. In the *transfer phase,* the teacher should provide new problems that can be solved with the same strategy, even though the problems appear different on the surface. To enhance motivation, point out to students how using the strategy will help them solve many problems and accomplish different tasks. These steps help build both procedural and conditional knowledge—how to use the strategy as well as when and why.

Newly mastered concepts, principles, and strategies must be practiced and applied in a wide variety of situations. Positive transfer is encouraged when skills are used under authentic conditions, similar to those that will exist when the skills are needed later. Students can learn about multiplication by figuring how many ways they can make $1.67 using only dimes and pennies. They can learn to write by corresponding with e-mail pen pals in other countries. They can learn historical research methods by researching their own families. Some of these applications should involve complex, ill-defined, unstructured problems, because many of the problems to be faced in later life, in school and out, will not come to students complete with instructions and applications should include situations outside school. The Guidelines give ideas for enlisting the support of families in encouraging transfer.

Focus on . . .

Transfer

- Distinguish between specific and general transfer.
- How do low-road and high-road transfer relate to the development of expertise?
- Why is it important to ask students to apply new knowledge to both well-defined and ill-defined problems?

Guidelines

Family and Community Partnerships for Encouraging Transfer

Keep families informed about their child's curriculum so they can support learning.

Examples

1. At the beginning of units or major projects, send a letter summarizing the key goals, a few of the major assignments, and some common problems students have in learning the material for that unit.
2. Ask parents for suggestions about how their child's interests could be connected to the curriculum topics.

Give families ideas for how they might practice, extend, or apply learning from school.

Examples

1. To extend writing, ask parents to encourage their children to write letters or e-mail to companies or civic organizations asking for information or free products. Provide a shell letter form for structure and ideas and include addresses of companies that provide free samples or information.
2. Ask family members to include their children in some projects that require measurement, halfing or doubling recipes, or estimating costs.
3. Suggest students work with grandparents to do a family memory book. Combine historical research and writing.

Show connections between learning in school and life outside.

Examples

1. Ask families to talk about and show how they use the skills their children are learning in jobs, hobbies, or community involvement projects.

(continued)

2. Ask family members to come to class to demonstrate how they use reading, writing, science, math, or other knowledge in their work.

Make families partners in practicing learning strategies.

Examples

1. Focus on one learning tactic at a time—ask families to simply remind their children to use a particular tactic with homework that week.

2. Develop a lending library of books and videotapes to teach families about learning strategies.

3. Give parents a copy of the Study Skills and Learning Strategies Guidelines on page 313, rewritten for your grade level.

This chapter has covered quite a bit of territory, partly because the cognitive perspective has so many implications for instruction. Although they are varied, you can see that most of the cognitive ideas for teaching concepts, problem-solving skills, and thinking emphasize the role of the student's prior knowledge in learning and the need for active, mindful learning.

SUMMARY

The Importance of Thinking and Understanding

The ultimate goal of teaching is student understanding. Students demonstrate understanding when they can use knowledge appropriately in new situations. Thinking, in the form of problem solving or critical analysis, is the avenue to understanding.

Learning and Teaching about Concepts

Concepts are categories used to group similar events, ideas, people, or objects. We probably learn concepts from prototypes or exemplars of the category, understand in terms of our schematic knowledge, and then refine concepts through our additional experience of relevant and irrelevant features. Lessons about concepts include four basic components: concept name, definition, attributes, and examples. The concept attainment model is one approach to teaching concepts that asks students to form hypotheses about why particular examples are members of a category and what that category (concept) might be.

Problem Solving

Problem solving is both general and domain-specific. The five stages of problem solving are: identifying the problem (and perhaps seeing the problem as an opportunity), understanding the problem through representation and setting goals, exploring possible solutions, anticipating possible consequences of the strategies and then implementing one strat-

egy, and evaluating the results and learning from the results. A critical element in solving problems in school is representing the problem accurately, showing understanding of both the whole problem and its discrete elements. Schema training may improve this ability. The application of algorithms and heuristics—such as means-ends analysis, analogical thinking, working backward, and verbalization—may help students solve problems. Factors that hinder problem solving include functional fixedness or rigidity (response set). These disallow the flexibility needed to represent problems accurately and to have insight into solutions.

Expert problem solvers have a rich store of declarative, procedural, and conditional knowledge. They organize this knowledge around general principles or patterns that apply to large classes of problems. The same is true for expert teachers. Accomplishing many classroom tasks has become automatic, so that routines are smooth. Less class time is wasted. Experts can apply well-practiced solutions or readily invent new ones. They have a rich store of well-organized knowledge about the many specific situations of teaching.

Becoming an Expert Student: Learning Strategies and Study Skills

Teachers also need to help students develop procedural knowledge by teaching learning strategies (plans) and learning tactics (techniques), including study skills. Examples of study skills that aid both memory and comprehension are underlining, note taking, concept mapping and other visual representations, and PQ4R. Good strategies help students focus attention and stay engaged; invest effort and think deeply about what they are learning; and monitor their own understanding as they study. Strategies must be practiced in different situations so students learn not only how to use different strategies, but when and why to apply them.

Teaching and Learning about Thinking

Two approaches to teaching thinking skills are to use stand-alone programs or to embed programs in the regular curriculum. In every class, teachers can use a rich language of thinking, develop critical thinking skills, model good thinking, and encourage the practice of specific skills.

Teaching for Transfer

The transfer of learning from one situation to another may be positive or negative, general or specific. Transfer involving spontaneity and automaticity in familiar situations has been called low-road transfer. High-road transfer involves reflection and conscious application of abstract knowledge to new situations. Teachers can promote thinking and learning skills by teaching for mastery, and for the positive, general transfer of knowledge. In addition, teachers can help students transfer learning strategies by teaching strategies directly, providing practice with feedback, and then expanding the application of the strategies to new and unfamiliar situations.

KEY TERMS

algorithm, p. 300
analogical thinking, p. 301
concept, p. 289
concept mapping, p. 293
critical thinking, p. 318
defining attributes, p. 289
exemplar, p. 290
functional fixedness, p. 302
graded membership, p. 289
heuristic, p. 300
high-road transfer, p. 320

insight, p. 303
learning strategies, p. 307
learning tactics, p. 307
linguistic comprehension, p. 296
low-road transfer, p. 320
means-ends analysis, p. 300
overgeneralization, p. 293
overlearning, p. 322
PQ4R, p. 311
problem, p. 294
problem solving, p. 295

prototype, p. 289
response set, p. 302
schema-driven problem solving, p. 299
stand-alone thinking skills programs, p. 315
transfer, p. 319
undergeneralization, p. 292
verbalization, p. 301
working-backward strategy, p. 300

CHECK YOUR UNDERSTANDING

Can you apply the ideas from this chapter on cognitive processes to solve the following problems of practice?

Preschool and Kindergarten

- Several students in your class still have trouble discriminating between simple shapes. What would you do to help them understand?

Elementary and Middle School

- Students in your class are having a really hard time with the concepts of heat and energy. What would you do?

Junior High and High School

- Students in your math class can solve problems for homework, but get confused on tests that cover several chapters. They don't seem to know when to apply one procedure and when to use another. How would you help them?

- You decide to give an essay test that requires creativity and critical thinking. Your students perform very badly and protest loudly that the test is "unfair." They want to use the definitions and facts they have so carefully memorized. What would you do?

Cooperative Learning Activity

- With four or five other members of your class, design a lesson or series of lessons that teach important content and thinking skills at the same time. How would you introduce the lessons, and how would you evaluate students' learning?

What Would They Do?

The directions seemed perfectly clear to you: Read two poems about nature (selected from the eight poems you read together last week), then write a one-page compare-and-contrast analysis of the two poems. The students enjoyed reading the poetry last week. But their first attempt to write about the poems is a disaster. They jot down a few lines, giving superficial descriptions of each poem and then tell which one they liked best. Most don't even give reasons why they chose one over the other. There is no comparison, no contrast, no critical thinking or analysis. The students must have spent all their time worrying about spelling and grammar. The form is fine, but the students don't really have anything to say. As you hand back the papers, you can see the disappointment in their faces. The grades are clearly lower than they expected.

MARTHA J. POND

Tenth Grade Teacher
Timberline Regional High School, Plaistow, New Hampshire

I f these students presented papers that are grammatically correct, without errors in spelling or form, they obviously care about their work. I would try to defuse a tense situation for them by speaking first to the class as a whole about how the grades are generally lower than expected, but that they will be given a chance to rewrite their papers after we discuss them. As I pass back the papers, I would speak briefly to each student, pointing out specific comments I had written on their papers, or making a more general comment, such as "Why did you like this poem better?" I would give them a chance to reread their papers and my comments, and then we would discuss just what "compare-and-contrast analysis" means. I would encourage them to take notes, so that they would have something to which they could refer when they sat down to rewrite their papers. I would try to center the discussion not on the poems, for they will need to do that for themselves later, but on some other interest, such as music, food, or TV. I would, through questions and answers, help them to realize that a summary and opinion doesn't explain much; that they need to give reasons for their opinions and try to make connections, as well as show differences, between whatever they are analyzing. They need to decide what they are trying to say, and then determine how best to support it through examples. I would spend as much class time as necessary on this, and then assign a due date for the rewrite. I would offer to read any and all rough drafts, perhaps even devoting any remaining class time to working on them. Most importantly, I would continue to ask students to use this and other critical analysis skills, both in class discussions and in their writing, for they will improve with practice and feedback.

ANDREA SANTORO

Fourth Grade Teacher
Snug Harbor Community School, Quincy, Massachusetts

If the majority of the class is disappointed with their papers, I'd start all over again. In this situation it appears that the delivery of the lesson was the problem, not the students. If you don't build a strong foundation first, the whole structure will fall apart. In this case, further exploration of poetry is necessary.

I'd encourage my students to think of poetry as a song without music. We'd start with what they know: analyzing words from popular musicians, comparing lyrics, reading songs instead of singing songs. The teacher should ask, "Does the meaning come from the words or the music?"

Teaching a student to *think* is not easy. *Critical thinking* needs to be coaxed. The quote, "A picture is worth a thousand words," can be rephrased for poetry as "A poem can be worth a thousand pictures." Visualizing the message of a poem is in the mind's eye.

Writing a compare-and-contrast analysis of two poems is a skill that needs to be practiced. Given examples, encouragement, group responses, partner reading, and time, the students can be motivated to rethink what was asked.

Learning and Instruction

Overview | *What Would You Do?*

CONTRIBUTIONS OF BEHAVIORAL LEARNING   330
Objectives for Learning | Kinds of Objectives | Are Objectives
Useful? | Mastery Learning | Direct Instruction

COGNITIVE MODELS OF TEACHING   338
Discovery Learning | Expository Teaching | Reception Learning |
The Instructional Events Model

CONSTRUCTIVIST AND SITUATED LEARNING   346
Elements of Constructivist Perspectives | Inquiry and Problem-Based
Learning | Group Work and Cooperation in Learning | Instructional
Conversations | Cognitive Apprenticeships

COGNITIVE AND CONSTRUCTIVIST APPROACHES TO READING,
MATHEMATICS, AND SCIENCE   357
Learning to Read and Write | Reciprocal Teaching | Learning and
Teaching Mathematics | Learning Science | Working with Families

Summary | *Key Terms* | *Check Your Understanding* |
Teachers' Casebook: What Would They Do?

W*hat have you heard about models of teaching today? Do you know about whole language? Apprenticeships? Inquiry? Cooperative learning? Reciprocal teaching? What comes to mind when you hear these terms?*

For the past three chapters we have examined different aspects of learning. We considered behavioral, social cognitive, information processing, constructivist, and social/situated explanations of what people learn and how they learn it. But many of you reading this book hope to teach in some setting, whether in schools or business or health care. What do these perspectives on learning tell us about teaching? The writings of psychologists and educators are filled with models of instruction—some derived from theory, others derived from common practices, and still others grounded in both theory and practice. We can't discuss all these approaches, so we will focus on several that are good representatives of the different explanations of learning.

Rather than debating the merits of each approach, we will consider the contributions of different models of instruction, grounded in different theories of learning. Don't feel that you must choose the "best" approach—there is no such thing. The goal of all the different models is to create situations in which students learn, understand, and remember. Even though theorists argue about which model is best, most excellent teachers learn from all the approaches and apply them as appropriate.

In the next pages, we will examine the contributions of behavioral, early cognitive, constructivist, and situated theories of learning. By the time you finish this chapter, you should be able to:

- Describe at least one model of teaching based on behavioral, cognitive, constructivist, and situated perspectives on learning.
- Contrast guided discovery and expository approaches.
- Explain when different teaching models are appropriate—match learning to teaching.
- Incorporate cooperative learning into your teaching.
- Debate the merits of whole language and code-based approaches to reading.

What Would You Do?

TEACHERS' CASEBOOK

Your school district has adopted a whole-language, integrated curriculum approach for grades K through six. Quite a bit of time and money was spent on workshops for teachers; buying big books and multiple copies of good children's literature; developing manipulatives for mathematics; building comfortable reading corners; making costumes, puppets, and other reading props; designing science projects; and generally supporting the innovations. Students and teachers are mostly pleased with the program. There seems to be more reading and more enjoyment of reading, at least for many children—but some students seem lost. The students' written work is longer and more creative. However, standardized tests indicate a drop in scores. The principal is clearly getting worried—this was her big project and she had to work hard to "sell it" to some members of the PTA and school board. Several parents of students in your class are complaining that they are having to hire tutors or buy commercial programs to teach their children to read.

- As a teacher, what would you do about the parents' complaints?
- Would you make any changes in your approach?
- What information would you need to make good decisions?
- Who should be involved in these decisions?

Contributions of Behavioral Learning

The behavioral approach to learning has made several important contributions to instruction, including systems for specifying learning objectives, mastery learning techniques, and direct instruction. These approaches are useful when the goal is to learn *explicit information* or new *behaviors* and when the material is *sequential* and *factual*.

Objectives for Learning

The items listed in the overview at the beginning of this chapter are examples of learning objectives. Although there are many different approaches to writing objectives, each assumes that the first step in teaching is to decide what changes should take place in the learner—what is the goal of teaching. This leads us to a general definition of an **instructional objective**: it is a clear and unambiguous description of your educational intentions for your students.

At a very general, abstract level are the grand goals society may have for graduates of public schools, such as increased intellectual development and effective citizenship. But very general goals become meaningless as potential guidelines for instruction. On the other hand, objectives that are too specific may teach poor study habits by focusing the students' attention on specific facts and encouraging them to skip anything that is not mentioned in the objective (Ten-Brink, 1986).

Instructional Objective Clear statement of what students are intended to learn through instruction.

Most psychologists and educators agree that we need something between grand generalities and specific item-by-item instructions for each student. But here the agreement ends. Objectives written by people with behavioral views focus on observable and measurable changes in the learner. **Behavioral objectives** use terms such as *list, define, add,* or *calculate.* **Cognitive objectives,** on the other hand, emphasize thinking and comprehension, so they are more likely to include words such as *understand, recognize, create,* or *apply.* Let's look at one well-developed method of writing specific objectives.

Mager: Start with the Specific.   Robert Mager has developed a very influential system for writing instructional objectives. Mager's idea is that objectives ought to describe what students will be doing when demonstrating their achievement and how you will know they are doing it (Mager, 1975). Mager's objectives are generally regarded as behavioral.

According to Mager, a good objective has three parts. First, it describes the intended student behavior—what must the student do? Second, it lists the conditions under which the behavior will occur—how will this behavior be recognized or tested? Third, it gives the criteria for acceptable performance on the test. Figure 9.1 shows how the system works. This system, with its emphasis on final behavior, requires a very explicit statement. Mager contends that often students can teach themselves if they are given well-stated objectives.

Gronlund: Start with the General.   Norman Gronlund (1993) offers a different approach, often used for writing cognitive objectives. He believes that

FIGURE 9.1

Mager's Three-Part System

Robert Mager believes that a good learning objective has three parts: the student behavior, the conditions under which the behavior will be performed, and the criteria for judging a performance.

Part	Central Question	Example
Student behavior	Do what?	Mark statements with an *F* for fact or an *O* for opinion
Conditions of performance	Under what conditions?	Given an article from a newspaper
Performance criteria	How well?	75% of the statements are correctly marked

Source: From R. F. Mager, *Preparing instructional objectives,* 1975, Fearon, Belmont, CA. Reprinted by permission of David S. Lake Publishers.

Behavioral Objectives Instructional objectives stated in terms of observable behaviors.

Cognitive Objectives Instructional objectives stated in terms of higher-level thinking operations.

TABLE 9.1   Gronlund's Combined Method for Creating Objectives

General Objective

For sixth-grade mathematics: Student can efficiently solve real-life problems that require finding sizes of surface areas.

Specific Examples

1. Discriminates between the surface area of a figure and other quantitative characteristics of that figure (e.g., height and volume).
2. States the formula for the area of a rectangle.
3. Given the dimensions of a rectangle, computes its area.
4. Given the dimensions of a right triangle, computes its area.
5. Given the dimensions of a right cylinder, computes its surface area.
6. When confronted with a real-life problem, determines whether computing the area of a surface will help solve that problem.

Source: From *Designing Tests for Evaluating Student Achievement* by James S. Cangelosi, p. 6. Copyright © 1990. Adapted by permission of Addison-Wesley Educational Publishers, Inc.

an objective should be stated first in general terms (*understand, solve, appreciate,* etc.). Then the teacher should clarify by listing a few sample behaviors that would provide evidence that the student has attained the objective.

Look at the example in Table 9.1, taken from Cangelosi (1990). The goal here really is problem solving. The teacher does not want the student to stop with discriminating, stating, computing, and so on. Instead, the teacher looks at performance on these sample tasks to decide if the student can solve real-life problems. The teacher could just as well have chosen six different tasks to indicate ability to solve problems.

Gronlund's emphasis on specific objectives as samples of more general student ability is important. A teacher could never list all the behaviors that might be involved in solving problems in the subject area, but stating an initial, general objective makes it clear that the ability to solve problems is the purpose.

The most recent research on instructional objectives tends to favor approaches similar to Gronlund's. It seems reasonable to state a few central objectives in general terms and clarify them with samples of specific behaviors, as in Table 9.1 (Hamilton, 1985; Popham, 1993).

Bloom's Taxonomy of Objectives.   As you will see when we discuss teacher planning in Chapter 13, years ago Benjamin Bloom and his colleagues developed a **taxonomy** or classification system of educational objectives in three different areas of learning: cognitive, affective, and psychomotor. The most developed and widely used objectives are in the cognitive domain. Cognitive objectives are classified from simple and factual to complex and conceptual, depending on the level of thinking and understanding required to reach the objective. The categories (from simple to complex) are *knowledge* (recalling information and facts), *comprehension* (understanding, translating the information in to your own words), *application* (using information to solve prob-

Taxonomy Classification system.

lems), *analysis* (breaking down information into parts and revealing organization), *synthesis* (creating a new idea, product, solution), and *evaluation* (judging something against a standard). Thinking about objectives using Bloom's taxonomies can be very helpful in planning, but we will go into depth on this point in Chapter 13 (Bloom, 1994).

Are Objectives Useful?

Providing objectives for students seems to improve achievement, but only under certain conditions. First, objectives can promote learning with loosely organized and less-structured activities such as lectures, films, and research projects. With very structured materials such as programmed instruction, objectives seem less important (Tobias & Duchastel, 1974). Second, if the importance of some information is not clear from the learning materials and activities themselves, instructional objectives will probably help focus students' attention and thus increase achievement (Duchastel, 1979). But when the task involves simply getting the gist of the passage or transferring the information to a new situation, objectives are not as effective. In these situations, it is better to use questions that focus on meaning, inserting the questions right before the passage to be read (Hamilton, 1985).

If the objectives are supplied in advance—and especially if students have a role designing objectives—both students and teacher will know what the performance criteria are. In thinking about objectives, both teachers and students must consider what is important, what is worth learning. I have found that teachers who have clear, appropriate goals for each student often are successful in helping the students learn. Finally, many school districts still require teachers to complete lesson plans that include learning objectives. The Guidelines should help you whether you decide to make thorough use of objectives or just to prepare them for certain assignments.

Guidelines

Developing Instructional Objectives

Avoid "word magic"—phrases that sound noble and important but say very little.

Examples

1. Keep the focus on specific changes that will take place in the students' knowledge of skills.

2. Ask students to explain the meaning of the objectives. If they can't give specific examples of what you mean, the objectives are not communicating your intentions to your students.

Suit the activities to the objectives.

Examples

1. If the goal is the memorization of vocabulary, give the students memory aids and practice exercises.

2. If the goal is the ability to develop well-thought-out positions, consider position papers, debates, projects, or mock trials.

3. If you want students to become better writers, give many opportunities for writing and rewriting.

(continued)

Make sure your tests are related to your objectives.

Examples

1. Write objectives and rough drafts for tests at the same time.
2. Weight the tests according to the importance of the various objectives and the time spent on each.

When the objectives and steps are clearly mapped, how might students go about learning? Mastery learning and direct instruction are two possibilities that are consistent with behavioral principles.

Mastery Learning

Mastery learning is based on the assumption that, given enough time and the proper instruction, most students can master any learning objective (Bloom, 1968; Guskey & Gates, 1986). To use the mastery approach, a teacher must break a course down into small units of study. Each unit might involve mastering several specific objectives. "Mastery" usually means a score of 80 to 90% on a test or other assessment. The teacher informs the students of the objectives and the criteria for meeting each. Students who do not reach the minimum level of mastery or who reach this minimum but want to improve their performance (thus raising their grade) can recycle through the unit. When they are ready, they take another form of the unit test.

The challenge in mastery learning is providing the appropriate extra help for students who don't attain mastery. There are many possibilities. Students can work with peer tutors or aides inside or outside class or they can get extra help from their team members in cooperative groups. If no extra time or staff is available, mastery learning can be adapted to a regular class time frame. For example, after explaining the mastery approach, the teacher teaches the lessons, then gives an ungraded assessment to determine students' levels of understanding. Those who have reached the mastery level are given enrichment activities such as independent or group work, computer simulations, research projects, or creative problems to solve. Those who need more help work with the teacher on corrective instruction (Block & Anderson, 1975). The Keller Plan, also called the Personalized System of Instruction (PSI), is a form of mastery learning used most often in college (Sherman, Ruskin, & Semb, 1982).

Advantages and Problems. Mastery learning makes the most sense when the focus is key concepts or skills that serve as a foundation for later learning. In mathematics, for example, some students will fall farther and farther behind if they have to move from addition of fractions to more advanced topics, before they ever really understand addition. By the time they reach division of fractions, they are lost. Mastery learning has been successful when students get the extra time and support they need to learn—especially through corrective instruction outside class or inside class from peer tutors or cooperative learning group members (Guskey, 1990; Kulick, Kulick, & Bangert-Drowns, 1990; Shuell, 1996). The effects of the Block and Anderson (1975) remediation/enrichment in-class model are less clear cut and probably depend on the quality of the remediation possible using class time alone (Ellis & Fouts, 1993).

Mastery Learning An approach to teaching and grading that focus on achieving specific objectives before moving to the next unit or topic. Based on the assumption that every student is capable of achieving most of the objectives if given enough time and proper instruction.

There are problems with the mastery learning approach. Teachers must have a variety of materials to allow students to recycle through objectives they failed to meet the first time. Usually, just repeating the same materials won't help. It is also important to have several assessments for each unit. In practice, mastery learning has not helped to erase achievement differences among students, as some proponents have hoped. Individual differences in achievement persist, unless the teacher holds back the faster students while the slower ones catch up—a practice that makes little sense (Arlin, 1984). Left to work at their own pace, some students will learn much more and leave a unit with much better understanding than others. Some will work much harder to take advantage of the learning opportunities. (Grabe & Latta, 1981). Some will be frustrated instead of encouraged by the chance to recycle ("You mean I have to do it *again*?").

There is another approach to teaching basic skills that focuses more on the whole group than on individuals—direct instruction.

Direct Instruction

The direct instruction models described in this section fit a specific set of circumstances because they are derived from a particular approach to research. Researchers identified these models by comparing teachers whose students learned more than expected (based on entering knowledge) with teachers whose students performed at an expected or average level. The researchers focused on teaching as it is—on existing practices in American classrooms. Because the focus was on traditional forms of teaching, the research could not identify successful innovations. Effectiveness was usually defined as average improvement in standardized test scores for a whole class or school. So the results hold for large groups, but not necessarily for every student in the group. Even when the average achievement of a group improves, the achievement of some individuals may decline (Brophy & Good, 1986; Good, 1996; Shuell, 1996).

Given these conditions, you can see that the models described below apply best to the teaching of **basic skills**—clearly structured knowledge and essential skills, such as science facts, mathematics computations, reading vocabulary, and grammar rules (Rosenshine & Stevens, 1986). These skills involve tasks that are relatively unambiguous; they can be taught step by step and tested by standardized tests. The teaching approaches described below are not necessarily appropriate for objectives such as helping students to write creatively, solve complex problems, or mature emotionally.

Several psychologists have identified a teaching approach that is related to improved student learning. Barak Rosenshine calls this approach **direct instruction** (1979) or **explicit teaching** (1986). Tom Good (1983a) uses the term **active teaching** for a similar approach. Ausubel's expository teaching, described later in this chapter, also shares many features of direct instruction, even though it is considered a cognitive approach to instruction. Weinert and Helmke describe direct instruction as having the following features:

> (a) the teachers' classroom management is especially effective and the rate of student interruptive behaviors is very low; (b) the teacher maintains a strong academic focus and uses available instructional time intensively to initiate and facilitate students' learning activities; (c) the teacher insures

Basic Skills Clearly structured knowledge that is needed for later learning and that can be taught step by step.

Direct Instruction/Explicit Teaching Instruction for mastery of basic skills.

Active Teaching Teaching characterized by high levels of teacher explanation, demonstration, and interaction with students.

Guided practice with feedback is at the heart of the direct instruction model.

that as many students as possible achieve good learning progress by carefully choosing appropriate tasks, clearly presenting subject-matter information and solution strategies, continuously diagnosing each student's learning progress and learning difficulties, and providing effective help through remedial instruction. (1995, p. 138)

How would a teacher turn these themes into actions?

Rosenshine's Six Teaching Functions.   Rosenshine and his colleagues (Rosenshine, 1988; Rosenshine & Stevens, 1986) have identified six teaching functions based on the research on effective instruction. These could serve as a checklist or framework for teaching basic skills.

1. *Review and check the previous day's work*. Reteach if students misunderstood or made errors.

2. *Present new material*. Make the purpose clear, teach in small steps, provide many examples and nonexamples.

3. *Provide guided practice*. Question students, give practice problems, and listen for misconceptions and misunderstandings. Reteach if necessary. Continue guided practice until students answer about 80% of the questions correctly.

4. *Give feedback and correctives* based on student answers. Reteach if necessary.

5. *Provide independent practice*. Let students apply the new learning on their own, in seatwork, cooperative groups, or homework. The success rate during independent practice should be about 95%. This means that students must be well prepared for the work by the presentation and guided practice and that assignments must not be too difficult. The point is for the students to practice until the skills become overlearned and automatic—until the students are confident. Hold students accountable for the work they do—check it.

6. *Review weekly and monthly* to consolidate learning. Include some review items as homework. Test often, and reteach material missed on the tests.

These six functions are not steps to be followed in a particular order, but all of them are elements of effective instruction. For example, feedback, review, or reteaching should occur whenever necessary and should match the abilities of the students. There are several other models of direct instruction, but most share the elements presented in Table 9.2. Missouri Math (Good, Grouws, & Ebmeier, 1983) is another example of direct instruction.

Criticisms of Direct Instruction.   Critics say that direct instruction is limited to lower-level objectives, and that it is based on traditional teaching methods, ignores innovative models, and discourages students' independent thinking. Some educational psychologists claim that the direct instruction model tells teachers to "do what works" without grounding the suggestions in a theory of student learning. Other critics disagree, saying that direct instruction is based on a theory of student learning—but it is the *wrong* theory. Teachers break material into small segments, present each segment clearly, and reinforce or correct, thus *transmitting* accurate understandings from teacher to student. The student is seen as an "empty vessel" waiting to be filled with knowledge, rather than an

---

Focus on...

Behavioral Learning and Instruction

- What are the three parts of Mager's learning objectives?
- How does Gronlund's approach to creating objectives differ from Mager's?
- Under what conditions might mastery learning be effective?
- Describe Rosenshine's six teaching functions.
- When is direct teaching effective?

TABLE 9.2   The Hunter Mastery Teaching Program: Selected Principles

---

Get students set to learn.

■ Make the best use of the prime time at the beginning of the lesson.

■ Give students a review question or two to consider while you call the roll, pass out papers, or do other "housekeeping" chores. Follow up—listen to their answers, and correct if necessary.

■ Create an *anticipatory set* to capture the students' attention. This might be an advance organizer, an intriguing question, or a brief exercise. For example, at the beginning of a lesson on categories of plants you could ask, "How is pumpkin pie similar to cherry pie but different from sweet potato pie?" Answer: Pumpkins and cherries are both fruits, unlike sweet potatoes.

■ Communicate the lesson objectives (unless withholding this information for a while is part of your overall plan).

Provide information effectively.

■ Determine the basic information and organize it. Use this basic structure as scaffolding for the lesson.

■ Present information clearly and simply. Use familiar terms, examples, illustrations.

■ Model what you mean. If appropriate, demonstrate or use analogies—"If the basketball Ann is holding were the sun, how far away do you think I would have to hold this pea to represent Pluto . . . ?"

Check for understanding, and give guided practice.

■ Ask a question and have every student signal an answer—"Thumbs up if this statement is true, down if it's false."

■ Ask for a choral response: "Everyone, is this a dependent or an independent clause?"

■ Sample individual responses: "Everyone, think of an example of a closed system. Jon, what's your example?

Allow for independent practice.

■ Get students started right by doing the first few few questions together.

■ Make independent practice brief. Monitor responses, giving feedback quickly.

---

active constructor of knowledge (Anderson, 1989a; Berg & Clough, 1991; Davis, Maher, & Noddings, 1990). These criticisms of direct instruction echo the criticisms of behavioral learning theories.

But there is ample evidence that direct instruction and explanation can help students learn actively, not passively. For younger and less prepared learners, student-controlled learning without teacher direction and instruction can lead to systematic deficits in the students' knowledge. Without guidance, the understandings that students construct can be incomplete and misleading (Weinert & Helmke, 1995). Deep understanding and fluid performance—whether in dance or mathematical problem solving or reading—require models of expert performance and extensive practice with feedback (Anderson, Reder, & Simon, 1995). Guided and independent practice with feedback are at the heart of the direct instruction model.

Cognitive Models of Teaching

Many instructional models are consistent with information processing and cognitive theories of learning. These approaches are especially helpful for learning new concepts and relations among concepts. We will consider Jerome Bruner's discovery learning, David Ausubel's expository teaching, and Robert Gagné's Instructional Events Model.

Discovery Learning

Jerome Bruner's early research on thinking (Bruner, Goodnow, & Austin, 1956) stirred his interest in educational approaches that encourage the development of thinking. Bruner's work emphasized the importance of understanding the structure of a subject being studied, the need for active learning as the basis for true understanding, and the value of inductive reasoning in learning.

Structure and Discovery.   **Subject structure** refers to the fundamental ideas, relationships, or patterns of the field—the essential information. Because structure does not include specific facts or details about the subject, the essential structure of an idea can be represented simply as a diagram, set of principles, or formula. According to Bruner, learning will be more meaningful, useful, and memorable for students if they focus on understanding the structure of the subject being studied. For example, if you learned the concepts *figure, plane, simple, closed, quadrilateral, isosceles, scalene, equilateral,* and *right,* you would be on your way to understanding one aspect of geometry. But how do these terms relate to one another? If you can place the terms into a coding system such as the one in Figure 9.2, you will have a better understanding of the basic structure of this part of geometry.

A **coding system** is a hierarchy of related concepts. At the top of the coding system is the most general concept, in this case *plane, simple, closed figure.* More specific concepts are arranged under the general concept.

In order to grasp the structure of information, Bruner believes, students must be active—they must identify key principles for themselves rather than simply accepting teachers' explanations. He believes that teachers should provide problem situations stimulating students to question, explore, and experiment. This process has been called discovery learning. In **discovery learning,** the teacher presents examples and the students work with the examples until they discover the interrelationships—the subject's structure. Thus, Bruner believes that classroom learning should take place through **inductive reasoning,** that is, by using specific examples to formulate a general principle. For instance, if students are presented with enough examples of triangles and nontriangles, they will eventually discover what the basic properties of any triangle must be. Encouraging inductive thinking in this way is sometimes called the **eg-rule method,** from the Latin e.g., meaning "for example."

Discovery in Action.   An inductive approach requires **intuitive thinking** on the part of students. Bruner suggests that teachers can nurture this intuitive thinking by encouraging students to make guesses based on incomplete evidence and then to confirm or disprove the guesses systematically (Bruner, 1960).

Subject Structure According to Bruner, the fundamental framework of ideas.

Coding System A hierarchy of ideas or concepts.

Discovery Learning Bruner's approach, in which students work on their own to discover basic principles.

Inductive Reasoning Formulating general principles based on knowledge of examples and details.

Eg-Rule Method Teaching or learning by moving from specific examples to general rules.

Intuitive Thinking Making imaginative leaps to correct perceptions or workable solutions.

FIGURE 9.2

A Coding System for Triangles

Place the concept in a hierarchy so you know what concepts are above and possibly below.

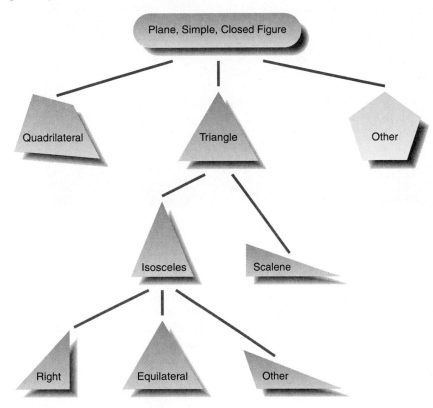

After learning about ocean currents and the shipping industry, for example, students might be shown old maps of three harbors and asked to guess which one became a major port. Then students could check their guesses through systematic research. Unfortunately, educational practices often discourage intuitive thinking by punishing wrong guesses and rewarding safe but uncreative answers.

Notice that in Bruner's discovery learning, a teacher organizes the class so that the students learn through their own active involvement. A distinction is usually made between discovery learning, in which the students work on their own to a very great extent, and **guided discovery,** in which the teacher provides some direction. Unguided discovery is appropriate for preschool children, but in a typical elementary or secondary classroom, unguided activities usually prove unmanageable and unproductive. For these situations, guided discovery is preferable. Students are presented with intriguing questions, baffling situations, or interesting problems: Why does the flame go out when we cover it with a jar? Why does this pencil seem to bend when you put it in water? What is the rule for grouping these words together? Instead of explaining how to solve the problem, the teacher provides the appropriate materials and encourages students to

Guided Discovery An adaptation of discovery learning, in which the teacher provides some direction.

Bruner's ideas about discovery learning emphasize the importance of active learning as a basis for true understanding.

make observations, form hypotheses, and test solutions. Feedback must be given at the optimal moment, when students can either use it to revise their approach or take it as encouragement to continue in the direction they've chosen. The Guidelines should help you apply Bruner's suggestions.

Guidelines

Applying Bruner's Ideas in the Classroom

Present both examples and nonexamples of the concepts you are teaching.

Examples

1. In teaching about mammals, include people, kangaroos, whales, cats, dolphins, and camels as examples, and chickens, fish, alligators, frogs, and penguins as nonexamples.
2. Ask students for additional examples and nonexamples.

Help students see connections among concepts.

Examples

1. Ask questions such as these: What else could you call this apple? (Fruit.) What do we do with fruit? (Eat.) What do we call things we eat? (Food.)
2. Use diagrams, outlines, and summaries to point out connections.

Pose a question and let students try to find the answer.

Examples

1. How could the human hand be improved?
2. What is the relation between the area of one tile and the area of the whole floor?

Encourage students to make intuitive guesses.

Examples

1. Instead of giving a word's definition, say, "Let's guess what it might mean by looking at the words around it."
2. Give students a map of ancient Greece and ask where they think the major cities were.
3. Don't comment after the first few guesses. Wait for several ideas before giving the answer.
4. Use guiding questions to focus students when their discovery has led them too far astray.

Discovery learning appears to have many advantages, but even Bruner believes that it is not appropriate in every situation. The Point/Counterpoint section on page 342 examines the pros and cons of this approach.

Expository Teaching/Reception Learning

David Ausubel's (1963, 1977) view of learning offers an interesting contrast to that of Bruner. According to Ausubel, people acquire knowledge primarily through reception rather than through discovery. Concepts, principles, and ideas are presented and understood, not discovered. As you saw in Chapter 7, the more organized and focused the presentation, the more thoroughly the person will learn.

Ausubel stresses what is known as **meaningful verbal learning**—verbal information, ideas, and relationships among ideas, taken together. Rote memorization is not considered meaningful learning, because material learned by rote is not connected with existing knowledge. Ausubel has proposed his **expository teaching** model to encourage meaningful rather than rote reception learning. (Here, exposition means *explanation,* or the setting forth of facts and ideas.) In this approach, teachers present materials in a carefully organized, sequenced, and somewhat finished form, and students thus receive the most usable material in the most efficient way. Ausubel does agree with Bruner that people learn by organizing new information into hierarchies or coding systems. Ausubel calls the general concept at the top of the system the *subsumer,* because all other concepts are subsumed under it, as in Figure 9.2. However, Ausubel believes that learning should progress, not inductively as Bruner recommends, but deductively: from the general to the specific, or from the rule or principle to examples. The **deductive reasoning** approach is sometimes called the **rule-eg method**.

Advance Organizers.   Optimal learning generally occurs when there is a potential fit between the student's schemas and the material to be learned. To make this fit more likely, a lesson following Ausubel's strategy always begins with an **advance organizer**. This is an introductory statement of a relationship or a high-level concept broad enough to encompass all the information that will follow.

The function of advance organizers is to provide scaffolding or support for the new information. You can also see the advance organizer as a kind of

Meaningful Verbal Learning Focused and organized relationships among ideas and verbal information.

Expository Teaching Ausubel's method—teachers present material in complete, organized form, moving from broadest to more specific concepts.

Deductive Reasoning Drawing conclusions by applying rules or principles; logically moving from a general rule or principle to a specific solution.

Rule-Eg Method Teaching or learning by moving from general principles to specific examples.

Advance Organizer Statement of inclusive concepts to introduce and sum up material that follows.

Is Discovery Learning Effective?

Most psychologists and educators agree that students must make sense of information in order to learn and remember it. Simply memorizing lists and facts leads to superficial understanding and rapid forgetting. When students struggle with perplexing problems, test possible solutions, and finally discover for themselves the fundamental structure of a key concept, they are more likely to understand and remember the information. But critics of discovery learning raise some important questions. Is discovery learning an effective method?

POINT Discovery learning matches cognitive development.

Educators favoring discovery learning note that this approach is consistent with the ways that people learn and develop. For example, Jerome Bruner (1966, 1971) identified three stages of cognitive growth, similar to the stages identified by Piaget. Bruner believes that children move from an *enactive* stage to an *iconic* stage and finally to a *symbolic* stage. In the enactive stage (similar to Piaget's sensorimotor stage), the child represents and understands the world through actions—to understand something is to manipulate it, taste it, throw it, break it and so on. At the iconic stage, the child represents the world in images—appearances dominate. This stage corresponds to Piaget's preoperational thinking, in

which the higher the water level, the more water there must be in the glass, because that's what appears to be true. At the final level, the child is able to use abstract ideas, symbols, language, and logic to understand and represent the world. Actions and images can still be used in thinking, but they do not dominate.

Discovery learning allows students to move through these three stages as they encounter new information. First the students manipulate and act on materials; then they form images as they note specific features and make observations; and finally they abstract general ideas and principles from these experiences and observations. Because they have experienced each stage of representation, Bruner believes, the students will have a better understanding of the topic. When students are motivated and really participate in the discovery project, discovery learning leads to superior learning (Strike, 1975).

COUNTERPOINT Discovery learning is impractical.

In theory, discovery learning seems ideal, but in practice there are problems. To be successful, discovery projects often require special materials and extensive preparations. And these preparations can't guarantee success. For example, a discovery lesson on the effects of light on plants takes many hours and often falls flat because the

plants grown in darkness and those grown in light don't always behave as they should— many factors other than light affect growth (Anderson & Smith, 1987).

In order to benefit from a discovery situation, students must have basic knowledge about the problem and must know how to apply problem-solving strategies. Without this knowledge and skill, they will flounder and grow frustrated. Instead of learning from the materials, they may simply play with them. The brightest students may make some discoveries, while the others lose interest or just wait passively for someone else to complete the project. Instead of benefiting from a teacher's organized explanation, these "nondiscovering" students may get an inadequate explanation from a fellow student who can't quite communicate his or her discoveries. Everyone may grow frustrated as the teacher seems to withhold the solutions and explanations needed.

Critics believe that discovery learning is so inefficient and so difficult to organize successfully that other methods are preferable. This seems especially true for lower-ability students. Discovery methods may make too many demands on these students, because they lack the background knowledge and problem-solving skills needed to benefit. Some research has shown that discovery methods are ineffective and even detrimental for lower-ability students (Corno & Snow, 1986; Slavin, Karweit, & Madden, 1989).

conceptual bridge between new material and students' current knowledge (Faw & Waller, 1976). Textbooks often contain advance organizers—the chapter overviews in this book are examples. The organizers can serve three purposes: they direct your attention to what is important in the coming material; they highlight relationships among ideas that will be presented; and they remind you of relevant information you already have.

In general, advance organizers fall into one of two categories, *comparative* and *expository* (Joyce & Weil, 1996; Mayer, 1979, 1984). Each fulfills an important function. Comparative organizers *activate* (bring into working memory) already existing schemas. They remind you of what you already know, but may not realize is relevant. A comparative advance organizer for a history lesson on revolutions might be a statement that contrasts military uprisings with the physical and social changes involved in the Industrial Revolution; you could also compare the common aspects of the French, English, Mexican, Russian, Iranian, and American revolutions (Salomon & Perkins, 1989).

In contrast, *expository organizers* provide *new* knowledge that students will need to understand the upcoming information. An expository organizer is thus a statement of a subsumer, a definition of a general concept. In an English class, you might begin a large thematic unit on rites of passage in literature with a very broad statement of the theme and why it has been so central in literature—something like, "A central character coming of age must learn to know himself or herself, often makes some kind of journey of self-discovery, and must decide what in the society is to be accepted and what rejected."

The general conclusion of research on advance organizers is that they do help students learn, especially when the material to be learned is quite unfamiliar, complex, or difficult (Corkill, 1992; Mayer, 1984; Shuell, 1981b). Of course, the effects of advance organizers depend on how good they are and how students actually use them. First, to be effective, the organizer must be processed and understood by the students. This was demonstrated dramatically in a study by Dinnel and Glover (1985). They found that instructing students to paraphrase an advance organizer—which, of course, requires them to understand its meaning—increased the effectiveness of the organizer. Second, the organizer must really be an organizer: It must indicate relations among the basic concepts and terms that will be used. In other words, a true organizer isn't just a statement of historical or background information. No amount of student processing can make a bad organizer more effective. Concrete models, diagrams, or analogies seem to be especially good organizers (Mayer 1983a, 1984).

Ausubel's principles of expository teaching and reception learning emphasize the concepts, principles, and ideas as presented by the teacher and then understood by students.

Steps in an Expository Lesson.   After presenting an advance organizer, the next step in a lesson using Ausubel's approach is to present content in terms of basic similarities and differences, using specific examples. To learn any new material, students must see not only the similarities between the material presented and what they already know but also the differences so that interference—the confusion of old and new material—can be avoided.

It is often helpful in an expository lesson to ask students to supply similarities and differences themselves. In a grammar lesson, you might ask, "What are the differences between the way commas and semicolons are used?" Or suppose in teaching the coming-of-age theme in literature, you choose *The Diary of Anne Frank* and *The Adventures of Huckleberry Finn* as the basic material for the

FIGURE 9.3

Phases of Expository Teaching

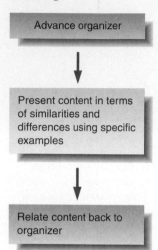

unit. As the students read the first book, you might ask them to compare the central character's growth, state of mind, and position in society with characters from other novels, plays, and films. When the class moves on to the second book, you can start by asking students to compare Anne Frank's inner journey with Huck Finn's trip down the Mississippi. As comparisons are made, whether within a single class lesson or during an entire unit, it is useful to underscore the goal of the lesson and occasionally to repeat the advance organizer (with amendments and elaborations).

Along with the comparisons, specific examples must come into play. You can see that the best way to point out similarities and differences is with examples. There must be specific examples of comma and semicolon usage; the specific elements of Huck Finn's and Anne Frank's dilemmas must be clear. Finally, when all the material has been presented, ask students to discuss how the examples can be used to expand on the original advance organizer. The phases of expository teaching are summarized in Figure 9.3.

Making the Most of Expository Teaching.   As with any teaching approach, expository teaching works better in some situations than in others. First, this approach is most appropriate when you want to teach about the relationships among several concepts. Students must have some knowledge of the actual concepts first. What if students in a history class had never heard of the French Revolution or the Industrial Revolution? How could they compare these specific events to get a better understanding of elements that characterize different kinds of revolutions? They might resort to memorizing definitions and lists, such as "the five characteristics of a revolution are. . . . " Even in a lesson on what poetry is, students who don't have a basic understanding of the concept of literature—why people write and why they read—will be at a loss.

Another consideration with expository teaching is the age of the students. This approach requires students to manipulate ideas mentally, even if the ideas are simple and based on physical realities such as rocks and minerals. This means that expository teaching is more developmentally appropriate for students at or above later elementary school, that is, around the fifth or sixth grade (Luiten, Ames, & Ackerson, 1980). The Guidelines should help you follow the main steps in expository teaching.

Guidelines

Applying Ausubel's Ideas in the Classroom

Use advance organizers.

Examples

1. English: Shakespeare used the social ideas of his time as a framework for his plays—*Julius Caesar, Hamlet,* and *Macbeth* dealt with concepts of natural order, a nation as the human body, etc.

2. Social studies: Geography dictates economy in preindustrialized regions or nations.

3. History: Important concepts during the Renaissance were symmetry, admiration of the classical world, the centrality of the human mind.

Use a number of examples.

Examples

1. In mathematics class, ask students to point out all the examples of right angles that they can find in the room.
2. In teaching about islands and peninsulas, use maps, slides, models, postcards.

Focus on both similarities and differences.

Examples

1. In a history class, ask students to list the ways in which the North and South were alike and different before the Civil War.
2. In a biology class, ask students how they would transform spiders into insects or an amphibian into a reptile.

The Instructional Events Model

Robert Gagné (1977; Gagné & Driscoll, 1988) has proposed a well-developed theory of instruction based on the information processing model of learning described in Chapter 7. He is less concerned about whether students learn by discovery or by reception and is more interested in the quality, permanence, and usefulness of their learning. Table 9.3 shows Gagné's phases of learning and the "instructional events" associated with each phase.

As you can see, in the instructional events model the first step in learning, and the first challenge for the teacher, is to gain the students' attention. The next step is to set an expectancy for learning by letting the students know the

TABLE 9.3 Gagné's Phases of Learning and the Instructional Events That Support Learning at Each Phase

Description	Learning Phase	Instructional Event
Preparation for learning	1. Attention; alertness	Gain learner's attention through unusual event, question, or change of stimulus
	2. Expectancy	Inform the learner of the objective; activate motivation
	3. Retrieval (of relevant information and/or skills) to working memory	Stimulate recall of prior knowledge
Acquisition and performance	4. Selective perception of stimulus features	Present material; highlight distinctive features
	5. Encoding; storage in LTM	Provide learning guidance
	6. Retrieval and responding	Elicit performance
	7. Reinforcement	Provide informative feedback
Transfer of learning	8. Cueing retrieval	Assess performance
	9. Generalizing	

Source: Adapted from *Learning and instruction: Theory into practice,* 3/e, by M. E. Gredler, p. 125. © 1997. Reprinted by permission of Prentice Hall, Inc. Saddle River, NJ.

goals of the lesson and perhaps arousing their curiosity or providing other motivation for learning (we will talk more about this in the next two chapters). When the students are paying attention and have the right expectations, they need to be reminded of what they already know that is related to the material to be learned. With this prior knowledge in their working memories, they are ready to make connections between new and old information. Now it is time to present the new material, highlighting the important aspects or key features. At this point the students should have the new material in their short-term or working memories, so they are ready to process the information and move it to long-term memory. The teacher's role now is to provide learning guidance, such as explanations and examples or a guided-discovery exercise.

But learning does not stop here. In Gagné's model, students have to demonstrate, to the teacher and to themselves, that they really understand the material. The students must respond in some way. These responses allow the teacher to check the students' understanding and provide reinforcement or corrections or both. Finally, to ensure that they can retrieve and apply their new knowledge readily, students should practice in a variety of situations. Reviews at the end of the lesson, week, and unit encourage transfer by extending practice over time. You can see that Gagné's model shares some features of direct instruction.

Constructivist and Situated Learning

As you saw in Chapter 7, constructivist perspectives on learning and teaching are increasingly influential today. Voices in favor of a **constructivist approach** come not only from the field of psychology but also from other arenas such as philosophy, anthropology, science and mathematics education, and educational technology. Constructivist perspectives on learning have definite implications for teaching. "While there are several interpretations of what [constructivist] theory means, most agree that it involves a dramatic change in the focus of teaching, putting the students' own efforts to understand at the center of the educational enterprise" (Prawat, 1992, p. 357).

Elements of Constructivist Perspectives

Many of the ideas we already have considered—including discussions of Piaget and Vygotsky, the constructive nature of memory, problem solving, creativity, thinking, and discovery learning—are consistent with constructivist perspectives. Even though there is no single constructivist theory, many constructivist approaches recommend:

- complex, challenging learning environments and authentic tasks;
- social negotiation and shared responsibility as a part of learning;
- multiple representations of content;
- understanding that knowledge is constructed;
- student-centered instruction (Driscoll, 1994; Marshall, 1992).

Before we discuss particular approaches, let's look more closely at these dimensions of constructivist teaching.

Constructivist Approach View that emphasizes the active role of the learner in building understanding and making sense of information.

Constructivist approaches may involve, among other things, authentic or real-life tasks, social negotiation, and shared responsibility as part of learning.

Complex Learning Environments and Authentic Tasks.   Constructivists believe that students should not be given stripped down, simplified problems and basic skills drills, but instead should deal with complex situations and "fuzzy," ill-structured problems. The world beyond school presents few simplified problems or step-by-step directions, so schools should be sure that *every* student has experience solving complex problems. These problems should be embedded in authentic tasks and activities, the kinds of situations that students will face as they apply what they are learning to real-world problems (J. S. Brown, 1990; Needles & Knapp, 1994; Resnick, 1987). Students may need support as they work on these complex problems, helping them find resources, keeping track of their progress, breaking larger problems down into smaller ones, and so on. This aspect of constructivist approaches is consistent with situated learning in emphasizing learning in *situations* where the learning will be applied.

Social Negotiation.   Many constructivists share Vygotsky's belief that higher mental processes develop through social interaction, so collaboration in learning is valued. The Language Development and Hypermedia Group (1992) suggests that a major goal of teaching is to develop students' abilities to establish and defend their own positions while respecting the positions of others. To accomplish this exchange, students must talk and listen to each other.

Multiple Representations of Content.   When students encounter only one model, one analogy, one way of understanding complex content, they often oversimplify as they try to apply that one approach to every situation. I saw this happen in my educational psychology class when six students were presenting an example of guided discovery learning. The students' presentation was a near copy of a guided discovery demonstration I had given earlier in the semester, but with some major misconceptions. My students knew only one way

Complex Learning Environments Problems and learning situations that mimic the ill-structured nature of real life.

Social Negotiation Aspect of learning process that relies on collaboration with others and respect for different perspectives.

Multiple Representations of Content Considering problems using various analogies, examples, and metaphors.

to represent discovery learning. Resources for the class should have provided multiple representations of guided discovery using different analogies, examples, and metaphors. We'll do better next semester.

Richard Spiro and his colleagues (1991) suggest that "revisiting the same material, at different times, in rearranged contexts, for different purposes, and from different conceptual perspectives is essential for attaining the goals of advanced knowledge acquisition" (p. 28). This idea is not entirely new. Years ago Jerome Bruner (1966) described the advantages of a *spiral curriculum*. This is a structure for teaching that introduces the fundamental structure of all subjects —the "big ideas"—early in the school years, then revisits the subjects in more and more complex forms over time.

Understanding the Knowledge Construction Process. Throughout this text you have encountered the concept of metacognition—knowledge of your own mental processes and how you learn. Constructivist approaches often go beyond helping students understand their own metacognitive processes to making them aware of their own role in constructing knowledge (Cunningham, 1992). The assumptions we make, our beliefs, and experiences shape what each of us comes to "know" about the world. Different assumptions and different experiences lead to different knowledge. Constructivists stress the importance of understanding the knowledge construction process so that students will be aware of the influences that shape their thinking; thus they will be able to choose, develop, and defend positions in a self-critical way while respecting the positions of others.

The last characteristic of constructivist teaching listed by Driscoll (1994) is *student-centered instruction*. Because instruction is the focus of this chapter, we will spend several pages discussing examples of student-centered instruction that are consistent with the other dimensions of constructivist teaching as well.

Inquiry and Problem-Based Learning

John Dewey described the basic **inquiry learning** format in 1910. There have been many adaptations of this strategy, but the form usually includes the elements listed next (Pasch, Sparks-Langer, Gardner, Starko, & Moody, 1991).

The teacher presents a puzzling event, question, or problem. The students:

- formulate hypotheses to explain the event or solve the problem;
- collect data to test the hypotheses;
- draw conclusions; and
- reflect on the original problem and the thinking processes needed to solve it.

At times, teachers present a problem and students ask yes/no questions to gather data and test hypotheses. This allows the teacher to monitor students' thinking and guide the process. Here is an example:

1. Teacher presents discrepant event (after clarifying ground rules). The teacher blows softly across the top of an 8-½" × 11" sheet of paper, and the paper rises. She tells students to figure out why it rises.

2. Students ask questions to gather more information and to isolate relevant variables. Teacher answers only "yes" or "no." Students ask if temperature is important (no). They ask if the paper is of a special kind (no). They ask if air pressure has anything to do with the paper rising (yes). Questions continue.

Inquiry Learning Approach in which the teacher presents a puzzling situation and students solve the problem by gathering data and testing their conclusions.

3. Students test causal relationships. In this case, they ask if the nature of the air on top causes the paper to rise (yes). They ask if the fast movement of the air results in less pressure on the top (yes). Then they test out the rule with other materials—for example, thin plastic.

4. Students form a generalization (principle): "If the air on the top moves faster than the air on the bottom of a surface, then the air pressure on top is lessened, and the object rises." Later lessons expand students' understanding of the principles and physical laws through further experiments.

5. The teacher leads students in a discussion of their thinking processes. What were the important variables? How did you put the causes and effects together? and so on. (Pasch et al., 1991, pp. 188–189)

Inquiry teaching allows students to learn content and process at the same time (Kindsvatter, Wilen, & Ishler, 1988). In the example above, students learned about the effects of air pressure and how airplanes fly. In addition, they learned the inquiry process itself—how to solve problems, evaluate solutions, and think critically.

The inquiry approach has much in common with guided discovery learning and shares its advantages and disadvantages. Like discovery learning, inquiry methods require great preparation, organization, and monitoring to be sure everyone is engaged and challenged.

Group Work and Cooperation in Learning

The terms "group learning" and "cooperative learning" often are used as if they meant the same thing. Actually, group work is simply several students working together—they may or may not be cooperating. Angela O'Donnell and Jim O'Kelly, colleagues of mine at Rutgers University, describe a teacher who claimed to be using "cooperative learning" by asking students to work in pairs on a paper, each writing one part. Unfortunately, the teacher allowed no time to work together and provided no guidance or preparation in cooperative social skills. Students got a grade for their individual part and a group grade for the whole project. One student received an A for his part, but a C for the group project because his partner earned an F—he never turned in any work. So one student was punished with a C for a situation he could not control while the other was given a C for doing no work at all. This was not cooperative learning—it was hardly even a group project (O'Donnell & O'Kelly, 1994).

Working in Groups.   Many activities can be completed in groups. For example, students can work together in conducting local surveys. How do people feel about the plan to build a new mall that will bring more shopping and more traffic? Would the community support or oppose the building of a nuclear power plant?

Judy Pitts (1992) describes a lesson about how to do library research that has a group format. The project for each group is to educate the class about a different country. Students have to decide what information to present and how to make it interesting for their classmates. In the library, each group member is responsible for mastering a particular resource and teaching other group members, if the need arises (this is similar to the Jigsaw format described below). Students help each other to use the actual resources—the *Readers' Guide, News-Bank,* reference sets, almanacs, and so on.

In this class, students confront complex, real-life problems, not simplified worksheets. They learn by doing and by teaching others. The students must take positions and argue for them while being open to the ideas of others. They may encounter different representations of the same information—graphs, databases, maps, interviews, or encyclopedia articles—and have to integrate information from different sources. So this lesson exemplifies many of the characteristics of constructivist approaches. But the most important characteristic of the lesson is that students have a good chance of learning how to do library research.

Many of the most ordinary assignments can be enhanced by working in groups. If students must learn 10 new definitions in a biology class, why not let students divide up the terms and definitions and teach one another? Be sure, however, that everyone in the group can handle the task. Sometimes a group effort ends with one or two students doing the work of the entire group.

Group work can be useful, but true **cooperative learning** requires much more than simply putting students in groups, as you will see in the next few pages.

Beyond Groups to Cooperation.   Collaboration and cooperative learning have a long history in American education. In the early 1900s, John Dewey criticized the use of competition in education and encouraged educators to structure schools as democratic learning communities. These ideas fell from favor in the 1940s and 1950s, replaced by a resurgence of competition. In the 1960s, there was a swing back to individualized and cooperative learning structures, stimulated in part by concern for civil rights and interracial relations (Webb & Palincsar, 1996).

Today, interest in collaboration and cooperative learning is fueled by evolving constructivist perspectives on learning. As you saw above, two characteristics of constructivist teaching are *complex, real-life learning environments* and *social interaction*. As educators focus on learning in real contexts, "there is a heightened interest in situations where elaboration, interpretation, explanation, and argumentation are integral to the activity of the group and where learning is supported by other individuals" (Webb & Palincsar, 1996, p. 844).

Different constructivist approaches favor cooperative learning for different reasons. Information processing (exogenous constructivist) theorists point to the value of group discussion in helping participants rehearse, elaborate, and expand their knowledge. As group members question and explain, they have to organize their knowledge, make connections, and review—all processes that support information processing and memory. Advocates of a Piagetian perspective (endogenous constructivists) suggest that the interactions in groups can create the cognitive conflict and disequilibrium that lead an individual to question his or her understanding and try out new ideas—or, as Piaget (1985) said, "to go beyond his current state and strike out in new directions" (p. 10). Constructivists who favor a dialectical or Vygotskian theory of learning and development suggest that social interaction is important for learning because higher mental functions such as reasoning, comprehension, and critical thinking originate in social interactions and are then internalized by individuals. Children can accomplish mental tasks with social support before they can do them alone. Thus cooperative learning provides the social support and scaffolding that students need to move learning forward. Table 9.4 summarizes the functions of cooperative learning from different constructivist perspectives, and describes some of the elements of each kind of group.

Cooperative Learning Arrangement in which students work in mixed-ability groups and are responsible for each other's learning.

TABLE 9.4	Different Forms of Cooperative Learning for Different Purposes		

Different forms of cooperative learning fit different purposes, need different structures, and have their own potential problems and possible solutions.

Considerations	Elaboration	Piagetian	Vygotskian
Group size	Small (2–4)	Small	Dyads
Group composition	Heterogeneous/ homogeneous	Heterogeneous	Heterogeneous
Tasks	Rehearsal/ integrative	Exploratory	Skills
Teacher role	Facilitator	Facilitator	Model/guide
Potential problems	Poor help-giving	Inactive	Poor help-giving
	Unequal participation	No cognitive conflict	Providing adequate time/dialogue
Averting problems	Direct instruction in help-giving	Structuring controversy	Direct instruction in help-giving
	Modeling help-giving		Modeling help-giving
	Scripting interaction		

Source: From A. M. O'Donnell and J. O'Kelly, "Learning from peers: Beyond the rhetoric of positive results." *Educational Psychology Review, 6,* 1994, p. 327. Reprinted by permission of Plenum Publishing Corporation.

To benefit from the dimensions of cooperative learning listed in Table 9.4, groups must *be cooperative*—all members must participate. But, as any teacher or parent knows, cooperation is not automatic when students are put into groups. The next sections examine how teachers can encourage true cooperation.

Elements of Cooperative Learning Groups. David and Roger Johnston (1994) list five elements that define true cooperative learning groups:

- Face-to-face interaction
- Positive interdependence
- Individual accountability
- Collaborative skills
- Group processing

Students *interact face to face* and close together, not across the room. Group members experience *positive interdependence*—they need each other for support, explanations, and guidance. Even though they work together and help each other, members of the group must ultimately demonstrate learning on their own—they are held *individually accountable* for learning. *Collaborative skills* are necessary for effective group functioning. Often these skills, such as giving constructive feedback, reaching consensus, and involving every member, must be taught and practiced before the groups tackle a learning task. Finally, members monitor *group processes* and relationships to make sure the group is working effectively and to learn about the dynamics of groups.

Setting Up Cooperative Groups.   How large should a cooperative group be? The answer depends on your learning goals. If the purpose is for the group members to review, rehearse information, or practice, 4 to 5 or 6 students is about the right size. But if the goal is to encourage each student to participate in discussions, problem solving, or computer learning, then groups of 2 to 4 members work best. Also, in setting up cooperative groups, it often makes sense to balance the number of boys and girls. Some research indicates that when there are just a few girls in a group, they tend to be left out of the discussions unless they are the most able or assertive members. By contrast, when there are only one or two boys in the group, they tend to dominate and be "interviewed" by the girls unless these boys are less able than the girls or very shy. In general, for very shy and introverted students, individual learning may be a better approach (O'Donnell & O'Kelly, 1994; Webb, 1985; Webb & Palincsar, 1996). Whatever the case, teachers must monitor groups to make sure everyone is contributing and learning.

In practice, the effects of learning in a group vary, depending on what actually happens in the group and who is in it. If only a few people take responsibility for the work, these people will learn, but the nonparticipating members probably will not. Students who ask questions, get answers, and attempt explanations are more likely to learn than students whose questions go unasked or unanswered. In fact, there is evidence that the more a student provides elaborated, thoughtful explanations to other students in a group, the more the *explainer* learns. Giving good explanations appears to be even more important for learning than receiving explanations (Webb & Palincsar, 1996). In order to explain, you have to organize the information, put it into your own words, think of examples and analogies (which connect the information to things you already know), and test your understanding by answering questions. These are excellent learning strategies (King, 1990; O'Donnell & O'Kelly, 1994).

Some teachers assign roles to students to encourage cooperation and full participation. Several roles are described in Table 9.5. If you use roles, be sure that the roles support learning. In groups that focus on practice, review, or mastery of basic skills, roles should support persistence, encouragement, and participation. In groups that focus on higher-order problem solving or complex learning, roles should encourage thoughtful discussion, sharing of explanations and insights, probing, brainstorming, and creativity. Make sure that you don't communicate to students that the major purpose of the groups is simply to do the procedures—the roles. Roles are supports for learning, not ends in themselves (Woolfolk Hoy & Tschannen-Moran, in press).

Jigsaw.   An early format for cooperative learning emphasizes high interdependence. Each group member is given part of the material to be learned by the whole group and becomes an "expert" on his or her piece. Students have to teach each other, so everyone's contribution is important. A more recent version, Jigsaw II, adds expert meetings where the students who have the same material confer to make sure they understand their assigned part and then plan ways to teach the information to their group members. Next, students return to their groups, bringing their expertise to the learning sessions. In the end, students take an individual test covering all the material and earn points for their learning team score. Teams can work for rewards or simply for recognition (Slavin, 1995).

TABLE 9.5 Possible Student Roles in Cooperative Learning Groups	

Depending on the purpose of the group and the age of the participants, having these assigned roles might help students cooperate and learn. Of course, students may have to be taught how to enact each role effectively, and roles should be rotated so students can participate in different aspects of group learning.

Role	Description
Encourager	Encourages reluctant or shy students to participate
Praiser/Cheerleader	Shows appreciation of other's contributions and recognizes accomplishments
Gate Keeper	Equalizes participation and makes sure no one dominates
Coach	Helps with the academic content, explains concepts
Question Commander	Makes sure all students' questions are asked and answered
Checker	Checks the group's understanding
Taskmaster	Keeps the group on task
Recorder	Writes down ideas, decisions and plans
Reflector	Keeps group aware of progress (or lack of progress)
Quiet Captain	Monitors noise level
Materials Monitor	Picks up and returns materials

Source: Adapted from Spencer Kagan, *Cooperative learning.* San Clemente, CA: Kagan Cooperative Learning, 1994, 1 (800) WEE CO-OP.

Reciprocal Questioning.   Another cooperative approach can be used with a wide range of ages and subjects. **Reciprocal questioning** requires no special materials or testing procedures. After a lesson or presentation by the teacher, students work in pairs or triads to ask and answer questions about the material (King, 1990, 1994). The teacher provides question stems (see Figure 9.4 on page 354), then students are taught how to develop specific questions on the lesson material using the generic question stems. The students create questions, then take turns asking and answering. This process has proved more effective than traditional discussion groups because it seems to encourage deeper thinking about the material. Questions like those on the "Prompt Cards" in Figure 9.4, which encourage students to make connections between the lesson and previous knowledge or experience, seems to be the most helpful.

Scripted Cooperation.   Donald Dansereau and his colleagues have developed a method for learning in pairs called *scripted cooperation.* Students work together on almost any task—reading a selection of text, solving math problems, editing writing drafts. For example, in reading, both partners read a passage, then one student gives an oral summary The other partner comments on the summary, noting omissions or errors. Next, the partners work together to elaborate on the information—create associations, images, mnemonics, ties to previous

Reciprocal Questioning Approach where groups of two or three students ask and answer each other's questions after a lesson or presentation.

FIGURE 9.4

Reciprocal Questioning Prompt Cards to Guide Dialogue

After studying material or participating in a lesson, pairs of students use the "Prompt Cards" below to develop questions and then share answers.

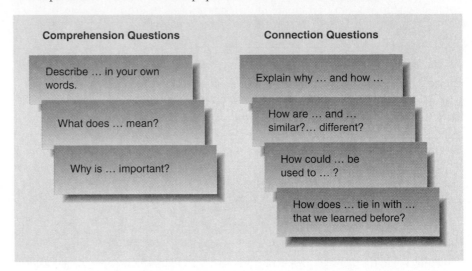

Source: Adapted from Anita King, "Guiding knowledge construction in the classroom: Effects of teaching children how to question and how to explain." *American Educational Research Journal, 31,* p. 345. Copyright 1994 by the American Educational Research Association. Reprinted by permission of the publisher.

work, examples, analogies, and so on. The partners switch roles of summarizer and listener for the next section of the reading, then continue to take turns until they finish the assignment (Dansereau, 1985, O'Donnell & O'Kelly, 1994).

There are many other forms of cooperative learning. In Chapter 11 you will find methods that emphasize increasing motivation through teamwork and interteam competition. Kagan (1994) has written extensively on the subject and developed many formats.

What Can Go Wrong: Misuses of Group Learning. Without careful planning and monitoring by the teacher, group interactions can hinder learning and reduce rather than improve social relations in classes. For example, if there is pressure in a group for conformity—perhaps because rewards are being misused or one student dominates the others—interactions can be unproductive and unreflective. Misconceptions might be reinforced or the worst, not the best, ideas may be combined to construct a superficial understanding (Battistich, Solomon, & Delucci, 1993). Also, the ideas of low status students may be ignored or even ridiculed while the contributions of high status students are accepted and reinforced, regardless of the merit of either set of ideas (Cohen, 1986). Mary Mc-Caslin and Tom Good (1996) list several other disadvantages of group learning:

- Students often value the process or procedures over the learning. Speed and finishing take precedence over thoughtfulness and learning.
- Rather than challenging and correcting misconceptions, students support and reinforce misunderstandings.
- Socializing and interpersonal relationships may take precedence over learning.

- Students may simply shift dependency from the teacher to the "expert" in the group—learning is still passive and what is learned can be wrong.
- Status differences may be increased rather than decreased. Some students learn to "loaf" because the group progresses with or without their contributions. Others are even more convinced that they are helpless to understand without the support of the group.

Another constructivist approach that relies heavily on interaction is instructional conversations.

Instructional Conversations

One implication of Vygotsky's theory of cognitive development is that important learning and understanding require interaction and conversation. Students need to grapple with problems in their zone of proximal development, and they need the scaffolding provided by interaction with a teacher or other students. Instructional conversations provide these opportunities. **Instructional conversations** are *instructional* because they are designed to promote learning, but they are *conversations,* not lectures or traditional discussions.

In instructional conversations, the teacher's goal is to keep everyone engaged in a substantive discussion. The teacher is a guide, helping students construct their own understandings (Putnam & Borko, in press). Table 9.6 on page 356 summarizes the elements of productive instructional conversations.

Cognitive Apprenticeships

Over the centuries, apprenticeships have proved to be an effective form of education. By working alongside a master and perhaps other apprentices, young people have learned many skills, trades, and crafts. Why are they so effective? Howard Gardner (1991) suggests that apprenticeships are rich in information because the master knows a great deal about the subject. Working with more knowledgeable guides provides models, demonstrations, and corrections, as well as a personal bond that is motivating. The performances required of the learner are real and important and grow more complex as the learner becomes more competent (Collins, Brown, & Holum, 1991; Collins, Brown, & Newman, 1989).

Allan Collins and his colleagues (1989) suggest that knowledge and skills learned in school have become too separated from their use in the world beyond school. To correct this imbalance, some educators recommend that schools adopt many of the features of apprenticeships. But rather than learning to sculpt or dance or build a cabinet, apprenticeships in school would focus on cognitive objectives such as reading comprehension or writing or mathematical problem solving. There are many cognitive apprenticeship models, but most share six features:

- Students observe an expert (usually the teacher) *model* the performance.
- Students get external support through *coaching* or tutoring (including hints, feedback, models, reminders).
- Conceptual *scaffolding* is provided and then gradually faded as the student becomes more competent and proficient.

> **Focus on...**
>
> ### Constructivist and Situated Learning
>
> - What are four common elements in most constructivist views of learning?
> - Give an example of inquiry learning.
> - Describe five elements that define true cooperative learning.
> - Compare cooperative learning and instructions conversations.
> - Describe six features that most cognitive apprenticeship approaches share.

Instructional Conversation Situation in which students learn through interactions with teachers and/or other students

- Students continually *articulate* their knowledge—putting into words their understanding of the processes and content being learned.
- Students *reflect* on their progress, comparing their problem solving to an expert's performance and to their own earlier performances.
- Students are required to *explore* new ways to apply what they are learning—ways that they have not practiced at the master's side.

As students learn, they are challenged to master more complex concepts and skills and to perform them in many different settings (Roth & Bowen, 1995; Shuell, 1996).

TABLE 9.6   Elements of the Instructional Conversation

Good instructional conversations must have elements of both instruction and conversation.

Instructional

1. *Thematic focus.* Teacher selects a theme on which to focus the discussion and has a general plan for how the theme will unfold, including how to "chunk" the text to permit optimal exploration of the theme.
2. *Activation and use of background knowledge.* Teacher either "hooks into" or provides students with pertinent background knowledge necessary for understanding a text, weaving the information into the discussion.
3. *Direct teaching.* When necessary, teacher provides direct teaching of a skill or concept.
4. *Promotion of more complex language and expression.* Teacher elicits more extended student contributions by using a variety of elicitation techniques: invitations to expand, questions, restatements, and pauses.
5. *Promotion of bases for statements or positions.* Teacher promotes students' use of text, pictures, and reasoning to support an argument or position, by gently probing: "What makes you think that?" or "Show us where it says _____."

Conversational

6. *Fewer "known-answer" questions.* Much of the discussion centers on questions for which there might be more than one correct answer.
7. *Responsiveness to student contributions.* While having an initial plan and maintaining the focus and coherence of the discussion, teacher is also responsive to students' statements and the opportunities they provide.
8. *Connected discourse.* The discussion is characterized by multiple, interactive, connected turns; succeeding utterances build on and extend previous ones.
9. *Challenging, but non-threatening, atmosphere.* Teacher creates a challenging atmosphere that is balanced by a positive affective climate. Teacher is more collaborator than evaluator and students are challenged to negotiate and construct the meaning of the text.
10. *General participation, including self-selected turns.* Teacher does not hold exclusive right to determine who talks; students are encouraged to volunteer or otherwise influence the selection of speaking turns.

Source: From Claude Goldenberg (1991). *Instructional Conversations and Their Classroom Application*, p. 7. Santa Cruz, CA and Washington, DC: National Center for Research on Cultural Diversity and Second Language Learning. Reprinted by permission.

How can teaching provide **cognitive apprenticeships?** In the Key School, an inner-city public elementary school in Indianapolis, Indiana, students of different ages work side by side for part of every day on a "pod" designed to have many of the qualities of an apprenticeship. The pods might focus on a craft or a discipline. Examples include gardening, architecture, and "making money." Many levels of expertise are evident in the students of different ages, so students can move at a comfortable pace, but still have the model of a master available. Community volunteers, including many parents, visit to demonstrate a skill that is related to the pod topic.

Another successful example of cognitive apprenticeships is the reciprocal teaching approach described later in this chapter.

Cognitive and Constructivist Approaches to Reading, Mathematics, and Science

In the last decade, psychologists have made great progress understanding how students learn different subjects (Mayer, 1992). Based on these findings, many approaches have been developed to teach reading, writing, science, mathematics, social studies, and all the other subjects. We will look at a few instructional models that are based on the explanations of learning discussed in this chapter.

Learning to Read and Write

For years, educators have debated whether students should be taught to read and write through code-based (phonics, skills) approaches that relate letters to sounds and sounds to words or through meaning-based (whole-language, literature-based, emergent literacy) approaches that do not dissect words and sentences into pieces, but instead focus on the meaning of the text (Goodman, 1986; Smith, 1994; Stahl & Miller, 1989; Symons, Woloshyn, & Pressley, 1994; Vellutino, 1991).

Whole Language. Advocates of whole-language approaches believe that learning to read is a natural process, very much like mastering your native language. Reading is a kind of guessing game in which students sample words and make predictions and guesses about meaning based on the context of other words in the passage and on their prior knowledge. Thus, words should not be presented out of context, and "sounding out" words and "breaking whole (natural) language into bite-size abstract little pieces" should be avoided (Goodman, 1986, p. 7). Rather, children should be immersed in a print-rich environment, surrounded by books worth reading and adults who read—to the children and for themselves.

Within this **whole-language perspective,** teaching and learning are seen as reciprocal and collaborative. The teacher becomes an astute observer of students, noticing what support or resources they need in order to learn. Teacher and students together make decisions about curriculum. When students write, they write for an audience; their goal is to communicate effectively. Writing is a relevant and meaningful activity. Vygotsky (1978) recognized the importance of

Cognitive Apprenticeship A relationship in which a less experienced learner acquires knowledge and skills under the guidance of an expert.

Whole-Language Perspective A philosophical approach to teaching and learning that stresses learning through authentic, real-life tasks. Emphasizes using language to learn, integrating learning across skills and subjects, and respecting the language abilities of student and teacher.

authentic writing tasks: "[W]riting should be incorporated into a task that is necessary and relevant for life. Only then can we be certain that it will develop not as a matter of hand and finger habits but as a really new and complex form of speech" (p. 118). David Pearson (1989) makes a similar point: "[We] should ask students to read and write for real reasons (the kind real people in the real world have) rather than fake reasons we give them in school. School is too school-like" (p. 235).

Integrated Curriculum.   The advocates of whole language insist that the curriculum should be integrated. There is no reason to work on spelling skills, then listening skills, then writing skills, and then social studies or science. All these abilities can be developed together if students work to solve authentic problems. For example, one teacher capitalized on current affairs to encourage student reading, writing, and social studies problem solving:

> Cathie's elementary class learned about the Alaskan oil spill. She brought a newspaper article to class that sequenced in logbook fashion the events of the oil spill in Prince William Sound. To prepare her students to understand the article, she had her students participate in several background-building experiences. First, they used a world map, an encyclopedia, and library books to gather and share relevant information. Next, she simulated an oil spill by coating an object with oil. By then, the class was eager to read the article. (Espe, Worner, & Hotkevich, 1990, p. 45)

After they read and discussed the newspaper article, the teacher asked the class to imagine how the problem might have been prevented. Students had to explain and support their proposed solutions. The next week the students read another newspaper article about how people in their state were helping with the cleanup efforts in Alaska. The teacher asked if the students wanted to help, and they replied with an enthusiastic "Yes!" The students designed posters and made speeches requesting donations of clean towels to be used to clean the oil-soaked animals in Prince William Sound. The class sent four large bags of towels to Alaska to help in the cleanup. The teacher's and the students' reading, writing, research, and speaking were directed toward solving a real-life problem (Espe, Worner, & Hotkevich, 1990).

There are many approaches to whole-language learning, but most share an emphasis on authentic tasks and integrated curricula. The Contoocook Valley (CoVal) District in New Hampshire has adopted a whole-language approach with ten elements, listed in Table 9.7. Clearly, there are many advantages of a whole language, integrated curriculum approach, but still . . . .

Do Students Need Skills and Phonics?   There are now two decades of research demonstrating that skill in recognizing sounds and words supports reading. Advocates of code-based approaches cite research showing that being able to identify many words as you read does not depend on using context to guess meaning. In fact, it is almost the other way around—knowing words helps you make sense of context. Identifying words as you read is a highly automatic process. The more fluent and automatic you are in identifying words, the more effective you will be in getting meaning from context (Vellutino, 1991). It is the poorest readers who resort to using context to help them understand meaning (Pressley, 1996).

Many studies support the code-based position. For example, three different groups reported similar findings in the *Journal of Educational Psychology* (De-

TABLE 9.7	Ten Elements of a Whole-Language Program

1. *Reading to children*—the teacher reads quality literature to children to encourage them to read.

2. *Shared book experience*—a cooperative language activity based on the bedtime story tradition; the teacher reads and rereads appealing rhymes, songs, poems, and stories.

3. *Sustained silent reading*—everyone, including the teacher, reads for an extended period of time.

4. *Guided reading*—the teacher assigns books to groups of eight to ten children for independent reading followed by reading conferences; books are selected to keep the children on the cutting edge of their reading ability.

5. *Individualized reading*—an organized alternative to guided reading; grows out of guided reading; careful monitoring of individual progress is done by both child and teacher.

6. *Language experience*—oral language is recorded by a scribe or on tape and made available to children in written format; firsthand or vicarious experience is translated into written language.

7. *Children's writing*—ConVal uses the writing process of rehearse, draft, revise, edit, publish, and receive responses.

8. *Modeled writing*—the teacher models writing process and behavior; children see and hear an "expert" writer in action.

9. *Opportunities for sharing*—a finished piece is presented to an audience; ConVal uses author's teas and published books as two methods.

10. *Content area reading and writing*—students see demonstrations of each type of text (by subject content) and learn about varying reading speed and looking for content clues.

Source: From P. A. Robbins. "Implementing whole language: Bridging children and books." *Educational Leadership, 47*(6) p. 53. Reprinted with permission of the Association for Supervision and Curriculum Development. Copyright © 1990 by ASCD. All rights reserved.

cember, 1991). Summarizing the results of these investigations, Frank Vellutino states:

> I think it is fair to say that the major theoretical assumptions on which whole-language approaches to instruction are based have simply not been verified in relevant research testing those assumptions. Aside from the fact that there are very sound reasons to reject the "natural" parallel between spoken and written language drawn by whole-language theorists, the research supports the following generalizations: (a) The most basic skill in learning to read is word identification; (b) an adequate degree of fluency in word identification is a basic prerequisite to successful reading comprehension; (c) word identification in skilled readers is a fast-acting, automatic, and in effect modular process that depends little on contextual information for execution; (d) even skilled readers can predict not more than one word out of four in sentence contexts, indicating that the predictive role of context must be extremely limited; (e) because of limited facility in word identification, beginning and poor readers are much more dependent on context than are more advanced readers. (p. 442)

Vellutino goes on to list two more generalizations, that alphabetic coding and awareness of letter sounds are essential skills for acquiring word identification, so some direct teaching of the alphabet and phonics is helpful in learning to read. The best approach probably makes sensible use of both phonics and whole language. After all, we want our students to be fluent *and* enthusiastic readers and writers.

Being Sensible about Reading and Writing. The results of high quality studies suggest that:

- Whole-language approaches to reading and writing are most effective in preschool and kindergarten. Whole language gives children a good conceptual basis for reading and writing. The social interactions around reading and writing—reading big books, writing shared stories, examining pictures, discussing meaning—are activities that support literacy and mirror the early home experiences of children who come to school prepared to learn. Whole language approaches seem to improve students' motivation, interest, and attitude toward reading and help children understand the nature and purposes of reading and writing (Graham & Harris, 1994; Morrow, 1992; Neuman & Roskos, 1992).

■ Phonemic awareness—the sense that words are composed of separate sounds and that sounds are combined to say words—in kindergarten and first grade predicts literacy in later grades. If children do not have phonemic awareness in the early grades, direct teaching can dramatically improve their chances of long-term achievement in literacy (Pressley, 1996).

■ Excellent primary school teachers use a *balance* of explicit decoding-skills teaching and whole-language instruction (Adams, Trieman, & Pressley, in press; Vellutino, 1991; Wharton-McDonald, Pressley, & Mistretta, 1996).

If students need help cracking the code—give them what they need. Don't let ideology get in the way. You will just send more students to private tutors—if their families can afford it. But don't forget that reading and writing are for a purpose. Surround students with good literature and create a community of readers and writers.

The above discussion applies to reading and writing in the early grades, but what about the later years when comprehending difficult texts becomes important? Here reciprocal teaching can be helpful.

Reciprocal Teaching

The goal of **reciprocal teaching** is to help students understand and think deeply about what they read (Palincsar, 1986; Palincsar & Brown, 1984, 1989). To accomplish this goal, students learn four strategies: *summarizing* the content of a passage, *asking a question* about the central point, *clarifying* the difficult parts of the material, and *predicting* what will come next. These are strategies that skilled readers apply almost automatically, but poor readers seldom do—or they don't know how. To use the strategies effectively, poorer readers need direct instruction, modeling, and practice in actual reading situations.

First, the teacher introduces these strategies, perhaps focusing on one strategy each day. The teacher explains and models each strategy and encourages students to practice. Next, the teacher and the students read a short passage silently. Then the teacher again provides a model by summarizing, questioning, clarifying, and predicting based on the reading. Everyone reads another passage, and the students gradually begin to assume the teacher's role. Often the students' first attempts are halting and incorrect. But the teacher gives clues, guidance, and encouragement (what Bruner might call "scaffolding") to help the students master these strategies. The goal is for students to learn to apply these strategies independently as they read so they can make sense of text.

An Example of Reciprocal Teaching. Let's look at some examples of reciprocal teaching in action. The first example is an early lesson. Here the teacher is guiding a student as he tries to formulate a question about the central point in a passage on spiders (Harvard University, March 1986, p. 6):

Text: Spinner's mate is much smaller than she, and his body is dull brown. He spends most of his time sitting at one side of her web.

Annemarie Palincsar's research has focused attention on strategies that improve reading comprehension.

Reciprocal Teaching A method, based on modeling, of teaching reading comprehension strategies.

Charles: (No question)

Teacher: What's this paragraph about?

Charles: Spinner's mate. How do spinner's mate. . . .

Teacher: That's good. Keep going.

Charles: How do spinner's mate is smaller than. . . . How am I going to say that?

Teacher: Take your time with it. You want to ask a question about spinner's mate and what he does, beginning with the word "how."

Charles: How do they spend most of his time sitting?

Teacher: You're very close. The question would be, "How does spinner's mate spend most of his time?" Now, you ask it.

Charles: How does spinner's mate spend most of his time?

After a while, students are usually able to take more and more responsibility for the teaching. In the following example, Laura shows how much progress she has made after about 12 lessons (Harvard University, March 1986, p. 6):

Text: The second oldest form of salt production is mining. Unlike early methods that made the work extremely dangerous and difficult, today's methods use special machinery, and salt mining is easier and safer. The old expression "back to the salt mine" no longer applies.

Laura: Name two words that often describe mining salt in the old days.

Kim: Back to the salt mines?

Laura: No. Angela?

Angela: Dangerous and difficult.

Laura: Correct. This paragraph is all about comparing the old mining of salt and today's mining of salt.

Teacher: Beautiful!

Laura: I have a prediction to make.

Teacher: Good.

Laura: I think it might tell when salt was first discovered . . . well, it might tell what salt is made of and how it's made.

Teacher: OK. Can we have another teacher?

Applying Reciprocal Teaching. Research on reciprocal teaching has shown some dramatic results. Although reciprocal teaching seems to work with almost any age student, most of the research has been done with younger adolescents who can read aloud fairly accurately, but who are far below average in reading comprehension. After 20 hours of practice with this approach, many students who were in the bottom quarter of their class moved up to the average level or above on tests of reading comprehension. Based on the results of several studies, Palincsar has identified three guidelines for effective reciprocal teaching (Harvard University, March 1986; Palincsar & Brown, 1984):

1. *Shift gradually.* The shift from teacher control to student responsibility must be gradual.

2. *Match demands to abilities.* The difficulty of the task and the responsibility must match the abilities of each student and grow as these abilities develop.

3. *Diagnose thinking.* Teachers should carefully observe the "teaching" of each student for clues about how the student is thinking and what kind of instruction the student needs.

In reciprocal teaching, Annemarie Palincsar and Ann Brown have made four significant contributions to education. First, they remind us that procedures for fostering and monitoring comprehension must be taught—not all students develop these strategies on their own. Second, Palincsar and Brown focused attention on four rather than 40 or more strategies, as some sources have suggested. Third, they emphasized practicing these four strategies in the context of actual reading—reading literature and reading texts. Finally, they refined and developed the idea of scaffolding and gradually moving the student toward independent and fluid reading comprehension (Rosenshine & Meister, 1994).

With a consideration of reciprocal teaching, we are moving toward instructional approaches that emphasize social interaction and students' active construction of meaning.

Learning and Teaching Mathematics

Some of the most compelling support for constructivist approaches to teaching comes from mathematics education. Critics of direct instruction believe that traditional mathematics instruction often teaches students an unintended lesson—that they "cannot understand mathematics," or worse, that mathematics doesn't have to make sense, you just have to memorize the formulas. Arthur Baroody and Herbert Ginsburg (1990, p. 62) give this example:

> Sherry, a junior high student, explained that her math class was learning how to convert measurements from one unit to another. The interviewer gave Sherry the following problem:
>
> > To feed data into the computer, the measurements in your report have to be converted to one unit of measurement: feet. Your first measurement, however, is 3 feet 6 inches. What are you going to feed into the computer?
>
> Sherry recognized immediately that the conversion algorithm taught in school applied. . . . However, because she really did not understand the rationale behind the conversion algorithm, Sherry had difficulty in remembering the steps and how to execute them. After some time she came up with an improbable answer (it was less than 3 feet). Sherry knew she was in trouble and became flustered. At this point, the interviewer tried to help by asking her if there was any other way of solving the problem. Sherry responded sharply, "No!" She explained, "That's the way it has to be done." The interviewer tried to give Sherry a hint: "Look at the numbers in the problem, is there another way we can think about them that might help us figure out the problem more easily?" Sherry grew even more impatient, "This is the way I learned in school, so it has to be the way."
>
> Sherry believed that there was only one way to solve a problem. Though Sherry knew that 6 inches was one-half a foot and that the fraction one-half was equivalent to the decimal expression .5, she did not use this knowledge to solve the problem informally and quickly ("3 feet 6 inches is 3-½ feet, or 3.5 feet"). Her beliefs prevented her from effectively using her existing mathematical knowledge to solve the problem.

Sherry had probably been taught to memorize the steps to convert one measurement to another. How would a constructivist approach teach the same material?

The following excerpt shows how a third-grade teacher, Ms. Coleman, uses a constructivist approach to teach negative numbers. Notice the use of dialogue and the way the teacher asks students to justify and explain their thinking. The class has been considering one problem: $-10 + 10 = ?$ A student, Marta, has just tried to explain, using a number line, why $-10 + 10 = 0$:

Teacher: Marta says that negative ten plus ten equals zero, so you have to count ten numbers to the right. What do you think, Harold?

Harold: I think it's easy, but I don't understand how she explained it.

Teacher: OK. Does anybody else have a comment or a response to that? Tessa? (Peterson, 1992, p. 165)

As the discussion progresses, Ms. Coleman encourages students to talk directly to each other:

Teacher: You said you don't understand what she is trying to say?

Chang: No.

Teacher: Do you want to ask her?

Chang: What do you mean by counting to the right?

This dialogue reveals three things about learning and teaching in a constructivist classroom: the thinking processes of the students are the focus of attention; one topic is considered in depth rather than attempting to "cover" many topics; and assessment is ongoing and mutually shared by teacher and students.

Jere Confrey (1990b) analyzed an expert mathematics teacher in a class for high school girls who had difficulty with mathematics. Confrey identified five components in a model of this teacher's approach to teaching. These components are summarized in Table 9.8.

TABLE 9.8   A Constructivist Approach to Mathematics: Five Components

1. Promote students' autonomy and commitment to their answers

Examples:

- Question both right and wrong student answers.
- Insist that students at least try to solve a problem and be able to explain what they tried.

2. Develop students' reflective processes

Examples:

- Question students to guide them to try different ways to resolve the problem.
- Ask students to restate the problem in their own words; to explain what they are doing and why; and to discuss what they mean by the terms they are using.

3. Construct a case history of each student

Examples:

- Note general tendencies in the way the student approaches problems, as well as common misconceptions and strengths.

4. If the student is unable to solve a problem, intervene to negotiate a possible solution with the student

Examples:

- Based on the case study and your understanding of how the student is thinking about the problem, guide the student to think about a possible solution.
- Ask questions such as "Is there anything you did in the last one that will help you here?" or "Can you explain your diagram?"
- If the student is becoming frustrated, ask more direct, product-oriented questions.

5. When the problem is solved, review the solution

Examples:

- Encourage students to reflect on what they did and why.
- Note what students did well and build confidence.

Source: Adapted by permission from J. Confrey (1990). What constructivism implies for teaching. In R. Davis, C. Maher, and N. Noddings (Eds.), *Constructivist views on the teaching and learning of mathematics.* Monograph 4 of the National Council of Teachers of Mathematics, Reston, VA.

Conceptual change teaching in science focuses teachers' and students' attention on students' understanding rather than on "covering the curriculum." Dialogue is a key.

Learning Science

We have seen a number of times that by high school many students have "learned" some unfortunate lessons in school. Like Sherry, described in the preceding section, they have learned that math is impossible to understand and you just have to apply the rules to get the answers. Or they may have developed some misconceptions about the world, such as the belief that the earth is warmer in the summer because it is closer to the sun.

Howard Gardner (1991, 1993a) and many other educators note that the key to understanding in science is for students to directly examine their own theories and confront the shortcomings. Only then can true learning and conceptual change happen. For change to take place, students must go through six stages: initial discomfort with their own ideas and beliefs, attempts to explain away inconsistencies between their theories and evidence presented to them, attempts to adjust measurements or observations to fit personal theories, doubt, vacillation, and finally conceptual change (Nissani & Hoefler-Nissani, 1992). You can see Piaget's notions of assimilation, disequilibrium, and accommodation operating here. Students try to make new information fit existing ideas (assimilation), but when the fit simply won't work and disequilibrium occurs, then accommodation or changes in cognitive structures follow.

The goal of **conceptual change teaching in science** is to help students pass through these six stages of learning. The two central features of conceptual change teaching are:

Conceptual Change Teaching in Science A method that helps students understand (rather than memorize) concepts in science by using and challenging the students' current ideas.

- Teachers are committed to teaching for student understanding rather than "covering the curriculum."
- Students are encouraged to make sense of science using their current ideas—they are challenged to describe, predict, explain, justify, debate, and defend the adequacy of their understanding. Dialogue is key. Only when intuitive ideas prove inadequate can new learning take hold (Anderson & Roth, 1989).

Conceptual change teaching has much in common with cognitive apprentice-ships, inquiry learning, and reciprocal teaching—with scaffolding and dialogue playing key roles (Shuell, 1996).

Working with Families

Many teachers using nontraditional approaches to learning find that they must explain these approaches to students' families. The Guidelines give ideas for communicating with parents about innovative teaching and learning.

Guidelines

Family and Community Partnerships for Innovative Teaching Approaches

Be confident and honest.

Examples

1. Write out your rationale for the methods you are using—consider likely objections and craft your responses.
2. Admit mistakes or oversights—explain what you have learned from them.

Treat parents as equal partners.

Examples

1. Listen carefully to parents' objections, take notes, and follow up on requests or suggestions—remember, you both want the best for the child.
2. Give parents the telephone number of an administrator who will answer their questions about a new program or initiative.
3. Invite families to visit your room or assist in the project in some way.

Communicate effectively.

Examples

1. Use plain language and avoid jargon. If you must use a technical term, define it in accessible ways. Use your best teaching skills to educate parents about the new approach.
2. Encourage local newspapers or television stations to do stories about the "great learning" going on in your classroom or school.
3. Create a lending library of articles and references about the new strategies.

Have examples of projects and assignments available for parents when they visit your class.

Examples

1. Encourage parents to try math activities. If they have trouble, show them how your students (and their child) are successful with the activities and highlight the strategies the students have learned.
2. Keep a library of students' favorite activities to demonstrate for parents.

(continued)

Develop family involvement packages.

Examples

1. Once a month, send families, via their children, descriptions and examples of the math, science, or language to be learned in the upcoming unit. Include activities children can do with their parents
2. Make the family project count, for example, as a homework grade.

Source: From M. Meyer, M. Delgardelle, and J. Middleton. "Addressing parents' concerns over curriculum reform." *Educational Leadership, 53*(7), p. 57. Adapted by permission of the Association for Supervision and Curriculum Development. Copyright © 1996 by ASCP. All rights reserved.

SUMMARY

Contributions of Behavioral Learning

When the goal is to learn facts, explicit information, sequenced steps, or rules, then behavioral principles of learning can guide teaching. Three contributions are instructional objectives, mastery learning, and direct instruction. Instructional objectives help provide structure, let students know what they are studying for or working toward, and help guide the teacher in writing fair and balanced tests. Two approaches to writing objectives are Mager's specific behavior objectives and Gronlund's combination of general and specific objectives. Many educators believe that Gronlund's approach is the most helpful. Bloom and others have developed taxonomies categorizing basic objectives in the cognitive, affective, and psychomotor domains.

Mastery learning breaks material down into small units that focus on specific objectives. Students may progress at their own rate and must master each unit before proceeding to the next. If they fail, they must recycle through the unit, ideally with extra help or by using new approaches. Mastery learning seems most effective when each unit builds on the one before and when high quality remediation is available for students who need extra help. Direct instruction is most appropriate when teaching basic skills to groups or the whole class. A framework for direct instruction might involve reviewing yesterday's work, presenting new material, giving guided practice, giving feedback and corrections, providing independent practice, and reviewing weekly and monthly. Hunter's Mastery Teaching and the Missouri Mathematics Program are elaborations on direct instruction.

Cognitive Models of Teaching

According to Jerome Bruner's discovery model of teaching, students learn best when they discover the structure of a subject through inductive reasoning (the eg-rule method) and intuitive thinking. In guided discovery, the teachers ask leading questions and give directive feedback. According to David Ausubel's reception model, learning should be primarily deductive (the rule-eg method) and based on meaningful verbal learning. In expository teaching, teachers present material that is fully organized and sequenced from the general (subsumers and advance organizers) to the specific. Gagné's Instructional Events Model is based on information processing and connects instruction with phases of learning such as attention, motivation, tying new information to prior knowledge, organizing, processing deeply, and reviewing.

Constructivist and Situated Learning

Educators and psychologists who take constructivist and situated approaches are among the strongest voices speaking in favor of student-centered teaching. They emphasize the importance of students' construction of knowledge and the difficulty of transferring learning from the situation in which it was learned to new applications. Constructivist approaches to teaching recommend: complex, challenging learning environments; social negotiation and shared responsibility as part of learning; multiple representations of content; understanding that knowledge is constructed; and student-centered instruction. Inquiry, group work and cooperative learning, instructional conversations, and cognitive apprenticeships are examples of teaching approaches based on constructivist and situated theories of learning. These methods make minimal use of rote memorization. An important part of many of the approaches is student discussion—asking questions and giving explanations. Cooperative learning is a potentially valuable approach, if groups are carefully planned and monitored and if students are taught how to cooperate for productive learning. There are many structures for cooperative learning, including jigsaw, reciprocal questioning, and scripted cooperation. Other structures emphasizing motivation are discussed in Chapter 11.

Cognitive and Constructivist Approaches to Reading, Mathematics, and Science

Today there is an ongoing debate between advocates of whole-language approaches to reading and writing and balanced approaches that include direct teaching of skills and phonics. Advocates of whole language believe children learn best when they are surrounded by good literature and read and write for authentic purposes. Advocates of a balanced approach cite extensive research indicating that skill in recognizing sounds and words—phonemic awareness—is fundamental in learning to read. Excellent primary teachers use a balanced approach combining authentic reading with skills instruction when needed. As children grow older, reciprocal teaching helps them understand what they read. Reciprocal teaching emphasizes direct teaching of comprehension strategies, modeling by the teacher, and a movement toward independence and self-regulated learning on the part of the students.

Constructivist approaches to mathematics and science emphasize deep understanding of concepts (as opposed to memorization), discussion and explanation, and exploration of students' implicit understandings. Success with any innovative approach to teaching often requires gaining and maintaining the cooperation of families.

KEY TERMS

active teaching, p. 335
advance organizer, p. 341
basic skills, p. 335
behavioral objectives, p. 331
coding system, p. 338
cognitive apprenticeship, p. 357
cognitive objectives, p. 331
complex learning environments, p. 347
conceptual change teaching in science, p. 364
constructivist approach, p. 346
cooperative learning, p. 350

deductive reasoning, p. 341
direct instruction/explicit teaching, p. 335
discovery learning, p. 338
eg-rule method, p. 338
expository teaching, p. 341
guided discovery, p. 339
inductive reasoning, p. 338
inquiry learning, p. 348
instructional conversation, p. 355
instructional objective, p. 330
intuitive thinking, p. 338

mastery learning, p. 334
meaningful verbal learning, p. 341
multiple representations of content, p. 347
reciprocal questioning, p. 353
reciprocal teaching, p. 360
rule-eg method, p. 341
social negotiation, p. 347
subject structure, p. 338
taxonomy, p. 332
whole-language perspective, p. 357

CHECK YOUR UNDERSTANDING

Can you apply the ideas from this chapter on learning and instruction to solve the following problems of practice?

Preschool and Kindergarten

- One of your students is very fearful of taking risks or attempting any task that does not have a right answer. The child tries to tell other students "the right way" to do everything. How would you help the student tolerate uncertainty and take risks in her thinking?

Elementary and Middle School

- How would you help third-grade students understand negative numbers?

- The principal and curriculum coordinator in your school have decided that study skills will be a high priority this year. How would you approach teaching study skills to your third-grade class? To your sixth-grade class?

Junior High and High School

- Your school librarian wants to help all the history classes learn to use the print and database resources in the library. How would you take advantage of this opportunity?

Cooperative Learning

- With three or four other members of your educational psychology class, brainstorm ways to "understand your students' understanding" in a particular content area. What would you do before, during, and after a class in this unit to make your students' knowledge and thinking processes visible to both you and them?

What Would They Do?

Your school district has adopted a whole-language, integrated curriculum approach for grades K through six. Students and teachers are mostly pleased with the program. There seems to be more reading and more enjoyment of reading, at least for many children—but some students seem lost. The students' written work is longer and more creative. However, standardized tests indicate a drop in scores. The principal is clearly getting worried—this was her big project and she had to work hard to "sell it" to some members of the PTA and school board. Several parents of students in your class are complaining that they are having to hire tutors or buy commercial programs to teach their children to read.

REGINA M. LAROSE

Second Grade Teacher
Hillside School, Needham, Massachusetts

The good news in this case is that the children appear to be productive learners with positive attitudes. I would remind parents of this as I respond to their questions and concerns. Parents need to be informed; therefore, I would approach their complaints with an open mind and offer explanations as directly and honestly as I could. Perhaps parent workshops could be held by the school's principal and teachers to further explain goals and to answer questions.

I believe that children are successful when they are offered a balance between an innovative approach and a structured plan for delivering skills. If children were not meeting the standards of a required test, I would take a serious look at my goals and methods. I would scrutinize my plans and make sure that I was offering students sufficient practice in those skills that seem to be the weakest. Because children have different learning styles, a variety of approaches should be used to introduce and practice skills. Discussions with fellow teachers often reveal new techniques that help to stimulate ideas.

After analyzing my program, I would supply my principal with concrete examples of methods that would provide more understanding and practice in the skills that I found lacking. I would include an explanation of these additional lessons in my weekly newsletter to parents.

VALERIE A. CHILCOAT

Fifth/Sixth Grade Advanced Academics
Glenmount School, Baltimore, Maryland

When addressing parent complaints, great care is needed, especially when they concern the decisions made by your administration. If the concern is widespread, I would set up a meeting with the parents that included your administrator. Perhaps other teachers would want to be involved. Discuss in detail with your administrator what you plan to say, and make sure you are clear on the position of the administration.

As a teacher who uses an integrated curriculum, I have much practical experience with the pros and cons of a whole-language approach. As educators, we know that all children do not learn in the same way. That is why I believe that a completely whole-language approach is an inappropriate teaching style. In keeping with the idea of an integrated curriculum, basic language and reading skills can be introduced in conjunction with the standard whole-language approach.

By first evaluating the learning styles of my students, I could discover which of my students learn better whole-to-part and which learn better part-to-whole. I could then provide all students with lessons designed to meet their needs as well as introduce alternative learning strategies to them.

By using an integrated curriculum approach, I believe that students learn and retain more of the major concepts and themes that run throughout the many disciplines. Issues are constantly visited and revisited from different perspectives and through the implementation of the dictates inherent in the disciplines of reading, math, science, and the social sciences. However, this many not be enough. Basic reading, language, and math skills must also be integrated into the program to best address the needs of all students.

FRANCES D. GARLAND

Third Grade Teacher
Winship School, Boston, Massachusetts

I would speak directly to individual parents about their concerns regarding whole language and lower test scores. While I certainly would validate their complaints, I would also point out that test scores are not the only indicators of progress. Whole-language teachers are kid watchers. Kid watching informs good teaching and provides insight into children's strengths, weaknesses, strategies, and skills. Test scores are only part of the overall assessment process.

During the dialogue with parents, I would invite them to visit my classroom so they could witness a meaning-based learning environment, where children are engaged in real reading and real writing activities. I would also provide some suggestions for them to use at home that would reinforce and support techniques employed in the classroom. I would recommend books for them to read to help them understand the whole-language philosophy, such as *The Foundations of Literacy* (Holdaway) or *Classrooms That Work* (Cunningham, Allington).

Motivation: Issues and Explanations

Overview | *What Would You Do?*

WHAT IS MOTIVATION? **372**
Intrinsic and Extrinsic Motivation | Four General Approaches to Motivation | Motivation to Learn in School

GOALS AND MOTIVATION **379**
Types of Goals | Feedback and Goal Acceptance | Goals: Lessons for Teachers

NEEDS AND MOTIVATION **382**
Maslow's Hierarchy | Achievement Motivation | The Need for Self-Determination | The Need for Relatedness | Needs and Motivation: Lessons for Teachers

ATTRIBUTIONS, BELIEFS, AND MOTIVATION **387**
Attribution Theory | Beliefs about Ability | Beliefs about Self-Efficacy | Attributions, Achievement Motivation, and Self-Worth | Attributions and Beliefs: Lessons for Teachers

ANXIETY AND COPING IN THE CLASSROOM **396**
What Causes Anxiety in School? | Helping Anxious Students | Anxiety: Lessons for Teachers

Summary | *Key Terms* | *Check Your Understanding* | *Teachers' Casebook: What Would They Do?*

W*hy are you reading this chapter? Did you open the book because you are curious about motivation and interested in the topic? Or is there a test in your near future? Do you need this course to earn a teaching certificate or to graduate? Maybe you believe that you have a good chance to do well in this class, and that belief keeps you working. Perhaps it is some combination of these reasons. What motivates you to study motivation?*

Most educators agree that motivating students is one of the critical tasks of teaching. We begin with the question "What is motivation?" and examine many of the answers that have been proposed. This leads to a discussion of intrinsic and extrinsic motivation and four general theories of motivation: behavioral, humanistic, cognitive, and social learning.

The remainder of the chapter examines more closely several personal factors that frequently appear in discussions of motivation: goals; needs for self-actualization, achievement, self-determination, and belonging; beliefs about the causes of success and failure in school; notions about ability and self-efficacy; and anxiety. In Chapter 11 we will complete the picture with an examination of the external factors that can affect motivation.

By the time you have completed this chapter, you should be able to:

- Give examples of intrinsic and extrinsic motivation and motivation to learn.
- Define the concept of motivation from the behavioral, humanistic, cognitive, and social learning points of view.
- Set motivating goals for yourself and your students.
- List Maslow's seven levels of needs and give a classroom example of each.
- Explain how to encourage the need for achievement in your class.
- Explain the relationship between self-determination and motivation.
- Discuss the possible motivational effects of success and failure and how these effects relate to beliefs about ability.
- Describe the characteristics of mastery-oriented, failure-avoiding, and failure-accepting students.
- Develop a plan for helping an anxious student improve.

What Would You Do?

For some reason this year, many of the students in your middle school classes seem defeated about learning. They look at an assignment and protest, "This is too long (too hard, too much)!" "We can't do this by tomorrow (Monday, next week)!" Because they don't exert much effort, of course, they prove themselves right every time—they can't do the work. Neither pep talks nor punishments for incomplete work are making a dent in the students' defeatist attitudes. And the "I can'ts" seem contagious. Even the better students are starting to drag their feet, protest longer assignments, and invest minimal effort in class. You suspect a few students have started to cheat on tests to save their sinking grades. A few teachers blame the negative attitudes on students from " projects" who are in school this year because the other middle school in the district was closed and those students had to be redistributed. A cloud of despair seems to be hovering over the whole school. You are starting to dread Mondays.

- Are these students "unmotivated"?
- Why might they be so pessimistic about learning?
- What could you do to change the attitudes in your class?
- How can you save your own sinking motivation?
- How will these issues affect the grades you will teach?

What Is Motivation?

Motivation is usually defined as an internal state that arouses, directs, and maintains behavior. Psychologists studying motivation have focused on five basic questions (Graham & Weiner, 1996; Pintrich, Marx, & Boyle, 1993). First, what *choices* do people make about their behavior? Why do some students, for example, focus on their homework while others watch television? Second, having made a decision, *how long* is it before the person actually gets started? Why do some students who chose to do their homework start right away, while others procrastinate? Third, what is the *intensity* or level of involvement in the chosen activity? Once the book bag is opened, is the student absorbed and focused or just going through the motions? Fourth, what causes a person to *persist* or to give up? Will a student read the entire Shakespeare assignment or just a few pages? Finally, what is the individual *thinking* and *feeling* while engaged in the activity? Is the student enjoying Shakespeare or worrying about an upcoming test?

Answering these questions about real students in classrooms is a challenge. As you will see in this chapter and the next, there are many factors that influence motivation. To get a sense of the complexity, let's step into a middle school general science classroom and survey the motivational problems that might confront you as the teacher. The students are taken from Stipek (1993).

The assignment: "In your lab notebook, describe the procedures for tomorrow's chemistry experiment. Indicate all the materials you will need and how you will set up the apparatus." As soon as you finish your instructions, the

Motivation An internal state that arouses, directs, and maintains behavior.

hands go up. "Do we have to write in paragraphs or can we outline?" "Do we have to draw the apparatus or just describe it?" "Can we work together?" Some students begin right away, while others wait for answers to these questions. A few students seem to be in another world.

Hopeless Henry won't even start the assignment—as usual. He just keeps saying, "I don't understand," or "This is too hard." When you try to help him, he answers your questions correctly, but then says he "guessed" and he "doesn't really know." Henry causes no management problems because he spends most of his time staring into space, but he is falling farther and farther behind.

Safe Sally checks with you about every step—she wants to be perfect. You once gave her bonus points for doing an excellent color drawing of the apparatus and now she produces a work of art for lab every time. But Sally never takes any chances. She does well in science, but plans to take only the required science courses so she won't risk getting a B. If it isn't required or on the test, Sally isn't interested.

Satisfied Sam on the other hand, is interested in this project. In fact, he knows more than you do about it. Evidently he has set up a lab in his garage and spends hours reading about chemistry and performing experiments. But his overall grade in your class is between B– and C+ because when you were studying biology, Sam couldn't have cared less. He was satisfied with the C he could get on tests without even trying. Homework didn't interest him. His only participation was to make jokes about the illustrations in the text. Judging by his standardized test scores, Sam could do much better.

Defensive Diana doesn't have her lab manual—again. You tell her that she may share with another student. Then Diana pretends to be working, but she spends most of her time making fun of the assignment or trying to get answers from other students when your back is turned. She wants everyone to know that she "isn't really trying." That way, if her grades are low she has an excuse. She is afraid to try because if she makes an effort and fails, she fears that everyone will know she is "dumb."

Anxious Amy is a good student in most subjects, but she freezes on science tests. She seems fine in group projects and doing her homework, but "forgets" everything she knows when she has to answer questions in class or take a test. Her parents are scientists and expect her to become one too, but her prospects for this future look dim.

Each student presents a different motivational problem, yet you have to teach the entire class. In the next few pages we will look more closely at the meaning of motivation so we can better understand these students.

Intrinsic and Extrinsic Motivation

We all know how it feels to be motivated, to move energetically toward a goal. We also know what it is like to work hard, even if we are not fascinated by the task. What energizes and directs our behavior? The explanation could be drives, needs, incentives, fears, goals, social pressure, self-confidence, interests, curiosity, beliefs, values, expectations, and more. Some psychologists have explained motivation in terms of personal *traits* or individual characteristics. Certain people, so the theory goes, have a strong need to achieve, a fear of tests, or an enduring interest in art, so they behave accordingly. They work hard to achieve,

"WHAT DO I GET FOR JUST NEATNESS?"

(© Glenn Bernhardt)

A basic question in motivation is "Where does it come from—within or outside the individual?" Why does this boy raise his hand in class—because he is interested in the subject or because he wants to earn a good grade? The answer is probably much more complicated than either alternative.

Intrinsic Motivation Motivation associated with activities that are their own reward.

Extrinsic Motivation Motivation created by external factors like rewards and punishments.

Locus of Causality The location—internal or external—of the cause of behavior.

avoid tests, or spend hours in art galleries. Other psychologists see motivation more as a *state,* a temporary situation. If, for example, you are reading this paragraph because you have a test tomorrow, you are motivated (at least for now) by the situation. Of course, the motivation we experience at any given time usually is a combination of trait and state. You may be studying because you value learning *and* because your professor often gives pop quizzes.

As you can see, some explanations of motivation rely on internal, personal factors such as needs, interests, curiosity, and enjoyment. Other explanations point to external, environmental factors—rewards, social pressure, punishment, and so on. Motivation that stems from factors such as interest or curiosity is called **intrinsic motivation**. Intrinsic motivation is the natural tendency to seek out and conquer challenges as we pursue personal interests and exercise capabilities (Deci & Ryan, 1985; Reeve, 1996). When we are intrinsically motivated, we do not need incentives or punishments, because *the activity itself is rewarding.*

James Raffini (1996) states simply that intrinsic motivation is "what motivates us to do something when we *don't have* to do anything (p. 3). Satisfied Sam studies chemistry outside school simply because he loves the activity; no one makes him do it. In contrast, when we do something in order to earn a grade or reward, avoid punishment, please the teacher, or for some other reason that has very little to do with the task itself, we experience **extrinsic motivation**. We are not really interested in the activity for its own sake; we care only about what it will gain us. Safe Sally works for the grade; she has little interest in the subject itself.

It is impossible to tell just by looking if a behavior is intrinsically or extrinsically motivated. The essential difference between the two types of motivation is the student's reason for acting, that is, whether the **locus of causality** for the action (the location of the cause) is internal or external—inside or outside the person. Students who read or practice their backstroke or paint may be reading, stroking, or painting because they freely chose the activity based on personal interests (*internal locus* of causality/intrinsic motivation), or because someone or something else outside is influencing them (*external locus* of causality/extrinsic motivation).

Is your motivation for reading this page intrinsic or extrinsic? Is your locus of causality internal or external? As you try to answer this question, you probably realize that the dichotomy between intrinsic and extrinsic motivation is too simple—too all-or-nothing. Our activities fall along a continuum from fully *self-determined* (internal locus of causality/intrinsic motivation) to fully *determined by others* (external locus of causality/extrinsic motivation). For example, students may freely choose to work hard on activities that they don't find particularly enjoyable, because they know the activities are important in reaching a valued goal—like spending hours studying anatomy in order to become a physician. Is this intrinsic or extrinsic motivation? Actually it is in between—the person is freely choosing to respond to outside causes such as medical school requirements. The person has *internalized an external cause.*

In school, both intrinsic and extrinsic motivation are important. Many activities are, or could be, interesting to students. Teaching can create intrinsic motivation by stimulating the students' curiosity and making them feel more competent as they learn. But you know this won't work all the time. Did you find long division or grammar inherently interesting? Was your curiosity piqued by the states and their capitals? If teachers count on intrinsic motivation to energize all their students all of the time, they will be disappointed. There are situations when incentives and external supports are necessary. Teachers must encourage and nurture intrinsic motivation while making sure that extrinsic motivation supports learning (Brophy, 1988; Ryan & Deci, 1996). To do this, they need to know about the factors that influence motivation.

Four General Approaches to Motivation

Motivation is a vast and complicated subject encompassing many theories. Some theories were developed through work with animals in laboratories. Others are based on research with humans in situations that used games or puzzles. Some theories grow out of the work done in clinical or industrial psychology. Our examination of the field will be selective; otherwise we would never finish the topic.

Behavioral Approaches to Motivation.   Behaviorists explain motivation with concepts such as "reward" and "incentive." A **reward** is an attractive object or event supplied as a consequence of a particular behavior. For example, Safe Sally was rewarded with bonus points when she drew an excellent apparatus diagram. An **incentive** is an object or event that encourages or discourages behavior. The promise of an A+ was an incentive to Sally. Actually receiving the grade was a reward. Thus, according to the behavioral view, an understanding of student motivation begins with a careful analysis of the incentives and rewards present in the classroom.

If we are consistently reinforced for certain behaviors, we may develop habits or tendencies to act in certain ways. For example, if a student is repeatedly rewarded with affection, money, praise, or privileges for earning letters in baseball, but receives little recognition for studying, the student will probably work longer and harder on perfecting her fastball than on understanding geometry. Providing grades, stars, and so on for learning—or demerits for misbehavior—is an attempt to motivate students by extrinsic means of incentives, rewards, and punishments. Of course, in any individual case, many other factors will affect how a person behaves.

Humanistic Approaches to Motivation.   The **humanistic view** is sometimes referred to as "third-force" psychology because it developed in the 1940s as a reaction against the two forces dominant at that time: behaviorism and Freudian psychoanalysis. Proponents of humanistic psychology such as Abraham Maslow and Carl Rogers felt that neither behavioral nor Freudian psychology adequately explained why people act as they do.

Humanistic interpretations of motivation emphasize such intrinsic sources of motivation as a person's needs for "self-actualization" (Maslow, 1968, 1970), the inborn "actualizing tendency" (Rogers & Freiberg, 1994), or the need for "self-determination" (Deci, Vallerand, Pelletier, & Ryan, 1991). What these theories have in common is the belief that people are continually motivated by the inborn need to fulfill their potential. So, from the humanistic perspective, to motivate students means to encourage their inner resources—their sense of competence, self-esteem, autonomy, and self-actualization. One current reflection of the humanistic perspective is the "self-esteem movement," a controversial approach to meeting students' needs for dignity and self-esteem. The Point/Counterpoint section on page 376 explores this issue. When we examine the role of *needs* in motivation, we will see two examples of the humanistic approach to motivation, Maslow's theory of the hierarchy of needs and Deci's self-determination theory.

Reward An attractive object or event supplied as a consequence of a behavior.

Incentive An object or event that encourages or discourages behavior.

Humanistic View Approach to motivation that emphasizes personal freedom, choice, self-determination, and striving for personal growth.

What Should Schools Do to Encourage Students' Self-Esteem?

James Beane (1991) begins his article "Sorting Out the Self-Esteem Controversy" with this statement: "In the '90s, the question is not whether schools should enhance students' self-esteem, but how they propose to do so" (p. 25). The attempts to improve students' self-esteem have taken three main forms: personal development activities such as sensitivity training; self-esteem programs where the curriculum focuses directly on improving self-esteem; and structural changes in schools that place greater emphasis on cooperation, student participation, community involvement, and ethnic pride.

POINT The self-esteem movement has problems.

Attempts to encourage self-esteem directly through sensitivity training or self-esteem courses have not proven very successful. As Beane notes, "Saying 'I like myself and others' in front of a group is not the same as actually feeling that way, especially if I am only doing it because I am supposed to. Being nice has a place in enhancing self-esteem, but it is not enough" (p. 26). Many of the self-esteem courses are commercial packages—costly for schools but without solid evidence that they make a difference for students (Crisci, 1986; Leming, 1981).

Sensitivity training and self-esteem courses share a common conceptual problem. They assume that we encourage self-esteem by changing the individual's beliefs, making the young person work harder against the odds. But what if the student's environment is truly unsafe, debilitating, and unsupportive? Some people have overcome tremendous problems, but to expect everyone to do so "ignores the fact that having positive self-esteem is almost impossible for many young people, given the deplorable conditions under which they are forced to live by the inequities in our society" (Beane, 1991, p. 27).

Because many attempts to encourage self-esteem have been superficial, commercial, and filled with "pop psychology," the self-esteem movement has become an easy target for critics in magazine articles such as "Education: Doing Bad and Feeling Good" (*Time*, February 5, 1990) and "The Trouble with Self-Esteem" (*U.S. News and World Report*, April 2, 1990).

COUNTERPOINT The self-esteem movement has promise.

Beyond the "feel-good psychology" of some aspects of the self-esteem movement is a basic truth: "Self-esteem is a central feature of human dignity and thus an inalienable human entitlement. As such, schools and other agencies have a moral obligation to help build

it and avoid debilitating it" (Beane, 1991, p. 28). If we view self-esteem accurately as a product of our thinking and our actions—our values, ideas, and beliefs as well as our interactions with others—then we see a significant role for the school. Practices that allow authentic participation, cooperation, problem solving, and accomplishment should replace policies that damage self-esteem, such as tracking and competitive grading.

Beane suggests four principles to guide educators:

First, being nice is surely a part of this effort, but it is not enough. Second, there is a place for some direct instruction regarding affective matters, but this is not enough either. Self-esteem and affect are not simply another school subject to be placed in set-aside time slots. Third, the negative affect of "get tough" policies is not a promising route to self-esteem and efficacy. This simply blames young people for problems that are largely not of their own making. Fourth, since self-perceptions are powerfully informed by culture, comparing self-esteem across cultures without clarifying cultural differences is distracting and unproductive. (pp. 29–30)

Source: From J. A. Beane. Sorting out the self-esteem controversy. *Educational Leadership, 49,* 1, pp. 25–30. Reprinted by permission of the Association for Supervision and Curriculum Development. Copyright © 1991 by ASCD. All rights reserved.

Cognitive Approaches to Motivation. In many ways, cognitive theories of motivation also developed as a reaction to the behavioral views. Cognitive theorists believe that behavior is determined by our thinking, not simply by whether we have been rewarded or punished for the behavior in the past (Schunk, 1996; Stipek, 1993). Behavior is initiated and regulated by plans (Miller, Galanter,

The hard work required to accomplish the goal of learning to play a musical instrument calls for a large measure of intrinsic motivation; if these children don't really care about learning to play the piano, they probably won't stick with it. But extrinsic motivation in the form of incentives and praise from others could help, too.

& Pribram, 1960), goals (Locke & Latham, 1990), schemas (Ortony, Clore, & Collins, 1988), expectations (Vroom, 1964), and attributions (Weiner, 1992). One of the central assumptions in cognitive approaches is that people respond not to external events or physical conditions like hunger, but rather to their interpretations of these events. You may have had the experience of being so involved in a project that you missed a meal, not realizing you were hungry until you noticed the time. Food deprivation did not automatically motivate you to seek food.

In cognitive theories, people are seen as active and curious, searching for information to solve personally relevant problems. People work hard because they enjoy the work and because they want to understand. Thus, cognitive theorists emphasize intrinsic motivation. We will see examples of cognitive theories of motivation when we examine Bernard Weiner's attribution theory and Martin Covington's self-worth theory.

Social Learning Approaches to Motivation. Social learning theories of motivation are integrations of behavioral and cognitive approaches: They take into account both the behaviorists' concern with the effects or outcomes of behavior and the cognitivists' interest in the impact of individual beliefs and expectations. Many influential social learning explanations of motivation can be characterized as **expectancy × value theories.** This means that motivation is seen as the product of two main forces, the individual's expectation of reaching a goal and the value of that goal to him or her. In other words, the important questions are, "If I try hard, can I succeed?" and "If I succeed, will the outcome be valuable or rewarding to me?" Motivation is a product of these two forces, because if either factor is zero, there is no motivation to work toward the goal. For example, if I believe I have a good chance of making the basket-

Expectancy × Value Theories Explanations of motivation that emphasize individuals' expectations for success combined with their valuing of the goal.

TABLE 10.1　Four Views of Motivation

	Behavioral	Humanistic	Cognitive	Social Learning
Source of Motivation	Extrinsic reinforcement	Intrinsic reinforcement	Intrinsic reinforcement	Extrinsic and intrinsic reinforcement
Important Influences	Reinforcers, rewards, incentives, and punishers	Need for self-esteem, self-fulfillment, and self-determination	Beliefs, attributions for success and failure, expectations	Value of goals, expectation of reaching goals
Key Theorists	Skinner	Maslow Deci	Weiner Covington	Bandura

ball team (high expectation), and if making the team is very important to me (high value), then my motivation should be strong. But if either factor is zero (I believe I haven't a prayer of making the team, or I couldn't care less about playing basketball), then my motivation will be zero, too. Bandura's social cognitive theory, discussed later in this chapter, is an example of an expectancy × value approach to motivation (Pintrich & Schunk, 1996).

The behavioral, humanistic, cognitive, and social learning approaches to motivation are summarized in Table 10.1. These theories differ in their answers to the question "What is motivation?" but each contributes in its own way toward a comprehensive understanding of human motivation.

Motivation to Learn in School

Teachers are concerned about developing a particular kind of motivation in their students—the motivation to learn. Jere Brophy (1988) describes **student motivation to learn** as "a student tendency to find academic activities meaningful and worthwhile and to try to derive the intended academic benefits from them. Motivation to learn can be construed as both a general trait and a situation-specific state" (pp. 205–206).

Many elements make up the motivation to learn. These include planning, concentration on the goal, metacognitive awareness of what you intend to learn and how you intend to learn it, the active search for new information, clear perceptions of feedback, pride and satisfaction in achievement, and no anxiety or fear of failure (Johnson & Johnson, 1985). Motivation to learn thus involves more than wanting or intending to learn. It includes the quality of the student's mental efforts. For example, reading the text 10 times may indicate persistence, but motivation to learn implies more thoughtful, active study strategies, like summarizing, elaborating the basic ideas, outlining in your own words, drawing graphs of the key relationships, and so on (Brophy, 1988).

It would be wonderful if all our students came to us filled with the motivation to learn, but they don't. And even if they did, work in school might still seem boring or unimportant to some students. As teachers, we have three major goals. The first is to get students productively involved with the work of the class; in other words, to create a *state* of motivation to learn. The second and longer-term goal is to develop in our students the *trait* of being

---

Motivation

- It is sometimes suggested that one way of improving education would be to pay students for successful school achievement. What would be the likely effects of doing this?
- Why would a student be motivated to study for a test according to a behavioral viewpoint? A cognitive viewpoint? A humanistic viewpoint?
- How might teachers' attempts to help students "find the fun in learning" undermine the long-term development of the trait of motivation to learn?

Student Motivation to Learn The tendency to work hard on academic activities because one believes they are worthwhile.

motivated to learn so they will be able "to educate themselves throughout their lifetime" (Bandura, 1993, p. 136). And finally, we want our students to be cognitively engaged—to think deeply about what they study. In other words, we want them to be *thoughtful* (Blumenfeld, Puro, & Mergendoller, 1992).

In the next pages we will examine the role of goals, needs, and beliefs in supporting motivation to learn. In fact, we will use the concept of motivation to learn to develop a chart summarizing the many factors that influence motivation. Table 10.4 on page 392 is the final version of that chart. Our first entry in the chart indicates that when the source of motivation is *intrinsic,* motivation to learn is *encouraged,* while *extrinsic* sources of motivation tend to *diminish* motivation to learn.

Goals and Motivation

A **goal** is what an individual is striving to accomplish (Locke & Latham, 1990). When students strive to read a chapter or make a 4.0 GPA, they are involved in *goal-directed behavior.* In pursuing goals, students are generally aware of some current condition (I haven't even opened my book), some ideal condition (I have read and understood every page), and the discrepancy between the current and ideal situations. Goals motivate people to act in order to reduce the discrepancy between "where they are" and "where they want to be." Goal setting is usually effective for me. In addition to the routine tasks, like eating lunch that will happen without much attention, I often set goals for each day. For example, today I intend to finish this chapter, jog, make soup for next week's lunches, and send a birthday gift to my father-in-law. Having decided to do these things, I will feel uncomfortable if I don't complete the list.

According to Locke and Latham (1990), there are four main reasons why goal setting improves performance. First, goals direct our attention to the task at hand. (Every time my mind wanders from this chapter, my goal of finishing helps direct my attention back to the writing.) Second, goals mobilize effort. (The harder the goal, to a point, the greater the effort.) Third, goals increase persistence. (When we have a clear goal we are less likely to be distracted or to give up until we reach the goal.) Finally, goals promote the development of new strategies when old strategies fall short. For example, if your goal is making an A and you don't reach that goal on your first quiz, you might drop the strategy of reading the text over and over and try a new study approach for the next quiz, such as explaining the key points to a friend.

Types of Goals

The types of goals we set influence the amount of motivation we have to reach them. Goals that are specific, moderately difficult, and likely to be reached in the near future tend to enhance motivation and persistence (Pintrich & Schunk, 1996; Stipek, 1996). Specific goals provide clear standards for judging performance. If performance falls short, we keep going. For example, I have decided to "finish this chapter" instead of deciding to "work on the book." Because it is clear when I am finished (the chapter is in the mail), I know when I have met the goal. Anything short of having the chapter in the mail means "keep working." Moderate difficulty provides a challenge, but not an unreasonable one. I can finish this chapter if I stay with it. Finally, goals that can be reached fairly soon are

Goal What an individual strives to accomplish.

not likely to be pushed aside by more immediate concerns. Groups like Alcoholics Anonymous show they are aware of the motivating value of short-term goals when they encourage their members to stop drinking "one day at a time."

In classrooms there are two main categories of goals—learning and performance. The point of a **learning goal** is to improve, to learn, no matter how many mistakes you make or how awkward you appear. Students who set learning goals tend to seek challenges and persist when they encounter difficulties. Nicholls and Miller (1984) call these students **task-involved learners** because they are concerned with mastering the task and are not worried about how their performance "measures up" compared to others in the class. We often say that these people "get lost in their work." In addition, task-involved learners are more likely to seek appropriate help (Butler & Neuman, 1995).

The second kind of goal is a **performance goal.** Students with performance goals are focused on how they are judged by others. They want to look smart and avoid seeming incompetent. If this seems impossible, they may adopt defensive, failure-avoiding strategies like Defensive Diana described earlier—they pretend not to care, make a show of "not really trying," or they may simply give up (Jagacinski & Nicholls, 1987; Pintrich & Schunk, 1996). The evaluation of their performance, not what they learn or how hard they try, is what matters. Nicholls and Miller (1984) refer to these students as **ego-involved learners** because they are preoccupied with themselves. Deborah Stipek (1996) lists these behaviors as indicative of a student who is ego-involved with classwork:

- Uses short cuts to complete tasks (tries to finish without doing the work it would take to really learn the material)
- Cheats/copies from classmates' papers
- Seeks attention for good performance
- Only works hard on graded assignments
- Is upset by and hides papers with low grades
- Compares grades with classmates
- Chooses tasks that are most likely to result in positive evaluations
- Is uncomfortable with assignments that have unclear evaluation criteria

As we will see later in this chapter, students' beliefs about ability and effort affect the kinds of goals they set. Table 10.4 on page 392 shows how goals and type of involvement fit the concept of motivation to learn. As you might expect, setting *learning goals* and being *task-involved* tends to *increase* motivation to learn, while working toward *performance goals* and being *ego-involved diminish* motivation to learn.

Feedback and Goal Acceptance

Besides having specific, challenging, attainable learning goals and focusing on the task, there are two additional factors that make goal-setting in the classroom effective. The first is *feedback*. In order to be motivated by a discrepancy between "where you are" and "where you want to be," you must have an accurate sense of where you are and how far you have to go. When feedback tells a student that current efforts have fallen short of the goal, the student can exert

Learning Goal A personal intention to improve abilities and understand, no matter how performance suffers.

Task-Involved Learners Students who focus on mastering the task or solving the problem.

Performance Goal A personal intention to seem competent or perform well in the eyes of others.

Ego-Involved Learners Students who focus on how well they are performing and how they are judged by others.

more effort or even try another strategy. When feedback tells the student that the goal is reached or exceeded, the student should feel satisfied and competent—competent enough perhaps to set a higher goal for the future. There is evidence that feedback emphasizing progress is the most effective. In one study, feedback to adults emphasized either that they had accomplished 75% of the standards set or that they had fallen short of the standards by 25%. When the feedback highlighted accomplishment, the subjects' self-confidence, analytic thinking, and performance were all enhanced (Bandura, 1993).

The second factor affecting motivation to pursue a goal is *goal acceptance*. When students accept the goals set by their teachers or establish their own goals, then the power of goal setting to motivate learning can be tapped. But if students reject goals set by others or refuse to set their own goals, then motivation will suffer. Generally, students are more willing to adopt the goals of others if the goals seem realistic, reasonably difficult, and meaningful (Erez & Zidon, 1984) and if good reasons are given for the value of the goals. Goal acceptance might be greater (and goals more appropriate) if you work with students' families to identify and monitor the goals. The Guidelines give some ideas.

Focus on...

Goals and Motivation

- Are students with learning goals more likely to (1) be internal or external in locus of control? (2) be failure avoiders or success seekers?

- A teacher says to the class, "I want all of you to study hard so you can make good scores on the state tests next spring." Predict the effects of this goal-setting statement. Are students likely to be motivated by the goal? Why or why not?

- How does feedback influence motivation?

Guidelines

Family and Community Partnerships for Setting Goals

Understand family goals for children.

Examples

1. In an informal setting, around a coffee pot or snacks, meet with families individually or in small groups to listen to what they want for their children.

2. Mail out questionnaires or send response cards home with students, asking what skills the families believe their children most need to work on. Pick one goal for each child and develop a plan for working toward the goal both inside and outside school. Share the plan with the families and ask for feedback.

Identify student and family interests that can be related to goals.

Examples

1. Ask a member of the family to share a skill or hobby with the class.

2. Identify "family favorites"—favorite foods, music, vacations, sports, colors, activities, hymns, movies, games, snacks, recipes, memories. Tie class lessons to interests.

Give families a way to track progress toward goals.

Examples

1. Provide simple "progress charts" or goal cards that can be posted on the refrigerator.

2. Ask for feedback (and mean it) about parents' perceptions of your effectiveness in helping students reach goals.

Goals: Lessons for Teachers

Students are more likely to work toward goals that are clear, specific, reasonable, moderately challenging, and attainable within a relatively short period of time. If teachers focus on student performance, high grades, competition, and achievement, they may encourage students to set performance goals. This will undermine the students' ability to learn and become task-involved (Anderman & Maehr, 1994). Students may not yet be expert at setting their own goals or keeping the goal in mind, so encouragement and accurate feedback are necessary. If you use any reward or incentive systems, be sure the goal you set is to *learn and improve* in some area, not just to perform well or look smart. And be sure the goal is not too difficult.

Needs and Motivation

A need can be defined as "a biological or psychological requirement; a state of deprivation that motivates a person to take action toward a goal" (Darley, Glucksberg, & Kinchla, 1991, p. 743). Our needs are seldom satisfied completely and perfectly; improvement is always possible. People are thus motivated by the tensions the needs create to move toward goals that could satisfy the needs. Let's look at one very influential *humanistic* theory of motivation that deals with this central concept.

Maslow's Hierarchy

Abraham Maslow has had a great impact on psychology in general and on the psychology of motivation in particular. Maslow (1970) suggested that humans have a **hierarchy of needs** ranging from lower-level needs for survival and safety to higher-level needs for intellectual achievement and finally **self-actualization.** Self-actualization is Maslow's term for self-fulfillment, the realization of personal potential. Figure 10.1 is a diagram of Maslow's model.

Hierarchy of Needs Maslow's model of seven levels of human needs, from basic physiological requirements to the need for self-actualization.

Self-Actualization Fulfilling one's potential.

The needs for safety and belonging are among Maslow's hierarchy of needs.

FIGURE 10.1

Maslow's Hierarchy of Needs

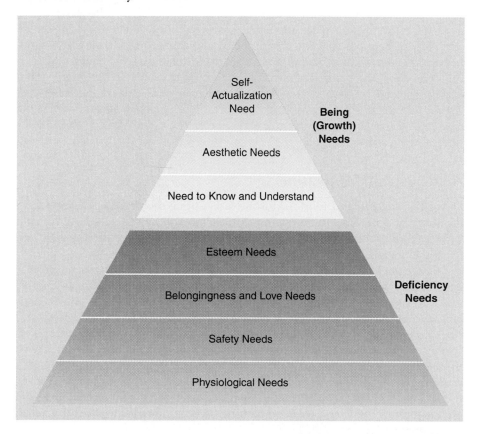

Source: Data for diagram based on Hierarchy of Needs from "A Theory of Human Motivation" *Motivation and Personality,* 2d ed. by Abraham Maslow. Copyright © 1970 by Abraham H. Maslow. Reprinted by permission of Harper & Row, Publishers, Inc.

Maslow (1968) called the four lower-level needs—survival, safety, belonging, and self-esteem—**deficiency needs.** When these needs are satisfied, the motivation for fulfilling them decreases. He labeled the three higher-level needs—intellectual achievement, aesthetic appreciation, and self-actualization—**being needs.** When they are met, a person's motivation does not cease; instead, it increases to seek further fulfillment. For example, the more successful you are in your efforts to know and understand, the harder you are likely to strive for even greater knowledge and understanding. Unlike the deficiency needs, these being needs can never be completely filled. The motivation to achieve them is endlessly renewed.

Maslow's theory has been criticized for the very obvious reason that people do not always appear to behave as the theory would predict. Most of us move back and forth among different types of needs and may even be motivated by many different needs at the same time. Some people deny themselves safety or friendship in order to achieve knowledge, understanding, or greater self-esteem.

Criticisms aside, Maslow's theory does give us a way of looking at the whole person, whose physical, emotional, and intellectual needs are all interrelated. This

Deficiency Needs Maslow's four lower-level needs, which must be satisfied first.

Being Needs Maslow's three higher-level needs, sometimes called *growth needs.*

has important implications for education. Students who come to school hungry, sick, or hurt are unlikely to be motivated to seek knowledge and understanding. A child whose feelings of safety and sense of belonging are threatened by divorce may have little interest in learning to divide fractions. If the classroom is a fearful, unpredictable place and students seldom know where they stand, they are likely to be more concerned with security and less with learning. Maslow's hierarchy can provide other insights into students' behavior. Students' desires to fill lower-level needs may at times conflict with a teacher's desire to have them achieve higher-level goals. Belonging to a social group and maintaining self-esteem within that group, for example, are important to students. If doing what the teacher says conflicts with group rules, students may choose to ignore the teacher's wishes or even defy the teacher.

Achievement Motivation

David McClelland and John Atkinson were among the first to concentrate on the study of **achievement motivation** (McClelland, Atkinson, Clark, & Lowell, 1953). People who strive for excellence in a field for the sake of achieving, not for some reward, are considered to have a high need for achievement.

There are two general explanations for the source of achievement motivation (Stipek, 1993). Some psychologists see achievement motivation as a stable and unconscious trait—something the individual has more or less of. The origins of high achievement motivation are assumed to be in the family and cultural group of the child. If achievement, initiative, and competitiveness are encouraged and reinforced in the home, and if parents let children solve problems on their own without becoming irritated by the children's initial failures, children are more likely to develop a high need for achievement (McClelland & Pilon, 1983). Children who see that their actions can have an impact and who are taught how to recognize a good performance are more likely to grow up with the desire to excel (Schunk, 1996).

Other theorists see achievement motivation as a set of conscious beliefs and values shaped mainly by recent experiences with success and failure and by factors in the immediate situation such as the difficulty of the task or the incentives available. Thus, you might have high achievement motivation in your educational psychology class because you are doing well and you value the material, but low achievement motivation in a required government class because you have had trouble with that subject in the past and the assignments seem unnecessarily long and difficult (Stipek, 1993).

Atkinson (1964) added a new consideration to the theory of achievement need when he noted that all people have a need to avoid failure as well as a need to achieve. If our need to achieve in a particular situation is greater than the need to avoid failure, the overall tendency, or **resultant motivation,** will be to take the risk and try to achieve. On the other hand, if the need to avoid failure is greater, the risk will be threatening rather than challenging, and the resultant motivation will be to avoid the situation.

If students' motivation to achieve is greater than their motivation to avoid failure, a moderate amount of failure can often enhance their desire to pursue a problem. They are determined to achieve, so they try again. On the other hand, success gained too easily can actually decrease motivation for those with high achievement needs. In contrast, students motivated by the need to avoid failure

Achievement Motivation Desire to excel; impetus to strive for excellence and success.

Resultant Motivation Whichever is the stronger tendency—the need to achieve or the need to avoid failure.

are usually discouraged by failure and encouraged by success. Table 10.4 on page 392 integrates achievement motivation into the idea of motivation to learn. Motivation to *achieve encourages* motivation to learn, while *anxiety* and *fear of failure diminish* motivation to learn.

The Need for Self-Determination

Self-determination is the need to experience choice in what we do and how we do it. It is the desire to have our own wishes, rather than external rewards or pressures, determine our actions (Deci & Ryan, 1985; Deci, Vallerand, Pelletier, & Ryan, 1991). People strive to be in charge of their own behavior. They constantly struggle against pressure from external controls such as the rules, schedules, deadlines, orders, and limits imposed by others. Sometimes even help is rejected so that the individual can remain in command (deCharms, 1976, 1983).

To capture the difference between self- and other-determination, deCharms used the metaphor of people as "origins" and "pawns." Origins perceive themselves as the origin or source of their intention to act in a certain way. As pawns, people see themselves as powerless participants in a game controlled by others. When people feel like pawns, play becomes work, leisure feels like obligation, and intrinsic motivation becomes extrinsic motivation (Lepper & Greene, 1978). For example, you may have had the experience of deciding to wash the car or clean your room, only to have your motivation dampened by a parent who insists that you tackle the chore. Your chance to be an origin seems spoiled by outside attempts at control. You don't want to wash the car anymore because your sense of self-determination is taken away.

Richard de Charms was struck by his observation that students are too little governed by their own intrinsic motivation and too powerless over external controls and demands. As origins, students are active and responsible, but as pawns, they are passive and they take little responsibility for school work. To deal with the issue, deCharms developed programs to help teachers support student self-determination. The programs emphasized setting realistic goals, personal planning of activities to reach the goals, personal responsibility for actions, and feelings of self-confidence. Results of some studies show that when students feel more like origins and less like pawns, they have higher self-esteem, feel more competent and in charge of their learning, score higher on standardized tests, and are absent less (deCharms, 1976; Ryan & Grolnick, 1986). The Guidelines give ideas about how to support students' self-determination.

Guidelines

Supporting Autonomy and Self-Determination

Allow and encourage students to make choices.

Examples

1. Design several different ways to meet a learning objective (e.g., a paper, a compilation of interviews, a test, a news broadcast) and let students choose one. Encourage them to explain the reasons for their choice.
2. Appoint student committees to make suggestions about streamlining procedures such as caring for class pets or distributing equipment.

(continued)

Help students plan actions to accomplish self-selected goals.

Examples

1. Experiment with goal cards. Students list their short- and long-term goals and then record 3 or 4 specific actions that will move them toward the goals. Goal cards are personal—like credit cards.
2. Encourage middle- and high school students to set goals in each subject area, record them in a goal book or on a floppy disk, and check progress toward the goals on a regular basis.

Hold students accountable for the consequences of their choices.

Examples

1. If students choose to work with friends and do not finish a project because too much time was spent socializing, grade the project as it deserves and help the students see the connection between lost time and poor performance.
2. When students choose a topic that captures their imagination, discuss the connections between their investment in the work and the quality products that follow.

Source: Adapted from J. P. Raffini (1996). *150 ways to increase intrinsic motivation in the classroom.* Boston: Allyn & Bacon.

The Need for Relatedness

Relatedness is the need to establish close emotional bonds and attachments with others and reflects the desire to be emotionally connected to the important people in our lives (Ryan, 1991). When teachers and parents are responsive and demonstrate that they care about the children's interests and well-being, the children show high intrinsic motivation. But, when children are denied the interpersonal involvement they seek from adults—when adults, for example, are unresponsive to their needs—the children lose intrinsic motivation (Grolnick, Ryan, & Deci, 1991). In addition, emotional and physical problems—ranging from eating disorders to suicide —are more common among people who lack social relationships (Baumeister & Leary, 1995).

Relatedness has two components, involvement and autonomy support. Involvement is the degree to which teachers and parents are interested in and knowledgeable about their childrens' activities and experiences and devote time to them. Autonomy support is the degree to which teachers and parents encourage children to make their own choices rather than applying pressure to control the children's behavior. When teachers and parents show high involvement and autonomy support, children show greater competence, academic achievement, and responsibility, as well as less aggression (Grolnick & Ryan, 1989; Grolnick, Ryan, & Deci, 1991).

Focus on...

Needs and Motivation

- Use Maslow's theory to explain why a student who is upset about events in his or her family might not be motivated to study.
- Do you believe the need to achieve is more a personal trait or a situation-specific state? Why?
- How can students' needs for self-determination be supported through goal setting?

Needs and Motivation: Lessons for Teachers

All people need to feel safe, secure, accepted, competent, effective, connected, and in charge of their own behavior. Some people may have developed a particularly strong need to achieve. Most people are more motivated when they are involved with tasks that give them a sense of achievement and a chance to form positive relationships with others. No one enjoys failure, and for some people it is crushing. Students, like adults, are unlikely to stick with tasks or respond well to teachers who make them feel insecure or incompetent and cause them to fail. They are less likely to take responsibility for learning if they feel like pawns rather than origins in the classroom or if they believe that the teacher doesn't really care about them.

Attributions, Beliefs, and Motivation

Thus far, we have talked about goals and needs, but there is another factor that must be considered in explaining motivation. Success will not encourage motivation if you believe it was "just lucky" and probably won't happen again. Failure is not threatening unless you believe that it implies something is "wrong" with you. In other words, our *beliefs* and *attributions* about what is happening and why—about why we succeed and why we fail—affect motivation.

Attribution Theory

Cognitive explanations of motivation, called **attribution theories,** begin with the assumption that we all ask "Why?" in our attempts to understand our successes and failures. Students may ask themselves, "Why did I flunk my midterm?" "What's wrong with my essay?" "Why did I do so well this grading period?" Students may *attribute* their successes and failures to ability, effort, mood, knowledge, luck, help, interest, clarity of instructions, the interference of others, unfair policies, and so on. Attribution theories of motivation describe how the individual's explanations, justifications, and excuses influence motivation.

Dimensions: Locus, Stability, Responsibility.   Bernard Weiner is one of the main educational psychologists responsible for relating attribution theory to school learning (Weiner, 1979, 1986, 1992, 1994a,b; Weiner & Graham, 1989). According to Weiner, most of the causes to which students attribute their successes or failures can be characterized in terms of three dimensions: *locus* (location of the cause internal or external to the person), *stability* (whether the cause stays the same or can change), and *responsibility* (whether the person can control the cause). Table 10.2 on page 388 shows how a student might explain failing a test using the eight possible combinations of these dimensions as causes.

Weiner (1992, 1994a,b) believes that these three dimensions have important implications for motivation. The *internal/external locus,* for example, seems to be closely related to feelings of self-esteem (Weiner, 1980). If success or failure is attributed to internal factors, success will lead to pride and increased motivation, whereas failure will diminish self-esteem.

The *stability* dimension seems to be closely related to expectations about the future. If, for example, students attribute their success (or failure) to stable factors such as the difficulty of the subject, they will expect to succeed (or fail) in that subject in the future. But if they attribute the outcome to unstable factors such as mood or luck, they will expect (or hope for) changes in the future when confronted with similar tasks. The *responsibility* dimension is related to emotions such as anger, pity, gratitude, or shame. If we fail at something that we

Attribution Theories Descriptions of how individuals' explanations, justifications, and excuses influence their motivation and behavior.

TABLE 10.2   Weiner's Theory of Causal Attribution

There are many explanations students can give for why they fail a test. Below are eight reasons representing the eight combinations of locus, stability, and responsibility in Weiner's model of attributions.

Dimension Classification	Reason for Failure
Internal-stable-uncontrollable	Low aptitude
Internal-stable-controllable	Never studies
Internal-unstable-uncontrollable	Sick the day of the exam
Internal-unstable-controllable	Did not study for this particular test
External-stable-uncontrollable	School has hard requirements
External-stable-controllable	Instructor is biased
External-unstable-uncontrollable	Bad luck
External-unstable-controllable	Friends failed to help

Source: From B. Weiner (1992). *Human motivation: Metaphors, theories and research,* p. 253. Adapted by permission of Sage Publications, Inc.

believe is controllable, we may feel guilt; if we succeed, we may feel proud. Failing at an uncontrollable task may lead to shame or to anger toward the person or institution in control, while succeeding leads to feeling lucky or grateful. Also, feeling in control of your own learning, seems to be related to choosing more difficult academic tasks, putting out more effort, and persisting longer in school work (Schunk, 1996; Weiner, 1994a,b).

Weiner (1994a) summarizes the sequence of motivation when failure is attributed to lack of ability and ability is considered uncontrollable:

$$\text{Failure} \rightarrow \frac{\text{Lack of}}{\text{Ability}} \rightarrow \text{Uncontrollable} \rightarrow \frac{\text{Not}}{\text{Responsible}} \rightarrow \frac{\text{Shame and}}{\text{Embarrassment}} \rightarrow \frac{\text{Performance}}{\text{Declines}}$$

When failure is attributed to lack of effort, the sequence is:

$$\text{Failure} \rightarrow \frac{\text{Lack of}}{\text{Effort}} \rightarrow \text{Controllable} \rightarrow \text{Responsible} \rightarrow \text{Guilt} \rightarrow \frac{\text{Performance}}{\text{Improves}}$$

Weiner's locus and responsibility dimensions are closely related to Deci's concept of *locus of causality* and deCharm's origin/pawn distinction, discussed earlier. J. B. Rotter's (1954) idea of **locus of control** also captures the distinction between self-determination and control by others. Rotter suggested that locus of control is a relatively stable trait. For example, some people have an internal locus of control and believe they are responsible for their own fate. They like to work in situations where skill and effort can lead to success. Other people tend to have an external locus of control, generally believing that people and forces outside themselves control their lives. These individuals prefer to work in situations where luck determines the outcome (Lefcourt, 1966). Locus of control can be influenced by the behavior of others. Continuing discrimination against women, people of color, and individuals with special needs can affect these individuals' perceptions of their own ability to control their lives (Beane, 1991). If people feel that they are not in control of their own lives, their self-esteem is likely to be diminished.

Locus of Control "Where" people locate responsibility for success and failures—inside or outside themselves.

Learned Helplessness.   Whatever the label, most theorists agree that a sense of choice, control, and self-determination is critical if people are to feel intrinsically motivated. When people come to believe that the events and outcomes in their lives are mostly uncontrollable, they have developed **learned helplessness** (Seligman, 1975). To understand the power of learned helplessness, consider this experiment (Hiroto & Seligman, 1975): Subjects receive either solvable or unsolvable puzzles. In the next phase of the experiment, all subjects are given a series of solvable puzzles. The subjects who struggled with unsolvable problems in the first phase of the experiment usually solve significantly fewer puzzles in the second phase. They have learned that they cannot control the outcome, so why should they even try?

Learned helplessness appears to cause three types of deficits: motivational, cognitive, and affective. Students who feel hopeless will be unmotivated and reluctant to attempt work. Like Helpless Henry described earlier, they expect to fail so why even try—thus motivation suffers. Because they are pessimistic about learning, these students miss opportunities to practice and improve skills and abilities, so they develop cognitive deficits. Finally, they often suffer from affective problems such as depression, anxiety, and listlessness (Alloy & Seligman, 1979). Once established, it is very difficult to reverse the effects of learned helplessness. As we saw in Chapters 4 and 5, learned helplessness is a particular danger for students with learning disabilities and students who are the victims of discrimination.

Attributions and Student Motivation.   Most students try to explain their failures to themselves. When usually successful students fail, they often make internal, controllable attributions: they misunderstood the directions, lacked the necessary knowledge, or simply did not study hard enough, for example. When students see themselves as capable and attribute failure to lack of effort or insufficient knowledge—controllable causes—they usually focus on strategies for succeeding next time. This is an adaptive, mastery-oriented response, one that often leads to achievement, pride, a greater feeling of control, and a sense of self-determination (Ames, 1992).

The greatest motivational problems arise when students attribute failures to stable, uncontrollable causes. Such students may seem resigned to failure, depressed, helpless—what we generally call "unmotivated" (Weiner, 1994a,b; Weiner, Russell, & Lerman, 1978). These students respond to failure by focusing even more on their own inadequacy; their attitudes toward schoolwork may deteriorate even further (Ames, 1992). Apathy is a logical reaction to failure if students believe the causes are stable, unlikely to change, and beyond their control. In addition, students who view their failures in this light are less likely to seek help—they believe nothing and no one can help (Ames & Lau, 1982). Table 10.4 on page 392 adds the role of attributions to motivation to learn. As you might guess, when students attribute outcomes to *controllable causes,* motivation to learn is *encouraged,* while attributing outcomes to *uncontrollable causes diminishes* motivation to learn.

Cues about Causes.   How do students determine the causes of their successes and failures? The behavior of their teachers is one cue. When teachers assume that student failure is attributable to forces beyond the students' control, they tend to respond with sympathy and to avoid giving punishments. If, however, the failures are attributed to a controllable factor such as lack of effort, the

Learned Helplessness The expectation, based on previous experiences with a lack of control, that all one's efforts will lead to failure.

teacher's response is more likely to be anger and punishments may follow. These tendencies seem to be consistent across time and cultures (Weiner, 1986).

What do students make of these reactions from their teachers? Sandra Graham (1991, 1996) gives some surprising answers. There is evidence that when teachers respond to students' mistakes with pity, praise for a "good try," or unsolicited help, the students are more likely to attribute their failure to an uncontrollable cause—usually lack of ability. For example, Graham and Barker (1990) asked subjects of various ages to rate the effort and ability of two boys on a videotape. On the tape was a teacher circulating around the class while students worked. The teacher stopped to look at the two boys' papers, did not comment to the first boy, but said to the second, "Let me give you a hint. Don't forget to carry your tens." The second boy had not asked for help and did not appear to be stumped by the problem. All the age groups watching the tapes, even the youngest, perceived the helped boy as lower in ability than the boy who did not get help. It is as if the subjects read the teacher's behavior as saying, "You poor child, you just don't have the ability to do this hard work, so I will help."

Does this mean that teachers should be critical and withhold help? Of course not! But it is a reminder that "praise as a consolation prize" for failing (Brophy, 1985) or oversolicitous help can give unintended messages. Graham (1991) suggests that many minority-group students could be the victims of well-meaning pity from teachers. Seeing the very real problems that the students face, teachers may "ease up" on requirements so the students will "experience success" and "feel good about themselves." But a subtle communication may accompany the pity, praise, and extra help: "You don't have the ability to do this, so I will overlook your failure." Graham says, "The . . . pertinent question for blacks is whether their own history of academic failure makes them more likely to be the targets of sympathetic feedback from teachers and thus the recipients of low-ability cues" (1991, p. 28). This kind of sympathetic feedback, even if well-intended, can be a subtle form of racism.

Beliefs about Ability

As you can see, some of the most powerful attributions affecting motivation in school are beliefs about *ability*. By examining these beliefs and how they affect motivation, we will understand why some people set inappropriate, unmotivating goals; why some students adopt self-defeating strategies; and why some students seem to give up altogether.

Adults use two basic concepts of ability. An **entity view of ability** assumes that ability is a *stable, uncontrollable* trait—a characteristic of the individual that cannot be changed. According to this view, some people have more ability than others, but the amount each person has is set. An **incremental view of ability**, on the other hand, suggests that ability is unstable and controllable—"an ever-expanding repertoire of skills and knowledge" (Dweck & Bempechat, 1983, p. 144). By hard work, study, or practice, knowledge can be increased and thus ability can be improved. Table 10.3 shows how these two conceptions of ability would fit into Weiner's model of causal attribution (Table 10.2).

Young children tend to hold an exclusively incremental view of ability (Nicholls & Miller, 1984). Through the early elementary grades, most students believe that effort is the same as intelligence. Smart people try hard and trying hard makes you smart. If you fail, you aren't smart and you didn't try hard; if

Entity View of Ability Belief that ability is a fixed characteristic that cannot be changed.

Incremental View of Ability Belief that ability is a set of skills that can be changed.

TABLE 10.3   A Revised View of the Internal Attribution Model with Two Kinds of Ability

	Internal Attribution	
	Stable	**Unstable**
Controllable	Never studies	Did not study for this particular test *Incremental ability*
Uncontrollable	*Entity ability*	Sick day of exam

you succeed, you must be a smart, hard worker (Stipek, 1993). Children are age 11 or 12 before they can differentiate among effort, ability, and performance. About this time, they come to believe that someone who succeeds without working at all must be really smart. This is when beliefs about ability begin to influence motivation (Anderman & Maehr, 1994).

Students who hold an entity view of intelligence tend to set performance goals. They seek situations where they can look smart and protect their self-esteem. Like Safe Sally, they keep doing what they can do well without expending too much effort or risking failure, since either one—working hard or failing—indicates (to them) low ability. And to work hard but still fail would be a devastating blow to their sense of competence.

Another strategy is to make a point of not trying at all, like Defensive Diana described earlier. If you don't try and fail, no one can accuse you of being dumb. Just before a test a student might say, "I didn't study at all!" or "All I want to do is pass." Then, any grade above passing is a success. Procrastination is another self-protective strategy. Low grades do not imply low ability if the student

Students' beliefs about their own ability to succeed influence achievement. These beliefs are affected in one way or another by family, teachers, and others.

TABLE 10.4   Building a Concept of Motivation to Learn

Motivation to learn is encouraged when the sources of motivation are intrinsic, the goals are personally challenging, and the individual is focused on the task, has a mastery orientation, attributes successes and failures to controllable causes, and believes ability can be improved.

	Optimum Characteristics of Motivation to Learn	Characteristics That Diminish Motivation to Learn
Source of Motivation	INTRINSIC: Personal factors such as needs, interests, curiosity, enjoyment	EXTRINSIC: Environmental factors such as rewards, social pressure, punishment
Type of Goal Set	LEARNING GOAL: Personal satisfaction in meeting challenges and improving; tendency to choose moderately difficult and challenging goals	PERFORMANCE GOAL: Desire for approval of performance in others' eyes; tendency to choose very easy or very difficult goals
Type of Involvement	TASK-INVOLVED: Concerned with mastering the task	EGO-INVOLVED: Concerned with self in others' eyes
Achievement Motivation	Motivation to ACHIEVE: mastery orientation	Motivation to AVOID FAILURE: prone to anxiety
Likely Attributions	Successes and failures attributed to CONTROLLABLE effort and ability	Successes and failures attributed to UNCONTROLLABLE causes
Beliefs about Ability	INCREMENTAL VIEW: Belief that ability can be improved through hard work and added knowledge and skills	ENTITY VIEW: Belief that ability is a stable, uncontrollable trait

---

can claim, "I did okay considering I didn't start the term paper until last night." Some evidence suggests that blaming anxiety for poor test performance can also be a self-protective strategy (Covington & Omelich, 1987). Of course, even though these strategies may help students avoid the negative implications of failure, very little learning is going on.

Incremental theorists, in contrast, tend to set learning goals and seek situations in which they can improve their skills, since improvement means getting smarter. Failure is not devastating; it simply indicates more work is needed. Ability is not threatened. Incremental theorists tend to set moderately difficult goals, the kind we have seen are the most motivating. Table 10.4 merges beliefs about ability into the concept of motivation to learn. Now our chart is complete and serves as a summary of the factors that support motivation to learn.

Beliefs about Self-Efficacy

Bandura (1986, 1995) suggests that one source of motivation is thoughts and predictions about possible outcomes of behavior. "Will I succeed or fail? Will I be liked or laughed at?" We imagine future consequences based on past experiences and our observations of others. These predictions are also affected by **self-efficacy**—our predictions about our personal efficacy (competence or effectiveness) *in a given area*. Bandura (1995) defines self-efficacy as "beliefs in one's

Self-Efficacy Beliefs about personal competence in a particular situation.

capabilities to organize and execute the courses of action required to manage prospective situations" (p. 2). A sense of efficacy has four main influences: mastery experiences (past successes or failures in a particular area), vicarious experiences (observing others who are like us succeed or fail), social persuasion (encouragement from others), and physiological or emotional feedback (sweaty palms or relaxed responses taken as signs of the ability to do the task). Of these four, the most powerful is our own experience.

Efficacy and Motivation.   Sense of self-efficacy not only affects expectations for success or failure, it also influences motivation through goal setting. If we have a high sense of efficacy in a given area, we will set higher goals, be less afraid of failure, and persist longer when we encounter difficulties. If our sense of efficacy is low, however, we may avoid a task altogether or give up easily when problems arise (Bandura, 1993, 1997; Zimmerman, 1995).

Self-efficacy also seems to be related to attributions. People with a strong sense of self-efficacy for a given task ("I'm good at math") attribute their failures to lack of effort ("I should have double-checked my work"). But people with a low sense of efficacy ("I'm terrible at math") tend to attribute their failures to lack of ability ("I'm just dumb"). You can see that if a student held an entity view (ability cannot be changed) and a low sense of self-efficacy, motivation would be destroyed when failures were attributed to lack of (unchangeable) ability ("I just can't do this and I'll never be able to learn") (Bandura, 1997; Pintrich & Schunk, 1996).

There is evidence that a high sense of self-efficacy supports motivation, even when the feeling of efficacy is unrealisticly high. Children and adults who are optimistic about the future, believe that they can be effective, and have high expectations are more mentally and physically healthy, less depressed, and more motivated to achieve (Flammer, 1995). After examining almost 140 studies of motivation, Sandra Graham concluded that these qualities characterize many African Americans. She found that the African Americans studied had strong self-concepts and high expectations, even in the face of difficulties (Graham, 1994, 1995).

Research on self-efficacy and achievement suggests that performance in school is improved and self-efficacy is increased when students (a) adopt short-term goals so it is easier to judge progress; (b) are taught to use specific learning strategies such as outlining or summarizing that help them focus attention; and (c) receive rewards based on performance, not just engagement, because performance rewards signal increasing competence (Graham & Weiner, 1996).

Teacher Efficacy.   Much of my own recent research has focused on a particular kind of self-efficacy—sense of efficacy in teaching (Hoy & Woolfolk, 1990, 1993; Woolfolk & Hoy, 1990; Woolfolk, Rosoff, & Hoy, 1990). **Teaching efficacy,** a teacher's belief that he or she can reach even difficult students to help them learn, appears to be one of the few personal characteristics of teachers that is correlated with student achievement (Ashton & Webb, 1986; Guskey & Passaro, 1994). Self-efficacy theory predicts that teachers with a high sense of efficacy work harder and persist longer even when students are difficult to teach, in part because these teachers believe in themselves and in their students.

Teaching Efficacy A teacher's belief that he or she can reach even the most difficult students and help them learn.

We have found that prospective teachers tend to increase in their personal sense of efficacy as a consequence of completing student teaching. Teachers' sense of personal efficacy is higher in schools where the other teachers and administrators have high expectations for students and where teachers receive help from their principals in solving instructional and management problems (Hoy & Woolfolk, 1993). Another important conclusion from our research is that efficacy grows from real success with students, not just from the moral support or cheerleading of professors and colleagues. Any experience or training that helps you succeed in the day-to-day tasks of teaching will give you a foundation for developing a sense of efficacy in your career.

Attributions, Achievement Motivation, and Self-Worth

What are the connections between our need for achievement, attributions for success and failure, beliefs about ability, self-efficacy, and self-worth? Covington and his colleagues suggest that these factors come together in three kinds of motivational sets: *mastery-oriented, failure-avoiding,* and *failure-accepting,* as shown in Table 10.5 (Covington, 1992; Covington & Omelich, 1984, 1987).

Mastery-oriented students tend to value achievement and see ability as improvable, so they focus on learning goals in order to increase their skills and abilities. They are not fearful of failure, because failing does not threaten their sense of competence and self-worth. This allows them to set moderately difficult goals, take risks, and cope with failure constructively. They generally attribute success to their own effort, and thus they assume responsibility for learning and have a strong sense of self-efficacy. They perform best in competitive situations, learn fast, have more self-confidence and energy, are more aroused, welcome concrete feedback (it does not threaten them), and are eager to learn "the rules

Mastery-Oriented Students
Students who focus on learning goals because they value achievement and see ability as improvable.

TABLE 10.5   Mastery-Oriented, Failure-Avoiding, and Failure-Accepting Students

	Need for Achievement	Goals Set	Attributions	View of Ability	Strategies
Mastery-oriented	High need for achievement; low fear of failure	Learning goals: moderately difficult and challenging	Effort, use of right strategy, sufficient knowledge is cause of success	Incremental; improvable	Adaptive strategies: e.g., try another way, seek help, practice/ study more
Failure-avoiding	High fear of failure	Performance goals; very hard or very easy	Lack of ability is cause of failure	Entity; set	Self-defeating strategies: e.g., make a feeble effort, pretend not to care
Failure-accepting	Expectation of failure; depression	Performance goals or no goals	Lack of ability is cause of failure	Entity; set	Learned helplessness; likely to give up

of the game" so that they can succeed. All of these factors make for persistent, successful learning (Alderman, 1985; McClelland, 1985; Morris, 1991).

Failure-avoiding students tend to hold an entity view of ability, so they set performance goals. They lack a strong sense of their own competence and self-worth separate from their performance. In other words, they feel only as smart as their last test grade, so they never develop a solid sense of self-efficacy. In order to feel competent, they must protect themselves (and their self-images) from failure. If they have been generally successful, they may avoid failure simply by taking few risks and "sticking with what they know." If, on the other hand, they have experienced some successes but also a good bit of failure, they may adopt the strategies we discussed earlier—procrastination, feeble efforts, setting very low or ridiculously high goals, or claiming not to care. Both Safe Sally and Defensive Diana are failure-avoiding students.

Unfortunately, as we have seen, failure-avoiding strategies are self-defeating, generally leading to the very failure the students were trying to avoid. If failures continue and excuses wear thin, the students may finally decide that they are incompetent. This is what they feared in the first place, but they come to accept it. Their sense of self-worth and self-efficacy deteriorate. They give up and thus become **failure-accepting students.** They are convinced that their problems are due to low ability, and they can no longer protect themselves from this conclusion. As we saw earlier, those students who attribute failure to low ability and believe ability is set are likely to become depressed, apathetic, and helpless. Like Hopeless Henry, they have little hope for change.

Teachers may be able to prevent some failure-avoiding students from becoming failure-accepting by helping them to find new and more realistic goals. Also, some students may need support in aspiring to higher levels in the face of sexual or ethnic stereotypes about what they "should" want or what they "should not" be able to do well. This kind of support could make all the difference. Instead of pitying or excusing these students, teachers can teach them how to learn and then hold them accountable.

> **Focus on...**
>
> ### Attributions, Beliefs, and Motivation
>
> - If a person has a strong sense of self-efficacy, what kind of goals would he or she set? Why?
> - Explain how beliefs about the nature of ability might be associated with students' self-protective, self-defeating behaviors such as procrastination or not trying.
> - Describe the development of learned helplessness. What kinds of goals would a student set if the student felt helpless?
> - Why are students more likely to learn if they attribute successes and failures to controllable causes? How does the attribution to controllable causes relate to the need for self-determination?

Attributions and Beliefs: Lessons for Teachers

At the heart of attribution theory is the notion of individual perception. If students believe they lack the ability to deal with higher mathematics, they will probably act on this belief even if their actual abilities are well above average. These students are likely to have little motivation to tackle trigonometry or calculus, because they expect to do poorly in these areas. If students believe that failing means they are stupid, they are likely to adopt many self-protective, but also self-defeating, strategies. Just telling students to "try harder" is not particularly effective. Students need real evidence that effort will pay off, that setting a higher goal will not lead to failure, that they can improve, and that abilities can be changed. The Guidelines on page 396 provide ideas for encouraging self-worth.

Failure-Avoiding Students Students who avoid failure by sticking to what they know, by not taking risks, or by claiming not to care about their performance.

Failure-Accepting Students Students who believe their failures are the result of low ability and there is little they can do about it.

Guidelines

Encouraging Students' Self-Worth

Emphasize students' progress in a particular area.

Examples

1. Return to earlier material in reviews and show how "easy" it is now.
2. Encourage students to improve projects when they have learned more.
3. Keep examples of particularly good work in portfolios.

Make specific suggestions for improvement, and revise grades when improvements are made.

Examples

1. Return work with comments noting what the students did right, what they did wrong, and why they might have made the mistakes.
2. Experiment with peer editing.
3. Show students how their revised, higher grade reflects greater competence and raises their class average.

Stress connections between past efforts and past accomplishments.

Examples

1. Have individual goal-setting and goal-review conferences with students, in which you ask students to reflect on how they solved difficult problems.
2. Confront self-defeating, failure-avoiding strategies directly.

Set learning goals for your students, and model a mastery orientation for them.

Examples

1. Recognize progress and improvement.
2. Share examples of how you have developed your abilities in a given area.
3. Read stories about students who overcame physical, mental, or economic challenges.
4. Don't excuse failure because a student has problems outside school. Help the student succeed inside school.

Anxiety and Coping in the Classroom

At one time or another, everyone has experienced **anxiety,** or "general uneasiness, a sense of foreboding, a feeling of tension" (Hansen, 1977, p. 91). The effects of anxiety on school achievement are clear. "From the time of the earliest work on this problem, starting with the pioneering work of Yerkes and Dodson (1908), to the present day, researchers have consistently reported a negative correlation between virtually every aspect of school achievement and a wide range of anxiety measures" (Covington & Omelich, 1987, p. 393). Anxiety can be both a cause and an effect of school failure—students do poorly because they are anxious, and their poor performance increases their anxiety. Anxiety probably is both a trait and a state. Some students tend to be anxious in many situations (trait anxiety), but some situations are especially anxiety-provoking (state anxiety) (Covington, 1992).

Anxiety seems to have both cognitive and affective components. The cognitive side includes worry and negative thoughts—thinking about how bad it

Anxiety General uneasiness, a feeling of tension.

would be to fail and worrying that you will, for example. The affective side involves physiological and emotional reactions such as sweaty palms, upset stomach, racing heartbeat, or fear (Schunk, 1996; Zeidner, 1995).

What Causes Anxiety in School?

In the classroom, the conditions surrounding a test can influence the performance of highly anxious individuals. For example, Hill and Eaton (1977) found that very anxious fifth and sixth graders worked as quickly and accurately as their less-anxious classmates when there was no time limit for solving arithmetic problems. With a time limit, however, the very anxious students made three times as many errors as their classmates, spent about twice as much time on each problem, and cheated twice as often as the less-anxious group. Whenever there are pressures to perform, severe consequences for failure, and competitive comparisons among students, anxiety may be encouraged (Wigfield & Eccles, 1989).

Sigmund Tobias (1985) suggests a model to explain how anxiety interferes with learning and test performance at three points in the learning and performance cycle. When students are learning new material, they must pay attention to it. Highly anxious students evidently divide their attention between the new material and their preoccupation with how nervous they are feeling. Instead of concentrating on a lecture or on what they are reading, they keep noticing the tight feelings in their chest, thinking, "I'm so tense, I'll never understand this stuff!" Much of their attention is taken up with negative thoughts about performing poorly, being criticized, and feeling embarrassed. From the beginning, anxious students may miss much of the information they are supposed to learn because their thoughts are focused on their own worries (Hill & Wigfield, 1984; Paulman & Kennelly, 1984).

But the problems do not end here. Even if they are paying attention, many anxious students have trouble learning material that is somewhat disorganized and difficult—material that requires them to rely on their memory. Unfortunately, much material in school could be described this way. Anxious students may be more easily distracted by irrelevant or incidental aspects of the task at hand. They seem to have trouble focusing on the significant details (Hill & Wigfield, 1984). In addition, many highly anxious students have poor study habits. Simply learning to be more relaxed will not automatically improve these students' performance; their learning strategies and study skills must be improved as well (Naveh-Benjamin, 1991).

Finally, anxious students often know more than they can demonstrate on a test. They may lack critical test-taking skills, or they may have learned the materials but "freeze and forget" on tests. So anxiety can interfere at one or all three points—attention, learning, and testing (Naveh-Benjamin, McKeachie, & Lin, 1987).

Helping Anxious Students

When students face stressful situations such as tests, they can use three kinds of coping strategies—*problem solving, emotional management,* and *avoidance.* Problem-focused strategies might include planning a study schedule, borrowing good notes, or finding a protected place to study. Emotion-focused strategies are attempts to reduce the anxious feelings, for example, by using relaxation exercises or describing the feelings to a friend. Of course, the latter might become an avoidance strategy, along with going out for pizza or suddenly launching an all out desk-cleaning attack (can't study till you get organized!). Different strategies are helpful at different points—for example, problem solving before and emotion management during an exam. Different strategies fit different people and situations (Zeidner, 1995).

Teachers should help highly anxious students to set realistic goals, because these individuals often have difficulty making wise choices. They tend to select either extremely difficult or extremely easy tasks. In the first case, they are likely to fail, which will increase their sense of hopelessness and anxiety about school. In the second case, they will probably succeed on the easy tasks, but they will miss the sense of satisfaction that could encourage greater effort, ease their fears about schoolwork, and nurture a sense of self-efficacy. Anxious students may need a good deal of guidance in choosing both short- and long-term goals. The goal cards or goal books described earlier may help here.

Anxious students may also need help working at a moderate pace, especially when taking tests. Often, these students either work too quickly and make many careless errors or work too slowly and are never able to finish the task. If possible, consider eliminating time limits on important tests.

Because anxiety appears to interfere with both attention and retention (Wittrock, 1978), highly anxious students (at least those of average or high ability) benefit most from instruction that is very structured and allows for repetition of parts of the lesson that are missed or forgotten (Seiber, O'Neil, & Tobias, 1977; Wigfield & Eccles, 1989).

| Focus on... |

Anxiety in the Classroom

- Name some sources of anxiety in typical classroom situations.
- How does anxiety interfere with learning?

Arousal Physical and psychological reactions causing a person to be alert, attentive, and wide awake.

Anxiety: Lessons for Teachers

You need to work at keeping the level of **arousal** right for the task at hand. If students are going to sleep, energize them by introducing variety, piquing their curiosity, surprising them, or giving them a brief chance to be physically active. If arousal is too great, follow the Guidelines for dealing with anxiety.

Guidelines

Dealing with Anxiety

Use competition carefully.

Examples
1. Monitor activities to make sure no students are being put under undue pressure.
2. During competitive games, make sure all students involved have a reasonable chance of succeeding.
3. Experiment with cooperative learning activities.

Avoid situations in which highly anxious students will have to perform in front of large groups.

Examples
1. Ask anxious students questions that can be answered with a simple yes or no, or some other brief reply.
2. Give anxious students practice in speaking before smaller groups.

Make sure all instructions are clear.

Examples

1. Write test instructions on the board or on the test itself instead of giving them orally.
2. Check with students to make sure they understand. Ask several students how they would do the first question or an exercise or the sample question on a test. Correct any misconceptions.
3. If you are using a new format or starting a new type of task, give students examples or models to show how it is done.

Avoid unnecessary time pressures.

Examples

1. Give occasional take-home tests.
2. Make sure all students can complete classroom tests within the period given.

Remove some of the pressures from major tests and exams.

Examples

1. Teach test-taking skills; give practice tests; provide study guides.
2. Avoid basing most of a report-card grade on one test.
3. Make extra-credit work available to add points to course grades.
4. Use different types of items in testing, since some students have difficulty with certain types.

Develop alternatives to written tests.

Examples

1. Try oral, open-book, or group tests.
2. Have students do projects, organize portfolios of their work, make oral presentations, or create a finished product.

SUMMARY

What Is Motivation?

The study of motivation focuses on how and why people initiate actions directed toward specific goals, how intensively they are involved in the activity, and how persistent they are in their attempts to reach these goals. Explanations of motivation include both personal and environmental factors as well as intrinsic and extrinsic sources of motivation.

Behaviorists tend to emphasize extrinsic motivation caused by incentives, rewards, and punishment. Humanistic views stress the intrinsic motivation created by the need for personal growth, fulfillment, and self determination. Cognitive psychologists stress a person's active search for meaning, understanding, and competence, and the power of the individual's beliefs and interpretations. Social learning views suggest that motivation to reach a goal is the product of our expectations for success and the value of the goal to us. If either is zero, our motivation is zero also. This general approach is called the expectancy × value theory of motivation. Teachers are interested in a particular kind of motivation—student motivation to learn. Student motivation to learn is both a trait and a state. It involves taking academic work seriously, trying to get the most from it, and applying appropriate learning strategies in the process.

Goals and Motivation

Many theories of motivation feature a prominent role for goals. Goals increase motivation if they are specific, moderately difficult, and able to be reached in the near future. The distinction between performance goals (the intention to appear smart or capable in the eyes of others) and learning goals (the intention to gain knowledge and master skills) is important. Students who are motivated to learn set learning rather than performance goals and are task-involved rather than ego-involved. In order for goal-setting to be effective in the classroom, students need accurate feedback about their progress toward goals and they must accept the goals rather than reject them.

Needs and Motivation

Needs are also an important component of many theories of motivation. Maslow has suggested that people are motivated by a hierarchy of needs, beginning with basic physiological requirements and moving up to the need for self-fulfillment. Lower-level needs must by met before higher-level needs can influence motivation. The need for achievement has been viewed as a personal characteristic nurtured by early experiences in the family and as a reaction to recent experiences with success or failure. The need to achieve is balanced by the need to avoid failure. Together, these are strong motivating forces. Several theorists emphasize the role of choice and self-determination in motivation and the need for positive relations with others.

Attributions, Beliefs, and Motivation

The attribution theory of motivation suggests that the explanations people give for behavior, particularly their own successes and failures, have strong influences on future plans and performance. One of the important features of an attribution is whether it is internal and within a person's control or external and beyond control. Teachers may cue attributions by the way they respond to students' work. Surprisingly, praise, sympathy, and unsolicited help can communicate to students that they lack the ability to do the work.

When people believe that ability is fixed, they tend to set performance goals and strive to protect themselves from failure. When they believe ability is improvable, however, they tend to set learning goals and handle failure constructively. A low sense of self-worth seems to be linked with the failure-avoiding and failure-accepting strategies intended to protect the individual from the consequences of failure. These strategies may seem to help in the short term, but are damaging to motivation and self-esteem in the long run.

Bandura suggests that sense of self-efficacy, the belief that you will be effective in a given situation, is a powerful influence on motivation. If an individual has a strong sense of self-efficacy, he or she tends to set more challenging goals and to persist even when obstacles are encountered.

Anxiety in the Classroom

Severe anxiety is an example of arousal that is too high for optimal learning. Anxiety can be the cause or the result of poor performance; it can interfere with attention to, learning of, and retrieval of information. Many anxious students need help in developing effective test-taking and study skills.

KEY TERMS

achievement motivation, p. 384
anxiety, p. 396
arousal, p. 398
attribution theories, p. 387
being needs, p. 383
deficiency needs, p. 383
ego-involved learners, p. 380
entity view of ability, p. 390
expectancy × value theories, p. 377
extrinsic motivation, p. 374
failure-accepting students, p. 395

failure-avoiding students, p. 395
goal, p. 379
hierarchy of needs, p. 382
humanistic view, p. 375
incentive, p. 375
incremental view of ability, p. 390
intrinsic motivation, p. 374
learned helplessness, p. 389
learning goal, p. 380
locus of causality, p. 374
locus of control, p. 388

mastery-oriented students, p. 394
motivation, p. 372
performance goal, p. 380
reward, p. 375
resultant motivation, p. 384
self-actualization, p. 382
self-efficacy, p. 392
student motivation to learn, p. 378
task-involved learners, p. 380
teaching efficacy, p. 393

Can you apply the ideas from this chapter on motivation to solve the following problems of practice?

Preschool and Kindergarten

- How would you create an environment that communicates the value of learning to young children without becoming too directive or academic in your teaching? How could you help students build a foundation for self-efficacy in school?

Elementary and Middle School

- Several of your students seem to have given up in science. They almost expect to fail. This is especially troubling because a number of the students are girls who believe that "girls are no good in science." What would you do?

Junior High and High School

- You are the faculty advisor for the student newspaper. Your students have grand ideas for stories and features, but they seem to run out of steam and never quite finish. The production of the paper is always last-minute and rush, rush. How would you help the students stay motivated and work steadily?

- As the time to take the PSAT nears, a few of your students are becoming so anxious that you wonder if they will make it through the test. What can you do to help them?

Cooperative Learning Activity

- With four or five other members of your class, identify ways you can respond to student mistakes without communicating to students that their mistakes are the result of low ability. You also want to avoid being unrealistic about what they can do or implying that the material is "easy."

What Would They Do?

For some reason this year, many of the students in your middle school classes seem defeated about learning. They look at an assignment and protest, "This is too long (too hard, too much)!" A few teachers blame the negative attitudes on students from " projects" who are in school this year because the other middle school in the district was closed and those students had to be redistributed. A cloud of despair seems to be hovering over the whole school. You are starting to dread Mondays.

PEGGY MCDONNELL

Sixth Grade Teacher
West Park School, Moscow, Idaho

It appears that the students in this middle school class have lost the motivation to work in school. Have they also lost the motivation to excel on the basketball court, in the video arcade or on their rollerblades? If not, it may help to see what rewards they reap from their efforts outside of school. Are these rewards all external? Probably not—many are intrinsic, such as the feelings of well-being and success. Outside of school these students are striving to meet higher, often self-imposed standards. What can we, as educators, do to parallel this in our classrooms?

First and foremost we can provide a sense of relevance to our assignments, an attachment to real-life situations and problems. If we are teaching about percentages, we should be taking students "shopping" to calculate sales prices. If we are exploring classification in science, we can visit a pet store or greenhouse to classify the animals or plants. We need to make the subjects we share with our students come alive by providing material in a variety of ways. We should also be giving students choices that allow them to share their understanding of subject matter in various ways. This would offer more opportunities for success.

Educators have made great strides in developing "shared-decision making models" in schools. In such models teachers share decision-making power with administrators. Somehow, many of us have left the students out of this process. Although we realize how much harder we work when we have an investment in a process, we tend to deny our students that right. This middle school class needs a project that they can plan and develop as a group and execute as a group to see if they can benefit from this model. It appears that the students need to have some ownership of their activities and that they need to help set the standards for performance.

JEFF HOVERMILL

Seventh–Twelfth Grade Teacher
Seabury Hall School, Makawao, Idaho

I would try to improve the environment for learning in the classroom by fostering intrinsic motivation in the students. I would look for topics in which the students are interested and incorporate those themes into assignments and activities. Keeping class fresh and interesting is particularly important in the middle grades. A wide variety of activities and assignments help to keep the students involved and motivated. I try to use such activities as group work, films, field trips, projects, speakers, drill and practice, and interdisciplinary themes to introduce assignments.

Some of their projects should have varying levels of difficulty. Students should have the option of selecting from the entire list the projects that most appeal to them and are most realistic in terms of meeting their goals. This is one way to help students experience success without having them feel they have been "tracked" into different ability levels. I also choose assignments of varying lengths, in different educational settings, and ones which will involve different learning styles.

Getting to know the students outside of the classroom is another way to demonstrate concern and model motivational behaviors. Participating with or observing students in extracurricular activities outside of class often enhances motivation inside of class. When a teacher expresses enough interest in the students to be a club sponsor or athletic coach and attends plays or recitals in which students are involved, this attention is often reciprocated with increased effort in the classroom.

Decreased motivation to learn can be a contagious inhibitor to learning in school. If students are apathetic and feel that the locus of causality for success in school is extrinsic to them and that they cannot succeed even if they do try, it will be very difficult to motivate them to learn. Careful attention by the teacher to the students' needs can help to alleviate decreased motivation. Helping the students to meet realistic goals and develop intrinsic reasons for learning will increase academic success and in turn increase self-esteem and motivation. Group and individual affect among the students within the classroom should also be improved by this attention, which in turn provides a better environment for learning.

NICOLE DEPALMA COBB AND SANDRA T. MCNEICE

Eighth Grade Teachers
Sterling Middle School, Quincy, Massachusetts

In a situation where the students seem defeated about learning, we must ask ourselves if the current curriculum fits the children and the times. We must remember the power of connecting their high interest and curiosity to our curriculum. Assuming that we have developed our curriculum to fit our students' needs and we still find there is a motivation problem, we must try to adopt certain strategies. In order to tap into the inner motivation of the students, groupings of students could be used to brainstorm about the current conflicts facing the class. We can entice students by modeling the inquiry process. To encourage our students to be vested and have a sense of ownership, inner motivation could also be stimulated by peer tutorials, educational games, project-based learning, oral presentations, videos or photo montages, student-peer teaching drama, newspaper or community magazine work, and the use of interdisciplinary connections.

Motivation, Teaching, and Learning

Overview | *What Would You Do?*

AN ULTIMATE GOAL OF TEACHING: LIFELONG LEARNING   406
Self-Regulated Learning | On TARGETT for Self-Regulated Learning

TASKS FOR LEARNING   409
Tapping Interests and Arousing Curiosity | Task Operations: Risk and Ambiguity | Task Value

SUPPORTING AUTONOMY AND RECOGNIZING ACCOMPLISHMENT   414
Advantages of Autonomy in the Classroom | Information and Control | Autonomy Supporting Class Climates | Recognizing Accomplishment

GROUPING, EVALUATION, AND TIME   416
Grouping and Goal Structures | Evaluation | Time

TEACHER EXPECTATIONS   421
Two Kinds of Expectation Effects | Sources of Expectations | Teacher Behavior and Student Reaction

STRATEGIES TO ENCOURAGE MOTIVATION AND THOUGHTFUL LEARNING   427
Necessary Conditions in Classrooms | Can I Do It? Building Confidence and Positive Expectations | Do I Want to Do It? Seeing the Value of Learning | What Do I Need to Do to Succeed? Staying Focused on the Task | How Do Beginning Teachers Motivate Students? | Students' Views of Motivation

Summary | *Key Terms* | *Check Your Understanding* | *Teachers' Casebook: What Would They Do?*

*W*hen you are facing a difficult task, what do you do? How do you handle distractions? Are there activities that you have no trouble doing—that you have to "make yourself quit"? What are they? Are you more motivated when you are a member of a team and others are counting on you or when you are on your own?

In the previous chapter we saw that motivation is an extremely complex concept. Many factors seem to affect the goals we choose and our energy and persistence in working toward them. We saw that goals, needs, beliefs, attributions, expectations, and anxiety can all affect motivation.

How do we put all this information together in teaching? How do we create environments, situations, and relationships that encourage motivation? These are the questions we will consider in the next several pages. First we focus on the overall goal in motivating students—the development of self-regulated learners. Then we examine how motivation is influenced by the academic work of the class, the value of the work, and the setting in which the work must be done. Having considered the task and the setting, we turn to a very important influence on student motivation—the teacher. Finally, we discuss a number of strategies for developing motivation as a constant state in your classroom and as a permanent trait in your students.

By the time you have completed this chapter, you should be able to:

- List some characteristics of a self-regulated learner, and describe how teachers can promote self-regulated learning in the classroom.
- Explain how the ambiguity and risk of the learning task affect motivation.
- Discuss how the value of a task affects motivation to learn.
- Describe the characteristics of classrooms that support students' autonomy.
- Explain how evaluation procedures and grouping arrangements, particularly cooperative learning, can influence motivation.
- Describe potential effects on students of teachers' expectations.
- Devise a strategy for teaching your subject to an uninterested student.

What Would You Do?

It is July and you have just been hired to teach third grade. Job openings were really tight, so you're pleased with your new position; many friends who graduated with you last May are still looking for work. Third grade wasn't your first choice. Neither was this district, for that matter. The teaching resources are slim to none. You have just been informed that the school has no money for new materials, and the only resources for one of your classes are some aging texts and the workbooks that go with them. Every idea you have suggested for software, simulation games, visual aids, or other more active teaching materials has been greeted with the same response, "There's no money in the budget for that." As you look over the texts and workbooks, you wonder how the students could be anything but bored by them. To make matters worse, the texts look pretty high-level for third grade. But the objectives in the workbooks are important—you agree that students need to understand the material. Besides, the district curriculum requires these units and students will be tested over them in district-wide assessments next spring.

- How would you arouse student curiosity and interest about the topics and tasks in the workbooks?

- How would you establish the value of learning this material?

- How would you handle the difficult level of the texts?

- What do you need to know about motivation to solve these problems?

An Ultimate Goal of Teaching: Lifelong Learning

Today, people change jobs an average of seven times before they retire. Many of these are career changes requiring new knowledge and skills (Weinstein, 1994). Students entering the workforce in the next 10 to 20 years probably will experience the same need for continuous learning. Thus, one goal of teaching should be to free students from the need for teachers so the students can continue to learn independently throughout their lives.

Self-Regulated Learning

To continue learning independently throughout life, you must be a self-regulated learner. **Self-regulated learners** have a combination of academic learning skills and self-control that makes learning easier, so they are more motivated; in other words, they have the *skill* and the *will* to learn (McCombs & Marzano, 1990; Weinstein & McCombs, in press). The concept of self-regulated learning integrates much of what is known about effective learning and motivation. Three factors influence skill and will: knowledge, motivation, and self-discipline or volition.

Knowledge.   To be self-regulated learners, students need *knowledge* about themselves, the subject, the task, strategies for learning, and the contexts in which

Self-Regulated Learners Students whose academic learning abilities and self-discipline make learning easier so motivation is maintained.

they will apply their learning. "Expert" students know about *themselves* and how they learn best. For example, they know their preferred learning styles, what is easy and what is hard for them, how to cope with the hard parts, what their interests and talents are, and how to use their strengths. These experts also know quite a bit about the *subject* being studied—and the more they know, the easier it is to learn more (Alexander, in press). They probably understand that different *learning tasks* require different approaches on their part. A simple memory task, for example, might require a mnemonic strategy, while a complex comprehension task might be approached by means of concept maps of the key ideas. Also, these self-regulated learners know that learning often is difficult and knowledge is seldom absolute—there usually are different ways of looking at problems as well as different solutions (Pressley, 1995; Winne, 1995).

These expert students not only know what each task requires, they can also apply the *strategy* needed. They can skim or read carefully. They can use mnemonics or reorganize the material. As they become more knowledgeable in a field, they apply many of these strategies automatically. In short, they have mastered a large, flexible repertoire of learning strategies and tactics.

Finally, expert learners think about the *contexts* where they will apply their knowledge—when and where they will use their learning—so they can set motivating goals and connect present work to future accomplishments (Wang & Palincsar, 1989; Weinstein, 1994, Winne, 1995).

Motivation.   Self-regulated learners are *motivated to learn*. They find many tasks in school interesting because they value learning, not just performing well in the eyes of others. But even if they are not intrinsically motivated by a particular task, they are serious about getting the intended benefit from it. They know *why* they are studying, so their actions and choices are self-determined and not controlled by others. However, knowledge and motivation are not always enough. Self-regulated learners need volition or self-discipline. "Where motivation denotes commitment, volition denotes follow-through" (Corno, 1992, p. 72).

Volition.   It is Friday night. I have been writing almost all day and my cold is getting worse. I want to keep writing because the deadline for this chapter is very near. I have knowledge and motivation, but to keep going I need a good dose of volition. **Volition** is an old-fashioned word for willpower. Self-regulated learners know how to protect themselves from distractions—where to study, for example, so they are not interrupted. They know how to cope when they feel anxious, drowsy, or lazy (Corno, 1992, 1995; Snow, Corno, & Jackson, 1997). And they know what to do when tempted to stop working and take a nap—the temptation I'm facing now—that, and a large bowl of (low fat) chips and salsa.

Obviously, not all of your students will be self-regulated learners. In fact, some psychologists suggest that you think of this capacity as an individual difference characteristic (Snow, Corno, & Jackson, 1997). Some students are much better at it than others. How can you help more students become self-regulated learners? We discussed the development of *knowledge,* particularly knowledge of learning strategies and tactics (the *skill* to learn) in earlier chapters, so in this chapter we will

Lyn Corno has written extensively about self-regulated learning.

Focus on...

Self-Regulated Learning

- Distinguish between motivation and volition.
- How does knowledge play a role in self-regulated learning?
- What are the TARGETT areas?

Volition Willpower; self-discipline.

TABLE 11.1 The TARGETT Model for Supporting Student Motivation to Learn

Teachers make decisions in many areas that can influence motivation to learn. The TARGETT acronym highlights task, autonomy, recognition, grouping, evaluation, time, and teacher expectations.

TARGETT Area	Focus	Objectives	Examples of Possible Strategies
Task	How learning tasks are structured—what the student is asked to do	Enhance intrinsic attractiveness of learning tasks Make learning meaningful	Encourage instruction that relates to students' backgrounds and experience Avoid payment (monetary or other) for attendance, grades, or achievement Foster goal setting and self-regulation
Autonomy/ Responsibility	Student participation in learning/school decisions	Provide optimal freedom for students to make choices and take responsibility	Give alternatives in making assignments Ask for student comments on school life—and take them seriously Encourage students to take initiatives and evaluate their own learning Establish leadership opportunities for *all* students
Recognition	The nature and use of recognition and reward in the school setting	Provide opportunities for *all* students to be recognized for learning Recognize *progress* in goal attainment Recognize challenge seeking and innovation	Foster "personal best" awards Reduce emphasis on "honor rolls" Recognize and publicize a wide range of school-related activities of students
Grouping	The organization of school learning and experiences	Build an environment of acceptance and appreciation of all students Broaden the range of social interaction, particularly of at-risk students Enhance social skills development	Provide opportunities for cooperative learning, problem solving, and decision making Encourage multiple group membership to increase range of peer interaction Eliminate ability-grouped classes

Source: From M. L. Maehr and E. M. Anderman. "Reinventing schools for early adolescents: Emphasizing task goals." *The Elementary School Journal, 93,* pp. 604–605. Copyright © 1993. Adapted by permission of The University of Chicago Press.

focus on *will*—motivation and volition. What can teachers do to encourage and support motivation to learn? To organize our discussion, we will use the TARGETT model.

On TARGETT for Self-Regulated Learning

Carol Ames (1990, 1992) has identified six areas where teachers make decisions that can influence student motivation to learn: the nature of the *task* that students are asked to do, the *autonomy* students are allowed in working, how students are *recognized* for their accomplishments, *grouping* practices, *evaluation* procedures, and the scheduling of *time* in the classroom. Epstein (1989)

TARGETT Area	Focus	Objectives	Examples of Possible Strategies
Evaluation	The nature and use of evaluation and assessment procedures	Grading and reporting processes Practices associated with use of standardized tests Definition of goals and standards	Reduce emphasis on social comparisons of achievement Give students opportunities to improve their performance (e.g., study skills, classes) Establish grading/reporting practices that portray student progress in learning Encourage student participation in the evaluation process
Time	The scheduling of the school day	Allow the learning task and student needs to dictate scheduling Provide opportunities for extended and significant student involvement in learning tasks	Allow students to *progress at their own rate* whenever possible Encourage flexibility in the scheduling of learning experiences Give teachers greater control over time usage through, for example, block scheduling
Teacher Expectations	Beliefs and predictions about students abilities	Hold appropriate but high expectations for all students Communicate that you expect growth	Give all students the chance to revise and improve their work Monitor who gets which opportunities Make sure materials show diversity in achievement

coined the acronym TARGET to organize these areas of possible teacher influence. We will add *teacher expectations* to the model, so ours will be a TARGETT for motivation to learn. Table 11.1 summarizes the model. In the following pages we will examine each of these areas more closely.

Tasks for Learning

To understand how an **academic task** can affect students' motivation, we need to analyze the task. Tasks can be interesting or boring for students. Tasks have a particular subject content and also involve certain cognitive operations such

Academic Tasks The work the student must accomplish, including the content covered and the mental operations required.

as *memorize, infer, classify, apply,* and so on. As students work on a task they are learning content and practicing operations. Tasks also vary in terms of how clear-cut or ambiguous they are and how much risk is involved in doing them (Doyle, 1983). Finally, tasks have a certain value to students, determined in part by how authentic and meaningful the tasks are for them. We will look at each of these aspects of tasks more closely.

Tapping Interests and Arousing Curiosity

When Walter Vispoel and James Austin (1995) asked over 200 junior high students to rate reasons for their successes and failures in different school subjects, lack of interest in the topic received the highest rating as an explanation for failures. Interest was second only to effort as a choice for explaining successes. It seems logical that learning experiences should be related to the interests of the students. However, this is not always an easy or even a desirable strategy; there are times when students must master basic skills that hold no intrinsic interest for them. Nevertheless, if a teacher knows what students' interests are, these can be part of many teaching strategies. For example, Cordova and Lepper (1996) found that students learned more math facts during a computer exercise when they were challenged, as captains of star ships, to navigate through space by solving math problems. The students got to name their ships, stock the (imaginary) galley with their favorite snacks, and name all the crew members after their friends.

For younger students, the chance to manipulate and explore objects relevant to what is being studied may be the most effective way to keep curiosity stimulated. For older students, well-constructed questions, logical puzzles, and paradoxes can have the same effect. Example: ranchers in an area killed the wolves on their land. The following spring they noticed that the deer population was much smaller. How could this be, since wolves hunt the deer and fewer wolves should mean more deer? In searching for a solution, students learn about ecology and the balance of nature: without wolves to eliminate the weaker and

Connecting the learning task to a puzzle or game can spark interest. What is in this box, and what does it have to do with learning to spell?

sicker deer, the deer population expanded so much that the winter food supply could not sustain the deer herds. Many deer died of starvation.

George Lowenstein (1994) suggests that curiosity arises when attention is focused on a gap in knowledge "Such information gaps produce the feeling of deprivation labeled *curiosity.* The curious person is motivated to obtain the missing information to reduce or eliminate the feeling of deprivation" (p. 87). This has a number of implications for teaching. First, students need some base of knowledge before they can experience gaps in knowledge leading to curiosity. Second, students must be aware of the gaps in order for curiosity to result. Asking students to make guesses, then providing feedback can be helpful. Also, mistakes, properly handled, can stimulate curiosity by pointing to missing knowledge. Finally, the more we learn about a topic, the more curious we may become about that subject. As Maslow (1970) predicted, fulfilling the need to know and understand increases, not decreases, the need to know more.

Task Operations: Risk and Ambiguity

Doyle (1983) has suggested that academic tasks can be categorized by the operations that they require: *memory, routine procedure, comprehension,* and *opinion.* Memory tasks require students to recognize or reproduce something they have encountered before, such as matching states and capitals. Routine procedures involve following steps or rules to solve a problem—using πr^2 to calculate the area of a circle, for example. Comprehension tasks require students to go beyond the information given—by combining several ideas, originating a procedure, or writing in a particular style. Opinion tasks ask students to state a personal preference or belief, such as which character in a story is the bravest. The kind of operation in a task determines how ambiguous and risky the task is, and this, in turn, affects student motivation, as you will see.

Some tasks involve less *risk* than others, because failure is unlikely. For example, opinion tasks are very low-risk tasks—there are no right or wrong answers. Simple memory or procedural tasks also involve few risks, because getting the right answer is easy: you just follow the steps. But the stakes can be very high with longer and more complex memory or procedural tasks. Reciting 100 lines from Shakespeare is risky, especially if you are graded on how well you do, because there is a great deal to memorize.

Another characteristic of tasks is level of *ambiguity*—how straightforward the expected answer is. Opinion and understanding tasks are ambiguous: it is hard to predict the right answer (if there is one) or how to find it. The "right" answer may involve the teacher's opinion. Memory and procedural tasks, on the other hand, are straightforward and unambiguous. If you are reciting a soliloquy from *Hamlet,* the "right" answer is clear, even though the task is difficult. Figure 11.1 on page 412 summarizes how tasks can be categorized by risk and ambiguity.

What does this have to do with motivation? Most students want to *lower the risk* and *decrease the ambiguity* involved in schoolwork, because their grades are at stake. This is especially true for highly anxious students or those who are trying to avoid failure. Many times teachers plan a complicated *comprehension* task that is both ambiguous and risky. They want their students to think and solve problems. But the students want more guidance. They may ask for models, rules, minimums, or formulas: "How many references do you want?" "How many pages?" "Will we have to know dates and names?" "Give us a model to follow."

FIGURE 11.1

Ambiguity and Risk Associated with Academic Tasks in Classrooms

Academic tasks can be characterized by their levels of risk and ambiguity. Because students often find high-ambiguity/high-risk tasks very threatening, they need extra support and fewer pressures when completing them.

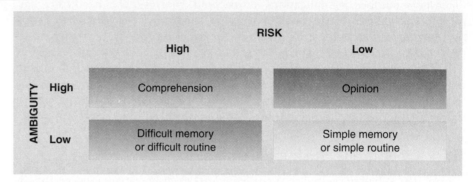

Source: From W. Doyle (1983). "Academic work." *Review of Educational Research, 53,* Figure p. 183. Copyright 1983 by the American Educational Research Association. Adapted by permission of the publisher.

In other words, students *negotiate the task.* These negotiations can lead to management problems. If the students are very confused, they may become restless, turn to other students for help, get discouraged, or lose interest in the task.

Under this kind of pressure, the teacher often responds by stating the three main points that should be addressed, giving a minimum number of references or a page limit, and providing books that would be helpful. This transforms the *comprehension* task into a *procedural* one. Risk and ambiguity are reduced and motivation may seem to increase, at least temporarily. But the task itself is not as interesting. Doing well on the procedural task is not as rewarding, because achievement does not lead to a sense of increased competence. So the results of the "task negotiation" may be a temporary *state* of motivation, but it is motivation to perform, to get the grade, not motivation to learn. And little has been done to foster the long-term development of the *trait* of motivation to learn. Furthermore, because students learn the operations that they practice, these students have learned how to do a procedure—and how to negotiate with teachers (Doyle, 1983). But they probably have not improved the problem-solving or critical-thinking skills that the teacher had intended to develop.

Obviously, some balance is needed. Teachers must make wise choices, then stick with them even when students try to negotiate changes. Instructions should be clear, but not too restricting. The penalties for taking a risk or making a mistake should not be too great. Finally, tasks must have some value to students. Let's take a closer look now at the value of classroom tasks.

Task Value

As you recall from the previous chapter, many theories suggest that the strength of our motivation in a particular situation is determined by our *expectation* that we can succeed and the *value* of that success to us. We can think of a task as having three kinds of value to the students (Eccles & Wigfield, 1985). **Attainment value** is the importance of doing well on the task. This aspect of value is closely tied to the needs of the individual (for example, the need to be competent, well-liked, etc.) and the meaning of success to that person. For instance, if someone has a strong need to appear smart and believes that a high grade on a test shows you are smart, then the test has high attainment value for that person. A second kind of value is **intrinsic or interest value.** This is simply the enjoyment one gets from the activity itself. Some people like the experience of learning. Others enjoy the feeling of hard physical effort or the challenge of solving puzzles. Finally, tasks have **utility value;** that is, they help us achieve a short-term or long-term goal.

You see from our discussion of task value that personal and environmental influences on motivation interact constantly. The task we ask students to accomplish is an aspect of the environment; it is external to the student. But the value of accomplishing the task is bound up with the internal needs, beliefs, and goals of the individual.

Recently there has been a great deal written about the use of authentic tasks in teaching. An **authentic task** is one that has some connection to the real-life problems and situations that students will face outside the classroom, now and in the future. If you ask students to do busywork, to memorize definitions they will never use, to learn the material only because it is on the test, or to repeat work they already understand, then there can be little motivation to learn. But if the tasks are authentic, students are more likely to see the genuine utility value of the work and are also more likely to find the tasks meaningful and interesting.

Problem-based learning is one example of the use of authentic tasks in teaching. According to William Stepien and Shelagh Gallagher (1993), "problem-based learning turns instruction topsy-turvy. Students meet an ill-structured problem before they receive any instruction. In place of covering the curriculum, learners probe deeply into issues searching for connections, grappling with complexity, and using knowledge to fashion solutions" (p. 26). Teachers act as coaches and tutors, asking questions, modeling thinking, helping students organize and monitor their own problem solving.

An example problem presented to one group of seventh and eighth graders in Illinois is, "What should be done about a nuclear waste dump site in our area?" The students soon learn that this real problem is not a simple one. Scientists disagree about the dangers. Environmental activists demand that the materials be removed, even if this bankrupts the company involved—one that employs many local residents. Some members of the state assembly want the material taken out of state, even though no place in the country is licensed to receive the toxic materials. The company believes the safest solution is to leave the materials buried. The students must research the situation, interview parties involved, and develop recommendations to be presented to state experts and community groups. "In problem-based learning students assume the roles of scientists, historians, doctors, or others who have a real stake in the proposed problem. Motivation soars because students realize it's their problem" (Stepien & Gallagher, 1993, p. 26).

Focus on...

Tasks for Learning

- What does it mean for students to "negotiate a task?"
- What makes a task risky?
- Name some ways other than problem-based learning to make learning tasks more authentic.

Attainment Value The importance of doing well on a task; how success on the task meets personal needs.

Intrinsic or Interest Value The enjoyment a person gets from a task.

Utility Value The contribution of a task to meeting one's goals.

Authentic Task Tasks that have some connection to real-life problems the students will face outside the classroom.

Problem-based Learning Methods that provide students with realistic problems that don't necessarily have "right" answers.

Calvin and Hobbes

by Bill Watterson

CALVIN AND HOBBES © 1991 Watterson. Dist. by Universal Press Syndicate. Reprinted with permission. All rights reserved.

Supporting Autonomy and Recognizing Accomplishment

The second area in the TARGETT model involves how much choice and autonomy students are allowed. We saw in the previous chapter that the need for self-determination—the need to be an *origin* not a *pawn*—is an important factor in motivation. There is no intrinsic motivation without self-determination.

Advantages of Autonomy in the Classroom

Classroom environments that support student autonomy are associated with greater student interest, sense of competence, self-esteem, creativity, conceptual learning, and preference for challenge. These relationships appear to hold from first grade through graduate school (Ryan & Grolnick, 1986; Williams, Wiener, Markakis, Reeve, & Deci, 1993). In autonomy-oriented classrooms, students are more likely to believe that the work is important, even if it is not "fun." Thus, they tend to internalize educational goals and take them as their own. For example, the problem-based project described above might encourage autonomy and self-determination as the students made choices about how best to solve the problem of toxic-waste dumps.

Controlling environments tend to improve performance only on rote recall tasks. When students are pressured to perform, they often seek the quickest, easiest solution. One discomforting finding, however, is that both students and parents seem to prefer more controlling teachers, even though the students learn more when their teachers support autonomy (Flink, Boggiano, & Barrett, 1990). Assuming you are willing to risk going against popular images, how can you support student autonomy? One answer is to focus on *information*, not *control*, in your interactions with students.

Information and Control

Many things happen to students throughout the school day. They are praised or criticized, reminded of deadlines, assigned grades, given choices, lectured about rules, and on and on. **Cognitive evaluation theory** (Deci & Ryan, 1985; Deci,

Cognitive Evaluation Theory Suggests that events affect motivation through the individual's perception of the events as controlling behavior or providing information.

Vallerand, Pelletier, & Ryan, 1991) explains how these events can influence the students' intrinsic motivation by affecting their sense of self-determination and competence. According to this theory, all events have two aspects, controlling and informational. If an event is highly controlling, that is, if it pressures students to act or feel a certain way, then students will experience less control and their *intrinsic motivation* will be diminished. If, on the other hand, the event provides information that increases the students' sense of competence and efficacy, then intrinsic motivation will increase. Of course, if the information provided makes students feel less competent, it is likely that motivation will decrease.

For example, a teacher might praise a student by saying, "Good for you! You got an A because you finally followed my instructions correctly." This is a highly controlling statement, giving the credit to the teacher and thus undermining the student's sense of self-determination and intrinsic motivation. The teacher could praise the same work by saying, "Good for you! Your understanding of the author's use of metaphors has improved tremendously. You earned an A." This statement provides information about the student's growing competence and should increase intrinsic motivation. But if the information is negative, as in "You still have not grasped the concept of metaphor and your grade shows it," then motivation is likely to diminish.

Autonomy Supporting Class Climates

What can teachers do to support student autonomy? An obvious first step is to limit their controlling messages to their students and make sure the information they provide highlights students' growing competence. Unfortunately, when teachers are under pressure and "controlled" by the school administration, they are likely to treat students the same way. In one study, teachers told to "make sure" their students performed well in solving problems were more critical and gave students more hints and less time for independent work than teachers who were told that their job was to "help" the students learn how to solve the problems themselves. And the students of the pressured teachers actually performed worse (Boggiano, Flink, Shields, Seelbach, & Barrett, 1995). The Guidelines describe five essential elements that support student autonomy.

Guidelines

Supporting Autonomy in the Classroom

Acknowledge the students' points-of-view.

Examples

1. Try to adopt the students' frame of reference as they encounter learning tasks.
2. Try to identify needs and feelings of students.

Encourage students' choice and initiative.

Examples

1. Create opportunities for initiative and choice in learning tasks, timing, and problem solving.
2. Provide time for independent and extended projects.

(continued)

Provide rationales for limits, rules, and constraints.

Examples

1. Explain reasons for rules.
2. Respect rules and constraints in your own behavior.

Acknowledge that negative emotions are valid reactions to teacher control.

Examples

1. Communicate that it is OK (and normal) to feel bored waiting for a turn, for example.
2. Communicate that sometimes important learning involves frustration, confusion, weariness.

Use noncontrolling, positive feedback.

Examples

1. See poor performance or behavior as a problem to be solved, not a target of criticism.
2. Avoid controlling language, "should," "must," "have to."

Source: Adapted from J. Reeve (1996). *Motivating others: Nurturing inner motivational resources.* Boston: Allyn & Bacon, pp. 29–31.

Recognizing Accomplishment

The third TARGETT area is *recognition*. How should students' accomplishments be acknowledged and rewarded? In Chapter 6 we discussed the importance of authentic praise that focuses on progress, growing competence, and independence. But nothing in teaching is simple. At times praise can have paradoxical effects. For example, if two students succeed and the teacher praises only one of them, the message, to older children at least, may be that the praised student had less ability and had to work harder to succeed, thus earning praise. The unpraised student was simply "doing what comes naturally," succeeding based on high ability. So students may use the teacher's praise or criticism as cues about capabilities—praise means I'm not very smart, so when I succeed, I deserve recognition. Criticism means my teacher thinks I'm smart and could do better (Stipek, 1996).

We have also seen that giving students rewards for activities that they already enjoy can undermine intrinsic motivation. Students should be recognized for improving on their own personal best, for tackling difficult tasks, for persistence, and for creativity—not just for performing better than others. The next section explains one way to use personal progress as a basis for recognition in classrooms.

> **Focus on...**
>
> ### Supporting Autonomy and Recognizing Accomplishment
>
> - Name three characteristics of a classroom environment that supports students' autonomy.
> - How can recognition undermine motivation and a sense of self-efficacy?
> - Why would providing rationales for class rules help students feel more autonomous?

Grouping, Evaluation, and Time

You may remember a teacher who made you want to work hard—someone who made a subject come alive. Or you may remember how many hours you spent practicing as a member of a team, orchestra, choir, or theater troupe. If you do, then you know the motivational power of relationships with other people. David and Roger Johnson (1985) describe the power this way:

> Motivation to learn is inherently interpersonal. It is through interaction with other people that students learn to value learning for its own sake, enjoy the process of learning, and take pride in their acquisition of knowledge and development of skill. Of the interpersonal relationships available in the classroom, peers may be the most influential on motivation to learn. (p. 250)

The ways that students relate to peers are influenced by the goal structure of the activities and tasks created by the teacher.

Grouping and Goal Structures

Students in the classroom function as part of a large group. Johnson and Johnson (1994) have given considerable attention to this in their work on motivation. They have found that motivation can be greatly influenced by the ways we relate to the other people who are also involved in accomplishing a particular goal. Johnson and Johnson have labeled this interpersonal factor the **goal structure** of the task. There are three such structures: cooperative, competitive, and individualistic, as shown in Figure 11.2.

We saw in Chapter 9 that there are many advantages for cooperative goal structures. Several studies have shown that when the task involves complex learning and problem-solving skills, cooperation leads to higher achievement than competition, especially for low-ability students (Johnson & Johnson, 1985; Slavin, 1995). In addition, well-designed **cooperative learning** seems to result in improved ability to see the world from another person's point of view, better re-

Goal Structure The way students relate to others who are also working toward a particular goal.

Cooperative Learning Arrangement in which students work in mixed-ability groups and are rewarded on the basis of the success of the group.

FIGURE 11.2

Different Goal Structures

Each goal structure is associated with a different relationship between the individual and the group. This relationship influences motivation to reach the goal.

	Cooperative	**Competitive**	**Individualistic**
Definition	Students believe their goal is attainable only if other students will also reach the goal.	Students believe they will reach their goal if and only if other students do not reach the goal.	Students believe that their own attempt to reach a goal is not related to other students' attempts to reach the goal.
Examples	Team victories—each player wins only if all the team members win; a relay race; a quilting bee; a barn raising; a symphony; a play.	Golf tournament, singles tennis match, a 100-yard dash; valedictorian; Miss America pageant.	Lowering your handicap in golf, jogging, learning a new language, enjoying a museum, losing or gaining weight, stopping smoking.

Source: From D. Johnson and R. Johnson (1975). *Learning together and alone: Cooperation, competition, and individualization.* Adapted by permission of Allyn & Bacon.

Students working in teams can support each others' learning and motivation. Immediate help is available for learning problems, and encouragement can help overcome lagging interest.

lations among different ethnic groups in schools and classrooms, increased self-esteem, greater willingness to help and encourage fellow students, and greater acceptance of handicapped and low-achieving students (Slavin, 1995; Stipek, 1996; Webb & Palincsar, 1996). Students learn to set attainable goals and negotiate. They become more altruistic. The interaction with peers that students enjoy so much becomes a part of the learning process. The result? The need for belonging described by Maslow is more likely to be met and motivation is increased.

There are many approaches to peer learning or group learning, as you saw in Chapter 9. Some approaches, such as STAD and TGT, are designed specifically to enhance motivation.

STAD.   Robert Slavin and his associates have developed a system for overcoming the disadvantages of the cooperative goal structure (lack of focus, off-task behaviors, unfair division of work) while maintaining its advantages. The system is called **Student Teams–Achievement Divisions,** or **STAD** (Slavin, 1995). Each team has about five members with a mix of abilities, ethnic backgrounds, and sexes. The teacher calculates an **individual learning expectation (ILE)** score, or base score, for each team member. This score represents the student's average level of performance. Details about how to determine the base scores are given in Table 11.2.

Students work in their teams to study and prepare for twice-weekly quizzes, but they take the quizzes individually, just as in a regular class. Based on test performance, each team member can earn from one to three points for the group. Table 11.2 shows how points are awarded by comparing each student's current test score to his or her base (ILE) score (Slavin, 1995). As you can see from the table, every student has an equal chance to contribute the maximum number of points to the team total. Thus, every student, not just the most able or motivated, has reason to work hard. This system avoids the problem of students' unequal contributions to a group project. Every week the group earning the greatest

Student Teams–Achievement Divisions (STAD) Cooperative learning with heterogeneous groups and elements of competition and reward.

Individual Learning Expectation (ILE) Constantly recomputed average score in a subject.

TABLE 11.2   Using Individual Learning Expectations

The idea behind individual learning expectations, or ILEs, is that students ought to be judged in relation to their own abilities and not compared to others. The focus is on improvement, not on comparisons among students.

To calculate an ILE score, the teacher simply averages the student's grades or test scores from previous work. These scores are usually on a 100-point scale. Letter grades can be converted to points based on the school's system—for example, A = 90 points, B = 80 points, and so on. The student's average score is her or his initial base score. The ILE score becomes the standard for judging each student's work.

If the teacher is using the STAD system of cooperative learning, then students earn points for their group based on the following system:

Test Score	Points Earned for Group
A perfect score	3
10 or more points above ILE score	3
5 to 9 points above ILE score	2
4 points below to 4 points above ILE score	1
5 or more points below ILE score	0

---

number of points is declared the winner. Team accomplishments should be recognized in a class newsletter or a bulletin board display.

Every few weeks the teams can be changed so that students have a chance to work with many different class members. Every two weeks or so the teacher must recompute each student's ILE score by averaging the old base score with grades on the recent tests. With this system, improvement pays off for all students. Those with less ability can still earn the maximum for their team by scoring 10 or more points above their own base score. Those with greater ability are still challenged because they must score well above their own average or make a perfect score to contribute the maximum to the group total.

TGT.   **Teams-Games-Tournaments** or **TGT** is similar to STAD. After the teacher's presentation, students move into their heterogeneous groups to help each other answer problems or questions about the material. Instead of taking written tests, however, each student meets once a week at a "tournament table" with two other students of comparable ability from the other teams. The three students at each tournament table compete, answering questions similar to the problems practiced in their study teams. The winner at each table earns 6 points for his or her team. Each week the participants at the tournament tables are adjusted—the winners are "bumped" up to a higher-ability table to keep the competition fair. This way, every student has the chance to contribute equally to the team's total score (Slavin, 1990).

Some recent research on TGT raises a caution. Bette Chambers and Philip Abrami (1991) found that members of successful teams did learn more than members of unsuccessful teams, but also they were happier about the outcome and

Teams-Games-Tournaments (TGT) Learning arrangement in which team members prepare cooperatively, then meet comparable individuals of competing teams in a tournament game to win points for their team.

rated their ability higher than members of losing teams. For low-achieving students who tend to be anxious, failure-accepting, or helpless, being on a losing team could make matters worse. Chambers and Abrami suggest experimenting with cooperation both within and between teams. For example, the whole class might earn recognition if each team reaches a specified level of learning.

Table 11.1 gave ideas for fostering motivation through peer relations. Besides using cooperative learning, other ideas include allowing time and opportunity for peer interaction in school, using project-based learning, and encouraging the development of teams and "schools within schools."

The nature of the goal structure—cooperative, competitive, or individualistic—has implications for the next two TARGETT areas, *evaluation* and *time*.

Evaluation

The greater the emphasis on competitive evaluation and grading, the more students will focus on performance goals rather than learning goals and the more they will be ego-involved as opposed to task-involved. Students must take tests, answer questions in class, and complete assignments, and they must perform within certain time limits. Doyle (1983) suggests that students look on most classroom work as "an exchange of performance for grades" (p. 181). Grading here refers to more than marks on a report card. It includes both the formal and informal evaluations of teachers.

Of course, not all students are caught up in an exchange of performance for grades. Low-achieving students who have little hope of either "making the grade" or mastering the task may simply want to finish. One study of first graders found that low-achieving students made up answers, filled in the page with patterns, or copied from other students, just to get through their seatwork. As one student said when she finished a word/definition matching exercise, "I don't know what it means, but I did it" (Anderson, Brubaker, Alleman-Brooks, & Duffy, 1985, p. 132). On closer examination, the researchers found that the work was much too hard for these students, so they connected words and definitions at random.

How can teachers prevent students from simply focusing on the grade or doing the work "just to get finished"? The most obvious answer is to de-emphasize grades and emphasize learning in the class. Students need to understand the value of the work. Instead of saying, "You will need to know this for the test," tell students how the information will be useful in solving problems they want to solve. Suggest that the lesson will answer some interesting questions. Communicate that understanding is more important than finishing.

Unfortunately, many teachers do not follow this advice. Brophy (1988) reports that when he and several colleagues spent about 100 hours observing how six teachers introduced their lessons, they found that most introductions were routine, apologetic, or unenthusiastic. The introductions described procedures, made threats, emphasized finishing, or promised tests on the material. A few examples are:

> "You don't expect me to give you baby work to do every day, do you?"
> "My talkers are going to get a third page to do during lunch."
> "If you are done by 10 o'clock, you can go outside." (Brophy, 1988, p. 204)

While many teachers are similar to the six Brophy studied, there are exceptions. Hermine Marshall (1987) described a few elementary-school teachers who seemed to establish a *learning orientation* in their classrooms. They stressed understanding instead of performing, being graded, or finishing work. Later in the chapter we will examine strategies for establishing such an orientation in your class.

Time

How does the use of time affect student motivation? Most experienced teachers know that there is too much work and not enough time in the school day. Students seldom have the opportunity to stick with an activity. Even if they become engrossed in a project, students must stop and turn their attention to another subject when the bell rings or the schedule demands. Furthermore, students must progress as a group. If particular individuals can move faster or if they need more time, they may still have to follow the pace of the whole group. So scheduling often interferes with motivation by making students move faster or slower than would be appropriate or by interrupting their involvement. It is difficult to develop persistence and a sense of efficacy in the face of difficulties when students are not allowed to stick with a difficult activity.

We have examined the TARGET influences on student motivation to learn, *task, autonomy, recognition, grouping, evaluation,* and *time.* Before we summarize strategies to encourage motivation let's add the last T—teacher expectations.

> **Focus on...**
>
> ### Grouping, Evaluation, and Time
>
> - What determines whether a goal structure is cooperative, competitive, or individualistic?
> - Describe a cooperative learning structure that is designed to support student motivation.
> - How can evaluation procedures help to create a learning-oriented classroom?

Teacher Expectations

Over 25 years ago, a study by Robert Rosenthal and Lenore Jacobson (1968) captured the attention of the national media in a way that few studies by psychologists have since. Articles in newspapers across the country reported the seemingly remarkable effects of "Pygmalion in the classroom," a term taken from the title of the book about the experiment. The study also caused great controversy within the professional community. Debate about the meaning of the results continues (Babad, 1995; Brophy, 1982; Cooper & Good, 1983; Elashoff & Snow, 1971; Good, 1988; Rosenthal, 1987, 1994; 1995; Snow, 1995).

What did Rosenthal and Jacobson say that caused such a stir? They chose several students at random in a number of elementary-school classrooms, then told the teachers that these students probably would make significant intellectual gains during the year. The students did indeed make larger gains than normal that year. The researchers presented data suggesting the existence of a self-fulfilling prophecy in the classroom. A **self-fulfilling prophecy** is a groundless expectation that comes true simply because it has been expected. In the classroom this means that a teacher's beliefs about students' abilities or behaviors bring about the very behaviors the teacher expects. The Point/Counterpoint on page 422 examines the debate over the existence of a self-fulfilling prophecy or **Pygmalion effect.**

Two Kinds of Expectation Effects

Actually, two kinds of expectation effects can occur in classrooms. The first is the self-fulfilling prophecy described above. In this situation the teacher's beliefs

Self-Fulfilling Prophecy A groundless expectation that is confirmed because it has been expected.

Pygmalion Effect Exceptional progress by a student as a result of high teacher expectations for that student; named for mythological king, Pygmalion, who made a statue, then caused it to be brought to life.

Do Teachers' Expectations Affect Students' Learning?

The answer to this question is more complicated than it might seem. There are two ways to investigate the question. One is to give teachers unfounded expectations about their students and note if these baseless expectations have any effects. The other approach is to identify the naturally occurring expectations of teachers and study the effects of these expectations. The answer to the question of whether teacher expectations affect student learning depends in part on which approach is taken to study the question.

POINT Teachers' expectations have less effect than we think.

The original Rosenthal and Jacobson experiment used the first approach—giving teachers groundless expectations and noting the effects. The study was heavily criticized for the experimental and statistical methods used (Elashoff & Snow, 1971; Snow, 1995; Weinberg, 1989). A careful analysis of the results revealed that even though first- through sixth-grade students participated in the study, the self-fulfilling prophecy effects were confined mostly to students in grades one and two. In these grades, the effects could be traced to just five students who changed dramatically. When

other researchers tried to replicate the study, they did not find evidence of a self-fulfilling prophecy effect, even for children in these lower grades (Claiborn, 1969; Wilkins & Glock, 1973). Critics argued that even if higher expectations do lead to greater learning in the early grades, this does not prove that lower expectations will lead to decreased learning. Besides, the critics pointed out, giving teachers false expectations is an unnatural situation. Several studies found that when teachers did not believe the information they were given, no expectation effects occurred. After reviewing the research on teacher expectations, Raudenbush (1984) concluded that these expectations have only a small effect on student IQ scores (the outcome measure used by Rosenthal and Jacobson) and only in the early years of a new school setting—in the first years of elementary school and then again in the first years of junior high school.

COUNTERPOINT Teachers' expectations can have powerful effects.

When researchers study the naturally occurring expectations of teachers, they find that teachers do indeed form beliefs about students' capabilities. Many

of these beliefs are accurate assessments based on the best available data and are corrected as new information is collected (Good & Brophy, 1994). Even so, some teachers do favor certain students (Babad, 1995; Rosenthal, 1987). For example, in a study of over 400 classrooms in the southwest United States, the Civil Rights Commission (1973) found that Hispanic-American students consistently received less praise and encouragement and fewer positive teacher responses and questions than Anglo-American students. In classes where teachers treat high-achieving students differently from lower-achieving students, the teachers' evaluation of students' ability appears to affect the students' achievement in the class. "Although the importance of teacher expectation effects has sometimes been overstated, it is clear that these effects are important, especially when considered with other teaching abilities" (Good & Brophy, 1994, p. 114). If teachers decide that some students are less able, and if the teachers lack effective strategies for working with lower-achieving students, then students may experience a double threat—low expectations and inadequate teaching. Just how powerful the expectation effect is depends on how differently a teacher treats high- versus low-expectation students.

about the students' abilities have no basis in fact, but student behavior comes to match the initially inaccurate expectation. The second kind of expectation effect occurs when teachers are fairly accurate in their initial reading of students' abilities and respond to students appropriately. So far, so good. There is nothing wrong with forming and acting on accurate estimates of student ability. Indeed, many teachers do this almost automatically. The problems arise when students show some improvement but teachers do not alter their expectations to take account of the improvement. This is called a **sustaining expectation effect,** because the teacher's unchanging expectation sustains the student's achievement at the expected level. The chance to raise expectations, provide more appropriate teaching, and thus encourage greater student achievement is lost. In practice, sustaining effects are more common than self-fulfilling prophecy effects (Cooper & Good, 1983).

Sources of Expectations

There are many possible sources of teachers' expectations (Braun, 1976). Intelligence test scores are an obvious source, especially if teachers do not interpret the scores appropriately. Sex also influences teachers; most teachers expect more behavior problems from boys than from girls. The notes from previous teachers and the medical or psychological reports found in cumulative folders (permanent record files) are another obvious source of expectations. Knowledge of ethnic background also seems to have an influence, as does knowledge of older brothers and sisters. The influence of students' physical characteristics is shown in several studies, indicating that teachers hold higher expectations for attractive students. Previous achievement, socioeconomic class, and the actual behaviors of the student are also often used as sources of information.

Expectations and beliefs focus attention and organize memory, so teachers may pay attention to and remember the information that fits the initial expectations (Fiske, 1993; Hewstone, 1989). Even when student performance does not fit expectations, the teacher may rationalize and attribute the performance to external causes beyond the student's control. For example, a teacher may assume that the low-ability student who did well on a test must have cheated and that the high-ability student who failed must have been upset that day. In both cases, behavior that seems out of character is dismissed. It may take many instances of supposedly uncharacteristic behavior to change the teacher's beliefs about a particular student's abilities. Thus, expectations often remain in the face of contradictory evidence (Brophy, 1982).

Teacher Behavior and Student Reaction

Table 11.3 on page 424 shows six dimensions of teacher communication toward students that may be influenced by expectations. These dimensions include both instructional practices and interpersonal interactions.

Instructional Strategies. As we have seen, different grouping processes may well have a marked effect on students. And some teachers leave little to the imagination; they make their expectations all too clear. For example, Alloway (1984) recorded comments like these directed to low-achieving groups:

> "I'll be over to help you slow ones in a minute."
> "The blue group will find this hard."

In these remarks the teacher not only tells the students that they lack ability, the teacher also communicates that finishing the work, not understanding, is the goal.

Sustaining Expectation Effect
Student performance maintained at a certain level because teachers don't recognize improvements.

TABLE 11.3	Six Dimensions of Teaching That Can Communicate Expectations	
Dimension	Students believed to be MORE capable have:	Students believed to be LESS capable have:
Task Environment Curriculum, procedures, task definition, pacing, qualities of environment	More opportunity to perform publicly on meaningful tasks.	Less opportunity to perform publicly, especially on meaningful tasks (supplying alternate endings to a story vs. learning to pronounce a word correctly).
	More opportunity to think.	Less opportunity to think, analyze (since much work is aimed at practice).
Grouping Practices	More assignments that deal with comprehension, understanding (in higher-ability groups).	Less choice on curriculum assignments—more work on drill-like assignments.
Locus of Responsibility for Learning	More autonomy (more choice in assignments, fewer interruptions).	Less autonomy (frequent teacher monitoring of work, frequent interruptions).
Feedback and Evaluation Practices	More opportunity for self-evaluation.	Less opportunity for self-evaluation.
Motivational Strategies	More honest/contingent feedback.	Less honest/more gratuitous/less contingent feedback.
Quality of Teacher Relationships	More respect for the learner as an individual with unique interests and needs.	Less respect for the learner as an individual with unique interests and needs.

Source: From T. Good and R. Weinstein, "Teacher expectations: A framework for exploring classrooms." In K. Zumwalt (Ed.), *Improving teaching* (The ASCD 1986 Yearbook). Reprinted by permission of the Association for Supervision and Curriculum Development. Copyright © 1986 by ASCD. All rights reserved.

Once teachers assign students to ability groups, they usually assign different learning activities. To the extent that teachers choose activities that challenge students and increase achievement, these differences are probably necessary. Activities become inappropriate, however, when students who are ready for more challenging work are not given the opportunity to try it because teachers believe they cannot handle it. This is an example of a sustaining expectation effect.

Teacher–Student Interactions. However the class is grouped and whatever the assignments, the quantity and the quality of teacher–student interactions are likely to affect the students. Students who are expected to achieve tend to be asked more and harder questions, to be given more chances and a longer time to respond, and to be interrupted less often than students who are expected to do poorly. Teachers also give these high-expectation students cues and prompts, communicating their belief that the students can answer the question (Allington, 1980; Good & Brophy, 1994; Rosenthal, 1994). Teachers tend to be more encouraging in general toward those students for whom they have high expectations. They smile at these students more often and show greater warmth through such nonverbal responses as leaning toward the students and nodding their heads as the students speak (Woolfolk & Brooks, 1983, 1985). In contrast, with low-expectation students, teachers ask easier questions, allow less time for answering, and are less likely to give prompts.

It appears that feedback and reinforcement are also somewhat dependent on teacher expectations. Good and Brophy (1994) have noted that teachers demand better performance from high-achieving students, are less likely to accept a poor answer from them, and praise them more for good answers. Teachers are more likely to respond with sympathetic acceptance or even praise to inadequate answers from low-achieving students, but to criticize these same students for wrong answers. Even more disturbing, low-achieving students receive less praise than high-achieving students for similar correct answers. On tests when an answer is "almost right," the teacher is more likely to give the benefit of the doubt (and thus the better grade) to high-achieving students (Finn, 1972).

This inconsistent feedback can be very confusing for low-ability students. Imagine how hard it would be to learn if your wrong answers were sometimes praised, sometimes ignored, and sometimes criticized, and your right answers received little recognition (Good 1983a, b).

You may be promising yourself that you will never communicate low expectations to your students, especially now that you know about the dangers involved. Of course, not all teachers form inappropriate expectations or act on their expectations in unconstructive ways (Babad, Inbar, & Rosenthal, 1982). But avoiding the problem may be more difficult than it seems. In general, low-expectation students also tend to be the most disruptive students. (Of course, low expectations can reinforce their desire to disrupt or misbehave.) Teachers may call on these students less, wait a shorter time for their answers, and give them less praise for right answers, partly to avoid the wrong, careless, or silly answers that can cause disruptions, delays, and digressions (Cooper, 1979). The challenge is to deal with these very real threats to classroom management without communicating low expectations to some students or fostering their own low expectations of themselves. And sometimes, low expectations become part of the culture of the school—beliefs shared by teachers and administrators alike (Weinstein, Madison, & Kuklinski, 1995). The Guidelines may help you avoid some of these problems.

Focus on...

Teacher Expectations

- What are some sources of teacher expectations?
- What are the two kinds of expectation effects and how do they happen?
- What are the different avenues for communicating teacher expectations?
- How can teacher expectations set up a cycle of expectation and confirmation?

Guidelines

Avoiding the Negative Effects of Teacher Expectations

Use information about students from tests, cumulative folders, and other teachers very carefully.

Examples

1. Some teachers avoid reading cumulative folders at the beginning of the year.
2. Be critical and objective about the reports you hear from other teachers.

Be flexible in your use of grouping strategies.

Examples

1. Review work of students often and experiment with new groupings.
2. Use different groups for different subjects.
3. Use mixed-ability groups in cooperative exercises.

(continued)

Make sure all the students are challenged.

Examples

1. Don't say, "This is easy, I know you can do it."
2. Offer a wide range of problems, and encourage all students to try a few of the harder ones for extra credit. Find something positive about these attempts.

Be especially careful about how you respond to low-achieving students during class discussions.

Examples

1. Give them prompts, cues, and time to answer.
2. Give ample praise for good answers.
3. Call on low achievers as often as high achievers.

Use materials that show a wide range of ethnic groups.

Examples

1. Check readers and library books. Is there ethnic diversity?
2. If few materials are available, ask students to research and create their own, based on community or family sources.

Make sure that your teaching does not reflect racial, ethnic, or sexual stereotypes or prejudice.

Examples

1. Use a checking system to be sure you call on and include all students.
2. Monitor the content of the tasks you assign. Do boys get the "hard" math problems to work at the board? Do you avoid having students with limited English give oral presentations?

Be fair in evaluation and disciplinary procedures.

Examples

1. Make sure equal offenses receive equal punishment. Find out from students in an anonymous questionnaire whether you seem to be favoring certain individuals.
2. Try to grade student work without knowing the identity of the student. Ask another teacher to give you a "second opinion" from time to time.

Communicate to all students that you believe they can learn—and mean it.

Examples

1. Return papers that do not meet standards with specific suggestions for improvements.
2. If students do not have the answers immediately, wait, probe, and then help them think through an answer.

Involve all students in learning tasks and in privileges.

Examples

1. Use some system to make sure you give each student practice in reading, speaking, and answering questions.
2. Keep track of who gets to do what job. Are some students always on the list while others seldom make it?

Monitor your nonverbal behavior.

Examples

1. Do you lean away or stand farther away from some students? Do some students get smiles when they approach your desk while others get only frowns?
2. Does your tone of voice vary with different students?

Strategies to Encourage Motivation and Thoughtful Learning

Until four basic conditions are met, no motivational strategies will succeed. Once these requirements are in place, there are many strategies to help students gain confidence, value learning, and stay involved with the task (Brophy, 1988; Lepper, 1988). Let's look at the necessary conditions.

Necessary Conditions in Classrooms

First, the classroom must be relatively organized and free from constant interruptions and disruptions. (Chapter 12 will give you the information you need to make sure this requirement is met.) Second, the teacher must be a patient, supportive person who never embarrasses students for mistakes. Everyone in the class should see mistakes as opportunities for learning (Clifford, 1990, 1991). Third, the work must be challenging but reasonable. If work is too easy or too difficult, students will have little motivation to learn. They will focus on finishing, not on learning. Finally, the learning tasks must be authentic (Brophy 1983; Brophy & Kher, 1986; Stipek, 1993).

Once these four basic conditions are met, the influences on students' motivation to learn in a particular situation can be summarized in three questions: Can I succeed at this task? Do I want to succeed? What do I need to do to succeed? (Eccles & Wigfield, 1985). As reflected in these questions, we want students to have confidence in their ability so they will approach learning with energy and enthusiasm. We want them to see the value of the tasks involved and work to learn, not just try to get the grade or get finished. We want students to believe that success will come when they apply good learning strategies instead of believing that their only option is to use self-defeating, failure-avoiding, face-saving strategies. When things get difficult, we want students to stay focused on the task, not get so worried about failure that they "freeze." Table 11.4 on page 428 summarizes the basic requirements and strategies for encouraging student motivation to learn, all of which are discussed at length in the next few pages.

Can I Do It? Building Confidence and Positive Expectations

One of the most important factors in building expectations for success is past success. No amount of encouragement or "cheerleading" will substitute for real accomplishment. To ensure genuine progress:

1. *Begin work at the students' level and move in small steps.* The pace should be brisk, but not so fast that students have to move to the next step before they understand the previous one. This may require assigning different tasks to different students. One possibility is to have very easy and very difficult questions on every test and assignment, so all students are both successful and challenged. When grades are required, make sure all the students in class have a chance to make at least a C if they work hard.

2. *Make sure learning goals are clear, specific, and possible to reach in the near future.* When long-term projects are planned, break the work into subgoals and

TABLE 11.4 Strategies to Encourage Motivation to Learn

Fulfill basic requirements
- Provide an organized class environment
- Be a supportive teacher
- Assign challenging work, but not too difficult
- Make tasks worthwhile

Build confidence and positive expectations
- Begin work at the students' level
- Make learning goals clear, specific, and attainable
- Stress self-comparison, not competition
- Communicate that academic ability is improvable
- Model good problem solving

Show the value of learning
- Connect the learning task to the needs of the students
- Tie class activities to the students' interests

- Arouse curiosity
- Make the learning task fun
- Make use of novelty and familiarity
- Explain connections between present learning and later life
- Provide incentives and rewards, if needed

Help students stay focused on the task
- Give students frequent opportunities to respond
- Provide opportunities for students to create a finished product
- Avoid heavy emphasis on grading
- Reduce task risk without oversimplifying the task
- Model motivation to learn
- Teach learning tactics

This table refers to the entire Strategies to Encourage Motivation and Thoughtful Learning section of the text.

help students feel a sense of progress toward the long-term goal. If possible, give students a range of goals at different levels of difficulty and let them choose.

3. *Stress self-comparison, not comparison with others.* Help students see the progress they are making by showing them how to use self-management strategies like those described in Chapter 6. Give specific feedback and corrections. Tell students what they are doing right as well as what is wrong and *why* it is wrong. Periodically, give students a question or problem that was once hard for them but now seems easy. Point out how much they have improved.

4. *Communicate to students that academic ability is improvable* and specific to the task at hand. In other words, the fact that a student has trouble in algebra doesn't necessarily mean that geometry will be difficult or that he or she is a bad English student. Don't undermine your efforts to stress improvement by displaying only the 100% papers on the bulletin board.

5. *Model good problem solving,* especially when *you* have to try several approaches to get a solution. Students need to see that learning is not smooth and error-free, even for the teacher.

Do I Want to Do It? Seeing the Value of Learning

Teachers can use intrinsic and extrinsic motivation strategies to help students see the value of the learning task. In this process the age of the student must be taken into consideration. For younger children, intrinsic or *interest value* is a greater determinant of motivation than attainment or utility value. Because younger students have a more immediate, concrete focus, they have trouble seeing the value of an activity that is linked to distant goals such as getting a good job—or even preparing for the next grade. Older students, on the other hand, have the cognitive ability to think more abstractly and connect what they are learning now with goals and future possibilities, so *utility value* becomes important to these students (Eccles & Wigfield, 1985).

Attainment and Intrinsic Value. To establish *attainment value,* we must connect the learning task with the needs of the students. First, it must be possible for students to meet their needs for safety, belonging, and achievement in our classes. The classroom should not be a frightening or lonely place. Second, we must be sure that sexual or ethnic stereotypes do not interfere with motivation. For example, if students subscribe to rigid notions of masculinity and femininity, we must make it clear that both women and men can be high achievers in all subjects and that no subjects are the territory of only one sex. It is not "unfeminine" to be strong in mathematics, science, shop, or sports. It is not "unmasculine" to be good in literature, art, music, or French.

There are many strategies for encouraging *intrinsic* (interest) motivation. Several of the following are taken from Brophy (1988).

1. *Tie class activities to student interests* in sports, music, current events, pets, common problems or conflicts with family and friends, fads, television and cinema personalities, or other significant features of their lives (Schiefele, 1991). But be sure you know what you are talking about. For example, if you use a verse from a Hootie and the Blowfish song to make a point, you had better have some knowledge of the music and the group members. When possible, give students choices of research paper or reading topics so they can follow their own interests.

2. *Arouse curiosity.* Point out puzzling discrepancies between students' beliefs and the facts. For example, Stipek (1993) describes a teacher who asked her fifth-grade class if there were "people" on some of the other planets. When the students said yes, the teacher asked if people needed oxygen to breathe. Since the students had just learned this fact, they responded yes to this question also. Then the teacher told them that there is no oxygen in the atmosphere of the other planets. This surprising discrepancy between what the children knew about oxygen and what they believed about life on other planets led to a rousing discussion of the atmospheres of other planets, the kinds of beings that could survive in these atmospheres, and so on. A straight lecture on the atmosphere of the planets might have put the students to sleep, but this discussion led to real interest in the subject.

3. *Make the learning task fun.* Many lessons can be taught through simulations or games. For example, when my daughter was in the eighth grade, all the students in her grade spent three days playing a game her teachers had designed called ULTRA. Students were divided into groups and formed their own "countries." Each country had to choose a name, symbol, national flower, and bird. They wrote and sang a national anthem and elected government officials. The teachers allocated different resources to the countries. To get all the materials needed for the completion of assigned projects, the countries had to establish trade with one another. There was a monetary system and a stock market. Students had to work with their fellow citizens to complete cooperative learning assignments. Some countries "cheated" in their trades with other nations, and this allowed debate about international relations, trust, and war. Liz says she had fun—but she also learned how to work in a group without the teacher's supervision and gained a deeper understanding of world economics and international conflicts.

4. *Make use of novelty and familiarity.* Don't overuse a few teaching approaches or motivational strategies. We all need some variety. Varying the goal structures of tasks (cooperative, competitive, individualistic) can help, as can using different teaching media. When the material being covered in class is abstract

Learning is more interesting when students are personally involved in the task.

or unfamiliar to students, try to connect it to something they know and understand. For example, talk about the size of a large area, such as the Acropolis in Athens, in terms of football fields. Brophy (1988) describes one teacher who read a brief passage from *Spartacus* to personalize the unit on slavery in the ancient world.

Instrumental Value. Sometimes it is difficult to encourage intrinsic motivation, and so teachers must rely on the utility or "instrumental" value of tasks. That is, it is important to learn many skills because they will be needed in more advanced classes or because they are necessary for life outside school.

1. When these connections are not obvious, you should *explain the connections to your students.* Jeanette Abi-Nader (1991) describes one project, the PLAN program, that makes these connections come alive for Hispanic high school students. The three major strategies used in the program to focus students' attention on their future are: (1) working with mentors and models—often PLAN graduates—who give advice about how to choose courses, budget time, take notes, and deal with cultural differences in college; (2) storytelling about the achievements of former students—sometimes the college term papers of former students are posted on PLAN bulletin boards; and (3) filling the classroom with future-oriented talk such as "When you go to college, you will encounter these situations . . . " or, "You're at a parents' meeting—you want a good education for your children—and you are the ones who must speak up; that's why it is important to learn public speaking skills" (p. 548).

2. In some situations teachers need to *provide incentives and rewards for learning.* Chapter 6 details the use of extrinsic reinforcement through the application of positive and negative consequences, self-management systems, and other behavioral approaches, so we need not spend time on those topics here. Remember, though, that giving rewards when students are already interested in the activity may undermine intrinsic motivation. As Stipek (1993) has noted, if teachers began testing and grading students on their memory of the television programs they watched the previous evening, even television viewing would lose some of its intrinsic appeal.

3. Use *ill-structured problems and authentic tasks* in teaching. Connect problems in school to real problems outside.

What Do I Need to Do to Succeed? Staying Focused on the Task

When students encounter difficulties, as they must if they are working at a challenging level, they need to keep their attention on the task. If the focus shifts to worries about performance, fear of failure, or concern with looking smart, then motivation to learn is lost. Here are some ideas for keeping the focus on learning.

1. *Give students frequent opportunities to respond* through questions and answers, short assignments, or demonstrations of skills. Make sure you check the students' answers so you can correct problems quickly. You don't want students to practice errors too long. Computer learning programs give students the immediate feedback they need to correct errors before they become habits.

2. When possible, *have students create a finished product.* They will be more persistent and focused on the task when the end is in sight. We all have experi-

enced the power of the need for closure. For example, I often begin a house-painting project thinking I will work for just an hour and then find myself still painting hours later because I want to see the finished product.

3. *Avoid heavy emphasis on grades and competition.* You will force students to be ego-involved rather than task-involved. Anxious students are especially hard hit by highly competitive evaluation.

4. *Reduce task risk without oversimplifying the task.* When tasks are risky (failure is likely and the consequences of failing are grave), student motivation suffers. For difficult, complex, or ambiguous tasks, provide students with plenty of time, support, resources, help, and the chance to revise or improve work.

5. *Model motivation to learn for your students.* Talk about your interest in the subject and how you deal with difficult learning problems.

6. *Teach the particular learning tactics* that students will need to master the material being studied. Show students how to learn and remember so they won't be forced to fall back on self-defeating strategies or rote memory.

Table 11.4 on page 428 summarizes these ideas for helping students to have confidence in their abilities, value learning, and stay focused on the right task. The support of families and the community can encourage motivation to learn. The Guidelines give ideas for working with families.

Guidelines

Family and Community Partnerships to Encourage Motivation to Learn

Work with families to build confidence and positive expectations.

Examples

1. Avoid comparing one child in a family to another during conferences and discussions with family members.

2. Ask family members to highlight strong points of homework assignments. They might attach a note to assignments describing the three best aspects of the work and one element that could be improved.

Make families partners in showing the value of learning.

Examples

1. Invite family members to the class to demonstrate how they use mathematics or writing in their work.

2. Involve parents in identifying skills and knowledge for the children to learn in school that could be applied at home and prove helpful to the family right now, for example, keeping records on service agencies, writing letters of complaint to department stores or landlords, or researching vacation destinations.

Provide resources that build skill and will for families.

Examples

1. Give family members simple strategies for helping their children improve study skills.

2. Involve older students in a "homework hotline" telephone network for helping younger students with class assignments.

(continued)

Have frequent celebrations of learning.

Examples

1. Invite families to a "museum" at the end of a unit on dinosaurs. Students create the museum in the auditorium, library, or cafeteria. After visiting the museum, families go to the classroom to examine their child's portfolio for the unit.[1]

2. Place mini-exhibits of student work at local grocery stores, libraries, or community centers.

[1]R. C. Fowler and K. K. Corley (1996). Linking families, building community. *Educational Leadership, 7*(7), 24–26

How Do Beginning Teachers Motivate Students?

Timothy Newby (1991) trained classroom observers to record the motivational strategies of 30 first-year elementary-school teachers over a 16-week period. He found that the teachers used about 10 different strategies per hour—half were rewards and punishments. Figure 11.3 gives examples of the four types of strategies used by these beginning teachers. As you can see, commenting on the rele-

FIGURE 11.3

Motivational Strategies of Beginning Teachers

First-year teachers tend to rely on reward and punishment strategies to motivate students, even though these are not necessarily the most effective approaches.

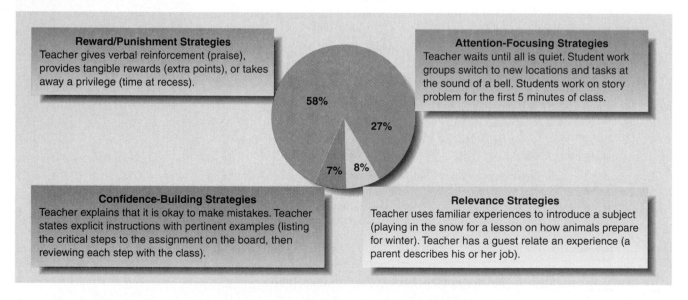

Source: From T. J. Newby. Classroom motivation: Strategies of first-year teachers. *Journal of Educational Psychology, 83* pp. 195–200. Copyright © 1991 by the American Psychological Association. Adapted by permission.

vance of the lessons accounted for 8% of strategies and building student confidence accounted for 7% of strategies, focusing student attention made up 27%, and rewards and punishments accounted for 58%.

Another interesting finding is that commenting on relevance was positively correlated with students being on task, while using rewards/punishments was negatively correlated. Thus, beginning teachers tended to use less effective strategies more often. It may be that these new teachers turned to extrinsic reinforcement (rewards and punishments) only when it became difficult to keep the students interested in their work.

Students' Views of Motivation

Let's let the students have the last word on motivation. Two recent studies examined students' beliefs about motivation and fairness. Theresa Thorkildsen and her colleagues interviewed 93 students (grades 2 through 5) from an urban and a suburban elementary school. The interviewers described four approaches to motivation: encouraging focus on the task, praising excellent performance, giving rewards for excellent performance, and giving rewards for high effort. Students were asked a number of questions, including how effective and fair each practice seemed to them. Analyses of the interviews showed that students seemed to hold different personal theories about motivation. One group valued meaningful learning and favored strategies that encourage the desire to understand. Another group valued learning as duty and liked practices that promote effort. A third group favored extrinsic rewards for either effort or good performance. In terms of fairness, 98% of the students thought that encouraging task focus is fair, 85% saw rewarding effort as fair, 50% viewed rewarding performance as fair, and only 30% believed public praise is fair (Thorkildsen, Nolen, & Fournier, 1994).

In a second study, John Nicholls and his colleagues interviewed 128 African American students, 8 boys and 8 girls randomly selected from each grade—1 through 8—in an urban school. The focus of the interviews was two types of teaching: collaborative inquiry about controversies, such as why dinosaurs died out, contrasted with traditional presentations of facts about dinosaurs, such as their names and sizes. One conclusion was that older students were more likely than younger students to see collaborative inquiry as fairer and more motivating. In addition, the older the students, the more strongly they agreed that schools should foster motivation and understanding, not just memory for facts (Nicholls, Nelson, & Gleaves, 1995).

What can the results of these studies offer teachers? First, it might be interesting to learn about your own students' theories of motivation and fairness. Second, expect there to be developmental and individual differences among students in their beliefs about these topics. Knowing what your students believe about motivation will help you to apply the TARGETT model and design strategies to encourage motivation to learn.

Focus on...

Motivation Strategies

- What are four conditions that must exist in a classroom before any motivational strategies can be successful?
- Give an example of a strategy to:
    build student confidence
    show the value of learning
    help students stay focused on the task
- What are the most commonly used motivational strategies of beginning teachers?

The Ultimate Goal of Teaching: Lifelong Learning

One important goal of teaching is to prepare students for lifelong learning. To reach this goal, students must be self-regulated learners, that is, they must have a combination of the knowledge, motivation to learn, and volition that provides the skill and will to learn independently and effectively. Knowledge includes an understanding of self, subject, task, learning strategy, and contexts for application. Motivation to learn provides the commitment, and volition is the follow-through that combats distraction and protects persistence.

Teachers make many decisions that influence student motivation to learn. The TARGETT acronym highlights decisions about tasks, autonomy, recognition, grouping, evaluation, time, and teacher expectations.

Tasks for Learning

The tasks that teachers set affect motivation. When students encounter tasks that are related to their interests, stimulate their curiosity, or are connected to real-life situations, the students are more likely to be motivated to learn. Tasks that are difficult and require critical thinking are risky and ambiguous. Students often seek to lower the risk and ambiguity in tasks through negotiation with the teacher.

Tasks can have attainment, intrinsic, or utility value for students. Attainment value is the importance to the student of succeeding. Intrinsic value is the enjoyment the student gets from the task. Utility value is determined by how much the task contributes to reaching short-term or long-term goals.

Supporting Autonomy and Recognizing Accomplishment

In order to experience intrinsic motivation, students must have a sense of self-determination about their activities in school. When students experience autonomy, they are more interested in their work, have a greater sense of self-esteem, and learn more. Whether students experience self-determination depends in part on if the teacher's communications with students provide information or seek to control them. In addition, teachers must acknowledge the students' perspective, offer choices, provide rationales for limits, and treat poor performance as a problem to be solved rather than a target for criticism.

Recognition and reward in the classroom will support motivation to learn if the recognition is for personal progress rather than competitive victories. Praise and rewards should focus on students' growing competence.

Grouping, Evaluation, and Time

Students may be motivated by their relationships with their peers. How students relate to their peers in the classroom is influenced by the goal structure of the activities and tasks created by the teacher. Cooperative learning arrangements can encourage motivation and increase learning, especially for low-achieving students. There are a number of approaches, including STAD and TGT. The evaluative climate of the class—that is, the relative emphasis on competition and grading—influences motivation. The more competitive the grading, the more students set performance goals and focus on "looking competent"; that is, the more they are ego-involved. When the focus is on performing rather than learning, students often see the goal of classroom tasks as simply finishing, especially if the work is difficult.

In order to foster motivation to learn and support volition, teachers should be flexible in their use of time in the classroom. Students who are forced to move faster or slower than they should or who are interrupted as they become involved in a project are not likely to develop the willpower for learning.

Teacher Expectations

Several studies have pointed to the important role teachers' expectations play in motivating students. Some teachers tend to treat students differently, depending on their own views of how well the students are likely to do. Differences in treatment toward low-expectation students may include setting less challenging tasks, focusing on lower-level learning, giving fewer choices, providing inconsistent feedback, and communicating less respect and trust. Students may behave accordingly, fulfilling teachers' predictions or staying at an expected level of achievement.

Strategies to Encourage Motivation and Thoughtful Learning

Before any strategies to encourage motivation can be effective, four conditions must exist in the classroom. The classroom must be organized and free from constant disruption, the teacher must be a supportive person who never embarrasses students for making mistakes, the work must be neither too easy nor too difficult, and finally, the tasks set for students must be authentic—not busy work. Once these conditions are met, teachers can use strategies that help students feel confident in their abilities to improve (e.g., set challenging but reachable goals, stress self- not other-comparisons, communicate that ability is improvable), strategies that highlight the value the learning tasks (e.g., tie tasks to student interests, arouse curiosity, show connections to the future and to real-world problems, provide incentives), and strategies that help students stay involved in the learning process without being threatened by fear of failure (e.g., provide opportunities to create a finished product, teach learning tactics, model motivation to learn for students, avoid emphasizing grades, reduce risk without oversimplifying the task).

KEY TERMS

academic tasks, p. 409
attainment value, p. 413
authentic task, p. 413
cognitive evaluation theory, p. 414
cooperative learning, p. 417
goal structure, p. 417

individual learning expectation (ILE), p. 418
intrinsic or interest value, p. 413
problem-based learning, p. 413
Pygmalion effect, p. 421
self-fulfilling prophecy, p. 421
self-regulated learners, p. 406

student teams-achievement divisions (STAD), p. 418
sustaining expectation effect, p. 423
teams-games-tournaments (TGT), p. 419
utility value, p. 413
volition, p. 407

CHECK YOUR UNDERSTANDING

Can you apply the ideas from this chapter on motivation to solve the following problems of practice?

Preschool and Kindergarten

■ What would you do to help your students develop persistence without discouraging their spontaneity and enthusiasm?

Elementary and Middle School

■ You are talking to the parents of one of your lower-achieving students. You really like the student, but he seems not to apply himself to the work. Suddenly the boy's mother says, "We think our son is doing badly in your class because you don't like him. You just seem to expect him to fail!" What would you do?

Junior High and High School

■ You want to prepare your senior classes for the kind of independent work they will face in college, so you assign a research project. As soon as you make the assignment, the questions begin: "How many sources?" "How many pages?" "What exactly do you mean by 'support your conclusions with evidence'?" "What kind of evidence?" How do you make the assignment clear without turning it into a "spoon feeding"?

■ How could you use cooperative learning strategies with ninth-grade students?

Cooperative Learning Activity

■ With four or five other members of your educational psychology class, develop a self-monitoring procedure for identifying the expectations that you communicate to your students.

What Would They Do?

It is July and you have just been hired to teach third grade. Job openings were really tight, so you're pleased with your new position; many friends who graduated with you last May are still looking for work. Third grade wasn't your first choice. Neither was this district, for that matter. The teaching resources are slim to none. You have just been informed that the school has no money for new materials, and the only resources for one of your classes are some aging texts and the workbooks that go with them. Every idea you have suggested for software, simulation games, visual aids, or other more active teaching materials has been greeted with the same response, "There's no money in the budget for that." As you look over the texts and workbooks, you wonder how the students could be anything but bored by them. To make matters worse, the texts look pretty high-level for third grade. But the objectives in the workbooks are important—you agree that students need to understand the material. Besides, the district curriculum requires these units and students will be tested over them in district-wide assessments next spring.

MARY ELLEN CASEY

First Grade Teacher
Snug Harbor Community School, Quincy, Massachusetts

I strongly feel that children learn best when they are personally vested in a topic. It is imperative to relate the subject matter to the students' daily lives or interests. The teacher should find a "hook" that leaves the children wanting to know more about a topic. There are several ways a teacher can arouse student curiosity: tapping prior knowledge through brainstorming activities; posing a question for discussion; conducting an experiment; predicting activities; presenting a scenario or problem to solve; and use of graphic organizers such as KWL strategy, webs, and so on. Integrated thematic units are also helpful in gaining and maintaining student interest. Visual displays such as bulletin boards or posters are motivating. Some teachers set aside a special table or shelf to display books or artifacts for the unit being studied. Additional books can be obtained from the Media Center or local library.

Students need to see how we use reading, writing, math, and science skills every day. Teachers can invite guest speakers from the community to demonstrate how the subject matter relates to their profession.

There are many things a teacher can do to aid students in reading a difficult textbook. First of all, children need to be taught how to read various kinds of texts including previewing, test set-up, reading captions, and reading headings and sub-headings. Often teachers need to spend more time developing vocabulary and concepts. This can be done with graphic organizers such as semantic maps, creation of word webs, crossword puzzles, and diagrams. The teacher can also make games to reinforce vocabulary and create study guides for each chapter. Cooperative learning activities (especially the Jigsaw method) can help students understand a difficult text.

In conclusion, teachers need to know that the most effective learning takes place when children are actively engaged in meaningful and relevant activities. Teachers need to take into account the interests and educational background of their students when planning lessons. Effective teachers vary their teaching methodologies to accommodate the many learning styles found within their classrooms.

AIMEE FREDETTE

Second Grade Teacher
Fisher Elementary School, Walpole, Massachusetts

In order to arouse student curiosity and interest, I would use the topics and implement them as themes. Theme studies integrate all discipline areas to help the children make connections and apply their knowledge. The teacher could create themes directly from the workbook, using the objectives from the workbooks. The teacher also pick a theme that directly interests the children and integrate the objectives into the activities. Children grasp and apply concepts better when they can relate them to real life. To help cover the objective required, the use of trade books (literature books) helps the children to make connections. To increase student interest, the use of current events (news articles and even news clips) is very effective. Teachers can also involve the local community by having guest speakers come into the classroom and discuss the specific theme.

A very effective way that I use to get the children curious and interested is to pose a question to the class before the start of a lesson. This gives the children a focus for the lesson. As the year progresses, the children begin coming up with questions of their own. Another very successful way to spark interest and curiosity is the use of three-column activators, a brainstorming activity that the teacher and students do together. The students brainstorm WHAT WE THINK WE KNOW about the topic. The teacher records *all* responses, writing them on chart paper. Then the children brainstorm WHAT WE WANT TO KNOW about the topic. Again the teacher would record their responses. The third column, titled WHAT WE HAVE LEARNED, is added to as the theme progresses. The first two columns are referred to as the children learn about the theme.

To help with the difficulty of the text, I would use the difficult words as vocabulary words. This way the words and their meanings can be pre-taught. For nonreaders, put the passages onto tape for them to listen to.

A teacher needs to implement activities in a thorough and enthusiastic way. Modeling is the most powerful way to affect a child's learning. If the teacher is excited, the children will follow. Children should enjoy the learning process almost to the extent that they don't realize they are learning.

Creating Learning Environments

Overview | *What Would You Do?*

THE NEED FOR ORGANIZATION **440**
The Ecology of Classrooms | The Goals of Classroom Management

CREATING A POSITIVE LEARNING ENVIRONMENT **445**
Some Research Results | Rules and Procedures Required | Planning
Spaces for Learning | Getting Started: The First Weeks of Class

MAINTAINING A GOOD ENVIRONMENT FOR LEARNING **455**
Encouraging Engagement | Prevention Is the Best Medicine | Dealing
with Discipline Problems | Special Problems with Secondary Students

SPECIAL PROGRAMS FOR CLASSROOM MANAGEMENT **461**
Group Consequences | Token Reinforcement Programs | Contingency
Contract Programs

THE NEED FOR COMMUNICATION **463**
Message Sent—Message Received | Diagnosis: Whose Problem Is It?
| Counseling: The Student's Problem | Confrontation and Assertive
Discipline | Student Conflicts and Confrontations | Communicating
with Families about Classroom Management

Summary | *Key Terms* | *Check Your Understanding* |
Teachers' Casebook: What Would They Do?

*W*hen you imagine facing 25 or 30 students on the first day of class, what are your concerns? List the management problems that you find most difficult. What are your strengths in dealing with classroom management problems?

This chapter examines the ways that teachers create social and physical environments for learning. We will look at classroom management—one of the main concerns of teachers, particularly beginning teachers.

The very nature of classes, teaching, and students makes good management a critical ingredient of success; we will look at why this is true. Next, we will turn to the goals of classroom management. Successful managers create more time for learning, involve more students, and help students to become self-managing.

A positive learning environment must be established and maintained throughout the year. One of the best ways to do this is to try to prevent problems from occurring at all. But when problems arise—as they always do—an appropriate response is important. What will you do when students challenge you openly in class, when one student asks your advice on a difficult personal problem, or when another withdraws from all participation? We will examine the ways that teachers can communicate effectively with their students in these and many other situations.

By the time you have completed this chapter, you should be able to:

- Describe the special managerial demands of classrooms and relate these demands to students of different ages.
- Create a list of rules and procedures for a class.
- Develop a plan for organizing your first week of teaching.
- Explain Kounin's suggestions for preventing management problems.
- Describe how you might respond to a student who seldom completes work.
- Describe how and when you might use group consequences, token economies, and contingency contracts to enhance classroom management.
- Suggest two different approaches for dealing with a conflict between teacher and student, or between two students.
- Arrange the physical environment of your classroom to fit your learning goals and teaching methods.

What Would You Do?

There are students from four different ethnic groups in the middle school "pod" you are working with this year. Last week, the principal added a student with pretty severe emotional/behavioral problems and a student with cerebral palsy to the group as part of an experiment in full inclusion. The boy with cerebral palsy is in a wheelchair and has some difficulties with language and hearing. Each of the four ethnic groups seems to stick together, never making friends with students from "outside." When you ask people to work together for projects, the divisions are strictly on ethnic lines. Many of the subgroups communicate in their native language—one you don't understand—and you assume that often the joke is on you because of the looks and laughs directed your way. Clarise, the emotionally disturbed student, is making matters worse by telling ethnic jokes to anyone who will listen in a voice loud enough to be overheard by half the class. There are rumors of an ambush after school to "teach Clarise a lesson." You agree she—and the whole class for that matter—needs a lesson, but not this kind.

- How would you structure the class to help the students feel more comfortable together?
- What are your first goals in working on this problem?
- Is conflict negotiation called for here? How would you handle the situation?
- How will these issues affect the grade-levels you will teach?

The Need for Organization

In 1996, *Phi Delta Kappa* published the 28th annual Gallup Poll of the public's attitude toward public schools. For 16 of the first 18 years of the poll, "lack of discipline" was named as the number one problem facing the schools. In the other years lack of discipline was the number two problem (Elam, Rose, & Gallup, 1996). Clearly, the public sees discipline as an important challenge for teachers. In order to understand the role of management in teaching, let's take a closer look at the classroom itself.

The Ecology of Classrooms

The word *ecology* is usually associated with nature. But classrooms are ecological systems, too. The environment of the classroom and the inhabitants of that environment—students and teachers—are constantly interacting. Each aspect of the system affects all others. The characteristics of classrooms, the tasks of teaching, and the needs of students all influence classroom management (Epanchin, Townsend, & Stoddard, 1994).

Characteristics of Classrooms. Classes are particular kinds of environments. They have "distinctive properties affecting participants regardless of how students are organized for learning or what educational philosophy the teacher espouses" (Doyle, 1986, p. 394). Let's look at six of the features described by Doyle.

So much is happening at any given moment in a typical classroom that a teacher needs to be "on" at every moment of the day.

Classrooms are *multidimensional.* They are crowded with people, tasks, and time pressures. Many individuals, all with differing goals, preferences, and abilities, must share resources, accomplish various tasks, use and reuse materials without losing them, move in and out of the room, keep track of what is happening, and so on. In addition, actions can have multiple effects. Calling on low-ability students may encourage their participation and thinking but may slow the discussion and lead to management problems if the students cannot answer.

There is *simultaneity.* Everything happens at once. A teacher explaining a concept must also notice if students are following the explanation, decide whether two whispering youngsters should be ignored or stopped, determine if there is enough time to start the next topic, and decide who should answer the question that Jill just asked.

The next characteristic, *immediacy,* refers to the fast pace of classroom life. Teachers have literally hundreds of exchanges with students during a single day. In this rapid-fire existence, events are *unpredictable.* Even when plans are carefully made, the overhead projector is in place, and the handouts are ready, the lesson can still be interrupted by a burned-out bulb in the projector, a child who suddenly becomes ill, or a loud, angry discussion right outside the classroom.

Because classrooms are *public,* the way the teacher handles these unexpected intrusions is seen and judged by all. Students are always noticing if the teacher is being "fair." Is there favoritism? What happens when a rule is broken? Finally, classrooms have *histories.* The meaning of a particular teacher's or student's actions depends in part on what has happened before. The 15th time a student arrives late requires a different response from the teacher than the first late arrival. In addition, the history of the first few weeks of school affects life in the class all year.

The Basic Task: Gain Their Cooperation.   No productive activity can take place in a group without the cooperation of all members. This obviously applies to classrooms. Even if some students don't participate, they must allow others to do so. (You have probably seen one or two students bring an entire class to a halt.) So the basic management task for teachers is to achieve order and harmony by gaining and maintaining student cooperation in class activities (Doyle, 1986). Given the multidimensional, simultaneous, immediate, unpredictable, public, and historical nature of classrooms, this is quite a challenge.

Gaining student cooperation means much more than dealing effectively with misbehavior. It means planning activities, having materials ready, making appropriate behavioral and academic demands on students, giving clear signals to students, accomplishing transitions smoothly, foreseeing problems and stopping them before they start, selecting and sequencing activities so that flow and interest are maintained—and much more. Also, different activities require different managerial skills. For example, a new or complicated activity may be a greater threat to classroom management than a familiar or simple activity.

Age-Related Needs. Obviously, gaining the cooperation of kindergartners is not the same task as gaining the cooperation of high school seniors. Jere Brophy and Carolyn Evertson (1978) have identified four general stages of classroom management, defined by age-related needs. Let's look briefly at each.

During kindergarten and the first few years of elementary school, children are learning how to go to school. They are being socialized into a new role. Direct teaching of classroom rules and procedures is important during this stage. Little learning will take place until the children master these basics.

Children in the middle elementary years are usually familiar with the student role, even if they are not always perfect examples of it. Many school and classroom routines have become relatively automatic. Specific new rules and procedures for a particular activity may have to be taught directly, however. And you may hear the familiar refrain, "My teacher last year didn't do it that way!" Still, at this stage you will spend more time monitoring and maintaining the management system than teaching it directly.

Toward the end of elementary school and the beginning of high school, friendships and status within peer groups take on tremendous importance. Pleasing the teacher may be replaced by pleasing peers. Some students begin to test and defy authority. The management challenges at this stage are to deal productively with these disruptions and to motivate students who are becoming less concerned with teachers' opinions and more interested in their social lives.

By the end of high school, the focus of most students returns to academics. By this time, unfortunately, many of the students with overwhelming behavioral problems have dropped out. At this stage the challenges are to manage the curriculum, fit academic material to students' interests and abilities, and help students become more self-managing in their learning. The first few classes each semester may be devoted to teaching particular procedures for using materials and equipment, or for keeping track of and submitting assignments. But most students know what is expected.

Classroom Management Techniques used to maintain a healthy learning environment, relatively free of behavior problems.

The Goals of Classroom Management

The aim of **classroom management** is to maintain a positive, productive learning environment. But order for its own sake is an empty goal. As we discussed in Chapter 6, it is unethical to use class management techniques just to keep students docile and quiet. What, then, is the point of working so hard to manage classrooms? There are at least three reasons why management is important.

More Time for Learning.   As a child, I once used a stopwatch to time the commercials during a TV quiz show. I was amazed to find that half of the program was devoted to commercials. Actually, very little quizzing took place. If you used a similar approach in classrooms, timing all the different activities throughout the day, you might be surprised by how little actual teaching takes place. Many minutes each day are lost through interruptions, disruptions, late starts, and rough transitions (Karweit, 1989; Karweit & Slavin, 1981).

Obviously, students will learn only the material they have a chance to learn. Almost every study examining time and learning has found a significant relationship between time spent on content and student learning (Berliner, 1988). In fact, the correlations between content studied and student learning are usually larger than the correlations between specific teacher behaviors and student learning (Rosenshine, 1979). So one important goal of classroom management is to expand the sheer number of minutes available for learning. This is sometimes called **allocated time.**

But simply making more time for learning will not automatically lead to achievement. To be valuable, time must be used effectively. As you saw in the chapters on cognitive learning, the way students process information is a central factor in what they learn and remember. Basically, students will learn what they practice and think about (Doyle, 1983). Time spent actively involved in specific learning tasks is often called **engaged time,** or sometimes **time on task.**

Again, however, engaged time doesn't guarantee learning. Students may be struggling with material that is too difficult or using the wrong learning strategies. When students are working with a high rate of success—really learning and understanding—we call the time spent **academic learning time.** A second goal of class management is to increase academic learning time by keeping students *actively engaged in worthwhile, appropriate learning activities.* Figure 12.1 on page 444 shows how the 1,000+ hours of time mandated for school in most states can become only about 333 hours of quality academic learning time for a typical student.

Access to Learning.   Each classroom activity has its own rules for participation. Sometimes these rules are clearly stated by the teacher, but often they are implicit and unstated. Teacher and students may not even be aware that they are following different rules for different activities (Berliner, 1983). And the differences are sometimes quite subtle. For example, in a reading group students may have to raise their hands to make a comment, but in a show-and-tell circle in the same class they may simply have to catch the teacher's eye.

As we saw in Chapter 5, the rules defining who can talk; what they can talk about; and when, to whom, and how long they can talk are often called **participation structures.** In order to participate successfully in a given activity, students must understand the participation structure. Some students, however, seem to come to school less able to participate than others. The participation structures they learn at home in interactions with siblings, parents, and other adults do not match the participation structures of school activities (Tharp, 1989). But teachers are not necessarily aware of this conflict. Instead, the teachers see that a child doesn't quite fit in, always seems to say the wrong thing at the wrong time, or is very reluctant to participate, and they are not sure why.

Allocated Time Time set aside for learning.

Engaged Time Time spent actively learning.

Time on Task Time spent actively engaged in the learning task at hand.

Academic Learning Time Time when students are actually succeeding at the learning task.

Participation Structures Rules defining how to participate in different activities.

FIGURE 12.1

Who Knows Where the Time Goes?

The over 1,000 hours per year of instruction mandated by most states can represent only 300 or 400 hours of quality academic learning time.

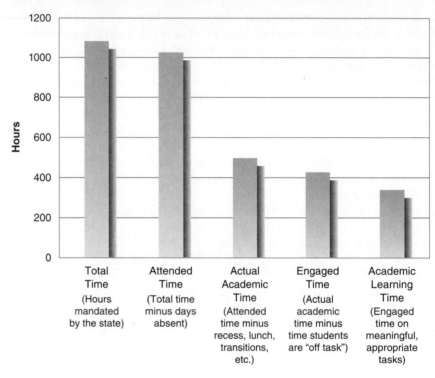

Source: From C. S. Weinstein and A. J. Mignano, Jr. *Elementary Classroom Management.* Copyright © 1993 by The McGraw-Hill Companies. Adapted with permission of The McGraw-Hill Companies.

What can we conclude? In order to involve all your students, you must make sure that everyone knows *how* to participate in each specific activity. The key is awareness. What are your rules and expectations? Are they understandable, given your students' cultural backgrounds and home experiences? What unspoken rules or values may be operating? Are you clear and consistent in signaling your students about how to participate? To reach the second goal of good classroom management—giving all students access to learning—you must make sure everyone knows how to participate in class activities. This means teaching and signaling appropriate ways to participate.

Management for Self-Management. The third goal of any management system is to help students become better able to manage themselves. Encouraging **self-management** requires extra time, but teaching students how to take responsibility is an investment well worth the effort. When elementary and secondary teachers have very effective class management systems but neglect to set student self-management as a goal, their students often

Self-Management Management of your own behavior and acceptance of responsibility for your own actions.

find that they have trouble working independently after they graduate from these "well-managed" classes.

Creating a Positive Learning Environment

In making plans for your class, much of what you have already learned in this book should prove helpful. You know, for example, that problems are prevented when individual variations, such as those discussed in Chapters 2, 3, 4, and 5, are taken into account in instructional planning. Sometimes students become disruptive because the work assigned is too difficult. And students who are bored by lessons well below their ability levels may be interested in finding more exciting activities to fill their time.

In one sense, teachers prevent discipline problems whenever they make an effort to motivate students. A student involved in learning is usually not involved in a clash with the teacher or other students at the same time. All plans for motivating students are steps toward preventing problems.

Some Research Results

What else can teachers do to be good managers? For several years, educational psychologists at the University of Texas at Austin studied classroom management quite thoroughly (Emmer, Evertson, & Anderson, 1980; Emmer, Evertson, Clements, & Worsham, 1997; Evertson, 1988; Evertson, Emmer, Clements, & Worsham, 1997). Their general approach was to study a large number of classrooms, making frequent observations the first weeks of school and less-frequent visits later in the year. After several months there were dramatic differences among the classes. Some had very few management problems, while others had many. The most and least effective teachers were identified on the basis of the quality of classroom management and student achievement later in the year.

Next, the researchers looked at their observation records of the first weeks of class to see how the effective teachers got started. Other comparisons were made between the teachers who ultimately had harmonious, high-achieving classes and those whose classes were fraught with problems. On the basis of these comparisons, management principles were developed. The researchers then taught these principles to a new group of teachers; the results were quite positive. Teachers who applied the principles had fewer problems; their students spent more time learning and less time disrupting; and achievement was higher. The findings of these studies formed the basis for two books on classroom management (Emmer et al., 1997; Evertson et al., 1997). Many of the ideas in the following pages are from these books.

Rules and Procedures Required

At the elementary-school level, teachers must lead 20 to 30 students of varying abilities through many different activities each day. Without efficient rules and procedures, a great deal of time is wasted answering the same question over and over. "My pencil broke. How can I do my math?" "I'm finished with my story. What should I do now?" "Steven hit me!" "I left my homework in my locker."

At the secondary-school level, teachers must deal daily with over 100 students who use dozens of materials and often change rooms for each class. Secondary-school students are also more likely to challenge teachers' authority. The effective managers studied by Emmer, Evertson, and their colleagues had planned procedures and rules for coping with these situations.

Procedures. How will materials and assignments be distributed and collected? Under what conditions can students leave the room? How will grades be determined? What are the special routines for handling equipment and supplies in science, art, or vocational classes? **Procedures** describe how activities are accomplished in classrooms, but they are seldom written down; they are simply the ways of getting things done in class. Carol Weinstein (1996) and Weinstein and Mignano (1997) suggest that teachers establish procedures to cover the following areas:

1. *Administrative routines,* such as taking attendance.
2. *Student movement,* such as entering and leaving or going to the bathroom.
3. *Housekeeping,* such as watering plants or storing personal items.
4. *Routines for accomplishing lessons,* such as how to collect assignments or return homework.
5. *Interactions between teacher and student,* such as how to get the teacher's attention when help is needed.
6. *Talk among students,* such as giving help or socializing.

You might use these six areas as a framework for planning your class procedures and routines. The Guidelines should help you as you plan.

Guidelines

Establishing Class Procedures

Determine procedures for student upkeep of desks, classroom equipment, and other facilities.

Examples

1. Some teachers set aside a cleanup time each day or once a week in self-contained classes.
2. You might demonstrate and have students practice how to push chairs under the desk, take and return materials stored on shelves, sharpen pencils, use the sink or water fountain, assemble lab equipment, and so on.
3. In some classes a rotating monitor is in charge of equipment or materials.

Decide how students will be expected to enter and leave the room.

Examples

1. How will students know what they should do as soon as they enter the room? Some teachers have a standard assignment ("Have your homework out and be checking it over").
2. Under what conditions can students leave the room? When do they need permission?
3. If students are late, how do they gain admission to the room?
4. Many teachers require students to be in their seats and quiet before they can leave at the end of class. The teacher, not the bell, dismisses class.

Establish a signal and teach it to your students.

Examples

1. In the classroom, some teachers flick the lights, sound a chord on a piano or recorder, move to the podium and stare silently at the class, use a phrase like "Eyes, please," take out their grade books, or move to the front of the class.

Procedures Prescribed steps for an activity.

2. In the halls, a raised hand, one clap, or some other signal may mean "Stop."
3. On the playground, a raised hand or whistle may mean "Line up."

Set procedures for student participation in class.

Examples

1. Will you have students raise their hands for permission to speak or simply require that they wait until the speaker has finished?
2. How will you signal that you want everyone to respond at once? Some teachers raise a cupped hand to their ear. Others preface the question with "Everyone . . . "
3. Make sure you are clear about differences in procedures for different activities: reading group, learning center, discussion, teacher presentation, seatwork, film, peer learning group, library, and so forth.
4. How many students at a time can be at the pencil sharpener, teacher's desk, learning center, sink, bookshelves, reading corner, or bathroom?

Determine how you will communicate, collect, and return assignments.

Examples

1. Some teachers reserve a particular corner of the board for listing assignments. Others write assignments in colored chalk. For younger students it may be better to prepare assignment sheets or folders, color-coding them for math workbook, reading packet, and science kit.
2. Some teachers collect assignments in a box or bin; others have a student collect work while they introduce the next activity.

Rules   **Rules** specify expected and forbidden actions in the class. They are the do's and don'ts of classroom life. Unlike procedures, rules are often written down and posted. In establishing rules, you should consider what kind of atmosphere you want to create. What student behaviors will help you teach effectively? What limits do the students need to guide their behavior? The rules you set should be consistent with school rules, and also in keeping with principles of learning. For example, we know from the research on small-group learning that students benefit when they explain work to peers. They learn as they teach. A rule that forbids students to help each other may be inconsistent with good learning principles. Or a rule that says, "No erasures when writing" may make students focus more on preventing mistakes than on communicating clearly in their writing (Burden, 1995; Weinstein & Mignano, 1997).

Having a few general rules that cover many specifics is better than listing all the do's and don'ts. But, if specific actions are forbidden, such as chewing gum in class or smoking in the bathrooms, then a rule should make this clear.

Rules for Elementary School.   Evertson and her colleagues (1997) give five examples of general rules for elementary-school classes:

1. *Be polite and helpful.* This applies to behavior toward adults (including substitute teachers) and children. Examples of polite behavior include waiting your turn, saying "please" and "thank you," and not fighting or calling names.
2. *Respect other people's property.* This might include picking up litter; returning library books; not marking on walls, desks, or buses; and getting permission before using other people's things.

Rules Statements specifying expected and forbidden behaviors; dos and don'ts.

3. *Listen quietly while others are speaking.* This applies to the teacher and other students, in large-class lessons or small-group discussions.

4. *Do not hit, shove, or hurt others.* Make sure you give clear explanations of what you mean by "hurt." Does this apply to hurt feelings as well as hurt bodies?

5. *Obey all school rules.* This reminds students that all school rules apply in your classroom. Then students cannot claim, for example, that they thought it was okay to chew gum or listen to a radio in your class, even though these are against school rules, "because you never made a rule against it for us."

Whatever the rule, students need to be taught the behaviors that the rule includes and excludes. Examples, practice, and discussion will be needed before learning is complete.

As you've seen, different activities often require different rules. This can be confusing for elementary students until they have thoroughly learned all the rules. To prevent confusion, you might consider making signs that list the rules for each activity. Then, before the activity, you can post the appropriate sign as a reminder. This provides clear and consistent cues about participation structures so all students, not just the "well-behaved," know what is expected. Of course, these rules must be explained and discussed before the signs can have their full effect.

Rules for Secondary School.   Emmer and colleagues (1997) suggest six examples of rules for secondary students:

1. *Bring all needed materials to class.* The teacher must specify the type of pen, pencil, paper, notebook, texts, and so on.

2. *Be in your seat and ready to work when the bell rings.* Many teachers combine this rule with a standard beginning procedure for the class, such as a warm-up exercise on the board or a requirement that students have paper with a proper heading ready when the bell rings.

3. *Respect and be polite to everyone.* This covers fighting, verbal abuse, and general troublemaking.

4. *Respect other people's property.* This means property belonging to the school, the teacher, or other students.

5. *Listen and stay seated while someone else is speaking.* This applies when the teacher or other students are talking.

6. *Obey all school rules.* As with the elementary class rules, this covers many behaviors and situations, so you do not have to repeat every school rule for your class. It also reminds the students that you will be monitoring them inside and outside your class. Make sure you know all the school rules. Some secondary students are very adept at convincing teachers that their misbehavior "really isn't against the rules."

Consequences.   As soon as you decide on your rules and procedures, you must consider what you will do when a student breaks a rule or does not follow a procedure. It is too late to make this decision after the rule has been broken. For many infractions, the logical consequence is having to go back and "do it right." Students who run in the hall may have to return to where

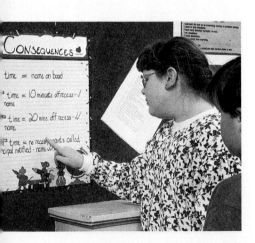

Consequences for breaking rules are posted in this classroom. How about consequences for following the rules?

TABLE 12.1   Seven Categories of Penalties for Students

1. *Expressions of disappointment.* If students like and respect their teacher, then a serious, sorrowful expression of disappointment may cause students to stop and think about their behavior.

2. *Loss of privileges.* Students can lose free time. If they have not completed homework, for example, they can be required to do it during a free period or recess.

3. *Exclusion from the group.* Students who distract their peers or fail to cooperate can be separated from the group until they are ready to cooperate. Some teachers give a student a pass for 10 to 15 minutes. The student must go to another class or study hall where the other students and teachers ignore the offending student for that time.

4. *Written reflections on the problem.* Students can write in journals, write essays about what they did and how it affected others, or write letters of apology—if this is appropriate. Another possibility is to ask students to describe objectively what they did; then the teacher and the student can sign and date this statement. These records are available if parents or administrators need evidence of the students' behavior.

5. *Detentions.* Detentions can be very brief meetings after school, during a free period, or at lunch. The main purpose is to talk about what has happened. (In high school, detentions are often used as punishments; suspensions and expulsions are available as more extreme measures.)

6. *Visits to the principal's office.* Expert teachers tend to use this penalty rarely, but they do use it when the situation warrants. Some schools require students to be sent to the office for certain offenses, such as fighting. If you tell a student to go to the office and the student refuses, you might call the office saying the student has been sent. Then the student has the choice of either going to the office or facing the principal's penalty for "disappearing" on the way.

7. *Contact with parents.* If problems become a repeated pattern, most teachers contact the student's family. This is done to seek support for helping the student, not to blame the parents or punish the student.

Source: From C. S. Weinstein and A. J. Mignano, Jr. *Elementary Classroom Management.* Copyright © 1993 by The McGraw-Hill Companies. Adapted with permission of The McGraw-Hill Companies.

---

they started and walk properly. Incomplete papers can be redone. Materials left out should be put back (Charles, 1996). Sometimes consequences are more complicated. In their case studies of four expert elementary-school teachers, Weinstein and Mignano (1997) found that the teachers' negative consequences fell into seven categories, as shown in Table 12.1.

In the first chapter I described Ken, an expert teacher who worked with his students to establish a students' and teacher's "Bill of Rights" instead of defining rules. These "rights" cover most situations that might require a "rule" and help the students move toward the goal of becoming self-managing. The rights for one recent year's class are listed in Table 12.2 on page 450. The main point here is that decisions about penalties (and rewards) must be made early on, so students know before they break a rule or use the wrong procedure what this will mean for them. I encourage my student teachers to get a copy of the school rules and their cooperating teacher's rules, then plan their own.

Another kind of planning that affects the learning environment is designing the physical arrangement of the class furniture, materials, and learning tools.

Planning Spaces for Learning

There are two basic ways of organizing space: interest areas and personal territories. These are not mutually exclusive; many teachers use a design that combines interest areas and personal territories. Individual students' desks—their

TABLE 12.2	A Bill of Rights for Students and Teachers

Students' Bill of Rights

Students in this class have the following rights:

To whisper when the teacher isn't talking or asking for silence.
To celebrate authorship or other work at least once a month.
To exercise outside on days there is no physical education class.
To have 2-minute breaks.
To have healthy snacks during snack time.
To participate in choosing a table.
To have privacy. Get permission to touch anyone else's possessions.
To be comfortable.
To chew gum without blowing bubbles or making a mess.
To make choices about the day's schedule.
To have free work time.
To work with partners.
To talk to the class without anyone else talking.
To work without being disturbed.

Teacher's Bill of Rights

The teacher has the following rights:

To talk without anyone else talking, or moving about, or disturbing the class.
To work without being disturbed.
To have everyone's attention while giving directions.
To punish someone who is not cooperating.
To send someone out of the group, or room, or to the office.

Source: From C. S. Weinstein and A. J. Mignano, Jr. *Elementary Classroom Management.* Copyright © 1993 by The McGraw-Hill Companies. Adapted with permission of The McGraw-Hill Companies.

territories—are placed in the center, with interest areas in the back or around the periphery of the room. This allows the flexibility needed for both large- and small-group activities. Figure 12.2 shows an elementary classroom that combines interest area and personal territory arrangements.

Interest-Area Arrangements. The design of interest areas can influence the way the areas are used by students. For example, working with a classroom teacher, Carol Weinstein (1977) was able to make changes in interest areas that helped the teacher meet her objectives of having more girls involved in the science center and having all students experiment more with a variety of manipulative materials. In a second study, changes in a library corner led to more involvement in literature activities throughout the class (Morrow & Weinstein, 1986).

To plan your classroom space, first decide what activities the classroom should accommodate. For example, if you are in a self-contained elementary classroom, you might set up interest areas for reading, arts and crafts, science, and math. If you are teaching one particular subject on the junior or senior high level, you might divide your room into several areas, perhaps for audiovisual activities, small-group instruction, quiet study, and projects.

FIGURE 12.2

An Elementary Classroom Arrangement

This 4th-grade teacher has designed a space that allows teacher presentations and demonstrations, small group work, computer interactions, math manipulatives activities, informal reading, art, and other projects without constant rearrangements required.

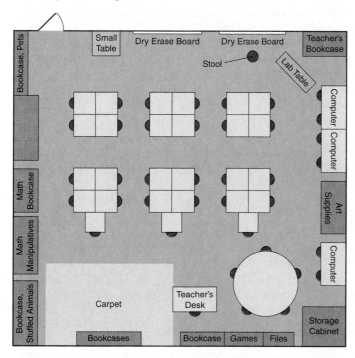

Source: From C. S. Weinstein and A. J. Mignano, Jr. *Elementary Classroom Management.* Copyright © 1993 by The McGraw-Hill Companies. Reproduced with permission of The McGraw-Hill Companies.

Next, you are ready to draw several possible floor plans. Use graph paper if possible, and draw to scale. As you work, keep the Guidelines in mind.

Guidelines

Designing
Learning Spaces

Note the fixed features and plan accordingly.

Examples

1. Remember that the audiovisual center and computers need an electrical outlet.

2. Keep art supplies near the sink, small group work by a blackboard.

Create easy access to materials and a well-organized place to store them.

Examples

1. Make sure materials are easy-to-reach and visible to students.

2. Have enough shelves so that materials need not be stacked.

(continued)

Provide students with clean, convenient surfaces for studying.

Examples

1. Put bookshelves next to reading area, games by game table.
2. Prevent fights by avoiding crowded work spaces.

Make sure work areas are private and quiet.

Examples

1. Make sure there are no tables or work areas in the middle of traffic lanes; a person should not have to pass through one area to get to another.
2. Keep noisy activities as far as possible from quiet ones. Increase the feeling of privacy by placing partitions, such as bookcases or pegboards, between areas or within large areas.

Arrange things so you can see your students and they can see all instructional presentations.

Examples

1. Make sure you can see over partitions.
2. Design seating so that students can see instruction without moving their chairs or desks.

Avoid dead spaces and "racetracks."

Examples

1. Don't have all the interest areas around the outside of the room, leaving a large dead space in the middle.
2. Avoid placing a few items of furniture right in the middle of this large space, creating a "racetrack" around the furniture.

Provide choices and flexibility.

Examples

1. Establish closed, small spaces, private cubicles for individual work; open tables for group work; and cushions on the floor for whole-class meetings.
2. Give students a place to keep their personal belongings. This is especially important if students don't have personal desks.

Try new arrangements, then evaluate and improve.

Examples

1. Have a "two-week arrangement," then evaluate.
2. Enlist the aid of your students. They have to live in the room, too, and designing a classroom can be a very challenging educational experience.

Personal Territories. Can the physical setting influence teaching and learning in classrooms organized by territories? Adams and Biddle (1970) found that verbal interaction between teacher and students was concentrated in the center front of the classroom and in a line directly up the center of the room. The data were so dramatic that Adams and Biddle coined the term **action zone** to refer to this area of the room. Later research modified this finding. Even though most rooms have an action zone where participation is greatest, this area may be on one side, or near a particular learning center (Good, 1983a).

Action Zone Area of a classroom where the greatest amount of interaction takes place.

Front-seat location does seem to increase participation for students who are predisposed to speak in class, whereas a seat in the back will make it more difficult to participate and easier to sit back and daydream (Woolfolk & Brooks, 1983). To "spread the action around," Weinstein and Mignano (1997) suggest that teachers move around the room when possible, establish eye contact with students seated far away, and direct comments to students seated at a distance.

Many teachers vary the seating so the same students are not always consigned to the back of the room or to make the arrangement more appropriate for particular objectives and activities. Figure 12.3 is a high school mathematics class with a seating arrangement that allows focus on teacher demonstration as well as small-group work.

Horizontal rows (like the front and back rows in Figure 12.3) share many of the advantages of the traditional row and column arrangements. Both are useful for independent seatwork and teacher, student, or media presentations; they encourage students to focus on the presenter and simplify housekeeping. Horizontal rows also permit students to work more easily in pairs. However, this is a poor arrangement for large-group discussion.

FIGURE 12.3

A High School Math Classroom

This high school teacher has designed a math classroom that allows teacher presentations and demonstrations as well as small group work. By moving 3 tables, the room can be transformed into 4 horizontal rows for independent work or testing.

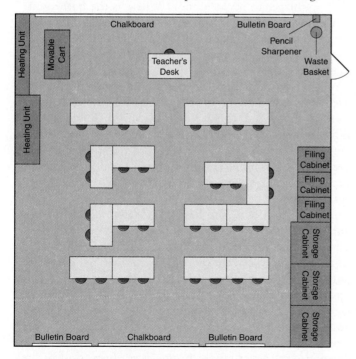

Source: From C. S. Weinstein and A. J. Mignano, Jr. *Elementary Classroom Management.* Copyright © 1993 by The McGraw-Hill Companies. Reproduced with permission of The McGraw-Hill Companies.

Clusters of four or circle arrangements are best for student interaction. Circles are especially useful for discussions but still allow for independent seatwork. Clusters permit students to talk, help one another, share materials, and work on group tasks. Both arrangements, however, are poor for whole-group presentations and may make class management more difficult.

The fishbowl or stack special formation, where students sit close together near the focus of attention (the back row may even be standing), should be used only for short periods of time, because it is not comfortable and can lead to discipline problems. On the other hand, the fishbowl can create a feeling of group cohesion and is helpful when the teacher wants students to watch a demonstration, brainstorm on a class problem, or see a small visual aid.

Getting Started: The First Weeks of Class

Determining a room design, rules, and procedures are first steps toward having a well-managed class—but how do effective teachers gain students' cooperation in those first critical days and weeks? One study carefully analyzed the first weeks' activities of effective and ineffective elementary teachers, and found striking differences (Emmer, Evertson, & Anderson, 1980).

Effective Managers for Elementary Students.   In the effective teachers' classrooms, the very first day was well organized. Name tags were ready. There was something interesting for each child to do right away. Materials were set up. The teachers had planned carefully to avoid any last-minute tasks that might take them away from their students. These teachers dealt with the children's pressing concerns first. "Where do I put my things? How do I pronounce my teacher's name? Can I whisper to my neighbor? Where is the bathroom?" The effective teachers had a workable, easily understood set of rules and taught the students the most important rules right away. They taught the rules like any other subject, with lots of explanation, examples, and practice.

Throughout the first weeks, the effective managers continued to spend quite a bit of time teaching rules and procedures. Some used guided practice to teach procedures; others used rewards to shape behavior. Most taught students to respond to a bell or some other signal to gain their attention. These teachers worked with the class as a whole on enjoyable academic activities. They did not rush to get students into small groups or to get them started in readers. This whole-class work gave the teachers a better opportunity to continue monitoring all students' learning of the rules and procedures. Misbehavior was stopped quickly and firmly, but not harshly.

In the poorly managed classrooms, the first weeks were quite different. Rules were not workable; they were either too vague or very complicated. For example, one teacher made a rule that students should "be in the right place at the right time." Students were not told what this meant, so their behavior could not be guided by the rule. Neither positive nor negative behaviors had clear, consistent consequences. After students broke a rule, ineffective managers might give a vague criticism, such as "Some of my children are too noisy," or issue a warning, but not follow through with the threatened consequence.

In the poorly managed classes, procedures for accomplishing routine tasks varied from day to day and were never taught or practiced. Instead of dealing with these obvious needs, ineffective managers spent time on procedures that could have waited. For example, one teacher had the class practice for a fire drill the first day, but left unexplained other procedures that would be needed every day. Students wandered aimlessly and had to ask each other what they should be doing. Often the students talked to one another because they had nothing productive to do. Ineffective teachers frequently left the room. Many became absorbed in paperwork or in helping just one student. They had not made plans for how to deal with late-arriving students or interruptions. One ineffective manager tried to teach students to respond to a bell as a signal for attention, but later let the students ignore it. All in all, the first weeks in these classrooms were disorganized and filled with surprises for teachers and students alike.

Effective Managers for Secondary Students.   What about getting started in a secondary-school class? It appears that many of the differences between effective and ineffective elementary-school teachers hold at the secondary level as well. Again, effective managers focus on establishing rules, procedures, and expectations on the first day of class. These standards for academic work and class behavior are clearly communicated to students and consistently enforced during the first weeks of class. Student behavior is closely monitored, and infractions of the rules are dealt with quickly. In classes with lower-ability students, work cycles are shorter; students are not required to spend long, unbroken periods on one type of activity. Instead, during each period they are moved smoothly through several different tasks. In general, effective teachers carefully follow each student's progress, so students cannot avoid work without facing consequences (Emmer & Evertson, 1982).

With all this close monitoring and consistent enforcement of the rules, you may wonder if effective secondary teachers have to be grim and humorless. Not necessarily. The effective managers in one study also smiled and joked more with their students (Moskowitz & Hayman, 1976). As any experienced teacher can tell you, there is much more to smile about when the class is cooperative.

> **Focus on...**
>
> ### Creating a Positive Learning Environment
>
> - Distinguish between rules and procedures.
> - What basic rules would you use for your students and how would you teach them?
> - Distinguish between personal territories and interest-area spatial arrangements.
> - How can the physical arrangement of the room promote learning?
> - Contrast the first school week of effective and ineffective classroom managers.

Maintaining a Good Environment for Learning

A good start is just that—a beginning. Effective teachers build on this beginning. They maintain their management system by preventing problems and keeping students engaged in productive learning activities. We have discussed several ways to keep students engaged. In the chapters on motivation, for example, we considered stimulating curiosity, relating lessons to student interests, encouraging cooperative learning, establishing learning goals instead of performance goals, and having positive expectations. What else can teachers do?

Encouraging Engagement

The format of a lesson affects student involvement. In general, as teacher supervision increases, students' engaged time also increases (Emmer & Evertson, 1981). A recent study, for example, found that elementary students working directly with a teacher were on task 97% of the time, while students working on their own were on task only 57% of the time (Frick, 1990). This does not mean that teachers should eliminate independent work for students. It simply means that this type of activity usually requires careful monitoring.

When the task provides continuous cues for the student about what to do next, involvement will be greater. Activities with clear steps are likely to be more absorbing, since one step leads naturally to the next. When students have all the materials they need to complete a task, they tend to stay involved (Kounin & Doyle, 1975). If their curiosity is piqued, students will be motivated to continue seeking an answer. And as you now know, students will be more engaged if they are involved in authentic tasks—activities that have connections to real life.

Of course, teachers can't supervise every student all the time or rely on curiosity. Something else must keep students working on their own. In their study of elementary and secondary teachers, Evertson, Emmer, and their colleagues found that effective class managers at both levels had well-planned systems for encouraging students to manage their own work (Evertson et al., 1997; Emmer et al., 1997). The Guidelines are based on their findings.

Guidelines

Keeping Students Engaged

Make basic work requirements clear.

Examples

1. Specify and post the routine work requirements for headings, paper size, pen or pencil use, and neatness.
2. Establish and explain rules about late or incomplete work and absences. If a pattern of incomplete work begins to develop, deal with it early; speak with parents if necessary.
3. Make due dates reasonable, and stick to them unless the student has a very good excuse for lateness.

Communicate the specifics of assignments.

Examples

1. With younger students, have a routine procedure for giving assignments, such as writing them on the board in the same place each day. With older students, assignments may be dictated, posted, or given in a syllabus.
2. Remind students of coming assignments.
3. With complicated assignments, give students a sheet describing what to do, what resources are available, due dates, and so on. Older students should also be told your grading criteria.
4. Demonstrate how to do the assignment, do the first few questions together, or provide a sample worksheet.

Monitor work in progress.

Examples

1. When you make an assignment in class, make sure each student gets started correctly. If you check only students who raise their hands for help, you will miss those who think they know what to do but don't really understand, those who are too shy to ask for help, and those who don't plan to do the work at all.
2. Check progress periodically. In discussions, make sure everyone has a chance to respond.

Give frequent academic feedback.

Examples

1. Elementary students should get papers back the day after they are handed in.
2. Good work can be displayed in class and graded papers sent home to parents each week.
3. Students of all ages can keep records of grades, projects completed, and extra credits earned.
4. For older students break up long-term assignments into several phases, giving feedback at each point.

Prevention Is the Best Medicine

What else can you do to maintain your management system? The ideal way to manage problems, of course, is to prevent them in the first place. In a classic study, Jacob Kounin (1970) examined classroom management by comparing effective teachers, whose classes were relatively free of problems, with ineffective teachers, whose classes were continually plagued by chaos and disruption. Observing both groups in action, Kounin found that they were not very different in the way they handled discipline once problems arose. The difference was that the successful managers were much better at preventing problems. Kounin concluded that effective classroom managers were especially skilled in four areas: *"withitness," overlapping activities, group focusing, and movement management* (Doyle, 1977). More recent research confirms the importance of these factors (Emmer & Evertson, 1981; Evertson, 1988).

Withitness.   **Withitness** means communicating to students that you are aware of everything that is happening in the classroom, that you aren't missing anything. "With-it" teachers seem to have eyes in the back of their heads. They avoid becoming absorbed or interacting with only a few students, because this encourages the rest of the class to wander. They are always scanning the room, making eye contact with individual students, so the students know they are being monitored (Brooks, 1985).

These teachers prevent minor disruptions from becoming major. They also know who instigated the problem, and they make sure the right people are dealt with. In other words, they do not make what Kounin called *timing errors* (waiting too long before intervening) or *target errors* (blaming the wrong student and letting the real perpetrators escape responsibility for their behavior).

If two problems occur at the same time, effective managers deal with the more serious one first. For example, a teacher who tells two students to stop whispering but ignores even a brief shoving match at the pencil sharpener communicates to students a lack of awareness. Students begin to believe they can get away with almost anything if they are clever (Charles, 1996).

Overlapping and Group Focus.   **Overlapping** means keeping track of and supervising several activities at the same time. For example, a teacher may have to check the work of an individual and at the same time keep a small group working by saying, "Right, go on," and stop an incident in another group with a quick "look" or reminder (Burden, 1995; Charles, 1996).

Withitness According to Kounin, awareness of everything happening in a classroom.

Overlapping Supervising several activities at once.

*W*hile this teacher is talking to a group of students does he know what else is happening in the class? Can he "overlap" activities and still be "withit"?

Maintaining a **group focus** means keeping as many students as possible involved in appropriate class activities and avoiding narrowing in on just one or two students. All students should have something to do during a lesson. For example, the teacher might ask everyone to write the answer to a question, then call on individuals to respond while the other students compare their answers. Choral responses might be required while the teacher moves around the room to make sure everyone is participating (Charles, 1996). Some teachers have their students use small blackboards or colored cards for responding in groups. This lets the teacher check for understanding as well. For example, during a grammar lesson the teacher might say, "Everyone who thinks the answer is *have run*, hold up the red side of your card. If you think the answer is *has run*, hold up the green side" (Hunter, 1982). This is one way teachers can ensure that all students are involved and check that they all understand the material.

Movement Management.   **Movement management** means keeping lessons and the group moving at an appropriate (and flexible) pace, with smooth transitions and variety. The effective teacher avoids abrupt transitions, such as announcing a new activity before gaining the students' attention or starting a new activity in the middle of something else. In these situations, one-third of the class will be doing the new activity, many will be on the old lesson, several will be asking other students what to do, some will be taking the opportunity to have a little fun, and most will be confused.

Another transition problem Kounin noted is the *slowdown,* or taking too much time to start a new activity. Sometimes teachers give too many directions. Problems also arise when teachers have students work one at a time while the rest of the class waits and watches. Charles (1985, p. 26) gives this example:

During a science lesson the teacher began, "Row 1 may get up and get their beakers. Row 2 may get theirs. Now Row 3. Now, Row 1 may line up to put some bicarbonate of soda in their beakers. Row 2 may follow them," and so forth. When each row had obtained their bicarbonate of

Group Focus The ability to keep as many students as possible involved in activities.

Movement Management Ability to keep lessons and groups moving smoothly.

soda the teacher had them go row by row to add water. This left the remainder of the class sitting at their desks with no direction, doing nothing
or else beginning to find something with which to entertain themselves.

A teacher who successfully demonstrates withitness, overlapping activities,
group focus, and movement management tends to have a class filled with actively engaged students who do not escape his or her all-seeing eye. This need
not be a grim classroom. It is more likely a busy place where students are actively learning and gaining a sense of self-worth rather than misbehaving in
order to get attention and achieve status.

Dealing with Discipline Problems

Being an effective manager does not mean publicly correcting every minor infraction of the rules. This kind of public attention may actually reinforce the
misbehavior, as we saw in Chapter 6. Teachers who frequently correct students
do not necessarily have the best behaved classes (Irving & Martin, 1982). The
key is to know what is happening and what is important so you can prevent
problems. Emmer and colleagues (1997) and Levin and Nolan (1996) suggest
four simple ways to stop misbehavior quickly:

1. *Make eye contact* with, or move closer to, the offender. Other nonverbal signals, such as pointing to the work students are supposed to be doing, might be
   helpful. Make sure the student actually stops the inappropriate behavior and
   gets back to work. If you do not, students will learn to ignore your signals.

2. If they are not performing a class procedure correctly, *remind the students* of
   the procedure and have them follow it correctly. You may need to quietly collect a toy, comb, magazine, or note that is competing with the learning activities, while privately informing the students that their possessions will be returned
   after class.

3. In a calm, unhostile way, *ask the student to state the correct rule or procedure*
   and then to follow it.

4. Tell the student in a clear, assertive, and unhostile way to *stop the misbehavior.*
   (Later in the chapter we will discuss assertive messages to students in more detail.)

If you must impose penalties, the Guidelines, taken from Weinstein and Mignano (1997; 1996), give ideas about how to do it. The examples are taken from
the actual words of the expert teachers described in their book.

Guidelines

Imposing Penalties

**Delay the discussion of the situation until you and the students involved are
calmer and more objective.**

Examples

1. Say calmly to a student, "Sit there and think about what happened. I'll talk
   to you in a few minutes," or, "I don't like what I just saw. Talk to me during
   your free period today."

2. Say, "I'm really angry about what just happened. Everybody take out journals; we are going to write about this." After a few minutes of writing, the class
   can discuss the incident.

(continued)

Impose penalties privately.

Examples

1. Make arrangements with students privately. Stand firm in enforcing arrangements.

2. Resist the temptation to "remind" students in public that they are not keeping their side of the bargain.

3. Move close to a student who must be disciplined and speak so that only the student can hear.

After imposing a penalty, reestablish a positive relationship with the student immediately.

Examples

1. Send the student on an errand or ask him or her for help.

2. Compliment the student's work or give a real or symbolic "pat on the back" when the student's behavior warrants. Look hard for such an opportunity.

Set up a graded list of penalties that will fit many occasions.

Example

1. For not turning in homework: (1) receive reminder; (2) receive warning; (3) hand homework in before close of school day; (4) stay after school to finish work; (5) participate in a teacher-student-parent conference to develop an action plan.

Special Problems with Secondary Students

Many secondary students never complete their work. Besides encouraging student responsibility, what else can teachers do to deal with this frustrating problem? Because students at this age have many assignments and teachers have many students, both teacher and students may lose track of what has and has not been completed. It often helps to teach students how to use a daily planner. In addition, the teacher must keep accurate records. But the most important thing is to enforce the established consequences for incomplete work. Do not pass a student because you know he or she is "bright enough" to pass. Make it clear to these students that the choice is theirs: they can do the work and pass, or they can refuse to do the work and face the consequences.

There is also the problem of students who continually break the same rules, always forgetting materials, for example, or getting into fights. What should you do? Seat these students away from others who might be influenced by them. Try to catch them before they break the rules, but if rules are broken, be consistent in applying established consequences. Do not accept promises to do better next time (Levin & Nolan, 1996). Teach the students how to monitor their own behavior; some of the self-management techniques described in Chapter 6 should be helpful. Finally, remain friendly with the students. Try to catch them in a good moment so you can talk to them about something other than their rule-breaking.

The defiant, hostile student can pose serious problems. If there is an outbreak, try to get out of the situation as soon as possible; everyone loses in a pub-

PRINCIPAL

"THEY'RE TESTING YOU."

(By permission of James Warren. From Phi Delta Kappan.*)*

lic power struggle. One possibility is to give the student a chance to save face and cool down by saying, "It's your choice to cooperate or not. You can take a minute to think about it." If the student complies, the two of you can talk later about controlling the outbursts. If the student refuses to co-operate, you can tell him or her to wait in the hall until you get the class started on work, then step outside for a private talk. If the student refuses to leave, send another class member for the assistant principal. Again, follow through. If the student complies before help arrives, do not let him or her off the hook. If outbursts occur frequently, you might have a conference with the counselor, parents, or other teachers. If the problem is an unreconcilable clash of personalities, the student should be transferred to another teacher.

It sometimes is useful to keep records of the incidents by logging the student's name, words and actions, date, time, place, and teachers' response. These records may help iden-tify patterns and can prove helpful in meeting with administrators, parents, or special services personnel (Burden, 1995). Some teachers have students sign each entry to verify the incidents.

Violence or destruction of property is a difficult and potentially dangerous problem. The first step is to send for help and get the names of participants and witnesses. Then get rid of any crowd that may have gathered; an audience will only make things worse. Do not try to break up a fight without help. Make sure the school office is aware of the incident; usually the school has a policy for deal-ing with these situations.

> **Focus on . . .**
>
> ### Maintaining a Good Environment for Learning
>
> - Explain the factors identified by Kounin that prevent management problems in the classroom.
> - Will you use penalties in your class when students violate rules? What kinds?

Special Programs for Classroom Management

In some situations you may want to consider using a much more formal class-room management system. Three possibilities, all based on behavioral princi-ples, are group consequences, token programs, and contingency contracts.

Group Consequences

A teacher can base reinforcement for the class on the cumulative behavior of all members of the class, usually by adding each student's points to a class or a team total. The **good behavior game** is an example of this approach. A class is divided into two teams. Specific rules for good behavior are cooperatively de-veloped. Each time a student breaks one of the rules, that student's team is given a mark. The team with the fewest marks at the end of the period receives a spe-cial reward or privilege (longer recess, first to lunch, and so on). If both teams earn fewer than a preestablished number of marks, both teams receive the re-ward. Most studies indicate that even though the game produces only small im-provements in academic achievement, it can produce definite improvements in the behaviors listed in the good behavior rules.

You can also use **group consequences** without dividing the class into teams, that is, you can base reinforcement on the behavior of the whole class. Wilson

Good Behavior Game Arrange-ment where a class is divided into teams and each team receives de-merit points for breaking agreed-on rules of good behavior.

Group Consequences Rewards or punishments given to a class as a whole for adhering to or vio-lating rules of conduct.

and Hopkins (1973) conducted a study using group consequences to reduce noise levels. Radio music served effectively as the reinforcer for students in a home economics class. Whenever noise in the class was below a predetermined level, students could listen to the radio; when the noise exceeded the level, the radio was turned off. Given the success of this simple method, such a procedure might be considered in any class where music does not interfere with the task at hand.

However, caution is needed in group approaches. The whole group should not suffer for the misbehavior or mistakes of one individual if the group has no real influence over that person (Epanchin, Townsend, & Stoddard, 1994; Jenson, Sloane, & Young, 1988). I saw an entire class break into cheers when the teacher announced that one boy was transferring to another school. The chant "No more points! No more points!" filled the room. The "points" referred to the teacher's system of giving one point to the whole class each time anyone broke a rule. Every point meant 5 minutes of recess lost. The boy who was transferring had been responsible for many losses. He was not very popular to begin with, and the point system, though quite effective in maintaining order, had led to rejection and even greater unpopularity.

Peer pressure in the form of support and encouragement, however, can be a positive influence. Group consequences are recommended for situations in which students care about the approval of their peers. If the misbehavior of several students seems to be encouraged by the attention and laughter of other students, then group consequences could be helpful. Teachers might show students how to give support and constructive feedback to classmates. If a few students seem to enjoy sabotaging the system, those students may need separate arrangements.

Token Reinforcement Programs

Often it is difficult to provide positive consequences for all the students who deserve them. A **token reinforcement system** can help solve this problem by allowing all students to earn tokens for both academic work and positive classroom behavior. The tokens may be points, checks, holes punched in a card, chips, play money, or anything else that is easily identified as the student's property. Periodically the students exchange the tokens they have earned for some desired reward (Martin & Pear, 1992).

Depending on the age of the student, the rewards could be small toys, school supplies, free time, special class jobs, or other privileges. When a "token economy," as this kind of system is called, is first established, the tokens should be given out on a fairly continuous schedule, with chances to exchange the tokens for rewards often available. Once the system is working well, however, tokens should be distributed on an intermittent schedule and saved for longer periods of time before they are exchanged for rewards.

Another variation is to allow students to earn tokens in the classroom and then exchange them for rewards at home. These plans are very successful when parents are willing to cooperate. Usually a note or report form is sent home daily or twice a week. The note indicates the number of points earned in the preceding time period. The points may be exchanged for minutes of television viewing, access to special toys, or private time with parents. Points can also be saved up for larger rewards such as trips. Do not use this procedure, however, if you suspect the child might be severely punished for poor reports.

Token Reinforcement System
System in which tokens earned for academic work and positive classroom behavior can be exchanged for some desired reward.

Token reinforcement systems are complicated and time-consuming. Generally, they should be used in only three situations: to motivate students who are completely uninterested in their work and have not responded to other approaches; to encourage students who have consistently failed to make academic progress; and to deal with a class that is out of control. Some groups of students seem to benefit more than others from token economies. Mentally retarded students, slow learners, children who have failed often, students with few academic skills, and students with behavior problems all seem to respond to the concrete, direct nature of token reinforcement.

Before you try a token system, you should be sure that your teaching methods and materials are right for the students. Sometimes class disruptions or lack of motivation indicate that teaching practices need to be changed. Maybe the class rules are unclear or are enforced inconsistently. Maybe the text is too easy or too hard. Maybe the pace is wrong. If these problems exist, a token system may improve the situation temporarily, but the students will still have trouble learning the academic material (Jenson, Sloane, & Young, 1988).

Contingency Contract Programs

In a **contingency contract** program, the teacher draws up an individual contract with each student, describing exactly what the student must do to earn a particular privilege or reward. In some programs, students participate in deciding on the behaviors to be reinforced and the rewards that can be gained. The negotiating process itself can be an educational experience, as students learn to set reasonable goals and abide by the terms of a contract.

An example of a contract for completing assignments that is appropriate for intermediate and upper-grade students is presented in Figure 12.4 on page 464. This chart serves as a contract, assignment sheet, and progress record. Something like this might even help you keep track of your assignments and due dates in college.

The few pages devoted here to token reinforcement and contingency contracts can offer only an introduction to these programs. If you want to set up a large-scale reward program in your classroom, you should probably seek professional advice. Often the school psychologist, counselor, or principal can help. In addition, remember that, applied inappropriately, external rewards can undermine the students' motivation to learn (Deci, 1975; Lepper & Greene, 1978).

> **Focus on...**
>
> ## Special Management Programs
>
> ■ What are the uses and limitations of group consequences?
> ■ Describe a situation in which you might use a contingency contract.

The Need for Communication

Communication between teacher and students is essential when problems arise. Communication is more than "teacher talks—student listens." It is more than the words exchanged between individuals. We communicate in many ways. Our actions, movements, voice tone, facial expressions, and many other nonverbal behaviors send messages to our students. Many times the messages we intend to send are not the messages our students receive.

Contingency Contract A contract between the teacher and an individual student specifying what the student must do to earn a particular privilege or reward.

FIGURE 12.4

A Contingency Contract for Completing Assignments

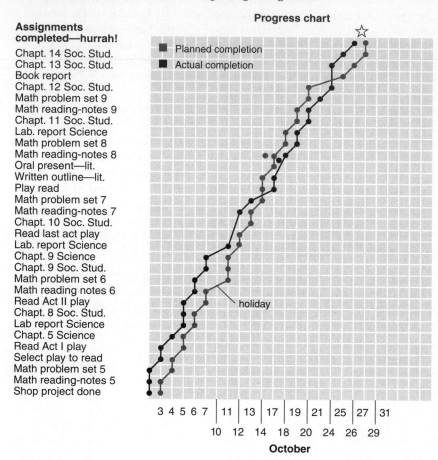

Assignments completed—hurrah!

Chapt. 14 Soc. Stud.
Chapt. 13 Soc. Stud.
Book report
Chapt. 12 Soc. Stud.
Math problem set 9
Math reading-notes 9
Chapt. 11 Soc. Stud.
Lab. report Science
Math problem set 8
Math reading-notes 8
Oral present—lit.
Written outline—lit.
Play read
Math problem set 7
Math reading-notes 7
Chapt. 10 Soc. Stud.
Read last act play
Lab. report Science
Chapt. 9 Science
Chapt. 9 Soc. Stud.
Math problem set 6
Math reading notes 6
Read Act II play
Chapt. 8 Soc. Stud.
Lab report Science
Chapt. 5 Science
Read Act I play
Select play to read
Math problem set 5
Math reading-notes 5
Shop project done

Progress chart

■ Planned completion
■ Actual completion

holiday

3 4 5 6 7 | 11 | 13 | 17 | 19 | 21 | 25 | 27 | 31
10 12 14 18 20 24 26 29

October

The teacher and student agree on the due dates for each assignment, marking them in blue on the chart. Each time an assignment is turned in, the date of completion is marked in black on the chart. As long as the actual completion line is above planned completion line, the student earns free time or other contracted rewards.

Source: From B. Sulzer-Azaroff and G. R. Mayer. Figure from *Achieving educational excellence. Behavior analysis for school personnel*, p. 89. Copyright © 1994 by Beth Sulzer-Azaroff and G. Roy Mayer (San Marcos, CA: Western Image, P.O. Box 427). Reprinted by permission of the authors.

Message Sent—Message Received

Teacher: Carl, where is your homework?

Carl: I left it in my Dad's car this morning.

Teacher: Again? You will have to bring me a note tomorrow from your father saying that you actually did the homework. No grade without the note.

Message Carl receives: I can't trust you. I need proof you did the work.

Teacher: Sit at every other desk. Put all your things under your desk. Jane and Laurel, you are sitting too close together. One of you move!

Message Jane and Laurel receive: I expect you two to cheat on this test.

A new student comes to Ms. Lincoln's kindergarten. The child is messy and unwashed. Ms. Lincoln puts her hand lightly on the girl's shoulder and says, "I'm glad you are here." Her muscles tense, and she leans away from the child.

Message student receives: I don't like you. I think you are bad.

In all interactions, a message is sent and a message is received. Sometimes teachers believe they are sending one message, but their voices, body positions, choices of words, and gestures may communicate a different message.

Students may hear the hidden message and respond to it. For example, a student may respond with hostility if she or he feels insulted by the teacher (or by another student), but may not be able to say exactly where the feeling of being insulted came from. Perhaps it was in the teacher's tone of voice, not the words actually spoken. In such cases, the teacher may feel attacked for no reason. "What did I say? All I said was . . . ." The first principle of communication is that people respond to what they *think* was said or meant, not necessarily to the speaker's intended message or actual words.

There are many exercises for practicing sending and receiving messages accurately. Students in my classes have told me about one instructor who encourages accurate communication by using the **paraphrase rule.** Before any participant, including the teacher, is allowed to respond to any other participant in a class discussion, he or she must summarize what the previous speaker said. If the summary is wrong, indicating the speaker was misunderstood, the speaker must explain again. The respondent then tries again to paraphrase. The process continues until the speaker agrees that the listener has heard the intended message.

Paraphrasing is more than a classroom exercise. It can be the first step in communicating with students. Before teachers can deal appropriately with any student problem, they must know what the real problem is. A student who says, "This book is really dumb! Why did we have to read it?" may really be saying, "The book was too difficult for me. I couldn't read it, and I feel dumb."

Diagnosis: Whose Problem Is It?

As a teacher, you may find many student behaviors unacceptable, unpleasant, or troubling. It is often difficult to stand back from these problems, take an objective look, and decide on an appropriate response. According to Thomas Gordon (1981), the key to good teacher–student relationships is determining why you are troubled by a particular behavior and whose problem it is. The teacher must begin by asking who "owns" the problem. The answer to this question is critical. If it is really the student's problem, the teacher must become a counselor and supporter, helping the student find his or her own solution. But if the teacher "owns" the problem, it is the teacher's responsibility to find a solution through problem solving with the student.

Diagnosing who owns the problem is not always straightforward. Let's look at three troubling situations to get some practice in this skill:

1. A student writes obscene words and draws sexually explicit illustrations in a school encyclopedia.

2. A student tells you that his parents had a bad fight and he hates his father.

3. A student quietly reads a newspaper in the back of the room.

Paraphrase Rule Policy whereby listeners must accurately summarize what a speaker has said before being allowed to respond.

Why are these behaviors troubling? If you cannot accept the student's behavior because it has a serious effect on you as a teacher—if you are blocked from reaching your goals by the student's action—then *you* own the problem. It is your responsibility to confront the student and seek a solution. A teacher-owned problem appears to be present in the first situation described above—the young pornographer—because teaching materials are damaged.

If you feel annoyed by the behavior because it is getting in the student's own way or because you are embarrassed for the child, but the behavior does not directly interfere with your teaching, then it is probably the student's problem. The test question is: Does this student's action tangibly affect you or prevent you from fulfilling your role as a teacher? The student who hates his father would not prevent you from teaching, even though you might wish the student felt differently. The problem is really the student's, and he must find his own solution.

Situation 3 is more difficult to diagnose. I have had lengthy debates in my class about whose problem it is when a student reads a newspaper in class. One argument is that the teacher is not interfered with in any way, so it is the student's problem. Another argument is that teachers might find reading the paper distracting during a lecture, so it is their problem, and they must find a solution. In a gray area such as this, the answer probably depends on how the teacher actually experiences the student's behavior. Having decided who owns the problem, it is time to act.

Counseling: The Student's Problem

Let's pick up the situation in which the student found the reading assignment "dumb." How might a teacher handle this positively?

Student: This book is really dumb! Why did we have to read it?

Teacher: You're pretty upset. This seemed like a worthless assignment to you. [Teacher paraphrases the student's statement, trying to hear the emotions as well as the words.]

Student: Yeah! Well, I guess it was worthless. I mean, I don't know if it was. I couldn't exactly read it.

Teacher: It was just too hard to read, and that bothers you.

Student: Sure, I felt really dumb. I know I can write a good report, but not with a book this tough.

Teacher: I think I can give you some hints that will make the book easier to understand. Can you see me after school today?

Student: Okay.

Here the teacher used **empathetic listening** to allow the student to find a solution. (As you can see, this approach relies heavily on paraphrasing.) By trying to hear the student and by avoiding the tendency to jump in too quickly with advice, solutions, criticisms, reprimands, or interrogations, the teacher keeps the communication lines open. Here are a few *unhelpful* responses the teacher might have made:

> I chose the book because it is the best example of _____ in our library. You will need to have read it before your English II class next year. (The teacher justifies the choice; this prevents the student from admitting that this "important" assignment is too difficult.)

Empathetic Listening Hearing the intent and emotions behind what another says and reflecting them back by paraphrasing.

Did you really read it? I bet you didn't do the work, and now you want out of the assignment. (The teacher accuses; the student hears, "The teacher doesn't trust me!" and must defend herself or himself or accept the teacher's view.)

Your job is to read the book, not ask me why. I know what's best. (The teacher pulls rank, and the student hears, "You can't possibly decide what is good for you!" The student can rebel or passively accept the teacher's judgment.)

Empathetic, active listening can be a helpful response when students bring problems to you. You must reflect back to the student what you hear him or her saying. This reflection is more than a parroting of the student's words; it should capture the emotions, intent, and meaning behind them. Sokolove, Garrett, Sadker, and Sadker (1986, p. 241) have summarized the components of active listening: (1) blocking out external stimuli; (2) attending carefully to both the verbal and nonverbal messages; (3) differentiating between the intellectual and the emotional content of the message; and (4) making inferences regarding the speaker's feelings.

When students realize they really have been heard and not evaluated negatively for what they have said or felt, they feel freer to trust the teacher and to talk more openly. Sometimes the true problem surfaces later in the conversation.

Confrontation and Assertive Discipline

Now let's assume a student is doing something that actively interferes with teaching. The teacher decides the student must stop. The problem is the teacher's. Confrontation, not counseling, is required.

"I" Messages.   Gordon (1974) recommends sending an **"I" message** in order to intervene and change a student's behavior. Basically, this means telling a student in a straightforward, assertive, and nonjudgmental way what she or he is doing, how it affects you as a teacher, and how you feel about it. The student is then free to change voluntarily, and often does so. Here are two "I" messages:

If you leave your book bags in the aisles, I might trip and hurt myself.

When you all call out, I can't concentrate on each answer, and I'm frustrated.

Assertive Discipline.   Lee and Marlene Canter (1992; Canter, 1989) suggest other approaches for dealing with a teacher-owned problem. They call their method **assertive discipline.** Teachers are assertive when they make their expectations clear and follow through with established consequences. Students then have a straightforward choice: they can follow the rules or accept the consequences. Many teachers are ineffective with students because they are either wishy-washy and passive or hostile and aggressive.

The *passive style* can take several forms. Instead of telling the student directly what to do, the teacher tells, or often asks, the student to *try* or to *think about* the appropriate action. The passive teacher might comment on the problem behavior without actually telling the child what to do differently: "Why are you doing that? Don't you know the rules?" or "Sam, are you disturbing the class?" Or teachers may clearly state what should happen, but never follow through with the established consequences, giving the students "one more chance" every time. Finally, teachers may ignore behavior that should receive a response or may wait too long before responding.

One of the challenges of managing elementary school children is to deal effectively with disruptive behavior and achieve a positive outcome.

"I" Message Clear, nonaccusatory statement of how something is affecting you.

Assertive Discipline Clear, firm, unhostile response style.

A *hostile response style* involves different mistakes. Teachers may make "you" statements that condemn the student without stating clearly what the student should be doing: "You should be ashamed of the way you're behaving!" or "You never listen!" or "You are acting like a baby!" Teachers may also threaten students angrily but follow through too seldom, perhaps because the threats are too vague—"You'll be very sorry you did that when I get through with you!"—or too severe. For example, a teacher tells a student in a physical education class that he will have to "sit on the bench for *three weeks*." A few days later the team is short one member and the teacher lets the student play, never returning him to the bench to complete the three-week sentence. Often a teacher who has been passive becomes hostile and explodes when students persist in misbehaving.

In contrast with both the passive and hostile styles, an *assertive response* communicates to the students that you care too much about them and the process of learning to allow inappropriate behavior to persist. Assertive teachers clearly state what they expect. To be most effective, the teachers often look into a student's eyes when speaking and address the student by name. Assertive teachers' voices are calm, firm, and confident. They are not sidetracked by accusations such as "You just don't understand!" or "You don't like me!" Assertive teachers do not get into a debate about the fairness of the rules. They expect changes, not promises or apologies.

Even though many teachers and school administrators have given enthusiastic testimonies about the assertive discipline approach, some educators and psychologists question its effectiveness. The Point/Counterpoint further explores the issue.

Confrontations and Negotiations.   If "I" messages or assertive responses fail and a student persists in misbehaving, teacher and student are in a conflict. Several pitfalls now loom. The two individuals become less able to perceive each other's behavior accurately. Research has shown that the angrier you get with another person, the more you see the other as the villain and yourself as an innocent victim. Because you feel the other person is in the wrong, and he or she feels just as strongly that the conflict is all your fault, very little mutual trust is possible. A cooperative solution to the problem is almost impossible. In fact, by the time the discussion has gone on a few minutes, the original problem is lost in a sea of charges, countercharges, and self-defense (Johnson & Johnson, 1994).

There are three methods of resolving a conflict between teacher and student. One is for the teacher to impose a solution. This may be necessary during an emergency, as when a defiant student refuses to go to the hall to discuss a public outbreak, but it is not a good solution for most conflicts. The second method is for the teacher to give in to the student's demands. You might be convinced by a particularly compelling student argument, but again, this should be used sparingly. It is generally a bad idea to be talked out of a position, unless the position was wrong in the first place. Problems arise when either the teacher or the student gives in completely.

Gordon recommends a third approach, which he calls the "no-lose method." Here the needs of both the teacher and the students are taken into account in the solution. No one person is expected to give in completely; all participants

Does Assertive Discipline Work?

Lee Canter, the developer of "assertive discipline," describes his observations of effective teachers:

> I found that, above all, the master teachers were assertive; that is they taught students how to behave. They established clear rules for the classroom, they communicated those rules to the students, and they taught students how to follow them. (1989, p. 58)

Is assertive discipline effective? There are strong opinions both against and in favor of the approach, as you will see. Researchers are skeptical, but some practitioners are committed to assertive discipline.

POINT   **Research results do not support assertive discipline.**

In an article entitled "What research really shows about Assertive Discipline," Gary Render, Je Neil Padilla, and H. Mark Krank (1989) note that very little unbiased information is available about the effectiveness of this approach. Even though reports claim that 500,000 people have been trained in assertive discipline, Render and his colleagues were able to find only 16 systematic studies of assertive discipline. Their analysis of these studies led them to conclude that:

> The claims made by Canter (1988) . . . are simply not supported by the existing and available literature. We would agree that Assertive Discipline could be helpful in severe cases where students are behaving inappropriately more than 96 percent of the time, as in the study by Mandlebaum et al. (1983). We would also argue that teachers such as the one in that study would benefit from any intervention. However, we can find no evidence that Assertive Discipline is an effective approach deserving schoolwide or districtwide adoption. (p. 72)

A second criticism of assertive discipline is that while it may stop misbehavior in the short run, the long-term effects on students are damaging. Richard Curwin and Allen Mendler (1988) remind teachers that classroom management systems not only manage behavior, they also teach students lessons about their own self-worth, their ability to act responsibly and solve problems, how much control they have over their own lives, and how to use that control. What lessons are taught by systems such as assertive discipline? "If Richard shapes up after the third mark on the chalkboard because the fourth means a call home to an abusive parent, did the program improve his self-control, or did it simply transfer the inner turmoil of a child caught in a dysfunctional family?" (Curwin & Mendler, 1988, p. 68). This concern is echoed by John Covaleskie (1992): "What helps children become moral is not knowledge of the rules, or even obedience to the rules, but discussions about the reasons for acting in certain ways (p. 56).

COUNTERPOINT   Practitioners know that assertive discipline works.

In response to the assertion by Render and his colleagues that research does not support assertive discipline, Sammie McCormack (1989) says, "The decision to implement a program should be based on many factors, in addition to research; from a practitioner's standpoint, Assertive Discipline works" (p. 77). McCormack reports the reactions of more than 8,700 teachers from four school districts and a confederation of schools in Oregon. In these schools, 78 to 99 percent of the teachers saw improvements in student behavior as a consequence of using assertive discipline. McCormack does not explain how these particular samples were selected or if teachers in other schools had different reactions.

In response to Curwin and Mendler's (1988) concerns that classroom management models such as assertive discipline may undermine students' self-worth and sense of responsibility, Lee Canter (1988) notes that several studies have found improvements in both teachers' and students' self-concepts after the introduction of assertive discipline. Further, Canter states that the basis of assertive discipline is giving students choices and that it is through making choices and accepting the consequences that students learn about responsibility.

retain respect for themselves and each other. The no-lose method is a six-step, problem-solving strategy:

1. *Define the problem.* What exactly are the behaviors involved? What does each person want? (Use active listening to help students pinpoint the real problem.)

2. *Generate many possible solutions.* Brainstorm, but remember, don't allow any evaluations of ideas yet.

3. *Evaluate each solution.* Any participant may veto any idea. If no solutions are found to be acceptable, brainstorm again.

4. *Make a decision.* Choose one solution through consensus—no voting. In the end, everyone must be satisfied with the solution.

5. *Determine how to implement the solution.* What will be needed? Who will be responsible for each task? What is the timetable?

6. *Evaluate the success of the solution.* After trying the solution for a while, ask, "are we satisfied with our decision? How well is it working? Should we make some changes?"

Many of the conflicts in classrooms are between students. These can be important learning experiences for all concerned.

Student Conflicts and Confrontations

Handling conflict is difficult for most of us—for young people it can be even harder. Given the public's concern about violence in schools, it is surprising how little we know about conflicts among students (Elam, Rose & Gallup, 1996; Johnson, Johnson, Dudley, Ward, & Magnuson, 1995). There is some evidence that in elementary schools, conflicts most often center on disputes over resources (school supplies, computers, athletic equipment, or toys) and over pref-

During a problem-solving session, it is important to brainstorm—list all possible solutions before evaluating any one solution.

TABLE 12.3	Strategies for Managing Conflict

Different situations call for different strategies. But any strategy can be used inappropriately. For example, withdrawing may be used inappropriately to avoid all conflict or appropriately to postpone confrontation until constructive discussions are possible.

Goal Important?	Relationship Important?	Strategy	Appropriate Uses	Inappropriate Use
No	No	Withdraw	Postpone until constructive discussion is possible	Avoid conflict, hide
No	Yes	Smooth/Give in	When other's needs are more important	Give in just to be liked
Yes	No	Force	Seldom appropriate, perhaps when others' safety is your responsibility	To intimidate, win at all costs, overpower
Yes	Yes	Confront	Resolve conflict—strengthen relationship—protect both parties' goals	Generally appropriate
Moderately	Moderately	Compromise	When mutual sacrifices are required for the common good	When confrontation could satisfy both parties' goals

erences (which activity to do first or what game to play). Over twenty years ago, a large study of more than 8,000 junior and senior high students and 500 faculty from three major cities concluded that 90% of the conflicts among students are resolved in destructive ways or never resolved at all (DeCecco & Richards, 1974). The few studies since that time have reached similar conclusions. Avoidance, force, and threats seem to be the major strategies for dealing with conflict (Johnson et al., 1995).

Conflicts: Goals and Needs. When people are in conflict, they have two major concerns. The first is to satisfy their needs and meet their goals. This usually is the source of the conflict—the needs or goals of one person or group clash with the needs or goals of others. The second concern is to maintain an appropriate relationship with the other party in the conflict. Both of these concerns can be placed on a continuum from not very important to critically important. Different strategies are called for, depending on the importance of the goals and the relationships, as shown in Table 12.3 (Johnson & Johnson, 1994).

The message here is that different strategies make sense in different situations. Without guidance and practice, however, students may always use the same strategy—they may not be able to fit strategy to situation.

Violence in the Schools. "Interpersonal violence among youth is a growing problem in many communities and schools across this nation" (Lowry, Sleet, Duncan, Powell, & Kolbe, 1995, p. 7). Young people ages 12 to 24 are the most likely victims of nonfatal violence in American society, and many of these attacks happen on school property. This problem has many causes; it is a challenge for every element of society. What can the schools do?

One answer is prevention. Some Chicano gang members in Chicago reported that they turned to gang activities when their teachers insulted them, called them names, humiliated them publicly, belittled their culture, ignored them in class, or blamed all negative incidents on particular students. The students reported joining gangs for security and to escape teachers who treated them badly or expected little of them because they were Latino (Padilla, 1992; Parks, 1995). Another two-year study in Ohio found that gang members respected teachers who insisted on academic performance is a caring way (Huff, 1989). I once asked a gifted educator in an urban New Jersey high school which teachers were most effective with the really tough students. He said there are two kinds, teachers who can't be intimidated or fooled and expect their students to learn, and teachers who really care about the students. When I asked, "Which kind are you?" and he answered "Both!"

Besides prevention, schools can also establish mentoring programs, conflict resolution training, social skills training, more relevant curricula, and parent and community involvement programs (Padilla, 1992; Parks, 1995). One intervention that seems to be helpful in peer mediation.

Peer Mediation.   David Johnson and his colleagues provided conflict resolution training to 227 students in second through fifth grade. Students learned a five-step negotiating strategy:

1. *Jointly define the conflict.* Separate the person from the problem and the actions involved, avoid win–lose thinking, get both parties' goals clear.

2. *Exchange positions and interests.* Present a tentative proposal and make a case for it; listen to the other person's proposal and feelings; and stay flexible and cooperative.

3. *Reverse perspectives.* See the situation from the other person's point of view and reverse roles and argue for that perspective.

4. *Invent at least three agreements that allow mutual gain.* Brainstorm, focus on goals, think creatively, and make sure everyone has power to invent solutions.

5. *Reach an integrative agreement.* Make sure both sets of goals are met. If all else fails, flip a coin, take turns, or call in a third party—a mediator.

In addition to learning conflict resolution, all students in Johnson and Johnson's study were trained in mediation strategies. The role of the mediator was rotated—every day the teacher chose two students to be the class mediators and to wear the mediator's T-shirt. Johnson and his colleagues found that students learned the conflict resolutions and mediation strategies and used them successfully, both in school and at home, to handle conflicts in a more productive way. For details of the strategies, see Johnson and Johnson (1994), Miller, (1994), or Smith (1993).

Peer mediation has also been successful with older students and serious problems (Sanchez & Anderson, 1990). In one program, selected gang members are given mediation training, then all members are invited to participate voluntarily in the mediation process, supervised by school counselors. Strict rules govern the process leading to written agreements signed by gang representatives. Sanchez and Anderson (1990) found that gang violence in

---

Focus on...

Communication

- What is meant by "empathetic listening"?
- Distinguish among assertive, passive, and hostile response styles.
- What are the steps in Gordon's problem-solving approach?

the school was reduced to a bare minimum—"The magic of the mediation process was communication" (p. 56).

Communicating with Families about Classroom Management

As we have seen throughout this book, families are important partners in education. This statement applies to classroom management as well. When parents and teachers share the same expectations and support each other, they can create a more positive classroom environment and more time for learning. The Guidelines give ideas for working with families and the community.

Guidelines

Family and Community Partnerships for Classroom Management

Make sure families know the expectations and rules of your class and school.

Examples

1. At a Family Fun Night, have your students do skits showing the rules—how to follow them and what breaking them "looks like" and "sounds like."

2. Make a poster for the refrigerator at home that describes, in a light way, the most important rules and expectations.

3. For older students, give families a list of due dates for the major assignments, along with tips about how to encourage quality work by pacing the effort—avoiding last minute panic.

4. Communicate in appropriate ways—use the family's first language when possible. Tailor messages to the reading level of the home.

Make families partners in recognizing good citizenship.

Examples

1. Send positive notes home when students, especially students who have had trouble with classroom management, work well in the classroom.

2. Give ideas for ways any family, even those with few economic resources, can celebrate accomplishment—a favorite food; the chance to choose a video to rent; a comment to a special person such as an aunt, grandparent, or minister; the chance to read to a younger sibling.

Identify talents in the community to help build a learning environment in your class.

Examples

1. Have students write letters to carpet and furniture stores asking for donations of remnants to carpet a reading corner.

2. Find family members who can build shelves or room dividers, paint, sew, laminate manipulatives, write stories, repot plants, or network computers.

3. Contact businesses for donations of computers, printers, or other equipment.

Seek cooperation from families when behavior problems arise.

Examples

1. Talk to families over the phone or in their home. Have good records about the problem behavior.

2. Listen to family members and solve problems with them.

The Need for Organization

Classrooms are by nature multidimensional, full of simultaneous activities, fast-paced and immediate, unpredictable, public, and affected by the history of students' and teachers' actions. A manager must juggle all these elements every day.

Productive classroom activity requires students' cooperation. Maintaining cooperation is different for each different age group. Young students are learning how to "go to school" and need to learn the general procedures of school. Older students need to learn the specifics required for working in different subjects. Working with adolescents requires teachers to understand the power of the adolescent peer group.

The goals of effective classroom management are to make ample time for learning; improve the quality of time use by keeping students actively engaged; make sure participation structures are clear, straightforward, and consistently signaled; and encourage student self-management.

Creating a Positive Learning Environment

The most effective teachers set rules and establish procedures for handling predictable problems. Procedures should cover administrative tasks, student movement, housekeeping, routines for running lessons, interactions between students and teachers, and interactions among students. Consequences should be established for following and breaking the rules and procedures so that the teacher and the students know what will happen.

There are two basic kinds of spatial organization, territorial (the traditional classroom arrangement) and functional (dividing space into interest or work areas). Flexibility is often the key. Access to materials, convenience, privacy when needed, ease of supervision, and a willingness to reevaluate plans are important considerations in the teacher's choice of physical arrangements.

Maintaining a Good Environment for Learning

For effective classroom management, it is essential to spend the first days of class teaching basic rules and procedures.

Students should be occupied with organized, enjoyable activities and learn to function cooperatively in the group. Quick, firm, clear, and consistent responses to infractions of the rules characterize effective teachers. To create a positive environment and prevent problems, teachers must take individual differences into account, maintain student motivation, and reinforce positive behavior. Successful problem preventers are skilled in four areas described by Kounin: "withitness," overlapping, group focusing, and movement management. When penalties have to be imposed, teachers should impose them calmly and privately.

Special Programs for Classroom Management

There are several special procedures that may be helpful in maintaining positive management, including group consequences, token economies, and contingency contracts. A teacher must use these programs with caution, emphasizing learning and not just "good" behavior.

The Need for Communication

Communication between teacher and student is essential when problems arise. All interactions between people, even silence or neglect, communicate some meaning.

Techniques such as paraphrasing, empathetic listening, determining whether the teacher or the student "owns" the problem, assertive discipline, avoidance of passive and hostile responses, and active problem solving with students help teachers open the lines of positive communication. Students need guidance in resolving conflicts. Different strategies are useful, depending on whether the goal, the relationship, or both are important to those experiencing conflict. It can help to reverse roles and see the situation through the eyes of the other. In dealing with serious problems, prevention and peer mediation might be useful. No matter what the situation, the cooperation of families can help to create a positive learning environment in your classroom and school.

KEY TERMS

academic learning time, p. 443

action zone, p. 452

allocated time, p. 443

assertive discipline, p. 467

classroom management, p. 442

contingency contract, p. 463

empathetic listening, p. 466

engaged time, p. 443

good behavior game, p. 461

group consequences, p. 461

group focus, p. 458

"I" message, p. 467
movement management, p. 458
overlapping, p. 457
paraphrase rule, p. 465

participation structures, p. 443
procedures, p. 446
rules, p. 447
self-management, p. 444

time on task, p. 443
token reinforcement system, p. 462
withitness, p. 457

CHECK YOUR UNDERSTANDING

Can you apply the ideas from this chapter on creating learning environments to solve the following problems of practice?

Preschool and Kindergarten

- Your class is larger than ever this year, and it is very difficult to get everyone dressed for play outside. How would you handle the situation?

Elementary and Middle School

- It takes your class 15 minutes to settle down each morning and begin work. What would you do?

- A few students in your class always seem to be out of step with the rest of the class. They call out when they shouldn't, interrupt others, and get up and walk around when they should be seated and working. What would you do?

Junior High and High School

- You tell a student to put away a radio, and she says, "Try and make me!" What would you do?

- One of your students who is bright and able has stopped doing homework. What would you do?

Cooperative Learning Activity

- With four or five other members in your educational psychology class, decide how you would determine the rules and procedures for a class you might teach.

What Would They Do?

There are students from four different ethnic groups in the middle school "pod" you are working with this year. Last week, the principal added a student with pretty severe emotional/behavioral problems and a student with cerebral palsy to the group as part of an experiment in full inclusion. The boy with cerebral palsy is in a wheelchair and has some difficulties with language and hearing. Each of the four ethnic groups seems to stick together, never making friends with students from "outside." Clarise, the emotionally disturbed student, is making matters worse by telling ethnic jokes to anyone who will listen in a voice loud enough to be overheard by half the class. There are rumors of an ambush after school to "teach Clarise a lesson." You agree she—and the whole class for that matter—needs a lesson, but not this kind.

ANN SANDE

Third Grade Teacher
Henry Viscardi School, Albertson, New York

In order to break down the barriers separating ethnic groups I would assign two children from different groups to perform a desirable task. It might be working together to find information on the computer's encyclopedia or the Internet and reporting it back to the class, or preparing materials for the class science experiments. It would depend on the grade level and the interests of the group. I would assure that the task was one in which the children would meet success together. This is time-consuming but must be done repeatedly with different students in a variety of situations. The children need to "see" each other in new ways and to learn to appreciate each other's strengths and talents beyond preconceived notions.

I would do a theme relating to a group that has suffered injustice. I would allow choice within a predetermined list of topics. One might be a study of the problems of the physically disabled in terms of access or discrimination. Hopefully the students would be able to draw comparisons between the group being studied and other ethnic groups who suffer discrimination and to see the experiences and challenges that each group has in common.

Modeling behavior is critical. When a group of students is speaking in another language and seemingly laughing at me I would "call them on it." I would express my dislike of the behavior in a firm manner and reiterate that it is unacceptable within our class community. By doing so, it gives the students another way and the appropriate language to deal with the objectionable behavior displayed by Clarise. I might also suggest that, as a fun activity, the entire class try to learn a language that is not part of the curriculum; we might learn some American Sign Language together.

NICOLE DEPALMA COBB AND SANDRA T. MCNEICE

Eighth Grade Teachers
Sterling Middle School, Quincy, Massachusetts

There are no constants in teaching, but there are many ways of bringing together different groupings of students. In this case, the groupings are ethnically divided. On the first day when we, as facilitators, are faced with new groups, we try to envision what might be possible particularly when the students are drawn to their own ethnic zone of comfort. Our vision for the future is harmony within our classroom, which includes respect for ourselves and each other in a safe environment.

A respect and feeling of self-worth can be enhanced by exposing all students to a variety of language, books, food, tapes, videos, games from around the world, and music; in this living "personal gallery," all voices and faces are represented and heard. The facilitator would initiate the sharing of her own culture by bringing in a plethora of artifacts and memorabilia. By participating in a group project along with our students, we model our own personal respect for our ethnic background by bringing in a representation of who we are and where we have come from. Once materials have been brought to class, the students will be divided into diverse pairings in order to conduct personal interviews about classmates of a different culture. These interviews create a woven fabric symbolizing the strength of a new bond.

From the beginning of our journey, we have been engaged in a process that has allowed all of us to explore and investigate the questions surrounding ourselves with regard to our ethnicity. Since our class was introduced at the beginning of the year with an open-ended project along with consistent reinforcement, we have circumvented potential conflicts. As facilitators it is our job to model for our students strategies that hopefully they will internalize and use outside the classroom. Our students then become the teachers of other students.

STEVEN P. RUDE

Guidance Counselor
John C. Fremont High School, Los Angeles, California

I would request that the school psychologist or special education teacher come to my class to prepare the class for the arrival of their new fellow students. I would also encourage the students with disabilities to explain their own individual differences in their own way. There are many classroom activities that encourage students to explore and acknowledge their own differences, whether it be the color of their skin or the type of disability they possess. I would expect to review the Individual Education Plan for each of the students involved in the transition. Also, it would be helpful to know what behavior interventions work for the emotionally disturbed child and what teaching methods are most effective for the student with cerebral palsy. I would speak with the parents of these children to explore their expectations and past experiences in inclusive settings. There would also need to be teachers' aides available to help the special education students and to assist in communicating with the children who do not speak English. The inclusion of special education students' into the classroom is a challenge, but it can ultimately encourage acceptance across all lines, including ethnicities and exceptionalities.

Teaching for Learning

Overview | *What Would You Do?*

THE FIRST STEP: PLANNING 480
   Flexible and Creative Planning: Using Taxonomies | Planning from a
   Constructivist Perspective

TEACHING: WHOLE GROUP AND DIRECTIVE 488
   Lecturing and Explaining | Recitation and Questioning | Seatwork
   and Homework

TEACHING: SMALL GROUP AND STUDENT-CENTERED 494
   An Example of Constructivist Teaching | Group Discussion |
   Humanistic Education | Computers, Videodiscs, and Beyond

SUCCESSFUL TEACHING: FOCUS ON THE TEACHER 502
   Characteristics of Effective Teachers | Putting It All Together: The
   Effective Teacher

SUCCESSFUL UNDERSTANDING: FOCUS ON THE STUDENT 506
   The New Zealand Studies | Learning Functions: The Effective Student

INTEGRATIONS: BEYOND MODELS TO
OUTSTANDING TEACHING 508
   Matching Methods to Learning Goals | APA's Learner-Centered
   Psychological Principles

Summary | *Key Terms* | *Check Your Understanding* |
Teachers' Casebook: What Would They Do?

I n the first chapter of this book I asked you to list the characteristics of those teachers you found truly outstanding. Consider what you now know about student learning and suggest why the teacher characteristics you listed might promote learning.

In this chapter we focus on the teachers—on their decisions, plans, knowledge, and actions. We look first at how teachers plan, including how to use taxonomies of learning objectives or themes as a basis for planning. With a sense of how to set goals and make plans, we move to a consideration of teaching strategies. First, we examine more directive and teacher-centered approaches such as lecturing, questioning, recitation, seatwork, and homework. Next, we discuss several methods that emphasize student-centered learning—group discussion, humanistic education, and technology such as computers and videodiscs.

What else do we know about teachers? Are there particular characteristics that distinguish effective from ineffective teachers? Recently, the study of teaching has taken a very logical turn to focus on the person being taught—the student. We explore what is known about how to encourage and support students' learning. We conclude by considering the American Psychological Association's Learner-Centered Psychological Principles as a summary and integration of this chapter and much of the text.

By the time you have completed this chapter you should be able to:

- Describe the functions and levels of teacher planning.
- Describe situations in which each of the following formats would be most appropriate: lecture-recitation, seatwork and homework, group discussion, humanistic education, and computer-based environments.
- Describe a number of characteristics that effective teachers seem to share.
- List steps that can ensure clarity in presentation.
- Connect teaching and learning through Shuell's Learning Functions.
- Summarize the American Psychological Association's 14 learner-centered psychological principles.

What Would You Do?

You have finally landed a job teaching English and writing in a high school. Over the summer, you plan your World Literature course. You pick books you really enjoyed in high school and some new selections that relate to recent films.

TEACHERS' CASEBOOK

The first day of class, you discover that a number of students in your class appear to be limited in their English proficiencies. You make a mental note to meet with them to determine how much and what kind of reading they can handle. To get a sense of the class's interest, you ask them to write a "review" of the last book they read, as if they were on TV doing a "Book Beat" program. There is a bit of grumbling, but the students seem to be writing, so you take a few minutes to try to talk with one of the students who has trouble with English.

That night you look over the "book reviews." Either the students are giving you a hard time, or no one has read anything lately. Two students try to write about the Bible, but they refuse to "review" it. Several mention a text from another class, but their reviews are one sentence evaluations—usually containing the words "lame" or "useless," (often misspelled). If the paragraphs are any indication, these students can't put four sentences together and stay on the same topic. In stark contrast are the papers of three students—they are a pleasure to read, and worthy of publication in the school literary magazine (if there were one), and reflect a fairly sophisticated understanding of some good literature.

- How would you adapt your plans for this group?

- What will you do tomorrow?

- What teaching approaches do you think will work with this class?

- How will you work with the three students who are more advanced?

The First Step: Planning

As you thought about what you would do in the World Literature class described above, you were planning. In the past few years, educational researchers have become very interested in teachers' planning. They have interviewed teachers about how they plan, asked teachers to "think out loud" while planning or to keep journals describing their plans, and even studied teachers intensively for months at a time. What have they found?

First, planning influences what students will learn, because planning transforms the available time and curriculum materials into activities, assignments, and tasks for students. When a teacher decides to devote 7 hours to language arts and 15 minutes to science in a given week, the students in that class will learn more language than science. In fact, differences as dramatic as this do occur. Nancy Karweit (1989) reported that in one school the time allocated to mathematics ranged from 2 hours and 50 minutes a week in one class to 5 hours and 55 minutes a week in a class down the hall (Clark & Peterson, 1986; Clark & Yinger, 1988; Doyle, 1983).

Second, teachers engage in several levels of planning—by the year, term, unit, week, and day. All the levels must be coordinated. Accomplishing the year's plan requires breaking the work into terms, the terms into units, and the units into weeks and days. Planning done at the beginning of the year is particularly important, because many routines and patterns are established early. For experienced teachers, unit planning seems to be the most important level, followed by weekly and then daily planning (Clark & Peterson, 1986; Clark & Yinger, 1988).

Third, plans reduce—but do not eliminate—uncertainty in teaching. Even the best plans cannot (and should not) control everything that happens in class—planning must allow flexibility (Calderhead, 1996). There is some evidence that when teachers "overplan"—fill every minute and stick to the plan no matter what—their students do not learn as much as students whose teachers are flexible (Shavelson, 1987). Chris Clark (1983) suggests that beginning teachers should think of their plans as "flexible frameworks for action, as devices for getting started in the right direction, as something to depart from or elaborate on, rather than as rigid scripts" (p. 13).

In order to plan creatively and flexibly, teachers need to have wide-ranging knowledge about students, their interests, and abilities; the subjects being taught; alternative ways to teach and assess understanding; working with groups; the expectations and limitations of the school and community; how to apply and adapt materials and texts; and how to pull all this knowledge together into meaningful activities. The plans of beginning teachers sometimes don't work because they lack knowledge about the students or the subject—they can't estimate how long it will take students to complete an activity, for example, or they stumble when asked for an explanation or a different example (Calderhead, 1996).

Finally, there is no one model for effective planning. For experienced teachers, planning is a creative problem-solving process (Shavelson, 1987). Experienced teachers know how to accomplish many lessons and segments of lessons. They know what to expect and how to proceed, so they don't necessarily continue to follow the detailed lesson-planning models they learned during their teacher-preparation programs. Planning is more informal—"in their heads." But many experienced teachers think it was helpful to learn this detailed system as a foundation (Clark & Peterson, 1986).

No matter how you plan, you must have a learning goal in mind. In Chapter 9 we talked about learning objectives. In the next section we consider the range of goals that you might have for your students.

"AND THEN, OF COURSE, THERE'S THE POSSIBILITY OF BEING JUST THE SLIGHTEST BIT TOO ORGANIZED."

(By permission of Glen Dines. From Phi Delta Kappan.*)*

Flexible and Creative Plans—Using Taxonomies

Several decades ago, a group of experts in educational evaluation led by Benjamin Bloom set out to improve college and university examinations. The impact of their work has touched education at all levels around the world (Anderson & Sosniak, 1994). Bloom and his colleagues developed a **taxonomy**, or classification system, of educational objectives. Objectives were divided into three domains: cognitive, affective, and psychomotor. A handbook describing the objectives in each area was eventually published. In real life, of course, behaviors from these three domains occur simultaneously. While students are writing (psychomotor), they are also remembering or reasoning (cognitive), and they are likely to have some emotional response to the task as well (affective).

Taxonomy Classification system.

Planning involves designating learning goals, making decisions about how to help students achieve them, and assessing their success. Tactics may or may not involve written tasks.

Cognitive Domain In Bloom's taxonomy, memory and reasoning objectives.

Affective Domain Objectives focusing on attitudes and feelings.

The Cognitive Domain.   Six basic objectives are listed in Bloom's taxonomy of the thinking or **cognitive domain** (Bloom, Engelhart, Frost, Hill, & Krathwohl, 1956):

1. *Knowledge:* Remembering or recognizing something without necessarily understanding, using, or changing it.

2. *Comprehension:* Understanding the material being communicated without necessarily relating it to anything else.

3. *Application:* Using a general concept to solve a particular problem.

4. *Analysis:* Breaking something down into its parts.

5. *Synthesis:* Creating something new by combining different ideas.

6. *Evaluation:* Judging the value of materials or methods as they might be applied in a particular situation.

It is common in education to consider these objectives as a hierarchy, each skill building on those below, but this is not entirely accurate (Seddon, 1978). Some subjects, such as mathematics, do not fit this structure very well (Pring, 1971). Still, you will hear many references to *lower-level* and *higher-level objectives,* with knowledge and comprehension considered lower level and the other categories considered higher level. As a rough way of thinking about objectives, this can be helpful.

Consider how Bloom's taxonomy might suggest objectives for a social studies/language arts class. At the *analysis* level an objective might be:

After reading an article from the local newspaper, mark each statement as F for fact or O for opinion.

At the *synthesis* level, an objective for the class could be written this way:

Given a list of three facts, write a two-paragraph news story taking a position on an issue and documenting the position with the facts.

At the *evaluation* level, the objective might be written like this:

Given two articles that present contradictory views of a recent event, decide which article gives the fairer presentation and justify your choice.

The taxonomy of objectives can also be helpful in planning assessments because different procedures are appropriate for objectives at the various levels. Gronlund (1993) suggests that knowledge-level objectives can best be measured by true-false, short-answer, matching, or multiple-choice tests. Such tests will also work with the comprehension, application, and analysis levels of the taxonomy. For measuring synthesis and evaluation objectives, however, essays, reports, projects, and portfolios are more appropriate. Essay tests will also work at the middle levels of the taxonomy.

The Affective Domain.   The objectives in the taxonomy of the **affective domain,** or domain of emotional response, run from least committed to most committed (Krathwohl, Bloom, & Masia, 1964). At the lowest level, a student would simply pay attention to a certain idea. At the highest level, the student would adopt an idea or a value and act consistently with that idea. There are five basic objectives in the affective domain.

1. *Receiving:* Being aware of or attending to something in the environment. This is the I'll-listen-to-the-concert-but-I-won't-promise-to-like-it level.

2. *Responding:* Showing some new behavior as a result of experience. At this level a person might applaud after the concert or hum some of the music the next day.

3. *Valuing:* Showing some definite involvement or commitment. At this point a person might choose to go to a concert instead of a film.

4. *Organization:* Integrating a new value into one's general set of values, giving it some ranking among one's general priorities. This is the level at which a person would begin to make long-range commitments to concert attendance.

5. *Characterization by value:* Acting consistently with the new value. At this highest level, a person would be firmly committed to a love of music and demonstrate it openly and consistently.

Like the basic objectives in the cognitive domain, these five objectives are very general. To write specific learning objectives, you must state what students will actually be doing when they are receiving, responding, valuing, and so on. For example, an objective for a nutrition class at the valuing level (showing involvement or commitment) might be stated: After completing the unit on food contents and labeling, at least 50% of the class will commit to the junk-food boycott project by giving up candy for a month.

How can the teacher in the nutrition example be sure that students have given up candy in support of a junk-food boycott? The best method may be to ask them to report anonymously on their candy consumption; if students have to sign their names to their responses, the process may counteract the desire to reach another affective goal, honesty. Also, if students are graded on their success, this process might really encourage the students to give false reports. In most cases, it is best not to grade the assessment of affective goals.

The Psychomotor Domain.   Until recently, the **psychomotor domain,** or realm of physical ability objectives, has been mostly overlooked by teachers not directly involved with physical education. There are several taxonomies in this domain (e.g., Harrow, 1972; Simpson, 1972) that generally move from basic perceptions and reflex actions to skilled, creative movements. James Cangelosi (1990) provides a useful way to think about objectives in the psychomotor domain as either voluntary muscle capabilities that require endurance, strength, flexibility, agility, or speed; or the ability to perform a specific skill.

Objectives in the psychomotor domain should be of interest to a wide range of educators, including those in fine arts, vocational-technical education, and special education. Many other subjects, such as chemistry, physics, and biology, also require specialized movements and well-developed hand and eye coordination. Using lab equipment, the "mouse" on a computer, or art materials means learning new physical skills. Here are two psychomotor objectives:

Four minutes after completing a one-mile run in eight minutes or under, your heart rate will be below 120.

Without referring to notes or diagrams, assemble the appropriate laboratory apparatus to distill _____.

Psychomotor Domain Physical ability and coordination objectives.

TABLE 13.1   Checklist to Evaluate Student's Performance of a Two-Arm Press

The student, stationed in front of a barbell with only a light weight that would offer little resistance, is directed to demonstrate one two-arm press.

Scoring key: (11 points possible) +1 for each blank checked on the following form:

_____ feet properly positioned under the bar throughout the entire lift

_____ proper grip and hand spread

_____ back straight throughout

_____ head facing forward throughout

_____ clean initiated with knees flexed

_____ clean initiated with elbows extended

_____ clean properly executed

_____ pauses with bar just above the chest

_____ executes press properly

_____ returns bar to position just above chest and pauses

_____ gently returns bar to floor, flexing knees on the way down

Source: From *Designing Tests for Evaluating Student Achievement* by James S. Cangelosi, p. 125. Copyright © 1990. Adapted by permission of Addison-Wesley Educational Publishers, Inc.

Learning in the psychomotor area means developing a particular performance ability. How do you assess a student's performance? The obvious answer is to ask the student to demonstrate the skill and then observe the student's proficiency. In some cases, the performance of the skill results in a product, so assessment of the product can be substituted for observation of the actual performance. An art student learning to use the potter's wheel, for example, should be able to produce a pot that is symmetrical, stands by itself, and doesn't crack when fired.

When students are actually demonstrating skills or performing, you need a checklist or rating scale to help you focus on the important aspects of the skill being evaluated. A checklist usually gives the measurable dimensions of performance, along with a series of blank spaces for judgments. Table 13.1 provides an example. A rating scale generally follows the same plan but has a numerical scale to rate each aspect of performance.

Planning from a Constructivist Perspective

Constructivist Approach View that emphasizes the active role of the learner in building understanding and making sense of information.

Traditionally, it has been the teacher's responsibility to do most of the planning for instruction, but new ways of planning are developing. In **constructivist approaches**, planning is shared and negotiated. The teacher and students together make decisions about content, activities, and approaches. Rather than having specific student behaviors and skills as objectives, the teacher has overarching goals—"big ideas"—that guide planning. These goals are understandings or abilities that the teacher returns to again and again.

An Example of Constructivist Planning.   Vito Perrone (1994) has these goals for his secondary history students. He wants his student to be able to:

- use primary sources, formulate hypotheses, and engage in systematic study
- handle multiple points of view
- be close readers and active writers
- pose and solve problems

The next step in the planning process is to create a learning environment that allows students to move toward these goals in ways that respect their individual interests and abilities. Perrone (1994) suggests identifying "those ideas, themes, and issues that provide the depth and variety of perspective that help students develop significant understandings" (p. 12). For a secondary history course, a theme might be "democracy and revolution," "fairness," or "slavery." In math or music a theme might be "patterns"; in literature, "personal identity" might be the theme. Perrone suggests mapping the topic as a way of thinking about how the theme can generate learning and understanding. An example of a topic map, using the theme of "Immigrants in the United States," is shown in Figure 13.1 on page 486.

With this topic map as a guide, teacher and students can work together to identify activities, materials, projects, and performances that will support the development of the students' understanding and abilities—the overarching goals of the class. The teacher spends less time planning specific presentations and assignments and more time gathering a variety of resources and facilitating students' learning. The focus is not so much on students' products as on the processes of learning and the thinking behind the products.

Integrated and Thematic Plans.   Perrone's planning map shows a way to use the theme of immigrants to the United States to integrate issues in a history class. Today, teaching with themes and integrated content are major elements in planning and designing lessons and units, from kindergarten (Roskos & Neuman, 1995) through high school (Clarke & Agne, 1997). For example, Elaine Homestead and Karen McGinnis (two middle-school teachers) and Elizabeth Pate (a college professor) (1995) designed a unit on "Human Interactions" that included studying racism, world hunger, pollution, and air and water quality. Students researched issues by reading textbooks and outside sources, learning to use databases, interviewing local officials, and inviting guest speakers into class. Students had to develop knowledge in science, mathematics, and social studies. They learned to write and speak persuasively, and in the process, raised money for hunger relief in Africa.

Some ideas for integrating themes with younger children are people, friendship, habitats, communities, patterns, and roots and wings. Possibilities for older children are given in Table 13.2 on page 487.

Assessment.   Assessment plans differ within a constructivist classroom. Assessment is ongoing as teachers and students comment on each others efforts.

> **Focus on . . .**
>
> ### Planning
>
> - How does planning affect teaching?
> - Identify a cognitive, affective, and psychomotor objective for yourself for this week.
> - Name a theme that could organize your planning for a grade you might teach.

FIGURE 13.1

Planning with a Topic Map

With this map of the topic, "Immigrants to the United States," a history teacher can identify themes, issues, and ideas for study. Rather than "cover" the whole map, a few areas are examined in depth.

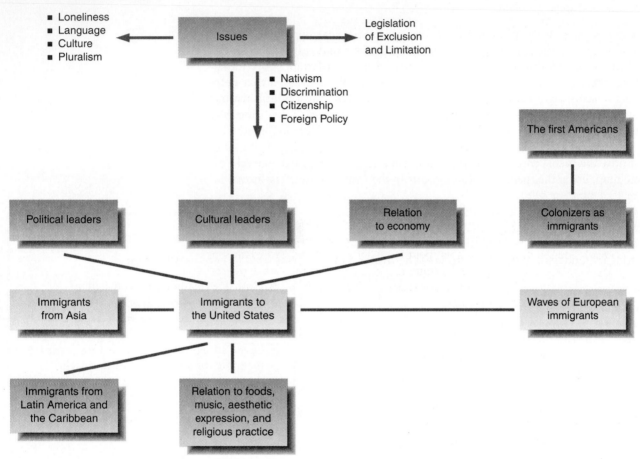

Source: From V. Perrone (1994). "How to engage students in learning." *Educational Leadership, 51, 5,* p. 13. Reprinted with permission of the Association for Supervision and Curriculum Development. Copyright 1990 by ASCD. All rights reserved.

Authentic assessment in the form of exhibitions, portfolios of work, and performances (described in Chapters 14 and 15) substitutes for traditional testing. But perhaps most important, teacher and students share the authority to evaluate work. The students have a responsibility to assess their own and each others' thinking, explanations, and performances. The teacher gives up control of "correctness" in the classroom and instead asks students, "Does that explanation make sense?" "Can you improve it?" "Do you agree?" "Why?" Students learn that self-assessment, judgment, and reflection is an important part of learning. Table 13.3 is a checklist that can be used to plan assessment in teaching with themes.

**TABLE 13.2   Some Themes for Integrated Planning
for Older Children**

Courage	Time and Space
Mystery	Groups and Institutions
Survival	Work
Human Interaction	Motion
Communities of the Future	Cause and Effect
Communication/Language	Probability and Prediction
Human Rights and Responsibilities	Change and Conservation
Identity/Coming of Age	Diversity and Variation
Interdependence	Autobiography

Source: Adapted from J. A. Beane (1995). (Ed.). *Toward a coherent curriculum.* Alexandria, VA: Association for Supervision and Curriculum Development; J. H. Clarke and R. M. Agne (1997). *Interdisciplinary high school teaching.* Boston: Allyn & Bacon; and G. Thompson (1991). *Teaching through themes.* New York: Scholastic. See Thompson for resources and strategies to develop some of these themes in elementary school and Clarke and Agne for ideas at the high school level.

Let's assume you and your students have valuable and interesting plans and learning objectives as well as some appropriate ways to assess learning. What next? You still need to decide what's happening on Monday. You need to design tasks and activities for teaching and learning that are appropriate for the objectives. You have an idea of *what* you want students to understand, but *how* do you teach to encourage understanding?

**TABLE 13.3   A Checklist to Guide Assessment in Teaching
with Themes**

You may want to use this checklist as one of your bases of evaluation for the children's discussions, writing, and projects.

_____ Displays knowledge of content
_____ Uses theme vocabulary
_____ Understands relationships explored in theme
_____ Notes the details of the theme information
_____ Classifies and categorizes theme information
_____ Compares and contrasts books in theme
_____ Assimilates and displays knowledge of books' relationships to theme
_____ Listens to discussions and responds accordingly
_____ Recognizes different curriculum areas explored in theme
_____ Is able to work in groups and individually on activities
_____ Clarifies theme information
_____ Completes projects on a timely basis
_____ Expands theme reading independently

Source: From *Teaching with Themes* by Gare Thompson, p. 176. Copyright © 1991 by Scholastic Inc. Reprinted by permission of Scholastic Inc.

"NOW THAT YOU'RE ALL
PRESENT AND ACCOUNTED
FOR, I'LL BEGIN
TODAY'S LECTURE."

*(By permission of Doug Redfern
—From* Phi Delta Kappan)

Teaching: Whole Group and Directive

This section describes a variety of general teaching strategies or formats for turning objectives into action in the classroom. These strategies are not complete models of teaching, but rather building blocks that can be used to construct lessons and units. We begin with the strategy many people associate most directly with teaching: lecturing.

Lecturing and Explaining

Some studies have found that teachers' presentations take up one-sixth to one-fourth of all classroom time. High school teachers, of course, lecture more than teachers in the lower grades. You will probably learn about how to lecture in your methods classes. Many different approaches are available, and the one you choose will depend on your objectives and the subject you are teaching. You will certainly want to keep in mind the age of your students, because the younger your students, the briefer and simpler your explanations should be. You may also want to follow a basic three-part format suggested by Kindsvatter, Wilen, and Ishler (1992), shown in Table 13.4.

Lecturing is appropriate for communicating a large amount of material to many students in a short period of time. The teacher can integrate information from many sources in less time than it would take for the students to integrate all the information themselves. Lecturing is a good method for introducing a new topic, giving background information, and motivating students to learn more on their own. Lecturing also helps students learn to listen accurately and critically and gives the teacher a chance to make on-the-spot changes to help students understand when they are confused (Gilstrap & Martin, 1975; Kindsvatter, Wilen, & Ishler, 1988). Lectures are therefore most appropriate for cognitive and affective objectives at the lower levels of the taxonomies described earlier: for knowledge, comprehension, application, receiving, responding, and valuing.

TABLE 13.4   Three Phases in the Lecture Method

Entry: Preparation for Learning
A. State objectives and rationale.
B. Provide a context for the new material to be presented.
C. Focus attention on key concept, generalization, or principle that encompasses the lecture.

Presentation
A. Sequence content from simpler to complex understandings.
B. Enhance presentation with visual aids.
C. Stimulate attention with verbal and nonverbal behaviors.

Closure: Review of Learning
A. Integrate with students' knowledge and experiences.
B. Transition to next lesson or activity.

Lecturing Organized explanation of a topic by a teacher.

Source: From *Dynamics of effective teaching, 2/e* by Richard Kindsvatter, William Wilen, and Margaret Ishler, p. 221. Copyright © 1988 and 1992. Reprinted with permission of Addison-Wesley Educational Publishers Inc.

TABLE 13.5   Active Learning and Teacher Presentations

Here are some ideas for keeping students cognitively engaged in lessons. They can be adapted for many ages.

Question, All Write: Pose a question, ask everyone to jot an answer, then ask, "How many students would be willing to share their thoughts?"

Outcome Sentences: After a segment of presentation, ask students to finish a sentence such as "I learned . . . , I'm beginning to wonder. . . , I was surprised. . . ." Share as above. Students may keep their outcome sentences in a learning log or portfolio.

Underexplain with Learning Pairs: Give a brief explanation, then ask students to work in pairs to figure out the process or idea.

Voting: Ask "How many of you . . . " questions and take a count. "How many of you agree with Raschon?" "How many of you are ready to move on?" "How many of you got 48 on this problem?"

Choral Response: Have the whole class restate in unison important facts and ideas, such as "The environment is one whole system" or " A 10-sided polygon is called a decagon."

Speak-Write: Tell students you will speak briefly, for 3 or 4 minutes. They are to listen, but not take notes. At the end of the time, ask them to write the main ideas, a summary, or questions they have about what you said.

Source: Adapted from M. Harmin (1994). *Inspiring active learning: A handbook for teachers.* Alexandria, VA: Association for Supervision and Curriculum Development.

Scripted cooperation, described in Chapter 9, is one way of incorporating active learning into lectures. Several times during the presentation, the teacher asks students to work in pairs. One person is the summarizer and the other critiques the summary. This give students a chance to check their understanding, organize their thinking, and translate ideas into their own words. Other possibilities are described in Table 13.5.

The lecture method also has disadvantages. You may find that some students have trouble listening for more than a few minutes at a time and that they simply tune you out. Lecturing puts the students in a passive position. It does much of the cognitive work for the students and may prevent them from asking or thinking of questions. Also, students learn and comprehend at different paces, whereas a lecture proceeds at the lecturer's own pace (Freiberg & Driscoll, 1996; Gilstrap & Martin, 1975). If your objectives include having students solve a problem; develop arguments; write essays, poems, or short stories; create paintings; or evaluate work, then you must go beyond lecturing to methods that require more active student involvement.

Recitation and Questioning

Recitation is a common approach to teaching that has been with us for many years (Stodolsky, 1988). Teachers pose questions, students answer. The teacher's questions generally follow some sort of plan to develop a framework for the subject matter involved. The students' answers are often followed by reactions from the teacher, such as praise, correction, or requests for further information. The

Scripted Cooperation Learning strategy in which two students take turns summarizing material and criticizing the summaries.

Recitation Format of teacher questioning, student response, and teacher feedback.

TABLE 13.6   Classroom Questions for Objectives in the Cognitive Domain

Questions can be posed that encourage thinking at every level of Bloom's taxonomy in the cognitive domain. Of course, the thinking required depends on what has gone before in the discussion.

Category	Type of Thinking Expected	Examples
Knowledge (recognition)	Recalling or recognizing information as learned	Define.... What is the capital of...? What did the text say about...?
Comprehension	Demonstrating understanding of the materials; transforming, reorganizing, or interpreting	Explain in your own words.... Compare.... What is the main idea of...? Describe what you saw....
Application	Using information to solve a problem with a single correct answer	Which principle is demonstrated in...? Calculate the area of.... Apply the rule of...to solve....
Analysis	Critical thinking; identifying reasons and motives; making inferences based on specific data; analyzing conclusions to see if supported by evidence	What influenced the writings of...? Why was Washington, D.C. chosen...? Which of the following are facts and which are opinions...? Based on your experiment, what is the chemical...?
Synthesis	Divergent, original thinking; original plan, proposal, design, or story	What's a good name for...? How could we raise money for...? What would the United States be like if the South had won...?
Evaluation	Judging the merits of ideas, offering opinions, applying standards	Which U.S. senator is the most effective? Which painting do you believe to be better? Why? Why would you favor...?

Source: Adapted by permission of D. C. Heath from M. Sadker and D. Sadker (1986), Questioning skills. In J. Cooper (Ed.), *Classroom teaching skills: A handbook* (3rd ed.), pp. 143–160.

pattern from the teacher's point of view consists of *structure* (setting a framework), *solicitation* (asking questions), and *reaction* (praising, correcting, and expanding) (Clark et al., 1979). These steps are repeated over and over.

Let us consider the heart of recitation, the soliciting or *questioning* phase, by looking at the different kinds of questions, when to ask them, and how to respond to student answers. Of course, an important goal of teaching should be to encourage students to ask questions, but for now we will focus on teachers' questions, to make them as helpful as possible for students. Many of the beginning teachers I work with are surprised to discover how valuable good questions can be and how difficult they are to create.

Kinds of Questions.   Some educators have estimated that high school teachers ask an average of 395 questions per day (Gall, 1970). What are these questions like? Many can be categorized in terms of Bloom's taxonomy of objectives in the cognitive domain. Table 13.6 offers examples of questions at the different taxonomic levels.

Another way to categorize questioning is in terms of **convergent questions** (only one right answer) or **divergent questions** (many possible answers). Questions about concrete facts are convergent: "Who ruled England in 1540?" "Who wrote the original *Peter Pan*?" Questions dealing with opinions or hypotheses are divergent: "In this story, which character is most like you and why?" "In 100 years, which of the past five presidents will be most admired?"

Quite a bit of space in education textbooks has been devoted to urging teachers to ask a greater number of higher-level (analysis, synthesis, and evaluation) and divergent questions. Is this really a better way of questioning? Research has provided several surprises.

Fitting the Questions to the Students.   Both high- and low-level questions can be effective (Gall, 1984; Redfield & Rousseau, 1981). Different patterns seem to be better for different students, however. The best pattern for younger students and for lower-ability students of all ages is simple questions that allow a high percentage of correct answers, ample encouragement, help when the student does not have the correct answer, and praise. For high-ability students, the successful pattern includes harder questions at both higher and lower levels and more critical feedback (Berliner, 1987; Good, 1988).

Whatever their age or ability, all students should have some experience with thought-provoking questions and, if necessary, help in learning how to answer them. As we saw in Chapter 8, to master critical thinking and problem-solving skills, students must have a chance to practice the skills. They also need time to think about their answers. But research shows that teachers wait an average of only one second for students to answer (Rowe, 1974). Consider the following slice of classroom life (Sadker & Sadker, 1986a, p. 170):

Teacher: Who wrote the poem "Stopping by Woods on a Snowy Evening"? Tom?

Tom: Robert Frost.

Teacher: Good. What action takes place in the poem? Sally?

Sally: A man stops his sleigh to watch the woods get filled with snow.

Teacher: Yes. Emma, what thoughts go through the man's mind?

Emma: He thinks how beautiful the woods are . . . (She pauses for a second.)

Teacher: What else does he think about? Joe?

Joe: He thinks how he would like to stay and watch. (Pauses for a second.)

Teacher: Yes—and what else? Rita? (Waits half a second.) Come on, Rita, you can get the answer to this. (Waits half a second.) Well, why does he feel he can't stay there indefinitely and watch the woods and the snow?

Sarah: Well, I think it might be—(Pauses a second.)

Teacher: Think, Sarah. (Teacher waits for half a second.) All right then—Mike? (Waits again for half a second.) John? (Waits half a second.) What's the matter with everyone today? Didn't you do the reading?

Very little thoughtful responding can take place in this situation. When teachers learn to pose a question, then wait at least 3 to 5 seconds before calling on a student to answer, students tend to give longer answers; more students are likely to participate, ask questions, and volunteer appropriate answers; student comments involving analysis, synthesis, inference, and speculation tend to increase; and the students generally appear more confident in their answers (Berliner, 1987; Rowe, 1974; Sadker & Sadker, 1986a; Tobin, 1987). This seems like

Convergent Questions Questions that have a single correct answer.

Divergent Questions Questions that have no single correct answer.

a simple improvement in teaching, but 5 seconds of silence is not that easy to handle. It takes practice. You might try asking students to jot down ideas or even discuss the question with another student and formulate an answer together. This makes the wait more comfortable and gives students a chance to think. Of course, if it is clear that students are lost or don't understand the question, waiting longer will not help. When your question is met with blank stares, rephrase the question or ask if anyone can explain the confusion. Another qualification—there is some evidence that extending wait times does not affect learning in university classes (Duell, 1994), so with advanced high school students, you might conduct your own evaluation of wait time.

A word about selecting students to answer questions. If you call only on volunteers, then you may get the wrong idea about how well students understand the material. Also, the same people volunteer over and over again. Many expert teachers have some systematic way of making sure that they call on everyone: They pull names from a jar or check names off a list as each student speaks (Weinstein, 1996; Weinstein & Mignano, 1997). Another possibility is to put each student's name on an index card, then shuffle the cards and go through the deck as you call on people. You can use the card to make notes about students' answers or extra help they may need.

Responding to Student Answers. What do you do after the student answers? The most common response, occurring about 50% of the time in most classrooms, is simple acceptance—"OK" or "Uh-huh" (Sadker & Sadker, 1986a). But there are better reactions, depending on whether the student's answer is correct, partially correct, or wrong. If the answer is quick, firm, and correct, simply accept the answer or ask another question. If the answer is correct but hesitant, give the student feedback about *why* the answer is correct: "That's right, Chris, the Senate is part of the legislative branch of government because the Senate . . . ." This allows you to explain the material again. If this student is unsure, others may be confused as well. If the answer is partially or completely wrong but the student has made an honest attempt, you should probe for more information, give clues, simplify the question, review the previous steps, or reteach the material. If the student's wrong answer is silly or careless, however, it is better simply to correct the answer and go on. (Good, 1988; Rosenshine & Stevens, 1986).

Seatwork and Homework

There is little research on the effects of **seatwork,** or independent classroom-desk work, but it is clear that this technique is often overused. In fact, a study found that American elementary students spend 51% of mathematics time in school working alone, while Japanese students spend 26% and Taiwanese students spend only 9% (Stigler, Lee, & Stevenson, 1987). Some educators point to these differences as part of the explanation for Asian students' superiority in mathematics. Seatwork should follow up a lesson and give students supervised practice. It should not be the main mode of instruction.

In the 1980s several studies reported strong positive correlations between the amount of *homework* students were assigned and their grades (Keith, 1982). Many schools responded by requiring more homework. But just assigning more homework is not necessarily a good idea. The homework must be meaningful extensions of class lessons, not just busywork. Unfortunately, many workbook

Seatwork Independent classroom work.

pages and "dittos" do little to support the learning of important objectives. Before you assign work, ask yourself, "Does doing this work help students learn anything that matters?" For example, consider this task, cited in the report of the Commission on Reading of the National Institute of Education (Anderson, Hiebert, Scott, & Wilkinson, 1985):

> Read each sentence. Decide which consonant letter is used the most. Underline it each time.

What's the point? This sort of activity communicates to students that reading isn't very important or useful. Students should see the connection between the seatwork or homework and the lesson. Tell them why they are doing the work. The objectives should be clear, all the materials that might be needed should be provided, and the work should be easy enough that students can succeed on their own. Success rates should be high—near 100%. When seatwork is too difficult, students often resort to guessing or copying just to finish (Anderson, 1985).

Individualized instruction does not necessarily mean students working alone; it refers to the idea of tailoring the pace, learning objectives, learning activities, level, and assessment approach so that each individual student benefits.

Carol Weinstein and Andy Mignano (1997) describe several alternatives to workbooks and dittos, such as reading silently and reading aloud to a partner; writing for a "real" audience; writing letters or journals; transcribing conversations and punctuating them properly; making up problems; working on long-term projects and reports; solving brainteasers and puzzles; and engaging in computer activities. One of my favorites is creating a group story. Two students begin a story on the computer. Then two more add a paragraph. The story grows with each new pair's addition. The students are reading and writing, editing and improving.

To benefit from individual or group seatwork or homework, students must stay involved and do the work. The first step toward involvement is getting students started correctly by making sure they understand the assignment. It may help to do the first few questions as a class, to clear up any misconceptions. This is especially important for homework assignments, because students may have no one at home to consult if they have problems with the assignment. A second way to keep students involved is to hold them accountable for completing the work correctly, not just for filling in the page. This means the work should be checked, the errors corrected, and the results counted toward the class grade (Brophy & Good, 1986). Expert teachers often have ways of correcting homework quickly during the first minutes of class by having students check each other's or their own work.

Seatwork particularly requires careful monitoring. Being available to students doing seatwork is more effective than offering students help before they ask for it. To be available, you should move around the class and avoid spending too much time with one or two students. Short, frequent contacts are best (Brophy & Good, 1986; Rosenshine, 1977).

Sometimes you may be working with a small group while other students do seatwork. In these situations it is especially important for students to know what to do if they need help. One expert teacher described by Weinstein and Mignano (1996) taught students a rule, "Ask three, then me." Students have to consult three classmates before seeking help from the teacher. This teacher also spends time early in the year showing students *how* to help each other—how to ask questions and how to explain.

Focus on...

Directive Teaching

- What are three phases of a lecture?
- Give examples of convergent and divergent questions.
- Describe some alternatives to seatwork.

What about monitoring homework? If students get stuck on homework, they need help at home, someone who can scaffold their work without just "giving the answer" (Pressley, 1995). But many parents don't know how to help (Hoover-Dempsey, Bassler, & Burow, 1995). The Guidelines give ideas for helping parents help with homework.

Guidelines

Family and Community Partnerships for Homework

Make sure families know what students are expected to learn.

Examples

1. At the beginning of a unit, send home a list of the main objectives, examples of major assignments, key due dates, homework "calendar," and a list of resources available free at libraries or on the Internet.
2. Provide a clear, concise description of your homework policy—how homework is counted toward class grades; consequences for late, forgotten, or missing homework, etc.

Help families find a comfortable and helpful role in their child's homework.

Examples

1. Remind families that "helping with homework" means encouraging, listening, monitoring, praising, discussing, brainstorming—not necessarily teaching and never doing the work for their child.
2. Encourage families to set aside a quiet time and place for everyone in the family to study. Make this time a regular part of the daily routine.
3. Have some homework assignments that are fun and involve the whole family—puzzles, family albums, watching a television program together and doing a "review."
4. At parent-teacher conferences, ask families what they need to play a more helpful role in their child's homework.

Solicit and use suggestions from families about homework.

Examples

1. Find out what responsibilities the child has at home—how much time is available for homework.
2. Periodically, have a "homework hotline" for call-in questions and suggestions.

In the preceding section, the teacher was in the center of the action—presenting, questioning, reacting, and correcting. For certain objectives and situations, these approaches are useful. In the next section we discuss practices that bring the students more closely into the center of decisions and interactions.

Teaching: Small Group and Student-Centered

In this section we will examine examples of student-centered teaching practices and methods that are consistent with constructivist and situated learning approaches. Like explanation, questioning, and seatwork described above, these are building blocks for teaching that can be combined with other strategies and assembled into lessons, units, and programs of teaching. Table 13.7 lists some characteristics of constructivist teaching practices described by Jacqueline Grennon Brooks and M. G. Brooks (1993). Most student-centered approaches share these characteristics.

An Example of Constructivist Teaching

If we apply the ideas in Table 13.7 to teach children about numbers, we would create an environment in which students can make sense of mathematics and use mathematics to make sense of the world. To accomplish these goals, teaching begins with the student's current understanding. A major challenge for teachers is to capitalize on the student's natural ways of thinking about mathematics. Young children can create concrete, direct representations of problems and use counting to solve problems. To answer the question, "Melissa has three cookies—how many more does she need to have six altogether?" young children might use counters (sticks, fingers, or pebbles) to represent three cookies, keep adding until there are six, then count how many were added (Peterson, Fennema, & Carpenter, 1989).

TABLE 13.7   Constructivist Teaching Practices

Many constructivist practices can be incorporated into any class.

1. Constructivist teachers encourage and accept student autonomy and initiative.
2. Constructivist teachers use raw data and primary sources, along with manipulative, interactive, and physical materials.
3. When framing tasks, constructivist teachers use cognitive terminology such as "classify," "analyze," "predict," and "create."
4. Constructivist teachers allow student responses to drive lessons, shift instructional strategies, and alter content.
5. Constructivist teachers inquire about students' understandings of concepts before sharing their own understandings of those concepts.
6. Constructivist teachers encourage students to engage in dialogue, both with the teacher and with one another.
7. Constructivist teachers encourage student inquiry by asking thoughtful, open-ended questions and encouraging students to ask questions of each other.
8. Constructivist teachers seek elaboration of students' initial responses.
9. Constructivist teachers engage students in experiences that might engender contradictions to their initial hypotheses and then encourage discussion.
10. Constructivist teachers allow wait-time after posing questions.
11. Constructivist teachers provide time for students to discover relationships and create metaphors.

Source: From J. G. Brooks and M. G. Brooks. "Becoming a Constructivist Teacher." *In Search of Understanding: The Case for Constructivist Classrooms,* excerpted from pp. 101–118. Reprinted with permission of the Association for Supervision and Curriculum Development. Copyright © 1993 by ASCD. All rights reserved.

Teachers can capitalize on the natural use of counting strategies to see how many different ways students can solve a problem. The emphasis is on mathematical thinking, not on math "facts" or on learning the one best (teacher's) way to solve the problem. Here is an example of how one teacher encouraged mathematical thinking while doing the lunch count:

> During the first few minutes of the day, Ms. White asked how many children wanted hot lunches that day. Eighteen children raised their hands. Six children were going to eat cold lunches. Ms. White asked, "How many children are going to eat lunch here today?"
>
> By starting with 18 and counting on, several children got to the answer of 24. One child got out counters and counted out a set of 18 and another set of 6. He then counted all of them and said "24."
>
> Ms. White then asked, "How many more children are eating hot lunch than are eating cold lunch?"
>
> Several children counted back from 18 to 12. The child with the blocks matched 18 blocks with 6 blocks and counted the blocks left over.
>
> Ms. White asked the children who volunteered to tell the rest of the class how they got the answer. Ms. White continued asking for different solutions until no one could think of a new way to solve the problem. (Peterson, Fennema, & Carpenter, 1989, p. 45)

Let's look more closely at a few other student-centered approaches: group discussion, humanistic education, and technology.

Group Discussion

Group discussion is in some ways similar to the recitation strategy described in a previous section, but should be more like the instructional conversations described in Chapter 9 (Tharp & Gallimore, 1991). A teacher may pose questions, listen to student answers, react, and probe for more information, but in a true group discussion, the teacher does not have a dominant role. Students ask questions, answer each other's questions, and respond to each other's answers.

There are many advantages to group discussions. The students are directly involved and have the chance to participate. Group discussion helps students learn to express themselves clearly, to justify opinions, and to tolerate different views. Group discussion also gives students a chance to ask for clarification, examine their own thinking, follow personal interests, and assume responsibility by taking leadership roles in the group. Thus, group discussions help students evaluate ideas and synthesize personal viewpoints. Discussions are also useful when students are trying to understand difficult concepts that go against common sense. As we saw in Chapters 8 and 9, many scientific concepts, like the role of light in vision or Newton's laws of motion, are difficult to grasp because they contradict commonsense notions. By thinking together, challenging each other, and suggesting and evaluating possible explanations, students are more likely to reach a genuine understanding.

Of course, there are disadvantages. Class discussions are quite unpredictable and may easily digress into exchanges of ignorance. Some members of the group may have great difficulty participating and may become anxious if forced to speak. In addition, you may have to do a good deal of preparation to ensure that participants have a background of knowledge on which to base the discussion. And large groups are often unwieldy. In many cases, a few students will dominate

Group Discussions Conversations in which the teacher does not have the dominant role; students pose and answer their own questions.

the discussion while the others daydream (Kindsvatter, Wilen, & Ishler, 1988). The Guidelines give some ideas for facilitating a productive group discussion.

Guidelines

Leading Class Discussions

Invite shy children to participate.

Examples

1. "What's your opinion, Joel? We need to hear from some other students."
2. Don't wait until there is a deadly silence to ask shy students to reply. Most people, even those who are confident, hate to break a silence.

Direct student comments and questions back to another student.

Examples

1. "That's an unusual idea, Steve. Kim, what do you think of Steve's idea?"
2. "That's an important question, John. Maura, do you have any thoughts about how you'd answer that?"
3. Encourage students to look at and talk to one another rather than wait for your opinion.

Make sure you understand what a student has said. If you are unsure, other students may be unsure as well.

Examples

1. Ask a second student to summarize what the first student said; then the first student can try again to explain if the summary is incorrect.
2. "Karen, I think you're saying. . . . Is that right, or have I misunderstood?"

Probe for more information.

Examples

1. "That's a strong statement. Do you have any evidence to back it up?"
2. "Tell us how you reached that conclusion. What steps did you go through?"

Bring the discussion back to the subject.

Examples

1. "Let's see, we were discussing . . . and Sarah made one suggestion. Does anyone have a different idea?"
2. "Before we continue, let me try to summarize what has happened thus far."

Give time for thought before asking for responses.

Example

"How would your life be different if television had never been invented? Jot down your ideas on paper, and we will share reactions in a minute." After a minute: "Jean, will you tell us what you wrote?"

When a student finishes speaking, look around the room to judge reactions.

Examples

1. If other students look puzzled, ask them to describe why they are confused.
2. If students are nodding assent, ask them to give an example of what was just said.

Humanistic Education

Years ago a group of psychologists and educators such as Carl Rogers (1969; Rogers & Freiberg, 1994), Abraham Maslow (1970), and Art Combs (1984) called for student-centered teaching. They were not identified as constructivist at the time, though their **humanistic** philosophy and approach surely was consistent with constructivism. The basic principles of humanism include a belief that each person constructs his or her own reality. What a person perceives as real and important *is* reality for that individual, and one person cannot fully know the reality of another.

Humanistic approaches to education stress the importance of feelings, open communication, and the value of every student. Humanistic education is a philosophy rather than a collection of strategies—an attitude of caring and respect for students. In their book, *Inviting School Success: A Self-Concept Approach to Teaching and Learning,* William Purkey and John Novak (1984) list many things that teachers can do to support self-esteem and make school an inviting place. A few of the ideas are listed in Table 13.8.

Computers, Videodiscs, and Beyond

No discussion of student-centered teaching strategies would be complete today without considering the role of technology in teaching and learning. Technology allows students to explore different worlds, access resources all over the world, and confront complex problems. The uses of computers and other instructional technology are so broad and varied that we can only touch on a few key points here. Because this is such an important topic for today's teachers, I encourage you to learn all you can about it. Some of my student teachers have gotten teaching positions in difficult times partly because they knew how to use computers in their classroom.

Many of your students will have used computers for word processing, graphic design, or games since their preschool years. Other students will have had little experience with computers. Some schools will have computers in every classroom. Videodisc encyclopedias will make a tremendous amount of information available to students. Communications networks will connect your class with students around the country and with museums, research labs, or colleges. But in other schools, there will be a few old computers in a lab down the hall. Given this wide range in students' sophistication and in schools' resources, what can we say about using technology to teach? There are three main roles of computers in schools: as *learning environments* to help students learn content and problem-solving skills, as *tools* to help students and teachers with such tasks as word processing, computing, locating and managing information, doing graphics, or programming computers; and as what Roger Taylor (1980) called *tutees.* In this last role, the student teaches the computer what to do through programming using BASIC, LOGO, Pascal, or some other language. We will focus first on the computer as a *learning environment.*

Computers as Learning Environments.   Computer games encourage learning and problem solving through motivating activities that resemble video games. An elementary school in upstate New York was faced with an all too

Humanistic View An approach to motivation that emphasizes personal freedom, choice, self-determination, and striving for personal growth.

TABLE 13.8   Inviting School Success

Here is a sample from the list of practices recommended to invite success in school.

Elementary Teachers

1. *Give an apple on opening day.* Instead of an apple for the teacher, put an apple on each student's desk on the first day of school.
2. *Build a loft.* Create a snug place for reading or small meetings.
3. *Rotate the seating.* Make sure everyone has a chance to be in the favorite seats—near the teacher, close to class pets, and so forth.
4. *Dial-a-parent.* Each week, call one parent with honest and positive comments about his or her child.
5. *Use the newspaper.* Watch for articles about students, their families, their interests, or course content. Share the articles with the class. Before a holiday, take out a classified ad to send a special greeting to your class.

Middle School

1. *Share decisions.* Whenever possible, get students involved in decisions about rules of conduct, activities, academic expectations, even textbook reviews.
2. *Start a trading library.* Set up a library in your classroom so students can share favorite books. Communicate that books are meant to be used and enjoyed, and the more people involved the better.
3. *Hold a fractions party.* Bring (or ask the class to bring) pies, cakes, and other goodies in various shapes. Ask students to recognize the difference between 3/4, 5/8, 1/2, and 1/3, and let them eat their answers.

4. *Build a poem.* Rather than having each student write a long poem (a daunting task for many students), ask everyone in the class to write a one-line poem about a particular topic (sunset is a good subject). A small group can assemble the lines into an outstanding class poem.
5. *Visit a graveyard.* Ask students to study the gravestones, imagine, then write about one of the people represented. What happened in this person's lifetime? What was life like in those days? Older students might even do some research in library files, old newspapers, etc.

High School

1. *Tap expertise.* Your school cafeteria worker may be a music buff, the school psychologist an amateur photographer. Have these people share their interests with your class.
2. *Invite participation.* When students are not joining in, divide into small discussion groups—first pairs, then fours, then eights, and so on.
3. *Arrange a Big-Pal program.* Organize tutoring programs for younger students.
4. *And now a word from our sponsor.* Divide the class into small groups and have each group write, design, and videotape a commercial for an academic concept to be shown to the entire class.
5. *Make and take.* Have students produce something—"invest" in the stock market and follow the outcome, design a better parking plan for the school, write letters to manufacturers to request donations for the class.

Source: From W. W. Purkey and J. M. Novak. *Inviting school success: A self-concept approach to teaching and learning,* 2nd ed., pp. 102–129. Copyright © 1984 by Wadsworth Publishing Co. Adapted by permission.

typical set of somewhat contradictory demands: improve students' knowledge of social studies and their ability to write and use reference skills, and get them computer literate while you're at it. Unfortunately, the school day was already filled and there were only 14 computers available. The school's computer coordinator put together a social studies unit built around the computer simulation program *Where in the World Is Carmen Sandiego?* The unit begins with the whole class playing the game as it is presented on a large monitor, practicing the note-taking and other fact-finding skills that will be useful in successfully "cap-

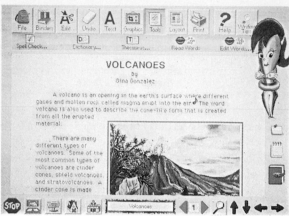

Two different computer learning environments: Where in the World Is Carmen Sandiego *(Broderbund) and The Learning Company's word processing and graphic program that emphasizes process writing.*

turing the criminal." After several days of guided instruction in using reference materials to unravel the clues that appear in the game, students pair off and, as a team, continue working with the program. The culminating activity for the student is the preparation of a report about the state he or she researched.

Computer simulations are simplified versions of situations that the student would encounter in real life. "In this simplified world, the student solves problems, learns procedures, comes to understand the characteristics of phenomena and how to control them, or learns what actions to take in different situations" (Alessi & Trollip, 1991, p. 119). One example is *SimCity,* which allows students to plan and build cities complete with transportation systems, law enforcement, and industrial, recreational, and residential development. Students must cope with problems as they build and plan—everything from mild discontent over traffic to major natural disasters. In the interactive videodisc world of *ScienceVision,* students can conduct experiments that would be too dangerous or costly to be accomplished in a typical middle-school laboratory (Tobin & Dawson, 1992). *Science 2000* is a multimedia, thematic science curriculum with a hypertext database that is tied into videodiscs. In one unit, for example, students study the ecosystem by participating in a simulated community that is concerned about the quality of water in a nearby lake. Working in cooperative groups, students play the roles of farmers, politicians, building developers, naturalists, and representatives from the Environmental Protection Agency. These groups use the database to research their positions and develop their cases. The unit involves more than science; social studies and language arts play a role as well as the groups debate and compromise (Coburn, 1993).

Microworlds are small but complete parts of real environments that encourage discovery through exploration (Papert, 1993). Working in the environments, students construct knowledge as they explore and experiment. For example, in LOGO, young children learn to program a computer by writing moves for a "Turtle" (Papert, 1980). *TinkerTools,* a series of microworlds that incorporate simulations and game-like features, allows students as young as 11 or 12 to explore the world of Newtonian physics (White, 1993). Microworlds pro-

Computer Simulations Programs that require students to apply knowledge and skills to solve lifelike problems.

Microworlds Simplified but complete computerized model of a real world working system.

vide tools to support and extend thinking or "objects-to-think-with" such as the Turtle in LOGO (Gargarian, 1996). By using these tools, students are supported or guided in discovering powerful ideas such as principles of geometry or Newtonian laws of motion, without spending endless hours on detours and dead ends. "Microworlds provide the means to control what is discoverable without giving up on discovery learning" (Gargarian, 1996, p. 151).

Computers and Learning. Are computers effective as learning environments? The answer in any given situation depends on the quality of the programs and how they are used, but in general, computer-assisted instruction appears to be moderately more effective than conventional methods (Niemiec & Walberg, 1987). And computers can provide back-up or extended instruction, allowing students to get help privately, without publicly exposing their limitations (Schofield, Eurch-Fulcer, & Britt, 1994). Given all the possibilities for using instructional technology and the rapid pace of advances in the field, it would be foolhardy to specify exactly how students should use computers. However, some general ideas are listed in the Guidelines.

Guidelines

Using Computers and Other Technology

Take advantage of the capacity to individualize.

Because teachers are concerned about being fair and equitable, they often have all their students use the same software at the same time. Yet one of the most important benefits of computers is the variety of ways they can be used to encourage children to develop different skills at different times. For some, this can be accomplished through the use of drill-and-practice programs; for others, through learning a programming language or word processing.

Involve students in decisions about hardware and software for the class.

Have student teams review software and make recommendations to the administration. Take students on visits to other schools to see how technology is working for them.

Give students experience with technology as a tool.

Computer experience for students should be consistent with the ways computers are currently used in the adult world outside of school. Have students do research for projects on databases and using videodisc encyclopedias. Incorporate word processing, page layout, and spreadsheet applications in assignments.

Use computers as tools for your own work.

Focus on those aspects of computing that will enable you to do your job well by making work easier, more interesting, and more effective. Use electronic gradebooks, test generators, spreadsheets, databases, and word processors.

The notion that computers individualize instruction has been interpreted by many educators to mean that the computer should be used by one student at a time. As a result, computers have been underutilized as a means of providing small-group and large-group learning experiences. Research on cooperative or collaborative learning indicates that this approach may have numerous benefits for both cognitive and social development (Webb & Palincsar, 1996).

Videodiscs.   Video technology offers an alternative or addition to computers in teaching and learning. For example, the Cognition and Technology Group at Vanderbilt University (CTGV, 1990, 1993) has developed a videodisc-based learning environment that focuses on mathematics instruction for the fifth and sixth grades. The series, called *The Adventures of Jasper Woodbury*, presents students with complex situations that require problem finding; subgoal setting; and the application of mathematics, science, history, and literature concepts to solve problems. Even though the situations are complex and lifelike, the problems can be solved using data embedded in the stories presented. For example, in one adventure, Jasper sets out in a small motorboat, headed to Cedar Creek to inspect an old cruiser he is thinking of buying. Along the way Jasper has to consult maps, use his marine radio, deal with fuel and repair problems, buy the cruiser, and finally determine if he has enough fuel and time to sail his purchase home before sundown.

The CTGV group plans to create 6 to 10 different adventures. Initial research indicates that students as young as fourth grade and as old as high school can work with the adventures (CTGV, 1990). Students are highly motivated as they work in groups to solve the problems; even group members with limited math skill can contribute to the solutions because they might notice key information in the videotape or suggest innovative ways to approach the situation.

The Vanderbilt group calls its problem-based approach **anchored instruction.** The *anchor* is the rich, authentic, and interesting situation. This anchor provides a focus—a reason for setting goals, planning, and using mathematical tools to solve problems. The intended outcome is to develop knowledge that is useful and flexible, not inert. Inert knowledge is information that is memorized but seldom applied. Anchored instruction is an example of cognitive apprenticeships described in Chapter 9 (De Corte, Greer, & Verschaffel, 1996).

So far we have talked about goals and teaching approaches. But what about the teacher? Is there more to teaching than objectives and strategies? Research has given us a number of answers over the years.

Successful Teaching: Focus on the Teacher

How would you go about identifying the keys to effective teaching? You might ask students, principals, college professors of education, or experienced teachers to list the characteristics of good teachers. Or you could do intensive case studies of a few classrooms over a long period. You might observe classrooms, rate different teachers on certain characteristics, and then see which characteristics were associated with teachers whose students either achieved the most or were the most motivated to learn. (To do this, of course, you would have to decide how to assess achievement and motivation.) You could identify teachers

---

Anchored Instruction Problem-based teaching that "anchors" or embeds the instruction in a real-life, interesting situation.

whose students, year after year, learned more than students working with other teachers; then you could watch the more successful teachers, and note what they do. You might also train teachers to apply several different strategies to teach the same lesson and then determine which strategy led to the greatest student learning. You could videotape teachers, then ask them to view the tapes and report what they were thinking about as they taught and what influenced their decisions while teaching. You might study transcripts of classroom dialogue to learn what helped students understand.

All these approaches and more have been used to investigate teaching. Often researchers conduct a series of studies by making careful observations and identifying relationships between teaching and learning. The researchers then use these relationships as the basis for developing teaching approaches and testing these approaches in design experiments (Brown, 1992; Greeno, Collins, and Resnick, 1996). Let's examine some of the specific knowledge about teaching gained from these projects.

Characteristics of Effective Teachers

Some of the earliest research on effective teaching focused on the personal qualities of the teachers themselves. Researchers thought that the key to success in teaching must lie in the characteristics of teachers (Medley, 1979). Although this assumption proved incorrect—or at least incomplete—it did teach us some lessons about three teacher characteristics: knowledge, clarity, and warmth.

Teachers' Knowledge.   Do teachers who know more about their subject have a more positive impact on their students? When we look at teachers' knowledge of facts and concepts, as measured by test scores and college grades, the relationship to student learning is unclear and may be indirect. Teachers who know more facts about their subject do not necessarily have students who learn more. But teachers who know more may make clearer presentations and recognize student difficulties more readily. They are ready for any student questions and do not have to be evasive or vague in their answers. Thus, knowledge is necessary but not sufficient for effective teaching because being more knowledgeable helps teachers be clearer and more organized.

Organization and Clarity.   Students discussing a teacher are likely to say things like, "Oh, she can really explain," or "He's so disorganized!" When Barak Rosenshine and Norma Furst (1973) reviewed about 50 studies of teaching, they concluded that clarity was the most promising teacher behavior for future research on effective teaching. Recent studies confirm the importance of clarity. Teachers who provide clear presentations and explanations tend to have students who learn more and who rate their teachers more positively (Hines, Cruickshank, & Kennedy, 1982, 1985; Land, 1987). Teachers with more knowledge of the subject tend to be less vague in their explanations to the class. The less vague the teacher, the more the students learn (Land, 1987).

Planning for Clarity.   Recent research offers guidelines for greater clarity in teaching (Berliner, 1987; Evertson et al., 1994; Hines, Cruickshank, & Kennedy, 1982, 1985). When planning a lesson, try to anticipate the problems your students will have with the material. Turn to teachers' manuals and expe-

Effective teachers must know how to transform their knowledge into examples, explanations, illustrations, and activities.

rienced teachers for help with this. You might also do the written parts of the lesson yourself to identify potential problems. Have definitions ready for new terms, and prepare several relevant examples for concepts. Think of analogies that will make ideas easier to understand. Organize the lesson in a logical sequence; include checkpoints that incorporate oral or written questions or problems to make sure the students are following the explanations.

Plan a clear introduction to the lesson. Tell students what they will be learning and how they could approach it. Often teachers are vague about both the "what" and the "how." For example, in a study by Duffy, Roehler, Meloth, and Vavrus (1986), an ineffective reading teacher began her lesson on using context in reading by saying, "Today we are going to learn about context. This skill will help you in your reading" (p. 206). This is a vague and general statement of "what" the students will learn. An effective teacher in the same study began her lesson with an explicit, precise description:

> At the end of today's lesson, you will be able to use the other words in a sentence to figure out the meaning of an unknown word. The skill is one that you use when you come to a word that you don't know and you have to figure out what the word means. (p. 206)

Being precise about "how" to do the work is even harder. One study found that teachers seldom, if ever, explain the cognitive processes they want their students to practice in a seatwork activity. Bright students figure out the right process, but slower students often guess or give up. For example, an *ineffective* teacher might introduce a seatwork activity on words with prefixes by saying, "Here are some words with prefixes. Write the meaning of each in the blanks." An *effective* teacher, on the other hand, would demonstrate how to divide the words into a prefix and a root; how to determine the meaning of the root and the prefix; and how to put the two meanings together to make sense of the whole word (Berliner, 1987).

Clarity during the Lesson.

Make clear connections between facts or concepts by using **explanatory links** such as *because, if . . . then,* or *therefore.* For example, when a teacher says, "The Northern economy was based on manufacturing and the North had an advantage in the Civil War," students are given two facts, but no connection between them. If there is a relationship between the two ideas, it should be indicated with an explanatory link as in, "The North had an advantage in the Civil War *because* its economy was based on manufacturing." Explanatory links tie ideas together and make them easier to learn (Berliner, 1987). Explanatory links are also helpful in labeling visual material such as graphs, concept maps, or illustrations.

In general, stick with your plan and do not digress. Signal transitions from one major topic to another with phrases such as *"The next area . . . ,"* *"Now we will turn to . . . ,"* or *"The second step is . . . ."* You might help students follow the lesson by outlining topics, listing key points, or drawing concept maps on the board or on an overhead projector. Continually monitor the group to see if everyone is following the lesson. Look for confident nods or puzzled stares. You should be able to tell if most students are keeping up.

Throughout the lesson, choose words that are familiar to the students. Define new terms and relate them to what the students already know. Be precise. Avoid vague words and ambiguous phrases: steer clear of "the somes"—*something, someone, sometime, somehow;* "the not verys"—*not very much, not very*

Explanatory Links Words and phrases such as "because" and "in order to" that specify the relationships between ideas.

well, not very hard, not very often; and other unspecific fillers, such as *most, not all, sort of, and so on, of course, as you know, I guess, in fact, or whatever,* and *more or less.* Use specific (and, if possible, colorful) names instead of *it, them,* and *thing.* Also, refrain from using pet phrases such as *you know, like,* and *Okay?* Another idea is to record a lesson on tape to check yourself for clarity.

Warmth and Enthusiasm.   As you are well aware, some teachers are much more enthusiastic than others. Some studies have found that ratings of teachers' enthusiasm for their subject are correlated with student achievement gains (Rosenshine & Furst, 1973).Warmth, friendliness, and understanding seem to be the teacher traits most strongly related to student attitudes (Murray, 1983; Ryans, 1960; Soar & Soar, 1979). In other words, teachers who are warm and friendly tend to have students who like them and the class in general. But notice, these are correlational studies. The results do not tell us that teacher enthusiasm causes student learning or that warmth causes positive attitudes, only that the two variables tend to occur together. Teachers trained to demonstrate their enthusiasm have students who are more attentive and involved but not necessarily more successful on tests of content (Gillett & Gall, 1982).

The research we have looked at has identified teacher knowledge, clarity, organization, and enthusiasm as important characteristics of effective teachers. The Guidelines summarize the practical implications of this work for the classroom.

Guidelines

Teaching Effectively

Organize your lessons carefully.

Examples

1. Provide objectives that help students focus on the purpose of the lesson.
2. Begin lessons by writing a brief outline on the board, or work on an outline with the class as part of the lesson.
3. If possible, break the presentation into clear steps or stages.
4. Review periodically.

Strive for clear explanations.

Examples

1. Use concrete examples or analogies that relate to the students' own lives. Have several examples for particularly difficult points.
2. Give explanations at several levels so all students, not just the brightest, will understand.
3. Focus on one idea at a time and avoid digressions.

Communicate an enthusiasm for your subject and the day's lesson.

Examples

1. Tell students why the lesson is important. Have a better reason than "This will be on the test" or "You will need to know it next year." Emphasize the value of the learning itself.
2. Be sure to make eye contact with the students.
3. Vary your pace and volume in speaking. Use silence for emphasis.

Putting It All Together: The Effective Teacher

Much of the research that focused on effective teaching in the 1970s and 1980s pointed toward a model of teaching described in Chapter 9—**direct instruction** or **active teaching.** By examining the best research on effective teaching, Rosenshine and Stevens (1986) identified the six *Teaching Functions* described in Chapter 9 on page 336:

> (1) Review and check the previous day's work; (2) Present new material; (3) Provide guided practice; (4) Give feedback and correctives; (5) Provide independent practice; (6) Review weekly and monthly.

The successful teacher in this model protects learning time with effective class management; makes clear and organized presentations; maintains an academic, learning-is-serious-business focus; expertly uses reviews, learning probes, understanding checks, and guided practice; asks higher- and lower-level questions with plenty of wait time for student answers; and moves at a steady pace to cover key topics. Study after study has associated these teacher actions with student learning (Brophy & Good, 1986; Weinert & Helmke, 1995).

What aspects of direct instruction might explain its success? Linda Anderson (1989b) suggests that lessons that help students perceive links among main ideas will help them construct accurate understandings. Well-organized presentations, clear explanations, the use of explanatory links, and reviews can all help students perceive connections among ideas. If done well, therefore, a direct instruction lesson could be a resource that students use to construct understanding. For example, reviews activate prior knowledge so the student is ready to understand. Brief, clear presentations and guided practice avoid overloading the students' information processing systems and taxing their working memories. Numerous examples and explanations give many pathways and associations for building networks of concepts. Guided practice can also give the teacher a snapshot of the students' thinking and of their misconceptions, so these can be addressed directly as misconceptions rather than simply as "wrong answers."

What direct instruction cannot do is *ensure* that students understand. If badly done, it may encourage students to memorize and mimic but never to "own" the knowledge. To help students reach this goal, Eleanor Duckworth believes that teachers must pay very close attention to understanding their students' understandings (Meek, 1991).

Focus on...

Successful Teaching

- What methods have been used to study teaching?
- How can a teacher be clear during lesson presentations?
- What aspects of direct instruction help students process information more effectively?

Direct Instruction/Explicit Teaching Systematic instruction for mastery of basic skills, facts, and information.

Active Teaching Teaching characterized by high levels of teacher explanation, demonstration, and interaction with students.

Successful Understanding: Focus on the Student

Recently, rather than focus on what the *teacher* is doing, some researchers turned their attention to what the *students* were doing. Results of these studies indicated that many different approaches and activities can be effective—if the activities create environments in which students think deeply.

The New Zealand Studies

Graham Nuthall and Adrienne Alton-Lee (1990, 1992, 1993, 1995) in New Zealand have conducted a series of studies focusing on how and what students learn. The researchers take a long-term view, trying to pinpoint what helps students construct accurate understandings and remember them a year later. The design of the studies includes careful development of *pretests* and *posttests* based on the actual material being taught in the class; *records* of everything that happens in class; and in-depth *case studies* of selected students.

Some Findings:

1. Students learn very different things from the same lesson. The class average test score "is more likely to misrepresent rather than reflect the learning of an individual student" (1990, p. 555).

2. Quantity of *academic learning time* (the amount of time students spend engaged with challenging but understandable tasks) is closely related to learning.

3. Watching demonstrations and looking at visual illustrations seem to be powerful influences on the students and promote learning that is remembered.

4. Students' prior knowledge in a subject area, including erroneous knowledge, is particularly important in shaping what they learn. For example, students' misconceptions make a significant difference in what they will learn and remember. Sometimes students in the study "learned" a concept temporarily, but remembered their initial misconception *as fact* a year later.

Conditions for Learning from Teaching.

Nuthall and Alton-Lee (1990) are developing a theory of student learning based on these and other findings. They believe that three clusters of factors must come together for memorable learning to be strong and enduring.

1. The student must have *resources* to learn. These might include such personal, social, and technical resources as sufficient prior knowledge, support from home, materials and equipment, and relevant experiences.

2. The student must have many *opportunities* to learn. This means sufficient time spent with demonstrations, discussions, and projects; opportunities to clarify concepts; and challenges that will displace misconceptions.

3. The student must take *advantage of these resources and opportunities*. The student must pay attention, talk to the teachers and other students, and express an understanding of key concepts orally or in writing.

Nuthall and Alton-Lee (1993) have extended their theory by relating classroom events to the students' cognitive processes. As students are involved in activities about a topic, they store a representation of information about the topic in their working memories. These representations become connected and integrated with other related information in semantic memory—the propositions, images, schemas described in Chapter 7. Any representations that do not get connected are lost, but if enough representations are integrated and connected, then the ideas become established in long-term memory. Sometimes information is misinterpreted. For example, on the test given right after the unit was taught and again months later, in answer to the question, "Why was William

Caxton famous?" one student answered, "He led the Peasants' Revolt." Looking back at the class transcripts, the researchers found that during a discussion of the Peasants' Revolt, the teacher described changes in society that brought about the collapse of the feudal system. One change was the printing press—invented by William Caxton. So the student had connected Caxton with the Peasants' Revolt and later "remembered" (or reconstructed) that Caxton *led* the revolt. This construction was strong and lasting.

We must provide resources and opportunities for learning, *and* we must help students benefit from resources and take advantage of learning opportunities. To do so, we have to focus on both teaching and learning—on what teachers think and say and do and on what their students think and say and do.

Focus on...

Successful Learning: The Student

- What three factors encourage durable learning according to the findings of the New Zealand studies?
- Relate the findings of the New Zealand studies to cognitive and information-processing view of learning.
- Describe four learning functions and explain how a teacher or a learner can activate each function.

Learning Functions: The Effective Student

If we turn our attention to what the student is thinking and doing, we turn from a focus on teaching to a focus on learning. You may remember that Rosenshine and Stevens (1986) identified six *Teaching Functions* by examining the research on teaching. Similarly, Tom Shuell has identified a set of *Learning Functions* by examining the research on classroom learning. These learning functions—expectations, motivation, prior knowledge activation, attention, encoding, comparison, hypothesis generation, repetition, feedback, evaluation, monitoring, and integration—are listed in the far left column of Table 13.9. No matter what kind of teaching is happening, students must engage these learning functions if they are to learn. No attention—no learning, no feedback—no learning, and so on. The focus on learning functions unites teaching and learning, and highlights that many kinds of teaching can support learning. As Nuthall and Alton-Lee point out, students must *use* resources to learn, but either the teacher or the student can trigger or activate a learning function, as indicated in Table 13.9. So, students have to do the learning, but teachers can create situations that guide, support, stimulate, and encourage learning.

Integrations: Beyond Models to Outstanding Teaching

We have examined two ways of studying teaching, one that centers on the teacher and another that focuses on the student. You may hear debates about the merits of these general approaches in many of your education courses. Often the debate about directive versus student-centered approaches is loudest when the students in question are at risk of failing, as you can see in the Point/ Counterpoint on page 510.

Matching Methods to Learning Goals

Penelope Peterson (1979) compared the more traditional teacher-centered direct instruction with more open, constructivist methods. She concluded that teacher-centered instruction leads to better performance on achievement tests; while the

TABLE 13.9 Learning Functions		

The learning functions listed in the far left column can be initiated by the teacher or by the student. The important thing is the function be engaged.

Function	Teacher Initiated	Learner Initiated
Expectations	Specify goal/purpose of lesson; provide overview of the material to be studied, etc.	Identify the purpose for doing an assigned project or homework, reading a chapter, etc.
Motivation	Provide opportunities for student inter-action; use interesting material	Look for ways to make material, lesson, or project personally relevant
Prior knowledge activation	Remind students of prerequisite infor-mation, relevant information in previ-ous lessons, etc.	Ask self what is already known about the topic and what information is needed to complete the assignment
Attention	Highlight important information and/or characteristics; use verbal emphasis	Identify key features of material being studied; underline key information; take notes
Encoding	Provide diagrams and/or multiple exam-ples/contexts; suggest mnemonics, etc.	Generate mnemonics, images, and/or multiple examples in multiple contexts
Comparison	Encourage comparison through the use of questions, diagrams, or charts	Look for similarities; draw diagrams or charts that compare the material being studied
Hypothesis generation	Ask "What if?" questions; encourage students to think of alternative courses of action	Generate possible alternatives and corres-ponding solutions
Repetition	Guide practice and/or reflection; multiple perspectives and/or examples	Systematically review and reflect on the material being studied
Feedback	Provide instructionally relevant feedback and correctives	Seek answers and/or reactions to self-posed questions
Evaluation	Encourage students to evaluate their performance and point of view on the basis of the feedback received	Ask "What do I currently know about what I am studying?" "What do I need to know and/or find out?"
Monitoring	Check for understanding	Monitor performance; self-testing
Combination, integration, synthesis	Suggest ways of combining and inte-grating information (e.g., by con-structing diagrams, graphs, etc.)	Establish categories; construct tables; seek higher order relationships

Source: Based on "The Role of the Student in Learning from Instruction" by T. J. Shuell (1988), *Contemporary Educational Psychology*, 13, pp. 276–295 and "Designing Instructional Computing Systems for Meaningful Learning" by T. J. Shuell (1992) in M. Jones and P. Winne (Eds.), *Adaptive Learning Environments: Foundations and Frontiers* (pp. 19–54), Springer. Adapted by permission. (This combined version was used in T. Shuell, "Teaching and Learning in a Classroom Context." In D. Berliner and R. Calfee (Eds.), *Handbook of Educational Psychology*, 1996, Macmillan).

open, informal methods like discovery learning or inquiry approaches are as-sociated with better performance on tests of creativity, abstract thinking, and problem solving. In addition, the open methods are better for improving attitudes toward school and for stimulating curiosity, cooperation among students, and lower absence rates (Walberg, 1990). According to these conclusions, when the goals of teaching involve problem solving, creativity, understanding, and master-ing processes, many approaches besides direct instruction should be effective.

POINT · COUNTERPOINT

What Is the Best Way to Help Students at Risk of Failing?

There are many ideas and models for teaching low-achieving students—students often referred to as "at risk" for failure. Some recommendations are based on direct instruction and basic skills teaching. Another approach bases its recommendations on cognitive theories of learning, and these recommendations question the value of direct instruction. What are the teaching strategies offered by each approach?

POINT Adapt direct instruction for students' needs.

Research on effective teachers of low achievers (Ebmeier & Ziomek, 1982; Emmer et al., 1997; Slavin, Karweit, & Madden, 1989) has identified these approaches as helpful:

> Break instruction into small steps and provide short activities, chosen and sequenced by the teacher.
>
> Cover material thoroughly and at a moderate pace. Give plenty of practice, immediate clear feedback, and specific praise.
>
> Have students work as a whole class or in groups so the teacher can supervise. Avoid individualized, self-paced, or independent work.
>
> Keep a level of difficulty that guarantees high rates of success.

> Ask convergent questions—one correct answer.
>
> Make sure to call on everyone and stay with a student until a question is answered.
>
> Avoid interruptions, open-ended questions, and nonacademic conversations.
>
> Emphasize short, frequent paper-and-pencil exercises, not games, arts, crafts, discovery learning activities, and interest centers. These are less helpful for learning.

COUNTERPOINT Move beyond the basics.

Educators and psychologists who hold a cognitive view of learning are critical of direct instruction. For example, Barbara Means and Michael Knapp (1991) decry the "basics" approach to teaching low achievers:

> A recent summary of critiques of conventional approaches to teaching academic skills to at-risk students, offered by a group of national experts in reading, writing, and mathematics education, concluded that such approaches tend to:
>
> > underestimate what students are capable of doing;
> >
> > postpone more challenging and interesting work for too long—in some cases, forever;

and deprive students of a meaningful or motivating context for learning or for employing the skills that are taught. (pp. 283–284)

What do critics of direct instruction offer in its place? The following are some principles recommended by Means and Knapp (1991):

> Focus on complex, meaningful problems. Keep the level of tasks high enough that the purpose of the task is apparent and makes sense to students.
>
> Embed basic skills instruction in the context of more global tasks such as class record keeping or letter writing.
>
> Make connections with students' out-of-school experience and culture.
>
> Model powerful thinking strategies for students; for example, think aloud as you try to figure out a difficult text passage.
>
> Encourage multiple approaches to academic tasks. Have students describe how they reached their answers.
>
> Provide scaffolding to enable students to accomplish complex tasks; for example, perform the calculations for students as they set up an algebra problem correctly.
>
> Make dialogue the central medium for teaching and learning. Reciprocal teaching is one example. (See Chapter 9.)

These guidelines are in keeping with Tom Good's conclusion that teaching should become less direct as students mature and when the goals involve affective development and problem solving or critical thinking (Good, 1983a). Of course, every subject, even college English or chemistry, can require some direct

Learning of complex subject matter in schools is most effective when it is an intentional process of constructing meaning from information and experience. Successful learners are goal-directed, self-regulating, persistent, and assume personal responsibility for their own learning.

instruction. If you are teaching when to use "who" and "whom," or how to set up laboratory apparatus, direct instruction may be the best approach. Noddings (1990) reminds teachers that students may need some direct instruction in how to use various manipulative materials to get the possible benefits from them. Students working in cooperative groups may need guidance, modeling, and practice in how to ask questions and give explanations. And to solve difficult problems, students may need some direct instruction in possible problem-solving strategies. The message for teachers is to match instructional methods to learning goals.

As a summary of this chapter on teaching for learning, let's consider 14 principles identified by an American Psychological Association task force. These 14 principles integrate ideas from the chapters on development, individual differences, and motivation and learning, and serve as guide to plan teaching that supports student learning.

APA's Learner-Centered Psychological Principles

In December of 1995, the American Psychological Association's Board of Educational Affairs circulated a draft of its *Learner-Centered Psychological Principles: A Framework for School Redesign and Reform.* (Revision prepared by a Work Group of the American Psychological Association's Board of Educational Affairs [BEA], 1995). The document was met with both praise and criticism. In fact, discussions and debate continue even as I write this paragraph. The authors of the document plan to continue revisions, but this draft is a concise statement from advocates of student-centered learning and motivation. The principles are:

Principle 1: The nature of the learning process. There are different types of learning—from learning habits in motor skills, to generating knowledge, to learning cognitive skills and strategies. Learning of complex subject matter in schools is most effective when it is an intentional process of constructing meaning from information and experience. Successful learners are active, goal-directed, self-regulating, persistent, and assume personal responsibility for contributing to their own learning.

Principle 2: Goals of the learning process. The successful learner, over time and with support and guidance, can create meaningful, coherent representations of knowledge. To learn, students must have a goal. To construct useful knowledge and acquire learning strategies for life-long learning, students need to pursue personally relevant goals. Teachers can help students set short- and long-term goals that are both personally meaningful and educationally sound.

Principle 3: The construction of knowledge. The successful learner can link new information with existing knowledge in meaningful ways. Because each student has different experiences and because the mind works to link information meaningfully, each student will organize information in a way that is unique. Teachers can help students develop shared understandings about important knowledge and skills. However, unless new knowledge becomes integrated with the learner's prior understandings, the new knowledge remains isolated and difficult to apply to new situations.

Principle 4: Strategic thinking. The successful learner can create and use a range of thinking and reasoning skills to achieve complex learning goals. Successful learners use strategic thinking in learning, reasoning, problem solving, and concept learning. They can use a variety of strategies and continue to expand their repertoire by reflecting on and changing their current strategies, observing others, and benefiting from instruction.

Principle 5: Thinking about thinking. Higher-order strategies for "thinking about thinking and learning"—for overseeing and monitoring mental operations—facilitate creative and critical thinking and the development of expertise. Successful learners can reflect on how they learn, set reasonable goals, select appropriate strategies, monitor progress toward goals, and change strategies when necessary. These abilities can be developed through instruction.

Principle 6: Context of learning. Learning is influenced by environmental factors, including culture, technology, and instruction. Teachers play major interactive roles with both learners and the learning environment. Instruction must fit the students' level or prior knowledge, cognitive abilities, and ways of thinking. The nurturing qualities of the classroom environment are particularly influential in student learning.

Principle 7: Motivational and emotional influences on learning. The depth and breadth of information processed, and what and how much is learned and remembered, are influenced by (a) self-awareness and beliefs about personal control, competence, and ability; (b) clarity and saliency of personal values, interests, and goals; (c) personal expectations for success or failure; (d) affect, emotion, and general states of mind; and (e) the resulting motivation to learn. The inner world of beliefs, goals, and expectations can enhance or interfere with learning. Intense negative cognitions and emotions (e.g., feeling insecure, worrying about failure, being self-conscious or shy, and fearing punishment, ridicule, or stigmatizing labels) thwart complex learning.

Principle 8: Intrinsic motivation to learn. Intrinsic motivation, creativity, and higher-order thinking are stimulated by relevant, authentic learning tasks of optimal difficulty and novelty for each student. Students need opportunities to make choices about learning in line with their personal interests. Students are more likely to be creative and think deeply about projects that are as complex as real-world situations.

Principle 9: Effects of motivation on effort. Learning complex skills and knowledge requires extended effort, persistence, and practice (with guidance and feedback). Learning of complex subject matter requires considerable investments of time and energy. Unless students are motivated to learn, they are unlikely to expend the needed effort without being coerced.

Principle 10: Developmental constraints and opportunities. Individuals progress through stages of physical, intellectual, emotional, and social development that are a function of unique genetic and environmental factors. Students learn best when materials are developmentally appropriate. Overemphasis on one kind of developmental readiness—such as reading readiness, for example—may interfere with development in other areas.

Principle 11: Social influences on learning. Learning is influenced by social interactions and communication with others. Learning can be enhanced when students have the opportunity to interact and collaborate with others on instructional tasks. Learning situations that allow for and respect diversity encourage flexible thinking, social competence, and moral development. Learning and self-esteem are heightened when individuals are in respected and caring relationships with others who see their potential, appreciate their unique talents, and accept them as individuals. Self-esteem and learning are mutually reinforcing.

Principle 12: Individual differences in learning. Individuals have different capabilities. These differences are a function of environment (what is learned and communicated in different cultures or other social groups) and heredity (what occurs naturally as a function of the genes). Through learning and social acculturation, learners have acquired preferences for how and at what pace they like to learn. But these preferences are not always useful in helping learners reach their goals. Teachers need to help students examine their learning preferences and expand or modify them if necessary, while respecting individual differences.

Principle 13: Learning and diversity. Learning is most effective when differences in learners' linguistic, cultural, and social behaviors are taken into account. Although basic principles of learning, motivation, and effective instruction may apply to all learners, language, ethnic group, race, beliefs, and socioeconomic status all can influence learning. When learners see that their individual differences in abilities, background, and cultures are valued and respected, then motivation is enhanced and learning supported.

Principle 14: Standards and assessment. Setting appropriately high and challenging standards and assessing both the learner and the learning process are integral parts of successful learning. Assessment provides important information to both the learner and the teacher at all stages of the learning process. Ongoing assessment can provide feedback of progress toward goals. Stan-

---

Focus on...

Integrations

- What learning goals match more direct instruction?
- What learning goals match more student-centered instruction?
- Relate the APA Learner-Centered psychological principles to self-regulated learning.

dardized, performance, and self-assessments—used appropriately—can guide instructional planning, support motivation, and provide necessary corrections to guide learning.

Teaching based on these learner-centered principles would make sure that students are active in solving problems, practicing learning strategies, making choices, and discovering important ideas.

SUMMARY

The First Step: Planning

Planning on several different levels is an important step in teaching. The plan determines how time and materials will be turned into activities for students. There is no single model of planning, but all plans should allow for flexibility. Bloom and others have developed taxonomies categorizing basic objectives in the cognitive, affective, and psychomotor domains. A taxonomy encourages systematic thinking about relevant objectives and ways to evaluate them.

In teacher-centered approaches, teachers select learning objectives and plan how to get students to meet those objectives. Teachers control the "what" and "how" of learning. In contrast, planning is shared and negotiated in student-centered, or constructivist, approaches. The teacher and students together make decisions about content, activities, and approaches. Rather than having specific student behaviors as objectives, the teacher has overarching goals or "big ideas" that guide planning. Integrated content and teaching with themes are often part of the planning. Assessment of learning is ongoing and mutually shared by teacher and students.

Teaching: Whole Group and Directive

The teaching format for putting objectives into action should be suited to the objectives. Lecturing is efficient for communicating a large amount of new material to a large group. There are three basic phases a lecture should follow: preparation of students; presentation of content; and review of content. However, lecturing may keep students too passive and ignore individual learning rates. The younger the student, the shorter the presentation should be. Recitation can involve various types of questions, and should fit students' abilities and motivation levels. Convergent questions have only one right answer. Divergent questions have many possible answers. Teacher responses to answers should not be too hasty in most cases and should provide appropriate feedback. Homework and seatwork should be extensions of class lessons, not busywork.

Teaching: Small Group and Student-Centered

Constructivist teaching practices include group discussion, humanistic education, and computers and hypermedia. These methods make minimal use of rote memorization and expose students to a variety of learning approaches. They strive instead to encourage in students an excitement about learning, a thrill in discovering how the world works.

Successful Teaching: Focus on the Teacher

For years, researchers have tried to unravel the mystery of effective teaching. Researchers have used a variety of methods including classroom observation, case studies, interviews, experimentation with different methods, and other approaches to study teaching in real classrooms. Results of research on teacher characteristics indicate that thorough and expert knowledge of a subject, organization and clarity in presentation, and enthusiasm all play important parts in effective teaching. But no one way of teaching has been found to be right for each class, lesson, or day.

Successful Understanding: Focus on the Student

Many researchers studying teaching today have turned their attention from a focus on teachers' behavior to an examination of student learning. Educators now see their main task to be helping their students become effective, motivated learners. Students must have adequate resources for learning and opportunities to use those resources, and must take advantage of learning opportunities.

Integrations: Beyond Models to Outstanding Teaching

Many educators feel that the careful use of direct instruction methods—well-organized presentations, clear explanations, carefully delivered prompts, and guided discovery—can be a resource for students as they construct understanding. In all cases, teaching methods should match learning. The American Psychological Association is drafting a set of principles designed to define and promote student-centered learning practices. Teaching based on these principles would ensure that students are active in solving problems, practicing learning strategies, making choices, and discovering important ideas.

KEY TERMS

active teaching, p. 506
affective domain, p. 482
anchored instruction, p. 502
cognitive domain, p. 482
computer simulations, p. 500
constructivist approach, p. 484
convergent questions, p. 491

direct instruction, p. 506
divergent questions, p. 491
explanatory links, p. 504
group discussion, p. 496
humanistic view, p. 498
lecturing, p. 488
microworlds, p. 500

psychomotor domain, p. 483
recitation, p. 489
scripted cooperation, p. 489
seatwork, p. 492
taxonomy, p. 481

CHECK YOUR UNDERSTANDING

Can you apply the ideas from this chapter on teaching to solve the following problems of practice?

Preschool and Kindergarten

- You have a very well-supplied science corner in your class, but your students seldom visit it. When they do, they don't seem to take advantage of the learning possibilities available with the manipulatives. How would you help students benefit from the materials?

Elementary and Middle School

- Your cooperating teacher wants a full lesson plan for each subject. What would you include in the plan to make it useful for you?
- You are given a math workbook and text series and told that you must use these materials as the basis for your math teaching. What would you do to incorporate these materials into lessons that help students understand mathematical thinking and problem solving?

Junior High and High School

- You have been assigned a "developmental" class—25 students who are several years behind their peers. How would you help them become better learners?
- Identify three instructional objectives for a lesson in your subject to be used in a mixed-ability tenth-grade class. How would you make these learning objectives clear to your students?

Cooperative Learning Activity

- With four or five other members of your educational psychology class, plan a unit. Include objectives, lesson formats, and room arrangements.

What Would They Do?

You have finally landed a job teaching English and writing in a high school. Over the summer, you plan your World Literature course. The first day of class, you discover that a number of your students have limited English proficiencies. You make a mental note to meet with them to determine how much and what kind of reading they can handle. To get a sense of the class's interest, you ask them to write a "review" of the last book they read.

That night you look over the "book reviews." If the paragraphs are any indication, these students can't put four sentences together and stay on the same topic. In stark contrast are the papers of three students—they are a pleasure to read, and worthy of publication in the school literary magazine (if there were one), and reflect a fairly sophisticated understanding of some good literature.

JEFF D. HORTON

Seventh–Tenth Grade Teacher
Colton School, Colton, Washington

This teacher may have set himself or herself up for problems from the start by assuming that all the students would be at the same learning level. Since this is clearly not the case, the course was delivered to a narrow range of students, and the majority are probably frustrated. The teacher needs to take another approach, though perhaps not abandon his or her original goals.

It appears that most of the students need some form of reteaching of the skills this teacher feels are necessary to complete the original plans. The teacher must determine which skills and knowledge are necessary for the students to successfully complete the course, and then assess the students in those areas. Once this is completed the teacher can develop several units that address those needs. This may take several days, but it is not wasted time. It will make life for all much easier in the long run.

Another problem may be the materials that the teacher planned to use. I do believe that students need to be introduced to the "classics" in literature. However, teachers are self-motivated to read and study these writings. We must remember that most students do not feel the same way. The teacher in this scenario must present the "classics" in a way that will hold the students' interest. Instead of reading a whole book, pick out parts that reflect the writing style or message of the author. Then present other parts of the book using other teaching tools. There are movies available that are presented in a more current style that will appeal to students. Whatever the teaching tool used, there must always be a learning activity connected to it.

Having students that excel in a subject is always rewarding to a teacher. It makes us feel that we have accomplished what we are setting out to do. These three students can help a teacher convey the skills and knowledge to the rest of the class. They should be required to complete all the assignments and activities along with the class. However, they will do this quickly while others struggle. The teacher should try and use them to help in conveying the material to the other students. Students that are finding the work easy could be used to help others by reviewing their work and offering suggestions on how to improve it. They could also offer the teacher some suggestions as to how to make the material more interesting to the rest of the class.

MICHAEL J. ELLIS

Tenth and Eleventh Grade English Teacher
Quincy High School, Quincy, Massachusetts

The problem here is one of mistaken assumption. The teacher has anticipated a certain level of ability and a certain degree of past knowledge, both of which seem to be abundantly lacking in this case. Obviously, the students are unfamiliar with the review as a literary form. Starting tomorrow, I'd begin teaching that. The first thing the students need to see is a well-written review, something they can begin to pattern their own responses on. Fortunately, I have three excellent examples already in hand, passed in by my own students. In the next class, I would have those three students read their reviews aloud and I'd pass out copies of them to the class. A discussion of what made those three papers so good would not only be instructive to the group, but would also positively reinforce the work done by those three students.

It seems the purpose behind the curriculum for this class is to expose the students to a wide array of great literature. That is a noble goal. In teaching, however, nobility must frequently give way to practicality. A teacher's first duty is to guide his students in the acquisition of necessary skills. Sometimes having them read Dickens isn't the best way to do that. The curriculum worked up over the summer will probably work well with the three standouts in the class. I'd try splintering them off from the rest. This can be a logistical nightmare and it effectively doubles your prep time for the class, but it's the best way to be sure that the students of a particular ability level don't stagnate while you cater to another group.

With the rest of the class, it's time to shift on the fly and ditch the original reading list. Emphasizing longer novels in a class dominated by poor readers is nothing less than a suicide attempt spread over 40 weeks. If you rely instead on shorter selections and young adult fiction titles with catchy plot lines, then you've at least given yourself a fighting chance at a class that actually finishes the books. It's also never a bad idea to throw video material into the mix. My first year of teaching I showed an episode of the *Mighty Morphin Power Rangers* to two classes of tenth graders, knowing they'd despise it. Kids can always write more effectively on things they hate than on things they like. The reviews they passed in were, from a technical standpoint, the best paragraphs most of them had ever written. That assignment really helped to etch the proper paragraph format in a lot of their minds. You can never allow yourself to forget that it's the skill itself, and not the means you use to convey it, that is ultimately most important.

14

Standardized Testing

Overview | *What Would You Do?*

MEASUREMENT AND EVALUATION   **520**
   Norm-Referenced Tests | Criterion-Referenced Tests

WHAT DO TEST SCORES MEAN?   **523**
   Basic Concepts | Types of Scores | Interpreting Test Scores

TYPES OF STANDARDIZED TESTS   **532**
   Achievement Tests: What Has the Student Learned? | Diagnostic
   Tests: What Are the Student's Strengths and Weaknesses? | Aptitude
   Tests: How Well Will the Student Do in the Future?

ISSUES IN STANDARDIZED TESTING   **539**
   The Uses of Testing in American Society | Advantages in Taking
   Tests—Fair and Unfair

NEW DIRECTIONS IN STANDARDIZED TESTING   **547**
   Assessing Learning Potential | Authentic Assessment

Summary | *Key Terms* | *Check Your Understanding* |
Teachers' Casebook: What Would They Do?

*H**ow has standardized testing affected your life so far? What opportunities have opened or closed to you based on test scores? Was the process fair? Propose a better way to make these decisions.*

Would it surprise you to learn that published tests, such as the college entrance exams and IQ tests, are creations of the 20th century? In the 19th and early 20th centuries, college entrance was generally based on grades, essays, and interviews. From your own experience, you know that testing has come a long way since then—too far say some critics. They want to reshape testing as a way of reshaping the curriculum and reforming education. We will explore these new ideas.

In spite of the criticisms, schools still use many standardized tests, so teachers must be knowledgeable about testing. This chapter focuses on preparing for and interpreting standardized tests. Understanding how standardized test scores are determined, what they really mean, and how they can be used (or misused) provides you a framework for ensuring that the tests you give are appropriate.

First, we consider testing in general, including the various methods of interpreting test scores. Then we look at the different kinds of standardized tests used in schools. Finally, we examine the criticisms of testing and the alternatives being proposed. By the time you have completed this chapter, you should be able to do the following:

- Calculate mean, median, mode, and standard deviation.
- Define percentile ranks, standard deviations, *z* scores, *T* scores, and stanine scores.
- Explain how to improve reliability and validity in testing.
- Interpret the results of achievement, aptitude, and diagnostic tests in a realistic manner.
- Take a position on the testing issue and defend your position.
- Describe how to prepare students (and yourself) for taking standardized tests.
- Explain the strengths and weaknesses of alternative forms of assessment such as portfolios.

What Would You Do?

It is nearing the end of school and the ninth grade achievement test results are finally in. The parents' report form went home last Friday, and Monday morning you get a call from the principal during your planning period. The parents of one of your math students are in the office and have asked to speak with you and the principal immediately. The father is a prominent businessman and the mother is a lawyer. Their daughter received a grade-equivalent score of 11.8 on her standardized math test. The girl has been making Bs and Cs in your class—she seldom completes homework and has trouble with your conceptual approach to math. She just wants to know the "steps" to solve the problems so she can finish. You have tried several times to get the parents to come in to talk about ways to support the girl's learning, but they never seem to have had the time—until today.

You smile as you enter the principals' office, but the parents are not smiling. As soon as you sit down, the father says, "Well, you can see from our daughter's scores that you have been totally wrong in the grades you have given her this year. We thought she was just weak in math, but now it is clear you have something against her! Or maybe you just don't know how to teach math to bright girls."

The mother chimes in, "Yes, we expect you to reconsider her final grades for the year in light of her obvious ability. In fact," she glances at the principal and then glares at you again, "we believe she should get credit for the tenth grade class you teach as well, because she obviously knows the material already."

- What would you say to the parents?

- What do you need to know about tests to deal with this situation?

- How will you approach working with this student?

- How will these issues affect the grade levels you will teach?

Measurement and Evaluation

All teaching involves **evaluation.** At the heart of evaluation is judgment, making decisions based on values. In the process of evaluation, we compare information to criteria and then make judgments. Teachers must make all kinds of judgments. "Should we use a different text this year?" "Is the film appropriate for my students?" "Will Sarah do better if she repeats the first grade?" "Should Terry get a B – or a C+ on the project?"

Measurement is evaluation put in quantitative terms—the numeric description of an event or characteristic. Measurement tells how much, how often, or how well by providing scores, ranks, or ratings. Instead of saying, "Sarah doesn't seem to understand addition," a teacher might say, "Sarah answered only 2 of the 15 problems correctly in her addition homework." Measurement also allows a teacher to compare one student's performance on one particular task with a standard or with the performances of the other students.

Not all the evaluative decisions made by teachers involve measurement. Some decisions are based on information that is difficult to express numerically:

Evaluation Decision making about student performance and about appropriate teaching strategies.

Measurement An evaluation expressed in quantitative (numerical) terms.

student preferences, information from parents, previous experiences, even intuition. But measurement does play a large role in many classroom decisions, and properly done, it can provide unbiased data for evaluations.

The answers given on any type of test have no meaning by themselves; we must make some kind of comparison to interpret test results. There are two basic types of comparison: In the first, a test score is compared to the scores obtained by other people who have taken the same test. (This is called a norm-referenced comparison.) The second type is criterion-referenced. Here, the comparison is to a fixed standard or minimum passing score.

Norm-Referenced Tests

In **norm-referenced testing,** the people who have taken the test provide the *norms* for determining the meaning of a given individual's score. You can think of a norm as being the typical level of performance for a particular group. By comparing the individual's raw score (the actual number correct) to the norm, we can determine if the score is above, below, or around the average for that group.

There are at least three types of **norm groups** (comparison groups) in education. One frequently used norm group is the class or school itself. Norm groups may also be drawn from wider areas. Sometimes, for example, school districts develop achievement tests. When students take this kind of test, their scores are compared to the scores of all other students at their grade level throughout the district. Finally, some tests have national norm groups. When students take the college entrance exam, their scores are compared with the scores of students all over the country.

Norm-referenced tests cover a wide range of general objectives rather than assessing a limited number of specific objectives. Norm-referenced tests are especially useful in measuring the overall achievement of students who have come to understand complex material by different routes. Norm-referenced tests are also appropriate when only the top few candidates can be admitted to a program.

However, norm-referenced measurement has its limitations. The results of a norm-referenced test do not tell you whether students are ready to move on to more advanced material. For instance, knowing that a student is in the top 3% of the class on a test of algebraic concepts will not tell you if he or she is ready to move on to trigonometry; everyone in the class may have a limited understanding of the algebraic concepts.

Nor are norm-referenced tests particularly appropriate for measuring affective and psychomotor objectives. To measure individuals' psychomotor learning, you need a clear description of standards. (Even the best gymnast in school performs certain exercises better than others and needs specific guidance about how to improve.) In the affective area, attitudes and values are personal; comparisons among individuals are not really appropriate. For example, how could we measure an "average" level of political values or opinions? Finally, norm-referenced tests tend to encourage competition and comparison of scores. Some students compete to be the best. Others, realizing that being the best is impossible, may compete to be the worst. Either goal has its casualties.

Criterion-Referenced Tests

When test scores are compared, not to those of others, but to a given criterion or standard of performance, this is **criterion-referenced testing.** To decide who

Norm-Referenced Testing Testing in which scores are compared with the average performance of others.

Norm Group A group whose average score serves as a standard for evaluating any student's score on a test.

Criterion-Referenced Testing Testing in which scores are compared to a set performance standard.

should be allowed to drive a car, it is important to determine just what standard of performance is appropriate for selecting safe drivers. It does not matter how your test results compare to the results of others. If your performance on the test was in the top 10% but you consistently ran through red lights, you would not be a good candidate for receiving a license, even though your score was high.

Criterion-referenced tests measure the mastery of very specific objectives. The results of a criterion-referenced test should tell the teacher exactly what the students can and cannot do, at least under certain conditions. For example, a criterion-referenced test would be useful in measuring the ability to add three-digit numbers. A test could be designed with 20 different problems, and the standard for mastery could be set at 17 correct out of 20. (The standard is often somewhat arbitrary and may be based on such things as the teacher's experience.) If two students receive scores of 7 and 11, it does not matter that one student did better than the other since neither met the standard of 17. Both need more help with addition.

In teaching basic skills there are many instances where comparison to a preset standard is more important than comparison to the performance of others. It is not very comforting to know, as a parent, that your child is better in reading than most of the students in class if none of the students is able to read material suited for their grade level. Sometimes standards for meeting the criterion must be set at 100% correct. You would not like to have your appendix removed by a surgeon who left surgical instruments inside the body *only* 10% of the time.

But criterion-referenced tests are not appropriate for every situation. Many subjects cannot be broken down into a set of specific objectives. Moreover, although standards are important in criterion-referenced testing, they can often be arbitrary, as you have already seen. When deciding whether a student has mastered the addition of three-digit numbers comes down to the difference between 16 or 17 correct answers, it seems difficult to justify one particular standard over another. Finally, at times it is valuable to know how the students in your class compare to other students at their grade level both locally and nationally. Table 14.1 offers a comparison of norm-referenced and criterion-referenced tests.

Focus on...

Measurement and Evaluation

- What is the difference between measurement and evaluation?
- What examples of criterion-referenced and norm-referenced tests have you experienced in the past year?
- The doctor tells you that your cholesterol level is above average. What would you like to know about the norm group?
- Would you prefer a criterion-referenced or norm-referenced measure of your blood pressure? Why?

TABLE 14.1   Deciding on the Type of Test to Use

Norm-referenced tests may work best when you are
- Measuring general ability in certain areas, such as English, algebra, general science, or American history.
- Assessing the range of abilities in a large group.
- Selecting top candidates when only a few openings are available.

Criterion-referenced tests may work best when you are
- Measuring mastery of basic skills.
- Determining if students have prerequisites to start a new unit.
- Assessing affective and psychomotor objectives.
- Grouping students for instruction.

You can see that each type of test is well suited for certain situations, but each also has its limitations.

What Do Test Scores Mean?

On the average, more than 1 million standardized tests are given per school day in classes throughout this country (Lyman, 1986). Most of these are norm-referenced standardized tests. **Standardized tests** are those official-looking pamphlets and piles of forms purchased by school systems and administered to students. More specifically, the tests are called standardized because "the same directions are used for administering them in all classrooms and standard procedures are used for scoring and interpreting them" (Carey, 1994, p. 443). The tests are meant to be given under carefully controlled conditions so that students all over the country undergo the same experience. Standard methods of developing items, administering the test, scoring it, and reporting the scores are all implied by the term *standardized test*.

Basic Concepts

In standardized testing the test items and instructions have been tried out to make sure they work and then rewritten and retested as necessary. The final version of the test is administered to a **norming sample,** a large sample of subjects as similar as possible to the students who will be taking the test in school systems throughout the country. This norming sample serves as a comparison group for all students who take the test.

The test publishers provide one or more ways of comparing each student's raw score (number of correct answers) with the norming sample. Let's look at some of the measurements on which comparisons and interpretations are based.

Frequency Distributions. A **frequency distribution** is simply a listing of the number of people who obtain each score or fall into each range of scores on a test or other measurement procedure. For example, on a spelling test 19 students made these scores: 100, 95, 90, 85, 85, 85, 80, 75, 75, 75, 70, 65, 60, 60, 55, 50, 50, 45, 40. A graph, in this case a **histogram** (bar graph), of the spelling test scores is shown in Figure 14.1 on page 524, where one axis (the x, or horizontal, axis) indicates the possible scores and the other axis (the y, or vertical, axis) indicates the number of subjects who attained each score. As you can see, one student made a score of 100, three made 85, and so on.

Measurements of Central Tendency and Standard Deviation. You have probably had a great deal of experience with means. A **mean** is simply the arithmetical average of a group of scores. To calculate the mean, you add the scores and divide the total by the number of scores in the distribution. For example, the total of the 19 spelling scores is 1,340, so the mean is 1,340/19, or 70.53. The mean offers one way of measuring **central tendency,** the score that is typical or representative of the whole distribution of scores.

Two other measures of central tendency are the median and the mode. The **median** is the middle score in the distribution, the point at which half the scores are larger and half are smaller. The median of the 19 scores is 75. Nine scores

Standardized Tests Tests given, usually nationwide, under uniform conditions and scored according to uniform procedures.

Norming Sample Large sample of students serving as a comparison group for scoring standardized tests.

Frequency Distribution Record showing how many scores fall into set groups.

Histogram Bar graph of a frequency distribution.

Mean Arithmetical average.

Central Tendency Typical score for a group of scores.

Median Middle score in a group of scores.

FIGURE 14.1

Histogram of a Frequency Distribution

This bar graph or histogram shows the number of people who earned each score on a test. You can quickly see, for example, that three people earned a 75 and three people earned an 85.

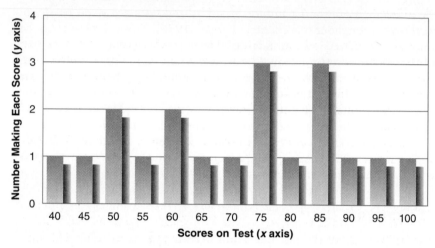

in the distribution are greater than or equal to 75, and nine are less. The **mode** is the score that occurs most often. The distribution in Figure 14.1 actually has two modes, 75 and 85, because each of these scores occurred three times. This makes it a **bimodal distribution.**

The measure of central tendency gives a score that is representative of the group of scores, but it does not tell you anything about how the scores are distributed. Two groups of scores may both have a mean of 50 but be alike in no other way. One group might contain the scores 50, 45, 55, 55, 45, 50, 50; the other group might contain the scores 100, 0, 50, 90, 10, 50, 50. In both cases the mean, median, and mode are all 50, but the distributions are quite different.

The **standard deviation** is a measure of how widely the scores vary from the mean. The larger the standard deviation, the more spread out the scores in the distribution. The smaller the standard deviation, the more the scores are clustered around the mean. For example, in the distribution 50, 45, 55, 55, 45, 50, 50, the standard deviation is much smaller than in the distribution 100, 0, 50, 90, 10, 50, 50. Another way of saying this is that distributions with very small standard deviations have less **variability** in the scores.

The standard deviation is relatively easy to calculate if you remember your high school math. It does take time, however. The process is similar to taking an average, but you use square roots. To calculate the standard deviation, you follow these steps:

1. Calculate the mean (written as $\overline{\chi}$) of the scores.

2. Subtract the mean from each of the scores. This is written as $(\chi - \overline{\chi})$.

3. Square each difference (multiply each difference by itself). This is written $(\chi - \overline{\chi})^2$.

Mode Most frequently occurring score.

Bimodal Distribution Frequency distribution with two modes.

Standard Deviation Measure of how widely scores vary from the mean.

Variability Degree of difference or deviation from the mean.

4. Add all the squared differences. This is written $\Sigma(\chi - \overline{\chi})^2$.

5. Divide this total by the number of scores. This is written $\dfrac{\Sigma(\chi - \overline{\chi})^2}{N}$.

6. Find the square root. This is written $\sqrt{\dfrac{\Sigma(\chi - \overline{\chi})^2}{N}}$, which is the formula for calculating the standard deviation.

Knowing the mean and the standard deviation of a group of scores gives you a better picture of the meaning of an individual score. For example, suppose you received a score of 78 on a test. You would be very pleased with the score if the mean of the test were 70 and the standard deviation were 4. In this case, your score would be 2 standard deviations above the mean, a score well above average.

Consider the difference if the mean of the test had remained at 70 but the standard deviation had been 20. In the second case, your score of 78 would be less than 1 standard deviation from the mean. You would be much closer to the middle of the group, with a score above average, but not high. Knowing the standard deviation tells you much more than simply knowing the **range** of scores. No matter how the majority scored on the tests, one or two students may do very well or very poorly and thus make the range very large.

The Normal Distribution.   Standard deviations are very useful in understanding test results. They are especially helpful if the results of the tests form a normal distribution. You may have met the **normal distribution** before. It is the bell-shaped curve, the most famous frequency distribution because it describes many naturally occurring physical and social phenomena. Many scores fall in the middle, giving the curve its puffed appearance. You find fewer and fewer scores as you look out toward the end points, or *tails,* of the distribution.

The normal distribution has been thoroughly analyzed by statisticians. The mean of a normal distribution is also its midpoint. Half the scores are above the mean, and half are below it. In a normal distribution, the mean, median, and mode are all the same point.

Another convenient property of the normal distribution is that the percentage of scores falling within each area of the curve is known, as you can see in Figure 14.2 on page 526. A person scoring within 1 standard deviation of the mean obviously has a lot of company. Many scores pile up here. In fact, 68% of all scores are located in the area of ±1 standard deviation from the mean. About 16% of the scores are higher than 1 standard deviation above the mean. Of this higher group, only 2% are better than 2 standard deviations above the mean. Similarly, only about 16% of the scores are less than 1 standard deviation below the mean, and of that group only about 2% are worse than 2 standard deviations below. At 2 standard deviations from the mean in either direction, the scorer has left the pack.

The SAT college entrance exam is one example of a normal distribution. The mean of the SAT is 500 and the standard deviation is 100. If you know people who made scores of 700, you know they did very well. Only about 2% of the people who take the test do that well, because only 2% of the scores are better than 2 standard deviations above the mean in a normal distribution.

Range Distance between the highest and the lowest score in a group.

Normal Distribution The most commonly occurring distribution, in which scores are distributed evenly around mean.

FIGURE 14.2

The Normal Distribution

The normal distribution or bell-shaped curve has certain predictable characteristics. For example, 68 percent of the scores are clustered within 1 standard deviation below to 1 standard deviation above the mean.

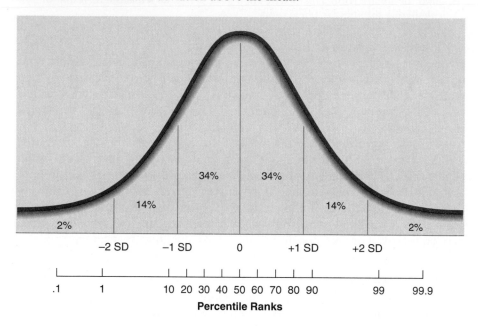

Types of Scores

Now you have enough background for a discussion of the different kinds of scores you may encounter in reports of results from standardized tests.

Percentile Rank Scores. The concept of ranking is the basis for one very useful kind of score reported on standardized tests, a **percentile rank** score. In percentile ranking, each student's raw score is compared with the raw scores of the students in the norming sample. The percentile rank shows the percentage of students in the norming sample who scored at or below a particular raw score. If a student's score is the same as or better than three-quarters of the students in the norming sample, the student would score in the 75th percentile or have a percentile rank of 75. You can see that this does *not* mean that the student had a raw score of 75 correct answers or even that the student answered 75% of the questions correctly. Rather, the 75 refers to the percentage of people in the norming sample whose scores on the test were equal to or below this student's score. A percentile rank of 50 means that a student has scored as well as or better than 50% of the norming sample and has achieved an average score.

Figure 14.3 illustrates one caution in interpreting percentile scores. Differences in percentile ranks do not mean the same thing in terms of raw score points in the middle of the scale as they do at the fringes. The graph shows Joan's and Alice's percentile scores on the fictitious Test of Excellence in Language and Arithmetic. Both students are about average in arithmetic skills. One equaled or sur-

Percentile Rank Percentage of those in the norming sample who scored at or below an individual's score.

FIGURE 14.3

Percentile Ranking on a Normal Distribution Curve

Percentile scores have different meanings at different places on the scale. For example, a difference of a few raw score points near the mean might translate into a 10 point percentile difference, while it would take 6 or 7 points to make a 10 point percentile difference farther out on the scale.

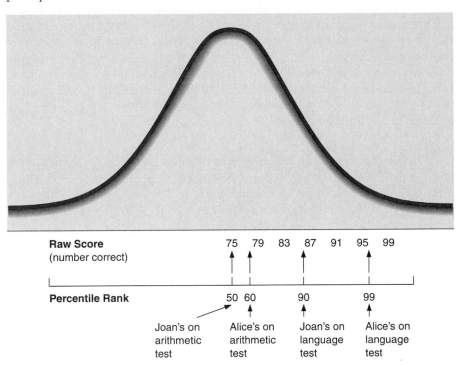

passed 50% of the norming sample; the other, 60%. However, because their scores are in the middle of the distribution, this difference in percentile ranks means a raw score difference of only a few points. Their raw scores were actually 75 and 77. In the language test, the difference in percentile ranks seems to be about the same as the difference in arithmetic, since one ranked at the 90th percentile and the other at the 99th. But the difference in their raw scores on the language test is much greater. It takes a greater difference in raw score points to make a difference in percentile rank at the extreme ends of the scale. On the language test the difference in raw scores is about 10 points.

Grade-Equivalent Scores.   **Grade-equivalent scores** are generally obtained from separate norming samples for each grade level. The average of the scores of all the 10th graders in the norming sample defines the 10th-grade equivalent score. Suppose the raw-score average of the 10th-grade norming sample is 38. Any student who attains a raw score of 38 on that test will be assigned a grade-equivalent score of 10th grade. Grade-equivalent scores are generally listed in numbers such as 8.3, 4.5, 7.6, 11.5, and so on. The whole number gives the grade. The decimals stand for tenths of a year, but they are usually interpreted as months.

Grade-Equivalent Score Measure of grade level based on comparison with norming samples from each grade.

Suppose a student with the grade-equivalent score of 10 is a 7th grader. Should this student be promoted immediately? Probably not. Different forms of tests are used at different grade levels, so the 7th grader may not have had to answer items that would be given to 10th graders. The high score may represent superior mastery of material at the 7th-grade level rather than a capacity for doing advanced work. Even though an average 10th grader could do as well as our 7th grader on this particular test, the 10th grader would certainly know much more than this test covered. Also, grade-equivalent score units do not mean the same thing at every grade level. For example, a 2nd grader reading at the 1st-grade level would have more trouble in school than an 11th grader who reads at the 10th-grade level.

Because grade-equivalent scores are misleading and are so often misinterpreted, especially by parents, most educators and psychologists strongly believe they should not be used at all. There are several other forms of reporting available that are more appropriate.

Standard Scores.   As you may remember, one problem with percentile ranks is the difficulty in making comparisons among ranks. A discrepancy of a certain number of raw-score points has a different meaning at different places on the scale. With standard scores, on the other hand, a difference of 10 points is the same everywhere on the scale.

Standard scores are based on the standard deviation. A very common standard score is called the *z* score. A *z* score tells how many standard deviations above or below the average a raw score is. In the example described earlier, in which you were fortunate enough to get a 78 on a test where the mean was 70 and the standard deviation was 4, your *z* score would be +2, or 2 standard deviations above the mean. If a person were to score 64 on this test, the score would be 1.5 standard deviation units *below* the mean, and the *z* score would be –1.5. A *z* score of 0 would be no standard deviations above the mean—in other words, right on the mean.

To calculate the *z* score for a given raw score, subtract the mean from the raw score and divide the difference by the standard deviation. The formula is:

$$z = \frac{X - \overline{X}}{SD}$$

Since it is often inconvenient to use negative numbers, other standard scores have been devised to eliminate this difficulty. The *T* **score** has a mean of 50 and uses a standard deviation of 10. Thus a *T* score of 50 indicates average performance. If you multiply the *z* score by 10 (which eliminates the decimal) and add 50 (which gets rid of the negative number), you get the equivalent *T* score as the answer. The person whose *z* score was –1.5 would have a *T* score of 35.

First multiply the *z* score by 10: $-1.5 \times 10 = -15$

Then add 50: $-15 + 50 = 35$

The scoring of the SAT test is based on a similar procedure. The mean of the scores is set at 500, and a standard deviation of 100 is used.

Standard Scores Scores based on the standard deviation.

z **Score** Standard score indicating the number of standard deviations above or below the mean.

T **Score** Standard score with a mean of 50 and a standard deviation of 10.

FIGURE 14.4

Four Types of Standard Scores on a Normal Distribution Curve

Using this figure, you can translate one type of standard into another.

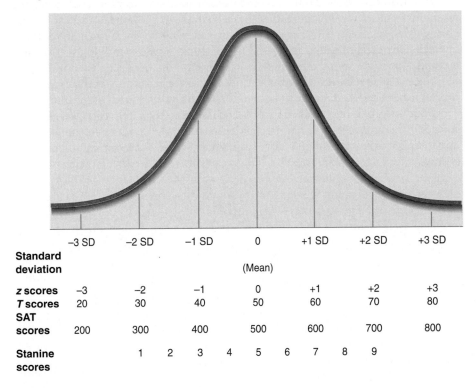

	−3 SD	−2 SD	−1 SD	0	+1 SD	+2 SD	+3 SD
Standard deviation				(Mean)			
z scores	−3	−2	−1	0	+1	+2	+3
T scores	20	30	40	50	60	70	80
SAT scores	200	300	400	500	600	700	800
Stanine scores		1 2	3 4	5 6	7 8	9	

Before we leave this section on types of scores, we should mention one other widely used method. **Stanine scores** (the name comes from "standard nine") are standard scores. There are only nine possible scores on the stanine scale, the whole numbers 1 through 9. The mean is 5, and the standard deviation is 2. Each unit from 2 to 8 is equal to half a standard deviation.

Stanine scores provide a method of considering a student's rank, since each of the nine scores includes a specific range of percentile scores in the normal distribution. For example, a stanine score of 1 is assigned to the bottom 4% of scores in a distribution. A stanine of 2 is assigned to the next 7%. Of course, some raw scores in this 7% range are better than others, but they all get a stanine score of 2.

Each stanine score represents a wide range of raw scores. This has the advantage of encouraging teachers and parents to view a student's score in more general terms instead of making fine distinctions based on a few points. Figure 14.4 compares the four types of standard scores we have considered, showing how each would fall on a normal distribution curve.

Interpreting Test Scores

One of the most common problems with the use of tests is misinterpretation of scores. This often happens because of the belief that numbers are precise mea-

Stanine Scores Whole-number scores from 1 to 9, each representing a wide range of raw scores.

surements of a student's ability. No test provides a perfect picture of a person's abilities; a test is only one small sample of behavior. Two factors are important in developing good tests and interpreting results: reliability and validity.

Reliability. If you took a standardized test on Monday, then took the same test again a week later, and you received about the same score each time, you would have reason to believe the test was reliable. If 100 people took the test one day, then repeated it the following week, and the ranking of the individual scores was about the same for both tests, you would be even more certain the test was reliable. (Of course, this assumes that no one looks up answers or studies before the second test.) A reliable test gives a consistent and stable "reading" of a person's ability from one occasion to the next, assuming the person's ability remains the same. A reliable thermometer works in a similar manner, giving you a reading of 100°C each time you measure the temperature of boiling water. Measuring a test's **reliability** in this way, by giving the test on two different occasions, indicates *stability* or *test-retest reliability.* If a group of people takes two equivalent versions of a test and the scores on both tests are comparable, this indicates *alternate-form reliability.*

Reliability can also refer to the internal consistency or the precision of a test. This type of reliability, known as *split-half reliability,* is calculated by comparing performance on half of the test questions with performance on the other half. If, for example, someone did quite well on all the odd-numbered items and not at all well on the even-numbered items, we could assume that the items were not very consistent or precise in measuring what they were intended to measure. The most effective way to improve reliability is to add more items to a test. Generally speaking, longer tests are more reliable than shorter ones.

True Score. All tests are imperfect estimators of the qualities or skills they are trying to measure. There are errors in every testing situation. Sometimes the errors are in your favor, and you score higher than your ability might warrant. This can occur when you happen to review a key section just before the test or are unusually well rested and alert the day of a pop quiz. Sometimes the errors go against you. You don't feel well the day of the examination, have just gotten bad news from home, or focused on the wrong material in your review. But if you could be tested over and over again without becoming tired and without memorizing the answers, your good luck and bad luck would even out, and the average of the test scores would bring you close to a **true score.** In other words, we can think of a student's true score as the mean of all the scores the student would receive if the test were repeated many times.

In reality, however, students take a test only once. That means that the score each student receives is made up of the hypothetical true score plus some amount of error. How can error be reduced so that the actual score can be brought closer to a true score? As you might guess, this returns us to the question of reliability. The more reliable the test, the less error in the score actually obtained. On standardized tests, test developers take this into consideration and make estimations of how much the students' scores would probably vary if they were tested repeatedly. This estimation is called the **standard error of measurement.** It represents the *standard deviation* of the distribution of scores from our hypothetical repeated testings. Thus a reliable test can also be defined as a test with a small standard error of measurement. In their interpretation of tests, teachers must also take into consideration the margin for error.

Reliability Consistency of test results.

True Score Hypothetical average of all of an individual's scores if repeated testing under ideal conditions were possible.

Standard Error of Measurement Hypothetical estimate of variation in scores if testing were repeated.

Confidence Interval.   Teachers should never base an opinion of a student's ability or achievement on the exact score the student obtains. Many test companies now report scores using a **confidence interval,** or "standard error band," that encloses the student's actual score. This makes use of the standard error of measurement and allows a teacher to consider the range of scores that might include a student's true score.

Let us assume, for example, that two students in your class take a standardized achievement test in Spanish. The standard error of measurement for this test is 5. One student receives a score of 79; the other, a score of 85. At first glance, these scores seem quite different. But when you consider the standard error bands around the scores, not just the scores alone, you see that the bands overlap. The first student's true score might be anywhere between 74 and 84 (that is, the actual score of 79 plus and minus the standard error of 5). The second student's true score might be anywhere between 80 and 90. If these two students took the test again, they might even switch rankings. It is crucial to keep in mind the idea of standard error bands when selecting students for special programs. No child should be rejected simply because the obtained score missed the cutoff by one or two points. The student's true score might well be above the cutoff point.

Validity.   If a test is sufficiently reliable, the next question is whether it is valid, or more accurately, whether the judgments and decisions based on the test are valid. To have **validity,** the decisions and inferences based on the test must be supported by evidence. This means that validity is judged in relation to a particular use or purpose, that is, in relation to the actual decision being made and the evidence for that decision (Gronlund, 1993).

Traditionally, psychologists described three different kinds of validity: content, criterion, and construct. The move today is toward viewing validity as a single quality. Instead of different kinds of validity, there are different kinds of evidence to support a particular judgment. If the purpose of a test is to measure the skills covered in a particular course or unit, then we would hope to see test questions on all the important topics and not on extraneous topics. If this condition is met, we would have *content-related evidence of validity.* Have you ever taken a test that dealt only with a few ideas from one lecture or just a few pages of the textbook? Then decisions based on that test (like your grade) certainly lacked content-related evidence of validity.

Some tests are designed to predict outcomes. The SATs, for example, are intended to predict performance in college. If SAT scores correlate with academic performance in college as measured by, say, grade-point average in the first year, then we have *criterion-related evidence of validity* for the use of the SAT in admissions decisions. In other words, the test scores are fairly accurate predictors of the criterion—how well the student will do in college.

Most standardized tests are designed to measure some psychological characteristic or "construct" such as reasoning ability, reading comprehension, achievement motivation, intelligence, creativity, and so on. It is a bit more difficult to gather *construct-related evidence of validity,* yet this is a very important requirement, probably the most important. Construct-related evidence of validity is gathered over many years. It is indicated by a pattern of scores. For example, older children can answer more questions on intelligence tests than younger children. This fits with our construct of intelligence. If the average 5-year-old answered as many questions correctly on a test as the average 13-year-old, we

Confidence Interval Range of scores within which an individual's particular score is likely to fall.

Validity Degree to which a test measures what it is intended to measure.

would doubt that the test really measured intelligence. Construct-related evidence for validity can also be demonstrated when the results of a test correlate with the results of other well-established, valid measures of the same construct.

Today, many psychologists suggest that construct validity is the broadest category and that gathering content- and criterion-related evidence is another way of determining if the test measures the construct it was designed to measure. And new questions are being raised about validity. What are the consequences of using a particular assessment procedure for teaching and learning? Twenty years ago Sam Messick (1975) raised two important questions to consider in making any decisions about using a test: Is the test a good measure of the characteristic it is assumed to assess? Should the test be used for the proposed purpose? The first question is about construct validity; the second is about ethics and values (Moss, 1992).

A number of factors may interfere with the validity of tests given in classroom situations. One problem has already been mentioned—a poorly planned test with little or no relation to the important topics. Standardized achievement tests must be chosen so that the items on the test actually measure knowledge gained in the classes. This match is absent more often than we might assume: one group of teachers in St. Louis found that fewer than 10% of the items in their curriculum overlapped in both the textbooks and the standardized tests they were using (Fiske, 1988). Also, students must have the necessary skills to take the test. If students score low on a science test not because they lack knowledge about science, but because they have difficulty reading the questions, do not understand the directions, or do not have enough time to finish, then the test is not a valid measure of science achievement for those students.

A test must be reliable in order to be valid. For example, if, over a few months, an intelligence test yields different results each time it is given to the same child, then by definition it is not reliable. Certainly it couldn't be a valid measure of intelligence because intelligence is assumed to be fairly stable, at least over a short period of time. However, reliability will not guarantee validity. If that intelligence test gave the same score every time for a particular child but didn't predict school achievement, speed of learning, or other characteristics associated with intelligence, then performance on the test would not be a true indicator of intelligence. The test would be reliable—but invalid. The Guidelines should help you increase the reliability and validity of the standardized tests you give.

Types of Standardized Tests

Several kinds of standardized tests are used in schools today. If you have seen the cumulative folders that include testing records for individual students over several years, then you know the many ways students are tested in this country. There are three broad categories of standardized tests: achievement, diagnostic, and aptitude (including interest). As a teacher, you will probably encounter achievement and aptitude tests most frequently.

Make sure the test actually covers the content of the unit of study.

Examples

1. Compare test questions to course objectives. A behavior-content matrix might be useful here (see Chapter 15).
2. Use local achievement tests and local norms when possible.
3. Check to see if the test is long enough to cover all important topics.
4. Are there any difficulties your students experience with the test, such as not enough time, level of reading, and so on? If so, discuss these problems with appropriate school personnel.

Make sure students know how to use all the test materials.

Examples

1. Several days before the testing, do a few practice questions with a similar format.
2. Demonstrate the use of the answer sheets, especially computer-scored answer sheets.
3. Check with new students, shy students, slower students, and students who have difficulty reading to make sure they understand the questions.
4. Make sure students know if and when guessing is appropriate.

Follow instructions for administering the test exactly.

Examples

1. Practice giving the test before you actually use it.
2. Follow the time limits exactly.

Make students as comfortable as possible during testing.

Examples

1. Do not create anxiety by making the test seem like the most important event of the year.
2. Help the class relax before beginning the test, perhaps by telling a joke or having everyone take a few deep breaths. Don't be tense yourself!
3. Make sure the room is quiet.
4. Discourage cheating by monitoring the room. Don't become absorbed in your own paper-work.

Remember that no test scores are perfect.

Examples

1. Interpret scores using bands instead of a single score.
2. Ignore small differences between scores.

Achievement Tests: What Has the Student Learned?

The most common standardized tests given to students are **achievement tests.** These are meant to measure how much a student has learned in specific content areas such as reading comprehension, language usage, computation, science, social studies, mathematics, and logical reasoning.

Achievement Tests Standardized tests measuring how much students have learned in a given content area.

"I HATE TAKING A TEST
WITHOUT AN ERASER."

(© Martha Campbell)

Achievement tests can be designed to be administered either to a group or individually. Group tests can be used for screening—to identify children who might need further testing or as a basis for grouping students according to achievement levels. Individual achievement tests are given to determine a child's academic level more precisely, or to help diagnose learning problems.

Norm-referenced achievement tests that are commonly given to groups include the California Achievement Test, the Metropolitan Achievement Test, the Stanford Achievement Test, the Comprehensive Test of Basic Skills, the SRA Achievement Series, and the Iowa Test of Basic Skills. Individually administered norm-referenced tests include Part II of the Woodcock-Johnson Psycho-Educational Battery: Tests of Achievement; the Wide-Range Achievement Test; the Peabody Individual Achievement Test; and the Kaufman Assessment Battery for Children. These tests vary in their reliability and validity.

Using Information from a Norm-Referenced Achievement Test.

What specific information can teachers expect from achievement test results? Test publishers usually provide individual profiles for each student, showing scores on each subtest. Figure 14.5 is an example of an individual profile for a fifth grader, Ken Allen, on the *California Achievement Test,* Fifth Edition. Note that the Individual Test Record reports the scores in many different ways. At the top of the form, after the identifying information about Ken's grade and birthday, is a list of the various tests—Reading Vocabulary, Reading Comprehension, Total Reading (Vocabulary and Comprehension combined), Language Mechanics, and so on. Beside each test are several different ways of reporting Ken's score:

NS: Ken's National Stanine Score (his stanine score based on a national norming sample comparison group).

NCE: Ken's Normal Curve Equivalent Score (a score used mostly for research purposes to evaluate certain compensatory education programs).

SS: Ken's Scale Score. This describes growth in achievement that typically occurs as a student progresses through the grades—the higher the grade the higher the expected scale score.

NCR: Ken's actual number correct—his raw score.

NP: Ken's National Percentile Score, telling us where he stands in relation to students at his grade level across the country.

RANGE: The range of national percentile scores in which Ken's *true score* is likely to fall. You may remember from our discussion of true scores that this range, or confidence interval, is determined by adding and subtracting the standard error of the test from Ken's actual score. There is a 95% chance that Ken's true score is within this range.

Beside the scores is a graph showing Ken's national percentile and stanine scores, with the standard error bands indicated around the scores. Bands that show any overlap are probably not significantly different. When there is no overlap between bands for two test scores, we can be reasonably certain that Ken's achievement levels in these two areas are actually different.

Interpreting Achievement Test Scores.

Let's look at Ken's scores more carefully. In language mechanics he has a stanine score of 5, which is equal to a scale score of 717. This is at the 49th percentile nationally. His true national percentile score is probably in the range from 37 to 61 (that is, plus and minus 1 standard error of measurement from the actual score of 49, so the standard error

FIGURE 14.5

An Individual Test Record

Test publishers provide several kinds of report forms for individual students and for entire classes. The form below gives both norm-referenced and criterion-referenced information about a fifth-grade boy.

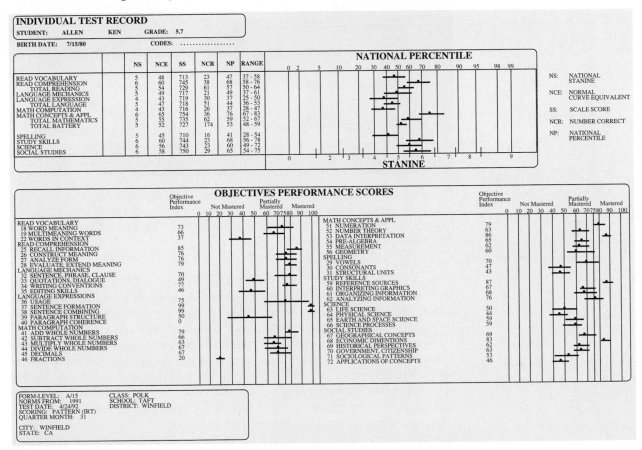

Source: Reproduced from the *California Achievement Test*, 5th edition, by permission of the publisher, CTB, a division of Macmillan/McGraw-Hill School Publishing Company. Copyright © 1992 CTB by Macmillan/McGraw-Hill School Publishing Company. All rights reserved.

of the language mechanics test must be 12). By looking at the graph, we can see that Ken's language mechanics and language expression score bands overlap. His achievement in these areas is probably similar, even though there seems to be a difference when you look at the NP scores alone. Comparing language expression with reading comprehension, on the other hand, we see that the bands do not overlap. Ken is stronger in reading comprehension than in language expression.

The profile in Figure 14.5 tells us a number of things. First, we can see that all Ken's scores are within the average range compared to the national norming sample. Ken's highest score is in math concepts and applications. However, this score band overlaps several other score bands, so we cannot say for sure that this is his strongest area. Ken's strength in math concepts and applications raises his total math battery score to a percentile of 59, but his math computation

*F*or a standardized test to be a valid measure of students' knowledge, the students must be familiar with procedures for taking the test— how to use the machine-scored sheets, what to do if they don't know an answer, and so on.

score is significantly lower than his math concepts score (the bands do not overlap). With some work on math computations, Ken would probably improve his overall math performance. We can also see that Ken is weak in spelling. Improving his spelling might improve his vocabulary score and vice versa.

The scores we have just described are all norm-referenced. However, results from standardized tests like the one Ken took can also be interpreted in a criterion-referenced way. The bottom portion of Ken's Individual Test Record in Figure 14.5 breaks down the larger categories of the top section (reading vocabulary, reading comprehension, etc.) and shows criterion-referenced scores that indicate mastered, partially mastered, or not mastered for specific skills. These include reading vocabulary skills such as the use of word meanings and words in context and study skills such as using reference sources and interpreting graphics. The Objective Performance Index score is an estimate of the percentage of all possible items that Ken could be expected to answer correctly in each performance area. In other words, based on his performance on these test items, what percentage of all possible questions in this area (at his level) should he get right? Teachers can use these results to get an idea of Ken's strengths and weaknesses with these specific skills and thus determine his progress toward objectives in a given subject. Be aware, though, that some of these specific skill areas may be measured with only a few items each, and the fewer the items, the more potential problems there can be with reliability.

Diagnostic Tests: What Are the Student's Strengths and Weaknesses?

If teachers want to identify specific learning problems, they may need to refer to results from the various diagnostic tests that have been developed. Most

diagnostic tests are given to students individually by a highly trained professional. The goal is usually to identify the specific problems a student is having. Achievement tests, both standardized and teacher-made, identify weaknesses in academic content areas like mathematics, computation, or reading. Individually administered diagnostic tests identify weaknesses in learning processes. There are diagnostic tests to assess the ability to hear differences among sounds, remember spoken words or sentences, recall a sequence of symbols, separate figures from their background, express relationships, coordinate eye and hand movements, describe objects orally, blend sounds to form words, recognize details in a picture, coordinate movements, and many other abilities needed to learn, remember, and communicate learning.

Elementary-school teachers are more likely than secondary-school teachers to receive information from diagnostic tests. There are few such tests for older students. If you become a high school teacher, your students are more likely to be given aptitude tests.

Aptitude Tests: How Well Will the Student Do in the Future?

Both achievement and aptitude tests measure developed abilities. Achievement tests may measure abilities developed over a short period of time, such as during a week-long unit on map reading, or over a longer period of time, such as a semester. **Aptitude tests** are meant to measure abilities developed over many years and to predict how well a student will do in the future at learning unfamiliar material. The greatest difference between the two types of tests is that they are used for different purposes. Achievement tests measure final performance (and perhaps give grades), and aptitude tests predict how well people will do in particular programs like college or professional school (Anastasi, 1988).

Scholastic Aptitude. The purpose of a scholastic aptitude test, such as the SAT (Scholastic Assessment Test) or ACT (American College Testing Program), is to predict how well a student is likely to do in college. Colleges use such scores to help decide on acceptances and rejections. The SAT may have seemed like an achievement test to you, measuring what you had learned in high school. Although the test is designed to avoid drawing too heavily on specific high school curricula, the questions are very similar to achievement test questions.

Standardized aptitude tests—such as the SAT, the School and College Ability Tests (SCAT), and the Preliminary Scholastic Assessment Test (PSAT) for younger students— seem to be reliable in predicting future achievement. Since standardized tests are less open to teacher bias, they may be even fairer predictors of future achievement than high school grades. Indeed, some psychologists believe grade inflation in high schools has made tests like the SAT even more important. Others believe that the SATs are not good predictors of success in college, particularly for women or members of cultural or ethnic minority groups. The controversy continues.

> **Focus on...**
>
> ### Standardized Tests
>
> - If you were Ken Allen's teacher (see Figure 14.5) how would you help him improve in reading? in math? in spelling?
> - What is the purpose of achievement testing? of aptitude testing? How do you tell the difference in the two kinds of tests?
> - Are the WISC III scores of 120 and 125 significantly different? Why or why not?
> - If there are 100 million adults in a country, and every one takes a Wechsler Intelligence Test, about how many should have IQ test scores above 130?

Diagnostic Tests Individually administered tests to identify special learning problems.

Aptitude Tests Tests meant to predict future performance.

IQ and Scholastic Aptitude.   In Chapter 4 we discussed one of the most influential aptitude tests of all, the IQ test. The IQ test as we know it could well be called a test of scholastic aptitude. Now that you understand the concept of standard deviation, you will be able to appreciate several statistical characteristics of the tests. For example, the IQ score is really a standard score with a mean of 100 and a standard deviation of 15 or 16, depending on the test. Thus about 68% of the general population would score between +1 and −1 standard deviations from the mean, or between about 85 and 115. Only about 2.5% of the general population would have a score higher than 2 standard deviations above the mean, that is, above 130 on the Wechsler Scales.

A difference of a few points between two students' IQ scores should not be viewed as important. Scores between 90 and 109 are within the average range. In fact, scores between 80 and 119 are considered within the range of low average to high average. To see the problems that may arise, consider the following conversation:

Parent: We came to speak with you today because we are shocked at our son's IQ score. We can't believe he has only a 99 IQ when his sister scored much higher on the same test. We know they are about the same. In fact, Sam has better marks than Lauren did in the fifth grade.

Teacher: What was Lauren's score?

Parent: Well, she did much better. She scored a 103!

Clearly, brother and sister have both scored within the average range. While the standard error of measurement on the WISC-III (Weschler Intelligence Scale for Children, third edition) varies slightly from one age to the next, the average standard error for the total score is 3.2. So the bands around Sam's and Lauren's IQ scores—about 96 to 102 and 100 to 106—are overlapping. Either child could have scored 100, 101, or 102. The scores are so close that on a second testing Sam might score slightly higher than Lauren.

Discussing Test Results with Families.   At times, you will be expected to explain or describe test results to your students' families. The Guidelines give some ideas.

Guidelines

Family and Community Partnerships for Discussing Standardized Test Results

Be ready to explain, in nontechnical terms, what each type of score on the test report means.

Examples

1. If the test is norm-referenced, know if the comparison group was national or local. Explain that the child's score shows how he or she performed *in relation to* the other students in the comparison group.

2. If the test is criterion-referenced, explain that the child's scores show how well he or she performs in specific areas.

If the test is norm-referenced, focus on the percentile scores. They are the easiest to understand.

Examples

1. Percentile scores tell what percent of students in the comparison group made the same score or lower—higher percentiles are better and 99 is as high as you can get. 50 is average.

2. Remind parents that percentile scores do not tell the "percent correct" so scores that would be bad on a classroom test (say 65% to 75% or so) are above average—even good—as percentile scores.

Avoid using grade-equivalent scores.

Examples

1. If parents want to focus on the "grade level– of their child, tell them that high grade-equivalent scores reflect a thorough understanding of the current grade level and NOT the capacity to do higher grade-level work.

2. Tell parents that the same grade-equivalent score has different meanings in different subjects—reading versus mathematics, for example.

Be aware of the error in testing.

Examples

1. Encourage parents to think of the score not as a single point but as a range or band that includes the score.

2. Ignore small differences between scores.

3. Note that sometimes individual skills on criterion-referenced tests are measured with just a few (2 or 3) items. Compare test scores to actual class work in the same areas.

Use conference time to plan a learning goal for the child, one that families can support.

Examples

1. Have example questions, similar to those on the test, to show parents what their child can do easily and what kinds of questions he or she found difficult.

2. Be prepared to suggest an important skill to target.

Issues in Standardized Testing

Today, many important decisions about students, teachers, and schools are based in part on the results of standardized tests. Test scores may affect "admission" to first grade, high school graduation, access to special programs, placement in special education classes, teacher certification and tenure, and school funding. Because the decisions affected by test scores are so critical, many educators call this process **high-stakes testing.** By 1991, 47 states had some form of statewide mandated testing for public school students (Ziomek & Maxey, 1993). Some groups are working to increase the role of testing—by establishing a national examination, for example—while others are working to cut back the use of standardized tests in schools (Madaus & Kellaghan, 1993).

In the next few pages we will consider two basic questions: What role should testing play in making decisions about people? Do some students have an unfair advantage in taking tests?

The Uses of Testing in American Society

Tests are not simply procedures used in research. Every day, there are many decisions made about individuals that are based on the results of tests. Should Liz

High-Stakes Testing Standardized tests whose results have powerful influences when used by school administrators, other officials, or employers to make decisions.

be issued a driver's license? How many and which students from the eighth grade would benefit from an accelerated program in science? Who belongs in a remedial class? Who will be admitted to college or professional school? Who will get a teaching certificate? In answering these questions, it is important to distinguish between the quality of the test itself and how the test is used. Even the best instruments can be, and have been, misused. In earlier years, for example, using otherwise valid and reliable individual intelligence tests, many students were inappropriately identified as having mental retardation. The problem was not with the tests, but with the fact that the test score was the only information used to classify students. Much more information must be considered.

Behind all the statistics and terminology are issues related to values and ethics. Who will be tested? What are the consequences of choosing one test over another for a particular purpose with a given group? What is the effect of the testing on the students? How will the test scores of minority-group students be interpreted? What do we really mean by intelligence, competence, and scholastic aptitude? Do our views agree with those implied by the tests we use to measure these constructs? How will test results be integrated with other information about the individual to make judgments? Answering these questions requires choices based on values as well as accurate information about what tests can and cannot tell us. As you can see in the Point/Counterpoint, the debate about testing continues.

Readiness Testing.   In 1988, Georgia became the first state to require that children pass a test before moving from kindergarten to first grade (Fiske, 1988; Linn, 1986). The test quickly became a symbol of the misuse of tests. Public outcry led to modifications of the policy and spurred many educators

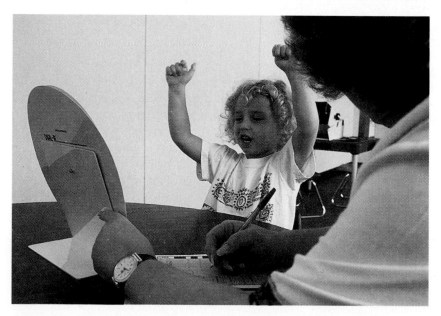

School "readiness" testing is a controversial procedure. Individualized assessment is one response to criticisms of group-administered, machine-scored, norm-referenced tests for kindergarten placement.

To Test or Not to Test?

Student teachers are often astounded by the amount of time they must spend every spring preparing their students for "test week." Schools have been known to abandon innovations such as "whole language" and hands-on science teaching and to adopt drill-and-practice test-based programs in their place, just because test scores fell when these innovations were introduced. Yet there is talk of more, not less, testing and the development of a National Curriculum. Should standardized testing be continued?

POINT Testing should be stopped.

Critics of standardized testing state that these tests measure disjointed facts and skills that have no use or meaning in the real world. Often test questions do not match the curriculum of the schools, so the tests can't measure how well students have learned the curriculum. Even so, there is great pressure on teachers to produce high test scores. Teachers' jobs, principals' raises, and even the value of real estate in the school district are affected by the schools' test scores. So teachers find themselves "teaching to the test." Because tests are best at measuring lower-level objectives, facts, and basic skills, these facts and skills become the content of the curriculum. Too often, the results of tests are used to label students as low achievers, and self-fulfilling prophecies are set into motion. Mary Lee Smith (1991) found the following effects of standardized testing on teachers:

When test scores are made public, teachers often feel embarrassed, angry, or ashamed. They sometimes change students' answers, excuse poor students from taking the test, drill students on the answers, or give unallowed "help" because the pressure for high scores is so great.

Teachers feel alienated from the test process, because when test scores are published, no one takes into account the fact that some of their students live in poverty or are just learning English.

Teachers are concerned that the tests take away valuable teaching time and make their students too anxious. Preparing for, giving, and recovering from the tests took an average of 100 hours of instructional time in the schools Smith studied.

COUNTERPOINT Tests can provide valuable information.

Defenders of standardized tests note that it is the responsibility of the school to select an appropriate test. Standardized tests are designed to sample what is typically taught, so the fit with any particular school's curriculum will not be perfect. Thus a standardized test is only one source of information. To redesign the curriculum so that it matches the test or to make placement decisions based only on a test score is to overuse and misuse the test. No test is reliable and valid enough to serve as the only basis for making important decisions. But tests do provide useful information.

To make good use of test results, Blaine Worthen and Vicki Spandel (1991) suggest the following:

Don't test unless there is an important decision to make. Then choose a good test that will give useful information about the decision.

Never use the test as the only basis for the decision. Supplement with other information, including the teacher's judgment.

Assume every test score is imperfect. Take the score as an estimate.

Know what the test actually measures. Just because it is called a test of reading comprehension does not mean that a test measures everything about reading comprehension.

Know your students. A test of math achievement that uses word problems can be a test of reading comprehension for students whose English is limited.

Don't use test results to compare students or foster competition. Use the results to benefit students.

to reform the **readiness testing** process. In fact, the uproar over this group-administered, machine-scored, norm-referenced test for kindergarten children "probably did more to advance readiness assessment reform in this country than all other causes combined" (Engel, 1991, p. 41).

Readiness Testing Testing procedures meant to determine if an individual is ready to proceed to the next level of education or training.

Critics of readiness tests (Meisels, 1989; Shepard & Smith, 1989) believe:

1. Group-administered paper-and-pencil tests are inappropriate for preschool children and thus should not be the basis for decisions about school entry.

2. The use of readiness tests narrows the preschool curriculum, making it more academic and less developmentally appropriate.

3. The evidence shows that delaying entry into first grade or retaining students in kindergarten is not effective. Students who are retained do no better than similar students who are not held back.

In spite of these criticisms, today almost every state uses testing at the state or district level to determine if a child is "ready" for first grade or to place a child in a special "developmental kindergarten" (Kirst, 1991a). Several states, as well as a few test publishers, are trying to develop appropriate ways to determine readiness. Engel (1991) suggests that such procedures could be ongoing assessments about many different aspects of readiness—cognitive, social/emotional, physical, and so on. These assessments would be indirect, that is, they would be completed by adults rather than requiring the children to answer questions directly on paper. The observations would provide useful information for teaching; they would be conducted in a comfortable natural setting, often as part of the preschool program itself.

Minimum and World-Class Standards.   In many studies comparing the United States with other industrialized nations, American students have placed low in academic achievement (Educational Testing Service, 1992). Even though these conclusions have been questioned (Berliner & Biddle, 1997), policymakers are concerned. One suggestion to improve student performance is minimum competency testing. A **minimum competency test** is a standardized test meant to determine whether an individual meets the minimum standard for moving to the next level or graduating. Almost every state in the United States has some kind of high school competency testing program. Some people have even suggested that a national examination would be helpful (O'Neil, 1991).

The push for a national test slowed, replaced by the idea of *national standards* (Lewis, 1995; Ziomek & Maxey, 1993). "Whether lauded as a sign of progress or scorned as anathema, the notion of national standards for what students learn in public schools is the hottest item in education reform today" (Lewis, 1995, p. 745). The public seems to agree that standards should be higher. In the 1995 Phi Delta Kappa/Gallup Poll of the Public's Attitude Toward the Public Schools, over 80% of the respondents favored higher standards for high school graduation and for promotion from grade to grade. But are *national* standards the answer? What are these standards and who will set them?

Actually, there are several kinds of standards. *Content standards* define what should be learned in particular subject areas such as mathematics or history. *Performance standards* specify the level or quality of student learning expected. *Opportunity-to-learn standards* describe the conditions and resources necessary to give every student an equal chance to reach the content and performance standards. Finally, you may hear about *world-class standards,* or the level of content and performance expected in other countries. National educational groups such as the National Council of Teachers of Mathematics (NCTM, 1991) have led the way in establishing standards (Hambleton, 1996; Lewis, 1995; Resnick & Nolan, 1995). At this point, standards are voluntary, but the debate continues about the value of adopting national standards.

Minimum Competency Tests
Standardized tests meant to determine if students meet minimum requirements to graduate or to proceed in school.

Testing Teachers.   New models of teacher assessment are in the planning and development stages. For example, the revised National Teachers Examination (NTE) is a battery of tests called the *Praxis Series* and is given in three phases. Early in the prospective teacher's education program, *Praxis I: Academic Skills Assessment* tests basic skills such as reading, writing, and mathematics. A computer-based package is available to remediate any weak areas identified by the test. *Praxis II: Subject Assessments,* given at the end of the undergraduate program, tests subject matter knowledge and principles of teaching and learning. *Praxis III: Classroom Performance Assessments* is based on the particular licensing requirements for each participating state. This assessment is conducted by trained local evaluators, mostly through classroom observations. Within each Praxis phase there are several modules from which to choose. States can require any one—or a combination of two or all three—of the Praxis phases for certification (Danielson & Dwyer, 1995; Dwyer & Villegas, 1993).

Like the alternatives to standardized tests we will examine shortly, the Praxis Series and other new teacher tests will make greater use of authentic performances and products. In *Praxis II,* teacher candidates analyze case studies and suggest solutions to teaching problems. In *Praxis III,* teachers might complete a lesson-planning exercise and then be interviewed about what they planned and why. They might be asked to submit a portfolio containing an overview of a unit, details of two consecutive lessons, copies of student handouts, lists of the resources selected for background, a videotape of teaching samples showing both large- and small-group lessons, and other examples of the teacher's actual work. Connecticut is developing a new system for assessing beginning science teachers that also relies on portfolios, including samples of teacher's writing, student work, and videotaped segments of classroom instruction, as shown in Table 14.2 on page 544. Results of these assessments will be used to determine eligibility for a provisional teaching certificate as well as to provide feedback for continuing professional development (Lomask, Pecheone, & Baron, 1995).

These procedures look promising. Of course, every innovation has its shortcomings. Can these portfolios and performances be evaluated objectively? Will we see an explosion of businesses that specialize in helping teachers build a beautiful portfolio? Will the wealthier teachers and teacher candidates have the best portfolios and videos (Kirst, 1991b)?

In addition to assessing beginning teachers, there is growing interest in setting standards for accomplished teaching. In 1986 the Carnegie Task Force on Teaching as a Profession called for the creation of a National Board for Professional Teaching Standards (NBPTS). This Board will offer experienced teachers advanced certification in more than 30 fields, categorized by subject matter and developmental level of students. Standards in all areas will be grounded in five general propositions about accomplished practice (Shapiro, 1995):

- Teachers are committed to students and their learning.
- Teachers know the subjects they teach and how to teach those subjects to their students.
- Teachers are responsible for managing and monitoring student learning.
- Teachers think systematically about their practice and learn from experience.
- Teachers are members of learning communities.

The process, which relies on portfolio assessment, is voluntary and still being refined. If you become a teacher, assessment awaits you at several points in your career.

TABLE 14.2   An Overview of a Science Teaching Portfolio

These are the entries expected in the portfolio of a beginning science teacher in Connecticut. Decisions about provisional certification as well as suggestions for improvement are based on the portfolio.

Task I—Planning for student learning

- Description of major concepts and goals for a two-week unit.
- Description of student characteristics relevant to learning this unit.
- Day-to-day journal entries for the unit.

Task II—Facilitating student learning

- Description of one student-centered lab activity during the unit.
- Description of one unit's topic dealing with science, technology, and society issues.
- Three 15-minute video segments of lab activity, post-lab discussion, and science-technology-society lesson.

Task III—Evaluation of student learning

- Entire work of three students during the unit.
- Detailed analysis of these students' learning.
- General analysis of whole class work and learning.
- Analysis of teaching and suggestions for future changes.

Source: From M. S. Lomask, R. L. Pecheone, and J. B. Baron. "Assessing new science teachers," *Educational Leadership, 52,* 6, 1995 p. 63. Adapted by permission of Connecticut State Department of Education.

Advantages in Taking Tests— Fair and Unfair

In this section we will consider three basic issues: Are standardized tests biased against minority students? Can students gain an advantage on admissions tests through coaching? Can they be taught test-taking skills?

Bias in Testing.   As you saw in Chapter 5, on most standardized measures of mental abilities the average performance of students of lower socioeconomic status and from minority groups is below that of middle-class white students, although the discrepancies are decreasing for some minority groups (Burton & Jones, 1982). Are tests such as the individual measures of intelligence or college admissions tests biased against minorities? This is a complex question.

Research on test bias shows that most standardized tests predict school achievement equally well across all groups of students. Items that might appear on the surface to be biased against minorities are not necessarily more difficult for minorities to answer correctly (Sattler, 1992). Even though standardized aptitude and achievement tests are not biased against minorities in predicting school performance, many people believe there are factors related to the specific content and procedures of such tests that put minority students at a disadvantage. Here are a few examples:

1. The language of the test and the tester is often different from the languages of the students.

2. The questions asked tend to center on experiences and facts more familiar to the dominant culture than to minority-group students.

3. Answers that support middle-class values are often rewarded with more points.

4. On individually administered intelligence tests, being very verbal and talking a lot is rewarded. This favors students who feel comfortable in that particular situation.

5. Minority-group children may not be oriented toward individual achievement and may not appreciate the value of doing well on tests.

Concern about cultural bias in testing has led some psychologists to try to develop **culture-fair** or **culture-free tests.** These efforts have not been very successful. On many of the so-called culture-fair tests, the performance of students from lower socioeconomic backgrounds and minority groups has been the same as or worse than their performance on the standard Wechsler and Binet Intelligence scales (Sattler, 1992).

Coaching and Test-Taking Skills. Courses to prepare students for college entrance exams are becoming more popular. As you probably know from experience, both commercial and public school coaching programs are available. It is difficult to evaluate the effects of these courses. In general, research has indicated that short high school training programs yield average gains of 10 points in SAT verbal scores and 15 points in SAT math scores, whereas longer commercial programs show gains of anywhere from 50 to as much as 200 points for some people (Owen, 1985). Kulik, Kulik, and Bangert (1984) analyzed the results of 40 different studies on aptitude and achievement test training and found that there were more substantial gains when students practiced on a parallel form of a test for brief periods. The design of the coaching program, therefore, may be the critical factor.

Two other types of training can make a difference in test scores. One is simple familiarity with the procedures of standardized tests. Students who have extensive experience with standardized tests do better than those who do not. Some of this advantage may be the result of greater self-confidence, less tendency to panic, familiarity with different kinds of questions (for example, analogies like house: garage:: _____ : car), and practice with the various answer sheets (Anastasi, 1988). Even brief orientations about how to take tests can help students who lack familiarity and confidence.

A second type of training that appears to be very promising is instruction in general cognitive skills such as solving problems, carefully analyzing questions, considering all alternatives, noticing details and deciding which are relevant, avoiding impulsive answers, and checking work. These are the kinds of metacognitive and study skills we have discussed before. Training in these skills is likely to generalize to many tasks (Anastasi, 1988). The Guidelines on page 546 give some ideas about how to be a more effective test-taker.

Focus on...

Issues in Testing

- What does high-stakes testing mean? What are some decisions that should *not* be based on standardized test scores?
- What are the most effective ways to help students learn to take tests?
- Describe at least three different kinds of standards.
- How would you determine readiness for school?

Culture-Fair/Culture-Free Test A test without cultural bias.

Taking a Test

Use the night before the test effectively.

Examples

1. Study the night before the exam, ending with a final look at a summary of the key points, concepts, and relationships.
2. Get a good night's sleep. If you know you generally have trouble sleeping the night before an exam, try getting extra sleep on several previous nights.

Set the situation so you can concentrate on the test.

Examples

1. Give yourself plenty of time to eat and get to the exam room.
2. Don't sit near a friend. It may make concentration difficult. If your friend leaves early, you may be tempted to do so too.

Make sure you know what the test is asking.

Examples

1. Read the directions carefully. If you are unsure, ask the instructor or proctor for clarification.
2. Read each question carefully to spot tricky words, such as *not, except, all of the following but one.*
3. On an essay test, read every question first, so you know the size of the job ahead of you and can make informed decisions about how much time to spend on each question.
4. On a multiple-choice test, read every alternative, even if an early one seems right.

Use time effectively.

Examples

1. Begin working right away and move as rapidly as possible while your energy is high.
2. Do the easy questions first.
3. Don't get stuck on one question. If you are stumped, mark the question so you can return to it easily later, and go on to questions you can answer more quickly.
4. If you are unsure about a question, answer it but mark it so you can go back if there is time.
5. On a multiple-choice test, if you know you will not have time to finish, fill in all the remaining questions with the same letter if there is no penalty for guessing.
6. If you are running out of time on an essay test, do not leave any questions blank. Briefly outline a few key points to show the instructor you "knew" the answer but needed more time.

Know when to guess on multiple-choice or true-false tests.

Examples

1. Always guess when only right answers are scored.
2. Always guess when you can eliminate some of the alternatives.
3. Don't guess if there is a penalty for guessing, unless you can confidently eliminate at least one alternative.
4. Are correct answers always longer? shorter? in the middle? more likely to be one letter? more often true than false?
5. Does the grammar give the right answer away or eliminate any alternatives?

Check your work.

Examples

1. Even if you can't stand to look at the test another minute, reread each question to make sure you answered the way you intended.
2. If you are using a machine-scored answer sheet, check occasionally to be sure the number of the question you are answering corresponds to the number of the answer on the sheet.

On essay tests, answer as directly as possible.

Examples

1. Avoid flowery introductions. Answer the question in the first sentence and then elaborate.
2. Don't save your best ideas till last. Give them early in the answer.
3. Unless the instructor requires complete sentences, consider listing points, arguments, and so on by number in your answer. It will help you organize your thoughts and concentrate on the important aspects of the answer.

Learn from the testing experience.

Examples

1. Pay attention when the teacher reviews the answers. You can learn from your mistakes, and the same question may reappear in a later test.
2. Notice if you are having trouble with a particular kind of item; adjust your study approach next time to handle this type of item better.

New Directions in Standardized Testing

Standardized tests continue to be controversial. In response to dissatisfaction with traditional forms of assessment, new approaches have emerged to deal with some of the most common testing problems. However, each of these approaches has its own problems. We will examine proposed procedures for measuring learning potential and for making assessment more "authentic."

Assessing Learning Potential

One criticism of traditional forms of intelligence testing is that such tests are merely samples of performance at one particular point in time. These tests, critics say, fail to capture the child's potential for future learning. An alternative view of cognitive assessment is based on the assumption that the goal of assessment is to reveal potential for learning and to identify the psychological and educational interventions that will help the person realize this potential. Procedures developed by Joe Campione and Ann Brown give graduated prompts as a child works to solve a problem. The prompts are scripted, beginning with a general hint and ending with a detailed instruction for how find the answer. The way the child uses the prompt and learns within the testing situation gives evidence of learning potential (Kozulin & Falik, 1995).

Reuven Feuerstein's **Learning Propensity Assessment Device** is another attempt to look at the process of learning rather than its product (Feuerstein, 1979; Kozulin & Falik, 1995). The assessment is a battery of 14 different in-

Learning Propensity Assessment Device Innovative method for testing the student's ability to benefit from teaching, consistent with Vygotsky's theory of cognitive development.

In many subjects, the most reasonable test is to demonstrate the ability to produce a finished product.

struments that include reasoning, numerical, verbal, figural, logical, and memory tasks. When necessary, the examiner teaches the child how to solve the problems and then assesses how well the child has benefited from instruction. The outcome of the assessment is not a score but descriptive information about practical teaching methods and materials for working with the child.

Both Feuerstein's and Campione and Brown's techniques reflect Vygotsky's ideas about the zone of proximal development—the range of functioning where a child cannot solve problems independently but can benefit from guidance. Results of these tests offer a thought-provoking and radically different approach to intelligence testing. Rather than focusing on where a child is, these approaches point toward where the child could go and give guidance for the journey.

Authentic Assessment

As the public and government demanded greater accountability in education in the 1980s and 1990s and as traditional standardized tests became the basis for high-stakes decisions, pressure to do well led many teachers and schools to "teach to the test." This tended to focus student learning on basic skills and facts. Even more troubling, say critics, the traditional tests assess skills that have no equivalent in the real world. Students are asked to solve problems or answer questions they will never encounter again; they are expected to do so alone, without relying on any tools or resources and while working under extreme time limits. Real life just isn't like this. Important problems take time to solve and often require using resources, consulting other people, and integrating basic skills with creativity and high-level thinking (Kirst, 1991a; Wolf, Bixby, Glenn, & Gardner, 1991).

In response to these criticisms, the **authentic assessment** movement was born. The goal was to create standardized tests that assess complex, important, real-life outcomes. The approach is also called *direct assessment, performance assessment,* or *alternative assessment.* These terms refer to procedures that are alternatives to traditional multiple-choice standardized tests because they directly assess student performance on "real-life" tasks (Hambleton, 1996; Worthen, 1993). Some states are developing procedures to conduct authentic assessments. For example, in 1990, Kentucky passed the Educational Reform Act. The act identifies six objectives for students, including such goals as applying knowledge from mathematics, the "hard" sciences, arts, humanities, and the social sciences to problems the students will encounter throughout their lives as they become self-sufficient individuals and responsible members of families, work groups, and communities.

Many of the suggestions for improving standardized tests will require new forms of testing, more thoughtful and time-consuming scoring, and perhaps new ways of judging the quality of the tests themselves. Standardized tests of the future may be more like the writing sample you may have submitted for college entrance and less like the multiple-choice college entrance tests you also had to take. Newer tests will feature more **constructed-response formats.** This means that students will create responses (essays, problem solutions, graphs, diagrams), rather than simply selecting the (one and only) correct answer. This will allow tests to measure higher-level and divergent thinking. For example, on the mathematical portion of the revised *Scholastic Assessment Test* students generate their own answers for 20% of the questions. Hand-held calculators are allowed, but not required. In addition, there is a writing test consisting of two-thirds multiple-choice questions and one-third essay.

Authentic Assessment Measurement of important abilities using procedures that simulate the application of these abilities to real-life problems.

Constructed-Response Format Assessment procedures that require the student to create an answer instead of selecting an answer from a set of choices.

In the excitement about authentic assessment, it is important to be sensible. Just being different from traditional standardized tests will not guarantee that the alternative tests are better. Many questions have to be answered. Assume, for example, that a new assessment requires students to complete a hands-on science project. If the student does well on one science project, does this mean the student "knows" science and would do well on other projects? One study found that students' performance on three different science tasks was quite variable: a student who did well on the absorbency experiment, for example, might have trouble with the electricity task. Thus, it was hard to generalize about a student's knowledge of science based on just the three tasks. Many more tasks would be needed to get a good sense of science knowledge. But a performance assessment with many different tasks would be expensive and time-consuming (Shavelson, Gao, & Baxter, 1993).

In addition, if high-stakes decisions are based on performance assessments, will teachers begin to "teach to the assessment" by giving students practice in these particular performances? Will being a good writer bias judges in favor of a performance? Will this make performance assessments even more prone to discriminate against some groups? And how will the projects be judged? Will different judges agree on the quality? When researchers examined the results of the 1992 Vermont Portfolio Assessment Program, they found that scorers assessing the same portfolio often gave very different ratings (Kotrez, Stecher, & Diebert, 1993). In other words, will judgments based on alternative assessments be reliable and valid? Will the assessment results generalize to tasks beyond those on the test itself? Will the new assessments have a positive effect on learning (Hambleton, 1997; Moss, 1992)?

Many state legislatures are drafting laws that will require direct assessment of student performance to determine how well the schools, districts, and even the whole state is doing. These new, authentic, or alternative assessment procedures could be used to make the same high-stakes decisions as the traditional standardized tests and thus create some of the same problems (Worthen, 1993). Because this is a new area, it will take time to develop high-quality alternative assessments for use by whole school districts or states. Until more is known, it may be best to focus on authentic assessment at the classroom level, as we will discuss in the next chapter.

Focus on...

New Directions in Testing

- How would you judge the reliability and validity of a performance test in which a student was asked to show a knowledge of geometry by designing a tile floor using tiles of different shapes and sizes?

- What are the possibilities for bias in alternative assessments?

- Relate the measurement of learning potential to Vygotsky's theory of zone of proximal development.

SUMMARY

Measurement and Evaluation

Evaluation of student learning can be based on measurements from norm-referenced tests in which a student's performance is compared to the average performance of others, or from criterion-referenced tests, in which scores are compared to a preestablished standard.

What Do Test Scores Mean?

Standardized tests are most often norm-referenced. They have been pilot-tested, revised, and then administered in final form to a norming sample, which becomes the comparison group for scoring. Important aspects of measurement in standardized testing are the frequency distribution, the central tendency, and the standard deviation. The mean (arithmetical average), median (middle score), and mode (most common score) are all measures of central tendency. The standard deviation reveals how scores spread out around the mean. A normal distribution is a frequency distribution represented as a bell-shaped curve. Many scores cluster in the middle; the farther from the midpoint, the fewer the scores. Half the scores are above the mean; half are below. There are several basic types of standardized test scores: percentile rankings, which indicate the percentage of others who scored at or below an individual's score; grade-equivalent scores, which indicate how closely a student's performance matches average scores for a given grade; and standard scores, which are based on the standard deviation. T and z scores are both common standard scores. A stanine score is a standard score that incorporates elements of percentile rankings.

Care must be taken in the interpretation of test results. Each test is only a sample of a student's performance on a given day. The score is only an estimate of a student's hypothetical true score. Some tests are more reliable than others, that is, they yield more stable and consistent estimates. The standard error of measurement takes into account the possibility for error and is one index of test reliability.

The most important consideration about a test is the validity of the decisions and judgments that are based on the test results. Some of these judgments are more valid than others because there is strong evidence for the interpretations and judgments made. Evidence of validity can be related to content, criterion, or construct. Construct-related evidence for validity is the broadest category and encompasses the other two categories of content and criterion. Tests must be reliable to be valid, but reliability does not guarantee validity.

Types of Standardized Tests

Three kinds of standardized tests are used frequently in schools: achievement, diagnostic, and aptitude. Profiles from norm-referenced achievement tests can also be used in a criterion-referenced way to help a teacher assess a student's strengths and weaknesses in a particular subject. Diagnostic tests usually are given individually to elementary school students when learning problems are suspected. Aptitude tests are designed to predict how a student will perform in the future. For example, the Scholastic Assessment Test (SAT) predicts performance in the first year of college.

Issues in Standardized Testing

Controversy over standardized testing has focused on the role and interpretation of tests, the validity of readiness tests as a guide for decisions about young children, the fairness and usefulness of minimum competency testing, the testing of teachers, and the degree of bias against minority-group students inherent in tests.

The way test results are used is a major issue for teachers. Teachers should use results to improve instruction, not to stereotype students or justify lowered expectations. Performance on standardized tests can be improved if students gain experience with this type of testing and training in study skills and problem solving.

New Directions in Standardized Testing

Today there is great interest in authentic assessment—designing procedures that assess students' abilities to solve important real-life problems, think creatively, and act responsibly. Such approaches assume that assessment should reveal the potential for future learning and help identify interventions for realizing that potential. Standardized tests of the future will be more varied and will use more constructed-response formats, requiring students to generate (rather than select) answers.

KEY TERMS

achievement tests, p. 533
aptitude tests, p. 537
authentic assessment, p. 548
bimodal distribution, p. 524
central tendency, p. 523
confidence interval, p. 531
constructed-response format, p. 548
criterion-referenced testing, p. 521
culture-fair/culture-free test, p. 545

diagnostic tests, p. 537
evaluation, p. 520
frequency distribution, p. 523
grade-equivalent score, p. 527
high-stakes testing, p. 539
histogram, p. 523
Learning Propensity Assessment
  Device, p. 547
mean, p. 523

measurement, p. 520
median, p. 523
minimum competency tests,
  p. 542
mode, p. 524
norm group, p. 521
norm-referenced testing, p. 521
normal distribution, p. 525
norming sample, p. 523

percentile rank, p. 526
range, p. 525
readiness testing, p. 541
reliability, p. 530
standard deviation, p. 524

standard error of measurement,
    p. 530
standard scores, p. 528
standardized tests, p. 523
stanine scores, p. 529

T score, p. 528
true score, p. 530
validity, p. 531
variability, p. 524
z score, p. 528

CHECK YOUR UNDERSTANDING

Can you apply the ideas from this chapter on standardized assessments to solve the following problems of practice?

Preschool and Kindergarten

- Your district is considering establishing a first-grade readiness testing program. As the lead teacher for the kindergarten, you are asked to speak to the school board about the issue—they are still open to various alternatives. What points would you make?

Elementary and Middle School

- Your students seem very nervous about the spring testing. The local paper has carried stories about the school's "low" scores last year, and there is pressure on everyone to do better this time. How would you prepare your students?

Junior High and High School

- The parents of one of your students are angry with you because their child was not selected for the special accelerated math group. Selection was based on both standardized test scores and class performance. How would you explain the school's decision?

Cooperative Learning Activity

- With four or five other members of your educational psychology class, analyze the test printout in Figure 14.5. If you were Ken's teacher, how would you use this information in teaching?

What Would They Do?

It is nearing the end of school and the ninth grade achievement test results are finally in. The parents' report form went home last Friday, and Monday morning you get a call from the principal during your planning period. The parents of one of your math students are in the office and have asked to speak with you and the principal immediately. The father is a prominent businessman and the mother is a lawyer. Their daughter received a grade-equivalent score of 11.8 on her standardized math test. The girl has been making Bs and Cs in your class—she seldom completes homework and has trouble with your conceptual approach to math. She just wants to know the "steps" to solve the problems so she can finish. You have tried several times to get the parents to come in to talk about ways to support the girl's learning, but they never seem to have had the time—until today.

You smile as you enter the principals' office, but the parents are not smiling. As soon as you sit down, the father says, "Well, you can see from our daughter's scores that you have been totally wrong in the grades you have given her this year. We thought she was just weak in math, but now it is clear you have something against her! Or maybe you just don't know how to teach math to bright girls."

The mother chimes in, "Yes, we expect you to reconsider her final grades for the year in light of her obvious ability. In fact," she glances at the principal and then glares at you again, "we believe she should get credit for the tenth grade class you teach as well, because she obviously knows the material already."

THOMAS O'DONNELL

Social Studies Chairperson, Grades 7–12
Malden High School, Malden, Massachusetts

The math achievement the girl took might not be a good device for measuring one's ability to go beyond high school math to the more abstract, conceptual approach needed for college-level math. You must explain your grading system to parents so they understand the needed combination of effort and achievement to achieve top grades.

Since the parent statements include two serious charges against you, make it clear you expect respect from them but that this issue will have no impact on your work with the student. You must reject their expectations of changing grades and credits.

SUZY L. BOSWELL

Art Teacher, Grades 6–8
Pickens County Middle School, Jasper, Georgia

One of the most challenging aspects of a teacher's job is often the task of communicating with the parents. Unfortunately, most parents begin to lose contact with the school system and the children's teachers when their child enters middle school or junior high. Parents may think that they are no longer needed or that their child prefers them to remain anonymous, so as not to embarrass them. However, the motivation and learning process are still very much a shared responsibility of school and home.

Concerned parents such as these who apparently could not seem to find the time until something happens, are at least showing up now. Whatever the reason that finally brings them to school, I think it is important for the teacher to first of all thank the parents for coming in to the school to discuss the education of their child. Make it clear to them that we want them to be involved in their child's education. We know that it is important to the child to have their support. Secondly, we are on the same team and together we can win. We all want the best possible education for the child and we are best able to accomplish that by working together.

The parents did not volunteer their time to listen to a lecture. In this particular case they may actually be coming to the school to give the teacher a lecture and to "set her straight." It may require a great deal of diplomacy to turn this into a positive and productive meeting, but we as teachers deal with unwilling students almost daily and this situation is not any different.

Once the tone is set and the parents are receptive, it may be helpful to explain to them the characteristics of the tests, including the various methods that are used to measure the results of the test. It is important to note that students may have the aptitude to learn and to perform in the classroom and yet simply choose not to apply themselves. Therefore, these students are still not meeting the requirements necessary to earn credit for a particular class.

Their daughter is apparently bright. If she would apply herself in class and do the homework, her grade in class should improve considerably. However, she must realize that it is her responsibility to complete the class requirements in order to earn a higher grade.

In closing, it is important to assure the parents that you do appreciate their concerns and that you are happy to work with them and their daughter to improve her grades. Assure them that working together, we can certainly expect their daughter's performance in school to reflect the abilities indicated in the standardized test score.

15

Classroom Assessment and Grading

Overview | *What Would You Do?*

FORMATIVE AND SUMMATIVE ASSESSMENT   556

GETTING THE MOST FROM TRADITIONAL
ASSESSMENT APPROACHES   558
Planning for Testing | Objective Testing | Evaluating Objective Test
Items | Essay Testing

INNOVATIONS IN ASSESSMENT   566
Authentic Classroom Tests | Performance in Context: Portfolios and
Exhibitions | Evaluating Portfolios and Performances

EFFECTS OF GRADES AND GRADING ON STUDENTS   575
Effects of Failure | Effects of Feedback | Grades and Motivation

GRADING AND REPORTING: NUTS AND BOLTS   578
Criterion-Referenced versus Norm-Referenced Grading | Preparing
Report Cards | The Point System | Percentage Grading | The
Contract System and Grading Rubrics | Grading on Effort and
Improvement | Cautions: Being Fair

BEYOND GRADING: COMMUNICATION   587

Summary | *Key Terms* | *Check Your Understanding* |
Teachers' Casebook: What Would They Do?

T *hink back on your report cards and grades over the years. Did you ever receive a grade that was lower than you expected? How did you feel about yourself, the teacher, the subject, and school in general as a result of the lower grade? What could the teacher have done to help you understand and profit from the experience?*

In this chapter, we will look at both tests and grades, focusing not only on the effects these are likely to have on students, but also on practical means of developing more efficient methods for testing and grading.

We begin with a consideration of the many types of tests teachers prepare each year and some new approaches to assessment. Then we examine the effects grades are likely to have on students. Because there are so many grading systems, we also spend some time identifying the advantages and disadvantages of one system over another. Finally, we turn to the very important topic of communication with students and parents. How will you justify the grades you give?

By the time you have completed this chapter, you should be able to:

- Make a plan for testing students on a unit of work.
- Evaluate tests that accompany textbooks and teachers' manuals.
- Create multiple-choice and essay test items for your subject area.
- Describe authentic assessment approaches, including portfolios, performances, exhibitions, and the development of scoring rubrics.
- Discuss the potential positive and negative effects of grades on students.
- Give examples of criterion-referenced and norm-referenced grading systems.
- Assign grades to a hypothetical group of students and defend your decisions in a class debate.
- Role-play a conference with parents who do not understand your grading system or their child's grades.

What Would You Do?

Your school requires that you give letter grades to your class. You can use any method you want, as long as an A, B, C, D, or F appears for each of the subject areas on every student's report card, every grading period. Some teachers use worksheets, quizzes, homework, and tests. Others are assigning group work and portfolios. A few teachers are individualizing standards by grading on progress and effort more than final achievement. Some are trying contract approaches and experimenting with longer term projects while others are relying almost completely on daily class work. Two teachers who use group work are considering giving credit toward grades for being a "good group member" or competitive bonus points for the top-scoring group. Others are planning to use improvement points for class rewards but not for grades. Your only experience with grading was using written comments and a mastery approach that rated the students as making satisfactory or unsatisfactory progress toward particular objectives. You want a system that is fair and manageable, but also encourages learning, not just performance.

- What would be your major graded assignments and projects?

- Would you include credit for behaviors like group participation or effort?

- How would you put all the elements together to determine a grade for every student for every marking period?

- How would you justify your system to the principal and to the parents?

- How will these issues affect the grades you will teach?

Formative and Summative Assessment

As a teacher, you may or may not help in designing the grading system for your school or your class. Many school districts have a standard approach to grading. Still, you will have choices about how you use your district's grading system and how you assess your students' learning. Will you give tests? How many? What kinds? Will students do projects or keep portfolios of their work? How will homework influence grades? Will you grade on students' current academic performance or on their degree of improvement? How will you use the information from standardized student assessments?

There are two general uses or functions for assessment: formative and summative. **Formative assessment** occurs before or during instruction. It has two basic purposes: to guide the teacher in planning and to help students identify areas that need work. In other words, formative assessment helps *form* instruction. Often students are given a formative test prior to instruction, a **pretest** that helps the teacher determine what students already know. Sometimes a test is given during instruction to see what areas of weakness remain so teaching can be directed toward the problem areas. This is generally called a **diagnostic test** but should not be confused with the standardized diagnostic tests of more general learning abil-

Formative Assessment Ungraded testing used before or during instruction to aid in planning and diagnosis.

Pretest Formative test for assessing students' knowledge, readiness, and abilities.

Diagnostic Test Formative test to determine students' areas of weakness.

Testing is formative or summative depending on what is done with the results: If the results are used to plan future instruction, then it is formative. If they're used to determine a final evaluation of a student, then it is summative.

ities. A classroom diagnostic test identifies a student's areas of achievement and weakness in a particular subject. Older students are often able to apply the information from diagnostic tests to "reteach" themselves. For example, armed with the knowledge that you have difficulty interpreting standardized test reports like the one shown in Figure 14.5 in the preceding chapter, you could reread the section on this topic in Chapter 14, read the interpretation section of a test manual, or ask another student or the instructor for an explanation.

Pretests and diagnostic tests are not graded. And since formative tests do not count toward the final grade, students who tend to be very anxious on "real" tests may find this low-pressure practice in test taking especially helpful.

A variation of formative measurement is ongoing measurement, often called **data-based instruction** or **curriculum-based assessment (CBA).** This approach uses frequent "probes," brief tests of specific skills and knowledge drawn from the curriculum, to give a precise picture of a student's current performance. Actually, CBA is not just one approach, but a whole family of approaches for linking teaching and assessment. CBA is "*any* set of measurement procedures that use direct observation and recording of a student's performance in the local curriculum as a basis for gathering information to make instructional decisions" (Deno, 1987, p. 41). This method has been used primarily with students who have learning problems, because it provides systematic assessment of both student performance and the teaching methods used. The assessment probes check to see if the difficulty level and the pace of instruction is right for the student. If a student shows inadequate progress on the assessment probes, the teacher

Data-Based Instruction Assessment method using daily probes of specific-skill mastery.

Curriculum-Based Assessment (CBA) Evaluation method using frequent tests of specific skills and knowledge.

should consider modifying or switching instructional strategies or pacing (Shapiro & Ager, 1992).

Summative assessment occurs at the end of instruction. Its purpose is to let the teacher and the students know the level of accomplishment attained. Summative assessment, therefore, provides a *summary* of accomplishment. The final exam is a classic example.

The distinction between formative and summative assessment is based on how the results are used. The same assessment procedure can be used for either purpose. If the goal is to obtain information about student learning for planning purposes, the assessment is formative. If the purpose is to determine final achievement (and help determine a course grade), the assessment is summative.

Getting the Most from Traditional Assessment Approaches

When most people think of assessment, they usually think of testing. As you will see shortly, teachers today have many other options, but testing is still a significant activity in most classrooms. Let's consider your options for assessing students using the traditional testing approach. In this section we will examine how to plan effective tests, how to evaluate the tests that accompany standard curriculum materials, and how to write your own test questions.

Planning for Testing

Both instruction and assessment are most effective when they are well organized and planned. Creating a behavior-content matrix can help teachers develop thoughtful learning objectives. The same process can be applied in planning classroom assessment. When you have a good plan, you are in a better position to judge the tests provided in teacher's manuals and texts and to write tests yourself.

Using a Behavior-Content Matrix.   Here is how you might use a behavior-content matrix to design a unit test. First you will need to decide how many items students can complete during the testing period, and then you must make sure that the items you write cover all the objectives you have set for the unit. More important objectives should have more items (Berliner, 1987).

An example of a plan that might be appropriate for a 40-question unit test in government is given in Table 15.1. From the test plan, you can see that this teacher has decided the most important topic is *major political issues* and has accordingly allotted a total of 15 questions to it. The least important topic is *methods of inquiry.* Also, the teacher wants to emphasize students' abilities to make *generalizations* (14 questions) while giving considerable attention to *understanding concepts* and *locating information. Interpreting graphs* is the least important skill, but it is not to be overlooked.

By preparing such a plan, you can avoid a situation where you have written 15 great questions (out of 40), only to discover that all 15 ask students to deal with the same concept or topic. Making a test plan will also improve the validity of tests. You will be able to ask a reasonable number of questions that measure the skills you hoped to develop about each key topic.

Summative Assessment Testing that follows instruction and assesses achievement.

TABLE 15.1   Test Plan for a Unit on Government

In making a test plan, begin by deciding on the totals (the numbers in bold) and then allocate the number of questions to each particular type and skill combination.

Topics	Skills Tested				
	Understanding Concepts	Making Generalizations	Locating Information	Interpreting Graphs	Total Questions
Social Trends	4	4	1	1	**10**
National Political Events	2	3	3	2	**10**
Methods of Inquiry	1	1	2	1	**5**
Major Political Issues	3	6	4	2	**15**
Total Questions	**10**	**14**	**10**	**6**	**4**

When to Test?   Frank Dempster (1991) examined the research on reviews and tests and reached these useful conclusions for teachers:

1. Frequent testing encourages the retention of information and appears to be more effective than a comparable amount of time spent reviewing and studying the material.

2. Tests are especially effective in promoting learning if you give students a test on the material soon after they learn it, then retest on the material later. The retestings should be spaced farther and farther apart.

3. The use of cumulative questions on tests is a key to effective learning. Cumulative questions ask students to apply information learned in previous units to solve a new problem.

Unfortunately, the curriculum in many schools is so full that there is little time for frequent tests and reviews. Dempster argues that students will learn more if we "teach them less," that is, if the curriculum includes fewer topics, but explores those topics in greater depth and allows more time for review, practice, testing, and feedback (Dempster, 1993).

Judging Textbook Tests.   Most elementary and secondary school texts today come complete with supplemental materials such as teaching manuals, handout masters, and ready-made tests. Using these tests can save time, but is this good teaching practice? The answer depends on your objectives for your students, the way you taught the material, and the quality of the tests provided (Airasian, 1996). If the textbook test matches your testing plan and the instruction you actually provided for your students, then it may be the right test to use. Table 15.2 on page 560 gives key points to consider in evaluating textbook tests.

What if there are no tests available for the material you want to cover, or the tests provided in your teacher's manuals are not appropriate for your students? Then it's time for you to create your own tests. We will consider the two major kinds of tests—objective and essay.

TABLE 15.2 Key Points to Consider in Judging Textbook Tests

The decision to use a textbook test must come *after* a teacher identifies the objectives that he or she taught and now wants to assess.

Textbook tests are designed for the typical classroom, but since few classrooms are typical, most teachers deviate somewhat from the text in order to accommodate their pupils' needs.

The more classroom instruction deviates from the textbook objectives and lesson plans, the less valid the textbook tests are likely to be.

The main consideration in judging the adequacy of a textbook test is the match between its test questions and what pupils were taught in their classes:

- Are questions similar to the teacher's objectives and instructional emphases?
- Do questions require pupils to perform the behaviors they were taught?
- Do questions cover all or most of the important objectives taught?
- Is the language level and terminology appropriate for pupils?
- Does the number of items for each objective provide a sufficient sample of pupil performance?

Source: From P. Airasian. *Assessment in the classroom,* p. 190. Copyright © 1996 by The McGraw-Hill Companies. Adapted with permission of The McGraw-Hill Companies.

Objective Testing

Multiple-choice questions, matching exercises, true/false statements, and short-answer or fill-in items are all types of **objective testing**. The word "objective" in relation to testing means "not open to many interpretations," or "not subjective." The scoring of these types of items is relatively straightforward compared to the scoring of essay questions because the answers are more clear-cut than essay answers.

Gronlund (1993) suggests that the guiding principle for deciding which item format is best is to "use the item types that provide the most direct measures of student performance specified by the intended learning outcome" (p. 28). In other words, if you want to see how well students can write a letter, have them write a letter, don't ask multiple-choice questions about letters. But if many different item formats will work equally well, then use multiple-choice questions because they are easier to score fairly and can cover many topics. Switch to other formats if writing good multiple-choice items for the material is not possible. For example, if related concepts need to be linked, such as terms and definitions, then a matching item is a better format than multiple-choice. If it is difficult to come up with several wrong answers for a multiple-choice item, try a true/false question instead. Alternatively, ask the student to supply a short answer that completes a statement (fill in the blank). Variety in objective testing can lower students' anxiety because the entire grade does not depend on one type of question that a particular student may find difficult. Here we look closely at the multiple-choice format, because it is the most versatile—and the most difficult to use well.

Using Multiple-Choice Tests. People often assume that multiple-choice items are appropriate only for asking factual questions. But multiple-choice items

Objective Testing Multiple-choice, matching, true-false, short-answer, and fill-in tests; scoring answers does not require interpretation.

can test higher-level objectives as well, although writing higher-level items is difficult. A multiple-choice item can assess more than recall and recognition if it requires the student to deal with new material by *applying* or *analyzing* the concept or principle being tested (Gronlund, 1993). For example, the following multiple-choice item is designed to assess students' ability to recognize unstated assumptions, one of the skills involved in analyzing an idea:

> An educational psychology professor states, "A *z* score of +1 on a test is equivalent to a percentile rank of approximately 84." Which of the following assumptions is the professor making?
>
> 1. The scores on the test range from 0 to 100.
> 2. The standard deviation of the test scores is equal to 3.4.
> 3. The distribution of scores on the test is normal. (correct answer)
> 4. The test is valid and reliable.

Writing Multiple-Choice Questions.   All test items require skillful construction, but good multiple-choice items are a real challenge. Some students jokingly refer to multiple-choice tests as "multiple-guess" tests—a sign that these tests are often poorly designed. Your goal in writing test items is to design them so that they measure student achievement, not test-taking and guessing skills.

The **stem** of a multiple-choice item is the part that asks the question or poses the problem. The choices that follow are called *alternatives*. The wrong answers are called **distractors** because their purpose is to distract students who have only a partial understanding of the material. If there were no good distractors, students with only a vague understanding would have no difficulty in finding the right answer.

The Guidelines adapted from Gronlund (1993), should make writing multiple-choice and other objective test questions easier.

Stem The question part of a multiple-choice item.

Distractors Wrong answers offered as choices in a multiple-choice item.

Guidelines

Writing Objective Test Items

The stem should be clear and simple, and present only a single problem. Unessential details should be left out.

Poor
> There are several different kinds of standard or derived scores. An IQ score is especially useful because . . .

Better
> An advantage of an IQ score is . . .

The problem in the stem should be stated in positive terms. Negative language is confusing. If you must use words such as *not, no,* or *except,* underline them or type them in all capitals.

Poor
> Which of the following is not a standard score?

Better
> Which of the following is NOT a standard score?

(continued)

Do not expect students to make extremely fine discrimination among answer choices.

Poor

The percentage of area in a normal curve falling between +1 and −1 standard deviations is about:

a. 66%.   b. 67%.   c. 68%.   d. 69%.

Better

The percentage of area in a normal curve falling between +1 and −1 standard deviations is about:

a. 14%   b. 34%   c. 68%.   d. 95%.

As much wording as possible should be included in the stem so that phrases will not have to be repeated in each alternative.

Poor

A percentile score

a. indicates the percentage of items answered correctly.
b. indicates the percent of correct answers divided by the percent of wrong answers.
c. indicates the percent of people who scored at or above a given raw score.
d. indicates the percent of people who scored at or below a given raw score.

Better

A percentile score indicates the percentage of

a. items answered correctly.
b. correct answers divided by the percent of wrong answers.
c. people who scored at or above a given raw score.
d. people who scored at or below a given raw score.

Each alternative answer should fit the grammatical form of the stem, so that no answers are obviously wrong.

Poor

The Stanford-Binet test yields an

a. IQ score.   c. vocational preference.
b. reading level.   d. mechanical aptitude.

Better

The Stanford-Binet is a test of

a. intelligence.   c. vocational preference.
b. reading level.   d. mechanical aptitude.

Categorical words such as *always, all, only,* or *never* should be avoided unless they can appear consistently in all the alternatives. Most smart test takers know the categorical answers are usually wrong.

Poor

A student's true score on a standardized test is

a. never equal to the obtained score.
b. always very close to the obtained score.
c. always determined by the standard error of measurement.
d. usually within a band that extends from +1 to −1 standard errors of measurement on each side of the obtained score.

Better

Which one of the statements below would most often be correct about a student's true score on a standardized test?

    a. It equals the obtained score.
    b. It will be very close to the obtained score.
    c. It is determined by the standard error of measurement.
    (d.) It could be above or below the obtained score.

You should also avoid including two distractors that have the same meaning. If only one answer can be right and if two answers are the same, then these two must both be wrong. This narrows down the choices considerably.

Poor

    The most frequently occurring score in a distribution is called the

    a. mode.   c. arithmetical average.
    b. median.   d. mean.

Better

    The most frequently occurring score in a distribution is called the

    (a.) mode.   c. standard deviation.
    b. median.   d. mean.

Using the exact wording found in the textbook is another technique to avoid. Poor students may recognize the answers without knowing what they mean.

Avoid overuse of *all of the above* and *none of the above*. Such choices may be helpful to students who are simply guessing. In addition, using *all of the above* may trick a quick student who sees that the first alternative is correct and does not read on to discover that the others are correct, too.

Obvious patterns on a test also aid students who are guessing. The position of the correct answer should be varied, as should its length.

Evaluating Objective Test Items

How will you evaluate the quality of the objective tests you give? One way is to conduct an item analysis to identify items that are performing well and those that should be changed or eliminated. There are many techniques for item analysis, but one simple approach is to calculate the difficulty and discrimination indices of the test. The difficulty index (p) of any item is simply the proportion or percentage of people who answered that item correctly. For norm-referenced tests, items with difficulty indices of around .50 are best. These items are most likely to identify individual differences in achievement levels. A simple way of calculating the difficulty index of an item when you have a large class is shown in Table 15.3 on page 564.

    The discrimination index (d) tells you how well each test item discriminated between people who performed well overall on the test and those who did poorly. The assumption here is that good items are those that are answered correctly by students who do well on the entire test but are missed by the students who get low scores on the test. A test item that was passed more often by the low scorers than by the high scorers would be suspect. Table 15.3 gives a simple way to estimate the discrimination index of an item.

TABLE 15.3   Calculating the Difficulty and Discrimination Indices for Test Items

---

To estimate the **Difficulty Index** (p) for each item:

■ Rank the scores on the test from highest to lowest.
■ Identify the people in the top one-third (the high-scoring group or HSG) and the people in the bottom one-third (the low-scoring group or LSG).
■ For each item, count the number of people who answered correctly the HSG and the LSG combined and divide by the total in the two groups. The formula is:

$$\text{Difficulty Index of an item} = \frac{\text{number correct in HSG} + \text{number correct in LSG}}{\text{number in HSG} + \text{number in LSG}}$$

This calculation is a reasonable estimate of the proportion of students in the whole class who answered correctly. Ideally, most of the items on a norm-referenced test would have difficulty indices of .40 to .59, with only a few hard (.00 to .25) or easy (.75 to 1.00) items.

To estimate the **Discrimination Index** (d) for each item:

■ Rank the scores on the test from highest to lowest.
■ Identify the people in the top one-third of the scores (high-scoring group or HSG) and the people in the bottom one-third (low-scoring group or LSG).

■ Subtract the percentage of students in the LSG who answered correctly from the percentage of students in the HSG who answered correctly. The formula is:

$$\text{Discrimination Index of an item} = \text{percent correct in HSG} - \text{percent correct in LSG}$$

The meaning of the discrimination index for any item is as follows:

$d = +.60$ to 1.00	*Very Strong* discriminator between high- and low-scoring students
$d = +.40$ to $.59$	*Strong* discriminator between high- and low-scoring students
$d = +.20$ to $.39$	*Moderate* discriminator between high- and low-scoring students (improve the item)
$d = -.19$ to $.19$	*Does Not* discriminate between high- and low-scoring students (improve or eliminate the item)
$d = -.20$ to -1.00	*Strong Negative* discriminator between high- and low-scoring students (check item for problems, miskeyed? two right answers? etc.)

Source: Adapted with permission from K. Linden (1992). *Cooperative learning and problem solving,* pp. 207–209. Published by Waveland Press.

Essay Testing

The best way to measure some learning objectives is to require students to create answers on their own. An essay question is appropriate in these cases. The most difficult part of essay testing is judging the quality of the answers, but writing good, clear questions is not particularly easy, either. We will look at writing, administering, and grading essay tests, with most of the specific suggestions taken from Gronlund (1993). We will also consider factors that can bias the scoring of essay questions and ways you can overcome these problems.

Constructing Essay Tests.   Because answering takes time, true essay tests cover less material than objective tests. Thus, for efficiency, essay tests should be limited to the assessment of the more complex learning outcomes.

An essay question should give students a clear and precise task and should indicate the elements to be covered in the answer. Gronlund suggests the following as an example of an essay question that might appear in an educational psychology course to measure an objective at the *synthesis* level of Bloom's taxonomy in the cognitive domain:

> For a course that you are teaching or expect to teach, prepare a complete plan for assessing student achievement. Be sure to include the procedures you would follow, the instruments you would use, and the reasons for your choices.

*O*ften the best way to measure students' learning is to have them create their own answers in essay tests; however, grading essay tests is less straightforward than grading objective tests.

This question requires students to apply information and values derived from course material to produce a complex new product.

Students should be given ample time for answering. If more than one essay is being completed in the same class period, you may want to suggest time limits for each. Remember, however, that time pressure increases anxiety and may prevent accurate assessment of some students. Whatever your approach, do not try to make up for the limited amount of material an essay test can cover by including a large number of essay questions. It would be better to plan on more frequent testing than to include more than two or three essay questions in a single class period. Combining an essay question with a number of objective items is one way to avoid the problem of limited sampling of course material (Gronlund 1993).

Evaluating Essays: Dangers. In 1912, Starch and Elliot began a classic series of experiments that shocked educators into critical consideration of subjectivity in testing. These researchers wanted to find out the extent to which teachers were influenced by personal values, standards, and expectations in scoring essay tests. For their initial study, they sent copies of English examination papers written by two high school students to English teachers in 200 high schools. Each teacher was asked to score the papers according to his or her school's standards. A percentage scale was to be used, with 75% as a passing grade.

The results? Neatness, spelling, punctuation, and communicative effectiveness were all valued to different degrees by different teachers. The scores on one of the papers ranged from 64 to 98%, with a mean of 88.2. The average score for the other paper was 80.2, with a range between 50 and 97. The following year, Starch and Elliot (1913a, b) published similar findings in a study involving history and geometry papers. The most important result of these studies was the discovery that the problem of subjectivity in grading was not confined to any particular subject area. The main difficulties were the individual standards of the grader and the unreliability of scoring procedures.

Certain qualities of an essay may influence grades. Teachers may reward quantity rather than quality in essays. In a series of studies described by Fiske (1981), many high school and college English teachers rated pairs of student essays that were identical in every way but linguistic style. One essay was quite verbose, with flowery language, complex sentences, and passive verbs. The other essay was written in the simple, straightforward language most teachers claim is the goal for students of writing. The teachers consistently rated the verbose essay higher.

Evaluating Essays: Methods. Gronlund (1993) offers several strategies for grading essays that avoid problems of subjectivity and inaccuracy. When possible, a good first step is to construct a model answer, then you can assign points to its various parts. You might also give points for the organization of

---

Focus on...

Traditional Assessment Approaches

- What is the most important consideration in deciding whether to use a test that comes with the text for your class?
- Write three multiple-choice items for this chapter and then evaluate them using the Guidelines: Writing Objective Test Items.
- Would an objective test or an essay test be more appropriate under these circumstances:
  1. You wish to test the students' knowledge of the terminology used in lab experiments.
  2. The test must be given and graded in the two days before the end of the six-week grading period.
  3. You want to test the students' ability to present a logical argument.
  4. Your aim is to balance subjective judgments with a highly reliable measure.
  5. You are seeking to test student understanding of a few major principles.
  6. You want to test students' knowledge of foreign countries' major export goods.
  7. You have limited time to construct the test.
  8. You are interested in students' ability to differentiate between the major philosophies of democracy and socialism.

TABLE 15.4 Comparing Objective and Essay Tests

Objective tests include any tests that ask the student to select the answer from a set of choices (multiple choice, true/false, matching).

	Selection-Type Items	Essay Questions
Learning Outcomes Measured	Good for measuring outcomes at the knowledge, comprehension, and application levels of learning; inadequate for organizing and expressing ideas.	Inefficient for measuring knowledge outcomes; best for ability to organize, integrate, and express ideas.
Sampling of Content	The use of a large number of items results in broad coverage which makes representative sampling of content feasible.	The use of a small number of items limits coverage which makes representative sampling of content infeasible.
Preparation of Items	Preparation of good items is difficult and time consuming.	Preparation of good items is difficult but easier than selection-type items.
Scoring	Objective, simple, and highly reliable.	Subjective, difficult, and less reliable.
Factors Distorting Scores	Reading ability and guessing.	Writing ability and bluffing.
Probable Effect on Learning	Encourages students to remember, interpret, and use the ideas of others.	Encourages students to organize, integrate, and express their own ideas.

Source: From Norman E. Gronlund, *How to Make Achievement Tests and Assessments 5/e,* p. 83. Copyright © 1993 by Allyn & Bacon. Reprinted by permission.

the answer and the internal consistency. You can then assign grades such as 1 to 5 or A, B, C, D, and F, and sort the papers into piles by grade. As a final step, skim the papers in each pile to see if they are comparable in quality. These techniques will help ensure fairness and accuracy in grading.

When grading essay tests with several questions, it makes sense to grade all responses to one question before moving on to the next. This helps prevent the quality of a student's answer to one question from influencing your reaction to the student's other answers. After you finish reading and scoring the first question, shuffle the papers so that no students end up having all their questions graded first, last, or in the middle.

You may achieve greater objectivity if you ask students to put their names on the back of the paper, so that grading is anonymous. A final check on your fairness as a grader is to have another teacher who is equally familiar with your goals and subject matter grade your tests without knowing what grades you have assigned. This can give you valuable insights into areas of bias in your grading practices.

Now that we have examined both objective and essay testing, we can compare the two approaches. Table 15.4 presents a summary of the important characteristics of each.

Innovations in Assessment

We have been considering how to make traditional testing more effective; now let's look at a few new approaches to classroom assessment. One of the main

To Test or Not to Test, Part II

We have seen the advantages and disadvantages of standardized tests, but what about classroom testing? Are traditional multiple-choice and essay tests useful in classroom assessment?

POINT Traditional tests are a poor basis for classroom assessment.

In his article "Standards, Not Standardization: Evoking Quality Student Work," Grant Wiggins (1991) makes a strong case for giving students standards of excellence against which they can judge their accomplishments. But these standards should not be higher scores on multiple-choice tests. When scores on traditional tests become the standard, the message to students is that only right answers matter and the thinking behind the answers is unimportant. Wiggins notes:

> We do not judge Xerox, the Boston Symphony, the Cincinnati Reds, or Dom Perignon vineyards on the basis of indirect, easy to test, and common indicators. Nor would the workers in those places likely produce quality if some generic, secure test served as the only measure of their success in meeting a standard. Demanding and getting quality, whether from students or adult workers, means framing standards in terms of the work that we undertake and value. And it means framing expectations about that work

which make quality a necessity, not an option. Consider:

- the English teacher who instructs peer-editors to mark the place in a student paper where they lost interest in it or found it slapdash and to hand it back for revision at that point;
- the professor who demands that all math homework be turned in with another student having signed off on it, where one earns the grade for one's work *and* the grade for the work that each person (willingly!) countersigned. (p. 22)

In a more recent article, Wiggins continues to argue for assessment that makes sense, that tests knowledge as it is applied in real-world situations. Understanding cannot be measured by tests that ask students to use skills and knowledge out of context. "In other words, we cannot be said to understand something unless we can employ our knowledge wisely, fluently, flexibly, and aptly in particular and diverse contexts" (Wiggins, 1993, p. 200).

COUNTERPOINT Traditional tests can play an important role.

Most psychologists and educators would agree with Wiggins that setting clear, high, authentic standards is important, but many also believe that traditional tests are useful in this process. Learning may be more than knowing the right answers, but right answers are im-

portant. While schooling is about learning to think and solve problems, it is also about knowledge. Students must have something to think about—facts, ideas, concepts, principles, theories, explanations, arguments, images, opinions. Well-designed traditional tests can evaluate students' knowledge effectively and efficiently (Airasian, 1996; Kirst, 1991b).

Some educators believe that traditional testing should play an even greater role than it currently does. Educational policy analysts suggest that American students, compared to students in many other developed countries, lack essential knowledge because American schools emphasize process—critical thinking, self-esteem, problem solving—more than content. In order to teach more about content, teachers will need to determine how well their students are learning the content, and traditional testing provides useful information about content learning.

Tests are also valuable in motivating and guiding students' learning. There is research evidence that frequent testing encourages learning and retention (Nungester & Duchastel, 1982). In fact, students generally learn more in classes with more rather than fewer tests (Dempster, 1991).

Source: From Grant Wiggins. "Standards not standardization." *Educational Leadership, 48,* 5, p. 18–25. Reprinted with permission of the Association for Supervision and Curriculum Development. Copyright © 1991 by ASCD. All rights reserved.

criticisms of standardized tests—that they control the curriculum, emphasizing recall of facts instead of thinking and problem solving—is a major criticism of classroom tests as well. Few teachers would dispute these criticisms. Even if you follow the guidelines we have been discussing, traditional testing can be limiting. What can be done? Should innovations in classroom assessment make traditional testing obsolete? The Point/Counterpoint section addresses this question.

One solution that has been proposed to solve the testing dilemma is to apply the concept of authentic assessment to classroom testing.

Authentic Classroom Tests

Authentic tests ask students to apply skills and abilities as they would in real life. For example, they might use fractions to enlarge or reduce recipes. Grant Wiggins makes this argument:

> If tests determine what teachers actually teach and what students will study for—and they do—then the road to reform is a straight but steep one: test those capabilities and habits we think are essential, and test them in context. Make [tests] replicate, within reason, the challenges at the heart of each academic discipline. Let them be—authentic. (1989, p. 41)

Wiggins goes on to say that if our instructional goals for students include the abilities to write, speak, listen, create, think critically, do research, solve problems, or apply knowledge, then our tests should ask students to write, speak, listen, create, think, solve, and apply. How can this happen?

Many educators suggest we look to the arts and sports for analogies to solve this problem. If we think of the "test" as being the recital, exhibition, game, mock court trial, or other performance, then teaching to the test is just fine. All coaches, artists, and musicians gladly "teach" to these "tests" because performing well on these tests is the whole point of instruction. Authentic assessment asks students to perform. The performances may be thinking performances, physical performances, creative performances, or other forms.

It may seem odd to talk of thinking as a performance, but there are many parallels. Serious thinking is risky, because real-life problems are not well defined. Often the outcomes of our thinking are public—our ideas are evaluated by others. Like a dancer auditioning for a Broadway show, we must cope with the consequences of being evaluated. Like a sculptor looking at a lump of clay, a student facing a difficult problem must experiment, observe, redo, imagine and test solutions, apply both basic skills and inventive techniques, make interpretations, decide how to communicate results to the intended audience, and often accept criticism and improve the solution (Wolf, in press; Wolf, Bixby, Glenn, & Gardner, 1991). Table 15.5 lists some characteristics of authentic tests.

Performance in Context: Portfolios and Exhibitions

The concern with authentic assessment has led to the development of several new approaches based on the goal of *performance in context*. Instead of circling answers to "factual" questions on nonexistent situations, students are required to solve real problems. Facts are used in a context where they apply—for example, the student uses grammar facts to write a persuasive letter to a software company requesting donations for the class computer center. The following example of a test of performance is taken from the Connecticut Core of Common Learning:

> Many local supermarkets claim to have the lowest prices. But what does this really mean? Does it mean that every item in their store is priced lower, or just some of them? How can you really tell which supermarket will save

Authentic Tests Assessment procedures that test skills and abilities as they would be applied in real-life situations.

TABLE 15.5   Characteristics of Authentic Tests

A. Structure and Logistics

1. Are more appropriately public; involve an audience, a panel, and so on.
2. Do not rely on unrealistic and arbitrary time constraints.
3. Offer known, not secret, questions or tasks.
4. Are more like portfolios or a *season* of games (not one-shot).
5. Require some collaboration with others.
6. Recur—and are *worth* practicing for, rehearsing, and retaking.
7. Make assessment and feedback to students so central that school schedules, structures, and policies are modified to support them.

B. Intellectual Design Features

1. Are "essential"—not needlessly intrusive, arbitrary, or contrived to "shake out" a grade.
2. Are "enabling"—constructed to point the student toward more sophisticated use of the skills or knowledge.
3. Are contextualized, complex intellectual challenges, not "atomized" tasks, corresponding to isolated "outcomes."
4. Involve the student's own research or use of knowledge, for which "content" is a means.
5. Assess student habits and repertoires, not mere recall or plug-in skills.
6. Are *representative* challenges—designed to emphasize *depth* more than breadth.

7. Are engaging and educational.
8. Involve somewhat ambiguous ("ill-structured") tasks or problems.

C. Grading and Scoring Standards

1. Involve criteria that assess essentials, not easily counted (but relatively unimportant) errors.
2. Are graded not on a "curve" but in reference to performance standards (criterion-referenced, not norm-referenced).
3. Involve demystified criteria of success that appear to *students* as inherent in successful activity.
4. Make self-assessment a part of the assessment.
5. Use a multifaceted scoring system instead of one aggregate grade.
6. Exhibit harmony with shared schoolwide aims—a *standard*.

D. Fairness and Equity

1. Ferret out and identify (perhaps hidden) strengths.
2. Strike a *constantly* examined balance between honoring achievement and native skill or fortunate prior training.
3. Minimize needless, unfair, and demoralizing comparisons.
4. Allow appropriate room for student learning styles, aptitudes, and interests.
5. Can be—should be—attempted by *all* students, with the test "scaffolded up," not "dumbed down," as necessary.

Source: From Grant Wiggins. "Teaching to the authentic test." *Educational Leadership, 45*(7), p. 44. Reprinted by permission of the Association of Supervision and Curriculum Development. Copyright © 1989 by ASCD. All rights reserved.

you the most money? Your assignment is to design and carry out a study to answer this question. What items and prices will you compare and why? How will you justify the choice of your "sample"? How reliable is the sample, etc.? (Wolf, Bixby, Glenn, & Gardner, 1991, p. 61)

Students completing this "test" will use mathematical facts and procedures in the context of solving a real-life problem. In addition, they will have to think critically and write persuasively.

Portfolios and exhibitions are two new approaches to assessment that require performance in context. With these new approaches, it is difficult to tell where instruction stops and assessment starts because the two processes are interwoven.

Portfolios.   According to Paulson, Paulson, and Meyer (1991), **portfolio** is:

a purposeful collection of student work that exhibits the student's efforts, progress, and achievements in one or more areas. The collection must in-

Portfolio A collection of the student's work in an area, showing growth, self reflection, and achievement.

FIGURE 15.1

A Student Reflects on Learning: Self-Analysis of Work in a Portfolio

Not only has this student's writing improved, but the student has become a more self-aware and self-critical writer.

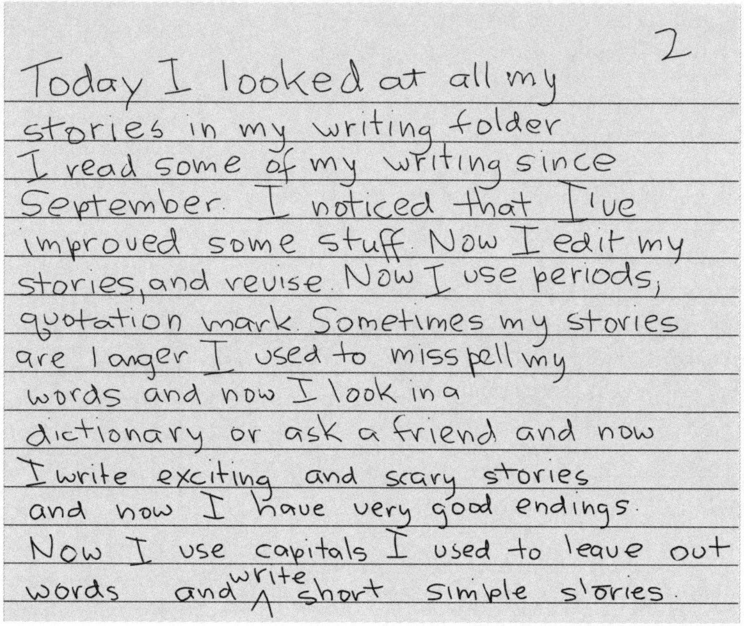

Today I looked at all my stories in my writing folder I read some of my writing since September. I noticed that I've improved some stuff. Now I edit my stories, and revise. Now I use periods, quotation mark. Sometimes my stories are longer I used to miss spell my words and now I look in a dictionary or ask a friend and now I write exciting and scary stories and now I have very good endings. Now I use capitals I used to leave out words and write short simple stories.

Source: From F. Leon Paulson, P. Paulson, and C. Meyers. "What makes a portfolio a portfolio?" *Educational Leadership, 48, 5,* p. 63. Reprinted with permission of the Association for Supervision and Curriculum Development. Copyright © 1991 by ASCD. All rights reserved.

clude student participation in selecting contents, the criteria for judging merit, and evidence of student self-reflection. (p. 60)

Portfolios often include work in progress, revisions, student self-analyses, and reflections on what the student has learned. For example, one student's self-reflection is presented in Figure 15.1.

Written work or artistic pieces are common contents of portfolios, but students might also include graphs, diagrams, snapshots of displays, peer comments, audio- or videotapes, laboratory reports, computer programs—anything that demonstrates learning in the area being taught and assessed (Belanoff & Dickson, 1991; Camp, 1990; Wolf, Bixby, Glenn, & Gardner, 1991). The Vermont Mathematics Portfolio, for example, has (a) five to seven of the student's "best pieces," including at least one puzzle, one investigation, one application, and no more than two examples of group work; (b) a letter to the portfolio examiner; and (c) a collection of other pieces of mathematics work (Abruscato, 1993). The Guidelines on the following page give some ideas for using portfolios in your teaching.

Students should be involved in selecting the pieces that will make up the portfolio.

Examples

1. During the unit or semester, ask each student to select work that fits certain criteria, such as "my most difficult problem," "my best work," "my most improved work," or "three approaches to. . . ."

2. For their final submissions, ask students to select pieces that best show how much they have learned.

A portfolio should include information that shows student self-reflection and self-criticism.

Examples

1. Ask students to include a rationale for their selections.

2. Have each student write a "guide" to his or her portfolio, explaining how strengths and weaknesses are reflected in the work included.

3. Include self- and peer critiques, indicating specifically what is good and what might be improved.

4. Model self-criticism of your own productions.

The portfolio should reflect the students' activities in learning.

Examples

1. Include a representative selection of projects, writings, drawings, and so forth.

2. Ask students to relate the goals of learning to the contents of their portfolios.

The portfolio can serve different functions at different times of the year.

Examples

1. Early in the year, it might hold unfinished work or "problem pieces."

2. At the end of the year, it should contain only what the student is willing to make public.

Portfolios should show growth.

Examples

1. Ask students to make a "history" of their progress along certain dimensions and to illustrate points in their growth with specific works.

2. Ask students to include descriptions of activities outside class that reflect the growth illustrated in the portfolio.

Teach students how to create and use portfolios.

Examples

1. Keep models of very well done portfolios as examples, but stress that each portfolio is an individual statement.

2. Examine your students' portfolios frequently, especially early in the year when they are just getting used to the idea. Give constructive feedback.

*T*o prepare for this performance, students may have conducted historical research, written scripts, and negotiated their roles in the oral presentation. How will the teacher assess individual learning?

Exhibitions.   An **exhibition** is a performance test that has two additional features. First, it is public, so students preparing exhibitions must take the audience into account; communication and understanding are essential. Second, an exhibition often requires many hours of preparation, because it is the culminating experience of a whole program of study. Ted Sizer (1984) proposed that "exhibitions of mastery" replace traditional tests in determining graduation or course completion requirements. Grant Wiggins (1989) believes that an exhibition of mastery "is meant to be more than a better test. Like the thesis and oral examination in graduate school, it indicates whether a student has earned a diploma, is ready to leave high school" (p. 47).

Evaluating Portfolios and Performances

Checklists, rating scales, and scoring rubrics are helpful when you assess performances, because assessments of performances, portfolios, and exhibitions are criterion-referenced, not norm-referenced. In other words, the students' products and performances are compared to established public standards, not ranked in relation to other students' work (Cambourne & Turbill, 1990; Wiggins, 1991). For example, Figure 15.2 gives three alternatives—numerical, graphic, and descriptive—for rating an oral presentation.

Scoring Rubrics.   A checklist or rating scale gives specific feedback about elements of a performance. **Scoring rubrics** are more general descriptions of overall performance. For example, a rubric describing an excellent oral presentation might be:

> Pupil consistently faces audience, stands straight, and maintains eye contact; voice projects well and clearly; pacing and tone variation appropriate; well-organized; points logically and completely presented; brief summary at end. (Airasian, 1996, p. 155)

Exhibition A performance test or demonstration of learning that is public and usually takes an extended time to prepare.

Scoring Rubric A general description of different levels of performance, equivalent to different scores or grades.

FIGURE 15.2

Three Ways of Rating an Oral Presentation

Numerical Rating Scale

Directions: Indicate how often the pupil performs each of these behaviors while giving an oral presentation. For each behavior circle **1** if the pupil **always** performs the behavior, **2** if the pupil **usually** performs the behavior, **3** if the pupil **seldom** performs the behavior, and **4** if the pupil **never** performs the behavior.

Physical Expression

A. Stand straight and faces audience.

    1 2 3 4

B. Changes facial expression with change in the tone of the presentation.

    1 2 3 4

Graphic Rating Scale

Directions: Place an **X** on the line which shows how often the pupil did each of the behaviors listed while giving an oral presentation.

Physical Expression

A. Stands straight and faces the audience.

    always   usually   seldom   never

B. Changes facial expressions with change in tone of the presentation.

    always   usually   seldom   never

Descriptive Rating Scale

Directions: Place an **X** on the line at the place which best describes the pupil's performance on each behavior.

Physical Expression

A. Stands straight and faces audience.

stands straight, always looks at audience	weaves, fidgets, eyes roam from audience to ceiling	constant, distracting movements, no eye contact with audience

B. Changes facial expressions with change in tone of the presentation.

matches facial expressions to content and emphasis	facial expressions usually appropriate, occasional lack of expression	no match between tone and facial expression; expression distracts

Source: From P. W. Airasian. *Assessment in the classroom,* p. 153. Copyright © 1996 by The McGraw-Hill Companies. Reproduced with permission of The McGraw-Hill Companies.

It is often helpful to have students join in the development of rating scales and scoring rubrics. When students participate, they are challenged to decide what quality work looks or sounds like in a particular area. They know in advance what is expected. As students gain practice in designing and applying scoring rubrics, their work and their learning often improve. Figure 15.3 on page 574 is an evaluation form for self- and peer assessment of contributions to cooperative learning groups.

FIGURE 15.3

Self and Peer Evaluation of Group Learning

STUDENT SELF- AND PEER EVALUATION FORM

This form will be used to assess the members of your learning group. Fill one form out on yourself. Fill one form out on each member of your group. During the group discussion, give each member the form you have filled out on them. Compare the way you rated yourself with the ways your groupmates have rated you. Ask for clarification when your rating differs from the ratings given you by your groupmates. Each member should set a goal for increasing his or her contribution to the academic learning of all group members.

Person Being Rated: _____

Write the number of points earned by the group member:
(4=Excellent, 3=Good, 2=Poor, 1=Inadequate)

____On time for class.

____Arrives prepared for class.

____Reliably completes all assigned work on time.

____Work is of high quality.

____Contributes to groupmates' learning daily.

____Asks for academic help and assistance when it is needed.

____Gives careful step-by-step explanations (doesn't just tell answers).

____Builds on others' reasoning.

____Relates what is being learned to previous knowledge.

____Helps draw a visual representation of what is being learned.

____Voluntarily extends a project.

Source: From D. W. Johnson and R. T. Johnson. "The role of cooperative learning in assessing and communicating student learning." In T. Guskey (Ed.), *ASCD 1996 Yearbook: Communicating student learning,* p. 41. Reprinted by permission of the Association for Supervision and Curriculum Development. Copyright © 1996 by ASCD. All rights reserved.

Performance assessment requires careful judgment on the part of teachers and clear communication to students about what is good and what needs improving. In some ways the approach is similar to the clinical method first introduced by Binet to assess intelligence: It is based on observing the student perform a variety of tasks and comparing his or her performance to a standard. Just as Binet never wanted to assign a single number to represent the child's intelligence, teachers who use authentic assessments do not try to assign one score to the student's performance. Even if rankings, ratings, and grades have to be given, these judgments are not the ultimate goals—improvement of learning is. If you look back to Table 15.5 you will see other grading characteristics of performance tests.

Reliability, Validity, and Equity.   Because judgment plays such a central role in evaluating performances, issues of reliability, validity, and equity are critical considerations. As we saw in the previous chapter, judges assessing the Vermont Portfolios often have not agreed on ratings, so reliability may not be adequate. When raters are experienced and scoring rubrics are well developed and refined, however, reliability may improve (Herman & Winters, 1994; LeMahieu,

Gitomer, & Eresh, 1993). In terms of validity, there is some evidence that students who are classified as "master" writers on the basis of portfolio assessment are judged less capable using standard writing assessment. Which form of assessment is the best reflection of enduring qualities? There is so little research on this question, it is hard to say. (Herman & Winters, 1994).

Equity is an issue in all assessment and no less so with performances and portfolios. With a public performance there could be bias effects based on a student's appearance and speech or the student's access to expensive audio, video, or graphic resources. Performance assessments have the same potential as other tests to discriminate unfairly against students who are not wealthy or who are culturally different (McDonald, 1993). And the extensive group work, peer editing, and out-of-class time devoted to portfolios means that some students may have access to more extensive networks of support and outright help. Many students in your classes will have families with sophisticated computer graphic and desktop publishing capabilities. Others may have little support from home. These differences can be sources of bias and inequity.

> **Focus on...**
>
> ### Authentic Assessment
>
> - Summarize the characteristics of authentic assessment.
> - How can checklists and rating scales be used to assess student portfolios and exhibitions? What should be included in the assessment?
> - How would you assure reliability, validity, and equity in your use of authentic assessment tasks?

Effects of Grades and Grading on Students

There is some evidence that high standards, a competitive class atmosphere, and a large percentage of lower grades are associated with increased absenteeism and dropout rates (Moos & Moos, 1978; Trickett & Moos, 1974). This seems especially likely with disadvantaged students (Wessman, 1972). Highly competitive classes may be particularly hard on anxious students or students who lack self-confidence. So, while high standards and competition do tend generally to be related to increased academic learning, it is clear that a balance must be struck between high standards and a reasonable chance to succeed.

Effects of Failure

It may sound as though low grades and failure should be avoided in school. But the situation is not that simple. After reviewing many years of research on the effects of failure from several perspectives, Margaret Clifford (1990, 1991) concluded that failure can have both positive and negative effects on subsequent performance, depending on the situation and the personality of the students involved.

For example, one study required subjects to complete three sets of problems. On the first set, the experimenters arranged for subjects to experience either zero, 50, or 100% success. On the second set, it was arranged for all subjects to fail completely. On the third set of problems, the experimenters merely recorded how well the subjects performed. Those who had succeeded only 50% of the time before the failure experience performed the best. It appears that a history of complete failure or 100% success may be bad preparation for learning to cope with failure, something we must all learn. Some level of failure may be helpful for most students, especially if teachers help the students see connections between hard work and improvement. Efforts to protect students from fail-

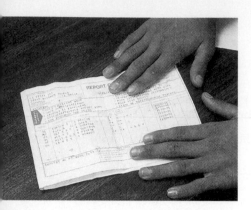

What effects will these grades have on the student? That depends in part on what grades the student expected and on his usual level of performance.

ure and guarantee success may be counterproductive. Clifford (1990) gives this advice to teachers:

> It is time for educators to replace easy success with challenge. We must encourage students to reach beyond their intellectual grasp and allow them the privilege of learning from mistakes. There must be a tolerance for error-making in every classroom, and gradual success rather than continual success must become the yardstick by which learning is judged. (p. 23)

The more able your students, the more challenging and important it will be to help them learn to "fail successfully" (Foster, 1981).

So far, we have been talking about the effects of failing a test or perhaps a course. But what about the effect of failing an entire grade—that is, of being "held back"? Some researchers believe that being held back injures students' self-esteem and increases the chances that they will drop out of school (Grissom & Smith, 1989; Roderick, 1994). In their view, students generally do better academically when promoted. Other researchers have found some advantage for children who are retained in first, second, or third grade (Pierson & Connell, 1992), but the advantage may not last. In one study that followed many students for several years, children who could have been retained, but who were promoted, did about as well as similar children who were held back. No matter what, students who have trouble should get help, whether they are promoted or retained. Just covering the same material again in the same way won't solve the students' academic or social problems. The best approach may be to promote the students along with their peers, but to give them special remediation during the summer or the next year (Mantzicopoulos & Morrison, 1992; Shepard & Smith, 1989).

Effects of Feedback

The results of several studies of feedback fit well with the notion of "successful" or constructive failure. These studies have concluded that it is more helpful to tell students *why* they are wrong so they can learn more appropriate strategies (Bangert-Drowns, Kulik, Kulik, & Morgan, 1991). Students often need help figuring out why their answers are incorrect. Without such feedback, they are likely to make the same mistakes again. Yet this type of feedback is rarely given. In one study, only about 8% of the teachers noticed a consistent type of error in a student's arithmetic computation and informed the student (Bloom & Bourdon, 1980).

Early research indicated that teachers' written comments on completed assignments can lead to improved performance in the future (Page, 1958). In more recent work the emphasis has been on identifying characteristics of effective written feedback. With older students (late elementary through high school), written comments are most helpful when they are personalized and when they provide constructive criticism. This means the teacher should make specific comments on errors or faulty strategies, but balance this criticism with suggestions about how to improve, and with comments on the positive aspects of the work (Butler & Nisan, 1986; Elawar & Corno, 1985). Working with sixth-grade teachers, Elawar and Corno (1985) found that feedback was dramatically improved when the teachers used these four questions as a guide: "What is the key error? What is

Focus on...

Feedback

- Summarize the characteristics of effective feedback.
- How can grading support student learning? Can authentic assessment play a role? How?

the probable reason the student made this error? How can I guide the student to avoid the error in the future? What did the student do well that could be noted?" (p. 166). Here are some examples of teachers' written comments that proved helpful (Elawar & Corno, 1985, p. 164):

> Juan, you know how to get a percent, but the computation is wrong in this instance. . . . Can you see where? (Teacher has underlined the location of errors.)

> You know how to solve the problem—the formula is correct—but you have not demonstrated that you understand how one fraction multiplied by another can give an answer that is smaller than either ($\frac{1}{2} \times \frac{1}{2} = \frac{1}{4}$).

Extensive written comments may be inappropriate for younger students, but brief written comments are a different matter. These comments should help students correct errors and should recognize good work, progress, and increasing skill.

Grades and Motivation

Is there really a difference between working for a grade and working to learn? The answer depends in part on how a grade is determined. As a teacher, you can use grades to motivate the kind of learning you intend students to achieve in your course. If you test only at a simple but detailed level of knowledge, you may force students to choose between higher aspects of learning and a good grade. But when a grade reflects meaningful learning, working for a grade and working to learn become the same thing. Finally, while high grades may have some value as rewards or incentives for meaningful engagement in learning, low grades generally do not encourage greater efforts. Students receiving low grades are more likely to withdraw, blame others, decide that the work is "dumb," or feel responsible for the low grade but helpless to make improvements. Rather than give a failing grade, you might consider the work incomplete and give students support in revising or improving. Maintain high standards and give students a chance to reach them (Guskey, 1994). The Guidelines summarize the effects grades can have on students.

Guidelines

Minimizing the Detrimental Effects of Grading

Avoid reserving high grades and high praise for answers that conform to your ideas or to those in the textbook.

Examples

1. Give extra points for correct and creative answers.
2. Withhold your opinions until all sides of an issue have been explored.
3. Reinforce students for disagreeing in a rational, productive manner.
4. Give partial credit for partially correct answers.

Make sure each student has a reasonable chance to be successful, especially at the beginning of a new task.

Examples

1. Pretest students to make sure they have prerequisite abilities.
2. When appropriate, provide opportunities for students to retest to raise their grades, but make sure the retest is as difficult as the original.

(continued)

3. Consider failing efforts as "incomplete" and encourage students to revise and improve.

Balance written and oral feedback.

Examples

1. Consider giving short, lively written comments with younger students and more extensive written comments with older students.
2. When the grade on a paper is lower than the student might have expected, be sure the reason for the lower grade is clear.
3. Tailor comments to the individual student's performance; avoid writing the same phrases over and over.
4. Note specific errors, possible reasons for errors, ideas for improvement, and work done well.

Make grades as meaningful as possible.

Examples

1. Tie grades to the mastery of important objectives.
2. Give ungraded assignments to encourage exploration.
3. Experiment with performances and portfolios.

Base grades on more than just one criterion.

Examples

1. Use essay questions as well as multiple-choice items on a test.
2. Grade oral reports and class participation.

Grading and Reporting: Nuts and Bolts

In determining a final grade, the teacher must make a major decision. Should a student's grade reflect the amount of material learned and how well it has been learned, or should the grade reflect the student's status in comparison with the rest of the class? In other words, should grading be criterion-referenced or norm-referenced?

Criterion-Referenced versus Norm-Referenced Grading

In **criterion-referenced grading,** the grade represents a list of accomplishments. If clear objectives have been set for the course, the grade may represent a certain number of objectives met satisfactorily. When a criterion-referenced system is used, criteria for each grade generally are spelled out in advance. It is then up to the student to earn the grade she or he wants to receive. Theoretically, in this system all students can achieve an A if they reach the criteria.

In **norm-referenced grading,** the major influence on a grade is the student's standing in comparison with others who also took the course. If a student studies very hard and almost everyone else does too, the student may receive a disappointing grade, perhaps a C.

Criterion-Referenced Systems. Criterion-referenced grading has the advantage of relating judgments about a student to the achievement of clearly de-

Criterion-Referenced Grading Assessment of each student's mastery of course objectives.

Norm-Referenced Grading Assessment of students' achievement in relation to one another.

fined instructional goals. Some school districts have developed reporting systems where report cards list objectives along with judgments about the student's attainment of each. Reporting is done at the end of each unit of instruction. The junior high report card shown in Figure 15.4 demonstrates the relationship between assessment and the goals of the unit.

FIGURE 15.4

A Criterion-Referenced Report Card

This is one example of a criterion-referenced report card. Other forms are possible, but all criterion-referenced reports indicate student progress toward specific goals.

LINCOLN ELEMENTARY SCHOOL
GRADE 5

Student _____   Teacher _____   Principal ___Muriel Simms___   Quarter 2 3 4

E = Excellent   S = Satisfactory   P = Making Progress   N = Needs improvement

READING PROGRAM
Materials Used: _____
_____

___ Reads with understanding
___ Is able to write about what is read
___ Completes reading group work accurately and on time
___ Shows interest in reading

Reading Skills
___ Decodes new words
___ Understands new words

Independent Reading Level
Below   At Grade Level   Above

LANGUAGE ARTS
___ Uses oral language effectively
___ Listens carefully
___ Masters weekly spelling

Writing skills
___ Understands writing as process
___ Creates a rough draft
___ Makes meaningful revisions
___ Creates edited, legible final draft

Editing skills
___ Capitalizes
___ Punctuates
___ Uses complete sentences
___ Uses paragraphs
___ Demonstrates dictionary skills

Writing skill level:
Below   At Grade Level   Above

MATHEMATICS
Problem Solving
___ Solves teacher-generated problems
___ Solves Self/Student-generated problems
___ Can create story problems

Interpreting Problems
___ Uses appropriate strategies
___ Can use more than one strategy
___ Can explain strategies in written form
___ Can explain strategies orally

Math Concepts
    Understands Base Ten
Beginning Developing Sophisticated
    Multiplication, Basic facts
Beginning Developing Sophisticated
    2 digit Multiplication
Beginning Developing Sophisticated
    Division
Beginning Developing Sophisticated
    Geometry
Beginning Developing Sophisticated

Overall Math Skill Level:
Beginning Developing Sophisticated

Attitude/Work Skills
___ Welcomes a challenge
___ Persistent
___ Takes advantage of learning from others
___ Listens to others
___ Participates in discussion

It Figures
Is working on: _____

Goals: _____
Is working on achieving goal: _____

SOCIAL STUDIES
___ Understands subject matter
___ Shows curiosity and enthusiasm
___ Contributes to class discussions
___ Uses map skills
___ Demonstrates control of reading skills by interpreting text
Topics covered: individual cultures, Columbus–first English colonies

SCIENCE
___ Shows curiosity about scientific subject matter
___ Asks good scientific questions
___ Shows knowledge of scientific method
___ Uses knowledge of scientific method to help set up and run experiment(s)
___ Makes good scientific observations
___ Has researched scientific topic(s)
    Topic(s) _____

I Wonder
Is currently working on _____
_____

WORKING SKILLS
___ Listens carefully
___ Follows directions
___ Works neatly and carefully
___ Checks work
___ Completes work on time
___ Uses time wisely
___ Works well independently
___ Works well in a group
___ Takes risks in learning
___ Welcomes a challenge

HOMEWORK
___ Self-selects homework
___ Completes work accurately
___ Completes work on time

PRESENTATIONS/PROJECTS
_____
_____

HUMAN RELATIONS
___ Shows courtesy
___ Respects rights of others
___ Shows self-control
___ Interacts well with peers
___ Shows a cooperative and positive attitude in class
___ Shows a cooperative attitude when asked to work with other students
___ Is willing to help other students
___ Works well with other adults (subs, student teacher, parents, etc.)

Attendance

	1st	2nd	3rd	4th
Present				
Absent				
Tardy				

Placement for next year:

In practice, many school systems would look askance at a teacher who turned in a roster filled with As and explained that all the students had reached the class objectives. Administrators might say that if all the objectives could be so easily attained by all the students, then more or tougher objectives would be needed. Nevertheless, a criterion-referenced system may be acceptable in some schools.

Norm-Referenced Systems.   One common type of norm-referenced grading is called **grading on the curve.** In grading on the curve, the middle of the normal distribution or "average" performance becomes the anchor on which grading is based. In other words, teachers look at the average level of performance, assign what they consider an "average grade" for this performance, and then grade superior performances higher and inferior performances lower.

If grading were done strictly on the normal curve, there would be an equal number of As and Fs, a larger number of Bs and Ds, and an even larger number of Cs. The grades would have to form a bell-shaped curve. For example, a teacher might decide to give 10 percent As and Fs, 20 percent Bs and Ds, and 40 percent Cs. This is a very strict interpretation of grading on the curve, and will discourage students who work hard, but always perform below average.

Grading on the curve can be done with varying levels of precision. The simplest approach is to rank-order the students' raw scores on a test and use this ranked list of scores as the basis for assigning grades. Knowing that two-thirds of the scores in a normal distribution should be in the middle, you might bracket off the middle two-thirds of the scores and plan to give those students C's (or B's, if you believed B was an average grade for the class in question). Some people prefer to use the middle one-third of the students rather than the middle two-thirds as the basis for the average grade. Based on this second approach, grades for the following scores might be:

Middle One-Third Assigned C's

A	B	C	D	F

92 | 91 91 90 83 80 78 76 | 72 68 65 61 57 54 53 49 | 48 47 46 43 38 36 | 29 29

In this example the distance between one letter grade and another is sometimes one point! Given the amount of error in testing, this assignment of grades is probably not fair. You can correct some of these problems by introducing common sense into the process. For example, you may believe the following grade assignment is fairer:

Adjusted Grades

A	B	C	D	F

92 91 91 90 | 83 80 78 76 72 | 68 65 61 57 54 53 | 49 48 47 46 43 38 36 | 29 29

In this case the instructor has used the natural gaps in the range of scores to locate boundaries between grades. Between the A and B categories are 7 points, between the B and C, 4 points, and so on. Even though this may seem fairer, many educators encourage teachers to avoid grading on the curve because this approach determines in advance that students must compete for the few good grades available (Guskey, 1994; Kohn, 1994).

Grading on the Curve Norm-referenced grading that compares students' performance to an average level.

	TABLE 15.6 Comparing Norm-Referenced and Criterion-Referenced Standards for Grading	

Norm-referenced systems use the performance of the rest of the class as the standard for determining grades. Criterion-referenced systems use standards of subject mastery and learning to determine grades.

Grade	Criterion-referenced	Norm-referenced
A	Firm command of knowledge domain High level of skill development Exceptional preparation for later learning	Far above class average
B	Command of knowledge beyond the minimum Advanced development of most skills Has prerequisites for later learning	Above class average
C	Command of only the basic concepts of knowledge Demonstrated ability to use basic skills Lacks a few prerequisites for later learning	At the class average
D	Lacks knowledge of some fundamental ideas Some important skills not attained Deficient in many of the prerequisites for later learning	Below class average
F	Most of the basic concepts and principles not learned Most essential skills cannot be demonstrated Lacks most prerequisites needed for later learning	Far below class average

Source: From D. A. Frisbie and K. K. Waltmen. Developing a personal grading plan. *Educational Measurement: Issues and practices*, p. 37. Copyright 1992 by the National Council on Measurement in Education. Reprinted by permission of the publisher.

Table 15.6 compares descriptions of a student's performance using criterion-referenced and norm-referenced standards and suggests a way to translate these descriptions into grades.

Preparing Report Cards

Whatever grading system you use, you will undoubtedly give several tests and you will probably assign homework or projects. Let's assume your unit assessment plan includes two short tests (mostly multiple-choice questions with one essay), homework, a portfolio, and a unit test. If you use a criterion-referenced system for testing and grading, how will you convert scores on these individual performances to the overall indications of mastery on a report card such as that in Figure 15.6 What about using a norm-referenced system? How do you combine results from individual tests and assignments to yield a final distribution of scores for the unit grade?

Let us consider criterion-referenced grading first. If you adopt this system, you cannot average or combine test scores or homework grades mathematically.

Since each test and assignment measures the mastery of a particular objective (or set of objectives), it would be meaningless to average, say, the students' mastery of addition of two-digit numbers with their mastery of measurement with a ruler, although both might be objectives in arithmetic. On the report card, the various objectives are listed and the student's level of proficiency in each is indicated.

Norm-referenced grading is a different story. In order to assign grades, the teacher must merge all the scores from tests and other assignments into one final score. Final grades are based on how each student's final score compares with that of the rest of the students. But the usual procedure of simply adding up all the scores and averaging the total is often not appropriate, and it can be misleading. For example, assume two students took two tests. The tests are equally important in the overall unit. The students' scores are shown below (from Chase, 1978, p. 328).

	Test 1 Class mean = 30 Standard deviation = 8	Test 2 Class mean = 50 Standard deviation = 16	Total Raw score
Leslie	38	50	88
Jason	30	66	96

If we compute an average or if we rank the students based on their totals, Jason will be ahead of Leslie. But if we look at the class mean and standard deviation for each test, we see a different picture. On one test, Leslie's score was 1 standard deviation above the mean, and on the other her score was at the mean; Jason's record is exactly the same.

If these two tests are really equally important, Jason and Leslie have identical records in relation to the rest of the class on these tests. To compare students' performances on several tests, the scores for each must be converted to a standard scale like a T score. As you may recall from Chapter 14, a T mean is automatically 50 and the standard deviation is 10. Most teachers do not calculate T scores for all their students, but the example illustrates the importance of using common sense in grading. Gross totals do not always reflect how well one student is doing in relation to others in the class.

The Point System

One popular system for combining grades from many assignments is a point system. Each test or assignment is given a certain number of total points, depending on its importance. A test worth 40% of the grade could be worth 40 points. A paper worth 20% could be worth 20 points. Points are then awarded on the test or paper based upon specific criteria. An A+ paper, one that meets all the criteria, could be given the full 20 points; an average paper might be given 10 points. If tests of comparable importance are worth the same number of points, are equally difficult, and cover a similar amount of material, we can ex-

TABLE 15.7	Points Earned on Five Assignments					
Student	Test 1 20% 20 points	Test 2 20% 20 points	Unit Test 30% 30 points	Homework 15% 15 points	Portfolio 15% 15 points	Total
Amy	10	12	16	6	7	___
Lee	12	10	14	7	6	___
Luis	20	19	30	15	13	___
Wayne	18	20	25	15	15	___
Étienne	6	5	12	4	10	___
Frieda	10	12	18	10	9	___
Grace	13	11	22	11	10	___
Houston	7	9	12	5	6	___
Isaac	14	16	26	12	12	___
Liz	20	18	28	10	15	___
Keith	19	20	25	11	12	___
Linda	14	12	20	13	9	___
Melody	15	13	24	8	10	___
Ned	8	7	12	8	6	___
Olivia	11	12	16	9	10	___
Peter	7	8	11	4	8	___

pect to avoid some of the problems encountered with Jason and Leslie, when the means and standard deviations of two supposedly comparable tests varied so greatly.

Let us assume a grade book indicates the scores shown in Table 15.7. How would you assign grades to students for this unit? The most common way is to find the total number of points for each student and rank the students. Assign grades by looking for natural gaps of several points or imposing a curve (a certain percentage of As, Bs, and so on).

Percentage Grading

There is another approach to assigning grades to a group of students like those in Table 15.6. Using **percentage grading** the teacher can assign grades based on how much knowledge each student has mastered—what percentage of the total knowledge he or she understands. To do this, the teacher might score tests and other classwork with percentage scores (based on how much is correct—50%, 85%, etc.) and then average these scores to reach a course score. These scores can then be converted into letter grades according to predetermined cutoff points. Any number of students can earn any grade. This procedure is very common; you may have experienced it yourself as a student. Let us look at it more closely, because it has some frequently overlooked problems.

The grading symbols of A, B, C, D, and F are probably the most popular means of reporting at the present time. School systems often establish equiva-

Percentage Grading System of converting class performances to percentage scores and assigning grades based on predetermined cutoff points.

lent percentage categories for each of these symbols. The percentages vary from school district to school district, but two typical ones are as follows:

90–100% = A; 80–89% = B; 70–79% = C; 60–69% = D; below 60% = F

94–100% = A; 85–93% = B; 76–83% = C; 70–75% = D; below 70% = F

As you can see, although both districts have an A to F five-point grading system, the average achievement required for each grade is different.

But can we really say what is the total amount of knowledge available in, for example, eighth-grade science? Are we sure we can accurately measure what percentage of this body of knowledge each student has attained? To use percentage grading appropriately, we would have to know exactly what there was to learn and exactly how much of that each student had learned. These conditions are seldom met, even though teachers use the cutoff points to assign grades as if measurement were so accurate that a one-point difference was meaningful: "In spite of decades of research in educational and psychological measurement, which has produced more defensible methods, the concept [of percentage grading], once established, has proved remarkably resistant to change" (Zimmerman, 1981, p. 178).

Any grading system prescribed or suggested by the school can be influenced by particular concerns of the teacher. So don't be fooled by the seeming security of absolute percentages. Your own grading philosophy will continue to operate, even in this system. Because there is more concern today with specifying objectives and criterion-referenced assessment, especially at the elementary-grade levels, several alternative methods for evaluating student progress against predetermined criteria have evolved. We will look at one: the contract system.

The Contract System and Grading Rubrics

When applied to the whole class, the **contract system** indicates the type, quantity, and quality of work required for each number or letter grade in the system. Rubrics describe the performance expected for each level. Students agree, or "contract," to work for particular grades by meeting the specified requirements and performing at the level specified. For example, the following standards might be established:

F: Not coming to class regularly or not turning in the required work.

D: Coming to class regularly and turning in the required work on time.

C: Coming to class regularly, turning in the required work on time, and receiving a check mark on all assignments to indicate they are satisfactory.

B: Coming to class regularly, turning in the required work on time, and receiving a check mark on all assignments except at least three that achieve a check-plus, indicating superior achievement.

A: As above, plus a successful oral or written report on one of the books listed for supplementary reading.

This example calls for more subjective judgment than would be ideal. However, contract systems reduce student anxiety about grades. The contract system can be applied to individual students, in which case it functions much like an independent study plan.

Contract System System in which each student works for a particular grade according to agreed-on standards.

Unfortunately, the system can lead to overemphasis on the quantity of work. Teachers may be too vague about the standards that differentiate acceptable from unacceptable work. This is where scoring rubrics for each assignment can be helpful. If clear and well-developed rubrics describe the performances expected for each assignment, and if students learn to use the rubrics to evaluate their own work, then quality, not quantity, will be at the center of grading. A teacher can modify the contract system by including a **revise option.** For example, a check mark might be worth 75 points and a check-plus 90 points; a check-plus earned after revision could be worth 85 points—more than a check, but less than a check-plus earned the first time around. This system allows students to improve their work, but also rewards getting it right the first time. Some quality control is possible, because students earn points not just for quantity but also for quality. In addition, the teacher may be less reluctant to judge a project unsatisfactory because students can improve their work (King, 1979). But beware, if a school system requires a five-point grading scale and all students contract for and achieve the highest grade (before or after revising), the teacher will wish that the principal had been consulted about the system before the grades came out.

"I HOPE THIS ISN'T ANOTHER PLOY TO UP YOUR GRADE, HASKELL."

(© Art Bouthillier)

Grading on Effort and Improvement

Grading on effort and improvement is not really a complete grading system but rather a theme that can run through most grading methods. Should teachers grade students based on how much they learn or on the final level of learning? One problem with using improvement as a standard for grading is that the best students improve the least, because they are already the most competent. Do you want to penalize these students because they knew quite a bit initially, and the teaching and testing have limited how much learning they can demonstrate? After all, unless you assign extra work, these students will run out of things to do.

One solution is to use the **individual learning expectation (ILE)** system. With this system students earn improvement points on tests or assignments for scoring above their personal base (average) score or for making a perfect score. The teacher can count these improvement points when figuring a final grade or simply use them as a basis for giving other classroom rewards.

Many teachers try to include some judgment of effort in final grades, but effort is difficult to assess. Are you certain your perception of each student's effort is correct? Clement (1978) suggests a system for including a judgment about effort in the final grade called the **dual marking system.** Students are assigned two grades. One, usually a letter, indicates the actual level of achievement. The other, a number, indicates the relationship of the achievement to the student's ability and effort. For example, a grade of B could be qualified as follows (Clement, 1978, p. 51):

B1: Outstanding effort, better achievement than expected, good attitude

B2: Average effort, satisfactory in terms of ability

B3: Lower achievement than ability would indicate, poor attitude

Of course, this system assumes that the teacher can adequately judge true ability and effort. A grade of D1, D2, or F2 could be quite insulting. A grade of

Revise Option In a contract system, the chance to revise and improve work.

Individual Learning Expectation (ILE) Personal average score.

Dual Marking System System of assigning two grades, one reflecting achievement, the other effort, attitude, and actual ability.

A3 or F1 should not be possible. But the system does have the advantage of recognizing hard work and giving feedback about a seeming lack of effort. An A2 or B2 might tell very bright students: "You're doing well, but I know you could do better." This could help the students to expect more of themselves and not slip by on high ability. The overall grade—A, B, C—still reflects achievement and is not changed (or biased) by teachers' subjective judgment of effort.

Focus on...

Grading Systems

- What grading systems are you experiencing right now in your college classes?
- What are the advantages and disadvantages of contract grading?
- What are the advantages and disadvantages of percentage grading?
- What are the advantages and disadvantages of grading on the curve?

Cautions: Being Fair

The attributions a teacher makes about the causes of student successes or failures can affect the grades that students receive. Teachers are more likely to give higher grades for effort (a controllable factor) than for ability (an uncontrollable factor). Lower grades are more likely when teachers attribute a student's failure to lack of effort instead of lack of ability (Weiner, 1979). It is also possible that grades can be influenced by a **halo effect**—that is, by the tendency to view particular aspects of a student based on a general impression, either positive or negative. As a teacher, you may find it difficult to avoid being affected by positive and negative halos. A very pleasant student who seems to work hard and causes little trouble may be given the benefit of the doubt (B- instead of C+), whereas a very difficult student who seems to refuse to try might be a loser at grading time (D instead of C-). The Guidelines give ideas for using any grading system in a fair and reasonable way.

Guidelines

Using Any Grading System

Explain your grading policies to students early in the course and remind them of the policies regularly.

Examples

1. Give older students a handout describing the assignments, tests, grading criteria, and schedule.
2. Explain to younger students in a low-pressure manner how their work will be evaluated.

Set reasonable standards.

Examples

1. Discuss workload and grading standards with more experienced teachers.
2. Give a few formative tests to get a sense of your students' abilities before you give a graded test.
3. Take tests yourself first to gauge the difficulty of the test and to estimate the time your students will need.

Base your grades on as much objective evidence as possible.

Examples

1. Plan in advance how and when you will test.
2. Keep a portfolio of student work. This may be useful in student or parent conferences.

Halo Effect The tendency for a general impression of a person to influence our perception of any aspect of that person.

Be sure students understand test directions.

Examples

1. Outline the directions on the board.
2. Ask several students to explain the directions.
3. Go over a sample question first.

Correct, return, and discuss test questions as soon as possible.

Examples

1. Have students who wrote good answers read their responses for the class; make sure they are not the same students each time.
2. Discuss why wrong answers, especially popular wrong choices, are incorrect.
3. As soon as students finish a test, give them the answers to questions and the page numbers where answers are discussed in the text.

As a rule, do not change a grade.

Examples

1. Make sure you can defend the grade in the first place.
2. DO change any clerical or calculation errors.

Guard against bias in grading.

Examples

1. Ask students to put their names on the backs of their papers.
2. Use an objective point system or model papers when grading essays.

Keep pupils informed of their standing in the class.

Examples

1. Write the distribution of scores on the board after tests.
2. Schedule periodic conferences to go over work from previous weeks.

Give students the benefit of the doubt. All measurement techniques involve error.

Examples

1. Unless there is a very good reason not to, give the higher grade in borderline cases.
2. If a large number of students miss the same question in the same way, revise the question for the future and consider throwing it out for that test.

Source: Adapted by permission of the author and publisher from A. M. Drayer (1979). *Problems in middle and high school teaching: A handbook for student teachers and beginning teachers,* pp. 182–187. Boston: Allyn & Bacon.

Beyond Grading: Communication

No number or letter grade conveys the totality of a student's experience in a class or course. Both students and teachers sometimes become too focused on the end point—the grade. But children and adolescents spend the majority of their waking hours for many months of the year in school, where teachers are the relevant adults. This gives teachers the opportunity and the responsibility to know their students as people.

The success of a parent–teacher conference depends largely on the teacher's communication skills. Here the student helps to lead the conference.

Conferences with parents are often expected of teachers in elementary school and can be equally important in junior high and high school. At every level, the success of the conference depends on a number of factors. At the simplest level, both parties must be present. Schedule conferences at a time convenient for parents; confirm appointments in writing or by phone.

Clearly, the more skilled teachers are at communicating, the more effective they will be at conducting these conferences. Listening and problem-solving skills such as those discussed in Chapter 12 can be particularly important. When you are dealing with parents or students who are angry or upset, make sure you really hear the concerns of the participants, not just their words.

The conference should not be a time for lecturing parents or students. As the professional, the teacher needs to take a leadership role and yet remain sensitive to the needs of the other participants. The atmosphere should be friendly and unrushed. Any observations about the student should be as factual as possible, based on observation or information from assignments. Information gained from a student or a parent should be kept confidential. The Guidelines on the following page offer some helpful ideas for planning and conducting conferences.

An important federal law, the Buckley Amendment, may affect you as a teacher. Also called the Family Educational Rights and Privacy Act of 1974 and the Educational Amendments Act of 1974, this law states that all educational agencies must make test results and any other information in students' records available to the students and/or their parents. If the records contain information students or parents believe is incorrect, they can challenge such entries and have the information removed if they win the challenge. This means that the information in a student's records must be based on firm, defensible evidence. Tests must be valid and reliable. Your grades must be justified by thorough testing and observation. Comments and anecdotes about students must be accurate and fair.

Guidelines

Family and Community Partnerships for Successful Parent–Teacher Conferences

Plan ahead.

Examples

What are your goals?

Problem solving?

Sharing test results?

Asking questions that you want answered?

Providing information you want to share? Emphasize the positive.

Describing your "next steps" in the classroom?

Making suggestions for use at home?

Begin with a positive statement.

Examples

"Howard has a great sense of humor."

"Giselle really enjoys materials that deal with animals."

"Sandy is sympathetic when somebody has a problem."

Listen actively.

Examples

Empathize with the parents.

Accept their feelings: "You seem to feel frustrated when Lee doesn't listen."

Establish a partnership.

Examples

Ask parents to follow through on class goals at home:

"If you ask to see the homework checklist and go over it at home with Iris, I'll review it and chart her progress at school."

Plan follow-up contacts.

Examples

Write notes or make phone calls to share successes.

Keep parents informed *before* problems develop.

End with a positive statement.

Examples

"José has made several friends this year."

"Courtney should be a big help in the social studies play that her group is developing."

Source: Adapted by permission from D. P. Fromberg & M. Driscoll (1985). *The successful classroom: Management strategies for regular and special education teachers*, p. 181. New York: Teachers College Press.

SUMMARY

Formative and Summative Assessment

Two important and challenging tasks for teachers are assessing students and assigning grades. Many schools have established policies about testing and grading practices, but individual teachers decide how these practices will be carried out. In the classroom, assessment may be formative (ungraded, diagnostic) or summative (graded). Formative assessment helps form instruction, and summative assessment summarizes students' accomplishments.

Getting the Most from Traditional Assessment Approaches

Assessment requires planning. Teachers can use a behavior-content matrix to plan tests so that test questions match course objectives. With the goals of assessment in mind, teachers are in a better position to design their own tests or evaluate the tests provided by textbook publishers.

Two traditional formats for testing are the objective test and the essay test. Objective tests, which can include multiple-choice, true/false, fill-in, and matching items, should be written with specific guidelines in mind. Writing and scoring essay questions requires careful planning plus criteria to discourage bias in scoring.

Innovations in Assessment

Critics of traditional testing believe that teachers should use authentic tests and other authentic assessment procedures. This approach requires students to perform tasks and solve problems that are similar to the real-life performances that will be expected of students outside of school. Portfolios and exhibitions are two examples of authentic assessment. With portfolios and exhibitions there is an emphasis on performing real-life tasks in meaningful contexts. Evaluating alternative assessments requires judgment and attention to validity, reliability, and equity, just as with all assessment.

Effects of Grades and Grading on Students

Students need experience in coping with failure, so standards must be high enough to encourage effort. Occasional failure can be positive if appropriate feedback is provided. Grades can encourage students' motivation to learn if grades are tied to meaningful learning.

Grading and Reporting: Nuts and Bolts

Grading can be either criterion-referenced or norm-referenced. Criterion-referenced report cards usually indicate how well each of several objectives has been met by the individual student. One popular norm-referenced system is grading on the curve, based on a ranking of students in relation to the average performance level.

Tests and papers are often scored on a point system. Many schools use percentage grading systems, but the difficulty of the tests and the scoring criteria often influence the results. The difference between a B and a C may only be a matter of one or two points on paper, but the effect of the difference can be large for a student.

Alternatives to traditional grading are the contract, ILE, and dual marking approaches. Whatever system you use, you will have to decide whether you want to grade on effort, improvement, or some combination and whether you want to limit the number of good grades available.

Many factors besides quality of work can influence grades: the teacher's beliefs about the student's ability or effort or the student's general classroom behavior, for example.

Beyond Grading: Communication

Not every communication from the teacher needs to be tied to a grade. Communication with students and parents can be important in helping a teacher understand students and create effective instruction. Students and parents have a legal right to see all the information in the students' records.

KEY TERMS

authentic tests, p. 568
contract system, p. 584
criterion-referenced grading, p. 578
curriculum-based assessment (CBA), p. 557
data-based instruction, p. 557
diagnostic test, p. 556
distractors, p. 561

dual marking system, p. 585
exhibition, p. 572
formative assessment, p. 556
grading on the curve, p. 580
halo effect, p. 586
individual learning expectation (ILE), p. 585
norm-referenced grading, p. 578

objective testing, p. 560
percentage grading, p. 583
portfolio, p. 569
pretest, p. 556
revise option, p. 585
scoring rubric, p. 572
stem, p. 561
summative assessment, p. 558

CHECK YOUR UNDERSTANDING

Can you apply the ideas from this chapter on classroom assessment and grading to solve the following problems of practice?

Preschool and Kindergarten

- The parents of several children in your class want a report about how their daughters and sons are "progressing" in preschool. How would you respond to their requests? What kind of assessment and reporting would be helpful for your young students?

Elementary and Middle School

- During a parent–teacher conference, a mother and father accuse you of playing favorites and giving their child low grades "just because he's different." How would you respond?

Junior High and High School

- Several students are very unhappy with the grades on their term projects. They come to you for an explanation and to try to get you to raise their grades. What would you do?

- Your school requires percentage grading, but you would prefer a different system. How would you make a case for your alternative?

Cooperative Learning Activity

- With four or five other members of your educational psychology class, plan how you would use portfolios in your teaching. What would be the content? How would you evaluate the work and give students feedback?

What Would They Do?

Your school requires that you give letter grades to your class. You can use any method you want, as long as an A, B, C, D, or F appears for each of the subject areas on every student's report card, every grading period. Your only experience with grading was using written comments and a mastery approach that rated the students as making satisfactory or unsatisfactory progress toward particular objectives. You want a system that is fair and manageable, but also encourages learning, not just performance.

KATIE PIEL

Kindergarten–Sixth Grade Teacher
West Park School, Moscow, Idaho

Grades have always been a debatable issue in K–12 classrooms. I will speak from the point of view of an elementary K–6 teacher. I have been faced with the same situation cited above. Like most educators, I would enjoy the freedom to be able to select the assessment and evaluation criteria that best suits both my teaching style and the learning style of my students each year. However, this is not the case, as "A–F" grades are still widely used. In this situation I would review the National Standards, the State Guidelines, and the School District Curriculum Goals. That review would assure me that my curriculum is aligned. I would establish a curriculum for the grading period based on acceptable academic behaviors established by the National, State, and District Guidelines. Then I would clearly spell out the expectations or criteria for each grade. For example, in social science to earn the grade of "A," *all* the listed criteria must be satisfactorily accomplished. In math, to earn a "B," 4/5 of the listed criteria must be satisfactorily met. A grade of "C" in science is earned when 3/5 of the expectations are satisfactorily completed. These standards, criteria, expectations, or rubric must be clearly delineated for the learner, the parent, and the administrator before the grading period begins. Students should be given the latitude to express achievement in different ways like group projects, daily class work, tests, and individual projects. All students would be held accountable for demonstrating their own learning. With each teacher grading on a different standard, the teachers must also take on the responsibility of collaborating with their peers. Communicating to other teachers the skills a student can be expected to bring with him or her to the next level is crucial.

ALLAN OSBORNE

Assistant Principal
Snug Harbor Community School, Quincy, Massachusetts

Any grading system should consider a student's progress and effort. Grading systems also should be individualized to account for a student's unique strengths and weaknesses. Thus, a mainstreamed special education student should not be held to the same expectations as a gifted student.

The final grade for each marking period should be based on a number of variables. Although tests and quizzes are important methods of ascertaining what has been learned, students should be given the opportunity to demonstrate knowledge through other vehicles as well. For this reason I would ask students to complete long-term projects that demonstrate knowledge in a practical, real-life way. In calculating a final grade for the term, I would place a greater emphasis on assignments that demonstrated practical knowledge on a topic.

Although group assignments can be an important learning experience, I would be reluctant to place too much emphasis on a group project grade. As we all know, each member of the group does not participate equally, and thus, a group grade does not reflect the contribution of each individual member.

The most critical aspect of any successful grading system is that it is fair. Fairness dictates that students and their parents be given information in advance about class requirements and expectations, along with a description of grading criteria. A system that is fair can be easily justified. It is also important to keep accurate and detailed records of student progress. In addition to recording grades on tests, quizzes, and projects, anecdotal records describing a student's typical performance should be kept. These records can be valuable if a report card grade is questioned.

AIMEE FREDETTE

Second Grade Teacher
Fisher Elementary School, Walpole, Massachusetts

I believe that students are not all smart in the same ways. I give the students a variety of ways to demonstrate their knowledge. I also focus on the students' ability to take their knowledge and integrate it into other subject areas across the curriculum.

I use a student portfolio for each child, compiled throughout the year and used to show growth and development. Each time I correct papers I choose a couple of pieces of work that each child has done. I put these papers in the portfolio folder. I try to choose a variety of work, not necessarily their "prize work." At the end of the year the children receive the entire folder to keep.

I individualize the grades for each student. Each child is compared only to himself or herself, using work samples from the portfolio. In order to do this type of assessment, teachers need the support of the school administration. To justify the portfolio type assessment I use, I would simply show the administration or parents the "proof" (the students' actual work) of what a particular student was able to do. Growth and development can be demonstrated more concretely by holding a work sample from September in one hand and a work sample from December in the other.

Glossary

Academic Learning Time Time when students are actually succeeding at the learning task.

Academic Tasks The work the student must accomplish, including the content covered and the mental operations required.

Accommodation Altering existing schemes or creating new ones in response to new information.

Achievement Motivation Desire to excel; impetus to strive for excellence and success.

Achievement Tests Standardized tests measuring how much students have learned in a given content area.

Acronym Technique for remembering names, phrases, or steps by using the first letter of each word to form a new, memorable word.

Action Zone Area of a classroom where the greatest amount of interaction takes place.

Active Teaching Teaching characterized by high levels of teacher explanation, demonstration, and interaction with students.

Adaptation Adjustment to the environment.

Adolescent Egocentrism Assumption that everyone else shares one's thoughts, feelings, and concerns.

Advance Organizer Statement of inclusive concepts to introduce and sum up material that follows.

Affective Domain Objectives focusing on attitudes and feelings.

Aggression Bold, direct action that is intended to hurt someone else or take property; unprovoked attack.

Algorithm Step-by-step procedure for solving a problem; prescription for solutions.

Allocated Time Time set aside for learning.

Americans with Disabilities Act (ADA) Legislation prohibiting discrimination against persons with disabilities in employment, transportation, public access, local government, and telecommunications.

Analogical Thinking Heuristic in which one limits the search for solutions to situations that are similar to the one at hand.

Anchored Instruction Problem-based teaching that "anchors" or embeds the instruction in a real-life, interesting situation.

Androgynous Having some typically male and some typically female characteristics apparent in one individual.

Anorexia Nervosa Eating disorder characterized by very limited food intake.

Antecedents Events that precede an action.

Anxiety General uneasiness, a feeling of tension.

Applied Behavior Analysis The application of behavioral learning principles to understand and change behavior.

Aptitude Tests Tests meant to predict future performance.

Arousal Physical and psychological reactions causing a person to be alert, attentive, and wide awake.

Articulation Disorders Any of a variety of pronunciation difficulties, such as the substitution, distortion, or omission of sounds.

Articulatory Loop A system for temporarily storing information that can hold as much information as can be repeated in about 1.5 seconds.

Assertive Discipline Clear, firm, unhostile response style.

Assimilation Fitting new information into existing schemes.

Assisted Learning Providing strategic help in the initial stages of learning, gradually diminishing as students gain independence.

Associative Stage Individual steps of a procedure are combined or "chunked" into larger units.

Attainment Value The importance of doing well on a task; how success on the task meets personal needs.

Attention-Deficit/Hyperactivity Disorder Current term for disruptive behavior disorders marked by overactivity, excessive difficulty sustaining attention, or impulsiveness.

Attention Focus on a stimulus.

Attribution Theories Descriptions of how individuals' explanations, justifications, and excuses influence their motivation and behavior.

Authentic Assessment Measurement of important abilities using procedures that simulate the application of these abilities to real-life problems.

Authentic Task Tasks that have some connection to real-life problems the students will face outside the classroom.

Authentic Tests Assessment procedures that test skills and abilities as they would be applied in real-life situations.

Authoritarian Personality Rigidly conforming to belief that society is naturally competitive, with "better" people reaping its rewards.

Automated Basic Skills Skills that are applied without conscious thought.

Automaticity The ability to perform thoroughly learned tasks without much mental effort.

Autonomous Stage Final stage in the learning of automated skills. The procedure is fine-tuned and becomes "automatic."

Autonomy Independence.

Aversive Irritating or unpleasant.

Basic Skills Clearly structured knowledge that is needed for later learning and that can be taught step by step.

Behavior Modification Systematic application of antecedents and consequences to change behavior.

Behavioral Learning Theories Explanations of learning that focus on external events as the cause of changes in observable behaviors.

Behavioral Objectives Instructional objectives stated in terms of observable behaviors.

Being Needs Maslow's three higher-level needs, sometimes called *growth needs*.

Between-Class Ability Grouping System of grouping in which students are assigned to classes based on their measured ability or their achievements.

Bilingualism The ability to speak two languages fluently.

Bimodal Distribution Frequency distribution with two modes.

Blended Families Parents, children, and stepchildren merged into families through remarriages.

Bottom-Up Processing Perceiving based on noticing separate defining features and assembling them into a recognizable pattern.

Brainstorming Generating many ideas without stopping to evaluate each one.

Bulimia Eating disorder characterized by overeating, then getting rid of the food by self-induced vomiting or laxatives.

Case Study Intensive study of one person or one situation.

Central Tendency Typical score for a group of scores.

Cerebral Palsy Condition involving a range of motor or co-ordination difficulties due to brain damage.

Chain Mnemonics Memory strategies that associate one element in a series with the next element.

Chunking Grouping individual bits of data into meaningful larger units.

Classical Conditioning Association of automatic responses with new stimuli.

Classification Grouping objects into categories.

Classroom Management Techniques used to maintain a healthy learning environment, relatively free of behavior problems.

Coding System A hierarchy of ideas or concepts.

Cognitive Apprenticeship A relationship in which a less experienced learner acquires knowledge and skills under the guidance of an expert.

Cognitive Behavior Modification Procedures based on both behavioral and cognitive learning principles for changing your own behavior by using self-talk and self-instruction.

Cognitive Development Gradual, orderly changes by which mental processes become more complex and sophisticated.

Cognitive Domain In Bloom's taxonomy, memory and reasoning objectives.

Cognitive Evaluation Theory Suggests that events affect motivation through the individual's perception of the events as controlling behavior or providing information.

Cognitive Objectives Instructional objectives stated in terms of higher-level thinking operations.

Cognitive Self-Instruction Approach in which students "talk themselves through" a learning task.

Cognitive Stage The initial learning of an automated skill when we rely on general problem-solving approaches to make sense of steps or procedures.

Cognitive Styles Different ways of perceiving and organizing information.

Cognitive View of Learning A general approach that views learning as an active mental process of acquiring, remembering, and using knowledge.

Collective Monologue Form of speech in which children in a group talk but do not really interact or communicate.

Collective Self-Esteem The sense of the value of a group, such as an ethnic group, that you belong to.

Community of Practice Social situation or context in which ideas are judged useful or true.

Compensation The principle that changes in one dimension can be offset by changes in another.

Complex Learning Environments Problems and learning situations which mimic the ill-structured nature of real life.

Components In an information-processing view, basic problem-solving processes underlying intelligence.

Computer Simulations Programs that require students to apply knowledge and skills to solve lifelike problems.

Concept A general category of ideas, objects, people, or experiences whose members share certain properties.

Concept Mapping Students' diagramming their understanding of a concept.

Conceptual Change Teaching in Science A method that helps students understand (rather than memorize) concepts in science by using and challenging the students' current ideas.

Concrete Operations Mental tasks tied to concrete objects and situations.

Conditional Knowledge "Knowing when and why" to use declarative and procedural knowledge.

Conditioned Response (CS) Learned response to a previously neutral stimulus.

Conditioned Stimulus (CS) Stimulus that evokes an emotional or physiological response after conditioning.

Confidence Interval Range of scores within which an individual's particular score is likely to fall.

Connectionist Models Views of knowledge as being stored in patterns of connections among basic processing units in the brain.

Consequences Events that are brought about by an action.

Conservation Principle that some characteristics of an object remain the same despite changes in appearance.

Constructed-Response Format Assessment procedures that require the student to create an answer instead of selecting an answer from a set of choices.

Constructivist Approach View that emphasizes the active role of the learner in building understanding and making sense of information.

Context The physical or emotional backdrop associated with an event.

Contiguity Association of two events because of repeated pairing.

Contingency Contract A contract between the teacher and an individual student specifying what the student must do to earn a particular privilege or reward.

Continuous Reinforcement Schedule Presenting a reinforcer after every appropriate response.

Contract System System in which each student works for a particular grade according to agreed-on standards.

Convergent Questions Questions that have a single correct answer.

Cooperative Learning Arrangement in which students work in mixed-ability groups and are rewarded on the basis of the success of the group.

Cooperative Teaching Collaboration between regular and special education teachers.

Correlation Statistical description of how closely two variables are related.

Creativity Imaginative, original thinking or problem solving.

Criterion-Referenced Grading Assessment of each student's mastery of course objectives.

Criterion-Referenced Testing Testing in which scores are compared to a set performance standard.

Critical Thinking Evaluating conclusions by logically and systematically examining the problem, the evidence, and the solution.

Cueing Providing a stimulus that "sets up" a desired behavior.

Cultural Deficit Model A model that explains the school achievement problems of ethnic minority students by assuming that their culture is inadequate and does not prepare them to succeed in school.

Culturally Compatible Classrooms Classrooms in which procedures, rules, grouping strategies, attitudes, and teaching methods do not cause conflicts with the students' culturally influenced ways of learning and interacting.

Culture The knowledge, values, attitudes, and traditions that guide the behavior of a group of people and allow them to solve the problems of living in their environment.

Culture-Fair/Culture-Free Test A test without cultural bias.

Curriculum-Based Assessment (CBA) Evaluation method using frequent tests of specific skills and knowledge.

Data-Based Instruction Assessment method using daily probes of specific-skill mastery.

Decay The weakening and fading of memories with the passage of time.

Decentering Focusing on more than one aspect at a time.

Declarative Knowledge Verbal information; facts; "knowing that" something is the case.

Deductive Reasoning Drawing conclusions by applying rules or principles; logically moving from a general rule or principle to a specific solution.

Deficiency Needs Maslow's four lower-level needs, which must be satisfied first.

Defining Attributes Distinctive features shared by members of a category.

Descriptive Research Studies that collect detailed information about specific situations, often using observation, surveys, interviews, recordings, or a combination of these methods.

Development Orderly, adaptive changes we go through from conception to death.

Developmental Crisis A specific conflict whose resolution prepares the way for the next stage.

Developmentally Appropriate Education Educational programs and activities designed to meet the cognitive, emotional, social, and physical needs of students.

Deviation IQ Score based on statistical comparison of individual's performance with the average performance of others in that age group.

Diagnostic Tests Formative tests to determine students' areas of weakness; also individually administered tests to identify special learning problems.

Dialect Rule-governed variation of a language spoken by a particular group.

Dialectical Constructivism View that locates the source of knowledge in the interaction between learners and the environment.

Direct Instruction/Explicit Teaching Systematic instruction for mastery of basic skills, facts, and information.

Disability The inability to do something specific such as walk or hear.

Discovery Learning Bruner's approach, in which students work on their own to discover basic principles.

Discrimination Responding differently to similar, but not identical stimuli.

Discrimination Treating particular categories of people unequally.

Disequilibrium In Piaget's theory, the "out-of-balance" state that occurs when a person realizes that his or her current ways of thinking are not working to solve a problem or understand a situation.

Distractors Wrong answers offered as choices in a multiple-choice item.

Distributed Practice Practice in brief periods with rest intervals.

Divergent Questions Questions that have no single correct answer.

Domain-Specific Knowledge Information that is useful in a particular situation or that applies only to one specific topic.

Domain-Specific Strategies Consciously applied skills to reach goals in a particular subject or problem area.

Dual Marking System System of assigning two grades, one reflecting achievement, the other effort, attitude, and actual ability.

Educational Psychology The discipline concerned with teaching and learning processes; applies the methods and theories of psychology and has its own as well.

Educationally Blind Needing Braille materials in order to learn.

Eg-Rule Method Teaching or learning by moving from specific examples to general rules.

Ego-Involved Learners Students who focus on how well they are performing and how they are judged by others.

Egocentric Assuming that others experience the world the way you do.

Elaboration Adding and extending meaning by connecting new information to existing knowledge.

Elaborative Rehearsal Keeping information in working memory by associating it with something else you already know.

Empathetic Listening Hearing the intent and emotions behind what another says and reflecting them back by paraphrasing.

Empathy Ability to feel emotion as experienced by others.

Endogenous Constructivism The view emphasizing that learners construct their own knowledge through transforming and reorganizing their existing cognitive structures.

Engaged Time Time spent actively learning.

English as a Second Language (ESL) Designation for programs and classes to teach English to students who are not native speakers of English.

Entity View of Ability Belief that ability is a fixed characteristic that cannot be changed.

Epilepsy Disorder marked by seizures and caused by abnormal electrical discharges in the brain.

Episodic Memory Long-term memory for information tied to a particular time and place, especially memory of the events in a person's life.

Equilibration Search for mental balance between cognitive schemes and information from the environment.

Ethnic Pride A positive self-concept about one's racial or ethnic heritage.

Ethnicity A cultural heritage shared by a group of people.

Ethnography A descriptive approach to research that focuses on life within a group and tries to understand the meaning of events to the people involved.

Evaluation Decision making about student performance and about appropriate teaching strategies.

Exceptional Students Students who have abilities or problems so significant that the students require special education or other services to reach their potential.

Executive Control Processes Processes such as selective attention, rehearsal, elaboration, and organization that influence encoding, storage, and retrieval of information in memory.

Exemplar A specific example of a given category that is used to classify an item.

Exhibition A performance test or demonstration of learning that is public and usually takes an extended time to prepare.

Exogenous Constructivism A perspective that considers knowledge to be the reconstruction of structures that really exist in the external world.

Expectancy × Value Theories Explanations of motivation that emphasize individuals' expectations for success combined with their valuing of the goal.

Experimentation Research method in which variables are manipulated and the effects recorded.

Expert Teachers Experienced, effective teachers who have developed solutions for common classroom problems. Their knowledge of teaching process and content is extensive and well organized.

Explanatory Links Words and phrases such as "because" and "in order to" that specify the relationships between ideas.

Expository Teaching Ausubel's method—teachers present material in complete, organized form, moving from broadest to more specific concepts.

Extinction Gradual disappearance of a learned response.

Extrinsic Motivation Motivation created by external factors like rewards and punishments.

Faces of Intellect In Guilford's theory, the three basic categories of thinking—operations, contents, and products.

Failure-Accepting Students Students who believe their failures are the result of low ability and there is little they can do about it.

Failure-Avoiding Students Students who avoid failure by sticking to what they know, by not taking risks, or by claiming not to care about their performance.

Field Dependence Cognitive style in which patterns are perceived as wholes.

Field Independence Cognitive style in which separate parts of a pattern are perceived and analyzed.

Fine-Motor Skills Voluntary body movements that involve the small muscles.

Finger Spelling Communication system that "spells out" each letter with a hand position.

Formal Operations Mental tasks involving abstract thinking and coordination of a number of variables.

Formative Assessment Ungraded testing used before or during instruction to aid in planning and diagnosis.

Frequency Distribution Record showing how many scores fall into set groups.

Full Inclusion The integration of all students, including those with severe disabilities, into regular classes.

Functional Fixedness Inability to use objects or tools in a new way.

Gender Biases Different views of males and females, often favoring one gender over the other.

Gender Schemas Organized networks of knowledge about what it means to be male or female.

Gender-Role Identity Beliefs about characteristics and behaviors associated with one sex as opposed to the other.

General Knowledge Information that is useful in many different kinds of tasks; information that applies to many situations.

Generalization Responding in the same way to similar stimuli.

Generalized Seizure A seizure involving a large portion of the brain.

Generativity Sense of concern for future generations.

Gifted Student A very bright, creative, and talented student.

Goal What an individual strives to accomplish.

Goal-Directed Actions Deliberate actions toward a goal.

Goal Structure The way students relate to others who are also working toward a particular goal.

Good Behavior Game Arrangement where a class is divided into teams and each team receives demerit points for breaking agreed-on rules of good behavior.

Grade-Equivalent Score Measure of grade level based on comparison with norming samples from each grade.

Graded Membership The extent to which something belongs to a category.

Grading on the Curve Norm-referenced grading that compares students' performance to an average level.

Gross-Motor Skills Voluntary body movements that involve the large muscles.

Group Consequences Rewards or punishments given to a class as a whole for adhering to or violating rules of conduct.

Group Discussions Conversations in which the teacher does not have the dominant role; students pose and answer their own questions.

Group Focus The ability to keep as many students as possible involved in activities.

Guided Discovery An adaptation of discovery learning, in which the teacher provides some direction.

Halo Effect The tendency for a general impression of a person to influence our perception of any aspect of that person.

Handicap A disadvantage in a particular situation, sometimes caused by a disability.

Heuristic General strategy used in attempting to solve problems.

Hierarchy of Needs Maslow's model of seven levels of human needs, from basic physiological requirements to the need for self-actualization.

High-Road Transfer Application of abstract knowledge learned in one situation to a different situation.

High-Stakes Testing Standardized tests whose results have powerful influences when used by school administrators, other officials, or employers to make decisions.

Histogram Bar graph of a frequency distribution.

Holophrases Single words that express complex ideas.

Humanistic View Approach to motivation that emphasizes personal freedom, choice, self-determination, and striving for personal growth.

Hyperactivity Behavior disorder marked by atypical, excessive restlessness and inattentiveness.

Hypothetico-Deductive Reasoning A formal-operations problem-solving strategy in which an individual begins by identifying all the factors that might affect a problem and then deduces and systematically evaluates specific solutions.

Identity Principle that a person or object remains the same over time (in Piaget's theory); also the complex answer to the question, "Who am I?"

Identity Achievement Strong sense of commitment to life choices after free consideration of alternatives.

Identity Diffusion Uncenteredness; confusion about who one is and what one wants.

Identity Foreclosure Acceptance of parental life choices without consideration of options.

Images Representations based on the physical attributes—the appearance—of information.

"I" Message Clear, nonaccusatory statement of how something is affecting you.

Impulsive Characterized by cognitive style of responding quickly but often inaccurately.

Incentive An object or event that encourages or discourages behavior.

Incremental View of Ability Belief that ability is a set of skills that can be changed.

Individual Learning Expectation (ILE) Constantly recomputed average score in a subject.

Individualized Education Program (IEP) Annually revised program for an exceptional student, detailing present achievement level, goals, and strategies, drawn up by teachers, parents, specialists, and (if possible) student.

Individuals with Disabilities Education Act (IDEA) Amendment to PL 94-142.

Inductive Reasoning Formulating general principles based on knowledge of examples and details.

Industry Eagerness to engage in productive work.

Information Processing Human mind's activity of taking in, storing, and using information.

Initiative Willingness to begin new activities and explore new directions.

Inquiry Learning Approach in which the teacher presents a puzzling situation and students solve the problem by gathering data and testing their conclusions.

Insight The ability to deal effectively with novel situations.

Instructional Conversation Situation in which students learn through interactions with teachers and/or other students

Instructional Objective Clear statement of what students are intended to learn through instruction.

Integrity Sense of self-acceptance and fulfillment.

Intelligence Ability or abilities to acquire and use knowledge for solving problems and adapting to the world.

Intelligence Quotient (IQ) Score comparing mental and chronological ages.

Interference The process that occurs when remembering certain information is hampered by the presence of other information.

Intermittent Reinforcement Schedule Presenting a reinforcer after some but not all responses.

Internalize Process whereby children adopt external standards as their own.

Interval Schedule Length of time between reinforcers.

Intrinsic Motivation Motivation associated with activities that are their own reward.

Intrinsic or Interest Value The enjoyment a person gets from a task.

Intuitive Thinking Making imaginative leaps to correct perceptions or workable solutions.

Keyword Method System of associating new words or concepts with similar-sounding cue words.

Learned Helplessness The expectation, based on previous experiences with a lack of control, that all one's efforts will lead to failure.

Learning Process through which experience causes permanent change in knowledge or behavior.

Learning Disability Problem with acquisition and use of language; may show up as difficulty with reading, writing, reasoning, and math.

Learning Goal A personal intention to improve abilities and understand, no matter how performance suffers.

Learning Preferences Preferred ways of studying and learning, such as using pictures instead of text, working with other people versus alone, learning in structured or in unstructured situations, and so on.

Learning Propensity Assessment Device Innovative method for testing the student's ability to benefit from teaching, consistent with Vygotsky's theory of cognitive development.

Learning Strategies General plans for approaching learning tasks.

Learning Styles An individual's characteristic approaches to learning and studying, usually involving deep versus superficial processing of information.

Learning Tactics Specific techniques for learning, such as using mnemonics or outlining a passage.

Least Restrictive Placement Placement of each child in as normal an educational setting as possible.

Lecturing Organized explanation of a topic by a teacher.

Levels of Processing Theory Theory that recall of information is based on how deeply it is processed.

Limited English Proficiency (LEP) Descriptive term for students who have limited mastery of English.

Linguistic Comprehension Understanding of the meaning of sentences.

Loci Method Technique of associating items with specific places in order to remember the items.

Locus of Causality The location—internal or external—of the cause of behavior.

Locus of Control "Where" people locate responsibility for success and failures—inside or outside themselves.

Long-Term Memory Permanent store of knowledge.

Low Vision Vision limited to close objects.

Low-Road Transfer Spontaneous and automatic transfer of highly practiced skills.

Mainstreaming Teaching disabled children in regular classes for part or all of their school day.

Maintenance Rehearsal Keeping information in working memory by repeating it to yourself.

Massed Practice Practice for a single extended period.

Mastery Learning An approach to teaching and grading that focuses on achieving specific objectives before moving to the next unit or topic. Based on the assumption that every student is capable of achieving most of the objectives if given enough time and proper instruction.

Mastery-Oriented Students Students who focus on learning goals because they value achievement and see ability as improvable.

Maturation Genetically programmed, naturally occurring changes over time.

Mean Arithmetical average.

Meaningful Verbal Learning Focused and organized relationships among ideas and verbal information.

Means-Ends Analysis Heuristic in which a goal is divided into subgoals.

Measurement An evaluation expressed in quantitative (numerical) terms.

Median Middle score in a group of scores.

Melting Pot A metaphor for the absorption and assimilation of immigrants into the mainstream of society so that ethnic differences vanish.

Mental Age In intelligence testing, a score based on average abilities for that age group.

Mental Retardation Significantly below-average intellectual and adaptive social behavior, evident before age 18.

Metacognition Knowledge about our own thinking processes.

Metalinguistic Awareness Understanding about one's own use of language.

Microworlds Simplified but complete computerized model of a real world working system.

Minimum Competency Tests Standardized tests meant to determine if students meet minimum requirements to graduate or to proceed in school.

Minority Group A group of people who have been socially disadvantaged—not always a minority in actual numbers.

Mnemonics Techniques for remembering; also, the art of memory.

Mode Most frequently occurring score.

Modeling Changes in behavior, thinking, or emotions that occur through observing another person —a model.

Monolinguals Individuals who speak only one language.

Moral Dilemmas Situations in which no choice is clearly and indisputably right.

Moral Realism Stage of development wherein children see rules as absolute.

Moral Reasoning The thinking processes involved in judgments about questions of right and wrong.

Morality of Cooperation Stage of development wherein children realize that people make rules and people can change them.

Moratorium Identity crisis; suspension of choices because of struggle.

Motivation An internal state that arouses, directs, and maintains behavior.

Movement Management Ability to keep lessons and groups moving smoothly.

Multicultural Education Education that teaches the value of cultural diversity.

Multiple Intelligences In Gardner's theory of intelligence, a person's seven separate abilities: logical-mathematical, verbal, musical, spatial, bodily-kinesthetic, interpersonal, intrapersonal.

Multiple Representations of Content Considering problems using various analogies, examples, and metaphors.

Negative Correlation A relationship between two variables in which a high value on one is associated with a low value on the other. Example: height and distance from top of head to the ceiling.

Negative Reinforcement Strengthening behavior by removing an aversive stimulus.

Neutral Stimulus Stimulus not connected to a response.

Nongraded Elementary School/The Joplin Plan Arrangement wherein students are grouped by ability in particular subjects, regardless of their ages or grades.

Norm Group A group whose average score serves as a standard for evaluating any student's score on a test.

Norm-Referenced Grading Assessment of students' achievement in relation to one another.

Norm-Referenced Testing Testing in which scores are compared with the average performance of others.

Normal Distribution The most commonly occurring distribution, in which scores are distributed evenly around the mean.

Norming Sample Large sample of students serving as a comparison group for scoring standardized tests.

Object Permanence The understanding that objects have a separate, permanent existence.

Objective Testing Multiple-choice, matching, true/false, short-answer, and fill-in tests; scoring answers does not require interpretation.

Observational Learning Learning by observation and imitation of others.

Operant Conditioning Learning in which voluntary behavior is strengthened or weakened by consequences or antecedents.

Operants Voluntary (and generally goal-directed) behaviors emitted by a person or an animal.

Operations Actions a person carries out by thinking them through instead of literally performing the actions.

Organization Ongoing process of arranging information and experience into mental systems or categories.

Orthopedic Devices Devices such as braces and wheelchairs that aid people with physical disabilities.

Overextension Using one word to cover a range of concepts.

Overgeneralization Inclusion of nonmembers in a category; overextending a concept.

Overlapping Supervising several activities at once.

Overlearning Practicing a task past the point of mastery to combat forgetting and improve transfer.

Overregularize Apply a learned rule to all situations, including inappropriate ones.

Parallel Distributed Processing (PDP) Connectionist model that uses the brain's physical network of neurons as a metaphor for memory networks.

Paraphrase Rule Policy whereby listeners must accurately summarize what a speaker has said before being allowed to respond.

Part Learning Breaking a list of rote items into shorter lists.

Partial Seizure A seizure beginning in a localized area and involving only a small part of the brain.

Participant Observation A method for conducting descriptive research in which the researcher becomes a participant in the situation in order to better understand life in that group.

Participation Structures The formal and informal rules for how to take part in a given activity.

Peg-Type Mnemonics Systems of associating items with cue words.

Percentage Grading System of converting class performances to percentage scores and assigning grades based on predetermined cutoff points.

Percentile Rank Percentage of those in the norming sample who scored at or below an individual's score.

Perception Interpretation of sensory information.

Performance Goal A personal intention to seem competent or perform well in the eyes of others.

Personal Development Changes in personality that take place as one grows.

Perspective-Taking Ability Understanding that others have different feelings and experiences.

Physical Development Changes in body structure and function over time.

Portfolio A collection of the student's work in an area, showing growth, self-reflection, and achievement.

Positive Correlation A relationship between two variables in which the two increase or decrease together. Example: calorie intake and weight gain.

Positive Practice Practicing correct responses immediately after errors.

Positive Reinforcement Strengthening behavior by presenting a desired stimulus after the behavior.

PQ4R A method for studying text that involves six steps: Preview, Question, Read, Reflect, Recite, Review.

Pragmatics Area of language involving the effects of contexts on meaning.

Prejudice Prejudgment, or irrational generalization about an entire category of people.

Premack Principle Principle stating that a more-preferred activity can serve as reinforcer for a less-preferred activity.

Preoperational The stage before a child masters logical mental operations.

Presentation Punishment Decreasing the chances that a behavior will occur again by presenting an aversive stimulus following the behavior; also called Type I punishment.

Pretest Formative test for assessing students' knowledge, readiness, and abilities.

Principle Established relationship between factors.

Private Speech Children's self-talk, which guides their thinking and action. Eventually these verbalizations are internalized as silent inner speech.

Problem Any situation in which you are trying to reach some goal and must find a means to do so.

Problem Solving Creating new solutions for problems.

Problem-based Learning Methods that provide students with realistic problems that don't necessarily have "right" answers.

Procedural Knowledge Knowledge that is demonstrated when we perform a task; "knowing how."

Procedural Memory Long-term memory for how to do things.

Procedures Prescribed steps for an activity.

Productions The contents of procedural memory; rules about what actions to take, given certain conditions.

Prompt A reminder that follows a cue to make sure the person reacts to the cue.

Propositional Network Set of interconnected concepts and relationships in which long-term knowledge is held.

Prototype Best representative of a category.

Psychomotor Domain Physical ability and coordination objectives.

Psychosocial Describing the relation of the individual's emotional needs to the social environment.

Puberty The period in early adolescence when individuals begin to reach physical and sexual maturity.

Punishment Process that weakens or suppresses behavior.

Pygmalion Effect Exceptional progress by a student as a result of high teacher expectations for that student; named for mythological king, Pygmalion, who made a statue, then caused it to be brought to life.

Race A group of people who share common biological traits that are seen as self-defining by the people of the group.

Random Without any definite pattern; following no rule.

Range Distance between the highest and the lowest score in a group.

Ratio Schedule Number of responses between reinforcers.

Readiness Testing Testing procedures meant to determine if an individual is ready to proceed to the next level of education or training.

Receptors Parts of the human body that receive sensory information.

Reciprocal Determinism An explanation of behavior that emphasizes the mutual effects of the individual and the environment on each other.

Reciprocal Questioning Approach where groups of two or three students ask and answer each other's questions after a lesson or presentation.

Reciprocal Teaching A method, based on modeling, of teaching reading comprehension strategies.

Recitation Format of teacher questioning, student response, and teacher feedback.

Reconstruction Recreating information by using memories, expectations, logic, and existing knowledge.

Reflective Characterized by cognitive style of responding slowly, carefully, and accurately.

Reflective Thoughtful and inventive. Reflective teachers think back over situations to analyze what they did and why and to consider how they might improve learning for their students.

Regular Education Initiative An educational movement that advocates giving regular education teachers, not special education teachers, responsibility for teaching mildly (and sometimes moderately) handicapped students.

Reinforcement Use of consequences to strengthen behavior.

Reinforcer Any event that follows a behavior and increases the chances that the behavior will occur again.

Reliability Consistency of test results.

Removal Punishment Decreasing the chances that a behavior will occur again by removing a pleasant stimulus following the behavior; also called Type II punishment.

Reprimands Criticisms for misbehavior; rebukes.

Resistance Culture Group values and beliefs about refusing to adopt the behaviors and attitudes of the majority culture.

Resource Room Classroom with special materials and a specially trained teacher.

Respondents Responses (generally automatic or involuntary) elicited by specific stimuli.

Response Observable reaction to a stimulus.

Response Cost Punishment by loss of reinforcers.

Response Set Rigidity; tendency to respond in the most familiar way.

Restructuring Conceiving of a problem in a new or different way.

Resultant Motivation Whichever is the stronger tendency—the need to achieve or the need to avoid failure.

Retrieval Process of searching for and finding information in long-term memory.

Reversibility A characteristic of Piagetian logical operations—the ability to think through a series of steps, then mentally reverse the steps and return to the starting point; also called reversible thinking.

Reversible Thinking Thinking backward, from the end to the beginning.

Revise Option In a contract system, the chance to revise and improve work.

Reward An attractive object or event supplied as a consequence of a behavior.

Ripple Effect "Contagious" spreading of behaviors through imitation.

Rote Memorization Remembering information by repetition without necessarily understanding the meaning of the information.

Rule-Eg Method Teaching or learning by moving from general principles to specific examples.

Rules Statements specifying expected and forbidden behaviors; dos and don'ts.

Satiation Requiring a person to repeat a problem behavior past the point of interest or motivation.

Scaffolding Support for learning and problem solving. The support could be clues, reminders, encouragement, breaking the problem down into steps, providing an example, or anything else that allows the student to grow in independence as a learner.

Schema-Driven Problem Solving Recognizing a problem as a "disguised" version of an old problem for which one already has a solution.

Schemas (singular, **Schema**) Basic structures for organizing information; concepts.

Schemes Mental systems or categories of perception and experience.

Scoring Rubric A general description of different levels of performance, equivalent to different scores or grades.

Script Schema or expected plan for the sequence of steps in a common event such as buying groceries or ordering take-out pizza.

Scripted Cooperation Learning strategy in which two students take turns summarizing material and criticizing the summaries.

Seatwork Independent classroom work.

Self-Actualization Fulfilling one's potential.

Self-Concept Our perceptions about ourselves.

Self-Efficacy A person's sense of being able to deal effectively with a particular task.

Self-Efficacy Beliefs about personal competence in a particular situation.

Self-Esteem The value each of us places on our own characteristics, abilities, and behaviors.

Self-Fulfilling Prophecy A groundless expectation that is confirmed because it has been expected.

Self-Instruction Talking oneself through the steps of a task.

Self-Management Management of your own behavior and acceptance of responsibility for your own actions.

Self-Regulated Learners Students whose academic learning abilities and self-discipline make learning easier so motivation is maintained.

Self-Reinforcement Providing yourself with positive consequences, contingent on accomplishing a particular behavior.

Semantic Memory Memory for meaning.

Semilingual Not proficient in any language; speaking one or more languages inadequately.

Semiotic Function The ability to use symbols—language, pictures, signs, or gestures—to represent actions or objects mentally.

Sensorimotor Involving the senses and motor activity.

Sensory Memory System of receptors holding sensory information very briefly.

Serial-Position Effect The tendency to remember the beginning and the end but not the middle of a list.

Seriation Arranging objects in sequential order according to one aspect, such as size, weight, or volume.

Shaping Reinforcing each small step of progress toward a desired goal or behavior.

Sign Language Communication system of hand movements that symbolize words and concepts.

Situated Learning The idea that skills and knowledge are tied to the situation in which they were learned and difficult to apply in new settings.

Social Cognitive Theory Theory that emphasizes learning through observation of others.

Social Development Changes over time in the ways we relate to others.

Social Isolation Removal of a disruptive student for 5 to 10 minutes.

Social Negotiation Aspect of learning process that relies on collaboration with others and respect for different perspectives.

Socialization The ways in which members of a society encourage positive development for the immature individuals of the group.

Sociocultural Theory Emphasizes role in development of cooperative dialogues between children and more knowledgeable members of society. Children learn the culture of their community (ways of thinking and behaving) through these interactions.

Socioeconomic Status (SES) Relative standing in the society based on income, power, background, and prestige.

Sociolinguistics The study of the formal and informal rules for how, when, about what, to whom, and how long to speak in conversations within cultural groups.

Spasticity Overly tight or tense muscles, characteristic of some forms of cerebral palsy.

Specific Learning Disability Problem with acquisition and use of language; may show up as difficulty with reading, writing, reasoning, or math.

Speech Impairment Inability to produce sounds effectively for speaking.

Speech Reading Using visual cues to understand language.

Spread of Activation Retrieval of pieces of information based on their relatedness to one another. Remembering one bit of information activates (stimulates) recall of associated information.

Stand-Alone Thinking Skills Programs Programs that teach thinking skills directly without need for extensive subject matter knowledge.

Standard Deviation Measure of how widely scores vary from the mean.

Standard Error of Measurement Hypothetical estimate of variation in scores if testing were repeated.

Standard Scores Scores based on the standard deviation.

Standard Speech The most generally accepted and used form of a given language.

Standardized Tests Tests given, usually nationwide, under uniform conditions and scored according to uniform procedures.

Stanine Scores Whole-number scores from 1 to 9, each representing a wide range of raw scores.

Statistically Significant Not likely to be a chance occurrence.

Stem The question part of a multiple-choice item.

Stereotype Schema that organizes knowledge or perceptions about a category.

Stimulus Event that activates behavior.

Stimulus Control Capacity for the presence or absence of antecedents to cause behaviors.

Story Grammar Typical structure or organization for a category of stories.

Student Motivation to Learn The tendency to work hard on academic activities because one believes they are worthwhile.

Student Teams–Achievement Divisions (STAD) Cooperative learning with heterogeneous groups and elements of competition and reward.

Stuttering Repetitions, prolongations, and hesitations that block flow of speech.

Subject Structure According to Bruner, the fundamental framework of ideas.

Subjects People or animals studied.

Successive Approximations Small components that make up a complex behavior.

Summative Assessment Testing that follows instruction and assesses achievement.

Sustaining Expectation Effect Student performance maintained at a certain level because teachers don't recognize improvements.

Syntax The order of words in phrases or sentences.

Task Analysis System for breaking down a task hierarchically into basic skills and subskills.

Task-Involved Learners Students who focus on mastering the task or solving the problem.

Taxonomy Classification system.

Teaching Efficacy A teacher's belief that he or she can reach even the most difficult students and help them learn.

Teams-Games-Tournaments (TGT) Learning arrangement in which team members prepare cooperatively, then meet comparable individuals of competing teams in a tournament game to win points for their team.

Telegraphic Speech Children's speech using only essential words, as in a telegram.

Theory Integrated statement of principles that attempts to explain a phenomenon and make predictions.

Time on Task Time spent actively engaged in the learning task at hand.

Time Out Technically, the removal of all reinforcement. In practice, isolation of a student from the rest of the class for a brief time.

Token Reinforcement System System in which tokens earned for academic work and positive classroom behavior can be exchanged for some desired reward.

Top-Down Processing Perceiving based on the context and the patterns you expect to occur in that situation.

Transfer Influence of previously learned material on new material.

Transition Programming Gradual preparation of exceptional students to move from high school into further education or training, employment, or community involvement.

Triarchic Theory of Intelligence A three-part description of the mental abilities (thinking processes, coping with new experiences, and adapting to context) that lead to more or less intelligent behavior.

True Score Hypothetical average of all of an individual's scores if repeated testing under ideal conditions were possible.

T **Score** Standard score with a mean of 50 and a standard deviation of 10.

Unconditioned Response (UR) Naturally occurring emotional or physiological response.

Unconditioned Stimulus (US) Stimulus that automatically produces an emotional or physiological response.

Underextension Being too specific in using a word, limiting the word's meaning to a narrow range of possible examples.

Undergeneralization Exclusion of some true members from a category; limiting a concept.

Utility Value The contribution of a task to meeting one's goals.

Validity Degree to which a test measures what it is intended to measure.

Variability Degree of difference or deviation from the mean.

Verbalization Putting your problem-solving plan and its logic into words.

Vicarious Reinforcement Increasing the chances that we will repeat a behavior by observing another person being reinforced for that behavior.

Voicing Problems Inappropriate pitch, quality, loudness, or intonation.

Volition Willpower; self-discipline.

Whole-Language Perspective A philosophical approach to teaching and learning that stresses learning through authentic, real-life tasks. Emphasizes using language to learn, integrating learning across skills and subjects, and respecting the language abilities of student and teacher.

Within-Class Ability Grouping System of grouping in which students in a class are divided into two or three groups based on ability in an attempt to accommodate student differences.

Withitness According to Kounin, awareness of everything happening in a classroom.

Working Memory The information that you are focusing on at a given moment.

Working-Backward Strategy Heuristic in which one starts with the goal and moves backward to solve the problem.

Zone of Proximal Development Phase at which a child can master a task if given appropriate help and support.

z **Score** Standard score indicating the number of standard deviations above or below the mean.

References

AAMD Ad Hoc Committee on Terminology and Classification. (1992). *Mental retardation: Definition, classification, and systems of support* (9th ed.). Washington, DC: American Association on Mental Retardation.

Abi-Nader, J. (1991). Creating a vision of the future: Strategies for motivating minority students. *Phi Delta Kappan, 72,* 546–549.

Aboud, F., & Skerry, S. (1984). The development of ethnic identification: A critical review. *Journal of Cross-Cultural Psychology, 15,* 3–34.

Abruscato, J. (1993). Early results and tentative implications from the Vermont Portfolio Project. *Phi Delta Kappan, 74,* 474–477.

Adams, M. J., Treiman, R., & Pressley, M. (in press). Reading, writing, and literacy. In I. Sigel & A. Renninger (Eds.) *Handbook of child psychology, Vol. 4, Child psychology in practice.* New York: Wiley.

Airasian, P. W. (1996). *Assessment in the classroom.* New York: McGraw-Hill.

Alberto, P., & Troutman, A. C. (1990). *Applied behavior analysis for teachers: Influencing student performance* (3rd ed.). Columbus, OH: Merrill.

Alderman, M. K. (1985). Achievement motivation and the preservice teacher. In M. Alderman & M. Cohen (Eds.), *Motivation theory and practice for preservice teachers* (pp. 37–49). Washington, DC: ERIC Clearinghouse on Teacher Education.

Alessi, S. M., & Trollip, S. R. (1991). *Computer-based instruction: Methods and development* (2nd ed.). Boston: Allyn & Bacon.

Alexander, P. (in press). Stages and phases of domain learning: The dynamics of subject-matter knowledge, strategy knowledge, and motivation. In C. Weinstein & B. McCombs (Eds.), *Strategic learning: Skill, will, and self-regulation.* Mahwah, NJ: Lawrence Erlbaum Associates.

Alexander, P. A. (1992). Domain knowledge: Evolving themes and emerging concerns. *Educational Psychologist, 27,* 33–51.

Alexander, P. A. (1995). Superimposing a situation-specific and domain specific perspective on an account of self-regulated learning. *Educational Psychologist, 30,* 189–194.

Alexander, P. A. (1996). The past, present, and future of knowledge research: A reexamination of the role of knowledge in learning and instruction. *Educational Psychologist, 31,* 89–92.

Alexander, P. A., Kulikowich, J. M., & Schulze, S. K. (1994). How subject-matter knowledge affects recall and interest. *American Educational Research Journal, 31,* 313–337.

Allington, R. (1980). Teacher interruption behaviors during primary-grade oral reading. *Journal of Educational Psychology, 71,* 371–377.

Alloway, N. (1984). *Teacher expectations.* Paper presented at the meetings of the Australian Association for Research in Education, Perth.

Alloy, L. B., & Seligman, M. E. P. (1979). On the cognitive component of learned helplessness and depression. *The Journal of Learning and Motivation, 13,* 219–276.

Alwin, D., & Thornton, A. (1984). Family origins and schooling processes: Early versus late influence of parental characteristics. *American Sociological Review, 49,* 784–802.

American Association for the Advancement of Science (AAAS) (1993). Benchmarks for science literacy. Washington, DC: Author.

American Association of University Women (1991). *Shortchanging girls, shortchanging America.* Washington, DC: AAUW.

Ames, C. (1990). Motivation: What teachers need to know. *Teachers College Record, 91,* 409–421.

Ames, C. (1992). Classrooms: Goals, structures, and student motivation. *Journal of Educational Psychology, 84,* 261–271.

Ames, R., & Lau, S. (1982). An attributional analysis of student help-seeking in academic settings. *Journal of Educational Psychology, 74,* 414–423.

Anastasi, A. (1988). *Psychological testing* (6th ed.). New York: Macmillan.

Anderman, E. M., & Maehr, M. L. (1994). Motivation and schooling in the middle grades. *Review of Educational Research, 64,* 287–310.

Anderson, C. W., & Roth, K. J. (1989). Teaching for meaningful and self-regulated learning of science. In J. Brophy (Ed.), *Advances in research on teaching,* (Vol. 1, pp. 265–306). Greenwich, CT: JAI Press.

Anderson, C. W., & Smith, E. L. (1983, April). *Children's conceptions of light and color: Developing the concept of unseen rays.* Paper presented at the annual meeting of the American Educational Research Association, Montreal.

Anderson, C. W., & Smith, E. L. (1987). Teaching science. In V. Richardson-Koehler (Ed.), *Educators' handbook: A research perspective* (pp. 84–111). New York: Longman.

Anderson, J. R. (1985). *Cognitive psychology and its implications* (2nd ed.). San Francisco: Freeman.

Anderson, J. R. (1993). *Problem solving and learning. American Psychologist, 48,* 35–44.

Anderson, J. R. (1995a). *Cognitive psychology and its implications* (4th ed.), New York: Freeman.

Anderson, J. R. (1995b). *Learning and memory,* New York: John Wiley & Sons.

Anderson, J. R., Reder, L. M., & Simon, H. A. (1995). Applications and misapplication of cognitive psychology to mathematics education. Unpublished manuscript (accessible at http://www.psy.cmu.edu/~mm4b/misapplied.html)

Anderson, J. R., Reder, L. M., & Simon, H. A. (1996). Situated learning and education. *Educational Researcher, 25,* 5–11.

Anderson, L. M. (1985). What are students doing when they do all that seatwork? In C. Fisher & D. Berliner (Eds.), *Perspectives on instructional time.* New York: Longman.

Anderson, L. M. (1989a). Learners and learning. In M. Reynolds (Ed.), *Knowledge base for beginning teachers* (pp. 85–100). New York: Pergamon.

Anderson, L. M. (1989b). Classroom instruction. In M. Reynolds (Ed.), *Knowledge base for beginning teachers* (pp. 101–116). New York: Pergamon.

Anderson, L. M., Brubaker, N. L., Alleman-Brooks, J., & Duffy, G. G. (1985). A qualitative study of seatwork in first-grade classrooms. *Elementary School Journal, 86,* 123–140.

Anderson, L. W., & Sosniak, L. A. (Eds.) (1994). *Bloom's Taxonomy: A forty-year retrospective.* Ninety-third yearbook for the National Society for the Study of Education: Part II. Chicago: University of Chicago Press.

Anderson, P. J., & Graham, S. M. (1994). Issues in second-language phonological acquisition among children and adults. *Topics in Language Disorders, 14,* 84–100.

Anderson, R., Hiebert, E., Scott, J., & Wilkinson, I. (1985). *Becoming a nation of readers: The report of the commission on reading.* Washington, DC: National Institute of Education.

Anderson, S. M., Klatzky, R. L., & Murray, J. (1990). Traits and social stereotypes: Efficiency differences in social information processing. *Journal of Personality and Social Psychology, 59,* 192–201.

Anglin, J. M. (1993). Vocabulary development: A morphological analysis. *Monographs of the Society for Research in Child Development, 58*(10, Serial No. 238).

Anyon, J. (1980). Social class and the hidden curriculum of work. *Journal of Education, 162,* 67–92.

APA Board of Educational Affairs. (1995). *Learner-Centered Psychological Principles: A Framework for School Redesign and Reform.* Washington, DC: American Psychological Association

Archer, S. L. (1982). The lower age boundaries of identity development. *Child Development, 53,* 1551.

Archer, S. L., & Waterman, A. S. (1990). Varieties of identity diffusions and foreclosures: An exploration of the subcategories of the identity statuses. *Journal of Adolescent Research, 5,* 96–111.

Arlin, M. (1984). Time, equality, and mastery learning. *Review of Educational Research, 54,* 65–86.

Armbruster, B. B., & Anderson, T. H. (1981). Research synthesis on study skills. *Educational Leadership, 39,* 154–156.

Armstrong, L. S. (1991, January 16). Racial, ethnic prejudice still prevalent, survey finds. *Education Week,* p. 7.

Artman, L., & Cahan, S. (1993). Schooling and the development of transitive inference. *Developmental Psychology, 29,* 753–759.

Ashton, P. T. (1978). Cross-cultural Piagetian research: An experimental perspective. *Harvard Educational Review* (Reprint Series No. 13).

Ashton, P. T., & Webb, R. B. (1986). *Making a difference: Teachers' sense of efficacy and student achievement.* New York: Longman.

Association for Supervision and Curriculum Development. (1990). Effective teaching redux. *ASCD Update, 32*(6), 5.

Association for Supervision and Curriculum Development. (1991). Issue. *ASCD Update, 33*(3), 7.

Atkinson, J. W. (1964). *An introduction to motivation.* Princeton, NJ: Van Nostrand.

Atkinson, R. C., & Shiffrin, R. M. (1968). Human memory: A proposed system and its control processes. In K. Spence & J. Spence (Eds.), *The psychology of learning and motivation* (Vol. 2). New York: Academic Press.

Au, K. H. (1980). Participation structures in a reading lesson with Hawaiian children: Analysis of a culturally appropriate instructional event. *Anthropology and Education Quarterly, 11,* 91–115.

Ausubel, D. P. (1963). *The psychology of meaningful verbal learning.* New York: Grune and Stratton.

Ausubel, D. P. (1977). The facilitation of meaningful verbal learning in the classroom. *Educational Psychologist, 12,* 162–178.

Babad, E. (1995). The "Teachers' Pet" phenomenon, students' perceptions of differential behavior, and students' morale. *Journal of Educational Psychology, 87,* 361–374.

Babad, E. Y., Inbar, J., & Rosenthal, R. (1982). Pygmalion, Galatea, and the Golem: Investigations of biased and unbiased teachers. *Journal of Educational Psychology, 74,* 459–474.

Baddeley, A. (1990). *Human memory: Theory and practice.* Boston: Allyn & Bacon.

Baddeley, A. D. (1986). *Working memory.* Oxford, UK: Claredon Books.

Baer, J. (1997). *Creative teachers, creative students.* Boston: Allyn & Bacon.

Bailey, S. M. (1993). The current status of gender equity research in American Schools. *Educational Psychologist, 28,* 321–339.

Baker, D. (1986). Sex differences in classroom interaction in secondary science. *Journal of Classroom Interaction, 22,* 212–218.

Bakerman, R., Adamson, L. B., Koner, M., & Barr, R. G. (1990). !Kung infancy: The social context of object exploration. *Child Development, 61,* 794–809.

Bandura, A. (1986). *Social foundations of thought and action.* Englewood Cliffs, NJ: Prentice-Hall.

Bandura, A. (1993). Perceived self-efficacy in cognitive development and functioning. *Educational Psychologist, 28,* 117–148.

Bandura, A. (1995). Exercise of personal and collective efficacy in changing societies. In A. Bandura, (Ed.). *Self-efficacy in changing societies* (pp. 1–45). New York: Cambridge University Press.

Bandura, A. (1997). *Self-efficacy: The exercise of control.* New York: Freeman.

Bandura, A., Ross, D., & Ross, S. A. (1963). Vicarious reinforcement and imitative learning. *Journal of Abnormal and Social Psychology, 67,* 601–607.

Bangert, R., Kulik, J., & Kulik, C. (1983). Individualized systems of instruction in secondary schools. *Review of Educational Research, 53,* 143–158.

Bangert-Drowns, R. L., Kulik, C. C., Kulik, J. A., & Morgan, M. (1991). The instructional effect of feedback in test-like events. *Review of Educational Research, 61,* 213–238.

Banks, J. A. (1993). Multicultural education: Characteristics and goals. In J. Banks & C. McGee Banks (Eds.), *Multicultural education: Issues and perspectives* (2nd ed.) (pp. 2–26). Boston: Allyn & Bacon.

Banks, J. A. (1993). Multicultural education: Development, dimensions, and challenges. *Phi Delta Kappan, 75,* 22–28.

Banks, J. A. (1994). *Multiethnic education: Theory and practice.* Boston: Allyn & Bacon.

Banks, J. A. (1997). *Teaching strategies for ethnic studies* (6th ed.). Boston: Allyn & Bacon.

Baron, J. (1990, July). *Blurring the edges of assessment, curriculum, and instruction.* Paper presented at the Institute on New Modes of Assessment, Cambridge, MA.

Baron, R. A. (1992). *Psychology* (2nd ed.) Boston: Allyn & Bacon.

Baroody, A. R., & Ginsburg, H. P. (1990). Children's learning: A cognitive view. In R. Davis, C. Maher, & N. Noddings (Eds.), *Constructivist views on the teaching and learning of mathematics* (pp. 51–64). Monograph 4 of the National Council of Teachers of Mathematics, Reston, VA.

Bartlett, F. C. (1932). *Remembering: A study in experimental and social psychology.* New York: Macmillan.

Barton, E. J. (1981). Developing sharing: An analysis of modeling and other behavioral techniques. *Behavior Modification, 5,* 386–398.

Battistich, V., Solomon, D., & Delucci, K. (1993). Interaction processes and student outcomes in cooperative groups. *Elementary School Journal, 94,* 19–32.

Baumeister, R. F. (1990). Identity crisis. In R. Lerner, A. Petersen, & J. Brooks-Gunn (Eds.), *The encyclopedia of adolescence* (Vol. 1, pp. 518–521). New York: Garland.

Baumeister, R. F., & Leary, M. R. (1995). The need to belong: Desire for interpersonal attachments as a fundamental human motivation. *Psychological Bulletin, 117,* 497–529.

Beane, J. A. (1991). Sorting out the self-esteem controversy. *Educational Leadership, 49*(1), 25–30.

Beane, J. A. (1995). (Ed.) *Toward a coherent curriculum.* Alexandria, VA: Association for Supervision and Curriculum Development.

Bear, T., Schenk, S., & Buckner, L. (1993). Supporting victims of child abuse. *Educational Leadership, 50*(4), 44.

Becker, W. C., Engelmann, S., & Thomas, D. R. (1975). *Teaching 1: Classroom management.* Chicago: Science Research Associates.

Bee, H. (1981). *The developing child* (3rd ed.). New York: Harper & Row.

Bee, H. (1992). *The developing child* (6th ed.). New York: Harper & Row.

Beezer, B. (1985). Reporting child abuse and neglect: Your responsibilities and your protections. *Phi Delta Kappan, 66,* 434–436.

Belanoff, P., & Dickson, M. (1991). *Portfolios: Process and product.* Portsmouth, NH: Heinemann, Boynton/Cook.

Bell, R. (1980). *Changing bodies, changing lives: A book for teens on sex and relationships.* New York: Random House.

Bem, S. L. (1974). The measurement of psychological androgyny. *Journal of Consulting and Clinical Psychology, 42,* 155–162.

Benbow, C. P., & Minor, L. L. (1986). Mathematically talented males and females and achievement in the high school sciences. *American Educational Research Journal, 23,* 425–436.

Benbow, C. P., & Stanley, J. C. (1980). Sex differences in mathematical ability: Fact or artifact? *Science, 210,* 1262–1264.

Benbow, C. P., & Stanley, J. C. (1983a). Sex differences in mathematical abilities: More facts. *Science, 222,* 1029–1031.

Benbow, C. P., & Stanley, J. C. (1983b). Differential course-taking hypothesis revisited. *American Educational Research Journal, 20,* 469–473.

Benenson, J. F. (1993). Greater preference among females than males for dyadic interaction in early childhood. *Child Development, 64,* 544–555.

Benjafield, J. G. (1992). *Cognition.* Englewood Cliffs, NJ: Prentice-Hall.

Bennett, C. I. (1995). *Comprehensive multicultural education: Theory and practice* (3rd ed.). Boston: Allyn & Bacon.

Bereiter, C. (1991). Implications of connectionism for thinking about rules. *Educational Researcher, 20*(3), 1016.

Berg, C. A., & Clough, M. (1991). Hunter lesson design: The wrong one for science teaching. *Educational Leadership, 48*(4), 73–78.

Berger, K. S. (1986). *The developing person through childhood and adolescence* (2nd ed.). New York: Worth.

Berk, L. E. (1993). *Infants, children, and adolescents.* Boston: Allyn & Bacon.

Berk, L. E. (1994). *Child development* (3d ed.). Boston: Allyn & Bacon.

Berk, L. (1996). *Infants, children, and adolescents* (2nd ed.). Boston: Allyn & Bacon.

Berk, L. (1997). *Child development* (4th ed.). Boston: Allyn & Bacon.

Berk, L. E., & Garvin, R. A. (1984). Development of private speech among low-income Appalachian children. *Developmental Psychology, 20,* 272.

Berk, L. E., & Spuhl, S. T. (1995). Maternal interaction, private speech, and task performance in preschool children. *Early Childhood Research Quarterly, 10,* 145–169.

Berliner, D. (1983). Developing concepts of classroom environments: Some light on the T in studies of ATI. *Educational Psychologist, 18,* 1–13.

Berliner, D. (1987). But do they understand? In V. Richardson-Koehler (Ed.), *Educators' handbook: A research perspective* (pp. 259–293). New York: Longman.

Berliner, D. (1988). Simple views of effective teaching and a simple theory of classroom instruction. In D. Berliner & B. Rosenshine (Eds.), *Talks to teachers* (pp. 93–110). New York: Random House.

Berliner, D. (1992). Telling the stories of educational psychology. *Educational Psychologist, 27,* 143–152.

Berliner, D., & Biddle, B. (1997). *The manufactured crisis: Myths, frauds, and the attack on America's public schools.* White Plains: Longman.

Berndt, T. J., & Perry, T. B. (1986). Children's perceptions of friendships as supportive relationships. *Developmental Psychology, 22,* 640–648.

Berndt, T. J., & Perry, T. B. (1990). Distinctive features and effects of early adolescent friendships. In R. Montemayor, G. Adams, & T. Gullotta (Eds.), *From childhood to adolescence: A transitional period?* (pp. 269–287). Newbury Park, CA: Sage.

Betancourt, H., & Lopez, S. R. (1993). The study of culture, ethnicity, and race in American psychology. *American Psychologist, 48,* 629–637.

Bivens, J. A., & Berk, L. E. (1990). A longitudinal study of elementary school children's private speech. *Merrill-Palmer Quarterly, 36,* 443–463.

Bjorklund, D. F. (1989). *Children's thinking: Developmental function and individual differences.* Pacific Grove, CA: Brooks/Cole.

Blackham, G., & Silberman, A. (1979). *Modification of child and adolescent behavior* (3rd ed.), Belmont, CA: Wadsworth.

Block, J. (1983). Differential premises arising from differential socialization of the sexes: Some conjectures. *Child Development, 54,* 1335–1354.

Block, J. H., & Anderson, L. W. (1975). *Mastery learning in classroom instruction.* New York: Macmillan.

Bloom, B. (1994). Reflections on the development and use of the taxonomy. In L. Anderson & L. Sosniak (Eds.), *Bloom's Taxonomy: A forty-year retrospective.* Ninety-third yearbook for the National Society for the Study of Education: Part II (pp. 1–8). Chicago: University of Chicago Press.

Bloom, B. S. (1968). *Learning for mastery. Evaluation Comment, 1(2).* Los Angeles: University of California, Center for the Study of Evaluation of Instructional Programs.

Bloom, B. S., Engelhart, M. D., Frost, E. J., Hill, W. H., & Krathwohl, D. R. (1956). *Taxonomy of educational objectives. Handbook I: Cognitive domain.* New York: David McKay.

Bloom, R., & Bourdon, L. (1980). Types and frequencies of teachers' written instructional feedback. *Journal of Educational Research, 74,* 13–15.

Blumenfeld, P. C. (1992). Classroom learning and motivation: Clarifying and expending goal theory. *Journal of Educational Psychology, 84,* 272–281.

Blumenfeld, P. C., Puro, P. & Mergendoiller, J. R. (1992). Translating motivation into thoughtfulness. In H. Marshall (Ed.) *Redefining student learning: Roots of educational change* (pp. 207–240). Norwood, NJ: Ablex.

Boggiano, A. K., Flink, C., Shields, A., Seelbach, A., & Barrett, M. (1993). Use of techniques promoting students' self-determination: Effects on students' analytic problem-solving skills. *Motivation and Education, 17* 319–336.

Bohannon, J. N., III, & Warren-Leubecker, A. (1989). Theoretical approaches to language acquisition. In J. Berko Gleason (Ed.), *The development of language* (pp. 167–223). Columbus, OH: Merrill.

Boldizar, J. P. (1991). Assessing sex typing and androgyny in children: The children's sex inventory. *Developmental Psychology, 27,* 505–515.

Borko, H. (1989). Research on learning to teach: Implications for graduate teacher preparation. In A. Woolfolk (Ed.), *Research perspectives on the graduate preparation of teachers* (pp. 69–87). Boston: Allyn & Bacon.

Borko, H., & Livingston, C. (1989). Cognition and improvisation: Differences in mathematics instruction by expert and novice teachers. *American Educational Research Journal, 26,* 473–498.

Borkowski, J. G., Johnston, M. B., & Reid, M. K. (1986). Metacognition, motivation, and the transfer of control processes. In S. J. Ceci (Ed.), *Handbook of cognition: Social and neurological aspects of learning disabilities.* Hillsdale, NJ: Erlbaum.

Bos, C. S., & Reyes, E. I. (1996). Conversations with a Latina teacher about education for language-minority students with special needs. *The Elementary School Journal, 96,* 344–351.

Brain and Education: Special Issue of *Educational Psychologist,* (1992, Fall), Iran-Nejad, A., Wittrock, M. C., & Hidi, S. (Eds.).

Brandt, R. (1994). On making sense: A conversation with Magdalene Lampert. *Educational Leadership, 51(5),* 26–32.

Brandt, R. On teaching for understanding: A conversation with Howard Gardner. *Educational Leadership, 50(7),* 4–7.

Bransford, J. D. & Stein, B. S. (1993). *The IDEAL problem solver: A guide for improving thinking, learning, and creativity* (2nd ed.). New York: Freemen.

Bransford, J. D., Stein, B. S., Vye, N. J., Franks, J. J., Auble, P. M., Mezynski, K. J., & Perfetto, G. A. (1982). Differences in approaches to learning: An overview. *Journal of Experimental Psychology: General, 111,* 390–398.

Brantlinger, E. A., & Guskin, S. L. (1987). Ethnocultural and social-psychological effects on learning characteristics of handicapped children. In M. Wang, M. Reynolds, & H. Walberg (eds.), *Handbook of special education: Research and practice. Vol. 1 Learner characteristics and adaptive education* (pp. 7–34). New York: Pergamon Press.

Braun, C. (1976). Teacher expectation: Sociopsychological dynamics. *Review of Educational Research, 46(2),* 185–212.

Bredekemp, S. (1986). *Developmentally appropriate practice in early childhood programs serving children from birth through age 8.* Washington, DC: National Association for the Education of Young Children.

Bredo, E. (1994). Reconstructing educational psychology: Situated cognition and Deweyian pragmatism. *Educational Psychologist, 29,* 23–36.

Bretherton, I., & Waters, E. (1985). Growing points of attachment theory and research. *Monographs of the Society for Research in Child Development, 50* (1, 2, Serial No. 209).

Brookhart, S. M., & Freeman, D. J. (1992). Characteristics of entering teacher candidates. *Review of Educational Research, 62,* 37–60.

Brooks, D. (1985). Beginning the year in junior high: The first day of school. *Educational Leadership, 42,* 76–78.

Brooks, J. G., & Brooks, M.G. (1993). Becoming a constructivist teacher. In ASCD (Ed.), *In search of understanding: The case for constructivist classrooms*. Alexandria, VA: The Association for Supervision and Curriculum Development.

Brooks-Gunn, J. (1988). The impact of puberty and sexual activity upon the health and education of adolescent boys and girls. *Peabody Journal of Education, 64,* 88–113.

Brooks-Gunn, J., & Furstenberg, F. F., Jr. (1989). Adolescent sexual behavior. *American Psychologist, 44,* 2249–2257.

Brophy, J. E. (1981). Teacher praise: A functional analysis. *Review of Educational Research, 51,* 5–21.

Brophy, J. E. (1982, March). *Research on the self-fulfilling prophecy and teacher expectations.* Paper presented at the annual meeting of the American Educational Research Association, New York.

Brophy, J. E. (1983). Conceptualizing student motivation to learn. *Educational Psychologist, 18,* 200–215.

Brophy, J. E. (1985). Teacher-student interaction. In J. Dusek (Ed.), *Teacher expectancies.* Hillsdale, NJ: Erlbaum.

Brophy, J. E. (1988). On motivating students. In D. Berliner & B. Rosenshine (Eds.), *Talks to teachers* (pp. 201–245). New York: Random House.

Brophy, J. E., & Evertson, C. (1978). Context variables in teaching. *Educational Psychologist, 12,* 310–316.

Brophy, J. E., & Good, T. (1986). Teacher behavior and student achievement. In M. Wittrock (Ed.), *Handbook of research on teaching* (3rd ed., pp. 328–375). New York: Macmillan.

Brophy, J., & Good, T. (1994). *Looking in classrooms* (6th ed.). New York: Harper Collins.

Brophy, J. E., & Kher, N. (1986). Teacher socialization as a mechanism for developing student motivation to learn. In R. Feldman (Ed.), *Social psychology applied to education* (pp. 256–288). New York: Cambridge University Press.

Brown, A. (1987). Metacognition, executive control, self-regulation, and other more mysterious mechanisms. In F. Weinert & R. Kluwe (Eds.), *Metacognition, motivation, and understanding* (pp. 65–116). Hillside, NJ: Erlbaum.

Brown, A. L. (1992). Design experiments: Theoretical and methodological challenges in creating complex interventions in classroom settings. *Journal of the Learning Sciences, 2,* 141–178.

Brown, A. L., Bransford, J., Ferrara, R., & Campione, J. (1983). Learning, remembering, and understanding. In P. Mussen (Ed.), *Handbook of child psychology* (Vol. 3). New York: Wiley.

Brown, J. S. (1990). Toward a new epistemology for learning. In C. Frasson & G. Gauthier (Eds.) *Intelligent tutoring systems: At the crossroads of artificial intelligence and education.* (pp. 266–282). Norwood, NJ: Ablex.

Brown, J. S., & Burton, R. R. (1979). Diagnostic models for procedural bugs in basic mathematical skills. *Cognitive Science, 2,* 155–192.

Brown, R. (1973). *A first language: The early stages.* Cambridge, MA: Harvard University Press.

Brown, R., & Hanlon, C. (1970). Derivational complexity and order of acquisition in child speech. In J. M. Hays (Ed.), *Cognition and the development of language.* New York: Wiley.

Bruner, J. S. (1960). *The process of education.* New York: Vintage Books.

Bruner, J. S. (1966). *Toward a theory of instruction.* New York: Norton.

Bruner, J. S. (1971). *The relevance of education.* New York: Norton.

Bruner, J. S. (1973). *Beyond the information given: Studies in the psychology of knowing.* New York: Norton.

Bruner, J. S., Goodnow, J. J., & Austin, G. A. (1956). *A study of thinking.* New York: Wiley.

Bruning, R. H., Schraw, G. J., & Ronning, R. R. (1995). *Cognitive psychology and instruction* (2nd ed.). Englewood Cliffs, NJ: Merrill/Prentice-Hall.

Buenning, M., & Tollefson, N. (1987). The cultural gap hypothesis as an explanation for the achievement patterns of Mexican-American students. *Psychology in the Schools, 14,* 264–271.

Burden, P. R. (1995). *Classroom management and discipline: Methods to facilitate cooperation and instruction.* White Plains, NY: Longman.

Burton, N. W., & Jones, L. V. (1982). Recent trends in achievement levels of black and white youth. *Educational Research, 11,* 10–14.

Burton, R. V. (1963). The generality of honesty reconsidered. *Psychological Review, 70,* 481–499.

Buss, D. M. (1995). Psychological sex differences: Origin through sexual selection. *American Psychologist, 50,* 164–168.

Butler, R., & Neuman, O. (1995). Effects of task and ego achievement goals on help-seeking behaviors and attitudes. *Journal of Educational Psychology, 87,* 261–271.

Butler, R., & Nisan, M. (1986). Effects of no feedback, task-related comments, and grades on intrinsic motivation and performance. *Journal of Educational Psychology, 78,* 210–224.

Byrne, B. M., & Worth Gavin, D. A. (1996). The Shavelson model revisited: Testing for structure of academic self concept across pre-, early, and late adolescents. *Journal of Educational Psychology, 88,* 215–229.

Calderhead, J. (1996) Teacher: Beliefs and knowledge. In D. Berliner & R. Calfee (Eds.), *Handbook of educational psychology* (pp. 709–725). New York: Macmillan.

Calderhead, J., & Robson, M. (1991). Images of teaching: Student teachers' early conceptions of classroom practice. *Teaching and Teacher Education, 7,* 1–8.

Calfee, R. (1992), Refining educational psychology: The case of the missing links. *Educational Psychologist, 27,* 163–176.

Calmore, J. A. (1986). National housing policy and black America: Trends, issues, and implications. In *The state of black America 1986* (pp. 115–149). New York: National Urban League.

Cambourne, B., & Turbill, J. (1990). Assessment in whole-language classrooms: Theory into practice. *Elementary School Journal, 90,* 337–349.

Cameron, J., & Pierce, W. D. (1994). Reinforcement, reward, and intrinsic motivation: A meta-analysis. *Review of Educational Research, 64,* 363–423.

Cameron, J., & Pierce, W. D. (1996). The debate about rewards and intrinsic motivation: Protests and accusations do not alter the results. *Review of Educational Research, 66,* 39–52.

Camp, R. (1990, Spring). Thinking together about portfolios. *The Quarterly of the National Writing Project, 27,* 8–14.

Campbell, F. A., & Ramey, C. T. (1994). Effects of early intervention on intellectual and academic achievement: A follow-up study of children from low-income families. *Child Development, 65,* 684–698.

Campbell, F. A., & Ramey, C. T. (1995). Cognitive and school outcomes for high-risk African-American students at middle adolescence: Positive effects of early interventions. *American Educational Research Journal, 32,* 743–772.

Canfield, J. (1990). Improving students' self-concepts. *Educational Leadership, 48*(1), 48–50.

Cangelosi, J. S. (1990). *Designing tests for evaluating student achievement.* New York: Longman.

Canter, L. (1988). Let the educator beware: A response to Curwin and Mendler. *Educational Leadership, 46*(2), 71–73.

Canter, L. (1989). Assertive discipline—More than names on the board and marbles in a jar. *Phi Delta Kappan, 71*(1), 41–56.

Canter, L., & Canter, M. (1992). *Lee Canter's Assertive Discipline: Positive behavior management for today's classroom.* Santa Monica: Lee Canter and Associates.

Carey, L. M. (1994). *Measuring and evaluating school learning* (2nd ed.). Boston: Allyn & Bacon.

Cariglia-Bull, T., & Pressley, M. (1990). Short-term memory differences between children predict imagery effects when sentences are read. *Journal of Experimental Child Psychology, 49,* 384–398.

Carnegie Forum on Education and the Economy. (1986). *A nation prepared: Teachers for the 21st century.* Washington, DC: Carnegie Forum on Education and the Economy.

Carnegie Foundation for the Advancement of Teaching (1987). *1987 national survey of public school teachers.* Princeton, NJ.

Caroll, J. (1993). *Human cognitive abilities: A survey of factor analytic studies.* Cambridge, England: Cambridge University Press.

Carter, K. (1984). Do teachers understand principles of writing tests? *Journal of Teacher Education, 35,* 57–60.

Cartwright, G. P., Cartwright, C. A., & Ward, M. E. (1981). *Educating special learners.* Belmont, CA: Wadsworth.

Casanova, U. (1987). Ethnic and cultural differences. In V. Richardson-Koehler (Ed.), *Educators' handbook: A research perspective* (pp. 370–393). New York: Longman.

Case, R. (1985a). *Intellectual development: Birth to adulthood.* New York: Academic Press.

Case, R. (1985b). A developmentally-based approach to the problem of instructional design. In R. Glaser, S. Chipman, & J. Segal (Eds.), *Teaching thinking skills* (Vol. 2, pp. 545–562). Hillsdale, NJ: Erlbaum.

Cauley, K., & Tyler, B. (1989). The relationship of self-concept to prosocial behavior in children. *Early Childhood Research Quarterly, 4,* 51–60.

Cazden, C. B. (1988). *Classroom discourse: The language of teaching and learning.* Portsmouth, NH: Heinemann.

Ceci, S. J. (1991). How much does schooling influence intelligence and its cognitive components? A reassessment of the evidence. *Developmental Psychology, 27,* 703–720.

Chambers, B., & Abrami, P. C. (1991). The relationship between student team learning outcomes and achievement, causal attributions, and affect. *Journal of Educational Psychology, 83,* 140–146.

Chamot, A. U., & O'Malley, J. M. (1996). The Cognitive Academic Language Learning Approach: A model for linguistically diverse classrooms. *The Elementary School Journal, 96,* 259–274.

Chance, P. (1991). Backtalk: a gross injustice. *Phi Delta Kappan, 72,* 803.

Chance, P. (1992). The rewards of learning. *Phi Delta Kappan, 73,* 200–207.

Chance, P. (1993). Sticking up for rewards. *Phi Delta Kappan, 74,* 787–790.

Chapman, M., Zahn-Waxler, C., Cooperman, G., & Iannotti, R. (1987). Empathy and responsibility in the motivation of children's helping. *Developmental Psychology, 23,* 140–145.

Charles, C. M. (1985). *Building classroom discipline: From models to practice* (2nd ed.). New York: Longman.

Charles, C. M. (1996). *Building classroom discipline* (5th ed.). White Plains, NY: Longman.

Chi, M. T. H. (1978). Knowledge structures and memory development. In R. Siegler (Ed.), *Children's thinking: What develops?* (pp. 73–96). Hillsdale, NJ: Erlbaum.

Chi, M. T. H., & Koeske, R. D. (1983). Network representation of a child's dinosaur knowledge. *Developmental Psychology, 19,* 29–39.

Chi, M. T. H., Glaser, R., & Farr, M. (Eds.) (1988). *The nature of expertise.* Hillsdale, NJ: Earlbaum.

Children's Defense Fund. (1994). *The state of America's children: Yearbook 1994.* Washington, DC: Author.

Childs, C. P., & Greenfield, P. M. (1982). Informal modes of learning and teaching: The case of Zinacanteco weaving. In N. Warren (Ed.), *Advances in cross-cultural psychology* (Vol. 2, pp. 269–316). London: Academic Press.

Chomsky, N. (1965). *Aspects of a theory of syntax.* Cambridge, MA: MIT Press.

Chomsky, N. (1980). *Rules and representations.* New York: Columbia University Press.

Chomsky, N. (1986). *Knowledge of language: Its nature, origin, and use.* New York: Praeger.

Civil Rights Commission. (1973). *Teacher and students: Differences in teacher interactions with Mexican-American and Anglo students.* Washington, DC: Government Printing Office.

Cizek, G. J. (1991). Innovation or enervation: Performance assessment in perspective. *Phi Delta Kappan, 72*(9), 695–699.

Claiborn, W. L. (1969). Expectancy effects in the classroom: A failure to replicate. *Journal of Education Psychology, 60,* 377–383.

Clark, C. M. (1983). Personal communication.

Clark, C. M., & Peterson, P. L. (1986). Teachers' thought processes. In M. Wittrock (Ed.), *Handbook of research on teaching* (3rd ed.) (pp. 255–296). New York: Macmillan.

Clark, C. M., & Yinger, R. (1988). Teacher planning. In D. Berliner & B. Rosenshine (Eds.), *Talks to teachers* (pp. 342–365). New York: Random House.

Clark, C. M., Gage, N. L., Marx, R. W., Peterson, P. L., Staybrook, N. G., & Winnie, P. H. (1979). A factorial experiment on teacher structuring, soliciting, and reacting. *Journal of Educational Psychology, 71,* 534–550.

Clark, D. L., & Astuto, T. A. (1994). Redirecting reform: Challenges to popular assumptions about teachers and students. *Phi Delta Kappan, 75,* 512–520.

Clark, J. M., & Paivio, A. (1991). Dual coding theory and education. *Educational Psychology Review, 3,* 149–210.

Clark, K., & Clark, M. (1939). The development of consciousness of self and the emergence of racial identification in Negro preschool children. *Journal of Social Psychology, 10,* 591–599.

Clarke, J. H., & Agne, R. M. (1997). *Interdisciplinary high school teaching.* Boston: Allyn & Bacon.

Clement, S. L. (1978). Dual marking system: Simple and effective. *American Secondary Education, 8,* 49–52.

Clements, D. H. (1991). Enhancement of creativity in computer environments. *American Educational Research Journal, 28,* 173–188.

Clifford, M. M. (1984a). Educational psychology. In *Encyclopedia of Education* (pp. 413–416). New York: Macmillan.

Clifford, M. M. (1990). Students need challenge, not easy success. *Educational Leadership, 48*(1), 22–26.

Clifford, M. M. (1991). Risk taking: Empirical and educational considerations. *Educational Psychologist, 26,* 263–298.

Coburn, J. (1993). Opening new technological horizons for middle and high school. *Technology & Learning* (Special Supplement).

Cognition and Technology Group at Vanderbilt. (1991). Some thoughts about constructivism and instructional design. *Educational Technology, 31* (5), 16–18.

Cognition and Technology Group at Vanderbilt. (1990). Anchored instruction and its relations to situated cognition. *Educational Researcher, 19*(6) 2–10.

Cognition and Technology Group at Vanderbilt. (1993). Anchored instruction and situated learning revisited. *Educational Technology, 33*(3), 52–70.

Cohen, E. G. (1986). *Designing groupwork: Strategies for the heterogeneous classroom.* New York: Teachers College Press.

Coles, R. (1990, September). Teachers who made a difference. *Instructor,* 58–59.

Collins, A., & Ferguson, W. (1993). Epistemic forms and epistemic games: Structures and strategies to guide inquiry. *Educational Psychologist, 28,* 35.

Collins, A., Brown, J. S., & Holum, A. (1991). Cognitive apprenticeship: Making thinking visible. *American Educator, 15*(3), 38–39.

Collins, A., Brown, J. S., & Newman, S. E. (1989). Cognitive apprenticeship: Teaching the crafts of reading, writing, and mathematics. In L. B. Resnick (Ed.), *Knowing, learning, and instruction: Essays in honor of Robert Galser.* Hillsdale, NJ: Lawrence Earlbaum.

Combs, A. W. (1984). *A personal approach to teaching: Beliefs that make a difference.* Boston: Allyn & Bacon.

Confrey, J. (1990a). A review of the research on students' conceptions in mathematics, science, and programming. *Review of Research in Education, 16,* 3–56.

Confrey, J. (1990b). What constructivism implies for teaching. In R. Davis, C. Maher, & N. Noddings (Eds.), *Constructivist views on the teaching and learning of mathematics* (pp. 107–122). Monograph 4 of the National Council of Teachers of Mathematics, Reston, VA.

Conley, S. (1991). Review of research on teacher participation in school decision making. *Review of Research in Education, 17,* 225–266.

Cooke, B. L., & Pang, K. C. (1991). Recent research on beginning teachers: Studies of trained and untrained novices. *Teaching and Teacher Education, 7,* 93–110.

Cooper, G., & Sweller, J. (1987). Effects of schema acquisition and rule automation on mathematical problem-solving transfer. *Journal of Educational Psychology, 79,* 347–362.

Cooper, H. (1979). Pygmalion grows up: A model for teacher expectation communication and performance influence. *Review of Educational Research, 49,* 389–410.

Cooper, H. M., & Good, T. (1983). *Pygmalion grows up: Studies in the expectation communication process.* New York: Longman.

Cordova, D. I., & Lepper, M. R. (1996). Intrinsic motivation and the process of learning: Beneficial effects of contextualization, personalization, and choice. *Journal of Educational Psychology, 88,* 715–730.

Corenblum, B. & Annis, R. C. (1987). Racial identity and preference among Canadian Indian and White children: Replication and extension. *Canadian Journal of Behavioural Science, 19,* 254–265.

Corkill, A. J. (1992). Advance organizers: Facilitators of recall. *Educational Psychology Review, 4,* 33–67.

Corno, L. (1992). Encouraging students to take responsibility for learning and performance. *The Elementary School Journal, 93,* 69–84.

Corno, L. (1995). Comments on Winne: Analytic and systemic research are both needed. *Educational Psychologist, 30,* 201–206.

Corno, L., & Snow, R. E. (1986). Adapting teaching to individual differences in learners. In M. Wittrock (Ed.), *Handbook of research on teaching* (3rd cd.) (pp. 605–629). New York: Macmillan.

Corwin, R. (1981). Patterns of organizational control and teacher militancy: Theoretical continuities in the idea of "loose coupling." In A. Kerckhoff (Ed.), *Research in the sociology of education and socialization* (Vol. 2, pp. 261–291). Greenwich, CT: JAI Press.

Costa, A. L. (Ed.). (1985). *Developing minds: A resource book for teaching thinking.* Alexandria, VA: Association for Supervision and Curriculum Development.

Covaleskie, J. F. (1992). Discipline and morality: Beyond rules and consequences. *The Educational Forum, 56*(2), 56–60.

Covington, M., & Omelich, C. L. (1984). An empirical examination of Weiner's critique of attribution research. *Journal of Educational Psychology, 76,* 1214–1225.

Covington, M., & Omelich, C. (1987). "I knew it cold before the exam": A test of the anxiety-blockage hypothesis. *Journal of Educational Psychology, 79,* 393–400.

Covington, M. V. (1992). *Making the grade: A self-worth perspective on motivation and school reform.* New York: Holt, Rinehart, & Winston.

Craik, F. I. M. (1979). Human memory. *Annual Review of Psychology, 30,* 63–102.

Craik, F. I. M., & Lockhart, R. S. (1972). Levels of processing: A framework for memory research. *Journal of Verbal Learning and Verbal Behavior, 11,* 671–684.

Crisci, P. E. (1986). The Quest National Center: A focus on prevention of alienation. *Phi Delta Kappan, 67,* 440–442.

Cronin, J. F. (1993). Four misconceptions about authentic learning. *Educational Leadership, 50*(7), 78–80.

Cummins, D. D. (1991). Children's interpretation of arithmetic word problems. *Cognition and Instruction, 8,* 261–289.

Cummins, J. (1984). *Bilingualism and special education.* San Diego: College Hill Press.

Cummins, J. (1994). *The acquisition of English as a second language.* In K. Spangenberg-Urbschat & R. Prichard (Eds.), *Kids come in all languages: Reading instruction for ESL students* (pp. 36–62). Newark, DE: International Reading Association.

Cunningham, D. J. (1992) Beyond educational psychology: Steps toward an educational semiotic. *Educational Psychology Review, 4,* 165–194.

Current Directions in Psychological Science. (1993). Special Section: Controversies, 2, 1–12.

Curwin, R. L., & Mendler, A. N. (1988). Packaged discipline programs: Let the buyer beware. *Educational Leadership, 46*(2), 68–71.

Damon, W. (1977). *The social world of the child.* San Francisco: Jossey-Bass.

Danielson, C., & Dwyer, C. (1995). How Praxis III supports beginning teachers. *Educational Leadership, 52*(6), 66–67.

Dansereau, D. F. (1985). Learning strategy research. In J. Segal, S. Chipman, & R. Glaser (Eds.), *Thinking and learning skills. Vol. I: Relating instruction to research.* Hillsdale, NJ: Erlbaum.

Dark, V. J., & Benbow, C. P. (1991). Differential enhancement of working memory with mathematical versus verbal precocity. *Journal of Educational Psychology, 83,* 48–60.

Darley, J. M., Glucksberg, S., & Kinchla, R. (1991). *Psychology* (5th ed.). Englewood Cliffs, NJ: Prentice-Hall.

Das, J. P. (1995). Some thought on two aspect of Vygotsky's Work. *Educational Psychologist, 30,* 93–97.

Davidson, J. (1982). The group mapping activity for instruction in reading and thinking. *Journal of Reading, 26,* 52–56.

Davis, J. K. (1991). Educational implications of field-dependence—independence. In S. Wapner & J. Demick (Eds.), *Field-dependence—independence: Cognitive styles across the life span.* (pp. 149–176). Hillsdale, NJ: Lawrence Erlbaum.

Davis, R. B., Maher, C. A., & Noddings, N. (Eds.) (1990). Constructivist views on the teaching and learning of mathematics. *Monograph 4 of the National Council of Teachers of Mathematics,* Reston, VA.

Davis, S. F., Grover, C. A., Becker, A. H., & McGregor, L. N. (1992). Academic dishonesty: Prevalence, determinants, techniques, and punishments. *Teaching of Psychology, 9,* 16–20.

De Corte, E., & Verschaffel, L. (1985). Beginning first graders' initial representation of arithmetic word problems. *Journal of Mathematical Behavior, 4,* 3021.

De Corte, E., Greer, B., Verschaffel, L. (1996). Mathematics learning and teaching. In D. Berliner & R. Calfee (Eds.), *Handbook of educational psychology* (pp. 491–549). New York: Macmillan.

De Mott, R. M. (1982). Visual impairments. In N. Haring (Ed.), *Exceptional children and youth.* Columbus, OH: Charles E. Merrill.

DeCecco, J., & Richards, A. (1974). *Growing pains: Uses of school conflicts.* New York: Aberdeen.

DeRidder, L. M. (1993). Teenage pregnancy: Etiology and educational interventions. *Educational Psychology Review, 5,* 87–107.

Deaux, K. (1993). Commentary: Sorry, wrong number: A reply to Gentile's call. *Psychological Science, 4,* 125–126.

deCharms, R. (1976). *Enhancing motivation.* New York: Irvington.

deCharms, R. (1983). Intrinsic motivation, peer tutoring, and cooperative learning: Practical maxims. In J. Levine & M. Wang (Eds.), *Teacher and student perceptions: Implications for learning* (pp. 391–398). Hillsdale, NJ: Erlbaum.

Deci, E. (1975). *Intrinsic motivation.* New York: Plenum.

Deci, E., & Ryan, R. M. (1985). *Intrinsic motivation and self-determination in human behavior.* New York: Plenum.

Deci, E., Vallerand, R. J., Pelletier, L. G., & Ryan, R. M. (1991). Motivation and education: The self-determination perspective. *Educational Psychologist, 26,* 325–346.

Dembo, M. H. (1994). *Applying educational psychology* (5th ed.). New York: Longman.

Demetras, M. J., & Post, K. N. (1985, April). *Negative feedback in mother-child dialogues.* Paper presented at the biennial meeting of the Society for Research in Child Development, Toronto.

Dempster, F. N. (1981). Memory span: Sources of individual and developmental differences. *Psychological Bulletin, 89,* 63–100.

Dempster, F. N. (1991). Synthesis of research on reviews and tests. *Educational Leadership, 48*(7), 71–76.

Dempster, F. N. (1993). Exposing our students to less should help them learn more. *Phi Delta Kappan, 74,* 432–437.

Deno, S. L. (1987). Curriculum-based measurement. *Teaching Exceptional Children, 20,* 41.

Derry, S. (1991). Beyond symbolic processing: Expanding horizons for educational psychology. *Journal of Educational Psychology, 84,* 413–418.

Derry, S. J. (1989). Putting learning strategies to work. *Educational Leadership, 47*(5) 4–10.

Derry, S. J. (1991). Strategy and expertise in solving word problems. In C. McCormick, G. Miller, & M. Pressley (Eds.), *Cognitive strategies research: From basic research to educational applications.* New York: Springer-Verlag.

Derry, S. J. (1992). Beyond symbolic processing: Expanding horizons for educational psychology. *Journal of Educational Psychology, 84,* 413–419.

Derry, S. J., & Murphy, D. A. (1986). Designing systems that train learning ability: From theory to practice. *Review of Educational Research, 56,* 1–39.

Deshler, D. D., & Schumaker, J. B. (1986). Learning strategies: An instructional alternative for low-achieving adolescents. *Exceptional Children, 52,* 583–590.

Dewey, J. (1910). *How we think.* Boston: D. C. Heath.

Dias, R. M. (1983). Thought and two languages: The impact of bilingualism on cognitive development. *Review of Research in Education, 10,* 23–54.

Diaz, R. M., & Berk, L. E. (1992) (Eds.). *Private speech: From social interaction to self-regulation.* Hillsdale, NJ: Erlbaum.

Dinnel, D., & Glover, J. A. (1985). Advance organizers: Encoding manipulations. *Journal of Educational Psychology, 77,* 514–522.

DiVesta, F. J., & Gray, G. S. (1972). Listening and notetaking. *Journal of Educational Psychology, 63,* 8–14.

Doctorow, M., Wittrock, M. C., & Marks, C. (1978). Generative processes in reading comprehension. *Journal of Educational Psychology, 70,* 109–118.

Dodge, K. A., & Somberg, D. R. (1987). Hostile attributional biases among aggressive boys are exacerbated under conditions of threats to the self. *Child Development, 58,* 213–224.

Dorval, R., & Eckerman, C. O. (1984). Developmental trends in the quality of conversation achieved by small groups of acquainted peers. *Monographs of the Society for Research in Child Development, 49* (2, Serial No. 206).

Doyle, W. (1977). The uses of nonverbal behaviors: Toward an ecological model of classrooms. *Merrill-Palmer Quarterly, 23,* 179–192.

Doyle, W. (1983). Academic work. *Review of Educational Research, 53,* 159–200.

Doyle, W. (1986). Classroom organization and management. In M. C. Wittrock (Ed.), *Handbook of research on teaching* (3rd ed., pp. 392–431). New York: Macmillan.

Drayer, A. M. (1979). *Problems in middle and high school training: A handbook for student teachers and beginning teachers.* Boston: Allyn & Bacon.

Driscoll, M. P. (1994). *Psychology of learning for instruction.* Boston: Allyn & Bacon.

Duchastel, P. (1979). Learning objectives and the organization of prose. *Journal of Educational Psychology, 71,* 100–106.

Duckitt, J. (1992). Psychology and prejudice: A historical analysis and integrative framework. *American Psychologist, 47,* 1182–1193.

Duckitt, J. (1994). *The social psychology of prejudice.* Westport, CN: Praeger.

Duell, O. K. (1994). Extended wait time and university student achievement. *American Educational Research Journal, 31,* 397–414.

Duffy, G., Roehler, L. R., Meloth, M. S., & Vavrus, L. G. (1986). Conceptualizing instructional explanation. *Teaching and Teacher Education, 2,* 197–214.

Duncker, K. (1945). On solving problems. *Psychological Monographs, 58* (5, Whole No. 270).

Dunkin, M. J., & Biddle, B. J. (1974). *The study of teaching.* New York: Holt, Rinehart & Winston.

Dunn, K., & Dunn, R. (1978). *Teaching students through their individual learning styles.* Reston, VA: National Council of Principals.

Dunn, K., & Dunn, R. (1987). Dispelling outmoded beliefs about student learning. *Educational Leadership, 44*(6), 55–63.

Dunn, R. (1987). Research on instructional environments: Implications for student achievement and attitudes. *Professional School Psychology, 2,* 43–52.

Dunn, R., Beaudry, J. S., & Klavas, A. (1989). Survey of research on learning styles. *Educational Leadership, 47*(7), 50–58.

Dunn, R., Dunn, K., & Price, G. E. (1984). *Learning Style Inventory.* Lawrence, KS: Price Systems.

Dweck, C. S. (1986). Motivational processes affecting learning. *American Psychologist, 41,* 1040–1047.

Dweck, C. S., & Bempechat, J. (1983). Children's theories on intelligence: Consequences for learning. In S. Paris, G. Olson, & W. Stevenson (Eds.), *Learning and motivation in the classroom* (pp. 239–256). Hillsdale, NJ: Erlbaum.

Dwyer, C. A., & Villegas, A. M. (1993, January). *Guiding conceptions and assessment principles for the Praxis Series: Professional assessments for beginning teachers.* Princeton, NJ: Educational Testing Service.

Eaton, J. F., Anderson, C. W., & Smith, E. L. (1984). Students' misconceptions interfere with science learning: Case studies of fifth-graders. *Elementary School Journal, 84,* 365–379.

Eccles, J., & Wigfield, A. (1985). Teacher expectations and student motivation. In J. Dusek (Ed.), *Teacher expectancies* (pp. 185–226). Hillsdale, NJ: Erlbaum.

Educational Testing Service. (1992). *The second international assessment of educational progress.* Princeton, NJ: ETS.

Eggen, P. D. & Kauchak, D. P. (1996). *Strategies for teachers: Teaching content and thinking skills* (3rd ed.) Boston: Allyn & Bacon.

Eimas, P. D. (1985). The perception of speech in early infancy. *Scientific American, 252,* 46–52.

Eiseman, J. W. (1981). What criteria should public school moral education programs meet? *The Review of Education, 7,* 213–230.

Eisenberg, N., & Miller, P. A. (1987). The relation of empathy to prosocial and related behaviors. *Psychological Bulletin, 101,* 91–119.

Eisenberg, N., Shell, R., Pasernack, J., Lennon, R., Beller, R., & Mathy, R. M. (1987). Prosocial development in middle childhood: A longitudinal study. *Developmental Psychology, 23,* 712–718.

Elam, S. M., & Rose, L. C. (1995). The 27th annual Phi Delta Kappa/Gallup Poll of the public's attitude toward the public schools. *Phi Delta Kappan, 77*(1), 41–59

Elashoff, J. D., & Snow, R. E. (1971). *Pygmalion reconsidered.* Worthington, OH: Charles A. Jones.

Elawar, M. C., & Corno, L. (1985). A factorial experiment in teachers' written feedback on student homework: Changing teacher behavior a little rather than a lot. *Journal of Educational Psychology, 77,* 162–173.

Elkind, D. (1981). Obituary—Jean Piaget (1896–1980). *American Psychologist, 36,* 911–913.

Elkind, D. (1986). *The miseducation of children: Superkids at risk.* New York: Knopf.

Elkind, D. (1989). Developmentally appropriate education for 4-year-olds. *Theory into Practice, 28*(1), 47–52.

Elkind, D. (1991). Formal education and early childhood education: An essential difference. In K. M. Cauley, F. Linder, & J. H. MacMillan (Eds.), *Annual Editions: Educational Psychology 91/92* (pp. 27–37). Guilford, CT: Duskin.

Ellis, A. K. & Fouts, J. T. (1993). *Research on educational innovations.* Princeton, NJ: Eye on Education.

Elrich, M. (1994). The stereotype within. *Educational Leadership, 51*(8), 12–15.

Emery, R. E. (1989). Family violence. *American Psychologist, 44,* 321–328.

Emmer, E. T., & Evertson, C. M. (1981). Synthesis of research on classroom management. *Educational Leadership, 38,* 342–345.

Emmer, E. T., & Evertson, C. M. (1982). Effective classroom management at the beginning of the school year in junior high school classes. *Journal of Educational Psychology, 74,* 485–498.

Emmer, E. T., Evertson, C., Clements, B., & Worsham, M. (1997). *Classroom management for secondary teachers* (4th ed.). Boston: Allyn & Bacon.

Emmer, E. T., Evertson, C. M., & Anderson, L. M. (1980). Effective classroom management at the beginning of the school year. *Elementary School Journal, 80,* 219–231.

Engel, P. (1991). Tracking progress toward the school readiness goal. *Educational Leadership, 48*(5), 39–42.

Engelmann, S., & Englemann, T. (1981). *Give your child a superior mind.* New York: Simon & Schuster.

Epanchin, B. C., Townsend, B., Stoddard, K. (1994). *Constructive classroom management: Strategies for creating positive learning environments.* Pacific Grove, CA: Brooks/Cole.

Epstein, H. (1978). Growth spurts during brain development: Implications for educational policy and practice. In J. Chall & A. Mirsky (Eds.), *Education and the brain. The seventy-seventh yearbook of the National Society for the Study of Education, Part II.* Chicago: University of Chicago Press.

Epstein, H. (1980). EEG developmental stages. *Developmental Psychobiology, 13,* 629–631.

Epstein, J. L. (1989). Family structure and student motivation. In R. E. Ames & C. Ames (Eds.), *Research on motivation in education: Vol 3. Goals and cognitions* (pp. 259–295). New York: Academic Press.

Epstein, J. L. (1995). School/Family/Community partnerships: Caring for the children we share. *Phi Delta Kappan, 76,* 701–712.

Erez, M., & Zidon, I. (1984). Effects of goal acceptance on the relationship of goal difficulty to performance. *Journal of Applied Psychology, 69,* 69–78.

Erickson, F., & Shultz, J. (1982). *The counselor as gatekeeper: Social interaction in interviews.* New York: Academic Press.

Erikson, E. (1963). *Childhood and society* (2nd ed.). New York: Norton.

Erikson, E. H. (1968). *Identity, youth, and crisis.* New York: Norton.

Erikson, E. H. (1980). *Identity and the life cycle* (2nd ed.). New York: Norton.

Espe, C., Worner, C., & Hotkevich, M. (1990). Whole language—What a bargain. *Educational Leadership, 47*(6), 45.

Estes, W. K. (1993). Concepts, categories, and psychological science. *Psychological Science, 4,* 143–153.

Evertson, C. M. (1988). Managing classrooms: A framework for teachers. In D. Berliner & B. Rosenshine (Eds.), *Talks to teachers* (pp. 54–74). New York: Random House.

Evertson, C. M., Emmer, E. T., Clements, B. S., & Worsham, M. E. (1997). *Classroom management for elementary teachers* (4th ed.). Boston: Allyn & Bacon.

Fagot, B. I., & Hagan, R. (1991). Observations of parent reactions to sex-stereotyped behaviors: Age and sex effects. *Child Development, 62,* 617–628.

Fagot, B. I., Hagan, R., Leinbach, M. D., & Kronsberg, S. (1985). Differential reactions to assertive and communicative acts of toddler boys and girls. *Child Development, 56,* 1499–1505.

Fantuzzo, J., Davis, G., & Ginsburg, M. (1995). Effects of parent involvement in isolation or in combination with peer tutoring on student self-concept and mathematics achievement. *Journal of Educational Psychology, 87,* 272–281.

Farnham-Diggory, S. (1994). Paradigms of knowledge and instruction. *Review of Educational Research, 64,* 463–477.

Farrar, M. J. (1990). Discourse and the acquisition of grammatical morphemes. *Journal of Child Language, 17,* 607–624.

Faw, H. W., & Waller, T. G. (1976). Mathemagenic behaviors and efficiency in learning from prose. *Review of Educational Research, 46,* 691–720.

Federal Register (1977, December 29). *Procedures for evaluating specific learning disabilities.* Washington, DC: Department of Health, Education, and Welfare.

Feiman-Nemser, S. (1983). Learning to teach. In L. Shulman & G. Sykes (Eds.), *Handbook of teaching and policy* (pp. 150–170). New York: Longman.

Feingold, A. (1995). Gender differences in personality: A meta-analysis. *Psychological Bulletin, 116,* 429–456.

Fennema, E., & Peterson, P. (1988). Effective teaching for boys and girls: The same or different? In D. Berliner & B. Rosenshine (Eds.), *Talks to teachers* (pp. 111–127). New York: Random House.

Fennema, E., & Sherman, J. (1977). Sex-related differences in mathematics achievement, spatial visualization and affective factors. *American Educational Research Journal, 14*(1), 51–71.

Ferguson, D. L., Ferguson, P. M., & Bogdan, R. C. (1987). If mainstreaming is the answer, what is the question? In V. Richardson-Koehler (Ed.), *Educators' handbook: A research perspective* (pp. 394–419). New York: Longman.

Fernald, A. (1993). Approval and disapproval: Infant responsiveness to vocal affect in familiar and unfamiliar languages. *Child Development, 64,* 657–674.

Feuerstein, R. (1979). *The dynamic assessment of retarded performers: The Learning Potential Assessment Device, theory, instruments, and techniques.* Baltimore: University Park Press.

Feuerstein, R. (1990). The theory of structural cognitive modifiability. In B. Presseisen (Ed.), *Learning and thinking styles: Classroom interaction* (pp. 68–134). Washington, DC: National Education Association.

Fielding, L. G., & Pearson, P. D. (1994). Synthesis of research: Reading comprehension: What works. *Educational Leadership, 51*(5), 62–68.

Finn, J. (1972). Expectations and the educational environment. *Review of Educational Research, 42,* 387–410.

Fiske, E. B. (1981, October 27). Teachers reward muddy prose, study finds. *New York Times,* p. C1.

Fiske, E. B. (1988, April 10). America's test mania. *New York Times* (Education Life Section), pp. 16–20.

Fiske, S. T. (1993). Social cognition and social perception. *Annual Review of Psychology, 44,* 155–194.

Fitts, P. M., & Posner, M. I. (1967). *Human performance.* Belmont, CA: Brooks Cole.

Fitzgerald, J. (1995). English-as-a-second-language learners' cognitive reading process: A review of the research in the United States. *Review of Educational Research, 62,* 145–190.

Flammer, A. (1995). Developmental analysis of control beliefs. In A. Bandura, (Ed.). *Self-efficacy in changing societies* (pp. 69–113). New York: Cambridge University Press.

Flavell, J. H. (1985). *Cognitive development* (2nd ed.). Englewood Cliffs, NJ: Prentice-Hall.

Flavell, J. H., Friedrichs, A. G., & Hoyt, J. D. (1970). Developmental changes in memorization processes. *Cognitive Psychology, 1,* 324–340.

Flavell, J. H., Green, F. L., & Flavell, E. R. (1995). Young children's knowledge about thinking. *Monographs of the Society for Research in Child Development, 60*(1) (Serial No. 243).

Flecter, J. D., Hawley, D. E., & Piele, P. K. (1990). Costs, effects, and utility of microcomputer assisted instruction in the classroom. *American Educational Research Journal, 27,* 783–806.

Flink, C. F., Boggiano, A. K., & Barrett, M. (1990). Controlling teaching strategies: Undermining children's self-determination and performance. *Journal of Personality and Social Psychology, 59,* 916–924.

Floden, R. E., & Klinzing, H. G. (1990). What can research on teacher thinking contribute to teacher preparation? A second opinion. *Educational Researcher, 19*(4), 15–20.

Forest, M. (1991). It's about relationships. In L. Meyer, C. Peck, & L. Brown (Eds.), *Critical issues in the lives of people with disabilities* (pp. 399–408). Baltimore: Paul H. Brookes.

Foster, J. D. (1991). The role of accountability in Kentucky's Educational Reform Act of 1990. *Educational Leadership, 48*(5), 34–36.

Foster, W. (1981, August). *Social and emotional development in gifted individuals.* Paper presented at the Fourth World Conference on Gifted and Talented, Montreal.

Fox, L. H. (1981). Identification of the academically gifted. *American Psychologist, 36,* 1103–1111.

Frank, S. J., Pirsch, L. A., & Wright, V. C. (1990). Late adolescents' perceptions of their parents: Relationships among deidealization, autonomy, relatedness, and insecurity and implications for adolescent adjustment and ego identity status. *Journal of Youth and Adolescence, 19,* 571–588.

Frederiksen, N. (1984). Implications of cognitive theory for instruction in problem solving. *Review of Educational Research 54,* 363–407.

Freiberg, H. J. & Driscoll, A. (1996). *Universal teaching strategies* (2nd ed.). Boston: Allyn & Bacon.

Freud, S. (1959). Creative writers and daydreaming. In J. Strachey (ed.), *The standard edition of the complete psychological works of Sigmund Freud* (vol. 9). London: Hogarth Press.

Frick, T. W. (1990). Analysis of patterns in time: A method of recording and quantifying temporal relations in education. *American Educational Research Journal, 27,* 180–204.

Friend, M., & Bursuck, W. (1996). *Including students with special needs: A practical guide for classroom teachers.* Boston: Allyn & Bacon, p. 87.

Frisbie, D. A., & Waltmen, K. K. (1992). Developing a personal grading plan. *Educational Measurement: Issues and practices* (pp. 35–42). Washington, DC: National Council on Measurement in Education.

Fromberg, D. P., & Driscoll, M. (1985). *The successful classroom: Management strategies for regular and special education teachers.* New York: Teachers College Press.

Fulk, C. L., & Smith, P. J. (1995). Students' perceptions of teachers' instructional and management adaptations for students with learning or behavior problems. *The Elementary School Journal, 95,* 409–419.

Fuller, F. G. (1969). Concerns of teachers: A developmental conceptualization. *American Educational Research Journal, 6,* 207–226.

Furman, W., & Bierman, K. L. (1984). Children's conceptions of friendship: A multimethod study of developmental changes. *Developmental Psychology, 20,* 925–931.

Furstenberg, F. F., & Cherlin, A. J. (1991). *Divided families.* Cambridge: Harvard University Press.

Gage, N. L. (1991). The obviousness of social and educational research results. *Educational Researcher, 20*(A), 10–16.

Gagné, E. D., Yekovich, C. W., & Yekovich, F. R. (1993). *The cognitive psychology of school learning* (2nd ed.). New York: HarperCollins.

Gagné, R. M. (1977). *The conditions of learning* (3rd ed.). New York: Holt, Rinehart & Winston.

Gagné, R. M. (1985). *The conditions of learning and theory of instruction* (4th ed.). New York: Holt, Rinehart & Winston.

Gagné, R. M., & Driscoll, M. P. (1988). *Essentials of learning for instruction* (2nd ed.). Englewood Cliffs, NJ: Prentice-Hall.

Gagné, R. M., & Smith, E. (1962). A study of the effects of verbalization on problem solving. *Journal of Experimental Psychology, 63,* 12–18.

Gaines, S. O., & Reed, E. S. (1995). Prejudice: From Allport to DuBois. *American Psychologist, 50,* 96–103.

Galambos, S. J., & Goldin-Meadow, S. (1990). The effects of learning two languages on metalinguistic development. *Cognition, 34,* 1–56.

Galbraith, J. (1985). The eight great gripes of gifted kids: Responding to special needs. *Roeper Review, 7,* 15–18.

Gall, M. D. (1970). The use of questions in teaching. *Review of Educational Research, 40,* 707–721.

Gall, M. D. (1984). Synthesis of research on teachers' questioning. *Educational Leadership, 41,* 40–47.

Gallini, J. K. (1991). Schema-based strategies and implications for instructional design in strategy training. In C. McCormick, G. Miller, & M. Pressley (Eds.), *Cognitive strategies research: From basic research to educational applications.* New York: Springer-Verlag.

Garcia, E. E. (1992). "Hispanic" children: Theoretical, empirical, and related policy issues. *Educational Psychology Review, 4,* 69–94.

Garcia, R. L. (1991). *Teaching in a pluralistic society: Concepts, models, and strategies.* New York: Harper-Collins.

Garcia, T., & Pintrich, P. (1994). Regulating motivation and cognition in the classroom: The role of self-schemas and self-regulatory strategies. In B. J. Zimmerman & D. Schunk (Eds.), *Self-regulation of learning and performance: Issues and educational applications* (pp. 127–153). Hillsdale, NJ: Erlbaum.

Gardner, H. (1982a). *Art, mind, and brain: A cognitive approach to creativity.* New York: Basic Books.

Gardner, H. (1982b). *Developmental psychology* (2nd ed.). Boston: Little, Brown.

Gardner, H. (1983). *Frames of mind: The theory of multiple intelligences.* New York: Basic Books.

Gardner, H. (1991). *The unschooled mind: How children think and how schools should teach.* New York: Basic Books.

Gardner, H. (1993a). *Creating minds: An anatomy of creativity seen through the lives of Freud, Einstein, Picasso, Stravinsky, Elliot, Graham, and Gandhi.* New York: Basic Books.

Gardner, H. (1993b). *Educating the unschooled mind: A science and public policy seminar.* Washington, DC: American Educational Research Association.

Gardner, H. (1993c). *Multiple intelligences: The theory in practice.* New York: Basic Books.

Gardner, H. (1995). Reflection on multiple intelligences: Myths & messages. *Phi Delta Kappan, 77,* 200–210.

Gardner, H., & Hatch, T. (1989). Multiple intelligences go to school. *Educational Researcher, 18*(8), 4–10.

Gargarian, G. (1996). The art of design. In Y. Kafai & M. Resnick (Eds.), *Constructivism in practice: Designing, thinking, and learning in a digital world.* (pp. 125–160). Mahwah, NJ: Erlbaum.

Garmon, A., Nystrand, M., Berends, M., & LePore. P. C. (1995). An organizational analysis of the effects of ability grouping. *American Educational Research Journal, 32,* 687–715.

Garner, R. (1990). When children and adults do not use learning strategies: Toward a theory of settings. *Review of Educational Psychology, 60,* 517–530.

Garner, R. (1992). Learning from school tests. *Educational Psychologist, 27,* 53–63.

Garrett, S. S., Sadker, M., & Sadker, D. (1986). Interpersonal communication skills. In J. Cooper (Ed.), *Classroom teaching skills* (3rd ed.). Lexington, MA: D. C. Heath.

Garrison, J. (1995). Deweyan pragmatism and the epistemology of contemporary social constructivism. *American Educational Research Journal, 32,* 716–741.

Garrod, A., Beal, C., & Shin, P. (1990). The development of moral orientation in elementary school children. *Sex Roles, 22,* 13–27.

Gartner, A., & Lipsky, D. K. (1987). Beyond special education: Toward a quality system for all students. *Harvard Educational Review, 57,* 367–395.

Geary, D. C. (1995). Sexual selection and sex differences in spatial cognition. *Learning and Individual Differences, 7,* 289–303.

Gelman, R. (1979). Preschool thought. *American Psychologist, 34,* 900–905.

Gelman, R., & Baillargeon, R. (1983). A review of some Piagetian concepts. In P. Mussen (Ed.), *Carmichael's manual of child psychology. Vol. 3: Cognitive development* (E. Markman & J. Flavell, Volume Eds.). New York: Wiley.

Gelman, R., Meck, E., & Merkin, S. (1986). Young children's numerical competence. *Cognitive Development, 1,* 1–29.

Gelman, S. A., & Ebeling, K. S. (1989). Children's use of nonegocentric standards in judgments of size. *Child Development, 60,* 920–932.

Gentner, D. (1975). Evidence for the psychological reality of semantic components: The verbs of possession. In D. Norman & D. Rumelhart (Eds.), *Explorations in cognition.* San Francisco: Freeman.

Gerbner, G., Gross, L. Signorelli, N., & Morgan, M. (1986). *Television's mean world: Violence Profile No. 14–15.* Philadelphia: Annenberg School of Communication, University of Pennsylvania.

Gersten, R. (1996a). The language-minority students in transition: Contemporary instructional research. *The Elementary School Journal, 96,* 217–220.

Gersten, R. (1996b). Literacy instruction for language-minority students: The transition years. *The Elementary School Journal, 96,* 217–220.

Giaconia, R. M., & Hedges, L. V. (1982). Identifying features of effective open education. *Review of Educational Research, 52,* 579–602.

Gibbs, J. W., & Luyben, P. D. (1985). Treatment of self-injurious behavior: Contingent versus noncontingent positive practice overcorrection. *Behavior Modification, 9,* 3–21.

Gick, M. L. (1986). Problem-solving strategies. *Educational Psychologist, 21,* 99–120.

Gick, M. L., & Holyoak, K. L. (1983). Schema induction and analogical transfer. *Cognitive Psychology, 15,* 1–38.

Gillett, M., & Gall, M. (1982, March). *The effects of teacher enthusiasm on the at-task behavior of students in the elementary grades.* Paper presented at the annual meeting of the American Educational Research Association, New York.

Gilligan, C. (1982). *In a different voice: Psychological theory and women's development.* Cambridge, MA: Harvard University Press.

Gilligan, C., & Attanucci, J. (1988). Two moral orientations: Gender differences and similarities. *Merrill-Palmer Quarterly, 34,* 223–237.

Gilstrap, R. L., & Martin, W. R. (1975). *Current strategies for teachers: A resource for personalizing education.* Pacific Palisades, CA: Goodyear.

Ginsburg, H., & Opper, S. (1988). *Piaget's theory of intellectual development* (3rd ed.). Englewood Cliffs, NJ: Prentice-Hall.

Glaser, R. (1981). The future of testing: A research agenda for cognitive psychology and psychometrics. *American Psychologist, 36,* 923–936.

Gleitman, H. (1991). *Psychology* (3rd ed.). New York: Norton.

Goldenberg, C. (1996). The education of language-minority students: Where are we, and where do we need to go? *The Elementary School Journal, 96,* 353–361.

Goleman, D. (1988, April 10). An emerging theory on blacks' I.Q. scores. *New York Times* (Education Life Section), 22–24.

Gollnick, D. A., & Chinn, P. C. (1994). *Multicultural education in a pluralistic society* (4th ed.). New York: Merrill.

Good, T. (1996). Teaching effects and teacher evaluation. In J. Sikula (Ed.) *Handbook of research on teacher education* (pp. 617–665). New York: Macmillan.

Good, T., & Weinstein, R. (1986). Schools make a difference: Evidence, criticisms, and new directions. *American Psychologist, 41,* 1090–1097.

Good, T. L. (1983a). Classroom research: A decade of progress. *Educational Psychologist, 18,* 127–144.

Good, T. L. (1983b). Research on classroom teaching. In L. Shulman & G. Sykes (Eds.), *Handbook of teaching and policy* (pp. 42–80). New York: Longman.

Good, T. L. (1988). Teacher expectations. In D. Berliner & B. Rosenshine (Eds.), *Talks to teachers* (pp. 159–200). New York: Random House.

Good, T. L., & Brophy, J. E. (1994). *Looking in classrooms* (6th Ed.). New York: HarperCollins.

Good, T. L., & Marshall, S. (1984). Do students learn more in heterogeneous or homogeneous groups? In P. Peterson, L. C. Wilkinson, & M. Hallinan (Eds.), *The social context of instruction: Group organization and group processes* (pp. 15–38). Orlando, FL: Academic Press.

Good, T. L., Grouws, D., & Ebmeier, H. (1983). *Active mathematics teaching.* New York: Longman.

Goodenow, C. (1992). Strengthening the links between educational psychology and the study of social contexts. *Educational Psychologist, 27,* 177–196

Goodman, K. S. (1986). *What's whole in whole language: A parent-teacher guide.* Portsmouth, NH: Heinemann.

Goodman, Y. M., & Goodman, K. S. (1990). Vygotsky in a whole-language perspective. In L. Moll (Ed.), *Vygotsky and education: Instructional implications and applications of sociohistorical psychology* (pp. 223–250). New York: Cambridge University Press.

Gordon, E. W. (1991). Human diversity and pluralism. *Educational Psychologist, 26,* 99–108.

Gordon, T. (1974). *Teacher effectiveness training.* New York: Peter H. Wyden.

Gordon, T. (1981). Crippling our children with discipline. *Journal of Education, 163,* 228–243.

Grabe, M., & Latta, R. M. (1981). Cumulative achievement in a mastery instructional system: The impact of differences in resultant achievement motivation and persistence. *American Educational Research Journal, 18,* 7–14.

Graham, S. (1991). A review of attribution theory in achievement contexts. *Educational Psychology Review, 3,* 5–39.

Graham, S. (1994). Motivation in African Americans. *Review of Educational Research, 64,* 55–117.

Graham, S. (1995). Narrative versus meta-analytic reviews of race differences in Motivation. *Review of Educational Research, 65,* 509–514.

Graham, S. (1996). How causal beliefs influence the academic and social motivation of African-American children. In G. G. Brannigan (Ed.), *The enlightened educator: Research adventures in the schools* (pp. 111–126). New York: McGraw-Hill.

Graham, S., & Golan, S. (1991). Motivational influences on cognition: Task involvement, ego involvement, and depth of information processing. *Journal of Educational Psychology, 83,* 187–194.

Graham, S., & Guskey, T. R. (1990). Cooperative mastery learning strategies. *The Elementary School Journal, 91,* 33–42.

Graham, S., & Harris, K. R. (1994). The effects of whole language on children's writing: A review of the literature. *Educational Psychologist, 29,* 187–192.

Grant, C. A., & Sleeter, C. E. (1989). Race, class, gender, exceptionality, and educational reform. In J. Banks & C. McGee Banks (Eds.), *Multicultural education: Issues and perspectives* (pp. 49–66). Boston: Allyn & Bacon.

Greeno, J. G., Collins, A. M., & Resnick, L. B. (1996). Cognition and learning. In D. Berliner & R. Calfee (Eds.), *Handbook of educational psychology* (pp. 15–46). New York: Macmillan.

Gregorc, A. F. (1982). *Gregorc Style Delineator: Development, technical, and administrative manual.* Maynard, MA: Gabriel Systems.

Gresham, F. (1981). Social skills training with handicapped children. *Review of Educational Research, 51,* 139–176.

Grinder, R. E. (1981). The "new" science of education: Educational psychology in search of a mission. In F. H. Farley & N. J. Gordon (Eds.), *Psychology and education: The state of the union.* Berkeley, CA: McCutchan.

Grissom, J. B., & Smith, L. A. (1989). Repeating and dropping out of school. In L. Shepard & M. Smith (Eds.), *Flunking grades: Research and policies on retention* (pp. 34–63). Philadelphia: Falmer Press.

Grolnick, W. S., & Ryan, R. M. (1989). Parent styles associated with children's self-regulation and competence in school. *Journal of Educational Psychology, 81,* 143–154.

Grolnick, W. S., Ryan, R. M., & Deci, E. L. (1991) Inner resources for school achievement: Motivational mediators of children's perceptions of their parents. *Journal of Educational Psychology, 83,* 508–517.

Gronlund, N. E. (1993). *How to make achievement tests and assessments* (5th ed.). Boston: Allyn & Bacon.

Gross, M. U. M. (1992). The use of radical acceleration in cases of extreme intellectual precocity. *Gifted Child Quarterly, 36,* 91–99.

Grossman, H., & Grossman, S. H. (1994). *Gender issues in education.* Boston: Allyn & Bacon.

Guilford, J. P. (1988). Some changes in the Structure-of-Intellect model. *Educational and Psychological Measurement, 48,* 1–4.

Guitierrez, R., & Slavin, R. E. (1992). Achievement effects of the nongraded elementary school: A best evidence synthesis. *Review of Educational Research, 62,* 333–376.

Guskey, T. (1994). Making the grade: What benefits students? *Educational Leadership, 52*(2), 14–21.

Guskey, T. R., & Gates, S. L. (1986). Synthesis of research on mastery learning. *Education Leadership, 43,* 73–81.

Guskey, T. R., & Passaro, P. D. (1994). Teacher efficacy: A study of construct dimensions. *American Educational Research Journal, 31,* 645–674.

Gustafsson, J-E., & Undheim, J. O. (1996) Individual differences in cognitive functioning. In D. Berliner & R. Calfee (Eds.), *Handbook of educational psychology* (pp. 186–242). New York: Macmillan.

Guttmacher (Alan) Institute (1991). *Issues in brief* (Vol. 11, No. 2). Washington, DC: Alan Guttmacher Institute.

Haertel, E. H. (1991). New forms of teacher assessment. *Review of Research in Education, 17,* 3–30.

Hakuta, K. (1986). *Mirror of language: The debate on bilingualism.* New York: Basic Books.

Hakuta, K., & Garcia, E. E. (1989). Bilingualism and education. *American Psychologist, 44,* 374–379.

Hakuta, K., & Gould, L. J. (1987). Synthesis of research on bilingual education. *Educational Leadership, 44*(6), 38–45.

Hale-Benson, J. E. (1986). *Black children: Their roots, culture, and learning styles* (rev. ed.). Baltimore: Johns Hopkins University Press.

Hall, J. W. (1991). More on the utility of the keyword method. *Journal of Educational Psychology, 83,* 171–172.

Hallahan, D. P., & Kauffman, J. M. (1997). *Exceptional learners: Introduction to special education* (7th ed.) Boston: Allyn & Bacon.

Hallahan, D. P., Kauffman, J. M., & Lloyd, J. W. (1995). *Introduction to learning disabilities.* Boston: Allyn & Bacon.

Hallowell, E. M., & Ratey, J. J. (1994). *Driven to distraction.* New York: Pantheon Books.

Hambleton, R. K. (1996). Advances in assessment models, methods, and practices. In D. C. Berliner & R. C. Calfee (Eds.), *Handbook of educational psychology* (pp. 899–925). New York: Macmillan.

Hamilton, R. J. (1985). A framework for the evaluation of the effectiveness of adjunct questions and objectives. *Review of Educational Research, 55,* 47–86.

Hansen, R. A. (1977). Anxiety. In S. Ball (Ed.), *Motivation in education.* New York: Academic Press.

Hansford, B. C., & Hattie, J. A. (1982). The relationship between self and achievement/performance measures. *Review of Educational Research, 52,* 123–142.

Hardiman, P. T., Dufresne, R., & Mestre, J. P. (1989). The relation between problem categorization and problem solving among experts and novices. *Memory & Cognition, 17,* 627–638.

Hardman, M. L. (1994). *Inclusion: Issues of educating students with disabilities in regular educational settings.* A booklet to accompany Hardman, M. L., Drew, C. J., Egan, M. W., & Wolf, B. (1993). *Human exceptionality: Society, school, and family* (4th ed.). Boston: Allyn & Bacon.

Hardman, M. L., Drew, C. J., & Egan, M. W. (1996). *Human exceptionality: Society, school, and family* (5th ed.) Boston: Allyn & Bacon.

Harmin, M. (1994). *Inspiring active learning: A handbook for teachers.* Alexandria, VA: Association for Supervision and Curriculum Development.

Harris, K. R. (1990). Developing self-regulated learners: The role of private speech and self-instruction. *Educational Psychologist, 25,* 35–50.

Harris, K. R., & Pressley, M. (1991). The nature of cognitive strategy instruction: Interactive strategy construction. *Exceptional Children, 57,* 392–404.

Harris, K. R., Graham, S., & Pressley, M. (1991). Cognitive-behavioral approaches in reading and written language: Developing self-regulated learners. In N. N. Singh & I. L. Beale (Eds.), *Learning disabilities: Nature, theory, and treatment* (pp. 415–451). New York: Springer-Verlag.

Harris, K. R., Graham, S., & Pressley, M. (in press). Cognitive strategies in reading and written language. In N. Singhh & I. Beale (Eds.), *Current perspectives in learning disabilities: Nature, theory, and treatment.* New York: Springer-Verlag.

Harris, L. (1989, June). *The ICD survey III: A report card on special education.* New York: Louis Harris & Associates.

Harris, R. T. (1991). Anorexia nervosa and bulimia nervosa in female adolescents. *Nutrition Today, 26*(2), 30–34.

Harrison, A. O., Wilson, M. N., Pine, C. J., & Buriel, R. (1990). Family ecologies of ethnic minority children. *Child Development, 61,* 347–362.

Harrow, A. J. (1972). *A taxonomy of the psychomotor domain: A guide for developing behavior objectives.* New York: David McKay.

Harter, S. (1990). Issues in the assessment of self-concept of children and adolescents. In A. LaGreca (Ed.), *Through the eyes of a child* (pp. 292–325). Boston: Allyn & Bacon.

Hartup, W. W. (1989). Social relationships and their developmental significance. *American Psychologist, 44,* 120–126.

Harvard University (1986, January). Girls' math achievement: What we do and don't know. *Harvard Education Letter, 2*(1), 1–5.

Harvard University (1986, March). When the student becomes the teacher. *Harvard Education Letter, 2*(3), 5–6.

Hayes, J. R., Waterman, D. A., & Robinson, C. S. (1977). Identifying relevant aspects of a problem text. *Cognitive Science, 1,* 297–313.

Hayes, S. C., Rosenfarb, I., Wulfert, E., Munt, E. D., Korn, Z., & Zettle, R. D. (1985). Self-reinforcement effects: An artifact of social standard setting? *Journal of Applied Behavior Analysis, 18,* 201–214.

Herman, J., & Winters. L. (1994). Portfolio research: A slim collection. *Educational Leadership, 52*(2), 48–55.

Herman, J. L., Aschbacher, P. R., & Winters, L. (1992). *A practical guide to alternative assessment.* Alexandria, VA: Association for Supervision and Curriculum Development.

Hernshaw, L. S. (1987). *The shaping of modern psychology: A historical introduction from dawn to present day.* London: Routledge & Kegan Paul.

Hess, R., & McDevitt, T. (1984). Some cognitive consequences of maternal intervention techniques. A longitudinal study. *Child Development, 55,* 1902–1912.

Hess, R., Chih-Mei, C., & McDevitt, T. M. (1987). Cultural variation in family beliefs about children's performance in mathematics: Comparisons among People's

Republic of China, Chinese-American, and Caucasian-American families. *Journal of Educational Psychology, 79,* 179–188.

Hess, R. D., & Shipman, V. C. (1965). Early experience and the socialization of cognitive modes in children. *Child Development, 36,* 869–886.

Hetherington, E. M. (1989). Coping with family transitions: Winners, losers, and survivors. *Child Development, 60,* 1–14.

Heward, W. L., & Orlansky, M. D. (1992). *Exceptional children* (4th ed.). Columbus, OH: Charles E. Merrill.

Hewstone, M. (1989). Changing stereotypes with disconfirming information. In D. Bar-Tal, C. Graumann, A. Kruglanski, & W. Stroebe (Eds.), *Stereotyping and prejudice: Changing conceptions* (pp. 207–223). New York: Springer-Verlag.

Hilgard, E. R., Atkinson, R. L., & Atkinson, R. C. (1979). *Introduction to psychology* (7th ed.). New York: Harcourt Brace Jovanovich.

Hill, K. T., & Eaton, W. O. (1977). The interaction of test anxiety and success-failure experiences in determining children's arithmetic performance. *Developmental Psychology, 13,* 205–211.

Hill, K. T., & Wigfield, A. (1984). Test anxiety: A major educational problem and what can be done about it. *Elementary School Journal, 85,* 105–126.

Hill, W. E. (1990). *Learning: A survey of psychological interpretations* (5th ed.). New York: Harper & Row.

Hilliard, A. G. (1991/1992). Why we must pluralize curriculum. *Educational Leadership, 49*(4), 12–16.

Hines, C. V., Cruickshank, D. R., & Kennedy, J. J. (1982, March). *Measures of teacher clarity and their relationships to student achievement and satisfaction.* Paper presented at the annual meeting of the American Educational Research Association, New York.

Hines, C. V., Cruickshank, D. R., & Kennedy, J. J. (1985). Teacher clarity and its relation to student achievement and satisfaction. *American Educational Research Journal, 22,* 87–99.

Hinsley, D., Hayes, J. R., & Simon, H. A. (1977). From words to equations. In P. Carpenter & M. Just (Eds.), *Cognitive processes in comprehension.* Hillsdale, NJ: Erlbaum.

Hiroto, D. S., & Seligmen, M. E. P. (1975). Generality of learned helplessness in man. *Journal of Personality and Social Psychology, 31,* 311–327.

Hirsch, E. D. Jr. (1996). *The schools we need—and why we don't have them.* New York: Doubleday.

Hodgkinson, H. L. (1985). *All one system: Demographics of education, kindergarten through graduate school.* Washington, DC: Institute of Educational Leadership.

Hoffman, L. W. (1984). Work, family, and the socialization of the child. In R. Parke (Ed.), *Review of child development research* (Vol. 7, pp. 223–282). Chicago: University of Chicago Press.

Hoffman, M. L. (1988). Moral development. In M. Bornstein & M. Lamb (Eds.) *Developmental psychology: An advanced textbook* (2nd ed., pp. 497–548). Hillsdale, NJ: Erlbaum.

Hoge, D. R., Smit, E. K., & Hanson, S. L. (1990). School experiences predicting changes in self-esteem of sixth- and seventh-grade students. *Journal of Educational Psychology, 82,* 117–126.

Holden, G. W., & Ritchie, K. L. (1991). Linking extreme marital discord, child rearing practices, and child behavior problems: Evidence from battered women. *Child Development, 62,* 311–327.

Holmes, C. T., (1989). Grade-level retention effects: A meta analysis of research studies. In L. Shepard & M. Smith (Eds.) *Flunking grades: Research and policies on retention* (pp. 16–33). Philadelphia: Falmer Press.

Hoover-Dempsey, K. V., Bassler, O. C., & Burow, R. (1995). Parents' reported involvement in students' homework: Strategies and practices. *The Elementary School Journal, 95,* 435–450.

Horgan, D. D. (1995). *Achieving gender equity: Strategies for the classroom.* Boston: Allyn & Bacon.

Howard, K. (1990, spring). Making the writing portfolio real. *The Quarterly of the National Writing Project, 27,* 4–8.

Hoy, W. K., & Woolfolk, A. E. (1990). Organizational socialization of student teachers. *American Educational Research Journal, 27,* 279–300.

Hoy, W. K., & Woolfolk, A. E. (1993). Teachers' sense of efficacy and the organizational health of schools. *Elementary School Journal, 93,* 355–372.

Huessman, L. R., Eron, L. D., Klein, R., Brice, P., & Fischer, P. (1983). Mitigating the imitation of aggressive behaviors by changing children's attitudes about media violence. *Journal of Personality and Social Psychology, 44,* 899–910.

Huff, C. R. (1989). Youth gangs and public policy. *Crime Del, 35,* 524–537.

Hundert, J., & Bucher, B. (1978). Pupil's self-scored arithmetic performance: A practical procedure for maintaining accuracy. *Journal of Applied Behavior Analysis, 11,* 304.

Hunt, J. McV. (1961). *Intelligence and experience.* New York: Ronald.

Hunter, M. (1982). *Mastery teaching.* El Segundo, CA: TIP Publications.

Hyde, J. S., Fennema, E., & Lamon, S. J. (1990). Gender differences in mathematical performance: A meta-analysis. *Psychological Bulletin, 107,* 139–155.

IIS Report (1990). Water Mill, NY: Educational Products Information Exchange Institute.

IRA (International Reading Association). (1985). *Literacy development.* Newark, DE: IRA (pre-K through 3rd grade).

Inclusive Education Programs. (1994, February). AFT President calls inclusion "Fad." *Inclusive Education Programs: Advice on Educating Students with Disabilities in Regular Settings.* LRP Publications, 1+.

Iran-Nejad, A. (1990). Active and dynamic self-regulation of learning processes. *Review of Educational Research, 60,* 573–602.

Iran-Nejad, A., Marsh, G. E., & Clements, A. C. (1992). The figure and ground of constructive brain functioning: Beyond explicit memory processes. *Educational Psychologist, 27,* 473–492.

Iran-Najad, A., Wittrock, M., & Hidi, S. (Eds.) (1992). Special Issue: Brain and Education: *Educational Psychologist, 27*(4), Washington, DC: American Psychological Association.

Irving, O., & Martin, J. (1982). Withitness: The confusing variable. *American Educational Research Journal, 19,* 313–319.

Irwin, J. W. (1991). *Teaching reading comprehension* (2nd ed.). Boston: Allyn & Bacon.

Isabella, R., & Belsky, J. (1991). Interactional synchrony and the origins of infant-mother attachment: A replication study. *Child Development, 62,* 373–384.

Isenberg, J. (1991). Societal influences on children. In K. M. Cauley, F. Linder, & J. H. MacMillan (Eds.), *Annual Editions: Educational Psychology 91/92* (pp. 38–44). Guilford, CT: Duskin.

Jacklin, C. N., Dipietro, J. A., & Maccoby, E. E. (1984). Sex-typing behavior and sex-typing pressure in child-parent interactions. *Sex Roles, 13,* 413–425.

Jagacinski, C. M., & Nicholls, J. G. (1987). Competence and affect in task involvement and ego involvement: The impact of social comparison information. *Journal of Educational Psychology, 76,* 107–114.

James, W. (1890). *The principles of psychology.* (Vol. 2). New York: Henry Holt.

James, W. (1912). *Talks to teachers on psychology: And to students on some of life's ideals.* New York: Holt.

Jenson, W. R., Sloane, H. N., & Young, K. R. (1988). *Applied behavior analysis in education: A structured teaching approach.* Englewood Cliffs, NJ: Prentice-Hall.

Johnson, D., & Johnson, R. (1985). Motivational processes in cooperative, competitive, and individualistic learning situations. In C. Ames & R. Ames (Eds.), *Research on motivation in education. Vol. 2: The classroom milieu* (pp. 249–286). New York: Academic Press.

Johnson, D., & Johnson, R. (1994). *Learning together and alone: Cooperation, competition, and individualization* (4th ed.). Boston: Allyn & Bacon.

Johnson, D. W. (1993). *Reaching out: Interpersonal effectiveness and self-actualization* (5th ed.) Boston: Allyn & Bacon.

Johnson, D. W., Johnson, R., Dudley, B, Ward, M., & Magnuson, D. (1995). The impact of peer mediation training on the management of school and home conflicts. *American Educational Research Journal, 32,* 829–844.

Johnson, J. S., & Newport, E. L. (1989). Critical period effects in second language learning: The influence of maturational state on the acquisition of English as a second language. *Cognitive Psychology, 21,* 60–69.

Johnson. D. W., & Johnson, R. T. (1996). The role of cooperative learning in assessing and communicating student learning. In T. Guskey (Ed.), *ASCD 1996 Yearbook: Communicating student learning* (pp. 25–46). Alexandria, VA: Association for Supervision and Curriculum Development.

Jones, E. D., & Southern, W. T. (1991). Conclusions about acceleration: Echoes of a debate. In W. Southern & E. Jones (Eds.), *The academic acceleration of gifted children* (pp. 223–228). New York: Teachers College Press.

Jones, V. F., & Jones, L. S. (1995). *Comprehensive classroom management: Creating positive learning environments* (4th ed.). Boston: Allyn & Bacon.

Jordan, N., & Goldsmith-Phillips, J. (1994). *Assessment of learning disabilities.* Boston: Allyn & Bacon.

Joshua, S., & Dupin, J. J. (1987). Taking into account students conceptions in instructional strategy: An example in physics. *Cognition and Instruction, 4,* 117–135.

Journal of Educational Psychology. (1991, December). Volume 83, pp. 437+.

Joyce, B. & Weil, M. (1996). *Models of teaching* (5th ed.). Boston: Allyn & Bacon.

Jurden, F. H. (1995). Individual differences in working memory and complex cognition. *Journal of Educational Psychology, 87,* 93–102.

Kagan, D. (1992). Implications of research on teacher belief. *Educational Psychologist, 27,* 65–90.

Kagan, S. (1983). Social orientation among Mexican-American children: A challenge to traditional classroom structures. In E. Garcia (Ed.), *The Mexican-American child: Language, cognition, and social development.* Tempe, AZ: Center for Bilingual Education.

Kagan, S. (1994). *Cooperative learning.* San Juan Capistrano, CA: Kagan Cooperative Learning.

Kanfer, F. H., & Gaelick, L. (1986). Self-management methods. In F. Kanfer & A. Goldstein (Eds.), *Helping people change: A textbook of methods* (3rd ed.). New York: Pergamon.

Kantor, H., & Lowe, R. (1995). Class, race, and the emergence of federal education policy: From the New Deal to the Great Society. *Educational Researcher, 24*(3), 4–11.

Kaplan, B. (1984). *Development and growth.* Hillsdale, NJ: Erlbaum.

Kaplan, J. S. (1991). *Beyond behavior modification* (2nd ed.). Austin, TX: Pro-Ed.

Karpov, Y. V., & Bransford, J. D. (1995). L. S. Vygotsky and the doctrine of empirical and theoretical learning. *Educational Psychologist, 30,* 61–66.

Karweit, N. (1989). Time and learning: A review. In R. E. Slavin (Ed.), *School and classroom organization.* Hillsdale, NJ: Erlbaum.

Karweit, N., & Slavin, R. (1981). Measurement and modeling choices in studies of time and learning. *American Educational Research Journal, 18,* 157–171.

Kash, M. M., & Borich, G. (1978). *Teacher behavior and pupil self-concept.* Reading, MA: Addison-Wesley.

Kazdin, A. E. (1984). *Behavior modification in applied settings.* Homewood, IL: Dorsey Press.

Keefe, J. W. (1982). Assessing student learning styles: An overview. In *Student learning styles and brain behavior.* Reston, VA: National Association of Secondary School Principals.

Keefe, J. W., & Monk, J. S. (1986). *Learning style profile examiner's manual.* Reston, VA: National Association of Secondary School Principals.

Keith, T. Z. (1982). Time spent on homework and high school grades: A large-sample path analysis. *Journal of Educational Psychology, 74,* 248–253.

Keogh, B. K., & MacMillan, D. L. (1996). Exceptionality. In D. Berliner & R. Calfee (Eds.), *Handbook of educational psychology* (pp. 311–330). New York: Macmillan.

Kiewra, K. A. (1985). Investigating notetaking and review: A depth of processing alternative. *Educational Psychologist, 20,* 23–32.

Kiewra, K. A. (1988). Cognitive aspects of autonomous note taking: Control processes, learning strategies, and prior knowledge. *Educational Psychologist, 23,* 39–56.

Kiewra, K. A. (1989). A review of note-taking: The encoding storage paradigm and beyond. *Educational Psychology Review, 1,* 147–172.

Kindsvatter, R., Wilen, W., & Ishler, M. (1988). *Dynamics of effective teaching.* New York: Longman.

King, A. (1990). Enhancing peer interaction and learning in the classroom through reciprocal questioning. *American Educational Research Journal, 27,* 664–687.

King, A. (1994). Guiding knowledge construction in the classroom: Effects of teaching children how to question and how to explain. *American Educational Research Journal, 31,* 338–368.

King, G. (1979, June). Personal communication. University of Texas at Austin.

Kintsch, E. (1990). Macroprocesses and microprocesses in the development of summarization skills. *Cognition and Instruction, 7,* 161–195.

Kirk, S., & Gallagher, J. J., & Anastasiow, N. J. (1993). *Educating exceptional children* (7th ed.). Boston: Houghton Mifflin.

Kirschenbaum, H. (1992). A comprehensive model for values education and morals education. *Phi Delta Kappan, 73,* 771–776.

Kirst, M. (1991a). Interview on assessment issues with Lorrie Shepard. *Educational Researcher, 20*(2), 21–23.

Kirst, M. (1991b). Interview on assessment issues with James Popham. *Educational Researcher, 20*(2), 24–27.

Klausmeier, H. J. (1976). Instructional design and the teaching of concepts. In J. Levin & V. Allen (Eds.), *Cognitive learning in children: Theories and strategies.* New York: Academic Press.

Klausmeier, H. J. (1992). Concept learning and concept teaching. *Educational Psychologist, 27,* 267–286.

Knapp, M., Turnbull, B. J., & Shields, P. M. (1990). New directions for educating children of poverty. *Educational Leadership, 48*(1), 4–9.

Kneedler, P. (1985). California assesses critical thinking. In A. Costa (Ed.), *Developing minds: A resource book for teaching thinking.* Alexandria, VA: Association for Supervision and Curriculum Development.

Kneedler, R. (1984). *Special education for today.* Englewood Cliffs, NJ: Prentice-Hall.

Kogan, N. (1983). Stylistic variation in childhood and adolescence: Creativity, metaphor, and cognitive style. In P. Mussen (Ed.), *Handbook of child psychology* (4th ed.), (Vol. 3, pp. 630–706). New York: Wiley.

Kohlberg, L. (1963). The development of children's orientations toward moral order: Sequence in the development of moral thought. *Vita Humana, 6,* 11–33.

Kohlberg, L. (1975). The cognitive-developmental approach to moral education. *Phi Delta Kappan, 56,* 670–677.

Kohlberg, L. (1981). *The philosophy of moral development.* New York: Harper & Row.

Kohlberg, L. (1984). *Essays on moral development.* San Francisco: Harper & Row.

Kohlberg, L., Yaeger, J., & Hjertholm, E. (1969). Private speech: Four studies and a review of theories. *Child Development, 39,* 691–736.

Kohn, A. (1991). Caring kids; The role of the schools. *Phi Delta Kappan, 72,* 496–506.

Kohn, A. (1993). Rewards versus learning: A response to Paul Chance. *Phi Delta Kappan, 74,* 783–787.

Kohn, A. (1996). By all available means: Cameron and Pierce's defense of extrinsic motivators. *Review of Educational Research, 66,* 1–4.

Kolata, G. B. (1980). Math and sex; Are girls born with less ability? *Science, 210,* 1234–1235.

Kotrez, D., Stecher, B., & Diebert, E. (1993). *The reliability of scores from the 1992 Vermont Portfolio Assessment Program.* CSE Technical Report 355. Los Angeles: UCLA Center for the Study of Evaluation.

Kounin, J. (1970). *Discipline and group management in classrooms.* New York: Holt, Rinehart & Winston.

Kounin, J. S., & Doyle, P. H. (1975). Degree of continuity of a lesson's signal system and task involvement of children. *Journal of Educational Psychology, 67,* 159–164.

Kozulin, A. (1990). *Vygotsky's psychology: A biography of ideas.* Cambridge, MA: Harvard University Press.

Kozulin, A., & Falik, L. (1995). Dynamic cognitive assessment of the child. *Current Directions, 4,* 192–195.

Kozulin, A., & Presseisen, B. Z. (1995). Mediated learning experience and psychological tools: Vygotsky's and Feuerstein's perspectives in a study of student learning. *Educational Psychologist, 30,* 67–75.

Krathwohl, D. R., Bloom, B. S., & Masia, B. B. (1964). *Taxonomy of educational objectives. Handbook II: Affective domain.* New York: David McKay.

Krumboltz, J. D., & Krumboltz, H. B. (1972). *Changing children's behavior.* Englewood Cliffs, NJ: Prentice-Hall.

Kulik, C. C., & Kulik, J. A. (1982). Effects of ability grouping on secondary school students: A meta-analysis of evaluation findings. *American Educational Research Journal, 19,* 415–428.

Kulik, C. L., Kulik, J. A., & Bangert-Drowns, R. L. (1990). Effectiveness of mastery learning programs: A meta-analysis. *Review of Educational Research, 60,* 265–299.

Kulik, J. A., & Kulik, C. C. (1984). Effects of accelerated instruction on students. *Review of Educational Research, 54,* 409–425.

Kulik, J. A., Kulik, C. C., & Bangert, R. L. (1984, April). Effects of practice on aptitude and achievement test scores. *American Educational Research Journal, 21,* 435–447.

Kupersmidt, J. B., Coie, J. D., & Dodge, K. A. (1990). The role of poor peer relations in the development of disorder. In S. Asher & J. Coie (Eds.), *Peer rejection in childhood* (pp. 274–305). New York: Cambridge.

Lake, K., & Kafka, K. (1996). Reporting methods in grades K-8. In T. Guskey (Ed.), *ASCD 1996 Yearbook: Communicating student learning* (pp. 90–118). Alexandria, VA: Association for Supervision and Curriculum Development.

Land, M. L. (1987). Vagueness and clarity. In M. Dunkin (Ed.), *The international encyclopedia of teaching and teacher education* (pp. 392–397). New York: Pergamon.

Langer, E. J. (1993). A mindful education. *Educational Psychologist, 28,* 43–51.

Language Development and Hypermedia Group (1992). "Open" software design: A case study. *Educational Technology, 32,* 43–55.

Languis, M. L., & Miller, D. C. (1992). Luria's theory of brain functioning: A model for research in cognitive psychophysiology. *Educational Psychologist, 27*, 493–512.

Laosa, L. (1984). Ethnic, socioeconomic, and home language influences on early performance on measures of ability. *Journal of Educational Psychology, 76*, 1178–1198.

Larrivee, B. (1985). *Effective teaching behaviors for successful mainstreaming.* New York: Longman.

Lave, J. (1988). *Cognition in practice: Mind, mathematics, and culture in everyday life.* New York: Cambridge University Press.

Lave, J., & Wenger, E. (1991). *Situated learning: Legitimate peripheral participation.* Cambridge, MA: Cambridge University Press.

LeMahieu, P., Gitomer, D. H., & Eresh, J. T. (1993). *Portfolios in large-scale assessment: Difficult but not impossible.* Unpublished manuscript, University of Delaware.

Leavy, J. (1996, March 18). Mother's little helper. *Newsweek, 127*, 51–56.

Lefcourt, H. (1966). Internal versus external control of reinforcement: A review. *Psychological Bulletin, 65*, 206–220.

Lefton, L. A. (1994). *Psychology* (5th ed.). Boston: Allyn & Bacon.

Leinhardt, G. (1986). Expertise in mathematics teaching. *Educational Leadership, 43*, 28–33.

Leinhardt, G. (1988). Situated knowledge and expertise in teaching. In J. Calderhead (Ed.), *Teachers' professional learning.* London: Farmer Press.

Leming, J. S. (1981). Curriculum effectiveness in value/moral education. *Journal of Moral Education, 10*, 147–164.

Lepper, M. (1995, August). *Intrinsic motivation and the process of learning.* Paper presented at the American Psychological Association, New York.

Lepper, M. R. (1988). Motivational considerations in the study of instruction. *Cognition and Instruction, 5*, 289–309.

Lepper, M. R., & Greene, D. (1978). *The hidden costs of rewards: New perspectives on the psychology of human motivation.* Hillsdale, NJ: Erlbaum.

Lepper, M. R., Keavney, M., & Drake, M. (1996). Intrinsic motivation and extrinsic reward: A commentary on Cameron and Pierce's meta-analysis. *Review of Educational Research, 66*, 5–32.

Levin, J., & Nolan, J. F. (1996) *Principles of classroom management: A professional decision-making model.* Boston: Allyn & Bacon.

Levin, J. R. (1985). Educational applications of mnemonic pictures: Possibilities beyond your wildest imagination. In A. A. Sheikh (Ed.), *Imagery in the educational process.* Farmingdale, NY: Baywood.

Levin, J. R. (1994) Mnemonic strategies and classroom learning: A twenty-year report card. *Elementary School Journal, 94*, 235–254.

Levin, J. R., McCormick, C. B., Miller, G. E., Kessler, J., & Pressley, M. (1981). *Mnemonic versus nonmnemonic vocabulary learning strategies for children.* Report from the Project on Studies in Language: Reading and Communication. University of Wisconsin.

Lewinsohn, P. M., Rohde, P. & Seeley, J. R. (1994). Psychological risk factors for future attempts. *Journal of Consulting and Clinical Psychology, 62*, 297–305.

Lewis, A. C. (1995). An overview of the standards movement. *Phi Delta Kappan, 76*, 744–750.

Liben, L. S., & Signorella, M. L. (1993). Gender-schematic processing in children: the role of initial interpretations of stimuli. *Developmental Psychology, 29*, 141–149.

Lieber, J., & Semmel, M. (1988, April). *The relationship of group configuration to educational outcomes using microcomputers.* Paper presented at the annual meeting of the American Educational Research Association, New Orleans.

Linden, K. (1992). *Cooperative learning and problem solving.* Prospect Heights, IL: Waveland Press.

Lindsay, P. H., & Norman, D. A. (1977). *Human information processing: An introduction to psychology* (2nd ed.). New York: Academic Press.

Linn, M. C., & Hyde, J. S. (1989). Gender, mathematics, and science. *Educational Researcher, 18*, 17–27.

Linn, R., Klein, S., & Hart, F. (1972). The nature and correlates of law school essay grades. *Educational and Psychological Measurement, 32*, 267–279.

Linn, R. L. (1986). Educational testing and assessment: Research needs and policy issues. *American Psychologist, 41*, 1153–1160.

Lipscomb, T. J., MacAllister, H. A., & Bregman, N. J. (1985). A developmental inquiry into the effects of multiple models on children's generosity. *Merrill-Palmer Quarterly, 31*, 335–344.

Locke, E. A., & Latham, G. P. (1990). *A theory of goal setting and task performance.* Englewood Cliffs, NJ: Prentice-Hall.

Loftus, E., & Palmer, J. C. (1974). Reconstruction of automobile destruction: An example of the interaction between language and memory. *Journal of Verbal Learning and Verbal Behavior, 13*, 585–589.

Lohman, D. L. (1989). Human intelligence: An introduction to advances in theory and research. *Review of Educational Research, 59*, 333–374.

Lomask, M. S., Pecheone, R. L., & Baron, J. B. (1995). Assessing new science teachers. *Educational Leadership, 52*(6), 62–65.

Lortie, D. (1975). *Schoolteachers: A sociological study.* Chicago: University of Chicago Press.

Lortie, D. (1977). The balance of control and autonomy in elementary school teaching. In D. Erickson (Ed.), *Educational organization and administration* (pp. 335–371). Berkeley, CA: McCutchan.

Lowenstein, G. (1994). The psychology of curiosity: A review and reinterpretation. *Psychological Bulletin, 117*, 75–98.

Lowry, R., Sleet, D., Duncan, C., Powell, K., & Kolbe, L. (1995). Adolescents at risk for violence. *Educational Psychology Review, 7*, 7–40.

Luiten, J., Ames, W., & Ackerson, G. (1980). A meta-analysis of the effects of advance organizers on learning and retention. *American Educational Research Journal, 17*, 211–218.

Lyman, H. B. (1986). *Test scores and what they mean* (4th ed.). Englewood Cliffs, NJ: Prentice-Hall.

Lytton, H., & Romney, D. M. (1991). Parents' sex-related differential socialization of boys and girls: A meta-analysis. *Psychological Bulletin, 109*, 267–296.

Maccoby, E. E. (1990). Gender and relationships. *American Psychologist, 45,* 513–520.

Macionis, J. J. (1991). *Sociology* (3rd ed.). Englewood Cliffs, NJ: Prentice-Hall.

Macionis, J. J. (1994). *Sociology* (4th ed.). Englewood Cliffs, NJ: Prentice-Hall.

Madaus, G. F., & Kellaghan, T. (1993). Testing as a mechanism of public policy: A brief history. *Measurement and Evaluation in Counseling and Development, 26,* 6–10.

Madsen, C. H., Becker, W. C., & Thomas, D. R. (1968). Rules, praise, and ignoring: Elements of elementary classroom control. *Journal of Applied Behavior Analysis, 1,* 139–150.

Madsen, C. H., Becker, W. C., Thomas, D. R., Koser, L., & Plager, E. (1968). An analysis of the reinforcing function of "sit down" commands. In R. K. Parker (Ed.), *Readings in educational psychology.* Boston: Allyn & Bacon.

Maehr, M. L. (1974). *Sociocultural origins of achievement.* Monterey, CA: Brooks/Cole.

Maehr, M. L., & Anderman, E.M. (1993). Reinventing schools for early adolescents: Emphasizing task goals. *The Elementary School Journal, 93,* 593–610.

Mager, R. (1975). *Preparing instructional objectives* (2nd ed.). Palo Alto, CA: Fearon.

Maier, N. R. F. (1933). An aspect of human reasoning. *British Journal of Psychology, 24,* 144–155.

Maker, C. J. (1987). Gifted and talented. In V. Richardson-Koehler (Ed.), *Educators' handbook: A research perspective* (pp. 420–455). New York: Longman.

Mandlebaum, L. H., Russell, S. C., Krouse, J., & Gonter, M. (1983). Assertive discipline: An effective classwide behavior management program. *Behavior Disorders, 8(4),* 258–264.

Manning, B. H. (1991). *Cognitive self-instruction of classroom processes.* Albany, NY: State University of New York Press.

Manning, B. H., & Payne, B. D. (1996). *Self-talk for teachers and students: Metacognitive strategies for personal and classroom use.* Boston: Allyn & Bacon.

Manning, M. L. & Baruth, L. G. (1996). *Multicultural education of children and adolescents* (2nd ed.). Boston: Allyn & Bacon.

Mantzicopolos, P., & Morrison, D. (1992). Kindergarten retention: Academic and behavioral outcomes through the end of second grade. *American Educational Research Journal, 29,* 182–198.

Maratsos, M. P. (1989). Innateness and plasticity in language acquisition. In M. L. Rice & R. L. Schiefelbusch (Eds.), *The teachability of language* (pp. 105–125). Baltimore, MD: Brooks/Cole.

Marcia, J. (1980). Ego identity development. In J. Adelson (Ed.), *The handbook of adolescent psychology.* New York: Wiley.

Marcia, J. (1987). The identity status approach to the study of ego identity development. In T. Honess & K. Yardley (Eds.), *Self and identity: Perspectives across the life span.* London: Routledge & Kagan Paul.

Marcus, N., Cooper, M., & Sweller, J. (1996). Understanding instructions. *Journal of Educational Psychology, 88,* 49–63.

Markman, E. M. (1977). Realizing that you don't understand: A preliminary investigation. *Child Development, 48,* 986–992.

Markman, E. M. (1979). Realizing that you don't understand: Elementary school children's awareness of inconsistencies. *Child Development, 50,* 643–655.

Markman, E. M. (1990). Constraints children place on word meanings. *Cognitive Science, 14,* 57–77.

Marsh, H. W. (1987). The big-fish-little-pond effect on academic self-concept. *Journal of Educational Psychology, 79,* 280–295.

Marsh, H. W. (1990). Influences of internal and external frames of reference on the formation of math and English self-concepts. *Journal of Educational Psychology, 82,* 107–116.

Marsh, H. W. (1993). The multidimensional structure of academic self-concept: Invariance over gender and age. *American Educational Research Journal, 30,* 841–860.

Marsh, H. W. (1994). Using the National Longitudinal Study of 1988 to evaluate theoretical models of self-concept: The Self-Description Questionnaire. *Journal of Educational Psychology, 86,* 439–456.

Marsh, H. W., & Holmes, I. W. M. (1990). Multidimensional self-concepts: Construct validation of responses by children. *American Educational Research Journal, 27,* 89–118.

Marsh, H. W., & Shavelson, R. (1985). Self-concept: Its multifaceted, hierarchical structure. *Educational Psychologist, 20,* 107–123.

Marsh, H. W., Chessor, D., Craven, R., & Roche, L. (1995). The effects of gifted and talented programs on academic self-concept: The big fish strikes again. *American Educational Research Journal, 32,* 285–321.

Marshall, H. H. (1987). Motivational strategies of three fifth-grade teachers. *Elementary School Journal, 88,* 135–150.

Marshall, H. H. (1989). The development of self-concept. *Young Children, 44(5),* 44–51.

Marshall, H. H. (Ed.) (1992). *Redefining student learning: Roots of educational change.* Norwood, NJ: Ablex.

Martin, C. L. (1989). Children's use of gender-related information in making social judgments. *Developmental Psychology, 25,* 80–88.

Martin, C. L., & Little, J. K. (1990). The relation of gender understanding to children's sex-typed preferences and gender stereotypes. *Child Development, 61,* 1427–1439.

Martin, G., & Pear, J. (1992). *Behavior modification: What it is and how to do it* (4th ed.). Englewood Cliffs, NJ: Prentice-Hall.

Martindale, C. (1991). *Cognitive psychology: A neural-network approach.* Pacific Grove, CA: Brooks/Cole.

Maslow, A. H. (1968). *Toward a psychology of being* (2nd ed.). New York: Van Nostrand.

Maslow, A. H. (1970). *Motivation and personality* (2nd ed.). New York: Harper and Row.

Mason, D. A., & Good, T. L. (1993). Effects of two-group and whole-class teaching on regrouped elementary students' mathematics achievement. *American Educational Research Journal, 30,* 328–360.

Mayer, R. (1991). Cognition and instruction: Their historic meeting within educational psychology. *Journal of Educational Psychology, 84,* 405–412.

Mayer, R. E. (1979). Can advance organizers influence meaningful learning? *Review of Educational Research, 49,* 371–383.

Mayer, R. E. (1982). Memory for algebra story problems. *Journal of Educational Psychology, 74,* 199–216.

Mayer, R. E. (1983a). Can you repeat that? Qualitative and quantitative effects of repetition and advance organizers on learning from science prose. *Journal of Educational Psychology, 75,* 40–49.

Mayer, R. E. (1983b). *Thinking, problem solving, cognition.* San Francisco: Freeman.

Mayer, R. E. (1984). Twenty-five years of research on advance organizers. *Instructional Science, 8,* 133–169.

Mayer, R. E. (1992). *Thinking, problem solving, cognition* (2nd ed.). New York: Freeman.

Mayer, R. E. (1992). Cognition and instruction: Their historic meeting within educational psychology. *Journal of Educational Psychology, 84,* 405–412.

Mayer, R. E., & Sims, V. K. (1994). For whom is a picture worth a thousand words? Extensions of a dual-coding theory of multimedia learning. *Journal of Educational Psychology, 86,* 389–401.

Mayer, R. E., & Wittrock, M. C. (1996). Problem-solving transfer. In D. Berliner & R. Calfee (Eds.), *Handbook of educational psychology* (pp. 47–62). New York: Macmillan.

McCaslin, M., & Good, T. (1996). The informal curriculum. In Berliner, D. & Calfee, R. (Eds.), *Handbook of educational psychology* (pp. 622–670). New York: Macmillan.

McClelland, D. (1985). *Human motivation.* Glenview, IL: Scott, Foresman.

McClelland, D., & Pilon, D. (1983). Sources of adult motives in patterns of parent behavior in early childhood. *Journal of Personality and Social Psychology, 44,* 564–574.

McClelland, D., Atkinson, J. W., Clark, R. W., & Lowell, E. L. (1953). *The achievement motive.* New York: Appleton-Century-Crofts.

McClelland, D. C. (1993). Intelligence is not the best predictor of job performance. *Current Directions in Psychological Science, 2,* 5–6.

McCombs, B. L., & Marzano, R. J. (1990). Putting the self in self-regulated learning: The self as agent in integrating skill and will. *Educational Psychologist, 25,* 51–70.

McCormack, S. (1989). Response to Render, Padilla, and Krank: But practitioners say it works! *Educational Leadership, 46*(6), 77–79.

McCormick, C. B., & Levin, J. R. (1987). Mnemonic prose-learning strategies. In M. Pressley & M. McDaniel (Eds.), *Imaginary and related mnemonic processes.* New York: Springer-Verlag.

McDonald, J. P. (1993). Three pictures of an exhibition: Warm, cool, and hard. *Phi Delta Kappan, 6,* 480–485.

McGee, L. M., & Richgels, D. J. (1990). *Literacy's beginnings.* Boston: Allyn & Bacon.

McGuire, J. (1988). Gender stereotypes of parents with two-year-olds and beliefs about gender differences in behavior. *Sex Roles, 19,* 233–240.

McKenzie, T. L., & Rushall, B. S. (1974). Effects of self-recording on attendance and performance in a competitive swimming training environment. *Journal of Applied Behavior Analysis, 7,* 199–206.

McLaughlin, J. (1991). Reconciling care and control: Authority in classroom relationships. *Journal of Teacher Education, 40*(3), 182–195.

McLaughlin, T. F., & Gnagey, W. J. (1981, April). *Self-management and pupil self-control.* Paper presented at the annual meeting of the American Educational Research Association, Los Angeles.

McNemar, Q. (1964). Lost: Our intelligence? Why? *American Psychologist, 19,* 871–882.

Means, B., & Knapp, M. S. (1991). Cognitive approaches to teaching advanced skills to educationally disadvantaged students. *Phi Delta Kappan, 73,* 282–289.

Medley, D. M. (1979). The effectiveness of teachers. In P. Peterson & H. Walberg (Eds.), *Research on teaching: Concepts, findings, and implications* (pp. 11–27). Berkeley, CA: McCutchan.

Meek, A. (1991). On thinking about teaching: A conversation with Eleanor Duckworth. *Educational Leadership, 48*(6), 30–34.

Meichenbaum, D. (1977). *Cognitive behavior modification: An integrative approach.* New York: Plenum.

Meichenbaum, D. (1986). Cognitive behavior modification. In F. Kanfer & A. Goldstein (Eds.), *Helping people change: A textbook of methods* (3rd ed., pp. 346–380). New York: Pergamon.

Meichenbaum, D., Burland, S., Gruson, L., & Cameron, R. (1985). Metacognitive assessment. In S. Yussen (Ed.), *The growth of reflection in children.* Orlando, FL: Academic Press.

Meisels, S. J. (1989). High-stakes testing in kindergarten. *Educational Leadership, 46*(7), 16–22.

Mendell, P. R. (1971). Retrieval and representation in long-term memory. *Psychonomic Science, 23,* 295–296.

Mercer, C. (1992). *Students with learning disabilities* (4th ed.), Columbus: Merrill.

Messick, S. (1975). The standard problem: Meaning and values in measurement and evaluation. *American Psychologist, 35,* 1012–1027.

Messick, S. (1994). The matter of style: Manifestations of personality in cognition, learning, and teaching. *Educational Psychologist, 29,* 121–136.

Metcalfe, B. (1981). Self-concept and attitude toward school. *British Journal of Educational Psychology, 51,* 66–76.

Meyer, D. R., & Garasky, S. (1993). Custodial fathers: Myths, realities, and child support. *Journal of Marriage and the Family, 55,* 73–79.

Meyer, M. Delgardelle, M. & Middleton, J. (1996). Addressing parents' concerns over curriculum reform. *Educational Leadership, 53*(7), 54–57.

Miller, E. (1994). Peer mediation catches on, but some adults don't. *Harvard Education Letter, 10*(3), 8.

Miller, G. A. (1956). The magical number seven, plus or minus two: Some limits on our capacity for processing information. *Psychological Review, 63,* 81–97.

Miller, G. A., Galanter, E., & Pribram, K. H. (1960). *Plans and the structure of behavior.* New York: Holt, Rinehart & Winston.

Miller, K., & Gelman, R. (1983). The child's representation of number: A multidimensional scaling analysis. *Child Development, 54,* 1470–1479.

Miller, R. B. (1962). Analysis and specification of behavior for training. In R. Glaser (Ed.), *Training research and education: Science edition.* New York: Wiley.

Mills, C. J., Ablard, K. E., & Stumpf, H. (1993). Gender differences in academically talented young students' mathematical reasoning: Patterns across age and subskills. *Journal of Educational Psychology, 85,* 340–346.

Mills, J. R., & Jackson, N. E. (1990). Predictive significance of early giftedness: The case of precocious reading. *Journal of Educational Psychology, 82,* 410–419.

Mitchell, B. M. (1984). An update on gifted and talented education in the U.S. *Roeper Review, 6,* 161–163.

Moely, B. E., Hart, S. S., Santulli, K., Leal, L., Johnson, T., Rao, N., & Burney, L. (1986). How do teachers teach memory skills? In J. Levin & M. Pressley (Eds.), *Educational Psychologist, 21* (Special issue on learning strategies), 55–72.

Moos, R. H., & Moos, B. S. (1978). Classroom social climate and student absences and grades. *Journal of Educational Psychology, 70,* 263–269.

Morine Dershimer, G. (1993). Tracing conceptual change in preservice teachers. *Teaching and Teacher Education, 9,* 15–26.

Morris, C. G. (1988). *Psychology: An introduction* (6th ed.). Englewood Cliffs, NJ: Prentice-Hall.

Morris, C. G. (1991). *Psychology: An introduction* (7th ed.). Englewood Cliffs, NJ: Prentice-Hall.

Morris, P. F. (1990). Metacognition. In M. W. Eysenck, (Ed.), *The Blackwell dictionary of cognitive psychology* (pp. 225–229). Oxford, UK: Basil Blackwell.

Morrow, L. (1983). Home and school correlates of early interest in literature. *Journal of Educational Research, 76,* 221–230.

Morrow, L., & Weinstein, C. (1986). Encouraging voluntary reading: The impact of a literature. *Reading Research Quarterly, 21,* 330–346.

Morrow, L. M. (1992). The impact of a literature-based program on literacy achievement, use of literature, and attitudes of children from minority backgrounds. *Reading Research Quarterly, 27,* 251–275.

Morrow, L. M. (1997). *Literacy development in the early years: Helping children to read and write* (3rd ed.). Boston: Allyn & Bacon.

Moshman, D. (1982). Exogenous, endogenous, and dialectical constructivism. *Developmental Review, 2,* 371–384.

Moshman, D., Glover, J. A., & Bruning, R. H. (1987). *Developmental psychology.* Boston: Little, Brown.

Moskowitz, G., & Hayman, M. L. (1976). Successful strategies of inner-city teachers: A year-long study. *Journal of Educational Research, 69,* 283–289.

Moss, P. A. (1992). Shifting conceptions of validity in educational measurement: Implications for performance assessment. *Review of Educational Research, 62,* 229–258.

Mumford, M. D., Costanza, D. P., Baughman, W. A., Threlfall, V., & Fleishman, E. A. (1994). Influence of abilities on performance during practice: Effects of massed and distributed practice. *Journal of Educational Psychology, 86,* 134–144.

Murray, H. G. (1983). Low inference classroom teaching behavior and student ratings of college teaching effectiveness. *Journal of Educational Psychology, 75,* 138–149.

Musgrave, G. R. (1975). *Individualized instruction: Teaching strategies focusing on the learner.* Boston, MA: Allyn & Bacon.

Mussen, P., Conger, J. J., & Kagan, J. (1984). *Child development and personality* (6th ed.). New York: Harper & Row.

National Center for Education Statistics. (1990). *Digest of Education Statistics.* Washington, DC: Center for Education Statistics.

National Center for Research on Cultural Diversity and Second Language Learning, Center for Applied Linguistics (1992). *Instructional conversations.* Washington, DC: ERIC Document #EDO-FL-92–01.

National Council of Teachers of Mathematics (NCTM) (1989). *Curriculum and evaluation standards for school mathematics.* Reston, VA: Author.

National Council for Teachers of Mathematics. (1991). *Professional standards for teaching mathematics.* Reston, VA: National Council for Teachers of Mathematics.

National Governors Association (1989). *Results in education: 1989.* Washington, DC: NGA.

National Joint Committee on Learning Disabilities (1989). *Letter from NJCLD to member organizations. Topic: Modifications to the NJCLD definition of learning disabilities.*

National Science Foundation (1988). *Women and minorities in science and engineering* (NSF 88–301). Washington, DC: National Science Foundation.

Naveh-Benjamin, M. (1991). A comparison of training programs intended for different types of test-anxious students: Further support for an information-processing model. *Journal of Educational Psychology, 83,* 134–139.

Naveh-Benjamin, M., McKeachie, W. J., & Lin, Y. (1987). Two types of test-anxious students: Support for an information processing model. *Journal of Educational Psychology, 79,* 131–136.

Needles, M., & Knapp, M. (1994). Teaching writing to children who are undeserved. *Journal of Educational Psychology, 86,* 339–349.

Neimark, E. (1975). Intellectual development during adolescence. In F. D. Horowitz (Ed.), *Review of child development research* (Vol. 4). Chicago: University of Chicago Press.

Neisser, U., Boodoo, G., Bouchard, A., Boykin, W., Brody, N., Ceci, S. J., Halpern, D. F., Loehlin, J. C., Perloff, R., Sternberg, R. J., & Urbina, S. (1996). Intelligence: Knowns and unknowns. *American Psychologist, 51,* 77–101.

Nelson, G. (1993). Risk, resistance, and self-esteem: A longitudinal study of elementary school-aged children from mother-custody and two-parent families. *Journal of Divorce and Remarriage, 19,* 99–119.

Nelson, K. (1981). Individual differences in language development: Implications for development and language. *Developmental Psychology, 17,* 170–187.

Nelson, K. (1986). *Event knowledge.* Hillsdale, NJ: Erlbaum.

Nelson, T. O. (1996). Consciousness and metacognition. *American Psychologist, 51,* 102–116.

Neuman, R. S., & Schwager, M. T. (1995). Students' help seeking during problem solving: Effects of grade, goal, and prior achievement. *American Educational Research Journal, 32,* 352–376.

Neuman, S. B., & Roskos, K. (1992). Literacy objects as cultural tools: Effects on children's literacy behaviors in play. *Reading Research Quarterly, 27,* 255–275.

Newby, T. J. (1991). Classroom motivation: Strategies of first-year teachers. *Journal of Educational Psychology, 83,* 195–200.

Newcomb, M. D., & Bentler, P. M. (1989). Substance use and abuse among children and teenagers. *American Psychologist, 44,* 242–248.

Newcombe, N., & Baenninger, M. (1990). The role of expectations in spatial test performance: A meta-analysis. *Sex Roles, 16,* 25–37.

Newmann, F. M., & Wehlage, G. G. (1993). Five standards of authentic instruction. *Educational Leadership, 50*(7), 8–12.

Newstead, S. E., Franklyn-Stokes, A., & Armstead, P. (1996). Individual differences in student cheating. *Journal of Educational Psychology, 88,* 229–241.

Newsweek (Summer, 1991). *The end of innocence,* pp. 62–64. Special Edition: How Kids Grow.

Nicholls, J. G., & Miller, A. (1984). Conceptions of ability and achievement motivation. In R. Ames & C. Ames (Eds.), *Research on motivation in education. Vol. 1: Student Motivation* (pp. 39–73). New York: Academic Press.

Nicholls, J. G., Nelson, J. R., Gleaves, K. (1995). Learning facts versus learning that most questions have many answers: Students' evaluations of contrasting curricula. *Journal of Educational Psychology, 87,* 253–260.

Nielsen, L. (1993). Students from divorced and blended families. *Educational Psychology Review, 5,* 177–199.

Niemiec, R., & Walberg, H. J. (1987). Comparative effects of computer-assisted instruction: A synthesis of reviews. *Journal of Educational Computing Research, 3,* 19–37.

Nissani, M., & Hoefler-Nissani, D. M. (1992). Experimental studies of belief dependence of observations and of resistance to conceptual change. *Cognition and Instruction, 9,* 97–111.

Noddings, N. (1990). Constructivism in mathematics education. In R. Davis, C. Maher, & N. Noddings (Eds.), *Constructivist views on the teaching and learning of mathematics* (pp. 7–18). Monograph 4 of the National Council of Teachers of Mathematics, Reston, VA.

Noddings, N. (1995). Teaching themes of care. *Phi Delta Kappan, 76,* 675–679.

Norman, D. P. (1982). *Learning and memory.* San Francisco: Freeman.

Novak, J. D., & Musonda, D. (1991). A twelve-year longitudinal study of science concept learning. *American Educational Research Journal, 28,* 117–154.

Nucci, L. (1987). Synthesis of research on moral development. *Educational Leadership, 44*(5), 86–92.

Nungester, R. J., & Duchastel, P. C. (1982). Testing versus review: Effects on retention. *Journal of Educational Psychology, 74,* 18–22.

Nuthall, G., & Alton-Lee, A. (1990). Research on teaching and learning: Thirty years of change. *Elementary School Journal, 90,* 546–570.

Nuthall, G., & Alton-Lee, A. (1992). Understanding how students learn in classrooms. In M. Pressley, K. Harris, &

J. Guthrie (Eds.), *Promoting academic competence and literacy in school* (pp. 57–87). San Diego: Academic Press.

Nuthall, G., & Alton-Lee, A. (1993). Predicting learning from student experience of teaching: A theory of student knowledge in classrooms. *American Educational Research Journal, 30,* 799–840.

Nuthall, G., & Alton-Lee, A. (1995). Assessing classroom knowledge: How students use their knowledge and experience to answer classroom achievement test questions in science and social studies. *American Educational Research Journal, 32,* 185–197.

O'Donnell, A. M., & O'Kelly, J. (1994). Learning from peers: Beyond the rhetoric of positive results. *Educational Psychology Review, 6,* 321–350.

O'Leary, K. D. (1980). Pills or skills for hyperactive children? *Journal of Applied Behavior Analysis, 13,* 191–204.

O'Leary, K. D., & O'Leary, S. (Eds.). (1977). *Classroom management: The successful use of behavior modification* (2nd ed.). Elmsford, NY: Pergamon.

O'Leary, K. D., & Wilson, G. T. (1987). *Behavior therapy: Application and outcome.* Englewood Cliffs, NJ: Prentice-Hall.

O'Leary, K. D., Kaufman, K. F., Kass, R. E., & Drabman, R. S. (1970). The effects of loud and soft reprimands on the behavior of disruptive students. *Exceptional Children, 37,* 145–155.

O'Leary, S. (1995). Parental discipline mistakes. *Current Directions in Psychological Science, 4,* 11–13.

O'Leary, S. G., & O'Leary, K. D. (1976). Behavior modification in the schools. In H. Leitenberg (Ed.), *Handbook of behavior modification and behavior therapy.* Englewood Cliffs, NJ: Prentice-Hall.

O'Neil, J. (1990a). Link between style, culture proves divisive. *Educational Leadership, 48*(2), 8.

O'Neil, J. (1990b). Piecing together the restructuring puzzle. *Educational Leadership, 47*(7), 4–10.

O'Neil, J. (1991). Drive for national standards picking up steam. *Educational Leadership, 48*(5), 4–8.

O'Neil, J. (1993). Can national standards make a difference? *Educational Leadership, 50*(5), 4–8.

Oakes, J. (1990). Opportunities, achievement, and choice: Women and minority students in science and math. *Review of Research in Education, 16,* 153–222.

Ogbu, J. (1987). Variability in minority school performance: A problem in search of an explanation. *Anthropology and Education Quarterly, 18,* 312–334.

Ogden, J. E., Brophy, J. E., & Evertson, C. M. (1977, April). *An experimental investigation of organization and management techniques in first-grade reading groups.* Paper presented at the annual meeting of the American Educational Research Association, New York.

Ollendick, T. H., Dailey, D., & Shapiro, E. S. (1983). Vicarious reinforcement: Expected and unexpected effects. *Journal of Applied Behavior Analysis, 16,* 485–491.

Olsen, L. (1988). *Crossing the schoolhouse border: Immigrant students and the California public schools.* San Francisco: California Tomorrow.

Onslow, M. (1992). Choosing a treatment program for early stuttering: Issues and future directions. *Journal of Speech and Hearing Research, 35,* 983–993.

Ortony, A., Clore, G. L., & Collins, A. (1988). *The cognitive structure of emotions.* Cambridge: Cambridge University Press.

Osborn, A. F. (1963). *Applied imagination* (3rd ed.). New York: Scribner's.

Ovando, C. J. (1989). Language diversity and education. In J. Banks & C. McGee Banks (Eds.), *Multicultural education: Issues and perspectives* (pp. 208–228). Boston: Allyn & Bacon.

Owen, L. (1985). *None of the above: Behind the myth of scholastic aptitude.* Boston: Houghton Mifflin.

Owens, R. E. (1995). *Language disorders* (2nd ed.) Boston: Allyn & Bacon.

Padilla, F. M. (1992). *The gang as an American enterprise.* New Brunswick, NJ: Rutgers University Press.

Page, E. B. (1958). Teacher comments and student performances: A 74-classroom experiment in school motivation. *Journal of Educational Psychology, 49,* 173–181.

Paivio, A. (1971). *Imagery and verbal processes.* New York: Holt, Rinehart & Winston.

Paivio, A. (1986). *Mental representations: A dual-coding approach.* New York: Oxford University Press.

Palincsar, A. S. (1986). The role of dialogue in providing scaffolded instruction. In J. Levin & M. Pressley (Eds.), *Educational Psychologist, 21* (Special issue on learning strategies), 73–98.

Palincsar, A. S., & Brown, A. L. (1984). Reciprocal teaching of comprehension-fostering and monitoring activities. *Cognition and Instruction, 1,* 117–175.

Palincsar, A. S., & Brown, A. L. (1989). Classroom dialogues to promote self-regulated comprehension. In J. Brophy (ed.), *Advances in research on teaching,* (Vol. 1, pp. 35–67). Greenwich, CT: JAI Press.

Pallas, A. M., & Alexander, K. (1983). Sex differences in quantitative SAT performance: New evidence on the differential coursework hypothesis. *American Educational Research Journal, 20,* 165–182.

Pallas, A. M., Natriello, G., & McDill, E. L. (1989). The changing nature of the disadvantaged population: Current dimensions and future trends. *Educational Researcher, 18*(5), 16–22.

Papert, S. (1980). *Mindstorms: Children, computers, and powerful ideas.* New York: Basic Books.

Papert, S. (1993). *The children's machine: Rethinking school in the age of the computer.* New York: Basic Books.

Paris, S. (1988, April). *Fusing skill and will: The integration of cognitive and motivational psychology.* Paper presented at the annual meeting of the American Educational Research Association, New Orleans.

Paris, S. G., & Cunningham, A. E. (1996). Children becoming students. In D. Berliner & R. Calfee, (Eds.), *Handbook of Educational Psychology* (pp. 117–146). New York. Macmillan.

Paris, S. G., Lipson, M. Y., & Wixson, K. K. (1983). Becoming a strategic reader. *Contemporary Educational Psychology, 8,* 293–316.

Parks, C. P. (1995). Gang behavior in the schools: Myth or reality? *Educational Psychology Review, 7,* 41–68.

Pasch, M., Sparks-Langer, G., Gardner, T. G., Starko, A. J., & Moody, C. D. (1991). *Teaching as decision making: In-*structional practices for the successful teacher. New York: Longman.

Pate, P. E., McGinnis, K., & Homestead, E. (1995). Creating coherence through curriculum integration. In M. Harmin (1994). *Inspiring active learning: A handbook for teachers* (pp. 62–70). Alexandria, VA: Association for Supervision and Curriculum Development.

Pauk, W. (1989). *How to study in college* (4th ed.). Boston: Houghton Mifflin.

Paulman, R. G., & Kennelly, K. J. (1984). Test anxiety and ineffective test taking: Different names, same construct? *Journal of Educational Psychology, 76,* 279–288.

Paulson, F. L., Paulson, P. R., & Meyer, C. A. (1991). What makes a portfolio a portfolio? *Educational Leadership, 48*(5), 60–63.

Pearson, P. D. (1989). Commentary: Reading the whole language movement. *Elementary School Journal, 90,* 231–241.

Pelham, W. E. (1981). Attention deficits in hyperactive and learning-disabled children. *Exceptional Education Quarterly, 2,* 13–23.

Pelham, W. E., & Murphy, H. A. (1986). Attention deficit and conduct disorders. In M. Hersen (Ed.), *Pharmacological and behavioral treatment: An integrative approach* (pp. 108–148). New York: Wiley.

Peneul, W. R., & Wertsch, J. V. (1995). Vygotsky and identity formation: A sociocultural approach. *Educational Psychologist, 30,* 83–92.

Peng, S. & Lee, R. (1992, April). *Home variables, parent-child activities, and academic achievement: A study of 1988 eighth graders.* Paper presented at the annual meeting of the American Educational Research Association, San Francisco.

Peper, R. J., & Mayer, R. E. (1986). Generative effects of note taking during science lectures. *Journal of Educational Psychology, 78,* 34–38.

Perkins, D., & Blythe, T. (1994). Putting understanding up front. *Educational Leadership, 51*(5), 4–7.

Perkins, D., Jay, E., & Tishman, S. (1993). New conceptions of thinking: From ontology to education. *Educational Psychologist, 28,* 67–85.

Perkins, D. N. (1986). Thinking frames. *Educational Leadership, 43,* 4–11.

Perkins, D. N. (1987). Thinking frames: An integrative perspective on teaching cognitive skills. In J. B. Baron & R. J. Sternberg (Eds.), *Teaching thinking skills: Theory and practice* (pp. 41–85). New York: Freeman.

Perkins, D. N. (1991, May). Technology meets constructivism: Do they make a marriage? *Educational Technology, 31,* 18–23.

Perkins, D. N., & Salomon, G. (1989). Are cognitive skills context-bound? *Educational Researcher, 18,* 16–25.

Perrone, V. (1994). How to engage students in learning. *Educational Leadership, 51*(5), 11–13.

Peterson, C., & Barrett, L. C. (1987). Explanatory style and academic performance among university freshmen. *Journal of Personality and Social Psychology, 53,* 603–607.

Peterson, M. P. (1993). Physical and sexual abuse among school children: Prevalence and prevention. *Educational Psychology Review, 5,* 63–86.

Peterson, P. (1979). Direct instruction reconsidered. In P. Peterson & H. Walberg (Eds.), *Research on teaching: Con-*

cepts, findings, and implications (pp. 57–69). Berkeley, CA: McCutchan.

Peterson, P., Fennema, E., & Carpenter, T. (1989). Using knowledge of how students think about mathematics. *Educational Leadership, 46*(4), 42–46.

Peterson, P. L. (1992). Revising their thinking: Keisha Coleman and her third-grade mathematics class. In H. Marshall (Ed.) *Redefining student learning: Roots of educational change* (pp. 151–176). Norwood, NJ: Ablex.

Peterson, P. L., & Comeaux, M. A. (1989). Assessing the teacher as a reflective professional: New perspectives on teacher evaluation. In A. Woolfolk (Ed.), *Research perspectives on the graduate preparation of teachers* (pp. 132–152). Englewood Cliffs, NJ: Prentice-Hall.

Peterson, S. E., DeGracie, J. S., & Ayabe, C. R. (1987). A longitudinal study of the effects of retention/promotion on academic achievement. *American Educational Research Journal, 24,* 107–118.

Pfeffer, C. R. (1981). Developmental issues among children of separation and divorce. In I. Stuart & L. Abt (Eds.), *Children of separation and divorce.* New York: Van Nostrand Reinhold.

Pfiffner, L. J., Rosen, L. A., & O'Leary, S. G. (1985). The efficacy of an all-positive approach to classroom management. *Journal of Applied Behavior Analysis, 18,* 257–261.

Phillips, D., & Zimmerman, M. (1990). The developmental course of perceived competence and incompetence among competent children. In R. Sternberg & J. Kolligian (Eds.), *Competence considered* (pp. 41–66). New Haven, CT: Yale University Press.

Phinney, J., & Alipiria, L. (1990). Ethnic identity in college students from four ethnic groups. *Journal of Adolescence, 13,* 171–183.

Phye, G. D. (1992). Strategic transfer: A tool for academic problem solving. *Educational Psychology Review, 4,* 393–421.

Phye, G. D., & Sanders, C. E. (1994). Advice and feedback: Elements of practice for problem solving. *Contemporary Educational Psychology, 17,* 211–223.

Piaget, J. (1954). *The construction of reality in the child* (M. Cook, Trans.). New York: Basic Books.

Piaget, J. (1962). *Comments on Vygotsky's critical remarks concerning "The language and thought of the child" and "Judgment and reasoning in the child."* Cambridge, MA: MIT Press.

Piaget, J. (1963). *Origins of intelligence in children.* New York: Norton.

Piaget, J. (1965). *The moral judgment of the child.* New York: Free Press.

Piaget, J. (1970a). Piaget's theory. In P. Mussen (Ed.), *Handbook of child psychology* (3rd ed.). New York: Wiley.

Piaget, J. (1970b). *The science of education and the psychology of the child.* New York: Orion Press.

Piaget, J. (1974). *Understanding causality* (D. Miles and M. Miles, Trans.). New York: Norton.

Piaget, J. (1985). *The equilibrium of cognitive structures: The central problem of intellectual development.* (T. Brown & K. L. Thampy, Trans.) Chicago: University of Chicago Press.

Pierson, L. H., & Connell, J. P. (1992). Effect of grade retention on self-system processes, school engagement, and academic performance. *Journal of Educational Psychology, 84,* 300–307.

Pine, G. J., & Hilliard, A. G., III (1990). Rx for racism: Imperatives for America's schools. *Phi Delta Kappan, 71,* 593–600.

Pintrich, P. (1994). Continuities and Discontinuities: Future directions for research in educational psychology. *Educational Psychologist, 29,* 137–148.

Pintrich, P., & Schrauben, B. (1992). Students' motivational beliefs and their cognitive engagement in academic tasks. In D. Schunk & J. Meece (Eds.) *Students' perceptions in the classroom: Causes and consequences* (pp. 149–183). Hillsdale, NJ: Erlbaum.

Pintrich, P. R., & Schunk, D. H. (1996). *Motivation in education: Theory, research, and applications.* Columbus, OH: Merrill.

Pintrich, P. R., Marx, R. W., & Boyle, R. A. (1993). Beyond cold conceptual change: The role of motivational beliefs and classroom contextual factors in the process of conceptual change. *Review of Educational Research, 63,* 167–199.

Pitts, J. M. (1992). Constructivism: Learning rethought. In J. B. Smith & J. C. Coleman, Jr. (Eds.), *School Library Media Annual* (Vol. 10, pp. 14–25). Englewood, CO: Libraries Unlimited.

Polson, P. G., & Jeffries, R. (1985). Instruction in general problem-solving skills: An analysis of four approaches. In J. Segal, S. Chipman, & R. Glaser (Eds.), *Thinking and learning skills* (Vol. 1, pp. 417–455). Mahwah, NJ: Erlbaum.

Popham, W. J. (1993). *Educational evaluation* (3rd ed.). Boston: Allyn & Bacon.

Posner, M. I. (1973). *Cognition: An introduction.* Glenview, IL: Scott, Foresman.

Powell, R. R., Garcia, J., & Denton, J. J. (1985, March). *The portrayal of minorities and women in selected elementary science series.* Paper presented at the annual meeting of the American Educational Research Association, Chicago.

Powers, S. I., Hauser, S. T., & Kilner, L. A. (1989). Adolescent mental health. *American Psychologist, 44,* 200–208.

Prawat, R. S. (1991). The value of ideas: The immersion approach to the development of thinking. *Educational Researcher, 20,* 3–10.

Prawat, R. S. (1992). Teachers beliefs about teaching and learning: A constructivist perspective. *American Journal of Education, 100,* 354–395.

Prawat, R. S., & Floden, R. E. (1994). Philosophical perspectives on constructivist view of learning. *Educational Psychologist, 29,* 37–48.

Premack, D. (1965). Reinforcement theory. In D. Levine (Ed.), *Nebraska symposium on motivation* (Vol. 13). Lincoln, NE: University of Nebraska Press.

Pressley, M. (1986). The relevance of the good strategy user model to the teaching of mathematics. In J. Levin & M. Pressley (Eds.), *Educational Psychologist, 21* (Special issue on learning strategies), 139–161.

Pressley, M. (1991). Comparing Hall (1988) with related research on elaborative mnemonics. *Journal of Educational Psychology, 83,* 165–170.

Pressley, M. (1995). More about the development of self-regulation: complex, long-term, and thoroughly social. *Educational Psychologist, 30,* 207–212.

Pressley, M. (1996, August). *Getting beyond whole language: Elementary reading instruction that makes sense in light of recent psychological research.* Paper presented at the Annual meeting of the American Psychological Association, Toronto.

Pressley, M., Barkowski, J. G., & Schneider, W. (1987). Cognitive strategies: Good strategy users coordinate metacognition and knowledge. In R. Vasta & G. Whitehurst (Eds.), *Annals of Child Development. Vol. 4.* Greenwich, CT: JAI Press.

Pressley, M., Levin, J., & Delaney, H. D. (1982). The mnemonic keyword method. *Review of Research in Education, 52,* 61–91.

Price, G., & O'Leary, K. D. (1974). *Teaching children to develop high performance standards.* Unpublished manuscript. State University of New York at Stony Brook.

Pring, R. (1971). Bloom's taxonomy: A philosophical critique. *Cambridge Journal of Education, 1,* 83–91.

Purcell, P., & Stewart, L. (1990). Dick and Jane in 1989. *Sex Roles, 22,* 177–185.

Purkey, W. W., & Novak, J. M. (1984). *Inviting school success: A self-concept approach to teaching and learning.* Belmont, CA: Wadsworth.

Putnam, R. T., & Borko, H. (in press). Teacher learning: Implications of new views of cognition. In B. J. Biddle, T. L. Good, & I. F. Goodson (Eds.), *The international handbook of teachers and teaching.* Dordrecht, the Netherlands: Kluwer.

Quay, H. C., & Peterson, D. R. (1987). *Manual for the revised behavior problem checklist.* Coral Cables, FL: Author.

Rachlin, H. (1991). *Introduction to modern behaviorism* (3rd ed.), New York: W. H. Freeman.

Raffini, J. P. (1996). *150 ways to increase intrinsic motivation in the classroom.* Boston: Allyn & Bacon.

Ramirez, J., Yuen, S., & Ramey, D. (1991). *Executive summary: Longitudinal study of structured English immersion strategy, early-exit, late-exit transitional bilingual education programs for language minority children.* San Mateo, CA: Aguirre International.

Range, L. M. (1993). Suicide prevention: Guidelines for schools. *Educational Psychology Review, 5,* 135–154.

Rathus, S. A. (1988). *Understanding child development.* New York: Holt, Rinehart & Winston.

Raudenbush, S. (1984). Magnitude of teacher expectancy effects on pupil IQ as a function of the credibility of expectancy induction: A synthesis of findings from 18 experiments. *Journal of Educational Psychology, 76,* 85–97.

Ravitch, D. (1995). National standards in American education: A citizens's guide. Washington, DC: Brookings Institution.

Recht, D. R., & Leslie, L. (1988). Effect of prior knowledge on good and poor readers' memory of text. *Journal of Educational Psychology, 80,* 16–20.

Redfield, D. L., & Rousseau, E. W. (1981). A meta-analysis of experimental research on teacher questioning behavior. *Review of Educational Research, 51,* 181–193.

Reed, S., & Sautter, R. C. (1990). Children of poverty: The status of 12 million Americans. *Phi Delta Kappan, 71*(10), K1–K12.

Reed, S. K. (1992). *Cognition* (3rd ed.). Pacific Grove, CA: Brooks/Cole.

Reeve, J. (1996). *Motivating others: Nurturing inner motivational resources.* Boston: Allyn & Bacon.

Reich, P. A. (1986). *Language development.* Englewood Cliffs, NJ: Prentice-Hall.

Reid, D. K., Hresko, W. P., & Swanson, H. L. (1991). *A cognitive approach to learning disabilities* (2nd ed.). Austin, TX: Pro-Ed.

Reid, M. K., & Borkowski, J. G. (1987). Causal attributions of hyperactive children: Implications for teaching strategies and self control. *Journal of Educational Psychology, 79,* 296–307.

Render, G. F., Padilla, J. N. M., & Krank, H. M. (1989). What research really shows about assertive discipline. *Educational Leadership, 46*(6), 72–75.

Rennie, L. J., & Parker, L. H. (1987). Detecting and accounting for gender differences in mixed-sex and single-sex groupings in science lessons. *Educational Review, 39*(1), 65–73.

Rentel, V. (1994). Preparing clinical faculty members: Research on teachers' reasoning. In K. Howey & N. Zimpher (Eds.) *The professional development of teacher educators.* Norwood, NJ: Ablex.

Renzulli, J. S., & Reis, S. M. (1991). The schoolwide enrichment model: A comprehensive plan for the development of creative productivity. In N. Colangelo & G. Davis (Eds.), *Handbook of gifted education* (pp. 111–141). Boston: Allyn & Bacon.

Renzulli, J. S., & Smith, L. H. (1978). *The Learning Styles Inventory: A measure of student preferences for instructional techniques.* Mansfield Center, CT: Creative Learning Press.

Resnick, L. (1987). Learning in school and out. *Educational Researcher, 16*(9), 13–20.

Resnick, L., & Nolan, K. (1995). Where in the world are world-class standards? *Educational Leadership, 52*(6), 6–11.

Resnick, L. B. (1981). Instructional psychology. *Annual Review of Psychology, 32,* 659–704.

Resnick, L. B., & Klopfer, L. E. (1989). Toward the thinking curriculum: An overview. In *Toward the thinking curriculum: Current cognitive research* (pp. 1–18). Alexandria, VA: Association for Supervision and Curriculum Development.

Reynolds, M. C., & Birch, J. W. (1988). *Adaptive mainstreaming: A primer for teachers and principals* (3rd ed.). New York: Longman.

Reynolds, W. M. (1980). Self-esteem and classroom behavior in elementary school children. *Psychology in the Schools, 17,* 273–277.

Rhode, G., Morgan, D. P., & Young, K. R. (1983). Generalization and maintenance of treatment gains of behaviorally handicapped students from resource rooms to regular classrooms using self-evaluation procedures. *Journal of Applied Behavior Analysis, 16,* 171–188.

Ricciardelli, L. A. (1992). Bilingualism and cognitive development: Relation to threshold theory. *Journal of Psycholinguistic Research, 21,* 301–316.

Rice, M. L. (1984). Cognitive aspects of communicative development. In R. Schiefelbusch & J. Pickar (Eds.), *The acquisition of communicative competence*. Baltimore: University Park Press.

Rice, M. L. (1989). Children's language acquisition. *American Psychologist, 44,* 149–156.

Richardson, T. M., & Benbow, C. P. (1990). Long-term effects of acceleration on the social-emotional adjustment of mathematically precocious youths. *Journal of Educational Psychology, 82,* 464–470.

Riley, M. S., & Greeno, J. G. (1991). Developmental analysis of understanding language about quantities and of solving problems. *Cognition and Instruction, 5,* 49–101.

Robbins, P. A. (1990). Implementing whole language: Bridging children and books. *Educational Leadership, 47*(6), 50–55.

Robert Wood Johnson (1988). *Serving handicapped children: A special report.* Princeton, NJ: Robert Wood Johnson Foundation.

Robinson, C. S., & Hayes, J. R. (1978). Making inferences about relevance in understanding problems. In R. Revlin & R. E. Mayer (Eds.), *Human reasoning.* Washington, DC: Winston.

Robinson, D. H., & Kiewra, K. A. (1995). Visual argument: Graphic outlines are superior to outlines in improving learning form text. *Journal of Educational Psychology, 87,* 455–467.

Robinson, F. P. (1961). *Effective study.* New York: Harper & Row.

Roderick, M. (1994). Grade retention and school dropout: Investigating an association, *American Educational Research Journal, 31,* 729–760.

Rodriguez, R. (1987, September 9). What is an American education? *Education Week, 7*(1).

Rogers, C. R. (1969). *Freedom to learn.* Columbus, OH: Charles E. Merrill.

Rogers, C. R., & Freiberg, H. J. (1994). *Freedom to learn* (3rd ed.). Columbus, OH: Charles E. Merrill.

Rogoff, B. (1990). *Apprenticeship in thinking: Cognitive development in social context.* New York: Oxford University Press.

Rogoff, B., & Chavajay, P. (1995). What's become of the research on the cultural basis of cognitive development? *American Psychologist, 50,* 859–877.

Rogoff, B., & Morelii, G. (1989). Perspectives on children's development from cultural psychology. *American Psychologist, 44,* 3 5–348.

Rogoff, B., & Wertsch, J. V. (Eds.). (1984). *Children's learning in the "zone of proximal development."* San Francisco: Jossey-Bass.

Rohwer, W. D. Jr., & Sloane, K. (1994). Psychological perspectives. In L. Anderson & L. Sosniak (Eds.), *Bloom's Taxonomy: A forty-year retrospective.* Ninety-third yearbook for the National Society for the Study of Education: Part II (pp. 41–63). Chicago: University of Chicago Press.

Rosch, E. H. (1973). On the internal structure of perceptual and semantic categories. In T. Moore (Ed.), *Cognitive development and the acquisition of language.* New York: Academic Press.

Rosch, E. H. (1975). Cognitive representations of semantic categories. *Journal of Experimental Psychology: General, 104,* 192–233.

Roschelle, J., & Clancey, W. J. (1992). Learning as social and neural. *Educational Psychologist, 27,* 435–454.

Rose, A. (1962). The causes of prejudice. In I. M. Barron (Ed.), *American cultural minorities: A textbook in intergroup relations.* New York: Alfred A. Knopf.

Rose, L. C., & Gallup, A. M. (1996). The 28th annual Phi Delta Kappa/Gallup Poll of the public's attitude toward the public schools. *Phi Delta Kappan, 78*(1), 41–59.

Rosen, L. A., O'Leary, S. G., Joyce, S. A., Conway, G., & Pfiffner, L. J. (1984). The importance of prudent negative consequences for maintaining the appropriate behavior of hyperactive students. *Journal of Abnormal Child Psychology, 12,* 581–604.

Rosenman, A. A. (1987, November 11). The value of multicultural curricula. *Education Week, 7*(10).

Rosenshine, B. (1977, April). *Primary grades instruction and student achievement.* Paper presented at the annual meeting of the American Educational Research Association, New York.

Rosenshine, B. (1979). Content, time, and direct instruction. In P. Peterson & H. Walberg (Eds.), *Research on teaching: Concepts, findings, and implications* (pp. 28–56). Berkeley, CA: McCutchan.

Rosenshine, B. (1986). Synthesis of research on explicit teaching. *Educational Leadership, 43*(7), 60–69.

Rosenshine, B. (1988). Explicit teaching. In D. Berliner & B. Rosenshine (Eds.), *Talks to teachers* (pp. 75–92). New York: Random House.

Rosenshine, B., & Furst, N. (1973). The use of direct observation to study teaching. In R. Travers (Ed.), *Second handbook of research on teaching.* Chicago: Rand McNally.

Rosenshine, B., & Meister, C. (1992, April). *The uses of scaffolds for teaching less structured academic tasks.* Paper presented at the annual meeting of the American Educational Research Association, San Francisco.

Rosenshine, B., & Meister, C. (1994). Reciprocal teaching: A review of the research. *Review of Educational Research, 64,* 479–530.

Rosenshine, B., & Stevens, R. (1986). Teaching functions. In M. Wittrock (Ed.), *Handbook of research on teaching* (3rd ed., pp. 376–391). New York: Macmillan.

Rosenthal, R. (1973). The Pygmalion effect lives. *Psychology Today,* pp. 56–63.

Rosenthal, R. (1987). Pygmalion effects: Existence, magnitude and social importance. A reply to Wineburg. *Educational Researcher, 16,* 37–41.

Rosenthal, R. (1995). Critiquing Pygmalion: A 25-year perspective. *Current Directions in Psychological Science, 4,* 171–172.

Rosenthal, R., and Jacobson, L. (1968). *Pygmalion in the classroom.* New York: Holt, Rinehart, Winston.

Roskos, K., & Neuman, S. B. (1993). Descriptive observation of adults' facilitation of literacy in young children's play. *Early Childhood Research Quarterly, 8,* 77–98.

Roskos, K., & Neuman, S. B. (1995). Two beginning kindergarten teachers' planning for integrated literacy instruction. *Elementary School Journal, 96,* 195–215.

Rosser, R. (1994). *Cognitive development: Psychological and biological perspectives*. Boston: Allyn & Bacon.

Roth, W-M., & Bowen, G. M. (1995). Knowing and interacting: A study of culture, practices, and resources in a grade 8 open-inquiry science guided by an apprenticeship metaphor. *Cognition and Instruction, 13,* 73–128.

Rothenberg, J. (1989), The open classroom reconsidered. *Elementary School Journal, 90,* 68–86.

Rotherham-Borus, M. J. (1994). Bicultural reference group orientations and adjustment. In M. Bernal & G. Knight (Eds.), *Ethnic identity*. Albany, NY: State University of New York Press.

Rotter, J. (1954). *Social learning and clinical psychology*. Englewood Cliffs, NJ: Prentice-Hall.

Rowe, M. B. (1974). Wait-time and rewards as instructional variables: Their influence on language, logic, and fate control. Part 1: Wait-time. *Journal of Research in Science Teaching, 11,* 81–94.

Rumelhart, D. & Ortony, A. (1977). The representation of knowledge in memory. In R. Anderson, R. Spiro, & W. Montague (Eds.), *Schooling and the acquisition of knowledge*. Hillsdale, NJ: Erlbaum.

Ruopp, F., & Driscoll, M. (1990, January/February). Access to algebra. *Harvard Education Letter, 6*(A), 4–5.

Ryan, R. M. (1991). The nature of the self in autonomy and relatedness. In G. R. Goethals & J. Strauss (Eds.), *Multidisciplinary perspectives on the self*. New York: Springer-Verlag.

Ryan, R. M., & Deci, E. L. (1996). When paradigms clash: Comments on Cameron and Pierce's claim that rewards do not undermine intrinsic motivation. *Review of Educational Research, 66,* 33–38.

Ryan, R. M., & Grolnick, W. S. (1986). Origins and pawns in the classroom: Self-report and projective assessments of individual differences in the children's perceptions. *Journal of Personality and Social Psychology, 50,* 550–558.

Ryans, D. G. (1960). *Characteristics of effective teachers, their descriptions, comparisons and appraisal: A research study*. Washington, DC: American Council on Education.

Sabers, D. S., Cushing, K. S., & Berliner, D. C. (1991). Differences among teachers in a task characterized by simultaneity, multidimensionality, and immediacy. *American Educational Research Journal, 28,* 68–87.

Sadker, M., & Sadker, D. (1985, March). Sexism in the schoolroom of the '80s. *Psychology Today,* 54–57.

Sadker, M., & Sadker, D. (1986a). Questioning skills. In J. Cooper (Ed.), *Classroom teaching skills* (3rd ed., pp. 143–180). Lexington, MA: D. C. Heath.

Sadker, M., & Sadker, D. (1986b). Sexism in the classroom: From grade school to graduate school. *Phi Delta Kappan, 68,* 512.

Sadker, M., Sadker, D., & Klein, S. (1991). The issue of gender in elementary and secondary education. *Review of Research in Education, 17,* 269–334.

Salomon, G., & Perkins, D. N. (1989). Rocky roads to transfer: Rethinking mechanisms of a neglected phenomenon. *Educational Psychologist, 24,* 113–142.

Sanchez, F., & Anderson, M. L. (1990, May). Gang mediation: A process that works. *Principal,* 54–56.

Sanchez, R. (1995, April 6). Educators reexamine the way teachers are taught. *The Washington Post,* pp. A1.

Sattler, J. (1992). *Assessment of children* (3rd ed. revised). San Diego: Jerome M. Sattler.

Sawyer, R. J., Graham, S., & Harris, K. R. (1992). Direct teaching, strategy instruction, and strategy instruction with explicit self-regulation: Effects on the composition skills and self-efficacy of learning disabled students. *Journal of Educational Psychology, 84,* 340–352.

Saxe, G. B. (1988). Candy selling and math learning. *Educational Researcher, 17*(6), 14–21.

Scarr, S., & Carter-Saltzman, L. (1982). Genetics and intelligence. In R. Sternberg (Ed.), *Handbook of human intelligence*. New York: Cambridge University Press.

Scarr, S., Weinberg, R. A., & Levine, A. (1986). *Understanding development*. New York: Harcourt Brace Jovanovich.

Schab, F. (1980). Cheating in high school: Differences between the sexes (revisited). *Adolescence, 15,* 959–965.

Scherer, M. (1993). On savage inequalities: A conversation with Jonathan Kozol. *Educational Leadership, 50*(4), 4–9.

Schiedel, D., & Marcia, J. (1985). Ego integrity, intimacy, sex role orientation, and gender. *Developmental Psychology, 21,* 149–160.

Schiefele, U. (1991). Interest, learning, and motivation. *Educational Psychologist, 26,* 299–324.

Schneider, W., & Bjorklund, D. F. (1992). Expertise, aptitude, and strategic remembering. *Child Development, 63,* 416–473.

Schoenfeld, A. H. (1979). Explicit heuristic training as a variable in problem solving performance. *Journal for Research in Mathematics Education, 10,* 173–187.

Schofield, J. W. (1991). School desegregation and intergroup relations. *Review of Research in Education, 17,* 235–412.

Schofield, J. W. (1995). Review of research on school desegregation's impact on elementary and secondary school students. In J. A. Banks & C. Banks (Eds.), *Handbook of research on multicultural education*. New York: Macmillan.

Schofield, J. W., Eurch-Fulcer, R. & Britt, C. L. (1994). Teachers, computer tutors, and teaching: The artificially intelligent tutor as an agent for classroom change. *American Educational Research Journal, 31,* 579–607.

Schon, D. (1983). *The reflective practitioner*. New York: Basic Books.

Schraw, G., & Moshman, D. (1995). Metacognitive theories. *Educational Psychology Review, 7,* 351–371.

Schuder, T. (1994). The genesis of transactional strategies for at-risk students. *Elementary School Journal, 94,* 235–254.

Schunk, D. H. (1987). Peer models and children's behavioral change. *Review of Educational Research, 57,* 149–174.

Schunk, D. H. (1991a). *Learning theories: An educational perspective*. New York: Merrill.

Schunk, D. H. (1991b). Self-efficacy and academic motivation. *Educational Psychologist, 26,* 207–232.

Schunk, D. H. (1996). *Learning theories: An educational perspective* (2nd ed.). Columbus, OH: Merrill.

Schunk, D. H. (1996). Goal and self-evaluative influences during childrens' cognitive skill learning. *American Educational Research Journal, 33,* 359–382.

Schunk, D. H., & Hanson, A. R. (1985). Peer models: Influence on children's self-efficacy and achievement. *Journal of Educational Psychology, 77,* 313–322.

Schwartz, B., & Reisberg, D. (1991). *Learning and memory.* New York: Norton.

Schwartz, B., & Robbins, S. J. (1995). *Psychology of learning and behavior* (4th ed.). New York, Norton.

Seddon, G. M. (1978). The properties of Bloom's taxonomy of educational objectives for the cognitive domain. *Review of Educational Research, 48,* 303–323.

Seiber, J. E., O'Neil, H. F., & Tobias, S. (1977). *Anxiety, learning, and instruction.* Hillsdale, NJ: Erlbaum.

Seifert, K. L., & Hoffnung, R. J. (1991). *Child and adolescent development.* Boston: Houghton Mifflin.

Seligman, M. E. P. (1975). *Helplessness: On depression, development, and death.* San Francisco: Freeman.

Selman, R. L. (1981). The child as a friendship philosopher. In S. Asher & J. Gottman (Eds.), *The development of children's friendships.* Cambridge: Cambridge University Press.

Selman, R. L., & Byrne, D. F. (1974). A structural-developmental analysis of levels of role taking in middle childhood. *Child Development, 45,* 803–806.

Semb, G. B., & Ellis, J. A. (1994). Knowledge taught in school: What is remembered? *Review of Educational Research, 64,* 253–286.

Serbin, L., & O'Leary, D. (1975, January). How nursery schools teach girls to shut up. *Psychology Today,* pp. 56–58.

Shapiro, B. C. (1995). The NBPTS sets standards for accomplished teaching. *Educational Leadership, 52*(6), 55–57.

Shapiro, E. S., & Ager, C. (1992). Assessment of special education students in regular education programs: Linking assessment to instruction. *The Elementary School Journal, 92,* 283–296.

Shavelson, R. J. (1987). Planning. In M. Dunkin (Ed.), *The international encyclopedia of teaching and teacher education* (pp. 483–486). New York: Pergamon Press.

Shavelson, R. J., & Bolus, R. (1982). Self-concept: The interplay of theory and methods. *Psychology, 74,* 3–17.

Shavelson, R. J., Gao, X., & Baxter, G. (1993). *Sampling variability of performance assessments.* CSE Technical Report 361. Los Angeles: UCLA Center for the Study of Evaluation.

Shepard, L. A., & Smith, M. L. (1989). Academic and emotional effects of kindergarten retention. In L. Shepard & M. Smith (Eds.), *Flunking grades: Research and policies on retention* (pp. 79–107). Philadelphia: Falmer Press.

Sherman, J. G., Ruskin, R. S., & Semb, G. B. (Eds.) (1982). *The Personalized System of Instruction: 48 seminal papers.* Lawrence, KS: TRI Publications.

Sherry, M. (1990). Implementing an integrated instructional system: Critical issues. *Phi Delta Kappan, 72,* 118–120.

Shields, P., Gordon, J., & Dupree, D. (1983). Influence of parent practices upon the reading achievement of good and poor readers. *Journal of Negro Education, 52,* 436–445.

Shuell, T. (1996). Teaching and learning in a classroom context. In D. Berliner & R. Calfee (eds.), *Handbook of educational psychology* (pp. 726–764). New York: Macmillan.

Shuell, T. J. (1981b, April). *Toward a model of learning from instruction.* Paper presented at a meeting of the American Educational Research Association, Los Angeles.

Shuell, T. J. (1986). Cognitive conceptions of learning. *Review of Educational Research, 56,* 411–436.

Shuell, T. J. (1990). Phases of meaningful learning. *Review of Educational Psychology, 60,* 531–548.

Shulman, L. S. (1987). Knowledge and teaching: Foundations of the new reform. *Harvard Educational Review, 19*(2), 4–14.

Shulman, L. S. (1992). Toward a pedagogy of cases. In J. Shulman (Ed.), *Case method in teacher education* (pp. 1–30) New York: Teachers College Press.

Shultz, J., & Florio, S. (1979). Stop and freeze: The negotiation of social and physical space in a kindergarten/first grade classroom. *Anthropology and Education Quarterly, 10,* 166–181.

Siedenberg, M. S. (1993). Connectionist models and cognitive theory. *Psychological Science, 4,* 228–235.

Siegel, J., & Shaughnessy, M. F. (1994). Educating for understanding: An interview with Howard Gardner. *Phi Delta Kappan, 75,* 536–566.

Siegler, R. S. (1986). *Children's thinking.* Englewood Cliffs: NJ: Prentice-Hall.

Siegler, R. S. (1991). *Children's thinking* (2nd ed.). Englewood Cliffs, NJ: Prentice-Hall.

Siegler, R. S. (1993). Adaptive and non-adaptive characteristics of low-income children's mathematical strategy use. In B. Penner (Ed.), *The challenge in mathematics and science education: Psychology's response* (pp. 341–366). Washington, DC: American Psychological Association.

Simmons, R. G. , & Blyth, D. A. (1987). *Moving into adolescence.* New York: Aldine De Gruyter.

Simon, D. P., & Chase, W. G. (1973). Skill in chess. *American Scientist, 61,* 394–403.

Simon, H. A. (1995). The information-processing view of mind. *American Psychologist, 50,* 507–508.

Simon, P. (1980). *The tongue-tied American: Confronting the foreign language crisis.* New York: Continuum.

Simpson, E. J. (1972). "The classification of educational objectives in the psychomotor domain." *The Psychomotor Domain. Vol 3.* Washington, Gryphon House.

Singley, K., & Anderson, J. R. (1989). *The transfer of cognitive skill.* Cambridge, MA: Harvard University Press.

Sisk, D. A. (1988). Children at risk: The identification of the gifted among the minority. *Gifted Education International, 5,* 138–141.

Sizer, T. (1984). *Horace's compromise: The dilemma of the American high school* (updated ed.). Princeton, NJ: Houghton Mifflin.

Skinner, B. F. (1950). Are theories of learning necessary? *Psychological Review, 57,* 193–216.

Skinner, B. F. (1953). *Science and human behavior.* New York: Macmillan.

Skinner, B. F. (1989). The origins of cognitive thought. *American Psychologist, 44,* 13–18.

Slavin, R. E. (1984). Students motivating students to excel: Cooperative incentives, cooperative tasks, and student achievement. *Elementary School Journal, 85,* 53–64.

Slavin, R. E. (1987). Ability grouping and student achievement in elementary schools: A best-evidence synthesis. *Review of Educational Research, 57,* 293–336.

Slavin, R. E. (1990). Achievement effects of ability grouping in secondary schools: A best-evidence synthesis. *Review of Educational Research, 60,* 471–500.

Slavin, R. E. (1995). *Cooperative learning* (2nd ed.). Boston: Allyn & Bacon.

Slavin, R. E., & Karweit, N. (1985). Effects of whole class, ability grouped, and individualized instruction on mathematics achievement. *American Educational Research Journal, 22,* 351–368.

Slavin, R. E., Karweit, N. L., & Madden, N. A. (1989). *Effective programs for students at risk.* Boston: Allyn & Bacon.

Sleeter, C. E. (1995). Curriculum controversies in multicultural education. In E. Flaxman & H. Passow (Eds.), *94th Yearbook of the National Society for the Study of Education: Part II: Changing populations, changing schools* (pp. 162–185). Chicago: University of Chicago Press.

Sleeter, C. E., & Grant, C. A. (1987). An analysis of multicultural education in the United States. *Harvard Educational Review, 57,* 421–444.

Smetana, J. G., & Braeges, J. L. (1990). The development of toddlers' moral and conventional judgments. *Merrill-Palmer Quarterly, 36,* 329–346.

Smith, C. B. (Moderator) (1994). *Whole language: The debate.* Bloomington, IN: EDINFO Press.

Smith, D. D., & Luckasson, R. (1995). *Introduction to special education* (2nd ed). Boston: Allyn & Bacon.

Smith, F. (1975). *Comprehension and learning: A conceptual framework for teachers.* New York: Holt, Rinehart & Winston.

Smith, F. (1992). Learning to read: The never-ending debate. *Phi Delta Kappan, 73,* 432–442.

Smith, J. D., & Caplan, J. (1988). Cultural differences in cognitive style development. *Developmental Psychology, 24,* 46–52.

Smith, M. (1993). Some school-based violence prevention strategies. *NASSP Bulletin, 77*(557), 70–75.

Smith, M. L. (1991). Put to the test: The effects of external testing on teachers. *Educational Researcher, 20*(5), 8–11.

Smith, S. M., & Neisworth, J. T. (1975). *The exceptional child: A functional approach.* New York: McGraw Hill.

Smith, S. M., Glenberg, A., & Bjork, R. A. (1978). Environmental context and human memory. *Memory and Cognition, 6,* 342–353.

Snider, V. E. (1990). What we know about learning styles from research in special education. *Educational Leadership, 48*(2), 53.

Snow, C. E. (1987). Beyond conversation: Second language learners' acquisition of description and explanation. In J. P. Lantolf & A. Labarca (Eds.), *Research in second language learning: Focus on the classroom* (pp. 3–16). Norwood, NJ: Ablex.

Snow, C. E. (1993). Families as social contexts for literacy development. In C. Daiute (Ed.) *New directions for child development* (No. 61, pp. 11–24). San Francisco: Jossey-Bass.

Snow, M. A. (1986). *Innovative second language education: Bilingual immersion programs* (Education Report 1). Los Angeles: Center of Language Education and Research, University of California.

Snow, R. E. (1995). Pygmalion and intelligence. *Current Directions in Psychological Science, 4,* 169–171.

Snow, R. E., Corno, L., & Jackson, D. (1996) Individual differences in affective and cognitive functions. In D. Berliner & R. Calfee (Eds.), *Handbook of educational psychology* (pp. 243–310). New York: Macmillan.

Snowman, J. (1984). Learning tactics and strategies. In G. Phye & T. Andre (Eds.), *Cognitive instructional psychology.* Orlando, FL: Academic Press.

Soar, R. S., & Soar, R. M. (1979). Emotional climate and management. In P. Peterson & H. Walberg (Eds.), *Research on teaching: Concepts, findings, and implications.* Berkeley, CA: McCutchan.

Sobesky, W. E. (1983). The effects of situational factors on moral judgment. *Child Development, 54,* 575–584.

Sokolove, S., Garrett, J., Sadker, D., & Sadker, M. (1986). Interpersonal communications skills. In J. Cooper (Ed.), *Classroom teaching skills: A handbook.* Lexington, MA: D. C. Heath.

Soloway, E., Lockhead, J., & Clement, J. (1982). Does computer programming enhance problem solving ability? Some positive evidence on algebra word problems. In R. J. Seidel, R. E. Anderson, & S. B. Hunter (Eds.), *Computer literacy.* New York: Academic Press.

Spearman, C. (1927). *The abilities of man: Their nature and measurement.* New York: Macmillan.

Spector, J. E. (1992). Predicting progress in beginning reading: Dynamic assessment of phonemic awareness. *Journal of Educational Psychology, 84,* 353–363.

Spencer, M. B., & Markstrom-Adams, C. (1990). Identity processes among racial and ethnic-minority children in America. *Child Development, 61,* 290–310.

Spiro, R. J., Feltovich, P. J., Jacobson, M. L., & Coulson, R. L. (1991). Cognitive flexibility, constructivism, and hypertext: Random access instruction for advanced knowledge acquisition in ill-structured domains. *Educational Technology, 31*(5), 24–33.

Stahl, S. A., & Miller, P. D. (1989). Whole language and language experience approaches for beginning reading: A quantitative research synthesis. *Review of Educational Research, 59,* 87–116.

Stainback, S., & Stainback, W. (1992). Schools as inclusive communities. In W. Stainback & S. Stainback (Eds.), *Controversial issues confronting special education: Divergent perspectives* (pp. 29–43). Boston: Allyn & Bacon.

Stanovich, K. E. (1991). Reading disability: Assessment issues. In H. Swanson (Ed.), *Handbook of assessment of learning disabilities: Theory, research, and practice* (pp. 147–175). Austin, TX: Pro-Ed.

Stanovich, K. E. (1992). *How to think straight about psychology* (3rd ed.). Glenview, IL: Scott, Foresman.

Starch, D., & Elliot, E. C. (1912). Reliability of grading high school work in English. *Scholastic Review, 20,* 442–457.

Starch, D., & Elliot, E. C. (1913a). Reliability of grading work in history. *Scholastic Review, 21,* 676–681.

Starch, D., & Elliot, E. C. (1913b). Reliability of grading work in mathematics. *Scholastic Review, 21,* 254–259.

Starr, R. H., Jr. (1979). Child abuse. *American Psychologist, 34,* 872–878.

Stein, B. S., Littlefield, J., Bransford, J. D., & Persampieri, M. (1984). Elaboration and knowledge acquisition. *Memory and Cognition, 12,* 522–529.

Stepien, W., & Gallagher, S. (1993). Problem-based learning: As authentic as it gets. *Educational Leadership, 50*(7), 25–28.

Sternberg, R. (1985). *Beyond IQ: A triarchic theory of human intelligence.* New York: Cambridge University Press.

Sternberg, R. (1986). *Intelligence applied: Understanding and increasing your own intellectual skills.* New York: Harcourt Brace Jovanovich.

Sternberg, R. (1990). *Metaphors of mind: Conceptions of the nature of intelligence.* New York: Cambridge University Press.

Sternberg, R., & Davidson, J. (1982, June). The mind of the puzzler. *Psychology Today,* pp. 37–44.

Sternberg, R. J., & Detterman, D. L. (Eds.). (1986). *What is intelligence? Contemporary viewpoints on its nature and definition.* Norwood, NJ: Ablex.

Sternberg, R. J., & Wagner, R. K. (1993). The *g*-ocentric view of intelligence and job performance is wrong. *Current Directions in Psychological Science, 2,* 1–5.

Sternberg, R. J., Wagner, R. K., Williams, W. M., & Horvath, J. A. (1995). Testing common sense. *American Psychologist, 50,* 912–927.

Stevenson, H. W, & Stigler, J. (1992). *The learning gap.* New York: Summit Books.

Stigler, J. W., Lee, S., & Stevenson, H. W. (1987). Mathematics classrooms in Japan, Taiwan, and the United States. *Child Development, 58,* 1272–1285.

Stipek, D. J. (1993). *Motivation to learn* (2nd ed.). Boston: Allyn & Bacon.

Stipek, D. J. (1996). Motivation and Instruction. In D. Berliner & R. Calfee (Eds.), *Handbook of educational psychology* (pp. 85–109). New York: Macmillan.

Stodolsky, S. S. (1988). *The subject matters: Classroom activity in math and social studies.* Chicago: University of Chicago Press.

Straus, M. A., Gelles, R. J., & Steinmetz, S. K. (1980). *Behind closed doors: Violence in the American family.* New York: Doubleday.

Strauss, S. (1993). Teachers' pedagogical content knowledge about children's minds and learning: Implications for teacher education. *Educational Psychologist, 28,* 279–290.

Strike, K. (1975). The logic of discovery. *Review of Educational Research, 45,* 461–483.

Stumpf, H. (1995). Gender differences on test of cognitive abilities: Experimental design issues and empirical results. *Learning and Individual Differences, 7,* 275–288.

Sulzby, E., & Teale, W. (1991). Emergent literacy. In R. Barr, M. L. Kamil, P. B. Mosenthal, & P. D. Pearson (eds.), *Handbook of reading research,* Vol. II (pp. 727–758). New York: Longman.

Sulzer-Azaroff, B., & Mayer, G. R. (1986). *Achieving educational excellence using behavioral strategies.* New York: Holt, Rinehart & Winston.

Suzuki, B. H. (1983). The education of Asian and Pacific Americans: An introductory overview. In D. Nakanishi & M. Hirano-Nakanishi (Eds.), *The education of Asian and Pacific Americans: Historical perspectives and prescriptions for the future.* Phoenix, AZ: Oryx Press.

Swanson, H. L. (1990). The influence of metacognitive knowledge and aptitude on problem solving. *Journal of Educational Psychology, 82,* 306–314.

Swanson, H. L., O'Conner, J. E., & Cooney, J. B. (1990). An information processing analysis of expert and novice teachers' problem solving. *American Educational Research Journal, 27,* 533–556.

Symons, S., Woloshyn, V., & Pressley, M. (1994). The scientific evaluation of the whole language approach to literacy development [Special Issue]. *Educational Psychologist, 29*(4).

Tait, H., & Enwistle, N. J. (in press). Identifying students at risk through ineffective study strategies. *Higher Education.*

Tal, Z., & Babad, E. (1990). The teachers' pet phenomenon: Rate of occurrence, correlates, and psychological costs. *Journal of Educational Psychology, 82,* 637–645.

Tanner, J. M. (1990). *Foetus to man* (2nd ed.). Cambridge: Harvard University Press.

Task Force on Pediatric AIDS: American Psychological Association. (1989). Pediatric AIDS and human immunodeficiency virus infection: Psychological issues. *American Psychologist, 44,* 258–264.

Taylor, J. B. (1983). Influence of speech variety on teachers' evaluation of reading comprehension. *Journal of Educational Psychology, 75,* 662–667.

Taylor, R. P. (Ed.) (1980). *The computer in the school: Tutor, tool, tutee.* New York: Teachers College Press.

Teacher Magazine (1991, April). *You and the system: Who you will teach,* p. 32H.

TenBrink, T. D. (1986). Writing instructional objectives. In J. Cooper (Ed.), *Classroom teaching skills* (3rd ed., pp. 71–110). Lexington, MA: D. C. Heath.

Tennyson, R. D. (1981, April). *Concept learning effectiveness using prototype and skill development presentation forms.* Paper presented at the annual meeting of the American Educational Research Association, Los Angeles.

Tennyson, R. D., & Cocchiarella, M. J. (1986). An empirically based instructional design theory for teaching concepts. *Review of Educational Research, 56,* 40–71.

Terman, L. M., & Oden, M. H. (1947). The gifted child grows up. In L. M. Terman (Ed.), *Genetic studies of genius* (Vol. 4). Stanford, CA: Stanford University Press.

Terman, L. M., & Oden, M. H. (1959). The gifted group in mid-life. In L. M. Terman (Ed.), *Genetic studies of genius* (Vol. 5). Stanford, CA: Stanford University Press.

Terman, L. M., Baldwin, B. T., & Bronson, E. (1925). Mental and physical traits of a thousand gifted children. In L. M. Terman (Ed.), *Genetic studies of genius* (Vol. 1). Stanford, CA: Stanford University Press.

Tharp, R. C., & Gallimore, R. (1988). *Rousing minds to life: Teaching, learning, and schooling in social context.* New York: Cambridge University Press.

Tharp, R. G. (1989). Psychocultural variables and constants: Effects on teaching and learning in schools. *American Psychologist, 44,* 349–359.

Tharp, R. G., & Gallimore, R. (1991). *The instructional conversation: Teaching and learning in social activity.* Washington, DC: National Center for Research on Cultural Diversity and Second Language Learning.

Thoma, S. J. (1986). Estimating gender differences in the comprehension and preference of moral issues. *Developmental Review, 6,* 165–180.

Thomas, E. L., & Robinson, H. A. (1972). *Improving reading in every class: A sourcebook for teachers.* Boston: Allyn & Bacon.

Thompson, G. (1991). *Teaching through themes.* New York: Scholastic.

Thorkildsen, T. A., Nolen, S. B., & Fournier, J. (1994). What is fair? Children's critiques of practices that influence motivation. *Journal of Educational Psychology, 86,* 475–486.

Thorndike, E. L. (1913). Educational psychology. In *The psychology of learning* (Vol. 2). New York: Teachers College, Columbia University.

Thorndike, R., Hagen, E., & Sattler, J. (1986). *The Stanford-Binet Intelligence Scale* (4th ed.). Chicago: Riverside.

Thurstone, L. L. (1938). Primary mental abilities. *Psychometric Monographs,* No. 1.

Tiedt, P. L., & Tiedt, I. M. (1990). *Multicultural education: A handbook of activities, information, and resources.* Boston: Allyn & Bacon.

Tierney, R. J., Readence, J. E., & Dishner, E. K. (1990). *Reading strategies and practices: A compendium,* (3rd ed.). Boston: Allyn & Bacon.

Timmer, S. G., Eccles, J., & O'Brien, K. (1988). How children use time. In F. Juster & F. Stafford (Eds.), *Time, goods, and well-being.* Ann Arbor, MI: Institute for Social Research, University of Michigan.

Tishman, S., Perkins, D., & Jay, E., (1995). *The thinking classroom: Creating a culture of thinking.* Boston: Allyn & Bacon.

Tobias, Sigmund, & Duchastel, P. (1974). Behavioral objectives, sequence, and anxiety in CAI. *Instructional Science, 3,* 232–242.

Tobias, Sigmund. (1982). When do instructional methods make a difference? *Educational Researcher, 11*(4), 4–10.

Tobias, Sigmund. (1985). Text anxiety: Interference, defective skills, and cognitive capacity. *Educational Psychologist, 20,* 135–142.

Tobin, (1990, April). *Metaphors in the construction of teacher knowledge.* Paper presented at the Annual Meeting of the American Educational Research Association, Boston.

Tobin, K. (1987). The role of wait time in higher cognitive learning. *Review of Educational Research, 56,* 69–95.

Tobin, K., & Dawson, G. (1992). Constraints to curriculum reform: Teachers and the myths of schooling. *Educational Technology Research and Development, 40*(1), 81–92.

Tochon, F., & Munby, H. (1993). Novice and expert teachers' time epistemology: A wave function from didactics to pedagogy. *Teaching and Teacher Education, 9,* 205–218.

Tomasello, M., Kruger, A. C., & Ratner, H. H. (1993). Cultural learning. *Behavioral and Brain Sciences, 16,* 495–552.

Tomlinson-Keasey, C. (1990). Developing our intellectual resources for the 21st century: Educating the gifted. *Journal of Educational Psychology, 82,* 399–403.

Tomlinson-Keasey, C., & Little, T. D. (1990). Predicting educational attainment, occupational achievement intellectual skill, and personal adjustment among gifted men and women. *Journal of Educational Psychology, 82,* 442–455.

Torrance, E. P. (1972). Predictive validity of the Torrance tests of creative thinking. *Journal of Creative Behavior, 6,* 236–262.

Torrance, E. P. (1986). Teaching creative and gifted learners. In M. Wittrock (Ed.), *Handbook of research on teaching* (3rd ed.) (pp. 630–647). New York: Macmillan.

Torrance, E. P., & Hall, L. K. (1980). Assessing the future reaches of creative potential. *Journal of Creative Behavior, 14,* 1–19.

Trickett, E., & Moos, R. (1974). Personal correlates of contrasting environments: Student satisfaction with high school classrooms. *American Journal of Community Psychology, 2,* 1–12.

Turiel E. (1983). *The development of social knowledge: Morality and convention.* New York: Cambridge University Press.

U.S. Bureau of the Census (1990). *Current Population Reports. Series P-20.* Washington, DC: U.S. Government Printing Office.

U.S. Bureau of the Census (1991). *Current Population Reports. Series P-20.* Washington, DC: U.S. Government Printing Office.

Ure, A. (1861). *The philosophy of manufactures: Or an exposition of the scientific, moral, and commercial economy of the factory system of Great Britain* (3rd ed.). London: H. G. Bohn.

Vacc, N. N. (1989). Writing evaluation: Examining four teachers' holistic and analytic scores. *Elementary School Journal, 90,* 88–95.

Van Houten, R., & Doleys, D. M. (1983). Are social reprimands effective? In S. Axelrod & J. Apsche (Eds.), *The effects of punishment on human behavior.* San Diego: Academic Press.

Van Metter, P., Yokoi, L., & Pressley, M. (1994). College students' theory of note-taking derived from their perceptions of note-taking. *Journal of Educational Psychology, 86,* 323–338.

Vasquez, J. A. (1990). Teaching to the distinctive traits of minority students. *The Clearing House, 63,* 299–304.

Vaughn, S., Bos, C. S., & Schumm, J. S. (1996). *Teaching mainstreamed, diverse, and at-risk students in the general education classroom.* Boston: Allyn & Bacon.

Veenman, S. (1984). Perceived problems of beginning teachers. *Review of Educational Research, 54,* 143–178.

Vellutino, F. R. (1991). Introduction to three studies on reading acquisition: Convergent findings on theoretical foundations of code-oriented versus whole-language approaches to reading instruction. *Journal of Educational Psychology, 83,* 437–443.

Vera, A. H., & Simon, H. A. (1993). Situated action: A symbolic interpretation. *Cognitive Science, 17,* 7–48.

Viadero, D. (1990). Battle over multicultural education rises in intensity. *Education Week, 10*(13), 1, 11, 13, 14.

Vispoel, W. P. (1995). Self-concept in artistic domains: An extension of the Shavelson, Hubmner, and Stanton (1976) model. *Journal of Educational Psychology, 87,* 134–153.

Vispoel, W. P. & Austin, J. R. (1995). Success and failure in junior high school: A critical incident approach to understanding students' attributional beliefs. *American Educational Research Journal, 32,* 377–412.

von Glaserfeld (1990). An Exposition of constructivism: Why some like it radical. In R. Davis, C. Maher, & N. Noddings (Eds.). *Constructivist views on the teaching and learning of mathematics* (pp. 19–30). Monograph 4 of the National Council of Teachers of Mathematics, Reston, VA.

Vroom, V. (1964). *Work and motivation.* New York: Wiley.

Vygotsky, L. S. (1978). *Mind in society: The development of higher mental process.* Cambridge, MA: Harvard University Press.

Vygotsky, L. S. (1986). *Thought and language.* Cambridge, MA: MIT Press.

Vygotsky, L. S. (1987). *Problems of general psychology.* New York: Plenum.

Vygotsky, L. S. (1993). *The collected works of L. S. Vygotsky: Vol. 2* (J. Knox & C. Stevens, Trans.). New York: Plenum.

Wadsworth, B. J. (1978). *Piaget for the classroom teacher.* New York: Longman.

Wadsworth, B. J. (1989). *Piaget's theory of cognitive development: An introduction for students of psychology and education* (4th ed.). New York: Longman.

Walberg, H. J. (1990). Productive teaching and instruction: Assessing the knowledge base. *Phi Delta Kappan, 72,* 470–478.

Walberg, H. J., Pascal, R. A., & Weinstein, T. (1985). Homework's powerful effects on learning. *Educational Leadership, 42*(7), 76–79.

Walker, C., & Shaw, W. (1988). Assessment of eating and elimination disorders. In P. Karoly (Ed.), *Handbook of child health assessment: Biosocial perspectives.* New York: Wiley.

Walker, L. J. (1989). A longitudinal study of moral reasoning. *Child Development, 60,* 157–166.

Walker, L. J. (1991). Sex differences in moral reasoning. In W. M. Kurtines & J. L. Gewirtz (Eds.), *Handbook of moral behavior and development* (Vol. 2, pp. 333–362). Hillsdale, NJ: Erlbaum.

Walker, L. J., de Vries, B., & Trevarthan, S. D. (1987). Moral stages and moral orientations in real-life and hypothetical dilemmas. *Child Development, 58,* 842–858.

Wallerstein, J., & Blakeslee, S. (1989). *Second chances: Men, women, and children a decade after divorce.* New York: Ticknor & Fields.

Wallerstein, J. S. (1991). The long-term effects of divorce on children: A review. *Journal of the American Academy of Child and Adolescent Psychiatry, 30,* 349–360.

Walton, G. *Identification of the intellectually gifted children in the public school kindergarten.* Unpublished doctoral dissertation, University of California, Los Angeles, 1961.

Wang, A. Y., & Thomas, M. H. (1995). Effects of keywords on long-term retention: Help or hindrance? *Journal of Educational Psychology, 87,* 468–475.

Wang, A. Y., Thomas, M. H., & Ouellette, J. A. (1992). Keyword mnemonic and retention of second-language vocabulary words. *Journal of Educational Psychology, 84,* 520–528.

Wang, M. C., & Palincsar, A. S. (1989). Teaching students to assume an active role in their learning. In M. Reynolds (Ed.), *Knowledge base for the beginning teacher* (pp. 71–84). New York: Pergamon.

Ward, M., & Sweller, J. (1990). Structuring effective worked examples. *Cognition and Instruction, 7,* 1–40.

Wasserman, S. (1993). *Getting down to cases.* New York: Teachers College Press.

Waters, H. F. (1993, July 12). Networks under the gun. *Newsweek,* pp. 64–66.

Webb, N. (1985). Verbal interaction and learning in peer-directed groups. *Theory into Practice, 24,* 32–39.

Webb, N., & Palincsar, A. (1996). Group processes in the classroom. In D. C. Berliner & R. C. Calfee (Eds.), *Handbook of educational psychology* (pp. 841–876). New York: Macmillan.

Weiland, A., & Coughlin, R. (1979). Self-identification and preferences: A comparison of White and Mexican-American first- and third-graders. *Journal of Cross-Cultural Psychology, 10,* 356–365.

Weinberg, R. A. (1989). Intelligence and IQ. *American Psychologist, 44,* 98–104.

Weiner, B. (1979). A theory of motivation for some classroom experiences. *Journal of Educational Psychology, 71,* 3–25.

Weiner, B. (1980). The role of affect in rational (attributional) approaches to human motivation. *Educational Researcher, 9,* 4–11.

Weiner, B. (1986). *An attributional theory of motivation and emotion.* New York: Springer.

Weiner, B. (1990). History of motivational research in education. *Journal of Educational Psychology, 82,* 616–622.

Weiner, B. (1992). *Human motivation: Metaphors, theories, and research.* Newbury Park, CA: Sage.

Weiner, B. (1994). Ability versus effort revisited: The moral determinants of achievement evaluation an achievement as a moral system. *Educational Psychologist, 29,* 163–172.

Weiner, B. (1994). Integrating social and persons theories of achievement striving. *Review of Educational Research, 64,* 557–575.

Weiner, B., & Graham, S. (1989). Understanding the motivational role of affect: Lifespan research from an attributional perspective. *Cognition and Emotion, 4,* 401–419.

Weiner, B., Russell, D., & Lerman, D. (1978). Affective consequences of causal ascriptions. In J. H. Harvey, W. J. Ickes, & R. F. Kidd (Eds.). *New directions in attribution research* (Vol. 2). Hillsdale, NJ: Erlbaum.

Weinert, F. E., & Helmke, A. (1995). Learning from wise mother nature or big brother instructor: The wrong choice as seen from an educational perspective. *Educational Psychologist, 30,* 135–143.

Weinstein, C., Woolfolk, A., Dittmeier, L. & Shanker, U. (1994). Protector or prison guard: Using metaphors and media to explore student teachers' thinking about classroom management. *Action in Teacher Education, 16*(1), 41–54.

Weinstein, C. E. (1994). Learning strategies and learning to learn. *Encyclopedia of Education.*

Weinstein, C. E., & Mayer, R. E. (1985). The teaching of learning strategies. In M. C. Wittrock (Ed.), *Handbook of research on teaching* (3rd ed.). New York: Macmillan.

Weinstein, C. E., & McCombs, B. (in press). A model of strategic learning. In C. Weinstein & B. McCombs (Eds.), *Strategic learning: Skill, will, and self-regulation.* Hillsdale, NJ: Erlbaum.

Weinstein, C. S. (1977). Modifying student behavior in an open classroom through changes in the physical design. *American Educational Research Journal, 14,* 249–262.

Weinstein, C. S. (1996). *Secondary classroom management: Lessons from research and practice.* New York: McGraw-Hill.

Weinstein, C. S., & Mignano, A. J. Jr. (1997). *Elementary classroom management: Lessons from research and practice* (2nd ed.) New York: McGraw-Hill.

Weinstein, R. S., Madison, S. M., & Kuklinski, M. R. (1995). Raising expectations in schools: Obstacles and opportunities for change. *American Educational Research Journal, 32,* 121–159.

Weisberg, R. W. (1993). *Creativity: Beyond the myth of genius.* New York: W. H. Freemen.

Weiss, G., & Hechtman, L. T. (1993). *Hyperactive children grow up: ADHD in children, adolescents, and adults* (2nd ed.). New York: Guilford Press.

Wells, A. S., & Crain, R. L. (1994). Perpetuation theory and the long-term effects of school desegregation. *Review of Educational Research, 64,* 531–55.

Wertsch, J. V. (1985). Adult-child interaction as a source of self-regulation in children. In S. Yussen (Ed.), *The growth of reflection in children.* Orlando, FL: Academic Press.

Wertsch, J. V. (1991). *Voices of the mind: A sociocultural approach to mediated action.* Cambridge, MA: Harvard University Press.

Wessells, M. G. (1982). *Cognitive psychology.* New York: Harper & Row.

Wessman, A. (1972). Scholastic and psychological effects of a compensatory education program for disadvantaged high school students: Project A B C. *American Educational Research Journal, 9,* 361–372.

Wharton-McDonald, R. Pressley, M., & Mistretta, J. (1996). *Outstanding literacy instruction in first grade: Teacher practices and student achievement.* Albany, NY: National Reading Research Center.

White, B. Y. (1993). TinkerTools: Causal models, conceptual change, and science education. *Cognition and Instruction, 10,* 1–100.

White, E. M. (1984). Holisticism. *College Composition and Communication, 35,* 400–409.

White, H. (1986). Damsels in distress: Dependency themes in fiction for children and adolescents. *Adolescence, 21,* 251–256.

White, K. R. (1982). The relation between socioeconomic status and academic achievement. *Psychological Bulletin, 91*(3), 461–481.

White, S., & Tharp, R. G. (1988, April). *Questioning and wait-time: A cross cultural analysis.* Paper presented at the annual meeting of the American Educational Research Association, New Orleans.

Whitehurst, G. J., Epstein, J. N., Angell, A. L., Payne, A. C., Crone, D. A., & Fischel, J. E. (1994). Outcomes of an emergent literacy program in headstart. *Journal of Educational Psychology, 86,* 542–555.

Wigfield, A., & Eccles, J. (1989). Test anxiety in elementary and secondary school students. *Educational Psychologist, 24,* 159–183.

Wigfield, A., Eccles, J. S., & Pintrich, P. R. (1996). Development between the ages of 11 and 25. In D. Berliner & R. Calfee, (Eds.), *Handbook of Educational Psychology* (pp. 148–185). New York: Macmillan.

Wiggins, G. (1989). Teaching to the authentic test. *Educational Leadership, 46*(7), 41–47.

Wiggins, G. (1991). Assessment, authenticity, context, and validity. *Phi Delta Kappan, 75,* 200–214.

Wiggins, G. (1991). Standards, not standardization: Evoking quality student work. *Educational Leadership, 48*(5), 18–25.

Wiggins, G. (1993). Assessment, authenticity, context, and validity. *Phi Delta Kappan, 75,* 200–214.

Wiig, E. H. (1982). Communication disorders. In H. Haring (Ed.), *Exceptional children and youth.* Columbus, OH: Charles E. Merrill.

Wilen, W. (1990). Forms and phases of discussion. In W. Wilen (Ed.), *Teaching and learning through discussion* (pp. 3–24). Springfield, IL: Charles C. Thomas.

Wilkins, W. E., & Glock, M. D. (1973). *Teacher expectations and student achievement: A replication and extension.* Ithaca, NY: Cornell University Press.

Willerman, L. (1979). *The psychology of individual and group differences.* San Francisco: Freeman.

Williams, C., & Bybee J. (1994). What do children feel guilty about? Developmental and gender differences. *Developmental Psychology, 30,* 617–623.

Williams, G. C., Wiener, M. W., Markakis, K. M., Reeve, J., & Deci, E. L. (1993). Medical student motivation for internal medicine. *Annals of Internal Medicine.*

Williams, M. D. (1991). Observations in Pittsburgh ghetto schools. *Anthropology and Education Quarterly, 12,* 211–220.

Willig, A. C. (1985). A meta-analysis of selected studies on the effectiveness of bilingual education. *Review of Educational Research, 55,* 269–317.

Willis, P. (1977). *Learning to labor.* Lexington, MA: D. C. Heath.

Wilson, C. W., & Hopkins, B. L. (1973). The effects of contingent music on the intensity of noise in junior high home economics classes. *Journal of Applied Behavior Analysis, 6,* 269–275.

Winett, R. A., & Winkler, R. C. (1972). Current behavior modification in the classroom: Be still, be quiet, be docile. *Journal of Applied Behavior Analysis, 15,* 499–504.

Wingate, N. (1986). Sexism in the classroom. *Equity and Excellence, 22,* 105–110.

Winne, P. H. (1995). Inherent details in self regulated learning. *Educational Psychologist, 30,* 173–188.

Winograd, P., & Johnston, P. (1982). Comprehension monitoring and the error-detection paradigm. *Journal of Reading Behavior, 14,* 61–76.

Witkin, H. A., Moore, C. A., Goodenough, D. R., & Cox, R. W. (1977). Field-dependent and field-independent cognitive styles and their educational implications. *Review of Educational Research, 47,* 1–64.

Wittrock, M. C. (1978). The cognitive movement in instruction. *Educational Psychologist, 13,* 15–30.

Wittrock, M. C. (1982, March). *Educational implications of recent research on learning and memory.* Paper presented at the annual meeting of the American Educational Research Association, New York.

Wittrock, M. C. (1992). An empowering conception of educational psychology. *Educational Psychologist, 27,* 129–142.

Wolf, D. (in press). *Presence of minds, performances of thought.* New York: College Entrance Examination Board.

Wolf, D., Bixby, J., Glenn, J., III, & Gardner, H. (1991). To use their minds well: New forms of student assessment. *Review of Research in Education, 17,* 31–74.

Women on Words and Images. (1975). *Dick and Jane as victims: Sex stereotyping in children's readers* (expanded ed.). Available from author, P. O. Box 2163, Princeton, NJ.

Wong, L. (1987). Reaction to research findings: Is the feeling of obviousness warranted? *Dissertation Abstracts International, 48/12,* 3709B (University Microfilms #DA 8801059).

Wood, D., Bruner, J., & Ross, S. (1976). The role of tutoring in problem solving. *British Journal of Psychology, 66,* 181–191.

Wood, E. R. G., & Wood, S. E. (1993). The world of psychology. Boston: Allyn & Bacon.

Woolfolk Hoy, A. & Tschannen-Moran, M. (in press). Implications of cognitive approaches to peer learning. In A. O'Donnell & A. King (Eds.), *Cognitive perspectives on peer learning.* Mahwah, NJ: Erlbaum.

Woolfolk, A. E., & Brooks, D. (1983). Nonverbal communication in teaching. In E. Gordon (Ed.), *Review of research in education* (Vol. 10 pp. 103–150). Washington, DC: American Educational Research Association.

Woolfolk, A. E., & Brooks, D. (1985). The influence of teachers' nonverbal behaviors on students' perceptions and performance. *Elementary School Journal, 85,* 514–528.

Woolfolk, A. E., & Hoy, W. K. (1990). Prospective teachers' sense of efficacy and beliefs about control. *Journal of Educational Psychology, 82,* 81–91.

Woolfolk, A. E., & Woolfolk, R. L. (1974). A contingency management technique for increasing student attention in a small group. *Journal of School Psychology, 12,* 204–212.

Woolfolk, A. E., Rosoff, B., & Hoy, W. K. (1990). Teachers' sense of efficacy and their beliefs about managing students. *Teaching and Teacher Education, 6,* 137–148.

Worthen, B. R. (1993). Critical issues that will determine the future of alternative assessment. *Phi Delta Kappan, 74,* 444–457.

Worthen, B. R., & Spandel, V. (1991). Putting the standardized text debate in perspective. *Educational Leadership, 48*(5), 65–70.

Wright, S. C., & Taylor, D. M. (1995). Identity and the language of the classroom: Investigating the impact of heritage versus second language instruction on personal and collective self-esteem. *Journal of Educational Psychology, 87,* 241–252.

Wyler, R. S. (1988). Social memory and social judgment. In P. Solomon, G. Goethals, C. Kelly, & B. Stephans (Eds.), *Perspectives on memory research.* New York: Springer-Verlag.

Wynne E. A. (1986). The great tradition in education: Transmitting moral values. *Educational Leadership, 43*(4), 4–9.

Yee, A. H. (1992). Asians as stereotypes and students: Misperceptions that persist. *Educational Psychology Review, 4,* 95–132.

Yerkes, R. M., & Dodson, J. D. (1908). The relation of strength of stimulus to rapidity of habit formation. *Journal of Comparative Neurology, 18,* 459–482.

Youniss, J. (1980). *Parents and peers in social development.* Chicago: University of Chicago Press.

Zeichner, K., & Gore, J. (1990). Teacher socialization. In W. R. Houston (Ed.), *Handbook of research on teacher education* (pp. 329–348). New York: Macmillan.

Zeidner, M. (1995). Adaptive coping with test situations. *Educational Psychologist, 30,* 123–134.

Zigmond, N., Jenkins, J., Fuchs, D., Deno, S., & Fuchs, L. S. (1995). When students fail to achieve satisfactorily: A reply to Leskey and Waldron. *Phi Delta Kappan, 77,* 303–306.

Zimmerman, B. J. (1990). Self-regulated learning and academic achievement: An overview. *Educational Psychologist, 21,* 3–18.

Zimmerman. B. J. (1995). Self-efficacy and educational development. In A. Bandura, (Ed.). *Self-efficacy in changing societies* (pp. 202–231). New York: Cambridge University Press.

Zimmerman, B. J., & Schunk, D. H. (Eds.). (1989). *Self-regulated learning and academic achievement: Theory, research, and practice.* New York: Springer-Verlag.

Zimmerman, B. J., Bandura, A., & Martinez-Pons, M. (1992). Self-motivation for academic attainment: The role of self-efficacy beliefs and goal-setting. *American Educational Research Journal, 29,* 663–676.

Zimmerman, D. W. (1981). On the perennial argument about grading "on the curve" in college courses. *Educational Psychologist, 16,* 175–178.

Ziomek, R. L., & Maxey, J. M. (1993). To nationally test or not to nationally test: That is the question! *Measurement and Evaluation in Counseling and Development, 26,* 64–68.

Name Index

AAMD Ad Hoc Committee on
Terminology and Classification, 123
Abi-Nader, J., 430
Ablard, K.E., 182, 183
Aboud, F., 78
Abrami, P.C., 419
Abruscato, J., 570
Ackerson, G., 344
Adams, M.J., 360
Ager, C., 558
Agne, R.M., 485
Airasian, P.W., 559
Alberto, P., 216
Alderman, M.K., 395
Alessi, S. M., 500
Alexander, K., 183
Alexander, P.A., 247, 248, 269, 270,
295, 305, 407
Alipiria, L., 78
Alleman-Brooks, J., 420
Allington, R., 424
Alloway, N., 423
Alloy, L.B., 389
Alton-Lee, A., 507
Alwin, D., 167
American Association for the
Advancement of Science, 280
American Association of University
Women, 77
Ames, C., 389, 408
Ames, R., 389
Ames, W., 344
Anastasi, A., 537, 545
Anastasiow, N.J., 138
Anderman, E.M., 382, 391
Anderson, C.W., 291, 306, 342, 365
Anderson, J.R., 26, 247, 250, 252,
253, 255, 257, 258, 261, 263, 264,
275, 280, 295, 300, 304, 313, 321,
337
Anderson, L.M., 337, 420, 445, 454,
493, 506
Anderson, L.W., 334, 481
Anderson, M.L., 472

Anderson, P.J., 188
Anderson, R., 493
Anderson, S.M., 177
Anderson, T.H., 311
Anglin, J.M., 55
Annis, R.C., 78
Anyon, J., 169
Archer, S.L., 71, 72
Arlin, M., 335
Armbruster, B.B., 311
Armstead, P., 89
Artman, L., 43
Ashton, P.T., 42, 393
Astuto, T.A., 9
Atkinson, J.W., 384
Atkinson, R.C., 73, 250
Atkinson, R.L., 73
Attanucci, J., 84
Au, K.H., 195
Auble, P.M., 262
Austin, G.A., 246, 338
Austin, J.R., 410
Ausubel, D.P., 246, 341

Babad, E.Y., 421, 422, 425
Baddeley, A.D., 254, 255
Baenninger, M., 182
Baer, J., 132
Bailey, S.M., 181
Baillargeon, R., 41
Baker, D., 181
Bakerman, R., 44
Bandura, A., 92, 225, 226, 228, 229,
234, 247, 379, 381, 392
Bangert, R.L., 545
Bangert-Drowns, R.L., 576
Banks, J.A., 162, 163, 164, 165, 166,
196
Barkowski, J.G., 316
Baron, J.B., 543
Baron, R.A., 177
Baroody, A.R., 362
Barrett, M., 414, 415
Barton, E.J., 227

Baruth, L.G., 193
Bassler, O.C., 494
Battistich, V., 354
Baughman, W.A., 271
Baumeister, R.F., 71, 386
Baxter, G., 549
Beane, J.A., 376, 388
Beaudry, J.S., 136
Becker, W.C., 12, 215, 216
Bee, H., 45, 90
Beezer, B., 101
Belanoff, P., 570
Belsky, J., 68
Bem, S.L., 178
Bempechat, J., 390
Benbow, C.P., 128, 183, 269
Benenson, J.F., 179
Benjafield, J.G., 289, 303
Bennett, C.I., 169, 193
Bentler, P.M., 104
Berends, M., 122
Berg, C.A., 337
Berger, K.S., 53
Berk, L., 26, 41, 43, 46, 57, 73, 79,
80, 89, 103, 104
Berliner, D., 11, 306, 443, 491, 503,
504, 542, 558
Berndt, T.J., 87
Betancourt, H., 164, 170, 171
Biddle, B., 542
Bierman, K.L., 87
Birch, J.W., 129, 154
Bivens, J.A., 46
Bjork, R.A., 262
Bjorklund, D.F., 26, 37, 130, 132,
134, 305
Blakeslee, S., 95
Block, J., 179, 180, 334
Bloom, B.S., 288, 334, 482
Bloom, R., 576
Blumenfeld, P.C., 379
Blyth, D.A., 99
Blythe, T., 288
Bogdan, R.C., 150

Boggiano, A.K., 414, 415
Bohannon, J.N., III, 51–52
Boldizar, J.P., 178
Bolus, R., 75, 76
Borko, H., 6, 8, 13, 305–306, 355
Borkowski, J.G., 142, 308
Bos, C.S., 195
Bourdon, L., 576
Bowen, G.M., 356
Boyle, R.A., 372
Braeges, J.L., 84
Bransford, J., 50, 262, 267, 295, 296
Braun, C., 423
Bredekemp, S., 94
Bregman, N.J., 89
Bretherton, I., 68
Brice, P., 90
Britt, C.L., 501
Brooks, D., 424, 453, 457
Brooks, J.G., 495
Brooks, M.G., 495
Brooks-Gunn, J., 99, 103
Brophy, J.E., 12, 15, 40, 122, 217,
    335, 375, 378, 390, 420, 421, 422,
    424, 425, 427, 429, 430, 442, 493,
    506
Brown, A.L., 267, 316, 360, 361, 503
Brown, J.S., 275, 347, 355
Brown, R., 51, 53
Brubaker, N.L., 420
Bruner, J., 47, 246, 289, 338, 342, 348
Bruning, R.H., 51, 54, 94, 278
Bucher, B., 233
Buenning, M., 192
Burden, P.R., 447, 457, 461
Burland, S., 267
Burow, R., 494
Bursuck, W., 146, 152
Burton, N.W., 544
Burton, R.V., 89
Buss, D.M., 182
Butler, R., 380, 576
Bybee, J., 85
Byrne, B.M., 75
Byrne, D.F., 80

Cahan, S., 43
Calderhead, J., 10, 481
Calmore, J.A., 176
Cambourne, B., 572
Cameron, J., 238
Cameron, R., 267
Camp, R., 570
Campbell, F.A., 125
Campione, J., 267

Cangelosi, J.S., 332, 483
Canter, L., 467, 469
Canter, M., 467
Caplan, J., 135
Carey, L.M., 523
Cariglia-Bull, T., 269
Carnegie Forum on Education and the
    Economy, 9
Caroll, J., 113
Carpenter, T., 495, 496
Carter-Saltzman, L., 175
Cartwright, C.A., 139, 143
Cartwright, G.P., 139, 143
Casanova, U., 163, 171, 172, 173
Case, R., 40, 268
Cauley, K., 75
Cazden, C.B., 58
Ceci, S.J., 121
Chambers, B., 419
Chamot, A.U., 191
Chance, P., 238, 239
Chapman, M., 85
Charles, C.M., 449, 457, 458
Chase, W.G., 304
Chavajay, P., 44
Cherlin, A.J., 94
Chessor, D., 75
Chi, M.T.H., 304, 305
Chih-Mei, C., 173
Children's Defense Fund, 94, 101
Childs, C.P., 44
Chinn, P.C., 166
Chomsky, N., 52
Civil Rights Commission, 422
Claiborn, W.L., 422
Clark, C.M., 480, 481, 490
Clark, D.L., 9
Clark, J.M., 257
Clark, K., 78
Clark, M., 78
Clark, R.W., 384
Clarke, J.H., 485
Clement, S.L., 585
Clements, A.C., 266
Clements, B.S., 445, 447
Clements, D.H., 133
Clifford, M.M., 11, 427, 575, 576
Clore, G.L., 377
Clough, M., 337
Coburn, J., 500
Cognition and Technology Group at
    Vanderbilt, 502
Cohen, E.G., 354
Coie, J.D., 87
Coles, R., 4

Collins, A., 247, 248, 275, 280, 355,
    377, 503
Combs, A.W., 498
Comeaux, M.A., 7, 8
Confrey, J., 40, 363
Conger, J.J., 24
Conley, S., 9
Connell, J.P., 576
Conway, G., 217
Cooke, B.L., 10
Cooney, J.B., 305
Cooper, G., 299, 301
Cooper, H., 421, 423, 425
Cooperman, G., 85
Corenblum, B., 78
Corkill, A.J., 343
Corno, L., 122, 135, 342, 407, 576,
    577
Corwin, R., 9
Costa, A.L., 315
Costanza, D.P., 271
Coughlin, R., 78
Coulson, R.L., 277
Covaleskie, J.F., 469
Covington, M., 392, 394, 396
Cox, R.W., 134
Craik, F.I.M., 255, 262
Crain, R.L., 176
Craven, R., 75
Crisci, P.E., 376
Cruickshank, D.R., 503
Cummins, D.D., 297
Cummins, J., 188, 189
Cunningham, A.E., 57, 76,
    248
Cunningham, D.J., 348
Curwin, R.L., 469
Cushing, K.S., 306

Dailey, D., 227
Damon, W., 86
Danielson, C., 543
Dansereau, D.F., 308, 354
Dark, V.J., 269
Darley, J.M., 382
Das, J.P., 45, 48
Davidson, J., 296, 311
Davis, G., 78
Davis, J.K., 134
Davis, R.B., 337
Davis, S.F., 89
Dawson, G., 500
Deaux, K., 178
DeCecco, J., 471
deCharms, R., 385

Deci, E., 237, 374, 375, 385, 386, 414–415, 463
De Corte, E., 297, 502
Delaney, H.D., 272
Delucci, K., 354
Demetras, M.J., 51
De Mott, R.M., 138
Dempster, F.N., 269, 559, 567
Deno, S.L., 557
Denton, J.J., 181
DeRidder, L.M., 103
Derry, S.J., 277, 279, 280, 295, 307, 308
Deshler, D.D., 145
Detterman, D.L., 113
de Vries, B., 84
Diaz, R.M., 46
Dickson, M., 570
Diebert, E., 549
Dinnel, D., 343
Dipietro, J.A., 179
Dishner, E.K., 12
DiVesta, F.J., 309
Doctorow, M., 313
Dodge, K.A., 79, 87
Dodson, J.D., 396
Doleys, D.M., 223
Dorval, R., 56
Doyle, P.H., 456
Doyle, W., 410, 411, 412, 440, 442, 443, 457
Drabman, R.S., 223
Drake, M., 237
Drew, C.J., 125, 154
Driscoll, A., 489
Driscoll, M., 6, 266, 277, 321, 345, 346, 348
Duchastel, P., 333, 567
Duckitt, J., 176, 177
Dudley, B., 470
Duell, O.K., 492
Duffy, G., 420, 504
Dufresne, R., 304
Duncan, C., 471
Duncker, K., 302
Dunn, K., 135, 136
Dunn, R., 135, 136
Dupin, J.J., 306
Dupree, D., 170
Dweck, C.S., 390
Dwyer, C., 543

Eaton, J.F., 306
Eaton, W.O., 397
Ebeling, K.S., 32

Ebmeier, H., 336
Eccles, J., 75, 90, 397, 398, 413, 427, 428
Eckerman, C.O., 56
Educational Testing Service, 542
Egan, M.W., 125, 154
Eggen, P.D., 290
Eimas, P.D., 52
Eisenberg, N., 83, 85
Elam, S.M., 440
Elashoff, J.D., 421, 422
Elawar, M.C., 576, 577
Elkind, D., 38, 42, 92, 93
Elliot, E.C., 565
Ellis, A.K., 335
Ellis, J.A., 264
Elrich, M., 168
Emery, R.E., 90
Emmer, E.T., 445, 447, 448, 454, 455, 456, 457, 459, 510
Engel, P., 541, 542
Engelhart, M.D., 288, 482
Engelmann, S., 42, 215
Englemann, T., 42
Enwistle, N.J., 135
Epanchin, B.C., 440, 462
Epstein, H., 41
Epstein, J.L., 173, 408
Eresh, J.T., 575
Erez, M., 381
Erickson, F., 172
Erikson, E., 66, 68
Eron, L.D., 90
Espe, C., 358
Eurch-Fulcer, R., 501
Evertson, C., 12, 15, 442, 445, 447, 454, 455, 456, 457, 503

Fagot, B.I., 179, 180
Falik, L., 547
Fantuzzo, J., 78
Farnaham-Diggory, S., 247, 248
Farr, M., 305
Farrar, M.J., 58
Faw, H.W., 343
Feiman-Nemser, S., 10
Feingold, A., 178
Feltovich, P.J., 277
Fennema, E., 182, 183, 184, 495, 496
Ferguson, D.L., 150
Ferguson, P.M., 150
Fernald, A., 52
Ferrara, R., 267
Feuerstein, R., 49, 547
Finn, J., 425

Fischer, P., 90
Fiske, E.B., 532, 565
Fiske, S.T., 423
Fitts, P.M., 275
Fitzgerald, J., 191
Flammer, A., 393
Flavell, E.R., 267
Flavell, J.H., 43, 267
Fleishman, E.A., 271
Flink, C., 414, 415
Floden, R.E., 7
Florio, S., 194
Foster, W., 576
Fournier, J., 433
Fouts, J.T., 335
Fox, L.H., 128
Frank, S.J., 72
Franklyn-Stokes, A., 89
Franks, J.J., 262
Frederiksen, N., 133
Freiberg, H.J., 375, 489, 498
Freud, S., 132
Frick, T.W., 456
Friedrichs, A.G., 267
Friend, M., 146, 152
Frost, E.J., 288, 482
Fulk, C.L., 239
Fuller, F.G., 10
Furman, W., 87
Furst, N., 503, 505
Furstenberg, F.F., 94, 103

Gaelick, L., 232
Gage, N.L., 13
Gagne, E.D., 248, 258, 259, 260, 263, 270, 275, 301, 305
Gagne, R.M., 248, 249, 250, 263, 294, 301, 345
Gaines, S.O., 178
Galambos, S.J., 188
Galanter, E., 246, 377
Gall, M., 490, 491, 505
Gallagher, J.J., 138
Gallagher, S., 413
Gallimore, R., 47, 496
Gallini, J.K., 295
Gao, X., 549
Garasky, S., 94
Garcia, E.E., 188, 190, 193
Garcia, J., 181
Garcia, R.L., 168, 171
Gardner, H., 55, 114, 115, 116, 126, 129, 130, 132, 172, 288, 355, 548, 568, 569, 570
Gardner, T.G., 348

Gargarian, G., 501
Garmon, A., 122
Garner, R., 267, 270
Garrett, J., 467
Garrison, J., 277, 280
Garrod, A., 84
Gartner, A., 143
Gates, S.L., 334
Geary, D.C., 182
Gelman, R., 32, 41, 42–43, 43
Gelman, S.A., 32
Gentner, D., 260
Gerbner, G., 177
Gersten, R., 187, 190, 191
Gibbs, J.W., 220
Gick, M.L., 295, 299
Gillett, M., 505
Gilligan, C., 84
Gilstrap, R.L., 488, 489
Ginsburg, H., 28, 30, 32, 40
Ginsburg, M., 78
Gitomer, D.H., 575
Glaser, R., 304, 305
Gleaves, K., 433
Gleitman, H., 130, 175
Glenberg, A., 262
Glenn J., III, 548, 568, 569, 570
Glock, M.D., 422
Glover, J.A., 51, 54, 94, 343
Glucksberg, S., 382
Gnagey, W.J., 233
Goldenberg, C., 189, 190, 191
Goldin-Meadow, S., 188
Goldsmith-Phillips, J., 27
Goleman, D., 167, 169
Gollnick, D.A., 166
Good, T., 40, 76, 122, 123, 335, 336, 354, 421, 422, 423, 424, 425, 452, 491, 492, 493, 506, 510
Goodenough, D.R., 134
Goodman, K.S., 357
Goodnow, J.J., 246, 338
Gordon, E.W., 194
Gordon, J., 170
Gordon, T., 465, 467
Gould, L.J., 190
Grabe, M., 335
Graham, S., 91, 145, 188, 236, 360, 387, 390, 393
Grant, C.A., 162
Gray, G.S., 309
Green, F.L., 267
Greene, D., 237, 385
Greenfield, P.M., 44

Greeno, J.G., 247, 248, 280, 503
Greer, B., 502
Gregorc, A.F., 135
Gresham, F., 141
Grinder, R.E., 11
Grissom, J.B., 576
Grolnick, W.S., 385, 386, 414
Gronlund, N.E., 331, 482, 531, 560, 561, 564, 565
Gross, L., 177
Gross, M.U.M., 129
Grossman, H., 77, 182, 195
Grossman, S.H., 77, 182, 195
Grouws, D., 336
Grover, C.A., 89
Gruson, L., 267
Guilford, J.P., 114, 126
Guitierrez, R., 122
Guskey, T., 334, 393, 577, 580
Gustafsson, J.E., 113
Guttmacher (Alan) Institute, 102

Hagan, R., 179
Hagen, E., 119
Hakuta, K., 188, 190
Hale-Benson, J.E., 193
Hall, J.W., 272
Hall, L.K., 130
Hallahan, D.P., 124, 126, 137, 138, 140, 143, 144, 154, 268
Hallowell, E.M., 142
Hambleton, R.K., 542, 548, 549
Hamilton, R.J., 313, 332, 333
Hanlon, C., 51
Hansen, R.A., 396
Hansford, B.C., 75
Hanson, A.R., 229
Hanson, S.L., 76
Hardiman, P.T., 304
Hardman, M.L., 125, 147, 154
Harris, K.R., 145, 236, 360
Harris, L., 147
Harris, R.T., 104
Harrow, A.J., 483
Harter, S., 76
Hartup, W.W., 87
Harvard University, 184, 360, 361
Hattie, J.A., 75
Hayes, J.R., 297, 298
Hayes, S.C., 233, 234
Hayman, M.L., 455
Hechtman, L.T., 142
Helmke, A., 335–336, 337, 506
Herman, J., 574, 575
Hernshaw, L.S., 246

Hess, R., 170, 173
Hetherington, E.M., 94, 95
Heward, W.L., 112
Hewstone, M., 423
Hiebert, E., 493
Hilgard, E.R., 73
Hill, K.T., 397
Hill, W.E., 226
Hill, W.H., 288, 482
Hilliard, A.G., 163, 176
Hines, C.V., 503
Hinsley, D., 297
Hiroto, D.S., 389
Hirsch, E.D., Jr., 316
Hjertholm, E., 46
Hodgkinson, H.L., 92
Hoefler-Nissani, D.M., 364
Hoffman, L.W., 170
Hoffman, M.L., 89
Hoffnung, R.J., 99, 104
Hoge, D.R., 76
Holden, G.W., 90
Holmes, I.W.M., 75
Homestead, E., 485
Hoover-Dempsey, K.V., 494
Hopkins, B.L., 461–462
Horgan, D.D., 184
Horvath, J.A., 118
Hotkevich, M., 358
Hoy, A., 352
Hoy, W.K., 393, 394
Hoyt, J.D., 267
Huessman, L.R., 90
Huff, C.R., 472
Hundert, J., 233
Hunt, J., 40
Hunter, M., 458
Hyde, J.S., 182, 183

Iannotti, R., 85
Inbar, J., 425
Inclusive Education Programs, 147
Insburg, H.P., 362
IRA (International Reading Association), 58
Iran-Nejad, A., 266, 271, 277
Irving, O., 459
Irwin, J.W., 309
Isabella, R., 68
Isenberg, J., 92
Ishler, M., 349, 488, 497

Jacklin, C.N., 179
Jackson, D., 135, 407
Jackson, N.E., 127

Jacobson, L., 421
Jacobson, M.L., 277
Jagacinski, C.M., 380
James, W., 76, 273
Jay, E., 315, 317, 318
Jeffries, R., 316
Jenson, W.R., 233, 462, 463
Johnson, D., 351, 378, 417, 468, 470, 471, 472
Johnson, J.S., 55
Johnson, R., 351, 378, 417, 468, 470, 471, 472
Johnston, M.B., 308
Jones, E.D., 128
Jones, L.V., 544
Jordan, N., 27
Joshua, S., 306
Journal of Educational Psychology, 358–359
Joyce, B., 290, 291, 292, 293, 343
Joyce, S.A., 217
Jurden, F.H., 255, 269

Kagan, J., 24
Kagan, S., 171, 354
Kanfer, F.H., 232
Kantor, H., 176
Kaplan, B., 99
Kaplan, J.S., 216, 232, 233
Karpov, Y.V., 50
Karweit, N., 342, 443, 480, 510
Kass, R.E., 223
Kauchak, D.P., 290
Kauffman, J.M., 124, 126, 137, 138, 140, 143, 144, 154, 268
Kaufman, K.F., 223
Kazdin, A.E., 220
Keavney, M., 237
Keefe, J.W., 135, 136
Keith, T.Z., 492
Kellaghan, T., 539
Kennedy, J.J., 503
Kennelly, K.J., 397
Keogh, B.K., 112, 127, 129
Kher, N., 427
Kiewra, K.A., 309, 311
Kinchla, R., 382
Kindsvatter, R., 349, 488, 497
King, A., 352, 353
King, G., 585
Kirk, S., 12, 138
Kirschenbaum, H., 87
Kirst, M., 542, 543, 548, 567
Klatzky, R.L., 177
Klausmeier, H.J., 290, 291

Klavas, A., 136
Klein, R., 90
Klein, S., 181
Klinzing, H.G., 7
Knapp, M., 196, 347, 510
Kneedler, R., 142
Kogan, N., 135
Kohlberg, L., 46, 81, 84
Kohn, A., 237, 238, 580
Kolata, G.B., 183, 184
Kolbe, L., 471
Korn, Z., 233
Koser, L., 12
Kotrez, D., 549
Kounin, J., 230, 456, 457
Kozulin, A., 45, 47, 50, 547
Krank, H.M., 469
Krathwohl, D.R., 288, 482
Kronsberg, S., 180
Kruger, A.C., 48
Krumboltz, H.B., 220, 222
Krumboltz, J.D., 220, 222
Kuklinski, M.R., 425
Kulik, C.C., 122, 128, 545, 576
Kulik, C.L., 334
Kulik, J.A., 122, 128, 334, 545
Kulikowich, J.M., 269
Kupersmidt, J.B., 87

Lamon, S.J., 182
Land, M.L., 503
Langer, E.J., 319
Language Development and Hypermedia Group, 347
Laosa, L., 168
Larrivee, B., 150
Latham, G.P., 377, 379
Latta, R.M., 335
Lau, S., 389
Lave, J., 280, 321
Leary, M.R., 386
Leavy, J., 142
Lee, R., 168, 170
Lee, S., 492
Lefcourt, H ., 388
Leinbach, M.D., 180
Leinhardt, G., 7, 305
LeMahieu, P., 575
Leming, J.S., 376
LePore, P.C., 122
Lepper, M., 237, 385, 410, 427
Lerman, D., 389
Leslie, L., 247
Levin, J., 271, 272, 459, 460
Levine, A., 103

Lewinsohn, P.M., 105
Lewis, A.C., 542
Liben, L.S., 179
Lin, Y., 397
Lindsay, P.H., 251
Linn, M.C., 182, 183
Linn, R.L., 540
Lipscomb, T.J., 89
Lipsky, D.K., 143
Lipson, M.Y., 248
Little, J.K., 179
Little, T.D., 127
Littlefield, J., 262
Livingston, C., 6, 13, 305–306
Lloyd, J.W., 144
Locke, E.A., 377, 379
Lockhart, R.S., 255, 262
Loftus, E., 264
Lohman, D.L., 113
Lomask, M.S., 543
Lopez, S.R., 164, 170, 171
Lortie, D., 9
Lowe, R., 176
Lowell, E.L., 384
Lowenstein, G., 411
Lowry, R., 471
Luckasson, R., 125
Luiten, J., 344
Luyben, P.D., 220
Lyman, H.B., 523
Lytton, H., 179

MacAllister, H.A., 89
McCaslin, M., 354
McClelland, D., 121, 384, 395
Maccoby, E.E., 179
McCombs, B., 136, 406
McCormick, S., 469
McCormick, C.B., 271
McDevitt, T., 170, 173
McDonald, J.P., 575
McGinnis, K., 485
MacGregor, L.N., 89
McGuire, J., 179
Macionis, J.J., 167, 171, 175, 176, 177
McKeachie, W.J., 397
McKenzie, T.L., 235
McLaughlin, T.F., 233
MacMillan, D.L., 112, 127, 129
McNemar, Q., 113
Madaus, G.F., 539
Madden, N.A., 342, 510
Madison, S.M., 425
Madsen, C.H., 12, 216

Maehr, M.L., 382, 391
Mager, R., 331
Magnuson, D., 470
Maher, C.A., 337
Maier, N.R.F., 302
Maker, C.J., 128
Mandlebaum, L.H., 469
Manning, B.H., 231, 232, 235
Manning, M.L., 193
Mantzicopolos, P., 576
Maratsos, M.P., 52
Marcia, J., 70
Markakis, K.M., 414
Markman, E.M., 52, 267
Marks, C., 313
Markstrom-Adams, C., 78
Marsh, G.E., 266
Marsh, H.W., 75, 76
Marshall, H.H., 346, 420
Marshall, S., 122
Martin, C.L., 179, 180
Martin, G., 462
Martin, J., 459
Martin, W.R., 488, 489
Martindale, C., 249, 250, 261
Marx, R.W., 372
Marzano, R.J., 406
Masia, B.B., 482
Maslow, A.H., 375, 382, 383, 411, 498
Mason, D.A., 123
Maxey, J.M., 539, 542
Mayer, G.R., 226
Mayer, R.E., 247, 257, 295, 296, 299, 315, 316, 319, 343, 357
Means, B., 510
Meck, E., 42–43
Medley, D.M., 503
Meek, A., 506
Meichenbaum, D., 46, 135, 232, 235, 267
Meisels, S.J., 542
Meister, C., 48, 316, 362
Meloth, M.S., 504
Mendell, P.R., 258
Mendler, A.N., 469
Mergendoiller, J.R., 379
Merkin, S., 42–43
Messick, S., 134, 532
Mestre, J.P., 304
Metcalfe, B., 75
Meyer, C.A., 569
Meyer, D.R., 94
Mezynski, K.J., 262

Mignano, A.J., Jr., 5, 446, 447, 449, 451, 453, 459, 492, 493
Miller, A., 380, 390
Miller, E., 472
Miller, G.A., 246, 254, 377
Miller, K., 43
Miller, P.A., 85
Miller, P.D., 357
Miller, R.B., 219–220
Mills, C.J., 182, 183
Mills, J.R., 127
Minor, L.L., 183
Mitchell, B.M., 129
Monk, J.S., 136
Moore, C.A., 134
Moos, B.S., 575
Moos, R., 575
Morelii, G., 43
Morgan, D.P., 233
Morgan, M., 177, 576
Morris, C.G., 395
Morris, P.F., 267
Morrison, D., 576
Morrow, L., 57, 58, 170, 209, 360, 450
Moshman, D., 51, 54, 94, 267, 277
Moskowitz, G., 455
Moss, P.A., 532, 549
Mumford, M.D., 271
Munby, H., 306
Munt, E.D., 233
Murphy, D.A., 295
Murphy, H.A., 142
Murray, H.G., 505
Murray, J., 177
Musonda, D., 293
Mussen, P., 24

National Center for Education Statistics, 182
National Council of Teachers of Mathematics, 280, 542
National Governors Association, 9
National Joint Committee on Learning Disabilities, 143
National Science Foundation, 177
Naveh-Benjamin, M., 397
Needles, M., 347
Neimark, E., 38
Neisser, U., 113, 121
Nelson, G., 94
Nelson, J.R., 433
Nelson, K., 52, 260
Nelson, T.O., 267
Neuman, O., 380

Neuman, S.B., 58, 360, 485
Newby, T.J., 432
Newcomb, M.D., 104
Newcombe, N., 182
Newman, S.E., 275, 355
Newport, E.L., 55
Newstead, S.E., 89
Newsweek, 92, 102
Nicholls, J.G., 380, 390, 433
Nielsen, L., 94, 95
Niemiec, R., 501
Nisan, M., 576
Nissani, M., 364
Noddings, N., 88, 337, 511
Nolan, J.F., 459, 460
Nolan, K., 542
Nolen, S.B., 433
Norman, D.A., 251
Norman, D.P., 304
Novak, J.D., 293
Novak, J.M., 498
Nucci, L., 84
Nungester, R.J., 567
Nuthall, G., 507
Nystrand, M., 122

Oakes, J., 177, 183
O'Brien, K., 90
O'Conner, J.E., 305
O'Donnell, A.M., 349, 352, 354
Ogbu, J., 169
Ogden, J.E., 12, 15
O'Kelly, J., 349, 352, 354
O'Leary, D., 181
O'Leary, K.D., 141, 142, 217, 223, 233
O'Leary, S., 217, 222, 223
Ollendick, T.H., 227
Olsen, L., 188
O'Malley, J.M., 191
Omelich, C., 392, 394, 396
O'Neil, H.F., 398
O'Neil, J., 9, 194, 542
Onslow, M., 140
Opper, S., 28, 30, 32, 40
Orlansky, M.D., 112
Ortony, A., 260, 377
Osborn, A.F., 132
Ouellette, J.A., 272, 273
Ovando, C.J., 189
Owen, L., 545
Owens, R.E., 140

Padilla, F.M., 472
Padilla, J.N.M., 469

Page, E.B., 576
Paivio, A., 257
Palincsar, A., 316, 350, 352, 360, 361, 407, 418, 502
Pallas, A.M., 183
Palmer, J.C., 264
Pang, K.C., 10
Papert, S., 316, 500
Paris, S., 57, 76, 142, 248
Parker, L.H., 182
Parks, C.P., 472
Pasch, M., 348, 349
Passaro, P.D., 393
Pate, P.E., 485
Paulman, R.G., 397
Paulson, F.L., 569
Paulson, P.R., 569
Payne, B.D., 231, 235
Pear, J., 462
Pearson, P.D., 358
Pecheone, R.L., 543
Pelham, W.E., 142, 268
Pelletier, L.G., 375, 385, 414–415
Peneul, W.R., 70
Peng, S., 168, 170
Perfetto, G.A., 262
Perkins, D., 270, 277, 288, 295, 315, 317, 318, 320, 322, 343
Perrone, V., 485
Perry, T.B., 87
Persampieri, M., 262
Peterson, D.R., 141
Peterson, P., 7, 8, 184, 363, 480, 481, 495, 496, 508
Pfeffer, C.R., 95
Pfiffner, L.J., 217
Phillips, D., 77
Phinney, J., 78
Phye, G.D., 322
Piaget, J., 27, 38, 46, 80, 247, 350
Pierce, W.D., 238
Pierson, L.H., 576
Pilon, D., 384
Pine, G.J., 176
Pintrich, P., 74, 75, 135, 226, 228, 233, 372, 378, 379, 380, 393
Pirsch, L.A., 72
Pitts, J.M., 349
Plager, E., 12
Polson, P.G., 316
Popham, W.J., 332
Posner, M.I., 275, 297
Post, K.N., 51
Powell, K., 471
Powell, R.R., 181

Prawat, R.S., 315, 346
Premack, D., 218
Presseisen, B.Z., 45, 50
Pressley, M., 59, 236, 269, 272, 308, 309, 310, 316, 357, 358, 360, 407, 494
Pribram, K.H., 246, 377
Price, G., 136, 233
Pring, R., 482
Purcell, P., 181
Purkey, W.W., 498
Puro, P., 379
Putnam, R.T., 355

Quay, H.C., 141

Rachlin, H., 207, 210
Raffini, J.P., 374
Ramey, C.T., 125
Range, L.M., 105
Ratey, J.J., 142
Rathus, S.A., 54
Ratner, H.H., 48
Raudenbush, S., 422
Readence, J.E., 12
Recht, D.R., 247
Reder, L.M., 247, 275, 280, 337
Redfield, D.L., 491
Reed, E.S., 178
Reed, S., 167, 169
Reeve, J., 233, 374, 414
Reich, P.A., 188
Reid, M.K., 142, 308
Reis, S.M., 126, 128
Reisberg, D., 205, 264, 289, 290
Render, G.F., 469
Rennie, L.J., 182
Renzulli, J.S., 126, 128, 135
Resnick, L., 247, 248, 260, 280, 298, 347, 503
Reyes, E.I., 195
Reynolds, M.C., 129, 154
Reynolds, W.M., 75
Rhode, G., 233
Ricciardelli, L.A., 188
Rice, M.L., 56, 58
Richards, A., 471
Richardson, T.M., 128
Ritchie, K.L., 90
Robinson, C.S., 298
Robinson, D.H., 311
Robinson, F.P., 311
Robinson, H.A., 311
Robson, M., 10
Roche, L., 75

Roderick, M., 576
Rodriguez, R., 164
Roehler, L.R., 504
Rogers, C.R., 375, 498
Rogoff, B., 43, 44, 47
Rohde, P., 105
Romney, D.M., 179
Ronning, R.R., 278
Rosch, E.H., 289
Rose, L.C., 440
Rosen, L.A., 217
Rosenfarb, I., 233
Rosenman, A.A., 164
Rosenshine, B., 48, 316, 335, 336, 362, 443, 492, 493, 503, 505, 506, 508
Rosenthal, R., 421, 425
Roskos, K., 58, 360, 485
Rosoff, B., 393
Ross, D., 90
Ross, S., 47, 90
Rosser, R., 52
Roth, K.J., 365
Roth, W.M., 356
Rotherham-Borus, M.J., 78
Rotter, J., 388
Rousseau, E.W., 491
Rowe, M.B., 491
Rumelhart, D., 260
Ruopp, F., 6
Rushall, B.S., 235
Ruskin, R.S., 334
Russell, B., 389
Ryan, R.M., 237, 374, 375, 385, 386, 414–415
Ryans, D.G., 505

Sabers, D.S., 306
Sadker, D., 181, 182, 467, 491, 492
Sadker, M., 181, 182, 467, 491, 492
Salomon, G., 270, 295, 320, 322, 343
Sanchez, F., 472
Sanders, C.E., 322
Sattler, J., 119, 120, 130, 133, 544, 545
Sautter, R.C., 167, 169
Sawyer, R.J., 145
Saxe, G.B., 44
Scarr, S., 103, 175
Schab, F., 89
Scherer, M., 169
Schiedel, D., 70
Schiefele, U., 429
Schneider, W., 305, 316
Schofield, J.W., 176, 501

Schon, D., 8
Schrauben, B., 135
Schraw, G., 267, 278
Schulze, S.K., 269
Schumaker, J.B., 145
Schunk, D.H., 74, 75, 225, 226, 228,
    229, 230, 231, 233, 248, 250, 258,
    261, 277, 278, 294, 376, 378, 379,
    380, 384, 388, 393, 397
Schwartz, B., 205, 264, 289, 290
Scott, J., 493
Seddon, G.M., 482
Seelbach, A., 415
Seeley, J.R., 105
Seiber, J.E., 398
Seifert, K.L., 99, 104
Seligman, M.E.P., 144, 389
Selman, R.L., 80, 86
Semb, G.B., 264, 334
Serbin, L., 181
Shapiro, B.C., 543
Shapiro, E.S., 227, 558
Shaughnessy, M.F., 273
Shavelson, R.J., 75, 76, 481, 549
Shepard, L.A., 542, 576
Sherman, J., 183, 334
Shields, A., 415
Shields, P., 170, 196
Shiffrin, R.M., 250
Shipman, V.C., 170
Shuell, T., 246, 247, 270, 295, 334,
    335, 343, 356, 365
Shulman, L.S., 7
Shultz, J., 172, 194
Siegel, J., 273
Siegler, R.S., 41, 43, 53, 268, 269, 316
Signorella, M.L., 179
Signorelli, N., 177
Simmons, R.G., 99
Simon, D.P., 304
Simon, H.A., 247, 275, 277, 280, 297,
    304, 337
Simpson, E.J., 483
Sims, V.K., 257
Singley, K., 321
Sisk, D.A., 128
Sizer, T., 572
Skerry, S., 78
Skinner, B.F., 210
Slavin, R., 122, 342, 352, 417, 418,
    419, 443, 510
Sleet, D., 471
Sleeter, C.E., 162, 163
Sloane, H.N., 233, 462, 463
Smetana, J.G., 84

Smit, E.K., 76
Smith, C.B., 357
Smith, D.D., 125
Smith, E., 301
Smith, E.L., 291, 306, 342
Smith, F., 251, 274
Smith, J.D., 135
Smith, L.A., 576
Smith, L.H., 135, 542
Smith, M., 472
Smith, M.L., 541, 542, 576
Smith, P.J., 239
Smith, S.M., 262
Snider, V.E., 136
Snow, C.E., 58, 189
Snow, M.A., 190
Snow, R.E., 122, 135, 342, 407, 421,
    422
Snowman, J., 308
Soar, R.M., 505
Soar, R.S., 505
Sobesky, W.E., 83
Sokolove, S., 467
Solomon, D., 354
Somberg, D.R.R., 79
Sosniak, L.A., 481
Southern, W.T., 128
Spandel, V., 541
Sparks-Langer, G., 348
Spearman, C., 113
Spector, J.E., 49
Spencer, M.B., 78
Spiro, R.J., 277, 348
Spuhl, S.T., 46
Stahl, S.A., 357
Stainback, S., 146
Stainback, W., 146
Stanley, J.C., 183
Stanovich, K.E., 16, 143
Starch, D., 565
Starko, A.J., 348
Starr, R.H., Jr., 101
Stecher, B., 549
Stein, B.S., 262, 295, 296
Stepien, W., 413
Sternberg, R., 113, 116, 118, 121, 296
Stevens, R., 335, 336, 492, 506, 508
Stevenson, H.W., 121, 492
Stewart, L., 181
Stigler, J., 121, 492
Stipek, D.J., 372, 377, 379, 380, 384,
    391, 416, 418, 427, 429, 430
Stoddard, K., 440, 462
Stodolsky, S.S., 489
Strike, K., 342

Stumpf, H., 182, 183
Sulzby, E., 59
Sulzer-Azaroff, B., 226
Suzuki, B.H., 193
Swanson, H.L., 268, 305
Sweller, J., 299, 301
Symons, S., 357

Tait, H., 135
Tanner, J.M., 99
Task Force on Pediatric AIDS:
    American Psychological Association,
    104–105
Taylor, D.M., 77, 78, 190
Taylor, J.B., 186
Taylor, R.P., 498
Teacher Magazine, 162
Teale, W., 59
TenBrink, T.D., 330
Tennyson, R.D., 290
Terman, L.M., 126
Tharp, R.C., 47
Tharp, R.G., 192, 193, 194, 195,
    496
Thoma, S.J., 84
Thomas, D.R., 12, 215, 216
Thomas, E.L., 311
Thomas, M.H., 272, 273
Thorkildsen, T.A., 433
Thorndike, E.L., 209
Thorndike, R., 119
Thornton, A., 167
Threlfall, V., 271
Thurstone, L.L., 114
Tierney, R.J., 12
Timmer, S.G., 90
Tishman, S., 315, 317, 318
Tobias, S., 397, 398
Tobin, K., 277, 491, 500
Tochon, F., 306
Tollefson, N., 192
Tomasello, M., 48
Tomlinson-Keasey, C., 126, 127
Torrance, E.P., 128, 130, 136
Townsend, B., 440, 462
Treiman, R., 360
Trevarthan, S.D., 84
Trickett, E., 575
Trollip, S.R., 500
Troutman, A.C., 216
Tschannen-Moran, M., 352
Turbill, J., 572
Turiel, E., 84
Turnbull, B.J., 196
Tyler, B., 75

Undheim, J.O., 113
U.S. Bureau of the Census, 92

Vallerand, R.J., 375, 385, 414–415
Van Houten, R., 223
Van Metter, P., 309, 310
Vasquez, J.A., 193
Vavrus, L.G., 504
Veenman, S., 8, 10
Vellutino, F.R., 357, 358, 360
Vera, A.H., 277
Verschaffel, L., 297, 502
Viadero, D., 164
Villegas, A.M., 543
Vispoel, W.P., 74, 410
von Glaserfeld, 277
Vroom, V., 377
Vye, N.J., 262
Vygotsky, L.S., 44, 47, 357

Wadsworth, B.J., 42
Wagner, R.K., 118, 121
Walberg, H.J., 501, 509
Walker, L.J., 84
Waller, T.G., 343
Wallerstein, J., 95
Walton, G., 128
Wang, A.Y., 272, 273
Wang, M.C., 407
Ward, M., 139, 143, 299, 470
Warren-Leubecker, A., 51–52
Waterman, A.S., 72
Waters, E., 68
Waters, H.F., 90
Webb, N., 350, 352, 418, 502
Webb, R.B., 393
Weil, M., 290, 291, 292, 293, 343
Weiland, A., 78
Weinberg, R.A., 103, 121, 422
Weiner, B., 377, 387, 388, 389, 390, 586
Weinert, F.E., 335–336, 337, 506

Weinstein, C., 209, 450
Weinstein, C.E., 136, 406, 407
Weinstein, C.S., 5, 446, 447, 449, 450, 451, 453, 459, 492, 493
Weinstein, R., 76, 425
Weisberg, R.W., 129
Weiss, G., 142
Wells, A.S., 176
Wenger, E., 280, 321
Wertsch, J.V., 49, 70
Wessells, M.G., 303
Wessman, A., 575
White, B.Y., 500
White, K.R., 167–168, 170
White, S., 195
Whitehurst, G.J., 58
Wiener, M.W., 414
Wigfield, A., 75, 397, 398, 413, 427, 428
Wiggins, G., 567, 568, 572
Wiig, E.H., 140
Wilen, W., 349, 488, 497
Wilkins, W.E., 422
Wilkinson, I., 493
Willerman, L., 170
Williams, C., 85
Williams, G.C., 414
Williams, W.M., 118
Willig, A.C., 190
Willis, P., 169
Wilson, C.W., 461–462
Wilson, G.T., 141
Winett, R.A., 237
Wingate, N., 181
Winkler, R.C., 237
Winne, P.H., 231, 407
Winters, L., 574, 575
Witkin, H.A., 134
Wittrock, M.C., 11, 245, 277, 295, 313, 315, 316, 319, 398
Wixson, K.K., 248
Wolf, D., 548, 568, 569, 570

Woloshyn, V., 357
Women on Words and Images, 181
Wong, L., 13
Wood, D., 47
Wood, E.R.G., 25
Wood, S.E., 25
Woolfolk, A.E., 232, 352, 393, 394, 424, 453
Woolfolk, R.L., 232
Worner, C., 358
Worsham, M.E., 445, 447
Worthen, B.R., 541, 548, 549
Worth Gavin, D.A., 75
Wright, S.C., 77, 78, 190
Wright, V.C., 72
Wulfert, E., 233
Wyler, R.S., 177
Wynne, E.A., 86

Yaeger, J., 46
Yee, A.H., 173, 182, 194
Yekovich, C.W., 248, 258, 259, 260, 263, 270, 275, 301
Yekovich, F.R., 248, 258, 259, 260, 263, 270, 275, 301
Yerkes, R.M., 396
Yinger, R., 480, 481
Yokoi, L., 309, 310
Young, K.R., 233, 462, 463
Youniss, J., 86

Zahn-Waxler, C., 85
Zeidner, M., 397, 398
Zettle, R.D., 233
Zidon, I., 381
Zigmond, N., 146
Zimmerman, B.J., 231, 393
Zimmerman, D.W., 584
Zimmerman, M., 77
Ziomek, R.L., 539, 542

Subject Index

Page numbers in boldface type indicate pages on which key terms and concepts are defined.

Abilities, 121–129
  beliefs about, 390–392
  cognitive. *See* Intelligence; Intelligence tests; IQ scores
  entity view of, **390**
  gifted and talented students and, 126–129
  grouping on basis of, 122–123
  incremental view of, **390**
  matching teaching strategies to, 40
  mental retardation and, 123–126
  sex differences in, 182–184
  underestimating, 42–43
Absence seizures, 137
Abstraction, mindful, 320
Abuse, 100–102
Academic learning time, **443**
Academic tasks, **409**, 409–413
  authentic, 413
  risk and ambiguity and, 411–412
  tapping interests and arousing curiosity and, 410–411
  task value and, 412–413
Accommodation, **29**
  in thinking, 29
Accomplishment, recognizing, 416
Achievement
  ethnicity and race and, 174–175
  intelligence tests and, 120–121
  socioeconomic status and, 167–170
Achievement motivation, **384**, 384–385
  attributions and self-worth and, 394–395
Achievement tests, **533**, 533–536
  interpreting scores on, 534–536
  norm-referenced, 534
Acquired immunodeficiency syndrome (AIDS), 104–105
Acquisition phase of strategic transfer, 322–323
Acronyms, **271**
Action zones, **452**, 452–454

Active teaching, **335**. *See also* Direct instruction
Activity, cognitive development and, 28
ADA (Americans with Disabilities Act), **146**
Adaptation, **28**
  in thinking, 28–29
ADHD (attention-deficit/hyperactivity disorder), **142**
Adolescent(s)
  physical development of, 99–100
  psychosocial development of, 67, 70–72
  sexuality and pregnancy among, 102–103
Adolescent egocentrism, **38**
Adults
  psychosocial development of, 67, 72–73
  role in cognitive development, 47
Advance organizers, **341**, 343
Affective domain, **482**, 482–483
African Americans, learning styles of, 193
Age. *See also specific age groups*
  mental, **119**
Age-related needs, 442
Aggression, **90**, 90–91
  socialized, 141
AIDS (acquired immunodeficiency syndrome), 104–105
Algorithms, **300**
Allocated time, **443**
Ambiguity, academic tasks and, 411–412
American Psychological Association, learner-centered psychological principles of, 511–514
Americans with Disabilities Act (ADA), **146**
Analogical thinking, **301**
Analytic intelligence, 116
Anchored instruction, **502**

Androgyny, **178**
Anorexia nervosa, **103**, 104
Antecedents, **210**
  behavior change and, 214–216
Anxiety, **396**, 396–399
  causes of, 397
  dealing with, 397–399
  teaching and, 398
Anxiety-withdrawal disorders, 141
Applied behavior analysis, **216**, 216–224
  discouraging behaviors with, 221–224
  encouraging behaviors with, 216–221
Apprenticeships, cognitive, 355–357
Aptitude tests, **537**, 537–539
  discussing results with families, 538–539
  IQ and, 538
Articulation disorders, **139**
Articulatory loop, **254**
Asian Americans, learning styles of, 193–194
Assertive discipline, **467**, 467–470
  effectiveness of, 469
  "I" messages and, 467
Assessment. *See also* Classroom tests; IQ scores; Standardized tests; Test(s); Test scores
  authentic, 486, **548**, 548–549
  curriculum-based, **557**, 557–558
  formative, **556**, 556–558
  plans for, 485–487
  summative, 558
Assignment propositions, 296
Assimilation, **28**
  in thinking, 28–29
Assisted learning, 48, **49**
Associative stage of automated skill development, **275**
Attainment value, **413**
  helping students to see, 429–430

Attention, **252**
    directing, 230
    focusing for problem solving, 296
    helping students to focus on task,
        430–431
    observational learning and, 226
    sensory memory and, 252–253
    from teacher, as reinforcement,
        216–218
    teaching and, 253
Attentional problems immaturity, 141
Attention-deficit/hyperactivity disorder
    (ADHD), **142**
Attention disorders, 141–142
Attributes, defining, **289**
Attribution theories, **387**, 387–390
    achievement motivation and self-
        worth and, 394–395
    cues about causes and, 389–390
    dimensions and, 387–388
    learned helplessness and, 389
    student motivation and, 389
    teaching and, 395
Authentic assessment, 486, 548,
    548–549
Authentic tasks, **413**
Authentic tests, **568**
Authoritarian personality, **176**,
    176–177
Automated basic skills, **275**
Automaticity, **118**, **253**
Autonomous stage of automated skill
    development, **275**
Autonomy, **68**, 414–416
    advantages of, 414
    class climates supporting, 415–416
    information and control and,
        414–415
Autonomy versus shame and doubt
    stage, 67, 68–69
Aversive situations, **211**

Backward-reaching transfer, 320
Basic skills, **335**
Beginning teachers. *See* Novice
    teachers
Behavioral approach to motivation,
    375
Behavioral disorders, 140–141
Behavioral learning theories, 202–240,
    205, 330–337
    applied behavior analysis, 216–224
    behavior modification and, 235–236
    classical conditioning, 207–208

cognitive view compared with,
    247
criticisms of methods based on,
    237–239
ethical issues related to, 237
instructional objectives and,
    330–334
mastery learning and, 334–337
operant conditioning, 208–216
self-instruction and, 235–236
self-management and, 231–235
social, 225–231
Behavioral objectives, **331**
Behavior-content matrix, for test
    design, 558
Behavior modification, **216**. *See also*
    Applied behavior analysis
    cognitive, **235**, 235–236
Being needs, **383**
Beliefs, 390–394
    about ability, 390–392
    about self-efficacy, 392–394
    teaching and, 395
Between-class ability grouping, **122**
Bias
    gender. *See* Gender bias
    in testing, 544–545
Bilingual education, 189–192
    research on, 190–192
Bilingualism, **187**, 187–192
    bilingual education and, 189–192
    definition of, 188
    development of, 188–189
Bimodal distributions, **524**
Blended families, **92**
Bottom-up processing, **252**
Brain, cognitive development and,
    25–27
Brain injury, 143
Brainstorming, **132**
Bulimia, **103**, 103–104

Caring, morality of, 84–88
Case studies, 14, **15**
Causality, locus of, **374**
CBA (curriculum-based assessment),
    557, 557–558
Central tendency measures, 523–524
Cerebral palsy, 137–138, *138*
Chain mnemonics, **271**
Cheating, 89–90
Child abuse, 100–102
Childrearing styles, socioeconomic
    status and, 170

Children. *See also specific age groups*
    latchkey, 92
Chunking, **256**
Clarity, of effective teachers, 503–505
Class, social. *See* Socioeconomic status
    (SES)
Classical conditioning, **207**, 207–208
    generalization, discrimination, and
        extinction and, 208
Classification, **35**
Classroom(s). *See also* Learning
    environments
    characteristics of, 440–441
    climates supporting autonomy in,
        415–416
    conditions necessary to encourage
        motivation in, 427
    creativity in, 131–133
    culturally compatible. *See* Culturally
        compatible classrooms
    ecology of, 440–442
    inclusive, 148, 150–153
    seatwork in, 492
    sex discrimination in, 181–182
Classroom assessment, 554–575. *See
    also* Classroom tests; Grading
    formative and summative, 556–
        558
Classroom management, **442**,
    461–463
    communicating with families about,
        473
    contingency contract programs for,
        463
    during first weeks of class, 454–455
    goals of, 442–445
    group consequences for, 461–462
    token reinforcement programs for,
        462–463
Classroom tests, 558–566
    authentic, 568
    behavior-content matrix for, 558
    essay, 564–566
    evaluation of, 567
    objective, 560–563
    textbook, 559
    timing of, 559
Coaching, for tests, 545
Coding systems, **338**
Cognitive apprenticeships, 355–357
Cognitive approaches to motivation,
    376–377
Cognitive behavior modification, **235**,
    235–236

Cognitive development, 24. *See also*
    Intelligence; Thinking
    acceleration of, 42
    brain and, 25–27
    Piaget's theory of. *See* Piaget's theory
        of cognitive development
    Vygotsky's sociocultural perspective
        on. *See* Vygotsky's sociocultural
        perspective
Cognitive domain, **482**
Cognitive evaluation theory, **414**
Cognitive objectives, **331**
Cognitive self-instruction, **46**
Cognitive stage of automated skill
    development, **275**
Cognitive strategies, 249
Cognitive styles, **134**, 134–135
Cognitive view of learning, 244–282,
    246, 338–346
    accuracy versus usefulness of
        knowledge and, 278–279
    behavioral view compared with, 247
    constructivist, 277–278
    declarative knowledge and, 270–274
    discovery learning and, 338–341,
        342
    elements of, 246–247
    expository teaching/reception
        learning and, 341, 343–345
    families and, 365–366
    importance of knowledge in learning
        and, 247–249
    individual differences and long-term
        memory and, 269
    information processing model. *See*
        Information processing
    instructional events model and,
        345–346
    for mathematics, 362–363
    metacognition and, 266–269
    procedural and conditional
        knowledge and, 274–276
    for reading and writing, 357–360
    reciprocal teaching and, 360–362
    for science, 364–365
    situated learning and, 279–280
Collaborative learning, 47–48
Collective monologue, **32**
Collective self-esteem, 77–78, **78**
Communication
    about grades, 587–589
    for classroom management,
        463–473
    confrontation and assertive
        discipline and, 467–470

counseling and, 466–467
diagnosing ownership of problems
    and, 465–466
with families, 365–366, 473,
    587–589
messages sent and received and,
    464–465
student conflicts and confrontations
    and, 470–473
Communication disorders, 139–140
Community of practice, **279**
Comparative organizers, 343
Compensation, **35**
Complex learning environments, 347
Comprehension, linguistic, **296**,
    296–297
Computers, 498–502
    exceptional students and, 153–154
    learning and, 501–502
    as learning environments, 498–501
Computer simulations, 499–501, **500**
Concept(s), **289**
Concept attainment, 290–291
Concept learning, 289–293
    teaching strategies for, 290–293
    views of, 289–290
Concept mapping, **293**
Conceptual change teaching in science,
    364, 364–365
Concrete-operational stage, 30, 34–36,
    35
Condition-action rules, 261
Conditional knowledge, **249**, 274–276
    automated basic skills and, 275
    domain-specific strategies and, 276
    learning outside school and, 276
Conditioned response (CR), **208**
Conditioned stimulus (CS), **208**
Conditioning
    classical, 207–208
    operant. *See* Operant conditioning
Conduct disorders, 141
Confidence, building, 427–428
Confidence intervals, **531**
Confrontation
    negotiations and, 468, 470
    student conflicts and, 470–473
Connectionist models, **266**
Consequences, **210**, 210–212
    group, **461**, 461–462
    for positive learning environments,
        448–449
    punishment, 211–212
    reinforcement, 210–211
Conservation, **32**

Constructed-response formats, **548**
Constructivism
    dialectical, **278**
    endogenous, **277**
    exogenous, **277**
Constructivist perspectives, **277**,
    277–278, **346**, 346–365, **484**
    cognitive apprenticeships and,
        355–357
    elements of, 346–348
    families and, 365–366
    group work and cooperation in
        learning and, 349–355
    inquiry and problem-based learning
        and, 348–349
    instructional conversations and, 355
    for mathematics, 362–363
    planning and, 484–487
    for reading and writing, 357–360
    reciprocal teaching and, 360–362
    for science, 364–365
    teaching and, 495–496
    types of constructivism and,
        277–278
Construct validity, 531–532
Content, multiple representations of,
    347, 347–348
Content standards, **542**
Content validity, **531**
Context, **262**
    performance in, 568–575
Contiguity, **207**
Contingency contracts, **463**
Continuous reinforcement schedule,
    212
Contract system, **584**, 584–585
Convergent questions, **491**
Convergent thinking, 130
Conversations, instructional, **355**
Cooperation
    scripted, **489**
    of students, gaining, 441–442
Cooperative learning, **350**, 350–354,
    417, 417–419
    group elements and, 351
    jigsaw for, 352
    reciprocal questioning and, 353
    scripted cooperation and, 353–354
    setting up groups for, 352
    STAD and, 418–419
    TGT and, 419–420
Cooperative teaching, **150**, 150–151
Correlations, 14, **15**
    negative, 14, **15**
    positive, 14, **15**

Counseling, 466–467
CR (conditioned response), **208**
Creativity, 117–118, **129**, 129–133
  assessing, 130–131
  in classrooms, 131–133
  cognition and, 129–130
Criterion-referenced grading, **478**,
  578–580
Criterion-referenced testing, **521**,
  521–523
Criterion validity, 531
Critical thinking, **318**
  teaching of, 316
CS (conditioned stimulus), **208**
Cueing, **214**, 214–215
Cultural deficit model, **163**
Cultural diversity, 162–166, 171–174
  American, 163–166
  cultural compatibility and, 173
  cultural conflicts and, 172–173
  individuals, groups, and society and,
    162–163
  learning styles and, 192–194
Culturally compatible classrooms, **192**,
  192–198
  learning styles and, 192–194
  social organization of, 192
  sociolinguistics and, 194–195
  teaching principles for, 195–198
Culture, **165**. *See also* Multicultural
  education
  cautions in interpreting differences
    in, 166
  cognitive development and, 43–44
  group membership and, 164–166
  moral reasoning and, 84
  resistance, **169**
  of thinking, 315
Culture-fair/culture-free tests, **545**
Curiosity, arousing, 410–411
Curricula
  gender bias in, 180–181
  integrated, for reading/writing
    instruction, 35
  regular, thinking in, 315, 317–319
  spiral, 348
Curriculum-based assessment (CBA),
  557, 557–558

Data-based instruction, **557**
Decay, **257**
Decentering, **32**
Declarative knowledge, **248**, 249,
  270–274
  meaningfulness and, 273–274

mnemonics and, 271–272
  rote memorization and, 270–
    271
Deductive reasoning, **341**
  hypothetico-deductive, **37**
Deep-processing approach to learning,
  135
Deficiency needs, **383**
Defining attributes, **289**
Descriptive research, **13**, 13–14
Development, **24**, 24–27
  cognitive. *See* Cognitive
    development; Piaget's theory of
    cognitive development
  general principles of, 25
  of language. *See* Language
    development
  moral. *See* Moral development
  personal, **24**
  physical, **24**, 98–100
  psychosocial. *See* Erikson's theory of
    psychosocial development; Moral
    development; Socialization
  social. *See* Social development
  of thinking, 314–319
  of working memory, 268–269
Developmental crises, **67**
Developmentally appropriate
  education, **93**, 93–94
Diagnostic tests, 536–537, **537**, **556**,
  556–557
Dialect(s), 185–186
  language skills and, 185
  teaching and, 185
Dialectical constructivism, **278**
Direct instruction, 315, **335**, 335–337,
  506
  criticisms of, 336–337
  teaching functions and, 336
Directive teaching, 488–494
  lecturing and explaining and,
    488–489
  recitation and questioning and,
    489–492
  seatwork and homework and,
    492–494
Disabilities, **136**, 136–154. *See also*
  Exceptional students; Inclusion of
  exceptional students
Discipline, assertive, **467**, 467–470
Discipline problems, 459–460
Discovery learning, **338**, 338–
  341
  effectiveness of, 342
  structure and, 338

Discrimination, **177**, **208**
  racial. *See* Racial discrimination
  sex, in classrooms, 181–182
Discussions, group, **496**, 496–497
Disequilibrium, **29**
  in thinking, 29
Distributed practice, **271**
Divergent questions, **491**
Divergent thinking, 130
Divorce, 94–96
Domain-specific strategies, **276**
Drug abuse, 104
Dual marking systems, **585**, 585–586

Eating disorders, 103–104
Education
  bilingual, 189–192
  developmentally appropriate, **93**,
    93–94
  as enculturation, 315
  multicultural. *See* Multicultural
    education
Educationally blind students, **138**
Educational psychology, **11**, 11–16
  research in. *See* Research
Education for All Handicapped
  Children Act, 146
Effective students, learning by, 508
Effective teachers, 502–506
  knowledge of, 503
  organization and clarity of, 503–505
  warmth and enthusiasm of, 505
Effective teaching, 508–514
  in inclusive classrooms, 148,
    150–153
  learner-centered psychological
    principles for, 511–514
  matching methods to learning goals
    for, 508–511
Effort, grading on, 585–586
Egocentrism, **32**
  adolescent, **38**
Ego-involved learners, **380**
Eg-rule method, **338**
Élaboration, **261**, 261–262
Elaborative rehearsal, **256**
Elementary schools
  effective teachers for, 454–455
  nongraded, **122**
  rules for positive learning
    environments in, 447–448
Emotion, arousing, 230
Emotional disorders, 140–141
Empathic listening, **466**, 466–467
Empathy, **85**, 85–86

Enculturation, education as, 315
Endogenous constructivism, **277**
Engaged time, **443**
Engagement, encouraging, 455–457
English as a second language (ESL),
    187, 187–188
Enthusiasm, of effective teachers, 505
Entity view of ability, **390**
Environment, intelligence and, 121
Epilepsy, **137**
Episodic memory, **261**
Equilibration, **29**
    in thinking, 29
Equity. *See* Fairness
Erikson's theory of psychosocial
        development, 66–73
    during adolescence, 70–72
    during adulthood, 72–73
    during elementary and middle
        school years, 69–70
    during preschool years, 67–69
ESL (English as a second language),
    187, 187–188
Essay testing, 564–566
    constructing, 564–565
    dangers in evaluating, 565
    evaluation methods for, 565–566
    objective tests compared with, 566
Ethical issues, with behavioral
        strategies, 237
Ethnicity, **170**. *See also* Cultural
        diversity
    of immigrants, 171
    school achievement and, 174–175
Ethnography, **13**
Evaluation, **520**
    metacognitive knowledge and, 267
    motivation and, 420–421
Event schemata, 260
Exceptional students, **112**
    with communication disorders,
        139–140
    with emotional and behavioral
        disorders, 140–141
    with hyperactivity and attention
        disorders, 141–142
    integration of. *See* Integration of
        exceptional students
    with learning disabilities, 142–145
    with physical and sensory disorders,
        137–139
Executive control processes, **267**
Exemplars, **290**
Exhibitions, **572**, 572–575
    evaluating, 572–575

Exogenous constructivism, **277**
Expectancy × value theories, **377**,
    377–378
Expectations
    positive, building, 427–428
    of socioeconomic status, 168–169
    of teachers. *See* Teacher expectations
Experimentation, **15**
Expert knowledge, problem solving
        and, 304–305
Expert teachers, 7, 7–8
    problem solving and, 305–306
Explaining, 488–489
Explanatory links, **504**, 504–505
Explicit teaching. *See* Direct
        instruction
Expository organizers, 343
Expository teaching, **341**, 343–345
    advance organizers and, 341, 343
    effective use of, 344
    steps in, 343–344
Extinction, **208**, 214
Extrinsic motivation, **374**, 374–375

Faces of intellect, **114**
Failure
    effects on students, 575–576
    helping students at risk for, 510
Failure-accepting students, **395**
Failure-avoiding students, **395**
Fairness
    of evaluating portfolios and
        exhibitions, 574–576
    in grading, 586
Families
    blended, **92**
    communicating with, 365–366,
        473
    discussing test results with, 538–539
    literacy and, 58–59
    socialization and, 92–96
Feature analysis, 252
Feedback
    effects on students, 576–577
    goal acceptance and, 380–381
Field dependence, **134**
Field independence, **134**
Fine-motor skills, **98**, 98–99
Finger spelling, **138**
First sentences, 53
First words, 52–53
Flexibility
    creativity and, 130
    for problem solving, 303
Fluency, creativity and, 130

Forgetting, 256–257
    long-term memory and, 264
Formal operations stage, 30, **37**,
    37–38, 39
Formative assessment, **556**, 556–558
Forward-reaching transfer, 320
Frequency distributions, **523**
Friendships, 86–88
Full inclusion, **146**, 147
Functional fixedness, **302**, 320

g (general intelligence), 113
Gender, 178–185
    eliminating bias based on, 184–185
    gender-role identity and, 178–182
    mental abilities and, 182–184
    self-esteem and, 77
Gender bias, **180**, 180–181
    eliminating, 184–185
Gender-role identity, **178**, 178–182
    gender bias in curriculum and,
        180–181
    sex discrimination in classrooms
        and, 181–182
    stereotyping in preschool years and,
        179–180
General intelligence (*g*), 113
Generalization, **208**
Generalized seizures, **137**
General knowledge, **248**
General transfer, 320
Generativity, **73**
Generativity versus stagnation stage,
    67, 73
Gestalt, 251–252
Gifted students, **126**, 126–129
    identification of, 126
    problems faced by, 126–127
    recognizing abilities of, 127–128
    teaching, 128–129
    testing of, 128
Goal(s), **379**, 379–382
    of behavioral strategies, ethical
        issues related to, 237
    conflicting, 471
    feedback and acceptance of,
        380–381
    learning, **380**
    matching methods to, 508–511
    performance, **380**
    for self-management, 233
    setting, 233, 382
    teaching and, 382
    types of, 379–380
Goal-directed actions, **31**

Goal structures, **417**, 417–418
Good behavior game, **461**
Graded membership, **289**
Grade-equivalent scores, **527**, 527–528
Grading, 575–587
   communication about grades and, 587–589
   contract system and grading rubrics and, 584–585
   criterion-referenced, **478**, 578–580
   effects of failure and, 575–576
   effects of feedback and, 576–577
   on effort and improvement, 585–586
   fairness and, 586
   motivation and, 577–578
   norm-referenced, **578**, 580–581
   percentage, 583–584
   point system and, 582–583
   report cards and, 581–582
Grading on the curve, **580**, 580–581
Grading rubrics, 584–585
Grammar
   learning, 53
   story, **260**
Grand mal seizures, 137
Gross-motor skills, **98**
Group(s)
   norm, **521**
   whole group teaching and, 488–494
Group consequences, **461**, 461–462
Group discussions, **496**, 496–497
Group focus, **458**
Grouping, 417–418
Group work, 349–355
   cooperation and, 350–354
   misuses of, 354–355
Guided discovery, **339**, 339–340

Halo effect, **586**
Handicaps, **136**, 136–137
Hearing impairment, 138
Heredity, intelligence and, 121
Heuristics, **300**, 300–301
Hierarchy of needs, **382**, 382–384
Highlighting, 308–309
High-road transfer, **320**
High-stakes testing, **539**
Hispanic Americans, learning styles of, 192–193
Histograms, **523**
Holophrases, **53**
Homework, 492–494
Hostile response style, 468

Humanistic view, **375**, **498**
   of motivation, 375
Hyperactivity, **141**, 141–142
Hypothetico-deductive reasoning, 37

IDEA (Individuals with Disabilities Education Act), **146**
Identity, 35, **70**
   gender-role. *See* Gender-role identity
Identity achievement, **70**, 70–71
Identity diffusion, **70**, 71
Identity foreclosure, **70**, 71
Identity versus role confusion stage, 67, 70–72
IEPs (individualized education programs), **148**
ILEs (individual learning expectations), **418**, 418–419, 585
Images, **258**
"I" Messages, **467**
Imitative learning, 47
Immigrants, 171
Improvement, grading on, 585–586
Impulsivity, **134**
Incentives, **375**
Inclusion of exceptional students, 146–154
   computers and, 153–154
   effective classrooms and, 148, 150–153
   legislation affecting, 146–148
Incremental view of ability, **390**
Incubation, 129
Individual differences
   in long-term memory, 269
   in metacognition, 267–268
   working memory and, 268–269
Individualized education programs (IEPs), **148**
Individual Learning Expectations (ILEs), **418**, 418–419, 585
Individuals with Disabilities Education Act (IDEA), **146**
Industry, **69**
Industry versus inferiority stage, 67, 69–70
Infancy, sensorimotor stage in, 30–31
Information, retaining in working memory, 255–256
Information processing, **249**, 249–266
   bottom-up, **252**
   cognitive development and, 43
   connectionist models of memory and, 266
   long-term memory and, 257–264

sensory memory and, 250–254
   top-down, **252**
   working memory and, 254–257
Initiative, **68**, 68–69
Inquiry learning, **348**, 348–349
Insight, **117**, 117–118, **303**
Instructed learning, 47
Instruction. *See also* Teaching
   anchored, **502**
   data-based, **557**
   direct. *See* Direct instruction
   student-centered, 348
Instructional conversations, **355**
Instructional events model, 345–346
Instructional objectives, **330**, 330–337
   behavioral, **331**
   Bloom's taxonomy of, 332–333
   cognitive, **331**
   usefulness of, 333–334
   writing of, 331–332
Instrumental value, helping students to see, 430
Integration of exceptional students, 146–154
   computers and, 153–154
   effective teaching and, 148, 150–153
   legislative changes affecting, 146–148
Integrity, **73**
Integrity versus despair stage, 67, 73
Intelligence, 113–121
   analytic, 116
   general, 113
   heredity versus environment and, 121
   measurement of. *See* Intelligence tests
   multiple, 114–116
   as process, 116–118
   triarchic theory of, **116**, 116–118
Intelligence quotient (IQ), **119**. *See also* IQ scores
Intelligence tests, 118–121
   achievement and, 120–121
   early development of, 118–119
   group versus individual, 119
   scores on. *See* IQ scores
Intention, 79
Interest(s), tapping, 410–411
Interest-area arrangements, 450–451
Interest value, **413**
Interference, **264**

Intermittent reinforcement schedule, **212**
Internalization, **89**
Interval reinforcement schedule, **213**
Intimacy versus isolation stage, 67, 72–73
Intrinsic motivation, 373–375, **374**
Intrinsic value, **413**, 429–430
  helping students to see, 429–430
Intuitive thinking, **338**, 338–339
IQ scores, **119**, 119–121
  of gifted students, 126
  mental retardation and, 124
  scholastic aptitude and, 538

Jigsaw, 352
Joplin plan, **122**

Keyword method, **271**, 271–272
Knowledge, 270–276
  accuracy versus usefulness of, 278–279
  conditional, **249**
  constructing, 40–41
  declarative, **248**, 249, 270–274
  of effective teachers, 503
  general, **248**
  importance in learning, 247–248
  metacognitive, regulation and, 267
  procedural, **248**, 248–249
  self-regulated learning and, 406–407
  specific, **248**

Labeling, 112–113
Language
  bilingualism and. *See* Bilingualism
  dialects and, 185–186
  literacy and, 57–59
  private speech and, 45–46
  sociolinguistics and, 194–195
  of thinking, 318
  Vygotsky's versus Piaget's views on, 45–46
Language development, 51–57
  process of, 51–52
  during school years, 54–57
  stages in, 52–54
Language disorders, 140
Latchkey children, 92
Learned helplessness, **144**, **389**
  attribution and, 389
  socioeconomic status and, 169
Learner-centered psychological principles, 511–514

Learning, 202–240
  access to, as goal of classroom management, 443–444
  assessing potential for, 547–548
  assisted, 48, **49**
  behavioral theories of. *See* Behavioral learning theories
  cognitive theories of. *See* Cognitive view of learning
  collaborative, 47–48
  computers and, 501–502
  of concepts, 289–293
  definition of, 204–205
  discovery, **338**, 338–341
  by effective students, 508
  imitative, 47
  inquiry, **348**, 348–349
  instructed, 47
  instructional objectives for, 330–334
  of language. *See* Language development
  mastery, **334**, 334–337
  motivation to learn and, 378–379
  observational, 226–231
  part, **271**
  problem-based, 348–349, **413**
  reception. *See* Expository teaching
  rewarding students for, 238
  outside school, **276**
  self-regulated, **406**, 406–409
  self-talk and, 46
  situated, **279**, 279–280
  spaces for, 449–454
  from teaching, conditions for, 507–508
  time for, as goal of classroom management, 443
  verbal, meaningful, **341**
Learning disabilities, **142**, 142–145
  teaching students with, 145
Learning environments, 438–474. *See also* Classroom(s)
  classroom management and, 461–463
  communication needed for, 463–473
  complex, **347**
  computers as, 498–501
  maintaining, 455–461
  organization needed for, 440–445
  positive, creating, 445–455
Learning goals, **380**
Learning preferences, **135**, 135–136
Learning Propensity Assessment Device, **547**, 547–548

Learning strategies, **307**, 307–311
  transfer of, 320–321, 322–324
Learning styles, **135**, 135–136
  cultural differences in, 192–194
  research on, criticisms of, 194
Learning tactics, **307**, 308–311
Least restrictive placement, **146**, 146–147
Lecturing, **488**, 488–489
LEP (limited English proficiency), **188**
Lessons, for teaching concepts, 290–293
Levels of processing theory, **262**
Limited English proficiency (LEP), **188**
Linguistic comprehension, **296**
  for problem solving, 296–297
Listening, empathic, **466**, 466–467
Literacy, 57–59
Loci method, **271**
Locus dimension, 387
Locus of causality, **374**
Locus of control, **388**
Long-term memory, **257**, 257–264
  capacity and duration of, 257
  contents of, 257–258
  episodic, **261**
  forgetting and, 264
  images and, 258
  individual differences in, 269
  levels of processing theories and, 262
  procedural, **261**
  propositions and propositional networks and, 258
  retrieving information from, 262–264
  schemas and, 259–260
  semantic, **258**
  storing information in, 261–262
Low-road transfer, **320**
Low vision, **138**

Mainstreaming, **146**
Maintenance rehearsal, **255**, 255–256
Massed practice, **271**
Mastery learning, **334**, 334–337
  advantages and problems with, 334–335
  direct instruction for, 335–337
Mastery-oriented students, **394**, 394–395
Mathematics
  instruction in, 362–363
  sex differences in ability and, 182–184

Maturation, **25**
  cognitive development and, 27–28
Mean, **523**
Meaningfulness, of lessons, 273–274
Meaningful verbal learning, **341**
Means-end analysis, **300**
Measurement, **520**, 520–521. *See also*
    Assessment; IQ scores;
    Standardized tests; Test(s); Test
    scores
  standard error of, **530**
Median, **523**, 523–524
Mediation, by peers, 472–473
Melting pot, **162**, 162–163
Memorization, rote, **270**, 270–271
  shortcomings of, 273
Memory
  connectionist models of, 266
  long-term, **257**, 257–264, 269
  sensory, **250**, 250–254
  working, **254**, 254–257, 268–269
Mental abilities. *See also* Cognitive
    development; Intelligence;
    Intelligence tests; IQ scores
  sex differences in, 182–184
Mental age, **119**
Mental retardation, **123**, 123–126
Metacognition, **267**, 267–268
  individual differences in, 267–268
  regulation and, 267
Metacognitive skills, 267
Metalinguistic awareness, **57**
Microworlds, **500**, 500–501
Mindful abstraction, 320
Mindfulness, 318–319
Minimal brain dysfunction, 143
Minimum competency testing, **542**
Minority groups, **171**
Mnemonics, **271**, 271–272
  chain, **271**
  peg-type, **271**
Mode, **524**
Modeling, **229**, 229–230
Monitoring, metacognitive knowledge
    and, 267
Monolinguals, **188**
Moral behavior, 89–91
Moral development, 80–91
  cultural differences in moral
    reasoning and, 84
  Kohlberg's stages of, 81–83
  moral behavior and, 89–91
  morality of caring and, 84–88
  social conventions versus moral
    issues and, 83–84

Moral dilemmas, **82**
Morality of cooperation, *80*
Moral realism, *80*
Moral reasoning, **81**. *See also* Moral
    development
Moratorium, **70**, 71
Motivation, 370–400, **372**, 404–435
  academic tasks and, 409–413
  achievement, **384**, 384–385,
    394–395
  anxiety and coping and, 396–399
  attribution theory and, 387–390,
    395
  by beginning teachers, 432–433
  behavioral approaches to, 375
  beliefs and, 390–394, 395
  cognitive approaches to, 376–377
  definition of, 372–373
  evaluation and, 420–421
  extrinsic, 374–375
  goals and, 379–382
  grades and, 577–578
  grouping and, 417–420
  humanistic approaches to, 375
  intrinsic, 373–375
  to learn in school, 378–379
  lifelong learning and, 406–409
  needs and, 382–387
  observational learning and, 227–
    228
  recognizing accomplishment and,
    416
  resultant, **384**
  self-efficacy and, 393
  self-regulated learning and, 407
  social learning approaches to,
    377–378
  strategies to encourage, 427–433
  students' views of, 433
  supporting autonomy and, 414–416
  teacher expectations and, 421–426
  time and, 421
Motor development, 98–99
Motor excess, 141
Movement management, **458**,
    458–459
Multicultural education, **163**
  emphasizing similarities versus
    differences in, 164
Multiple-choice tests. *See* Objective
    testing
Multiple intelligences, 114–116,
    115
Multiple representations of content,
    347, 347–348

National standards, **542**
Native Americans, learning styles of,
    193
Needs, 382–387
  achievement motivation and,
    384–385
  age-related, 442
  being, **383**
  conflicting, 471
  deficiency, **383**
  Maslow's hierarchy of, 382–384
  for relatedness, 386
  for self-determination, 385–386
  teaching and, 386–387
Negative correlations, 14, **15**
Negative reinforcement, **211**, 222
Negotiation, confrontation and, 468,
    470
Neutral stimuli, **207**
Nongraded elementary schools,
    122
Normal distribution, **525**
Norm groups, **521**
Norming samples, **523**
Norm-referenced grading, **578**,
    580–581
Norm-referenced tests, **521**
Note taking, 309–311
Novice teachers
  concerns of, 8, 10
  motivation of students by, 432–
    433
  problem solving and, 306

Objectives. *See* Instructional objectives
Objective testing, **560**, 560–563
  essay testing compared with, 566
  evaluating items for, 563
  using, 560–561
  writing, 561–563
Observation, participant, 14, **15**
Observational learning, **226**, 226–231
  elements of, 226–228
  factors influencing, 228
  in teaching, 228–231
Operant(s), **208**, 208–209
Operant conditioning, **208**, 208–216
  antecedents and behavior change
    and, 214–216
  consequences and, 210–212
  reinforcement schedules and,
    212–214
  Thorndike's and Skinner's work on,
    209–210
Operations, **31**

Opportunity-to-learn standards, **542**
Organization, **28**, **262**
  of effective teachers, 503
  for learning environments, 440–445
  of long-term memory, 262
  in thinking, 28
Originality, creativity and, 130
Orthopedic devices, **137**
Overextension, **53**
Overgeneralization, **293**
Overlapping, **457**, 457–458
Overlearning, **322**
Overregularization, **53**

Parallel Distributed Processing (PDP), **266**
Paraphrase rule, **465**
Parents. *See also* Families
  rights of, 148
Partial seizures, **137**
Participant observation, **14**, **15**
Participation structures, **194**, **443**
Part learning, **271**
Part-whole relations, 297
Passive style, **467**
PDP (Parallel Distributed Processing), **266**
Peer(s)
  friendships and, 86–88
  role in cognitive development, 47
Peer mediation, 472–473
Peg-type mnemonics, **271**
Penalties, 459–460
Percentage grading, **583**, 583–584
Percentile rank scores, **526**, 526–527
Perception(s)
  images and, 258
  sensory memory and, 251–252
Performance, in context, 568–575
Performance goals, **380**
Performance in context, 568–575
Performance standards, **542**
Personal development, **24**
Personality, authoritarian, **176**, 176–177
Personal territories, 452–454
Perspective-taking ability, **80**
Petit mal seizures, 137
Phonics, 358–359
Physical abuse, 102
Physical development, **24**, 98–100
Physical disabilities, 127–129
Physical neglect, 102

Piaget's theory of cognitive development, 27–44
  implications for teachers, 39–44
  influences on development and, 27–28
  limitations of, 41–44
  stages of development and, 29–39
  thinking and, 28–29
  Vygotsky's theory compared with, 45–46
Planning, 480–487
  for classroom testing, 558–559
  from constructivist perspective, 484–487
  metacognitive knowledge and, 267
  taxonomies for, 481–484
Point system, 582–583
Portfolios, **569**, 569–570, 572–575
  evaluating, 572–575
Positive correlations, **14**, **15**
Positive practice, 220, **221**
Positive reinforcement, **210**, 210–211
Poverty, 167
PQ4R, **311**, 311–313
Practice
  distributed, **271**
  massed, **271**
  positive, 220, **221**
Pragmatics, **56**
Praise-and-ignore approach, 217
Preadolescence, formal operations stage and, 30, **37**, 37–38, 39
Pregnancy, teenage, 102–103
Prejudice, **176**, 176–177
  continuing, 176
  development of, 176–177
Premack principle, **218**, 218–219
Preoperational stage, 30, **31**, 31–33
Preschool(s), developmentally appropriate, **93**, 93–94
Preschool children
  gender-role stereotyping and, 179–180
  physical development of, 98–99
  preoperational stage and, 30, 31–33
  psychosocial development of, 67–69
Presentation punishment, **211**, 211–212
Pretests, **556**
Principles, **15**
Private speech, **45**, 45–46
Problem(s), **294**
  understanding, 297–298
Problem-based learning, 348–349, **413**

Problem solving, 294–307, **295**
  anticipating, acting, and looking back and, 301–302
  expert, 304–307
  factors hindering, 302–303
  general strategy for, 295–296
  general versus domain-specific, 295
  goals and problem representation for, 296–299
  schema-driven, **299**
  solution strategies for, 300–301
  teaching of, 316
Procedural knowledge, **248**, 248–249, 274–276
  automated basic skills and, 275
  domain-specific strategies and, 276
  learning outside school and, 276
Procedural memory, **261**
Procedures, for positive learning environments, 446–447
Production, observational learning and, 227
Productions, **261**, 275
Prompting, 215–216, **216**
Pronunciation, 54
Proposition(s), 258
Propositional networks, **258**
Prototypes, **289**
Proximal development, zone of, **49**, 49–50
Psychomotor domain, **483**, 483–484
Psychosocial development. *See* Erikson's theory of psychosocial development; Moral development; Socialization
Psychotic behavior, 141
Puberty, **99**, 99–100
Punishment, **211**, 211–212
  presentation, **211**, 211–212
Pygmalion effect, **421**

Question(s)
  convergent, **491**
  divergent, **491**
  multiple-choice. *See* Objective testing
Questioning, 490–492
  fitting questions to students and, 491–492
  kinds of questions and, 490–491
  reciprocal, **353**
  responding to student answers and, 492

Race, **170**, 170–171. *See also* Cultural diversity
  school achievement and, 174–175
Racial discrimination, 175–178
  continuing, 177–178
  continuing prejudice and, 176
  development of prejudice and, 176–177
Random procedure, **15**
Range, **525**
Ratio reinforcement schedule, **213**
Readiness testing, 540–542, **541**
Reading, literacy and, 57–59
Reading/writing instruction, 357–360
  integrated curriculum for, 358
  sensible approach to, 359–360
  skills and phonics and, 358–359
  whole language approach to, 357–358
Reasoning
  deductive, **341**
  hypothetico-deductive, **37**
Reception learning. *See* Expository teaching
Receptors, **250**
Reciprocal determinism, **225**
Reciprocal questioning, **353**
Reciprocal teaching, **360**, 360–362
  applying, 361–362
  example of, 360–361
Recitation, **489**, 489–490
Reconstruction, **264**
Reflectiveness, **8**
Reflectivity, **134**, 134–135
Regular education initiative, **146**
Regulation, metacognitive knowledge and, 267
Rehearsal
  elaborative, **256**
  maintenance, **255**, 255–256
Reinforcement, **210**, 210–211
  negative, **211**, 222
  observational learning and, 227–228
  positive, **210**, 210–211
  removal, **212**
  of self, 233–234
  teacher attention as, 216–218
  vicarious, **226**
Reinforcement schedules, 212–214
Reinforcers, **210**, 210–211
  selecting, 218–219
Relatedness, need for, 386
Relational propositions, 296

Reliability, **530**
  of evaluating portfolios and exhibitions, 574–576
  of tests, 530
Removal reinforcement, **212**
Report cards, 581–582
Reprimands, **223**
Research, 13–16
  on bilingual education, 190–192
  correlations and, 14
  on creating positive learning environments, 445
  descriptive, **13**, 13–14
  experimentation and, 15
  on learning styles, criticisms of, 194
  teaching theories and, 15–16
Resistance cultures, **169**
Resource rooms, **150**
Respect, for students, 196
Respondents, **208**
Response(s), **207**
  conditioned, **208**
  unconditioned, **207**
Response cost, 223, **224**
Response sets, **302**, 302–303, 320
Responsibility dimension, 387–388
Restructuring, 9, **129**
Resultant motivation, **384**
Retention, observational learning and, 227
Retention phase of strategic transfer, 322–323
Retrieval, **263**
  form long-term memory, 262–264
Reversibility, **35**
Reversible thinking, **32**
Revise options, **585**
Rewards, **375**
  for learning, 238
Rights, of students and parents, 148
Ripple effect, **230**
Risk, academic tasks and, 411–412
Rote memorization, **270**, 270–271
  shortcomings of, 273
Rule(s), for positive learning environments, 445–446, 447–449
Rule-eg method, **341**

Samples, norming, **523**
Satiation, **222**, 222–223
Scaffolding, **47**
SCAT (School and College Ability Tests), 537
Schema-driven problem solving, **299**

Schemata, **259**, 259–260
  concept learning and, 290
  event, 260
  training in use of, 298–299
Scholastic aptitude tests. *See* Aptitude tests
School(s)
  developmentally appropriate education and, 93–94
  elementary. *See* Elementary schools
  encouragement of students' self-esteem by, 376
  secondary. *See* Secondary schools
  self-esteem and, 75–76
  teaching values in, 86–87
  violence in, 471–472
School-age children
  concrete-operational stage and, 30, 34–36, **35**
  language development in, 54–57
  physical development of, 99
  preoperational stage and, 30, 31–33
  psychosocial development of, 67, 69–70
School and College Ability Tests (SCAT), 537
Science instruction, 364–365
Scoring rubrics, **572**, 572–574
Script(s), **260**
Scripted cooperation, 353–354, **489**
Seatwork, **492**
Secondary schools
  effective teachers for, 455
  rules for positive learning environments in, 448
  special problems in, 460–461
Seizures, **137**
  absence, 137
  generalized, **137**
  partial, **137**
Self-actualization, **382**
Self-concept, **73**, 73–80
  development of, 75
  gender and ethnicity and, 76–79
  others and, 79–80
  school life and, 75–76
  self-esteem and, 73–75, 76–79
Self-determination, need for, 385–386
Self-efficacy, **228**, **392**
  beliefs about, 392–394
  motivation and, 393
  of teachers, 393–394
Self-esteem, **73**, 73–79
  encouraging, 376
  gender and, 77

Self-esteem, (continued)
  low expectations and, 168–169
  personal and collective, 77–78
  school life and, 75–76
  self-concept and, 73–75
Self-fulfilling prophecy, **421**
Self-instruction, **135**, **235**, 235–236
  cognitive, **46**
Self-management, **231**, 231–235,
    444
  classroom management for,
    444–445
  goal setting for, 233
  recording and evaluating progress
    in, 233
  self-reinforcement for, 233–234
Self-regulated learners, **406**, 406–
    409
  knowledge and, 406–407
  motivation and, 407
  TARGETT for, 408–409
  volition and, 407–408
Self-reinforcement, 233–234
Self-worth, attributions and
    achievement motivation and,
    394–395
Semantic memory, **258**
Semilingual approach, **190**
Semiotic function, **31**
Sensorimotor stage, **30**, 30–31
Sensory impairment, 138–139
Sensory memory, **250**, 250–254
  attention and, 252–253, 253
  capacity, duration, and contents of,
    250–251
  perception and, 251–252
  teaching and, 253
Sentences, first, 53
Serial-position effect, **271**
Seriation, **35**
SES. See Socioeconomic status (SES)
Sex discrimination, in classrooms,
    181–182
Sexual abuse, 102
Sexuality, adolescent, 102–103
Shaping, **219**, 219–220
Sign language, **138**
Situated learning, **279**, 279–280
Small group teaching, 494–502
  constructivist, 495–496
  group discussion for, 496–497
  humanistic, 498
  technology and, 498–502
Social class. See Socioeconomic status
    (SES)

Social cognitive theory, **225**, 225–
    231
  elements of, 225
  observational learning and, 226–231
Social conventions, moral issues
    versus, 83–84
Social development, **24**
Social isolation, 223, **224**
Socialization, **91**, 91–97
  families and, 92–96
  teachers' roles in, 96–97
Socialized aggression, 141
Social learning approaches to
    motivation, 377–378
Social negotiation, **347**, **500**
Social transmission, cognitive
    development and, 28
Sociocultural theory, **44**. See also
    Vygotsky's sociocultural
    perspective
Socioeconomic status (SES), **166**
  achievement and, 167–170
  poverty and, 167
Sociolinguistics, **194**, 194–195
  misunderstandings and, 194–195
  participation structures and, 194
Spaces, for learning, 449–454
Spasticity, **138**
Specific knowledge, **248**
Specific learning disabilities, **142**,
    142–145
Speech
  private, **45**, 45–46
  telegraphic, **53**
Speech impairments, **139**, 139–140
Speech reading, **138**
Spiral curricula, 348
Spreading of activation, 270
Spread of activation, **263**
Stability dimension, 387
STAD (Student Teams–Achievement
    Divisions), **418**, 418–419
Stand-alone thinking skills programs,
    315
Standard deviation, **524**, 524–525
Standard error of measurement, **530**
Standardized tests, 518–550, **523**
  achievement, 533–536
  aptitude, 537–539
  for assessing learning potential,
    547–548
  authentic assessment and, 548–549
  bias and, 544–545
  coaching and test-taking skills and,
    545

controversy regarding use of, 541
  criterion-referenced, 521–523
  diagnostic, 536–537
  high-stakes, 539
  measurement and evaluation and,
    520–521
  minimum and world-class standards
    and, 542
  norm-referenced, 521
  for readiness testing, 540–542
  scores on. See Test scores
  for testing teachers, 543
  uses in American society, 539–543
Standard scores, **528**, 528–529
Standard speech, **186**
Stanine scores, **529**
Statistical significance, **15**
Stereotypes, **177**
  gender-role, in preschool years,
    179–180
Stimuli, **207**
  conditioned, **208**
  neutral, **207**
  unconditioned, **207**
Stimulus control, **214**
Story grammar, **260**
Student(s)
  conflicts among, confrontation and,
    470–473
  effects of grading on. See Grading
  ego-involved learners, **380**
  failure-accepting, **395**
  failure-avoiding, **395**
  fitting questions to, 491–492
  gaining cooperation of, 441–442
  gifted, **126**, 126–129
  helping to see value of learning,
    428–430
  interactions with teachers, 424–425
  knowledge construction by, 40–41
  mastery-oriented, **394**, 394–395
  need to understand, 10–11,
    195–196
  New Zealand studies of, 507–508
  respecting, 196
  rights of, 148
  self-regulated, **406**, 406–409
  task-involved learners, **380**
  teacher expectations effects on,
    421–423
  thinking of, 39–40
  views on motivation, 433
Student-centered teaching, 348,
    494–502
  constructivist, 495–496

group discussion for, 496–497
humanistic, 498
technology and, 498–502
Student motivation to learn, **378**, 378–379
Student Teams–Achievement Divisions (STAD), **418**, 418–419
Stuttering, **140**
Subjects, **15**
Subject structure, **338**
Successive approximations, **219**
Suicide, **105**
Summative assessment, **558**
Surface-processing approach to learning, 135
Syntax, **54**

TARGETT, 408–409
Task(s)
academic, **409**, 409–413
helping students to focus on, 430–431
time on, **443**
Task analysis, **219**, 219–220
Task-involved learners, **380**
Taxonomies, **332**, **481**, 481–484
affective domain and, 482–483
cognitive domain and, 482
of objectives, 332–333
psychomotor domain and, 483–484
Teacher(s)
attention from, as reinforcement, 216–218
beginning. *See* Novice teachers
creativity judgments of, 130–131
expert. *See* Expert teachers
interactions with students, 424–425
self-efficacy of, 393–394
socialization and, 96–97
testing of, 543
understanding of students needed by, 10–11
Teacher expectations, 421–426
effects of, 421–423
instructional strategies and, 423–424
sources of, 423
teacher-student interactions and, 424–425
Teaching, 478–514. *See also* Instruction
active, **335**. *See also* Direct instruction
anxiety and, 398
attention and, 253

attributions and, 395
beliefs and, 395
complex nature of, 8
conditions for learning from, 507–508
cooperative, **150**, 150–151
in culturally compatible classrooms, 196–197
dialects and, 185
directive, 488–494
effective. *See* Effective teachers; Effective teaching
excellence in, 4–8
explicit. *See* Direct instruction
expository, **341**, 343–345
of gifted students, 128–129
goals and, 382
literacy and, 58
of mathematics, 362–363
needs and, 386–387
observational learning in, 228–231
planning for. *See* Planning
of reading. *See* Reading/writing instruction
reciprocal, **360**, 360–362
Rosenshine's functions of, 336
of science, 364–365
small group, 494–502
strategies for. *See* Teaching strategies
student-centered, 494–502
students' thinking and, 39–40
theories for, 15–16
for transfer, 319–324
of values in schools, 86–87
whole group, 488–494
of writing. *See* Reading/writing instruction
Teaching efficacy, **393**, 393–394
Teaching strategies, 488–494
behavioral, ethical issues related to, 237
lecturing and explaining, 488–489
matching to abilities, 40
matching to learning goals, 508–511
recitation and questioning, 489–492
seatwork and homework, 493–494
teacher expectations and, 423–424
for teaching concepts, 290–293
Teams-Games-Tournaments (TGT), **419**, 419–420
Technology, 498–502
computers, 498–502
videodiscs, 502
Teenagers. *See* Adolescent(s)
Telegraphic speech, **53**

Test(s)
authentic, **568**
classroom. *See* Classroom tests
for creativity, 130–131
diagnostic, **556**, 556–557
gifted students and, 128
objective. *See* Objective testing
performance in context and, 568–575
standardized. *See* Standardized tests
Test scores, 523–532
on achievement tests, 534–536
central tendency and standard deviation of, 523–525
confidence intervals and, 531
frequency distributions of, 523
grade-equivalent, 527–528
interpreting, 529–532
normal distribution of, 525
percentile rank, 526–527
reliability of, 530
standard, 528–529
true, 530
validity of, 531–532
Test-taking skills, 545
TGT (Teams-Games-Tournaments), **419**, 419–420
Theories, **15**, 15–16. *See also specific theories*
Thinking, 286–325
analogical, **301**
concept learning and, 289–293
convergent, 130
critical, 316, 318, **318**
divergent, 130
importance of, 288–289
intuitive, **338**, 338–339
language of, 318
learning strategies and study skills and, 307–314
Piaget's views on, 28–29
problem solving and, 294–307
in regular curriculum, 315, 317–319
reversible, **32**
stand-alone programs for developing, **315**
as "state of mind," 318–319
of students, understanding, 39–40
teaching and learning about, 314–319
teaching for transfer and, 319–324
Time
academic learning, **443**
allocated, **443**
engaged, **443**

Time, *(continued)*
  for learning, as goal of classroom
    management, 443
  motivation and, 421
Time on task, **443**
Time out, 223, **224**
Token reinforcement system, **462**,
  462–463
Top-down processing, **252**
Tracking, socioeconomic status and,
  169
Transfer, **319**, 319–324
  backward-reaching, **320**
  definition of, 319–320
  forward-reaching, **320**
  general, **320**
  high-road, **320**
  of learning strategies, 320–321,
    322–324
  low-road, **320**
Transfer phase of strategic transfer,
  322–323
Transition programming, **125**
Tree diagrams, 311
Triarchic theory of intelligence, **116**,
  116–118
True scores, **530**
Trust versus mistrust stage, 67–
  68
T scores, **528**

Unconditioned response (UR), **207**
Unconditioned stimulus (US), **207**
Underextension, **53**
Undergeneralization, **292**
Underlining, 308–309
UR (unconditioned response), **207**

US (unconditioned stimulus), **207**
Utility value, **413**

Validity, **531**
  of evaluating portfolios and
    exhibitions, 574–576
  of tests, 531–532
Value
  of academic tasks, 412–413
  attainment, **413**, 429–430
  instrumental, 430
  interest, **413**
  intrinsic, **413**, 429–430
  of learning, helping students see,
    428–430
  utility, **413**
Values, teaching in schools, 86–87
Variability, **524**, 524–525
Venn diagrams, 311
Verbalizations, **301**
Verbal learning, meaningful, **341**
Vicarious reinforcement, **226**
Videodiscs, 502
Violence, in schools, 471–472
Vision, low, **138**
Vision impairment, 138–139
Visual learning strategies, 311
Vocabulary, learning, 53–55
Voicing problems, **140**
Volition, self-regulated learning and,
  407–408
Vygotsky's sociocultural perspective,
  44–51
  adults and peers and, 47
  implications for teachers, 47–51
  language and private speech and,
    45–46

Piaget's theory compared with,
  45–46
zone of proximal development and,
  49–50

Warmth, of effective teachers,
  505
Whole group teaching, 488–494
  lecturing and explaining and,
    488–489
  recitation and questioning and,
    489–492
  seatwork and homework and,
    492–494
Whole-language perspective, **357**,
  357–358
Within-class ability grouping, **122**,
  122–123
Withitness, **457**
Words, first, 52–53
Working-backward strategy, **300**,
  300–301
Working memory, **254**, 254–257
  capacity, duration, and contents of,
    254–255
  development of, 268–269
  forgetting and, 256–257
  individual differences in, 268–269
  retaining information in, 255–256
World-class standards, **542**
Writing instruction. *See*
  Reading/writing instruction

Zone of proximal development, **49**,
  49–50
z scores, **528**